PHARMACY

LAW DIGEST

Facts &
Comparisons™

part of Wolters Kluwer Health

PHARMACY

LAW DIGEST

Authors

Joseph L. Fink III, BSPharm, JD
Professor of Pharmacy Administration
College of Pharmacy
University of Kentucky
Lexington, Kentucky

Jesse C. Vivian, BSPharm, JD
Professor of Pharmacy Practice
Eugene Applebaum College of Pharmacy and Health Sciences
Wayne State University
Detroit, Michigan

Kim Keller Reid, BSPharm, JD
Special Government Employee
Food and Drug Administration
Consultant
Germantown, Maryland

38th Edition
2004

Facts and Comparisons®
part of Wolters Kluwer Health
111 West Port Plaza Drive, Suite 300
St. Louis, Missouri 63146-3098
Toll free customer service 1-800-223-0554
www.drugfacts.com

PHARMACY LAW DIGEST
FACTS AND COMPARISONS® PUBLISHING GROUP:

Kenneth H. Killion
executive vice president

Cathy H. Reilly
publisher

Renée M. Wickersham
senior managing editor

Kirsten K. Novak
managing editor

Sara L. Schweain
associate editor

Kevin D. Harms
assistant editor

Joseph R. Horenkamp
assistant editor

Jennifer K. Walsh
senior composition specialist

Linda M. Jones
senior sgml specialist

Teri H. Burnham
acquisitions editor

Susan H. Sunderman
quality control editor

Mark L. Wickersham
cover design

Mark A. Sohasky
director of marketing

Cindy A. Meilink
marketing manager

Sara E. Heideman
product and market analyst

Susan L. Polcyn
manufacturing services manager

Indexing by Brooke Graves of Graves Editorial Services in Colorado Springs, Colorado.

This publication is designed to provide accurate and authoritative information in regard to the subject matter covered. It is sold with the understanding that the publisher is not engaged in rendering legal, accounting, or other professional services. If legal advice or other expert assistance is required, the services of a competent professional should be sought.

> From a declaration of principles jointly adopted by a committee of the American Bar Association and a committee of publishers and associations.

ISBN 1-57439-167-4

Library of Congress Catalog Card Number 72-115322

BURGUNDA V. SWEET, PharmD
Director, Drug Information and Investigational Drug Services
Clinical Associate Professor of Pharmacy
University of Michigan Health System and College of Pharmacy
Ann Arbor, Michigan

DAVID S. TATRO, PharmD
Drug Information Analyst
San Carlos, California

THOMAS L. WHITSETT, MD
Professor of Medicine
Director, Vascular Medicine
University of Oklahoma Health Sciences Center

TABLE OF CONTENTS

Publisher's Preface,   viii
Foreword,   ix
How to Use This Book,   x
Authors' Biographies,   xi

Chapter 1
Introduction,   1

Chapter 2
Regulation of Pharmaceuticals,   21

Chapter 3
Controlled Substances,   129

Chapter 4
Pharmacy Inspection,   173

Chapter 5
Business Law,   195

Chapter 6
Civil Liability,   241

Chapter 7
Court Cases,   321

Appendix,   797
        Glossary of Terms,   799
        State Boards of Pharmacy,   807
        State Laws Affecting Pharmacy Practice,   813
        National Association of
            Boards of Pharmacy –
            Survey of Pharmacy Law,   815
        Answer Key,   901

Index,   927

PREFACE

Pharmacy Law Digest (*PLD*), a publication dedicated to providing up-to-date information on pharmacy law, continues the tradition Facts and Comparisons® has established and refined in providing timely, accurate, useful information to its customers. Written and updated by a distinguished group of pharmacists/attorneys with multi-faceted experience, *PLD* remains the comprehensive source of information in this field. These authors, preeminent in their field, do an excellent job of presenting a complex and intricate body of information.

Intended to meet the needs of a wide audience, the broad scope of the material in *PLD* is useful for pharmacy law instructors, students, practicing pharmacists, and attorneys. Each group benefits from the exhaustive, yet concise, material provided in this reference.

Pharmacy Law Digest is published as a bound edition that is updated annually and is intended to be a useful and convenient reference. The popular court cases are arranged by topic with a detailed table of contents, making it easy to locate the specific cases and providing a useful teaching tool. A series of study questions that follow some chapters, are intended to enhance the classroom experience. The information within other chapters and sections are continuously updated with each new edition.

Although we consider *PLD* to be the premier source for pharmacy law information, we are always looking for ways to improve this publication to make it more useful. We are constantly reviewing each and every section, evaluating its scope and utility, in an effort to keep it as the most comprehensive pharmacy law book available. However, this can only be done with feedback from our customers. We welcome any comments and suggestions to help us continue to produce the quality publication you have come to expect.

Cathy H. Reilly
Publisher

FOREWORD

Pharmacy Law Digest was first published in 1965 by Eugene L. Kaluzny, a pharmacist-lawyer in Milwaukee, Wisconsin. Since that time, it has undergone numerous revisions and become recognized as the leading text and reference in the field of pharmacy law. The evolution of this book is continual because statutes and regulations in pharmacy law change frequently as do court interpretations of their meaning. The editors intend to carry on the tradition of excellence by staying up-to-date on developments and incorporating new material into subsequent editions.

Pharmacy Law Digest is divided into seven main sections: (1) The Introduction orients the reader to the legal system of the United States as well as to the law in its various forms. A discussion of how to read legal citations (references) is presented in this section. (2) The Regulation of Pharmaceuticals chapter includes a discussion of the Federal Food, Drug, and Cosmetic Act, with particular emphasis on the impact of this statute on the practice of pharmacy. (3) The Controlled Substances chapter provides detailed information regarding this important segment of the law that imposes substantial responsibilities on the pharmacist. (4) The Pharmacy Inspection chapter reviews the law in that field and includes general recommendations for dealing with pharmacy inspections. (5) The Business Law chapter discusses many principles that are relevant to modern pharmacy practice. (6) The Civil Liability chapter focuses on the expanding role of the pharmacist and emphasizes avoidance of legal entanglements. (7) Synopses of lawsuits pertaining to pharmacy practice are presented in the Court Cases chapter.

A glossary of terms and list of the state boards of pharmacy can be found in the Appendix. Excerpts from *Survey of Pharmacy Law*, published by the National Association of Boards of Pharmacy, are also included to provide profiles of the regulatory schemes in the various states on topics of legal interest. Substantial time has been invested in creating a valuable indexing system to assist the reader. Moreover, a list of reference sources featuring additional information about the topics discussed is included at the end of certain chapters.

At appropriate points, the authors have included references or citations to works where additional information can be obtained. There is not, however, a full accounting of the works consulted because it could run as long as the text itself. The *Pharmacy Law Digest* is a compilation based on the authors' work at the juncture of pharmacy and law over a cumulative period of more than 50 years.

We hope that you will find this book both interesting and relevant. The editors and the *Facts and Comparisons*® staff encourage your comments and suggestions.

Joseph L. Fink III   Kim Keller Reid   Jesse C. Vivian
Lexington, KY   Germantown, MD   Plymouth, MI

HOW TO USE THIS BOOK

Pharmacy Law Digest consists of explanatory text material and actual reproduction of applicable portions of statutes and regulations. With reference to specific questions or topics, consult the Index.

This book exists at the interface of pharmacy and law. Hence, legal citations follow *A Uniform System of Citation* (12th Edition) and references from the literature of pharmacy follow "*Uniform Requirements for Manuscripts Submitted to Biomedical Journals.*"

THE PURPOSE OF THIS BOOK IS TO INFORM and NOT TO ADVISE. In case of specific legal problems, consult an attorney familiar with the statutes and regulations in your state. Information in this book should be read in light of current legislative enactments and current judicial interpretations affecting such information. Therefore, the material in this book may not always be the latest information on a particular matter.

The Authors

AUTHORS' BIOGRAPHIES

Joseph L. Fink III, BSPharm, JD

Joseph L. Fink III is Vice President for Corporate Relations and Economic Outreach and Associate Vice President for Research at the University of Kentucky in Lexington. He is Professor of Pharmacy Administration at the UK College of Pharmacy. He is also Professor of Health Administration, Professor of Public Health, and Professor of Public Policy and Administration at UK. A native of Tyrone, Pennsylvania, he received his professional education in pharmacy at the Philadelphia College of Pharmacy and Science, graduating in 1970. He received the Juris Doctor degree from Georgetown University in 1973. He served on the faculty of the Philadelphia College of Pharmacy and Science from 1973 to 1981 when he moved to Kentucky. He is licensed to practice pharmacy in Kentucky and Pennsylvania and is a member of the Kentucky and Pennsylvania Bars and the Bar of the United States Supreme Court. He holds membership in a number of organizations in both pharmacy and law, and while he was a pharmacy student, he served as National President of the Student American Pharmaceutical Association. He has also served as President of the American Society for Pharmacy Law, an organization he founded in 1974. The UK National Alumni Association twice has honored him with a university-wide "Great Teacher Award."

Jesse C. Vivian, BSPharm, JD

Jesse C. Vivian is a Professor in the Pharmacy Practice Department at Wayne State University, Eugene Applebaum College of Pharmacy and Health Sciences. Professor Vivian received his B.S. in Pharmacy from the University of Michigan College of Pharmacy in 1975 and earned his Juris Doctor degree from the Wayne State University School of Law in 1983. He has practiced pharmacy in a variety of community and institutional settings. In his legal career, Professor Vivian has been employed in the law department of a large metropolitan hospital corporation and practiced health care law with private firms in the Detroit area. He presently serves as General Counsel to the Michigan Pharmacists Association and has been Chairman of its Peer Review and Ethics and Practice Commissions for several years. He is also Of Counsel to the law firm of Cummings, McClorey, Davis and Acho, PC where his practice focuses on pharmacy and health care law. He was named Pharmacist of the Year by the Michigan Pharmacists Association in 1992 and was inducted into its Hall of Honor in 1993 in recognition of his service and dedication to the practice of pharmacy. The association also bestowed its Board Medalist award to him in 2002 in further recognition of his dedication to advancement of the pharmacy profession. He also served as a member of the APhA Code of Ethics Revision Committee that produced the 1994 Code of Ethics for Pharmacists and is an editorial reviewer for APhA's Journal. Professor Vivian is a Past President of the American Society for Pharmacy Law, a national organization dedicated to educating lawyers and pharmacists about legal issues affecting the practice of pharmacy. He is also the author of several publications dealing with pharmacy law and ethics. For the past nine years, he has been featured in a monthly US Pharmacist legal perspectives series. Professor Vivian is also the co-author of Ethical Perspectives: Guidelines for Dealing with Ethics in Pharmacy Practice, a teaching manual used extensively in the colleges of pharmacy throughout this country and Canada. In 1997, he was named co-editor of *Pharmacy Law Digest* published by Facts and Comparisons. He is also co-author, along with Joseph L. Fink of the legal issues chapter in the 20th edition of *Remington: The Science and Practice of Pharmacy*. At Wayne State University, Professor Vivian teaches courses on professional ethics, drug regulation, health care law, and health care policy for pharmacy students and interdisciplinary groups. He is the recipient of the college's first Excellence in Teaching Award and has been named Professor of the Year by eight different graduating classes of students.

Kim Keller Reid, BSPharm, JD

Kim Keller Reid received her B.S. in Pharmacy, *cum laude*, in 1986 from Samford University, where she served as president of the student chapter of APhA. She received her law degree, *cum laude*, in 1993 from the University of Louisville, where she served as president of the Brandeis Society (the honor society). Prior to attending law school, Ms. Reid worked in pharmaceutical sales for the Dista division of Eli Lilly, where she was named "Rookie of the Year." She also has several years of experience in the practice of community pharmacy. Ms. Reid worked as a staff attorney for the United States Pharmacopeia for more than four years, where she advised management on Food and Drug Law issues, served as liason with the State Boards of Pharmacy and the FDA, and served as counsel to USP's Practitioner Reporting Network. She has served as a faculty member for the Food and Drug Law Institute's Seminar for Pharmacy Law Professors. She served as a member of the Board of Directors of the American Society for Pharmacy Law from 1996 to 2000 and as the Executive Director of ASPL from January 2000 through February 2001. She also serves as a special government employee in the FDA's Office of Compliance assisting in the promulgation of regulations persuant to the compounding provisions of the Food and Drug Administration Modernization Act. In addition, she serves as a consultant to various groups and organizations on issues related to pharmacy and food and drug law. She speaks frequently on several pharmacy law topics and has served as editor of the *Pharmacy Law Annual*. Ms. Reid is also a member of the American Pharmaceutical Association and the American Society of Law, Medicine, and Ethics.

Chapter 1

Introduction

The Law, 3
    Law Defined and Differentiated, 3
    Forms of Law, 3
    Law versus Equity, 5
    Substantive versus Procedural Law, 5
    Criminal versus Civil Law, 5

Legal Systems, 6
    Legislative System, 6
    Executive System, 8
    Freedom of Information Act, 9
    Judicial System, 9
        Civil Trial Procedure, 10
        Criminal Trial Procedure, 13
        Appeal, 14
        Conclusion, 15

The Attorney-Client Relationship, 15

Power of Attorney, 15

How to Find and Read the Law, 15
    Legal Citation Forms, 15
        Court Cases, 16
        Statutes, 16
        Regulations, 17

Information about Law School, 18

Sources of Additional Information, 20

INTRODUCTION

THE LAW

Law Defined and Differentiated

What is the law? Although there are numerous definitions, one that suits the purposes of this book is the following:

> The law is that body of principles that govern conduct and the observance of which can be enforced in courts, or that which must be obeyed and followed by citizens subject to legal sanctions or consequences.

Law was developed in order that relationships among individuals would conform to certain standards. For example, imagine the chaos that would ensue if there was no law that required operators of motor vehicles in this country to drive on the right side of the road. Without this requirement, some operators would drive on the right side, some on the left side, and some down the middle of the road. The highway system would not function smoothly. Drivers know that under the law they are to drive on the right side of the road and can expect that other drivers will also. Hence, they can pass an oncoming vehicle without a collision.

Law is used to enforce the minimum value system that is considered necessary to govern, and it establishes freedoms, if any, that are guaranteed to the people being governed. It is often disconcerting to pharmacists and others that the law is not exact and that the legal answers are not often easily derived. Because the law does not exist in a vacuum, it is not static. The law is a reflection of society, and it changes and grows as society changes. The legal system often adopts a rather negative view of human behavior. It restricts undesirable behavior, but it may not reward good and ethical behavior.

It should be noted that an important element in the definition of law is the possibility of governmentally imposed penalties for transgressions. This governmental role serves to differentiate law from ethics and mores. Ethics are rules promulgated by a profession or other group, and imposed upon all members of the profession by its own organization. Hence, ethical standards are enforced by the profession itself, not by the government. Codes of ethics are a tool of self-regulation and represent what "ought to be," whereas law represents what "must be." The concept of mores is sociological. They are customs that establish standards of conduct enforceable by social pressure, not by government. Laws often originate in ethical codes and mores.

Forms of Law

Law occurs in a variety of hierarchical forms:

(1) A **constitution** is a broad statement of powers of the government and its branches. Constitutions deal with matters of fundamental and enduring importance rather than details of a particular program or regulatory activity. Under the U.S. Constitution, a power rests with the states unless it is specifically assigned to the federal government. A constitution is the highest form of law, and all other forms of law must be consistent with it. For example, to state that something is "unconstitutional" means that the statute or regulation under consideration is not consistent with the constitution and consequently is declared invalid by a court. In this country, 2 constitutions are in force: the federal Constitution and the state constitution. While most challenges to the constitutionality of a statute or regulation are based on the provisions of the federal Constitution, the same challenges could be based sometimes on provisions of the state constitution.

(2) The next level of law is a **treaty** – an agreement between or among nations. Because all treaties are authorized by the U.S. Constitution, they override all laws but the Constitution. The treaties that the U.S. has formed with other nations

regarding narcotics are obviously applicable to pharmacy. The U.S. statutes regulating narcotics must be consistent with the treaties of this country or they will be invalid. For example, if the U.S. has a treaty requiring that marijuana and its constituents be considered as Schedule I substances for purposes of regulation, the government could not reschedule the drugs by statute or regulation without violating the treaty. Hence, the treaty would prevail over inconsistent statutes or regulations.

(3) **Statutes** are laws enacted by Congress at the federal level or by legislature at the state level. Under the American form of government, the concurrence of the head of the executive branch (ie, the president or governor) usually is required before the statute can go into effect. States have the authority to legislate in areas not prohibited or reserved for the federal government in the U.S. Constitution. As a result, states have broad "police power" to enact laws that protect the public's health, safety, and welfare. As stated, statutes must be consistent with the higher forms of law. An example of the potential for conflict between federal and state statutes exists with those laws designed to ensure drug product quality. The U.S. Congress has adopted the Food, Drug, and Cosmetic Act (FDCA) at the federal level to achieve this goal based on its authority over interstate commerce. All states also have adopted statutes designed to ensure drug product quality based on the concept of police power discussed above. Over the years, a situation has evolved where the greatest activity on this is at the federal level rather than the state level. The same is true with antitrust statutes, laws designed to protect economic competition, which exist at both the federal and state levels. Again, most activity is at the federal level because of resources available for enforcement. It also may be that a federal statute will be worded in a way to pre-empt state laws not consistent with it. An example of this is the Employee Retirement Income Security Act (ERISA), a federal statute designed to protect employees' fringe benefits of employment. This statute has had great impact on prescription drug insurance programs, also known as "third-party plans."

(4) **Regulations** are administrative enactments of the executive branch of government that fulfill statutory policies and procedures. For example, the Drug Enforcement Administration (DEA) issues detailed regulations to effect the requirements of the Comprehensive Drug Abuse Prevention and Control Act. State boards of pharmacy issue detailed regulations to carry out the policy and procedures of the state pharmacy acts. The regulations must be consistent with the authorizing statute, as well as with the constitution and any relevant treaties. They also must bear reasonable relationship to the public health, safety, and welfare.

Sometimes a question will arise regarding whether a change in law pertaining to pharmacy practice should be accomplished through enactment of a statute by the legislature or adoption of a regulation by an administrative agency, such as a board of pharmacy. Assuming that an option exists for taking either route to effect the change, the following points may be relevant: Statutes are more difficult to challenge than the regulations; however, regulations can be changed more easily than statutes. Thus, if a pharmacy organization is seeking to change the law, it must determine whether the change is to be sought at the administrative agency level (where it may be effected more easily but is more subject to challenge) or at the legislative level (where the change itself may be more difficult to secure). Importantly, it should be noted that some changes may only be made in a certain way (eg, the authority to prescribe may only be conferred by the legislature). Action of an administrative agency attempting to confer such authority without statutory authorization would be without legal basis and, therefore, invalid (see discussion regarding the executive branch of government under Legal Systems).

Another type of law is **Common Law**. The Common Law is a body of principles based on custom and usage in England between the Norman invasion and the establishment of the American colonies. Rather than start anew to develop a legal system, the colonists adopted the body of English law as the basis for American law. Therefore, British legal principles formed the underpinnings of the American legal system and have been carried to this day in the form of the Common Law.

Judicial or **case law** is law derived from judicial decisions and interpretations of statutes and regulations. Courts have the final say of what the law really means. An important principle of judicial or case law is **stare decisis**, literally translated as "the decision stands." Decisions made in prior cases are followed in current cases and will be followed in future cases where the same facts exist. This rule enables lawyers to anticipate how courts will decide legal cases in the future, which is how attorneys advise clients to avoid legal problems. The application of stare decisis has one important limitation: A prior decision is binding only in courts of the same jurisdiction. For example, a decision reached by an Illinois court would not be binding in a Wisconsin court, although the Wisconsin court is free to follow the Illinois decision if there is no contrary precedent in Wisconsin.

Large portions of U.S. law remain largely the product of judicial precedent. Precedents are always subject to being overruled. For example, in a 1972 decision, the U.S. Supreme Court reversed a 1928 ruling which had upheld a Pennsylvania statute restricting ownership of pharmacies to licensed pharmacists. In the later case (see *North Dakota Board of Pharmacy v. Snyder's Drug Stores, Inc.*, 414 U.S. 156 [1973]), the justices concluded that pharmacy ownership restrictions were constitutional if such requirements were deemed by the state legislature to be reasonably related to public health and safety.

The legislature is free to change the effects of case law decisions. In the case of a conflict between legislation and the case law, the statute will usually prevail. In some instances, the legislature will actually codify common law or case law principles in statutes.

Courts are often called upon to interpret the meaning of statutes because it is not always possible for the legislature to write a law that is clear and unambiguous. Courts will presume, if possible, the validity and constitutionality of a statute. When interpreting statutes, courts must often examine committee reports and other historical documents to determine the legislative intent behind the statute.

Law versus Equity

The distinction between law and equity is important. The law provides remedies that are rigid and limited; equitable remedies are more flexible and are capable of being customized to the needs of the individual case. The same court can order a legal or an equitable remedy. If a contract held by 2 parties is breached by one party, the only legal remedy is to sue for monetary damages resulting from the breach. An equitable remedy is more adaptable. For example, the court can order one party to perform the contract obligations in certain limited situations. This is "specific performance," and it is not a legal remedy but an equitable remedy. A common form of equitable remedy is the injunction, an order directing someone to refrain from doing something.

Substantive versus Procedural Law

Substantive law is law that creates, defines, and regulates rights. For example, the right of an injured party to sue a pharmacist for malpractice is substantive law. **Procedural law** is law that prescribes methods of enforcing rights and obtaining redress for the invasion of those rights. It is the machinery for conducting a law suit (ie, rules that must be followed to enforce legal rights). The distinction between substantive and procedural law can be critical.

Criminal versus Civil Law

One way of classifying law is on the basis of what it is regulating. **Criminal law** defines the limitations of the relationship between the individual and society. An individual who commits murder has wronged society by breaking one of its rules. Hence, the suit is brought by society acting through a district attorney or U.S. attorney. **Civil law**, on the other hand, pertains to the relationship among individuals within society. If an individual steals a book, that person could be sued by the owner, who has been wronged. The government is not a party in the suit. However, note that both a civil suit and a criminal suit could coexist. The thief could be sued by the owner for taking the book (wrong against the individual), and the government could criminally charge the thief for committing a wrong against society (the theft itself). An example from pharmacy practice would be if a pharmacist were to dispense a prescription drug without having authorization. Further assume that a patient is injured as a result of having taken this unlawfully dispensed medication. Here, the pharmacist has committed a crime (ie, dispensing the medication without a prescription) and a tort (negligently causing the injury to the patient). Both the criminal charge brought by the government and the civil claim brought by the injured patient can coexist; they are not mutually exclusive.

Civil law has 2 major subdivisions: contracts and torts. **Contract law** deals with duties that individuals have because they entered into an agreement. If an individual agrees to sell a car and then does not follow through, he could be sued for breach of contract. The subject matter of the suit is the breach of duty that was created when the parties entered into the contract. Conversely, **tort law** deals with duties created by law, not duties created by parties themselves. For example, the law has created a duty that a pharmacist dispensing medication must dispense the right drug as prescribed. If a wrong drug is dispensed, it is possible for the pharmacist to be sued for professional negligence (a tort), assuming other facets exist as well (see the Civil Liability chapter). Hence, the pharmacist who made the error may have committed a tort or a breach of the duty created by law.

Administrative law is civil in nature. It includes the vast number of state and federal regulations that govern the relationship between government and some regulated profession, trade, or industry. This area of the law governs much of the daily activities of a pharmacist.

It is easy to see that a pharmacist's wrongful conduct could result in a criminal, civil, or administrative action or any combination of these. For example, selling a prescription drug to a patient without a prescription is a criminal act against society and could result in a fine or prison sentence. Because the act is proscribed by board of pharmacy regulations, the pharmacist also will face possible license suspension, revocation, or probation. If the patient were injured by the drug, a civil lawsuit for damages could result.

LEGAL SYSTEMS

The purpose of this section is to present a brief discussion of some important principles related to the operations of the 3 subdivisions of government in the U.S. Most of this discussion will be applicable to activities at the state level, although there may be variations from jurisdiction to jurisdiction.

The U.S. government is based on a system of checks and balances, sometimes referred to as countervailing powers, between the legislative, executive, and judicial branches. The 3 branches of government each have authority that tends to balance that authority given to other branches. It is worth noting that, while administrative agencies are part of the executive branch, they are sometimes considered a fourth branch of government because in the view of some commentators they perform all three types of governmental functions – legislative, executive and judicial. These agencies are pervasive at both the state and federal levels, and they often have broad authority (described later). Two statutes that greatly affect pharmacy are the FDCA and the Controlled Substances Act (CSA), both of which will be referred to frequently in this book.

Legislative System

The legislative branch of government makes the law. By enacting legislation, the Congress or the state legislatures set into motion the operation of government and the rule of law. Pharmacy is affected heavily by legislation, and an understanding of the legislative system is necessary if pharmacists are to modify the legal framework within which they practice.

Generally, a bill may be introduced into either house of the legislature by a member. However, in some instances there is a requirement that appropriations bills (those that make government funds available) must originate in the House of Representatives. Once a bill is introduced, it is referred to a committee for consideration. The committee to which it is referred may be critical. For example, in some states, drug product selection legislation was referred to the committee dealing with health affairs, whereas in others it is referred to consumer protection committees. The orientations of the 2 committees are quite different, and the differences are reflected in the wording of the various statutes enacted, evidence of the committee referral decision having a profound affect on the outcome of the legislative process.

The committee may hold hearings or conduct an investigation to determine whether the legislation is needed. Often, the bill will be assigned to a subcommittee for consideration.

In some instances, the bill may never be considered by the full committee. One very effective way to deal with undesirable legislation is to have it "put on the back burner" by the committee so it will not be enacted.

Once the committee has completed its deliberations and reported the bill out, it comes for a vote before the branch of the legislature (House of Representatives or Senate) in which it was introduced. In the process of voting, members of the House or Senate may suggest amendments. Each amendment usually will be voted on separately. A "rider" may also be attached. A rider is an unrelated piece of legislation that is attached to the primary legislation in hope of getting it enacted along with the primary bill. If one branch of the legislature passes the bill, it will then be referred to the other branch where the process begins anew with referral to committee, etc.

When the second branch of the legislature considers the bill, it may be passed but with different provisions. If so, the bill will be referred to a joint conference committee composed of members of both houses of the legislature. If the differences are negotiated to a point of reconciliation, the agreed-upon version of the bill then will have to be passed by both houses.

After both houses have passed the bill, it goes to the head of the executive branch (president or governor) for consideration. In most cases, the president or governor has 3 options: (1) Sign the bill, making it law; (2) allow the bill to become law without signing it; or (3) veto the bill. Most governmental systems have a provision whereby a bill passed by the legislature will become law after a period of time if the president or governor has not signed it. This is especially useful when the president or governor is sympathetic toward the legislation but for political or other reasons does not want to concur affirmatively with the decision. Emotionally charged legislation is sometimes treated in this way so that the executive will not be placed in the position of approving or disapproving a highly controversial piece of legislation, such as abortion funding.

If the president or governor vetoes a bill, it is returned to the legislature where the opportunity exists to override the veto. It takes a two-thirds majority in both houses of the legislature to override the veto. Both the veto and the opportunity to override it are examples of the system of checks and balances between the various branches of government.

A special type of veto is seen at the end of a legislative session in some governmental systems. As stated, the president or governor often has a time limit within which a bill must be vetoed, or it will become law without his or her concurrence. If the time limit has not expired, but the legislature has adjourned (rather than merely recessing), the bill does not become law by virtue of what is known as a "pocket veto." Ordinarily, the president or governor would still have the option of vetoing the bill because the time limit has not expired. However, the bill cannot be vetoed if the legislature has adjourned; there is no legislature to which it can be returned. Hence, if the legislature adjourns before the president or governor signs the bill and it is not signed within the time limit, the bill will not go into effect. If the bill is signed, it will go into effect even though the legislature has adjourned.

Because legislation has been enacted and the head of the executive branch has signed the legislation, does not mean it will go into effect. Money still must be appropriated to effect the legislation; often, the bill itself does not include an appropriations clause. In such cases, a separate appropriations bill is needed. A bill can be enacted, yet the same legislature that enacted it may fail to provide money for it. For example, all states have legislation authorizing coverage of prescription drugs under state Medicaid programs. Still, these state programs sometimes run out of money to pay for the medication, and in such circumstances the program comes to a halt, even though the legislature mandated that the program exist. Hence, the legislature has control at 2 levels: Establishment of a program and funding of the program.

Executive System

Once a bill has been enacted by the legislature and has gone into effect, it is up to the executive branch of government to administer and enforce the legislation. The bill assigns this responsibility to a subdivision of the executive branch. For example, responsibility for the FDCA has been assigned to the Secretary of the Department of Health and Human Services, who in turn assigns the responsibility to the Food and Drug Administration (FDA).

Administrative agencies participate in 3 types of activity: (1) Executive action when enforcing the law; (2) legislative action when making rules and regulations; and (3) judicial action when interpreting the law to decide when violations have occurred. Thus, administrative agencies are sometimes referred to as minigovernments, engaging in the functions of all 3 branches of government, although they fall under the executive branch. An example will clarify this. Congress enacted a provision in the FDCA that states it is unlawful to render a drug misbranded while in interstate commerce. The FDA promulgated detailed regulations specifying what actions will violate this section (a legislative-type function). If the FDA considers the regulation as violated, the agency will take steps to enforce the regulation (an executive-type function). If the enforcement is challenged, the FDA may hold a hearing to determine whether a violation has indeed occurred (a judicial-type function).

The regulations adopted by administrative agencies are subject to public comment before they go into effect. They are released in an official government publication (the *Federal Register*) with a stated time period during which public comments are accepted. The agency then considers the comments received prior to finalizing the rule by giving public notice again in the same publication, stating the effective date of the regulation. Once finalized, it is printed in the compilation of administrative rules for the government (*Code of Federal Regulations*). However, at the state level Administrative Procedure Acts may vary regarding how this is done.

Actions of administrative agencies are subject to review by the courts. However, in order to secure a court review of an adverse ruling, the following 3 attributes of the case must be demonstrated: Standing, exhaustion, and ripeness. **Standing** means that there must be at least arguable invasion of an individual's interests by the agency action. **Exhaustion** means that every available remedy at the administrative agency level has been used before appeal is allowed. For example, if the agency has extended an opportunity for a rehearing, the individual must have the rehearing before appealing to a court. **Ripeness** means that the facts of the case must be developed fully before a court will review the agency decision. For example, in a classic case a group of pharmaceutical manufacturers attempted to challenge FDA regulation that had been finalized but not enforced (no manufacturer had been cited for violating the regulation). The court ruled that the case lacked ripeness because the agency had not attempted to enforce the rule (*Abbott Laboratories v. Gardner*, 387 U.S. 136 [1967]).

The chances of winning run in favor of the agency when a ruling of an administrative agency is challenged. An administrative ruling on a matter involving agency discretion will not be reversed unless there is a legal mistake, an abuse of discretion, or arbitrary or capricious action by the agency. This is so because the agency is considered an expert in its field, possessing more expertise than the judge. Judges are reluctant to second guess an administrative agency without a showing of one of the transgressions listed above.

Two basic principles of administrative law bear mentioning. The **nondelegation doctrine** refers to the fact that certain acts may be performed only by the legislature, and the legislature cannot delegate authority or responsibility for those acts to an administrative agency. If legislation purports to confer authority that cannot be delegated by the legislature, the delegation of authority is invalid (*Revco Southeast Drug Centers, Inc. v. North Carolina Board of Pharmacy*, 204 S.E.2d 38 [N.C. 1971]).

The other basic principle is known as **ultra vires**. The phrase refers to actions of an agency or organization that extend beyond its legal authority as defined by the legislature. When the legislature enacts law, it must provide both policy and standards in the statute. A good example is the Federal CSA. At the outset, the policy states that drug abuse is detrimental to the health of Americans. The standards in the CSA are found in the provisions in which Congress has stated the criteria for placing controlled drugs in schedules I–V. If Congress did not provide these standards, and the DEA placed drugs in various schedules, such action would be ultra vires, that is, outside the authority of the DEA.

Freedom of Information Act

The Freedom of Information Act (FOIA) was enacted during 1966 and extended the right to request federal agency records or information to any person. It can be found at 5 U.S.C. §552. Upon receipt of a written request, the agency must release the information requested unless it falls within 1 of the 9 exemptions or 3 exclusions of the Act.

There is no central office serving all federal agencies for FOIA purposes; each agency must be contacted individually. Agencies are required to respond to FOIA requests within 20 business days, but that time period does not start until the request is received at the FOIA office of the affected agency unit where the records are maintained. A fee may be assessed for charges associated with copying the requested records.

The publication *A Citizen's Guide on Using the Freedom of Information Act and the Privacy Act of 1974 to Request Government Records* is available at http://thomas.loc.gov/cgi-bin/cpquery/1?cp.

Judicial System

The judicial system is responsible for interpreting the law. This is accomplished at both federal and state levels.

There are 2 types of courts: those of original jurisdiction (also known as trial courts) and appellate courts. The judicial process is initiated in courts of original jurisdiction. They are where trials are held and where testimony and evidence are received. They have a variety of designations in the states, but in the federal court systems they are known as U.S. District Courts (see Figures 1 and 2).

Every state has one highest appellate court, usually called the supreme court. Additionally, many states have intermediate appellate courts to handle the ever-increasing caseload. State trial courts have very broad jurisdiction and may be designated county courts, superior courts, or district courts, depending on the state. There are also courts with limited jurisdiction in specific fields (eg, tax courts, traffic courts, small claims courts).

As a general rule, federal courts will only hear cases that involve either: (1) A federal question (ie, issues arising out of the U.S. Constitution, a federal treaty, a federal statute or regulation) or (2) diversity of citizenship (ie, the lawsuit involves citizens from different states). In a case featuring diversity jurisdiction, a certain minimum amount must be at issue, ie, $75,000. The U.S. Supreme Court has considerable discretion as to what cases it will hear, but it generally reviews cases from federal appellate courts and final judgments from a state's highest court when an important legal issue is involved.

When addressing issues involving the U.S. Constitution, federal courts generally engage in a balancing of competing interests. For example, how important is it for the government to do what it is attempting to do vs how important is it for the individual whose Constitutional rights are being invaded to be protected from the government? A good example from pharmacy is the case of *Virginia Board of Pharmacy v. Virginia Citizens Consumer Council*, a case decided by the U.S. Supreme Court involving freedom of speech of pharmacists. At issue was whether a state agency can enforce a state statute prohibiting all prescription drug price advertising to consumers. Here the Court had to balance (as on the pans of a balance, a good pharmacy metaphor) how important it was to the Commonwealth of Virginia to ban all such advertising against how important it was to pharmacists to have freedom of speech to disseminate this information and, by corollary, whether there was a constitutionally protected right of the citizens to freedom to receive speech. The ban on prescription drug advertising was struck down with a few limited exceptions (425 U.S. 748[1976]).

The American system of justice can be described as an adversarial system; that is, testimony and evidence for both sides of an issue are presented in court. The theory is that truth will best be found when both sides attempt to present the case in the best light for their perspective on the issues.

At trial, the jury has responsibility for answering questions of fact (eg, did the pharmacist indeed dispense the incorrect medication?). The judge answers questions of law (eg, should certain evidence be permitted to be introduced or should a particular person be considered an "expert witness"?).

Civil Trial Procedure

A civil law suit is initiated by the filing of a complaint with the appropriate governmental authorities (eg, the clerk of the court) by the attorney representing the person bringing the lawsuit, known as the plaintiff. A copy of the complaint is required to be delivered to the defendant. Therefore, the first indication someone has that they are being sued could be when the sheriff or marshall serves a complaint. Upon receipt of this important legal document, one should notify his/her attorney and liability insurance company as soon as possible. This is so because, in most jurisdictions, one must respond to the allegation in the complaint within a specified number of days.

One of the first things a plaintiff's attorney must do is decide the proper court or **venue** in which to file the complaint. As described above, cases may be heard in either the federal or state court system. Although there are many exceptions, cases in the state system are usually filed in the county in which the plaintiff or defendant resides.

The time of commencement of a lawsuit is very important because most legal actions must be brought within a certain time limit as prescribed in a **statute of limitations**. This period of time will vary from state to state and will also depend on the nature of the lawsuit. In most situations, negligence actions must be filed within 1 or 2 years, but actions based on contract are often accorded a longer time period.

Usually after initiation of a lawsuit, the judge assigned to the case will have a pretrial conference with the 2 parties in an attempt to determine whether there is any possibility of an out-of-court negotiated settlement. This step is included in an attempt to divert from the overburdened court system cases that do not really require judicial attention. Settlement negotiations that begin here may well continue in parallel with preparation for trial. Research has shown that the vast majority of claims filed against pharmacists and pharmacies are settled out-of-court, usually with the insurer making a modest payment to the potential plaintiff in exchange for an agreement not to proceed with the suit.

Prior to the beginning of trial, a pretrial process known as **discovery** will be carried out. The purpose of this is for each side to have an opportunity to ferret out exactly what testimony and evidence the other side will present at trial. Note, that if it is concluded during the process of discovery that the other side has a really strong case, that may facilitate settlement discussions.

Discovery includes 3 types of activities. A **deposition** is an interview of the other party or one of the witnesses for the other side conducted under oath just as it would be in court.

FEDERAL COURTS:

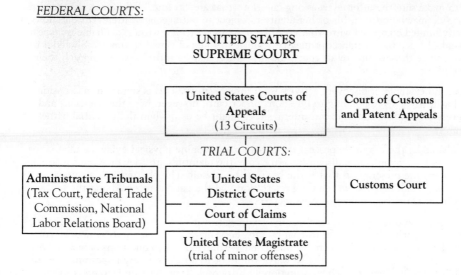

Figure 1. Chart of the federal court system.

STATE COURTS:

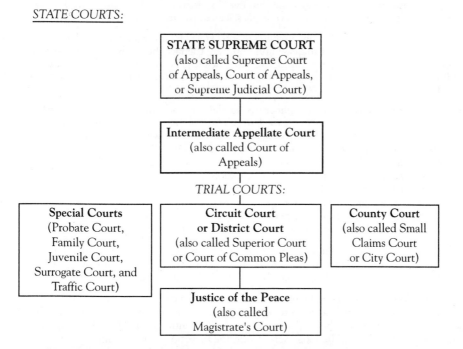

Figure 2. Chart of a typical state court system. In some states, an appeal can be
taken from county court or a specialty court to the circuit court or district court.

However, an important difference lies in the fact that depositions are typically conducted in
a law office, not in a courtroom, and there is no judge present. The absence of a judge can
make a deposition most unpleasant for the party being deposed; there is no one in author-

ity to make sure the attorney is asking questions that are "in line." While the attorney for your side may be present, his or her ability to object to outrageous or irrelevant questions is greatly limited compared with what could be done in court. If a witness is unable to appear at trial, the deposition transcript may be admitted in lieu of actual testimony. Should a witness deviate their testimony in court, the deposition may be introduced to impeach their credibility.

A second example of discovery activity is an **interrogatory**. This is similar to a deposition in that it involves responding to questions under oath; however, here the questions and answers are written, not oral. An interrogatory might be used when the potential witness is far away.

Finally, under the discovery process the parties may **examine physical evidence** related to the case. For example, in a dispensing error case, the plaintiff's attorney may want to see and photocopy the prescription that is the basis of the lawsuit. The pharmacist's attorney, on the other hand, may like to see the prescription vial the patient received and the medication it contains that is alleged to be incorrect.

If no settlement agreement is reached, the trial begins with selection of a jury. While in most states both parties have a right to trial by jury, both may agree that the trial may be conducted without a jury. In such an event, the judge will handle both questions of fact and questions of law. The issue of whether to waive the right to a jury is a very important one and should be made after thorough consultation with counsel. If the decision is to proceed with a jury then **voir dire** begins. This is the part of jury selection where potential jurors are called to be questioned to determine whether they have any biases that may affect their decision. Typical questions in a pharmacy-related case might include whether the prospective juror is a pharmacist or is related to one, has ever experienced a dispensing error by a pharmacist, and so on. Once the jurors have been selected, the trial can begin.

The initial phase of the trial is opening arguments. Here the attorney for the plaintiff goes first, telling the jury the gist of the case and outlining the facts he or she will try to prove from the perspective of the person initiating the lawsuit. The attorney for the plaintiff goes first because the defendant will follow, doing the same but from the perspective of the opposite side.

Following completion of opening arguments, the plaintiff's attorney begins to present his case, calling witnesses and introducing evidence. Witnesses are of 2 types: **fact witnesses** and **expert witnesses**. Fact witnesses testify regarding facts that are within their knowledge (eg, the prescription was presented for dispensing at Neighborhood Pharmacy and John Doe, RPh, was on duty at the time). On the other hand, expert witnesses are permitted to testify regarding their opinions, not facts. The question of whether a particular person has the appropriate background (ie, education, training, knowledge, experience) to be deemed an expert witness is a question of law for the judge to decide. Note that pharmacists could be called as expert witnesses on matters pertaining to medications in cases where they are not a party (plaintiff or defendant) to the lawsuit.

Evidence is introduced at trial, but there must be a basis for it in the testimony of a witness (eg, "Mrs. Smith, is this the prescription vial you received from Pharmacist Doe at Neighborhood Pharmacy?"). If so, then the vial could be introduced as evidence.

During the process of witnesses being examined and evidence being introduced, the attorney for the opposing party may wish to ask the judge to rule on whether the question being asked is proper or whether the evidence can be properly introduced. This is accomplished by making an objection. If the judge agrees with the objection, it is "sustained" and if not, it is "overruled." Motions also may be made during this process, being "granted" or "denied" by the judge as he or she deems appropriate. These objections and motions are critical because they lay the foundation for arguments to be made on appeal should the case be lost at the trial court level. The objections must be made in timely fashion or the right to object is lost. Moreover, if the objection is not made during the trial, the point at issue cannot be raised if the case is appealed.

When an attorney is asking questions of a witness who was called by the side the attorney represents, that is known as "direct examination." Upon conclusion, the attorney for the opposing party can ask questions during "cross examination." If desirable, the plaintiff's attorney can ask further questions of the same witness during "redirect," followed by "recross" by the other side. Generally speaking, the attorneys will try to avoid redirect and recross because it can be confusing to the jury and may even make it appear that the attorneys are badgering the witness, creating ill will with the jury.

Once the plaintiff's attorney has completed presenting his or her case, the defendant's attorney begins to call witnesses for his or her side and the process begins anew.

At the conclusion of both sides presenting their cases, each has an opportunity for a closing argument. This is their opportunity to summarize the facts for the jury and tie their points into a nice, neat bundle for the jury. Following that, the judge gives the jury its instructions. Here the judge provides the jury with essential legal definitions it needs to do its job (eg, the legal definition of negligence). He or she also tells the jury what standard of proof should be applied to the case. The following is a list of the hierarchy of levels of proof:

Highest	Proof beyond a reasonable doubt
Intermediate	Proof by clear and convincing evidence
Lowest	Proof by a preponderance of the evidence

Generally speaking, a civil trial uses the "preponderance" standard whereas a criminal trial requires the "beyond a reasonable doubt" standard.

After receiving instructions, the jury will retire to the jury room to deliberate. When a conclusion has been reached, they will report it to the judge as the verdict. However, note that should the verdict be in favor of the plaintiff who is seeking money damages for injuries suffered, the plaintiff cannot recover funds based on the verdict alone. The judge must enter a judgment in favor of the plaintiff in order for the recovery of money to occur.

Criminal Trial Procedure

The criminal trial process may be initiated in 2 ways: arrest by a governmental agent (eg, police officer, agency investigator with arrest authority) or by **indictment**. An indictment is issued by a grand jury (so designated because it is larger than the petit jury that hears a case trial) that has had evidence presented to it by an attorney for the government. An indictment means that the grand jury has heard sufficient evidence for a trial to be held, which is not surprising because they have heard only the government or prosecution's version of the case. The indictment means that probable cause exists that a crime was committed and that the charged individual should be arrested for trial.

A parallel procedure exists to determine probable cause when the process is initiated by an arrest rather than by indictment. Here, the arrested person must be given a **preliminary hearing**, usually before a magistrate or other minor judicial officer, for there to be an independent determination of whether probable cause existed for the arrest. A preliminary hearing is a test of the evidence to make an early determination of whether the prosecution has a reasonable case and had probable cause to make the arrest. The purpose is to prevent abuse of the governmental power to arrest individuals.

The next phase of the process is **arraignment** where the individual being charged is called forth by name in open court and given the opportunity to enter a plea to the various charges being leveled against him or her. The defendant has 3 options: guilty, not guilty, or nolo contendere (no contest). The last requires the consent of the judge and has the same effect as a plea of guilty but does not admit to the facts charged. Such a plea might be used when admitting to the facts charged has the possibility of subjecting the defendant to a civil suit. It might also be that entering a plea of "nolo" could preserve one's professional license in states where revocation of professional licensure can be based on "conviction of a felony." In some states, a plea of nolo may not equate to conviction. Obviously, close consultation with counsel is needed in such situations.

Prior to the criminal trial beginning, there may be a number of pretrial motions that are appropriate. Such motions may raise legal issues related to the indictment, the arrest, or to other procedures used by the government in prosecuting the case. An example of a common pretrial motion in a criminal case is a motion to suppress physical evidence collected (ie, to ban it from use at trial) because the government agents violated the defendant's constitutional rights by collecting it without a proper search warrant. A motion for discovery also may commonly be seen.

A pretrial process in criminal cases that is similar to negotiations for out-of-court settlement in civil cases is known as **plea bargaining**. Knowing the strengths and weaknesses of each other's arguments and facts, the offer is usually for the prosecution to accept a guilty plea to a lesser charge if the defendant will waive the right to trial by pleading guilty. While such practices are sometimes controversial, they do speed up sanctions against criminals while preserving judicial resources for cases where they are truly needed.

As with a civil case, both sides have a right to jury trial and may waive that right if they desire, therefore, trying the case to clarify issues and eliminate irrelevant or uncontested issues. Both sides present their cases (ie, witnesses, evidence) just as in a civil case.

Another similarity to a civil case lies in the fact that just as a jury verdict in a civil case may not serve as the basis for recovering money damages, a jury verdict in a criminal case is not sufficient to send the defendant to jail. The judge must enter a judgment of conviction.

Because the standard of proof applied in a criminal case is "proof beyond a reasonable doubt," and because the burden of proving the case rests with the prosecution (government), it is possible that the defendant did the nefarious act in question but still goes free because the prosecution could not prove its case. A verdict of not guilty by the jury does not necessarily mean the defendant did not break the law; it may merely reflect the fact that the government could not prove "beyond a reasonable doubt" that the defendant broke the law. This standard has been defined this way:

> A reasonable doubt is a doubt based on reason and common sense – the kind of doubt that would make a reasonable person hesitate to act. Proof beyond a reasonable doubt must, therefore, be proof of such a convincing character that a reasonable person would not hesitate to rely and act upon it in the most important of his or her own affairs.

Appeal

The defendant who has been convicted in a criminal trial has the right to one appeal. The same is true for the plaintiff or defendant who lost a civil case. The appeal can be based on one of 2 arguments: (1) There were procedural errors committed by the judge at the trial court level; or (2) the judge misapplied the law to facts of the case or erred in responding to an objection or a motion, thereby permitting information to be presented at trial that should not have been. Thus, the appeal is almost always based on errors of law and not on questions of fact. Points may be raised on appeal only if the appropriate objection or motion was made in timely fashion during trial. If no objection was made at trial or if it was not timely, the right to argue that point is forfeited.

The right to one appeal generally takes the appellant (the party who lost at trial court level and who, therefore, initiated appeal) to the court of appeals (see Figures 1 and 2). If unsuccessful there, that is the end of the road with regard to appeals by right. To proceed to the Supreme Court, one must petition the court to hear the case. Typically the highest courts in the judicial systems (federal or state) hear arguments in many fewer cases than they are asked to review. With the U.S. Supreme Court, if the Court agrees to hear the case, it is said that the Court has **granted certiorari**, meaning that it has certified that it will review the case.

Conclusion

The judicial system is a creation of humans, not divine; consequently, it has imperfections. There are individuals in prison who did not commit the crimes they have been convicted of, just as there are people walking the streets who should be incarcerated. While it does have defects, the system in current use has obvious advantages over those adopted in earlier times (eg, dunking alleged Salem witches, walking across hot coals, keelhauling sailors). When you are asked to participate in the system as a witness or juror, please do not attempt to escape this responsibility of citizenship; it is an important one that makes the system work as well as it does.

THE ATTORNEY-CLIENT RELATIONSHIP

When a person asks that someone serve as his or her attorney-at-law and the second person accepts that relationship, a special affiliation is created. Over the centuries, special rules have evolved to govern the attorney-client relationship. One example is what a client tells his or her attorney is absolutely confidential and may not be disclosed without the permission of the client. This is similar to the completely confidential relationship existing between physician and patient, as well as between clergyman and parishioner.

Selecting an attorney is a very important decision. Attorneys have areas of focus in their practices just as do other professionals. Some may specialize in tax or business matters while others may be litigators or estate planning specialists. It may be that the attorney who handles the transfer of title when you purchase your home may not be the best selection should you find yourself facing a civil suit or criminal charges.

POWER OF ATTORNEY

In its most basic form, the word "attorney" means one who acts on behalf of another, such as an agent. Thus, when the qualifier "attorney-at-law" is added, it is clear that the individual acts on your behalf on legal matters.

A "power of attorney" is a grant of authority to another to act on your behalf. The person creating the power is designated the "principal," and the agent who is to act on his or her behalf is called the "attorney-in-fact." Generally, there are 2 types of powers of attorney: (1) General Power of Attorney authorizes the agent or attorney to conduct all business and all other affairs of the principal; and (2) Special or Limited Power of Attorney grants authority to perform a specific transaction in a specific manner. An example of the latter would be a power of attorney executed to authorize another to sign DEA order forms in your name (see Executing Order Forms).

In recent years, a good deal of interest has focused on **"durable" powers of attorney**. These are documents containing words such as, "This power of attorney shall not be affected by disability of the principal." Language such as that is useful when designating others to make health care decisions on your behalf should you become mentally incapacitated.

HOW TO FIND AND READ THE LAW

Legal Citation Forms

In reading legal materials, one encounters legal terminology and symbols. This discussion is included to provide the reader with a brief introduction to legal citation forms so that the citations (references) found in this book, as well as in other materials, will not appear intimidating.

Official guidance about the format for legal citations is available in *The Bluebook: A Uniform System of Citation* (17th ed.). Cambridge, MA: The Harvard Law Review Association (2000).

Court Cases

Case titles are usually the names of the parties involved separated by a small "v" meaning versus (eg, *Smith v. Jones*). At the trial court level, the name of the party bringing the suit appears first; in the example just given, Smith (the plaintiff) has brought suit against Jones (the defendant). If one of the parties appeals the decision after judgment at the trial court level, the name of the party pursuing appeal will appear first. So it would be entered as *Smith v. Jones* or *Jones v. Smith*, depending on who appealed the decision. Notice that it is the same lawsuit, but the names of the parties may be reversed. Sometimes, a case will be decided under different names. This often occurs with suits brought against federal officials. A case might be filed as *Miller v. Bates*, the latter being the secretary of a federal agency. If Bates leaves office, the new secretary might be substituted as a defendant, resulting in the same case being known as *Miller v. Walker* (the new secretary).

A court can have 2 types of jurisdiction (the authority of the court to decide cases). **In personam** jurisdiction applies to persons. **In rem** jurisdiction, on the other hand, is jurisdiction over things. Under the FDCA, jurisdiction exists both ways, and strange case names are often encountered. When in rem jurisdiction occurs, the name of the thing appears in the case title (eg, *United States v. An Artice of Drug...Labeled...Colchicine*).

Some abbreviations commonly encountered in case titles are:

In re	In the matter of or concerning an inanimate object (eg, a suit brought to condemn or destroy some adulterated or misbranded pharmaceuticals).
Ex rel.	Upon relation or information (eg, legal proceedings instituted by the attorney general or other governmental official on the information of and at the instigation of a person who has a private interest in the matter).
Re.	In the case of (eg, where there is only one person involved, such as might exist where a person with Alzheimer's disease is being declared legally incompetent).

When a citation is to a case report (the written opinion of the court), the name of the case will be followed by the citation. For example, *United States v. Johnson*, 221 U.S. 488 (1911) means that the report of this case is found in volume 221 of *United States Reports* (the reports of cases in the U.S. Supreme Court) on page 488. Additionally, the date of the decision is given. Some common abbreviations used for the case reporters are included in the Common Abbreviations for Case Reporters table.

Included in parentheses after the case name, volume number, volume name, and page number may be other information of importance. With case reports in *United States Reports*, the date alone will appear in parentheses. With other decisions, the parentheses will contain an indication of what court issued the decision. The U.S. Courts of Appeals cases in the *Federal Reporter* series will indicate which of the 13 circuit courts of appeals issued the decision. For example, 298 F.3d 1217 (11th Cir. 2002) means that the U.S. Court of Appeals for the Eleventh Circuit decided the case in 2002 (see The 13 United States Judicial Circuits table). The circuit is indicated in a U.S. Court of Appeals decision because, under stare decisis, the court ruling is binding only in that circuit.

If a decision has been made by a U.S. District Court, the parenthetical statement will indicate which district court was involved. For example, *Reinert v. Larkin*, 211 F.Supp. 2d 589 (E.D. Pa. 2002) means that the U.S. District Court for the Eastern District of Pennsylvania rendered the decision during 2002.

Statutes

Statutes follow the same basic style of citation. Statutes are arranged into **titles** and are divided into **sections**. For example, the FDCA begins at 21 U.S. Code §321 - Title 21 of the U.S. Code, Section 321. The mark § means section. The marks §§ mean sections.

Regulations

Regulations are proposed by federal administrative agencies in the *Federal Register*, a daily publication of substantial size. Citations in the *Federal Register* use volume number and page number, for example, 65 Fed. Reg. 82462 (2000).

Once regulations have been finalized and adopted by the agency, they appear in the *Code of Federal Regulations* (CFR). The citations here refer to title number and section, for example 21 CFR §120.200.

Electronic access to legal information is expanding at a great rate. Westlaw and Lexis are 2 national electronic services to which law offices and law libraries can subscribe to locate court decisions. In addition, publications emanating from the federal government may be available electronically. For example, the following are World Wide Web addresses for federal sources:

Status of bills or hearing in Congress
http://thomas.loc.gov

Federal Register
http://www.access.gpo.gov/su_docs/aces/
aces140.html

Code of Federal Regulations
http://www.access.gpo.gov/nara/cfr/cfr-table-
search.html
http://www.findlaw.com

U.S. Code
http://uscode.house.gov/
http://www.findlaw.com/casecode/

State governments are also becoming active in this area so that statutes and regulations at that level may be accessible electronically.

Common Abbreviations for Case Reporters		
Abbreviation	Title	Courts included
U.S.	*United States Reports*	United States Supreme Court
F. F.2d[1], F.3d[2]	*Federal Reporter*	Federal circuit courts of appeals
F.Supp.	*Federal Supplement*	United States district courts
A. A.2d	*Atlantic Reporter*[2]	CT, DE, MD, ME, NH, NJ, PA, RI, VT
N.E. N.E.2d	*Northeastern Reporter*[2]	IL, IN, MA, NY, OH
N.W. N.W.2d	*Northwestern Reporter*[2]	IA, MI, MN, ND, NE, SD, WI
P. P.2d	*Pacific Reporter*[2]	AK, AZ, CA, CO, HI, ID, KS, MT, NM, NV, OK, OR, UT, WA, WY
So. So.2d	*Southern Reporter*[2]	AL, FL, LA, MS
S.E. S.E.2d	*Southeastern Reporter*[2]	GA, NC, SC, VA, WV
S.W. S.W.2d	*Southwestern Reporter*[2]	AR, KY, MO, TN, TX,

[1] The abbreviation 2d means the second series of volumens collecting specific reports (eg, F.2d means *Federal Reporter*, second series.
[2] The same is true for 3d (which indicates third series).

These regional reporters include decisions of all appellate courts in these states.

The 13 United States Judicial Circuits	
Circuit	States included
1st	MA, ME, NH, PR, RI
2nd	CT, NY, VT
3rd	DE, NJ, PA, VI
4th	MD, NC, SC, VA, WV
5th	LA, MS, TX
6th	KY, MI, OH, TN
7th	IL, IN, WI
8th	AR, IA, MN, MO, ND, NE, SD
9th	AK, AZ, CA, HI, ID, MT, NV, OR, WA
10th	CO, KS, NM, OK, UT, WY
11th	AL, FL, GA
D.C.	DC
Federal	Federal

INFORMATION ABOUT LAW SCHOOL

Some pharmacy students or pharmacists have an interest in attending law school. The purpose of this brief section is to give them some introductory information about this and to refer them to more detailed sources of insight.

Admission to law school requires a baccalaureate degree from an accredited institution of higher education. Contrary to common opinion, there is no "prelaw" major as an undergraduate. "Prelaw" is an intention, not an academic field of study. While many who go to law school have studied political science, history, or English while an undergraduate, no particular major is required for admission into law school. Consequently, one with a degree in pharmacy would meet the criteria for admission.

Law schools base their admission decisions heavily on 2 factors: cumulative grade-point average on prior academic work and a score on the Law School Admission Test (LSAT). This admission test is administered numerous times per year at colleges and universities around the country. For information about the examination, a list of test sites, or to request a current copy of the LSAT/LSDAS Registration and Information Book, write or call:

Law School Admissions Council
P.O. Box 2000
Newtown, PA 18940-2000
215/968-1001

Information is also available on the Internet at: http://www.lsac.org/.

The Law School Admissions Council (at the same address) also publishes a valuable book entitled The Official Guide to U.S. Law Schools. One main value of this book is that it provides a grid that indicates how many students with a certain GPA/LSAT profile applied to each school the prior year and how many were admitted. This enables one to focus on applying to law schools where a reasonable possibility of gaining admission exists.

While the cumulative GPA and LSAT score are the primary factors law school admission committees focus on, they also take other factors into account while attempting to create an academically talented and diverse entering class. As a result, the application essay can be quite important as can be the letters of reference submitted to the Admissions Committee.

There are over 175 law schools accredited by the American Bar Association. For a list of accredited law schools in the United States, write to:

American Bar Association
750 North Lake Shore Drive
Chicago, IL 60611-4497

The list is also available on the Internet at: http://www.abanet.org/legaled/approved.html.

Note that there are a number of law schools in this country that are not accredited by the ABA but are accredited by an agency of the state government in the jurisdiction where the school is located. Graduates of these schools may only practice law in the state that accredits the lawyer's alma mater.

The law school curriculum is 3 years in length. Usually, the first year consists of all required courses. After that, course decisions are left to the student. For this reason, it is usually advantageous to attend law school with a large number of course offerings. For example, pharmacists attending law school might be interested in enrolling in courses such as Health Law or Food and Drug Law. Not all law schools in the United States offer these courses. In response to the commonly asked question—no, there is no law school which specializes in "pharmacy law." Application of the legal principles and doctrines to pharmacy must be done by the student.

Here is a list of sources of further information about law school for pharmacists and careers in pharmacy law:

Woods WE. Career opportunities as a pharmacist-attorney. *The Squibb Review for Pharmacy Students*. 1965;IV(1):1-4.

Steeves RF. Pharmacist-lawyers. *Journal of the American Pharmaceutical Association*. 1967;NS7:145, 151.

Fink JL III. Pharmacist-lawyers. *Journal of the American Pharmaceutical Association*. 1974;NS14:565-569.

Anonymous. Pharmacists who are lawyers. *American Druggist*. 1974:34-35, 39-40.

Fink JL III. Law school for pharmacists? *American Pharmacy*. 1981;NS21:492-493.

Brushwood DB, Cole MG. The case of pharmacy law as a career. *Legal Aspects of Pharmacy Practice*. 1985;(Aug/Sept):1-2.

Brushwood DB. Career opportunities for lawyer-pharmacists. *Tomorrow's Pharmacist*. 1986;8:4-5.

Readers may also be interested to know that there is a national organization of pharmacist-lawyers and others who have an interest in issues involving the 2 professions. Pharmacists and students may become members if interested. The mailing address for the organization is:

American Society for Pharmacy Law
1224 Centre West (Suite 400B)
Springfield, IL 62704-2185
217/391-0219
217/793-0041 (fax)
Website: http://www.aspl.org

Once one graduates from law school, he or she must sit for the examination to determine whether sufficient competence in the law exists for the law school graduate to be admitted to the practice of law. The examination is known as the "bar exam" and is a multi-day exercise composed of both multiple choice and essay questions. As for pharmacy, many states have established continuing education requirements for law. Typically, an attorney must complete 15 hours of continuing education coursework each year to be eligible to continue in active practice.

SOURCES OF ADDITIONAL INFORMATION

Angorn RA. Manslaughter and the pharmacist. *Leg Asp Pharm Pract*. 1987;10:1-3.

Brushwood DB. State's right to treat a prisoner forcibly with anti-psychotic drugs without a judicial hearing. *Am J Hosp Pharm*. 1991;48:309-310.

Brushwood DB, Myers MJ. The statute of limitations. *US Pharm*. 1983;8:10.

Fern FH. Anatomy of a lawsuit. *US Pharm*. 1989;14:6.

Fink JL III. Giving legal references a fair trial. *Leg Asp Pharm Pract*. 1983;6:2-3.

Fink JL III. What to expect when a lawsuit is started. *US Pharm*. 1979;4:17-22.

Fink JL III. Your rights when you're wronged. *Leg Asp Pharm Pract*. 1985;8:3-4.

Fox LA. If you are served with a complaint ... do not panic. *South Drug/South Pharm J*. 1977;69:34-35.

Fox LA. The logistics of a lawsuit. *US Pharm*. 1985;10:28-29, 32, 61.

Fraser GL, Davis TD. The pharmacist as an expert witness. *Am J Hosp Pharm*. 1990;47:2082-2085.

Metzger JP, Pomerance RM. Guidelines to presenting testimony in court. *US Pharm*. 1987;12:69-72.

Metzger JP, Gardner RE. How to become a better defendant in a lawsuit. *US Pharm*. 1988;13:29-30, 53.

Montagne M, Pugh CB, Fink JL III. Testing for drug use, part 2: legal, social, and ethical concerns. *Am J Hosp Pharm*. 1988;45:1509-1522.

Simonsmeier LM, Fink JL III. Legal implications of drug testing in the workplace. *Am Pharm*. 1988;NS28:454-461.

Simonsmeier LM. Pharmacists and the First Amendment. *Leg Asp Pharm Pract*. 1988;11:8-12.

Strauss S. The federal register system. *US Pharm*. 1983;8:27-29, 32-34, 24.

Strauss S. Useful facts about the law and lawyers. *US Pharm*. 1984;9:33-34.

Strauss S. What to expect when a lawsuit is started. II: the appeal. *US Pharm*. 1979;4:20-24.

Strauss S, Forbes DS. Enactment of a federal law. *US Pharm*. 1982;7:17-19, 22-23.

Thomisen JT. Public policy protects hospital quality assurance documents from discovery in litigation. *Am J Hosp Pharm*. 1991;48:1989-1991.

Vivian JC. Experts and evidence. *US Pharm*. 2002;27:86-88.

Vivian JC. Forum shopping. *US Pharm*. 1995;20:81-82.

Vivian JC. How to prepare for a deposition. *Am J Hosp Pharm*. 1992;49:820, 822, 828.

Vivian JC. Necessity for expert witnesses. *US Pharm*. 1999;24:48, 54-55.

Vivian JC. States rights v. federal rights in assisted suicide. *US Pharm*. 27:06. http://www.uspharmacist.com/oldformat.asp?url=newlook/files/Phar/ACFA8DC.htm&pub_id=8&article_id=901

Chapter 2

Regulation of Pharmaceuticals

Introduction, 27
 Authority for Federal Regulation of Drug Products, 27
Food, Drug, and Cosmetic Act, 27
 Historical Background of the Act, 27
 The Sulfanilamide Tragedy, 28
 The Durham-Humphrey Amendment, 29
 The Thalidomide Tragedy, 29
 Kefauver-Harris Amendment, 30
 Efficacy and the Definition of a "New Drug," 30
 Further Case Law on What Constitutes a New Drug, 31
 New Drugs, 31
 Drug Efficacy Study, 32
 Further Amendments to the Act, 32
  Drug Price Competition and Patent Term Restoration Act of 1984, 32
  The Prescription Drug User Fee Act of 1992, 33
  The Food and Drug Administration Modernization Act of 1997, 33
   (1) Pediatric Studies of Drugs, 33
   (2) Pharmacy Compounding, 33
   (3) Positron Emission Tomography Compounding, 34
   (4) Expediting Study and Approval of Fast Track Drugs, 34
   (5) Information Program on Clinical Trials for Serious or Life-
    Threatening Diseases, 34
   (6) Elimination of Certain Labeling Requirements, 34
   (7) Dissemination of Off-Label Treatment Information, 34
 Liability Under the FD&C Act, 35
 Doctrine of Respondeat Superior, 35
  Dotterweich, 35
  Park, 36
 Recordkeeping under the FD&C Act, 37
  Statute of Limitations, 37
  Labels on Commercial Containers, 38
  Package Inserts/Professional Product Labeling, 38
   FDA New Regulations, 38
  Patient Package Inserts, 39
   Historical Background of Patient Package Inserts, 39
  MedGuides, 41
  Unit-Dose Labeling, 42
  Labeling of Customized Medication Packages, 43
 Regulation of Dietary Supplements, 43
  Historically, 43
  Dietary Supplement Health and Education Act of 1994, 43
 Drug Approval Process, 44
  Synopsis of New Drug Application Procedures, 44
   Drug Recall, 45

Food, Drug, and Cosmetic Act *(cont.)*
    Drug Approval Process *(cont.)*
        Labeling of Drugs, 46
            Special Labeling, 46
            Labeling of Nonprescription Drugs, 46
        Current Good Manufacturing Practices (CGMP), 48
        Important Points about the FD&C Act, 49

Regulation of Pharmaceutical Products, 50
    Definition of Drug, 50
    Intended Use, 50
        Prescription Drug Marketing Act, 50
        Drug Price Competition and Patent Term Restoration Act of 1984, 52
        FDA, 53
        Misbranding and Adulteration, 53
            United States Pharmacopeia Role, 54
            Adulterated Drugs, 54
            Misbranded Drugs, 55
            The Prescription Label, 58
        Receipt of Misbranded or Adulterated Drugs, 59
        Prescription Drugs, 59
        Nonprescription (Over-the-Counter) Drugs, 60
            Pharmacy Labeling of Bulk Products, 60
            Veterinary Prescription Labeling, 61

Dispensing of Pharmaceuticals, 61
    Prescription Requirements, 61
        Authority to Prescribe, 61
            Prescribing by Pharmacists, 62
            Collaborative Drug Therapy Management, 62
        Physician Dispensing, 63
        Generic Substitution, 64
            Drug Product Selection, 64
                Controversies Surrounding Drug Product Selection, 66
                Brand Name vs Generic Drugs, 66
                Bioavailability and Bioequivalency, 67
                Therapeutic Substitution, 68
                Hospital Formulary System, 68
                The Concept of Prior Consent, 68
                Medicaid Prescriptions and Product Selection, 69
            The Orange Book, 70
                The FDA Center for Drug Evaluation and Research – Approved Drug Products with Therapeutic Equivalence Evaluations, 70

Dispensing of Pharmaceuticals *(cont.)*
    Prescriptions Transmitted via Fax or Electronically, 72
        Prescription Refills, 73
            Recording of Prescription Refills, 73
            Refill Authorization, 73
        Out-of-State Prescriptions, 74
        Foreign Prescriptions, 74
        Mail-Order Pharmacies, 75
            Federal Antitrust Lawsuit, 76
        Burden on Interstate Commerce, 77

Postal Regulations, 78
    Nonmailable Items, 78
    Mailing of Prescription Medicines, 79
    Shipment of Chemicals, 79
    Other Nonmailable Items, 79
    Package Shipping or Courier Services, 79

Repackaging, 80
    Repackaging of Injectables for In-Hospital Use, 80
    Expiration Dating on Drugs Repackaged into Unit-Dose Containers, 80
    Historical Background of Pharmacy Compounding, 80
    Compliance Policy Guide, 81
    FDA Modernization Act—503A—Compounding—Current Status, 83
    Regulatory Action Guidance, 85
    Compounding *otc* Products, 85
    Compounding Bulk Chemicals, 85
        PET Compounding, 87
            CGMPs for PET Compounding, 87

Drug Exporting and Importing, 87
    Drug Exporting, 87
        Shipping Regulations, 88
        Specific Exporting Procedures, 88
        Export/Import Firms, 88
    Importing Drugs for Personal Use, 88

Marketing of Pharmaceuticals, 89
    Promotion for "Off-Label" Uses, 89
    Advertising, 90
        Advertising Prescription Drugs to Health Care Professionals, 90
        Direct-to-Consumer Advertising, 90
        Advertising of *otcs*, 90
            False Advertising, 91

Miscellaneous Issues, 92
  A Third Class of Drug Products, 92
  Veterinary Pharmaceuticals, 92
  Use of Approved Drugs for Nonapproved Uses, 94
  History of FDA Policy, 94
  Labeling of Ipecac Syrup, 96
  Drug Product Identification, 96
  National Drug Code, 96
  Reporting of Drug Product Problems/Medication Errors, 97

Other Relevant Legislation, 97
  Health Insurance Portability and Accountability Act of 1996, 97
      Health Insurance Reform, 97
      Administrative Simplification, 98
      Enforcement, 98
      Privacy Regulations, 98
      Sources of Information, 98
  Department for Health and Human Services (HHS) CMS, 99
      HIPAA Information, Compliance and Enforcement, 99
  OBRA '90, 99
      Drug Use Review, 100
      Counseling, 100
      Patient Medication Records, 101
      Impact of OBRA '90, 101
  Federal Hazardous Substances Act, 101
      Historical Background, 101
      Hazardous Substances Defined, 102
      Required Labeling, 102
      Pre-emption, 103
  Poison Prevention Packaging Act of 1970, 104
      Substances Requiring Special Packaging, 105
      Substances Covered under the Poison Prevention Packaging Act and
          Exemptions from the Act, 106
  Consumer Product Safety Act, 106
  Poison Sale Laws, 107
  Federal Anti-Tampering Act, 107
  Electronic Signatures in Global and National Commerce Act (E-Sign), 108
      Electronic Signatures, 108
      Electronic Recordkeeping, 108
  Federal Alcohol Regulations, 109
      Taxing of Retail Dealers, 109
  Kinds of Alcohol, 109
      Ethyl Alcohol, 109
      Denatured Alcohols, 109
      Isopropyl Alcohol, 110
  Use of Tax-Free Alcohol, 110
      Summary of Federal Rules for the Purchase and Use of Tax-Free
          Alcohol, 110
      Proof Gallon Measures, 111
      Storage of Tax-Free Alcohol, 111

Pharmacy Practice and the Health Care System, 111
   Medicare and Medicaid, 111
      Medicare, 111
         Part A Hospitalization Insurance, 112
         Part B Medical Insurance, 112
      Medicare — Conditions of Participation, 112
         Hospital Standards, 113
         Long-Term Care Facility Standards, 113
      Medicaid, 113
         Outpatient Prescription Drug Coverage, 114
      Medicare and Medicaid Fraud and Abuse Legislation, 114
   National Practitioner Databank, 114
   Health Maintenance Organizations, 115
      Medicare and HMOs, 115
      The Federal HMO Act, 115
      HMO Regulations, 116

Study Questions, 117

Regulation of Pharmaceuticals

INTRODUCTION

Pharmaceuticals are products subject to an extensive regulatory framework. From the production line where the product is created and on through the channels of distribution, special rules apply to these items that set them apart from other commercial goods. The regulatory environment within which pharmaceutical manufacturers and pharmacists work with these products can be complex and even daunting. It is the purpose of this chapter/section to provide the reader with an introduction to and overview of regulation of pharmaceuticals.

Authority for Federal Regulation of Drug Products

States derive their authority to regulate intrastate (within one state's borders) commerce, such as drug distribution, from the Tenth Amendment to the US Constitution. The powers granted to or reserved for the states are those that are not assigned specifically to the federal government or those that are prohibited specifically from the states.

FEDERAL FOOD, DRUG, AND COSMETIC ACT (FD&C)

The FD&C Act (21 U.S.C. §301 et seq.) is divided into 9 chapters, some of which are not discussed in *Pharmacy Law Digest* because they deal exclusively with food and cosmetics. Only specific provisions of the Act concerning the pharmacist and pharmacy practice are discussed. Selected portions of the Act are reproduced in *Pharmacy Law Digest* within the applicable text. The entire Act may be found on the Internet at http://www.gpo.gov.

Historical Background of the Act

Congress has the authority to regulate drugs pursuant to its powers under the "commerce clause" (Article 1, Section 8) of the US Constitution, which grants Congress authority to regulate commerce among the states. This type of commerce is known as interstate commerce. The federal government's control over interstate commerce extends to control over intrastate commerce in many instances. For example, the FD&C Act regulates the distribution of drugs between states, but it also regulates the distribution of drugs within a state (eg, the selling and dispensing of drugs by a neighborhood pharmacist whose transactions are entirely intrastate). The federal intrastate regulation is constitutional because the courts have decided that intrastate transactions may have a significant effect on interstate commerce.

The first federal statute designed to protect US citizens from harmful drugs was the Import Drug Act of 1848 (9 Stat. 237), which prohibited the importation of adulterated drugs. It was passed because antimalarial medication for US troops in Mexico was found to be grossly adulterated and lacking in potency.

The next federal legislation concerning adulterated articles was enacted on August 30, 1890, when Congress enacted a law to prevent importation of dangerously adulterated articles for food and drink. The law worked by the simple process that the President of the United States, upon assumption that adulterated articles were-to be imported, could issue a proclamation prohibiting their entry. In 1902, Congress passed a law (32 Stat. 632) prohibiting the introduction of falsely labeled dairy products into interstate commerce (21 U.S.C. §16).

The initial state legislation, an 1848 Virginia statute, imposed a jail sentence on anyone who fraudulently adulterated drugs that were intended for sale. Ohio passed a similar law in 1858.

However, the primary forerunner of today's Food Drug and Cosmetic Act, was enacted on June 30, 1906, with the passing of the Wiley-Heyburn Act, or the Federal Pure Food and Drug Act of 1906, which took effect in 1907. The Act was prompted, in part, by public concern over unsanitary practices in the drug and food industries, resulting in lack of purity.

The 1906 Federal Pure Food and Drug Act was a major advancement in prohibiting adulteration and misbranding of food and drugs in interstate commerce. Drug adulteration was defined in the 1906 Act to the extent that it prohibited drugs of substandard strength or purity (below USP or NF standards) unless the drugs were labeled to show how their strength, quality, and purity differed from those of the formulary standard. This concept of adulteration is carried through to today's law (see §501 [b] of the Act). The 1906 Act, with several minor amendments, lasted until 1938 (shortly after what has become known as the sulfanilamide tragedy, described below) — when Congress adopted new legislation.

The Sulfanilamide Tragedy

In 1937, the S.E. Massengill Company marketed *Sulfanilamide Elixir*, which contained 40 grains of sulfanilamide per fluid ounce in a solution with diethylene glycol. The diethylene glycol solvent was suggested by the firm's chief chemist in response to its marketing department's demand for a liquid preparation of sulfanilamide, a "sulfa" drug used to treat hemolytic streptococcal infections. Toxicity tests of the product were not made, and very little was known about the inherent toxicity of diethylene glycol (a deadly poison now used as a type of permanent automotive antifreeze). More than 100 individuals reportedly died from *Sulfanilamide Elixir* before the FDA pulled it from the market, acting pursuant to a technical labeling violation under the 1906 Act. This incident propelled the passage of the 1938 FD&C Act.

The 1938 Federal FC&C Act is the basis of today's law. It required anyone who wished to market a drug product to prove its safety to the FDA before it could be sold. This was the beginning of the "approval process" for drugs in the United States — the process requiring the submission of a New Drug Application (NDA). Any compound that fell within the definition of a "new drug" under the act required an NDA to be submitted to the FDA. The Act, as it was originally passed, did not require a manufacturer to prove the effectiveness of the drug product. That requirement came about in a later amendment to the Act.

The 1938 Act contains a loophole of sorts known as the "grandfather clause," It exempts certain drugs that were on the market on the day prior to the effective date of the Act (in 1938) from having to meet the FDA's preapproval requirements. Although few of those drugs are still marketed, today, many of those have already obtained an "approval" via NDA or Abbreviated New Drug Application (ANDA).

Before the 1938 FD&C Act, there was very limited federal or state control over the retail sale of nonnarcotic and nonpoisonous drugs. There was the 1914 Harrison Narcotic Act that regulated the distribution of narcotics, and there were various state laws restricting the retail sale of poisons. However, there was no federal comprehensive law that regulated the dispensing of controlled substances or other drugs.

The effects of the 1938 Act were on the 1890 federal statute prohibiting the import of adulterated drugs and the 1906 Federal Pure Food and Drug Act. These Acts did not appreciably affect intrastate commerce, and the community pharmacist in general was at legal liberty to dispense all manner of nonnarcotic and nonpoisonous drugs without a prescription. In the absence of state restrictions, the pharmacist, prior to the 1939 effective date of the 1938 Federal Act, could sell even barbiturates without a prescription.

In the 1930s, sensational drug abuse cases contributed to the enactment of the Food, Drug, and Cosmetic Act by Congress. The Act restricted certain drugs to be dispensed only by the pharmacist and dispensed pursuant to a prescription only. The prescriptions were nonrefillable. However, some pharmacists did not take the Act too seriously, especially in light of their history of relatively free dispensing powers. Furthermore, it was believed that the Act's labeling requirements only applied to interstate drug distribution as opposed to intrastate distribution.

The 1948 US Supreme Court case of *United States v. Sullivan*, 332 U.S. 689 (1948), helped to clarify the real effect of the Act. That case involved a community pharmacist who sold sulfathiazole tablets over-the-counter, labeled with only the drug name and dispensed in the pharmacist's own container. The Court held that his action, in effect dispensing without a prescription, violated a misbranding provision of the FD&C Act (§301[k]). More importantly, the Act in that case was applied judicially to an intrastate transaction, which extended the powers of the Federal Act over intrastate as well as interstate commerce.

The Durham-Humphrey Amendment

After the Sullivan case, pharmaceutical organizations worked for an amendment to the Act to elucidate the dispensing obligations of the pharmacist. The amendment was enacted in 1951 as the Durham-Humphrey Amendment, named for Carl Durham, a pharmacist representing North Carolina in the US House of Representatives, and Hubert Humphrey, a pharmacist representing Minnesota in the US Senate.

The Durham-Humphrey Amendment (FDCA §503[b][1]; 21 U.S.C. §353[b][1]) was enacted in 1951 and took effect in 1952. At the federal level, the amendment distinguished drugs requiring a prescription from drugs not requiring a prescription (otc drugs). The amendment did this by defining the kinds of drugs that cannot be used safely without medical supervision. The amendment restricted the sale of such drugs by requiring a prescription from a licensed practitioner and dispensing only pursuant to that prescription.

In addition to requiring a prescription for specific drugs, the Durham-Humphrey Amendment also provided statutory provisions for the receipt of oral prescriptions as well as provisions allowing for the refilling of prescriptions.

The Durham-Humphrey Amendment also provided that prescription drugs be dispensed:

(1) Upon the written prescription of a practitioner licensed by law to administer such drugs;
(2) upon the practitioner's oral prescription, to be promptly reduced to writing and filed by the pharmacist;
(3) by refilling a written or oral prescription if the refill was authorized by the prescriber either on the original prescription or orally, and then reduced to writing and filed by the pharmacist; or
(4) by administration (dispensing) directly by the practitioner.

The provision of drug regulation most likely to be violated (usually through carelessness) by the practicing pharmacist is the Durham-Humphrey Amendment or a comparable state law, which prohibits unauthorized refills of legend drug prescriptions. It is important to note that retail sale and distribution of prescription drugs require that a practitioner prescribe or dispense the drug.

Refilling the prescription is allowed only if it specifically is authorized in the prescription or if authorization is obtained subsequently from the prescribing practitioner or from another licensed practitioner. If the original prescription does not contain an indication of refills, it is by law deemed to be a "no refill" prescription and express authorization must be obtained prior to refilling it. Prescriptions for controlled substances have additional refill restrictions.

The terms "physician," "prescriber," and "practitioner," when used in this discussion, refer to the individual who is permitted by the jurisdiction or state in which he or she practices to prescribe or administer drugs in the course of professional practice. The determination of who may prescribe/administer is made by the state, not by the federal government. (See Civil Liability chapter.)

The Thalidomide Tragedy

In late 1961, the "thalidomide disaster" began to unfold. Thalidomide was marketed in West Germany under the trade name Contergan by Chemie Grünenthal in 1958 and was sold without prescription as a tranquilizer in the German Federal Republic until April 1961, when the drug was recognized as causing polyneuritis in adults. In November 1961, the drug first was believed to cause the severe birth defect phocomelia, or "seal limbs," and by that time thousands of infants had been born in West Germany without one or both arms or legs or with only partially formed extremities. Grünenthal withdrew the drug from the West German market on November 26, 1961.

A number of drug firms had obtained licenses to make thalidomide, and its distribution was worldwide. In the United States, the William S. Merrell Company had distributed the drug experimentally in 1960 under the trade name *Kevadon*, but the FDA never gave final approval to the NDA the company had submitted. The FDA's timely action in withholding *Kevadon* approval was because of the judgment of FDA medical officer, Dr. Frances Kelsey, who insisted on further proof of safety. Even so, 29,413 patients in the United States had been involved in the human clinical trial testing of *Kevadon*. When the evidence that thalidomide was teratogenic (causing harm to the human fetus) was established, the FDA agents picked up almost all of the *Kevadon* in circulation. Consequently, only a very small number of phocomelia cases were reported in this country.

Thalidomide had been widely tested around the world as a sedative and tranquilizer. It was later found to act as an antinauseant in pregnancy, and its widespread use for that indication brought the horrible side effect to the surface. The lesson of the thalidomide tragedy is that serious side effects caused by certain new drugs, or caused by new uses for old drugs, may not be discovered until the drug has had very wide clinical use — after some damage already has occurred.

In 1962, the thalidomide tragedy was the impetus for the Kefauver-Harris Amendment, otherwise known as the 1962 Drug Amendments, to the Food, Drug, and Cosmetic Act.

Kefauver-Harris Amendment

In the late 1950s and early 1960s, Senator Estes Kefauver of Tennessee led Congressional hearings concerning antitrust legislation and drug pricing. However, the hearings conditioned public attitudes toward a move for more stringent federal regulation of the drug industry.

The Kefauver-Harris Amendment, which became effective in 1963, required substantiation to the FDA of both the safety and efficacy of all drugs introduced after 1962 and of drugs for which NDAs had been approved between 1938 and 1962. Any compound falling under the revised definition of a "new drug" as defined in §201(p) of the Act required such substantiation. The amendments required a positive act of approval by the FDA (as opposed to automatic approval if not disapproved by the FDA under the previous version of the Act). The amendments also contained a typical grandfather clause exempting from both safety and efficacy requirements the drugs on the market from 1906 to the day prior to the effective date of the 1938 Act, as those drugs were never subject to NDAs.

Efficacy and the Definition of a "New Drug"

Dispute arose between the pharmaceutical firms and the FDA as to how the 1962 Drug Amendments affected the efficacy requirement for drugs approved by the FDA between 1938 and 1962. The issue was determined, somewhat, in three separate United States Supreme Court cases all decided on the same day-June 18, 1973. In *Weinberger v. Hynson, Wescott and Dunning*, 412 U.S. 609 (1973), the Court ruled that the 1962 efficacy proof requirement (well-controlled and adequate clinical studies) retrospectively applied to all NDAs approved from 1938 to 1962. The Court also held that the FDA had the power to decide the question of whether a drug is a new drug as defined in §201(p) of the Food, Drug, and Cosmetic Act. Thus, the Court held that the FDA had the authority to withdraw the NDA of any drug on the market, but only subject to court review.

In *Weinberger v. Bentex Pharmaceutical, Inc.*, 412 U.S. 645 (1973), the issues were similar to the *Hynson, Wescott and Dunning* case. The Court reinforced its position that the "me-too" drugs were subject to the FDA's determination of new drug status and efficacy proof. The drug firm only could seek a court review after the FDA's determination. The Court's ruling had the effect that each drug firm intending to market a "me-too" drug would be required by the FDA to submit proof of therapeutic efficacy. Of importance is how the Bentex Court described a "new drug".

> But the 'new drug' definition under Section 201(p) encompasses a drug 'not generally recognized, among experts qualified by scientific training and experience to evaluate the safety and effectiveness of drugs, as safe and effective for use.' Whether a particular drug is a 'new drug' depends, in part, on the expert knowledge and experience of scientists based on controlled clinical experimentation and backed by substantial support in scientific literature ... It may be, of course, true that in some cases general recognition that a drug is efficacious might be made without the kind of scientific support necessary to obtain approval of an NDA.

In the third case that was decided on June 18, 1973, *Ciba Corp. v. Weinberger*, 412 U.S. 640 (1973), the Court reached conclusions similar to the other cases: The FDA has authority to determine what encompasses a "new drug" under the Act.

Further Case Law on What Constitutes a New Drug

In the late 1970s and early 1980s, a series of cases arose that challenged the FDA's authority to determine the "new drug" status of "me-too" (generic) versions of drug products. FDA policy at the time allowed the continued marketing of the products as long as an Abbreviated New Drug Application (ANDA) had been filed, although it had not been "officially" approved (this was referred to in the agency as a "paper NDA"). An ANDA at the time contained only data on labeling and manufacturing, not data relating to safety and efficacy. This policy was based on the theory that the active ingredients in such products had become generally recognized as safe and effective and therefore, the FDA need only require assurance of proper labeling and manufacturing. However, there was concern by some about bioavailability and bioequivalence of these generic drugs and eventually this policy was challenged. In *Hoffman-LaRoche v. Weinberger*, 425 F.Supp. 890 (D.D.C. 1975) the court ruled that the FDA should not permit drugs to be marketed unless an NDA or ANDA had been approved. The manufacturers of generic products then challenged the policy adopted in *Hoffman-LaRoche*. For example, in *United States v. Lannett Co.*, 585 F.2d 575 (3rd Cir. 1978), and in *Premo Pharmaceutical Laboratories, Inc. v. United States*, 629 F. 2d 795 (2nd Cir. 1978) the courts split on the issue of whether a generic version of an approved pioneer drug was considered a "new drug" under the Act, therefore subject to the "new drug" requirements including the filing and approval of an NDA or ANDA.

Because of this split among the circuits, the issue ended up in the United States Supreme Court.

The landmark Supreme Court case of *United States v. Generix Drug Corp.*, U.S. 453 (1983) resolved the issue. The Court held that the definition of "drug" under the Act included inactive as well as active ingredients, and, therefore, a generic version of a pioneer drug would require its own NDA or ANDA if it differed in any significant aspect from the pioneer drug.

New Drugs

New drugs simply refer to those that have not yet received general recognition by medical experts as being both safe and effective for the intended use. The official definition is in §201(p) of the Act which states:

> The term "new drug" means — (1) any new drug (except a new animal drug or an animal feed bearing or containing a new animal drug) the composition of which is such that such drug is not generally recognized, among experts qualified by scientific training and experience to evaluate the safety and effectiveness of drugs, as safe and

effective for use under the conditions prescribed, recommended, or suggested in the labeling thereof, except that such a drug not so recognized shall not be deemed to be a "new drug" if at any time prior to the enactment of this Act it was subject to the Food and Drug Act of June 30, 1906, as amended, and if at such time its labeling contained the same representations concerning the conditions of its use; or (2) any drug (except a new animal drug or an animal feed bearing or containing a new animal drug) the composition of which is such that such drug, as a result of investigations to determine its safety and effectiveness for use under such conditions, has become so recognized, but which has not, otherwise than in such investigations, been used to a material extent or for a material time under such conditions.

A new drug may not be commercially marketed in the United States unless it has been approved as safe and effective. Such approval is based upon an NDA, which must contain acceptable scientific data, including the results of tests, to evaluate its safety. There must be substantial evidence of effectiveness for the conditions for which the drug is to be sold. Often, the question of whether a drug is recognized as "safe and effective" is a question of fact that must be decided in a legal action.

Newly discovered chemicals are not the only subjects of NDAs. A drug may be legally regarded as a "new drug" if it is an old, established drug (pre-1938 FD&C) which is offered in a new dosage form, with new medical claims, in new dosage levels, or if the drug is to be used on a different patient population. An NDA may also be required if a new combination of old drugs is used.

Drug Efficacy Study

As mentioned above, the 1962 Kefauver-Harris Amendment to the Act required proof of efficacy in addition to proof of safety before a drug product could be introduced into interstate commerce. The issue of how these provisions should be applied to drugs approved between 1938 and 1962 was controversial.

In 1966, the FDA commissioned the National Academy of Sciences/National Research Council to evaluate drug products introduced between 1938 and 1962. Some 16,000 claims for 4000 drug products (15% *otc* and 85% prescription) were reviewed, and 14.7% were reported to be ineffective (ie, lack of substantial evidence of effectiveness), 34.9% were reported to be possibly effective, 7.3% were reported to be probably effective, 19.1% were reported to be effective, and 24% were reported to be "effective, but ...." Subsequent to the 1966 studies, other efficacy studies were ordered.

The FDA initiated an action to remove from the market those drug products that lacked proof of efficacy. This process was known as the Drug Efficacy Study Implementation (DESI) project. The process has taken a number of years, but by most accounts is now complete.

Further Amendments to the Act

Since 1962, the Act has been amended several more times. Sometimes an amendment only covers a few provisions of the Act, as in the case of the Durham-Humphrey Amendment of 1951. At other times, it can be in the form of an entire Congressional act with many provisions, as in the FDA Modernization Act of 1997. Some of the more noted amendments are described briefly below.

The Drug Price Competition and Patent Term Restoration Act of 1984

This legislation, otherwise known as the Waxman-Hatch Act (Pub. L. No. 98-417, and 98-427, 98 Stat 1585 (1984) (codified at 21 USC Section 355 [j], FDCA Section 505 [j]) was a congressional effort to strike a balance between the competing forces of generic firms and innovator (pioneer or brand name) drug firms.

Title I of the Act extended the ANDA process to generic versions of drugs first approved and marketed after 1962. It required the FDA to approve generic drugs shown to be "bioequivalent" to a previously approved drug. This eliminated the requirement for generic manufacturers to duplicate expensive clinical and animal research to demonstrate the safety and efficacy of the products.

Title II of the Act compensated pioneer companies for losses caused by competition from the generic companies by extending the patent terms of some pioneer drugs.

The Prescription Drug User Fee Act of 1992

The Prescription Drug User Fee Act of 1992 (PDUFA) (Pub. L. 102-571, 106 Stat. 4491) authorized the FDA to charge fees to cover the costs incurred for review of human drug applications and supplements, inspection of prescription drug establishments, and other activities. The intent of this legislation was to make additional funds available to the FDA in order to expedite the review of human drug applications. The PDUFA authorized three different types of user fees: drug application fees, annual establishment fees, and annual product fees. Fees are assessed at different rates depending on whether an application requires a review of clinical data on safety and efficacy as opposed to review of only bioavailability or bioequivalence studies. All or part of the fees may be waived at the FDA's discretion.

The Food and Drug Administration Modernization Act of 1997 (FDAMA)

The first major overhaul of the Food, Drug, and Cosmetic Act in over 30 years occurred with the passage of the Food and Drug Administration Modernization Act of 1997 (FDAMA) (Pub. L. No. 105-115, 111 Stat. 2296). One of the major goals of FDAMA was to reenact the provisions of the Prescription Drug User Fee Act, which was to expire in fiscal year 1997. In addition to reenactment of the prescription drug user fees, FDAMA also made major changes in the regulation of foods, drugs, and devices. Documents related to FDAMA implementation can be found on the Internet as part of FDA's Web site, http://www.fda.gov, or more specifically at http://www.fda.gov/cder/fdama. Some of the major changes of FDAMA that impact pharmacy include:

(1) Pediatric Studies of Drugs

Section 111 of FDAMA Section 505A of the Act authorized the FDA to determine that a particular drug may produce health benefits in a pediatric population. The first step in this process required that the FDA, after consultation with experts in pediatric research, develop, prioritize, and publish a list of approved drugs for which additional pediatric information may produce health benefits in the pediatric population. If such a determination was made, the FDA could then request pediatric studies of the drug from the manufacturer. Once the manufacturer completed these studies and they were accepted by the FDA, the FDA had the ability to grant an additional 6 months of marketing exclusivity for the drug. The additional 6 months of marketing exclusivity did not apply to drugs for which an NDA was submitted after January 1, 2002.

The FDA began to implement these provisions. For example, on May 20, 1998, [(63 Fed. Reg. 27733] the FDA announced the availability of a *List of Drugs for Which Additional Pediatric Information May Produce Health Benefits in the Pediatric Population*. In addition, in June 1998, the FDA made available a *Guidance for Industry Qualifying for Pediatric Exclusivity Under Section 505A of the Federal Food, Drug, and Cosmetic Act*.

(2) Pharmacy Compounding

Section 127 of FDAMA clarified that compounding of pharmaceutical products was appropriately regulated by the states and exempted pharmacies from requirements for compliance with NDAs and current good manufacturing requirements when compounding drugs for an identified individual patient.

This section of FDAMA has been the subject of much litigation. In the case of *Western States v. Henney*, the 9th Circuit Court of Appeals struck the law down because it found two of its provisions unconstitutional. The United States Supreme Court granted and heard arguments in February, 2000. The Court's decision was released on April 29, 2002, under the case title of *Thompson, et al. v. Western States Medical Center, et al.* Briefly, the Court agreed with the lower court and found that legislation unconstitutional. The details of the litigation are discussed later in this chapter under the section discussing pharmacy compounding.

(3) Positron Emission Tomography (PET) Compounding

Section 121 of FDAMA required the FDA to establish a PET approval process within two years and prohibited the FDA from requiring an NDA or abbreviated NDA for these products for four years (or two years after the approval process was in place). The FDA has made several initiatives relating to this provision. See discussion of PET compounding in the Compounding section for further information.

(4) Expediting Study and Approval of Fast Track Drugs

Section 112 of the FDAMA established requirements for designation of a drug as a "fast track" product to facilitate the development and expedite the review of drugs that treat a serious or life-threatening condition and demonstrate the potential to address unmet medical needs for such a condition. The FDA issued a *Guidance to Industry Fast Track Drug Development Programs — Designation, Development, and Application Review*, which can be found at http://www.fda.gov/cder/guidance.htm. The FDA recently released a summary of its approval times, comparing the past few years.

(5) Information Program on Clinical Trials for Serious or Life-Threatening Diseases

Section 113 of FDAMA required the FDA to work through the National Institutes of Health to develop and maintain a databank of information on clinical trials for drugs for serious or life-threatening diseases and conditions.

(6) Elimination of Certain Labeling Requirements

Section 126 of FDAMA changed the requirement for the prescription "legend" on prescription drug packaging. A drug is now required to bear, at a minimum, the symbol "Rx only." In addition, this provision repealed Section 502(d) of the FDC Act which required the labels of certain habit-forming drugs to bear the statement, "Warning — May Be Habit Forming."

(7) Dissemination of Off-Label Treatment Information

Section 551 of FDAMA provided incentives for manufacturers to conduct research on new uses of drugs and to file supplemental NDAs for these uses by allowing manufacturers to disseminate limited information on unapproved uses of drugs. It required that information on an unapproved use must be in the form of a peer-reviewed article, and the information must include a statement disclosing, among other things, that the information concerns a use that has not been approved or cleared by the FDA. In addition, it required that notice was to be provided to the FDA 60 days before any information was disseminated under these provisions. A manufacturer could not disseminate information under this section unless it had submitted a supplemental NDA for the new use or certified that studies to support the new use had been done or were going to be done, and an application had been submitted. The application was to be submitted no later than 6 months after the date of the initial dissemination of the information if the studies had already been completed and no later than 36 months if studies had yet to be completed.

These provisions have been found to be unconstitutional by the courts under the First Amendment right to commercial speech. In a series of cCourt decisions involving the Washington Legal Foundation, these provisions, as well as previously issued guidance documents on the subject have been found to violate a manufacturer's right to free speech. (See discussion in Marketing of Pharmaceuticals and in the Court Cases chapter for further information.)

Liability Under the FD&C Act

The FD&C Act imposes a form of strict liability (liability without fault) on all who are affected by its provisions. (The specific prohibited acts involving misbranding and adulteration of drugs are discussed in the next section.) This concept is illustrated in the case of *United States v. Vitamin Industries, Inc.*, 130 F.Supp. 755 (D.Neb. 1955), which indicated that criminal intention is not essential for one to violate the Act. In other words, it is not a defense for the accused to claim lack of knowledge or lack of intent to violate the law. Although this may seem rather harsh, if lack of knowledge or specific intent were an acceptable defense, every violator would avail himself or herself of this claim and the Act would become unenforceable (see *United States v. Dotterweich*, 320 U.S. 277 [1943] and *United States v. Park*, 421 U.S. 658 [1975]).

Doctrine of Respondeat Superior

Under the FD&C Act, an employer can be convicted for a violation committed by an employee. The legal term for this doctrine is **Respondeat Superior**. There are several situations where this doctrine applies: (1) The employer has knowledge or should have knowledge of the employee's illegal action; (2) the employer participated in or willfully authorized or consented to the employee's illegal act; or (3) the employer has a responsible share in the employee's illegal act. Any one of these situations will impute liability to the employer; all three need not be present.

Dotterweich

The landmark court case in this area is *United States v. Dotterweich*, 320 U.S. 277 (1943), involving a drug repackaging firm that operated under the corporate form of a business organization.

In **Dotterweich**, the drug firm was repackaging and relabeling nonprescription drugs and shipping them through interstate commerce. It was alleged by the government that certain drugs were misbranded and adulterated in violation of §301 (a) of the Act (21 U.S.C. §331 [a]). At trial, the jury found the corporation not guilty, but found its president/general manager guilty of two counts of misbranding and one count of drug adulteration.

There was no evidence in the case that the president/general manager was personally guilty, nor was it proven that he even knew that the adulterated drugs were introduced into interstate commerce — in fact, he was out of the country when the shipments were made.

Eventually, the case was heard by the United States Supreme Court, which upheld the conviction on a narrow 5 to 4 vote. Justice Frankfurter justified the Strict Liability principle in enforcing the FD&C Act:

> To speak with technical accuracy, under §301 a corporation may commit an offense and all persons who aid and abet its commission are equally guilty. Whether an accused shares responsibility in the business process resulting in unlawful distribution depends on the evidence produced at trial .... Hardship there doubtless may be under a statute which thus penalizes the transaction though consciousness of wrongdoing be totally wanting. Balancing relative hardship, Congress has preferred to place it upon those who have at least the opportunity of informing themselves of the existence of conditions imposed for the protection of consumers before sharing in illicit commerce, rather than to throw the hazard on the innocent public who are wholly helpless.

In other words, the Court believes that the public, being totally helpless and without even the possibility of knowledge of what could go wrong, should be held harmless. Even though an employer/ee has neither specific intent nor knowledge of the prohibited act, he/she at least has/had the opportunity to inform themselves of critical conditions and are aware of the potential seriousness that could be caused by such conditions, it is fair for an employer/ee to take on that liability rather than the innocent public.

In *Dotterweich*, it is conceivable that the drugs received by the repackaging firm were already adulterated and misbranded by the firm that furnished them. Liability for subsequent reintroduction into interstate commerce might have been avoided by securing a guaranty of the type mentioned in §303(c) of the act. However, the guaranty only works as a defense if the shipment into commerce is in good faith (where the defect is not known), and if the relabeling contains the same information that is on the drugs that are received. In *Dotterweich*, the court did not say if any such guarantee was furnished to the firm; it can be assumed that it was not.

Park

In *United States v. Park*, 421 U.S. 658 (1975), the *Dotterweich* rule was reaffirmed and clarified. In *Park*, the president of a national food chain was convicted of several violations of the act stemming from unsanitary conditions at one of the corporation's food warehouses. He was fined only $50 on each count, but he appealed the convictions because a second violation under the FD&C Act would mean a felony penalty and the convictions were criminal convictions. Eventually, the case reached the US Supreme Court, which decided to hear it because it perceived a conflict in the courts as to the standard of liability for corporate officers under the FD&C Act. The Court upheld the convictions.

The defense in the case took the position that the corporate officer was "responsible for the entire operation of the company." However, sanitation was one of the many phases of the company's operation that the officer assigned to "dependable subordinates." The defense was not successful. Instead, the court spelled out the following rule, applicable to all corporate agents or employees.

> The Act imposes not only a positive duty to seek and remedy violations when they occur, but also, and primarily, a duty to implement measures that will ensure that violations will not occur.

In reaffirming *Dotterweich*, Justice Stewart crystallized the rule as:

> The *Dotterweich* case stands for two propositions, and I accept them both. First 'any person' within the meaning of 21 U.S.C. §333 may include any corporate officer or employee 'standing in responsible relation' to a condition or transaction forbidden by the Act. Second, a person may be convicted of a criminal offense under the Act even in the absence of 'the conventional requirement for criminal conduct — awareness of some wrongdoing.'

Both *Dotterweich* and *Park* deal with a corporate officer's liability for violations committed by subordinates. This principle is one of employer liability for employee violations. As such, the principle applies to sole proprietorship, where the proprietor-employer is liable for acts of employees that are committed within the scope of their employment. General partners are liable for the acts of each other; hence, one partner could share in the liability of a violation committed by another partner. (See discussion of this concept in the Civil Liability chapter.)

In the enforcement of state drug control laws, the doctrine of respondeat superior has been used to impute an employee's violation to the employer (see *Randle v. California Board of Pharmacy*, 49 Cal. Rptr. 485 [1966]). Usually, the doctrine that the master is liable for the acts of the servants is confined to civil liability for torts. However, the application has spilled over into the criminal liability area with respect to public safety laws. This type of liability, which exists without the actual guilt of wrongdoing, is sometimes called "vicarious liability." The courts invented this doctrine as a matter of public policy; the employer is usually financially better able to pay for the employee's wrongdoing than the employee. However, the relationship of employment between the employer and the person committing the wrongdoing must be established before liability can attach.

Strict liability of a proprietor under the FD&C Act exists if it is proven in court the defendant is the sole proprietor of a business, and the offense committed was committed by an employee of that business during the course of business duties. Although the proprietor may not have violated the law personally, he or she may still be found guilty. Responsibility for the acts of the employee rests with the proprietor.

Strict liability of the member of a partnership under the FD&C Act exists if it can be proven in court the defendant is a member of a partnership and is responsible, in part, for the conduct of its activities. If it can be proven that an employee of the partnership, during the course of business duties, violated the law, the defendant will be found guilty, although he or she did not personally commit the offense.

Recordkeeping Under the FD&C Act

Recordkeeping for the pharmacist under the FD&C Act is similar to the recordkeeping required under the Controlled Substances Act (CSA) but is not so precisely defined or detailed. Probably the most important distinction between the recordkeeping under the CSA as opposed to that under the FD&C Act is, for the pharmacist, that the required documents for the CSA are more quantitative while those for the FD&C Act are more qualitative. The recordkeeping under the CSA is concerned with accountability for the receipt and disposition of drugs, whereas recordkeeping under the FD&C Act is concerned with the ability to trace a specific drug product, usually in response to drug recall.

Nonetheless, the basic type of records is the same under the two Acts. For example, purchase invoices are considered records of drug receipt, prescriptions are records of drug disposition, and inventories furnish a record of drugs on hand. Sales or other disposals of drugs to physicians or pharmacists, returns to wholesalers or manufacturers, drug destruction, and thefts should be documented by some type of written or other reliable memorandum.

Statute of Limitations

The statute of limitations is a law that provides a specific period of time after which a criminal prosecution or civil lawsuit cannot be maintained. Although a criminal prosecution or civil suit might be commenced, the defendant could successfully plead the statute of limitations as a defense if it is applicable to the case at hand. The law was established because after a lapse of time, the facts of an alleged violation can become confused or forgotten; therefore, a cutoff date is necessary. This period varies with the type of crime or civil action involved. For civil negligence suits, it is usually 2 years from the date of injury. In some professional malpractice situations, the statute runs from the date that the affected individual discovers or should have discovered the resulting medical dysfunction or injury. In a criminal case, the statute of limitations runs from the date of the alleged crime to the date that the prosecutor files the complaint, indictment, or information. For some criminal offenses, such as murder, there is no statute of limitations. In most states, felony crimes have 5- or 6-year statutes of limitations.

Drug records should be kept at least for the running of state or federal statute of limitations on crimes. In most cases, this is a period of 5 or 6 years from the date of the alleged felony offense. Although federal or state drug control laws often provide for a lesser period of time (usually 3 years) for retention of drug records, the reason for preserving the records for the length of the statute of limitations is that they furnish proof of the transactions involved in a lawsuit, some of which may provide a valid defense to a prosecution arising out of an alleged drug law violation.

Labels on Commercial Containers

FDA regulations require that the following information appear on the manufacturer's or distributor's container of prescription drugs (see 21 CFR §§201.1 to 201.55):

(1) The name and address of the manufacturer, packager, or distributor;
(2) ingredient information;
(3) a statement of identity (ie, the generic and the proprietary names);
(4) quantity in terms of weight or measure applicable to drug (eg, 0.5 g);
(5) the net quantity of the package contents (eg, 100 tablets);
(6) a statement of dosage or a reference to the package insert for dosage information;
(7) the expiration date of the drug;
(8) the lot number; and
(9) the National Drug Code (NDC) number (requested, not required, by FDA regulations).

Package Inserts/Professional Product Labeling

The package insert is the part of a prescription drug product's approved labeling directed to health care professionals. It is the primary mechanism by which the FDA and drug manufacturers communicate essential, science-based prescribing information to health care practitioners.

Historically, the contents and format of package insert labeling are imposed by FDA regulations (21 CFR §201.56). FDA regulations §§201 .56 and 201.57, as they affect the prescription drug labeling described in FDA regulation 201.100 (d) (21 CFR §201.100 [d]), were revised in June 1979. Under the regulations, the package insert labeling must contain a summary of essential scientific information that is needed for the safe and effective use of the drug. The labeling must be informative, accurate, and neither promotional in tone nor false or misleading. The labeling must be based, whenever possible, on data derived from human experiments. Implied claims and suggestions for drug use may not be made if there is inadequate evidence of safety or lack of substantial evidence of effectiveness. Conclusions that are based on animal data are permitted if they are necessary for safe and effective use of the drug in humans; however, they must be identified as animal data.

There is no law or regulation that prohibits the pharmacist from giving a package insert to a patient.

Twenty-one CFR §201.56 required that the package insert for a prescription drug product contain the following specific information under the following section headings and in the following order:

(1) Description (proprietary and generic names);
(2) Clinical pharmacology;
(3) Indications and usage (the use of the drug in the treatment, prevention, or diagnosis of a recognized disease or condition);
(4) Contraindications;
(5) Warnings;
(6) Precautions;
(7) Adverse reactions;
(8) Drug abuse and dependence;
(9) Overdosage;
(10) Dosage and administration; and
(11) How supplied.

FDA New Regulations

On December 22, 2000, the FDA proposed new regulations that would significantly change the "labeling" (ie, the package insert) of prescription drugs. The proposal may be found at 65 FR 81082 or at http://www.fda.gov/OHRMS/DOCKETS/98fr/122200a.pdf.

The FDA's intent in making this proposal is to "make it easier for health care practitioners to access, read, and use" the package insert information, and to "enhance the safe and effective use of prescription drug products." By making the information easier to find, read, and use, the FDA hopes to reduce medical errors caused by inadequate communication.

The proposed labeling would require the addition (at the beginning of the insert) of a "Highlights of Prescribing Information" section. This section is intended to be a concise extract of the most important information that is contained in the "Comprehensive Information" section that would follow.

The Highlights section would contain the following categories:

(1) boxed warnings;
(2) recent substantive labeling changes;
(3) indications and usage;
(4) dosage and administration;
(5) how supplied;
(6) contraindications;
(7) warnings/precautions, including a subsection for the most common adverse reactions;
(8) drug interactions; and
(9) use in specific populations.

In addition, "Rx" should be present to indicate the product is sold only by prescription. A triangular icon appears for drugs that have been approved for marketing within the past 3 years.

An index to the Comprehensive Prescribing Information would be next, followed by that section itself.

In addition to proposing changes to the package insert, the proposal also provides for some changes to the label of the prescription drug itself. The agency hopes that by reducing the amount of required information on product labels and simplifying them, the number of medications errors will be reduced.

Patient Package Inserts

Historical Background of Patient Package Inserts

The first patient warning of a prescription drug was in 1968 when the FDA required that the following statement appear on the dispensing package of an isoproterenol inhalation drug product (21 CFR §201.306).

> "Warning: Do not exceed the dose prescribed by your physician. If difficulty in breathing persists, contact your physician immediately."

Isoproterenol aerosols and nebulizer solutions (eg, *Aerolone Solution*, *Isuprel Hydrochloride Solution*, *Medihaler-Iso*) are prescription-only drugs. The package warnings were required because repeated use of isoproterenol inhalation preparations occasionally causes airway resistance or a refractory state (commonly known as "concrete of the nasal passages"). Cardiac arrest and death also were noted in several instances of excessive use of the drug therapy.

In 1970, the FDA issued a regulation (21 CFR §310.501) requiring that certain information about oral contraceptive drugs be included in each package of the prescription drug dispensed to the patient. Again, the patient labeling informed the patient of the possible adverse effects (eg, thrombophlebitis, pulmonary embolism, retinal artery thrombosis, MI, benign hepatic adenomas, induction of fetal abnormalities, gallbladder disease).

In 1977, a regulation (21 CFR §310.515) was issued requiring that information regarding the newly discovered hazards of estrogen be provided for estrogenic drug products (eg, diethylstilbestrol, *Premarin*, *Tace*, and *Estinyl* tablets) and for combination preparations containing estrogens. Essentially, the PPI listed the risk of estrogens leading to endometrial carcinoma and risks encountered when estrogens are taken during pregnancy. Similar labeling requirements were promulgated for contraceptive intrauterine devices (IUDs), which were regulated as prescription drugs or medical devices, and for progestational drug products (see 21 CFR §310.516). (When diethylstilbestrol or progestational drug products are intended for contraceptive use, labeling requirements under 21 CFR §310.501 apply.)

In 1979, the FDA proposed a rule that would have required manufacturers to produce and distribute patient package inserts for 10 drug classes or about 375 different drugs. The proposed rule was withdrawn in 1982.

It is required that the manufacturer of a drug requiring a PPI provide the pharmacist with a sufficient amount of PPIs to provide one to each patient to whom the drug is dispensed. Sample forms of PPIs are provided by the FDA, and the manufacturer is, additionally, obligated to provide a PPI in Spanish upon the request of the distributor or dispenser.

The FDA requires the pharmacist to provide the PPI to the patient upon dispensing of the drug that is subject to the PPI requirements. PPIs for products dispensed in acute care hospitals or long-term care facilities are considered to have been provided if given to the patient before the first administration of the drug and every 30 days thereafter. Outpatient prescriptions are subject to the same requirements as are applicable to those dispensed by the community pharmacist.

In a 1989 action, the US District Court for the District of New Mexico addressed the dispensing of *Premarin* to a patient without the PPI. The plaintiff in this medical malpractice action was prescribed *Premarin* in conjunction with surgery performed at the Los Alamos Medical Center, but she did not receive the PPI as required by FDA regulations. The Medical Center moved for summary judgment on the claim that the regulations did not impose a duty on the institution to distribute a PPI when it was the institution's policy that this was to be done by the prescribing physician.

The FDA's regulations regarding estrogenic products state:

> Patient labeling for each estrogen drug product shall be provided in or with each package of the drug product intended to be dispensed or administered to the patient. However, patient labeling for drug products in acute care hospitals or long-term care facilities will be considered to have been provided in accordance with this section if provided to the patient prior to administration of the first dose of estrogen and every thirty days thereafter, as long as the therapy continues.

The Medical Center argued that the FDA later realized that inpatients and outpatients of institutions have different needs and that the Agency allows hospital pharmacies greater flexibility in devising a system for distributing this information. Therefore, the Medical Center concluded it could rely upon attending physicians to give this information to the patient. The defendant made its arguments by relying on comments accompanying the final regulation that established a pilot project for PPI requirements for all prescription drugs in 1980.

The court reviewed the FDA final rule published in 1980 and its subsequent history and concluded that it had no bearing on the issue before the court. Instead, the duty of the Medical Center to distribute a PPI for *Premarin* to the plaintiff was based upon the specific regulations pertaining to estrogen, which were finalized in 1977. Even if the pilot project rules were relevant in this case, those rules fully supported the notion that a dispenser cannot delegate the duty to distribute the PPI to the physician as a general matter. The only exception is where the physician, in handwriting, specifically requests in the prescription that a certain PPI not be given to a certain patient.

The thrust of the regulation is that patients, not physicians, must be given certain information concerning the use of estrogen-based drugs. This is to be accomplished by requiring all those who dispense drugs, whether a physician, a community pharmacist, or a hospital pharmacist, to also provide patients with a separate printed leaflet containing the specific information set out in the regulation. As to acute care hospitals, the regulation does exempt such institutions from providing a PPI each time the drug is dispensed. The patient labeling must only be provided prior to the administration of the first dose of estrogen and every 30 days thereafter as long as the therapy continues. There was no indication that the FDA intended distribution of this information to be left up to the prescribing physician. (*Schleiter v. Carlos et al*, No. 87-0955 [D.C.N.M. August 31, 1989].)

MedGuides

The issue of patient package inserts was revived in August of 1995 when the FDA published a proposed rule in the Federal Register entitled "Prescription Drug Product Labeling: Medication Guide Requirements" (61 Fed. Reg. 43769 [1996]). This proposal became known as the MedGuide proposal. It called for manufacturers to provide "MedGuides" for certain prescription drugs that posed a serious and significant public health concern. It also called for "useful" written patient information for all drugs to be delivered each time a new prescription is dispensed. The goal of the MedGuide proposal was to meet the Healthy People 2000 objective of having 75% of all new prescriptions accompanied by written information by the year 2000 and 95% by the year 2006. The FDA indicated that if these goals were not achieved by voluntary private efforts, then a mandatory FDA-prescribed program would be implemented.

In August 1996, President Bill Clinton signed the FDA appropriations bill (P.L. 104-180), which included requirements for the DHHS to take immediate action on the MedGuide proposal. The bill gave the Secretary of DHHS 30 days to evaluate the effectiveness of private-sector drug information efforts and to request national organizations representing health care professionals, consumer organizations, voluntary health agencies, the pharmaceutical industry, drug wholesalers, patient drug information databases, and other relevant parties to develop a long-range action plan to meet the goals of the MedGuide proposal. The law gave these private-sector groups 120 days to develop this plan and submit it to the secretary of DHHS. The secretary then had 30 days to accept, reject, or modify the plan. The plan was to address 6 specific issues:

(1) Identify the plan goals.
(2) Assess the effectiveness of the current private-sector approaches used to provide oral and written prescription information to consumers.
(3) Develop guidelines for providing effective oral and written prescription information consistent with the findings of such assessment.
(4) Contain elements necessary to ensure transmittal of useful information to the consuming public, including being scientifically accurate, non-promotional in tone and content, sufficiently specific and comprehensive to adequately inform consumers about the use of the product, and in an understandable, legible format that is readily comprehensible and not confusing to consumers expected to use the product.
(5) Develop a mechanism to periodically assess the quality of the oral and written prescription information and the frequency with which the information is provided to consumers.
(6) Provide for compliance with relevant state board regulations.

Interested parties from 34 groups formed the Steering Committee for the Collaborative Development of a Long-Range Action Plan for the Provision of Useful Prescription Drug Information to develop this plan. Although there was some disagreement on some points in the plan, the Steering Committee was able to reach consensus on most of the critical issues and submitted its action plan to the Secretary in December 1996. The plan was accepted by the Secretary in January 1997. In accepting the plan, the Secretary assigned responsibility for evaluating the quantity and quality of the information to the private-sector groups. The FDA will continue its periodic efforts to determine the quantity of information provided, as well as providing general reviews of the quality of that information; however, responsibility for ensuring the stated goals are met remains with the private sector. The private sector now has 4 years to meet those goals, or the FDA may implement the original government-mandated MedGuide proposal.

Several groups including the National Council on Patient Information and Education (NCPIE) are implementing this private-sector plan.

On December 1, 1998, the FDA issued a Final Rule entitled "Prescription Drug Product Labeling: Medication Guide Requirements." (See 63 Fed. Reg. 66378.) The regulation was effective June 1, 1999. This rule finalized a portion of the proposal made by the FDA in August 1995. However, because the FDA Appropriations Bill signed by President Clinton in August 1996 (discussed above) limits the authority of the FDA to implement the portion of the proposed rule regarding written information voluntarily provided (the private-sector initiative), the final rule deletes the provisions in the proposal that applied to the "private-sector" (voluntary) effort.

The final rule establishes a patient medication information program under which Medication Guides (FDA-approved patient information) will be required if the FDA determines it is necessary for the patients' safe and effective use of the product. Patient labeling will be required for drug products that "pose a serious and significant public health concern." The requirement applies to both new and refill prescriptions. The rule dictates the content and format of the required patient information. The manufacturer of the drug product must obtain FDA approval of the Medication Guide, and is responsible for ensuring that Medication Guides are available for distribution to patients.

The licensed practitioner who prescribes the drug product may direct that a Medication Guide not be provided to a particular patient. However, the "authorized dispenser" (the pharmacist) is mandated to provide a Medication Guide to any patient who requests the information regardless of any such direction by the licensed practitioner. The rule does not give any such request to the pharmacist.

Initially, the FDA will apply the rule only to drug classes where it has already asked for patient-directed labeling (eg, benzodiazepine hypnotics, nonsedating antihistamines). The FDA anticipates that, on average, no more than 5 to 10 products per year will require such information.

Unit-Dose Labeling

Unit-dose (or individual-dose) packaging of drug products is done routinely, especially in the institutional setting. Individually wrapped and labeled single doses of drug products in tablet or capsule form have resulted in an efficient institutional drug distribution system. The main advantages of the unit-dose system are: it reduces errors because each dose is labeled with the drug identity and strength, and it permits the return and recycling of unused doses provided the sealed package has not been opened. However, the unit-dose system is more expensive than multidose drug distribution systems.

The FDA, in Compliance Policy Guide 7132b.10, specifies its requirements for unit dose labeling for solid and liquid oral dosage forms of both prescription and nonprescription drugs. For prescription drugs, the label of the actual unit-dose container must contain:

(1) The established name of the drug and the quantity of active ingredient per dosage unit;

(2) the expiration date (see 21 CFR §§201.17, 211.137)

(3) the lot or control number (see 21 CFR §§201.100[b], 211.130);

(4) the name and place of business of the manufacturer, packer, or distributor as provided for in 21 CFR §201.1;

(5) for official drugs, any statement required by the compendia; for unofficial drugs, any pertinent statement bearing on special characteristics of the dosage form.

The Compliance Policy Guide (CPG) does not require, but strongly recommends, that the label contain:

(1) Any pertinent statement bearing on the need for special storage conditions;

(2) information to alert a health professional that a procedure(s) is necessary prior to patient administration;

(3) if more than one dosage unit is contained, the number of dosage units per container and the strength per dosage unit.

Because most commonly prescribed drugs are available in commercially marketed unit-dose packaging, it is prudent the pharmacist use the commercial unit-dose drug product, rather than repackaging the drug.

Labeling of Customized Medication Packages

In lieu of dispensing 2 or more drug products in separate containers, a pharmacist may, with the consent of the patient, his or her caregiver, or prescriber, provide a customized medication package (Patient Med Pak). Guidelines for the labeling of such packaging are given in USP Chapter 661.

Regulation of Dietary Supplements

Historically

Traditionally, the FDA considered dietary supplements to be foods and regulated them accordingly. The focus of the agency was on ensuring safety and wholesomeness as well as ensuring the labeling was truthful and not misleading.

Dietary Supplement Health and Education Act of 1994

In 1994 Congress enacted the Dietary Supplement Health and Education Act (DSHEA), amending several portions of the FD&C pertaining to dietary supplements and ingredients of dietary supplements.

DSHEA defines "dietary supplements" and treats them as a special class of foods. The legislation prohibits Congress from regulating "dietary supplements" as food additives or as drugs. It places the burden on the FDA to prove a dietary supplement is unsafe before it can be removed from the market. The intent of Congress in passing this legislation was to protect "the right of access of consumers to safe dietary supplements" and to remove "unreasonable regulatory barriers limiting or slowing the flow of safe products and accurate information to consumers." The passage of this legislation has had a significant impact on the marketing of dietary supplements in this country.

Under DSHEA (Section 201[ff]), a "dietary supplement" is defined as:

(1) A product (other than tobacco) intended to supplement the diet that bears or contains one or more of the following dietary ingredients: A vitamin; a mineral; an herb or other botanical; an amino acid; a dietary substance for use by man to supplement the diet by increasing the total dietary intake; or a concentrate, metabolite, constituent, extract, or combination of any ingredient above;

(2) a product intended for ingestion in tablet, capsule, powder, softgel, gelcap, or liquid form; or if not intended for ingestion in such a form, is not represented as conventional food and is not represented for use as a sole item of a meal or of the diet; and

(3) labeled as a dietary supplement.

Probably the most significant result of DSHEA is it allows for dietary supplement manufacturers to make certain claims on their products' labels. These claims cannot constitute a "disease claim" (ie, the type of claim made for a drug that claims it is effective to treat a disease). However, certain "structure/function" claims are allowed under the law. This type of claim describes, for example, the role the nutrient or dietary supplement plays in affecting the normal structure or function of the human body (as opposed to affecting the structure or function of the human body in a disease state). When such a claim is made on the label, the following "disclaimer" must also appear: "This statement has not been evaluated by the Food and Drug Administration. This product is not intended to diagnose, treat, cure, or prevent any disease." The manufacturer must have substantiation that such a statement is truthful and not misleading, and must notify the FDA within 30 days of the marketing of the dietary supplement with such a statement.

DSHEA also modified the law with regard to what constitutes "labeling" of a dietary supplement. Scientific publications and other types of information marketed along with dietary supplements are not defined as "labeling" as long as certain conditions are met.

Under DSHEA, a dietary supplement manufacturer may place a claim that the product affects the "structure/function" of the body on its product without preapproval of the FDA. On January 6, 2000, the FDA issued final regulations regarding types of "structure/function" claims allowed to be made under DSHEA (see 65 FFR 1000). In general, claims that a product affects the normal structure or function of the human body are allowed. Any claim that explicitly or implicitly says the product can be used to "prevent, treat, cure, mitigate, or diagnose disease" are considered "disease claims" and would subject the product to the drug requirements under the Act. The rule clarifies that such prohibited express or implied claims are made through the name of a product, through a statement about the formulation of a product (contains aspirin) or through the use of pictures, vignettes, or symbols (EKG tracings). The rule allows for claims that do not relate to disease, including health maintenance claims ("maintains a healthy circulatory system"), other nondisease claims ("for muscle enhancement," "helps you relax"), and claims for common, minor symptoms often associated with life stages ("for common symptoms of PMS," "for hot flashes").

Drug Approval Process

Synopsis of New Drug Application Procedures

Before a new drug can be marketed, federal law requires the submission and approval of form FDA-356h. Before the NDA is filed, an Investigational New Drug (IND) form (form FDA-1571) for the drug must be filed. The specific FDA regulations regarding INDs and NDAs are contained in 21 CFR 312 and 314. The FDA also has provided for the electronic submission of NDAs. A Guidance Document entitled *Guidance for Industry Providing Regulatory Submissions in Electronic Format-NDAs* may be found on the Internet at http://www.fda.gov/cder/guidance/index.htm. In addition, copies of forms required for such submissions may also be found on the Internet at http://aosweb.psc.dhhs.gov/forms/fdaforms.htm. If the FDA does not reject the IND request within 30 days of submission, clinical testing of the investigational drug on humans may begin by the IND sponsor. The IND application must include proof of preclinical testing of the new drug on animals to substantiate the safety of clinical testing in humans.

The sponsor of the IND can be a drug manufacturer, hospital, pharmacy, physician, pharmacist, or anyone who submits the application. However, the individuals (investigators) who conduct the clinical trials must be trained and experienced, and a statement of their respective qualifications must be attached to the IND. The investigators submit to the IND sponsor a completed and signed "Statement of Investigator" Form FDA-1572.

Phase 1 of clinical investigation involves a small number of patients in carefully controlled studies of the drug toxicity, metabolism, absorption, and elimination, to determine the preferred route of administration and safe dosage.

Phase 2 involves use of the investigational drug on a limited number of patients for specific disease treatment or prevention, along with additional pharmacology studies on animals to further determine the drug's safety.

Phase 3 trials evaluate whether information obtained from phase 1 and 2 studies can reasonably ensure the safety and efficacy of the drug or if the drug has a potential value outweighing its possible hazards.

"Phase 4," as it is unofficially termed, involves postmarketing surveillance of approved drugs to detect adverse effects or other problems not encountered in the 3 prior phases of drug testing due to the limited number of patients using the medication (see 21 CFR 314.80).

Before a human being may be involved as a subject in research, the investigator must obtain legally effective "informed consent" of the patient or his or her representative (see 21 CFR Part 50).

In April of 1996, the FDA released a Guidance Document entitled *Guidance for Industry E6 Good Clinical Practice: Consolidated Guidance* that may be obtained on the Internet at http://www.fda.gov/cder/guidance/index.htm or from the Drug Information Branch CDER, 5600 Fishers Lane, Rockville, MD 20857, telephone 301-827-4573. This guidance discusses the informed consent process of "trial subjects" in depth.

If, during the clinical testing of a new drug, the data furnished to the FDA indicate that the drug is too toxic under the criteria of the FDA's risk/benefit ratio, the FDA will terminate the IND approval. In this instance, the FDA's action is not subject to court review or appeal and, as such, it is one of the rare examples in the law in which administrative action is not judicially reviewable. If all goes well with the clinical testing, the sponsor of the drug (usually the manufacturer or supplier at this point) submits a voluminous NDA (form FD-356H) to the FDA wherein the proposed labeling (package insert) is contained. If approved by the FDA, the package insert will accompany the marketed drug product in its package.

After the NDA is approved by the FDA, the drug is marketed, but the drug manufacturer's reporting does not end there. The 1962 amendment to the Act requires that the manufacturer submit periodic reports to the FDA, containing samples of current labeling and advertisements, summaries of medical journal articles on the drug, and information on adverse reactions.

Drug Recall

It frequently is asked on the jurisprudence test of the pharmacy board examinations to discuss the FDA's recall classification system. There are essentially 3 classifications of FDA drug recall:

(1) Class I exists where there is a reasonable possibility that the use of or exposure to a violative product will cause either serious adverse effects on health or death.
(2) Class II exists where the use of or exposure to a violative product may cause temporary or medically reversible adverse effects on health or where the probability of serious adverse effects on health is remote.
(3) Class III exists where the use of or exposure to a violative product is not likely to cause adverse health consequences.

Note that no specific statutory provision expressly authorizes the FDA to order a drug product recall. Manufacturers do know, however, that if the FDA requests or suggests a drug product recall, and the manufacturer does not comply, the product is subject to the ultimate FDA sanction and seizure.

Labeling of Drugs

The regulations for drug labeling are contained in §§502 and 503 of the FD&C or 21 U.S.C. §§352 and 353. Labeling of controlled substances is discussed in detail in the Controlled Substances chapter. The emphasis in this section is on the basic labeling required for both prescription and *otc* drugs.

The FDA regulations differentiate between the terms "label" and "labeling." Label means the printed, written, or graphic material that is literally affixed to the container of the drug (see 21 CFR §1.3[b]). Labeling means the printed, written, or graphic material that is enclosed with or accompanies the drug once it enters interstate commerce and is put up for sale after shipment (see 21 CFR §1.3[a]).

Much of the authority of the FD&C over the manufacture and distribution of food, drugs, medical devices, and cosmetics is through the labeling requirements of the FDA regulations implementing the statute. To violate the labeling requirements of the Act and the FDA regulations, thereto, is to violate the essential spirit and letter of the law governing the purity, safety, and efficacy of food, drugs, medical devices, and cosmetics. Under the authority delegated by the DHHS, the FDA promulgates regulations dealing with specific labeling requirements. In addition, the FDA now issues labeling requirements pursuant to the authority of the Fair Packaging and Labeling Act (15 U.S.C. §1047 et seq.), which concern truthfulness in labeling as applicable to consumer packaging (eg, defining "economy size," "king size," etc.).

Of importance to the pharmacist are those FDA regulations relating to the general labeling of drugs and to specific labeling of prescription and nonprescription drugs. The FDA also has specific labeling requirements applicable to veterinary drugs. Applicable FDA regulations on labeling can be found at 21 CFR § 201.

"Adequate directions for use" refers to the labeling of nonprescription drugs. The directions must be written clearly so the layperson can use a drug safely for the purposes for which it is intended (see 21 CFR §201.5).

"Adequate information for its use" differs from the term previously discussed. It is defined in 21 CFR §201.100(c)(1) in reference to prescription drugs and applies to the promotional labeling and the package inserts accompanying the drugs in commercial containers. The labeling must include the medical indication, effects, and dosage; the route, method, frequency, and duration of administration; and any relevant hazards, contraindications, side effects, and precautions.

Special Labeling

Special labeling for certain drugs is contained in 21 CFR Part 201 Subpart G. These include specific requirements for certain prescription and certain *otc* drugs. One example is the statement required by 21 CFR §201.314 for salicylate preparations that says: "Warning: Keep out of reach of children." (See discussion of Proposed New Labeling Requirements in this chapter.)

Labeling of Nonprescription Drugs

On March 17, 1999, the FDA issued new final regulations regarding the labeling of *otc* drug products. The proposal for this regulation was released in February 1997. The new regulation is based on the FDA's success with standardizing food labeling.

The General Requirements for the *otc* label are contained in 21 CFR Part 210 Subparts A and C. Generally, the label of an *otc* drug must contain:

(1) A principal display panel, including a statement of identity of the product (21 CFR §201.60 and 201.61);

(2) the name and address of the manufacturer, packager, or distributor (21 CFR §201.1);

(3) the net quantity of contents (21 CFR §201.62);

(4) the National Drug Code number is requested, but not required, to be on the label (21 CFR §201.2);

(5) cautions and warnings that are needed for the protection of the user (this requirement varies by the type of product);

(6) adequate directions for safe and effective use (201 CFR §201.5);

(7) content and format of *otc* product labeling in "Drug Facts" panel format (21 CFR §201.66).

The regulations adopted in March 1999 are designed to simplify *otc* drug product labeling to enable consumers to make informed decisions about the medications they use and give their families. The regulations require the labeling to be in a standardized format that clearly shows the drug's active ingredients, uses, warnings, directions, and inactive ingredients. The FDA also recommends that manufacturers include a phone number for consumers to call for more information. The regulations set requirements for minimum type sizes and other graphic features for the standardized format, including options for modifying the format for various package sizes and shapes.

The Drug Facts panel must contain the following information in the following order:

- **Drug Facts** – title
- **Active ingredient(s)** – including amount in each dosage unit
- **Purpose** – pharmacologic class
- **Use(s)** – indications
- **Warnings:**
- Do not use – absolute contraindications, when the product should not be used under any circumstances
- Ask a doctor before use if you have – warnings for persons with certain pre-existing conditions and for persons experiencing certain symptoms
- Ask a doctor or pharmacist before use if you are – drug-drug and food-drug interactions
- When using this product – side effects that could occur and substances or activities to avoid
- Stop use and ask a doctor if – signs of toxicity and other serious reactions that would require consumers to stop using the product immediately
- Pregnancy/breast-feeding warning
- Keep out of reach of children/Accidental overdose warnings
- **Direction** – dosage when, how, or how often to take
- **Other information**
- **Inactive ingredients**
- **Questions? (Optional)** – followed by telephone number

On December 1, 1999, the FDA announced the availability of a Guidance Document entitled "Draft Guidance for Industry on Labeling of Over-the-Counter Human Drug Products Using a Column Format." It can be found on the Internet at http://www.fda.gov/cder/guidance/index.htm.

21 CFR §201.5 entitled: Drugs; adequate directions for use; remains unchanged by the new labeling requirements. By way of a "negative prohibition," it requires *otc* drug labeling to contain the following information:

(1) Statements of all cases, conditions, and purposes for which the drug is intended, except those restricted under medical supervision;

(2) the normal dose for each intended use of the drug and the doses for individuals of different ages and different physical conditions;

(3) both the frequency and duration of administration or application;

(4) the administration or application in relation to meals, onset of symptoms, or other time factors;

(5) the route or method of administration or application; and

(6) the preparation for use (ie, shaking, dilution, etc.).

When adequate directions for common use of an *otc* drug are known to the ordinary individual (which would be unlikely) there is an exemption under 21 CFR §201.116 from both the adequate directions for use requirement of labeling and from the prescription-only requirement, although not from the other labeling requirements of law, such as ingredient information and the manufacturer's name.

The individual who repackages or relabels an *otc* drug from bulk supply must comply with all of the FDA labeling regulations that are applicable to labeling *otc* drugs. (Or the product will be misbranded under the Act). With the new requirement for standardized labels, this will be much more difficult for the practicing pharmacist to do. 21 CFR 201.66 (e) provides a mechanism to request an exemption or deferral from the standardized format. It requires documentation of why a particular requirement is inapplicable or contrary to public health and requires a copy of the proposed labeling also be submitted.

Because a pharmacist is licensed, he or she is considered an expert on drugs and, as such, must be able to professionally answer all queries that his or her patients may have concerning the active ingredients and the labeling of the *otc* drugs sold in the pharmacy. The patient is ultimately responsible for reading and following the drug labeling; however, the pharmacist should draw attention to the directions for and warnings on use of the drugs.

While the pharmacist may not legally diagnose or prescribe in most states, he or she may recommend a nonprescription drug product in response to the patient's request for a remedy. When recommending a drug product, the pharmacist must be careful not to give an express warranty or guarantee for the preparation so as not to be involved in a civil liability suit should the "guaranteed remedy" prove ineffective (see the discussion of warranties in the Civil Liability chapter).

When nonprescription drugs are dispensed pursuant to a prescription, the prescription label satisfies the FDA labeling requirements applicable to consumer self-medication labeling.

Current Good Manufacturing Practices (CGMP)

The FDA's CGMP regulations apply to a pharmacy only if it is engaged in repackaging and relabeling drugs beyond the usual conduct of dispensing and selling them at retail. Such activities outside the usual scope of pharmacy practice would subject the pharmacy to FDA registration (FDCA §510) and to FDA inspection at regular intervals.

The FDA, in its introductory comments to the CGMP regulations, gave 3 situations in pharmacy practice that require the pharmacy to comply with FDA registration, inspections, and CGMPs:

(1) If the pharmacy in hospital "A" repackages drug products for its own use as well as for that in hospitals "B" and "C";

(2) if a pharmacy chain repackages and relabels quantities of drug products from the manufacturer's original commercial containers for shipment to an individual chain location; and

(3) if similar repackaging and relabeling are conducted by individual pharmacists as members of an informal buying group (43 Fed. Reg. 45028 [1978]).

If a hospital pharmacy confines repackaging of drug products to those used solely within the hospital, it appears the hospital would not be subject to the FDA registration, regular inspections, and CGMP compliance requirements. Similarly, the usual type of repackaging and relabeling of drug products done for on-premises dispensing or retail sale would not subject a pharmacy to FDA registration, regular inspections, and CGMP compliance requirements.

The FDA has also stated that CGMP requirements apply to shared service operations servicing HMOs and hospital groups. FDA Guideline 7356.002B (1993) states:

> For the purposes of differentiating whether an establishment is acting as a pharmacy or as a repackager/relabeler, the repackaging of drug products by licensed pharmacists, (ie, filling prescriptions for identified patients), is within the regular practice of pharmacy. The repackaging of drug products by pharmacists, or any other entity, for resale or distribution to hospitals, other pharmacies, nursing homes, health care facilities, etc., are beyond the practice of pharmacy, and these repackaging/relabeling facilities are thus required to register and list all such products with the FDA.

Thus, hospitals packaging drugs provided to other hospitals, nursing homes, or other entities are subject to the FDA's CGMP requirements.

The FDA's authority for its position on manufacturing practices can be found in the FD&C. Section 501(a)(2)(B) of the Act (21 U.S.C. §351[a][2][B]) provides that a drug will be deemed adulterated if the methods used in or the facilities or controls used for its manufacture, processing, packing, or holding do not conform to current good manufacturing practice. This section of the law can be made applicable to wholesalers, retailers, pharmacies, and hospitals as well as to drug manufacturers. However, the FDA states the CGMP regulations only apply to organizations engaged in the preparation of a drug product and, therefore, do not apply to wholesalers, retailers, pharmacies, and hospitals engaged in activities that are traditional to them. Pharmacies are exempt from FDA manufacturer registration only if they do not manufacture, prepare, propagate, compound, or process drugs for sale other than in the regular course of dispensing and selling drugs at retail (21 U.S.C. §510[g][1]). The exemption from regular FDA factory inspection is given to pharmacies by 21 U.S.C. §704(a)(2)(A); again, the pharmacy may engage only in the regular business of dispensing and selling drugs at retail. Consequently, repackaging and relabeling of drugs for off-premises sale can be interpreted as out of the regular course of the pharmacy's business and, hence, nullify the exemptions in §§510(g) and 704(a) and the FDA exemption of the pharmacy from CGMP compliance.

Important Points About the FD&C Act

The FD&C is designed to protect the public health by requiring that:

(1) Only safe, effective, and properly labeled drugs may be introduced into interstate commerce.
(2) The food and cosmetic preparations subject to the Act be safe and properly labeled.
(3) The manufacturing, processing, packaging, and holding of drugs comply with the Current Good Manufacturing Practices (CGMP) set by the FDA.
(4) The FD&C Act be enforced by the FDA.
(5) *otc* (nonprescription) drugs be labeled for safe use by consumers in self-medication.
(6) Prescription drugs be dispensed to an individual only pursuant to a prescription or administered directly by the physician or other authorized prescriber.
(7) Drug prescriptions be refilled only as authorized by a physician or other authorized prescriber.
(8) Specific labeling be used for both prescription and nonprescription drugs.
(9) Dispensing a drug for distribution in violation of the Act's labeling requirements is "misbranding" the drug.
(10) Drugs containing filthy, putrid, and decomposed substances and drugs packed and held under unsanitary conditions be deemed "adulterated."

(11) Seizures of misbranded or adulterated drugs can be made by the FDA.
(12) Interpretations of the Act show that lack of knowledge or lack of criminal intent will not excuse a violation.
(13) An employer or other responsible person may be prosecuted for violations of the Act committed by an employee.
(14) FDA has broad inspection powers over factories, warehouses, and establishments where drugs, food, medical devices, and cosmetics are made or processed.
(15) The FDA is authorized to perform limited inspection of pharmacies in certain circumstances.
(16) Manufacturers or repackagers of drugs must register with the FDA.

REGULATION OF PHARMACEUTICAL PRODUCTS

Definition of Drug

What constitutes a "drug" for legal purposes is set forth in Section 201 (g)(1), the FD&C (21 U.S.C. §321[g][1]). The definition of a "drug" does not differentiate between prescription and nonprescription drugs, nor does it distinguish legal or lawful drugs from illicit ones:

> The term "drug" means (A) articles recognized in the official United States Pharmacopeia, official Homeopathic Pharmacopeia of the United States, or official National Formulary, or any supplement to any of them; and (B) articles intended for use in the diagnosis, cure, mitigation, treatment, or prevention of disease in man or other animals; and (C) articles (other than food) intended to affect the structure or any function of the body of man or other animals; and (D) articles intended for use as a component of any articles specified in clause (A), (B), or (C). A food or dietary supplement for which a claim, subject to Sections 403(r)(1)(B) and 403(r)(3) or Sections 403(r)(1)(B) and 403(r)(5)(D), is made in accordance with the requirements of Section 403(r) is not a drug solely because the label or the labeling contains such a claim. A food, dietary ingredient, or dietary supplement for which a truthful and not misleading statement is made in accordance with Section 403(r)(6) is not a drug under clause (C) solely because the label or the labeling contains such a statement.

Intended Use

Often, a key element in determining whether a particular item is a drug is the "intended use" of the manufacturer or distributor of the article. The classifications under the FD&C are not mutually exclusive. For example, an item may meet the criteria to be classified as both a drug and a cosmetic under the legal framework of this statute.

Prescription Drug Marketing Act

The Prescription Drug Marketing Act of 1987 (PDMA), which became law in 1988 (P.L. 100-293), amended the FD&C to reduce the potential public health risks that may result from diversion of prescription drugs from legitimate commercial channels (see 21 U.S.C. §353[c]-[e]). Congress found the reintroduction of these drugs into commercial channels could lead to the distribution of mislabeled, adulterated, and subpotent or counterfeit drugs to the American public. The PDMA requires states license wholesale distributors of prescription human drugs in conformance with federal guidelines that will provide minimum standards for prescription drug storage, handling, and recordkeeping. It also requires wholesale distributors who are not authorized manufacturers' distributors to provide a written statement to the purchaser identifying each prior sale.

The PDMA, sometimes known as the Drug Diversion Act, amended several sections of the FD&C to:

(1) Ban the reimportation of federal legend human drugs manufactured in the United States, except when reimported by the manufacturer or for emergency medical care with permission of the Secretary;

(2) prohibit, with certain exceptions, the sale, purchase, or trade (including the offer to sell, purchase, or trade) federal legend human drugs by hospitals or health care entities;

(3) prohibit, with certain exceptions, the sale, trade, or purchase (including the offer to sell, purchase, or trade) federal legend human drugs donated or sold at reduced cost to charitable institutions;

(4) ban the sale, purchase, or trade, and the counterfeiting of drug coupons;

(5) ban the sale, purchase, or trade (including the offer to sell, purchase, or trade) of drug samples;

(6) require practitioners to request samples in writing;

(7) mandate storage, handling, and recordkeeping requirements for drug samples;

(8) require state licensing of wholesale distributors of federal legend human drugs under federal guidelines that include minimum standards for storage, handling, and recordkeeping;

(9) require unauthorized drug distributors to provide a statement of origin ("pedigree") as part of certain sales of drugs; and

(10) set forth criminal and civil penalties for violations of these provisions.

The effective date for most provisions was July 22, 1988, except that the sample distribution requirements became effective October 20, 1988, and the requirement for state licensing of wholesale distributors became effective September 14, 1992.

The reimportation of prescription human drugs produced in the United States is banned, except when reimported by the manufacturer or, after FDA approval, for emergency use. The PDMA also bans sale, trade, or purchase of drug samples and the trafficking in and counterfeiting of drug coupons (forms that may be redeemed for a prescription drug at no cost or reduced cost). For purposes of this legislation, a drug sample is defined as "a unit of drug, which is not intended to be sold, that is intended to promote the sale of the drug." The PDMA requires all requests for drug samples be made in writing by licensed practitioners. It also requires drug samples be properly stored and handled, and certain recordkeeping be followed. With certain specific exceptions, the resale of prescription drugs purchased by hospitals or health care facilities or donated or supplied to charitable institutions is prohibited.

The FDA on December 3, 1999, finally issued its final regulations implementing this legislation (see 64 Fed. Reg. 67720–67731). The proposed regulations to implement the PDMA of 1987 were published by the FDA in the *Federal Register* on March 14, 1994 (Fed. Reg. 11842). The final rule set forth requirements for reimportation and wholesale distribution of prescription drugs, the offer of, or the sale, purchase, or trade of prescription drugs purchased by hospitals or health care entities, or donated to charitable organizations, and the distribution of prescription drug samples. In this rulemaking, the FDA also amended certain sections of the regulations entitled "Guidelines for State Licensing of Wholesale Prescription Drug Distributors." However, on May 3, 2000, at 65 FR 25639, the FDA announced it was delaying the effective date for certain requirements related to wholesale distribution of prescription drugs by distributors who were not authorized distributors of record. Another portion of the final regulation being stayed was one prohibiting blood centers functioning as "health care entities" to act as wholesale distributors of blood derivatives. The proposed rule on state licensing of wholesale drug distributors was published in the *Federal Register* on September 13, 1988 (53 Fed. Reg. 35325). The proposal prescribed minimum requirements for the storage and handling of prescription drugs and for the establishment and maintenance of distribution records. The PDMA provision prohibits wholesale distribution of drugs in interstate commerce unless the wholesaler is licensed by a state in accordance with the guidelines, became effective September 14, 1992.

Prior to issuance of the regulations, the FDA had issued guidance letters interpreting sections of the PDMA not covered by the proposed state licensing. The FDA's views on sample distribution, sales by hospitals and health care entities, and distribution by secondary distributors were disseminated by letters to the industry and other interested persons. These letters discussed many sections of the PDMA and provided insight into the agency's current regulatory approach. They were extremely controversial and engendered substantial comment.

On November 3, 1988, the FDA sent a clarification letter to help hospitals return mistakenly ordered or delivered drugs to the wholesale distributor. The letter stated a return to a wholesale distributor by a hospital or health care entity would not be considered a sale, provided the return was made within 10 days of delivery and the hospital or health care entity notified the manufacturer of the return. On January 26, 1990, the FDA issued a letter that permits legitimate returns of prescription drugs by a hospital or health care entity to the manufacturer or wholesale distributor from which they were purchased, provided they are properly stored and handled, certain notifications are made, and records are kept and any credit refund or exchange does not exceed the purchase price.

In addition, a January 19, 1989, letter gave the agency's preliminary interpretation that the PDMA does not prohibit drug sales by hospitals to rescue squads and emergency medical services. Penalties for violation of this amendment to the FD&C are set forth in 21 U.S.C. §331(t).

Key points with regard to the PDMA and its final implementing regulations with regard to samples and pharmacies are:

(1) A "drug sample" is defined as "a unit of a prescription drug that is not intended to be sold and is intended to promote the sale of the drug."

(2) The FDA's position is that starter packs, which are distributed free to pharmacies, are not samples because they are intended to be sold by the pharmacy. Also, vouchers or other similar systems for indigent patients filled out of pharmacy's stock at the manufacturer's expense are not considered samples.

(3) Samples only may be distributed by a practitioner licensed to prescribe, or to the pharmacy of a hospitals or health care entity (at the written request of a prescriber).

(4) The proposed rule stated that drug samples found in a retail pharmacy would be considered evidence that the sample was obtained by the pharmacy in violation of the Act. The final rule excludes this provision, but if the pharmacy is not part of a health care entity, the presumption probably can still be made.

Drug Price Competition and Patent Term Restoration Act of 1984

When President Ronald Reagan signed the Drug Price Competition and Patent Term Restoration Act (DPCPTRA) into law on September 24, 1984, he stated "this legislation will speed up the process of federal approval of inexpensive generic versions of many brandname drugs, make the generic versions more widely available to consumers, and grant pharmaceutical firms added incentives to develop new drugs." The Act was the result of intense negotiations which involved generic drug manufacturers as well as the Pharmaceutical Manufacturers Association (PMA), now known as the Pharmaceutical. The law converts the drug approval process that had been used for pre-1962 generic drugs and makes that process a formal requirement for moving post-1962 drugs to ANDA status. All generic drugs approved under this process must be bioequivalent to the brand name reference drug.

During the legislative hearings, the PMA argued that the effective patent life of pharmaceuticals had been "cut in half" by government regulations when the Kefauver-Harris Amendments to the FD&C required new drugs to be proven effective and safe. The DPCPTRA provides pioneer drug firms 5 years of patent restoration or at least 5 years of exclusive marketing once their drug is approved. Generic companies may not submit an application until 5 years after the approval of the brand-name product.

The 1984 legislation specifically limited information the FDA could demand of would-be generic producers before they received marketing approval. The new law codified existing requirements for ANDAs in Section 505(j), clauses (i) through (viii) of the FD&C:

(1) Information must show dosage, routes of administration, strength, and conditions of use previously have been approved for the pioneer product;

(2) active ingredients are the same as those in the pioneer product (if one of the active ingredients is different, a petition must demonstrate the different substance is already in another approved product); and

(3) certification must be given that the innovator holds no in-force patent. "The Secretary may not require that an abbreviated application contain information in addition to that required by clauses (i) through (viii)."

The legislation also granted 10 years of exclusive marketing, regardless of patent status, to 50 drugs approved by the FDA from the period of January 1982 to September 1984, the transition period during which the legislation was in the making.

Some pharmacists and consumers have raised concerns about the equivalence of generic copies marketed under the new law. Particular concerns have been raised regarding substituting generic drug products for brand name products that still have exclusivity over certain indications. One pharmacy organization wrote, "Although the various brands of propranolol may be equivalent/bioavailable, they are not equivalent in that only one brand has been approved by the FDA for postmyocardial infarction."

Rep. Henry Waxman, D-Calif., one of the main proponents of the new legislation, became so concerned about such allegations that he wrote "Under no circumstances would the dispensing of a generic drug found by the FDA to be therapeutically equivalent to a brand name drug, even if the generic were not approved for all of the indications approved for the brand name, be considered a willful violation of a criminal statute." The only reason generic propranolol labeling differs from the brand name version is that certain new indications approved for existing products between 1982 and 1984 were available exclusively to the original manufacturer for 2 years. The FDA has asked brand name companies to point out to pharmacists that the new law does not prohibit a pharmacist from substituting a generic copy of a pioneer drug having exclusivity, even if the physician has written for that exclusive indication.

FDA

The FDA has the primary responsibility of enforcing the FD&C Act.

The FDA was an outgrowth of the Chemistry Bureau within the Department of Agriculture. In 1912, the Bureau expanded, and in 1927 it became known as the Food, Drug, and Insecticide Administration and had law enforcement powers when the Caustic Poison Act was passed by Congress. In 1930, it adopted the name of the FDA. In 1940, the FDA was transferred from the Department of Agriculture to the Federal Security Agency, which in turn became the Department of Health, Education, and Welfare in 1953.

The FDA now is a component of the Department of Health and Human Services (DHHS). The FD&C Act designates the DHHS and its Secretary as responsible for the Act's administration. The Secretary has, in turn, delegated the majority of authority under the Act to the Commissioner of the FDA. The Commissioner of the FDA reports to the Secretary. In 1988 the Act was modified to require that the FDA Commissioner be appointed by the President and confirmed by the Senate. (Prior to that time, the Secretary chose the Commissioner).

Misbranding and Adulteration

Sections 501 and 502 of the Act prohibit the introduction into interstate commerce of any article that is "misbranded" or "adulterated," as those terms are defined under the Act. The misbranding and adulteration provisions in the Act apply to action taken after shipment in interstate commerce, whereas the new drug provisions of the Act apply only at the moment of shipment (see *United States v. Phelps Dodge Mercantile Co.*, 157 F.2d 453 [9th Cir. 1946]).

United States Pharmacopeia Role

The majority of drugs marketed in the United States have monographs in The United States Pharmacopeia/National Formulary (USP/NF). The FD&C (the Act) recognizes the USP/NF as an "official compendia." If a drug product that appears in a monograph in the USP/NF fails to meet the standards for strength, quality, purity, packaging, or labeling contained in the monograph, the drug may be deemed "misbranded" or "adulterated" under the Act. For example, USP's monograph for nitroglycerin tablets requires that prescriptions be labeled for sublingual use and that they be dispensed in the original unopened container. In addition, the USP/NF's standards for packaging and storage of prescription drugs are widely recognized by individual state Food, Drug, and Cosmetic acts as well as by state pharmacy practice acts and regulations.

Adulterated Drugs

In most instances, adulteration violations would be committed by the pharmaceutical manufacturer. For example, if a drug is manufactured under conditions that do not conform to Current Good Manufacturing Practices, the drug is deemed adulterated under the Act. Section 502(a)-(d) of the Act states that:

> A drug or device shall be deemed to be adulterated —
>
> (a)(1) If it consists in whole or in part of any filthy, putrid, or decomposed substance; or (2)(A) if it has been prepared, packed, or held under unsanitary conditions whereby it may have been contaminated with filth, or whereby it may have been rendered injurious to health; or (B) if it is a drug and the methods used in, or the facilities or controls used for, its manufacture, processing, packing, or holding do not conform to or are not operated or administered in conformity with current good manufacturing practice to assure that such drug meets the requirements of this Act as to safety and has the identity and strength, and meets the quality and purity characteristics, which it purports or is represented to possess; or (C) if it is a compounded positron emission tomography drug, and the methods used in, or the facilities and controls used for, its compounding, processing, packing, or holding do not conform to or are not operated or administered in conformity with the positron emission tomography compounding standards and the official monographs of the United States Pharmacopeia to assure that such drug meets the requirements of this Act as to safety and has the identity and strength, and meets the quality and purity characteristics, that it purports or is represented to possess; or (3) if its container is composed, in whole or in part, of any poisonous or deleterious substance which may render the contents injurious to health; or (4) if (A) it bears or contains, for purposes of coloring only, a color additive which is unsafe within the meaning of Section 721(a), or (B) it is a color additive the intended use of which in or on drugs or devices is for purposes of coloring only and is unsafe within the meaning of Section 721(a); or (5) if it is a new animal drug which is unsafe within the meaning of Section 512; or (6) if it is an animal feed bearing or containing a new animal drug, and such animal feed is unsafe within the meaning of Section 512.
>
> (b) If it purports to be or is represented as a drug the name of which is recognized in an official compendium, and its strength differs from, or its quality or purity falls below, the standards set forth in such compendium. Such determination as to strength, quality, or purity shall be made in accordance with the tests or methods of assay set forth in such compendium, except that whenever tests or methods of assay have not been prescribed in such compendium, or such tests or methods of assay as are prescribed are, in the judgment of the Secretary, insufficient for the making of such determination, the Secretary shall bring such fact to the attention of the appropriate body charged with the revision of such compendium, and if such body fails within a reasonable time to prescribe tests or methods of assay which, in the judgment of the Secretary, are sufficient for purposes of this paragraph, then the Secretary shall promulgate

regulations prescribing appropriate tests or methods of assay in accordance with which such determination as to strength, quality, or purity shall be made. No drug defined in an official compendium shall be deemed to be adulterated under this paragraph because it differs from the standard of strength, quality, or purity therefore set forth in such compendium, if its difference in strength, quality, or purity from such standards is plainly stated on its label. Whenever a drug is recognized in both the United States Pharmacopeia and the Homeopathic Pharmacopeia of the United States it shall be subject to the requirements of the United States Pharmacopeia unless it is labeled and offered for sale as a homeopathic drug, in which case it shall be subject to the provisions of the Homeopathic Pharmacopeia of the United States and not to those of the United States Pharmacopeia.

(c) If it is not subject to the provisions of paragraph (b) of this section and its strength differs from, or its purity or quality falls below, that which it purports or is represented to possess.

(d) If it is a drug and any substance has been (1) mixed or packed therewith so as to reduce its quality or strength or (2) substituted wholly or in part thereof.

Misbranded Drugs

Misbranded or mislabeled drugs are those that are sold, dispensed, or distributed in violation of the labeling requirements of the FD&C. The courts have held that when a pharmacist sells a prescription drug at retail without a prescription or refills a prescription without the prescriber's authorization, he or she has in effect "misbranded" the drug (see *United States v. Carlisle*, 234 F.2d 196 [5th Cir. 1956]). Therefore, to violate the Durham-Humphrey Amendment is to misbrand a drug within the meaning of the term "misbrand" in the FD&C §301(k) or in 21 U.S.C. §331(k).

Section 502 (a)-(p) of the Act provides that:

A drug or device shall be deemed misbranded —

(a) If its labeling is false or misleading in any particular. Health care economic information provided to a formulary committee, or other similar entity, in the course of the committee or the entity carrying out its responsibilities for the selection of drugs for managed care or other similar organizations, shall not be considered to be false or misleading under this paragraph if the health care economic information directly relates to an indication approved under Section 505 or under Section 351(a) of the Public Health Service Act for such drug and is based on competent and reliable scientific evidence. The requirements set forth in Section 505(a) or in Section 351(a) of the Public Health Service Act shall not apply to health care economic information provided to such a committee or entity in accordance with this paragraph. Information that is relevant to the substantiation of the health care economic information presented pursuant to this paragraph shall be made available to the Secretary upon request. In this paragraph, the term "health care economic information" means any analysis that identifies, measures, or compares the economic consequences, including the costs of the represented health outcomes, of the use of a drug to the use of another drug, to another health care intervention, or to no intervention.

(b) If in a package form unless it bears a label containing (1) the name and place of business of the manufacturer, packer, or distributor; and (2) an accurate statement of the quantity of the contents in terms of weight, measure, or numerical count: *Provided*, That under clause (2) of this paragraph reasonable variations shall be permitted, and exemptions as to small packages shall be established, by regulations prescribed by the Secretary.

(c) If any word, statement, or other information required by or under authority of this Act to appear on the label or labeling is not prominently placed theron with such conspicuousness (as compared with other words, statements, designs, or devices, in the labeling) and in such terms as to render it likely to be read and understood by the ordinary individual under customary conditions of purchase and use.

(d) (Repealed by Pub. L. 105-115, November 21, 1997.)

(e)(1)(A) If it is a drug, unless its label bears, to the exclusion of any other nonproprietary name (except the applicable systematic chemical name or the chemical formula) — (i) the established name (as defined in subparagraph (3)) of the drug, if there is such a name; (ii) the established name and quantity, or, if determined to be appropriate by the Secretary, the proportion of each active ingredient, including the quantity, kind, and proportion of any alcohol, and also including whether active or not the established name and quantity or if determined to be appropriate by the Secretary, the proportion of any bromides, ether, chloroform, acetanilide, acetophenetidin, amidopyrine, antipyrine, atropine, hyoscine, hyoscyamine, arsenic, digitalis, digitalis glucosides, mercury, ouabain, strophanthin, strychnine, thyroid, or any derivative or preparation of any such substances, contained therein, except that the requirement for stating the quantity of the active ingredients, other than the quantity of those specifically named in this subclause, shall not apply to nonprescription drugs not intended for human use; and (iii) the established name of each inactive ingredient listed in alphabetical order on the outside container of the retail package and, if determined to be appropriate by the Secretary, on the immediate container, as prescribed in regulation promulgated by the Secretary, except that nothing in this subclause shall be deemed to require that any trade secret be divulged, and except that the requirements of this subclause with respect to alphabetical order shall apply only to nonprescription drugs that are not also cosmetics and that this subclause shall not apply to nonprescription drugs not intended for human use.

(e)(1)(B) For any prescription drug the established name of such drug or ingredient, as the case may be, on such label (and on any labeling on which a name for such drug or ingredient is used) shall be printed prominently and in type at least half as large as that used thereon for any proprietary name or designation for such drug or ingredient, except that to the extent that compliance with the requirements of subclause (ii) or (iii) of clause (A) or this clause is impracticable, exemptions shall be established by regulations promulgated by the Secretary.

(e)(2) If it is a device and it has an established name, unless its label bears, to the exclusion of any other nonproprietary name, its established name (as defined in subparagraph (4)) prominently printed in type at least half as large as that used thereon for any proprietary name or designation for such device, except that to the extent compliance with the requirements of this subparagraph is impracticable, exemptions shall be established by regulations promulgated by the Secretary.

(e)(3) As used in subparagraph (1), the term "established name" with respect to a drug or ingredient thereof, means (A) the applicable official name designated pursuant to Section 508, or (B) if there is no such name and such drug, or such ingredient, is an article recognized in an official compendium, then the official title thereof in such compendium, or (C) if neither clause (A) nor clause (B) of this subparagraph applies, then the common or usual name, if any, of such drug or of such ingredient, except that where clause (B) of this subparagraph applies to an article recognized in the United States Pharmacopeia and in the Homeopathic Pharamcopeia under different official titles, the official title used in the United States Pharmacopeia shall apply unless it is labeled and offered for sale as a homeopathic drug, in which case the official title used in the Homeopathic Pharmacopeia shall apply.

(e)(4) As used in subparagraph (2), the term "established name" with respect to a device means (A) the applicable official name of the device designated pursuant to Section 508, (B) if there is no such name and such device is an article recognized in an official compendium, then the official title thereof in such compendium, or (C) if neither clause (A) nor clause (B) of this subparagraph applies, then any common or usual name of such device.

(f) Unless its labeling bears (1) adequate directions for use; and (2) such adequate warnings against use in those pathological conditions or by children where its use may be dangerous to health, or against unsafe dosage or methods or duration of administration or application, in such manner and form, as are necessary for the protection of users, except that where any requirement of clause 1 of this paragraph, as applied to any drug or device, is not necessary for the protection of the public health, the Secretary shall promulgate regulations exempting such drug or device from such requirement.

(g) If it purports to be a drug the name of which is recognized in an official compendium, unless it is packaged and labeled as prescribed therein. The method of packing may be modified with the consent of the Secretary. Whenever a drug is recognized in both the United States Pharmacopeia and the Homeopathic Pharmacopeia of the United States, it shall be subject to the requirements of the United States Pharmacopeia with respect to packaging and labeling unless it is labeled and offered for sale as a homeopathic drug, in which case it shall be subject to the provisions of the Homeopathic Pharmacopeia of the United States, and not to those of the United States Pharmacopeia, except that in the event of inconsistency between the requirements of this paragraph and those of paragraph (e) as to the name by which the drug or its ingredients shall be designated, the requirements of paragraph (e) shall prevail.

(h) If it has been found by the Secretary to be a drug liable to deterioration, unless it is packaged in such form and manner, and its label bears a statement of such precautions, as the Secretary shall by regulations require as necessary for the protection of the public health. No such regulation shall be established for any drug recognized in an official compendium until the Secretary shall have informed the appropriate body charged with the revision of such compendium of the need for such packaging or labeling requirements and such body shall have failed within a reasonable time to prescribe such requirements.

(i)(1) If it is a drug and its container is so made, formed, or filled as to be misleading; or (2) if it is an imitation of another drug; or (3) if it is offered for sale under the name of another drug.

(j) If it is dangerous to health when used in the dosage or manner; or with the frequency or duration prescribed, recommended, or suggested in the labeling thereof.

(k) (Repealed by Pub. L. 105-115, November 21, 1997.)

(l) (Repealed by Pub. L. 105-115, November 21, 1997.)

(m) If it is a color additive the intended use of which is for the purpose of coloring only, unless its packaging and labeling are in conformity with such packaging and labeling requirements applicable to such color additive, as may be contained in regulations issued under Section 721.

(n) In the case of any prescription drug distributed or offered for sale in any State, unless the manufacturer, packer, or distributor thereof includes in all advertisements and other descriptive printed matter issued or caused to be issued by the manufacturer, packer, or distributor with respect to that drug a true statement of (1) the established name as defined in Section 502(e), printed prominently and in type at least half as large as that used for any trade or brand name thereof, (2) the formula showing quantitatively each ingredient of such drug to the extent required for labels under Section 502(e), and (3) such other information in brief summary relating to side effects, contraindications, and effectiveness as shall be required in regulations which shall be issued by the Secretary in accordance with the procedure specified in

Section 701(e) of this Act, except (A) in extraordinary circumstances, no regulation issued under this paragraph shall require prior approval by the Secretary of the content of any advertisement, and (B) no advertisement of a prescription drug, published after the effective date of regulations issued under this paragraph applicable to advertisements of prescription drugs, shall, with respect to the matters specified in this paragraph or covered by such regulations, be subject to the provisions of Sections 12 through 17 of the Federal Trade Commission Act, as amended (15 U.S.C. 52-57). This paragraph (n) shall not be applicable to any printed matter which the Secretary determines to be labeling as defined in Section 201(m) of this Act. Nothing in the Convention on Psychotropic Substances, signed at Vienna, Austria, on February 21, 1971, shall be construed to prevent drug price communications to consumers.

(o) If it was manufactured, prepared, propagated, compounded, or processed in an establishment in any State not duly registered under Section 510, if it was not included in a list required by Section 510(j), if a notice or other information respecting it was not provided as required by such section or Section 510(k), or if it does not bear such symbols from the uniform system for identification of devices prescribed under Section 510(e) as the Secretary by regulation requires.

(p) If it is a drug and its packaging or labeling is in violation of an applicable regulation issued pursuant to Section 3 and 4 of the Poison Prevention Packaging Act of 1970.

To understand the meaning of the term "misbranded," the term must be read in light of the requirement of §502(f)(1) of the Act (21 U.S.C. §352[f][1]) that the labeling of a drug contain "adequate directions for use." That is to say, prescription drugs are such because medical experts agree adequate directions for consumer self-medication cannot be provided for these drugs. Regardless of what directions a pharmacist or other dispenser might give when a legend drug is dispensed in absence of a prescription, the directions are, by law, not adequate for consumer use. Only the practitioner licensed to prescribe drugs is allowed to give directions adequate for the patient's safe and effective use of the federal legend drug product.

The Prescription Label

The directions and supervision of the prescribing or administering prescriber suffice in lieu of the adequate directions for use requirements of §502(f)(1) of the FD&C. However, this does not mean a drug may be dispensed without labeling by the pharmacist. Section 503(b)(2) of the Act (21 U.S.C. §353[b][2]) requires the prescription label have the following information:

(1) The name and address of the dispenser (pharmacy);
(2) the serial number of the prescription;
(3) the date of the prescription or the date of its filling (or refilling) — state law often determines which date is to be used;
(4) the name of the prescriber;
(5) the name of the patient, if stated in the prescription; and
(6) directions for use, including precautions, if any, as indicated on the prescription.

State law may require the following further information:

(1) The address of the patient;
(2) the initials or name of the dispensing pharmacist;
(3) the telephone number of the pharmacy;
(4) the drug name, strength, and manufacturer's lot or control number;
(5) the beyond-use date, if any; and
(6) the name of the manufacturer or distributor.

Receipt of Misbranded or Adulterated Drugs

If a pharmacy receives a misbranded or adulterated drug from a manufacturer or drug wholesaler, there is protection from federal penalty if the drug is then sold to a consumer. The FD&C provides a number of exemptions from prosecution for the sale of misbranded or adulterated products that are received from outside sources, although civil liability may not be avoided because of implied warranty under state laws.

Section 303(c) of the Act states that a retail dealer can escape criminal penalty for receipt in interstate commerce and subsequent delivery (sale) of misbranded or adulterated drugs if the delivery is in good faith and if, on request, he or she furnishes the FDA with records of the source of the interstate shipment. When the pharmacist purchases drugs from a wholesaler or manufacturer, he or she should look for a guaranty that the drugs are not adulterated or misbranded on the invoice. 21 CFR §7.13 suggests the following forms of guarantee.

(1) Limited form for use on invoice or bill of sale.

(Name of person giving the guaranty or undertaking) hereby guarantees that no article listed herein is adulterated or misbranded within the meaning of the FD&C, or is an article which may not, under the provisions of Section 404, 505, or 512 of the Act, be introduced into interstate commerce.

(Signature and post office address of person giving the guarantee or undertaking.)

(2) General and continuing form.

The article comprising each shipment or other delivery hereafter made by (name of person giving the guarantee or undertaking) to, or in the order of (name and post office address of person to whom the guaranty or undertaking is given) is hereby guaranteed, as of the date of such shipment or delivery, to be, on such date, not adulterated or misbranded within the meaning of the FD&C, and not an article which may not, under the provisions of Section 404, 505, or 512 of the Act, be introduced into interstate commerce.

(Signature and post office address of person giving the guarantee or undertaking.)

The "escape hatch" of §303(c)(1) does not apply to intrastate shipments of drugs; for reference consult *United States v. American Stores Co.*, 183 F.Supp 852 (D.Md. 1960).

Consequently, a pharmacy may obtain protection from its drug suppliers by obtaining a "continuing guaranty" (as part of its original purchase contracts) in the language outlined in 21 CFR §7.13. Again, if the guaranty is not obtained, the retailer has some protection under §303(c)(1). The drug wholesaler generally is limited to obtaining a guaranty from its suppliers since the §303(c)(1) exemption usually does not apply because the wholesaler puts drugs into interstate commerce (for reference, read *United States v. Moore Drug Exchange*, 239 F.Supp. 256 [D.Conn. 1965]).

Prescription Drugs

FDA regulations define "prescription drugs" as drugs subject to the requirement of §503(b)(1) of the FD&C, which states:

A drug intended for use by man which (A) because of its toxicity or other potentiality for harmful effect, or the method of its use, or the collateral measures necessary to its use, is not safe for use except under the supervision of a practitioner licensed by law to administer such drug; or (B) is limited by an approved application under Section 505 to use under the professional supervision of a practitioner licensed by law to administer such drug; shall be dispensed only (i) upon a written prescription of a practitioner licensed by law to administer such drug, or (ii) upon an oral prescription of such practitioner, which is reduced promptly to writing and filed by the pharmacist, or (iii) by refilling any such written or oral prescription if such refilling is authorized by the prescriber either in the original prescription or by oral order which is reduced promptly to writing and filed by the pharmacist. The act of dispensing a drug contrary to the provisions of this paragraph shall be deemed to be an act which results in the drug being misbranded while held for sale.

FDA regulations also define "prescription drugs" as those exempt from the requirement of §502(f)(1), which states that drugs must bear adequate directions for use or be considered misbranded and subject to seizure under certain conditions. A drug is limited by the Act to dispensing by or upon a prescription because it is habit-forming, toxic, or has a potential for harm, or the NDA limits it to use under a physician's supervision. (See also the corresponding FDA regulations found in 21 CFR Part 201 Subpart D.)

Previously, one of the conditions of the FDA regulations for exempting a prescription-only drug from the §502(f)(1) requirement of adequate directions for safe use was that the label of the prescription drug, prior to dispensing, required the statement: "Caution: Federal law prohibits dispensing without a prescription." (This phrase is known as the "federal legend," and, hence, prescription drugs have historically been known as "legend" drugs.) Section 126 of the FDAMA amended Section 503(b)(4) of the FD&C to require, at a minimum, that prior to dispensing, the label of prescription products contain the phrase "Rx only." The intent of this change was to simplify the labeling of prescription drug products in an effort to help reduce the incidence of medication errors in which product labeling and package design had been identified as a contributing factor. While the new requirement does not prohibit manufacturers from including other language on the label (ie, the "old" federal legend), the FDA believes that in the interest of simplification, it is preferable to have only the "Rx only" statement. The FDA has published a Guidance for Industry addressing the implementation of Section 126 of FDAMA. The Guidance Document (which can be found at http://www.fda.gov/cder/guidance/index.htm) states the FDA intends to exercise its enforcement discretion and not object if a manufacturer does not comply with the labeling provisions until the next revision of its labels, or by February 19, 2003, whichever comes first.

Nonprescription (Over-the-Counter) Drugs

Nonprescription drugs are defined as drugs recognized among experts to be safe and effective for use (21 CFR §330.10). These drugs must be manufactured in accordance with the FDA's current good manufacturing standards and be labeled with directions for the layperson that indicate their safe and effective use.

Such drugs are sold "over-the-counter" without a prescription; thus, they are called "*otc*" drugs.

Pharmacy Labeling of Bulk Drug Products

A pharmacist may legally repackage or relabel (under the pharmacy label) *otc* and prescription drugs purchased in bulk, but it is a risky business. When a pharmacy places its own label on a nonprescription drug container, it takes legal responsibility for compliance with all the general and applicable specific labeling requirements of both federal and state law and for compliance with state law prohibiting the sale of adulterated or substandard drugs. Moreover, in the preamble comments to the Current Good Manufacturing Practices (CGMP), the FDA indicates that pharmacies engaged in drug repackaging or relabeling operations beyond the usual dispensing and selling of drugs at retail will face liability for registration as a manufacturer, be subject to regular inspections, and must heed the detailed requirements of the CGMPs (43 Fed. Reg. 45028 [1978]).

Whether a pharmacy's relabeling and repackaging operation exceeds the usual practice of a pharmacy depends on the distribution of the relabeled and repackaged drugs. If the drugs are intended for distribution to other pharmacies or locations, then the CGMP regulations and FDA registration would apply. If the drugs are sold at retail only from the pharmacy that is engaged in the relabeling and repackaging, the CGMP and FDA registration would not apply. Hospital pharmacies regularly repackage bulk products into unit doses, and providing the unit doses are restricted to dispensing within the hospital, the pharmacy is not required to register with the FDA.

For more information regarding the applicability of CGMPs to repackaging and relabeling, see FDA Compliance Policy Guidances 7132.13 — Repacking of Drug Products — Testing/Examination under CGMPs and 7132.06 Hospital Pharmacies — Status as Drug Manufacturer. These can be found on the Internet at http://www.fda.gov/ora under the subject, Compliance Policy Guides. For further discussion of this issue, see Repackaging in the next section.

In community pharmacy practice, an occasion may arise when an *otc* drug needs to be dispensed at retail from a bulk container. Whenever the pharmacist relabels *otc* drugs, the safe rule is to include on the label all of the identical information, including directions, warnings, contents, control numbers, expiration date, and the manufacturer or distributor name, as is included on the manufacturer's or distributor's commercial package label. However, as stated above, this will be difficult to do with the requirements for standardized labels contained in 21 CFR §201.66. If this can be done, the labeling requirements of the FDA have probably been met and also the §303(c) prohibition against delivery for remuneration of a misbranded or adulterated drug has been heeded, provided the sale is in good faith (ie, provided no actual knowledge of adulteration or misbranding exists).

Veterinary Prescription Labeling

While the FD&C does not contain an explicit provision regarding prescription veterinary drugs, federal courts have interpreted Section 502(f)(1) as authority for restricting some veterinary drug products to prescription status. Under federal regulations (21 CFR §201.105), veterinary prescription drugs must be labeled with the legend: "Caution: Federal law restricts this drug to use by or on the order of a licensed veterinarian." The Center for Veterinary Medicine within the FDA decides which veterinary drugs require the veterinary prescription legend. The primary basis for distinguishing prescription from *otc* veterinary drug products is whether adequate directions for lay use can be developed for a product. If so, the drug may be sold without the order of a licensed veterinarian.

The sales policies of some manufacturers may require that veterinary products be sold only to licensed veterinarians. This statement has no basis under the law, but reflects the manufacturer's own sales policy.

A veterinarian may prescribe human legend drugs for use in animals. A drug product which has prescription-only status for humans may be an *otc* drug for veterinary purposes. However, such human prescription drugs that may be *otc* may not be sold for veterinary use without a prescription because they do not bear adequate directions for use in animals.

Federal law does not restrict the sale of veterinary prescription products to pharmacies or veterinarians' offices. Such products may be sold in feed stores or via catalogs. Persons who distribute animal drugs are responsible under federal law for ensuring that veterinary products bearing the "Caution" legend on their label are sold only to authorized recipients.

DISPENSING OF PHARMACEUTICALS

Prescription Requirements

Authority to Prescribe

The FD&C (21 U.S.C. Section 353[b][1]) states that federal legend drugs may be prescribed by a practitioner licensed by law to administer such drugs. However, the primary determination of whether a prescriber is authorized to prescribe for a given condition is based on state law, not federal law. Similarly, the Controlled Substances Act does not establish specific criteria regarding who may prescribe. Instead, the Act requires the prescriber be licensed to prescribe under state law and be registered with the Drug Enforcement Administration.

Once the classes of practitioners who are authorized to write prescriptions have been identified under state law, the pharmacist must next determine the scope of their prescribing authority. The physician, whether allopathic (MD) or osteopathic (DO), has the widest possible practice authority and consequently the widest latitude with respect to prescription-writing activities. All medical specialists (eg, obstetricians, psychiatrists, ophthalmologists) fall under the general category of physician and thus enjoy broad privileges when writing prescriptions. While prescriptions written outside the specialist's realm of expertise legally are authorized, the pharmacist may want to scrutinize the prescription for any medical-legal concerns.

Various states also have licensed other prescribers who have limited scopes of practice. For example, a veterinarian may prescribe only for animals; a podiatrist can prescribe only for ailments of the human foot or lower extremities; a dentist may treat disorders of the oral cavity or maxillofacial area. In some states, optometrists have been given authority to use drugs for diagnostic purposes, while in others, they have received the authority to both use and prescribe drugs for the treatment of eye disorders. Again, state law must be consulted to determine the scope of practice for each of these prescribers, as well as the prescribing limitations placed on chiropractors, nurse practitioners, midwives, and other health care providers. A pharmacist who dispenses a drug on a prescription order which exceeds the legal limits of the practitioner may be in violation of the state pharmacy practice statutes because the prescription is not within the course of professional practice.

Prescribing by Pharmacists

Just as other prescribers receive their authority under state law, pharmacists must also obtain authorization to prescribe under state "police powers." The authorization to prescribe should arise in the form of a statute from the state legislature, as opposed to a board of pharmacy regulation. A regulation that attempts to confer on pharmacists the right to prescribe without a statutory foundation most likely will be challenged as exceeding the agency's statutory authority. The pharmacist may be provided with independent or dependent authority to prescribe. Dependent functions are those the pharmacist performs under the authority of some other licensed independent health care practitioner. This delegation of authority is most effective when supported by statutory authorization and often includes a system of standing orders or protocols under which pharmacists perform their prescribing activities.

Collaborative Drug Therapy Management

A number of states have enacted legislation that expands the practice of pharmacy to include collaborative drug therapy management. While the details of collaborative drug therapy management vary from state to state, all involve the pharmacist and the physician working in collaboration to manage a patient's drug therapy. Such collaboration usually is accomplished through written protocols and may include authority for the pharmacist to collect and review patient drug histories, initiate and modify drug therapy, order and evaluate laboratory tests relating to drug therapy, and order and perform drug-related patient assessments. Collaborative drug therapy management programs that authorize pharmacists to initiate and modify drug therapy, in effect, give the pharmacist dependent prescribing authority.

State law may give the pharmacist the independent right to prescribe. Usually, such an independent right will be limited to certain drugs or categories of drugs. Pharmacists have no legal right to prescribe or administer drugs unless there is specific statutory authorization creating independent prescribing activity or where there is a legally authorized delegation of authority from another practitioner. A pharmacist who prescribes drugs without authorization not only violates the state's Pharmacy Practice Act but also is guilty of rendering a drug misbranded under the FD&C (21 U.S.C. §352).

Physician Dispensing

The professions of pharmacy and medicine have long been intertwined, but in the 20th century, pharmacy clearly established itself as a separate profession. Because pharmacy grew out of medicine, physicians traditionally have maintained the right to dispense the drugs they prescribe. While dispensing physicians have had an economic impact on some pharmacies in smaller communities, pharmacy as a whole was not particularly concerned about the physician dispenser until the 1980s, when a number of factors encouraged a dramatic increase in dispensing by physicians.

Pharmacists long have felt that physicians hold an unfair advantage because under the present law, physicians are not subject to the same FDA labeling requirements as pharmacists. The FDA has gone on record stating, "that although Section 503(b) is applicable to physicians, we have long considered physicians who have dispensed drugs to patients pursuant to a bona fide doctor-patient relationship to be exempt from strict compliance with the labeling requirements for prescription drugs." In a 1984 statement, FDA officials concluded that Congress did not intend to interfere with the dispensing practice of physicians and that the agency's present policy had not contributed to problems affecting the public health or safety. This position apparently applies to the labeling requirements of Section 503(b) of the FD&C but not the packaging requirements, which are applicable to the drug whether dispensed by a pharmacist or a physician. However, the FDA has deferred most of the enforcement of the packaging requirements, as well as the labeling requirements, to the individual states. Various states have enacted statutes outlining labeling requirements for practitioners who dispense, but as a general rule, these statutes are poorly enforced.

Because of an alleged concern for the public's health, boards of pharmacy in some states have proposed regulations setting forth conditions that physicians must meet when they dispense pharmaceuticals to their patients. These proposals have come under scrutiny by the staff of the Federal Trade Commission who argue that these proposals impose discriminatory restraints on practitioners without any justification.

In 1986, the Georgia Board of Pharmacy proposed practitioners who dispense must personally perform the complete act of dispensing and an assistant only may type a label or count or pour ingredients under the direct supervision of the physician. The prescriber would also be personally responsible for patient counseling and only could dispense from privately owned medication supplies for his or her own patients. The FTC staff argued that any action undertaken by a board composed largely of competing professionals that excludes another group of competitors from the market (such as physicians) could constitute a violation of the Federal antitrust laws.

The staff of the FTC further contended the Georgia requirement that a physician personally perform the complete act of dispensing could "frustrate efficient use of practitioner time and expertise in group practices." The FTC also took issue with this requirement because there was not a similar requirement for pharmacists. In addition, there was no apparent justification for imposing a counseling requirement on physicians, when Georgia pharmacists did not have such a requirement. The Georgia Board of Pharmacy agreed to reconsider its proposals.

Pharmacy organizations have responded to FTC allegations by claiming that statutes and regulations that permit physicians to dispense are more anticompetitive in nature than those currently being proposed by pharmacy boards. It is further alleged that the patient's health and safety and the checks and balances provided by pharmacists dispensing prescriptions are compromised when physicians dispense medications to patients.

The Pharmacy Practice Act in Texas was carefully drafted to place limitations on who may practice pharmacy. In 1985, the Attorney General of Texas issued an opinion, which concluded that physicians in that state who dispense drugs and charge a separate fee for the drugs are engaged in the practice of pharmacy and may not do so unless licensed by the Texas Board of Pharmacy. Exceptions are provided for physicians who practice in rural communities without pharmacies. The Texas Board of Pharmacy has been successful in its initial enforcement of the Act's provisions. Texas courts have permanently restrained and enjoined at least 5 physicians from charging a separate fee for dispensing or distributing drugs to patients.

Generic Substitution

Drug Product Selection

It is a basic tenet of pharmacy law that the pharmacist is obligated to his or her patrons, when filling a prescription, to dispense the exact drug prescribed. Physicians prescribe drugs either by reference to the brand name or trade name of the drug or by a generic or chemical name (eg, ferrous sulfate) or chemical formula (eg, $FeSO_4$).

Until the 1970s, almost every state had a statute or an administrative rule strictly forbidding prescription drug substitution. Typically, these statutes restricted the substitution of a drug brand different from the one prescribed. For example, a pharmacist would violate the prohibition if he or she dispensed cephalexin made by Barr when the prescription was for *Keflex*, Eli Lilly's brand, unless first obtaining authority for the substitution from the prescriber, an exception written into most of the old antisubstitution laws.

There were several underlying reasons for the original prohibition against substitution of brand name drugs. Many of the laws had been passed 25 years earlier to control the distribution of substandard counterfeit drugs. The prohibition also assured the patient of receiving the exact drug prescribed by his or her physician; it assured the medical profession of a more or less exclusive right to control drug selection; and it assured the pharmaceutical manufacturer of a captive market for its trademarked product.

The cost of drugs in the Medicaid program was the impetus to the re-evaluating of the antisubstitution laws. In 1975, the DHHS implemented the concept of maximum allowable costs (MAC) for reimbursement of selected generic drugs covered by the Medicaid program. Through this program, states with antisubstitution laws could not participate in the Medicaid program because the cost for the innovator's brand name product almost always was higher than the MAC.

In addition, there were several pharmaceutical societies that maintained that if the pharmacist had a greater say in the selection of prescription drug products, the image of the pharmacist would be enhanced. On the other hand, some legalists warned (and still warn) that pharmacist responsibility for drug product selection subjects the pharmacist to greater civil liability for therapeutic failure if the product selected has bioavailability problems or in some other way injures the particular patient.

Therefore, in the mid-1970s, states began repealing their antisubstitution laws and replacing them with product selection laws that eventually became applicable to all prescriptions.

Now every state has a drug product selection law that repeals, in part or in whole, its former drug antisubstitution law. A model Drug Product Selection Act was published by the Federal Trade Commission (FTC) in 1979.

In a number of states, the law was changed to the extent that not only was the brand name drug substitution prohibition modified or dropped, but the pharmacist was actually encouraged or even mandated to substitute or select a different product in the appropriate circumstances. In the court case of *Pharmaceutical Society of the State of New York v. Lefkowitz*, 586 F.2d 953 (2nd Cir. 1978), a US court of appeals sustained the constitutional validity of a New York generic drug act. This act provided that the health commissioner establish a list of drug products approved by the FDA as safe and effective and meet the FDA bioequivalency requirements. The state law further provided that every prescription blank must have 2 signature lines, one for "substitution permissible" and the other for "dispense as written." If the former line is signed, the prescriber is required to inform the patient that the pharmacist will substitute a generic drug on the commissioner's list.

A number of constitutional challenges were argued by opponents of this law, the most significant of which was that it forced a pharmacist to sell drugs in which he or she did not have confidence — running the risk of suits for defects in those drugs. In addition, a pharmacist could not sell the brand name drug when substitution was indicated, even though he or she did not have the less expensive generic equivalent in stock.

In answer to these issues, the federal appeals court first made it clear the New York act was not mandatory in the sense that the decision to substitute or not to substitute is initially set by the prescribing physician, who is free to sign either line. That is, the physician could sign the line "dispense as written" and the pharmacist would have no need (or requirement) to substitute. The claim that the law forces the selling of drugs in which the pharmacist has no confidence and considers unsafe was cited as speculative. The pharmacists could not prove that FDA-approved generic equivalents are less safe than brand name drugs. As to the problem of having only the brand name drug in stock, the easy solution, in the court's viewpoint, is to stock at least one lower priced generic equivalent.

The FTC's model Drug Product Selection Act (an optional type of product selection law) provides that the pharmacist filling a prescription written for a particular brand name drug product may select an equivalent drug product listed in the drug formulary. There are exceptions. The patient may instruct the pharmacist otherwise, or the prescriber may indicate that the specific brand prescribed is medically necessary.

The model act contained a provision designed to limit the pharmacist's civil liability when substituting a generically equivalent drug in place of the brand name drug product. The pharmacist liability limitation section is worded as follows:

> Any pharmacist who selects an equivalent drug pursuant to this section incurs no greater liability in filling the prescription by dispensing the equivalent drug product than would be incurred in filling the prescription by dispensing the brand name drug prescribed.

Some pharmacists took the position that it was in the patient's best interest for a generic drug prescription to be filled with the brand name product of a reputable drug firm. However, even reputable drug firms have occasional drug recalls for mislabeling or subpotency.

As is done in other cases of liability exposure, the pharmacist could ask the patient to consent to accept the lower priced generic drug at the patient's own risk, or the pharmacist could disclaim liability due to any therapeutically significant difference between the generic drug and the drug prescribed in a brand name. However, in either case, the courts probably would invalidate any consent that would hold the seller guiltless because of the public policy to protect the consumer.

Even if the consumer signs a consent to the substitution of brand A for brand B, the pharmacist probably is not relieved of liability. In *Spry v. Kiser* (179 N.C. 417; 102 S.E. 708 [1920]), the court stated the following:

> A person engaged in the business of pharmacy holds himself out to the public as one having the peculiar learning and skill necessary to a safe and proper conducting of the business, while the general customer is not supposed to be skilled in the matter, and frequently does not know one drug from another, but relies on the druggist to furnish the article called for....

The consumer is not in a position to appreciate bioavailability and bioequivalence. How then can he or she give an intelligent consent to a substitution in a prescription? Governmental agency determination of bioequivalent drug products probably would not insulate from liability the pharmacist who substitutes drug product equivalent A for the prescribed brand name drug product B. Regulations issued by administrative agencies set minimal standards and compliance with them does not, as a matter of law and in all cases, mean that the pharmacist is free from negligence (see the cases of *Bristol Myers Co. v. Gonzales*, 548 S.W.2d 416 [Tex.Civ.App.1977], *McEwen v. Ortho Pharmaceutical*, 528 P.2d 522 [Ore.1974], and *Stevens v. Parke, Davis and Co.*, 507 P.2d 653 [Cal.1973]).

Controversies Surrounding Drug Product Selection

By the end of the 1970s, many individuals were ready to close the file on the case of generic substitution. While there were those who were unhappy with the concept, they seemed resigned to the fact the substitution laws were in place and were working. State legislators were convinced they had met the responsibility of ensuring the citizens of their state were offered the benefit of quality pharmaceutical products at competitive prices.

Then, in the early 1980s, 2 things happened that caused drug product selection to become a topic of controversy again. The first was the formal advent of therapeutic substitution, a prerogative that had long been exercised by many hospital pharmacists. The second was the enactment of the 1984 Drug Price Competition and Patent Term Restoration Act. This federal legislation was designed to foster competition by generic manufacturers and encourage research by pioneer pharmaceutical firms. However, what was begun as a political compromise turned into the "generic drug wars" of the 1980s.

Before examining the controversies surrounding therapeutic substitution and recent claims of bioinequivalence of generic drugs, it is important to have a common understanding of basic terms. The American Pharmaceutical Association (APhA) and the American Medical Association (AMA) cooperated to work out terms in an interprofessional dialogue. The terms pertinent for this discussion include:

Drug Product Selection. The act of selecting the source of supply of a drug product in a specific dosage form.

Chemical Equivalents. Those multiple-source drug products that contain essentially identical amounts of the identical active ingredients in identical dosage forms.

Generic Substitution. The act of dispensing a different brand or an unbranded drug product for the drug product described (ie, chemically the exact drug entity in the same dosage form, but distributed by different companies).

Therapeutic Alternates. Drug products containing different therapeutic moieties but that are of the same pharmacological or therapeutic class that can be expected to have similar therapeutic effects when administered to patients in therapeutically equivalent doses.

Therapeutic Substitution. The act of dispensing a therapeutic alternate for the drug product prescribed.

Brand Name vs Generic Drugs

The Drug Price Competition and Patent Term Restoration Act of 1984 provided patent extensions and guarantees of market exclusivity to innovator drug companies. Generic companies, in turn, won the right to market generic copies by submitting Abbreviated New Drug Applications (ANDAs) showing that the generic formulation is bioequivalent to the brand name drug. Thus, the generic company does not need to submit data on the safety or effectiveness of their drug because these factors have already been proven by the innovator drug firm. (See the Regulation of Pharmaceuticals chapter for further discussion of this Act.)

After the enactment of the 1984 legislation, one of its authors, Rep. Henry Waxman (D-Calif.) declared that "the war between generics and brands is over." But in reality, the exchange of gunfire between the brand name manufacturers and generic drug firms was just beginning. The warfare that has developed centers on the issue of bioequivalence. The economic and political forces in this controversy are often stronger than the legal considerations. The FDA, the agency responsible for approving the marketing of drug products, has been caught in the middle of the "generic wars" at times.

Certain brand name manufacturers were accused of initiating the controversy by propagating antigeneric claims. These companies were accused of confusing or intimidating pharmacists into dispensing only the brand name drug for fear of increased liability if the generic version were dispensed. Other manufacturers were accused of launching scare campaigns to try to convince the public that generic drugs were not as safe or effective as brand name products. In turn, consumer groups have accused some brand name manufacturers of covert funding to underwrite the speaking tours and media appearances by supposedly independent physicians, pharmacologists, and academicians to allegedly raise fears about generic drugs. It also has been claimed that brand name manufacturers have changed the color or shape of their products (particularly when they are about to go off patent) and then warn physicians the patient may become confused if the doctor permits substitution of a different-looking generic product.

Sometimes the exchange between generic and brand name drug manufacturers has placed the FDA in an awkward position. Early in the controversy, the FDA assumed what appeared to be a somewhat defensive stance. The FDA was quick to the point out that although hundreds of new generic drug products had been approved, the agency had not received a documented instance of a serious problem with a generic drug. The FDA went so far as to publish 10 myths about generic drug quality in the April 1986 National Association of Boards of Pharmacy Newsletter.

Bioavailability and Bioequivalency

As a result of this controversy, the FDA increasingly has been called upon to defend the process by which it determines that the generic versions of brand name drug products are safe, effective, and bioequivalent. The bioavailability problems associated with certain drugs and the need to have some way of ensuring bioequivalent (generically equivalent) drugs really are equivalent prompted government action on the national level. As a result, an attempt to clarify the situation resulted in the FDA promulgating bioavailability/bioequivalence regulations in January 1977. The regulations are found in Title 21 CFR, §320 et seq.

Bioavailability is defined as the rate and the extent to which the active drug ingredient or therapeutic moiety is absorbed from the drug product and becomes available at the site of drug action. Bioequivalent drug products are defined as pharmaceutical equivalents or pharmaceutical alternatives whose rate and extent of absorption do not show a significant difference when administered at the same molar dose of the therapeutic moiety under similar experimental conditions, either as a single dose or as multiple doses.

A number of sources have objected to the fact that the bioavailability of generic products usually is tested only in a small group of healthy males. The FDA believes testing healthy volunteers is a strong indicator the 2 tested dosage forms will behave the same under the same conditions, and even though the metabolism and absorption rate of drugs in healthy volunteers will differ from the elderly, this does not invalidate the bioequivalence test.

The FDA also faces constant attack on its "± 20% rule" which requires generic drug products to have a rate and extent of absorption that, from a statistical standpoint, will not vary more than 20% in bioavailability when compared with the innovator's product. It is argued that the 20/25 rule allows bioavailability variances of as much as 45%. It is claimed a patient might receive a drug product that is 20% less bioavailable than the reference standard on one prescription and that is 20% on the plus side the next time. The FDA points out that it would be very difficult for a generic product to pass the test requirements if, in fact, the drug's bioavailability differed by 20% from the standard product. The FDA has noted that the average difference of the brand name and generic drug products is closer to 3.5%.

Therapeutic Substitution

The substitution of drugs which are not the same chemical entity but are in the same thera-peutic class is just as controversial as generic substitution. However, therapeutic substitu-tion is gaining increasing popularity as hospitals, health maintenance organizations, and third-party payers consider this process to aid in cost containment. While many hospital phar-macists long have engaged in therapeutic substitution, it is expected that this type of sub-stitution will increase outside the hospital environment as more third-party payers realize financial benefits even when a single source drug is prescribed because often a less expen-sive therapeutic equivalent could be dispensed in its place.

The state of Washington is the only state that has specific legislation permitting therapeu-tic substitution. During the 1987 legislative session, efforts were made to remove this authority from the practice of pharmacy. While lobbying efforts were not successful in Wash-ington, the pharmaceutical industry and physicians were successful in getting the state of Wisconsin to limit therapeutic substitution to hospital inpatients. The American Society of Hospital Pharmacists (ASHP) felt compelled to submit testimony at the Wisconsin hear-ing supporting therapeutic interchange because they felt that the Pharmaceutical Manufac-turers Association's (PMA) campaign to resist therapeutic substitution could significantly damage not only the concept of therapeutic interchange, but also that it could threaten hos-pital formularies and the profession of pharmacy itself. The PMA is now known as the Pharmaceutical Research and Manufacturers Association (PhRMA), a trade association rep-resenting brand-name manufacturers. A number of pharmacy organizations including APhA, ASHP, NCPA, and others have tried to reach an agreement with the PMA on the issue of therapeutic substitution. A negotiated statement in 1986 held that therapeutic substitu-tion is appropriate when pharmacists and physicians interrelate on behalf of the patient, but some pharmacy groups concluded that this language was not always in the best interest of the patient or the profession. The PMA also rejected the statement because some members did not want any therapeutic substitution conducted beyond hospital walls.

The medical profession believes that therapeutic substitution is a "usurpation of the physi-cian's professional prerogatives." Physicians argue that they are in the best clinical posi-tion to make critical decisions regarding a patient's drug therapy because they have access to the patient history, physical exam, and diagnosis.

Hospital Formulary System

If very few states provide direct or indirect statutory authorization of therapeutic substitu-tion, one may question the pervasiveness of such substitution in hospitals and other institu-tions. In absence of statutory authority, hospital pharmacists usually cite as legal authority the physician's agreement to abide by hospital policies and procedures when joining the hos-pital staff. These policies include the use of the hospital formulary. The hospital formulary system is a method whereby the medical staff of a hospital, working through a pharmacy and therapeutics (P & T) committee, evaluates, appraises, and selects from numerous therapeu-tic agents and dosage forms those which are considered most useful in the patient popu-lation. (Doering PL, et al. Therapeutic substitution and the hospital formulary system. *Am J Hosp Pharm.* 1981;38:1949.) Under the hospital formulary, the pharmacist has the authority to select the brand of medication dispensed unless the prescriber makes a specific nota-tion to the contrary. This product selection, in many institutions, may permit the auto-matic interchange of chemically inequivalent products deemed to be therapeutically equivalent by the P & T committee.

The Concept of Prior Consent

Those who support the concepts of generic and therapeutic substitution within institu-tional settings claim the physician has given prior consent to such drug product selection by agreeing to adhere to the procedures of the institution. An assumption is made that as long as prescribers are fully aware that there is the possibility of drug product selection, their prior consent will carry the same legal weight as if the prescriber were to authorize the substitution at the same time the medication order was issued. As an alternative to this process, the practitioners may give their concurrent consent by checking a box or signing their name on a given line if substitution is to be permitted. Some would claim that concurrent consent is the preferred mechanism, although it is probably not the system most often utilized.

There are no known court decisions that address the issues of therapeutic substitution and the legality of the hospital formulary system. However, the Oregan State Attorney General's Office has issued 2 opinions on the subject. In the first, the Attorney General's opinion was that a hospital pharmacist cannot perform therapeutic substitution, even though the hospital staff physicians may have agreed to abide by hospital rules; the substitution mandated by the hospital would not be equivalent to a prescription as required by Oregon law.

Later, the Attorney General of Oregon was asked if the laws of the state would permit any procedure by which a physician could, in advance, authorize a pharmacist to dispense a therapeutically equivalent drug in place of another product. In the opinion, the Attorney General stated that a prescription need not take any particular form. In the opinion of the Attorney General, there was nothing to preclude 2 statements separated in time from being deemed to constitute a prescription. Thus, the prescription might take the form of (a) a practitioner's advanced written authorization to substitute one drug for another, and (b) the later prescription order itself. Of particular interest, the opinion indicated the response to this issue was not limited to institutional settings. While an attorney general's opinion is simply that, it does demonstrate the current thinking in the area of drug product selection.

It is interesting to note the Office of General Counsel of the ASHP also issued an opinion holding that the operation of the formulary system is grounded in the states' Medical Practice Acts and not the Pharmacy Practice Acts. A pharmacist cannot alter or modify the medication eventually dispensed without first obtaining the physician's consent to such action or without direct statutory authority. The ASHP legal opinion concluded that any arguments that would claim the operation of the formulary system is restricted under the pharmacy practice statutes are inconsistent because the formulary's actual source of authority is in the Medical Practice Act.

It should also be noted that in the state of Washington, which has provided pharmacists with the authority to substitute therapeutically equivalent drug products, the substitution cannot occur without the practitioner's prior consent. The statute did not specify which mechanisms for obtaining prior consent are acceptable. Although there are still some questions about whether the agreement of prescribers to abide by hospital policies and procedures constitutes the consent necessary for a therapeutic substitution, the system seems to be working. The prerogatives of the Washington statute are available to all pharmacists whether or not they practice in an institutional setting.

Medicaid Prescriptions and Product Selection

Under the typical state Medicaid system, the pharmacist is reimbursed for filling Medicaid prescriptions on the basis of a state-determined estimated acquisition cost (EAC), the maximum allowable cost (MAC), plus a dispensing fee (which varies from state to state) or the pharmacist's customary charge, whichever figure is lower. Most states have rules governing generic substitution when a physician indicates the brand is "medically necessary" or "DAW." Pharmacists should follow the rules of the jurisdiction where the practice is located to ensure proper reimbursement.

The Orange Book

The FDA Center For Drug Evaluation and Research — Approved Drug Products with Therapeutic Equivalence Evaluations

The above publication, *Approved Drug Products with Therapeutic Equivalence Evaluations* (the List), identifies drug products approved on the basis of safety and effectiveness by the FDA under the FD&C (the Act). Drugs on the market approved only on the basis of safety (covered by the ongoing Drug Efficacy Study Implementation or pre-1938 drugs) are not included in the publication. The main criterion for the inclusion of any product is that the product is the subject of an application with an effective approval that has not been withdrawn for safety or efficacy reasons. In addition, the List contains therapeutic equivalence evaluations for approved multisource prescription drug products. Copies of FDA's *Approved Drug Products with Therapeutic Equivalence Evaluations* are available from: Superintendent of Documents, US Government Printing Office, Washington, DC 20402, telephone 202–783-3238. An online version of the FDA's Approved Drug Products with Therapeutic Equivalents can be viewed on the FDA's Web site at http://www.fda.gov/cder/ob/.

This List is a result of requests to the FDA from federal, state, and local health-related agencies, private institutions, pharmacists, and consumers to provide information on the availability of relatively inexpensive, therapeutically equivalent drug products. State agencies responsible for administering their own drug product selection laws were particularly interested.

The List was distributed as a proposal on January 12, 1979 (44 Fed. Reg. 2932), and a complete discussion of the background and basis of FDA's therapeutic equivalence evaluation policy is described there. The final rule, which includes the FDA's responses to the public comments on the proposal was published in the *Federal Register* on October 31, 1980 (35 Fed. Reg. 72582). At that time, it included only currently marketed prescription drug products approved by the FDA through NDAs and ANDAs under the provisions of Section 505 of the Act.

In 1984, the Drug Price Competition and Patent Term Restoration Act ("1984 Amendments," described in more detail below) required the agency to, among other things, begin publishing an up-to-date list of all marketed drug products, *otc* as well as prescription, that have been approved for safety and efficacy and for which new drug applications are required. The 6th edition of the publication began to include *otc* products, as well as drug products with approval under Section 505 of the Act administered by the Center for Biologics Evaluation and Research. An addendum to the publication identifies drugs that qualify under the 1984 amendments for periods of exclusivity and provides patent information concerning the listed drugs which also may delay the approval of ANDAs or Section 505(b)(2) applications (explained in more detail below).

The List is composed of 4 parts:

(1) Approved prescription drug products with therapeutic equivalence evaluations;
(2) approved *otc* drug products for those drugs that may not be marketed without NDAs or ANDAs because they are not covered under existing *otc* monographs;
(3) drug products with approval under Section 505 of the Act administered by the Center for Biologics; and
(4) a cumulative list of approved products that have never been marketed, have been discontinued from marketing, or have had their approvals withdrawn for reasons other than safety or efficacy subsequent to being discontinued from marketing.

The List only identifies the holder of the approved drug product application in the FDA files. It does not identify the distributor or repackager of drug products. At times, when there are drug products on the market that are generic copies of drugs for which the patent has expired, the FDA-approved application on file has been submitted only by the original drug firm that marketed the drug product or by a few other firms marketing the drug. The FDA's position is that every firm marketing generic drug products must have an FDA-approved application on file. The FDA has cautioned there is a certain degree of risk involved (as far as quality is concerned) in the use of drug products for which there is no FDA approval.

The FDA's list entitled *Approved Drug Products with Therapeutic Equivalence Evaluations* is commonly referred to as "The Orange Book" due to the color of the cover of the publication. The FDA Orange Book serves as the primary source for generic equivalency information and is used by many states as the standard for determining when drug products may be substituted with generic equivalents. Drug products are considered therapeutic equivalents if they are pharmaceutical equivalents (that is, they contain the same active ingredients, same dosage form, same route of administration, and same strength or concentration), and if they can be expected to have the same clinical effect and safety profile when administered to patients under conditions specified in the labeling. To meet this requirement, the products must be considered bioequivalent. The term bioequivalent describes pharmaceutical equivalent or pharmaceutical alternative products that display comparable bioavailability when studied under similar experimental conditions. Section 505(j)(7)(B) of the Act describes one set of conditions under which 2 products are considered bioequivalent. Under the Drug Price Competition and Patent Term Restoration Act of 1984, manufacturers seeking approval to market a generic drug must submit data demonstrating the drug product is bioequivalent to the pioneer (innovator) drug product. (This drug is referred to as the "reference listed drug" (See 21 CFR §314.94[a][3]) and is identified by the FDA as the drug product upon which an applicant relies in seeking approval of its ANDA.) A major premise underlying the 1984 law is that bioequivalent drug products are therapeutically equivalent and, therefore, interchangeable.

The FDA Orange Book uses a 2-letter coding system to allow users to easily determine whether an approved product is considered therapeutically equivalent to other approved products. The 2 basic categories into which multisource drugs are placed are indicated by the first letter of the code.

A - Drug products the FDA considers to be therapeutically equivalent to other pharmaceutically equivalent products.

B - Drug products the FDA considers NOT to be therapeutically equivalent to other pharmaceutically equivalent products.

To be therapeutically equivalent and thus substitutable, a drug product must have an "A" rating for the first part of the code. Among these "A" rated products, there are 2 subcategories. Those products for which there are no known or suspected in vivo bioequivalence issue are given a code of AA, AN, AO, AP, or AT depending on the dosage form as described below:

AA – Products in conventional dosage forms.
AN – Solutions and powders for aerosolization.
AO – Injectable oil solutions.
AP – Injectable aqueous solutions and certain IV non-aqueous solutions.
AT – Topical products.

The other subcategory of "A" rated products is for those products containing active ingredients or dosage forms that have been identified by the FDA as having actual or potential bioequivalence problems, but for which adequate scientific evidence has established bioequivalence. Such products are given a rating of "AB." For a drug product to obtain an "AB" rating, it must be shown through in vivo and in vitro studies to have the same rate and extent of absorption of the selected reference product. In certain instances, a number is added to the end of the AB code to make a 3-character code (ie, AB1, AB2, AB3, etc.). Three-character codes are assigned only in situations when more than one reference-listed drug of the same strength has been designated under the same heading. Two or more reference-listed drugs are generally selected only when there are at least 2 potential reference drug products that are not bioequivalent to each other. For example, *Adalat* CC (Bayer) and *Procardia* XL (Pfizer) extended release tablets are listed under the active ingredient nifedipine. These drug products, listed under the same heading, are not bioequivalent to each other. When generic products deemed to be bioequivalent to either of them are approved, *Adalat* CC and *Procardia* XL would be assigned ratings of AB1 and AB2 respectively. The generic drug products bioequivalent to *Adalat* CC would be assigned a rating of AB1 and those bioequivalent to *Procardia* XL would be assigned a rating of AB2.

Those products for which actual or potential bioequivalence problems have not been resolved are given a "B" rating and are not considered therapeutically equivalent. These products fall into 3 main types:

   (1) Drug products that contain active ingredients or are in dosage forms that have been identified by the FDA as having documented bioequivalence problems and for which no adequate studies demonstrating bioequivalence have been submitted;
   (2) drug products for which quality standards are inadequate or for which the FDA has an insufficient basis to determine therapeutic equivalency; and
   (3) drug products under regulatory review. A subcode again is used to provide further information.

B* –   Drug products requiring further FDA investigation and review to determine therapeutic equivalency.
BC –   Extended release dosage forms (capsules, injectables, and tablets).
BD –   Active ingredients and dosage forms with documented bioequivalence problems.
BE –   Delayed-release oral dosage forms.
BN –   Products in aerosol-nebulizer drug delivery systems.
BP –   Active ingredients and dosage forms with potential bioequivalence problems.
BR –   Suppositories or enemas that deliver drugs for systemic absorption.
BS –   Products having drug standard deficiencies.
BT –   Topical products with bioequivalence issues.
BX –   Drug products for which data are insufficient to determine therapeutic equivalence.

Pharmacists should be familiar with the drug product selection laws of the state in which they practice. Many states require a drug product to have an "A" rating in "The Orange Book" before it can be substituted for the brand name product.

Prescriptions Transmitted Via Fax or Electronically

The majority of states have adopted specific regulations regarding the transmission of prescriptions by facsimile machines. In addition, DEA regulations now allow prescriptions for controlled substances to be faxed as well (see discussion in the Controlled Substances chapter under Facsimile Prescriptions). It is recommended that pharmacy practitioners consult with their state pharmacy practice act or regulations regarding the faxing of prescriptions, as the requirements vary greatly from state to state.

Another issue that many state boards of pharmacy have been addressing recently involves the transmission of prescriptions electronically (computer-to-computer). The states' specific requirements vary widely. Some states only allow the transmission of these prescriptions from prescribers in the same state, while others also allow them from out-of-state prescribers. The rules regarding the transfer of prescriptions between computers are similar. While DEA regulations typically limit the transfer of a prescription for refill at another pharmacy to one time, 21 CFR §1306.25(a) allows pharmacies that share an electronic real-time, online database system to transfer up to the maximum number of refills permitted by law.

Prescription Refills

As previously stated, only legend drug prescriptions need refill authorization. Prescriptions for *otc* drugs are usually refillable; however, there are some exceptions:

(1) If an *otc* or nonprescription drug prescription calls for a dosage higher than that recommended on the label of the commercial container, the FDA's position is that the prescription should be refilled only as authorized by the prescriber.

(2) If the *otc* or nonprescription drug prescription contains prescriber's refill instructions, the pharmacist is obligated to follow them.

(3) If the *otc* or nonprescription drug prescription is for a Schedule V drug, the Federal Controlled Substances Act (CSA) requires that refills must be authorized by the prescriber.

(4) State law may dictate specific refill limitations on *otc* or nonprescription drug prescriptions, such as time limitations (usually 1 year from the issuance date). However, the pharmacist is not prohibited from selling an *otc* drug or nonprescription drug product in the commercial package as an *otc* transaction after the prescription refills have expired.

Recording of Prescription Refills

In regard to all legend drug prescriptions, the FDA's position always has been that a refill record is required for compliance with the law, and failure to record refills could result in prosecution. State laws also require such refill records.

Refill Authorization

An oral refill authorization may be handled as a new prescription or the authorization may be recorded on the back of the original prescription. If a controlled drug is involved, a new prescription may be composed. If a physician other than the original prescriber approves the refill, a new prescription is required.

A physician's office assistant or nurse has no authority in his or her own right to authorize a refill of a prescription, nor can the physician legally delegate such authority. DEA regulations (21 CFR §1306.03) do permit an agent of the physician to communicate a prescription from the physician; apparently this also applies to refill authorizations, and probably applies to situations when specific prescription refill instructions are left on the patient's office chart. However, any prescription or prescription refill communication from anyone other than the physician is subject to risk. Too often, the office assistant gives refill authorization without asking for or having the authorization from the prescriber. At least one court case has been decided against the office assistant in this type of situation (*Randle v. California Board of Pharmacy*, 49 Cal. Rptr. 485 [1966]).

Section 503(b)(1) of the FD&C also states that prescriptions can be refilled only if they are authorized by the prescriber. However, the prescriber may advise the agent, office nurse, or office assistant concerning the details of refills, which then may be communicated to the pharmacist. This is similar to the authority granted by DEA regulation §1306.03(b). A pharmacist may contact another prescriber who is covering for an out-of-town colleague and receive authorization for a refill. This authorization should be treated as a new prescription.

Many states have adopted specific provisions regarding the refilling of prescriptions marked "PRN," "refill ad lib," or some similar designation. It is recommended the practicing pharmacist follow these state statutes or regulations.

Although this kind of refill authorization is to be discouraged, it is sometimes used. The best advice to a pharmacist who receives a prescription so marked is that he or she use care and professional judgment in handling it; that he or she refill it only with a frequency consistent with the directions for use, and that he or she check with the physician after a reasonable time to make certain whether the physician wants the medication continued. The pharmacist should encourage the prescriber to indicate the number of refills desired. If a pharmacist does that, the legal status of the prescription will not be litigated with him.

A direction to the patient to take as needed (Sig: PRN) should not, of course, be confused with the prescriber's authorization to refill. It should be noted, too, that a state law or regulation may deal specifically with this question.

It often happens that a patient needs a legend drug prescription refill and the prescribing physician cannot be reached for authorization. This situation results when either the physician has not indicated refill instructions on the prescription or when the authorized refills all have been used. If a legend drug is involved in such a situation, the pharmacist should use professional judgment to supply the patient with the minimum amount of the drug that is necessary until the prescriber can be contacted.

In regard to controlled drugs (with the exception of Schedule II drugs), until a formal statement is issued by the DEA to the contrary, the US Attorney's office probably would not prosecute a pharmacist for dispensing the minimum amount of a drug required to last a patient until the physician can be reached for refill authorization in a true emergency situation. If a Schedule II drug is involved, provision in the law exists for an emergency oral prescription (see 21 C.F.R. §1306.11[d]). When the prescribing physician cannot be reached, the prudent course is that no amount of controlled drug be dispensed and that the patient should be directed to a hospital emergency room. Schedule II analgesics generally are indicated for pain relief rather than for life sustenance; greater abuse potential exists with Schedule II than with the other scheduled drugs.

A pharmacist legally may fill the prescription of a veterinarian who is prescribing a drug intended for human use in the treatment of an animal if the drug prescribed is on the market under a currently FDA-approved NDA, unless state law is to the contrary. FDA regulation §201.105 applies to the manufacturer's labeling of veterinary drugs, and subpart (f) of the regulation provides that drugs intended for both human and animal use must be labeled by the manufacturer accordingly.

Out-of-State Prescriptions

Legend drugs can be prescribed only by a practitioner who is licensed by law to administer them. Therefore, a pharmacist can dispense legend drugs only upon the prescription of such a practitioner (see §503[b][1] of the FD&C).

Physician licensure in one state does not allow practice in another; however, a number of states extend licensure to physicians in contiguous states as a professional courtesy. A physician who is licensed to practice in one particular state may, of course, treat out-of-state patients. A problem arises for the pharmacist when these patients take the prescriptions to be dispensed home with them rather than having them dispensed in the state where they were issued.

The wording of the drug control laws in the state where the pharmacist practices determines if he or she is permitted to fill out-of-state prescriptions, particularly if the prescriptions are for controlled substances. The boards of pharmacy in a number of states interpret the state laws as not prohibiting the honoring of out-of-state prescriptions for controlled drugs. For example, *State v. Rasmussen*, 213 N.W.2d 661 (Iowa, 1973), held that prescriptions emanating outside of Iowa could be dispensed by authorized pharmacists.

Foreign Prescriptions

It is rare that a patron may ask the pharmacist to dispense a drug based on a foreign prescription. Shortly after World War II, this type of request was fairly common because many countries were in short supply of modern medicines, particularly antibiotics. Today, the pharmaceutical industries of many foreign countries are as well developed as those of the United States. Furthermore, American drug manufacturers have made their drug products available to foreign markets either by direct export or by licensing foreign concerns to market the product. Consequently, the need for the pharmacist to provide a drug for a foreign consumer is infrequent.

In most states it is not legal for pharmacists to fill foreign prescriptions. However, a few states do allow limited filling of foreign prescriptions. For example, Texas allows pharmacists to fill prescriptions written by practitioners in Mexico and Canada for noncontrolled substances if the pharmacist has the original written prescription. No verbal prescriptions are allowed. State laws and regulations must be checked before a decision can be made whether or not a foreign prescription is legal, and therefore permitted to be filled.

Mail-Order Pharmacies

In an effort to control health care expenditures, many insurance companies, employers, and other third-party payers are looking to mail-order pharmacies to provide prescription drug benefits to consumer members at an allegedly lower cost. Because it is conceivable that mail-order pharmacies could capture a substantial share of the prescription market, pharmacists have placed political pressure on state legislatures and boards of pharmacy to regulate such out-of-state pharmacies. By contrast, the attorney general of the state of Ohio, in a May 1982 opinion, found that the Commerce Clause of the US Constitution could preclude state regulation of out-of-state pharmacies. The opinion stated that even though state regulation of out-of-state pharmacies serves a legitimate public interest and is evenhandedly applied, it appears the burden certain regulations would impose on interstate commerce could outweigh their benefits. The attorney general of the state of Nebraska concluded in an April 1985 opinion that state regulation of out-of-state pharmacies could be constitutionally suspect under the Commerce Clause of the US Constitution.

Two cases frequently are cited for guidance as to the impact of the Commerce Clause on state licensure and regulation of out-of-state pharmacies. The US Supreme Court, in *Pike v. Bruce Church, Inc.*, 397 U.S. 137 (1970), has established the following criteria for determining the validity of state statutes affecting interstate commerce:

> Where the statute regulates evenhandedly to effectuate a legitimate local public interest and its effects on interstate commerce are only incidental, it will be upheld unless the burden imposed on such commerce is clearly excessive in relation to the putative local benefits. If a legitimate local purpose is found, then the question becomes one of degree. And the extent of the burden that will be tolerated will of course depend on the nature of the local interest involved and on whether it could be promoted as well with a lesser impact on interstate activities.

Federal law does not determine who is authorized to prescribe or dispense drugs. One must examine state law to reach any conclusion on the issues created by mail-order prescriptions. The Wisconsin Board of Pharmacy requested an opinion from the state's Attorney General regarding the regulation of out-of-state pharmacies that solicit mail orders for prescription drugs from Wisconsin residents. The opinion stated there was an implied power to regulate out-of-state pharmacies when they continually solicit mail-order sales of prescription drugs from Wisconsin residents. The attorney general concluded that the protection of the health of the citizens of the state of Wisconsin could include regulation of out-of-state pharmacies. The opinion recognized there were many practical problems in trying to enforce state laws against mail-order firms. The attorney general of the state of California also has concluded, in an October 1984 opinion, that California may legally enforce its licensure, packaging, and labeling laws against out-of-state mail-order pharmacies.

Many take issue with the opinions described above, claiming that they ignore a large body of constitutional law supporting the argument that to extend state statutes to out-of-state pharmacies would impose an undue burden on interstate commerce. The Interstate Commerce Clause of the US Constitution does not forbid burdens being imposed on interstate commerce; the burden simply cannot be "undue." Proponents of such regulations argue the effects of the regulations on interstate commerce would only be incidental because similar regulations also are applied to in-state drug distributors.

In *State v. Rasmussen*, 213 N.W. 2d 661 (Iowa 1973), the state of Iowa was prevented from barring out-of-state practitioners from having their prescriptions filled in Iowa without being licensed in Iowa. The Rasmussen court clearly was concerned with the burden of requiring any prescriber who sent even one prescription into Iowa to be licensed beforehand. The court did not question the right of the state of Iowa to regulate for the health and safety of its citizens, but the law could act to insulate in-state businesses against interstate competition. The court concluded that controlled substance prescriptions emanating from out of state may be filled by Iowa pharmacies even though the practitioner was not licensed in that state.

Federal Antitrust Lawsuit

In June 1968, the Massachusetts State Pharmaceutical Association and some of its members filed a lawsuit in the state of Massachusetts against Federal Prescription Service (Federal), Inc., an Iowa-based mail-order prescription service. The defendant mailed to its customers circulars listing prescription drug prices, and it also advertised its availability to fill prescriptions by mail. The complaint alleged that Federal's mail-order solicitation in Massachusetts of prescription drug orders was illegal under state law because the sale of such orders was restricted by statute to pharmacists licensed by the state of Massachusetts.

Federal did not file an answer to the charges nor did it appear in the Massachusetts action. Therefore, a default judgment was obtained against the defendant, but Federal continued to pursue sales within Massachusetts.

Some time later, the plaintiffs filed an action in an Iowa court asking it to enforce the default judgment entered earlier by the Massachusetts court, and thus restrained Federal from the mail-order selling or soliciting sales of prescription drugs to Massachusetts residents. Federal conceded it received notice of the first proceeding, but it refused to appear because it felt the Massachusetts courts lacked proper jurisdiction. In the later case, filed in Iowa, Federal claimed the Massachusetts action was full of procedural and substantive errors.

Federal first claimed a professional association lacks standing to directly enforce a penal licensing statute, such as that which was relied on by the plaintiffs. Using Massachusetts law, the Iowa court came to the same conclusion.

Federal also alleged it was not doing business within the state of Massachusetts so it could not be subject to the jurisdiction of its courts. Again basing its decision upon Massachusetts law, the Iowa court found that Federal was not doing the character of business that would justify jurisdiction by the Massachusetts courts. Certain "minimum contacts" must be established before jurisdiction exists. The record showed "the total activities of Federal that relate to Massachusetts were the mailing of circulars to residents of that state, the receipt in Iowa of Massachusetts prescriptions to be filled, and the receipt of payment by mail in Iowa. Federal neither owned nor leased any property in Massachusetts, kept no bank accounts there, held no meetings there."

In addition, the mail-order company questioned the validity of the Massachusetts court decree because of its apparent conflict with federal statutes governing the sale of prescription drugs. If the conflict could be established, the decree would be in violation of the supremacy clause of the US Constitution. The Massachusetts judgment prohibited the defendant from selling prescription drugs by mail in interstate commerce to Massachusetts residents unless Federal obtained a Massachusetts pharmacy license; however, the Iowa court found that federal law authorized the defendant to fill prescriptions in interstate commerce under its Iowa license simply on the condition that they be "dispensed ... upon a prescription of a practitioner licensed by law to administer such drugs." 21 U.S.C. §353(b)(1)(c). Iowa law permitted the interstate mailing of prescription drugs as long as the Iowa-licensed pharmacist had been presented with prescriptions from physicians who are licensed in the state in which they practice. Because of the direct conflict between Massachusetts and federal law, the Massachusetts decree was found invalid.

The association plaintiff stated it had suffered no injury, but the individual pharmacist plaintiffs claimed competitive injuries because of Federal's business within Massachusetts. However, at the trial, the plaintiffs could not prove lost sales to Federal nor could they show any published Federal drug price that was lower than some other pharmacy within the state of Massachusetts. The Iowa court found that a general allegation of competitive damage was not enough to establish an irreparable injury.

The Iowa court found in favor of the defendant and dismissed the plaintiff's petition on June 28, 1977, but the court did not act on one of Federal's claims. Federal showed the American Pharmaceutical Association (AILA) had financially supported the plaintiffs in this action. Federal's expert witness testified this financial support was intended to restrain mail-order pharmacy business in favor of local pharmacies — in violation of state and federal antitrust laws. The court found that such a claim would require more specialized proceedings and a more appropriate forum.

Federal filed a complaint in the US District Court for the District of Columbia against the APhA, National Association of Boards of Pharmacy (NABP), and National Community Pharmacist Association (NCPA) on July 6, 1977. This complaint alleged that the defendants had conspired together for the "purpose of monopolizing the interstate retail sale of prescription drugs by restraining mail-order competition."

The APhA answered the complaint by denying the allegations, but it also filed a counterclaim against Federal. The counterclaim alleged that Federal had conspired with mail-order organizations to deprive the APhA of its First Amendment rights of free speech and free association. The APhA claimed that Federal wanted to silence any public expression of opposition to mail-order prescription service and that such a move would violate the APhA's right of free speech.

The trial court awarded the mail-order pharmacy $102,000 in damages, but this award was later overturned on appeal. (*Federal Prescription Serv. v. American Pharmaceutical Assn.*, 484 F. Supp. 1195 [1980], Aff'd in part and rev'd in part, 663 F.2d 253 [D.C. Cir., 1981].) The Appellate Court found that pharmacy associations may make legitimate attempts to secure governmental action, to lobby the legislature, and to petition licensing boards. Such political activity is protected from antitrust laws. While there was some evidence the pharmacy organizations were not entirely innocent in this matter, the mail-order company was not able to prove that it had suffered actual injury (see *Federal Prescription Service, Inc. v. American Pharmaceutical Association*).

Burden on Interstate Commerce

The federal government has left the issue of prescribing and dispensing to the states under their authority to protect the public's health, safety, and welfare, but the US Constitution provides that there shall not be undue restrictions on interstate commerce. It is suggested that state laws, to be constitutional, (1) must not constitute economic protectionism; (2) the state interest must not produce a significant burden or impact on interstate commerce; and (3) the state must consider whether there are reasonable alternatives to achieve the same goal with a lesser burden on interstate commerce.

The issue often becomes whether the state is trying to protect the public health or protect in-state pharmacies. The governor of Mississippi vetoed legislation that required a 24-hour WATS line for out-of-state pharmacies that dispensed prescriptions to Mississippi residents, but Mississippi pharmacists did not have to provide 24-hour service. The general rule is that where statutes regulate evenhandedly to effectuate a legitimate local public interest and the effects on interstate commerce are only incidental, it will be upheld unless the burden is clearly excessive in relation to the local benefits. For example, 1988 Utah legislation required mail-order pharmacies doing business in Utah to submit quarterly reports on Utah prescriptions, but Utah pharmacies also were required to file reports to detect patterns of abuse.

Furthermore, in 1988, the state of California enacted S.B. No. 2213 to require registration of out-of-state pharmacies dispensing prescription medication into the state. The California law also requires out-of-state pharmacies to disclose information to the California Board of Pharmacy and to meet certain other requirements.

It is generally recognized that the California legislation comports with the Commerce Clause. This is because that law recognizes that the primary responsibility for pharmacy regulation rests with the board of pharmacy of the state where the pharmacy is located. (As a matter of law, because only a pharmacist may dispense prescription medications, dispensing occurs in the state where the pharmacy is located rather than in the state where the patient may reside.) The California law thereby protects the health and safety of its residents in a reasonable manner without subjecting an out-of-state pharmacy to overlapping and potentially conflicting provisions of the state laws and regulations of the various states where its patients may be located. In the several years because enactment of the California legislation, numerous other states have adopted similar registration and disclosure statutes and regulations.

The 1988 death of an Idaho woman who allegedly received *Coumadin* (warfarin sodium) rather than her prescribed prednisone from a Nevada mail-order pharmacy resulted in national attention on this issue. An Idaho prosecutor filed charges of involuntary manslaughter against Medco, alleging that the company's high-speed automation created unsafe conditions for dispensing prescriptions and exhibited a reckless disregard for human life. After a preliminary hearing in which the judge found there was enough evidence of probable cause, the case was set for trial. However, the criminal matter was eventually settled. The county prosecutor admitted that local resources were inadequate to fight a large-scale criminal action against a national pharmacy mail-order firm. As a compromise, the state of Idaho and Medco agreed to cooperate in the development of legislation dealing with mail-order pharmacy in that state.

The NABP passed a resolution in 1988 that pharmacies should be licensed and registered in states where located and in all states to which they mail, ship, or distribute prescription drugs on a regular and customary basis. The resolution also encourages states in which mail-order pharmacies are located to establish procedures for processing complaints by individuals or entities not situated in that state. Some observers believe the resolution encourages states to study and control pharmacist stress in high-volume pharmacies and the rate at which prescriptions are filled per hour. While there have been some congressional hearings to examine mail-order pharmacies, it is expected that most of the action on this topic will take place at the state level.

On November 29, 1990, for example, the FDA rejected a citizen petition that had called for the FDA to regulate mail-service pharmacies. The FDA disputed the petitioner's contention that the states have not been effective in regulating mail-service pharmacies.

POSTAL REGULATIONS

Nonmailable Items

In general, potentially harmful or dangerous substances are nonmailable under federal law. Postal regulations permit some substances to be mailed if they are prepared specially for mailing or if they are mailed between specific classes of individuals.

Section 1716 of Title 18 of the US Code prohibits the mailing of articles that may injure or kill an individual or injure the mails or other property. Under the category of nonmailable articles are poisons; substances that contain poison; all poisonous animals, insects, and reptiles; explosives; flammable materials; bombs; devices or compositions that can ignite or explode; and all disease germs and scabs. Also prohibited from the mail are intoxicating liquors; however, exceptions are made for products conforming to the requirements of both the Internal Revenue Service and FDA alcohol regulations and for products that are neither alcoholic beverages, poisons, nor flammable substances (Postal Regulation 124.8).

Mailing of Prescription Medicines

For quite a long time, the postal regulations prohibited mailing narcotic-containing medications. It is an interesting historical note that the ban was based on whether the medication contained a particular category of medications, not the level of control. Thus certain Schedule II substances (those containing narcotics) could not be mailed while others in the same restricted category (nonnarcotic Schedule II medications such as methylphenidate) could be mailed. In October 1994, the US Postal Service amended its regulations to permit mailing of all medications, whether narcotic or nonnarcotic.

Powders, which could escape from their containers and cause damage, discomfort, destruction, and soiling, must be packed either in leak-proof receptacles or sealed in durable, leak-proof outer containers.

Shipment of Chemicals

The shipment of certain chemicals through the mail generally comes under the classification of the nonmailable, harmful matter that is regulated by §1716, Title 18 of the US Code, and by Postal Regulation 124.2. However, the regulations provide for exceptions, and a procedure has been established for mailing chemicals, including poisons and other hazardous items, if the packaging, labeling, and identification of the contents comply with the requirements. Consult the post office for specific information.

Similarly, any chemical substance or dangerous device that is shipped through a common carrier must comply with federal regulations. The carrier should be consulted for specific information. Federal regulations require the use of internationally recognized labels on domestic and foreign packages of explosives, radioactive materials, compressed gases, flammable liquids and solids, corrosives, poisons, water-reactive materials, spontaneously combustible materials, irritating materials, and etiologic agents. Department of Transportation regulation 173.404 (a) requires the appropriate labels to be on each package of hazardous material that is shipped unless the package is exempt. A sample of labels and general requirements may be obtained from the US Department of Transportation, Office of Hazardous Materials, Washington, DC 20590, or from the US Postal Service in major cities.

Other Nonmailable Items

Federal law (39 U.S.C. §3001) and postal regulations (124.7 and 123.434) prohibit the unsolicited mailing of contraceptives (eg, condoms) and the unsolicited mailing of contraceptive advertisements, except when they are sent to a licensed physician, nurse, pharmacist, hospital, or clinic. Another federal law (18 U.S.C. §1461) prohibits the mailing of abortive drugs or devices, any advertisements thereof, obscene matter, and any article intended for indecent or immoral purposes.

Package Shipping or Courier Services

Package shipping or courier services such as United Parcel Service (UPS) or Federal Express (FedEx) may be used by the pharmacist to return both narcotic and nonnarcotic controlled drugs to the manufacturer or wholesaler. They also may be used to ship narcotic drugs from the pharmacist to the ultimate user.

REPACKAGING

For more information on repackaging or relabeling of bulk drug products by pharmacists, see Pharmacy Labeling of Bulk Drug Products section in this chapter.

Repackaging of Injectables for In-Hospital Use

Hospital pharmacists sometimes repackage or prefill injectable drugs into unit-dose syringes for in-hospital use. The prefilled injectables can be used for immediate administration to hospital inpatients or outpatients treated in the emergency room. The repackaging process consists of prefilling individual injection syringes from multidose vials or ampules of the desired drug; this is done in a laminar airflow hood under aseptic conditions. The individual injectables are then labeled for unit-dose use. There are potential hazards in repackaging unit-dose injectables, such as incorrect labeling. The pharmacist must follow the FDA's suggested labeling procedures and must indicate the drug strength and quantity in such a way that misinterpretation by the individual administering the drug does not occur. Some hospital pharmacists assign an internal code number to each batch of prefilled syringes and log the prefilled data for future identification if the need should arise.

Drug deterioration with resultant drug product adulteration (in violation of the FD&C) can happen if the materials used in repackaging are not compatible with the drug to be repackaged. For example, paraldehyde quickly reacts with plastic and, therefore, must be packaged for injection in glass syringes only.

The safest procedure is for the pharmacist to stock the manufacturer's commercially marketed prefilled injectable drug whenever possible in preference to repackaging. The FDA has indicated if a hospital is not equipped for proper repackaging, it is advisable it obtain the drug from a supplier who is equipped and who can be expected to undertake tests to ensure the integrity of the drugs packaged.

Expiration Dating on Drugs Repackaged into Unit-Dose Containers

When drug items are repackaged into unit-dose containers, the expiration date stated on the manufacturer's or distributor's label is no longer applicable as it has been determined for the drug in that particular package and is not intended to be applicable to the product when it has been repackaged in a different container. Both Chapter 661 of the USP and CPG 7132b.10 of the FDA require the expiration date (or "beyond-use" date) on the label of a drug product repackaged into a unit-dose container for dispensing to be: 1) 6 months from the date of repacking; or 2) 25% of the remaining time between the date of repackaging and the expiration date on the original bulk container, whichever is earlier.

Historical Background of Pharmacy Compounding

Community and hospital pharmacy practitioners often are called upon to perform extemporaneous compounding. This includes not only the formulation of traditional ointments and creams, but also hyperalimentation and IV fluids, inhalation solutions, children's dosage forms, and nuclear pharmacy specialties.

The question often has arisen in the past whether these activities constitute "manufacturing." While manufacturing is regulated by the federal government under the FD&C, compounding is considered part of the practice of pharmacy and, therefore, is regulated by the states through the state boards of pharmacy. The distinction is important because pharmacies are exempt from registration with the FDA and exempt from FDA inspection, as long as they confine their activities to compounding. Section 510 (g)(1) of the Act states pharmacies are exempt from registration under the Act "if they do not manufacture, prepare, propagate, compound, or process drugs or devices for sale other than in the regular course of their business of dispensing or selling drugs or devices at retail."

The exact demarcation between compounding and manufacturing always has been subject to question. Historically, it was thought that the exemption would apply to pharmacies that prepare and compound drugs intended for use by their own patients and that were not being sold to other persons intending to sell or distribute them to the ultimate user. The exemption would not apply if a pharmacy were supplying compounded or repackaged drugs to other pharmacies, hospitals, doctors' offices, or other establishments that would then, in turn, dispense the product.

Another factor considered in determining whether a pharmacy was compounding or manufacturing was whether the product was being prepared to meet immediate demands (eg, a patient at the prescription counter awaiting preparation of the medication), or if the product was being made in anticipation of future demand. The latter situation was more likely to be considered manufacturing.

The FDA began to take regulatory action against some pharmacies it believed to be "manufacturing." For example, the FDA issued warning letters to several firms that were clearly manufacturing drugs for human use under the guise of traditional pharmacy practice. For example, one establishment manufactured over 300,000 dosage units of albuterol sulfate and other inhalation therapy drugs per month for 6000 patients, most of whom lived out of state. Another firm manufactured a large quantity of a drug product at dosage levels that have not been determined by adequate and well-controlled studies to be effective for the indicated use.

An inspection of another company operating with a pharmacy license revealed the firm had hundreds of bulk drug ingredients on hand to manufacture about 165 different products. A review of the manufacturing dates of the "compounded" drugs on hand during the inspection of this firm revealed that 37 products had been produced over 1 year prior to the inspection, 6 products had been made between 6 and 11 months prior to the inspection, and 111 products had no recorded manufacturing date.

In a Florida case, a pharmacy, in collaboration with a local physician, filled bulk orders for the physician's private dermatological preparation that was dispensed to other physicians pursuant to signed prescriptions indicated "For Office Use Only." The court found against Cedars North Towers Pharmacy (Federal Food Drug, and Cosmetic Law Reports, Section 38,200, August 20, 1978). The court noted that a number of factors are relevant in deciding whether a pharmacy qualifies for an exemption from registration as a manufacturer under federal law:

(1) Whether particular drugs are being compounded on a regular basis as opposed to periodic compounding of different drugs;
(2) whether drugs are being compounded primarily for individual patient prescriptions as opposed to orders contemplating larger amounts for office use;
(3) the geographic area of distribution;
(4) whether any form of advertising or promotion is being utilized;
(5) the percentage of gross income received from sales of particular compounded drugs; and
(6) whether particular compounded drugs are being offered at wholesale prices.

Compliance Policy Guide

Discussion of the CPG is for historical purposes only as it has been rescinded by the FDA in light of the passage of the Section 503A of the FD&C related to pharmacy compounding (discussed later in this section).

Compliance Policy Guide 7132.16 stated, in part:

FDA recognizes that a licensed pharmacist may compound drugs extemporaneously after receipt of a valid prescription for an individual patient (ie, an oral or written order of a practitioner licensed by state law to administer or order the administration of the drug to an individual patient identified and treated by the practitioner in the course of his or her professional practice).

Pharmacies that do not otherwise engage in practices that extend beyond the limits set forth in this CPG may prepare drugs in very limited quantities before receiving a valid prescription, provided they can document a history of receiving valid prescriptions that have been generated solely within an established professional practitioner-patient-pharmacy relationship, and provided further that they maintain the prescription on file for all such products dispensed at the pharmacy as required by state law.

If a pharmacy compounds finished drugs from bulk active ingredient materials considered to be unapproved new drug substances, as defined in 21 CFR §310.3(g), such activity must be covered by an FDA-sanctioned investigational new drug application (IND) that is, in effect, in accordance with 21 U.S.C. §355(i) and 21 CFR §312.

In certain circumstances, it may be appropriate for a pharmacist to compound a small quantity of a drug that is only slightly different than an FDA-approved drug that is commercially available. In these circumstances, patient-by-patient consultation between physician and pharmacist must result in documentation that substantiates the medical need for the particular variation of the compound.

Pharmacies may not, without losing their status as retail entities, compound, provide, and dispense drugs to third parties for resale to individual patients.

The FDA generally will continue to defer the regulation of the day-to-day practice of retail pharmacy and related activities to state and local officials. The FDA anticipates that cooperative efforts between the states and the agency will result in coordinated investigations, referrals, and follow-up actions by the states.

The FDA may, in the exercise of its enforcement discretion, initiate federal enforcement actions against entities and responsible persons when the scope and nature of a pharmacy's activity raises the kinds of concerns normally associated with a manufacturer and results in significant violations of the new drug, adulteration, or misbranding provisions of the Act. In determining whether to initiate such an action, the agency will consider whether the pharmacy engages in any of the following acts:

(1) Soliciting business (eg, promoting, advertising, or using sales persons) to compound specific drug products, product classes, or therapeutic classes of drug products;

(2) compounding, regularly or in inordinate amounts, drug products commercially available in the marketplace and essentially generic copies of commercially available, FDA-approved drug products;

(3) receiving, storing, or using drug substances without first obtaining written assurance from the supplier that each lot of the drug substance has been made in an FDA-approved facility;

(4) receiving, storing, or using drug components not guaranteed or otherwise determined to meet official compendia requirements;

(5) using commercial scale manufacturing or testing equipment for compounding drug products;

(6) compounding inordinate amounts of drugs in anticipation of receiving prescriptions in relation to the amounts of drugs compounded after receiving valid prescriptions;

(7) offering compounded drug products at wholesale to other state licensed persons or commercial entities for resale;

(8) distributing inordinate amounts of compounded products out of state; or

(9) failing to operate in conformance with applicable state law regulating the practice of pharmacy.

The foregoing list of factors is not intended to be exhaustive and other factors may be appropriate for consideration in a particular case.

This compliance policy guideline was the subject of litigation in *Professionals and Patients for Customized Care (P2C2) v. Shalala* 56 F3d (5th Cir. 1995). In that case, the plaintiffs contended that the guideline was in essence a substantive rule the FDA could not enact without the usual notice and comment requirements. The court held that the guideline was not a substantive rule because it did not create binding norms; therefore, the notice and comment rulemaking requirements did not apply.

FDA Modernization Act—503A—Compounding—Current Status

Despite the FDA's statement in the compliance guideline that it had no intention of regulating traditional pharmacy compounding, pharmacy groups remained concerned. A grass-roots movement in the pharmacy profession led to passage of language in the Food and Drug Administration Modernization Act of 1997 (Pub. L. No. 105-115, 111 Stat. 2296) which clarifies compounding is appropriately regulated at the state level by state boards of pharmacy and medicine. The FD&C in Section 503A now specifically exempts pharmacists from the new drug application procedures, the current good manufacturing practices, and the misbranding (adequate directions for use) provisions of the Act as long as certain conditions are met. Prior to these changes, the FD&C only exempted pharmacy compounding from the registration and inspection requirements. Technically, all compounded products constituted "new drugs" under the Act.

This provision took effect on November 21, 1998.

In order to qualify for these exemptions to the Act, certain conditions must be met. First, the prescription must be compounded for an identified patient based on a valid prescription order issued by a state-licensed prescriber. Second, the prescription must be compounded in a state-licensed pharmacy or by a state-licensed physician. Allowance is made for the compounding of limited quantities in advance of the receipt of a prescription if it is based on a history of receiving valid prescription orders from a prescriber, and there is a valid patient-pharmacist-physician relationship.

The drug product to be compounded must:

(1) Comply with an applicable USP or NF monograph (if one exists), and the USP chapter on pharmacy compounding; or
(2) be a component of an approved drug product; or
(3) if neither (1) nor (2) apply, the substance must appear on a list of bulk drug substances issued by the FDA and published in the *Federal Register*.

In addition, the bulk drug substance must be accompanied by a valid certificate of analysis and be manufactured in an FDA-registered establishment.

The drug product compounded must not:

(1) Appear on a list published by the FDA of drug products that have been withdrawn or removed from the market: or
(2) be essentially a copy of a commercially available drug product compounded regularly or in inordinate amounts; or
(3) be identified by the FDA as a drug product that presents demonstrable difficulty for compounding that reasonably demonstrate an adverse effect on the safety or effectiveness of the drug product.

This section of the Act also requires the FDA, in consultation with the NABP, develop a standard memorandum of understanding (MOU) that addresses the interstate distribution of inordinate amounts of compounded drug products and provides for appropriate investigation by a state agency of complaints relating to compounded drug products distributed outside the state. Pharmacies licensed in a state that has entered into such an MOU will be bound to the provisions contained in it. Those pharmacies in states not having entered into such an MOU are limited from out-of-state distribution of compounded drug products that exceed 5% of the total prescription orders dispensed or distributed by the pharmacy.

There has been a draft memorandum released upon which many comments have been received. It can be found at the Web site: http://www.fda.gov/cder/pharmcomp.

Finally, 503A provides for the formation of an advisory committee on compounding to aid in issuance of regulations pursuant to these provisions. The agency has established a pharmacy compounding advisory committee that has met and will continue to meet to advise the FDA regarding specific matters.

To date, the FDA has taken several steps in the implementation of Section 503A. Actions taken to date by the agency can be found on the Internet at http://www.fda.gov/cder/pharmcomp.

In addition, in November 1998, the agency published a *Guidance for Industry Enforcement Policy During Implementation of Section 503A of the FD&C*. In January 1999 (64 Fed. Reg. 996), the FDA published a proposed rule bearing a *List of Bulk Drug Substances That May Be Used in Pharmacy Compounding*. Also in January 1999 (64 Fed. Reg. 3301), the FDA announced the availability of a draft standard memorandum of understanding that states may enter into with the FDA. Finally, on March 8, 1999 (64 Fed. Reg. 10944), the FDA published a final rule of a *List of Drug Products That Have Been Withdrawn or Removed From the Market for Reasons of Safety or Effectiveness*.

Section 503A also has a provision that requires a prescription to be "unsolicited" and prohibits the advertising or promotion of the compounding of any particular drug, class of drug, or type of drug. However, the advertising and promotion of compounding services in general is allowed. These provisions were overturned in a lawsuit in federal court (*Western States Pharmacy v. Shalala*) based on the First Amendment to the US Constitution (commercial free speech). The FDA has been restrained from enforcing those provisions of the law.

The FDA appealed the decision to the 9th Circuit, where it argued the 2 provisions did not, in fact, place restrictions on "commercial speech." It argued that those provisions advanced the government interest in protecting the public health and safety, promoting the integrity of the drug approval process, and balancing the need for individual access to compounded drugs while preventing widespread distribution of unapproved drugs. The 9th Circuit disagreed with the FDA and found no evidence the public needs protection from compounding services.

At the same time, the FDA argued the 2 provisions at issue were not severable from the rest of 503A. The lower court had deemed the 2 provisions severable ... meaning all but the 2 provisions at issue could be enforced. The FDA argued on appeal that the provisions were not severable from the rest of the law. They argued that those provisions were an integral part of the law, and without them, the legislation did not meet Congressional intent. The court agreed with the FDA on that point — which means that 503A as a whole is no longer valid.

By a margin of 5–4, the majority of the United States Supreme Court affirmed the Court of Appeals. The majority reasoned that even if it were assumed that the ban directly advanced the government's interest, the government failed to demonstrate that the restrictions on the pharmacies' commercial speech were not more extensive than necessary to serve those interests. The majority noted that there are non-speech-related means to achieve the government's goal, such as regulating large-scale manufacturing, prohibiting wholesale sales, or limiting manufacturing to prescriptions received. The majority also read the ban as prohibiting the pharmacies' beneficial speech such as advising physicians concerning available compounded drugs for special medical needs.

Within days of the *Thompson* Decision by the Supreme Court, the Food and Drug Administration (FDA) "re-issued" a Compliance Policy Guidance (Guidance) (CPG Ch. 4 § 460.200 (May 2002) to give the FDA and pharmacists notice of what factors will be taken into account to determine whether the pharmacy is engaged in legal compounding as opposed to unlawful manufacturing of drugs under the guise of compounding. It is noteworthy that the Guidance was published as FDA policy without any advance public notice or comment period. The irony of that action is that it was the original 1992 Guidance on compounding issued by the FDA (CPG Ch. 4 § 7132.16 [March 1992] renumbered to § 460.200) that underlies the compounding case discussed at the beginning of this subchapter. The facts surrounding that case created such a furor that Congress had to step in and adopt the compounding statute in FDAMA — the section that the Supreme Court just days earlier had held unconstitutional. Taking these developments into account, it should be clear the pharmacies may advertise compounding services but still not "manufacture" large quantities of drugs under the guise of compounding. For more information, see *Thompson v. Western States Medical Center* in the Court Cases chapter. For a much more detailed explanation, see the article online addressing this subject at http://www.uspharmacist.com/index.asp?page=ce/2654/default.htm.

Regulatory Action Guidance

Pharmacies engaged in promotion and other activities analogous to manufacturing and distributing drugs for human use are subject to the same provisions of the Act as manufacturers. District FDA offices are encouraged to consult with state regulatory authorities to ensure that pharmacists not abuse their right to compound in situations determined to be manufacturing.

FDA-initiated regulatory action may include issuing a warning letter, seizure, injunction, or prosecution. Charges may include, but need not be limited to, violations of 21 U.S.C. §§ 351(a)(2)(B), 352(a), 352(f)(1), 352(o), and 355(a) of the Act.

All establishments registered as manufacturers must comply with the Current Good Manufacturing Practice regulations. For example, all firms, including pharmacies that manufacture large volume parenterals and distribute them without a prescription or conduct activities beyond the usual dispensing or selling of drugs at retail, are required to register with the FDA and comply with CGMP regulations. Pharmacies that prepare large volume parenterals pursuant to a prescription are within the practice of pharmacy and exempt from registration requirements but are not subject to biennial inspection or CGMP regulations.

Compounding *otc* Products

While pharmacists are exempt from registration as a manufacturer if they compound drugs under the direction of a prescription from a licensed practitioner, another question arises when the pharmacist is requested to compound an *otc* product. If the pharmacist is compounding the drug at the request of a consumer, the product still must comply with the labeling requirements of the FD&C. If these labeling requirements are not met, the product would be misbranded.

In a 1979 letter to state drug officials, the FDA noted that it was aware that pharmacists occasionally are asked to compound *otc* drugs at the request of a consumer, and the final drug product is not properly labeled. As a practical matter, the agency did not consider this a serious violation of the FD&C that would warrant regulatory action by the FDA unless the newly compounded drug was a health hazard or unless *otc* compounding becomes a widespread practice. The agency recommended the state boards of pharmacy handle situations in which such compounded drugs are inadequately labeled or are new drugs.

Compounding Bulk Chemicals

To understand the FDA regulations applicable to bulk chemicals, it is necessary to review certain legal concepts. A drug is allowed in interstate commerce if:

(1) It is labeled with adequate directions for use as is required by §502(f)(1) of the Act; or

(2) it is exempt from §502(f)(1) labeling requirements by §503(b)(2) if it is dispensed pursuant to a prescription and is labeled accordingly; or

(3) it is a new drug that is exempt from §502(f)(1) labeling, but it is limited to investigational use only, and a current IND application is on file with the FDA; or

(4) it is exempt from §502(f)(1) labeling because of a special FDA regulation to that effect.

A pharmacist legally can use bulk chemicals for prescription compounding provided the particular chemical is not restricted to investigational use only or has some other restrictive labeling. A pharmacist legally can use bulk chemicals for *otc* sales if the chemical is not restricted to dispensing on prescription only. FDA regulations provide for 2 basic classes of bulk chemicals for compounding and dispensing.

(1) "For prescription compounding" is the labeling statement required by FDA regulation 21 CFR §201.120 to be on the manufacturer's commercial container of chemicals to be used for prescription compounding, to be used if the chemical is for a nonlegend drug, and to be used for *otc* drugs. If the chemical is to be used as a nonprescription drug, the manufacturer must provide adequate directions for use in its labeling as required by §201.120(b)(3) in order to assist the pharmacist in dispensing the drug. In *otc* dispensing, the pharmacist must place all of the manufacturer's labeling information on his or her label. In order to obtain the §201.120 exemption from §502(f)(1) of the Act, the chemical must not be in dosage unit form (ie, tablets or capsules) except for liquid acids or alkalies.

(2) "Caution: For manufacturing, processing, or repacking" is the labeling statement required by 21 CFR §201.122 to be used by the manufacturer on the commercial container of chemicals marketed specifically for processing, repacking, or for the making of other drugs. These chemicals may be used in prescription compounding but may not be used for *otc* sales.

Chemicals labeled under FDA regulation §201.122, in substantially all dosage forms in which they are dispensed, are those that are subject to the prescription-only dispensing requirement. The regulation exempts the chemicals from the labeling required under §502(f)(1), but an exemption also may be claimed under FDA regulation §201.120.

The pharmacist must use adequate judgment when deciding what chemicals to use in compounded prescriptions. Section 503A of the FDC Act required the pharmacist to have on hand a Certificate of Analysis from the supplier. Chemicals generally are rated in the following order of increasing quality: Technical grade, USP or NF, CP, American Chemical Society (ACS), and AR, which is supposedly the exceptionally pure form. The technical grade should not be used in prescription compounding for obvious reasons. In some states, a pharmacy practice act may prohibit compounding with anything but USP or NF chemicals. USP's General Chapter 795 contains a section regarding ingredient selection.

In vitro diagnostic products are reagents used in diagnosing a disease or in determining a state of health. FDA regulation §201.119 states these products are in compliance with §502(f)(1) of the Act if they are labeled under the requirements of FDA regulation §809.10. The general requirement of this regulation is the labeling of a reagent with the statement, "for in vitro diagnostic use," plus its chemical name and intended uses, hazardous warning statements, quality assurance information and results of tests, lot number, and the manufacturer's or distributor's name.

A pharmacist legally may not use a chemical labeled "for in vitro diagnostic use" in prescription compounding unless the product also is labeled in conformance with the FDA regulations cited in §201.120 and §201.122.

PET Compounding

In a separate but related issue, the FDA sought to regulate the compounding of positron emission tomograph (PET) radiopharmaceuticals by nuclear pharmacists by classifying such products as new drugs. A 1995 FDA notice in the *Federal Register* stated the FDA's intent to require nuclear pharmacies compounding PET drugs to register with the FDA as drug manufacturers and to receive premarketing approval of compounded PET drugs. This action would have superseded a 1984 FDA guideline that had specifically allowed pharmacists to compound PET drugs pursuant to a prescription. This proposed action was challenged in court by radiopharmaceutical distributors and other interested parties in *Syncor v. Shalala.* Syncor and other plaintiffs argued the FDA was not authorized to regulate PET drugs because an NDA is not required for drugs compounded by a pharmacy pursuant to a physician's prescription. They also argued the FDA's action was invalid because it was a substantive rule and did not comply with the Administrative Procedure Act's notice and comment requirements. The district court ruled in favor of the FDA, finding that the FDA's action was an "interpretive rule" and thus was not subject to the notice and comment requirements. On appeal, a 3-judge panel reversed the district court and instead ruled the proposed action was substantive rule and was thus a new regulation subject to the notice and comment requirements The case was sent back to the lower court with instructions to enter a judgment in favor of Syncor on the procedural issue. The court did not rule on the issue of whether or not the FDA had authority to regulate PET drugs as new drugs. This left open the possibility the FDA could promulgate rules in an attempt to regulate PET drugs as new drugs. However, Section 121 of the 1997 FDA Modernization Act makes it clear that compounding of pharmaceutical products is appropriately regulated at the state level and prohibits the FDA from requiring NDAs for PET drugs that are not adulterated. In addition, FDAMA also established a specific time frame and guidelines for the development of regulations for PET compounding. In compliance with Section 121 of FDAMA, the FDA has revoked previous Guidance Documents on PET Drugs (62 Fed. Reg. 66636) and the Final Rule that required PET compounders to follow GMP requirements (62 Fed. Reg. 66522).

The FDA has made significant progress on the issue of compounding of PET drugs in 2000. It has published several documents — all of which may be found on the Internet at http://www.fda.gov/cder/fdama.

CGMPs for PET Compounding

The FDA has published a "Preliminary Draft of Regulations on Current Good Manufacturing Practices for PET Drugs." This may be found on the Internet at http://www.fda.gov/cder/fdama/212draft.htm.

On March 10, 2000, the FDA in the *Federal Register* published a document entitled "Positron Emission Tomography Drug Products: Safety and Effectiveness of Certain PET Drugs for Specific Indications" (65 FR 12999). At the same time, the agency released a document entitled "Guidance for Industry PET Drug Applications — Content and Format for NDAs and ANDAs." This document deals with the most commonly used products in PET compounding: (1) Fludeoxyglucose F 18 injection; (2) Ammonia N 13 injection; and (3) Sodium fluoride F 18 injection. Links to these documents may be found on the FDA's Web site on the implementation of FDAMA requirements.

For recent action taken by the FDA in implementing these FDAMA provisions see http://www.fda.gov at the FDAMA home page.

DRUG EXPORTING AND IMPORTING

Drug Exporting

The FDA recommends drugs being exported to other countries, including drugs intended for charitable distribution, either be packaged in their original container and bear the manufacturer's label or, if the drugs are no longer in their original container, the pharmacist must comply with all FDA regulations applicable to the repacking of drugs. Drugs that do not comply with FDA standards or are packaged differently are considered adulterated or misbranded under the FD&C.

Section 801(e) of the Act (21 U.S.C. §381) provides that a food, drug, medical device, or cosmetic intended for export will not be deemed adulterated or misbranded if:

  (1) It is in accordance with the foreign purchaser's specifications;
  (2) it is not in conflict with the laws of the country to which it is exported;
  (3) it is labeled on the outside package that it is intended for export;
  (4) it is not sold or offered for sale in domestic commerce.

Shipping Regulations

Before attempting to export a drug through the mail to a foreign country, it is imperative for the pharmacist to check with the US Postal Service regarding postal regulations. A knowledgeable postal clerk should be contacted, and the pharmacist must state that the drug is intended for consumer use. If the drug is to be shipped by common carrier (plane or ship), the applicable federal regulations may be obtained from the Treasury Department or from the cargo carrier firm.

Specific Exporting Procedures

  (1) A DEA district office or the Washington office should be consulted for specific directions on exporting controlled substances. DEA regulations §§1312.21 through 1312.32 are applicable. The exporting procedure differs depending on whether the controlled drug is narcotic or nonnarcotic.
  (2) If the drug intended for export is a legend drug, it should be shipped directly by the pharmacist to the patient or the patient's physician in order to prevent drug diversion into domestic channels.
  (3) The drug intended for export should be shipped in the manufacturer's or distributor's original commercial container with its labeling intact.
  (4) If the drug intended for export is requested upon a foreign prescription, the prescription should be shipped in the same package as the drug and a copy of the prescription should be retained for recordkeeping.
  (5) The outer shipping container or carton should be marked "medicines" and "for export." If the drug is shipped through the mail, the postal service instructions should be followed. Usually, a custom sticker or tag listing its contents is attached to the parcel.
  (6) A pharmacist should not export a drug pursuant to an oral request; a written document should be insisted upon, either a prescription or a letter from the foreign physician.

Export/Import Firms

There are several export/import agencies in the United States, mainly in New York and Chicago, that can arrange to have prescription medication delivered to a foreign recipient, usually through facilities in England, from which point the drug actually is exported. These agencies specialize in providing American-made pharmaceuticals for foreign customers, particularly for those in Eastern Europe. The use of or referral to a private export/import firm may be an alternative for a pharmacist who is asked to fill a foreign prescription. Information on the location of specific export/import firms sometimes may be obtained from the consulate office of the country to which the drug is intended to be exported.

Importing Drugs for Personal Use

The FDA has permitted the importation of medications for personal use for a number of years. This is true with pharmaceuticals commercially marketed in other countries but not available in the United States. During July 1988, the FDA issued procedures to be used by its officials in the field to handle such situations. If there is no fraud evident or evidence of unreasonable risk to health, drugs lawfully marketed in other countries may be imported into the United States if these criteria are met:

(1) The drug is not for commercial distribution and the quantity is not excessive (usually not more than a 3-month supply);
(2) the product is for personal use;
(3) the intended use of the product is clearly identified; and
(4) the patient declares it is for personal use and lists the practitioner in the United States under whose care it will be used.

If these criteria are met, the product may be shipped to the patient or his or her physician or pharmacist.

Each request is judged on a case-by-case basis. Contact an FDA field office or FDA's Division of Import Operations and Policy at 301-443-6553.

MARKETING OF PHARMACEUTICALS

Promotion for "Off-Label" Uses

The FDA Modernization Act of 1997 added provisions to the FD&C (Sections 551 to 557) that allow for manufacturers of drug products to disseminate information about certain "unapproved" uses under certain conditions. Such dissemination was previously prohibited (see 21 CFR §202.1[e][4]). This new provision of the Act is described in more detail under Dissemination of Off-Label Treatment Information.

The FDA then issued final regulations (see 63 Fed. Reg. 64555, effective November 20, 1998) implementing these provisions of the Act. The regulations described the type and content of information a manufacturer could disseminate. In general, it was required that the information be in the form of a peer-reviewed article and include a statement the information concerned a use not yet approved by the FDA. The regulations established the procedures for a manufacturer's submission to the FDA before it could begin disseminating such information and how manufacturers must agree to submit a supplemental application for the unapproved use within a specified period of time (generally 6 to 36 months after dissemination of information, depending on whether any studies have been completed).

Section 551(a), as it was passed by Congress, provides that information about these "unapproved uses" may be disseminated to:

(1) A health care practitioner;
(2) a pharmacy benefit manager;
(3) a health insurance issuer;
(4) a group health plan; or
(5) a federal or state governmental agency.

However, the term "health care practitioner" is defined in §556(1) as "a physician or other individual who is a provider of health care, who is licensed under the law of a state to prescribe drugs or devices." In most states, this definition would not include a pharmacist. Therefore, this provision of the law does not allow manufacturers to distribute this kind of information to pharmacists unless they fall under the definition of one of the above classifications.

The policies and regulations the FDA has promulgated in the form of guidance documents (prior to the FDAMA) and the FDAMA provisions themselves, have been the ongoing subject of litigation by representatives of pharmaceutical manufacturers alleging they violate the right of commercial free speech under the First Amendment to the US Constitution (see *Washington Legal Foundation v. Henny*). They recently were struck down by the

9th Circuit on the basis that the advertising and solicitation portions of the act are unconstitutional. It is interesting to consider the similarities in this case and the compounding case — advertising, free speech, the first amendment. This litigation is not over.

Advertising

Advertising Prescription Drugs to Health Care Professionals

The pharmacist may have little involvement with prescription drug advertising other than that of advertising drug prices. "Reminder advertising" of price information to the consumer is exempt from the detailed FDA regulations governing prescription drug advertising if certain conditions are met (see 21 CFR §200.200).

"Promotional labeling" aptly describes the advertising of prescription drugs by the manufacturer or distributor. One question sometimes asked on pharmacy licensure examinations is to discuss the concepts of "full disclosure" and "fair balance" as they apply to drug promotion.

FDA regulations require a brief summary ("true statement") of information relating to side effects, contraindications, and effectiveness in all advertising for any prescription drug. An exemption is made for certain reminder advertisements, which merely call attention to the name of the drug product (see 21 CFR §202.1 et seq.). The term "full disclosure" in relation to promotional advertising and labeling (package inserts) of prescription drugs means the advertising must include the conclusions of the National Academy of Sciences that a drug product is ineffective, possibly effective, probably effective, or ineffective as a fixed combination (see 21 CFR §201.200). Prescription drug advertisements require a "true statement of information in brief summary relating to side effects, contraindications, and effectiveness" (ie, fair balance). (See 21 CFR §202.1[e].) 21 CFR §202.1(e)(6) cites 20 ways an advertisement is false, lacking in fair balance, or otherwise misleading. 21 CFR §202.1(e)(7) gives another 13 examples of how an advertisement may be false, lacking in fair balance, or otherwise misleading.

Direct-To-Consumer Advertising

Traditionally, prescription drugs were advertised exclusively to health professionals. Early in the 1980s, it was suggested to the FDA that prescription drugs should be advertised directly to the consumer. Proponents claimed such advertising would increase patient information and encourage patients to seek medical treatment. Those opposed to consumer advertising argue it may be confusing and misleading to patients and could adversely affect the doctor-patient relationship and increase the demand for drugs.

The FDA is responsible for prescription drug advertising while the Drug Enforcement Administration has no direct statutory authority in this area. The FDA originally had serious reservations about direct-to-consumer prescription drug advertising and placed a moratorium in 1983 on all such advertisements until the issue could be thoroughly studied. This moratorium was lifted after $2\frac{1}{2}$ years when the FDA concluded "for the time being, current regulations governing prescription drug advertising provide sufficient safeguards to protect consumers. The agency will continue to regulate prescription drug advertising in accordance with the FD&C and applicable regulations." Prescription drug advertising continued to be guided in accordance with §502(n) of the FD&C (21 U.S.C. §353[n]) and the implementing regulations (21 CFR Part 202).

Under previous FDA regulations, advertisements that mentioned a product's name and indication were required to include a "brief summary" of the drug's adverse effects, contraindications, and effectiveness. Manufacturers found it difficult to meet the "brief summary" requirements particularly in broadcast (eg, radio, television) advertisements. FDA responded by modifying the regulations somewhat for broadcast advertisements. The regulations required broadcast advertisements to include information about the major risks of the advertised drug (often referred to as the "major statement") in either the audio or audio and visual parts of the presentation. However, instead of presenting the "brief summary" information, the manufacturer could make "adequate provision" for the dissemination of the drug's approved labeling (21 CFR §202.1[e][1]).

In August 1999, the FDA published a final version of its *Guidance for Industry–Consumer-Directed Broadcast Advertisements*. It can be found at http://www.fda.gov/cder/guidance/index.htm. This document clarifies how manufacturers can fulfill the "adequate provision" requirements for broadcast advertisements. This document does not differ substantially from its draft, which was released in August 1997.

The *Guidance* states a manufacturer using direct-to-consumer broadcast ads may meet the "adequate provision" requirement "through an approach that will allow most of a potentially diverse audience to receive the advertised product's approved labeling." The *Guidance* describes an approach consisting of the following 4 components:

(1) Disclosure in the advertisement of an operating toll-free telephone number for consumers to call for approved package labeling. Consumers should be given the choice of having the labeling mailed to them in a timely manner or having the labeling read to them over the phone.
(2) Reference in the advertisement to a mechanism to provide package labeling to consumers with restricted access to sophisticated technology, such as the Internet, or who are uncomfortable in requesting additional information. This could be accomplished by referring patients to print advertisements containing "brief summary" information or by providing brochures containing package labeling in a variety of publicly accessible sites (eg, pharmacies, physicians' offices, grocery stores, libraries).
(3) Disclosure in the advertisement of an Internet web page address (URL) that provides access to the package labeling.
(4) Disclosure in the advertisement that pharmacists, physicians (or other health care providers), or veterinarians (in the case of animal drugs) may provide additional product information to consumers.

The *Guidance* also briefly distinguishes telephone advertisements from broadcast ads and encourages sponsors to consider the benefits of also providing patients with nonpromotional, consumer-friendly product information in addition to the required labeling.

Finally, the *Guidance* encourages sponsors to collect relevant data and research and to make the research related to the overall effects of direct-to-consumer promotion on the public health publicly known.

Advertising of *otcs*

Over-the-counter drug advertising is regulated by the Federal Trade Commission (FTC) (15 U.S.C. §55). The general objective of the regulations is to prohibit false or misleading drug advertising. The principal targets are television advertisements that are misleading or that make unsubstantiated claims for an *otc* drug.

False Advertising

Conceivably, the FTC could prosecute the community pharmacist who uses misleading advertising to promote the sale of nonprescription drugs. A state false advertising statute would be a more appropriate vehicle, however, because the FTC Act relates more to interstate than to intrastate commerce. The pharmacist is cautioned against using any type of promotional approach in drug advertising that sounds like an express warranty, thereby exposing himself or herself to liability (see discussion of warranties in the Business Law chapter).

MISCELLANEOUS ISSUES

A Third Class of Drug Products

From time to time there is interest expressed in pharmacy circles in creating a "third class" of drugs — one that would create an intermediate level of control between prescription and *otc* drugs. Proposals call for certain drug products to be available only from a pharmacist.

The FDA takes the position that such a category of drugs would not be authorized by the current wording of the FD&C, and hence, the FDA cannot create the category by regulation; legislation would be required. There are, however, limitations placed upon certain categories of drug products.

The FDA has approved a statement for use on labels of products containing stramonium. The statement warns the pharmacist that stramonium should not be displayed or kept on open shelves due to its history of misuse and abuse.

The law in some states permits certain Schedule V-controlled substances to be distributed without a prescription, providing that certain recordkeeping and quantity limitations are met. In nearly all cases, only a pharmacist can distribute these products.

Hence, both the FDA and the Drug Enforcement Administration (DEA) have created de facto third classes of drugs. However, the number of products affected is small, and an attempt to increase that number would probably meet with vigorous opposition from the manufacturers of the affected products.

Some measure of success in this area has been achieved in certain states where pharmacists are permitted to prescribe in certain situations, often under collaborative practice agreements. Currently, nearly 16 states authorize prescribing by pharmacists in certain circumstances. This prescriptive authority for pharmacists in essence creates a third class of drug products.

Veterinary Pharmaceuticals

The FD&C governs the safety and effectiveness of new animal drugs. It provides that a new animal drug shall be considered unsafe unless there is, in effect, an approved new animal drug application (NADA), and unless the use and intended use of the drug, and its labeling, conform to the approved application. Virtually all animal drugs are "new" within the meaning of the term in the Act, and thus are subject to Section 512.

Just as with drugs for human use, before a new animal drug may receive agency approval, the drug product's sponsor must establish by scientific testing that the drug is safe and effective. If the product is intended for use in a food-producing animal, the data must show the edible animal products are free of unsafe residues. The sponsor must also develop analytical methods to detect and measure drug residues in edible animal products.

"Safe use," for purposes of determining the prescription or nonprescription status of a new animal drug, includes safety to the animal, safety of food products derived from the animals, safety to the person administering the drug, safety to persons associated with the animal, and safety in terms of the drug's effect on the environment. "Effective use," for the same purpose, assumes an accurate diagnosis can be made (with a reasonable degree of certainty), the drug can be properly administered, and the course of the disease can be followed so the success or lack of success of the product can be observed.

Just as with drugs for human use, the FDA has the responsibility for determining the marketing status (prescription or *otc*) of animal drug products on the basis of whether it is possible to prepare "adequate directions for use" under which a layperson can use the drugs safely and effectively. Products for which adequate directions for lay use can be written may be labeled for *otc* use under existing law. If adequate directions cannot be written, the prescription system provides a method of distribution and control is intended to ensure that the product is used only under a licensed practitioner's supervision.

Prescription veterinary products must bear the legend: "Caution: Federal law restricts this drug to use by or on the order of a licensed veterinarian." Because adequate directions for safe and effective lay use cannot be written for some veterinary prescription drug products, such products can only be distributed to or on the prescription or other order of a licensed veterinarian. Before being sold or dispensed, they must remain in the possession of a person or firm regularly and lawfully engaged in the manufacture, transportation, storage, or wholesale or retail distribution of veterinary prescription drug products. The drug products may be distributed only by persons or firms authorized by state and local laws.

The same drug substances (ie, active ingredient) can be marketed in a number of different dosage forms intended for use by different routes of administration, and in various species of animals. Thus, different drug products containing the same active ingredient may be prescription-only and otc, depending on the circumstances.

Distribution (dispensing, shipping, or otherwise making available for use in animals) to the layperson of a veterinary prescription drug product may be made only by or on the bona fide prescription or other order of a licensed veterinarian. The FDA has interpreted the word "prescription" to apply only to the practitioner's direction to a pharmacist. Because some states authorize persons other than pharmacists to dispense prescription drug products on a veterinarian's instructions, the term "other order" is used when instructions are for a legally authorized dispenser who is not a pharmacist. In both cases, the required instructions are the same and the dispenser may not dispense a prescription veterinary drug product without a veterinarian's explicit authorization.

Sale of a veterinary prescription legend drug product to a layperson, except on a prescription or other order of a licensed practitioner, causes the product to be misbranded because it fails to bear adequate directions for lay use and does not meet all of the requirements for exemption for the "adequate directions for use" requirement. It subjects the seller to civil and criminal provisions of the Act.

A licensed veterinarian may legally use or dispense a veterinary prescription drug product only within the course of his or her professional practice where a valid veterinarian-client-patient relationship exists. Veterinarians employed by drug manufacturers or distributors may not legally dispense prescription drug products to laypersons unless they meet the criteria listed above. Similarly, practicing veterinarians or their employees may not legally sell veterinary prescription drug products to walk-in customers unless the same criteria are met. The FDA is responsible for regulating animal feeds and pet foods and most animal health products. For example, pet foods are subject to the requirements of the Act, and pet food manufacturers are subject to individual annual product registration in most states. Pet foods are also subject to the labeling requirements of the Fair Packaging and Labeling Act, which governs certain aspects of consumer product labeling.

Some products used to control external pests are intended to act systemically and, therefore, are regulated as drugs by the FDA and not as pesticides by the Environmental Protection Agency (EPA). For example, topical flea-control products are usually regulated by the EPA, whereas oral flea-control products generally fall under the FDA's jurisdiction.

The animal counterpart of a cosmetic is commonly referred to as a "grooming aid." Section 201(i) of the Act defines a cosmetic as pertaining only to human use. Therefore, products intended solely for cleansing or promoting attractiveness of animals are not subject to FDA control. If such products are represented for any therapeutic purpose or if they contain an active drug ingredient, they are subject to regulation under the Act as animal drugs. They may also be subject to regulation under the Act as medical devices.

Use of Approved Drugs for Nonapproved Uses

The definition of a new drug is in §201(p) of the FD&C. A new drug can be defined summarily as one that generally is not recognized by experts as safe and effective for its recommended uses. A drug is considered new if it is:

(1) A new chemical for medical use;
(2) an established drug that is available in new dosage forms or at new dosage levels or is packaged in novel materials such as plastic; or
(3) an established drug with new medical claims. Without FDA approval, a new drug cannot be distributed in interstate commerce for use in humans, and an exemption is required for interstate shipment of drugs for investigational use.

The term "approved drug" can be defined as a new drug for which an NDA has been approved by the FDA and is still valid or as a drug in use prior to the effective date of the 1938 FD&C and, therefore, is not subject to the NDA requirement, provided the drug is distributed and promoted in accordance with the labeling and established use as then existed.

Sometimes, "approved" and "established" drugs are understood as the pre-1938 drugs, and "approved new drugs" are understood as post-1938 drugs for which FDA-approved NDAs are in force. In this discussion, the term "approved drug" refers to both the pre- and post-1938 drugs as defined above. The term "use," when it is applied in reference to an approved drug in this discussion, means the prescribing and administering of a drug within the limits of the required dosage and route of administration, therapeutic indications, precautions, warnings, and contraindications. Therefore, to use an approved drug for an approved use medically is to prescribe and administer the drug within the limits of the package insert information. Conversely, to use an approved drug for an unapproved use is to prescribe or administer the drug outside of the limits of the package insert information. This is commonly referred to as "off-label," "unlabeled," nonapproved, or "unapproved" use of a drug.

History of FDA Policy

It now has become accepted policy that a physician is free to prescribe a drug for uses that are not included in the official product labeling. However, historically, this was a contentious issue. For those interested, the following FDA public statements regarding the use of approved drugs for nonapproved uses should be considered:

> The requirements of the law are satisfied when an approved new drug is shipped in interstate commerce with the approved package insert, and neither the shipper nor the recipient intends it be used for an unapproved purpose. Once the drug is in the pharmacy, the physician may, as part of the practice of medicine, lawfully prescribe a different dosage for his patient or may otherwise vary the conditions or use from those approved in the package insert, without informing or obtaining approval of the Food and Drug Administration.[1]

> A physician's experimental use of an approved drug — without the submission of an IND (claimed exemption for investigational use of new drug) — does not violate federal law because the drug has been lawfully shipped in interstate commerce for the approved uses.[2]

> Although the law does not require the physician to file an investigational new drug plan before prescribing an approved drug for unapproved uses it is sometimes in the best interest of the physician and the public that this be done.[1]

Previously, there was an opinion that if a physician routinely used an approved drug in doses or methods outside of the approved uses, the physician was experimenting with the drug

[1] Use of drugs for unapproved indications: Your legal responsibility. FDA *Drug Bull.* 1972;Oct. 1-2.
[2] Jennings J. The Rx label: basis for all prescribing information. FDA *Papers.* 1967-1968;1:10.

and, therefore, was subject to the IND requirement. However, the FDA's current position is that a physician's experimental use of an approved drug does not violate federal law, even though it may violate a state law. It is obvious from the intent of the 1962 Federal FDCA amendment, and from the thalidomide episode, that public safety would be served best by the filing of an IND application (or by acting pursuant to the authority of an IND application filed by a drug firm or other sponsor) by the physician who experiments with unapproved uses for an approved drug.

On August 15, 1972, the FDA published in the *Federal Register* (37 Fed. Reg. 16503[1972]) certain proposed regulations to deal with the unapproved use of approved new drugs. The proposals generated some controversy, and as of this date have not been finalized. The proposed regulations would give the FDA 8 possible options, ranging from revocation of the NDA of the involved drug to adding the unapproved use to the package insert. It is noteworthy that the wording of the regulation proposed by the FDA would prohibit a pharmacist from recommending an unapproved use because the pharmacist is "in the chain of distribution." The inability of the FDA to draft a clear prohibition of activity by manufacturers that would not interfere with the lawful practice of pharmacy is one of the reasons the proposed regulation has never been finalized.

A pharmacist legally may dispense a prescription for an approved drug prescribed for an unapproved use. The prescription must comply with the labeling requirements of §503(b)(2), and any other requirements of federal and state law must be met as they relate to the drug dispensed. The general negligence law should be followed; that is, a pharmacist never should dispense a drug if the prescribed dose is obviously fatal; if the prescribed dose or administration is unusual, the prescriber should be contacted to ascertain if an error has been made. Controlled substances may be prescribed and dispensed legally for legitimate medical purposes (a violation of DEA regulation §1306.04 would occur if a narcotic were prescribed and dispensed solely to satisfy an addiction). At least one court has held that once a drug is lawfully in interstate commerce, a physician may prescribe it for any use at all without the constraints of the package insert (*United States v. Evers*, 453 F.Supp. 1141 [D.Ala. 1978]).

The difference between the use of an approved drug for a nonapproved purpose and the use of a nonapproved drug for a medical purpose should be noted. A nonapproved drug may be defined for the intention of this discussion either as a drug banned from commerce because of its hazards or because it is ineffective, or as a chemical or substance that has not been used previously in humans for the treatment of disease. If the banner substance or untried chemical is put to a drug use, it is obviously a new drug, within the meaning of the term in §201(p) of the Act; more precisely, it is an unapproved new drug or an investigational new drug.

The terminology can be confusing because not every new drug is a nonapproved drug. An approved drug becomes a new drug when and where it is put to new medical use, but it still remains an approved drug and legally on the market for other medical uses. The finite distinctions are important in light of the following statement:

> The use of an investigational new drug — a nonapproved drug that is shipped interstate — requires submission of an IND by the physician, although he uses the drug only in his practice of medicine.[1]

A nonapproved drug shipped interstate is illegally in interstate commerce unless compliance with the IND procedure is first met.

---

[1] Gyarfas WJ, Welch J. The IND procedure: assuring safe and effective drugs. FDA Papers. 1969-1970;3:27.

Labeling of Ipecac Syrup

The current FDA regulations pertaining to the labeling of ipecac syrup are in 21 CFR §§201.308 and 369.21. Ipecac syrup is used in the emergency treatment of certain kinds of poisonings where an emetic is indicated. While experts agree ipecac syrup should be used only under medical supervision, the need for the immediate availability of this drug is critical because rapid treatment may mean the difference between life and death. Consequently, ipecac is available *otc*, and the labeling for retail packages (containing no more than 1 fluid ounce or 30 mL) is as follows:

The following statements must appear in a conspicuous manner (boxed and in red letters):

(1) For emergency use to cause vomiting in poisoning. Before using, call physician, the Poison Control Center, or hospital emergency room immediately for advice.
(2) The following warning must also be on the label: "Warning: Keep out of reach of children. Do not use in unconscious persons. Ordinarily, this drug should not be used if strychnine; corrosives such as alkalies (lye) and strong acids; or petroleum distillates such as kerosene, gasoline, coal oil, fuel oil, paint thinner, or cleaning fluids have been ingested."
(3) The dosage indication must appear. The usual dosage is 1 tablespoon (15 mL) in individuals older than 1 year of age.

Anyone who dispenses ipecac syrup into a 1 oz. bottle from a bulk container must never confuse ipecac fluid extract with ipecac syrup. The fluid extract of ipecac is far more concentrated than the syrup; if overdosed, it could cause death. The FDA-approved, labeled ipecac syrup is widely available in commercial consumer packaging and should be stocked as such rather than purchased in bulk. The fluid extract of ipecac probably should not be stocked at all because it is almost never prescribed. At least one lawsuit has been based on this error (see *Sullivan v. Sisters of St. Francis*, 374 S.W.2d 294 [Tex Civ App 1963]).

Drug Product Identification

21 CFR §206 requires the imprinting of solid oral dosage forms. This requirement applies to both prescription and nonprescription medications. The imprinted code in conjunction with the product's size, shape, and color must allow identification of the drug product and the manufacturer or distributor of the product.

National Drug Code

The NDC system facilitates automated processing of drug data by government agencies, drug manufacturers and wholesalers, fiscal intermediaries for Medicare and Medicaid, private insurance companies, and drug providers.

The NDC number consists of at least 10 characters. The code is divided into 3 segments: A labeler code, a drug product code, and a package code. Formerly, a 9-character code was used, but the FDA has added a lead zero to the code for all of the drugs listed under the older code. Therefore, drug products coded in the older editions of the NDC system will have the 10-character code broken down into a 4-character labeler part, a 4-character drug identity part, and a 2-character package segment. Although the older drug code may have alpha-numerical characters, the FDA permits changeover to all numerical digits, as is used in the new drug code.

New participants in the NDC system will have a 10-digit code assigned to drug products, the first 5 digits of which identify a drug manufacturer or distributor; the last 5 digits identify the drug name, package size, and type of drug. An 11-digit code will be used when the available 5-digit labeler portions of the code have been exhausted.

Drug manufacturers or distributors must register with the FDA by submitting form FDA-2656; they must submit a list of their drug products on form FDA-2657. From these drug lists, a national drug code directory is prepared.

To obtain a copy of the National Drug Code Directory, write to the Superintendent of Documents, US Government Printing Office, Washington, DC 20402. This information is also available on magnetic tape from the Technical Information Service, US Department of Commerce, Springfield, VA 22151.

The NDC number is requested, but not required, in and on all drug labeling (see FDA regulation §207.35[b][3]).

The existence of an NDC number on the label of a drug product does not necessarily mean the product has an approved NDA. There is no relationship between the NDC number and the NDA. The NDC number is simply a number assigned for data processing purposes.

Reporting of Drug Product Problems/Medication Errors

Both the FDA and the USP operate voluntary reporting programs to which pharmacists may report drug product problems, adverse events, or medication errors. The FDA's MedWatch program encourages the voluntary reporting of adverse events or product problems. Such reports may be telephoned to 1-800-FDA-1088, faxed to 1-800-FDA-0178, or through the Internet at http://www.fda.gov/medwatch/index.html.

USP's Practitioner's Reporting Networks™ (USP PRN®) is an FDA MedWatch partner and operates the Drug Product Problem Reporting Program (DPPR) and the USP Medication Errors Reporting (MER) Program. The DPPR reporting form can be found on page DC-94b. In addition, reports may be phoned to 1-800-4-USP PRN (1-800-487-7776) or faxed to 301-816-8532. USP's home page, located at http://www.usp.org/prn has additional information about reporting electronically.

USP's MER Program, which is presented in cooperation with the Institute for Safe Medication Practices (ISMP), provides the opportunity for practitioners to share medication error experiences through a nationwide network to help gain an understanding of why errors occur and how to prevent them. Educational information gained from the program assists health care professionals to avoid errors by recognizing circumstances and causes of actual and potential errors. Reports may be phoned to 1-800-23-ERROR (1-800-233-7767) or faxed to 301-816-8532. USP's home page, located at http://www.usp.org, has additional information about reporting errors electronically.

OTHER RELEVANT LEGISLATION

Health Insurance Portability and Accountability Act of 1996 (HIPAA)

This legislation was passed in 1996, and was known as the Kassenbaum Kennedy Bill.

Health Insurance Reform

Title I of the legislation created a new title XXVII of the Public Health Service (PHS) Act (42 U.S.C. 300gg, et seq.) that requires group health plans and health insurance issuers to provide certain guarantees for availability and renewability of health coverage in the group and individual health insurance markets. Title I also contains some preemption provisions that prevent state law from differing in any way from the Federal requirements, except to expand HIPAA's protections in certain ways and to the extent that any state law prevents the application of any requirement of HIPAA. In more plain language, while HIPAA confirms that the states are the primary regulators of health insurance coverage in each state, the Federal government, if necessary, has the authority and will step in to the state to enforce the HIPAA provisions in Title I if necessary. This portion of the legislation is often referred to as HIPAA Health Insurance Reform. Its provisions have been in effect for several years, and relate to "preexisting health conditions" and to protection of health insurance coverage for workers and their families when they change or lose their jobs. This section of the legislation is beyond the scope of this textbook. However, regulations enforcing these provisions can be found at 45 CFR Parts 144, 146, 148, and 150.

Administrative Simplification

Title II of HIPAA is referred to as the Administrative Simplification portion of the legislation. This portion requires the Department of Health and Human Services (HHS) to establish national standards for electronic health care transactions and national identifiers for providers, health plans, and employers. These standardized electronic transmissions of administrative and financial transactions are intended to reduce the cost and administrative burdens of health care. This Administrative Simplication portion protects the *security* and *privacy* of health data. More information about the HIPAA standards is available at http://www.aspe.hhs.gov/adminsimp/.

The final Security regulations for HIPAA were published in the Federal Register on February 20, 2003.

Enforcement

The Centers for Medicare and Medicaid Services (CMS) has been chosen to enforce the HIPAA transaction and code set standards, while the HHS Office for Civil Rights is the agency responsible for enforcing the Privacy standards contained in the HIPAA statute and regulations.

Privacy Regulations

The portion of the HIPAA statute and regulations that is currently being established is the Privacy portion of the legislation. The final Privacy regulations adopted in accordance with the statute may be found at: 45 CFR Parts 160 and 164 or 67 FR 53182. These regulations go into effect on April 14th, 2003, at which time all applicable parties must be compliant.

For an overview and answers to frequently asked questions about the privacy regulations see www.hhs.gov/ocr/hipaa/finalmaster.html.

Sources of Information

There are many sources of information on this section of the legislation. For example, the American Medical Association, on its website at amednews.com contains a section entitled the *HIPAA Minute* which contains information on how to be compliant with the Privacy Regulations that take effect in April 2003. The CMS website contains a wealth of information on the enforcement of the Administrative Simplification Provisions of the statute. On the CMS website under the HIPAA Administrative Simplification section, a Provider HIPAA Readiness Checklist is available to get started towards compliance with the Electronic Transactions and Code Set Requirements.

The HHS website at www.hhs.gov/policies/index.shtml contains all the legislation and regulations that HHS is involved in. The final updated Privacy Rule is published at the Federal Register Vol.67, No.157/Wednesday, August 14, 2002. The proposed rule was published November 3, 1999 (64 FR 59918). After receiving over 52,000 public comments, HHS issued a final rule (65 FR 82462) on December 28, 2000, establishing "Standards for Privacy of Individually Identifiable Health Information". After publication of that rule, there seemed to be a fair amount of confusion and misunderstanding due to the complexity of the regulations as established. In response to those communications and to ensure that the provisions of the Privacy Rule would protect patients' access to health care or quality of healthcare, the Secretary opened the Privacy Rule for further comment in March 2001 (66 FR 12738). On March 27th, 2002, the Department proposed modifications to the Privacy Rule (67 FR 14776). Public comment was solicited on the proposed modifications (a 30 day only comment period) and the final rule was published, as stated above, on April 14, 2002. Therefore, there is a lot of material discussing the HIPAA privacy rule that predates the final rule.

Department for Health and Human Services (HHS) CMS

HIPAA Information, Compliance and Enforcement

A booklet entitled "Protecting Your Health Insurance Coverage" is available through the government on the internet. It was originally published by the Health Care Financing Administration (HFCA). Secretary of HHS, Tommy Thompson, under the Bush administration, announced that as of July 1, 2001, the government agency (HCFA) would be changed to the Center for Medicare and Medicaid Services (CMS). Emphasizing that the move was more than just a name change, he stated that

> These sweeping reforms will strengthen our programs and enable our dedicated employees to better serve Medicare and Medicaid beneficiaries, as well as health care providers. The agency has enforcement power over some of HIPAA's provisions. The CMS website contains a wealth of information on HIPAA in general, as well as on compliance and enforcement of the statute. The CMS website can be found at http://www.hhs.cms.gov. Go to the section named HIPAA. There, under the title HIPAA, you will find a site entitled *HIPAA Online*. HIPAA Online is an interactive tool provided by the federal government to help answer questions about health coverage and persons' rights and protections under the HIPAA legislation.

CMS is a federal agency within the U.S. Department of Health and Human Services. It runs the Medicare and Medicaid programs-health care programs that benefit about 75 million Americans. Along with the Health Resources and Services Administration, CMS runs the State Children's Health Insurance Program (SCHIP), a program that is expected to cover many of the approximately 10 million uninsured children in the United States. CMS also regulates all laboratory testing (except research) performed on humans in the United States. CMS, with the Departments of Labor and Treasury, helps millions of Americans and small companies get and keep health insurance coverage, while helping to eliminate discrimination based on health status for people buying health insurance.

Three new business centers have been formed as a result of this reform effort. They are:

(1) The Center for Beneficiary Choices, which focuses on the beneficiary education, providing beneficiaries with the information they need to make their health care decisions. It also manages the Medicare + Choice program, consumer research and demonstrations, and grievances and appeals.

(2) The Center for Medicare Management, which focuses on the management of the traditional fee for service Medicare program, including the development and implementation of payment policy and management of the Medicare carriers and fiscal intermediaries.

(3) The Center for Medicaid and State Operations, which focuses on programs administered by the states, including Medicaid, the State Children's Health Insurance Program, private insurance, survey and certification and the Clinical Laboratory Improvement Amendments (CLIA).

On October 1, 2001, the Medicare 800 number (1-800-633-4227) was enhanced, and now provides service to beneficiaries 24 hours per day, seven days per week. Recently, CMS' Office of Research, Development and Information (ORDI) published its sixth report involving the finances of its contractors, health providers, and other related businesses that provide services to its beneficiaries.

OBRA '90

On November 5, 1990, President Bush signed the Omnibus Budget Reconciliation Act of 1990 (P.L. 101-508) commonly known as OBRA '90. This huge appropriations legislation contained a few pages that made changes in the Medicaid program. However, these few pages have dramatically altered the standard of pharmacy practice in the United States. Part of the reason for this is, although the federal OBRA '90 requirements only were applicable to Medicaid patients, most states have made them applicable to all patients receiving prescription drugs. A 1993 survey of the 50 states, the District of Columbia, and Puerto Rico by the APhA revealed that 37 jurisdictions have made the OBRA requirements applicable to all patients while 7 jurisdictions have made them applicable to Medicaid patients only. Eight other jurisdictions have made the requirements applicable to other specified patients such as third-party patients and HMO patients in addition to Medicaid patients.

OBRA '90 directs that in order to participate in the Medicaid program, states must have in place drug use review (DUR) programs, and they also must enact requirements that pharmacists offer to counsel Medicaid beneficiaries receiving prescription drugs. Additionally, it requires states establish programs for manufacturers to pay rebates to the states for pharmaceuticals used in Medicaid programs, thereby reducing the cost of those medications to the lowest price charged to any purchaser from the manufacturer. Finally, the statute also mandates that states require pharmacists to make a reasonable effort to obtain, record, and maintain patient medication records containing specified information.

Drug Use Review

The drug use review programs were required to be in place by January 1, 1993, and had to include both prospective and retrospective components. The purpose of the DUR programs are to improve the quality of pharmaceutical care by ensuring prescriptions are appropriate, medically necessary, and they are not likely to result in adverse medical results. Under the prospective DUR program, pharmacists are required to screen prescriptions for potential problems. The review must include screening for potential drug therapy problems because of therapeutic duplication, drug disease contraindications, adverse drug-drug interactions, incorrect drug dosage, incorrect duration of drug therapy, drug-allergy interactions, and clinical abuse or misuse.

Counseling

State Medicaid programs and state boards of pharmacy took different approaches to implementing the OBRA '90 counseling requirements. In some states, the "offer to counsel" must be made by the pharmacist. Other states allow the pharmacist's agent or designee to make the offer or allow the offer to counsel to be made by use of a sign or by notation on the prescription bag or label. Many states have disposed with the "offer" to counsel altogether and have imposed mandatory patient counseling requirements. Although OBRA '90 does not mandate the type of information a pharmacist must provide patients, both the statute and accompanying regulations state that such information should include at least the following:

(1) The name and description of the medication.
(2) The dosage form, dosage, route of administration, and duration of drug therapy.
(3) Special directions and precautions for preparation, administration, and use by the patient.
(4) Common severe side or adverse effects or interactions and therapeutic contraindications that may be encountered, including their avoidance, and the action required if they occur.
(5) Techniques for self-monitoring drug therapy.
(6) Proper storage.
(7) Prescription refill information.
(8) Action to be taken in the event of a missed dose.

Most states have adopted this same language into their statutes or regulations. Thus, the type of information pharmacists are to provide to patients is set forth with particular detail in most states. OBRA '90 does state that a pharmacist is not obligated to counsel a patient if the patient refuses such counseling. In implementing the law, some states require such refusal of counseling to be documented in writing. Even if it is not required by state law however, it is probably best to have written documentation of such refusals in order to demonstrate compliance with the counseling provisions.

Patient Medication Records

The intent of OBRA '90 is for pharmacists to perform a comprehensive drug use evaluation each time a prescription is dispensed. In order to do this, pharmacists must have adequate information. OBRA '90 requires pharmacists to make a reasonable effort to obtain, record, and maintain at least the following information regarding patients:

- Name, address, telephone number, date of birth (or age), and sex.
- Individual history where significant, including disease state or states, known allergies and drug reactions and a comprehensive list of medications and relevant devices.
- Pharmacist comments relevant to the individual's drug therapy.

These requirements contemplate more than just a drug profile, which many states had previously required pharmacists to keep. Of particular note is the requirement for pharmacist comments relevant to drug therapy. Here, a pharmacist may document any findings from the drug use review and counseling information provided to the patient.

Impact of OBRA '90

Although many pharmacists were performing drug use review and were counseling patients prior to the enactment of OBRA '90, many courts had refused to recognize that pharmacists had any legal duty to provide these services (see Minimizing Liability in the Civil Liability chapter). Now, because of the OBRA '90 mandates, nearly all states have statutes and regulations that require pharmacists to perform these functions. In essence, OBRA '90 has statutorily raised the legal standard of conduct required of pharmacists. It will take time before we see the full effect of OBRA '90 on pharmacists' liability in reported cases, but at least one court already noted it may alter the legal landscape. In the case of *Walker v. Jack Eckerd Corp.* (434 S.E.2d 63 [Ga.App. 1993]), the court took care to note its holding that pharmacists have no duty to warn a patient about potential complications from overuse of medications does not serve as controlling precedent for cases arising after January 1, 1993, the effective date of the OBRA '90 regulations. As more courts are asked to address the legal standard of pharmacy practice, they will turn to OBRA '90 to assist them in defining those standards. OBRA '90 mandates that pharmacists take on additional responsibilities, and with those expanded responsibilities come expanded legal expectations and liability.

Federal Hazardous Substances Act

Historical Background

The first federal attempt at regulating caustic and corrosive poisons was the 1927 Federal Caustic Poison Act. This legislation was known colloquially as the "Lye Law." The Act covered only 12 caustic substances, and major revision did not take place until 1960 when the Federal Hazardous Substances Labeling Act was enacted. The 1960 Act repealed only sections of the Caustic Poison Act. It applied to household-sized containers of dangerous substances and required the labeling of precautions, directions for safe use and storage, and appropriate first aid and medical treatment by a physician in case of accidental injury. The 1960 Act had loopholes because it only applied to hazardous items that are distributed only in household containers, and it did not ban substances that are so dangerous they preclude any safe labeling for household consumer use.

In 1966, Congress passed the Child Protection Act, which amended the Federal Hazardous Substances Labeling Act, and it then became known simply as the Federal Hazardous Substances Act (15 U.S.C. §1261 et seq). The 1966 amendments made the following changes in the Act:

(1) All hazardous substances were regulated regardless of their packaging and wrapping;
(2) hazardous items that could not be labeled safely for household use were banned from interstate commerce; and
(3) the sale of toys and other children's articles containing hazardous substances was banned.

However, the 1966 amendments still did not adequately protect the consumer, and in 1970, Congress enacted the Poison Prevention Packaging Act and, in 1972, the Consumer Product Safety Act.

Hazardous Substances Defined

A hazardous substance can be defined as a substance or a mixture of substances that can cause injury or illness through handling and that can cause potential danger, especially to children, if misused. A hazardous substance can be a toxicant, corrosive, or irritant, and it can be flammable or can generate pressure through heat or decomposition.

The Act differentiates hazardous substances according to the nature of the potential danger. For example, the Act defines a toxic substance as "any substance (other than a radioactive substance) which has the capacity to produce personal injury or illness to man through ingestion, inhalation, or absorption through any body surface." A highly toxic substance is one in which "a single oral dose of 50 mg or less per kilogram body weight would kill half or more of the white rats to which it is fed."

The Hazardous Substances Act affects pharmacy practice in that it does not regulate the economic poisons subject to the Federal Insecticide, Fungicide, and Rodenticide Act, nor does it regulate drugs subject to the FD&C (although the unrepealed portions of the Caustic Poison Act still apply to certain provisions in the FD&C). Essentially, the Act regulates household items such as bleach, cleaning fluids, antifreeze, and drainpipe cleaners. Many of these and similar items are stocked in the community pharmacy. While many state poison-sale laws do not apply to poisonous items sold for nonmedical use (eg, muriatic acid used for soldering), the Federal Hazardous Substances Act does apply. The pharmacist selling such hazardous items should sell them only in the original containers, as labeled by the manufacturer or supplier with the required cautions and warnings, or label the products as required by the Act. The regulations for labeling are available from the Consumer Product Safety Commission, Washington, DC 20207, or the Internet at http://www.cpsc.gov.

Required Labeling

The Hazardous Substances Act requires labeling of hazardous substances with:

(1) The name and address of the manufacturer, distributor, or seller;
(2) the common name (the chemical name is only permitted if there is no common name);
(3) the signal word "danger" on extremely flammable, corrosive, or highly toxic substances;
(4) the signal words "warning" or "caution" on all other hazardous substances;
(5) a statement of the hazardous properties, including "flammable," "vapor harmful," "causes burns," "harmful or fatal if swallowed," or similar wording as prescribed by the regulations;
(6) precautionary statements;
(7) first-aid instructions followed by the statement, "Call a physician immediately";
(8) the signal word "poison" and the skull and crossbones symbol on highly toxic substances or when required by the regulations; or
(9) the signal word "poison" for certain substances that were formerly regulated by the Federal Caustic Poison Act.

Formerly, the FDA enforced the Act and issued regulations implementing it. As of May 14, 1973, however, it has been enforced by the Consumer Product Safety Commission, which also enforces several other federal consumer protection laws.

Pre-emption

Pre-emption is a legal doctrine by which one set of laws takes precedence over or excludes another. The most common illustration of this is when Congress specifically legislates in an area usually reserved for the states, and a Congressional act specifically excludes or pre-empts the states from legislation to the contrary.

In 1976, Public Law 94-284 made specific changes in the Federal Hazardous Substances Act (21 U.S.C. §1261 et seq), the net effect of which provided the Federal Act's labeling requirements are the standard and any state or municipal labeling requirements are inapplicable unless they are identical to the federal requirements or provide a higher degree of protection.

The pre-emption provision of Public Law 94-284 is summarized as follows:

(1) If a hazardous substance or its packaging is subject to cautionary labeling requirements under 15 U.S.C. §§1261(p) and 1262(b), which are designed to protect against the risk of illness or injury associated with the substance, no state or political subdivision of a state may establish or continue to effect a cautionary labeling requirement applicable to the substance or packaging unless the requirement is identical to that of the federal regulations.

(2) If the regulations of the Federal Consumer Product Safety Commission were promulgated under, or were for the enforcement of, the Federal Hazardous Substances Act, which protects against the risk of illness or injury associated with a hazardous substance, no state or political subdivision of a state may establish or continue to effect a requirement applicable to a hazardous substance unless the requirement is identical to the federal regulations.

(3) The federal government and the government of any state or political subdivision thereof could, however, establish or continue to effect requirements for the labeling of hazardous substances for their individual uses if the requirements provide a higher degree of protection from risk of illness or injury then the labeling requirements of 15 U.S.C. §§1261(p) and 1262(b).

Provision also has been made for a state or its political subdivisions for exemption from federal pre-emption through application to the Commission. Exemption is granted if the state requirement provides significantly higher degrees of protection than the federal and does not unduly burden interstate commerce. In other words, a state can ask the Commission that its own hazardous substance labeling requirements be the applicable standard within the state.

The pre-emption provision of the Federal Hazardous Substances Act was not taken too seriously by the states until the advent of a 1978 court case. In *Moore v. B & C Family Center, Inc.*, 272 N.W.2d 150 (Mich. App. 1978), a Michigan appeals court held that the warnings required by the Michigan Poison Sale Law were pre-empted by the Federal Hazardous Substances Act. The case involved a negligence suit in which the plaintiff claimed she wanted castor oil and was sold camphorated oil. She later ingested the camphorated oil and suffered injuries. The jury voted in favor of the defendant, and the plaintiff appealed. The appeal was based on the trial judge's refusal to give certain requested instructions to the jury; the appeals court reversed the trial court on those grounds and sent the case back for a new trial. However, the significance of the case is that in its written decision, the Michigan Court of Appeals indicated the Federal Hazardous Substances Act pre-empted the Michigan Poison Sale Law.

Poison Prevention Packaging Act of 1970

The Federal Caustic Poison Act and the Hazardous Substances Labeling Act, reported on the previous pages, were early attempts at trying to prevent accidental poisoning, particularly among young children. These laws primarily provided a uniform system for labeling and requirements for inclusion of cautionary statements. When studies indicated that childhood ingestion of poisons could be reduced through the use of child-resistant packaging, Congress enacted the Poison Prevention Packaging Act (PPPA) in 1970. This law has been administered by the US Consumer Product Safety Commission since 1973 when jurisdiction was transferred from the FDA.

The PPPA (15 U.S.C. §1471 to 1476, Public Law 91-601) regulates certain substances (defined as "hazardous household substances") and requires they be packaged for consumer use in special packaging that will make them significantly difficult for children under 5 years of age to open (see Prescription Drugs section of Substances Covered under the PPPA and Exemptions from the Act). This packaging is referred to in the common parlance as "child-resistant containers." One of the main purposes of the Act is to extend the special packaging requirements to both prescription and certain nonprescription drugs. These requirements are set forth at 16CFR§1700.

The PPPA requires that a number of findings be made before a special packaging standard can be required by the Consumer Product Safety Commission. The agency must show the potential involvement of the packaging in the injury. While some human oral prescription drugs do not have significant levels of toxicity, the PPPA still requires all human oral prescription drugs, with a few limited exceptions, to be dispensed in safety packaging. To do otherwise would have placed a significant burden on individual pharmacists to check each drug, dosage, and amount before dispensing. Pharmacists would also have to maintain extensive listings of regulated and nonregulated drugs. Because of these significant burdens, the issue was resolved by regulating all human oral prescription drugs and then establishing a relatively small list of exempted products.

Prescription drugs intended for topical application or in a dosage form not intended for oral administration are not required to be dispensed with child-resistant packaging. Investigational New Drugs (INDs) are subject to the PPPA standards if the drug is intended for oral administration to humans, can be dispensed only on or by an order of a licensed medical practitioner, and is to be dispensed directly to the patient. The Commission currently permits pharmacists to use reversible or other types of dual-purpose packaging for dispensing prescription drugs as long as the drug is dispensed in such a package using the child-resistant mode.

Pharmacists should not confuse the child-resistant packaging requirements with the FDA's tamper-resistant packaging requirements for *otc* drugs. The 2 systems are separate. Although some child-resistant packages are also tamper resistant (blister packs and unit-of-use), a child-resistant package is not necessarily tamper resistant.

Pharmacists who violate the PPPA regulations may be criminally prosecuted and imprisoned for not more than 1 year, or pay a fine or not more than $1000, or both. Penalties are increased on second or subsequent offenses.

Section 4(b) of the PPPA exempts from the special packaging requirement those drugs that are dispensed on prescription or on a medical practitioner's order if the prescriber requests a noncomplying container in the prescription or if the patient receiving the drug requests a noncomplying container. The request from the prescriber or patient is not required to be in writing, although documentation may be of value later. The Commission has taken the position that pharmacists may advise patients that they have the option of having their prescription dispensed in noncomplying packaging, but the final choice must be that of the patient. The Consumer Product Safety Commission has ruled, while it is permissible for a pharmacist to accept and honor a blanket request from a patient that child-resistant closures never be used on his or her medication, it is not permissible for the pharmacist to honor such a request from a prescriber (eg, "Never use safety caps for any of my patients"). Another exemption is made in the Act for *otc* items for elderly or handicapped individuals; the manufacturer is allowed to market one size of a consumer container with noncomplying packaging. In order for the exemption to apply, the noncomplying package must contain the printed statement, "This package is for households without young children." The manufacturer must also market popular sizes of the product in the special packaging as required.

To meet PPPA approval standards, not all children need to be prevented from gaining entry into child-resistant packaging, nor do all adults have to be able to gain entry into the package. In general, for a package to meet the child-resistant packaging requirements, not more than 20% of a test group of children should be able to gain entry (after a visual demonstration of the proper way to open the package), and not more than 10% of adults should be unable to gain entry. In response to complaints from consumers, particularly older consumers, CPSC amended the testing requirements to include greater representation of senior adults 50 to 70 years of age to determine whether they can open packages more easily. Requirements for senior-adult packaging became effective January 21, 1998. Both the child-resistant and senior-adult testing procedures can be found at 16 CFR §1700.20.

Regulations under the Act prohibit the reuse of special packaging containers. This prohibition is based on the wear associated with a plastic vial, which would compromise the effectiveness of the safety container. Because such wear with a glass container is negligible, the Consumer Product Safety Commission has indicated it would have no objections to the reuse of a glass prescription container, provided a new safety closure is used. Drugs dispensed to institutionalized patients may be packaged in a conventional container to be administered by institutional personnel.

While the Act requires specific child-resistant containers for consumer household items, the bulk containers shipped to manufacturers, wholesalers, and retailers are exempted from the special packaging (eg, stock bottles). The outside container of a household product shipped by the retailer to the consumer (eg, a box surrounding a bottle) is exempted from requirements of the Act unless it is the only container of the substance.

Substances Requiring Special Packaging

The products that are subject to special packaging standards under the PPPA cover a broad category because the law applies to many items produced for use in or around the household. Drugs, cosmetics, hazardous substances (including certain corrosive products), and prepackaged fuels are within the scope of the legislation. It should be noted that the responsibility for enacting child-resistant packaging standards for pesticides lies with the Environmental Protection Agency. While a significant number of substances theoretically could be subject to regulation under the PPPA, only 19 categories of household substances have been made subject to a child-resistant packaging standard.

Section 4(a) of the PPPA provides for the marketing of "non-complying" packages of regulated substances other than prescription drugs in order to facilitate access to regulated products by the elderly and handicapped.

"... the manufacturer or packer ... may package any household substance (subject to a PPPA standard), in packaging of a single size, which does not comply with such standard if:

(1) The manufacturer (or packer) also supplies such substance in packages which comply with such standard; and
(2) the packages of such substance, which do not meet such standard, bear conspicuous labeling stating: 'This package is for households without young children'; (or a similar substitute statement for small packages)."

As a result, except for prescription drugs, all household products regulated under the PPPA, may have one size marketed in a conventional package, so long as the same product is supplied by the manufacturer in popular-size packages that are child-resistant.

Substances Covered under the PPPA and Exemptions from the Act

A complete list of products may be found at http://www.cpsc.gov.

The Consumer Product Safety Commission's publication *Poison Prevention Packaging: A Text for Pharmacists and Physicians* can also be viewed at http://www.cpsc.gov. Frequently asked questions by practicing pharmacists are also featured on the Web site.

Consumer Product Safety Act

The Consumer Product Safety Act (Public Law 92-573, 15 U.S.C. §2151 et seq) transferred the FDA functions under the Federal Hazardous Substances Act and under the PPPA to the Consumer Product Safety Commission. The unique provision of the Act is its preemption of local and state consumer product safety standards unless these standards are identical with the federal or excepted by applicable federal regulations.

Under the Act, the Consumer Product Safety Commission may impose criminal sanctions on violators. The statute also expressly provides for a private right of action to any person who has been injured by a violation of a consumer products safety rule.

For example, in a 1991 action, the parents of a child who sustained severe and permanent injuries as a result of ingesting a prescription drug that was not dispensed in a child-proof container brought an action under the Consumer Product Safety Act against the pharmacy and the dispensing pharmacist.

In July 1986, Rita Deck had a prescription for *Asendin* dispensed by Terry McBrien, a pharmacist employed by Sullivan Drugs, Inc. The drug was not dispensed in a child-proof container as required by federal law. One month later, Rita's 2-year-old daughter ingested the drug and, as a result, sustained severe injuries.

The Decks brought this lawsuit under the Consumer Product Safety Act seeking $6 million in damages against the defendants. The defendants moved to dismiss the lawsuit on the basis this federal law does not provide for a private cause of action and, therefore, the court had no jurisdiction.

In resolving the issue, the court examined the Consumer Product Safety Act, the FD&C, and the PPPA, and concluded any person who is injured by a violation of a consumer product safety rule or any rule of the Consumer Product Safety Commission may sue any person who knowingly violated any such rule. The statute does not provide a private cause of action for a violation of the act itself but only for a violation of the rules or regulations.

The Consumer Product Safety Act expressly excluded rugs, devices, or cosmetics from the definition of a consumer product. Therefore, by its own terms, the act does not regulate prescription drugs.

However, the plaintiffs argued that a private cause of action under the act exists because the statute provides for a cause of action for violation of a consumer product safety rule (which did not apply in this case) and any other rule or order of the Consumer Product Safety Commission.

One such "rule or order" required that prescription drugs be dispensed only in special or child-proof packaging, but this requirement is based on the PPPA of 1970. This pre-existing statute was brought under the jurisdiction of the Commission rather than being repealed in favor of the more general Consumer Product Safety Act passed 2 years later. The existing PPPA legislation represented explicit findings by Congress as to specific hazards of prescription drugs.

With the enactment of the Consumer Product Safety Act, the Commission identified several products that it regulated under the new law rather than the pre-existing statutes. Prescription drugs were not included among those identified products because of their inclusion in the PPPA.

Thus, the plaintiff's case turned on whether a cause of action exists by applying the regulations issued pursuant to the PPPA through the Consumer Product Safety Act. Because no private cause of action is provided for under the Consumer Product Safety Act and the Commission has not acted to regulate prescription drugs under the said act, the Court concluded that the plaintiff's lawsuit must be dismissed. (*Deck v. McBrien*, 759 F. Supp. 454 [C.D.IL. 1991].)

Poison Sale Laws

The Federal Hazardous Substances Act is the standard for the cautionary labeling of hazardous substances, including poisons. The Act, as amended, provides that no state or political subdivision (municipality) may establish or continue to effect a cautionary labeling requirement that is applicable to hazardous substances or their packaging unless the cautionary labeling requirement is identical to that of the federal act, or unless the state labeling requirements provide a higher degree of protection than the federal requirements (15 U.S.C. §1261 [p] and §1262 [b]).

Not all requirements of state poison sale laws are pre-empted by federal law; only the labeling requirements are affected by the federal pre-emption. A number of state poison control laws contained provisions for the recording of the sale and inquiry into the purchaser's intended use and knowledge of the substance. These provisions may still be the legal standard, although the author does not know of a current court case illustrating the point. The practicing pharmacist should be aware of the general nature of the recording and warning proviso and should be knowledgeable of the exact requirement in the state in which he or she practices.

Federal Anti-Tampering Act

The Federal Anti-Tampering Act, passed by Congress as a result of a deliberate contamination of *Tylenol* capsules in 1982, makes it a federal offense to tamper with consumer products and gives regulatory authority to the Federal Bureau of Investigation, US Department of Agriculture, and FDA. The term tamper, when used in a criminal statute, has the limited meaning of improper interference "as for the purpose of alteration and to make objectionable or unauthorized changes." Tampering involves changing a product from what it was intended to be by the manufacturer. There are 5 sections of the Act:

(1) Tampering with a consumer product that affects interstate or foreign commerce with reckless disregard for the risk of death or bodily injury to another person;
(2) tainting a consumer product with the intent of injuring a business;
(3) communicating false information that a consumer product has been tainted;
(4) threatening to tamper with a consumer product; and
(5) conspiring to tamper.

By regulation, tamper-resistant packaging is required for certain otc drug products, cosmetics, and medical devices (contact lens solutions and lubricants). Dentifrices, dermatologics, lozenges, and insulin are excluded.

A tamper-resistant package is defined as "one having an indicator or barrier to entry which, if breached or missing, can reasonably be expected to provide visible evidence to consumers that tampering has occurred." The regulations do not require the use of specific packaging technologies; any technology that achieves the required effect is acceptable.

For tamper-resistant packaging to be fully effective, consumers need to examine the packaging carefully before consuming the contents, and they must be aware of the specific tamper-resistant features that have been used. FDA regulations require that the labeling of products with tamper-resistant packaging bear a statement alerting the consumer to the tamper-resistant feature. This labeling statement must be placed so it remains intact even if the tamper-resistant feature is breached or missing. If tampering is suspected, the closest FDA district office should be immediately notified.

The tamper-resistant packaging regulations for *otc* drug products (21 CFR §211.132) are part of the CGMP's for finished drug products. For devices, the tamper-resistant packaging regulations are in 21 CFR §800.12, and those for cosmetics are in 21 CFR §700.25. A Compliance Policy Guide (7132a.17) that describes specific tamper-resistant packaging technologies is available from the National Technical Information Service, 5285 Port Royal Road, Springfield, VA 22161.

Electronic Signatures in Global and National Commerce Act (E-Sign)

In June 2000, President Bill Clinton signed the "E-Sign" Law (Public Law 106-229). Most of its provisions went into effect on October 1, 2000. While this law is not pharmacy specific, it may have great impact on the way pharmacy is practiced. The essence of the law is to spur the growth of electronic commerce by ensuring electronic contracts, signatures, and records will have the same legal status and effect as their ink and paper counterparts.

Because E-Sign applies to all (there are a few exceptions) "transactions" in interstate commerce, it applies to the filling of prescriptions. This legislation has the potential to propel the electronic transmission of prescriptions. It is also important to note that the legislation is "technology neutral." It does not predetermine what technology to use or standards for such technology.

The legislation has 2 parts — one addressing primarily electronic signatures, and the other addressing electronic records. E-Sign states that electronic contracts, **signatures**, and **records** cannot be denied legal effect because the signature or record is in electronic form. E-Sign also declares that all other statutes, regulations, or rules of law requiring written signatures or written records are invalid or "pre-empted" in most circumstances. However, E-Sign does not *require* anyone (except governmental agencies) to accept an electronic signature or record. So, individuals still have a choice in determining whether to conduct business electronically.

Electronic Signatures

By declaring that an electronic prescription "may not be denied legal effect, validity, or enforceability solely because it is in electronic form," E-Sign effectively voids requirements that prescriptions be on paper or printed as a hard copy. In addition, E-Sign eliminates requirements that prescriptions be "hand-signed" or signed by the practitioner "in writing" or in the practitioner's "own handwriting." These types of handwriting requirements often are contained in state pharmacy practice acts and regulations but also appear in federal law through DEA requirements. (See section in Controlled Substances chapter about the effect of this law on DEA provisions). As of October 1, 2000, these laws are no longer enforceable.

Electronic Recordkeeping

The recordkeeping portion of E-Sign states that any recordkeeping requirement related to transactions involving interstate commerce may be met by keeping electronic records — as long as the record accurately reflects the information to be retained and that it remains accessible to all who have a right to see the information. This portion of E-Sign is in direct conflict with many or most state pharmacy regulations. That portion of E-Sign took effect March 1, 2001. Agencies working on, but have not completed, new state rulemaking activities related to record retention have the opportunity to extend the provision's effect until June 1, 2001. In order to avoid the provisions of E-Sign, a federal agency that attempts to require written signatures or records must show there is a "substantial justification" for making an exception.

Federal Alcohol Regulations

Taxing of Retail Dealers

Federal law (26 U.S.C. §5121) requires the annual taxing of alcoholic beverage retailers. In addition, a license from the Bureau of Alcohol, Tobacco, and Firearms (ATF) is required to handle any type of alcohol.

Retail liquor stores, grocery stores selling liquor, and taverns selling take-home liquors are required to obtain a federal retail liquor dealer's stamp. In a community pharmacy, if the retail alcohol is sold only for medicinal purposes, a federal medicinal spirits dealer's stamp may be obtained and used in place of the retail liquor dealer's stamp. However, if alcohol also is sold as a beverage, the retail liquor dealer's stamp must be obtained and will cover both purposes.

The federal retail liquor dealer's stamp and medicinal spirits dealer's stamp are not licenses to sell liquor. A retail license is obtained from the appropriate state agency or municipal subdivision. In some parts of the country, state law or municipal ordinances prohibit retail liquor sales or restrict them to sale by state-operated stores only.

Tax-paid 95% (190 proof) ethyl alcohol may be obtained by the community pharmacy from a liquor wholesaler, a drug wholesaler that is licensed as a liquor dealer, or from another pharmacy where it is stocked by authority of the retail liquor dealer's stamp. Certain hospital pharmacies may stock tax-free 95% ethyl alcohol pursuant to applicable federal regulation; however, the federal regulations prohibit these pharmacies from selling or distributing tax-free alcohol to off-premise outlets.

Kinds of Alcohol

Ethyl Alcohol

Ethyl alcohol is used in making medicines, food product flavors, various flavoring agents, and other preparations intended for internal consumption. Tax-free ethyl alcohol can be used in the preparation of medicines if compliance with the applicable federal regulations is met.

Denatured Alcohols

Regulations concerning the distribution and use of denatured alcohol and rum can be found at 27 CFR Part 20. Formulas for the denatured alcohols can be found in 27 CFR Part 20 Subpart F. Those individuals and manufacturers who use denatured alcohol in the preparation of commercial articles should obtain an industrial-use permit as provided in 27 CFR Part 20 Subpart D.

Specially denatured alcohol is used in the preparation of external-use only medicines and in products that are not intended for human consumption. Specially denatured alcohol is ethyl alcohol with the additions of denaturants (eg, benzene, methyl isobutyl ketone, methyl alcohol). No specially denatured alcohol remains in the finished product. 27 CFR Part 20 Subpart I regulates the operations by dealers and users of specially denatured spirits.

Completely denatured alcohol can be defined as ethyl alcohol containing denaturants of the type that preclude any successful attempt to remove them. Completely denatured alcohol with rust inhibitor added sometimes is used as an antifreeze. Similarly, the poisonous methanol is marketed as a radiator antifreeze, although it is far less popular than permanent antifreezes made with ethylene glycol. Ethylene glycol is extremely poisonous and should never be confused with propylene glycol, which is a solvent and drug preservative and is only as toxic as ordinary glycerin.

Rubbing alcohol is a specially denatured alcohol that is 70% in volume a specially denatured absolute alcohol plus other denaturants in accordance with the formulas listed in regulation 27 CFR.

Isopropyl Alcohol

Isopropyl alcohol needs no denaturants because it is poisonous if taken internally. Isopropyl alcohol is marketed as a type of "rubbing alcohol" unless it is modified so as to distinguish it from the official rubbing alcohol. Usually, this is done by labeling it as "isopropyl rubbing alcohol" or "isopropyl alcohol."

Use of Tax-Free Alcohol

"Alcohol" is defined in the federal regulations (27 CFR §22.11) as "spirits having a proof of 190 degrees or more when withdrawn from bond, including all subsequent dilutions and mixtures thereof, from whatever source or by whatever process produced." The term "spirits" is defined as "... ethyl alcohol, ethanol or spirits of wine ...." The term "proof" is defined as the ethyl alcohol content stated as twice the percent of ethyl alcohol by volume.

Hospitals may obtain a permit to purchase and use tax-free alcohol but only for medicinal, mechanical, and scientific purposes and for the treatment of patients. The regulations for obtaining such a permit can be found at 27 CFR Part 22 Subpart H.

Tax-free alcohol only may be used legally for nonbeverage purposes and for medicinal, mechanical, and scientific purposes. (27 CFR §§22.101-105-106) Medicines made with tax-free alcohol may not be sold, but a separate charge may be made for the medicines compounded on hospital premises for the use of patients on the premises (27 CFR §22.105). Nonprofit or charity clinics may furnish medicines compounded with tax-free alcohol to outpatients (whether charity or noncharity patients) provided such furnishing is not conditioned upon payment.

Hospitals may not furnish tax-free alcohol for use of physicians in private practice.

A hospital holding a form ATF-1447 permit may use tax-free alcohol in its pathology laboratory for tests and analyses if it is used exclusively for hospital patients (both inpatients and outpatients).

Any laboratory in a permit-holding hospital other than the pathology laboratory may use tax-free alcohol; however, it is restricted to scientific use, and the alcohol itself and its products are limited to the permit premises.

Federal regulations provide that permit-holding independent pathology laboratories may purchase tax-free alcohol but only if they are engaged exclusively in conducting analyses and tests for hospitals and sanitariums.

Summary of Federal Rules for the Purchase and Use of Tax-Free Alcohol

Title 27 CFR Part 22 regulates the distribution and use of tax-free alcohol. The following organizations are allowed to purchase (withdraw) tax-free alcohol (95% ethyl alcohol or absolute ethyl alcohol) from a bonded distilled spirits plant if the alcohol is used for nonbeverage purposes, is not for resale, and is used in compliance with the permit.

(1) A state, political subdivision thereof, and the District of Columbia may use tax-free alcohol for scientific and mechanical purposes only.
(2) Certain educational organizations, colleges of learning, and scientific universities may use tax-free alcohol for scientific and mechanical purposes only.
(3) Any laboratory may withdraw tax-free alcohol for use exclusively in scientific research (27 CFR 22.108).
(4) Hospitals, blood banks, and sanitariums may withdraw tax-free alcohol for medicinal, mechanical, and scientific purposes and for the treatment of patients.
(5) Pathology or other laboratories operated in connection with a hospital or sanitarium, or operated exclusively for hospital or sanitarium patients, may withdraw

tax-free alcohol for the same uses (in conducting patient tests and analyses) and to the extent as a hospital or sanitarium.

(6) Nonprofit clinics may withdraw tax-free alcohol for medicinal, scientific, and mechanical purposes and for the treatment of patients. Medicines compounded with tax-free alcohol and are used off-premises may not be sold legally nor may a fee be extracted for supplying them. A separate charge may be made for medicine compounded with tax-free alcohol on the clinic premises for the on-premises use of an inpatient (27 CFR 22.106).

Regulations for obtaining permits for tax-free alcohol can be found at 27 CFR Part 22 Subpart D.

Withdrawal (Purchase) and Receipt of Tax-Free Alcohol is regulated under 27 CFR Part 22 Subpart H.

27 CFR Part 22 Subpart M regulates the Records of Transactions involving tax-free alcohol.

Proof Gallon Measures

A standard US drum contains 54 US gallons or 102.6 proof gallons of ethyl alcohol (95% or 190 proof). If the drum contains absolute alcohol (100% ethyl alcohol or 200 proof), it would contain 108 proof gallons. However, absolute ethyl alcohol often is purchased in cases of pint bottles (see Table 1).

Table 1. Absolute (100%) Ethyl Alcohol			
Proof gallonsfluid ounces	Proof gallonsvolume measures	190 Proof	200 Proof
4	1/4 pint	.059	.062
8	1/2 pint	.119	.126
16	1 pint	.238	.250
32	1 quart	.475	.500
64	1/2 gallon	.950	1.000
96	3 quarts	1.425	1.500
128	1 gallon	1.900	2.000

Storage of Tax-Free Alcohol

Tax-free alcohol must be kept in a storeroom or compartment that is constructed and secured to prevent unauthorized access to the alcohol. The facility must be of sufficient capacity to hold the maximum quantity of alcohol that the permittee may have on hand, in transit, and unaccounted for at any one time. Containers of tax-free alcohol in use must have labels and identifying marks intact, but when they are empty, labels and markings must be effaced or obliterated before discarding the containers.

PHARMACY PRACTICE AND THE HEALTH CARE SYSTEM

Medicare and Medicaid

Medicare

Medicare is Title XVIII of the Social Security Act of 1935, as amended by Public Laws 89-97, 92-603, and 90-248. The "Medicare Law" is Title 42 U.S. Code §§1395 and 1396; the federal regulations for Medicare are published in 42 CFR §405.1 et seq. Medicare is federal health insurance for individuals 65 years of age and over and for certain other disabled individuals, regardless of age.

The Social Security Act of August 14, 1935 (49 Stat. 623), was a federal insurance trust program intended to provide cash benefits or continued income in the form of monthly checks for retired workers. In 1939, the Social Security system was expanded to provide benefits to the survivors of retired workers who died and to provide benefits to the dependents of retired workers. In 1954, coverage for disabled people was added. The Medicare program was enacted as a part of Social Security in 1965.

Medicare is a 2-part health insurance program: Part A is hospitalization insurance provided without charge to those eligible; Part B is medical insurance for which a beneficiary must pay a monthly premium. The premium is usually deducted from the beneficiary's social security check or railroad retirement check. Those eligible for Part A are automatically enrolled in Part B but may elect not to have Part B.

Part A typically covers institutional health care services provided by hospitals, skilled nursing facilities, home health agencies, renal dialysis, and hospice services. Part B provides coverage for outpatient services, physician services, clinical laboratory and diagnostic tests provided outside the hospital, durable medical equipment, and other products provided to patients for use in the home.

Part A Hospitalization Insurance

Application for Part A hospitalization insurance should be made 3 months prior to the applicant's 65th birthday so that the insurance will be in effect on that date.

Under Part A, Medicare covers drugs ordinarily provided by hospitals and skilled nursing facilities for the care and treatment of inpatients (see 42 CFR §409.13). Inpatient hospital services covered by Medicare Part A include medical equipment, drugs, and biologicals, if they are listed in the *USP-NF, New Drugs, U.S. Homeopathic Pharmacopoeia,* or *Accepted Dental Remedies* (except for any drugs or biologicals unfavorably evaluated therein), or if the drugs and biologicals are approved by the hospital pharmacy and the therapeutics committee or its equivalent.

Part B Medical Insurance

With a few exceptions, Part B covers only prescription drugs furnished to a patient "incident to" a physician's services. Therefore, outpatient drugs are covered only if: they cannot be self administered by the patient; administered by a physician (or under a physician's supervision) on an outpatient basis; are reasonable and necessary according to accepted standards of practice; and are furnished as part of a physician's services not charged for separately (see 42 U.S.C. §1395[s][2][A]).

As stated above, some exceptions to the general rules exist. At times, Part B covers antigens, blood clotting factors, immunosuppressive drugs, erythropoietin, drugs used for osteoporosis, and oral anticancer drugs (see 42 U.S.C. §§1395[s][2][G],[I],[J],[O]-[Q]; 1395[s][10][A]-[B]).

In addition, Part B also covers some drugs required for the effective use of durable medical equipment. Examples include respiratory medications used with nebulizers and some pain management drugs administered through covered durable medical equipment.

Medicare-Conditions of Participation

Medicare regulations specify the conditions under which hospitals (42 C.F.R. §482) and long-term care facilities (42 C.F.R. §483) must be certified for payment of services rendered to Medicare patients. Of particular interest to the pharmacist are the regulations dealing with pharmaceutical services and drugs (see Code of Regulations Title 42 — Public Health Medicare Regulations and Medicaid Regulations).

Hospital Standards

Medicare regulations provide that a hospital must have a pharmacy directed by a registered pharmacist or a drug storage area under competent supervision (42 C.F.R. §482.25). In the case of some smaller or specialty hospitals, pharmaceutical services may be provided by a consultant pharmacist whose primary operating location is off-site.

(The Medicare conditions of participation regarding pharmaceutical services are reproduced in the appendix to this section on pages DC-324 to DC-325.)

Government surveyors evaluate a number of factors when certifying a hospital or skilled nursing facility for Medicare participation. Included in the evaluation is, of course, compliance with the Medicare participation regulations. In addition to those covering pharmaceutical service, there are Medicare regulations for most hospital departments. Despite the wide differences among hospitals in departmental procedures, most hospitals in the United States participate in Medicare.

Long-Term Care Facility Standards

The Medicare regulations pertaining to pharmacy service in long-term care facilities are listed in 42 CFR §483.60 and are broader than are the Medicare regulations applying to pharmacy service in hospitals. Regulation §483.60(c) requires the pharmacist review monthly the drug regimen of each patient and report any irregularities to the attending physician and the director of nursing. Other regulations pertaining to services in long-term care facilities provide standards on drug administration, storage, and prescribing procedures.

A question sometimes arises regarding application of the "freedom of choice" provisions in the Medicare and Medicaid statutes to the rights of patients in long-term care facilities. In the context of pharmacy, this translates to whether patients are free to procure their medications from a pharmacy other than that selected by the institution to be the primary provider of pharmaceuticals. HCFA officials have issued an opinion stating that such long-term care facilities are required by law to provide pharmaceutical services, either directly or pursuant to a contractual relationship with an outside pharmacy. The facility is responsible for seeing that the medications are accurately administered and, as a result, the facility certainly may establish uniform standards for packaging, labeling, storing, distributing, and administering drugs. While a long-term care facility could opt to use multiple pharmacies to meet the needs of their patients, establishment of safety and accuracy standards certainly are within the expectations for the facility.

Medicaid

Medicaid, or Title XIX of the Social Security Act of 1935, provides federal grants of money to approved state medical assistance programs. The provisions of the law are found in Title 42 of the U.S. Code §1396 et seq. Medicaid came into being in 1965, along with the Medicare Law, and was an outgrowth of the federal Kerr-Mills Act, which provided federal monies to county health care programs.

Medicaid provides federal funds to be used by each state (along with state funds) for a medical assistance program that pays part or all of the costs of health care for aged or disabled individuals and families with dependent children — all of whom, in order to be eligible for benefits, must have income and assets that are insufficient to meet such health care costs.

There may be individuals who qualify for both Medicare and Medicaid (eg, a retired worker in the Social Security program who is 65 years of age or over and has limited assets and income). The assets and income limitations are established by each individual state in administering its own Medicaid program; however, the state program must meet federal approval in order to obtain the federal monies and federal regulation under the authority of HCFA. The Medicaid patient does not pay premium costs or fees in order to be entitled to benefits, but the patient sometimes must pay a nominal portion of the costs of the services that are furnished (copayment). Medicaid covers many more health services than does Medicare (eg, prescriptions that are dispensed in community or hospital pharmacies for outpatients may be covered by Medicaid but not by Medicare).

Outpatient Prescription Drug Coverage

An optional service of the Medicaid program is the coverage of prescription drugs (for outpatients). Although the program is optional, all states currently provide such coverage. When a state elects to provide such coverage, it must meet a number of provisions adopted as a part of the OBRA '90 legislation.

In a state medical assistance program, the usual benefits are payment of all or part of the patient's costs of inpatient hospital services, outpatient hospital services, laboratory and x-ray services, skilled nursing facility services, physician services (at the hospital, office, or home), home health care services, private nursing services, clinic services, dental services, physical therapy, prescribed drugs, dentures, prosthetic devices, eyeglasses, certain diagnostic screening, preventive and rehabilitative services, certain intermediate care facility services (ie, a nursing home) for individuals 65 years of age and over, inpatient psychiatric services for those under 21 years of age, and certain other medical or remedial care services. In the Medicaid program, the provider of the health services directly bills the Medicaid fiscal intermediary for payment of the services rendered; the patient pays the provider of the service for the copayment portion, if any.

Medicare and Medicaid Fraud and Abuse Legislation

The Medicare and Medicaid Patient and Program Protection Act of 1987 has served to consolidate provisions in earlier legislation and add new sections to the federal laws governing fraud and abuse in the Medicare and Medicaid programs. The legislation addresses 4 primary topics:

- It defines the types of activities that can result in a provider being banned from participating in Medicare or Medicaid;
- it defines the types of activities that can result in assessment of civil monetary penalties for fraud or abuse by a provider;
- it assigns authority to the DHHS for defining which forms of "kick-back" arrangements violate the law; and
- it authorizes DHHS to create a central database for the country of disciplinary actions taken by state licensing agencies to prevent those who have been disciplined in one state from relocating to another resuming practice.

The legislation addresses both civil and criminal penalties. In the civil area, the legislation specifies that an individual convicted of submitting a false claim is liable for:

- Double the amount of damages suffered by the government;
- $2000 per false claim; and
- the cost of the court action.

In the criminal area, the maximum penalty has been increased to a fine of $25,000, imprisonment for 5 years, or both.

These very significant penalties re-emphasize the importance of being very circumspect in dealing with these governmental programs.

National Practitioner Databank

The Health Care Quality Improvement Act of 1986 (Title IV of P.L. 99-660) directed the secretary of DHHS to establish a national data bank to receive and disseminate information on certain adverse actions taken against licensed health practitioners. The final regulation for the data bank was published in the *Federal Register* on October 17, 1989. A contract to operate the NPDB was awarded December 30, 1988, to Unisys Corporation, a private-sector contractor. The data bank opened September 1, 1990.

The purpose of the NPDB is to contribute to the improvement of the quality of health care by restricting the ability of incompetent and unethical practitioners to move from state to state without disclosure or discovery of their previous poor performance. Insurance companies and other entities must report to the NPDB any payment they make on medical malpractice actions or claims. State medical and dental boards must report to the NPDB disciplinary actions taken against physicians and dentists. The Medicare and Medicaid Patient and Program Protection Act of 1987 (P.L. 100-93) requires reporting of licensure disciplinary actions taken against all licensed health care practitioners and health care entities. This information also will be reported and disseminated by the NPDB.

Health care entities must report decisions that adversely affect, for more than 30 days, the clinical privileges of the physician or dentist. Professional societies must report adverse actions regarding membership of physicians and dentists. These decisions must have been reached through formal peer review.

Each hospital must query the data bank at the time a physician, dentist, or other health care practitioner applies for clinical privileges or a position on its medical staff and each 2 years thereafter. Other health care entities may query the data bank when entering into an employment or affiliation agreement with a physician, dentist, or other health care practitioner.

The Public Health Service Amendments of 1987 (P.L. 100-177) amended Title IV by authorizing the establishment and imposition of user fees, providing immunity from civil damages for the operator of the NPDB, restricting attorney access to information in the bank, and authorizing release of data stripped of personal identifiers.

Health Maintenance Organizations (HMO's)

An HMO can be defined as a private or public medical foundation or organization that provides comprehensive prepaid health care, with an emphasis on preventive services, to its enrolled subscribers.

The Federal Medicare Law defines HMOs, in part, as public or private organizations that furnish health services to enrollees at a predetermined periodic rate regardless of the frequency or the extent of services provided to any one enrollee. The type of health care insurance provided by an HMO differs from the traditional type in that the health service itself is actually delivered by the HMO directly to the insured individual. The traditional insurance company only pays the insured individual's health care bills; it does not actually deliver care.

Medicare and HMOs

A 1972 amendment to the Federal Medicare Law provided that payments could be made to HMOs under Part A and Part B of Medicare. Payment is made to the HMO on a per capita or reasonable cost reimbursement basis for Medicare patients enrolled in the HMO. In either case, a contract for payment must be drawn between the particular HMO and DHHS. Title 42 U.S.C. §1395 mm provides for payment adjustments in both the per capita cost rate system and the reasonable cost reimbursement system. The adjustment in payment can take place when the HMO furnishes Medicare with data on its actual health care cost experiences. However, any part of the incurred cost that is determined unnecessary to the efficient delivery of health care is not calculated by law as part of the actual reasonable cost.

The Federal HMO Act

Public Law 93-222, enacted on December 29, 1973, provided $375 million of federal monies for: (1) Grants to public or nonprofit private organizations to determine the feasibility of developing, operating, and expanding HMOs; (2) making loans to public or nonprofit private HMOs to assist them in meeting the amount by which their operating costs in the first 36 months of operation exceed their revenues or to aid in their expansion to serve medically deprived populations; and (3) guarantees nonfederal lenders payment of the principal and interest on loans made to any private organization for initial development of an HMO that will service a medically deprived population and, similarly, guarantees loans made by nonfederal lenders to private HMOs to help them meet current operating cost deficits and expand (but only) in areas with medically deprived populations. The federal HMO monies are not for complete funding of an HMO; the HMO must charge a fee to its enrollees. The HMO federal funds are only for initial HMO development, expansion, and study of the HMO concept of health care delivery. The $375 million in federal HMO money sometimes is referred to as "seed money" in that it is provided to help HMOs get started. However, the seed money is not without strings, and a set of qualifying requirements is detailed in the Act. Essentially, the HMO or proposed HMO project must provide its enrollees with certain basic health services and, at their option, certain additional supplemental health services, which are defined in the HMO Act.

Prescription drugs are one of the supplemental health services that a federally funded HMO may provide its enrollees as an option. Pharmacy organizations, particularly the ASHP, tried to persuade Congress to rule pharmaceutical services as basic health services in the HMO Act, but they did not succeed.

HMO Regulations

The HMO receiving federal funding under the HMO Act must deliver a comprehensive package of health care. The HMO Act states that these basic health care services must include:

(1) Physician services, including consulting and referral services;
(2) inpatient and outpatient hospital services;
(3) medically necessary emergency health services;
(4) short-term (not exceeding 20 visits) outpatient evaluative crisis intervention mental health services;
(5) medical treatment and referral services to appropriate ancillary organizations for abuse of and addiction to alcohol and drugs;
(6) diagnostic laboratory and diagnostic and therapeutic radiologic services; and
(7) preventive health services, including voluntary family planning services, infertility services, preventive dental care, and eye examinations for children.

The supplemental health services that may be offered include:

(1) Facilities for intermediate and long-term care;
(2) vision care that is not included as a basic service;
(3) dental care that is not included as a basic service;
(4) mental health care that is not included as a basic health service;
(5) long-term physical medicine and rehabilitative services, including physical therapy; and
(6) prescription drugs are prescribed by the HMO prescribers in the course of a basic or supplemental health service.

An HMO is authorized, in connection with the prescription or provision of prescription drugs, to maintain, review, and evaluate (in accordance with regulations of the Secretary) a drug use profile of its members receiving such services, evaluate patterns of drug utilization to assure optimum drug therapy, and provide for instruction of its members and of health professionals in the use of prescription and nonprescription drugs.

Prescriptions are covered through an HMO that offers prescription services by an inhouse pharmacy (a pharmacy that is operated by the HMO on its premises) or by community pharmacies contracted (often through a fiscal intermediary) for prescription services.

SOURCES OF ADDITIONAL INFORMATION

Vivian, JC. Compounding and the Supreme Court. *US Pharm*. 27:7. http://www.uspharmacist.com/oldformat.asp?url=newlook/files/Phar/ACF626F.htm&pub_id=8&article_id=903.

Vivian, JC. Compounding law invalidated. *US Pharm*. 26:03. http://www.uspharmacist.com/oldformat.asp?url=newlook/files/Phar/law.htm&pub_id=8&article_id=684.

Vivian, JC. Federal limits on gifts from pharmaceutical companies. *US Pharm*. 27:11. http://www.uspharmacist.com/index.asp?show=article&page=8_992.htm.

Vivian, JC. Pharmacy compounding and the FDA. *US Pharm*. 28;1:32-48. http://www.uspharmacist.com/index.asp?page=ce/2654/default.htm.

Vivian, JC. Physician-owned pharmacies. *US Pharm*. 27:08. http://www.uspharmacist.com/oldformat.asp?url=newlook/files/Phar/ACFB85.htm&pub_id=8&article_id=923.

Study Questions

REGULATION OF PHARMACEUTICALS

(1) Enacted in response to concern over unsanitary practices and lack of purity in the drug and food industries, the primary forerunner of today's FD&C was the:
(a) Import Drug Act of 1848.
(b) Wiley-Heyburn Act.
(c) 1906 Federal Pure Food and Drug Act.
(d) Durham-Humphrey Amendment
(e) b and c

(2) The law establishing the necessity of a New Drug Application (NDA) approval process was the:
(a) 1938 FD&C.
(b) Wiley-Heyburn Act.
(c) 1906 Federal Pure Food and Drug Act.
(d) Harrison Narcotic Act.
(e) b and c

(3) The thalidomide tragedy was the impetus for the:
(a) Harrison Narcotic Act.
(b) Kefauver-Harris Amendment.
(c) 1906 Federal Pure Food and Drug Act.
(d) FD&C.
(e) Durham-Humphrey Amendment.

(4) The Kefauver-Harris Amendment to the FD&C requires:
(a) proof of drug safety.
(b) specifics in pharmacist recordkeeping.
(c) proof of a drug's efficacy.
(d) a and c
(e) all of the above

(5) Under the FD&C, an employer can be convicted for a violation committed by an employee if the employer:
(a) has knowledge or should have knowledge of the employee's illegal action.
(b) participated in or willfully authorized or consented to the illegal act.
(c) has a responsible share in the employee's illegal act.
(d) b and/or c.
(e) any or all of the above.

(6) Compared with recordkeeping regulations under the FD&C, recordkeeping under the CSA is:
(a) more qualitative.
(b) more quantitative.
(c) more concerned with tracing a specific drug, usually in response to drug recall.
(d) a and c
(e) b and c

(7) According to the FD&C, drugs are "misbranded" if:

(a) their labels claim to be brand names while their contents are generic.

(b) their manufacturing, processing, packaging, or storage does not comply with the Current Good Manufacturing Practices (CGMP).

(c) they are dispensed for distribution in violation of the Act's labeling requirements.

(d) they are used by consumers in self-medication.

(e) they contain filthy, putrid, and/or decomposed substances or are held under unsanitary conditions.

(8) The definition of "drug":

(a) does not differentiate between prescription and *otc* drugs.

(b) distinguishes legal or lawful drugs from illicit ones.

(c) is not influenced by the manufacturer's intended use.

(d) a and c

(e) all of the above

(9) A sometimes proposed third class of drugs:

(a) would create an intermediate level of control between prescription and *otc* drugs.

(b) would be authorized by the current wording of the FD&C.

(c) has been created, de facto, by the FDA and DEA to categorize a large number of products currently on the market.

(d) a and b

(e) all of the above

(10) Phase 2 of clinical investigation of a new drug involves:

(a) postmarketing surveillance of approved drugs to detect adverse effects or other problems not encountered in earlier trials because of the limited number of patients.

(b) a small number of patients in carefully controlled studies of the drug toxicity, metabolism, absorption, and elimination, to determine route and safe dosage.

(c) use of the investigational drug on a limited number of patients for specific disease treatment or prevention.

(d) investigators submitting to an IND sponsor a completed, signed "Statement of Investigator" form.

(e) none of the above

(11) Class I of the FDA's recall classification system exists where:

(a) there is a reasonable possibility that the use of or exposure to a violative product will cause either serious adverse health effects or death.

(b) the use of or exposure to a violative product may cause temporary or medically reversible adverse effects.

(c) where the probability of serious adverse effects from the use of exposure of a violative product is remote.

(d) the use of or exposure to a violative product is not likely to cause adverse health consequences.

(e) b and c

(12) FDA regulations that require "adequate directions for use":
   (a) refer to the labeling of prescription drugs.
   (b) mandate that directions must be written clearly so that the layperson can use the drug safely and for appropriate purposes.
   (c) apply to the promotional labeling and package inserts, which must include the medical indication, effects, and dosage.
   (d) must include route, method, frequency, and duration of administration
   (e) all of the above.

(13) The National Drug Code (NDC) number includes:
   (a) a labeler code.
   (b) a drug product code.
   (c) a package code.
   (d) b and c
   (e) all of the above

(14) New participants in the NDC system will have a 10-digit code assigned to drug products, the first 5 digits of which identify:
   (a) a labeler code.
   (b) a drug product.
   (c) a drug manufacturer.
   (d) a package code.
   (e) drug name, size, and type.

(15) Prescriptions for *otc* drugs usually are refillable without additional authorization by the prescriber unless:
   (a) the prescription calls for a dosage higher than that recommended on the label of the commercial container.
   (b) the prescription is for a Schedule V drug.
   (c) the prescription is for a Schedule I drug.
   (d) a and b
   (e) a and c

(16) In order to be constitutional and not put undue restrictions on interstate commerce, state laws:
   (a) must not constitute economic protectionism.
   (b) must not produce a significant impact on interstate commerce in pursuit of the state's interest.
   (c) must consider whether there are reasonable alternatives to achieve a goal with minimal burden on interstate commerce.
   (d) b and c
   (e) all of the above

(17) A pharmacy is subject to FDA registration, inspections, and CGMP compliance requirements:

   (a) if the pharmacy chain repackages and relabels quantities of drug products from the manufacturer's original commercial containers for shipment to the individual franchises of the chain.

   (b) if individual pharmacists conduct similar repackaging and relabeling as members of an informal buying group.

   (c) if a hospital pharmacy repackages drug products to use within the hospital.

   (d) a and b

   (e) all of the above

(18) The FDA Modernization Act of 1997 broadened the exemptions allowed for pharmacy compounding. In order to qualify for these exemptions, the drug to be compounded must not:

   (a) be essentially a copy of a commercially available drug product compounded regularly.

   (b) be a component of an approved drug product.

   (c) appear on a list published by the FDA of drug products that have been withdrawn or removed from the market.

   (d) b and c

   (e) a and c

(19) A food, drug, medical device, or cosmetic intended for export will not be deemed adulterated or misbranded if:

   (a) it is specifically labeled on the package insert that it is intended for export.

   (b) it complies with the laws of the country to which it is exported.

   (c) it is sold or offered for sale in domestic commerce.

   (d) a and b

   (e) b and c

(20) Yvonne and Camille are both new on the job at a local pharmacy. On Friday, they decide to have dinner together so they can compare notes on their first week. When the appetizers arrive, the women decide to quiz each other on some of the terminology they have encountered. "What does a 'B' rating mean?" Camille asks. After her first bite of nachos, Yvonne responds, correctly, that a drug product is given a "B" rating and is not considered therapeutically equivalent if:

   (a) quality standards for the drug product are inadequate or the FDA has an insufficient basis to determine the product's therapeutic equivalency.

   (b) the drug product is under regulatory review.

   (c) the drug product contains an active ingredient identified by the FDA as having a documented bioequivalence problem.

   (d) a and c

   (e) all of the above

(21) As their entrees are served, Yvonne turns the tables and asks Camille to explain what constitutes a "new" drug. Camille hesitates at first but then remembers that a drug is considered "new" if it is:

   (a) an established drug that is available in new dosage forms or at new dosage levels or packaged in novel materials.

   (b) an established drug with established medical claims.

   (c) an established chemical for medical use.

   (d) a and c

   (e) none of the above

(22) Before Camille has a chance to try her pasta, Yvonne bombards her with another question: "What kind of drug would be considered an 'approved drug'?" Determined to answer quickly — and to get to her food — Camille answers, accurately, that an "approved drug" would be:

(a) a new drug for which a still-valid NDA has been approved by the FDA.

(b) a drug that was not in use until after 1938 and, therefore, not subject to the NDA requirement.

(c) a drug that was in use before 1938 and was distributed and promoted in accordance with the labeling and established use in existence at that time.

(d) a and b

(e) a and c

(23) Camille is considerate enough to let Yvonne eat her dinner and order dessert before quizzing her again. Once the coffee and cheesecake arrive, though, Camille insists Yvonne explain what is meant by an "off-label" or "unlabeled" use of a drug. Yvonne has no trouble remembering that these terms refer to:

(a) the prescription or administering of an unapproved drug within the limits of the packet insert information.

(b) the approved use of an unapproved drug.

(c) the unapproved use of an approved drug.

(d) a and b

(e) none of the above

(24) Which of the following are considered consumer products under the Consumer Product Safety Act?

(a) Cosmetics

(b) Devices

(c) Drugs

(d) a and b

(e) none of the above

(25) State poison control laws are pre-empted by federal law when dealing with:

(a) cautionary labeling.

(b) recording of the sale.

(c) inquiry into the purchaser's intended use and knowledge.

(d) a and c

(e) all of the above

(26) According to the Federal Anti-Tampering Act, tamper-resistant packaging is required for:

(a) certain *otc* drug products.

(b) dermatologics.

(c) contact lens solutions and lubricants.

(d) insulin.

(e) a and c

(27) Molly is a pharmacist in a hospital that has just begun to use unit-dose (or individual-dose) packaging of medications for inpatients. As Molly finishes labeling a medication order, her coworker Frank returns from lunch. Glancing over Molly's work, Frank says, "Wait a minute. This can't be dispensed yet. You've forgotten to include the quantity of active ingredients and the control number for this drug. That information is required by the FDA." Is Frank right? Explain.

(28) Nora's pharmacy needs to restock its supply of *otc* ipecac syrup. Harvey, who works at the pharmacy, prepares to dispense the ipecac into 60-mL bottles. Can these bottles of ipecac syrup be sold *otc* or is a prescription required? Explain your answer.

(29) Nora finds and begins bringing Harvey some 1-oz bottles she has found. But as she hands him the bottles, she shouts, "Stop. That's ipecac fluid extract, not syrup! We can't use that. In fact, we shouldn't even keep that in stock." Harvey seems shaken but replies, "No, we can substitute the fluid extract for the syrup. It seems like a waste to throw it out." Who is right? Explain why.

(30) What clarification concerning drug compounding was made in the FDA Modernization Act of 1997? What specific exemptions did this amendment add to the FD&C? What exemptions were allowed prior to this change?

(31) During July 1988 the FDA issued procedures to be used by its officials in handling the importation of medications for personal use. Fill in the blanks in the following statement, outlining those procedures: If there is no _____ evident or no evidence of unreasonable risk to health, drugs _____ marketed in other countries may be imported into the United States if these criteria are met: (1) The drug is not for _____ distribution, and the quantity is not excessive (usually not more than a _____ supply); (2) The product is for _____ use; (3) The intended use of the product is clearly _____; and (4) The _____ declares it is for _____ use and lists the practitioner in the United States under whose care it will be used.

(32) Discuss the concepts of "full disclosure" and "fair balance" as they apply to the promotion and advertising of prescription drugs directly to the consumer.

(33) Identify some of the key bans and prohibitions established by the Prescription Drug Marketing Act, sometimes known as the Drug Diversion Act.

(34) Discuss various concerns raised by pharmacists and consumers about the equivalence of generic copies marketed under the Drug Price Competition and Patent Term Restoration Act of 1984.

(35) What is the difference between the use of an approved drug for a nonapproved (ie, off-label) purpose and the use of a nonapproved drug for a medical purpose?

(36) A distributing company is holding a promotional meeting to discuss the marketing of a new dietary supplement. The company hopes this product will become widely used in efforts to alleviate certain symptoms of arthritis. Can the company mention that claim on the supplement's label? Exactly what can and cannot be claimed by diet supplements? What disclaimer must be included with any claim the supplement is allowed to make?

(37) Nikisha is working as a pharmacist for the first time, and although she is enjoying her job, she is unsure of the extent of some of her responsibilities. While having lunch with her colleagues Brock and Danielle, Nikisha voices her concerns: "I just don't feel comfortable answering some of the questions I'm asked. I mean, I'm not a doctor. Am I supposed to be counseling patients about drug use?" Brock answers, "Not only are you supposed to, you are required to — ever since OBRA '90.""Uh, I don't think that's true," says Danielle. "Pharmacists are allowed to counsel patients on drug use, but according to OBRA '90, we have no legal duty to do so."Help clear this up for Nikisha. Are either of her coworkers right? Did the Omnibus Budget Reconciliation Act of 1990 (OBRA '90) raise or lower the level of responsibility held by pharmacists?

(38) Brock decides he'd better ask Nikisha about some other regulations that she might not realize are part of her responsibility. "You won't always just be filling prescriptions, you know. If a customer wants to buy cleaning supplies while at the pharmacy, you have to be sure we are in compliance with the Hazardous Substances Act." What, specifically, is Brock referring to? Why must pharmacists be aware of the regulations of this act?

(39) Nikisha seems concerned about all these "new" responsibilities. "Quick," she says to her coworkers as she takes out a notepad. "Help me make a list of the information that's required on the label of a hazardous substance." What information should be on Nikisha's list?

(40) Once her coworkers have helped Nikisha understand the Hazardous Substance Act, Danielle adds, "Don't forget about the Poison Prevention Packaging Act." What does this Act regulate, and what specific packaging issue is it concerned with? Does this Act apply only to prescription drugs?

(41) Brock tries to reassure Nikisha about handling the PPPA regulations. "Don't worry," he says, "some drugs are exempt from PPPA standards." How can Nikisha find out which drugs are exempt?

(42) Later that day at the pharmacy, Nikisha helps a customer who specifically requests that his prescription be packaged in conventional packaging — not child-resistant packaging. Can Nikisha fulfill this request?

(43) Now that Nikisha is aware of her customer's preference for conventional packaging, can she use noncomplying packaging when filling this customer's prescriptions in the future without a specific request?

(44) What if a patient's physician simply checks a box on the prescription blank to indicate that a drug should be dispensed in noncomplying packaging? Can Nikisha use conventional packaging based on this?

(45) What consequences could Nikisha face if she improperly dispenses a prescription drug in conventional packaging?

(46) Nikisha receives a call from a mother who suspects that her 3-year-old son may have ingested the mother's prescription medication. What action should Nikisha take?

(47) Does the FDA requirement for tamper-evident packaging of otc drugs replace the requirement for child-resistant packaging?

(48) What is the unique provision of the Consumer Product Safety Act?

(49) Identify the specific types of tampering described in the 5 sections of the Federal Anti-Tampering Act.

(50) How are the terms alcohol, spirits, and proof defined for the purposes of federal regulations? Under what circumstances are hospitals allowed to purchase and use tax-free alcohol?

(51) What is the purpose of the National Practitioner Databank (NPDB)?

(52) Explain how the health care insurance provided by a Health Maintenance Organization (HMO) differs from traditional health care insurance.

Critical Thinking Activities

(1) Form 4 teams with each team responsible for creating a table on one of the following topics: (a) information required by the FD&C to appear on a prescription label; (b) additional information that may be required by state law to appear on the prescription label; (c) information required by the FDA to appear on the manufacturer's or distributor's prescription drug container; and (d) information required by the FDA to be included in the package insert for a prescription drug.

To make this activity more challenging, leave out some information or make some mistakes in your table; then exchange with another team and challenge each other to "fix" the tables. Continue passing the tables on to other teams until all have had a chance to check each table for accuracy. Hint: the FDA requirements for package inserts (d) must be listed under specifically worded headings and in a particular order.

Case Study 1: Drug Labeling

Fahad and Tim own a pharmacy as a partnership. Over the past several weeks they have begun purchasing several *otc* drugs in bulk. The same day the first shipment arrives, Tim begins to repackage these in new containers bearing the pharmacy's label, but Fahad is uncomfortable with this procedure. He appreciates the money saved by buying these drugs in bulk, but it is the repackaging and relabeling that has him worried. "Actually," he says, "I don't even think it's legal to do that." "It's legal," Tim says. "It's still just dispensing." "Tim, listen to me," Fahad says. "Don't repackage those yet till you can tell me this: Have you registered in compliance with the Current Good Manufacturing Practice regulations?" Tim looks up. "Do you think we have to?"

Answer Tim's question. Address other issues regarding what risks, if any, Fahad and Tim should really be concerned about.

One morning just as Fahad arrives for work, Tim says, "We're in trouble." "Is this about the relabeling?" Fahad says, hanging up his coat. "Because if it is, I told you —" "No, no, no," Tim says. "That's not it. That's fine. No, I just discovered that those drugs we got in from that Arizona company are misbranded. And we've sold some already." "Is that a criminal act?" Fahad says. "I don't know. Maybe ...."

(1)   What chances, if any, do Tim and Fahad have of escaping criminal penalty for receipt in interstate commerce (and subsequent sale) of misbranded drugs? How can they protect themselves?

(2)   What kind of guarantee can Tim and Fahad look for in their next interstate purchase?

Case Study 2: Prescription Requirements

Mandy is a pharmacist in a small town. It is a Tuesday morning, and she seems to be having an unusual day. First, she notices a prominent gynecologist in her community has written his patient a prescription for antidepressants. She comments on the oddness of this, but fills the order anyway. Then a patient comes into her shop and asks her to prescribe something for her arthritis pain, and Mandy does just that. A third patient brings in an empty pill bottle and says, "I'd like a refill of these, please. My doctor said it's all right." Mandy phones the physician's office, where a nurse assures her that it's all right to refill the drug. Finally, a fourth patient arrives with an empty container of yet another legend drug, requesting a refill also. Mandy checks the original prescription on this one and discovers that it has been marked by the physician as "refill ad lib."

Take time now to review Mandy's morning.

(1)   Is it legal for a gynecologist to write a prescription outside his or her realm of expertise? Did Mandy handle this situation correctly? What should she have done?

(2)   Is it possible for Mandy, as a pharmacist, to legally prescribe a drug as she does for the arthritis patient?

(3)   Should Mandy have accepted the nurse's authority to refill that third patient's drug prescription? What risks are associated with this, if any?

(4)   Is it legal to prescribe (and legal to dispense) drugs labeled "refill ad lib" or "PRN," etc.? What should Mandy have done in response to that?

(5)   Suppose a patient had come in needing a legend drug prescription refill and Mandy was not able to reach the prescribing physician for authorization. What options would Mandy have in such a situation?

Case Study 3: Compounding

An FDA inspector has been asked to investigate the compounding activities recently reported regarding 4 different pharmacists. She arrives in the pharmacists' community and visits each. As a result of her investigation, she is able to report the following evidence:

1) Phil, the first pharmacist she visits, occasionally compounds a small quantity of a drug that is only slightly different from an FDA-approved drug that is commercially available. The adult children of the elderly patient who receives this drug are the ones who originally reported it. Though the children live out of state, one daughter is herself a pharmacist. 2) Ana, the second pharmacist, is compounding and dispensing these resultant compounds to other pharmacists for resale. 3) Jack, the third pharmacist, is advertising to drum up more business for specific drugs he is compounding. 4) Mary, the fourth pharmacist, regularly is compounding drugs that are essentially generic copies of commercially available products; she is also purchasing this type of compound from 2 colleagues. When questioned by the investigator about the origin of each substance she receives in this way, Mary is unsure of how she can prove that they have been made at an FDA-approved facility.

(1) Without knowing further information, who of these 4 may be in the least trouble? Why?

(2) What risk is Ana running?

(3) Cite FDA concerns about the activities of the last 2 pharmacists.

Case Study 4: Pharmacy Practice and the Health Care System

As a new pharmacist, Carlos is trying to understand the basic principles of working with a health care system, namely HMOs. Because a large number of his patients are also receiving Medicare and Medicaid, he feels he should understand the basics of reimbursement and payment through those systems as well. Besides that, a number of the clientele in his pharmacy's community are elderly people on fixed incomes, and a surprising number of them ask him how to use Medicare for his services. With a little light research into each, answer each of the following questions from Carlos' clients:

(1) Mrs. Jenkins asks Carlos, "I have Part A Medicare insurance, but my neighbor has Part B. What's the difference? And she says I can have hers, but she doesn't have mine. What's she talking about?"

(2) Mrs. Jenkins asks, "What kind of drugs are covered under my Part A? If I get Part B, what drugs will get covered? Should I get it for my prescriptions?"

(3) Mr. Juarez has Medicare but is also part of an HMO that has contracted with Medicare. Mr. Juarez asks Carlos, "What am I getting with this new plan? This is so confusing." What basic health care services must be provided by any HMO receiving federal funding?

(4) Mr. Juarez comes in a couple of weeks later and tells Carlos, "My HMO is telling me what drugs I can keep taking. My doctor told me they won't let me have the drug I used to take for my joints. Can they do that?"

Chapter 3

Controlled Substances

Introduction to the Controlled Substances Act, 131
    Background, 131
    Enforcement by the DEA, 131
    Relationship to State Law, 132

Controlled Substances, 133
    Introduction to Schedules I-V, 133
    Schedule I Substances, 134
    Schedule II Substances, 134
    Schedule III Substances, 135
    Schedule IV Substances, 135
    Schedule V Substances, 135

Registration Under the CSA, 136
    Classification of Registrants and DEA Registration Forms, 136
    Registration Classes and Fee Amounts, 136
    Exempt Officials, 137
    Reregistration, Transfer, Suspension, Revocation, and Termination, 137

Labeling of Controlled Substances, 138
    Commercial Containers, 138
    Prescription Containers, 138

Recordkeeping, 139
    Contents of Records, 139
    Inventory Records, 141
    Central Recordkeeping and Computerized Systems, 142
        Computerized Recordkeeping, 142
    Theft or Loss of Controlled Substances, 144

Order Forms, 144
    Obtaining Order Forms, 144
    Executing Order Forms—Form 222, 145
    Filling Order Forms, 146
    Other Distribution Between Registrants, 146

Prescriptions, 146
    General Issuance Requirements, 146
        Purpose for Issuance, 147
        Who May Prescribe Controlled Substances, 149
        Manner of Issuance, 150
        Electronic Transmission, 151
        Special Considerations for Schedule II Prescriptions, 151
            Partial Filling of Prescriptions for Schedule II Drugs, 151
            Partial Filling of Prescriptions for Long-Term Care Facility Patients
                or Terminally Ill Patients, 151
            Provisions for Emergency Schedule II Prescriptions, 152
        Facsimile Prescriptions, 152
        Hospital Medication Orders, 153
    Filling Prescriptions for Controlled Substances, 154

Prescriptions (cont.),
    Quantity and Dating, 154
    Sale of Controlled Drugs Without a Prescription, 155
    Refilling Prescriptions for Controlled Substances, 155
        Transfers of Controlled Substance Prescription Information
            for Refills, 156
    Treatment of Opioid Addictions, 156
        Methadone Distribution, 156
        Other Treatments for Opioid Addictions, 157

Miscellaneous, 157
    The Internet and Controlled Substances, 157
    Comprehensive Methamphetamine Control Act of 1996, 158
    More Methamphetamine Legislation, 158
    Emergency Kits, 159
        Ocean Vessels, 159
        Commercial Aircraft, 159
        Long-Term Care Facilities, 159
    Storage and Security Requirements, 159
    Disposal of Excess Controlled Substances, 160
    Self-Prescribing, 160
    Compliance, 160
    Mailing Controlled Substances, 160
    Manufacturing Quotas, 160

Enforcement and Penalties for Violations of the Controlled
       Substances Act, 161
    Violations by Nonregistrant and Registrant, 161
    Violations by Registrants, 161
        Violations Committed Knowingly or Intentionally, 162
        Examples of Court Cases, 163
    Specific Guidelines for the Pharmacist in Filling Prescriptions for Controlled
        Drugs, 164
    Consumer Violations, 166
        Penalties, 166

Study Questions, 167

Controlled Substances

INTRODUCTION TO THE CONTROLLED SUBSTANCES ACT

Background

Congress enacted the CSA under its constitutional authority to regulate interstate commerce (Article I, Section 8, Clause 3, US Constitution). Federal courts have held that Congress acted within its commerce power when it enacted the CSA to provide a system for control of drug traffic and to prevent the abuse of drugs.

The Controlled Substances Act (CSA) is the principal federal law regulating the manufacture, distribution, dispensing, and delivery of drugs or substances that are subject to, or have the potential for, abuse or physical or psychological dependence. This law, also known as Title II of the Federal Comprehensive Drug Abuse Prevention and Control Act of 1970, was enacted as Public Law 91-513. These drugs or substances are designated as **controlled substances** because they come under the jurisdiction of the CSA. They are commonly referred to as "controlled drugs."

Title I of the Federal Comprehensive Drug Abuse Prevention and Control Act of 1970 establishes rehabilitation programs for drug abusers, and Title III of the law was meant to regulate the export and import of controlled substances.

The CSA was enacted by Congress in 1970 and became effective in May 1971. The CSA differs substantially from earlier drug control laws in its approach to controlling access to regulated substances. Control is achieved through federal **registration** of all persons in the legitimate chain of manufacture, distribution, or dispensing of controlled drugs. Even ultimate users of controlled drugs are affected by the Act because it sets forth conditions under which they may possess controlled drugs. In contrast, its predecessor, the Harrison Narcotic Act, exerted control over narcotic drugs by imposition of a tax. The Harrison Act regulated only narcotic drugs. The CSA regulates narcotics as well as stimulants, depressants, hallucinogens, anabolic steroids, and chemicals used in the illicit production of controlled substances.

Enforcement by the DEA

While there are very many federal laws that have an impact on pharmacy practice (see Regulation of Pharmaceuticals chapter for examples), this chapter deals primarily with the CSA. The CSA is codified along with the Food, Drug, and Cosmetic Act in Title 21, U.S.C., but it is enforced and regulated by the Drug Enforcement Administration (DEA) rather than the Food and Drug Administration (FDA). The CSA (Title II of the FCDAPC) may be found at 21 U.S.C. §801 et. seq. It also may be found on the Internet at http://www.access.gpo.gov, or on the DEA website at http://www.usdoj.gov:80/dea/agency/csa.htm.

The DEA is a unit of the Federal Bureau of Investigation (FBI), which is within the US Department of Justice. It was established in July 1973 under an executive reorganization plan when it took over the functions of the former Bureau of Narcotics and Dangerous Drugs (BNDD) and several other agencies having drug investigative and drug law enforcement responsibilities. A published reference to BNDD about controlled substance laws, unless it is solely historical, is designated properly as DEA.

DEA regulations implement the CSA and, in many instances, restate the law and apply it to specific situations. Those regulations can be found at 21 CFR §1300 et. seq. They also may be found on the Internet at the GPO *Federal Register* web site: http://www.access.gpo.gov/nara/cfr/index.html, as well as on the DEA website.

It is absolutely critical for the practicing pharmacist to have a working knowledge and understanding of the requirements of the CSA as described and detailed in DEA regulations. The following text discusses the authors' interpretation of both the DEA regulations and the CSA.

The DEA also has provided extensive helpful information on its web site. It provides the *Pharmacist's Manual – An Informational Outline of the Controlled Substances Act of 1970*. Published in March 2001, it provides comprehensive coverage of the DEA regulations as they apply to the practicing pharmacist. It may be found on the DEA's Diversion Control Program web site, http://www.deadiversion.usdoj.gov, under the heading "Publications." The DEA plans to update the manual periodically so that current information is available on the DEA web site. The manual can be downloaded and reproduced without having to request a print copy from the DEA. Manuals also will be available for physicians, mid-level practitioners, researchers, and chemical handlers.

The general DEA web site can be found at http://www.usdoj.gov/dea. The diversion control site may be accessed from there by hyperlink. This site also includes newsletters, *Federal Register* notices, DEA manuals and publications, and progress reports on DEA's electronic commerce initiative, as well as listings of field offices, etc.

However, it is so important to remember that when an issue is litigated, it is the precise wording of the CSA and DEA regulations that a court examines when interpreting the law and making a ruling. Therefore, it is prudent to read the regulations cited along with the text discussion. In the final analysis, the judiciary has the last word on interpretation of the law. Even the DEA must follow the court's interpretation.

The CSA establishes interagency responsibilities between FDA and DEA concerning drug regulation. For example, the CSA (at 21 U.S.C. §811 [b]) requires the DEA through the attorney general, to request a scientific and medical evaluation from the secretary of the Department of Health and Human Services (DHHS) before any substance may be added to a schedule, transferred between schedules, or removed entirely from the schedules. In addition to HHS's medical evaluation, factors considered by the attorney general include the following:

(1) Its actual or relative potential for abuse;
(2) scientific evidence of its pharmacologic effect, if shown;
(3) the state of current scientific knowledge regarding the drug or other substances;
(4) its history and current pattern of abuse;
(5) the scope, duration, and significance of abuse;
(6) what, if any, risk there is to the public;
(7) its psychic or physiologic dependence liability; and
(8) whether the substance is an immediate precursor of a substance already controlled under the Title.

Relationship to State Law

Pharmacists and other health care providers are subject to federal drug control laws as well as to drug control laws of the state in which they are licensed and practicing—unless the practice is exclusively in a federal facility, eg, a Veterans Administration hospital.

Each state has enacted various laws that control the manufacture, distribution, and sale of drugs within the state, as well as the practice of pharmacy and other health care professions. Most states have enacted their own version of a controlled substances act that regulates the manufacturing, distribution, and dispensing of controlled substances within that state. It often is based on provisions in the State Uniform Controlled Substances Act.

State controlled substance law is beyond the scope of this text. However, there is an organization as well as some references that may prove useful in the study of state law. The National Association of Controlled Substance Authorities (NASCSA) is a nonprofit educational organization, established in 1985, whose members are comprised primarily of state agencies that have responsibility concerning controlled substance scheduling, treatment, regulation, and other related activities. Its web site, located at http://www.nascsa.org contains useful information and links to other web sites concerning state (and some federal) regulation of controlled substances, as well as other timely topics about controlled substances.

One topic that is being discussed now is the implementation of State Prescription Monitoring Programs. Currently, 15 states have implemented such programs. Simply stated, these plans keep track of patients who receive controlled substances from physicians, as well as tracking the physicians who prescribe such drugs. They allow the state to identify people who may be "doctor shopping" and help state authorities identify unscrupulous physicians who may be prescribing controlled substances in violation of state or federal law. Proponents of such laws argue that they aid in enforcement of drug control laws. The DEA is one entity that supports these programs. In Congressional testimony given on December 11, 2001, DEA Administrator Asa Hutchinson stated that "It is clear that the presence of prescription monitoring programs play an integral role in addressing the illegal diversion and improper dispensing and acquisition of controlled substances. . . ." Opponents of these programs contend that there are privacy issues. In addition, it is believed that these programs may have a "chilling effect" on the legitimate prescribing of controlled substances for patients truly in need of pain relief. Further information about these programs may be found on the DEA's diversion web site at http://www.deadiversion.usdoj.gov. From there, go to "Publications," then to "Program Reports." The site has a multitude of information about state tracking systems. For access to Congressional testimony, see http://www.usdoj.gov/dea/pubs/testimony.htm.

Federal drug control laws or regulations may vary from state drug control laws, and a pharmacist is responsible to the same degree for compliance with federal and state laws and regulations governing the practice of pharmacy. A state drug control statute or regulation may be more stringent than its federal counterpart, or vice versa. Therefore, what should a pharmacist do when the federal and state law differ? The Supremacy Clause in Article VI of the US Constitution states:

"This Constitution, and the Laws of the United States which shall be made in Pursuance thereof . . . shall be the supreme Law of the Land; and the Judges in every State shall be bound thereby, anything in the Constitution or Laws of any State to the Contrary notwithstanding."

From the earliest US Supreme Court case of *Marbury v. Madison*, 1 Cr. 137, 2 L. Ed. 60, (1803), courts have declared the basic principle that the federal judiciary is supreme in the exposition of the law of the Constitution, and Article VI makes this supremacy binding on the states. Therefore, a state law that contravenes or conflicts with a federal law is unconstitutional and therefore void. In the area of controlled substances, there are many instances where a state law is more stringent than the comparable federal statute, but there are few instances of state law actually contravening federal law. (See *State v. Rasmussen*). Therefore, a pharmacist must comply with a state statute or regulation when it is more strict or when there is no similar prohibition or requirement under the federal law. If a federal law or regulation is more stringent than the comparable state law or regulation, the federal requirement must be followed. Simply put, the more stringent law or regulation is to be followed in all cases, unless a state law or regulation contravenes or conflicts with a valid federal law or regulation so that the two cannot consistently stand together, in which case the federal is followed.

CONTROLLED SUBSTANCES

Introduction to Schedules I through V

Drugs and other substances which come under the jurisdiction of the federal CSA are classified into 5 schedules, defined in 21 USC §812(b). (Some states have 6 schedules under their modified version of the State Uniform Controlled Substances Act.) The federal CSA schedules are as follows.†

---

† For a comprehensive list of Controlled Substances by schedule, see http://www.deadiversion.usdoj.gov.

Schedule I Substances

Schedule I includes drugs that have a high potential for abuse, no currently accepted medical use in the United States, and a lack of accepted safety for use under medical supervision. Those drugs included in this schedule are listed in 21 CFR §1308.11. Examples of substances contained in Schedule I include the following: Heroin, propiram, marijuana, lysergic acid diethylamide (LSD), peyote, mescaline, psilocybin, tetrahydrocannabinol, benzylmorphine, dihydromorphine, nicocodeine, nicomorphine, MDMA (Ecstasy), and methcathinone.

Because Schedule I controlled substances have no currently accepted medical use in the United States, they cannot be prescribed by practitioners and generally will not be found in pharmacies. The only exception to this law is that the use of Schedule I controlled substances for research purposes is allowed. However, this research does require a separate registration. This basically is the same conclusion that the Supreme Court reached in the case of US vs Oakland Cannabis Buyers Cooperative, 532 U.S. 483 (2001). In that case, the Court relied heavily on the fact that under the CSA, marijuana is classified as a Schedule I substance, which means it is addictive and has "no recognized medical benefits." This case originated from a federal case in which 6 California organizations were distributing marijuana under California legislation known as Proposition 215. This legislation allowed the use of marijuana with a doctor's prescription (several other states had passed similar legislation). The Court held that the DEA did have the right to prosecute the purchase, sale, distribution, ownership, or use of marijuana. This ruling (which comprises federal law), then, directly conflicts with state law. In this case, as we discussed above, the state law, then, must yield to the federal law, and the federal law must be upheld. By simply ruling that the DEA's actions were legal, the Court did not reach the issue of whether the legislation (Proposition 215) or the smoking of marijuana itself are constitutional. For example, what may happen if the DEA rescheduled marijuana to a Schedule II substance? Might the Court ruling be different then? If so, why?

There are some web sites that deal with the legalization of marijuana. One may be found at http://www.nap.edu. One on the history of federal investigation into the medicinal use of marijuana is at the National Institutes of Health (NIH) fact page, http://www.nih.gov/news/medmarijuana/hhsfact.htm. The full text report of an NIH workshop on the medical utility of marijuana may be found at http://www.nih.gov/news/medmarijuana/MedicalMarijuana.htm. There also is an Institute of Medicine report on the subject at http://pompeii.nap.edu/books/0309071550/html/index.html.

In 1999, the National Institues of Health conducted studies on possible medical uses of marijuana. A summary of this work was published July 13, 1999 in an HHS fact sheet titled "Investigating Possible Uses of Medical Marijuana." It may be found at http://www.nih.gov/news/medmarijuana/hhsfact.htm.

There is another group of substances that are treated as Schedules I and II substances for purposes of the CSA. These substances are called "controlled substance analogs." The term is defined in 21 U.S.C. §802(32) as a substance intended for human consumption that is substantially similar to a controlled substance in Schedules I or II in its chemical structure; its stimulant, depressant, or hallucinogenic effect on the CNS; and in a person's representation or intention of such effect. Not included in the meaning of the term are core compounds listed as controlled substances, substances for which there are approved new drug applications, substances falling under an exemption for investigational use, and substances not intended for human consumption before such an exemption takes effect.

Schedule II Substances

Schedule II includes drugs having a currently accepted medical use in the United States and a high abuse potential, with the potential for severe psychological or physical dependence. 21 CFR §1308.12 lists the drugs contained in this schedule. Some of the drugs contained in Schedule II that typically are used for pain include the following: Opium; morphine; codeine; hydromorphone (*Dilaudid*); methadone; meperidine; cocaine and its salts, isomers, derivatives, and salts of isomers and derivatives; oxycodone (eg, *Percocet, OxyContin*); and oxymorphone. Stimulant drug products also are in Schedule II and include the following: Amphetamine, methamphetamine, and methylphenidate (eg, *Ritalin*). Examples of depressant drug products classified in Schedule II include amobarbital (*Amytal*), pentobarbital (eg, *Nembutal*), and secobarbital (*Seconal*). Schedule II also includes bulk dextropropoxyphene (nondosage forms) as an opiate. However, various dosage formulations of this drug are classified as a narcotic and are included in Schedule IV. Some drugs are included in Schedule II if they are formulated as single entity products. They also may be found in other schedules when they are combined with different drugs or when marketed in the suppository form. For example, codeine formulated with one or more active nonnarcotic ingredient (eg, acetaminophen) is classified in Schedule III.

Schedule III Substances

Schedule III includes drugs having an abuse potential less than that of drugs listed in Schedules I and II. They all have a currently accepted medical use in the United States. However, abuse of the drug may be dangerous (eg, anabolic steroids) or lead to moderate or low physical dependence or high psychological dependence. 21 CFR §1308.13 lists drugs included in Schedule III. They include compounds containing limited quantities of certain narcotic drugs formulated with active nonnarcotic drugs, eg, acetaminophen with codeine. Also included are barbiturates combined with one or more other active medicinal ingredients that are not listed in any schedule and certain other depressants and narcotics. Some stimulant drugs such as benzphetamine (*Didrex*) and phendimetrazine also are listed in Schedule III. The Anabolic Steroids Control Act of 1990 required anabolic steroids to be placed in Schedule III. That legislation was passed by Congress in response to increased use of the drugs by athletes, bodybuilders, and adolescents in hopes of enhancing their athletic performance or physical appearance. The term "anabolic steroid" is defined in 21 CFR §1308.02(b). Also included here is the drug *Marinol* (dronabinol), which contains the active ingredient in marijuana in oral form.

Schedule IV Substances

Schedule IV includes drugs having a lesser potential for abuse than those listed in Schedule III. Like Schedules II and III, Schedule IV drugs have a currently accepted medical use in the United States. Abuse of these drugs may lead to a limited physical or psychological dependence. 21 CFR §1308.14 lists drugs contained in Schedule IV; they include the following: Depressants, including chloral hydrate, phenobarbital, meprobamate, and various benzodiazepine drug products; stimulants, including diethylpropion, mazindol, phentermine; and other products, including pentazocine.

Schedule V Substances

Schedule V includes drugs with low abuse potential and limited physical or psychological dependence relative to those listed in Schedule IV and with an accepted medical use in the United States. They are listed in 21 CFR §1308.15. Drugs in Schedule V mainly consist of preparations containing limited quantities of certain narcotic drugs in combination with nonnarcotic active medicinal ingredients, some of which are narcotic drugs containing a limited amount of diphenoxylate in combination with atropine sulfate (*Lomotil*). Another example is promethazine expectorant with codeine.

Drug preparations or chemicals excluded or exempted from some, but not all, of the controls applicable to controlled substances are set forth in 21 CFR §1308.22-24 and §1308.33-34.

REGISTRATION UNDER THE CSA

Every person or firm that manufactures, distributes, dispenses (including prescribing and administering), conducts instructional activity with, exports, imports, or conducts narcotic maintenance or detoxification programs with any controlled drugs, or that proposes to engage in the same, must register with the federal DEA unless such a person or firm is exempted by law or under the CSA regulations (21 CFR §1301.22-1301.24).

Classification of Registrants and DEA Registration Forms

Registrants are divided into 9 groups by activities (21 CFR §1301.13). Each group of activities requires a separate registration, but activities within certain groups are considered coincidental and need no additional registration for the added group(s), provided all other requirements prescribed by law are met. For example, a person registered to dispense controlled substances in Schedules II through V also may conduct research (other than narcotic treatment research programs) and conduct instructional activities with those substances (21 CFR §1301.22[b][6]) without further registration.

The independent groups of activities for which separate registration generally is required are as follows:

(1) Manufacturing controlled substances.
(2) Distributing controlled substances.
(3) Dispensing controlled substances listed in Schedules II through V.
(4) Conducting research with controlled substances listed in Schedule I.
(5) Conducting research with controlled substances listed in Schedules II through V.
(6) Conducting a narcotic treatment program using any narcotic drug listed in Schedules II through V.
(7) Importing controlled substances.
(8) Exporting controlled substances.
(9) Conducting chemical analysis with controlled substances.

A pharmacy registers under the CSA as a dispenser of controlled substances. (Notice that it is the pharmacy, not the pharmacist.) One registration covers the dispensing of controlled substances in Schedules II through V. Form DEA-224 is used for the initial registration, while form DEA-224a is used for the annual reregistration. Manufacturers, distributors, importers, exporters, and most research activities use form DEA-225 for initial registration and form DEA-225a for reregistration. Most of these forms may be found on the Internet at http://www.deadiversion.usdoj.gov.

Hospitals or institutional practitioners also register as dispensers of controlled substances. A single DEA registration covers both hospital inpatient and outpatient dispensing activities from its on-premise pharmacy. An employee pharmacist is not required to register with the DEA, providing that the pharmacy in which the pharmacist is employed is registered to dispense controlled substances. (See 21 CFR §1301.22[a].)

21 CFR §1312(a) requires separate registrations for each principal place of business for individual pharmacies regardless of the fact that they are owned by the same individual or corporation. However, a hospital registered with the DEA generally does not need to have separate DEA registrations for decentralized pharmacy services or for satellite pharmacies if they are all part of the same physical structure.

Registration Classes and Fee Amounts

Pharmacies, hospitals, clinics, practitioners, or teaching institutions register to dispense controlled substances using form DEA-224. The registration (or reregistration) period is 3 years and the total registration fee is $210 (payable in full at the time of filing). Manufacturers and distributors register using form DEA-225. The registration (or reregistration) period is 1 year and the annual fee is $875 for manufacturers; $438 for distributors. DEA registration forms and information on registration may be obtained from the registration branch of the DEA or on the Internet at www.deadiversion.usdoj.gov.

An affidavit that a new state pharmacy permit was issued or ownership of an existing pharmacy was transferred may be submitted with form DEA-224 for the purpose of expediting issuance of a DEA registration number. A sample affidavit is shown in 21 CFR §1301.17.

An application for DEA registration must be signed by the applicant if the applicant is an individual or sole proprietor, by a partner of the applicant if a partnership, or by an officer of the applicant if a corporation or other authorized business entity. For a corporate-owned pharmacy or a limited partnership (a limited partnership only has certain members exercising control and responsibility), it may be prudent to spell out in the corporate minutes or partnership agreement the person (designated by title or position rather than by name) who is to have the responsibility for handling controlled drugs. This procedure could help avoid a situation where a nonparticipating member may face liability exposure for the acts of the participating members. (See *United States v. Duggan Drug Stores*.)

Most hospitals are operated as corporations, and an officer of the corporation signs form DEA-224. Hospital registration also covers the registration of the pharmacy operated by the hospital on its premises. Usually a hospital operated by a religious order also is operated in the corporate form under state law providing for religious or nonprofit corporations. The hospital administrator is usually an officer of such a corporation or is given a corporate power of attorney, and therefore is the person who signs form DEA-224.

Exempt Officials

Under the CSA regulations the following categories of medical practitioners are exempt from registration:

(1) US Army, Navy, Marine Corps, Air Force, Coast Guard, and Public Health Service officials (medical doctors) who prescribe, dispense, or administer (but do not procure) controlled drugs in the course of their official duties are not required to register with DEA unless they also engage in private practice. (See 21 CFR §1301.25.) Prescriptions written by these exempt officials must conform to 21 CFR §1306.01-1306.32 and their service identification number is inserted in lieu of the DEA registration number.

(2) Certain law enforcement officials are exempt from registration when procuring controlled substances for possession during official duties. (See 21 CFR §1301.26.)

The DEA registration requirement is waived for civil defense or disaster relief agency officials during times of emergency or disaster as proclaimed by the President or Congress. The civil defense emergency order form, which is furnished by the US Office of Emergency Preparedness, may be filled by a registrant (including a pharmacy registrant) during a state of national emergency or disaster in order to provide civil defense or disaster relief officials with an immediate source of controlled drugs.

Reregistration, Transfer, Modification, Suspension, Revocation and Termination

A registration certificate (DEA form 223) is issued upon the DEA granting initial authorization to engage in a specified regulated activity. The expiration date of the registration is stated on the certificate. Approximately 60 days prior to the expiration date, the DEA will mail a reregistration form to the registrant. Pharmacies, hospitals, practitioners, and teaching institutions reregister every 3 years on form DEA-224a. Drug manufacturers and distributors register annually and use form DEA-225a. If the registrant does not receive the reregistration form within 45 days prior to the expiration date, DEA regulations require the registrant to give notice of this fact and request a reregistration form by writing to the registration branch of the DEA. (See 21 CFR §1301.13[e][3].)

Modification in a registration may be accomplished by writing to the registration branch of the DEA to request a change of the registrant's name or address or to receive authorization for handling additional schedules of controlled drugs. If the modification is approved, a new registration certificate is issued that should be kept with the old certificate of registration until expiration. (See 21 CFR §1301.51.)

Transfer or assignment of a registration is allowed only pursuant to the DEA's written consent. (See 21 CFR §1301.52.) If a registrant dies, goes out of business, discontinues professional practice, or, as in the case of a corporation or partnership, ceases legal existence, the registration automatically terminates unless the registration is requested to be transferred. (See 2C CFR §1301.52[a].) The transfer of the registration and the subsequent distribution of controlled substances is covered under 21 CFR §1301.52(d) and (e).

The DEA administrator may deny, suspend, or revoke a DEA registration for cause. Such action can be taken upon a finding that registration is inconsistent with the public interest, that the registrant has falsified the application, has been convicted of a felony violation concerning controlled substances, has had a state license or registration suspended, revoked, or denied, or has had such suspension, revocation, or denial recommended. (See 21 CFR §1301.36-1301.37 and §304 of the CSA, 21 U.S.C. §824.) A DEA suspension was involved in the *Norman Bridge Drug Company* case.

LABELING OF CONTROLLED SUBSTANCES

Commercial Containers

Commercial containers of controlled substances require labeling with the appropriate symbol designating its schedule (see below). The symbol must be prominently located on the label and must be clear and large enough to afford easy identification of the schedule of the controlled substance without removal from the dispenser's shelf. (See 21 CFR §1302.03-1302.06.)

Schedule I	CI or C-I
Schedule II	CII or C-II
Schedule III	CIII or C-III
Schedule IV	CIV or C-IV
Schedule V	CV or C-V

DEA regulations provide exceptions to the symbol labeling requirement for certain commercial containers. It is not required on a carton or wrapper in which a commercial container is held if the symbol is legible through such carton or wrapper. The symbols also are not required if the commercial container is too small, if the commercial container is used in clinical research involving blind or double-blind studies, and if the drug is intended for export. (See 21 CFR §§1302.03[d]-[f], and 1302.07[b].) There is no exception made for imported controlled substances. Substances that become scheduled or are rescheduled must be labeled 180 days following the effective date of the scheduling.

Prescription Containers

DEA regulations (21 CFR §§1306.14 and 1306.24) require the prescription label for a controlled substance to contain: (1) Name and address of the pharmacy; (2) patient's name; (3) prescription serial number; (4) date of dispensing; (5) name of the prescriber; (6) directions for use; and (7) cautionary statements, if any, as contained in the prescription or required by law. Schedules II, III, and IV controlled substances also must carry the "transfer warning" statement required under 21 U.S.C. §825(c) and 21 CFR §290.5. This warning is as follows:

Caution: Federal law prohibits the transfer of this drug to any person other than the patient for whom it was prescribed.

State regulations regarding prescription labels may require additional information, including the following: Pharmacy telephone number, pharmacist's initials; drug name, strength, lot number, and expiration date, if any; manufacturer's name; prescribing physician's address and DEA number; and pharmacy DEA number. Additionally, there are certain states that require veterinary prescription labels to carry the name and address of the owner of the animal and the species of the animal. An optional item often included on the prescription label is refill information, for example, "no refill," "may refill 5 times," or "may refill."

RECORDKEEPING

Contents of Records

Recordkeeping requirements under state and federal law are affected by—in fact, pre-empted by—the E-Sign legislation discussed in the previous chapter. The statute states that statutes or regulations may be met by keeping electronic records—as long as the information is accurate and it remains accessible to anyone with the right to see such records. The DEA takes the position that the E-sign legislation does not apply to the distribution of controlled substances but does apply to the recordkeeping requirements.

The CSA generally requires every dispenser (ie, pharmacies, physicians, and other individual practitioners and hospitals) registered with the DEA to maintain complete and accurate records of sales, receipts, dispensing deliveries, or other disposition of controlled substances. The starting record is an inventory, coinciding with the initial registration. Continuing records include biennial inventories thereafter, as well as current records that reflect the inflow and outflow of controlled drugs between each successive inventory. However, §307 of the CSA specifically states that a perpetual inventory where additions and subtractions are entered in the records on a daily basis is not required. (See 21 U.S.C. §827[a][3].) Regulations issued by the DEA set forth recordkeeping requirements in more specific terms in 21 CFR §1304 et. al. Recordkeeping requirements fall under the new legislation. That certainly will decrease the flowing papers that exist now.

A pharmacy registered under the Act as a dispenser is required to keep and maintain records reflecting all transactions with controlled substances. Other types of registrants are required to maintain records as well. DEA regulations define "individual practitioner" as a physician, dentist, veterinarian, or other individual licensed or permitted to dispense controlled substances in the course of professional practice. An individual practitioner need not keep records of Schedule II through V drugs that are prescribed or administered, but must keep records of such drugs that are dispensed. In other words, if the physician regularly dispenses controlled drugs as a substitute for the services of a pharmacist, the physician then must keep the same records required of pharmacies. (See 21 CFR §1304.03.)

Pharmacy registrants are required under the CSA to keep the following records: The initial and subsequent biennial **inventory** records of controlled drugs; records of **receipt** of controlled drugs; and records of **dispensing** and **disposal** of controlled drugs. 21 CFR §1304.22(c) sets forth the details of the requirements for the record content for pharmacy registrants. The records must contain: (1) The **name** of the controlled substance; (2) the **dosage form** (eg, tablets, capsules, ampules); (3) the **strength** or concentration of the substance per dosage unit (eg, 10 mg tablet, 1 mg/mL); and (4) the amount of **dosage units** per commercial container or volume per container (eg, 100 tablet bottle, 10 fluid ounces). In addition, the receipt record of controlled drugs must include the number of commercial containers received, the date of receipt, and the name, address, and DEA registration number of the supplier. For records of controlled drugs dispensed, the number of dosage units or volume dispensed, the name and address of the person to whom the drug is dispensed, the date of dispensing, and the name or initials of the pharmacist who actually dispensed the item are required. For controlled drugs disposed of in any other manner, a record of the number of dosage units or volume of the drug disposed, the number of commercial containers disposed, as well as the date and manner of disposal are required.

The disposal records referred to in the recordkeeping provisions of 21 CFR §1304-22(a)(2)(ix)(e) apply to disposals pursuant to DEA Form 41 procedures (21 CFR §1307.21) and to disposals of small residues or wasted controlled drugs.

The third copy of an official order form (DEA Form 222c) will suffice as a record of receipt of Schedule II drugs, provided the pharmacist indicates the supplier's DEA registration number and records the number of commercial containers received and the date of receipt on the third copy, as required by 21 CFR §1305.09(e). DEA Form 222c is a triplicate form for the purchase and acquisition of Schedule II controlled drugs. The third copy is retained by the pharmacy registrant.

A commercial invoice serves as a record of receipt for Schedules III, IV, and V drugs as long as the required information is contained therein. The pharmacist should place the actual date of receipt and the supplier's DEA registration number on the invoice (usually the number is printed on the invoice); indicate controlled drugs on the invoice by an asterisk or similar method of identification; and file the invoice appropriately. (Schedule II drug invoices should be in a separate file; Schedules III, IV, and V drug invoices should be in another separate file or filed with other commercial invoices.) The filing system should be such that controlled drug data are readily retrievable.

The following documents serve as records of disposition of controlled substances for the community pharmacist. A **prescription** is the basic written record of controlled substances dispensed. An **order form** (DEA form 222c) is the disposition record when controlled substances in Schedule II are sold or delivered to other DEA dispenser registrants or when they are returned to the manufacturer or distributor. Special written records are needed to account for disposition of Schedules III, IV, and V controlled substances sold or delivered to other DEA dispenser registrants or returned to the manufacturer or distributor. An invoice prepared by the pharmacist can suffice as this type of record if a copy is retained and appropriately filed. DEA Form 106 is used to account for controlled substances stolen or lost, and DEA Form 41 to account for outdated or controlled substances no longer required disposed of pursuant to 21 CFR §1307.21.

Hospital pharmacy registrants need a recordkeeping system to account for controlled substances dispensed and actually administered to patients pursuant to an individual practitioner's medication order. In institutional pharmacy practice, the patient's hospital chart is the basic original record of controlled substances ordered for and actually administered to the patient. It is standard procedure for the nurse to chart the medications actually administered to the patient. Medications that are ordered and dispensed for a hospital patient may sometimes, for various legitimate reasons, not be administered. In these circumstances, hospital dispensing and administration records must be reconciled to provide accountability for the institution's controlled substances.

Having ward stock or a nursing unit stock of controlled substances is a common practice in institutional pharmacy practice. A controlled substances "proof-of-use" sheet is an ancillary disposition record of the drugs for which the record is kept. The patient's chart also can contain a nurse's notation of drugs actually administered, but a proof-of-use record contains the identical information on the ward stock of controlled drugs, classified by the name of the drug rather than the name of the patient.

Medication profile sheets, which are used in some hospital pharmacies, indicate both controlled and noncontrolled drugs dispensed for an individual patient. The medication profile is prepared in a hospital directly from a copy of the patient's chart orders or from a drug order requisition written by the nurse or unit clerk who transcribes the order from the patient's chart. In most instances a medication profile system is a reasonably accurate record of the drugs dispensed to a patient.

In some hospitals, prescriptions written by staff physicians are used as the dispensing authorization for most medications for inpatients. The patient's chart again is the controlling record of drug disposition because doses actually administered to an inpatient are charted by the nurse.

All records and inventories (including prescriptions) of Schedules I and II controlled substances must be filed and maintained separately from all other business records of the registrant. (See 21 CFR §1304.04[f], [g], and [h].) Records and inventories (including prescriptions) of Schedules III, IV, and V controlled drugs must either be filed separately from other business records or in such form as to be readily retrievable. (See 21CFR §1304.04[h]). 21 CFR §1304.04(h)(2) gives the pharmacy registrant the option of filing these records in a separate file, or in a file with the noncontrolled prescriptions, or in a file with the Schedules I and II prescriptions. If they are not filed separately, they must be "readily retrievable." Not too long ago, prescriptions were deemed "readily retrievable" if, at the time of filing, the face of the prescription was stamped in red ink with the letter "C" in the lower right corner, not less than 1 inch high. In 1997, that regulation was amended to allow an exception to the requirement that prescriptions in Schedules III through V be marked with a red "C" as long as the pharmacy has a computer system that permits identification by prescription number and retrieval of the original documents. However, the red "C" still may be used if it is preferred.

Inventory Records

When a registrant first engages in practice or business, and every 2 years thereafter, a complete and accurate inventory of all stocks of controlled substances must be taken. It is not necessary to submit a copy of the inventory to the DEA. However, the inventory and other records must be kept for at least 2 years under 21 CFR §1304.04.

Inventories by pharmacies and other dispenser registrants require an exact count or measure of all controlled substances in Schedules I and II. For Schedules III, IV, and V controlled substances, an estimated count or measure is permitted unless the container holds more than 1000 tablets or capsules, in which case an exact count must be taken if the container has been opened. The inventory must include all controlled substances "on hand" on the day the inventory is taken. "On hand" is defined as in the possession or control of the registrant. This includes controlled substances returned by patients, ordered for patients but not yet invoiced, stored in a warehouse on behalf of the registrant, and expired drugs marked for return or destruction. The biennial inventory may be taken on any date that is within 2 years of the previous inventory. (21 CFR §1304.11[c].)

21 CFR §1304.11(d) requires registrants to take a physical inventory of any drug newly added to any schedule of controlled substances or when a controlled substance has been moved from one schedule to another. The inventory of all stock of such a drug must be taken on the effective date of the DEA regulation that made the drug a controlled substance or made the change in schedule.

A pharmacy registrant's inventory format should contain the following information: (1) The name, address, and DEA registration number of the registrant; (2) the date and time the inventory is taken (opening or close of a business day); (3) the signature of the person or persons responsible for taking the inventory; (4) an indication that the inventory is maintained for at least 2 years at the location appearing on the DEA registration certificate; and (5) an indication that inventory records of Schedule II drugs, as well as all other records of Schedule II drugs, are kept separately from all other controlled substances.

The inventory record is not to be sent to the DEA; it should be retained by the registrant. Pharmacy registrants must comply with the provisions of 21 CFR §1304.11(e)(1)(iii) and (iv). The inventory record for each controlled substance in a finished form must contain the following:

   (1) The **name** of the controlled substance;
   (2) the **dosage form** and **unit strength** (eg, mg per tablet or capsule, mg concentration per fluid ounce or mL);
   (3) the **number of units** or **volume** in each commercial container (eg, 100 tablet bottle, 5 mL vial);

(4) the **number of commercial containers** of each finished form (eg, 4 × 100 tablet bottles, 6 × 5 mL vials).

For each controlled substance maintained for extemporaneous compounding, the record should list the following: (1) The name of the controlled substance; (2) the total quantity to the nearest metric unit weight or the total number of units of finished form; and (3) the reason the controlled substance is maintained by the registrant and whether the substance is capable of use in the manufacture of any controlled substance in finished form. For example, 1 g in a 1 oz bulk container of codeine phosphate powder would be in stock usually for extemporaneous compounding of prescriptions written as cough medicines. In taking an inventory of this item, a pharmacist would weigh the contents in grams in an open receptacle and note the quantity in the inventory record, indicating that it is stocked for prescription compounding.

Central Recordkeeping and Computerized Systems

The DEA allows for central recordkeeping and computerized prescription refill dispensing. 21 CFR §1304.04 provides for a written notification system. The notification system allows certain records required of registrants to be kept at a central location rather than at the registered location.

Under a central recordkeeping system, only certain records may be maintained at the central location. The records required to remain at the registered pharmacy location are executed order forms, prescriptions, and inventories.

To use centralized recordkeeping under the DEA regulation, the registrant must send written notification in triplicate by registered or certified mail with return receipt requested to the regional director of the DEA. The notification of intent to keep central records of controlled substances must contain the nature of the records to be kept centrally; the exact location where the records will be kept; the name, address, DEA number, and type of DEA registration of the registrant; and whether the central records will be computerized. Fourteen days after receipt of the notification by the DEA regional director, the registrant may commence to maintain the central recordkeeping unless the registrant is informed by the DEA regional director prior to that date that permission to keep central records has been denied.

In addition to the notification requirement, the registrant also must agree to deliver all or any part of its central records to the DEA within 2 business days upon request from the DEA or, at the option of the DEA, to allow inspection of the records at the central location without warrant of any kind.

Requirements relating to computerized, microfilm, or other special recordkeeping systems are discussed below. In the event a registrant fails to comply with any of the central recordkeeping requirements (including the regulation relating to computerized records), the DEA may cancel the registrant's central recordkeeping authorization.

Computerized Recordkeeping

If records are kept on microfilm, in a computer, or in any form requiring special equipment to render the records readily retrievable, 21 CFR §1304.04(b)(2) requires the registrant to provide access to the equipment. If a code system is used for information other than pricing information, a key to the code also must be provided.

Computerized recordkeeping at the registered location does not require DEA notification or approval. If the registrant keeps all controlled substance records at the registered location and such records are readily retrievable, the records may be computerized without notifying the regional director.

The term "readily retrievable," is defined in 21 CFR §1300.02(b)(22) to mean that records can be separated out from all other records (noncontrolled drugs) in a reasonable time. It applies to computer records or other electronic recordkeeping systems as well as to printed records. For printed records, controlled substances must be asterisked, redlined, or in some other manner made visually identifiable from prescriptions for noncontrolled drugs or other records.

A record is required of each authorized refill of a controlled substance dispensed by a pharmacy. The pharmacy registrant may elect 1 of the following ways to maintain these records: (1) Records of refills may be kept in a paper format. Either each authorized refill of a prescription for a controlled substance must be documented by a notation on the back of the prescription, initialed and dated by the pharmacist, with the quantity dispensed included. If the quantity is not included, and only the pharmacist's initials and the date are included, it is assumed that the full amount on the face of the prescription was dispensed when it was refilled. In lieu of indicating the refills on the back of the prescription, refills may be indicated on a separate appropriate and uniformly maintained record (eg, medication profile records) as long as the records are readily retrievable and contain the prescription number, the name and dosage form of the controlled substance, the date of each refilling, the quantity dispensed, the initials or identity of the dispensing pharmacist for each refill, and the total number of refills for that prescription; or (2) A computer may be used for refill recordkeeping. A pharmacy may use only 1 of the 2 systems described above for recording refill information. (See 21 CFR§1306.22[b].)

21 CFR §1306.22(b) allows for the use of a computerized data processing system for refill recordkeeping of prescriptions for Schedules III and IV drugs only if the following conditions are met:

(1) The system must provide the following: Online retrieval (via cathode ray tube [CRT] display or hard copy printout) of the original prescription order information for those prescription orders currently authorized for refilling. The data must include, but are not limited to, the prescription number; the date of issuance of the original prescription order; the full name and address of the patient; the name, address, and DEA registration number of the prescribing practitioner; the name, strength, dosage form, and quantity of the controlled substance prescribed; the quantity dispensed if different from the quantity prescribed; and the total number of refills authorized by the prescribing practitioner; and

(2) The system must provide immediate retrieval of the current refill history for Schedules III and IV controlled drug prescription orders that have been authorized for refills during the previous 6 months and certain backup documentation to show that the refill information is correct. The backup documentation can consist of a hard copy printout of each day's controlled substances prescription refill data, which must be verified, dated, and signed by the pharmacist who refilled the prescription order. This verification document must be maintained in a separate file at the pharmacy for 2 years from the dispensing date. If the pharmacy data processing is linked into an off-premises computer center, the printout must be provided within 72 hours of the dispensing date. In lieu of the printout, a separate bound log book or separate file may be maintained for verification by the pharmacist that the refill data fed into the computer that day was reviewed and found correct; and

(3) A data processing refill recordkeeping system must be able to provide the DEA with a refill-by-refill audit trail for any specific dosage form of a controlled substance by brand name, generic name, or both. This audit trail must be on a printout that includes the information described in the method for manual refill recordkeeping and the name or identification code of the dispensing pharmacist. This information must be in such a form that it can be retrieved and available to the DEA in 48 hours; and

(4) The system must include a backup procedure for refilling prescriptions during computer downtime. The procedure must ensure that only those prescriptions with refill authorizations are refilled by the pharmacy and that the data on refills for input into the system is collected and retained for entry as soon as the computerized system is back in operation.

Prescription refill recordkeeping seems to be as complex and stringent for automated data systems, as for manual systems. Therefore it is important that systems that are set up are DEA compliant.

Theft or Loss of Controlled Substances

21 CFR §1301.76(b) requires a pharmacy registrant, upon discovery of theft or loss of controlled substances from the pharmacy, to immediately notify the nearest DEA Diversion Field Office. The pharmacy also should notify local police, as may be required by state law. Then the pharmacy is required to complete DEA Form 106 regarding such loss or theft. This report must contain: (1) The name and address of the firm; (2) the DEA registration number; (3) the date of the theft; (4) the fact that the local police department was notified; (5) the type of theft (break-in, armed robbery); (6) a list of the symbols or cost code used by the pharmacy in marking containers (if any); and (7) a list of the controlled substances missing through the loss or theft. The report is made in triplicate. The pharmacy keeps the original copy for its records and forwards the remaining 2 copies to the appropriate DEA Diversion Field Office.

ORDER FORMS

Obtaining Order Forms

DEA Form 222 is the controlled substance order form issued by the US Department of Justice/ DEA pursuant to the authority of §308 of the CSA (21 U.S.C. §828) and 21 CFR §1305.01-1305.16. It is used for the legal distribution of Schedules I and II controlled substances among persons registered with the DEA to handle such substances.

Order forms are used by DEA registrants such as pharmacies, physicians, hospitals, researchers, and exporters for the procurement or purchase of Schedules I and II drugs from DEA-registered manufacturers, importers and distributors (drug wholesalers). Under certain conditions, order forms are used by DEA dispenser registrants to procure Schedule II substances from other DEA dispenser registrants.

DEA Form 222 initially is obtained when a DEA registrant submits an order form requisition (DEA Form 222d), which is furnished to a DEA registrant when the original DEA registration application is submitted and the registrant asks for order forms by checking "block 3" on the application. After the initial set of order forms is obtained, subsequent order forms are obtained by submitting DEA Form 222b to the registration branch of the DEA. This requisition form is a separate form and is in each book of order forms (DEA Form 222). Such requests may be mailed to the DEA registration branch. However, the registrant also may request order forms by calling DEA headquarters or (800) 882-9539. In addition, many of the forms are available on the DEA's web site.

21 CFR §1305.05(c) requires that the order form requisition be signed by the same person who signed the most recent DEA registration, or by a person who is designated as a power of attorney previously submitted to the DEA pursuant to 21 CFR §1305.07. The wording of such a power of attorney authorization is in that section of the CFRs. DEA's *Pharmacist's Manual*, found on the DEA web site, also contains an example of a power of attorney form.

It is important to note that the DEA receives the second copy of the triplicate order form from the manufacturer or distributor filling the order. Hence, the DEA knows the quantity and kind of Schedule II substances purchased by each dispenser registrant. Unusually large purchases of certain kinds of Schedule II controlled substances by a pharmacy registrant will trigger a drug accountability audit, and recordkeeping inaccuracies can be detected on accountability audits. Improper recordkeeping could lead a pharmacist to criminal liability under the federal CSA and similar state laws. Therefore, pharmacy registrants should implement recordkeeping which has reasonable procedures to ensure accuracy.

Executing Order Forms—Form 222

(1) Order forms (DEA form 222) are designed only for ordering or transferring Schedules I and II controlled substances; all transfers of Schedules I and II substances must be made on order forms. If an item that is not in Schedule I or II is placed on the order form item line, the item will be voided by the supplier and will not be filled pursuant to the order.

(2) All copies of the triplicate form are prepared simultaneously by use of a typewriter, pen, or indelible pencil. Copies 1 and 2 must not be separated or the carbon removed. Suppliers will refuse to fill orders unless copies 1 and 2 are received with carbon intact.

(3) The dispenser registrant's name, address, and DEA number, the order form serial number and date of issue, schedules, and registrant's classification are preprinted by the DEA on the forms when ordered by the registrant.

(4) Only one item may be ordered per line, but multiple units of the same finished or bulk form and quantity of the same substance may be ordered as one item. Inserting the item's National Drug Code (NDC) number or manufacturer's catalog number is optional.

(5) Each order form has 10 lines, and the total number of items ordered should correspond to the number of lines filled on the order form. (See 21 CFR §1305.06.)

(6) The name and address of the supplier (drug manufacturer or drug wholesaler) to whom the order form is sent must be filled in by the ordering registrant. The purchaser must date and sign the form. The signature must match the one on the application for registration. A person properly authorized by a power of attorney, on file at the registered location as set forth in 21 CFR §1305.07, may sign for the purchasing registrant. The supplier will fill in its DEA registration number.

(7) Erasures or alterations cannot be made when filling out the order form. A supplier cannot fill the order if it contains any erasure or alteration. If an error is made by the purchaser, all copies of the form should be voided and kept on file.

(8) If an order form is unacceptable to the supplier, copies 1 and 2 will be returned to the purchaser with an explanation. This material is attached to copy 3 and retained in the purchaser's files. A partial filling of the order is permitted provided that the supplier sends the balance within 60 days. An exception is made for military facilities. (See 21 CFR §1305.09[f].)

(9) Copies 1 and 2 of the form with the carbon intact are sent to the supplier. Copy 3 is retained by the purchaser and, upon receipt of the items ordered, the number of containers received and the date of receipt must be inserted by the purchasing registrant. Order forms must be filed and maintained separately from all other records kept by the registrant.

(10) Copy 1 of the order form is retained by the supplier, and Copy 2 is sent by the supplier to the regional administrator of the DEA at the end of the month during which the order is filled, or when final shipment of a partially filled order has occurred.

(11) If an unfilled order form is lost, the purchaser should execute a new order form and send it to the same supplier together with the statement stating, among other things, the serial number and date of lost form under 21 CFR §1305.12(a). If order forms, used or unused, are lost or stolen (other than lost in transit), the registrant immediately should notify the DEA in writing by sending a written statement of facts to the registration branch of the DEA in Washington, D.C. If a registrant discontinues business, send all unused order forms to the nearest DEA office.

(12) If a registrant has several registered locations, Copy 3 of executed order forms and related documents may be kept only at the registered location. (See 21 CFR §1305.13[c].)

Filling Order Forms

Generally speaking, a person registered with the DEA to manufacture or distribute Schedules I and II controlled substances may fill orders submitted on a DEA order form. This person is identified as the "supplier" in the regulations. However, under certain specified conditions, a dispenser registrant also may act as a supplier in filing a DEA order form.

21 CFR §1305.08 sets forth the following situations in which a pharmacy registered with the DEA in the dispenser category legally is permitted to fill orders submitted on DEA order forms:

(1) **Return** of unused, partial, or full containers of controlled substances in Schedules I and II by a pharmacy registrant to a manufacturer or distributor places a pharmacy in the role of a "supplier." For example, if a pharmacy returns outdated codeine sulfate vials to the wholesaler from whom they were originally procured, the wholesaler would furnish the pharmacy with copies 1 and 2 of an order form. The date and the containers shipped (returned) are recorded by the pharmacy on copies 1 and 2. Copy 1 is retained by the pharmacy/supplier and copy 2 is sent to the regional administrator of the DEA.

(2) **Distribution by dispenser to another practitioner** is permitted under 21 CFR §1307.11, provided the registrant receiving the Schedules I and II controlled substances furnishes the registrant supplying them an executed order form. This allows a pharmacy registrant to supply Schedule II drugs to a physician registrant for his office practice, provided the physician obtains the drugs pursuant to an order form furnished to the pharmacy. Similarly, Schedule II drugs may be supplied by one pharmacy registrant to another pharmacy registrant pursuant to an order form executed by the recipient. If the number of dosage units of all controlled substances distributed under authority of 21 CFR §1307.11 is more than 5% of the total number of dosage units of all controlled substances distributed and dispensed by the pharmacy in a 12-month period, the pharmacy dispenser must register with the DEA as a distributor. (See 21 CFR §1307.11[a][4].) A physician is prohibited by 21 CFR §1306.04(b) from issuing a prescription as a means of obtaining any controlled substance for use in an office practice. The physician registrant must use an order form to obtain Schedule II drugs for office use. Unless prohibited by state law, a physician registrant may issue a prescription to obtain a controlled substance for a specific patient and personally deliver or administer the drug to the patient; however, the complete prescription must be delivered or administered to the specific patient named in the prescription. (See the *Richardson* case cited below.)

Other Distribution Between Registrants

Distribution of Schedules III, IV, and V controlled drugs between dispenser registrants (pharmacy to pharmacy, pharmacy to manufacturer, or pharmacy to physician) also is permitted, but the distributions must be evidenced by records conforming to the requirements for records for dispensers contained in 21 CFR §1304.22(c) described above. A commercial invoice containing the required data will comply if one copy is retained by the distributing registrant and the original or a copy is retained by the recipient registrant.

In addition, 21 CFR §1307.12 provides for the distribution to the original supplier of a controlled substance provided that a written record is maintained.

PRESCRIPTIONS

General Issuance Requirements

21 CFR §1306.01 through §1306.06 contain the general requirements for issuance of prescriptions for controlled drugs. These requirements may be summarized under 4 major topics: 1) Purpose of issuance of prescriptions for controlled substances; 2) Person permitted to issue such prescriptions; 3) Manner in which the prescription is issued; and 4) Person permitted to fill the prescriptions.

Purpose for Issuance of Prescriptions for Controlled Substances

21 CFR §1306.04(a) states: "A prescription for a controlled substance to be effective must be issued for a legitimate medical purpose by an individual practitioner acting in the usual course of his professional practice. The responsibility for the proper prescribing and dispensing of controlled substances is upon the prescribing practitioner, but a corresponding responsibility rests with the pharmacist who fills the prescription. . . ."

This language requires that a prescription for a controlled substance be issued for a "legitimate medical purpose" by an individual practitioner acting within the usual course of his professional practice. Samples of purported or invalid prescriptions include the following: A forged or false prescription issued by a person not licensed to prescribe drugs; a narcotic-controlled drug prescription issued for the purpose of abetting the habit of a narcotic addict or for continuing the addict's drug dependence; a prescription issued for a fictitious person or for a person other than the one named as the patient on the prescription; a prescription issued for controlled substances for the prescriber's office use; a prescription issued not in the usual course of the prescriber's medical practice (eg, a podiatrist issuing a prescription in treatment of a patient's gallbladder disease).

A review of several court cases may provide a clear understanding of the meaning of the phrases "legitimate medical purpose" and "usual course of prescriber's professional practice."

In *Richardson v. Florida State Board of Dentistry*, 326 So.2d 231 (1976), a disciplinary action was brought against a dentist who issued prescriptions for 20 mL vials of morphine sulfate in the name of a person (his dental assistant) for whom the medication was not intended and by whom it was not used. The morphine was used instead by the dentist to relieve his patients' anxiety and to make complex dental procedures less unpleasant. The dentist used prescriptions to obtain the morphine because he found it inconvenient to order the drug from a supplier via order forms.

The pharmacists dispensing such prescriptions apparently were not misled by the fact that the prescriptions were issued in the name of the dental assistant because on their face the "Sig" read "PRN in office," "PRN office use," or "PRN by Dr." One pharmacist did think it unusual for the dentist to order the drug by means of a prescription rather than the narcotic order form, but he testified in court to dispensing at least 7 such prescriptions.

A number of charges were brought against the dentist by the Board of Dentistry, but the two most important to the discussion here are the following: (1) The administration of morphine was not necessary to the practice of dentistry and by inference violated Florida law, which permitted dentists to prescribe drugs; and (2) the dentist obtained the drug by fraud, forgery, deception, or subterfuge in violation of another state law. As to the first charge, the court did not sustain the Board because there was no evidence in the record that the dentist's use of morphine was unnecessary or improper, even though most dentists used a less potent nonnarcotic drug, or no drug at all for the stated purposes. As to the second charge, the court found the evidence did not support the Board's suspension order because there was no intent on the part of the dentist to conceal. The court did state that the dentist's conduct "offends state and federal law . . ." but there was no evidence of moral turpitude to support the Board's license suspension.

If a pharmacist has actual knowledge or if the surrounding circumstances show that a pharmacist should have had knowledge that a prescription for a controlled substance is invalid, the CSA is violated by the dispensing of medication on a purported prescription. Accordingly, there may be some legal exposure for the pharmacist in such a transaction. (See the discussion of *United States v. Hayes*, 595 F.2d 258 [1979].)

In *United States v. Collier*, 478 F.2d 268 (1973), a physician registrant pleaded guilty in federal court to 6 counts of violating §401(a)(1), CSA (21 U.S.C. §841[a][1]) by dispensing methadone while not in the usual course of his professional practice. The physician was fined $20,000 and appealed. On appeal, he attacked the constitutionality of §401(a)(1) and, in effect, the regulations issued thereunder. The argument made was that the words "in the course of his professional practice" did not tell the physician what was legal in objective terms. The court ruled against the physician and, in so doing, restated the holding developed over the years in cases adjudicating the federal narcotic laws. "A physician is restricted to dispensing or prescribing drugs in the bona fide treatment of a patient's disease, including a dispensing of a moderate amount of drugs to a known addict in a good-faith attempt to treat the addiction or relieve conditions of suffering incident to addiction." (*Linder v. United States*, 268 U.S. 5 [1925] and other cases were cited.)

"In making a medical judgment concerning the right treatment for an individual patient, physicians require a certain latitude of available options. Hence, what constitutes bona fide medical practice must be determined upon consideration of evidence and attending circumstances." (*Linder v. United States*, 268 U.S. 5 [1925].)

In *United States v. Bartee*, 479 F.2d 484 (1973), a physician was convicted of dispensing controlled substances in violation of §401(a)(1), CSA (21 U.S.C. §841[a][1]) in that he knowingly and intentionally dispensed *Percodan* and *Seconal* by issuing prescriptions for them that were not for a legitimate medical purpose, nor were they issued in the usual course of professional practice. The reported facts are summarized as follows:

A DEA undercover agent visited the doctor and made complaints of persistent headaches. The physician, without giving a physical examination to the patient, prescribed *Parafon Forte*, a noncontrolled drug. Later, the agent returned to the physician, asked for something stronger, and told the physician that he, the patient, had traded the *Parafon Forte* for *Tuinal*, a barbiturate controlled drug. The physician then prescribed *Percodan*. Then the patient asked for a larger supply, and the physician wrote 3 prescriptions for *Percodan*.

Another undercover agent visited the same physician and complained of nervousness and insomnia. The physician prescribed *Librium* (a noncontrolled drug at that time). Again the patient/undercover agent returned and told the physician that he had traded the *Librium* for some "reds" because the *Librium* was ineffective. The physician dispensed *Triavil* (a noncontrolled drug) directly to the patient. The patient returned and told the physician that he had traded the *Triavil* for *Seconal*. The physician then prescribed *Seconal* for him, subsequently wrote several prescriptions, and postdated them for the patient. The physician told the patient to be careful as DEA personnel checked drugstores to see which physicians were heavily prescribing drugs. The patient/undercover agent replied that he would have the prescriptions filled in Denver, but the physician advised that it would not be necessary as long as the prescriptions were taken to different drugstores and not filled all at once.

On appeal from conviction by the trial court, the physician argued that the law only prohibited illegal dispensing of controlled drugs to the "ultimate consumer," and an undercover agent was not such a consumer because he did not use the drugs prescribed. The physician also contended that he did not violate §401(a)(1), CSA (21 U.S.C. §841[a][1]) because he prescribed the drugs rather than dispensed them. Section 401(a)(1) prohibits unlawful dispensing. The appellate court affirmed the trial court's conviction of the physician.

The court pointed out that the term "dispense" includes "prescribe" and "administer" as defined in §102(10), CSA (21 U.S.C. §802[10]). The court also pointed out that the term "ultimate consumer" as defined in §102(25), CSA (21 U.S.C. §805[25]) means that the person only must obtain the drug for his own use or for use by a member of his household and does not mean that the recipient actually must ingest the drug. Furthermore, the conviction of the physician was sustained because the doctor had actual knowledge that the patients were dealing in drugs or disposing of drugs to others.

In the *Bartee* case, the pharmacists who filled the prescriptions could not be prosecuted unless it could be shown that they had knowledge or should have had knowledge that the prescriptions were not issued in the prescriber's usual course of professional practice. Normally, the pharmacist does not have this type of knowledge unless the prescriptions are postdated (which is illegal) or some indication is present to alert the pharmacist to a bogus prescription. Usually, if the pharmacist suspects an invalid prescription, checks with the prescribing doctor and receives a satisfactory explanation, the pharmacist's duty has been fulfilled under the law. The consultation with the prescriber should be documented.

In *United States v. Nocerino*, 474 F.2d 993 (Cir. 1973), a pharmacist illegally sold drugs. The pharmacist transferred a cardboard box containing 17,000 amphetamines and barbiturates to a man; the transfer took place in the pharmacist's garage next to his home. The court reasoned that unless some plausible explanation could be shown, a jury normally was sophisticated enough to conclude, not unreasonably, that the vast amount of drugs transferred in a garage represented a "sale" where the transferee was intending to resell the drugs for enormous profits.

Who May Prescribe Controlled Substances

21 CFR §1306.03(a)(1) and (2) states:

> A prescription for a controlled substance may be issued only by an individual prescriber who is: (1) authorized to prescribe controlled substances by the jurisdiction in which he is licensed to practice his profession and (2) either registered or exempted from registration pursuant to Secs. 1301.22(c) and 1301.23 of this chapter.

21 CFR §1300.01(b)(17) defines "individual practitioner" as a physician, dentist, veterinarian, or other individual licensed, registered or otherwise permitted by the United States or the jurisdiction in which he or she practices to dispense a controlled substance in the course of professional practice. This definition does not include a pharmacist, a pharmacy, or an institutional practitioner. However, individual practitioners do include the category of health care providers known as mid-level practitioners. 21 CFR §1300.01(b)(28) defines a mid-level practitioner as "an individual practitioner other than a physician, dentist, veterinarian, or podiatrist, who is licensed, registered or otherwise permitted by the jurisdiction where the practice is located, to dispense a controlled substance in the course of professional practice." Examples of mid-level practitioners include, but are not limited to, health care providers such as nurse practitioners, nurse midwives, nurse anesthetists, clinical nurse specialists, and physician assistants who are authorized to dispense controlled substances by the state in which they practice, as well as pharmacists in states where they are authorized to prescribe.

DEA requires each registered mid-level practitioner to maintain, in a readily retrievable manner, the documents required by the state in which the person practices that describe the conditions and extent of the mid-level practitioner's authorization to dispense controlled substances. Examples of documentation include protocols or algorithm, practice guidelines or practice agreements. The documents must be made available for inspection and copying by authorized DEA personnel.

A veterinarian may legally prescribe drugs only in the treatment of animals. Generally, an osteopathic physician (DO) has the same prescribing authority as an allopathic physician (MD) under state law.

An osteopathic physician differs from an allopathic physician in that the osteopathic physician may treat certain diseases by bone manipulation or spinal manipulation in a fashion somewhat similar to that of the chiropractor. In other respects, his treatment of disease is the same as the allopathic physician.

Generally, state law prohibits chiropractors, psychologists, opticians, and other allied health persons from prescribing drugs. A psychologist (PhD) cannot prescribe drugs; a psychiatrist (MD) can. A chiropractor (DC) cannot prescribe drugs; a podiatrist or chiropodist (DPM) can (for foot diseases). A majority of states now permit optometrists (ODs) to prescribe for either diagnostic or therapeutic purposes.

It is important to remember that neither the CSA nor the DEA regulations confer authority to prescribe controlled drugs on a person who did not otherwise have the authority to do so under either state or federal law.

Manner of Issuing Prescriptions for Controlled Substances

The requirements for issuing prescriptions for controlled substances are set forth under 21 CFR §1306 et seq. A prescription for a Schedule II controlled drug may be prepared by the prescribing physician, by a nurse or office employee, or by another person acting as the prescriber's agent (which could include the pharmacist), but a written Schedule II prescription actually must be signed by the prescribing practitioner. He or she may sign it in the same way that he would sign a check or legal document. The emergency oral Schedule II prescription provision is the only exception to the signature requirement for Schedule II substances. (See 21 CFR §1306.11.) A physician cannot legally issue signed blank prescriptions for an agent to complete to avoid the prohibition on postdated Schedule II prescriptions.

21 CFR §1306.03(b) also states that a prescription for a controlled substance issued by an individual practitioner may be communicated to a pharmacist by an employee or agent of the individual practitioner. The usual application of this provision is when a physician's nurse or office employee transmits the physician's prescription to the pharmacist by telephone. The physician's nurse or office employee may act only on his specific instructions and has no authority or legal right to issue prescriptions or to authorize prescription refills. (See the discussion of the *Randle* case.)

21 CFR §1306.05(a) requires that all controlled substance prescriptions must be dated as of and signed on the day when issued and must bear the full name and address of the patient, the drug name, strength, dosage form, quantity prescribed, directions for use, and the name, address, and DEA number of the practitioner. In the situation of an oral prescription, the pharmacist transcribing the prescription "signs" the prescriber's name to it by simply placing the physician's name on the prescription. One method for doing this is to precede the physician's name by the letter "s" enclosed by diagonal lines in the manner that a transcribed signature is shown on copies of legal documents (eg, /s/Maxwell Makewell, MD).

A question may arise as to the propriety for insertion of the corrected or missing information after the physician has issued and signed the prescription, particularly in a Schedule II prescription. For example, suppose the prescriber wrote *Demerol* 50 mg ampules and then orally stated that he meant *Demerol* 50 mg tablets. The DEA has interpreted the regulation to permit the pharmacist to insert the necessary prescription content information even after the prescription is signed, provided that the insertions are correct and no serious question exists as to the validity of the prescription. It is legal for the pharmacist to insert omitted or corrected items on the controlled drug prescription, with the exception of the written signature of the prescriber in Schedule II prescriptions. The responsibility for the completeness of the prescription rests with both the prescriber and the pharmacist (21CFR §1306.05[a]).

It is actually the law of agency that gives a pharmacist authority to correct information on a prescription or insert missing information. Because the dispensing pharmacist is responsible under the law for the completeness of the prescription, in both implied agency and agency by operation of law (or necessity), no oral or written agreement is needed. The conduct of the parties and the circumstances creates the agency. (See 3 Am. Jur.2d. Agency, §18 and §19.)

Each prescription problem or omission must be reviewed carefully by the pharmacist using his best professional judgment and acting in good faith. In addition, a pharmacist has the legal right and responsibility to refuse to dispense a controlled substance when he believes that the prescription for it is not issued in good faith. A pharmacist has the right and duty to ascertain from the prescriber the purpose for issuing the prescription when in doubt as to its legitimate purpose.

Electronic Transmission of Prescriptions for Controlled Substances

For a general discussion of the "E-Sign" legislation that was signed in June 2000 and took effect on October 1, 2000, see the Other Relevant Legislation section of the Regulation of Pharmaceuticals chapter.

Technically, current DEA regulations requiring the handwritten signature of a prescriber and current recordkeeping requirements requiring paper copies of prescriptions are not enforceable because of the passage of the E-Sign legislation. However, the DEA takes the stand that the E-Sign legislation is not applicable to prescriptions—but does apply to recordkeeping provisions. Others dispute that stance, saying there is no exception in the E-Sign statute for prescriptions.

Since September 1999, the DEA has been developing standards for electronic transmission of prescriptions using digital security technology. Two concurrent projects are being conducted with Performance Engineering Corporation. They involve standards to be adopted to allow electronic transmission of prescriptions for controlled substances from prescriber to dispenser, and the supplement of the DEA Schedule II order form (222). The DEA has been working to make these standards more clearly defined. As a result, the DEA released a Notice of Proposed Rulemaking. On January 11, 2002, the DEA published in the *Federal Register* a *Notice of Intent to Conduct Performance Verification Testing of Public Key Infrastructure Enabled Controlled Substance Orders*. It is being done as a part of its Electronic Commerce Initiatives, and in partnership with the Health Care Distribution Management Association (HCDMA) and the National Association of Chain Drugstores (NACDS) See 67 FR no. 8 pg 1507.

The DEA is aware that physicians and pharmacists in many states already are using Electronic Data Interchange technology to transmit prescriptions using digital security technology. The standards developed by the DEA will involve the use of Public Key Infrastructures that use cryptographic algorithms to make encryption and digital signature rather than electronic signature. For an overview and more details about the DEA's efforts in this area, see http://www.deadiversion.usdoj.gov.

Special Considerations for Schedule II Prescriptions

Partial Filling of Prescriptions for Schedule II Drugs

A pharmacist may partially fill a written or emergency oral prescription for a Schedule II controlled substance if he is unable to supply the full face amount of the prescription. The quantity dispensed must be noted on the face of the prescription document, and the remaining portion of the quantity prescribed must be provided within 72 hours of the first partial filling. However, if the remaining portion is not or cannot be supplied within the 72-hour period, the pharmacist must notify the prescriber. No further quantity can be dispensed on the prescription. A new prescription is needed if the patient requests the balance of the prescription after the 72-hour period.

Partial Filling of Prescriptions for Long-Term Care Facility (LTCF) or Terminally Ill Patients

In 1980, the DEA adopted new regulations providing for partial filling of prescriptions for Schedule II drugs for patients in LTCF. (See 21 CFR §1306.13[b] and [c].) An LTCF is defined in 21 CFR §1306.02(e) as a nursing home, retirement care, mental care, or other facility or institution that provides extended health care to resident patients.

The regulations were amended in 1991 to extend the partial dispensing option in prescription services for patients with a medical diagnosis documenting a terminal illness. If there is any question whether a patient may be classified as having a terminal illness, the pharmacist must contact the practitioner prior to partially filling the prescription. Both the pharmacist and the prescribing practitioner are responsible for ensuring that the controlled substance is for a terminally ill patient. 21 CFR §1306.13(b) and (c) permits partial filling of prescriptions for Schedule II controlled substances and extends the 72-hour limit to a period of 60 days to prescriptions written for patients in an LTCF or patients with a medical diagnosis documenting a terminal illness. The regulation permits individual doses as part of the partial filling and requires recordkeeping of such partial fillings on the back of the prescription or on another appropriate record uniformly maintained and readily retrievable. The total quantity dispensed on all such partial fillings cannot exceed the total quantity prescribed. Schedule II prescriptions for LTCF patients or patients with a medical diagnosis documenting a terminal illness are valid for no longer than 60 days after the date of issuance unless they are cancelled sooner by discontinuation of the medication.

Information pertaining to current Schedule II prescriptions for LTCF patients or patients with a medical diagnosis documenting a terminal illness may be computerized if the system permits CRT display or produces a printout of the data (see 21 CFR §1306.13[c]).

Provisions for Emergency Schedule II Prescriptions

Among the requirements for emergency oral prescriptions for Schedule II drugs (see 21 CFR §1306.11[d]), it is important to note that the amount dispensed is required to be limited to that quantity necessary to cover only the emergency period. A written prescription for that amount must be provided by the prescribing physician to the dispensing pharmacist within 7 days; if the physician fails to provide the written prescription, the pharmacist shall notify the nearest DEA office. Another written prescription is necessary to cover any amounts of the drug needed in excess of the emergency amount.

21 CFR §1306.11(d), relating to Schedule II emergency oral prescriptions, should be read in conjunction with 21 CFR §290.10. The CSA requires the secretary of DHHS (in effect, the FDA) to define an emergency situation for purposes of authorizing an oral prescription of a controlled substance listed in Schedule II. Prescriptions for Schedule II drugs are not refillable.

Facsimile Prescriptions

DEA regulations permit prescriptions for Schedules II, III, IV and V drugs to be sent via fax from the practitioner directly to the pharmacy.

Before dispensing a Schedule II prescription, the original written, signed prescription must be presented to the pharmacist for review, except in the following 3 instances: (1) A faxed prescription for a Schedule II narcotic to be compounded for direct administration to a patient by parenteral, IV, IM, SC, or intraspinal infusion serves as legal authority for a home infusion pharmacy to dispense the product in the same manner as an original written prescription; (2) a faxed prescription for any Schedule II substance for a patient in a long-term care facility may be considered a "written" prescription; (3) a faxed prescription for any Schedule II narcotic substance for patients in hospice settings that are hospice certified under Medicare or licensed by the state may be considered an original written prescription. The pharmacy under these exceptions must retain the facsimile copy as file documentation of its dispensing action. (See 21 CFR §1306.1 1[e]-[g]).

In addition to written or oral prescribing of Schedules III, IV, and V substances, DEA regulations permit the facsimile of a written signed prescription transmitted by the prescribing practitioner or the practitioner's agent to serve as the authority for, and record of, the dispensing of a Schedule III, IV, or V substance. (See 21 CFR §1306.21[a]).

Although federal DEA regulations allow for facsimile prescriptions for controlled substances, they do not authorize a practitioner to prescribe, or a pharmacist to dispense, controlled substances via faxed prescriptions unless **expressly provided for under the state law** in the jurisdiction in which the health care providers practice.

Hospital Medication Orders

Hospitals register with the DEA as institutional practitioners, but the box checked on the DEA registration form (DEA Form 224) is "hospital/clinic." A hospital's DEA registration to dispense drugs in Schedules II through V also covers the dispensing activities of its on-premises pharmacy. A separate pharmacy DEA registration or DEA number is not required; the hospital's pharmacy uses the hospital's DEA number. Certain DEA regulations apply specifically to the dispensing of controlled drugs in hospitals. (See 21 CFR §1301.22, §1306.11[c] and §1306.21[c].)

A hospital's DEA registration will permit its employed medical interns and residents as well as foreign-trained physicians to dispense, administer, or prescribe controlled substances for hospital patients if the requirements of 21 CFR §1301.22(c) are met. Individual medical practitioners with hospital staff privileges who are not "employees" of the hospital may prescribe, administer, or dispense controlled drug to hospital patients only if the practitioner possesses a DEA registration as a dispenser. Normally, all nonemployee staff physicians have a personal DEA registration number. In fact, many residents and foreign physicians also have their own personal DEA registration.

Any physician who is an agent or employee of a hospital or other institution may dispense, administer, and prescribe controlled drugs under the DEA registration of the hospital or other institution by which the physician is employed, provided that:

(1) the dispensing, administering, and prescribing are in the usual course of professional practice;
(2) the practitioner is authorized or permitted to do so by the jurisdiction in which he is practicing;
(3) the hospital or institution has verified that the practitioner is permitted to dispense, administer, and prescribe drugs within the jurisdiction;
(4) the practitioner acts only within the scope of his employment in the hospital or institution;
(5) the hospital or institution authorizes the practitioner to dispense and prescribe under its registration and assigns a specific internal code number for each practitioner so authorized. The code number shall be a suffix to the institution's DEA number; and
(6) a current list of internal codes and the corresponding individual practitioners is kept by the hospital or other institution and is made available at all times to other registrants and law enforcement agencies upon request for the purpose of verifying the authority of the prescribing individual practitioner. (See 21 CFR §1301.22[c].)

Pharmacists should contact the hospital or institution for verification if they have any doubts in dispensing such prescription orders.

Hospital interns, residents, or foreign physicians may issue outpatient controlled drug prescriptions or inpatient controlled drug medication orders provided that all the requirements of 21 CFR §1301.22(c) listed above are met or physicians have individual DEA regulations as dispensers.

21 CFR §1300.01(b)(35) defines "prescription" as an order for medication to be dispensed to or for an ultimate user. Not included in the definition is an order for medication dispensed for immediate administration to the user. The exclusion is significant when read together with 21 CFR §1306.11(c) and §1306.21(c), which permit administration of controlled drugs to hospital patients either by prescription or by an order for medication for immediate administration. The typical hospital chart drug order for an inpatient or outpatient, when medication administration is immediate, is an example of the "order for medication" referred to in the regulations.

A physician may not order "take-home" controlled drugs via a chart order. Medication orders within the context of the DEA regulations are for medications dispensed for immediate administration, not for a supply of take-home medications, which should be handled by issuance of a prescription. However, there are some exceptions. Dispensing pursuant to a medication order of a single dose of a controlled drug to be taken home by a patient treated and released from a hospital emergency room might qualify as "immediate administration." This practice is used to provide medication to a patient until he or she can have a prescription dispensed. The immediate administration obviously encompasses the traditional hospital drug distribution system whereby a 3- or 4-day supply of drugs is dispensed from the hospital nursing station for a particular patient. The drugs are under hospital control until the immediate administration by the nurse to the patient.

An exemption from the full labeling of prescriptions for Schedule II controlled drugs is provided in 21 CFR §1306.14(b). If more than a 7-day supply of controlled drugs is dispensed to be administered to an institutionalized patient, the dispensing must be pursuant to a prescription.

The definition of prescription does not include a hospital medication order in the regulation quoted above because of the special treatment given to hospital medication orders by DEA regulations. (See 21 CFR §1306.11[c] and §1306.21[c].) In a context outside of CSA regulations, the hospital medication order, when given by the prescribing physician and entered on the patient's chart, has the same practical and often legal effect as a prescription.

Filling Prescriptions for Controlled Substances

21 CFR §1306.06 provides that only a pharmacist acting in the usual course of professional practice or an institutional practitioner may fill prescriptions for controlled substances. The pharmacist either must be registered individually with the DEA as a dispenser or be employed in a DEA-registered pharmacy or by a DEA-registered institutional practitioner (hospital).

The term "pharmacist" is defined in 21 CFR §1300.01 (33) to mean any pharmacist licensed by a "state to dispense controlled substances and includes any other person (eg, pharmacist intern) authorized by a state to dispense controlled substances under the supervision of a pharmacist licensed by the state."

Pharmacy technicians legally may dispense controlled drugs under a pharmacist's supervision, depending on the exact wording of the particular state law or regulation. Few states, if any, have specific provisions in their controlled substance law or regulation providing authority for pharmacy technicians or aides to handle controlled substances under a pharmacist's supervision. In states having a specific statutory provision permitting nonpharmacists to dispense drugs under a pharmacist's supervision, the provision is of a general nature and does not refer specifically to controlled substances.

Quantity and Dating

A pharmacist legally may fill a controlled substance prescription issued for a large quantity under certain conditions. First, laws or regulations in some states may limit the quantity of controlled substances that may be dispensed. Some states limit the controlled drug dispensed to a 34-day supply or 120 doses. Second, dispensing a prescription for an unreasonably large quantity of controlled substances may raise the issue of lack of good faith on the part of the pharmacist filling the prescription. However, the fact that a large quantity of a drug is prescribed does not necessarily indicate that the prescription is not legitimate. In such a case, the pharmacist should check with the prescriber to verify the quantity and to ascertain the reason for it. This fact should be documented on the prescription or on another readily retrievable record. If the same practitioner continues to prescribe excessive quantities, the pharmacist may refuse to fill the prescription in compliance with 21 CFR §1306.04(a). However, the pharmacist must use professional judgment, because a patient's medical condition may necessitate a large quantity of the drug.

A controlled substance prescription may not be legally predated or postdated. 21 CFR §1306.05 requires that a prescription be dated as of the date of issuance. Although federal regulations require a controlled substance prescription to be dated on the date issued, there is no prohibition against filling a controlled substance prescription several days after its issuance provided that good faith is present. In the case of a prescription for a controlled substance presented for filling several days or weeks after issuance, the pharmacist may use his/her discretion in determining whether it may be necessary to contact the prescriber to ascertain whether a legitimate medical purpose exists to support filling the prescription.

Sale of Controlled Drugs without a Prescription

A controlled drug in Schedule V or in Schedules II, III, and IV that is not a prescription (legend) drug under federal or state law may be sold over the counter provided that: (1) the sale is made only by a pharmacist; although after the pharmacist has completed the professional and legal responsibilities of the sale, the actual cash transfer and delivery of the drug may be done by a nonpharmacist employee; (2) no more than 240 mL (8 oz) or 48 dosage units of an opium-containing controlled substance or 120 mL (4 oz) or 24 dosage units of any other controlled substance may be sold or dispensed to the same buyer in any 48-hour period; (3) the purchaser must be at least 18 years of age and any purchaser not known to the pharmacist must furnish identification and proof of age (when appropriate); and (4) over-the-counter (otc) sales for Schedule V drugs must be recorded in a bound record book or registry containing name and quantity of the item sold, name and address of purchaser, date of purchase, and name or initials of the pharmacist seller. (See 21 CFR §1306.26.)

Refilling Prescriptions for Controlled Substances

Schedules III and IV drug prescriptions may be refilled up to 5 times within 6 months of the date on which the prescription is issued, if so authorized by the prescribing physician. After 5 authorized refills are received or after the expiration of 6 months from the issue date, whichever comes first, the prescription is not refillable. A new and separate prescription, written or oral, is required. If less than 5 refills originally are authorized, additional refills of an original prescription may be authorized by the prescribing practitioner and be added to the original prescription order as long as the number of refills, including those authorized on the original prescription, do not exceed the 5 refill limitation nor extend beyond 6 months from the date of issue of the original prescription.

Refills of all legend drug prescriptions may be dispensed only as authorized by the prescriber. If a prescription contains no instructions to refill, it is legally a "no refill" prescription, for which refill authorization must be obtained. If a controlled drug is involved, a new prescription must be made.

The recording of refills for Schedules III and IV prescriptions was discussed in the section regarding recordkeeping (see also 21 CFR §1306.22). It is sufficient here to restate that a pharmacist must record each refill dispensed by recording his initials, the date of refilling and the quantity dispensed on the back of the prescription or on another appropriate, uniformly maintained and readily retrievable record, such as a medication profile record. The registrant may use data processing or computerized systems for refill recording, subject to the rules in 21 CFR §1306.22.

If a prescription for a Schedule III, IV, or V controlled drug contains an authorization for refill and the patient requests to have all refills dispensed at once, is it legal for the pharmacist to honor the request? Some state drug control statutes or regulations prohibit dispensing more than a 34-day supply or 120 doses of a controlled substance. In those instances, the pharmacist legally cannot honor the request if the quantity dispensed would exceed the maximum allowed by state statute or regulation.

If there is no prohibition under state drug control statutes, then the pharmacist dispensing more than the face amount of the prescription may be acting in bad faith. Possibly, the patient is requesting all the refills at once in order to sell the drug or to provide some or all of the drug to another individual as an accommodation. However, often the question of dispensing all the authorized refills at once arises when the patient is leaving the area for an extended period of time. Where a bona fide reason exists for dispensing more than the face amount of the prescription, the safe thing for the pharmacist to do is to contact the prescriber and obtain a new prescription for a larger amount if permitted under state statute.

Any refills that a prescriber may indicate on a prescription for a Schedule II controlled drug are void. The CSA regulations are quite clear that prescriptions for Schedule II controlled drugs are not refillable, regardless of what the prescriber may indicate to the contrary.

Transfers of Controlled Substance Prescription Information for Refills

Unless otherwise prohibited by state statutes or regulations, federal regulations allow transfer of original prescription information for a controlled substance listed in Schedules III, IV, and V for the purpose of refill dispensing. Generally, the transfer is permissable between pharmacies on a one-time basis subject to the requirements of 21 CFR §1306.25. However, a 1997 regulation allows pharmacies that share a "real-time, on-line electronic database" to transfer prescription information for controlled substances up to the maximum refills permitted by law and the prescriber's authorization.

Treatment of Opioid Addictions

Methadone Distribution

Methadone HCl, a Schedule II controlled substance, is a synthetic narcotic analgesic indicated for relief of severe pain, for detoxification treatment of narcotic addiction, and for temporary maintenance treatment of narcotic addiction. In the past, the FDA and DEA jointly adopted criteria and guidelines for medical treatment of narcotic addicts with methadone. The relevant federal regulations were contained in 21 CFR §291. These actually were FDA regulations rather than DEA regulations and were, therefore, enforceable by FDA.

In July 1999, the Clinton administration proposed new regulations that would revise the system for dispensing methadone. These regulations were published as final on January 17, 2001 (see 66 FR 4076). They originally were to take effect on March 19, 2001. They were further delayed in taking effect upon the entrance of the Bush administration and took effect May 18, 2001 (see 66 FR 15347).

The most drastic change in regulation of the distribution of methadone is that responsibility its for enforcement it has been transferred from the FDA to the Substance Abuse and Mental Health Services Administration (SAMHSA). The FDA regulations contained in 21 CFR 291 are repealed. The new rule provides for a new regulatory system based on an accreditation model. The stated purpose is to allow for increased medical judgment in the treatment of opioid addiction. The new regulations are contained in 42 CFR Part 8.

Some important definitions are essential to understanding the conditions for use of methadone for detoxification and maintenance purposes.

"Detoxification treatment" is defined as "the dispensing of an opioid agonist treatment medication in decreasing doses to an individual to alleviate adverse physical or psychological effects incident to withdrawal from the continuous or sustained use of an opioid drug and as a method of bringing the individual to a drug-free state within such period."

On the other hand, "maintenance treatment" is defined as "the dispensing of an opioid agonist treatment medication at stable dosage levels for a period in excess of 21 days in the treatment of an individual for opioid addiction."

The new regulation defines opiate addiction as "a cluster of cognitive, behavioral, and physiological symptoms in which the individual continues use of opiates despite significant opiate-induced problems. Opiate dependence is characterized by repeated self-administration that usually results in opiate tolerance, withdrawal symptoms, and compulsive drug taking. Dependence may occur with or without the physiological symptoms of tolerance and withdrawal." The regulation goes on to define "detoxification treatment," "maintenance treatment," and many other relevant terms.

Under the new regulations, private nonprofit organizations or state governmental entities or any political subdivisions thereof are eligible for accreditation. Requirements for accreditation are quite comprehensive and are described in Subpart B of the regulations.

When used as an analgesic, a methadone product may be dispensed in any licensed pharmacy in accordance with the prescription requirements for Schedule II controlled drugs.

Other Treatments for Opioid Addictions

Along with changes in how methadone is distributed for opioid addiction (as opposed to "narcotic addiction"), there seems to be a movement to "decentralize" the treatment of such addiction—perhaps in an effort to encourage people to begin and continue treatment. The Narcotic Addict Treatment Act of 1974 (21 [USC 821g]) requires registration with the DEA and licensure with the attorney general. However, in the Drug Abuse Treatment Act of 2000, which is buried in the Children's Health Act of 2000, a waiver of such registration with the DEA and licensure with the attorney general is given to practitioners who dispense narcotic drugs in Schedules III, IV or V, or combinations of such to individuals for maintenance of detoxification if the practitioners and drugs meet specific conditions. While there may be a bit of argument by those who are uninformed, this legislation was meant to provide for physicians to treat patients for detoxification and maintenance with a drug called buprenorphine that apparently has been used with some success. This legislation provides a 3-year window (state law is pre-empted for 3 years) to see how it works. Now, there are those who may argue that the legislation states that any drug used in this treatment be approved by the FDA for maintenance and detoxification. Buprenorphine has not yet been approved by the FDA for this specific indication. (The only drug to have such approval is methadone.) However, the legislation contains the clause, "Nothing in such regulations or practice guidelines may authorize any federal official or employee to exercise supervision or control over the 'practice of medicine' or the manner in which medical services are provided." It is this clause that permits the practitioner to prescribe buprenorphine for maintenance or detoxification, as that constitutes the practice of medicine.

The legislation took effect on October 17, 2000; however, its contents are not widely known. On March 21, 2002 the DEA at 67 FR 13114 et.seq. issued a proposed rule to increase regulatory controls on buprenorphine by rescheduling it from a Schedule V Narcotic to a Schedule III narcotic. If finalized, it will impose the regulatory controls and criminal sanctions of a Schedule III narcotic on those persons who handle buprenorphine or products containing such.

The proposed rule contains some frequently asked questions that would be of interest to many. This proposal with this information may be found at http://www.deadiversion.usdoj.gov/fed_regs/rules/2002/fr0321.htm

MISCELLANEOUS

The Internet and Controlled Substances

With the onset of e-commerce and Internet pharmacies (see Regulation of Pharmaceuticals chapter) comes the question of how Internet pharmacies fit into existing DEA requirements for the prescribing and dispensing of controlled substances. On April 27, 2001 in the *Federal Register* (66 FR 82) the DEA published a guidance document entitled *Dispensing and Purchasing Controlled Substances over the Internet*. The document is intended to provide guidance not only to pharmacists but also to prescribers, law enforcement authorities, regulatory authorities, and the public about the application of current laws and regulations as they relate to dispensing, purchasing, or importing controlled substances. The document stresses that while the DEA is working on revisions to its regulations, currently, prescriptions for controlled substances may not be electronically transmitted and that current regulations (ie, written and manually signed prescriptions required for Schedule II substances still apply).

The notice generally clarifies that consumers must have valid prescriptions to obtain controlled substances legally. It also emphasizes that consumers or any other entity cannot legally purchase controlled substances from foreign supplier Internet sites and have them shipped to the United States, unless the consumer or entity is registered with the DEA as a controlled substance importer and is in compliance with all other DEA requirements. The document clarifies that the Personal Use Exemption for Controlled Substances Purchased Abroad does not apply to controlled substances purchased from a foreign Internet site. That exemption allows individuals to bring a limited quantity of controlled substances into the US for their use only when they bring them across the border in their possession. It does not apply to controlled substances being shipped into the United States.

Comprehensive Methamphetamine Control Act of 1996

The Comprehensive Methamphetamine Control Act of 1996 was signed into law on October 3, 1996. The primary purpose of this law was to control the distribution of certain precursor chemicals used in the production of methamphetamine. The law also sought to increase the penalties for trafficking and manufacture of methamphetamine and its precursor chemicals. The law sets forth registration requirements, transaction limits, recordkeeping requirements, and reporting requirements for persons possessing or distributing certain "listed chemicals." These listed chemicals are precursor chemicals used in the manufacture of methamphetamine and include ephedrine, pseudoephedrine, and phenylpropanolamine. All of these chemicals also are active ingredients found in many lawfully marketed nonprescription drug products. The intent of the law was not to regulate normal *otc* sales of these products, but to regulate sales of any significant quantities of these chemicals. For example, in July 1997, law enforcement personnel arrested 3 subjects and seized 144 cases of pseudoephedrine tablets that contained a total of 1,244,160 tablets. Each case (8640 tablets) contained enough pseudoephedrine to manufacture 11 oz of methamphetamine. In an effort not to interfere with legitimate *otc* sales of these chemicals, the Act exempts from the regulations "ordinary" *otc* sales. This includes products sold in blister packs and products containing no more than 3 g of pseudoephedrine or phenylpropanolamine. Sales of pseudoephedrine or phenylpropanolamine not in blister packs or containing more than 3 g per pack are limited to 24 g per single transaction. Sales of combination ephedrine products also are limited to 24 g per single transaction.

More Methamphetamine Legislation

In a large piece of legislation called the Children's Health Act of 2000 lie bits of legislation that further act to control the existence and proliferation of methamphetamine use and trafficking.

The first of these, the Methamphetamine Anti-Proliferation Act of 2000, directs the US Sentencing Commission to amend the federal sentencing guidelines with respect to any offense relating to manufacture, importation, exportation, or trafficking in amphetamine by reviewing and amending its guidelines to make the base level of penalities for amphetamine comparable to the base offense level for methamphetamine. This act also provides for mandatory restitution for CSA violations. This includes restitution for cleanup of clandestine laboratory sites and reimbursement for costs incurred for the manufacture of amphetamine (as well as methamphetamine). It expands reimbursement to state and local governments, as well as the United States. Illicit substance manufacturing operations are treated as crimes against property. The legislation also attempts to decrease the retail sales threshold for non-safe harbor products containing pseudoephedrine and phenylpropanolamine.

To the author's knowledge, there is no indication that this has been initiated yet. In addition, the legislation directs the commission to amend sentencing guidelines to provide enhanced penalties for CSA violations involving 1) ephedrine, phenylpropanolamine, and pseudoephedrine; and 2) other list I chemicals.

Emergency Kits

Controlled Substances Maintained Aboard Ocean Vessels

Special provisions apply to maintenance of controlled drugs in medicine chests or dispensaries aboard ocean vessels. (See 21 CFR §1301.25.) The controlled drugs are held aboard ship under the supervision of the ship's medical officer, who must register with the DEA. If no medical officer is employed by the owner of the ship, the master of the ship may procure controlled drugs on approval and with order forms furnished by the Public Health Service. The term "ocean vessels" as used in §1301.28 encompasses any vessel engaged in international trade or in trade between ports of the United States and any merchant vessel belonging to the US government.

Controlled Substances Maintained Aboard Commercial Aircraft

Special provisions apply to maintenance of controlled drugs in medicine chests or first-aid kits aboard aircraft operating under a certificate from the Federal Aviation Administration (FAA). The controlled drugs must be purchased by, and stored and dispensed under, the supervision of a medical officer employed by the airline and registered with the DEA. (See 21 CFR §1301.25.)

Controlled Substances Maintained at LTCFs

Controlled substances may be placed in emergency kits in an LTCF that is not registered if the appropriate state agency or regulatory authority specifically approves the placement of the drugs and promulgates procedures which delineate the following:

(1) The source of the controlled drugs must be a DEA-registered pharmacy, hospital, or practitioner.
(2) Both the LTCF and the supplier must maintain accountability records for the controlled drugs and take periodic inventories.
(3) Security safeguards must be instituted, including designation of individuals having access to the kits.
(4) Administration of the controlled drugs to LTCF patients must be by authorized personnel only and only as expressly authorized by 21 CFR §1306.11(c) and §1306.21(c).
(5) State authority must outline prohibited activities that can result in revocation, denial, or suspension of the privilege of having controlled drugs in the LTCF emergency kit.

These requirements were not adopted as a DEA regulation in the CFR but were issued as a DEA Statement of Policy in 1980 (45 Fed. Reg. 24128)].

Storage and Security Requirements

Storage and physical security requirements for controlled substances for pharmacies and institutions are found in 21 CFR §1301.75. Schedule I controlled substances must be stored in a securely locked, substantially constructed cabinet. Schedules II, III, IV, and V substances must be stored in a securely locked, substantially constructed cabinet or distributed throughout the inventory of noncontrolled drugs in a manner which will obstruct theft or diversion of the controlled substances.

Disposal of Excess Controlled Substances

A registrant wishing to dispose of excess or undesirable controlled substances in any schedule should request DEA form 41, and upon receipt, list the substances and submit 3 copies of the completed form to the DEA regional director. The regional director will send instructions for disposal pursuant to 21 CFR §1307.21.

Disposal of excessive amounts of residual and wasted controlled substances in the hospital setting is provided for in the regulations. In a situation typical of hospital medication administration, a physician may order a 60 mg dose of *Demerol* (meperidine) injection, but only a 75 mg ampule is available. Pursuant to state law or regulation, the hospital nurse is permitted to dispose of the 15 mg residual *Demerol* provided a written report is made in the hospital narcotic records. This procedure is permitted under 21 CFR §1307.21(c).

Self-Prescribing

Some states prohibit a physician from self-prescribing controlled substances, while others do not. A prescriber should not issue a controlled substance or legend drug prescription in the name of another person when he intends the prescription for his own use. Such a prescription is invalid as a purported prescription because it misrepresents the name of the patient. A pharmacist having actual knowledge of such misrepresentation cannot legally fill the purported prescription. Another view of the same situation would be that a physician is not acting in the usual course of professional practice when he is treating himself, and thus a self-prescribed prescription is not valid.

Compliance

Compliance with DEA regulations will not necessarily constitute compliance with state drug control laws or regulations. 21 CFR §1307.02 specifically states that compliance with the federal controlled substance regulations is not construed as compliance with other federal or state laws unless expressly provided in other such laws.

In many instances, state controlled substances statutes and regulations are almost identical to their federal counterparts. Hence, compliance with DEA regulations equates compliance with the state controlled drug statutes and regulations. In most instances, however, the state controlled drug statutes and regulations have a few unique provisions that impose stricter controls than the federal law. If the restrictive provision is not in conflict with the federal law and regulations, it must be followed by the practitioner in that state.

Mailing Controlled Substances

The US Postal Service regulations formerly allowed only prescription medicines containing nonnarcotic controlled substances to be mailed from a practitioner or dispenser to an ultimate user and prohibited the mailing of narcotic controlled substances. In October 1994, the regulations were amended to allow the use of mail service to carry prescription medicines containing narcotic drugs or other controlled substances. (See Postal Service 39 CFR §111.) Of course, courier services such as United Parcel Service or Federal Express also could be used. To see more information on this subject, refer to DEA's *Pharmacist's Manual*, located on its web site.

Manufacturing Quotas for Controlled Substances

21 CFR §1303.01-1303.37 deal with production, procurement, and manufacturing quotas applicable to people registered with DEA as manufacturers of controlled substances. Manufacturers apply on or before May 1 of each year for a quota that is set July 1 for the next calendar year. The purpose of the quota is to limit the total quantity of Schedules I and II

substances to an amount needed to provide for the estimated medical, scientific, research, and industrial needs of the United States, for lawful export, and for the establishment and maintenance of reserve stocks.

ENFORCEMENT AND PENALTIES FOR VIOLATIONS OF THE CONTROLLED SUBSTANCES ACT

The DEA enforces the CSA. In addition to its regulatory powers, the DEA can enforce the law by its inspection, seizure, and arrest powers. Pharmacy inspection and drug accountability audits are discussed in detail in the Pharmacy Inspection chapter.

The DEA investigates alleged CSA violations committed by nonregistrants and registrants alike. Most DEA activity, however, is directed toward illicit street drug traffic. The DEA also focuses attention on practitioners who distribute or sell controlled drugs outside of the usual course of their professional practice in violation of the law. If the DEA has evidence of a registrant's alleged violations, it may conduct an administrative hearing to determine if a violation has occurred, or it may bypass the hearing and immediately turn the evidence over to the office of the US Attorney for civil or criminal prosecution.

Violations by Nonregistrants and Registrants

Section 401(a) of the CSA (21 U.S.C. §841[a]) provides that "except as authorized by this subchapter, it shall be unlawful for any person knowingly or intentionally:

(1) To manufacture, distribute or dispense, or possess with intent to manufacture, distribute or dispense, a controlled substance; or

(2) To create, distribute or dispense, or possess with intent to create, distribute or dispense, a counterfeit substance."

A counterfeit substance is a "controlled substance" that because of identifying marks falsely purports to be or is represented to be the product of the original manufacturer. (See 21 U.S.C. §802[7] for exact definition.)

Violations by Registrants

Section 402(a) of the CSA (21 U.S.C. §842[a]) makes it unlawful for any person who is a registrant or an employee of a registrant to distribute or dispense a controlled substance in violation of 21 U.S.C. §829 (the prescription dispensing section). Other violations under this section are summarized as follows:

(1) Distribution and dispensing of a controlled substance by registrants unauthorized by their registration (eg, a dispenser acting as a wholesaler of controlled drugs or a manufacturer making a controlled substance that he or she is unauthorized to make);

(2) a registrant distributing a controlled substance in violation of the labeling and packaging requirements of §825;

(3) violation of the recordkeeping requirements; and

(4) violation of the inspection requirements.

In October 1998, as a part of an Omnibus Consolidated and Emergency Supplemental Appropriations Act, the portion of the CSA dealing with civil violations for recordkeeping was amended (Public Law 105-277, Oct. 21, 1998). The legal standard was changed from a "strict liability" standard to a "negligence" standard and the maximum civil penalty was reduced from $25,000 per penalty to $10,000 per penalty. The government now has to prove that a recordkeeping violation was due to a negligent act rather than an unintended mistake or omission. In addition, the conference report on the bill gives factors that the attorney general should consider in assessing whether to pursue civil penalties and in determining the appropriate amount of the fine to be assessed associated with recordkeeping violations. They are:

(1) Whether diversion actually occurred or if the recordkeeping violations are of such a nature that it cannot be determined whether diversion occurred;

(2) whether actual or potential harm to the public resulted;

(3) whether the violations were intentional or negligent in nature;

(4) whether the violations were a first-time offense;

(5) time intervals between inspections where no or any serious violations were found;

(6) whether violations were multiple occurrences of the same type of violation;

(7) whether and to what extent the defendant profited from the illegal activity; and

(8) the financial capacity of the defendant to pay the fine assessed.

In addition, the attorney general may take into account whether the violator has taken immediate and effective corrective actions. In appropriate situations, the attorney general shall act through informal procedures such as warning letters. The civil penalty limit of $10,000 per violation is a ceiling and the attorney general has the discretion to request and the courts the discretion to waive or impose amounts less than this limit as the circumstances warrant.

Other violations under §842(a) and (b) include removal, alteration, or obliteration of a symbol or label required on controlled substances and a manufacturer making controlled substances in excess of an assigned quota.

Section 403(a) of the CSA (21 U.S.C. §843) prohibits any person who is a distributor registrant of Schedules I and II controlled substances to distribute knowingly and intentionally such substances except pursuant to an order or order form as required under 21 U.S.C. §828. Other prohibitions under this section relate to using a fictitious, revoked, or suspended DEA number; obtaining a controlled drug by fraud, misrepresentation, or deception; furnishing false or fraudulent material information in or omitting material information from an application, report, record, or document required under the CSA; and making, distributing, or possessing any device designed to make or render a drug a counterfeit substance. Subsection (b) prohibits knowingly or intentionally using any communication facility in the commission of a CSA violation.

Violations Committed Knowingly or Intentionally

Violations of §842(a), if not committed knowingly or intentionally, are punishable by a civil penalty of up to $25,000, but violations committed with knowledge or intent incur a criminal penalty of up to 1 year in jail, a fine of up to $25,000, or both, for the first offense. Subsequent convictions will incur a penalty of up to 2 years in jail, a fine of up to $50,000, or both.

Violations of §843(a) are punishable by up to 4 years in jail, a fine of up to $30,000, or both, for the first offense. A violator with a prior conviction will receive a higher penalty.

Violations of §844(a) are punishable by up to 1 year imprisonment, a fine of up to $5000, or both. A second offense is subject to a higher penalty. See 21 U.S.C. §844(b) for details concerning conditional discharge and expunging of records for a first offense.

The illegal distribution of controlled substances to minors or pregnant women doubles the penalty that would otherwise attach to the violation, as does the employment or use of minors in drug operations. Special penalties are provided for distributing or manufacturing a controlled substance in or near a school (see 21 U.S.C. §845 [A]).

Several comments concerning the penalties for violations discussed above are appropriate. First, in reference to the higher penalty for a subsequent conviction, the prior conviction can be for a violation of either the same or a different provision of the federal CSA or any state controlled substances act or narcotic control law. The second observation is that the federal CSA does not prescribe mandatory imprisonment; the sentence may be stayed or suspended, and probation may be given for all violations except those under §848 involving a continuing criminal enterprise. The term "continuing criminal enterprise" means that the violator is acting in concert with 5 or more persons in a position of supervisor, manager, or organizer and that the violator receives substantial income from the illegal activity. In addition, §845 prescribes twice the authorized penalties for violations of §841(a)(1) if the unlawful distribution is to a person under 21 years of age.

If a pharmacist violates the federal CSA, the penalty section that will apply to the violation will depend essentially on whether the violation was committed knowingly and intentionally or, conversely, if it was unintentional or merely a "technical" violation. An unintentional recordkeeping violation without evidence of illegal drug distribution is punishable under §842(c)(1), where the first conviction is subject to a civil penalty. Similarly, if the offense involves a few isolated instances of inadvertently refilling a Schedule III or IV prescription beyond its 6-month issuance date or refilling it more times than the number of authorized refills, the violator, if prosecuted, probably would be prosecuted under the same §842(c); however, there is no guarantee that the violator would not be prosecuted under the more severe §841(a)(1) or §842(c)(2)(A).

Violations of the CSA committed knowingly or intentionally can subject the violator to prosecution under the more harsh penalties of 21 U.S.C. §841(a), the criminal sanctions of §842(c)(2)(A), or other applicable criminal penalty sections.

How are the terms "knowingly" and "intentionally" defined in reference to violations of federal law? The term "knowingly," when used to prove that a defendant knowingly committed an act which the law forbids, generally is defined as an act done voluntarily and intentionally and not because of a mistake, accident, or other innocent reason. The purpose of adding the word "knowingly" to statutory prohibitions is to ensure that no one will be convicted of an act done because of a mistake, accident, or other innocent reason.

The term "intentionally," when used to prove that a defendant intentionally committed an act which the law forbids, is more difficult to define precisely, and often the terms "knowingly" and "intentionally" have been used interchangeably. However, the term "intent" is definable. The following explanation regarding intent as used in a judge's instruction to the jury was approved in *U.S. v. Lawson*, 483 F.2d 535 (1973):

Intent may be proved by circumstantial evidence. It rarely can be established by any other means. While witnesses may see and hear and thus be able to give direct evidence of what the defendant does or fails to do, there can be no eyewitness account of the state of mind with which the acts were done or omitted. But what the defendant does or fails to do may indicate intent or lack of intent to commit the offense charged.

It should be kept in mind that a federal or state violation involving controlled substances could also have severe and very negative implications for a pharmacist's licence with the board of pharmacy to practice pharmacy.

Examples of Court Cases

In *U.S. v. Kershman*, 555 F.2d 198 (1977), a pharmacist was convicted both of knowingly and intentionally distributing *Dilaudid* (a Schedule II narcotic drug) in violation of 21 U.S.C. §841(a)(1) and conspiracy in violation of §846.

The reported facts are that the defendant had been a pharmacist for 39 years and had owned a pharmacy for the previous 10 years. An undercover operation by police authorities resulted in the arrest of 2 suspects leaving the defendant's pharmacy with 3 bottles of *Dilaudid*. When the police immediately approached the pharmacist, he produced 3 prescriptions for the *Dilaudid*. Later, a search warrant was served and numerous order forms and prescriptions were seized pursuant to it. The controversy in the case was whether the pharmacist in good faith believed that the prescriptions were for a legitimate medical purpose and were issued in the usual course of the physician's professional practice.

More specifically, the question put to the jury was framed in the following language: ". . . if you find that the prescriptions for *Dilaudid* which the defendant filled . . . . were not issued for a legitimate medical purpose by a physician during the usual course of his professional practice and that under the facts and circumstances known to him the defendant had every reason to believe that such purported prescriptions had not been issued for a legitimate medical purpose, and that the defendant deliberately and consciously closed his eyes to what he had every reason to believe was the fact, such a studied avoidance of positive knowledge is a circumstance from which you may reasonably draw the inference and find, in the light of the surrounding circumstances shown by the evidence in this case, that the defendant knew that such purported prescriptions had not been issued for a legitimate medical purpose, and hence were knowingly filled by him."

Surrounding circumstances in this case were that the defendant received 1600 *Dilaudid* tablets from June 17 to July 13, 1976 and that *Dilaudid* is prescribed very rarely and used almost exclusively for terminal cancer patients. Furthermore, a police undercover agent had arranged for a $4000 purchase of 425 *Dilaudid* tablets from one of the suspects. The suspect was followed to the pharmacy and was arrested with the *Dilaudid* after leaving. These events took place in September 1976, shortly after the 1600 *Dilaudid* tablets were received by the pharmacy. The conviction was affirmed.

In *U.S. v. Hayes*, 595 F.2d. 258 (1979), a pharmacist was convicted of violating 21 U.S.C. §841(a)(1) and 21 CFR §1306.04(a). The regulation places the responsibility for the proper prescribing and dispensing of controlled drugs upon the prescribing physician, but a corresponding responsibility rests with the pharmacist filling the prescription.

In the *Hayes* case, the pharmacist's argument was stated succinctly that, in fulfilling the requirements of 21 CFR §1306.04, all that a pharmacist can do to verify the bona fide status of the prescription is to check with the issuing practitioner; action beyond that would require the pharmacist to examine the patient, which he is neither qualified nor legally permitted to do. (This is a good argument; past court cases have held that a pharmacist is not to second-guess the physician in the prescribing of large quantities of a narcotic drug.) However, the court argued that the facts of this case show that a pharmacist can know when prescriptions are not issued for a legitimate medical purpose. The reported facts were that the defendant had filled 34 prescriptions for a total of 3400 *Dilaudid* tablets in 1 month for the same individual who paid $3400 for them.

Additionally, the pharmacist had filled 75 prescriptions for *Preludin* at $75 each (or $5625) for the same person. The pharmacist had a supply of the individual physician's prescription blanks, which he gave customers to have filled and signed by the physician. The physician testified that at the time he had no legitimate patients (the physician was an alcoholic who moved from one temporary lodging to another) and that the prescriptions written by him were not in the usual course of medical practice or for a legitimate medical purpose.

Under those facts, the circumstantial evidence was sufficient to prove that the pharmacist knew that the prescriptions were not issued for a legitimate medical purpose. The Court of Appeals, in affirming the conviction, held that ". . . when a pharmacist fills a prescription that he knows is not a prescription within the meaning of the regulations, he is subject to the penalties of §841."

Specific Guidelines for the Pharmacist in Filling Prescriptions for Controlled Drugs

The cases previously discussed are extreme examples of bad faith on the part of the pharmacist in dispensing controlled drugs pursuant to an obvious purported prescription. There are numerous situations in pharmacy practice in which the conscientious pharmacist has a difficult judgment call as to the validity of the controlled drug prescription. A state case clarifies professional standards in this gray area.

In *Talman v. Dept. of Registration and Education*, 397 N.E.2d 151 (1979), a pharmacist appealed to the court an order of the state licensing department revoking his pharmacist's license. The revocation was based on pharmacy board findings and conclusions that he was guilty of "gross immorality" for billing an insurance company for services not provided, for violating the good faith requirement in dispensing controlled drugs under the state CSA, and for failing to follow CSA recordkeeping requirements "in conformance with federal law" and "any additional rules and forms issued by the Department."

The reported facts are that an accountability audit showed shortages; the pharmacist dispensed 194 bottles of *Hycomine* syrup (a controlled drug) to a single family in an 8-month period; he dispensed 1000 *Preludin* tablets during the year; and certain wholesaler invoices were missing from his records. In rebuttal, the pharmacist testified that the several missing invoices were destroyed in a basement flood of his pharmacy; he had had one robbery and burglary of controlled substances (supported by police reports, one of which showed 400 *Preludin* tablets stolen), and he was able to locate prescriptions for many of the shortages on the audit.

In reference to dispensing the alleged excessive amounts of *Hycomine* syrup, the pharmacist testified that he called the prescribing physician and that he also spoke to a physician at the hospital to verify whether the family required such large amounts of the drug. The hospital physician confirmed that the family suffered from a condition requiring *Hycomine*.

On the issue of good faith, the court upheld the pharmacy board on the grounds that it is made up of pharmacists and "we must assume the Board possesses the necessary knowledge and expertise to determine when a lack of good faith is shown by a pharmacist in the dispensing of large quantities of controlled substances to a single family." The Illinois statute that set forth the accepted professional standards for dispensing controlled substances included, but was not limited by, the following considerations:

(1) Lack of consistency in the physician-patient relationship;
(2) frequency of prescription for the same drug by one prescriber for large numbers of patients;
(3) quantities beyond those normally prescribed;
(4) unusual dosages;
(5) unusual geographical distances between patient, pharmacist, and prescriber; and
(6) consistent prescribing of habit-forming drugs.

The court indicated that these standards set forth in the statute served as guidelines to the pharmacist as to what might constitute lack of good faith. As to the pharmacist in this case, the court's reported facts were that 400 stolen *Preludin* tablets represented only a small portion of the controlled substances shortages shown by the audit. Because of that and a lack of good faith finding by the pharmacy board on the *Hycomine* dispensing, the court upheld a lower circuit court's ruling that the pharmacist violated the Pharmacy Practice Act. However, the same lower court held that the pharmacy board's finding of "gross immorality" had to be dismissed because earlier Illinois cases held the term to be unconstitutionally vague. The case was remanded to the lower court, which, in turn, sent the matter back to the pharmacy board for reconsideration of the "revocation" penalty because the "gross immorality" charge was dismissed.

In the *Talman* case, it would appear that a stronger argument could be made that the pharmacist acted in good faith in attempting to verify the legitimacy of the *Hycomine* prescriptions. He consulted the prescriber as well as another physician who had apparent knowledge of the family's condition. However, the *Hycomine* situation was not the only damaging evidence against the pharmacist in *Talman*. In the *Hayes* case, the court considered the merits of the argument that the pharmacist checked with the prescriber, and thereby, the pharmacist lacked the knowledge that the prescription was outside the scope of professional practice since the prescriber verified it. The court said such verification was evidence of good faith but was not insurance that a jury would find that the verification was false. That is, the prescriber might lie about the legitimacy of his reason for issuance of the prescription, making the prescription a purported prescription only. The court stated that ". . . a pharmacist can either fill a prescription or decline to do so."

There is no hard and fast assurance to the pharmacist, who must use professional judgment in determining if a controlled substance prescription is issued in the usual course of the practitioner's medical practice. However, the *Talman* case at least provides some guidelines.

Consumer Violations (Illegal Possession)

Section 404 of the CSA (21 U.S.C. §844) prohibits any person from knowingly or intentionally possessing a controlled substance except pursuant to a valid prescription or order of a practitioner issued in the course of professional practice or except as otherwise authorized under the CSA.

Penalties

A sentence of imprisonment of from 10 years to life, or a fine of $4,000,000, or both, could be imposed on a person convicted of manufacturing, distributing, or dispensing the following amounts or more of controlled substances:

1 kg of a mixture or substance containing heroin;

5 kg of a mixture or substance containing coca leaves (unless cocaine, ecgonine, and their derivatives and salts have been removed); cocaine, its salts, optical and geometric isomers, and salts of isomers; or ecgonine, its derivatives, their salts, and salts of isomers;

50 g of the above with a cocaine base;

100 g of PCP;

1 kg of a mixture or substance containing PCP;

10 g of a mixture or substance containing LSD;

400 g of a mixture or substance containing N-phenyl-N-[1]-(2-phenylethyl)-4-piperidinyl) propanamide or 100 g of a mixture or substance containing an analog of the substance;

or 1000 kg or more of a mixture or substance containing marijuana.

The penalty is imprisonment of from 5 to 40 years or a $2,000,000 fine, or both, for violations involving certain smaller amounts of those substances. For other controlled substances in Schedule I or II, the penalty is not more than 20 years in prison, $1,000,000, or both. These penalties are greater if death or serious bodily injury results from the use of such substances or if the defendant is a repeat offender or other than an individual.

The preceding penalties were enacted through the Narcotic Penalties and Enforcement Act of 1986, which is subtitle A of the Anti-Drug Abuse Act of 1986 (P.L. 99-570), October 27, 1986.

SOURCES OF ADDITIONAL INFORMATION

Vivian JC. Changing Schedules. *US Pharm.* 2002;27:9 (http://www.uspharmacist.com/ index.asp?show=article&page=8_940.htm).

Study Questions

CONTROLLED SUBSTANCES

(1) Exactly how does the Controlled Substances Act (CSA) differ from earlier drug control laws in its approach to controlling access to regulated substances?

(2) Finish this sentence: "The _____ is the federal agency responsible for enforcement of the _____; it is a unit of the _____ within the US Department of _____."

(3) The term "controlled substance analog" is defined as a substance, intended for human consumption, that is substantially similar to a controlled substance in:
(a) its chemical structure.
(b) its effect on the CNS.
(c) a person's representation or intention of effect.
(d) b and c
(e) all of the above

(4) Schedule I drugs:
(a) have a high potential for abuse.
(b) have a currently accepted medical use in the United States.
(c) include drugs such as methadone.
(d) a and b
(e) all of the above

(5) Schedule II drugs:
(a) have a high potential for abuse.
(b) have a currently accepted medical use in the United States.
(c) include drugs such as nicocodeine.
(d) a and b
(e) all of the above

(6) Schedule III drugs:
(a) have the potential for severe psychological or physical dependence.
(b) include drugs such as anabolic steroids.
(c) include drugs such as phenobarbital.
(d) a and b
(e) all of the above

(7) Schedule IV drugs include:
(a) anabolic steroids.
(b) diphenoxylate.
(c) benzodiazepines.
(d) b and c
(e) all of the above

(8) Schedule V combination drugs most often are used for:
(a) antidiarrheal action.
(b) antiemetic action.
(c) antitussive action.
(d) a and c
(e) all of the above

(9) List 9 independent activities for which separate registration generally is required by the DEA.

(10) DEA regulations require the prescription label for a controlled substance to contain the name and address of the pharmacy, the patient's name, date of dispensing, directions for use, and:
(a) prescription serial number.
(b) pharmacy registration number.
(c) cautionary statements.
(d) a and c
(e) all of the above

(11) According to the CSA, an individual practitioner:
(a) is any individual licensed or permitted to dispense controlled substances in the course of professional practice.
(b) must keep records of Schedule II to V drugs that are prescribed or administered.
(c) need not keep records of all dispensed Schedule II to V drugs.
(d) a and b
(e) a and c

(12) Fill in the blanks in the following statement the following: Pharmacy registrants are required under the CSA to keep records of: Initial and subsequent biennial _____ records of controlled drugs _____ of controlled drugs and records of their _____ and _____.

(13) List 4 items of information that must be included in the records kept on any specific controlled substance.

(14) What constitutes a record of receipt for Schedule II drugs? Under what conditions? What constitutes a record of receipt for Schedules III, IV, and V drugs? Under what stipulation?

(15) Janice's pharmacy is installing a computerized data processing system, and she would like to use this system to keep refill records for Schedules III and IV drugs. Can she do this? If no, why not? If yes, what basic conditions must apply?

(16) Janice discovers that a colleague has distributed controlled substances to his original supplier. Can he do that? Explain. (Cite the law to prove your answer either way.)

(17) Suppose that Janice discovers that a physician, whose prescriptions she has been filling, is being charged with issuing controlled substance prescriptions to patients, knowing that these patients were dispensing these drugs to others. Janice remembers thinking that one prescription could be invalid, but when she had called this physician, he had given her a satisfactory explanation, so she had filled the prescription. Has Janice fulfilled her responsibilities in this physician's case? How liable is she?

(18) Give examples of mid-level practitioners who may prescribe controlled substances.

(19) A midwife claims that she has authority "under DEA regulations" to prescribe controlled drugs. What's the catch?

(20) Dr. Jeremy Castillo has his nurse phone in a prescription. Demonstrate on the line below how you might "sign" the prescriber's name on the prescription form.

_____

(21) Which of the following statements is not true?
  (a) A partially filled prescription for a Schedule II drug must be filled within 72 hours.
  (b) Partial filling of Schedule II prescriptions can be filled for a period of up to 60 days for a patient with a terminal illness.
  (c) When an emergency oral prescription is written for a Schedule II drug, the amount dispensed is limited to the quantity necessary to cover a period of 60 days only.
  (d) a and b
  (e) b and c

(22) Which of the following statements is not true?
  (a) Hospital physicians may order "take-home" controlled drugs via a chart order when releasing a patient after a long-term stay.
  (b) A single dose of a controlled drug may be dispensed pursuant to a medication order for a patient treated and released from a hospital emergency room.
  (c) As a rule, a controlled substance prescription may not be legally predated or post-dated.
  (d) a and b
  (e) b and c

(23) Methadone detoxification treatment is the:
  (a) continued administering or dispensing of methadone in conjunction with provision of social and medical services at relatively stable dosage levels for a period in excess of 21 days.
  (b) the administering or dispensing of methadone as a substitute narcotic drug in decreasing doses to reach a drug-free state in a period not to exceed 21 days.
  (c) use of the drug as an oral substitute for heroin or other morphine-like drugs for an individual dependent on one or more of these drugs.
  (d) b and c
  (e) all of the above

(24) The 1998 Omnibus Consolidated and Emergency Supplemental Appropriations Act:
  (a) changed the legal standard for recordkeeping violations from a "strict liability" standard to a "negligence" standard.
  (b) changed the legal standard for recordkeeping violations from a "negligence" standard to a "strict liability" standard.
  (c) changed the legal standard for distribution violations from a "strict liability" standard to a "negligence" standard.
  (d) changed the legal standard for distribution violations from a "negligence" standard to a "strict liability" standard.

(25) The illegal distribution of controlled substances to minors or pregnant women:
  (a) doubles the penalty otherwise attached to the violation.
  (b) is defined as a "continuing criminal enterprise."
  (c) is defined as a "technical violation."
  (d) a and b
  (e) a and c

(26) Intent:
 (a) may be proved by circumstantial evidence.
 (b) must be determined by more than circumstantial evidence.
 (c) is not definable.
 (d) a and c
 (e) b and c

Critical Thinking Applications

(1) Daryl represents a well-known drug company. One of his responsibilities is to manage a team of researchers who monitor efficacy studies, adverse reaction reports, and contract hospitals' research uses of specific substances manufactured by his company. One day, several members of Daryl's team report that a drug used in a long-term 8-hospital study has been shown to be more appropriately categorized in a different schedule of substances than the one it is currently assigned to. What initial step could Daryl take in attempting to get this substance transferred to a different schedule?

(2) Jackie is a pharmacist in a Veterans Administration hospital. She finds it rewarding to provide services in this facility but becomes frustrated when her state government contacts her to say that she must be reviewed by the state board; it is one official's belief that Jackie's pharmacy is not operating according to all state pharmacy law regulations. When she reports this to her administrator, he says, "You're in compliance with all regulations that you're bound to. These other people have no need to review you." Assuming that Jackie's supervisor knows what he's talking about, comment on the particular aspects of Jackie's subjectivity to specific drug control laws. What is unusual about Jackie's case that might not apply to all pharmacists in her state?

(3) Becca and her fiancé Roberto both work in small community pharmacies in neighborhood shopping centers. Becca is in Baltimore; Roberto is in San Diego. Both pharmacies discover contradictions between federal and state laws for pharmacy operations. Roberto's pharmacy chooses (correctly) to comply with state law; Becca's chooses (correctly) to comply with the federal statute. How can both pharmacies be right—or can they? Give every possible explanation in your answer.

(4) Create a table that will show the differences in CSA registration and reregistration guidelines for the following types of activities: Opening a pharmacy in a mall as a limited partnership; opening a pharmacy in a hospital; transferring ownership of a pharmacy; modification of a registration.

(5) Using the headings below, create a table that contrasts information needed in an inventory record for (a) each controlled substance in a finished form and for (b) a controlled substance maintained for extemporaneous compounding. Controlled Substance Inventory Data; Finished Form; Bulk Form for Compounding

(6) Three pharmacists, Jack, Jess, and Imani, are discovered to have sold or distributed Schedule II drugs to other registrants. Jack has distributed such drugs to other pharmacy registrants, as well as physician registrants; Imani, only to pharmacy registrants. At the end of the year, Jack is notified that he must register with the DEA as a distributor. Imani is not so notified. Jess is investigated for dispensing controlled substances to a physician, even though these drugs were only for office use. a. Under what conditions can Jack and Imani distribute Schedule II drugs to other registrants? Cite the law as well. b. Why does Jack receive a directive to register as a distributor, whereas Imani does not? c. Why is Jess in trouble?

(7) Form teams with your colleagues, with each team researching and presenting one of the court cases presented under the section "General Issuance Requirements" for prescriptions. Prepare a list of questions in which your team asks the rest of the class to predict the outcome. Tell the other students to leave space between each of their predictions to take notes on how close their predictions were. Then present your case. As you approach the answer to each question, pause and remind the other students to reflect on their predictions and then correct or add notes to each predicted answer. This activity reinforces matters of law for you as you prepare your case in an entertaining way; it also reinforces these points for the other class participants because prediction has been acknowledged as an excellent way to focus and thus take in new information and immediately apply it (by evaluating one's predictions).

(8) Jeff, a licensed pharmacist, receives a faxed prescription for a Schedule II drug for a patient in an LTCF. He is preparing to fill this prescription when Anne, his new supervisor, says, "I don't know if state law will permit you to fill a faxed prescription." Carrie, a third pharmacist, overhears this and says, "He's okay. DEA regulations permit faxed prescriptions of Schedule II drugs for patients in long-term care." "Maybe so," Anne says, "but I still can't let him do it, because I don't know what state law says." "Doesn't matter," Carrie smiles. "DEA is a federal agency. Federal law overrides state law. Go ahead and fill it. You'll be all right." "I don't think we can make that assumption," Anne says. Without knowing anything else about this case, who do you think is correct?

(9) Anne's pharmacy is asked to accept a transfer of information for an original prescription refill for a Schedule III drug; the customer is not able to get the refill at the original pharmacy. Oddly enough, Phil's and Leo's pharmacies receive similar requests on the very same day. Anne, Leo, and Phil reside and are licensed to dispense in the same community. However, while Phil and Anne are each permitted to accept and provide these refills (for different reasons, by the way), Leo is not. Explain what Leo's situation must be. Also, what might be the 2 "different reasons" for Phil's and Anne's participation in these transfers.

(10) To aid your own understanding of the law cases presented in this unit, divide yourselves into teams to each prepare a presentation and in-class quiz over one of the following cases: *U.S. v. Kershman*, 555 F. 2d 198 (1977); *U.S. v. Hayes*, 595 F. 2d 258 (1979); *Talman v. Dept. of Registration and Education*, 397 N.E. 2d 151 (1979). Researching and preparing one of these cases, including an in-class quiz, does more to help the student "teachers" learn the case than it does those who will listen (although they also benefit considerably from the student-led presentations).

Chapter 4

Pharmacy Inspection

Constitutional Considerations, 175
    Probable Cause, 176
    Exclusionary Rule, 177
    Inspections without Warrants, 178
    Licensing Exception, 179
    Arrest Situations, 179
    Consent to Inspection or Search, 180
    Emergency Situations, 180
    Inspections of Areas Open to the Public, 180

Types of Inspections, 181
    State Board Inspections, 181
    Food and Drug Administration Inspections, 182
    Drug Enforcement Administration Inspections (Drug Accountability
        Audits), 182
    Special Inspection Situations, 183

Practical Applications, 184
    Inspection Formats, 184
        FDA Inspections, 184
        DEA Inspections, 185
            Miranda Warning, 185
        Municipal Inspections, 186
        Special Situations, 187

What to Do and Not Do When the Inspector Comes, 187

Conclusion, 188
    Proper Method for Challenging an Unlawful Inspection, 188

Sources of Additional Information, 189

Study Questions, 191

Pharmacy Inspection

CONSTITUTIONAL CONSIDERATIONS

The Fourth Amendment of the U.S. Constitution provides protection from an unreasonable governmental search in that it guarantees that "the right of the people to be secure in their persons, houses, papers, and effects, against unreasonable searches and seizures, shall not be violated, and no warrant shall issue, but upon probable cause, supported by oath or affirmation, and particularly describing the place to be searched, and the persons or things to be seized."

The Fourth Amendment has been characterized as "the one procedural safeguard in the Constitution that grew directly out of the events that immediately preceded the revolutionary struggle with England." Prior to the Declaration of Independence, the British used a legal device called a "general warrant" to search the premises and products of colonial merchants and businessmen for noncompliance with Parliamentary revenue acts (notably the Stamp Act of 1765). The general warrant was issued on whim; it was not necessary to support the warrant with evidence that the revenue law was being violated. Equally irritating to the colonists was the "writ of assistance" document, which gave the King's customs officials power to search at large for smuggled goods.

Therefore, the framers of the Fourth Amendment were concerned with protection of both home and business from "unreasonable searches and seizures" and were concerned that "... no warrants shall issue, but upon probable cause...." Most court cases dealing with Fourth Amendment rights center around the application of the key provisions "unreasonable" and "probable cause."

The safeguards of the Fourth Amendment applied only to criminal searches until 1967 when the U.S. Supreme Court extended Fourth Amendment protection to administrative inspections. Prior to 1967, the courts held the opinion that **searches by administrative agencies** were noncriminal in nature and that such searches represented only a minimal intrusion into personal privacy. The companion cases of *See v. City of Seattle*, 387 U.S. 541 (1967) and *Camara v. Municipal Court*, 387 U.S. 523 (1967) initiated a new era of judicial thinking in the area of governmental inspection. Based on the decisions in these two cases, a search warrant is required, as a general rule, when an administrative inspection is to be conducted, even if commercial premises like a pharmacy are involved. Justice White, writing for the Court in *See v. City of Seattle*, stated the following:

> ... a search of private houses is presumptively unreasonable if conducted without a warrant. The businessman, like the occupant of a residence, has a constitutional right to go about his business free from unreasonable official entries upon his private commercial property. The businessman, too, has that right placed in jeopardy, if the decision to enter and inspect for violation of regulatory laws can be made and enforced by the inspector in the field without official authority evidenced by a search warrant.

The protection accorded by the *Camara* and *See* cases was expanded by the U.S. Supreme Court with its 1978 decision in the case of *Marshall v. Barlow's, Inc.*, 436 U.S. 307, where the Court had the opportunity to comment on the basic purpose of the Fourth Amendment:

> ... the Fourth Amendment prohibition against unreasonable searches protects against warrantless intrusions during civil as well as criminal investigations (citing *See v. City of Seattle*, 387 U.S. 541 [1967]). The reason is found in the "basic purpose of this Amendment ... (which) is to safeguard the privacy and security of individuals against arbitrary invasions by governmental officials."

The *Barlow's* decision also reiterated the general rule that, "... warrantless searches are generally unreasonable and this rule applies to commercial premises as well as homes... Except in certain carefully defined classes of cases, a search of private property without proper consent is 'unreasonable' unless it has been authorized by a valid search warrant."

Constitutionally recognized rights, such as the requirement of a **search warrant**, must be balanced with the government's duty to protect public health, safety, and welfare. The courts have not had an easy time balancing these two basic considerations, and a number of exceptions have arisen from the general rule requiring a search warrant. This discussion focuses on the **governmental inspection** of commercial premises, but many of the principles apply to the search of private, residential quarters. The inspection of private businesses by government agencies is an intrusion that is often necessary and is frequently authorized by statute. The search may be conducted pursuant to a warrant, or the situation may permit a warrantless search.

Probable Cause

The U.S. Constitution states that no search warrant may be issued except upon **probable cause**. Such a requirement demands more than suspicion on the part of the investigating agency. **Probable cause** exists when the circumstances would convince a reasonable person to believe that a crime has been committed or that the property to be searched will contain items related to a criminal act. Probable cause is concerned with probabilities—the factual and practical considerations of everyday life on which reasonable and prudent men act. The underlying circumstances or evidence to establish probable cause are usually presented in the form of an affidavit to the judicial officer who has been petitioned to issue a search warrant.

Because of the nature of an **administrative inspection**, it has been difficult for courts to require the stringent probable cause standards of a criminal case. For example, it is highly unlikely that board of pharmacy inspectors, hoping to conduct a routine inspection of a pharmacy, would have evidence that a crime has been committed. One by-product of *See v. City of Seattle* is, to use the terminology of Justice Clark, a "new-fangled warrant" in the form of the **administrative inspection warrant**. The inspection warrant differs from the traditional search warrant in that a judge or magistrate issues an inspection warrant merely upon application, with supporting affidavits showing that a substantial period of time has passed since the last inspection (*United States v. Prendergast*, 436 F.Supp. 931 [W.D.Pa. 1977]). In contrast, a traditional search warrant is issued only on affidavits establishing probable cause that evidence of a crime will be found at the place to be searched.

The two 1967 Supreme Court decisions helped define the criteria necessary to provide a right of entry for purposes of an administrative inspection. The Supreme Court, realizing that the inspector usually will not possess evidence of a code or regulatory violation, concluded that "... if a valid public interest justifies the intrusion contemplated, then there is probable cause." Administrative searches or inspections can be predicated on a number of reasonable standards, such as the simple passage of time since the last inspection. Thus, the administrative inspection warrant is easier to justify legally but is more limited in scope than a search warrant.

The new probable cause standards have been applied in cases involving pharmacy inspections. In *United States v. Anile*, special agents of the Bureau of Narcotics and Dangerous Drugs (BNDD) (now called the Drug Enforcement Administration [DEA]) visited a West Virginia pharmacy to conduct an inspection. As a result of the inspection, the pharmacy owner was arrested because of discrepancies in the pharmacy's controlled substances records. Although the case primarily focused on the voluntariness of the pharmacist's consent to a warrantless search, the court also stated that "the standards that apply to administrative inspections are not, by their very nature, the same that apply to criminal searches and seizures." (352 F. Supp. 14 [N.D.W.Va. 1973]).

The legality of a pharmacy inspection under the Controlled Substances Act (CSA) was tested in *United States v. Greenberg (334 F. Supp. 364 [W.D.Pa. 1971])*. The court reasoned that in the usual probable cause situation, the issuance of a warrant was supported with evidence that a crime had been committed, and that the premises to be inspected contained the fruits of the criminal act. The court noted that an inspection warrant under the CSA is different:

... We believe that in the absence of any evidence of the commission of some violation of the Act, a valid public interest in the enforcement of the Act could still be shown. For instance, there is a valid public interest in ensuring compliance with the record keeping requirements of the Act. To this end it would seem entirely proper to conduct an inspection of a particular premises simply because a substantial period of time had passed since the last inspection. In the instant case no inspection had ever been made of the premises in question.

Although the search warrant and the inspection warrant have some similarities, it is important to recognize the difference in probable cause standards as described above. Other differences should also be noted. A search warrant may be served night or day, although the *Federal Rules of Criminal Procedure* impose special requirements on nighttime warrants. A search warrant permits forcible entry; officers executing the search warrant must announce their purpose and authority. Admittance must be denied, or denial must be implied from the circumstances before entry may be forced. A search warrant delineates, with particularity, the items sought and the place to be searched; it is restrictive as to whom it is directed.

In contrast, the administrative inspection warrant usually is servable only during normal business hours. It is less specific than the search warrant in describing the scope of inspection. It does not allow forcible entry. "Regular business hours" does not mean at the convenience of the owner or the pharmacist in charge of the premises to be inspected. It means the time when the establishment is normally open for business. If a pharmacy were open on a 24-hour basis, an inspection could occur at any time even though the manager may not be present all the time.

Exclusionary Rule

A discussion of the Fourth Amendment is important because of the impact of the **exclusionary rule**, which has developed in the area of search and seizure. This rule states that evidence obtained against a defendant by law enforcement officers (either state or federal) in a search or inspection that was later judicially determined illegal on constitutional grounds cannot be used in court against the defendant. The exclusionary rule was first established in *Weeks v. United States*, 232 U.S. 383 (1914), where it applied only to federal courts. Later, it was made equally applicable to state prosecutions by the ruling in *Mapp v. Ohio*, 387 U.S. 643 (1961).

The exclusionary rule can have considerable impact on the course of a trial. If all the incriminating evidence that the prosecution has against a defendant is inadmissible, then the defendant will probably not be prosecuted. The case likely will be dropped for lack of evidence.

The exclusionary rule has been enforced in certain cases of pharmacy inspections. In *United States v. Pugh*, 417 F.Supp. 1019 (W.D.Mich. 1976) the court ruled certain evidence inadmissible because it was seized by the DEA acting only on an inspection notice (Form DEA-82) when an inspection warrant was constitutionally required. In *United States v. Anile*, 352 F.Supp. 14 (N.D.W.Va.1973), a motion to suppress evidence seized during a federal agency inspection was granted by the court, and the court ordered the evidence returned to the defendant. The basis for this decision was the fact that the government agents did not present a search warrant to the pharmacist when they arrived at the pharmacy to conduct the search and the pharmacist was told he had no choice but to submit to the search. This invalidated the search.

In *United States v. Enserro*, 401 F.Supp. 460 (W.D.N.Y. 1975), DEA agents threatened the pharmacist on duty with criminal penalties unless he signed a consent form permitting the inspection. The pharmacist agreed to the search, and the agents uncovered discrepancies in the controlled substances inventory. During the subsequent legal action, the court ruled that the representations made by the agents were erroneous and the consent to search was not legally effective. Thus, evidence obtained as a result of the inspection was suppressed; it was not permitted to be used at the trial.

The exclusionary rule has been criticized for "deflecting the truthfinding process" and "freeing the guilty." Those involved in law enforcement think that it frustrates justice because it occasionally allows a criminal to go free from prosecution. The courts have found some disfavor with the rule, which was formulated as a deterrent against unlawful police practices. There has been a movement in the judiciary and in Congress to soften the impact of the exclusionary rule to limit evidence excluded from a trial only when an officer has knowingly broken the law in collecting that evidence.

Inspections without Warrants

A search warrant or administrative inspection warrant is not required in all instances: (1) If the search is incidental to a lawful arrest and is confined to an area in the immediate control of the arrestee; (2) in emergency situations presenting imminent danger to health and safety; (3) in exigent circumstances where immediate action is needed to prevent removal or destruction of the evidence or to prevent danger to the inspectors; (4) when entry and inspection are limited to areas of commercial premises open to the public; (5) when the search is in an "open field," when the inspector is in pursuit of an escaping suspect, or if the item sought is in plain view (provided that the inspector is legally in the place where he sees the item and its discovery is inadvertent); (6) in situations when the warrant is not constitutionally required as decided by the U.S. Supreme Court on a case-by-case basis; and (7) when consent to the search is freely, voluntarily, knowingly, and understandingly given.

The *Camara* and *See* cases required search warrants for administrative inspections, but there are a number of important exceptions to this requirement. The first significant case holding a warrantless inspection constitutional was *Colonnade Catering v. United States*, 397 U.S. 72 (1970). The case involved confiscated liquor and other evidence obtained by agents of the Federal Alcohol and Tobacco Tax Division during a search without a warrant. The agents were acting under the authority of a federal law that allowed such inspections in the liquor industry. The U.S. Supreme Court held the relevant statute valid because it did not authorize forcible entries without a warrant and because the liquor industry had a long history of "close (governmental) supervision and inspection."

In another important case, *United States v. Biswell*, 406 U.S. 311 (1972), the U.S. Supreme Court upheld an inspection without warrant of a firearms dealer under the Federal Gun Control Act of 1968. The Court's reasoning was that, while the gun industry was not as governmentally regulated as the liquor industry, inspections were a "crucial part of the regulatory scheme," and a person choosing to deal in firearms knows ahead of time that "his business will be subject to inspection." The rule stated by the Court in *Biswell* was that "Congress could constitutionally authorize warrantless regulatory inspections as long as they are carefully limited in time, place, and scope."

Both the *Colonnade* and *Biswell* cases set the stage for a number of case rulings interpreting the inspection provisions applicable to pharmacies. In *United States v. Business Builders, Inc.*, 354 F.Supp. 141 (N.D.Okla. 1973), a federal court upheld warrantless inspections under Section 704 of the Federal Food, Drug and Cosmetic Act. The court indicated that consent to an inspection is immaterial because the inspection statute took the place of a valid search warrant.

In the area of state cases, *United States ex rel. Terraciano v. Montayne*, 493 F.2d. 682 (2nd Cir. 1974), a New York statute allowing warrantless inspections of pharmacies was upheld, but the court suggested that New York amend its law to incorporate the inspection warrant safeguard. In contrast, the Supreme Court of Florida held that information obtained from warrantless inspections of pharmacies under a Florida statute could not be used in a state criminal prosecution (see *Olson v. State*, 287 So.2d. 313 [Fla. 1973]).

A 1984 New Jersey trial court decision confirmed the state's right to conduct warrantless administrative searches of a pharmacy. The pharmacist challenged the constitutionality of routine, unannounced inspections by the New Jersey Board of Pharmacy. The court concluded that the pharmacist had no expectation of privacy because state statutes required a review of prescription records and included special rules for dispensing poisons and controlled substances. Furthermore, the pharmacy had been inspected 4 times in the last 3 years. The judge found it unrealistic to conclude that the owner had no expectations that the pharmacy would, from time to time, be inspected by government officials (see Greenblatt v. New Jersey Board of Pharmacy, 518 A.2d 1116 [N.J. Super. App. Div. 1986]).

Licensing Exception

The Colonnade and Biswell decisions gave rise to what has been termed the licensing exception to the general rule. This is also known at times as the "highly regulated industry" exception. These cases fall into that category of situations where warrants are not constitutionally required based on a case-by-case analysis by the U.S. Supreme Court. The licensing exception has been used by the courts in upholding warrantless searches of businesses and industries that are regulated heavily by the federal government.

Businesses with histories of close governmental regulation are subject to warrantless searches as long as the searches are specifically authorized by statutes limiting the time, place, and scope of inspection. The courts have ruled that those businesses that are licensed and extensively regulated have few expectations of privacy; thus, judges have justified the creation of an exception to the general rule. It is claimed that the exception is actually a situation of **implied consent**, inasmuch as the licensee expects frequent inspections and gives implied consent to a warrantless search when the license is granted.

The implied consent theory has been applied in some legal actions involving pharmacy inspections. In McKaba v. Board of Regents of the State of New York (294 N.Y.S.2d 382 [1968]), a pharmacist's failure to object to a warrantless inspection raised questions regarding the admissibility of the evidence obtained. The court stated, "In accepting his license, the petitioner accepted the incident obligation of keeping the required records and permitting their inspection. The dangers and hazards of narcotics to health and public safety are known to all. Such records are nonprivileged records required by statute to be kept for proper regulation and protection of the general public, and their inspection without a search warrant was constitutionally valid."

In Olson v. State of Florida, 287 So.2d 313 (Fla. 1973), a Florida court ruled that a warrant was required to search a pharmacy, unless the situation fit within defined statutory exceptions. However, the dissenting justice wrote that a "pharmacist agrees to all reasonable drug inspections by the state when licensed, and waives the right to object...." The U.S. Supreme Court has not yet specifically ruled whether an applicant's acceptance of a pharmacy license implies consent to warrantless regulatory inspections.

The Ohio Supreme Court has concluded in the case of Stone v. City of Stow, et al., 593 N.E. 2d 294 (Ohio 1992) that because pharmacy is a pervasively regulated profession, a pharmacist has a reduced expectation of privacy in the prescription records he or she keeps. Therefore, an administrative search warrant was not required.

The implied consent or licensing exception to the general rule appears to have some acceptance based upon existing cases, but there is no strong move by the judiciary to adopt the exception. The courts are expected to continue to scrutinize carefully situations in which a warrant may not be constitutionally required.

Arrest Situations

In the usual sense, an arrest occurs when a law enforcement officer stops an individual and restrains him or her from walking away. An **arrest** is an intentional taking into custody of a person by taking, seizing, or detaining them. Sometimes all that is needed to effect an arrest is the officer declaring to the suspect that they are "under arrest" and the suspect then acquiescing to the officer's custody.

Not every detention is an arrest. Police questioning without forced detention is not an arrest. Furthermore, reasonable detection and frisking by police on the suspicion that the person stopped has committed a crime and is armed is permissible based on the ruling in *Terry v. Ohio*, 392 U.S. 1 (1968).

When a warrantless search is made incidental to an arrest, the issue of whether there was, in fact, an arrest becomes crucial. If the arrest was not legal, there could not be a legal search. In a case involving temporary street detention, a federal court ruled that an arrest occurred when the stop was totally arbitrary, and the detention was too long. A New York law provides that police may stop any person for temporary questioning in a public place whom the officer reasonably suspects is committing, has committed, or is about to commit a felony. However, in *People v. Anonymous*, 265 N.Y.S.2d 705 (1965), the court made the adroit ruling that an officer could not stop a defendant simply because he was "carrying books in Hicksville."

Consent to Inspection or Search

Consent that is freely given has been well recognized as an exception to the warrant requirement of the Fourth Amendment. The courts have insisted that any relinquishment of constitutional rights must be made clear, must be intentional, and that individuals in control of premises to be inspected must not be misled by inspectors. In the case of *United States v. Anile*, a pharmacy owner asked BNDD inspectors, "Do I have a choice?" or words to that effect. The agents replied that the owner did not, and a search was made. In the subsequent legal action, the Court concluded that, "Having not been fully advised of the circumstances of his rights, the defendant's consent was not valid. Mere acquiescence to authority is not consent."

Any **waiver of Fourth Amendment rights** by a pharmacist must be knowledgeable and freely given in order to be legally enforceable. However, it should be noted that consent standards are less stringent in administrative inspections than in those relating to criminal cases.

Emergency Situations

In *See v. City of Seattle*, it was indicated that warrantless inspections are permissible when there is imminent public danger to health or safety. In the case of *Norman Bridge Drug Co. v. Banner et al.*, 529 F.2d 822 (5th Cir. 1976), the DEA seized a pharmacist's stock of controlled drugs on a claim of "imminent public danger." The court rejected the claim, and upon application by the pharmacist, a restraining order was issued to limit government action. However, there seems to be little doubt that in a case presenting a true imminent public danger (eg, contaminated food or drugs), a warrantless seizure and inspection would be upheld.

Inspection of Areas Open to the Public

The search of the public areas of business premises is exempt from the requirement of a warrant because privacy in these areas is not expected. In the California case of *People v. White*, 65 Cal. Rptr. 923 (1968), the court held that an inspection of areas on hospital premises open to the public was not subject to the warrant requirements enunciated by the U.S. Supreme Court. Furthermore, in the same case, it was held that an implied consent to the warrantless inspection existed because in accepting a license to operate a hospital, consent to supervision and inspection, as required by licensing statutes, was implied. In *White*, the violation was flagrant; no nurse or other qualified person was on duty when the inspector came.

The exceptions discussed above have been fashioned to balance the public's interest in regulating certain business activities against the constitutional protection from unreasonable searches and seizures. In 1978, the U.S. Supreme Court again examined the question of warrantless searches in *Marshall v. Barlow's, Inc.*, 436 U.S. 307. The *Barlow's* case centered around the constitutionality of a section of the Occupational Safety and Health Act (OSHA) that permitted Occupational Safety and Health Administration inspectors to search premises without a warrant. Barlow, the owner of an electrical and plumbing installation business, refused to allow an OSHA inspector to enter the nonpublic area of the premises for a routine inspection. The ensuing legal controversy ended in the U.S. Supreme Court with the Court concluding that OSHA inspections conducted without a warrant violate the Fourth Amendment unless consent to search has been obtained. This is so despite the fact that the federal statute in question specified that it was a crime to prohibit an OSHA inspector to enter the premises to conduct an inspection (29 U.S.C. §657[a]). This is a classic example of a conflict between a statute and the Constitution, with the latter prevailing because it is the higher form of law. It is also a good example of the clear wording of a statute that should not be taken at face value.

In the *Barlow's* case, the government argued that searches by OSHA investigators should be included within the licensing exception that had been developed for closely regulated businesses. The Supreme Court rejected the government's contention that all businesses involved in interstate commerce had given implied consent to OSHA inspections. Even though the court reaffirmed the general rule against warrantless inspections, it did not answer the question of what types of business are regulated so pervasively as not to require a warrant for inspection. Because it has a tradition of governmental regulation, the practice of pharmacy qualifies for inclusion in the carefully defined cases in the licensing exception. There is little expectation of privacy by those who handle controlled substances and poisons, but no U.S. Supreme Court decision has yet addressed the issue of pharmacy inspections. Readers are reminded that even though warrantless inspections of pervasively regulated businesses or professions may be permissible, such inspections must be authorized by statute and the administrative inspection warrant must specify the time, location, and scope of the inspection; and describe the items to be inspected. For example, a New York case (*State of New York v. Loorie, et al.*, 630 N.Y.S.2d 483 [1995]) focused on a warrant issued to seize computers and disks believed to be used in an alleged insurance fraud scheme. The court there ruled that the warrant did, by implication, authorize the searching of the information on the hard drive and the diskettes.

TYPES OF INSPECTIONS

State Board Inspections

The most common governmental intrusion endured by the pharmacist is the periodic visit to the pharmacy by the pharmacy board inspector. Usually, the inspection is not traumatic and is routine; it is more educational than investigative. The inspector will check pharmacy compliance with the laws and regulations pertaining to pharmacy staffing, sanitary conditions, and professional equipment, as well as perhaps compliance with mandatory continuing education requirements of the state. The State Pharmacy Act may well contain a provision similar to that found in the Model Pharmacy Act promulgated by the National Association of Boards of Pharmacy:

> The Board of Pharmacy shall be responsible for the control and regulation of the practice of pharmacy in this state, including, but not limited to, the following:
>
> Inspection of any licensed person and appropriate records at all reasonable hours for the purpose of determining if any provisions of the law governing the legal distribution of drugs or devices or the practice of pharmacy are being violated. The Board of Pharmacy, its officers, inspectors, and representatives shall cooperate with all agencies charged with enforcement of the laws of the United States, of this state, and of all other states relating to drugs, devices, and the practice of pharmacy (§213[a][12]).

Most pharmacists freely consent to the state board inspection, unless a personality clash arises between the pharmacist and the inspector. Although this type of inspection is usually innocuous, the pharmacist should be aware of a situation where the inspection becomes a search for incriminating evidence.

Food and Drug Administration Inspections

Food and Drug Administration **(FDA) inspections** of pharmacies are rare. This is because the Federal Food, Drug, and Cosmetic Act (FDCA) contains an exemption from the authorization given to the FDA to conduct inspections for the following:

> Pharmacies which maintain establishments in conformance with any applicable local laws regulating the practice of pharmacy and medicine and which are regularly engaged in dispensing prescription drugs or devices, upon prescriptions of practitioners licensed to administer such drugs or devices to patients under the care of such practitioners in the course of their professional practice, and which do not, either through a subsidiary or otherwise, manufacture, prepare, propagate, compound, or process drugs or devices for sale other than in the regular course of their business of dispensing or selling drugs or devices at retail (21 U.S.C. §374[a][2][A]).

Usually, the FDA agent only calls at the pharmacy to inquire about or look for the presence of a recalled drug or drug banned from the market. The FDA might inspect a pharmacy on the basis of some complaint lodged with the agency on the basis of Prescription Drug Marketing Act investigations involving alleged sales of samples (see discussion in Regulation of Pharmaceuticals chapter) or the investigation of pharmacies engaged in manufacturing or repackaging. In case of the last situation, the FDA will be inspecting the pharmacy's operation as it relates to current good manufacturing practices requirements (see Recordkeeping Under the FDCA).

The FDCA (21 U.S.C. §374) gives the FDA inspection powers that at least one court has characterized as taking the place of a search warrant (*United States v. Business Builders, Inc.*, 354 F.Supp. 141 [N.D.Okla. 1973]). However, the inspection must always satisfy **reasonable time** and, more importantly, **reasonable limit** tests.

The FDCA provides that FDA inspectors are authorized "to inspect, at reasonable times and within reasonable limits and in a reasonable manner, such factory, warehouse, establishment, or vehicle, and pertinent equipment, finished and unfinished materials, containers, and labeling therein ... Each such inspection shall be commenced and completed with reasonable promptness." (See 21 U.S.C. §374.)

The FDA apparently has taken the position that its inspections fall within the boundaries of those cases that permit warrantless searches of heavily regulated businesses. It is felt that there is little expectation of privacy by those who deal with food and drugs. The statutory limitations on the time, manner, and scope of FDA inspections fit in well with the dictates of the cases espousing the implied consent or licensing exception. The various federal courts have reached different conclusions when deciding whether FDA agents must obtain a warrant prior to an inspection. Though considerable uncertainty exists in this area, the weight of authority seems to support warrantless FDA inspections, even in light of the *Barlow's* decision. In *United States v. New England Grocers Supply Co.*, 488 F.Supp. 230 (D.Mass. 1980), the court stated that it did not read *Barlow's* as requiring a "knee-jerk invalidation of the warrantless inspections authorized by Section 374 (of the FDCA)." However, the nation's highest court has not specifically addressed the point. Questions remain as to the legality of **warrantless FDA inspections**.

Drug Enforcement Administration Inspections (Drug Accountability Audits)

The type of inspection often feared by pharmacists is the Drug Enforcement Administration **(DEA) inspection**, in particular the drug accountability audit. This audit determines if the purchase records, inventory, and disposition records (prescriptions and invoices) accurately account for a pharmacy's stock of controlled substances. If the audit shows substantial discrepancies, the involved pharmacist may be charged with illegally distributing controlled drugs, failing to keep and maintain controlled drug records, or furnishing false information in such records.

The **accountability audit inspection** is not limited to the DEA. In some states, a state authority has the power, under the Uniform State Controlled Substances Act, to conduct this type of pharmacy inspection. The state inspectors or DEA compliance investigators may come armed with an administrative inspection warrant issued by a magistrate or judge. An audit may be conducted pursuant to "voluntary consent," and the DEA Notice of Inspection (Form DEA-82) provides for such. However, the courts sometimes find that the consent is not voluntary, especially if prescriptions or other records are seized by the inspectors (see the case of *United States v. Pugh*, 417 F.Supp. 1019 [W.D.Mich. 1976]).

An accountability audit made pursuant to an administrative inspection warrant was upheld as valid in *United States v. Schiffman*, 572 F.2d 1137 (5th Cir. 1978) and in *United States v. Prendergast*, 436 F.Supp. 931 (W.D.Pa. 1977). In the *Schiffman* case, the pharmacist argued that there was no "probable cause" to support the issuance of the warrant. The court held that large purchases of controlled substances by a pharmacy was enough to create a valid public interest or probable cause to issue an administrative inspection warrant.

The provisions of the Controlled Substances Act of 1970 (CSA) were drafted by Congress shortly after the *Camara* and *See* cases were handed down by the U.S. Supreme Court. Even though DEA inspections might have fallen into the exception of heavily regulated businesses, Congress chose specifically to require an administrative inspection warrant in nonconsensual searches. The CSA outlines certain situations in which an inspection warrant is not required, such as initial registration inspections, emergencies, and dangerous health situations. The inspection of financial data, pricing data, and sales data by DEA agents is prohibited by statute unless the owner or pharmacist in charge consents in writing.

Special Inspection Situations

The pharmacist as a person in charge of business premises may be inspected by OSHA agents. However, inspections by OSHA are more or less on a random basis, except in instances of a complaint. The *Marshall v. Barlow's* case held that, in the absence of voluntary consent, the OSHA agent needed an administrative inspection warrant to gain entry and inspect the nonpublic portions of the business.

Some pharmacies have been faced with inspections by a state agency responsible for administering the Medicaid program. These inspections must comply with the general rules previously described because the inspections are being conducted by those representing the government. In a Louisiana action, an inspector for the Medicaid Fraud Control Unit of that state discovered prescription vials labeled with the drug's brand name but containing a generic version in a nursing home. During the investigation, it was found that the pharmacy had billed the state for the brand name product but had dispensed a cheaper generic version. The pharmacy refused to allow an administrative inspection of its prescription records, but the court held that the pharmacy clearly understood that when it began to participate in the Medicaid program, its records might be inspected by the state. The pharmacy could have no reasonable expectation of privacy regarding prescriptions dispensed to Medicaid patients (*Matter of Rozas Gibson Pharmacy of Eunice, Inc.*, 383 So.2d 929 [La. 1980]). Bear in mind that pharmacies participating in Medicaid prescription drug programs may also have consented to the search or inspection when signing and submitting the participating provider contract to the state.

State pharmacy practice acts require the pharmacist to make available certain records for copying and inspection by board inspectors and other designated law enforcement officers. For example, the state laws regarding the sale of poisons often require the pharmacist to maintain a poison sale register and to open it to inspection by designated law enforcement personnel. Similarly, the state Uniform Controlled Substances Act requires the pharmacist to maintain a Schedule V record book and to have it available for inspection along with other controlled substance records. There is no known court case challenging the constitutionality of such laws. Apparently, this type of record inspection has not caused significant problems. If challenged, the courts might uphold such inspections without warrants on the basis of both the implied consent theory and the necessity of inspection and copying as means of enforcing the law.

PRACTICAL APPLICATIONS

Inspection Formats

Despite Fourth Amendment protection, various federal and state statutes authorize entry and inspection without warrant in certain defined circumstances. Failure to permit such entry and inspection may be penalized by imposition of a fine, imprisonment, or loss of license.

FDA Inspections

Section 704 of the Federal FDCA (21 U.S.C. §374) permits FDA entry and inspection of establishments where drugs are held. However, it should be borne in mind that there is a major exemption for pharmacies engaging in traditional functions (see Food and Drug Administration Inspections). The FDA can gain such entry merely upon presentation of credentials and a Notice of Inspection, but the inspection must be made at a reasonable time, in a reasonable manner, and be reasonably limited. Section 301(f) of the FDCA (21 U.S.C. §331[f]) prohibits anyone from refusing entry and inspection as authorized by §704; §303(a) authorizes a penalty of up to 1 year in jail, a $1000 fine, or both for anyone violating §301.

FDA inspectors will show their credentials and state their purpose, which may be merely to inquire about a drug illegally on the market. The pharmacist should insist on seeing credentials, including a photo identification. However, federal law prohibits photocopying, counterfeiting, or misuse of official credentials (18 U.S.C. §201). Therefore, one may examine the credentials and record the official's name, badge number, ID number, etc, but do not photocopy them. If the FDA intends to conduct an inspection or to take samples from the drug inventory, the agent will present a Notice of Inspection (Form FD-482). A copy of the inspection notice does not need to be provided by the agents, and more importantly, the reason for the inspection or what is hoped will be found does not need to be stated (see *Daley v. Weinberger* 400 F.Supp. 1288 [E.D.N.Y. 1975]).

The person in charge of the pharmacy is required to allow entry and inspection upon the presentation of the FDA Notice of Inspection. However, if that person refuses, the FDA will usually obtain an inspection warrant from the U.S. District Court. Refusal in the face of this warrant may result in arrest.

There are limits to what the FDA may do in conducting an inspection. To help ensure that the agency does not exceed its jurisdiction, the pharmacist should ask to consult with an attorney (preferably, of course, one with experience with administrative inspections) before the inspection begins. If the inspector refuses to delay the inspection, the pharmacist should permit it to start but contact an attorney as soon as possible.

Upon inspection, if the FDA finds fault with the establishment, a written Inspection Observation (FDA Form FD-483) will be provided to the person in charge. If samples of drugs are taken during the inspection, the FDA agent will leave a receipt for the samples (FDA Form FD-484) and pay for them. The person receiving payment must sign one copy of the receipt.

The pharmacist should not take Form-483 lightly. If not properly handled, the document could lead to an enforcement action or prosecution. Unclear or inaccurate statements on Form-483 should be pointed out immediately. With the assistance of counsel, the pharmacist should respond to the FDA and identify the steps being taken to correct any deficiencies.

DEA Inspections

Section 510 of the CSA (21 U.S.C. §880) authorizes DEA entry and inspection of controlled premises. The term "controlled premises" is defined as including places where controlled substances are manufactured, held, distributed, or dispensed.

DEA inspections are made either pursuant to voluntary consent and Notice of Inspection, or to an administrative inspection warrant. The person in charge of controlled premises has a constitutional (Fourth Amendment) right to refuse consent to inspection and to insist that the DEA obtain an administrative inspection warrant (see DEA regulation §1316.08.)

Once the DEA has the administrative inspection warrant, entry and inspection must be permitted. Refusal to heed the warrant and to permit entry and inspection and impeding the inspection are violations of §402(a) of the CSA (21 U.S.C. §842[a][6]), which carry a civil penalty of up to a $25,000 fine or, if the violations are committed "knowingly," the penalty is up to one year in jail, up to a $25,000 fine, or both. The word "knowingly," when used in a criminal statute, means an action was committed voluntarily and intentionally—not because of mistake, accident, or other innocent purpose.

The DEA inspector or compliance investigator will show his credentials, state his purpose, and either (1) present a Notice of Inspection, which asks the person in charge to submit voluntarily to inspection and entry (to sign a waiver or right to inspection warrant) or (2) announce that he has an administrative inspection warrant. A copy of the inspection warrant usually is not left unless items are seized; in that event, a copy of the warrant as a receipt for the seized items is left at the premises inspected. The inspection warrant must be returned to the court within 10 days.

There is a difference between the FDA Notice of Inspection (Form FD-482), which requires mandatory submission to inspection, and the DEA Notice of Inspection (Form DEA-82), which asks for voluntary submission to inspection. Furthermore, the DEA Notice of Inspection of Controlled Premises informs the owner or pharmacist in charge that (1) there is a constitutional right not to have an administrative inspection made without an administrative inspection warrant; (2) there is a right to refuse to consent to the inspection; (3) anything said or found of an incriminating nature may be seized and used against the owner or pharmacist in charge; (4) a copy of the Notice of Inspection has been presented to the party being inspected; and (5) consent may be withdrawn at any time during the course of the inspection.

The owner or pharmacist in charge may want to give limited consent for only a certain portion of the premises or for particular records. In such cases, the limited consent should be documented and signed by both parties.

A court-issued administrative inspection warrant (federal or state) requires entry and inspection under pain of penalty. In such cases, the Miranda warning usually is given but may not be required.

Miranda Warning

In *Miranda v. Arizona*, 384 U.S. 436 (1966), the U.S. Supreme Court laid down the rule that under the Fifth Amendment a law enforcement officer's custodial interrogation of an accused individual must be preceded by the following warning:

- The accused or person in custodial interrogation has a right to remain silent.
- Any statement that the accused makes may be used against him or her.
- The accused has a right to have a lawyer present before he or she is questioned.
- If the accused cannot afford to hire a lawyer, a lawyer will be provided for him or her at the expense of the government.

In addition, later cases indicate that an individual does not need to deny any untrue accusation made against him under the penalty that his silence will be interpreted as an admission of the accusation (*Commonwealth v. Dravaecz*, 227 A.2d 904 [Pa. 1967] and *United States v. Hale*, 422 U.S. 171 [1975]).

If the law enforcement officer does not give the requisite warnings, the statements of the person in custodial interrogation may not be admitted into evidence at a trial.

The Miranda warning, when given, is given either orally, in writing, or both. It is addressed to the accused in the second person (eg, "You have the right to remain silent.") The people receiving the warning then may either waive their rights or refuse to waive them. If the person being interrogated refuses to waive his or her rights, the law enforcement officer may not continue the questioning. However, if the questioning continues, the statements are inadmissible in court. If the accused gives the officer background information or answers some questions, it may later be determined, judicially, that he or she had waived his/her right to remain silent.

What is "custodial interrogation"? The courts are not in complete agreement on the meaning of this term. In the Miranda case, the court said that custodial interrogation is "... questioning initiated by law enforcement officers after a person has been taken into custody or otherwise deprived of his freedom of action in any significant way." A number of federal courts have defined the term as meaning the time when the accused becomes the focus of a criminal investigation.

In general, the Miranda warning is not applicable to a pharmacy inspection. In a pharmacy inspection, the pharmacists are not in custody. They are free to depart; if necessary, they may close the pharmacy for the day and leave. If the inspection is focusing on the pharmacist as a suspect, the inspector often will give the Miranda warning; the warning may be required if the suspect is being questioned in the investigator's office, if the suspect is free to leave (*Beckwith v. U.S.*, 425 U.S. 341 [1976]).

The importance of the Miranda warning can be exemplified by a pharmacy inspection case, *United States v. Goldfine*, 538 F.2d 815 (9th Cir. 1976). During the course of an investigation, a DEA compliance investigator, after giving the Miranda warning, asked the pharmacist if he made any out-of-state purchases. The pharmacist stated that he had not. The answer proved false, and the pharmacist was convicted of violating a federal law (18 U.S.C. §1001) because of his false answer. In *Goldfine*, the court pointed out that the accused can say nothing or plead the Fifth Amendment, and either action cannot be used against him. However, in this case, the DEA investigator took the precaution of giving the warning, and the accused pharmacist apparently failed to heed it. The pharmacist waived his rights by answering the question, and giving a false answer to a federal official opened him to criminal prosecution.

The **pharmacy board inspectors** will usually show only their credentials and state their purpose when making a routine inspection. They may ask permission to enter and inspect, unless consent to the inspection is obvious, as in cases of initial inspections on applications for new pharmacy permits. Sometimes the board inspector will leave a copy of a report indicating items in need of correction or improvement and may ask the pharmacist in charge to sign for receipt of the report.

Municipal Inspections

Business establishments are subject to a variety of municipal inspections, including those by health officials, building inspectors, fire inspectors, and weights and measures inspectors. Usually, municipal inspectors show their badges and ask permission to inspect. If permission is refused, a judicial administrative inspection warrant is necessary before penalties can be invoked against the individual denying entry, except in emergency situations or upon the opening of new establishments.

Special Situations

Special situations include inspections by designated law enforcement officials of poison sale records and narcotic sale records. Various statutes authorize such inspections and copying of records and require the pharmacist to permit them. Usually, an inspection of this type is not focused on the pharmacist as a suspect but is conducted to gain evidence on a suspected drug abuser or narcotic addict. Consequently, in most instances a court would find that the authorizing statute takes the place of a warrant, but again, the ultimate test is the reasonableness or unreasonableness of the intrusion.

What To Do and Not Do When the Inspector Comes

Pharmacists who want to assert or protect their constitutional rights when a government agent comes to inspect should examine and ascertain the agent's credentials and purpose. The pharmacist should make a notation of the agent's name, agency, and badge number. If the agent's purpose is to conduct a drug accountability audit, the pharmacist should demand that the agent present an administrative inspection warrant. If the agent has an administrative inspection warrant, this need only be announced.

A DEA Notice of Inspection (Form DEA-82) is not an administrative inspection warrant. If an FDA agent presents Form FD-482, he or she is entitled to entry and inspection because the FDA notice takes the place of the administrative inspection warrant if the inspection is limited in scope. If the FDA agent wants to conduct an accountability audit of a pharmacy, he or she probably will need an administrative inspection warrant (and the pharmacist could insist on such) because the authorizing law (§704 of the FDCA) limits the scope of pharmacy inspections. If the agent has no administrative inspection warrant but insists on conducting a drug accountability audit, the pharmacist should not resist. The audit should be submitted to after first asserting a demand for the administrative inspection warrant.

The U.S. Supreme Court in *United States v. DiRe* (332 U.S. 581 [1947]) stated,

> Courts will hardly penalize failure to display a spirit of resistance or to hold futile debates on legal issues ... with an officer of the law. A layman may not find it expedient to hazard resistance on his own judgment of the law at a time when he cannot know what information, correct or incorrect, the officers may be acting upon... It is the right of (any)one...to reserve his defense for the neutral tribunals erected by the law for the purpose of judging his case.

If an inspector announces that there is an administrative inspection or search warrant but will not present it, the pharmacist should yield and allow entry and inspection. However, the pharmacist may assert that the inspection is being allowed **under protest**.

Refusal to permit execution of an administrative inspection warrant or to impede the inspector in the execution of the same violates §402(a)(6) of the CSA or 21 U.S.C. §842(a)(6) and may lead to the arrest of the violator (see DEA regulation §1316.12. Also refer to 18 U.S.C. §1501 or applicable state law).

The pharmacist, in that case, should not interfere with the inspection, audit, or seizure of records or prescriptions. If items are seized, a copy of the warrant will be left. Again, it is sufficient to state verbally to the agent that the inspection is allowed under protest and upon reliance that the administrative inspection warrant (or search warrant) is valid.

An inspection or search can be contested later in a court action for emergency injunction, quashing the warrant and suppressing any seized evidence (see *Weyerhauser v. Marshall*, 452 F.Supp. 1375 [E.D.Wisc. 1978]).

If the agent asks questions or the audit shows substantial discrepancies, the agent must be shown where drug records are kept; otherwise, the search could extend throughout the premises. However, specific compliance questions or explanations of audit shortages and overages should be referred to a conference when the pharmacist's attorney is present. It is better that an individual remain silent than to lie to the inspector. A **lie to a federal officer** in the course of an investigation could violate 18 U.S.C. §1001 (see *United States v. Goldfine*). The pharmacist has the right to refuse to answer others; however, any answers given can be held against the pharmacist if the agent has given the Miranda warning. A lie to a state officer conducting an investigation can be a crime of obstructing justice under applicable state law.

Silence is preferable to incriminating statements even if the statements are inadmissible in court. Once the secret is out, the inspectors know what they are looking for. In *United States v. Bayer*, 331 U.S. 532 (1947), the court said, "... after the accused has once let the cat out of the bag... he can never get the cat back into the bag. The secret is out for good."

The old rule that silence is an admission of guilt no longer applies. An individual's silence during interrogation cannot be used against him or her (see *United States v. Hale*, 422 U.S. 171 [1975]).

An individual may tape-record anything he or she says to the inspector. Although there is a federal law (18 U.S.C. §2511) that prohibits the interception of communications, the law applies to illegal wire taps, not to a party to the conversation. In *Stamatiou v. US Gypsum Co.*, 400 F.Supp. 431 (N.D. Ill. 1975), the court held that the federal law did not prohibit the "party to ... conversation from recording conversation or publishing without consent of other party" (accord *U.S. v. Nerber*, 222 F.3d 597 [9th Cir. 2000]).

The pharmacist should make written notes of everything said or done by the agent during the inspection. If the pharmacist is not a party to the conversation (by exercising the right of silence), it cannot be recorded without permission, and the agent is not likely to give permission. Additionally, a tape recording will not pick up all of the activity. Written observations of the events will provide an accurate picture if it is needed later.

It is not necessary to sign anything without first conferring with an attorney. A receipt for drug samples taken by the FDA or a receipt for a state board inspection report are exceptions to the above; however, it is advisable that an individual be wary of signing anything that looks like a waiver of rights. In one case, a defendant signed a government agent's prepared statement of facts, which amounted to a confession of guilt. The confession was allowed in court because the court felt that the defendant had ample opportunity to seek a lawyer's advice before signing the statement.

In the *Greenblatt* case previously cited, a pharmacist refused to surrender 28 original prescriptions and 11 patient profile cards to the pharmacy inspector. Although the court concluded that the government could enter a highly regulated business such as a pharmacy without a warrant, private citizens should not be asked to part with records that may be essential to their defense. The New Jersey statute permitted the inspector to seize pharmacy records with only verbal assurances that the pharmacy would, in time, receive a file copy. The court concluded that a copy of the prescription must be placed in the file when the original is removed. This replacement would further assure the continued well-being of the innocent patient who might be deprived of this vital information when requesting a refill. However, once the Board's representatives were able to photocopy the records and provide an accurate copy, the originals had to be released.

Conclusion

Proper Method for Challenging an Unlawful Inspection

Two court cases have produced some judicial wisdom on the proper approach to contesting an inspection or search. The cases were decided in 1978 by federal district courts. The cases were decided in reliance on the U.S. Supreme Court decision in *Marshall v. Barlow's, Inc.*, 436 U.S. 307 (1978), and on that basis, the decisions speak with authority because *Barlow's* involved an administrative inspection issue.

In *Becton, Dickinson and Co., v. FDA*, 448 F.Supp. 776 (N.D.N.Y. 1978), a manufacturer refused to permit the FDA access to certain records and files, despite the fact that the FDA agents had a court-issued inspection warrant. Although the court later invalidated the warrant, it admonished the manufacturer defendants for the improper procedure. The court stated, "The defendants' actions in resisting the Warrant of Inspection could have subjected them to liability for Criminal Contempt ... the Court feels that the proper presearch remedy available to the defendants would have been to seek emergency injunctive relief...."

In *Weyerhauser v. Marshall*, 452 F.Supp. 1375 (E.D.Wisc. 1978), an employer permitted OSHA compliance officers to enter and inspect after they showed an administrative inspection warrant but only under protest. Later, the employer went to federal court, seeking to challenge the administrative inspection warrant and the evidence seized during the inspection. The employer asked the court for a preliminary injunction prohibiting further inspection, an order quashing the inspection warrant, and an order suppressing evidence obtained pursuant to the warrant.

The employer's position was that the search pursuant to the administrative inspection warrant was under protest and this nullified the government's later claim that he had consented to the inspection. Furthermore, for reasons too detailed to discuss here (the case is discussed in detail in the Court Cases section), the court granted all of the employer's requests. The case is mentioned here because it illustrates the principle that the proper procedure is to yield to entry and inspection in the face of an inspection warrant and later challenge the validity of the warrant in court.

SOURCES OF ADDITIONAL INFORMATION

Fox LA, Smotherman IJ. The impact of the Barlow's decision. *American Pharmacy.* 1979;NS19:82.

Fox LA. Warrantless FDA inspections: an update. *US Pharm.* 1981;6:18-19.

Gibbs JN. FDA inspections of pharmacies: what should you do? *Am Pharm.* 1995;NS35:32-33, 35.

Norton DB. The constitutionality of warrantless inspections by the Food and Drug Administration. *Food Drug Cosmetic Law Journal.* 1980;35:25-43.

Patterson FT. Entrapment. *J Am Pharm Assoc.* 1968;NS8:256.

Pinco RG. Right of privacy in routine pharmacy inspections. *J Am Pharm Assoc.* 1969:NS9:380.

Simonsmeier LM. Governmental inspection of pharmacies. *US Pharm.* 1978;3:18-20, 22.

Simonsmeier LM. Pharmacy inspections: constitutional without a warrant? *Am J Hosp Pharm.* 1979;36:85-88.

White BD, Hamner ME. Entrapment. *US Pharm.* 1981;6:17-19, 24.

Study Questions

PHARMACY INSPECTION

(1) The Constitution states that no search warrant may be issued except:
  (a) upon probable cause.
  (b) when circumstances would convince a reasonable person to believe that a crime has been committed or that searching this property will reveal items related to a criminal act.
  (c) in the case of administrative searches.
  (d) a and b
  (e) all of the above

(2) The administrative inspection warrant:
  (a) is not as easy to justify legally as a search warrant.
  (b) is less limited in scope than a search warrant.
  (c) can be predicated on the passage of time since the last inspection.
  (d) a and c
  (e) all of the above

(3) Adam has never had his pharmacy inspected before and is surprised to hear from an employee that the inspector is there while Adam is not! Before protesting, he speculates on whether or not his rights are being violated. He remembers, correctly, that an administrative inspection warrant:
  (a) is servable only during business hours.
  (b) must take place in the presence of the owner or pharmacist in charge.
  (c) must be as specific as a search warrant in describing the scope of inspection.
  (d) a and b
  (e) all of the above

(4) Adam's nephew, a pharmacy student, is eating breakfast with him at the time Adam's employee calls to say an inspection is in progress. His nephew suggests, "Maybe this is a situation that reflects a licensing exception." Adam thinks about this and nods, remembering that a licensing exception:
  (a) means that pharmacists should expect frequent inspections once a license is granted.
  (b) is not the same as a situation of implied consent.
  (c) has been used by the courts in upholding warrantless searches of businesses.
  (d) a and c
  (e) all of the above

(5) As he looks for his car keys, Adam wonders what the rules are in this new situation. His nephew reminds him, accurately, that if this is a DEA inspection (drug accountability audit), it:
  (a) determines whether the pharmacy's stock of controlled substances is accurately accounted for.
  (b) is limited to the DEA.
  (c) may not be conducted without voluntary consent.
  (d) a and b
  (e) a and c

(6)   When Adam gets to work, he discovers that these inspectors are from the FDA, and not from the DEA after all. Adam's pharmacy does not engage in manufacturing or repackaging. Supposing we can eliminate that as a cause of FDA presence in his shop, which of the following is/are true?
      (a) Usually, FDA agents call only to inquire about or look for a recalled or banned drug.
      (b) The FDA might inspect his pharmacy on the basis of some complaint lodged with the agency or on the basis of Prescription Drug Marketing Act investigations.
      (c) Questions remain as to the legality of warrantless FDA inspections.
      (d) a and b
      (e) all of the above

(7)   As Adam approaches the inspectors, what can he expect? In other words, which of the following is/are not true? FDA inspectors:
      (a) must show their credentials and state their purpose (inspection).
      (b) must present a Notice of Inspection to take samples from the drug inventory.
      (c) must provide a copy of the Notice of Inspection for the pharmacist.
      (d) must state the reason for the inspection itself.
      (e) c and d

(8)   As Adam's inspectors introduce themselves, they keep referring to a "controlled premise." He knows that this is a place where controlled substances are:
      (a) manufactured.
      (b) held.
      (c) distributed.
      (d) dispensed.
      (e) all of the above

(9)   One of the agents shows Adam an FDA Notice of Inspection. This form:
      (a) asks for voluntary submission to inspection.
      (b) requires mandatory submission to inspection.
      (c) informs the pharmacist in charge that there is a right to refuse the inspection without an administrative inspection warrant.
      (d) b and c
      (e) none of the above

(10) Everything goes wrong in Adam's inspection, and he is given the Miranda warning. This warning:
      (a) must always be given at least orally.
      (b) informs the person that they have a right to an attorney present before being questioned.
      (c) informs the person that any statement he or she makes can be used against him or her.
      (d) b and c
      (e) all of the above

(11) A DEA Notice of Inspection:
      (a) is an inspection warrant.
      (b) takes the place of a warrant if the inspection is limited in scope.
      (c) authorizes the law enforcement official who carries it permission to inspect poison sale records and narcotic sale records.
      (d) b and c
      (e) none of the above

Critical Thinking Activities

(1) You have been asked to appear at a symposium to discuss the history of pharmacists' rights in the case of pharmacy inspections. Research and prepare a presentation on how the companion cases of *See v. City of Seattle*, 387 U.S. 541 (1967) and *Camara v. Municipal Court*, 387 U.S. 23 (1967) ultimately affected the way we approach pharmacy inspections. Why are these cases important? What did they change?

(2) Claudia, a pharmacist, is being prosecuted for evidence found during a pharmacy inspection conducted by the DEA. Although the evidence is incriminating, Claudia's attorney points out that the DEA acted "only on an inspection notice." She argues that this constitutes implementing the exclusionary rule. Do you agree or disagree? Cite a precedent case to back up your answer.

(3) Dan, a pharmacist, calls you. He believes an inspection of his pharmacy was done improperly, and he wants to challenge the notion of warrantless inspections. He asks for your help in getting some background information together because he knows you're studying pharmacy law. This is the friend who helped you get an internship when they were scarce, so of course, you agree. "I am interested in finding a precedent," he says, but he will not tell you what has happened. Knowing nothing else about Dan's case, contrast these 2 cases:

- *Norman Bridge Drug Co. v. Banner et al.*, 529 F. 2d 822 (5th Cir. 1976)
- *People v. White*, 65 Cal. Rptr. 923 (1968)

How do they differ in regard to warrantless inspections?

Case Study 1: Search and Seizure

For the first time ever, a government agent arrives to inspect Melanie's pharmacy. He tells her that he is an FDA agent. He shows her no papers but is very polite. He asks to inspect her pharmacy. Guide Melanie in her decision making as the dilemmas below arise:

(1) As soon as the agent enters her business, what is the first thing Melanie should do to protect her constitutional rights?

(2) Suppose Melanie is offered Form FD-482. Explain what this means.

(3) Suppose Melanie demands an inspection warrant, but the agent fails to produce one and insists on conducting the drug accountability audit anyway. What should Melanie do then?

(4) To Melanie's surprise, the agent actually confiscates several items. What should she demand? Does she have any further recourse against this?

(5) What will happen to Melanie if she refuses to answer this inspector's questions?

(6) Melanie decides she will answer the inspector, but only if she can tape-record their conversation. How is her ability to do so affected by the federal law that prohibits the interception of communications?

(7) In the end, Melanie decides not to speak at all, but instead to record everything said or done by the agent during the inspection. He tells her she does not have his permission. Does she need it or not? Explain your answer.

(8) Finally, at the conclusion of his inspection, the agent asks Melanie to sign a few papers. What should she sign or not sign?

Chapter 5

Business Law

Chapter Overview, 197

Contracts, Sales, and the Uniform Commercial Code, 197
    Introduction, 197
    Contracts, 197
        Requirements of a Contract, 197
            Mutual Assent, 197
            Consideration, 198
            Competent Parties, 198
            Legal Purpose or Object, 199
        Statute of Frauds, 199
            Parol Evidence Rule, 200
            Modification of a Written Agreement, 201
            Partial Performance, 201
            Full Performance, 201
        Types of Contracts, 201
            Express and Implied Contracts, 201
            Executory and Executed Contracts, 201
            Quasi Contract, 202
            Void Contract, 202
            Voidable Contract, 202
    Sales, 202
        Types of Sales, 202
        The Sales Contract, 203
            Breach of Sales Contract, 203
            Seller's Remedies on Buyer's Breach, 203
            Buyer's Remedies on Seller's Breach, 204
    Employment Law, 204
        Discharge for Cause, 205
        Wrongful Discharge for Complying with Public Policy, 206
        Covenants Not to Compete, 207
    Federal Laws Pertaining to Employment Discrimination, 208
        Religious Discrimination, 208
        Sexual Harassment, 208
        Wage Discrimination, 209
        Retaliatory Discharge, 210
        Handicap Discrimination, 210
        AIDS Discrimination, 212
        Polygraph Testing, 213
        Screening for Illicit Drug Use, 214
        Workers' Compensation, 215

Types of Business Organizations, 216
   Introduction, 216
      Sole Proprietorship, 216
      Partnership, 216
      Corporation, 216
   Sole Proprietorship, 216
   Partnership, 217
      General Partnership Agreements, 217
         Partner Liability, 218
      Limited Partnership Agreements, 218
   Corporation, 218
      Formation of a Business Corporation, 219
         Articles of Incorporation, 219
         Board of Directors, 219
         Liability of Stockholders, 220
         Corporate Stock, 220
         Preferred Stock, 221
         Reasons for Incorporation, 221
         Reasons Against Incorporation, 221
         S Corporations, 221
      Corporations for Professional Practice, 222
   Limited Liability Companies and Limited Liability Partnerships, 222

Regulation of Competition, 222
   Sherman Antitrust Act, 223
   Clayton Antitrust Act, 223
   Two Approaches by the Courts, 224
   Robinson-Patman Price Discrimination Act, 224
   Antitrust Laws and the Pharmacist, 225
      Treble-Damage Suits and the Pharmacist, 225
      Price-Fixing and Third Party Payment Plans, 226
      Exclusive Contracts, 227
      Discriminatory Pricing, 227
      Refusal to Deal, 228
         Community Pharmacist Networks, 228
      Prohibitions Against Corporate Mergers, 229
      Enforcement of the Antitrust Laws, 229

Federal Trade Commission, 229
      Corrective Advertisements, 230
      Deceptive Trade Practices, 230
      Retailer's Liability for Manufacturer's Claims, 231
      Below-Cost Sales, 231
      Unrelated Business Income Tax, 232

Sources of Additional Information, 232

Study Questions, 235

Business Law

CHAPTER OVERVIEW

As was emphasized in the Introduction, the law is very pervasive—affecting nearly all of our relationships with others. This is especially true in the business realm, be it an employment contract with the pharmacist in either the employee or employer role, a contract for purchase or sale of an item or service, or an attempt to steer clear of legal entanglements related to antitrust or trade regulation concerns. This section presents a brief overview of selected business law topics of importance to pharmacists. It is by no means exhaustive or complete; topics for discussion have been selected based on their prevalence in practice or importance to practicing pharmacists. There is no substitute for the advice of competent legal counsel familiar with the intricacies of the laws of your jurisdiction. Sitting down to discuss the facts of your specific situation with an attorney is highly recommended.

CONTRACTS, SALES, AND THE UNIFORM COMMERCIAL CODE

Introduction

A **contract** is a legally enforceable agreement between 2 or more individuals. An agreement is merely a meeting of the minds. It becomes a contract when there is sufficient consideration—doing or refraining from doing a particular lawful act. A **sale** is the transfer of property for a fixed price.

The Uniform Commercial Code (UCC) is a relatively similar set of statutes that are enacted in every state to regulate commercial (business) transactions. The UCC regulates certain sales, contracts, and transactions that are neither sales nor contracts.

Contracts

Requirements of a Contract

The essential elements of a contract are mutual assent; consideration that is sufficient; legal, competent parties (the parties must have the legal capacity to make a contract); and legal purpose or object—that which is agreed upon must be allowed by law and must not be against public policy.

Mutual Assent

Mutual assent is simply an offer and acceptance. This can be in the form of one promise for another. For example, a contractor promises to build a certain house for a landowner who promises to pay $195,000 for it. The offer and acceptance also can be an act for a promise. For example, a truck driver pays $50,000 to an individual who promises not to sue the truck driver for injuries suffered when the truck was driven into the car in which the individual was riding.

The mutual assent must be communicated. That is to say, it must be communicated by means of words or conduct that indicate an intent to contract. In some cases, silence or inaction can be an acceptance of an offer, but the instances are rare. Generally, if an individual receives a written or oral offer to buy goods or services, mere silence or inaction will suffice as a rejection of the offer.

An advertisement in a newspaper or magazine for sale of goods is not an offer; it is a solicitation for an offer. When a customer sends in an order for a catalogue item, that order is an offer. When the item is shipped, the offer is accepted by the firm that advertised the item.

Generally, an offer must be accepted on the terms offered. If the terms are changed by the other party, a counteroffer, in effect, has been made. A request for a price quotation is not an offer, but the reply to the quotation request can be an offer to be accepted or rejected by the individual or firm who asked for the quotation.

An offer is open for acceptance for a definite time, which is usually indicated in the offer; if there is no indication, the law will imply a reasonable time for acceptance, based on the circumstances of the situation.

Acceptance of the offer makes a contract valid, provided that all the other elements of the contract are present. The acceptor usually cannot rescind the acceptance without being liable for breach of contract, nor can the individual making the offer withdraw it after acceptance unless he or she is willing to pay the penalty, although in some instances a court may force the individual to carry out his or part of the contract. This occurs in cases of specific performance, an equitable remedy for breach of a contract to convey a particular piece of land or other unique property. The UCC also gives certain rights of cancellation of a contract to buyers and sellers under the conditions specified in the code.

Mutual consent must be free from fraud, misrepresentation, duress, undue influence, coercion, intimidation, and threats. For a valid contract, the consent of the parties must be of their own free will.

Fraud is a lie or false statement of a fact with knowledge of the falsity, or it is a reckless disregard for the truth. In order for fraud to invalidate a contract, usually the party on whom the fraud is perpetrated must have relied on it to his or her detriment. **Misrepresentation** is the same as fraud, except that the element of knowledge of the falsity and the intent to deceive are absent. Duress, coercion, intimidation, and threats are nearly synonymous; if proven, they indicate a lack of real consent to an agreement. Undue influence, on the other hand, indicates a situation in which the parties are not equal and in which the dominant party uses his or position to pressure the subservient party into an agreement.

Generally, a mistake in the nature of a contract may void it, but a mistake as to the terms of the contract will not. In this regard, the failure to read a contract before signing usually is not an excuse for voiding it to escape its obligations.

Consideration

Consideration to support a valid contract must be legal and sufficient. Consideration can be defined as a right, interest, profit, or benefit given to one party from the loss, detriment, forbearance, or responsibility suffered or undertaken by the other party. It has also been defined as a benefit to one party and a loss to the other, but a better definition might be a mutual benefit and mutual detriment. For example, a buyer pays $190,000 for a seller's house. The buyer's loss or detriment is the $190,000, and the benefit is the house. Conversely, the seller's loss is the house that is turned over to the buyer, and the benefit is the $190,000 received.

Adequacy of the consideration is immaterial except in situations in which the disparity is so gross as to presume fraud. The law does not examine the adequacy of the consideration but leaves it up to the parties to make their bargain. A contract is not void or voidable on the grounds of being a poor bargain alone. There is a distinction between adequacy and sufficiency. Payment of $100 for a painting that is worth $1000 is sufficient consideration, although not adequate. There are certain situations in which mutual consideration is not required in order for the contract to be enforceable, such as charitable pledges.

Competent Parties

It takes at least two individuals to make a contract. A limited exception exists in cases in which an individual is acting in two different capacities—personal and representative. An individual might enter into a contract with a corporation in which he or she is a corporate officer and in such cases would, conceivably, be signing the contract in one instance as an individual apart from the corporation and in another instance as a corporate officer acting for the corporation.

Parties to a contract must be competent to make a contract. Some legal authorities have ruled that a contract is void or is not a contract at all for want of legal capacity to contract on the part of one or both of the parties to the agreement. An agreement by an insane individual or an intoxicated individual is void. An insane individual is one adjudged to be so by a court or one declared incompetent in a legal guardianship proceeding. However, courts have found individuals to be insane for the purposes of voiding a contract, although the individuals were not declared so by a court.

Contracts by minors are voidable at their option. However, a minor may be legally liable in a quasi contract for the reasonable value (not the contracted price) of necessities that were actually furnished. The reason for this is that a minor might be deprived of the necessities of life unless some legal security for payment was given to the merchant dealing with the minor. Similarly, a merchant furnishing goods to an insane individual has some recourse for the reasonable value of the goods furnished if he or she did not know that the individual was insane, or if the goods were necessities of life.

Generally, parents have no legal liability for their children's contracts, whether the children are minors or adults, unless the parents are party to the contract as cosigners or unless they otherwise expressly obligate themselves in the contract. However, parents may have liability for the reasonable value of necessities that are furnished to minor children in situations in which the parents have the legal obligation to furnish them. In some states, the law makes parents liable for torts committed by their minor children.

A minor may legally ratify a contract made during minority by word or conduct upon reaching majority. If, on attaining majority, the minor accepts the benefit of a contract made during minority, he or she has ratified it. If, in a contract for services, the minor continues to furnish services after attaining majority, he or she has ratified the contract, and the ratification prevents him or her from avoiding the contract on grounds of it being made by a minor.

Legal Purpose or Object

A contract is void in cases in which there is illegality in the consideration or promise made or in its performance. The illegality is that which is contrary to the US Constitution, a state constitution, a federal or state statute, a municipal ordinance, or a public policy. Such agreements are unenforceable in court. However, in the case of some void agreements, the court can aid in restoring any payments already made in conjunction with the agreement.

Agreements against public policy have been defined by some courts as being against common conscience in matters of morals, health, safety, and welfare. In other words, the effect of a contract on the public at large is considered, rather than just its effect on the parties to the agreement.

An example of an agreement that is unenforceable because of illegal purpose is an agreement between a pharmacy owner and a physician in which the pharmacist splits the professional prescription fee with the physician on all prescriptions written by the physician and dispensed by the pharmacist. The agreement would be unenforceable in some states because it violates the pharmacy board regulations dealing with professional ethics.

A contract, illegal in part because of some provision that violates a statute or that is against public policy, may be salvageable if its legal portions can be separated from, and made independent of, the illegal matter.

Statute of Frauds

Each state has a statute of frauds, which requires that certain agreements must be written and signed by the party to be charged (the party against whom enforcement is sought). The purpose of the statute of frauds is to prevent fraud and to prevent the perjury of individuals who may lie about the terms of their oral agreements. If the subject matter of the agreement comes within the statute of frauds, unless it is in writing and signed by the party to be charged, the agreement is void, voidable, or unenforceable, depending upon the particular state statute.

Agreements that typically fall within the scope of the statute of frauds include agreements that cannot be performed within 1 year from the date that the agreement is made. On the other hand, if the contract could be performed within 1 year, it is outside of the scope of the statute of frauds, even though it takes more than 1 year to perform. For example, a contract for 1 year's services that will commence 1 week from the contract date is within the statute since it will take more than 1 year from the contract date to perform the services fully. However, a contract to build a boat with a maximum allowable construction time of 15 months from the contract date is not within the statute because the contract conceivably could be performed within the 1 year. Employment contracts for an undetermined period of time are outside the statute since the employee may quit or be fired after as little as 1 day's work. Most states require real estate agreements to be in writing or to provide that a broker cannot enforce an agreement to collect his or her commission on the sale of realty unless it is in writing. However, this requirement generally is not a part of the statute of frauds but is a separate statute applicable to real estate brokers.

Agreements for the sale of goods for $500 or more are within the statute of frauds even if a barter or exchange is contemplated, but they are not within the statute if personal services only are involved. The rule for performance within 1 year applies to the service contract. In most states, a separate statute requires a written agreement for the sale of personal property for $5000 or more.

Under the UCC, partial payment of goods, for which payment has been accepted, validates an otherwise invalid contract under the statute of frauds (see UCC §201). Similarly, the UCC validates an oral contract only for goods received and accepted by the buyer. For example, Fairfield Surgical Company, Inc., ordered 100 catheters at $1.59 each from a wholesaler, and the order was placed by telephone and was not evidenced by a written memorandum. Fairfield Surgical received 30 catheters and then canceled the rest of the order because the catheters could be purchased from another wholesaler at $1.29 each. Fairfield must pay the contracted price for the original 30 catheters unless they are returned to the wholesaler within a reasonable time.

A promise to pay the debt of another is within the statute of frauds and must be evidenced in writing, and that document must be signed by the promisor when the promise is made to the creditor. For example, individual A owes money to individual C on a promissory note that A gave to C. Individual B promises C that if A does not pay his debt to C, B will pay it. B's promise comes within the statute and must be in writing. If B's promise was made only to A and not to C, it would be outside the statute and enforceable by A against B, provided that the other essential elements for a valid contract were present.

In order to satisfy the requirements of the statute of frauds, any written memorandum should contain the names of the involved parties, the terms of the agreement, the description of the subject matter of the agreement, and the signature of the party to be charged. The memorandum does not need to be on a special form, nor must it be titled "Contract" or "Agreement" as long as it contains the elements outlined above.

Parol Evidence Rule

The parol evidence rule states that a written agreement must be sufficient in itself and cannot require parol (oral) evidence to supply an essential element; however, oral evidence may be used in court to clarify an ambiguity in the written agreement. An agreement may not be part oral and part written and satisfy the statute, but oral evidence may be used in court to show that a written memorandum of an oral agreement is inaccurate or incomplete. Oral evidence may be admitted in court to correct a typing error or misspelling; however, such errors usually are disregarded when the intended meaning is apparent. Oral evidence also can be used to show that a contract was obtained by fraud or duress.

Modification of a Written Agreement

In general, an agreement that is required to be in writing by the statute of frauds cannot be modified or changed by an oral agreement. While the required written agreement cannot be changed orally, in certain cases a written contract can be rescinded if it does not result in a retransfer of property. Rescission refers to the equitable cancellation of a contract, with the involved parties placed in the positions that they held prior to making the contract. Although an oral rescission may be valid in some instances, scratching out a signature or otherwise defacing a written agreement will not serve as a valid rescission.

Partial Performance

Most states follow the rule that partial performance of an oral agreement for sale of real estate exempts the transaction from application of the statute of frauds so that a court may enforce the contract even without a written agreement. Similarly, partial payment or partial delivery and acceptance of goods will take the oral agreement out of the statute's realm. In some cases in which goods have been ordered for manufacture according to the customer's particular specifications, the statute of frauds does not apply.

Full Performance

Full performance of an agreement by one of the involved parties will exempt it from application of the statute of frauds to the extent that the party who fulfilled part of the contract can enforce the agreement against the other party. In some cases, one party is "equitably estopped" from asserting the invalidity of the oral agreement as a defense against a suit brought by the party who has been induced to act on the agreement to his or her detriment.

Types of Contracts

Express and Implied Contracts

Essentially, there are 2 types of contracts—express and implied. An **express contract** is one in which the terms of the contract actually are stated, either orally or in writing, by the involved parties. The terms of an **implied contract** are set from the conduct of the parties and the circumstances.

The differences between express and implied contracts are illustrated by the following examples.

The patient asks the pharmacist, "How much is a *Hankscraft* vaporizer?" The pharmacist answers, "I have one for $25.95." The patient's response is, "I will take it. Please have it delivered to me, and bill me for it." The pharmacist promises, "It will go out to you this afternoon." The contract is an **express contract** because of the stated mutual promises of the patient to pay for the vaporizer and the pharmacist to deliver it.

A patient presents the pharmacist with a prescription, "May I have this filled?" The pharmacist dispenses the prescription. Without anything further said, there is an **implied contract** that the pharmacist dispensed the correct medication in an appropriately labeled container and that the patient will pay for the prescription, even though the price was not mentioned.

Executory and Executed Contracts

An executory contract is one that is not yet completed; in contrast, an executed contract is one in which all contractual obligations have been performed. In the previous example, if the pharmacist delivered the vaporizer and the patient paid for it, the contract would be executed. Prior to the delivery and payment, it would be an executory contract.

Quasi Contract

In a situation in which an agreement lacks the requisites to make it legally enforceable as a contract, the law may give a legal effect to it, making it a quasi contract based on reason and fairness in order to prevent a wrongdoing or unjust enrichment at the expense of another individual.

Void Contract

A void contract is an agreement without legal obligation. In fact, an agreement that is void is not a contract; it is a nullity. It is, in the eyes of the law, a contract that is nonexistent, a mere agreement or promise without consideration. For example, if a person has been formally judged by a court to be insane or incompetent, all personal rights are given to a guardian or conservator. The insane person would not be capable of entering into a legal contract, and any such attempted agreement would be void. Contracts also may be void if they propose an illegal act or are against public policy. Thus, a contract that requires one to commit an assault would be void; the same would be true of any agreement that restrains trade or promotes discrimination.

Voidable Contract

A voidable contract is an enforceable contract until one of the parties to it voids it or avoids it. Some contracts can be avoided by only one involved party, and other contracts can be avoided by all of the involved parties. The law distinguishes between a void contract (which is not legally recognized as a contract) and a voidable contract, which is a legally valid and binding contract in which one or more parties to it can get out of it without any legal consequences. For example, under usury laws, a loan agreement with an interest rate over the maximum allowable rate would, in some states, be void. Hence, such a loan agreement would not be a contract. The party charged with the loan might make the payments, but there would be no obligation to do so. An example of a voidable contract would be a minor's contract for a nonnecessity. A young girl, who is 15 years of age, signs a contract to purchase 50 CDs by mail. After purchasing 5, she decides to avoid the contract. The law gives her the right to disaffirm or avoid any contracts she makes for nonnecessities. Up until the time the minor avoids the contract by telling the CD company that she wants no more CDs and her money back, the contract is a valid contract but voidable at her option. In most states, the minor would not be legally entitled to a complete refund as she did receive 5 CDs, but she would not be held to the full contract price. Although a minor may, in most states, disaffirm any contract that he or she makes, the minor can be held liable for the benefit received, whether or not the benefit was a necessity.

Sales

The law of sales revolves around the following issues: When the title (ownership) to the goods actually passes from seller to buyer; who bears the risk of loss in the interim; the seller's liability for furnishing the contracted goods; the buyer's liability for paying the contracted price; the seller's remedies for the buyer's breach of contract; and the buyer's remedies for the seller's breach of contract.

Types of Sales

A **consignment sale** is that for the purpose of resale by a buyer, who may return any of the unsold goods. The consignment transaction differs from a sale on approval in that the latter is a sale of goods for the buyer's own use with the privilege of return even if the goods conform to the contract terms. In either type of transaction, the time allowed for the return of the goods is stated in the contract, or, if no time is specified, is a reasonable time.

In the consignment sale, title to the goods passes to the buyer, who attempts to resell the goods. If he or she does not sell the goods, they are returned to the seller, and title reverts back to the seller when the goods are actually received. The buyer's title to the goods while they are in his or her possession is good, and when he or she sells them, a good title is passed on to the purchaser. Because the buyer has title to goods that are in his or her possession, creditors can make claims against the goods.

In a **sale on approval**, title to the goods does not pass to the buyer until he or she accepts the goods—either by paying for them or by retaining them past the time allowed for return. The buyer's creditors cannot make claims against the goods until the buyer accepts them.

The Sales Contract

The performance of the sales contract is determined by the terms of the contract. In general, however, the performance includes the seller's obligation to transfer and deliver the goods and the buyer's obligation to accept and pay the price of the goods in accordance with the contract.

If the seller delivers nonconforming goods to the buyer, the buyer may reject all of the goods, accept all the goods, or accept some and reject some by commercial unit lots.

Breach of Sales Contract

Breach of contract can be defined as failure to perform a contract in whole or in part. Under provisions of the UCC, substantial performance of the contract is complying with its terms except for minor deviations. In some instances, before one party can perform, it becomes apparent that the other party is not going to or cannot perform. This is termed an anticipatory breach. Also known as anticipatory repudiation, anticipatory breach exists where words or acts of a party in regard to a sales contract indicate an intent not to perform or indicate that substantial performance is impossible or near impossible. For example, Fairfield Surgical entered into a sales contract with St. James' Hospital for 10 custom-built wheelchairs. However, no sooner was the ink dry on the sales contract than Fairfield turned around and sold the chairs for more money to Monticello Hospice. Fairfield's act of selling the wheelchairs to a third party constitutes anticipatory breach, which suspends St. James' Hospital's duty to render payment. In addition, St. James' could sue for breach of contract.

In cases in which one party to a sales contract has reasonable grounds to believe that the other party will not fulfill his or her part of the bargain or has breached the contract, the performing party may demand, in writing, that the other party give adequate assurance of performance. Adequate assurance may consist of a promise on the part of the breaching party, or it may consist of correcting the delivery of nonconforming goods. The UCC requires adequate assurance within a reasonable time not exceeding 30 days (see UCC §2-609).

Seller's Remedies on Buyer's Breach

When the buyer wrongfully rejects the goods, fails to make payment, or before delivery repudiates part or all of the contracted goods, the seller has the following remedies: Withholding delivery of the goods, stopping delivery of the goods in transit, and locating conforming goods that are not already committed and reselling them. When the goods are unfinished, the seller may finish the goods, exercising reasonable commercial judgment to avoid loss and resell them, or the seller may stop finishing the goods and resell the unfinished goods for scrap or salvage. The seller may resell the goods and sue for the difference between the resale price and the contract price plus incidental costs but less any expenses saved by buyer's breach. The seller may sue for damages for repudiation by the buyer (damages are the difference between the market price of the goods at time of tender and the unpaid contract price plus incidentals but less expenses saved) or sue for the profit that would have been made from the buyer's full performance. Finally, the seller may cancel the contract. The seller retains any remedy for breach of whole or part of the contract, but he or she must notify the buyer of cancellation (see UCC §§2-703 and 2-708.)

Buyer's Remedies on Seller's Breach

When the seller fails to make delivery under a sales contract or the buyer rightfully rejects goods or justifiably refuses acceptance, the buyer has several options: Cancel the contract, and, in addition to recovering what has been paid, purchase substitute goods and recover damages (measured by the difference between the cost of the substitute goods and the contract price plus incidentals but less any expenses saved by the seller's breach); or, simply recover damages for nondelivery (measured by the difference between the market price when the buyer learned of the breach and the contract price plus incidentals but less expenses paid). If the goods have been identified, the buyer may recover them if the seller becomes insolvent within 10 days after receipt of the first payment installment. If the goods are identified as the buyer's special property, the buyer has the right to recover the goods only if they conform to the contract price. In certain situations, the buyer may obtain specific performance or replevin (see below) of the goods identified in the contract if, after a reasonable effort, he or she is unable to acquire substitute goods or if circumstances indicate that he or she will be unable to get substitute goods.

Specific performance is only allowed by the court in cases in which monetary damages will not suffice (eg, when the sales contract is for priceless art or antiques). **Replevin** is a civil action to recover property wrongfully in possession of another. Again, this remedy is permitted by the court only when the buyer is unable to obtain substitute goods for a reasonable price.

Upon rightful rejection, a buyer has security interest in the goods in his or her possession or control for any payment for them and for any expenses reasonably incurred in their inspection, receipt, transportation, care, and custody. He or she may resell them (see UCC §2-711).

Under the Uniform Sales Act, when the seller breaches, a buyer cannot revoke acceptance and also recover damages. The UCC gives the buyer the option either of cover (purchase of substitute goods plus damages) or to sue for damages on nondelivery of contracted goods. However, the buyer is not obligated to obtain substitute goods, and failure to do so will not bar the use of other remedies.

Employment Law

The relationship between an employer and employee may be governed by an express agreement, such as an oral or written employment contract, or its terms may be implied by the circumstances. Some employment contracts are for a stated period of time (eg, 1 year). A written contract for a specific time period may be insisted upon by an employee pharmacist who is seeking some manner of job security. However, the typical employee pharmacist has only an oral contract for employment at will. This type of employment relationship is usually for an indefinite period of time, and it may be terminated by either party for any reason. It is customary for the employee to give the employer 2 weeks notice when the employee desires to terminate an employment-at-will relationship, but notice is not required unless it was a condition of the employment. Union rules or policies of the employing organization may require notice of some type.

Although most pharmacy employment situations are "at will," a Minnesota court awarded limited damages to a pharmacist whose offer of employment was revoked prior to the time he began work. This community pharmacist received a job offer from a health maintenance organization, but he informed the HMO that he wanted to give 2 weeks notice to his current employer. During the next few days, the chief pharmacist for the HMO learned that the organization's hiring requirements included written references, a background check, and approval of the general manager. The HMO was unable to obtain recommendations from the faculty at the pharmacist's alma mater, so another individual was hired for the position. Ten days later, the pharmacist reported for work, but he was informed that someone else had been hired. The pharmacist filed a lawsuit and the HMO defended itself by contending that it could terminate "at will" even if the pharmacist had not started work. The court agreed that the employer could discharge at will, but under the theory of promissory estoppel, limited damages could be awarded because the pharmacist had quit another job in reliance on the new position. Because the new employment could have been terminated at any time, the measure of damages was not what the pharmacist would have earned from the HMO, but what he lost in quitting his previous job and in declining at least one other offer of employment. (*Grouse v. Group Health Plan, Inc.*, 306 N.W.2d 114 [Minn. 1981]).

Some jurisdictions have used the theory of breach of an implied contract to establish a wrongful discharge. In these situations, employees usually allege that statements in the employee job manual, personnel handbook, or employment application serve as an implied promise prohibiting discharge except for cause. A pharmaceutical company employee sued his former employer, claiming that the company had breached his contractual rights as established by the company's employment manual. The manual stated that the company would retain the services of all employees who performed their duties efficiently and effectively. There was an implied promise that an employee would be fired only for cause. The New Jersey Supreme Court concluded that the manual was not a mere expression of the company's "philosophy" but represented the most reliable statement of their employment terms, and it gave employees a reasonable expectation that job security was a term of their employment. This was true even though the employment was for an indefinite term and would otherwise be terminable at will. (*Woolley v. Hoffman-LaRoche, Inc.*, 491 A.2d 1257 [N.J. 1985].)

When pharmacist Jack Loomstein was discharged from his position as pharmacist and manager with Medicare Pharmacies, he filed an action for retaliatory discharge and breach of contract. Loomstein presented 3 incidents in which he claimed his employer allegedly demanded that he violate the law and then fired him because of his refusal to do so. Loomstein contended that his employer requested that he return the original of a prescription back to a physician who had made an error in prescribing. Loomstein also questioned the authenticity of the signature of a physician on another prescription, but when the physician told him that he had in fact signed the prescription, Loomstein testified that he still thought that the doctor had not told the truth. The third incident involved a dispute between Loomstein and his supervisor regarding the dispensing of generic drugs that were no longer on a formulary. The court was not convinced that these 3 incidents, standing alone, provided enough evidence to establish a case for retaliatory discharge (*Loomstein v. Medicare Pharmacies, Inc.* 750 S.W.2d 106 [Mo. App. 1988]).

The court record was filled with testimony that the pharmacist had difficulties relating to his superiors and that he had a condescending manner and was sarcastic and rude to customers. A State Board of Pharmacy inspector also had a "run in" with Loomstein. The defendant claimed that these instances formed the basis of the company's discharge.

Loomstein further contended that the pharmacy's handbook contained rules and regulations that created contractual rights between him and the pharmacy. He claimed that the pharmacy had not given him oral or written warnings as required by the employee handbook. Yet, the file included a written employment report stating, "If Jack Loomstein had one more complaint of this type his services would no longer be needed." The evidence also showed that Loomstein had been verbally reprimanded for speaking rudely to a customer. Loomstein received 14 days severance pay as required by the handbook. The court concluded that the pharmacy had not breached its employment contract and was not in violation of the company handbook.

Discharge for Cause

In another employment contract dispute, pharmaceutical sales representative Edwin Brannan sued Wyeth Laboratories for breach of employment contract when he was terminated after 18 years of employment. He claimed that he was concerned about job security when he first interviewed with the pharmaceutical company. He alleged that it was made clear to him that he was applying for a permanent position and that he would be able to keep the job as long as he performed satisfactorily. Brannan also claimed that Wyeth had a policy not to terminate without reasonable just cause.

However, over the years, the company received complaints that Brannan did not call upon the physicians in his territory on a regular basis. The company conducted a 2-day surveillance of the plaintiff. This investigation resulted in the plaintiff's termination for falsifying physician call reports. The court found that the oral contract of employment was terminable at will.

In addition, the company had established just cause for termination because there was considerable evidence of complaints from physicians about the plaintiff not calling on them regularly. In light of this evidence, even if there had been a contract that could have run until the plaintiff's retirement, the company still had just cause to terminate his employment (see *Brannan v. Wyeth Laboratories, Inc.* 526 So.2d 1101 [La. 1988]).

When the employment is for a definite period of time, either party (employer or employee) can be liable in damages to the other party for terminating the employment without just cause. Generally, the grounds that permit an employer to discharge an employee prior to expiration of the term of employment are dishonesty, neglect of duty, incompetency, inefficiency, failure to follow instructions, insolence, disrespect, and breach of confidence or loyalty. However, an employer cannot discharge an employee for union activity or on the basis of race, sex, religion, national origin, or age. Generally, temporary illness of the employee is not valid ground for discharge prior to the end of a stated employment term, but a prolonged illness may be.

Wrongful Discharge for Complying with Public Policy

Pharmacists should not have to fear job loss because they exercise their professional judgment for the benefit of the public. A New Jersey pharmacist filed suit against his former employer because he was discharged for refusing to violate a law of the state of New Jersey pertaining to the operation of the pharmacy. The corporate employer notified the pharmacist that it intended to open the pharmacy on a holiday without a pharmacist on duty. The pharmacist lost his job when he insisted that this was not the correct procedure, and contacted the state board of pharmacy to inquire if the employer's actions were proper. The trial court granted the employer's motion for summary judgment because it questioned whether the board of pharmacy regulations qualified as a clear mandate of public policy or whether they simply served only the interest of the pharmacy profession. The pharmacist argued persuasively, on appeal, that the requirement that the pharmacy area be open and tended by a pharmacist whenever the premises were open was, indeed, an expression of public policy. The appellate court agreed that an unsecured, unsupervised pharmacy created a risk that potentially dangerous substances would be dispensed by unqualified persons or would be stolen. The court ruled that the pharmacist's discharge conflicted with 2 sources of public policy: (1) The statutory and regulatory scheme of requiring a pharmacist to be on duty whenever the premises were open, and (2) the pharmacist's professional code of ethics. (*Kalman v. Grand Union Co.*, 443 A.2d 728 [N.J. Super.App.Div. 1982].)

The New Jersey Supreme Court has also concluded that the right of an employer to fire an employee at will is limited. The plaintiff in this action was a physician who served as the director of medical research for a major drug manufacturer. Because of the controversial use of saccharin, the physician opposed its inclusion in the formula of a new drug being developed in the manufacturer's research laboratories. The physician felt that this would force her to violate her professional ethics. The plaintiff was removed from the project, and she brought suit against her employer.

The court held that, as a matter of law, there was no public policy against conducting research on drugs that may be controversial, particularly in cases in which the continuation of the research is subject to approval by the Food and Drug Administration. Consequently, the court found in favor of the pharmaceutical manufacturer. (*Pierce v. Ortho Pharmaceutical Corporation*, 417 A.2d 505, [N.J., 1980].) However, the court did find a need to protect employees who are wrongfully discharged by their employer for reasons that violate public policy. A common law cause of action based on contract law was found to exist in such instances. An employee who is wrongfully discharged for complying with public policy as stated in legislation, administrative rules, judicial decisions, and professional codes of ethics is provided with the right to maintain an action against the employer.

Thirty-two states recognize exceptions to the employment-at-will doctrine. While the rule has not been totally discarded, there has been some erosion as a result of court decisions and legislative mandate. Some examples of wrongful termination of employment involve employees who refused to take a polygraph examination, filed a worker's compensation claim, refused to testify falsely in a trial, accepted jury duty, participated in labor union activities, or were simply exercising their civil rights.

Covenants Not to Compete

The buyer of a pharmacy business often wants a covenant or promise by the seller not to compete with the buyer. Such promise is termed a covenant not to compete or a noncompetition clause. If a pharmacist sold his or her pharmacy and then opened another across the street from the one sold, the purchaser would be in the undesirable position of competing with an individual who had an established rapport with the neighborhood clientele. Similarly, there are anticompetition clauses in pharmacist employment contracts because an employee pharmacist is in a position to develop a following among the pharmacy patrons. Hence, if he or she left the employment and immediately opened a competing pharmacy nearby, or was employed by a nearby pharmacy, he or she would pose an economic threat to the former employer.

A covenant not to compete is a restraint to trade, which violates the Sherman Antitrust Act, but the courts will allow it when it is reasonable, supported by contract consideration, and ancillary to a lawful contract. In *Allen v. Rose Park Pharmacy*, 237 P.2d 823 (Utah 1951), a case involving an agreement by an employee pharmacist not to compete within a 2-mile radius for 5 years, the court upheld the agreement as valid. In the Allen case, the employee pharmacist worked under an employment contract with the corporate-owned pharmacy. The contract terms provided that the pharmacist be employed as manager at a set salary per week with a 10% bonus of net profits plus an option to acquire 25% of the corporate stock. The employee agreed to the contract, including the anticompetition clause. The employer could terminate the contract for any reason on a 30-day notice, and the employee could do so on a 60-day notice. After 1 year of service, the employer terminated the contract on a 30-day notice, and the son of one of the corporate directors was given the manager's job. The discharged pharmacist sued to have the anticompetition clause declared invalid. The trial court ruled against him.

On appeal, the Supreme Court of Utah upheld the trial court decision. The court ruled that the anticompetition clause was supported by sufficient consideration—the mutual promises of the parties. The employee pharmacist argued that the clause was a negative covenant, which was invalid for lack of mutuality of obligation because the employer could terminate the pharmacist's job after a few months and the pharmacist would be obliged not to compete for 5 years. The court did not agree. The mutuality of promises was present in the contract in which each promised the other something that was detrimental to the promisor and beneficial to the promisee, although not necessarily of equal exchange. The court stated, "Moreover a contract does not lack mutuality merely because its terms are harsh or its obligations unequal or because every obligation of one party is not met by an equivalent counter obligation of the other party."

Federal Laws Pertaining to Employment Discrimination

There is a wide variety of federal legislation pertaining to employment discrimination as well as a multitude of state laws that prohibit discrimination in the workplace. In addition, there are a number of constitutional provisions that prohibit employment discrimination.

The most significant piece of federal legislation in the area of employment discrimination is the Civil Rights Acts of 1964, as amended by the Equal Employment Opportunity Act of 1972. These laws preclude discrimination in employment on the basis of race, color, religion, sex, and national origin. These statutes apply to any private employer in an industry affecting interstate commerce with at least 15 employees and the laws also protect federal, state, and local government employees. These acts also prohibit retaliation for asserting rights guaranteed under the law or for opposing practices prohibited by the statutes. These laws are administered primarily by the Equal Employment Opportunity Commission (EEOC) and provisions are included for enforcement by a lawsuit in the federal court system brought by a private individual or the EEOC. The Supreme Court also has recognized that these laws prohibit sexual harassment, which causes emotional harm even though unaccompanied by economic consequences. Another important piece of federal legislation is the Age Discrimination in Employment Act. This law has been amended to remove the upper age limit of 70 for age protection so that coverage is now extended in all aspects of employment to those over 40 years of age.

Religious Discrimination

The Civil Rights Act of 1964, as amended, prohibits an employer from discriminating against an employee because of any "religious observance and practice" unless the employer is unable to reasonably accommodate the employee's religious practice without undue hardship on the conduct of the business. In a 1982 case, a hospital was accused of religious discrimination when it refused to continue to accommodate the work schedule of a pharmacist who would not work on Saturdays for religious reasons. The 5 staff pharmacists at the hospital were responsible for arranging their own schedules, and they were permitted to trade shifts with one another. The pharmacist in question failed to arrange an exchange of shifts and did not appear for work on Saturdays or certain other religious holidays. After one warning, he again failed to report to work on Saturday and failed to arrange an exchange of shifts.

The pharmacist brought an action in federal court claiming that he had been discharged because of his religion. At the trial, the hospital conceded that the pharmacist had established a case of religious discrimination by demonstrating that his bona fide religious practice conflicted with an employment requirement but argued that the hospital had made significant efforts to accommodate the pharmacist's needs. The court concluded that although there is a burden on the employer to accommodate the employee's religious beliefs, there is a corresponding duty on the employee to act in good faith and cooperate with the employer. A reasonable accommodation need not be on the employee's terms only. (*Brener v. Diagnostic Center Hospital*, 671 F.2d 141 [5th Cir. 1982].)

Sexual Harassment

Congress and the federal courts have defined sexual harassment to include unwelcomed sexual advances by supervisory personnel and the creation of a hostile working environment. Sexual harassment occurs when unwelcomed sexual advances are an implied or express condition for receiving job benefits. The loss of employment because of one's failure to submit to sexual demands also constitutes sexual harassment.

Sexual harassment that results from a hostile working environment may involve harassing conduct by a coworker or supervisor, such as sexually suggestive remarks or physical contact of a sexual nature. The victim must prove that the offensive action altered the victim's condition of employment and created an abrasive working environment.

The conduct and reaction of the victim will be very important in determining whether the sexual advances were unwelcome. The person being harassed should orally object to the offensive behavior and physically move away from the initiator to leave no doubt that the behavior is unacceptable.

In the case of *Meritor Savings Bank v. Vinson*, 477 U.S. 57 (1986), the US Supreme Court addressed previously unresolved issues regarding employer liability for sexually harassing conduct by supervisors. For the first time, the court dealt with "environmental harassment" or the creation of a hostile, intimidating, or offensive working environment through words or conduct of a sexual nature. The court ruled that the working environment itself is a term of employment, and that an employee can file a sexual harassment complaint even if she or he has suffered no economic detriment or other measurable damages. The court chose to rely upon a case-by-case analysis using traditional principles of agency law when deciding if the employer is liable. One of the circumstances to be considered is whether the employer has specific policies condemning sexual harassment. Long-standing and pervasive conduct would put the employer on constructive notice of sexual harassment.

In 1993, the US Supreme Court decided *Harris v. Forklift Systems, Inc.* 510 U.S. 17 (1993), the second major case in this area to reach that level. Here the Court identified the following list of factors to be evaluated in determining whether a "hostile working environment" case exists: (1) frequency of the conduct; (2) severity of the conduct; (3) whether the conduct was physically threatening or humiliating; and (4) whether it unreasonably interferes with the employee's work performance.

The employer may be held liable for sexual harassment by a supervisor who has authority over hiring, promotion, and dismissal of the employee alleging the act. The employer may be held liable irrespective of fault on his or her part. In cases involving hostile working environments, it must be shown that the employer, through his supervisory personnel, knew or should have known of the sexual harassment.

Wage Discrimination

The Equal Pay Act of 1963 precludes any wage irregularity on account of sex in substantially equal jobs. The law applies to any private employer who is engaged in interstate commerce and has 2 or more employees, subject to certain monetary standards. In the case of *Pedreyra v. Cornell Prescription Pharmacies*, 465 F. Supp. 936 (D.Colo. 1979), the plaintiff pharmacist brought an employment discrimination action alleging that the defendant pharmacy engaged in discriminatory activities including gender-based wage discrimination. Pedreya was able to show that she was paid a salary of $1,100 per month for the pay period February 1973 through April 1974, while the male pharmacists employed during the same time period earned from $100 to $150 more per month. The plaintiff was designated as a manager of one of the defendant's pharmacies. She also served as a preceptor and was responsible for supervising the pharmacy interns. When the plaintiff filed a charge of sex-based wage discrimination with the Equal Employment Opportunity Commission, her employer gave her 2 weeks notice of termination.

The plaintiff was able to show that she had consistently been paid less than the defendant's male pharmacist employees. She brought her action under the Civil Rights Act and the Equal Pay Act. The Equal Pay Act has the narrow purpose of prohibiting sex discrimination in pay between employees doing equal work. The plaintiff alleged that the wage differential was due solely to her sex. The court found that there was no question that the plaintiff had at least equal skills to all the male pharmacists. All were required to have a degree in pharmacy; to have served as interns; and to have passed the state board of pharmacy licensure examination. The plaintiff met all of these professional requirements and also was a designated preceptor. The defendant claimed that the plaintiff exerted less effort than the male pharmacists who performed additional duties. The defendant sought to prove that the plaintiff never worked on Saturdays, never took emergency night calls, never filled physician orders, and never stocked shelves. These differences were cited as examples of less than equal effort that justified a lower salary to the plaintiff.

However, the evidence showed that the plaintiff was hired by the defendant to manage his Denver pharmacy. The plaintiff agreed to work, but only Monday through Friday. She was never requested to work on Saturdays and the defendant had never explained to the plaintiff that she would be paid less than those who did. The court noted "the defendant's presentation had a distinct aura of hindsight associated with it." While she never worked Saturdays, she was responsible for opening the pharmacy and often was the only pharmacist on duty. The early morning openings also imposed an additional hazard for her because the pharmacy was robbed on occasions when she was the only employee present. Shift differentials alone would not justify a wage differential between a female and a male pharmacist. It was shown that the plaintiff stocked shelves when necessary and that she filled as many prescriptions as any other pharmacist employed by the defendant. The court concluded that the plaintiff's sex was a major factor in the pharmacy's decision to compensate her at a lower rate than that paid the male pharmacists.

In order to overcome the burden of proof, the defendant had to show that the differential salary was justified because of (1) seniority, (2) merit, (3) a system that measured earnings by quantity or quality of production, or (4) a differential based on any factor other than sex. The defendant was not able to meet any of these criteria and the court found that the plaintiff was a victim of wage discrimination. The court further found that the plaintiff had been discharged from her employment as a result of her filing charges with the EEOC. The plaintiff was awarded $23,000 in back wages along with other damages and lost fringe benefits.

Retaliatory Discharge

Retaliatory discharge also may form the basis of claims filed with the EEOC. A hospital pharmacist claimed that she was discharged for reporting alleged racial discrimination in the hiring practices of the hospital's director of pharmacy. The pharmacist, who was responsible for the IV services, was instructed to hire a staff pharmacist and pay different wages to a black pharmacist than would be paid to a white pharmacist. After complaining to the hospital administration, the pharmacist received a number of verbal and written reprimands regarding alleged errors in her job performance. Prior to her filing the complaint, she had no written reports in her personnel file detailing any problems with her services. The plaintiff was eventually terminated by the director of pharmacy for an incident that allegedly endangered a patient.

The appellate court found that the trial court did not make sufficient findings to evaluate the plaintiff's claims of retaliatory discharge. The court noted that the plaintiff did not need to prove that the discriminatory hiring practices really existed. She only had to show that she had a reasonable belief that such practices existed in order to be protected by the Civil Rights Act. The law provides that it is an unlawful employment practice for an employer to discriminate against employees who oppose allegedly discriminatory practices by the employer. (*De Anda v. St. Joseph Hospital*, 671 F2d 850 [5th Cir. 1982].)

In claims of wage-based sex discrimination, the issue of "comparable worth" has failed to obtain judicial support even though some states have taken statutory initiatives in this area. The comparison of jobs that are substantially equal, not merely similar, is required to establish wage-based sex discrimination. Reliance on the fact that the jobs had the same title, code, or even job description may be inadequate. Payment of traditionally female jobs at a salary rate that is less than traditionally male jobs is not evidence of discrimination even if the female jobs require more skill, effort, and responsibility. The mere predominance of persons of one sex in a job classification is not evidence of sex discrimination in setting wages.

Handicap Discrimination

The Americans with Disabilities Act (ADA) and the Rehabilitation Act of 1973 are the primary federal laws that prohibit discrimination on the basis of handicap. Under these pieces of legislation, a handicapped person is defined as one who: (1) has a physical or mental impairment that substantially limits one or more major life activities; (2) has a record of such impairment; and (3) is regarded as having such an impairment.

The Rehabilitation Act assures that truly disabled, but genuinely capable, individuals will not face discrimination in employment because of stereotypes about the insurmountability of their handicaps. However, the courts will insist that the statutory protection not be extended to individuals whose disability is minor and whose severity of impairment is widely shared by others. In *Marten v. Derwinski*, 1991 WL 255113 (N.D.N.Y.), a Veterans Administration pharmacist alleged that he was discharged because of his handicap. Marten offered evidence that he had a sprained shoulder, but he provided the court no indication that this affected his major life activities. The Veterans Administration stated that reasons for his dismissal included insubordination, input of false medication orders into the pharmacy computer, and refusal to perform assigned duties. The case was dismissed when the plaintiff could produce no evidence that he was unable to perform a major life activity, such as caring for himself, performing manual tasks, walking, seeing, hearing, speaking, breathing, learning, or working.

These 2 federal acts seek to integrate disabled individuals into the economic and social mainstream of the United States, and to ensure that the truly disabled will not face discrimination because of stereotypes or their insurmountable impairments. However, there is a clear line of demarcation between extending the statutory protection to a truly disabled individual and allowing an individual with marginal impairment to use disability laws as bargaining chips to gain a competitive advantage.

In a case on point, a pharmacist-attorney-physician filed a lawsuit against a hospital when he was denied admission to its pediatric residency program. The plaintiff, who had an eye disorder, alleged that the hospital and various members of the resident selection committee discriminated against him in their selection process and also retaliated against him for exercising his rights under the ADA.

Following the receipt of his pharmacy degree, the plaintiff entered law school as a full-time student and worked 15 to 35 hours per week as a pharmacist. While in law school, he experienced eye strain and was fitted with a contact lens that improved the visual acuity in his right eye. According to the plaintiff, during the years following his adjustment, he perceived no problems with his vision and functioned very well, both as a registered pharmacist and as an attorney.

When the plaintiff was admitted to the University of Illinois Medical School, he referred to his visual condition as a "former" problem, stating that the condition no longer confronted him and that it had been cured. During his first quarter at medical school, the plaintiff experienced eye strain and had some difficulty using a binocular microscope. He was examined by an ophthalmologist who concluded that his visual condition was congenital. Any laboratory tests requiring fine perception of depth would be difficult for the plaintiff, but the examining physician concluded that the plaintiff had adapted well to daily activities and should have visual capacity to function in most medical specialties.

When the pharmacist/attorney, now a medical student, received a below-average grade in an obstetrics/gynecology clerkship program, he filed a complaint alleging discrimination. The US Department of Education found that the plaintiff was disabled under the Rehabilitation Act and the ADA and that his grade in the clerkship likely was tainted by bias. The medical school eventually re-evaluated his grade and ultimately gave him a passing score.

Following medical school, the plaintiff applied to a number of pediatric residency programs. In his application, he stated that he no longer considered his visual problem an obstacle because he had been fitted with a contact lens which corrected his visual acuity. During his interview for the pediatric residency program at the defendant hospital, the plaintiff informed the director about his eye problem and asked to be excused from being on call for 36 hours at a time and from night call. His visual impairment was not mentioned to the remainder of the interviewers, some of whom found the plaintiff to be insolent and arrogant during the interviews. However, a hospital administrator agreed to accommodate the plaintiff by providing additional help if he were selected as a resident.

The admissions committee decided not to rank the plaintiff at all and despite his threats of legal action, remained firm in its decision not to admit him to the pediatric residency program. In the lawsuit that ensued, the United States Court of Appeals found that the plaintiff had failed to establish some likelihood that he was an individual with a disability within the meaning of the statutes. It concluded that his impairment did not rise to the level of substantially limiting one or more of the major life activities. The court could not conclude that an inability to fulfill long shifts necessarily proved that the plaintiff was disabled within the meaning of the law. More importantly, no objective medical finding supported the plaintiff's assertion that he is so significantly restricted by his visual impairment that he is incapable of performing night calls.

The court noted that the plaintiff was able to successfully complete both his pharmacy and law degrees without any accommodation. While medical school may be more demanding than law school or pharmacy school, the court noted that the plaintiff went to law school full time while being employed as a pharmacist for up to 35 hours a week. It was noted that when it was beneficial and opportune for the plaintiff to disclose his alleged disability, he would do so, and then he would advise that the failure to accommodate him would violate disability laws. The court noted that one could very well conclude that the admission committee's initial decision not to rank the plaintiff was motivated by its concern about his attitude, maturation, and questionable personality traits rather than by any alleged prejudice on the part of the program. (*Roth v. Lutheran General Hospital et al.*, 47 F.3d 1446 [7th Cir, 1975].)

AIDS Discrimination

Any consideration of employment law must take into account the impact of AIDS on the workplace. Individuals with AIDS have been provided protection under most existing state and federal laws prohibiting employment discrimination of the handicapped. The Rehabilitation Act of 1973 provides protection against discrimination on the basis of handicap by programs receiving federal financial assistance.

The courts have ruled that, under the law, an otherwise qualified handicapped individual is one who is able to meet all other requirements of the job in spite of the handicap. In the decision of *School Board of Nassau County v. Arline*, 480 U.S 273 (1987), the US Supreme Court ruled that a person suffering from tuberculosis can be a handicapped individual within the meaning of the law and the question of qualification depends to a large degree upon medical judgment. The court held that an employer has an affirmative obligation to make a reasonable accommodation of a handicapped person.

The New York City Human Rights Commission fined a dental clinic $37,000 for refusing to treat AIDS patients. The decision was based upon the city's ban on discrimination against handicapped persons. The dentist informed an AIDS patient that the clinic would not treat him because the clinic did not have the proper facilities. The patient called the reaction to his HIV status absurd because the clinic observed standard infection-control procedures.

Pharmacists have been discharged from their employment after testing positive for exposure to the AIDS virus. These cases generally have been settled out of court. In a Pennsylvania action, a hospital found that one of its pharmacists had tested positive to exposure to the AIDS virus. He was told that he could not continue to work unless he was further examined and submitted to a series of medical tests. No other hospital employee had been required to submit to such tests.

In his complaint, the pharmacist stated that his responsibilities involved no invasive procedures on patients and that he was physically and mentally capable of performing his job functions. The hospital argued that it had a duty, when confronted with acts that may pose a risk to hospital patients, to investigate and balance the rights of employees with the rights of patients. The hospital also noted that the pharmacist did perform procedures on fluids that were intended to be given to patients intravenously. The hospital settled out of court for an undisclosed sum.

Employers are encouraged to evaluate each AIDS case on an individual basis. It generally is accepted that the disease should be treated as a handicap, and employers are urged not to have a blanket policy against hiring anyone with AIDS. Reasonable accommodations should be made for individuals suffering from the disease. However, employers should remember that they need not hire or retain someone who cannot presently perform the job. Employers must be prepared to deal with unfounded fears and concerns from co-employees who may be asked to work with an AIDS victim. The employee with AIDS should be provided as much privacy and confidentiality as possible.

Polygraph Testing

Because of increasing instances of employee theft, prospective and current employees are being asked to submit to polygraph tests as a condition of employment. While the Constitution protects private citizens from intrusive government action, there is much less protection in actions between private individuals. Thus, a pharmacist may not be compelled to be a witness against himself in an investigation by a government agency, but there is little that an employee can do when faced with a private employer who offers the choice of a polygraph test or job termination. A handful of states have enacted statutes that make it unlawful for an employer to require an employee or prospective employee to take a lie detector or similar test as a condition of employment. However, some of these statutes contain exceptions for employees who dispense controlled substances.

In 1977, the American Pharmaceutical Association House of Delegates went on record as opposing polygraph testing in employment situations, but many pharmacy employers support the use of the polygraph because of financially devastating employee pilferage. An increasing number of lawsuits are being filed by employees because of polygraph testing. It has been reported that one pharmacy employer paid $57,241 in an out-of-court settlement to 22 employees who were fired because they would not take lie detector tests.

There was considerable interest in Congress in 1986 regarding the use of polygraphs by employers. Legislation was introduced that would virtually eliminate the use of the polygraph test in the workplace. While this bill had the support of employee pharmacists and certain professional organizations, there was strong opposition to the proposal by corporate pharmacy employers who amended the legislation to include an exemption for firms who employ individuals handling controlled substances.

On June 27, 1988, President Ronald Reagan signed into law the Employee Polygraph Protection Act of 1988 (29 U.S.C. §2001 et seq.), which prohibits private sector employers from using a polygraph to test job applicants or current employees on a random basis. This legislation bans about 85% of the previous use of polygraph examinations in this country. However, companies authorized to manufacture, dispense, or sell controlled substances can require polygraph tests from employees who will have direct access to controlled substances. A prospective employee would have direct access if the position has responsibilities that include contact with or affect disposition of a controlled substance. A current employee could be subject to a polygraph exam only if he has infrequent, random, or opportunist access to controlled substances. Thus, while the legislation does not prohibit polygraph testing of pharmacists, it does place a series of restrictions on when and how the polygraph test can be given.

Polygraph tests are allowed for all companies in connection with an ongoing criminal investigation if the employer has a reasonable suspicion that one of the workers was involved in a crime affecting the company. The test results cannot be the sole basis for an adverse employment action against an employee. The Act requires employers to post a notice informing employees of their rights under the legislation.

Screening for Illicit Drug Use

Biomedical tests in employee screening programs provide tremendous diagnostic tools, but also present a host of ethical, social, political, economic, and legal questions. Pharmacist-ethicist Robert Veatch has warned that we may become so infatuated with our technical abilities to accumulate data and tally scores that we run the risk of seriously misunderstanding the nature of the difficult decisions that must be made.

The legal defensibility of the analytical methods used in drug testing is of concern both to those challenging the procedures and those who are in the business of conducting such tests. Experts have reported wide differences in the defensibility of the tests that are currently available and almost all agree that single-procedure methods are the least defensible. Urine samples that test positive for drug use should be retested using a different procedure.

The accuracy of drug testing programs continues to be seriously debated. While the tests rarely miss detecting drugs in the urine, they will, on occasion, misidentify other substances as an illegal drug. This is referred to as a false-positive test result. Depending on the drug being tested, the screening method being used, and other factors, false-positive rates may vary from 1% or less to 50% or more. False-positives may be the result of human error or may be caused by cross-reactivity with legal over-the-counter (OTC) drugs or even certain foods.

OTC cold medications may create a false-positive for amphetamine use; cough syrups containing dextromethorphan can result in a positive test for morphine; herbal tea, aspirin, or poppyseed bagels may result in a positive result for marijuana. The possibility of even a small number of false-positive tests has prompted one pharmacist-attorney to state that drug testing is an inversion of the criminal justice system. That system says that some guilty may go free to ensure that the innocent are not convicted. This policy says lots of innocents may get fired to ensure that every guilty person is fired as well.

Many of the challenges to drug testing are based on Constitutional considerations, such as right to privacy, due process, and freedom from illegal searches. The Constitution's protection of individual freedoms is primarily against interference by state and federal governments. It is important to note that, as a general rule, employers in the private sector are not bound by Fourth Amendment restrictions because of the absence of any so-called "state action." It is not likely that there will be a significant judicial movement to impose Fourth Amendment prohibitions on private employers unless they are involved in activities with a high degree of governmental regulation.

Some would argue that submitting a urine sample does not constitute a seizure within the framework of the Constitution because there is no touching or invasion of the body, but merely an analysis of a human waste product. The courts generally have not accepted this argument. The taking of a blood sample from an allegedly drunk driver has been held to be a search and seizure within the context of the Constitution, and most courts have found little distinction between testing blood and testing a urine specimen.

Although it seems clear that drug testing constitutes a search or seizure, the Fourth Amendment prohibits only *unreasonable* searches and seizures. A search generally is not considered to be unreasonable unless there is no probable cause to believe that the individual was guilty of any misconduct. Public-sector employees who are responsible for the health and safety of others will most likely be subject to close scrutiny for drug use. These employees have been viewed by the courts as having a lesser expectation of privacy because they knowingly engage in a work involving public safety.

The preferability of some reasonable suspicion of drug use has caused courts generally to look with disfavor on random, blanket, or dragnet searches. Many employers argue that they cannot achieve a drug-free workplace without relying on the deterrent effect of random testing. While such tests are particularly suspect under the law, those employees involved in positions affecting public health and safety again are the most likely to be confronted with these tests.

Although the right to privacy is not directly articulated in the US Constitution, it permeates the Fourth Amendment. This Constitutional right to privacy is not absolute and the courts must again balance a variety of competing interests. Some drug-testing programs require employees to submit a urine specimen only under direct supervision to prevent counterfeit samples from being provided. The elimination of body wastes is one of the most private of human functions and the mandatory observation by others has been held to constitute an invasion of privacy. While some courts have shown a great deal of sensitivity to these intrusive searches, others have given more weight to the employer's needs.

While the rights of current employees continue to evolve through court decisions, little legal or economic protection has been provided to individuals seeking employment. Job applicants do not have the benefits of collective bargaining agreements, nor do they possess the vested rights of an employee. It is not unusual for many employers to require pre-employment physical and medical examinations that include both blood and urine tests. One could argue that employers have greater latitude to conduct such exams on prospective employees because the applicant has implicitly consented to the intrusion as a condition of obtaining employment.

The employer must be careful to develop policies that uniformly test all job applicants or that define certain job categories that require pre-employment screening. In all cases, the test results must be treated in a confidential manner to avoid charges of defamation or invasion of privacy.

The Rehabilitation Act of 1973 prohibits any employer receiving federal funds from discriminating against "otherwise qualified handicapped individuals." Alcoholics and drug users who are rehabilitated are protected as handicapped individuals under the Act, but employees who are currently drug abusers or alcoholics are specifically excluded. To be handicapped under the Act, a person must have a physical impairment that substantially limits one or more of the person's major life activities. This definition does not include the casual or recreational use of drugs because no major life activity is impaired.

Workers' Compensation

The state and federal workers' compensation laws are closely associated with express or implied employment contracts. Workers' compensation provides medical and cash benefits to employees who are injured or who incur a disease as a result of their employment.

At common law, an injured employee had to pay for his or her own medical care and was not compensated for time lost from work because of the injury. Furthermore, the employer would frequently fire an injured employee if the injury decreased the employee's ability to work. If a worker was injured because of the employer's negligence (a frequent occurrence), he or she could sue the employer, but such suits were frequently lost. As a legal defense, the employer would claim that the employee assumed the risks of the job, the employee's negligence was the cause of the injury, the injury was caused by a fellow employee, or the injury or disease was not related to the job. Consequently, as the United States became more industrialized and job-related injuries and deaths became more prevalent, social justice demanded that the employer's moral duty to compensate the employee for work injuries be turned into a legal duty. Wisconsin was the first state to enact a workers' compensation law in 1911. Every state now has such a law, and the federal government has several such laws covering federal employees, employees in the District of Columbia, and longshoremen and dock workers at all ports in the United States.

One of the underlying principles supporting the workers' compensation system is that industrial accidents are inevitable. Therefore, industry, not the employee, should bear the cost of accidents. Generally, workers' compensation provides payment of benefits without regard to the fault of the employee or employer; however, in some states, an employee who is injured because the employer violated a safety code receives more compensation.

TYPES OF BUSINESS ORGANIZATIONS

Introduction

There are 3 traditional types of business organizations: Sole proprietorship, partnership, and corporation. An additional option of more recent origin is the limited liability company (L.L.C.) or limited liability partnership (L.L.P.). A pharmacy that is operated for profit can be established within the legal structure of any of these. An institutional pharmacy, usually a department or service unit within the institution, may be run as a sole proprietorship, partnership, or corporation if it is operated for profit. Most nonprofit hospitals are operated as nonprofit or charitable corporations, and public hospitals are operated under the auspices of the municipal, state, or federal governments.

Sole Proprietorship

A proprietorship is individual ownership and operation of a business. It is the simplest way to operate a business because it does not require prior governmental approval with the exception of applicable municipal business permits and professional licensure. The proprietor is entirely in control, and this responsibility extends to liability for both the operation and debts of the business. The owner's personal assets are liable for proprietorship debts regardless of whether the assets are used in the business. Business net profits are taxed to the proprietor as personal income whether or not profit actually is taken out of the business.

Partnership

A partnership is the legal relationship between individuals who jointly own and operate a business for profit. The operation of a partnership differs from the sole proprietorship mainly in that it requires the mutual agreement of the partners. Usually, each partner in a general partnership is jointly liable for the debts, torts, and management of the partnership. In a limited partnership, the limited partner has limited liability. Although an oral agreement for general partnerships is often legal, a written agreement, which must be recorded in the appropriate government office, usually is required by state law for a limited partnership. A partnership is not taxed as a business entity for income; however, a partner's individual share of the partnership income is taxed as personal income.

Corporation

A corporation is a legal body that is comprised of one or more individuals or entities who operate a business under a charter or articles of incorporation executed in compliance with state law. In a sense, a corporation is recognized legally as an entity that is separate from its owners. It is the most complicated of the types of business organizations, and it requires a certain formality of creation and operation. It is managed by a board of directors who act in accordance with the corporation charter, bylaws, and resolutions.

Corporate net profits are first taxed to the corporation; when the profits are distributed (as dividends), they are taxed again to the stockholders. Closely held small business corporations, which are under subchapter S of the Internal Revenue Service (IRS) Code and Regulations, are not double-taxed. The officers, directors, and stockholders of the corporation are, to a certain extent, insulated from personal liability for corporate debts and activities.

Sole Proprietorship

The sole proprietorship is a one-person operation; therefore, the liabilities, business decisions, and net profits of the proprietorship are the proprietor's. The proprietor is responsible for the actions of employees acting within the scope of their employment. Personal and business assets are put on the line when money is borrowed. Hence, credit often is more difficult for a proprietorship to obtain than it is for the other types of business.

When the proprietor dies, the proprietorship ends unless provision for carrying on the business is made in the proprietor's will. An executor who is empowered by the will to carry on the proprietorship is, in a sense, an interim proprietor. An ongoing business that is left to a new owner or sold under provisions of the will is more valuable than one that must be closed because no provisions were made to continue the business after the death of the owner.

Although a proprietorship is often operated under the full name of the owner, it may also be run under a trade name or an assumed name. If a trade name or an assumed name is used, some states require that a document with the full name and address of the proprietor be filed with the government. On legal documents, the proprietorship is often designated by the term "doing business as" (dba) (eg, John Hetrick, dba Fairfield Surgical).

Partnership

The legal relationships designated by the participants as a partnership or a joint venture, association, group, pool, or syndicate, which often is considered by the IRS as a partnership, must file a tax return. This return is treated as informative because tax is not levied on a partnership itself. The partnership profits are taxed as the personal income of the partners. The mere sharing of profits or expenses, or the mere co-ownership of nonrented property is not necessarily a partnership. In some cases, the IRS will classify a partnership as a corporation when its operations are akin to that of a corporation.

There are 2 types of partnerships—the general partnership and the limited partnership. In the general partnership, all of the partners share in the duties, profits, and liabilities. The limited partnership consists of one or more general partners and one or more limited partners. The limited partners have limited liability, usually only to the extent of their dollar investment in the partnership; they usually cannot take an active part in the management and operation of the partnership.

General Partnership Agreements

Partnership agreements may be oral, although this is not recommended, except in states that require a written agreement for limited partnerships. If the partnership agreement is written, it usually is recorded in the register of deeds or with the government official who keeps title records. In the absence of a written agreement, partnership rights and duties are governed completely by the Uniform Partnership Act, which has been enacted in most states.

It also should be noted that the law of agency (one individual acting on behalf of another) applies to partnerships. In a general partnership, each partner is an agent of the partnership and of all the partners. That is to say, in the absence of a written agreement to the contrary, each partner individually may bind the partnership to a transaction.

The agreement for a general partnership usually is written because it provides evidence of the mutual understanding of the partners. In addition, by means of a written agreement, the partners can modify their various rights and duties, which otherwise would be governed strictly by statute. The agreement contains information such as the names and addresses of the partners; the purpose of the partnership; the location of the partnership; the amount of money, property, or services that each partner will contribute; compensation, if any, for the services rendered by the partners in the management of the firm; the procedure on dissolution of the firm upon the retirement or death of a partner; and how the profits and losses are to be shared.

Partnership decisions are made by majority rule unless they are otherwise modified by written agreement. Without agreement to the contrary, all partners have an equal vote regardless of the size of their contribution to the partnership. Each partner also shares equally in the profits regardless of his or her contribution, unless this is modified by written agreement.

Partner Liability

Partners are jointly liable for the debts of the partnership in those states where the Uniform Partnership Act is in effect. However, the statutes of certain other states hold that the liability of partners for the debts and contract obligations of the partnership is both joint and several. A joint obligation means that all of the partners in the firm are liable as a group. If an obligation is joint and several, all of the partners are liable together and each partner is liable individually for the entire debt or contractual agreement.

Tort liability of a partnership is joint and several, meaning that all partners are fully liable, provided that the tort is committed within the scope of the partnership activity.

There is some legal authority supporting the position that the individual authority of a partner to bind the firm contractually, by a provision to that effect, can be restricted in the partnership agreement (eg, the agreement may require all of the partners to sign a contract for sale of partnership real estate). The restriction of liability in a partnership agreement is effective against a third person dealing with the partnership only if that individual has notice of the restriction.

Generally speaking, a partnership is a separate entity, and it may be held liable for the criminal acts of a partner when those acts are committed within the scope of the partnership activity. However, criminal liability will not be imputed to the individual partners unless they have participated in the crime, have knowledge of it and have consented to it, or have received benefit from it.

In cases of license violations, if the license is held in the partnership's name, each partner may be held liable for the violation of a copartner when it is committed in the usual course of partnership business. It does not matter whether the partner had knowledge of the act.

Limited Partnership Agreements

In a limited partnership, one or more of the partners has limited liability, usually only to the extent of the monetary or property contribution to the partnership. A limited partner may not contribute services to the partnership. Generally, a limited partner may not exercise any control in the management of the partnership, but if he or she does share in the control, he or she becomes as liable as a general partner.

A number of states have enacted the Uniform Limited Partnership Act, which gives the limited partner the right to a share in the partnership income, a right to financial information relative to the partnership income, and certain rights upon dissolution of the partnership.

Usually the limited partners are in a better position than the general partners upon the dissolution of a partnership. However, the partners in a limited partnership may set up a different preference of payment priorities in their written agreement.

Corporation

A business corporation is an organization that is operated for profit with capital stock (the amount of money, property, or both that is contributed by the stockholders to the corporation to finance its operation). A business corporation is called a domestic corporation if it conducts business in the state in which it was organized. If it operates in states other than that in which it was organized, it is termed a foreign corporation by such states.

A business corporation can be closely held when it has only a few stockholders, or it can be public with numerous stockholders. However, the term "public corporation" often means a corporation that is established by the municipal, state, or federal government to perform a public service (eg, the Federal Deposit Insurance Corporation [FDIC]).

A corporation can be operated as a regular, functioning business or it can be formed for tax-saving reasons, as are some professional corporations and S corporations.

For federal income tax purposes, the IRS sometimes classifies certain unincorporated associations, insurance companies, trusts, joint stock companies, and even some partnerships as corporations when they operate as such. That is, when they have attributes of a corporation, including continuity of existence, centralized management, limited liability, and free transferability of interest (ownership).

A nonstock, nonprofit organization, which exists and operates under and by virtue of the specific laws of the state in which it is organized, may be operated for religious, charitable, social, educational, or scientific purposes.

Formation of a Business Corporation

The mechanics of incorporation vary among the states; however, the Model Business Incorporation Act has provided a degree of continuity from state to state.

The **corporate promoter** is an individual who brings about the formation of a business corporation by generating sufficient interest to invest in it. The promoter usually works prior to the formation of the corporation to circulate a capital stock subscription agreement, which binds the signers to purchase stock once the corporation is formed. In a number of states, if the corporate stock is to be sold to more than 10 or 15 individuals, the subscription agreement must be approved by the state securities bureau. Similarly, interstate sale of stock often requires registration of the subscription agreement with the federal Securities and Exchange Commission (SEC).

The **incorporator** is the individual who executes the articles of incorporation—the initiating document in the formation of the corporation. It is not necessary to have a prior stock subscription agreement in order to form a corporation. Some states no longer require a minimum capital before a corporation may commence business.

Articles of Incorporation

The articles of incorporation usually include the name of the corporation, the period of existence (usually perpetual), the purpose for the formation of the corporation, the location of the initial office, the name and address of the initial registered agent (the individual to whom legal papers may be served), the number of directors (in some cases, the names and addresses of the initial board of directors), the number and titles of the officers, and the number and type of shares of capital stock (eg, 100,000 shares of common stock).

State law prohibits corporations that are organized in the state from having the same corporate name. Therefore, the proposed corporate name must be approved by the state corporation office; the selected name may be held on reserve pending filing of the articles of incorporation. Usually, the state business corporation law requires that the name of a corporation include the word "corporation," "incorporated," "limited," or the abbreviated form (ie, "Corp.," "Inc.," or "Ltd."). The word "company" can refer to a corporation or it can refer to a partnership or proprietorship in which an assumed name is used. If it refers to a corporation, in some states the abbreviations "Corp.," "Inc.," or "Ltd." must follow the word "company" in the corporation name (eg, Fairfield Surgical Company, Inc.).

Board of Directors

After the articles of incorporation are executed and recorded, a certificate of incorporation is issued. The corporation is now in existence. The incorporator calls a meeting of the stock subscribers, and the stock subscribers name the initial board of directors at the meeting. In some states, the initial directors may be named in the articles of incorporation and the subscriber meeting is bypassed. The directors adopt bylaws (the procedures for operating the corporation). The bylaws also describe the duties of each corporate officer.

The board of directors manages the affairs of the corporation; the officers of the corporation carry out the directives of the board of directors. Major directives are in the form of resolutions that are adopted by majority vote at a board of directors meeting. The resolutions are entered by the corporate secretary in a minute book. The directors are answerable to the corporate stockholders, who can vote out the directors and vote in new directors at the annual meeting of corporation stockholders or at a meeting called specifically for that purpose.

A corporation operates upon strict formality. In fact, a corporation can lose its tax status as a corporation for failure to maintain the corporate form of operation.

Liability of Stockholders

One of the main reasons for incorporating a small business is to protect the stockholders' personal assets from business liabilities. In a proprietorship, for example, if the business fails, its creditors can attach claims to both the business assets and the personal assets (eg, car, home, and bank accounts) of the proprietor. In a corporation, the creditors usually can only attach claims to the corporate assets.

Stockholder insulation from corporate liability is not absolute. Stockholder liability is limited, but it is not nonexistent. It is usually true that if an individual owns stock in General Motors, he or she will not be liable for any corporate mismanagement. The case may be different if that individual is a majority stockholder in a closely held (small) corporation.

A court of law can charge the individual stockholders with, for example, fraud or misrepresentation on the part of the corporation. The corporate entity will be disregarded and the stockholders will be held personally liable in the following instances:

(1) When stockholders treat the assets of the corporation as their own personal assets—taking from the corporation at will to the injury of creditors;
(2) when stockholders personally sign or otherwise obligate themselves for corporate debts; and
(3) when stockholders substantially undercapitalize the corporation and actively participate in the corporate management.

Corporate Stock

Stock or shares are units of interest or ownership in a corporation. Stockholders are individuals who own stock in the corporation. In effect, they are the owners of the corporation. A stock certificate is evidence of stock ownership and is issued by the corporate officers to a stockholder. In some states, it is not necessary for a corporation to issue a stock certificate to stockholders, but it is required by law that the corporate records show the names and addresses of the stockholders and the amount of stock held by each. Authorized stock is the amount of stock that a corporation is authorized to issue. Outstanding shares mean the stock issued by the corporation and held by the stockholders. Treasury shares are the stock originally issued by the corporation, but subsequently acquired by the corporation.

A par or dollar value per share of stock can be listed in the articles of incorporation. However, in the closely held corporation, the stock usually is listed without par value. This gives the corporation more flexibility in that the board of directors is able to establish the stock value for sale purposes. In larger corporations, the par value of the stock value on the the stock exchange is subject to speculation.

In the small corporation, there is usually only one class of stock—common stock. Each outstanding share of common stock is entitled to one vote on each subject that is submitted to a vote at a stockholder meeting unless the articles of incorporation state otherwise. However, after a corporation is in business, any attempt by the directors or stockholders to diminish existing voting rights is void. A corporation may issue a new class of stock without voting rights.

Preferred Stock

This is a class of stock that sometimes does not have voting rights. However, it does have a preferred or priority right to distribution of capital assets upon liquidation of the corporation and, in some instances, a priority right to dividend distribution. Often, preferred stock has a stipulated dividend printed on the stock certificate. However, the usual rule is that the preferred stock dividend is payable only from corporate earnings: If there are no earnings, there are no dividends. A few courts have held that agreed payments are enforceable out of corporate capital assets.

In some closely held corporations, a provision in the articles of incorporation restricts transfer of stock. For example, a restriction may stipulate that a stockholder must first offer to sell the stock back to the corporation or to a fellow stockholder before it can be sold to a member of the general public. Any restriction on the transfer of corporate stock must be printed on the stock certificate or it is invalid.

Reasons for Incorporation

If a sole proprietorship or partnership incorporates, the transfer of the proprietorship or partnership business property to the new corporation is tax free if the proprietor or partners control the new corporation. Additional reasons for incorporation include limited personal liability, the perpetual existence of the corporation, and the flexibility of the transfer of interest (ownership is transferred by exchange of stock). A corporation can be a tax shelter, and qualified pension and profit-sharing plans can be established. Group life insurance and group health, accident, and medical insurance are advantages that a corporation can offer its employees. In a closely held corporation, the principal stockholder's estate can benefit from a stock redemption funded by life insurance proceeds, with the premium paid by the corporation, which is also the beneficiary.

Reasons Against Incorporation

Although incorporation offers many advantages, there are several disadvantages that should be evaluated. A corporation faces a double tax in that corporate income is first taxed to the corporation and then again when it is distributed as dividends to stockholders. Because the IRS looks very carefully at closely held corporations, the formalities of a corporation must be reasonably maintained or any tax advantages may be lost by reclassification of the firm by the IRS.

S Corporations

There is another way in which the closely held corporation can avoid double taxation. If the corporation has 35 or fewer stockholders and only one class of stock, it may apply for S status. If the business qualifies under federal law, the net profit is not subject to tax. Instead, the net profit is taxed directly to the individual stockholder in proportion to his or her stock holdings whether the profit is actually distributed to the stockholder or not. The profits that are actually distributed from the S corporation are called dividends. Again, the stockholder is taxed on his or her pro rata share of the net profit, regardless of whether or not he or she received the share of profit.

There are 6 qualifications for an S corporation:

(1) The corporation must be domestic (ie, it must exist under the laws of one of the states in the United States);
(2) it must not be a member of an affiliated group (except as an inactive subsidiary);
(3) it must have only one class of stock;
(4) the corporation must not have more than 35 stockholders;
(5) it may have only individuals or estates as stockholders, although certain trusts may also qualify; and
(6) the corporation must not have a nonresident alien as a stockholder.

Corporations for Professional Practice

Most states have enacted statutes authorizing creation of a special type of corporation to be used by professionals in practice. These are variously referred to as "professional service corporations" (P.S.C.) or "professional associations" (P.A.). An example of this would be the business entity that employs John Smith, M.D. The business organization would likely be known as "John Smith, M.D., P.S.C." or "John Smith, M.D., P.A." Notice that these designations apply to the business firm, taking the place of "Inc." that would typically be seen with a standard or traditional corporation; John Smith, M.D., is an employee of that firm.

The primary motivation for organization of a professional practice in this fashion is the tax advantages that accrue. The business entity can pay for fringe benefits (retirement plans, etc.) for the employee and then deduct those costs as a legitimate business expense for tax purposes.

Pharmacists should be careful to distinguish between "P.A." used to indicate the professional association form of business organization and "P.A.-C.," the professional designation used by certified physician assistants.

Limited Liability Companies and Limited Liability Partnerships

The last quarter of the twentieth century saw the development of 2 additional forms of business organizations—limited liability company (L.L.C.) and limited liability partnership (L.L.P.). These have been described as "a non-corporate business form that provides its owners ('members') with limited liability and allows them to participate actively in the entity's management." In some ways these organizational forms resemble corporations and in others they resemble partnerships. Both are based on state statutes.

The I.R.S. will treat an L.L.C. as a partnership for tax purposes (ie, no double taxation) if it meets 3 of these 4 criteria:

    (1) Limited liability;
    (2) free transferability of ownership interest;
    (3) unlimited life of the business entity; and
    (4) centralized management.

One who owns an interest in an L.L.C. is known as a "member." The contract that creates the L.L.C. among the members generally is known as the "operating agreement," although it may be referred to as the member control agreement, regulations, or limited liability company agreement. Articles of organization must be filed with the state to create an L.L.C. One commentator has noted that "the concept of a contractual arrangement that affords limited liability like a corporation but also provides the freedom to establish ownership and management relationships based on the contract of the parties and that is treated as a partnership for tax purposes has long been considered to be an ideal business vehicle . . ."

L.L.P.s are similar to a traditional partnership with one major difference and several more modest ones. The major difference is that the potential liability exposure of a general partner in an L.L.P. is less than that of a general partner in a traditional partnership. Some states have required, as a tradeoff for the limited liability exposure, that the partnership hold a certain minimum amount of liability insurance. Another difference is that the statutes that authorize L.L.P.'s dictate that they be registered with the state government, something not required of a traditional partnership.

REGULATION OF COMPETITION

The economy of the United States is based on free competition. Yet this relationship between competitors cannot go unfettered because history has shown that some will accumulate so much market power that they will be able to dominate all others, or that others will engage in unscrupulous, and therefore illegal, activities in order to further advance their competitive edge. Consequently, the government has had to effect some rules regulating activities by competitors to ensure that free competition continues to be the hallmark of the US economic system.

Sherman Antitrust Act

Toward the end of the nineteenth century, a movement developed to control the growth of industrial power and wealth, which was concentrated in a few large corporations. Congress enacted the Sherman Antitrust Act of 1890 (15 U.S.C. §1, et seq). The purpose of the Sherman Antitrust Act was to promote free competition and to prevent undue restriction of trade and commerce. The Act prohibited any contract, combination, or conspiracy that would restrain interstate or foreign trade. It prohibited any individual from monopolizing or combining with others to monopolize interstate or foreign trade. However, the original Sherman Antitrust Act had a soft spot in that its language was too broad to accomplish its aims. In a number of cases, the government was unsuccessful in attempting to enforce the Act. However, it enjoyed some success, and it is still in effect today. Most of the success has been in the prohibition of price-fixing.

The courts have read the term "price-fixing" into the Sherman Antitrust Act's prohibitions. The US Supreme Court ruled in the case of *United States v. Socony-Vacuum Oil*, 310 U.S. 150 (1940), that all forms of price-fixing are illegal per se (on their face, presumptively) under the Sherman Antitrust Act. In a more recent case, the Court held that an exchange of price information among competitors violates the Act even if the resultant price stabilization is lower. The Court ruled that an exchange of price information by competitors is illegal if its stabilizes or creates uniform prices.

Although the Sherman Antitrust Act was somewhat effective in curbing price-fixing, it did not enjoy much success in cases involving monopoly. On several occasions, the courts held that the mere size of a company or its share of the market alone does not make it an illegal monopoly. Furthermore, even if dominance of a market is present, it must be shown that the accused violator has used the position of dominance to destroy competition. As a result of its shortcomings, the Sherman Antitrust Act was augmented by the Clayton Antitrust Act in 1914.

Clayton Antitrust Act

The purpose of the Clayton Antitrust Act of 1914 (15 U.S.C.§12, et seq) was to strengthen the Sherman Antitrust Act and to obviate the Sherman Antitrust Act's application to unions. The Clayton Antitrust Act provides the following.

It prohibits tying arrangements whereby a sale, lease, or contract forces the purchaser, lessee, or contracting party to refrain from using a competitor's goods to the effect that such an arrangement substantially lessens competition or tends to create a monopoly.

It prohibits the same individual from serving as a director or officer of 2 or more corporations if the corporations have capital of $1 million each and if they are competitors; therefore, the elimination of competition by agreement between the corporations would violate the antitrust laws.

The Clayton Antitrust Act prohibits direct or indirect price discrimination in selling the same commodity in like grade, quality, and quantity to different purchasers unless the price differentials result from different purchasing methods. This provision within the Clayton Act is known as the Robinson-Patman Act.

It provides a right to sue in federal court for treble damages if an individual is injured in his or her business by reason of anything forbidden by the antitrust laws.

It specifically provides that antitrust laws do not prohibit the existence and operation of labor organizations.

The Act prohibits one commercial corporation from directly or indirectly acquiring another when the effect is to lessen competition substantially or to create a monopoly. Certain types of corporations are excepted; the scope of the prohibition is extended to certain corporate mergers and conglomerates. Late in the twentieth century, this provision was used by the federal government to block proposed mergers of pharmacy chains.

Two Approaches by the Courts

Through a series of cases decided over nearly a century, the courts have fashioned 2 approaches to deciding whether the conduct alleged to violate the antitrust laws does *unreasonably* harm competition. Some anticompetitive conduct is inherently unreasonable and will be considered unlawful despite any beneficial effects. Such conduct, labeled "illegal per se," includes:

    (1) Price-fixing;
    (2) agreements to divide markets;
    (3) group boycotts intending an anticompetitive effect; and
    (4) tying arrangements that require a buyer to purchase one product in order to be able to buy another.

The "rule of reason" standard is the other approach. Here the court will weigh anticompetitive effects against the procompetitive effects and purposes. This rule is applied to many situations more numerous and varied than with the *per se* rule.

Robinson-Patman Price Discrimination Act

After the Clayton Antitrust Act was in effect for some time, it was noticed that the price discrimination prohibition was circumvented by certain large commodity buyers. The original Clayton Act amendment to Title 15 of the US Code allowed price differentials on the basis of quantity purchases. The large buyers, including chain stores, would exact a price break so large from a supplier of goods that it had no bearing on the quantity purchased. Another scheme was to charge brokerage fees to the supplier when there were no broker services rendered.

Consequently, in 1936, Congress reacted by passing the Robinson-Patman Price Discrimination Act, which provided that price savings on quantity purchases had to relate to quantitative differences and nothing more. The Act also permitted a variation in price to different customers when the price difference was made in order that the customer might meet competition. Additionally, an amendment 2 years after initial enactment exempted purchase of supplies by schools, churches, hospitals, public libraries, and other nonprofit institutions when those supplies were for the use of the institution. This amendment was known as the Nonprofit Institutions Act. More importantly, the Robinson-Patman Act prohibited buyers from knowingly inducing and receiving discriminatory prices.

The interpretation of words "for their own use" in reference to the purchase of supplies by a nonprofit organization was the primary issue in a significant lawsuit involving the pharmacy profession and the Robinson-Patman Price Discrimination Act. A pharmaceutical association, on behalf of over 60 community pharmacies, brought suit against 12 manufacturers who allegedly sold drugs to nonprofit hospital pharmacies at lower prices than those charged to community pharmacies. The drug manufacturers argued that the hospitals purchased the drugs "for their own use" and, consequently, they were exempt from the provisions of the Robinson-Patman Act.

The case eventually went to the US Supreme Court. In *Abbott Laboratories, et al v. Portland Retail Druggists Association*, 425 U.S. 1 (1976), the Supreme Court ruled that not all of a nonprofit hospital's purchases are exempt from the provisions of the Robinson-Patman Act. In order for purchases to be regarded as for the institution's own use, the purchases must be part of the hospital's intended institutional operation in the care of individuals who are its patients. Therefore, manufacturers and others can sell drugs to nonprofit institutions at a lower price and not violate antitrust laws if the drugs are dispensed in the following situations:

(1) To an inpatient for use in his or her treatment in the hospital;
(2) to a patient who is treated in the hospital's emergency facility;
(3) to an outpatient for personal use on the hospital premises;
(4) to an inpatient, outpatient, or emergency facility patient upon discharge and for his or her personal use away from the premises provided that the take-home prescription is intended for use as a continuation of, or supplement to, the treatment administered at the hospital;
(5) to a hospital employee or student for personal use or for the use of his or her dependents; and
(6) to a staff physician for his or her personal use or for the use of his or her dependents.

The exemption does not cover drugs dispensed by the hospital pharmacies to refill the prescription of the discharged inpatient, outpatient, or emergency facility patient who lacks a continuing relationship with the institution; to fill the prescription of the walk-in patient who has no present connection with the hospital or its pharmacy (except for obtaining the occasional emergency prescription); or for use by physicians for their private practice or for use by nondependents.

In its written opinion, the Court indicated that a drug supplier could avoid antitrust liability by a reasonable and noncollusive reliance on the proper certification by the nonprofit hospital as to its disposition of the products purchased from the supplier.

In a later case, the U.S. Supreme Court ruled that government hospitals are subject to the same restrictions as other nonprofit hospitals in the resale of drug products purchased at preferential prices. (*Jefferson County Pharmaceutical Assn., Inc. v. Abbott Laboratories*, et al, 461 U.S. 150 [1980].) More recently, the US Court of Appeals for the Ninth Circuit ruled that a nonprofit HMO is considered a "charitable institution" for purposes of the Robinson-Patman Act and, thus, can use drugs purchased at preferential prices the same way a non profit hospital can. (*DeModena v. Kaiser Foundation Health Plan*, 743 F.2d 1388 [9th Cir. 1984].)

Antitrust Laws and the Pharmacist

Treble-Damage Suits and the Pharmacist

The Clayton Antitrust Act gave anyone injured by an antitrust law violation the right to sue the responsible party for triple damages.

In *West Virginia v. Pfizer*, 440 F.2d 1079 (2nd Cir. 1971), 66 civil suits were brought against various pharmaceutical manufacturers of tetracycline, a broad-spectrum antibiotic, alleging price-fixing in violation of the Sherman and Clayton Antitrust Acts. The plaintiffs in the suits included states, counties, cities and their political subdivisions, drug wholesalers, community pharmacies, and individual consumers. In 1969, a settlement was approved by the court whereby the suits were dismissed when the manufacturers agreed to pay $100 million (later adjusted to $82,615,030) as follows: $50 million to government institutions; $10 million to state welfare drug reimbursement programs; $3 million to the wholesale and community pharmacies; and $37 million to consumers who filed claims.

A US district court approved the settlement, but certain drug wholesalers and retailers (in a class action on behalf of others) appealed the district court settlement approval to a federal court of appeals. One of the issues was the mere $3 million nuisance value amount earmarked for the wholesalers and retailers.

The federal court of appeals affirmed the settlement order and found no real merit to the objections raised by the wholesalers and retailers. The court found that the wholesalers' average markup on the cost price of the antibiotic was $16\frac{2}{3}$%, and the retailers' markup was about $66\frac{2}{3}$%, even though some pharmacies used a professional fee system. The higher the cost of the drug, the higher the gross profit from the markup. Therefore, the wholesalers and retailers actually profited from the higher cost that was charged to them for the drugs. It was the consumer who paid for the inflated cost of the antibiotic.

The drug wholesalers and retailers passed on the price that was charged to them whether by markup or by professional fee plus cost. The passing-on procedure was referred to by the court as a valid defense to a charge of price-fixing if such was made against the wholesalers and retailers, but it did not entitle them to triple damages. The only real damage suffered by the wholesalers and retailers was an increase in inventory cost because of stocking the antibiotics.

In another suit, the US Justice Department brought a criminal antitrust action against the same tetracycline manufacturers (*United States v. Pfizer*, 367 F.Supp. 91 [S.D.N.Y. 1973]), but the government lost the suit. The government failed to prove that parallel pricing resulted from illegal price-fixing. In defense, the drug manufacturers claimed that each lowered its tetracycline price in response to a competitor's price.

Price-Fixing and Third-Party Payment Plans

A problem encountered by pharmacy owners as a group in dealing with a third-party prescription payment plans in the early days of such arrangements was the possibility that the plan might be invalidated as violating antitrust laws (ie, the plan may tend to establish a uniform prescription charge in a given geographical area). The leading case in this area is *Blue Cross v. Commonwealth*, 176 S.E.2d 439 (Va. 1970).

In the Blue Cross case, Blue Cross of Virginia entered into a prepaid prescription plan where participating pharmacies would furnish prescription drugs to Blue Cross subscribers at cost plus a professional fee of $1.85. The $1.85 fee was unilaterally determined by Blue Cross. Although it held discussions on the matter with the Virginia Pharmaceutical Association, and the association members voted to accept the $1.85 fee, there was no holding by the court that the association and Blue Cross had any agreement on a fixed fee.

The agreements that were made were between Blue Cross and the individual pharmacies. The court found that an antitrust violation occurred. "The evidence shows not only that the 519 cooperating pharmacies charge a uniform price for drugs furnished under plan, but indicates also that the same uniform price will be charged their customers who are not Blue Cross subscribers."

Hence, the plan, in effect, established a uniform prescription charge in violation of the antitrust price-fixing prohibitions. The fact that the uniform charge could keep drug costs down for the consumer did not lessen the illegal nature of the price-fixing. This is so because of the "per se" rule mentioned above, whereby price-fixing is deemed to be so inimical to free competition that nothing can justify it.

The pharmacists in this case probably would have avoided the invalidation of the prepayment plan if they had not adjusted their nonsubscriber prescription charge to coincide with the Blue Cross fee. Third-party prescription payment plans are in widespread use throughout the country. In many, if not most instances, the prescription fee charged to nonsubscribers is the customary price, which is substantially different from that of other pharmacists and different from the fee agreed to with third-party payment plans.

This nation's highest court has not decided whether agreements between pharmacies and third-party payers are illegal under antitrust laws. In *Group Life and Health Insurance Company, et al v. Royal Drug Company, et al*, 440 U.S. 205 (1979), the US Supreme Court held that pharmacy agreements between Blue Cross/Blue Shield and prescription drug providers were not the business of insurance. These agreements were found to be actually agreements to reduce the insurer's costs; while this is the business of insurance companies, it is not the business of insurance, a phrase related to pooling risk, the basic concept of insurance. Therefore, the agreements are not exempt from antitrust laws.

The *Royal Drug* case did not decide whether the pharmacy agreements actually involved antitrust violations. It simply ruled that such agreements were not exempt as the business of insurance. The case was returned to the lower courts for a trial on the issues and the pharmacy owners did not prevail in the end. The US Justice Department filed a brief in the case in which it stated its opinion that the pharmacy agreements probably did not violate antitrust laws, but such an opinion should not be considered definitive on the matter.

Pharmacists may run afoul of the antitrust laws if they collectively withdraw or refuse to participate in a third-party program in an attempt to influence levels of reimbursement. In 1978, a number of New York City pharmacists simply withdrew from the Medicaid system; they, in effect, boycotted the system. Although a pharmacist is not required to fill or refill any and all prescriptions, his or her refusal must be for a good reason. However, once a pharmacist has joined the Medicaid prescription system, an abrupt boycott may not be permissable.

In the New York case, the state of New York brought suit against the Empire City Pharmaceutical Society, Inc., which had apparently prompted the Medicaid boycott, and obtained a settlement from the society for violation of antitrust laws.

Exclusive Contracts

A legal issue that has come to the fore with proliferation of prescription drug insurance programs and health maintenance organizations is whether it is lawful for an insurance plan or HMO purchaser of pharmacy services to enter into an "exclusive contract." A typical arrangement would involve an HMO contracting with a pharmacy chain in a particular locale to use these pharmacies exclusively to serve the HMO enrollees. Two possibilities exist. First, enrollees may only receive pharmacy services at outlets of the chain if they want the HMO to pay for the medication (otherwise they must bear the expense out-of-pocket, giving up a significant benefit of enrollment); or second, enrollees will be given a direct financial incentive to deal with pharmacies of the chain (eg, go to the "participating" chain pharmacy and the deductible amount per prescription amount to be paid by the patient will be $5.00, or go to a "nonparticipating" pharmacy where the deductible will be $15.00).

Such arrangements were upheld by the US Supreme Court and other federal courts in the case of *Group Life and Health Insurance, et al v. Royal Drug Co., et al*, 440 U.S. 205 (1979). Moreover, it is a basic principle of contract law that one is free to deal with, or not deal with, whomever he or she wishes (eg, I may choose to sell my car to "A" rather than to "B") so long as it is not discriminatory or anticompetitive (see Refusal to Deal below). Nonetheless, some pharmacists continue to view these exclusive contracts as anticompetitive and seek to have legislation enacted at the state level to require that such prescription drug insurance programs be "open" to all pharmacy providers who are willing to accept the level of reimbursement established by the plan, be it an HMO or a traditional health insurance company. Such legislation has been designated "any willing provider" or "freedom of choice legislation" because it preserves the patient's option of selecting a pharmacist.

Discriminatory Pricing

Discriminatory pricing, forbidden by the Robinson-Patman Act, is pricing by a manufacturer or supplier of commodities charged to purchasers who are competitors of each other. A manufacturer can charge one price to a wholesaler and another price to a retailer since the two are normally not competitors. Similarly, a tire manufacturer can charge one price for tires sold to the automobile manufacturer and another for tires sold to its dealers because the dealers and the automobile manufacturer are not competitors.

During 1994, a major nationwide class action lawsuit alleging price discrimination by pharmaceutical manufacturers and distributors was filed in the US District Court for the Northern District of Illinois in Chicago. The allegations in the suit were numerous, but the thrust was that the defendants unlawfully discriminated in price between community pharmacies and mail-order pharmacies, HMOs, and hospital pharmacies by selling drug products of like grade and quality at widely differing prices. There also was a price-fixing allegation in that case that was not established at trial by the plaintiffs.

Discriminatory practices prohibited by federal antitrust laws include not only price discrimination but also discrimination in furnishing services or promotional aids.

Refusal to Deal

Generally, a businessperson can refuse to deal with a supplier or customer for good reason or for no reason at all, unless he or she is prohibited by some special statute or administrative regulation. However, a conspiracy or a concentrated effort on the part of a group of retailers, manufacturers, or wholesalers to refrain from dealing with an individual or firm usually violates antitrust laws or, in some cases, the federal Civil Rights Act (see 42 U.S.C. §2000a et seq). However, most civil rights cases involve discrimination in the furnishing of services, use of public facilities, employment, or housing.

A pharmacy case on refusal to deal is *Klingel's Pharmacy v. Sharp & Dohme et al*, 64 A. 1029 (Md. 1906). In *Klingel's*, a pharmacy association blacklisted a certain pharmacy because of its failure to join in a minimum price rate scheme. Several drug suppliers then refused to furnish drugs to the pharmacy, and the pharmacy sued under a common law rule of restraint of trade. The court ruled in favor of the pharmacy and found that an obvious conspiracy existed to the damage of the affected pharmacy.

The refusal to deal issue is surfacing in pharmacy today in light of the development of preferred provider organizations (PPOs) and HMOs. Such entities sometimes will be interested in granting exclusive contracts for pharmacy services for health plan enrollees to one pharmacy chain, excluding all other pharmacies from the possibility of dispensing medications to plan enrollees. This is legally permissible, as long as there is no conspiracy or concerted refusal to deal. However, some states have enacted statutory mandates that participation as providers in health insurance programs be open to "any willing provider." Sponsored by pharmacy groups in many states, such statutes require that the insurer accept any provider who is willing to abide by the program requirements pertaining to reimbursement, submission of claims, utilization review, and so forth. A closely related form of statute is that designated "freedom of choice laws." These statutes permit a person enrolled in a managed health care plan to be reimbursed for health care services even if the provider has not signed a contract with the managed care plan to be a participating provider. Typically, these laws require managed care plans to pay the same amount to a nonnetwork provider chosen by the enrollee as would be paid to a participating provider, but this does not guarantee that the enrollee will incur the same out-of-pocket expense. "Open bidding laws" require managed care organizations to send requests for proposals to every provider located in their service area. "Disclosure laws" merely require managed care organizations to disclose their criteria for provider selection. Finally, "mandated provider," "essential community provider," or "provider access" laws require managed care organizations to enter into contracts with at least one provider.

Community Pharmacy Networks

During the late 1990s, the Federal Trade Commission (FTC) issued two Opinion Letters to community pharmacy groups, the first in New Jersey and the other in California, regarding patient education or disease state management programs to be conducted by groups of pharmacists and pharmacies who ordinarily would be viewed as competitors for purposes of the antitrust laws. As long as they conducted their affairs in accord with the plans submitted to the FTC, the agency informed the 2 groups that they would not pursue antitrust enforcement against the groups. Details of the plans can be found in the FTC web site for

New Jersey at: http://www.ftc.gov/os/1997/9708/newjerad.htm and for California at: http://www.ftc.gov/bc/adops/openadop.htm. See also http://www.ftc.gov/bc/rxupdate.htm

Prohibitions Against Corporate Mergers

An interesting aspect of the antitrust laws is the prohibition against corporate amalgamations (mergers or consolidations) when the effect of the amalgamation may substantially lessen competition or tend to make a monopoly. A merger exists when one corporation buys out another so that the identity of the other is, for practical purposes, lost. The buyout can be through purchase of controlling stock or assets (the plant and equipment). A vertical merger exists when a product seller buys out one of its buyers. A horizontal merger is one competitor buying out the other. A conglomerate is formed when one corporation buys out a noncompeting firm as an investment or for diversification. Such mergers or consolidations are quite rampant now with regard to for-profit hospital chains, home health agencies, nursing home corporations, and other entities in the health care field.

Only mergers that have an anticompetitive effect on interstate commerce run afoul of the antitrust laws. A merger of 2 small companies or a small firm and a large firm is lawful when the overall effect on competition is not detrimental. Conglomerate mergers can be lawful if the effect is not anticompetitive.

Enforcement of the Antitrust Laws

The US Justice Department enforces the criminal sanctions of the federal antitrust laws. Enforcement can be in the form of criminal prosecution, court injunctions, or by a private suit for damages sustained from antitrust violations. To a certain extent, the FTC enforces or shares enforcement of the Clayton Antitrust Act provisions. The FTC's mode of enforcement is by administrative orders backed up by a court order or by civil forfeiture fines. It should be noted that states often have their own antitrust statutes, frequently with wording directly parallel to that of the federal statutes.

Criminal penalties for antitrust violations are:

(1) Sherman Act – fine of up to $350,000 for individuals or up to $10,000,000 for corporations and/or up to 3 years imprisonment.
(2) Clayton Act – fine of up to $3,000 and/or imprisonment for not more than 1 year.

Federal Trade Commission (FTC)

Certain methods of competition and unfair or deceptive practices are unlawful under 15 U.S.C. §45. Section 45 gives the FTC power to prevent individuals, partnerships, and corporations from using unfair trade practices.

The FTC was created as the expert agency in the antitrust field. The Federal Trade Commission Act was designed to supplement and improve 2 other pieces of antitrust legislation: The Sherman Antitrust Act and the Clayton Antitrust Act. The FTC enforces the acts by investigating unfair trade practice complaints, conducting administrative hearings, and issuing cease-and-desist orders to curb illegal trade practices. A cease-and-desist order is the administrative agency equivalent of a court injunction.

Once the FTC staff has investigated an alleged violation, it may attempt to settle the matter with a consent order. Parties who consent to an FTC order do not admit to any wrongdoing, but any party who enters into a consent order with the agency waives all rights to seek review. The consent procedure saves considerable time and expense, and the majority of proceedings handled by the agency result in the issuance of consent orders rather than in formal hearings. Decisions of the FTC may be appealed to the US Court of Appeals.

In addition to these quasi-judicial functions, the FTC also may enact trade regulation rules, which regulate entire professions or industries. The agency at one time published a proposed trade regulation rule that would have preempted state laws prohibiting the advertising of prescription drug price information. However, the US Supreme Court decision in a Virginia drug price advertising case (*Virginia State Board of Pharmacy, et al v. Virginia Citizens Consumer Council, Inc., et al*, 425 U.S. 748 [1976]), established pharmacists' legal rights to advertise prescription drug prices; the FTC staff concluded that there was no further need to proceed with a trade regulation rule in this area.

The FTC also has developed a Model Drug Product Selection Act, which was recommended to the states to assist them in enacting or amending laws to promote the selection of generic drug products. In addition, the agency has become involved in a number of other matters that have considerable impact on the practice of pharmacy, particularly in the areas of corrective advertising, deceptive trade practices, and the retailer's liability for the manufacturer's claims.

Corrective Advertisements

The FTC has taken some rather monumental strides in the regulation of false and deceptive advertising, particularly in the area of OTC drugs. A few years ago, an FTC administrative law judge ruled that advertisements for *Listerine* were false, misleading, and deceptive. The manufacturer was ordered to stop claiming that its product would cure, prevent, or result in fewer colds and sore throats. The manufacturer also was required to include a statement to this effect in its next $10 million worth of advertising. The FTC felt that it was necessary to include a statement remedying previous claims or the consumer would never receive the truthful information. The FTC decision was upheld by a federal court of appeals, and the US Supreme Court rejected the manufacturer's appeal without comment.

More recently, an FTC hearing examiner ruled that the manufacturer of *Anacin* falsely advertised the analgesic as a tension reliever and as a product that would enable individuals to cope with the stress of everyday life. The decision also included a recommendation that 1 year's advertising budget be spent by the manufacturer to correct the false impression. The case had been appealed to the full FTC.

National advertisers and manufacturers are not the only parties to feel the wrath of the FTC in the area of corrective advertisements. The FTC ordered a community pharmacy to buy seven 60-second television spots to retract its earlier claims about a vitamin B-complex tablet. The pharmacist claimed on television that the vitamins made the user feel and work better and that the product would build up the blood and would improve the user's physical and mental condition.

Deceptive Trade Practices

The FTC spends a substantial amount of time in protecting consumers from deceptive trade practices. The agency's efforts are directed at business activities that mislead consumers into thinking that they will get a good deal if they purchase the product. The advertiser should be prepared to back up any claims (ie, "lowest prices in town") and also should include in the advertisements all details regarding guarantees, discounts, sale prices, and free goods.

Because their services and products relate to the basic necessities of life, pharmacy and food chains have proven likely targets for FTC action in the area of deceptive trade practices. The Commission has ruled that it is deceptive to refer to "the regular price" unless the defendant actually sold items at that price previously. It also was held to be deceptive to refer to the "manufacturer's list price" when that list price is not the ordinary retail sales price of the item.

When a retailer advertises a product at a particular price in the newspapers or other media, the retailer has an obligation to have the product available for sale. When this was not so, a pharmacy chain found it necessary to consent to an FTC cease-and-desist order in which it agreed to have all sale items readily available and clearly and conspicuously marked with a price at or below the advertised price. Products are not deemed unavailable if adequate quantities are on hand to meet the anticipated demands or if, through no fault of the retailer, the ordered items are not delivered, as long as a rain check is offered to the consumer in these instances. The rain check should allow the customer to purchase the product in the near future at or below the advertised price, or the retailer may offer a similar product of equal or better quality at or below the advertised price. Also prohibited as deceptive acts are bait-and-switch promotions in which the seller lures consumers with a low price on an item and then switches their attention to higher-tagged items that the baiter really hoped from the beginning to sell.

Retailer's Liability for Manufacturer's Claims

Many pharmacies are provided with advertising copy prepared for them by the manufacturer; the pharmacy simply inserts its own name under the manufacturer's statements and claims in the advertisement. The FTC became particularly interested in this process when a northwestern drug chain used its name under an advertisement for weight reduction tablets. The copy for the piece had been supplied to the drug chain by the manufacturer and its advertising agency.

The FTC alleged that the claims in the advertisement were false and misleading, and the agency included the retailer as a defendant in the case. An administrative law judge ruled that the drug chain shared full responsibility for the deceptive advertising because it supplied the copy to the media and the advertisements were printed over its name. The judge concluded that if the drug chain was permitted to avoid responsibility for the advertisement because it had been prepared by the manufacturer, then a retailer could disseminate false advertising over his or her name with impunity as long as the advertisement had come from the supplier.

The drug chain appealed the decision to the full FTC bench. Counsel for the FTC argued that a retailer who places his or her name on a supplier's prepared advertising has an obligation to scrutinize the copy carefully, check questionable claims against standard references, and take the necessary steps to substantiate the claims.

It was further contended that the retailer would not have to test each product that he or she advertised independently, but that the retailer did have an obligation to scrutinize the proposed copy carefully in light of common sense and general trade knowledge. If questionable claims are uncovered, the chain or any other retailer should obtain substantiation from the supplier or some other source.

The Commission unanimously agreed with the administrative law judge's opinion that the chain had full responsibility along with the product's manufacturer and advertising agency. It concluded that the FTC law does not exempt from responsibility those retailers who disseminate advertisements that have been prepared by others. The use of deceptive advertisements is prohibited under the law, and it does not matter who originates the claims.

Below-Cost Sales

In some states, the law prohibits a retailer or anyone else from selling an item below cost or 6% below cost. This practice is referred to as the loss leader sale, in which the seller sells a name brand item below wholesale cost in order to attract customers who will probably buy other merchandise at the usual or above-average cost. Such sales often are prohibited by state fair trade laws. However, below-cost sales are permitted if:

> (1) Merchandise is on a bona fide clearance sale;
> (2) merchandise is perishable and must be sold to avoid immediate loss;
> (3) merchandise is imperfect or damaged;
> (4) merchandise is sold to charities or government units; or
> (5) merchandise is sold upon liquidation of the business.

Unrelated Business Income Tax

A great number of hospitals and some ambulatory care pharmacies in community clinics are operated as tax exempt entities under the US Internal Revenue Code, often under Section 501(c)(3). This section applies to entities "organized and operated exclusively for religious, charitable, scientific, testing for public safety, literary, or education purposes." The business activities of these organizations will be exempt from taxation as long as they are conducted to further the nonprofit purpose of the organization. However, if the activity is unrelated to the charitable purpose it may lead to tax liability for the operation. Note that such activities are not prohibited; they are merely an exception to the general rule of tax exemption. The Internal Revenue Code defines unrelated trade or business as:

> any trade or business the conduct of which is not substantially related to the exercise or performance by such organization of its charitable, educational, or other purpose constituting the basis for its exemption.

I.R.S. Announcement 92-83, issued during 1992, sets forth how the agency will apply this to the activities of hospital pharmacies.

SOURCES OF ADDITIONAL INFORMATION

A look at third-party prepaid prescription plans. *J Am Pharm Assoc.* 1970;NS10:52.

Abood RR. Report on third party prescription programs. Indianapolis IN: National Council of State Pharmaceutical Association Executives, 1984.

Abood RR. Third-party prescription program litigation. *Leg Asp Pharm Pract.* 1985;8:3-4.

Barton KJ. Expand your knowledge of contracts in pharmacy practice. *Legal Asp Pharm Pract.* 1985;8:3-4.

Breakenridge MA. Immigration requirements for hiring a foreign-trained pharmacist. *Am J Hosp Pharm.* 1992;49:2680, 2682.

Brushwood DB. Hospital and pharmacist liability for sexual harassment of a pharmacy technician. *Am J Hosp Pharm.* 1994;51:397-399.

Brushwood DB. Hospital's refusal to hire HIV-infected pharmacist without restrictions violates Rehabilitation Act. *Am J Hosp Pharm.* 1992;49:1959-1961.

Brushwood DB. Women of childbearing capacity may not be excluded from working with hazardous substances because of their gender. *Am J Hosp Pharm.* 1991;48:1281-1283.

Brushwood DB, Fern F. *Clozaril* and the threat of products liability: Defensive drug distribution invites regulatory reform. *J Products Toxics Liab.* 1993;15:45.

Butler DC. Buying and selling a pharmacy. *Leg Asp Pharm Pract.* 1984;7:1-3.

Campbell NA. Legal implications for the community pharmacist distributing nonprescription drug products. *Contemp Pharm Pract.* 1981;4:216-219.

Carlson J. Prepaid prescription drug plans under antitrust scrutiny: A stern challenge to health care cost containment. 75 *Nw. U.L. Rev* 506 (1980).

Cerullo T. The polygraph and the practicing pharmacist. *J Am Pharm Assoc.* 1976;NS16:178.

Cerullo TC. Employment discrimination—it can happen in a pharmacy. *Leg Asp Pharm Pract.* 1983;6:1-3.

DeMarco CT. Some legal considerations in the formation of a group practice. Part 1. *Am J Hosp Pharm.* 1972;29:168-171.

DeMarco CT. Some legal considerations in the formation of a group practice. Part 2. *Am J Hosp Pharm.* 1972;29:774-779.

Fink JL III. Employment contracts for pharmacists. *Pharm Manag.* 1980;152:199-200.

Fink JL III. Evaluating third party prescription program contracts. *Pharm Manag.* 1979;151:114-119.

Fink JL III. Fair employment practices and the pharmacist. *Am J Pharm.* 1975;147:129-134.

Fink JL III. How antitrust laws apply to pharmacy practice. *Leg Asp Pharm Pract.* 1984;7:2-4.

Fink JL III. Special uses for drugs purchased at special prices: The Portland and Jefferson County cases. *Leg Asp Pharm Pract.* 1984;7:1-2.

Fink JL III, Whitman JA. Overtime pay for pharmacists. *Pharm Manag.* 1980;152:237-238.

Fox LA. Business aspects of pharmacy practice. *Leg Asp Pharm Pract.* 1980;3:2.

Fox LA. Georgia's new third-party legislation: A unique solution. *Leg Asp Pharm Pract.* 1980;3:2.

Fox LA. Third-party legislation: The judicial response. *Leg Asp Pharm Pract.* 1984;7:2-3.

Greenberg RB. Legal aspects of termination of employment. *Am J Hosp Pharm.* 1984;41:2074-2077.

Greenberg RB. Legal implications of home health care by nonprofit hospitals. *Am J Hosp Pharm.* 1986;43:386.

Greenberg RB. *Portland Retail Druggists Association v. Abbott Laboratories, et al.* Part 1. *Am J Hosp Pharm.* 1976;33:572-573.

Greenberg RB. Robinson-Patman update: *DeModena v. Kaiser Foundation Health Plan. Am J Hosp Pharm.* 1985;42:1572-1574.

Greenberg RB, Mandl FL. *Portland Retail Druggists Association v. Abbott Laboratories, et al.* Part 2. *Am J Hosp Pharm.* 1976;33:648-651.

Greenberg RB, Ross RS. Effect of NLRB rulings on collective bargaining by hospital pharmacists. *Am J Hosp Pharm.* 1977;34:541-544.

Hann C. Random drug screenings: nothing to lose? *Am Pharm.* 1987;NS27:34.

Hospital discriminated against HIV-positive pharmacist, New York ruling says. *Am J Hosp Pharm.* 1991;48:606, 610.

Hoyt D. Drug testing in the workplace—are methods legally defensible? *JAMA.* 1987;258:504.

Kaluzny El. Legal liability for failure to dispense or refill a prescription. *US Pharm.* 1978;3:24, 26, 28, 96.

Meyers MJ. Do exclusive dealing contracts violate antitrust laws? *Leg Asp Pharm Pract.* 1983;6:2-3.

Myers MJ, Fink JL III. Recent antitrust developments affecting third party prescription programs. *US Pharm.* 1978;3:11, 12, 14.

Podell LB. Recent supreme court antitrust rulings in health care. *Am J Hosp Pharm.* 1983;40:639-641.

Professional service corporations: An overview. *J Am Pharm Assoc.* 1970;NS10:86.

Roberts C. The pharmacist's primer in price discrimination. *Am Pharm* 1980;NS20:584.

Rosoff AJ, Fink JL III. Supreme court scrutinizes nonprofit hospital drug sales. *Hosp Form.* 1977;12:613-615, 618.

Schmitz TM. Retail druggist's warranty of drugs. 15 *Cleve Mar L Rev* 285(1966).

Simonsmeier LM. Closing the door on premises liability. *Leg Asp Pharm Pract.* 1983;6:3-4.

Simonsmeier LM. The federal trade commission and pharmacy practice. *Leg Asp Pharm Pract.* 1985;8:1-3.

Simonsmeier LM, Fink JL III. Legal implications of drug testing in the workplace. *Am Pharm.* 1988;NS28:454.

Simonsmeier LM. Your rights as an 'employee-at-will.' *Leg Asp Pharm Pract.* 1982;5:3-4.

Spies AR. Fraud, pharmacy and the law. *Drug Topics.* 2001;145:65-72.

Stonitsch J. What to look for in a business structure. *Leg Asp Pharm Pract.* 1979;2:12.

Stonitsch JR. The ins and outs of pharmacy ownership. *Leg Asp Pharm Pract.* 1985;8:3-4.

Susina SV. Supreme Court bars discriminatory sales by makers of drugs. *Leg Asp Pharm Pract.* 1983;6:3-4.

Tyson P, Vaughn R. Drug testing in the workplace. *Occup Health Safety.* 1987;56:24.

Veatch R. The technical criteria fallacy. *Hastings Center Rep.* 1977;7:15-16.

Vivian JC. Antitrust developments. *US Pharm.* 1995;20:76,79.

Vivian JC. Conspiracy to boycott. *US Pharm.* 1999;24:106-109.

Vivian JC. Employment law labyrinths. *US Pharm.* 1996;21:80,82-83,96.

Vivian JC. Employment restraints. *US Pharm.* 1996;21:116,118-119.

Vivian JC. Freedom of choice. *US Pharm.* 1997;22:82,84-85.

Vivian JC. Hospital's exclusive contract arrangement with venders of durable medical equipment violates antitrust laws. *Am J Hosp Pharm.* 1991;48:1542-1543.

Vivian JC. Ownership of customer lists. *US Pharm.* 1998;23:96-98.

Vivian JC. Pharmacy law: sexual harrassment. *US Pharm.* 1994;19:87-88.

Vivian JC. Sale of a pharmacy. *US Pharm.* 2002;27:68-74.

Vivian JC. Taxes and more taxes. *US Pharm.* 2002;27:49-52.

Vivian JC. Two-tier pricing. *US Pharm.* 2000;25:72-74.

Weinstein BD, Brushwood DB. Ethical and legal issues when employer and employee disagree. *US Pharm.* 1991;16:80-81.

Williams KG. Hospital pharmacists and collective bargaining. *Am J Hosp Pharm.* 1994;51:2711-13.

Williams KG. Impact of federal law on dispensing activities in hospital pharmacies. *J Pharm Technology.* 1996;12:265-270.

Willig SH. Can you be fired before you're hired? *Leg Asp Pharm Pract.* 1982;5:1-2.

Study Questions

BUSINESS LAW

(1) An express contract is one in which the terms are:
   (a) stated in writing by the involved parties.
   (b) set from the conduct of the parties and the circumstances.
   (c) stated orally by the involved parties.
   (d) a and c
   (e) all of the above

(2) A(n) _____ contract is one in which all contractual obligations have been performed.
   (a) executory
   (b) quasi
   (c) executed
   (d) voidable
   (e) none of the above

(3) In a situation in which an agreement lacks the requisites to make it legally enforceable as a contract, the law may give a legal effect to it, making it a(n):
   (a) voidable contract.
   (b) quasi contract.
   (c) void contract.
   (d) executory contract.
   (e) none of the above

(4) Essential elements of a contract include:
   (a) competent parties.
   (b) mutual assent.
   (c) legal purpose or object.
   (d) sufficient and legal consideration.
   (e) all of the above

(5) An offer:
   (a) is open for acceptance for an unlimited period of time.
   (b) must be accepted on the terms offered; otherwise it becomes a counteroffer.
   (c) once accepted, becomes a valid contract.
   (d) b and c
   (e) all of the above

(6) Fraud is:
   (a) a reckless disregard for the truth.
   (b) a lie or false statement of a fact with knowledge of the falsity.
   (c) identical to misrepresentation.
   (d) a and b
   (e) all of the above

(7) Consideration can be defined as:
     (a) a mutual benefit and mutual detriment.
     (b) a benefit to both parties.
     (c) a right, interest, profit, or benefit given to one party from the loss, detriment, for-
         bearance, or responsibility suffered or undertaken by the other party.
     (d) a and b
     (e) a and c

(8) The parol evidence rule states that a written agreement:
     (a) may be part verbal and part written.
     (b) must be sufficient in itself.
     (c) can require oral evidence to supply an essential element.
     (d) a and b
     (e) b and c

(9) A bill of lading:
     (a) can be negotiable.
     (b) can be nonnegotiable.
     (c) is similar to a check, which is payable to the order of a named individual.
     (d) a and c
     (e) all of the above

(10) Howard's pharmacy sues a manufacturer for breach of contract. Jahna, one of his
     employees, asks him what this means. Howard explains, correctly, that breach of con-
     tract:
     (a) exists where words or acts of a party in regard to a sales contract indicate an intent
         to perform.
     (b) can be defined as failure to perform a contract in part.
     (c) can be defined as failure to perform a contract in whole.
     (d) a and c
     (e) b and c

(11) Howard decides to sell his pharmacy. The buyer of his business asks Howard to agree
     to a covenant not to compete. Again, Jahna wants to understand exactly what this
     means. A covenant not to compete:
     (a) possibly can violate the Sherman Antitrust Act if too broad or runs for too long.
     (b) is allowed when it is reasonable, supported by contract consideration and ancil-
         lary to a lawful contract.
     (c) is a restraint of trade, which can be legal.
     (d) a and c
     (e) all of the above

(12) Jahna continues to work at the pharmacy for the new owner. However, soon after, she
     quits coming to work and files a sexual harassment complaint against her new employer.
     A worried coworker wonders whether Jahna's claim is legitimate, so she does research
     to find out exactly what constitutes sexual harassment. She finds out that sexual harass-
     ment occurs when unwelcomed sexual advances are:
     (a) a cause of loss of employment because of one's failure to submit.
     (b) an implied condition for receiving job benefits.
     (c) an express condition for receiving job benefits.
     (d) a and c
     (e) all of the above

(13) Jahna applies for work elsewhere and is required to submit a urine sample to test for illegal drugs. She is alarmed to discover that her test results are positive. However, a friend tells her that she may have had a "false-positive" test result. A false-positive test is one that:

(a) misidentifies other substances as an illegal drug.

(b) detects drugs in sterile fluids.

(c) fails to detect a drug that is present.

(d) a and b

(e) a and c

(14) Meanwhile, Howard, who sold his pharmacy, enters into a business partnership with his friend Safah. A partnership:

(a) is taxed as a business entity for income.

(b) is recognized legally as an entity that is separate from its owners.

(c) is the legal relationship between individuals who jointly own and operate a business for profit.

(d) a and c

(e) b and c

(15) _____ is (are) considered unlawful despite any beneficial effects.

(a) Price fixing

(b) Agreements to divide markets

(c) Group boycotts intending an anticompetitive effect

(d) Tying arrangements that require a buyer to purchase one product to be able to buy another

(e) all of the above

(16) A vertical merger:

(a) exists when one competitor buys out another.

(b) exists when a product seller buys out one of its buyers.

(c) is formed when one corporation buys out a noncompeting firm as an investment or for diversification.

(d) b or c

(e) none of the above

(17) The Federal Trade Commission (FTC) enforces the Clayton Antitrust Act provision by:

(a) court injunction.

(b) civil forfeiture.

(c) administrative orders backed up by a court order.

(d) criminal prosecution.

(e) b and c

(18) Christine, a merchant, enters into a contract with Theodore. However, the contract is voided when Theodore is declared legally insane. Does Christine have any recourse in this case?

(19) Christine enters into a written contract with a different person. Later she decides that she wants to rescind the agreement. Can a written agreement be rescinded? If no, why not? If yes, how?

(20) Describe the function of a statute of frauds.

(21) How does a consignment transaction differ from a sale on approval?

(22) Explain how some jurisdictions have used the theory of breach of an implied contract to establish a wrongful discharge.

(23) Discuss the issue of "comparable worth" in claims of wage-based sex discrimination.

(24) (a) What group of individuals has the least legal protection in the issue of drug screening? Why?(b) Summarize both sides of this issue.

(25) What usually is included in the articles of incorporation?

(26) Rhesa has a sole proprietorship with 2 part-time employees. She is thinking about incorporating. List the advantages and disadvantages of incorporation.

(27) Can Rhesa's business qualify as an S corporation? List the 6 qualifications she must meet to do so.

(28) Rhesa decides to take on a partner. Describe the major difference between a limited liability partnership (L.L.P.) and a traditional partnership.

(29) Describe 2 forms of "exclusive contracts" that HMOs and pharmacies have sometimes engaged in. Are these legal?

(30) What is a fair trade agreement? What is the purpose of such an agreement?

(31) What is a "loss leader sale"? Discuss its legal implications.

Critical Thinking Applications

(1) Arman and George are both stockholders, but in different companies. Unfortunately, both companies go bankrupt because of mismanagement. (a) Arman is held liable, but George is not. Why? What is the most likely explanation? (b) Describe 3 situations in which stockholders can be held personally liable.

(2) A problem encountered by pharmacy owners as a group in dealing with a third-party prescription payment plan is the possibility that the plan might dictate a reimbursement level that is too low. Prepare a debate, panel discussion, or planning association meeting in which this will be discussed to be presented to the class to show how the courts have responded to this issue.

(3) A pharmaceutical manufacturer charges different prices to community pharmacies and hospital pharmacies, selling drug products of like grade and quality at different prices. The manufacturer claims that it has the right to charge different prices because the 2 types of pharmacies are normally not competitors. The plaintiffs disagree. Who is most likely to win? Why?

(4) Rebecca's pharmacy refuses to join in a minimum price rate scheme. Several drug suppliers then refuse to furnish drugs to her pharmacy. (a) Can Rebecca's pharmacy sue? If no, explain how the suppliers are protected. If yes, on what grounds? (b) How are PPOs and HMOs complicating this issue?

Case Study 1: Remedies on Breach

Liz, a pharmacist, and Jackie, a distributor, do business with each other on a regular basis. Usually, their transactions are completed without complications. However, lately things have not gone so smoothly. Discuss possible action in the following situations.

(1) The 2 women enter into a contract that states that Jackie will deliver certain goods to Liz's pharmacy. Eventually, Liz has reason to believe that Jackie's company will not fulfill its part of their contract. What can Liz do?

(2) Eventually, Jackie's company begins to deliver the contracted goods to Liz's pharmacy. However, Liz fails to make payment. What recourse does Jackie have? Can she resell any of the contracted goods?

(3)   Despite their previous problems, Liz and Jackie enter into another contract. This time, when Jackie's company delivers goods, Liz justifiably refuses to accept them. What options does Liz have for further action in this case?

Case Study 2: Employment Screening

An advisory board for a private hospital is discussing the hospital's current practices of employee polygraph and biomedical testing to decide whether any changes need to be made in these procedures. Help the board members evaluate the hospital's performance, outlined below.

(1)   Throughout the past year, the hospital administered random polygraph tests to various job applicants, including hospital pharmacists as well as food service and custodial workers. Has the hospital violated any laws?

(2)   The hospital also engages in single-procedure testing of employee urine samples to test for illicit drug use. Is this the best method they could use?

(3)   Three hospital pharmacy employees discover one afternoon that they will each be required to submit a urine sample for drug testing before leaving work. Alice, who has been fighting a sinus infection, took cough syrup and an OTC cold medication the night before and that morning. An hour ago, Matthew took 2 aspirin for a headache. At lunch, Maria had a cup of herbal tea and a poppyseed muffin for dessert. Could any potential problems result with these employees' tests?

(4)   Matthew, whose headache has not improved, flies into a rage and refuses to submit a urine sample. He tells Alice and Maria that he is going to look for pharmacy work in the public sector, where he would have Fourth Amendment protection against drug testing, because it constitutes a search or seizure against his body. Alice says he wouldn't be protected in the public sector either because submitting a urine sample does not constitute a search or seizure since there is no touching or invasion of the body, merely analysis of a human waste product. Maria says that neither of them is completely right. With whom do you agree? Explain.

Case Study 3: Partnership

Wallace and Julia each have owned their own pharmacies for years. Recently, the two have been considering forming a partnership. Julia thinks they should enter into a general partnership, whereas Wallace wants to form a limited partnership. Help them decide.

(1)   Explain the difference between a general and a limited partnership.

(2)   Julia eventually convinces Wallace that she is right, and they form a general partnership. Unfortunately, Julia soon makes a poor decision that results in serious debt. Discuss Wallace's liability potential as it would be affected by state law variations.

(3)   Julia's actions turn out to have been criminal in nature. What is Wallace's liability in this case?

(4)   What if Julia had committed a license violation? What would Wallace's liability be in such a case?

Case Study 4: Forming a Business Corporation

Jerod and Miguel want to form a new corporation. Jerod volunteers to be corporate promoter; Miguel agrees to be incorporator and registered agent.

(1)   Explain the different duties for which Miguel and Jerod will be responsible.

(2)   After the articles of incorporation have been executed and recorded, a certificate of incorporation is issued. Miguel and Jerod's corporation is now in existence. Who acts next, Jerod or Miguel? What will he do first?

(3)   Jerod and Miguel meet to discuss corporate stock. Jerod wants to list par value per share; Miguel does not. What might be Miguel's rationale?

Chapter 6
Civil Liability

Background: Civil, Criminal, and Administrative Liabilities, 245

Torts, 246

    Negligence, 246

        Malpractice vs Negligence, 247

        Mistake Differentiated from Negligence, 248

        Elements of Negligence, 248

            Duty, 248

                The "Expert Witness," 249

                The "Locality Rule," 249

                Court Imposed Duties, 250

                Negligence Per Se, 252

                Codes of Ethics and Standards of Practice, 252

                Changing and Evolving Duties, 253

                Intellectual vs Mechanical Claims, 253

                Black Letter Rules for Pharmacists, 254

                Standard of Due Care Expected of Pharmacists, 255

                Specific Duties Associated with Pharmacy Practice, 256

                      Duty to Counsel Patients, 256

                      Liability for Drug Product Selection, 259

                      Minimizing Liability for Product Selection, 260

                      Clinical Pharmacy Liability Exposure, 261

                      Prescribing by Pharmacists, 262

                      Counseling vs Prescribing, 262

                      Authority to Prescribe, 263

                      Pharmacists as Therapeutic Consultants, 264

                      Ownership of the Prescription, 266

                      Liability Aspects of Patient Profiles, 266

                      Delegation to Pharmacy Technicians, 267

            Breach of Duty, 268

                Mechanical Errors, 269

                  Dispensing Errors, 269

                      Inadvertence, 269

                      Inexperience, 269

                  Labeling Errors, 270

                Intellectual Errors, 271

                  Drug Product Selection Errors, 271

                  Civil Liability for Ineffective Supervision of Technicians, 271

            Proximate Cause, 272

                Direct Causation, 272

                Independent Intervening Causes, 272

                Comparative and Contributory Negligence, 273

            Damages, 273

                Punitive Damages, 274

                Wrongful Death Statutes, 275

Negligence *(cont.)*
    Defenses, 275
        The Sealed Container Doctrine, 275
        Comparative Negligence, 276
        Voluntary Assumption of the Risk, 276
        Statute of Limitations, 276
        Improper Parties, 277
    Strict Liability, 277
        Res Ipsa Loquitur, 277
        Strict Liability Contrasted with Implied Warranty, 278

Risk Management, 278
    Unit Dose System, 278
        Recordkeeping for Unit Dose Drug Products, 279
        Advantages of the Unit Dose System, 279
        Disadvantages of the Unit Dose System, 279
    Reduction of Distractions, 280
    Recording the Lot Number, 280
    Minimizing Liability, 280
    Summary of Suggestions for Minimizing Dispensing Errors, 283

Professional Liability Insurance, 283
    Extent of Coverage, 284
    Types of Policy Clauses, 285
    Other Policy Clauses of Which the Pharmacist Should Be Aware, 286
        Defense and Settlement Clauses, 286
        Exclusion Clause, 286
    Limitations on Amount of Coverage, 287
    Policy Conditions, 287
    Giving Notice of Claim, 288

Contractual Agreements, 288
    Sales Transactions, 288
    Warranties, 289
        Express Warranties, 289
        Implied Warranties, 290
    Applications to Pharmacy Practice, 290
        Over-the-Counter Products, 290
        Labeling Nonprescription Drugs, 291
        Warranty and Drug Product Selection, 292
    Removal of Warranties, 292
    Privity of Contract, 293
    Notice of Breach of Warranty, 293

Administrative Actions, 293
    The State Board of Pharmacy, 293
    Powers and Functions of the Board of Pharmacy, 294
    Enforcement Powers, 294
    Pharmacy Board Disciplinary Hearings, 295
    Challenging an Administrative Action, 295
        Declaratory Judgment, 296
        Collateral Attack, 296
        Suits in Equity, 297
        Petitions, 297
        Civil Suit Against the Pharmacy Board, 297
        Direct Judicial Review, 297
    Rights of the Pharmacist, 298
    Continuing Education, 299

Standards of the Joint Commission on the Accreditation of Healthcare Organizations, 300

APhA Code of Ethics, 301
    Code of Ethics for Pharmacists, 301

Sources of Additional Information, 302

Study Questions, 311

Civil Liability

BACKGROUND: CIVIL, CRIMINAL, AND ADMINISTRATIVE LIABILITIES

Civil liability refers to the class of cases where the law requires individuals, corporations, and other legal entities to take responsibility for their behavior toward each other in a civilized society. Another main branch of the law, **criminal liability**, is concerned with how society as a whole expects individuals and others to act. A third part of the law deals with administrative (sometimes called "regulatory") liabilities and how the government interacts with people who are licensed or otherwise authorized to engage in certain conduct. Administrative laws are a hybrid of criminal and civil laws. As pharmacists are required to obtain a license before engaging in the practice of pharmacy, and because many licensure issues are related to civil liabilities, discussion of these topics is included in this chapter. Similarities and distinctions between civil, criminal, and administrative laws should help the reader understand why these branches exist.

Violations of criminal laws may result in police investigation, prosecution, conviction, and the imposition by a court of penalties including fines, probation, or imprisonment. Civil liability is imposed after someone sues someone else and a judgment, usually for monetary damages, is entered by a court. Administrative prosecutions occur when a state believes a person has violated the rules governing the right to engage in a practice. Licensure revocation or suspension are typical administrative penalties.

The goal of civil laws, for the most part, is to make the injured party "whole" after a wrong has been inflicted. In most instances, the vehicle for achieving this result is money. For example, if a patient receives the wrong drug from the pharmacist and is hurt by this negligent act, the patient might sue for the compensation needed to remedy the situation. The amount claimed would be any health care costs incurred, such as doctor or hospital costs, as well as money to compensate for pain and suffering, lost wages, and any other form of injury that reasonably could be expected. If the patient died from the pharmacist's negligence, the family or estate would sue and seek additional amounts for wrongful death and loss of companionship. It might be hard to imagine how a monetary amount could be set to compensate for the loss of a loved one, but this is the only method recognized by civil laws.

The goal of criminal laws, on the other hand, is to punish a wrongdoer and rehabilitate the offender. If the patient who receives the wrong drug from a pharmacist has reason to believe the pharmacist gave the wrong drug intentionally for the purpose of causing injury or death, the pharmacist might be prosecuted and convicted of a variety of criminal laws, such as reckless endangerment or murder. A sentence of imprisonment might be imposed to punish the pharmacist.

The goal of administrative laws is to protect the public from those who are given special permission to interact with the public in some special way. The licensed pharmacist who acts in a negligent or criminal manner may have his or her license revoked or suspended for a period of time to protect other members of the public from further harm.

It should be noted that a single act may violate administrative, criminal, *and* civil laws. In the example of the wrong drug being dispensed, the pharmacist could be convicted criminally and could be sued by the patient for civil damages. A third consequence could be the suspension or revocation of the pharmacist's license in an administrative action brought by the state for the licensing agency, such as the board of pharmacy.

Many pharmacists have wondered whether these multiple legal actions violate the "double jeopardy" clause of the US Constitution. They do not because that clause only prohibits an individual from being tried more than once on criminal charges arising from a single act.

Different standards of proof are required in the different law forums and different rules of evidence and procedure apply. While there are significant exceptions, most criminal laws require evidence of **intent** before an accused may be convicted and require that the accused be **guilty beyond a reasonable doubt**. A minority of civil laws require proof of intent. Negligence laws only require that an event is foreseeable. For the most part, civil laws may be violated by a showing of a **preponderance of the evidence**, a standard much easier to satisfy. The rules of procedure and evidence in administrative actions are far less formal.

In the vast majority of cases, criminal laws are written down as sets of statutes or codes that have been adopted by a legislature and enacted into law. Civil liability may be imposed for violations of statutes but many cases involve violations of the **common law**. These often are court- or judge-made rules that depend on **precedent**, or application of earlier cases with similar facts. This often requires analysis and interpretation to determine which precedent or rules should be applied to the case at hand. Negligence laws, one of the main subjects of this chapter, are derived mainly from the common law. Administrative actions usually involve either statutory laws or regulations promulgated by an administrative agency, such as a board of pharmacy. However, common law standards of care and negligence concepts often are used as well.

This background should help in keeping the ideas involved in the separate but related areas of the law in perspective.

TORTS

The branch of civil liability that deals with remedies for wrongs suffered by people who have no formal relationship with those who caused the alleged harm is called *torts*. The other primary branch, where there is some kind of relationship between the parties to a lawsuit, deals with contractual agreements. Torts can be divided into the following 3 subdivisions: Negligent torts, intentional torts, and strict liability. Negligent torts occur when someone deviates from an established standard of care and causes damage to another as a direct result of that lack of due care. The vast majority of cases involving pharmacists involve the branch of torts known as *negligence* when someone either did something that should not have been done or failed to do something that should have been done. Another branch called *strict liability* or *products liability* impacts pharmacy practice to a lesser but important extent. Strict liability is the area of torts of most recent origin wherein the law has fashioned rules governing relationships where one party is injured, not through a lack of care by the other party as with negligence, but by a product or through some other way. In an attempt to achieve fairness, the courts rule that the party most able to bear the financial cost of an injury shall bear that cost. Therefore, strict liability is liability without fault. A party will be held liable in strict liability even though it was not lacking in care at all. There are a host of other torts, usually involving an element of intent to cause injury, that attempt to provide legal remedies to those harmed. These include the following: Defamation, such as libel, slander, and injurious falsehoods; invasion of privacy; breach of confidentiality; and infliction (either negligently or intentionally) of emotional distress.

It was noted above that the goal of civil law is to make the injured party "whole" in an economic sense for the damages suffered at the hands of others. Different goals and considerations also are possible in tort litigation as the needs arise. Punitive or exemplary damages, for example, may be awarded to an injured party where the defendant's conduct is particularly egregious or willful and wanton. In addition, monetary damages are not always available to remedy certain anticipated injuries. When appropriate, courts may enter orders for injunctive relief that bars the defendant from engaging in conduct that is likely to harm the plaintiff in the future. Punitive damages and injunctive relief also are discussed in this chapter where appropriate.

Negligence

There are many ways to define and explain the concept of negligence. None of them are totally satisfactory when taken out of context. However, once certain elements and aspects of the laws surrounding this area of the law are appreciated, it can be managed more easily.

In simple terms, negligence is failing to do something that a reasonable person, guided by those ordinary considerations that normally regulate human affairs, would do, or the doing of something that a reasonable and prudent person would not do.

There are 2 important points to remember from this description. The first is that one may be negligent in 2 ways. First, a person may be negligent by omitting or failing to do something, and second, a person may be negligent by doing something incorrectly. There is a common misconception among pharmacists and others that the only way a person can be negligent is by doing something incorrectly. This colloquial but erroneous understanding would indicate that as long as one opts not to do something, he or she cannot be judged negligent. A review of the above definition will make it obvious that this is not the case. Just as one can be negligent by failing to do something, one can be negligent by doing something.

The pharmacist's maintenance of patient profiles is a classic example. An argument heard decades ago was that a pharmacist would be held liable for missing a drug interaction if he or she maintained patient profiles, whereas if those patient profiles were not maintained, the same liability would not exist. Obviously, this argument is without merit because of the above definition. A pharmacist who fails to maintain patient profiles could be held liable for failure to detect a potentially dangerous drug-drug interaction that causes damage to the patient. One way to view this situation is that the pharmacist's obligation is to be aware of and diligently seek out potentially hazardous drug-drug interactions because the pharmacist is the drug expert on the health care team. Under this approach, it would be logical to say that patient profiles are merely a tool used to collect in one place all of the information the pharmacist needs to review prior to judging whether a potential drug-drug interaction is clinically significant. Consequently, one view is that the duty to detect drug-drug interactions is derived from the pharmacist's status as a health professional knowledgeable about drugs rather than from the existence of computer or other systems making the detection of such interactions more convenient. Further, patient profiles are in such commonplace use today that it is very realistic to believe failure to employ and use profiles violates a standard of care.

The other point to take away from the above definition is that attention should be focused on the person mentioned at the end, the reasonable and prudent person. The reasonable and prudent person does not exist in real life; he or she is a fictional character created by the law to facilitate the handling of negligence cases. While fictional in nature, the reasonable and prudent person plays a critical role in the determination of negligence. Applied to pharmacy cases, the question becomes, "What would a reasonable pharmacist do (or not do) under the same or similar circumstances?"

A second definition of negligence is more descriptive: Negligence occurs when a person who is under a duty to another to use due care breaches that duty and the second person suffers damages as a direct result of that breach. This definition is a little more concrete and offers more information for specific guidance to the pharmacist. This definition indicates that there is a finite number of elements to the concept of negligence. In order to have negligence there must be a person who is under a duty to another to use due care, a breach of that duty, and a second person suffering damages, and those damages must flow as a direct result of the breach of duty. This suggests that negligence is composed of 4 distinct elements and that all elements must be present. Before describing each of these elements in detail, there are unique semantics issues that need to be understood.

Malpractice vs Negligence

Many states recognize a special form of negligence lawsuit called **malpractice** when allegations are brought against a person holding a professional license. Malpractice is professional negligence, or negligence performed by a professional. More precisely, malpractice involves a professional person, whether pharmacist, podiatrist, optometrist, nurse, physician, dentist, lawyer, or architect, who, while acting within the scope of his or her profession, has performed in a fashion that is substandard and as a direct result of that substandard performance causes damages to another person. Malpractice cases usually are subject to rules of evidence and procedure not applicable to allegations of ordinary negligence. For example, the **statute of limitations**, or time in which a lawsuit must be initiated after a negligent act occurs, usually is shorter in malpractice cases (see *Steele v. Organon* and *Koderick v. Snyder Brothers Drug*) Another difference is that expert testimony usually is required from a professional working in the same field as the defendant to establish the applicable standard of care (see *Docken v. Ciba-Geigy*). In malpractice cases, the standard of care expected from the defendant usually is determined by the profession.

Mistake Differentiated from Negligence

The terms "mistake" and "negligence" sometimes are used interchangeably, but in the eyes of the law they are very different. To prove negligence, one must have all 4 required elements. Moreover, they must exist in a specified relationship to one another. Negligence is a concept that is much more specific than is the concept of mistake. In fact, in the cases reviewed above, there have been a number of instances where pharmacists made mistakes but clearly were not negligent. Dispensing the wrong drug, wrong strength, or wrong dosage form may be a breach of duty but not constitute negligence if no harm is done. It is merely a mistake. One cannot sue and recover for only a mistake; in order to sue and recover, there must be negligence. The vast majority of instances in pharmacy practice where dispensing errors are made are mistakes, not negligence.

Elements of Negligence

In a simplistic sense, the elements of negligence may be described as the following:

(1) Duty;
(2) Breach of duty;
(3) Proximate cause; and
(4) Damages.

The plaintiff has the responsibility of proving the existence of each of these elements with a degree of proof known as a preponderance of the evidence. At trial, the plaintiff will introduce witnesses who will give testimony, physical evidence may be introduced, and oral arguments will be made by the plaintiff's attorney. All of this is designed to establish the existence of each element of negligence. Of course, the defendant will be given an opportunity to disprove the elements or, alternatively, to establish legal defenses to the allegations.

The second major point with regard to the elements of negligence is that in order to establish negligence, all 4 elements must be present in a given factual situation. Negligence is an absolute concept. If all 4 elements are present, the person is negligent; if any one or more of the elements is missing, the defendant is not negligent. The concept of negligence is analogous to the concept of sterility in a drug product. A drug product cannot be 90% sterile. It is either sterile or not sterile. The same is true with negligence. A person is either negligent or not negligent. It is all or nothing.

Duty

As was mentioned above, duty ordinarily will be created by one's professional peers. One side in the trial will call to the witness stand expert witnesses who will be asked to testify about how they would handle the incident in question. There are several issues here. The first such issue is determining one's peers. In pharmacy practice, this may not be as clearcut as in medical practice. In medical practice, a physician's standard of care will be derived from testimony of other physicians who practice in the specialty of the defendant. If the defendant is a general surgeon, other general surgeons will testify to establish standard of care. If the defendant is a nephrologist, other nephrologists will be called to the stand to testify. And so, duty or standard of care is created by one's professional peers.

But in recent years, some pharmacists have begun to limit or focus their practices in ways that give them a special level of expertise. The pharmacist's role in detecting potentially hazardous drug-drug interactions has been alluded to above. Assume for the moment that the pharmacist misses a potentially hazardous drug-drug interaction and the patient suffers damages as a direct result. The pharmacist is sued by the patient who has suffered these damages and the plaintiff will try to establish that the pharmacist should have detected this drug-drug interaction. A likely issue in the trial is determining if the pharmacist has the duty to do this and if his professional peers perform this function. Assume further that the plaintiff brings in as an "expert witness" a pharmacist who has specialized in the study of drug-drug interactions. Will this pharmacist be allowed to testify to create the standard of expected performance of the defendant pharmacist? The law on this point does not appear to be well settled and solid arguments exist both ways.

The "Expert Witness"

In order for a jury to determine whether an individual who is alleged to have performed negligently did indeed do so, the jury needs to be able to measure and evaluate the defendant's performance. However, evaluation of professional performance can be problematic, particularly with health professionals. It is not possible to measure the performance of practitioners in any quantifiable or easily measured units. As a result, the legal system has devised a process whereby the jury will receive information about what reasonable and prudent practitioners in the defendant's field would have done in a given situation. Other reputable practitioners of the profession come to court and testify from the witness stand about how they would have handled a situation such as has given rise to the lawsuit.

After hearing the testimony of these other "expert witnesses," the jury takes their testimony and opinions into account in determining what standard of care will be expected of the defendant professional. Members of the jury will take into consideration the testimony received from other health professionals and arrive at a decision about what the mythical reasonable and prudent person or, in this case, reasonable and prudent health professional, would have done under the circumstances. Then, the jury sets off to one side (at least in its mind or its thinking) this mythical reasonable and prudent professional and focuses attention on the performance of the defendant in the case. The question then becomes, "Did the defendant in his or her handling of the situation perform in a fashion that measures up to the standard existing in the minds of the jurors as the mythical reasonable and prudent health professional?" If the answer to that question is "No, the performance of the health professional does not measure up," then the individual will be viewed as having breached his duty, the first step to liability for professional negligence.

It is important to emphasize at this point that the final determination of what constitutes appropriate professional performance under the circumstances is made by the jury, a small number of nonprofessionals who may know very little about pharmacy practice. Certainly they receive testimony from other practitioners of pharmacy and take into account this information from professional peers. This highlights the importance of projecting a positive image for pharmacy to patients and members of the general public.

The "Locality Rule"

An additional issue related to establishment of duty and breach of duty relates to the doctrine known as the "community rule" or "locality rule." The court created this rule in the latter part of the nineteenth century when the law of professional negligence in this country was in its formative stages. If a lawsuit were filed challenging the performance of a practitioner in a remote or rural area, the courts reasoned that it was not proper to have the parties import practitioners from the same professional field as the defendant from, say, East Coast centers of learning as expert witnesses in the trial. The reasoning was that medical information and information about advances in diagnosis of disease treatment was not rapidly disseminated in that era. As a result, professional practitioners in urban communities might have access to the very latest information by virtue of their location, whereas the rural practitioner might not have access to that same information. Therefore, courts would not permit these "out of town" experts to testify to establish standard of care for a local practitioner. The courts put this rule into play through adoption of the locality rule or the community rule, with both designations used for the same legal policy. Basically, the local defendant practitioner would have his or her standard of performance evaluated in light of the performance of other professional peers in the same or similar communities or in the same locality.

Over the decades since this rule was fashioned, the underpinnings of the rule, slow dissemination of information about scientific and technological advancements, have disappeared. As a result, the locality or community rule has disappeared. Hence, in the United States today, a practitioner in Madison, Wis., most likely will be held to the same standard of care as a practitioner in Philadelphia, Pa.; Orlando, Fla.; Tucson, Ariz.; or Seattle, Wash. The courts today apply a national standard of care to the performance of health professionals. Notice that health professionals today have tremendous access to the latest information. With computer linkages, the Internet, sophisticated telephone and satellite hookups, and a highly sophisticated transportation system, health professionals can communicate with someone who has the latest information or attend meetings to gain the latest information from primary sources. Therefore, it seems reasonable that the locality or community rule has faded from the picture.

Court-Imposed Duties

If the standard of care is established by one's professional peers, then why doesn't the profession get together and establish the standard of care and the standard of practice at a low level so that no one ever breaches that standard of care? The courts are one step ahead.

The first case in which the court imposed a duty on an industry in which the technology was available to prevent an accident but was not widely used because of its expense is *The T.J. Hooper*, 60 F.2d 737 (2nd Cir. 1932); cert. denied, 287 U.S. 662. While the facts may seem hardly relevant to pharmacy practice, cases decided afterward, using the common law rule it announced, show that it is of utmost importance.

The facts showed that an ocean-going tugboat was pushing a barge loaded with coal up the East Coast of the United States. A gale came up suddenly but the captain of the tugboat had no warning about this inclement weather. The barge sank and the coal was lost. The owner of the coal sued the owner of the tug, claiming that it was a negligent breach of duty for the tug operator not to have a radio receiver on board. His argument was that if the tug had had a radio receiver on board, the captain would have been in a position to get advance warning of the adverse weather and could have directed the barge into an inlet until conditions were more favorable. Because he did not have a radio receiver on board he couldn't get this advance warning and as a direct result, according to the owner of the coal, the coal was lost.

The attorney representing the defendant tug operator, on the other hand, introduced evidence that no tug operator on the East or Gulf coasts of the United States had a radio receiver on board to get weather forecasts. In essence, his argument was that because the tugboat operator's peers did not have radio receivers on board, he, the defendant tugboat operator in this case, had no legal duty to have a radio receiver. The trial court agreed with that proposition and ruled that the tugboat operator had no duty in these circumstances. Therefore, the case was thrown out at the trial court level because of the plaintiff's inability to prove any duty existed.

The case was appealed to the US Court of Appeals for the Second Circuit by the owner of the coal. The judge who wrote the opinion for the Court was Learned Hand, a highly regarded jurist. The opinion stated that in the vast majority of cases it will be the responsibility of the members of a trade, occupation, or profession to establish the standard of care for those engaged in that particular calling. Those involved in a particular line of work will obviously know much more about the day-to-day needs of operation in that field and, as a result, judges will defer to the standards created by the members of the trade industry, trade occupation, or profession. However, Judge Hand emphasized, there will be instances in which the members of a trade, occupation, or profession will lag in adopting some innovation. In such instances, he said, it will become necessary for the courts and judges to step in and establish the standard for that particular specialty so that the standards in the field do not lag. Judge Hand established the following 3-pronged test to be used to determine whether the members of a given occupation or profession had unduly lagged in adopting an innovation:

- Is the innovation low-cost?
- Does the innovation have a documented positive impact or benefit?
- Would the innovation have prevented the type of harm that occurred in this case?

In Judge Hand's view, the tugboat industry had lagged in adopting an innovation. He applied his 3-pronged test and the tugboat industry's standards were found wanting. In reversing the trial court's dismissal, the Court of Appeals, in essence, imposed a duty on the industry to have radio receivers available on board tugboats. Therefore, assuming that the plaintiff could prove the other 3 elements of negligence, he could recover damages for the loss of his coal.

For many years, the case was regarded by many as an aberration in the law. However, a professional negligence case in the state of Washington breathed new life into the analysis developed by Judge Hand. This later case also shows how important the rule announced in the earlier case could be to the practice of pharmacy.

The case of *Helling v. Carey*, 83 Wash.2d 514 (1974) arose when a young woman went to an ophthalmologist for the fitting of contact lenses. She returned for follow-up visits at regular intervals to have her adaptation to these lenses monitored. On each visit over a number of years, she complained to the ophthalmologist of a burning sensation in her eyes, and each time he assured her that it was merely the eye adjusting to the foreign body and that the condition would resolve itself. The young woman finally consulted a different ophthalmologist who conducted a relatively easy test and determined that she was suffering from glaucoma, an ophthalmologic condition characterized by increased intraocular pressure that over time can cause damage to the retina in the back of the eye, compromising eye sight. In fact, she had experienced a great diminution in her peripheral vision as a result of the glaucoma going untreated for a prolonged period of time. She filed a lawsuit alleging professional negligence against the original ophthalmologist.

When the case came to trial, the first issue was whether there was a legal duty on the part of the ophthalmologist to check this young woman for glaucoma as part of her routine eye examination associated with the fitting of contact lenses. The defendant ophthalmologist had done a survey of his professional peers in Washington and found that no ophthalmologist, as a routine matter, screened patients under 40 years of age for glaucoma as part of a regular eye exam. Based on that information, the court concluded that the defendant ophthalmologist had no legal duty and therefore had breached no legal duty. The case was dismissed. The young woman appealed to the Supreme Court of the state of Washington using as a basis for her argument the 3-pronged test from *The T.J. Hooper*. Here the court reviewed each of the 3 aspects of Judge Hand's decision and found the answers to be affirmative for each one and, as a result, ruled that the ophthalmologist could be held negligent for failing to screen this young woman for glaucoma. (It is noteworthy that subsequent to this decision, the legislature of that state adopted statutory changes to essentially nullify the Supreme Court ruling regarding imposed legal duty.)

To summarize, courts will defer to the members of a trade, occupation, or profession to establish the standards of performance in their field in the vast majority of cases. However, if the members of that calling allow those standards to slip, the courts will step in and establish standards for them. For this reason, pharmacists must stay at the forefront of professional education and maintain a knowledge of innovative practice techniques as well as technological developments in order to avoid negligence claims.

Negligence Per Se

As emphasized, duty will be derived primarily from the standards established by one's professional peers. The rule known as **statutory negligence** or **negligence per se** also can be used to establish duty, and it has particular applicability to pharmacy practice. In order to satisfy the requirements of this doctrine, there must be a statute which is (1) punitive in nature; that is, one for which an individual may be fined or incarcerated for violating; (2) designed to protect an identifiable group of people; (3) from an identifiable type of harm; and (4) which establishes an affirmative responsibility on someone to do something. If all elements are present, then the statute may be used to establish duty in a negligence case.

This rule applies in most jurisdictions only if the standards described are in a statute. There is wide variance between states and the federal courts as to whether a regulation, such as those adopted by the Food and Drug Administration (FDA), the Drug Enforcement Administration (DEA), or the state board of pharmacy, will suffice.

The federal Poison Prevention Packaging Act is a good example of how a statute meeting these 4 criteria could be used to establish duty on the part of a pharmacist. (See Poison Prevention Packaging Act of 1970 in the Regulation of Pharmaceuticals chapter.) The Poison Prevention Packaging Act is a statute that:

(1) Is punitive in nature (ie, a pharmacist who violates its provisions can be fined or incarcerated);
(2) is designed to protect an identifiable group of people (eg, children under 5 years of age);
(3) from an identifiable type of harm (eg, from ingestion of dangerous household substances including prescription drugs); and
(4) imposes an affirmative responsibility upon the pharmacist (eg, requiring child-resistant closures on containers of prescription drugs unless the patient or prescriber requests otherwise).

If a pharmacist were to dispense federal legend medication in a container without a safety closure when neither the prescriber nor the patient had requested a standard cap and then a child were to gain access to that medication and suffer damages as a result, in a lawsuit for negligence, a copy of the poison packaging act could be introduced at trial to establish negligence per se or statutory negligence. Since the statute meets the 4-pronged test here, it likely would be accepted by the court as establishing duty on the part of the pharmacist. Notice that testimony of professional peers would not necessarily be required in this case. Hence, one may view statutory negligence or negligence per se as an easier way for the plaintiff's attorney to establish duty.

It remains to be seen how the courts will view the mandatory patient consultation mandates of the Omnibus Budget Reconciliation Act of 1990 (OBRA '90) (discussed in the Regulation of Pharmaceuticals chapter). In one case decided after OBRA '90 requirements went into effect, a Georgia court ruled that a pharmacist did not have a "duty to warn" the patient but noted that OBRA '90 had been enacted after the factual situation that gave rise to the suit occurred. The court noted that the outcome might have been different had the mandate of OBRA '90 been in effect on the date of the transaction that gave rise to the suit (see *Huggins v. Long Drug Stores*). Another court, however, indicated that OBRA '90 and a state regulation enacting its counseling mandate did not create a private cause of action for failure to warn (see *Johnson v. Walgreen*).

Codes of Ethics and Standards of Practice

Codes of ethics and standards of practice as adopted by professional associations or organizations are offered in some cases by plaintiffs to establish a legal duty. Documents such as these are not sufficient in and of themselves to establish a specific duty, as the case with a statute under a negligence per se theory (see *Adkins v. Mong*, et al). Nonetheless, standards of practice of professional associations and codes of ethics may be used at trial to support the testimony of experts on a particular point (see *Lasley v. Shrake's Country Club Pharmacy*). For example, several pharmacy organizations have adopted standards of or guidelines for practice that could be used in concert with the testimony of expert witnesses to establish that a pharmacist should perform at a certain level. Consequently, pharmacists who engage in areas of practice where such standards have been prepared and adopted should be familiar with those documents and attempt to conform their performance to those standards. (See APhA Code of Ethics and Standards of the Joint Commission on the Accreditation of Healthcare Organizations at the end of this chapter.)

Changing and Evolving Duties

This concept of a pharmacist's legal duty to use due care does not result in standards of professional practice that are absolute, unchanging, or written in stone. Rather, these professional standards are dynamic and ever-evolving. As the profession advances, so do the standards to which professional practitioners are held. Therefore, it is important for pharmacists to attend professional meetings at the local, state, regional, or national level and to talk with colleagues about innovations that have been adopted in professional practice.

Contemporary pharmacy practice calls upon the pharmacist to engage in a wide variety of activities and to provide a wide array of services to patients and other health care professionals. Because the law deals so much with precedent, as pharmacy moves into unprecedented areas, it will not be possible to lay down broad statements concerning the pharmacist's legal duty that would be applicable in all cases. It is useful, however, to look at some trends in recent years to develop a picture of where the law is going with respect to establishing a normative duty for pharmacists.

Intellectual vs Mechanical Claims

The number and variety of malpractice claims against pharmacists are considerably less than those against physicians if the premium rates for liability insurance are used as criteria. Pharmacists' liability insurance usually costs from $100 to $300 per year for the employee pharmacist, while physicians' annual liability insurance premiums may be several thousand dollars, depending on the field of practice. However, liability suits against pharmacists appear to be increasing at a dramatic rate. For a short period of time in the late 1980s and early 1990s, claims were escalating so fast that no insurer would issue any pharmacy liability policies. As of now, however, there are several companies willing to insure pharmacists and pharmacies.

Until relatively recently, courts have not wanted to impose liability on pharmacists for anything other than mechanical dispensing errors. That reluctance seems to be changing at a rapid pace as courts are allowing new and unprecedented theories of liability claims to move forward. In fact, the growth of intellectual claims over the last decade seriously has changed the way that courts, lawyers, and patients view the role of pharmacists. Several sections of this chapter examine these "new" duties in detail. It is useful to review the kinds of claims that are being made against pharmacists to quantify the nature and types of legal risks pharmacists might face in practice.

In a study of all claims against pharmacists and pharmacies submitted to an insurance company, 83% involved "mechanical errors" in which the wrong drugs or wrong strength of drugs were dispensed or the correct strength and drug were dispensed but with the wrong directions. The other 17% of the claims involved "intellectual errors" in which the correct strength of the correct drugs with the correct directions were dispensed but the pharmacist did something or failed to do something else that allegedly caused harm to the claimant. These claims involved failure to warn the patient or physician about something that is known or should be known to cause a potential problem for the patient, failure to properly review the patient profile for drug interactions, inappropriate use of the drugs (overdosage, underdosage, or inappropriate utilization), generic selection, dispensing drugs illegally (usually without a valid prescription), excessive refills, failure to use child safety caps, and nonbodily injuries (libel, slander, invasion of privacy, breach of confidentiality, false arrest, and other personal torts). As a percentage of the total, intellectual error claims are increasing significantly. Within this category, the fastest growing types of claims involve failure to perform proper drug use review.

Black Letter Rules for Pharmacists

These data suggest that new duties are being imposed on pharmacists at a rapidly increasing rate. There are guidelines that can be suggested as duties that could be regarded as grounds for imposing liability if they are violated. Below is a list of rules and guidelines that Eugene L. Kaluzny, former editor of this publication (see Preface), included in prior editions of this book. Although somewhat dated for failure to include newer theories of liability, it is reproduced here under Kaluzny's original designation, "Black Letter Rules."

The standards of care or duties of the pharmacist are summarized below from the American Law Reports. The summary is in a form that lawyers call "black letter rules." These rules are helpful to the practicing pharmacist in that they provide a guide to a specific situation.

(1) *A pharmacist must employ individuals who are capable of discriminating among drugs sold.*

(2) *A pharmacist must know the purposes of the drugs that he or she sells.*

(3) *A pharmacist must know the properties of the medicines that he or she sells.*

(4) *A pharmacist is not bound to fill any and all prescriptions, and his or her legal duty to a purchaser goes beyond merely dispensing the identical substance for which a prescription calls. As a pharmacist, he or she may know that the physician has erred in the prescription and filling it might cause death or serious injury to the patient.*

(5) *A pharmacist cannot safely dispense a prescription calling for doses that are obviously fatal, nor can he or she, when the doses prescribed by the prescriber appear to be unusual, safely fill the prescription without questioning the prescriber to make sure that no error has been made.*

(6) *It would be a dangerous principle to establish that a pharmacist cannot safely fill a prescription merely because it is out of the ordinary. If that were done, patients conceivably could die from being denied unusual remedies in extreme cases.*

(7) *Upon the discovery of a mistake, the pharmacist must see that it is promptly rectified.*

(8) *Illegibility of a prescriber's prescription is no defense for a pharmacist who uses a different drug from the one prescribed in dispensing the prescription.*

(9) *If there is any doubt as to the identity of the drug ordered, it is the pharmacist's duty to take all reasonable precautions to be certain that one drug is not sold when another has been prescribed.*

(10) *A pharmacist has a duty to exercise ordinary care to discover defects in the drugs and medicines that he or she sells.*

(11) *A pharmacist is not required to analyze the contents of each individual bottle or package of nonprescription medicines furnished by the manufacturer.*

(12) *A pharmacist who, in dispensing a prescription, replaces the manufacturer's label on a prepackaged preparation with his or her own, must exercise an extremely high standard of care to ascertain that the drug dispensed is exactly that prescribed. The pharmacist is responsible for any observable deterioration of a prepackaged pharmaceutical.*

(13) *A pharmacist who knows that a drug, harmless in itself, is to be mixed or used in conjunction with another and the combination would have an injurious effect of which the patient has no knowledge, should advise the patient. Failure to do so makes the pharmacist liable for the consequences.*

(14) *A pharmacist dealing in dangerous drugs owes to the public a duty to limit the danger by labeling or otherwise conveying the potential hazards.*

(15) *It is obvious that a pharmacist's standard of care involves warning of dangers connected with the drugs and medicines that he or she compounds and sells.*

(16) *A seller of drugs is required only to give a warning if he or she has knowledge of a dangerous ingredient or side effect or if, by the application of reasonable, developed skill and foresight, he or she might suspect a hazard. This does not mean that a pharmacist is under any obligation to test independently the drug's chemical structure for side effects or other possible risks.*

The essence of these rules is that in a dispensing situation, the pharmacist has a legal obligation to provide the right drug in the correct strength and the correct dosage form to the correct patient. While this statement certainly summarizes the pharmacist's responsibility in a vast majority of situations, it is not enough to protect the pharmacist from all forms of civil liability. As illustrated above, even when the pharmacist dispenses the correct drug to the correct patient in the correct strength and with the correct instructions, liabilities could still be encountered if the patient is harmed by a foreseeable event that the pharmacist knew or should have known could occur but did not take steps to prevent. In summary, it is the duty of a pharmacist to do whatever is necessary to protect the patient.

Standard of Due Care Expected of Pharmacists

At various times, courts have taken opportunities to comment on the standard of care required of those who engage in the practice of pharmacy. Court opinions on the standard of due care as it applies to pharmacists are presented in no particular order but as a representative sample of how courts view the responsibility of the pharmacist.

The first statement comes from the 1978 case of *French Drug Company, Inc. v. Jones*, 367 So.2d. 431 (Miss. 1978):

> All courts have held that a druggist (sic) is required to use a high standard of care in dispensing drugs on prescriptions of physicians, and when he negligently supplies a drug other than the drug requested, he is liable for resulting harm to the purchaser.

Burke v. Bean, 363 S.W.2d 366 (Texas Civ. App. 1962) contains this statement about the standard of care for pharmacists:

> The very high degree of thoughtfulness and vigilance in the original filling of the prescription placed by law upon the druggist (sic) must also enjoin him to exercise the same vigilance and care for his customer upon discovery of a mistake to see that it is promptly rectified.

The 1981 case *Speevy v. United States*, 512 F.Supp. 670 (N.D. Texas 1981), states that:

> In filling and refilling prescriptions, a pharmacist is required to exercise that high degree of care which a very prudent and cautious person would exercise under the same or similar circumstances.

In *Tombari v. Connors* 82 A.640 (Conn. 1912), the Court wrote:

> The legal measure of the duty of druggists (sic) toward their patrons, as in all other relations of life, is properly expressed by the phrase 'ordinary care' with reference to that special and peculiar business. In determining what degree of prudence, vigilance, and thoughtfulness will fill the requirements of ordinary care in compounding medicines and filling prescriptions, it is necessary to consider the poisonous character of so many of the drugs with which the apothecary deals, and the grave and fatal consequence which may follow the want of care. In such case 'ordinary care' calls for a degree of vigilance and prudence commensurate with the dangers involved.

Another case from the same era, *Tremblay v. Kimball*, 77 A.405 (Maine 1910), provides:

> The law does not require the pharmacist to have the highest degree of skill attainable in the profession, only the degree exercised by other qualified pharmacists . . . in situations requiring judgment and discretion, a pharmacist is not necessarily liable for an error of judgment consistent with the exercise of ordinary skill . . . he does not

guarantee that no error will ever be committed and not all errors are actionable negligence. The degree of prudence and ordinary care commensurate with the dangers involved . . . care involved is proportioned to the danger involved.

Finally, in *Hoar v. Rasmussen*, 282 N.W. 652 (Wisc. 1938) the Court opined:

> The circumstances of a pharmacist's or druggist's (sic) calling demand the exercise of a high degree of care and skill, such care and skill as an ordinarily prudent person would exercise under those circumstances, the highest degree of care and prudence consistent with the reasonable conduct of business. The effect of a mistake may be swift and disastrous. There are many cases in which druggists have been held liable for injuries resulting from negligence in filling a prescription or supplying a remedy.

There are a number of other cases wherein courts have had opportunities to discuss the standard of care expected of pharmacists. Again, the standard of care to which a pharmacist is held would be derived, in general circumstances, from the performance of his or her professional peers.

Later in this section, civil liability considerations related to a variety of contemporary pharmacy legal issues such as drug product selection, patient consultation, and so forth are discussed. There are numerous examples of the point made above that pharmacists' legal duties are always changing, always evolving, and that new duties are always coming into being as rapidly as old ones are being modified.

Specific Duties Associated with Pharmacy Practice

The duty to use due care or to act as a reasonable pharmacist would in the same or similar circumstances are *general* duties that exist for all pharmacists at all times. It is usually up to the jury or finder of fact to decide whether the general duty has been breached in the malpractice case. However, whether certain *specific* duties exist are questions reserved for the courts or judges to decide. There are numerous specific duties ascribed to pharmacists.

Duty to Counsel Patients – Prescription drugs have become the most common form of medical care in the United States with an estimated 1.5 billion prescriptions written each year. Although there are vast benefits and cost savings associated with pharmaceuticals, there also is a down side. It is estimated that 5% of all hospital admissions in this country are caused by drug reactions or complications and that as many as 30,000 Americans die each year as a result of adverse drug reactions. Add to that an estimate that 7000 people die in the United States from preventable drug errors each year. The personal tragedy and health care costs associated with these deaths and injuries are enormous, but in today's litigious society, the legal implications also are far reaching. It may appear that there are legions of health care organizations, consumer groups, and governmental agencies promoting the benefits of patient education about the potential hazards of prescription drugs, but there is much that remains to be done. While patient education by pharmacists has been promoted by pharmacy organizations and colleges of pharmacy, the legal responsibility of the pharmacist to provide drug information remains unclear.

The general rule holds that a prescription drug manufacturer has the legal duty to warn prescribers of those side effects and adverse reactions about which it knows or should know. Although there has been some erosion of this principle, the courts generally have concluded that the prescriber is in the best position to decide which warnings to communicate to the patient. A manufacturer's duty to warn is fulfilled by providing precautions to the prescriber who is termed the "learned intermediary." The prescriber, as the individual between the patient and the manufacturer, is in the best position to know the patient's complete medical history and to decide which facts to tell the patient.

In the profession of pharmacy it generally has been felt that pharmacists share responsibility with prescribers to provide drug education to patients, but there is an extensive body of case law that suggests that the pharmacist does not have a legal duty to counsel. One of the first courts to consider the issue (*Vuhs v. Barber*, 36 P.2d 962 [Kans. 1934]) provided powerful language when a pharmacist failed to warn a patient that 2 skin preparations could interact. The syllabus of the case states that a "registered pharmacist should always exercise great care, and where a drug, harmless in itself, is to be mixed or used in conjunction with another, which would then have an injurious effect, and the purchaser has no knowledge of this effect, he should exercise a great deal of care in advising the purchaser of this injurious effect." This rationale was then used in the 1961 Minnesota case of *Krueger v. Knutson* (111 N.W. 2d 526) in which a 16-year-old boy who purchased potassium chlorate from a pharmacist was injured when he combined the product with other chemicals to make rocket fuel. While both of these early cases suggest a duty to warn on the part of the pharmacist, they both contain rather unusual facts and the legal theories may not extend beyond each of the particular cases.

In the mid 1970s, 2 trial court decisions were claimed by pharmacy literature to firmly establish the pharmacist's duty to warn. A pharmacist who placed his own label over the manufacturer's label on a package of methoxalen was jointly liable with a physician for $7500 in damages because both failed to provide a warning about exposure to sunlight. In the 1974 case of *Mahaffey v. Sandoz* (No. C20275, Dist Ct. Sedgwick County, Kansas) a pharmacist and drug manufacturer entered into a $350,000 settlement with a patient who claimed she had not been warned about the side effects of prolonged use of *Sansert*. It must be noted that the first case was a trial court decision and the latter was an out-of-court settlement, and very little emphasis can be placed on either of these decisions as legal precedents.

An appellate case in 1982, *Hand v. Krakowski* (453 N.Y.S.2d 121), provided an indication of a change in the courts' perception of the pharmacist's duty to warn patients. In the Hand case, the estate of a deceased patient filed a negligence action against a pharmacy for failing to warn the deceased of the adverse consequences of mixing alcohol with certain psychotropic drugs. The pharmacy's patient profile on the deceased identified her as an alcoholic, but the pharmacist failed to provide any warning about the possibility of an interaction between the drugs and alcohol. The court ruled that the pharmacist knew or should have known of the possible dangers and may have had a duty to warn the deceased.

However, any movement toward a duty to warn by a pharmacist was short-lived with the advent of a series of cases in the 1980s. The first case to deny the pharmacist's duty to counsel patients was *Pysz v. Henry's Drug Store* (457 So.2d 561 [Flat Dist. Ct. App.1984]). The plaintiff in this case alleged that he became addicted to *Quaalude* because the pharmacist failed to warn him of the addictive properties of the drug and also failed to warn the physician that the patient's use of the drug over a 9-year period of time could lead to physical and psychological dependence. The court concluded that the pharmacist does not have a duty to warn a customer of the dangerous properties of a prescription drug, but only has a duty to properly dispense the prescription.

The patient argued that the profession of pharmacy had changed dramatically in the past 20 years. He urged the court to take a new look at the duty of a pharmacist to either warn the patient or the physician of the adverse consequences of drug therapy. The patient argued that a pharmacist has greater knowledge of the pharmacology of drugs than does the physician. The court concluded that although this may be factually true in some instances, it is physicians who have the duty to know the drug that they are prescribing and to properly monitor the patient.

In *Jones v. Irwin* (602 F. Supp. 399 [S.D.111.1985]), a court was again faced with the issue of whether a pharmacist who correctly fills a prescription is negligent for failing to warn the patient or notify the physician that a drug is being prescribed in dangerous amounts. The plaintiff alleged that *Placidyl* was a drug of abuse and that it was being prescribed for her in massive amounts. The court concluded that a pharmacist has no duty to warn a patient that he or she is being overmedicated. "It is the duty of the prescribing physician to know the characteristics of the drug he is prescribing, to know how much of the drug he can give the patient . . . to warn the patient of any dangers associated with taking the drug . . . placing these duties to warn on the pharmacist would only serve to compel the pharmacist to second guess every prescription a doctor ordered in an attempt to escape liability." The court recognized the Hand decision as the only recent case upholding a pharmacist's duty to warn, but it found that the specific facts in the Hand case involving a known alcoholic were not alleged in the Jones case. Therefore, it felt no compulsion to follow the previous decision.

A case that gathered much attention in the pharmacy community involved an injury following a pharmacist's dispensing *Valium* without providing any warnings concerning its possible side effects. In the case of *Ingram v. Hook's Drugs* (476 N.E. 2d 881 [Inc. App. 1985]), the patient experienced an adverse reaction to *Valium* and fell off a ladder and fractured his leg. In his lawsuit against the pharmacy, the patient alleged that the pharmacist failed to warn him of the side effects associated with *Valium*, including dizziness and drowsiness. The court decided to follow the large number of cases already described that concluded that the duty to warn is part of the medical examination. The court felt that the decision of weighing the benefits of a medication against potential dangers was the function of the physician who has the benefit of a medical history and the medical examination. The injection of the pharmacist into the physician-patient relationship would "undercut the effectiveness of the ongoing medical treatment."

Brushwood and Simonsmeier (Drug Information Patients. *J Legal Med.* 1986;7.) contend that the courts have misconstrued the pharmacist's responsibility in various situations. They argue that the Ingram case is one involving risk management. Simply telling a patient that a drug may cause drowsiness does not require a medical history and extensive medical examinations. This information would not undercut the effectiveness of the ongoing medical treatment and it does not threaten the physician-patient relationship. These authors distinguish between risk management situations and risk assessment situations, with the latter being the physician's responsibility.

Risk assessment is a highly judgmental process that occurs prior to prescribing. Since decisions on whether to use drugs raise questions about personal values, lifestyle, and attitudes toward risk, physicians often cannot make the decision to prescribe without patient input. To participate intelligently, patients need information about drugs so they can properly assess the risk to which they may be exposed. The consequence of providing risk assessment information to a patient might be a decision by the patient to forego use of the drug. If this were to happen, the patient and the physician would then select an appropriate alternative form of therapy.

Risk management is nonjudgmental and occurs after prescribing. No drug is completely free from the risk of certain side effects or adverse reactions, even if it has been determined to be the most appropriate form of therapy for a particular patient.

Information concerning both proper drug use and potential problems can lead to more successful therapy and to early recognition of adverse effects. The consequence of providing risk management information to a patient would be a decision by the patient to use a drug in a manner that maximizes the benefits and minimizes the risks. Risk management information does not result in a decision to forego drug therapy; thus, it does not interfere with the physician-patient relationship.

A case that is better reasoned and consistent with the risk management/risk assessment theory described above is *Riff v. Morgan Pharmacy* (508 A.2d 1247 [Pa. Super. 1986]). There, the plaintiff contacted her physician because she was experiencing excruciating migraine headaches. The doctor prescribed *Cafergot* suppositories with instructions to "insert one in the rectum every four hours for headache." During the next 3 or 4 months, the plaintiff experienced several episodes of migraine headaches during which she used 15 to 17 suppositories on occasion. Neither the physician nor the pharmacist gave the appropriate warning to the patient to use no more than 2 suppositories per headache and no more than 5 suppositories per week.

The plaintiff began to experience discomfort in her right foot. It was later determined that her condition was the result of the toxic effects of an overdose of *Cafergot*. While the plaintiff initially was advised by her physicians that she was likely to die, the severity of the problem lessened, but the plaintiff suffered permanent damage to her foot. The defendant pharmacy argued that it was the physician's function and duty to determine the number of suppositories to be used by the plaintiff. The court found such an argument to be unprofessional. In the opinion of the Pennsylvania court, there was sufficient evidence to establish that Morgan Pharmacy had breached its duty of care by failing to warn the patient of the obvious inadequacies in the instructions. The court makes a powerful statement regarding the responsibilities of a pharmacist:

> Fallibility is a condition of the human existence. Doctors, like other mortals, will from time to time err through ignorance or inadvertence. An error in the practice of medicine can be fatal; and so, it is reasonable that the medical community including physicians, pharmacists, anesthesiologists, nurses, and support staff have established professional standards which require vigilance not only with respect to primary functions, but also regarding the acts and omissions of other professionals and support personnel in the health care team. Each has an affirmative duty to be, to a limited extent, his brother's keeper . . . If the consensus of the medical community is that a safety net of overlapping responsibilities is necessary to serve the best interests of patients, it is not for the judiciary to dismantle the safety net and leave patients at the peril of one man's frailty.

Many courts have been unwilling to recognize the pharmacist's duty to warn. This may be because they are applying risk assessment principles to risk management facts, but they also have chosen to deny the existence of a legal duty to warn in the pharmacist-patient relationship. There is a special relationship between pharmacist and patient just as there is between physician and patient. A party in control has a legal obligation to keep the other from foreseeable harm. The Riff case may be the first to fully appreciate the significant, positive impact that patient consultation by pharmacists can have on the quality of health care and to recognize an elevated duty of care based on the pharmacist's relationship with the patient.

Liability for Drug Product Selection – In the early days of generic substitution, writers claimed that statutes that authorized drug product selection for pharmacists constituted a judicial mine field. Yet, after all these years, there are no reported appellate court decisions against pharmacists for drug product selection. However, this does not mean that claims are not being filed against pharmacists. Counsel for insurance companies assert that claims are being made against pharmacists alleging that the product selected was not appropriate or was not bioequivalent.

Dispensing from the FDA's approved prescription drug products list will not insulate the pharmacist from liability in drug product selection. There are a number of variables affecting liability of the pharmacist under the drug product selection laws and failure in any one of them could cause civil liability, criminal liability, or both. These variables include the following:

- The pharmacist must correctly follow the state product selection law, ie, substitute when permitted or required and in the exact manner set forth in the law.
- The pharmacist must label the prescription so as to indicate whether a therapeutic equivalent or the brand name drug prescribed was dispensed. Again, state laws vary on labeling requirements, and some product selection laws contain labeling guidelines.
- The pharmacist should properly document whose generic drug actually was dispensed and note the lot number on the prescription document.

The most likely claims that pharmacists will have to face in cases involving drug product selection are negligence, breach of warranty, and strict liability. In brief, the pharmacist has always had the responsibility to exercise due care in selecting products for his or her patients. The standard of care that pharmacists must exercise is that degree of care that would be used by another reasonably prudent pharmacist under the same or similar circumstances.

Upon what standards should reasonably prudent pharmacists base their drug product selection decisions? Should pharmacists select products based upon cost? Upon reliance on FDA regulations? On bioequivalence data? On the decision of a formulary committee? These questions are not easy to answer because there are no court decisions that directly analyze the pharmacist's standard of care in drug product selection. One case that does address the issue indicates that the plaintiff would have to show that there is some difference between the prescribed brand name drug and the dispensed generic drug and that this difference is the proximate cause of the alleged damages.

In *Lejeune v. Trend Services*, the plaintiff was given generic medications instead of the brand prescribed. The insurance provider, who paid for the medications, determined that a generic should be substituted. The patient was not told by his physician, the pharmacist, or his employer who paid for the prescription benefit program that the insurance company would pay for the prescribed brand if the physician indicated "dispense as written," or DAW, on the prescription. The patient claimed that by being forced to take the generics, the defendants withheld prescribed treatment. The court agreed in principle because no one informed the patient about his therapeutic options, but held in favor of the defendants because the patient could not show that he suffered any damages.

One easily can see that pharmacists will be placed in a difficult legal position if they base their decision solely on cost. Institutional pharmacists have the benefit of relying upon the decision of the pharmacy and therapeutics committee which, hopefully, makes careful and deliberate decisions based upon data presented to it.

This issue is discussed further in the Breach of Duty. The notion of liability associated with drug product selection under theories of strict liability and breach of warranty also are addressed in later sections.

Pharmacists also must be prepared to face claims of breach of warranty and strict liability, which are traditional theories of recovery in the area of "product liability." In these cases, pharmacists have been joined as defendants in the lawsuit not because of their failure to exercise due care in selecting the product, but because they are involved in the chain of distribution of the drug. When pharmacists select a drug product, they also are selecting a potential co-defendant manufacturer. While primary responsibility usually rests with the manufacturer of the product selected, it is possible for the pharmacist to be "left holding the bag" if the product manufacturer does not have adequate assets or insurance to cover liability claims.

Finally, it should be noted that there is the remote possibility that pharmacists could face criminal charges for certain violations involving drug product selection. For example, an Ohio pharmacist was criminally charged with involuntary manslaughter for substituting a generic furosemide drug product, not approved by the FDA, for the FDA-approved *Lasix*. The patient, a 62-year-old woman, died. This was the first time a felony charge was brought against a pharmacist for dispensing a drug not approved by the FDA. The FDA issued a nationwide alert in 1979 advising patients who were on *Lasix* of the illegal, potentially unsafe furosemide tablets. A jury later acquitted the pharmacist when it concluded that the death was unrelated to the use of the generic product.

The reader should not confuse FDA-approved drugs for nonapproved uses with FDA-nonapproved drugs. This case involved a nonapproved drug, that is, a drug for which no FDA-approved NDA was effective.

Minimizing Liability for Product Selection —
Pharmacists have been concerned about their liability when third-party drug plans require that they substitute drugs which are not recognized as therapeutically equivalent to the brand name product. There is little case law in this area, but a California appellate court has addressed the issue of third-party liability. In the case of *Wickline v. State of California* (228 Cal, Rptr. 661 [Cal. App. 2 Dist. 1986]), a physician decided that the plaintiff, a welfare patient, needed to remain in the hospital following surgery for an additional 8 days. However, a consultant for the state welfare system authorized only 4 additional days of hospital stay. The plaintiff's physicians did not appeal this decision and discharged the plaintiff after the 4 days. She immediately developed additional com-

plications that required readmission to the hospital and eventually had to have her leg amputated. She brought suit against the state of California claiming that her premature discharge caused the loss of her leg. The court noted that cost consciousness has become a permanent feature of the health care system. It is essential that cost-limitation programs not be permitted to corrupt medical judgment. The court further stated:

> Third-party payers of health care services can be held legally accountable when medically inappropriate decisions result from defects in the design or implementation of cost containment mechanisms as, for example, when appeals made on a patient's behalf for medical or hospital care are arbitrarily ignored or unreasonably disregarded or overridden. However, the physician who complies without protest with the limitations imposed by a third-party payer, when his medical judgment dictates otherwise, cannot avoid his ultimate responsibility for his patient's care. He cannot point to the health care payer as the liability scapegoat when the consequences of his own determinative medical decisions go sour.

Although the Wickline decision does not involve the practice of pharmacy, it is likely that this case will be used by attorneys representing patients who have been injured by health care providers' compliance with cost-containment measures.

Pharmacists need not avoid performing drug product selection, even if not mandated by law, as long as they provide patients with high-quality pharmaceutical products at costs that benefit the consumer. The pharmacist should select a generic equivalent marketed by a reputable manufacturer that has a product liability protection plan extending to the dispenser.

The major drug manufacturers now market low-cost generic lines of certain drug products. Many brand name and generic drug firms have a product liability policy that will indemnify or defend the pharmacist who dispenses their products if a suit or claim is brought against the pharmacist because a product defect occurs. This protection for the pharmacist has some strings attached. The drug product usually must be dispensed strictly in accordance with federal, state, and local regulations and the applicable provisions of the package insert. Furthermore, the pharmacist must adequately document that the manufacturer's drug product was the one dispensed.

Clinical Pharmacy Liability Exposure – Clinical pharmacy and the concepts associated with pharmaceutical care are patient oriented. These services include advising patients on drug selection and proper use of both prescription and otc medications. Clinical pharmacy emphasizes patient care with drug therapy. The pharmacist provides information on all aspects of drugs to other health professionals, as well as to patients. Clinical pharmacy often is identified with hospital pharmacy practice, although most facets also are applicable to community pharmacy practice.

The establishment and use of a patient medication profile is a clinical pharmacy function that has substantial use in community pharmacy. The medication profile used in retail pharmacy practice is a listing of the prescription and otc medications that the patient is receiving. From this profile, the pharmacist can monitor or detect drug interactions and contraindications and call these to the attention of the prescribing physician. In hospital pharmacy practice, the patient drug profile often is more elaborate and can monitor (to a limited degree) drug interactions with diagnostic tests.

Providing advice, recommendations, and warnings for self-medication with otc drugs is an aspect of community pharmacy that can be considered a clinical pharmacy function. Frequently, the community pharmacist is asked by a patron to recommend a preparation for an ailment that the customer has self-diagnosed. The community pharmacist often informs the patient of the warnings and precautions applicable to the patient's prescribed medications, a practice that may be considered an element of dispensing the prescription.

Clinical pharmacy as practiced in a hospital pharmacy is much more involved than that practiced in a community pharmacy. Recently, pharmacists have been encouraged to deal more closely with patients in clinical settings. However, the degree of interaction varies with the needs of individual hospitals. In general, the pharmacist keeps patient medication profile records and functions as a consultant.

Liability exposure in clinical pharmacy practice is essentially the same as that in traditional pharmacy practice, except that the overall exposure is quantitatively (and possibly qualitatively) greater because the clinical pharmacist has added responsibilities that entail legal obligations of proper performance. Willig long ago stated the case succinctly:

> If you voluntarily offer and create a higher standard of careful practice, the public has a legal right to assume that pharmacists can and will consistently perform according to that standard. Colleagues in the associated professions of medicine and nursing will be similarly disposed and similarly expectant. (Legal considerations for the pharmacist undertaking new drug consultation responsibilities. 25 *Food Drug & Cosmetic Law Journal* 444[1970].)

While there is little case law involving the clinical activities of pharmacists, questions have arisen regarding the pharmacist's liability when serving as a therapeutic consultant, when administering drugs, when prescribing drugs under statutory authorization, when monitoring drug therapy by using a patient profile, and when providing drug information to the patient or to the prescriber. As pharmacists increase their clinical activities, it will become more necessary for them to use pharmacy technicians to facilitate the dispensing process. This also raises questions of increased liability exposure. Each of these issues will be examined on the following pages, but the reader is reminded that liability issues need to be kept in perspective and not permitted to dominate considerations of improving patient care. These issues raise the potential for liability and not actual liability. It should be further noted that there is the potential for clinical pharmacy services not only to improve patient care, but to reduce the liability of the institutions and personnel who provide such care.

Prescribing by Pharmacists – The practice of clinical pharmacy does not infringe illegally on the practice of medicine. The clinical pharmacist, whether in community or hospital practice, recommends the use or nonuse of a drug or drug therapy program; the pharmacist does not diagnose, prescribe, or treat the patient, and hence, does not transgress into the realm of medicine unless given specific statutory authority to do so. The ultimate decision of what drug or drug therapy program to use belongs to the patient's physician or, in the case of self-medication, to the patient. It is arguable that in recommending a drug, pharmacy practice encompasses elements of diagnosis and treatment. However, the situation must, from a legal standpoint, be viewed against the historical background of pharmacy practice in this country and the very limited, but still existent, court case law on the issue.

Counseling vs Prescribing – In the past, the typical community pharmacist did a substantial amount of recommendation and provided medication in response to a customer's request for something to relieve a particular ailment. This situation became known colloquially as "counterprescribing." It was not prescribing in the strict medical sense, providing that no examination was made of the patient. To clarify what constitutes prescribing, the reader should consult some of the criminal cases involving a "sale" of amphetamines by a physician (see *Brown v. United States*, 250 F.2d 745 [5th Cir. 1958] and *De Feese v. United States*, 270 F.2d 730, [5th Cir. 1959]).

Cases involving the specific issue of errors in counterprescribing are few. In the case of *Rudman et al v. Bancheri*, 23 N.Y.S.2d 584 (1940), the court stated the following rule:

> Under the facts alleged in the complaint, the defendant, a pharmacist, was practicing medicine . . . although not qualified or licensed as a physician. Recovery may be had in such an action as this only if the defendant's treatment of the plaintiff fell short of the professional standards of skill and care prevailing among those who offer treatment lawfully.

The action in the Rudman case was a civil action in malpractice against the pharmacist. If the action was a criminal action for violation of the Medical Practice Act, the skill of the violator would be no defense. Also, a court might invoke the negligence per se doctrine against a pharmacist who caused injury by violating the medical practice laws.

In an interesting Georgia case that took place in 1878 (*Ray v. Burbank and Jones*, 61 Ga. 506), a customer asked the pharmacist for a prescription for his horse. The medicine that was furnished injured the horse, and the customer sued. The court held for the pharmacist on the reasoning that the owner of the horse could choose the medication for his horse and if he chose the pharmacist's recommendation, then, in the absence of evidence of want of skill on the part of the pharmacist, the mere failure of the medication was simply a misfortune.

A more detailed analysis of the prescribe-vs-recommend controversy is found in the 1948 case of *State v. Baker*, 48 S.E.2d 61 (N.C. 1948). In *Baker*, an osteopath who gave hypodermic injections and gave oral orders to pharmacists for delivery of preparations to his patients in containers bearing his directions was convicted of illegally practicing medicine. Today, osteopathic physicians are licensed as are medical physicians to prescribe and diagnose; however, the osteopath involved in the Baker case was not.

In *Baker*, the court stated that "the giving of any direction to a patient for the use or application by him of any drugs for the cure of any bodily disease is prescribing drugs." The osteopath claimed that he only recommended drugs and, like any private citizen, he had a legal right to do so. However, the evidence showed that he did more than recommend drugs; he had "held himself out as an expert in medical affairs, and in determining the proper remedies for ailments diagnosed by himself on the examination of his patients . . . he charged his patients a fee for so doing."

Encroachment into areas formerly reserved for physicians is not new and now is becoming commonplace. Physicians' assistants and nurses have taken over functions formerly performed only by physicians. Terminology may be a controlling factor; for example, "patient drug counseling" is a more appropriate term than "counterprescribing," and "patient assessment" is more appropriate than "diagnosis."

Authority to Prescribe – While both the Federal Food, Drug, and Cosmetic Act and the Controlled Substances Act have had a significant impact on the use of drugs, neither of these statutes determines who may or may not engage in prescribing such drugs. This authority has been reserved to the states under their "police powers," which give them the authority to protect the public's health, safety, and welfare. Thus, the legislature of each state has the responsibility to determine who may prescribe and dispense legend drugs. The authority to prescribe should be provided in the form of a statute, as opposed to a board of pharmacy rule or regulation. For example, pharmacists in the state of Washington have been given the right to prescribe in the Pharmacy Practice Act as long as they are acting under protocol from a prescriber. A board of pharmacy regulation that attempts to confer the authority to prescribe on a certain class of individuals without a statutory basis most likely will be challenged because it exceeds the agency's statutory authority.

Pharmacists must practice within the clear boundaries of their statutory authority or they may face criminal charges. However, it is more likely that a lawsuit brought against a pharmacist who is prescribing will be in the area of civil liability than criminal liability. There is much that can be learned from the medical profession and its long history of writing prescriptions. Physicians have been found liable when they have failed to determine if a drug reaction was likely to occur or when they did not obtain an adequate medical history from the patient. All prescribers must make certain that patients are adequately informed of all relevant information regarding the proposed drug therapy.

The physician or other prescriber who elects to delegate (with statutory permission) prescribing authority to a pharmacist may share some legal responsibility. Under certain legal theories, it is possible for the physician to be held vicariously liable for the pharmacist's negligent acts. Society demands that a person who employs others for his or her profit should be expected to bear the risk of liability for harm caused by their negligent acts.

However, the theory of vicarious liability only governs those relationships in which one individual has the right to control the physical activities of another. This may not be the case in most instances of the delegation of prescribing authority. The pharmacist is not likely to be an employee of the physician but instead may be the physician's agent or even an independent contractor. Without the right to control the physical activities of the pharmacist, it is unlikely that the courts would hold the physician financially responsible for any of the pharmacist's negligent acts in the area of prescribing.

Pharmacists as Therapeutic Consultants — There are a number of legal issues when a pharmacist serves as a therapeutic consultant to other health professionals such as physicians, dentists, nurses, veterinarians, and other prescribers. Primary health care providers remain responsible for their patients' care, but on occasion it may be necessary for them to secure the consultation of other informed health practitioners. The primary physician must use "due care" when selecting a consultant, and, in a majority of states, the physician may be held liable for following negligent recommendations made by the consultant if the physician knew or should have known that the recommendations were improper.

In providing therapeutic information, the pharmacist must recognize that the health professional receiving the information is relying on the pharmacist's expertise and judgment. If pharmacists were to present inaccurate or potentially dangerous information to a health professional, they may be liable for the consequences, either alone or jointly with the individual to whom the information was provided.

As described earlier, the pharmacist's performance in any professional act normally is assessed against the performance of other reasonably prudent pharmacists in the same or similar circumstances. However, there is reason for some caution in this area. One might make the argument that in the area of therapeutic consultation, pharmacists should be measured against the standard of due care exercised by physicians. In at least 2 cases, nonphysicians were subjected to the standard of care established by physicians because they were performing medical functions. In the case of *Butler v. Louisiana State Board of Education*, 331 So.2d 192 (La. Ct. App., 1976), a biology student was injured while her professor was drawing blood samples. The Louisiana court compared the actions of the biology professor to a physician taking blood samples. In the case of *Steele v. U.S.*, 463 F. Supp. 321 (D. Alas. 1978), an optometrist treated a patient's eye problems by prescribing eyeglasses when in fact a pathological condition existed that eventually resulted in the removal of the patient's eye. The optometrist's performance was compared with that of an ophthalmologist. The question remains whether providing therapeutic information and prescribing are medical functions and as a result pharmacists could be compared with physicians when determining the standard of care.

In receiving the drug information requests, pharmacists also should be certain that the question is developed completely. Steps should be taken to assure that the question is not misinterpreted. In some instances, the pharmacist may have the duty to initiate consultation if the facts indicate such a precaution. The cases that pharmacists encounter on a daily basis are ones in which the prescriber has requested a medication or a combination of medications that may harm the patient either because of the dosage, route of administration, or drug-drug interaction. In many cases the response must be given orally because the demands on patient care prohibit any lengthy delays. A written consultation provides the advantage of having the communication documented including literature references. It should be noted that physicians have been reported to prefer oral responses to therapeutic inquiries. This is particularly true when the physician decides not to follow the consultant's recommendation.

It must be remembered that the pharmacist-consultant also has the potential to reduce liability. Pharmacists have the potential to identify patients at risk from specific drugs and thus may reduce or eliminate the possibility of adverse consequences of certain drug therapy. Individuals who are most likely to benefit from monitoring by a pharmacist include patients who are prescribed a number of different drugs, patients with a large number of laboratory tests, and patients with long periods of hospitalization. Geriatric and pediatric patients also would be well served by having their drug therapy monitored by pharmacists. Many hospital pharmacy directors have argued that therapeutic monitoring of patients by pharmacists has had a positive impact by reducing the institution's liability through the improvement of patient care.

A question that often arises in institutional settings is whether the pharmacist's therapeutic consultation should be placed in the patient's chart. The issue has been debated and discussed at length and the resolution of the issue appears to be best handled by the establishment of a medical staff policy.

Pharmacists and other health professionals employed by drug information and poison centers face drug information liability concerns similar to their colleagues in community and hospital settings, but the question arises whether drug information centers have a higher standard of care. It is unlikely that a drug information or poison control center could effectively argue that it owes no duty of care to the patient on whose behalf the center is called. A duty of care exists whenever performance has begun. This is true whether or not the center provides its services free of charge.

In an Arizona case, a 10-year-old child accidentally was administered 10% cocaine solution by a physician's office nurse instead of acetaminophen. The cocaine solution had been prepared by a community pharmacy and labeled "red solution" to avoid pilferage. As soon as the nurse realized her error, the physician called the Arizona Poison Control Center. He was told by the pharmacists who responded to the call that there was no specific antidote for cocaine. The pharmacist described the signs of a cocaine overdose and the importance of carefully monitoring the patient's vital signs. The child suffered seizures in the physician's office before he was taken to the hospital, where he experienced cardiopulmonary arrest. The child will require 24-hour nursing care for the rest of his life.

The jury awarded the boy and his parents $6.5 million with the physician and nurse paying $2.2 million; the local pharmacy that prepared the improperly labeled cocaine solution paying $650,000 in an out-of-court settlement; and the state of Arizona, representing the Poison Control Center, paying the remaining $3.6 million. *Reben v. Ely*, 2 Ca-CIV 5174 (Az Ct. App. 1985). Apparently, the jury was convinced that the Poison Control Center operated below the standard of practice of such centers because the physician who called was not offered a consultation by the Center's medical director. One expert testified that the pharmacist should have recommended that the child be taken to an emergency room immediately. Expert witnesses for the Center claimed that it only had a duty to provide consultation services to the physician, and that the physician himself was responsible for making the final decision regarding patient care.

Davis (*Hosp Pharm.* 1969;4:26) raises the question of whether the hospital nurse and pharmacist illegally practice medicine when they are forced to make decisions on routes of administration, dosage forms, dosage strengths, and dosage schedules because of incomplete drug orders given by the physician. Davis points to a survey of 6036 medication orders that showed that 67% lacked specification of the route of administration and 19.9% had no specification for dosage form. The problem easily is solved by calling the prescriber for the missing data. However, when the prescriber cannot be reached and the patient might suffer if administration of the drug is unduly delayed, the pharmacist or nurse decides upon the administration route, dosage form, or dosage strength from patient data and knowledge of the prescriber's usual preferences. Although these assumptions increase the liability exposure of the pharmacist and the nurse, there is no reasonable alternative.

The liability exposure of the pharmacist when providing drug information or recommending a drug concerns concepts of negligence and warranty. It should be noted that merely providing drug information is a service, not a sale. Therefore, the implied warranty rules should not apply in cases when the pharmacist merely provides drug information. If a sale results (directly or indirectly) from recommending a drug, there is no way of avoiding the implied warranty of fitness for a particular or intended purpose (see the warranty discussion earlier in this chapter). The obvious solution is for the pharmacist to recommend the correct drug for the intended purpose. The pharmacist can best avoid the attachment of any express warranty in the sale or use of drugs by never promising or guaranteeing any therapeutic action or inaction.

The most substantial liability for the pharmacist who provides drug information or recommends drug products lies in the area of negligence. If a negligence suit is commenced against a pharmacist for an injury alleged to have been caused by an error in providing drug information or in recommending a drug, the pharmacist's liability would depend on whether the error or misinformation was a mistake in judgment (in contrast to carelessness or inadvertence), and if it was a mistake in judgment, whether the judgment was reconcilable with the degree of skill and knowledge possessed by other pharmacists.

Generally, unless lack of skill or due care is demonstrated, a mistake in judgment is not actionable as malpractice. A pharmacist is not liable for a mere failure of the medication that he or she recommends; there must be additional evidence of lack of skill or care on the part of the pharmacist.

Ownership of the Prescription – The general rule regarding ownership of the prescription was formulated in a 1905 Mississippi case, *White v. McComb City Drug Co.*, (88 So. 739 [Miss. 1905]). When presented with a prescription for filling, the pharmacist should "either deliver the medicines or return the prescription." Once the written prescription (or oral prescription reduced to writing) has been dispensed, federal and state laws require the pharmacist to maintain the written prescription on file for a period of 3 to 5 years.

The pharmacist has a right to refuse to fill or refill a prescription for good reason (see the *Jones v. Walgreen Co.* case in the Court Cases chapter). A good reason may be any of the following. The pharmacist may:

(1) Not have the prescribed drug in stock;
(2) suspect that the prescription is forged or is fictitious writing;
(3) distrust his or her ability to fill the prescription;
(4) believe that the prescription will be harmful to the patient because of error on part of the prescriber; and
(5) know that the refilling of the prescription violates the law (in the case of a refill).

It should be noted that if refusing to fill a prescription for reason of prescriber error, it is imperative that the pharmacist refrain from making any comment to the patient as to the professional ability of the prescriber. An adverse comment could incur liability for slander, as in an 1894 Louisiana case, *Tarlton v. LaGarde*, 16 So. 180.

Liability Aspects of Patient Profiles – Pharmacists have maintained records of one type or another for almost as long as they have been engaged in professional practice. However, the advent of the patient medication record in the 1960s, also known as the patient profile, has caused many pharmacists to express concern about increased liability.

While it is true that by maintaining a patient profile, the pharmacist may be subject to legal action, it also is true that failure to maintain such records could subject the pharmacist to liability. A number of states require pharmacies to maintain patient medication records to protect the public's health. By monitoring a patient's drug therapy, pharmacists can detect significant drug hazards, problems associated with compliance, drug interactions, and many other therapeutic problems. Even in states that do not mandate patient profiles, evidence suggests that the majority of pharmacists within those states maintain profiles. Thus, one could argue that today's standard of pharmacy practice includes the accepted use of patient profiles whether mandated by law or by the pharmacist's peers.

If pharmacists dispense a medication without noting an allergy or other possible contraindication, they may be subject to a suit for negligence should the patient suffer an adverse reaction. In states where pharmacists are required by law to maintain patient medication profiles, failure to comply could constitute negligence per se. The fact that the patient medication record is maintained on a pharmacy's computer does not relieve the pharmacist from liability. The computer is simply an aid to pharmacists and does not substitute for their professional judgment.

Besides liability in tort for negligence, pharmacists also must be aware of the patient's right to privacy. The pharmacist should not divulge information in the patient profile to other individuals without the patient's consent. Most states have an exception to this general rule which permits inspection of prescription records by state board of pharmacy inspectors and officers of the law. In addition, pharmacists may, as a general rule, communicate information about one physician's prescriptions for a patient to another prescriber. The pharmacist probably would not be liable for invading the patient's right to privacy as long as the information transmitted is limited to that necessary for any prescriber to make a decision in the best interest of the patient.

Because of restraints on time and space, most pharmacists prefer family medication records which include an entire family's prescription records on one profile. This can lead to both embarrassing situations and legal encounters. Minor children, particularly those taking medications about which they do not want their parents to be aware, should understand that the family may have access to the profile information. This also is true when one spouse desires to know information about the other's medication. These questions often arise during the dissolution of a marriage or child custody battles. Pharmacists should consider the possibility of creating separate profiles on each individual in the family, not only to protect a patient's right of privacy, but also to improve the ease of monitoring drug therapy.

Delegation to Pharmacy Technicians – A pharmacy technician is a nonlicensed individual who assists the registered pharmacist in drug packaging, labeling, stocking, distribution, record-keeping, and storage. In *The Manual for Pharmacy Technicians*, Durgin states:

> The role of the pharmacy technician will soon be necessary to the profession if the pharmacy practitioner is to fulfill his contemporary role. This has already occurred in other fields, such as radiology and pathology, in which the technicians carry out the functional aspects of the profession under the supervision of the professional practitioner, who in turn is responsible for the directions, evaluations, and decisions that are made in his particular area of responsibility.

The concept of the pharmacy technician is not really new; the pharmacist always has had assistants of one type or another. In the community pharmacy, a number of routine, nonjudgmental tasks often were performed by clerks (nonlicensed personnel) (eg, shelf stocking, delivering, selling proprietary medicines, and so forth).

The current interest in a specific designation or title for the clerk in the pharmacy results from hospital pharmacy practice, where the use of clerks or pharmacy technicians is expanding in order to free the pharmacist to function more in the area of clinical pharmacy.

In the ASHP training guidelines, the term 'pharmacy technician' is defined as ". . . someone who, under the supervision of a licensed pharmacist, assists in the nonprofessional aspects of preparing and dispensing such medications . . ." The ASHP manual lists rather comprehensive guidelines for inservice training of supportive personnel.

"The Policy Statement on Supportive Personnel of the APhA" states that the APhA:

> Endorses the term, pharmacy aside, as the accepted term to designate . . . supportive personnel . . . who are trained to perform routine nonjudgmental functions under the supervision of a pharmacist. The Association advocates the training of pharmacy aides via in-service or on-the-job training programs. The Association advocates that pharmacy aides function under written procedures which specify functions and supervisory controls which assure the efficiency of pharmacy practice while not compromising the quality of pharmaceutical service, and further that no more than one nonpharmacist (excluding registered intern pharmacists) be involved in the nonjudgmental prescription dispensing functions under the direct supervision of a pharmacist at any given time.

The adoption of the term pharmacy aide (in preference to technician) coupled with the plea for on-the-job training (in preference to a formal academic curriculum) indicated an attempt to avert a situation in which supportive personnel could gain legal status of the type enjoyed 50 years ago by registered assistant pharmacists. This further substantiated by the statement that "current APhA policy opposes the licensure or certification of supportive personnel."

Pumpian points out in an article (*US Pharm.* 1977;2:22) that while some pharmacists limit the responsibilities of the pharmacy aide to accepting the written prescription from the patient and typing the label, other pharmacists permit the aide to select the product to be dispensed. In regard to the latter procedure, Pumpian warns:

> Pharmacists who permit their nonlicensed assistants to complete all steps involved in the dispensing and merely verify that the dispensed product and label conform to the prescription are following a procedure . . . fraught with danger, especially in a prescription department in which large numbers of prescriptions are dispensed. This danger results from the ever present possibility of an aide or clerk dispensing the product without determining whether or not the pharmacist had checked the dispensed product against the physician's prescription.

Extensive use of pharmacy technicians is taking place in hospital pharmacies. Under Kentucky law, a nonlicensed individual may compound and dispense drugs under the immediate supervision and presence of a licensed pharmacist. Ralph W. Kendall states:

> Non-pharmacist personnel perform essentially all of the traditional pharmacy tasks at the University of Kentucky Hospital. Pharmacists have delegated tasks and some responsibilities but not the ultimate responsibility of how and whether or not they are performed. This is not to say that the pharmacist must 'stand over' the technician to ensure that a task is accomplished. We interpret direct supervision and statements such as '. . . only under the direct supervision of the pharmacist . . .' in a broad sense. (*Am J Hosp Pharm.* 1972;29:496)

Kendall further points out that pharmacist supervision of technicians may vary from 1 pharmacist supervising 1 technician to 1 pharmacist supervising 10 technicians. The statutes of the state of Washington (ROW 18.64A.040) permit a pharmacist to supervise 3 "level A pharmacy assistants" when they are preparing medication for use by institutionalized patients. The pharmacist may supervise only 1 pharmacy assistant when dispensing medications on an outpatient basis. The statutes further provide that the pharmacy assistant may perform only under the immediate supervision of a licensed pharmacist, but immediate supervision is defined to include the visual or physical proximity that will ensure adequate safety controls.

The pharmacist on duty is responsible for the supervision of nonpharmacist supportive personnel. This duty applies, in particular, to the supervision of the technician and also extends to the supervision of the pharmacy intern or apprentice pharmacist.

When duties are delegated in a negligent manner or when the delegated person performs properly delegated duties in a negligent manner, the pharmacist may be found liable. In the eyes of the law, while tasks and functions may be delegated, responsibility and duty cannot be delegated. For cases dealing with liabilities associated with delegation, see the next section on breach of duty.

Breach of Duty

Once a plaintiff establishes that a specific duty of care exists, the next element of negligence that must be addressed is whether that duty was breached. There are any number of ways that a pharmacist might breach a legal duty of due care owed to a patient or caregiver. This section focuses on the mechanisms and methods that could create a situation in which the pharmacist fails to do what ought to be done or does something that ought not be done. This is, after all, what constitutes a breach of duty.

As mentioned in the prior section, most of the duties ascribed to a pharmacist fall into the "mechanical" and "intellectual" categories. Accordingly, the errors that may be alleged against pharmacists may also be analyzed by these classifications.

Mechanical Errors

Mechanical errors occur when the pharmacist does something wrong with respect to the prescription itself. Dispensing the wrong drug, the correct drug in the wrong strength, or dispensing the correct drug and correct strength but with the wrong directions are typical mechanical errors or, in legal terms, breaches of duty.

Dispensing Errors – Pharmacist dispensing errors do occur, probably more often than pharmacists would like to admit. Fortunately for the patient and the pharmacist, the vast majority of errors cause little or no harm and, in certain rare instances, even may benefit the patient. In other rare instances, the dispensing error could harm the patient and the patient may not be aware of it or simply does not want to bring a claim against the pharmacist. Of course, in some cases, claims have been made for redress.

There are 2 basic types of pharmacist dispensing errors. One is caused by inadvertence and the other by inexperience. Both may be the source of a breach of duty of due care.

Inadvertence. In an error caused by inadvertence, the pharmacist fails to see what he or she should see when reading the prescription or hospital medication order. For example, a pharmacist may have filled over a short period of time several prescriptions or hospital medication orders for *Elavil*, a commonly prescribed antidepressant drug, in 25 mg tablets. A prescription or drug order for *Edecrin*, a potent diuretic, in 25 mg tablets then is presented. When glancing at it, the pharmacist could conceivably and inadvertently dispense *Elavil* on the *Edecrin* order. Although the spelling *Elavil* and *Edecrin* are significantly different, both drugs are marketed by the same drug firm and are packaged in similar containers with similar labels. However, even where distinctive packaging is present, inattentiveness can lead to such errors as dispensing *Isordil* 10 mg tablets for *Inderal* 10 mg tablets, or as used to be the case when both strengths were distributed, dispensing *Coumadin* 25 mg when *Coumadin* 2.5 mg was ordered.

Inexperience. In an error caused by inexperience or lack of knowledge, the pharmacist reads the prescription or drug order correctly but does not recognize a problem inherent in the prescription or order. For example, a prescription is written for *Dilantin* oral suspension, an anticonvulsant drug, without any indication of the concentration per dosage unit. *Dilantin* oral suspension is marketed in 2 different preparations: *Dilantin 30*, which contains 30 mg of *Dilantin* per 5 mL and *Dilantin 125*, which contains 125 mg of *Dilantin* per 5 mL. If the pharmacist who is presented with the prescription has only the *Dilantin 125* in stock, he or she might automatically dispense it if he or she is unaware that *Dilantin* is available in 30 mg per 5 mL. The experienced pharmacist would, of course, know of the 2 *Dilantin* oral suspension concentrations and would contact the prescriber to clarify the order.

In another example, a hospital pharmacist receives an inpatient medication order for *Mycifradin* (neomycin sulfate) injection 100 mg to be administered IM every 6 hours; the order is written for an 8-year-old child. The pharmacist filling the order is reasonably satisfied that the dosage is not excessive for a child but he or she may not know that *Mycifradin* injection is not recommended for use in children and infants. Not knowing this and not making the effort to discover it, the pharmacist is not even in the position to alert the physician to the problem. Neomycin IM injection is an aminoglycoside, which is reported in the drug literature as being potentially nephrotoxic. Furthermore, neomycin can be ototoxic and can cause deafness. The liability would be substantial if the child is harmed by the drug's side effects.

In another illustration, a physician writes a prescription for iodine and starch to be mixed in equal amounts to make 30 g and gives directions for application to the affected skin area.

If prepared as directed, the resulting preparation would contain 50% elemental iodine, which is intensely irritating to the skin. Although starch paste is a known antidote for internal iodine poisoning, the current medical literature does not recommend topical elemental iodine concentrations greater than 5% to 10%. The pharmacist should know this or make the effort to find it out. If the pharmacist compounds and dispenses this prescription as written, he or she would be just as liable as the prescriber for any injury to the patient.

Labeling Errors – In an article that appeared in the *Journal of the American Pharmaceutical Association*, a Massachusetts Consumers Council study showed various shortcomings in the labels of prescriptions dispensed at 69 randomly selected pharmacies (*J Am Pharm Assoc.* 1977;NS17:62). The survey claimed that 100% of the pharmacies surveyed "failed to label the drug correctly or completely." It also claimed that 41% failed to use child-resistant safety tops on the containers and 100% failed to advise the patients to consult their physicians if specified symptoms should occur.

Fleckenstein reported a study of 232 labels from prescription drugs purchased at random from 33 pharmacies; "six labels (2.6%) had directions for use other than those intended by the prescribers and were considered gross errors" (*Guidelines to Professional Pharmacy.* 1978;5:1). The study also reported that 153 labels omitted the patient's address (often required by state law); 124 labels did not identify the drug manufacturer; 68 labels had spelling errors; and none of the labels indicated the number of tablets or capsules dispensed, which is helpful information and is vital in emergency situations (in accidental or suspected suicidal ingestion of the medication). (See Standard V of the JCAH standards for pharmaceutical service.)

In the August 1979 issue of *The White Sheet*, a report was made of a study by the University of Cincinnati Department of Pediatrics. Nurses, pediatricians, and pharmacists were required to calculate 10 dosages based on a physician's drug order, the weight of an infant, and the concentration of stock solution of a drug available for the preparation. The pharmacist mean test score was 96% correct, and none of the pharmacist errors "would have resulted in administration of doses more than or less than 1% of the dose prescribed." The mean score for the physicians was 89.1%, with a 10 times overdose or underdose occurring in 38.5% of the tabulated errors. The nurses scored 75.6% correct, but 56% of their errors would have been doses 10 times greater or less than those ordered.

A.F. Southwick stated that between the prescribing and administration of drugs there are many opportunities for error. As the number and potency of drugs increase, mistakes become more common and relatively more serious. It would seem that the hospital pharmacist is less likely to err than the doctor or nurse for the rather straightforward reason that the pharmacist is not preoccupied with so many other responsibilities. One study has shown that the pharmacist is responsible for only 3% of errors. Mistakes include misreading prescriptions, poor labeling of drugs, and supplying or dispensing drugs of poor quality. Nevertheless, the vast majority of mistakes seem to rest with the medical and nursing personnel on the floor of the hospital. The doctor's mistakes include poor handwriting, incomplete prescriptions, the signing of blank prescription forms, and the signing of prescriptions written by others. The hospital's mistakes often result from the storage of special drugs on the floor for particular patients, even after they have left the hospital, the breakdown of patient identification systems, and the general problem of an overburdened nursing staff. In the vast majority of errors, of course, the patient is caused no harm. Furthermore, the nurse generally is not aware that he or she has made an error.

The "errors" referenced in the article include those such as an omitted dose, the wrong dose, the wrong dosage form, the dose given at the wrong time, an unordered drug administered, or an extra dose administered.

When such criteria are used, the number of medication errors can be as high as 1 out of 7, but the significance of the error is a different matter. Often, when a medication dose is given late, the nurse blames it on the pharmacy department, eg, "the pharmacy did not send up the medication," and with the initial dosage, the nurse is often right. One of the most difficult problems to solve in hospital pharmacy practice is how to shorten the time gap between the physician's order and the delivery of the medication for administration. R.R. Wolfert and R.M. Stevens observed (*Hosp Pharm.* 1971;6:12) that:

> Throughout this 1-year period only 134 errors were reported and interpreted as being errors of pharmacists. This was out of 153,693 instances of possible error, or a percentage of error of 0.087. If we assume that not all errors were reported, we still have an error rate far less than one percent.

More significantly, the Wolfert and Stevens study listed the reasons for and percentage of occurrence of pharmacist error. Lack of concentration was listed as 51%; similarity of drug names was 16%; inexperience or lack of knowledge was 10%; interpretation (misread medication order) was 9%; storage (location of drug) was 8%; and the wrong assumption (the pharmacist did not investigate the order) was 5%.

Most pharmacist dispensing errors are the result of inattentiveness, which is caused by distractions, lack of sufficient sleep, boredom, and haste. In addition, pharmacists make certain dispensing errors out of laziness: The dispensing pharmacist does not take the time and effort to call the prescriber or take other steps to investigate the problem when a prescription or drug order is incomplete or contains a discrepancy. It is the nature of the error that counts. A pharmacist might conceivably dispense 499,999 prescriptions without a mistake and make a serious dispensing error on the 500,000th prescription, killing the patient and causing his or her own financial and reputation ruin. As the court stated in the case of *Tremblay v. Kimball*, which was discussed previously:

> Although the defendant may have been a skillful and competent druggist, he unfortunately omitted on the occasion in question to exercise such care and prudence and to take such reasonable precautions as the safety of his customer and the measure of his own legal duty required.

Intellectual Errors

Should a pharmacist be held liable for breaching a duty of due care when a prescription is filled and dispensed exactly as ordered by the prescriber if the patient suffers damages from a foreseeable harm that the pharmacist could have prevented by counseling or warning either the patient or the prescriber? As indicated in the prior section, older cases held that there was no duty to warn, so there was no duty to breach. That policy is changing in some jurisdictions to the point where there may be a recognizable duty. As an extensive discussion of the pharmacist's duty to warn and counsel patients and physicians about foreseeable risks associated with prescribed medicine is offered under the Specific Duties section above, it is not necessary to analyze whether the duty can be breached. There are, of course, several other intellectual duties that a pharmacist might fail to carry out.

Drug Product Selection Errors — Once the standard of practice or duty has been established, the plaintiff still must show that the pharmacist's product selection was breached. It will be a difficult task for the plaintiff to show that the product selected was not appropriate or was not equivalent with the prescribed drug. Considerable expert testimony will be required to convince the court that the scientific and regulatory standards were not followed. In all cases, damages must occur. Without damages, there is no negligence.

Civil Liability for Ineffective Supervision of Technicians — In a 1981 Illinois case, *Knop v. The Department of Registration and Education of State of Illinois*, (421 N.E.2d 1091 [Ill. 1981]), a pharmacist's license was suspended and an apprentice pharmacist's license revoked because the apprentice pharmacist dispensed a prescription without supervision. The prescription dispensed was *Mysoline*, an anticonvulsant drug, in a dose that was 5 times more than that prescribed. The apprentice pharmacist had 30 years of on-the-job experience. He claimed that he never once filled a prescription without pharmacist supervision. However, the isolated incident of dispensing in the absence of supervision coupled with the dispensing error was sufficient to sustain the revocation action. (Under Illinois law, no knowledge of pharmacy is required to be registered as an apprentice pharmacist; it is a situation similar to that of the pharmacy technician in many states.)

In *Duensing v. Huscher*, (431 S.W.2nd 169 [Mo. 1968]), which is discussed in the Court Cases chapter, a pharmacy owner was liable for actual and punitive damages for an injury caused by a nonlicensed individual dispensing *Seconal* suppositories on a prescription that called for aspirin suppositories. The same liability principles of the Duensing ruling could very well apply to situations in which a chief pharmacist or staff pharmacists improperly supervise a pharmacy technician and an injury results that was proximately caused by technician error.

Proximate Cause

Direct Causation

The third element required to successfully establish a claim of professional negligence is direct causation, which means that the breach of the duty (element number 1) must have led directly and without interruption to the damages (element number 2). It may help to visualize this as a chain composed of a number of links running from element number 1, the breach of duty, to element number 2, the damages. If any link in the chain is broken or missing, we don't have direct causation. In many drug-related negligence claims, this element is the most difficult to establish. It involves a battle of scientific expert witnesses who testify about the element of causation.

In another handwriting case, the pharmacists received a prescription for a drug called *Lutrexin*, a hormone product used to support pregnancy in women who had difficulty carrying pregnancy to term. The pharmacists misread the request of the prescriber and dispensed *Lactinex*, which is not intended for that use. The woman had a miscarriage and sued the pharmacist, alleging negligence.

Examine the elements of negligence as they exist in this case. There was a duty breached because the pharmacist dispensed the incorrect product, and there were clearly damages because the woman suffered a miscarriage with all the attendant physical and emotional trauma. But the third element of direct causation was unclear. In his instructions to the jury regarding how they were to apply the law to the facts of the case, the trial court judge indicated that the question regarding the issue of direct causation could be propounded 2 ways: First, if the woman had received the intended *Lutrexin*, would she have not had the miscarriage, or second, did she have the miscarriage because she received the *Lactinex*. The judge indicated to the jury that to phrase the issue the first way (ie, if she had received the intended *Lutrexin*, would she not have had the miscarriage) would require the jury to engage in pure speculation about the effectiveness of the drug for this patient. There is evidence at trial that the drug was not 100% effective (ie, some women took the drug and received benefit and had healthy complete pregnancies). Others took the medication but did not receive the benefit (ie, the drug was not effective for their condition). If the question were phrased the second way, did she have the miscarriage because she received the *Lactinex*, that approach to the issue enables the jury to answer the question in the context of available scientific evidence. Therefore, the second wording of the question was the one to be used by the jury. The outcome was that there is nothing in *Lactinex* that would cause the miscarriage and, therefore, the woman could not prove direct causation. Therefore, she could not recover. (*Sanders v. Marigold Drug Co*, Cir Ct., Cook Co., Docket No 64L5582 [111, 1969]).

Independent Intervening Causes

One other concept related to direct causation is known as independent intervening force. The rule here is that even if someone were negligent, if their negligence was not the direct cause of the damages, but rather the damages flowed from an independent intervening force, then the negligence suit will not be successful. An example involving prescription medications was a case in which a man was skiing and broke his ankle. His broken ankle was set by a local physician and he was given a potent narcotic analgesic to relieve the pain of his injury. When his ankle was healed, he found he had a limp and filed suit against the manufacturer of the pain medication, claiming that it had caused his limp. It was established at trial that the direct cause of his limp was not related to the medication, but rather a mis-setting of the broken bone by the physician or surgeon. Hence, the man could not establish direct causation and therefore could not recover.

Comparative and Contributory Negligence

One additional doctrine related to direct causation is the doctrine known as contributory negligence. Contributory negligence is the rule that if a plaintiff in some way contributed to his own injury through his own negligence, then he will be totally barred from recovery. In other words, the negligence of the plaintiff is regarded as the direct cause of the injury rather than the negligence of the defendant. Another case from pharmacy practice serves as an example of this doctrine.

A patient suffering from hypertension went to his physican and received a prescription for *Reserpoid* 0.1 mg. The prescription was taken to the pharmacist and by error, the pharmacist dispensed *Reserpoid* 1.0 mg (10 times the requested strength). The patient had never used this medication before and, hence, did not know he had received the incorrect strength of the product. He went home and consumed the medication as directed on the prescription label of the container. He experienced lightheadedness, vertigo, and a fainting spell, but he continued to consume the medication as indicated on the label of the container. After consuming the medication for several days, he had a spell while standing at the top of the steps and fell, injuring himself. Upon being taken to the hospital, the dispensing error was uncovered and a lawsuit was filed against the pharmacist alleging negligence. Obviously, a breach of duty and damages occurred, but is there direct causation? The attorney representing the pharmacist concluded that the best defense was a good offense, and therefore, followed the pact that the failure of the patient to contact either his prescriber or pharmacist when he noticed these bizarre side effects of the medication constituted negligence on the part of the patient. Thus, the patient was contributorially negligent and, as a result, should be barred from recovery. It was ruled that the patient had been contributorially negligent and could not recover. (*McKay v. Crown Drug Co.*, 420 P.2d 883 [Okla. 1966])

Under the doctrine of contributory negligence, the patient plaintiff's contribution to his or her own injury serves as a total bar to recovery. This is the traditional rule. The more modern rule, which now appears to have been adopted in the majority of states, is comparative negligence. With comparative negligence, the jury receives testimony about the relative contribution of the plaintiff and the defendant to causing the damages and then the jury engages in the activity of apportioning blame. For example, the jury might say that the plaintiff was 40% to blame and the defendant 60% to blame, or 70/30 or 80/20. The amount of the recovery is reduced in line with that apportionment of blame. So under this modern rule, contribution by the plaintiff to his own injury will not serve as a total bar to recovery.

In terms of legal theory, both the doctrine of independent intervening force and the doctrine of contributory negligence relate to the third element, direct causation. But with regard to impact on the case, these doctrines serve as a defense if the defendant can establish either an independent intervening force or contributory negligence on the part of the patient.

Damages

The second element that must be established by the plaintiff in order to prove professional negligence is that damages occurred and that they were substantial. The law does not provide any blanket guidance regarding what constitutes substantial damages (eg, damages exceeding $500). On the contrary, the assessment of damages must be performed on a case by case basis and in each case, the issue of whether the damages are substantial will be a question to be resolved.

A case from California may illustrate this concept of substantial damages. A patient suffering from a skin condition went to a dermatologist and received a prescription calling for *Synalar* cream in propylene glycol, with the intention that the pharmacist prepare a lotion. (Perhaps this predates the commercial availability of *Synalar* lotion.) The patient presented the prescription at the pharmacy and the pharmacist did not compound *Synalar* lotion as requested by the prescriber. Rather, the pharmacist dispensed straight *Synalar* cream in the proper strength, but the wrong dosage form. The patient went home and began to think about the transaction and realized that what he had received from the pharmacist was a semi-solid in a tube, whereas his discussion with the dermatologist had led him to conclude that what he should receive was a liquid in a bottle that he would have to shake prior to application. The patient filed a lawsuit against the pharmacist alleging negligence.

The first question to be asked is did the pharmacist in this case breach his duty. Clearly he did. He dispensed the right drug and the right strength but the wrong dosage form; therefore, he did breach his duty. The second question becomes did the patient suffer damages and were they substantial? At trial the plaintiff testified about a change in the texture of his skin occasioned by use of the *Synalar* cream. At the conclusion of the testimony, the judge inquired whether he had suffered any other damages as a result of receiving the wrong dosage form of the medication. The patient replied that he had not. The judge ruled that the patient had not shown substantial damages, the change in the texture of the skin not constituting "substantial damages." The judge threw the case out because the plaintiff was unable to meet his responsibility of establishing that substantial damages had in fact occurred. (*Wilson v. Lee*, [Cal.Mun.Ct., Alameda Co., Docket No. 222998, 1970]).

One other case demonstrative of the concept of a substantial damage involves a prescriber's poor handwriting and a pharmacist's failure to contact the prescriber to clarify exactly what drug is involved in the request for the dispensing. A woman received a prescription from her physician for a drug called *Norinyl*, which is an oral contraceptive preparation. The pharmacist misinterpreted the prescriber's handwriting and dispensed *Nardil*, a potent antidepressant. The woman thought she was protected from pregnancy. Later, a pregnancy resulted. She sued the pharmacist, alleging negligence in dispensing her medication. The pharmacist did breach his duty in that he dispensed the wrong drug, so patently we have the first element. Resolving the issue about damages though, is a little more problematic. At trial, the judge ruled that he could not in good conscience as an officer of the court take the position that the birth of a child qualified as legally cognizable damages. Rather, he said that having a child is a blessed event, when children are born we rejoice, we let children get away with things in our society we do not permit adults to get away with, and so forth. Therefore, he did not consider the birth of a child to be damage. The mother did not agree. She filed an appeal to the Michigan Court of Appeals where the appellate court said, "We agree. Having a child is a blessed event. However, these parents are not going to have to pay some money to raise this child that otherwise they would not have had to have paid, so viewed in that light, viewed from a financial perspective, it can be said that they did indeed suffer legally cognizable damages." They sent the case back to the trial court for resumption of the trial. In essence, the appellate court reversed the position of the trial court, saying that yes, there was a sufficient showing of damages here and the case should go forward and that the trial court judge erred in dismissing the case. (*Troppi v. Scarf*, 187 N.W.2d 511 [Mich.Ct.App. 1971]).

Punitive Damages

Punitive damages sometimes are permitted in civil cases to punish or make an example of a defendant when the conduct complained about is so egregious it amounts to intentional. It is rare for courts to award punitive or exemplary damages in pharmacy malpractice cases.

he jurisdictional requirements, it may be very difficult for a plaintiff to show
ist was "willful and wanton" or acted in callous disregard for the patient's
en a dispensing error is made in order to qualify for damages in excess of the
ry damages. There are, however, some cases where this has occurred.

Drugs v. Holloway, a jury awarded the plaintiff approximately $100,000 in compen-
damages and $150,000 in punitive damages when a pharmacist incorrectly filled a
ription issued by an oncologist for the treatment of breast cancer with a drug used to
t heart problems. The error was compounded because the wrong drug name was entered
to the pharmacy's computer and the computer records were used to refill the prescription 3 times over a 4-month period. The jury was permitted to hear evidence that the chain
store had 233 incident reports for the prior 3 years dealing with pharmacy complaints did
nothing to correct any of the identified problems. This evidence is sufficient according to the
Court to sustain punitive damages.

In *Schroeder v. Cox Medical Center*, the Court of Appeals let stand a $400,000 punitive dam-
ages award (in addition to over $92,000 in compensatory damages) against a hospital phar-
macy on evidence that a pharmacist failed to properly monitor a device that makes
compounded heart solutions. The pharmacist testified that she did not monitor the machine
closely and that she should have known something had gone wrong because the machine
was not turning during part of its regular cycle. Her failure to do anything at that point constituted "reckless disregard" for the patient according to the Court.

Wrongful Death Statutes

Another issue of relevance is a wrongful death statute. In contrast to the rule about survival statutes where the lawsuit is maintained in the name of the now-deceased plaintiff, with
a wrongful death action, one sees a lawsuit maintained by the surviving relatives of the
deceased injured party. For example, a wrongful death action could be maintained by a spouse
or by a child or children of a patient who perished as the result of consuming medication.
Note, however, that the lawsuit is not to recover for the damages done to the deceased
patient, but rather the lawsuit is seeking to recover the damages suffered by the survivors, the
spouse, or children, because of the the lack of having a spouse or parent.

An interesting sidelight to this designation of wrongful death actions is that in recent years
a category of lawsuits known as wrongful birth actions has been created. An example of this
would be the *Troppi v. Scarf* case above, where the pharmacist failed to dispense the requested
oral contraceptive tablet and the birth of a child resulted.

Defenses to Negligence

The Sealed Container Doctrine

Generally, this rule states that if the pharmacist merely dispenses a drug in the manufacturer's or distributor's sealed container, the pharmacist is not liable for any inherent product
defects excluding any knowledge or action that would constitute negligence (or excluding any
express warranty made). For example, in *Batiste v. American Home Products Corp.*, 231
S.E.2nd 269 (N.C.Ct.App. 1977), the plaintiff sued both the drug manufacturer and the dispensing pharmacy for damages resulting from a stroke alleged to be caused by taking *Ovral*,
an oral contraceptive. The drug was prescribed by brand name and the pharmacist filled it
with the exact drug product prescribed, but he placed his pharmacy label over the label on
the manufacturer's sealed container. The plaintiff's claim against the pharmacy was based
on an alleged failure to warn her of the hazards, risks, side effects, and dangerous adverse reactions that were inherent in the ingestion of the oral contraceptive. She also claimed that
the pharmacy should be held in strict liability and for breach of its implied warranty of fitness and merchantability of the product sold. The court held in favor of the pharmacy.

Concerning the pharmacist's responsibility to warn of hazards, the court found no lapse on
the part of the pharmacist who filled the prescription since he did not compound, add, or

subtract anything from the manufacturer's sealed containe
drug prescribed. Furthermore, the court indicated that t'
cian and, hence, not qualified ". . . to advise plaintiff wi'
tive for her . . ."

As to the strict liability claim, the court found that '
tion of the Restatement of Torts, 2d Sec. 402 A, co
in strict compliance with the physician's order, and there
would constitute negligence.

The court did not find breach of implied warranties for fitness and merci.
case because the plaintiff did not rely on the pharmacist's judgment, but relio,
scribing physician for product selection. The physician was also named a party defend..
in the suit.

In *Bichler v. Willing* 397 N.Y.S.2d 57 (1977), the court stated ". . . it appears he (the pharmacist) filled the prescription precisely as he was directed." However, the court added "and,
in view of the absence of any showing of a difference between the DES chosen by the druggist and other available brands, his choice of the particular brand of DES cannot be classified as negligence. Accordingly the negligence cause of action must be dismissed."

In *Bichler*, the court obviously was relying on the sealed container doctrine. This rule applies
if the dispensed prescription is an unopened full bottle or if the amount dispensed is counted
or poured from the manufacturer's container. The sealed container rule applies when the
pharmacist neither compounds, adds, nor takes anything away from the drug product as it is
prepared by the manufacturer.

Comparative Negligence

While comparative negligence is discussed above as it relates to direct causation, it is easily
mentioned here as well, since it is a defense because of its impact on the case in eliminating or reducing the liability of the defendant.

Voluntary Assumption of the Risk

The next defense is voluntary assumption of the risk, the doctrine that if a patient has
explained to him or her the risk inherent in a given procedure or transaction and voluntarily gives informed consent to assume that risk, then if something within that defined risk
does occur, the patient may not sue for negligence. Sometimes this doctrine is referred to in
health care circles as the doctrine of informed consent. Technically, that is incorrect because
the correct name of the doctrine is voluntary assumption of the risk.

Notice that the doctrine of voluntary assumption of the risk is critical to the advance of
therapeutics. If clinical researchers and pharmaceutical manufacturers did not have the doctrine of voluntary assumption of the risk to provide the underpinnings for clinical trials of
investigational drugs, it is likely that no insurance underwriter would assume the financial risk
associated with testing unknown drug products in humans. But because of this doctrine of
voluntary assumption of the risk, patients can give their acknowledgment of information
about the risks and agree to participate in clinical drug trials. Pharmacists in institutional
practice will also encounter this doctrine as it relates to surgical consent forms signed by
patients undergoing that form of treatment in a hospital.

Statute of Limitations

A statute of limitations is a legislatively imposed time limit within which a lawsuit must be
commenced or the plaintiff will lose forever the right to sue. In most states the statute of
limitations for a professional negligence claim is 1 or 2 years. However, at what point does the
clock begin for purposes of determining whether the statute of limitations has been exceeded?

The traditional rule has been that the statute of limitations time starts to run at the date of the transaction. For example, with the dispensing of medication in an outpatient setting, the date on which the patient received the medication would traditionally be the date of the transaction or on which time starts to run. However, the courts have come to realize over the years that there are a number of instances in which patients suffer damages and yet those damages may not be discoverable for quite some time. The courts reason that it would be unfair to deny recovery to the patients whose damages have rested concealed for some time. Hence, the courts have adopted the contemporary rule that an individual who suffers damages has the statutorily established time to initiate a lawsuit from either the date of the transactions or the date on which the plaintiff did or could have through the exercise of reasonable diligence discovered the damages. A classic example of this in pharmacy practice is the myriad of lawsuits filed by daughters of women who received diethylstilbestrol (DES) in the 1950s and 1960s. This medication was used by women to support pregnancy in which a hormonal imbalance was thought to threaten a successful pregnancy. Complications arose 18 to 22 years later when these female children began to experience precancerous lesions in their reproductive organs. In some cases, the young women could be treated with minimally invasive procedures, whereas in others, radical surgical procedures that permanently interfered with their ability to bear children were necessary. Some DES daughters filed lawsuits against the pharmaceutical manufacturers who sold DES. Because the damages in the young women did not appear until 18 to 22 years after the mother had consumed the medication, under the normal or traditional application of the statute of limitations rule, these young women would have been foreclosed any recourse. However, under the contemporary approach to the statute of limitations, they have 1 or 2 years, depending on state law, to commence the lawsuit from the time when they discovered, or through the exercise of reasonable diligence could have discovered, that they suffered this damage. This means that such lawsuits can be filed 20 to 25 years after the medication was actually consumed by the patient. An interesting aspect to these cases is that the patient for whom the medication was prescribed and who paid for the medication was not the patient who was suing; instead it was the daughter, not the mother, who was the plaintiff.

Improper Parties

Another possible defense is improper parties. The rule here is that a lawsuit must be filed by a person who has the right to file that lawsuit and there are a number of issues that are relevant. First, the patient (potential plaintiff) may be a minor under the approach used in most states and the minor will not get the right to sue in his or her own name until he reaches the age of majority, usually 18 years of age. This could mean a tremendous delay in initiation of a lawsuit because the plaintiff is minor. Another issue here is a survival statute. A survival statute is a law adopted by the legislature that says that even though a person has been killed by the negligence of another, a lawsuit may be maintained in the name of the now-deceased plaintiff. Therefore, it is conceivable that a negligence claim could be mounted by a plaintiff whose death was caused by a medication.

Strict Liability

Res Ipsa Loquitur

Res ipsa loquitur translated literally means "the act speaks for itself." It is a legal theory of recovery which is applied in a negligence suit in which the plaintiff cannot prove the defendant's negligence, but the resulting injury could only have happened as a result of the defendant's negligence. For example, if the defendant's flower pot falls from his window sill and hits the plaintiff, the defendant is negligent unless he can come up with a plausible explanation. Normally, flower pots do not fall from window sills unless they are pushed off or placed on a sill in such a careless fashion that they might fall. In comparison, in strict liability the element of negligence is not inferred or imputed; the object or product itself is inherently defective or unreasonably dangerous. If the defendant's flower pot were filled with liquid nitroglycerin instead of flowers, it would be unreasonably dangerous and could explode and cause injury without any action or inaction on the part of the defendant. The defendant's liability is then predicated on his or her creating the inherently dangerous object or, merely, on possessing it.

Strict Liability Contrasted With Implied Warranty

Some writers discuss strict liability as a concept of the warranty doctrines. However, the distinction between claims of strict liability and warranty in tort is that warranty (express or implied) involves the sale of goods; strict liability can exist whether or not a sale has occurred. A practice sometimes followed in drug liability cases is that the plaintiff's lawyer will assert multiple theories of recovery, hoping to collect on at least one. An illustration of the multiple action or "shotgun technique" is the case of *Holbrook v. Rose*, 458 S.W.2d 155 (Ky.Ct.App. 1970). Various charges of liability were brought against the drug firm: Negligence for improper preparation of the product and failure to warn adequately of its dangers, breach of warranty for failure of the product to fit a particular purpose, and strict liability for an inherently dangerous drug and inadequate warning of the danger.

In *Adams v. American Druggist Insurance Co.*, 245 So.2d 809 (La. Ct.App. 1971), a woman was suffering from a facial dermatological ailment. Her physician prescribed a compounded solution of 0.5% mercury bichloride and 1% salicylic acid. The pharmacist compounded a preparation, which on later analysis was found to contain 6.56% mercury bichloride and 4.08% salicylic acid. Unaware, the patient had used the preparation, and her facial condition became aggravated, resulting in disfigurement. She sued the pharmacist, claiming that the prescription was improperly compounded and caused her condition to become worse. She also sued the pharmacy owner and his insurance underwriter in the same action. The insurance company then brought a third-party action (or cross-complaint) against the pharmacist who compounded the prescription. In effect, the fact that the insurance company brought suit meant that if the insurance was paid, the pharmacist would have to reimburse the company because the liability insurance policy only covered the owner of the pharmacy and not his employee. This is known as subrogation. The court's decision was for the plaintiff and the insurance company; the pharmacist paid the damages plus all of the court costs. In the Adams case, the legal theory supporting the plaintiff's suit was not indicated in the court's published case report. It easily could have been a case in negligence if the facts had shown that the pharmacist misread the prescription or carelessly compounded it; or it could have been considered a case in strict liability premised on an inherently dangerous product if it could have been shown that any individual who used the prescription as compounded by the defendant would have been harmed by it. More likely, the pharmacist's liability in *Adams* was predicated on his implied warranty to compound the prescription properly, but the court did not state this.

RISK MANAGEMENT

Unit Dose System

The unit dose system in institutional practice has reduced dispensing errors substantially. Tablet or capsule dosage forms are packaged in single-dose blister wrappers with the name, strength, and lot or control number on the label. The system is bulky, expensive, and generally suitable only in institutional or hospital pharmacy practice. Most commonly prescribed drugs are available from the drug manufacturer in unit dose packaging; however, some hospitals do their own unit dose packaging. In these cases, the hospitals run additional risks of mislabeling or misfilling the drugs. Therefore, when unit dose packaging is prepared on the premises rather than procured from the manufacturer, adequate controls and documentation must be maintained to avoid packaging or labeling errors.

Liquid drug products also are available in unit dose packaging but not to the degree that the tablet and capsule drug products are. Hence, most hospital pharmacies prepare their own unit dose liquid drugs in special 5 or 10 mL oral syringes. Similarly, a number of injectable drugs are available from the manufacturer in prefilled, single-dose injectable syringes ready for use. Again, not all of the injectable drugs are available in this form, and most hospitals prepare some of their own single dose injectables. Care must be taken that the drug is properly labeled and measured in the ready-use syringe. The pharmacist also must be alert as to which drugs react to plastic syringes and must then be dispensed only in the more expensive glass syringes. (See Regulation of Pharmaceuticals chapter.)

Recordkeeping for Unit Dose Drug Products

Hospital pharmacy directors differ on the amount, type, and need for recordkeeping of the prepackaged unit dose drugs for inpatient dispensing. If the prepackaging operation is solely for in-hospital use, the FDA's Current Good Manufacturing Practices (CGMP) regulations do not have to be followed. (See Regulation of Pharmaceuticals chapter.) However, the CGMP regulations do contain guidelines that are worth following for the documentation and monitoring of prepackaging. Furthermore, good recordkeeping procedures in prepackaging are a method of proving quality control. Drug prepackaging records should contain, at a minimum, a record of the drug product, its manufacturer, the National Drug Code (NDC) number, the manufacturer's lot number, the drug expiration date, the pharmacy control number assigned to the particular batch prepackaged, and the identification or signature of the packer and the pharmacist.

Advantages of the Unit Dose System

The unit dose drug dispensing system can identify the drug product and dosage (by individual labeling) to the moment that the drug is administered to the patient. This is significant in a hospital or skilled nursing facility where the nurse is an intermediate between the pharmacist and the patient in drug delivery. The traditional system consisted of the pharmacist dispensing the drug in an individual container labeled for the patient and containing a 4- to 7-day supply of medication. Hence, an error in dispensing or administration might not be detected for 4 to 7 days.

Many studies have shown that the unit dose system reduces medication error. One 1977 study showed that the error of unordered medications dropped from 1.7% to 0.0063% when the unit dose system was adopted.

Disadvantages of the Unit Dose System

As more institutional pharmacy practitioners work with the unit dose system or a hybrid form (part unit dose/traditional dispensing), certain problems have come to light. Although each medication dose is labeled individually with the name and dose of the drug product, the pharmacist still can dispense the wrong medication, which may go undetected by the administering nurse, or the correct drug product can be dispensed, but the nurse might administer it to the wrong patient. A nurse borrows a drug from another patient's supply on a stat order without waiting for the pharmacist to interpret the order and dispense it. The nurse may err in his or her interpretation of the order and administer the wrong drug.

Other errors consist of "missing doses" and "extra doses" because new drug orders are not yet noted by the nurse or the nurse fails to note the discontinuation of prior drug orders. Nonpharmacist personnel fill the medication trays, bins, and carts with unit doses, and the pharmacist checks this procedure. Inattention on the part of the pharmacist also could result in missing doses. Another disappointing feature of the unit dose system is the time lag between a new drug order and when the drug actually is dispensed to the patient. Under a unit dose system, a patient's drug supply is dispensed approximately every day or every half-day. Smaller but more frequent dispensing increases the amount of paperwork required by the pharmacist resulting in great lag time between the drug order and when the drug is actually dispensed. However, if an error is made, it may be detected and corrected sooner than under a non-unit dose system.

Although a number of hospital pharmacies have begun to investigate and to take steps to minimize the problem areas in the unit dose system, attention should be called to a reported colchicine fatality. In an article, Cohen (*Hosp Pharm.* 1981;16:494) reported that colchicine was ordered in a 0.6 mg dose every 2 hours until diarrhea occurred and then was to be discontinued; a common prescription for colchicine treatment of gout. Six tablets of colchicine were dispensed initially, and 6 more were dispensed when the night nurse requested them. On the morning cart exchange, 12 colchicine tablets were dispensed; on the third day, 6 more were sent, and the patient died in a pool of diarrhea. The patient may have received 25 tablets or 15 mg of colchicine (as little as 7 mg has proved fatal).

Cohen commented, "the pharmacists acted as thoughtless robots. Did they expect the diarrhea to leak through the ceiling before they questioned the amount dispensed? There is more to pharmacy than checking to see whether the correct number of doses has been placed in the patient's bin."

Reduction of Distractions

Interference with the pharmacist's ability to concentrate must be minimized if error and liability are to be minimized. Formerly, a Mississippi Pharmacy Board rule required that the pharmacist or pharmacy intern could not be subject to any conditions that might cause error but the rule was repealed (it was probably too ambiguous to be enforceable). Some state boards prohibit placement of television sets in locations where they can be viewed from the prescription laboratory.

Attempts have been made to limit working hours so that the pharmacist is not overworked and errors caused by lack of alertness can be avoided. A Colorado statute limits the number of hours per day and total hours per 2-week period that a pharmacist may work. In the February 1979 issue of *American Druggist*, it was reported that the California Pharmacy Board was considering regulations that would "limit the number of pharmacists who may work in a given space, and bar pharmacists 'productivity standards' that are conducive to erroneous filling of prescriptions." There must be some data supporting the end that this type of administrative or legislative approach seeks to attain. Constitutionally, an unwarranted infringement on the employer's "freedom of contract right" (a right that is not written in the Constitution but is derived from the broad Fourteenth Amendment property right protection) could be claimed. However, if there are adequate data to support the need for this type of regulation, the courts may very well sustain it.

Recording the Lot Number

The lot or manufacturer's control number of the drug that is actually dispensed should be placed on the written prescription (or on the backside if it is a refill); this practice helps to reduce error. It somehow seems to help the pharmacist concentrate better on what he or she is dispensing. In addition, if a question should arise several months or years later involving the prescription, the pharmacist will have no difficulty in identifying the drug dispensed because lot numbers are available from the manufacturer. The lot number also can trace a problem to a bad batch of drug products. Rule 405.1027 (d) (3) of the hospital Medicare participation standards requires the recording of the lot number of the drug dispensed on the prescription. It also is wise to note the NDC number along with the lot number.

Minimizing Liability

Upon detecting an error in dispensing, the pharmacist must take all necessary steps to rectify it promptly; failure to do so can subject the pharmacist to punitive damage liability in addition to actual damages for the injury caused. The pharmacist should inform the patient and the prescribing physician regarding the prescription error immediately upon discovery. In instances where the potential harm resulting from a prescription error is slight, the pharmacist could inform the prescribing physician without alarming the patient. For example, if a prescription for 200,000 units of penicillin G was filled incorrectly with 400,000 units, the error may actually benefit the patient because there usually is more harm in the under-dosage of an antibiotic than in overdosage (because of the development of resistant strains of bacteria from underdosages). In such a situation, a call to the physician may result in the authorization to change the prescription to the higher strength. The pharmacist should not assume that a prescription error is harmless; the prescriber always should be informed of it, and where harm may be substantial, the patient should be alerted immediately.

Reports issued by professional liability insurers seem to indicate that a substantial number of claims against pharmacists for prescription errors involve prescriptions for children. The usual error is that an adult strength dose is dispensed for a child.

For example, in *Tolan v. S.S. Kresge Co.*, d/b/a KMart Stores, Case #75E, Circuit Court for Escambia County, Florida (1977), a prescription for 50 mg of aminophylline was written for a 2-year-old infant. The pharmacist who filled the prescription did so negligently with 500 mg aminophylline suppositories. The child suffered extensive injury from the suppositories. The suit against the pharmacy owner and the negligent pharmacist resulted in a $2,150,000 judgment against both.

A pharmacist assumes a risk when drugs are identified quickly, particularly when similarities exist. It could be easy to fill an order for *Cortisporin Otic Solution* when *Cortisporin Ophthalmic Suspension* is called for, especially if the pharmacist is in a hurry or is distracted. The only way to avoid this type of error is for the pharmacist to carefully check that the prescription label is consistent with the directions in the prescription; the auxiliary labels and the name of the drug product compared with the drug named in the prescription also should be checked. Consultation with the patient to ascertain his or her understanding of the directions and application of the medication often is helpful in avoiding errors, particularly errors when the prescription of one patient is mistakenly placed in the prescription container of another patient.

Although acceptable variances in inpatient drug labeling exist among hospitals because of the different medication delivery systems and particular needs of the individual hospital, medication labeling directions should be written unambiguously so that they convey only the correct meaning. In hospital inpatient drug labeling, the strength of the drug should be indicated to leave no mistake in interpretation by the nurse who administers the drug. For example, an inpatient container that is labeled "Digoxin 0.25 mg (4) tablets" should be labeled "Digoxin 0.25 mg each tablet content: (4) tablets."

Directions on prescription labels in community practice or on hospital outpatient prescriptions often are written using both words and figures to indicate numbers. For example, the prescription directions of "one tablet t.i.d." often are typed on the prescription label as "take one (1) tablet three (3) times a day." It is important to use Arabic numerals in parentheses following the written number in prescription labels to avoid any possible confusion.

Some drug names are spelled in a similar fashion to other drug names or sound like other drug names (eg, *Phenaphen-Phenergan*, *Inderal-Isordil*, *Inderal-Iberol*, *Paregoric-Percogesic*, and *Doriden-Doxidan*).

The problem is compounded further by the poor penmanship of some prescribers.

To distinguish between similar drug names, the pharmacist should consider the strength prescribed, the dosage prescribed, the patient's age, and diagnosis (when known). Then, if there still is substantial doubt, the prescribing physician must be contacted to verify the name of the drug ordered.

Despite the emphasis on reading labels, on occasion the wrong drug is dispensed simply because it is packaged by the manufacturer or distributor in the same style as the drug ordered. The practicing pharmacist is well aware that drug products with sound-alike names are sometimes marketed in look-alike packages. While some drug manufacturers use color-coded packaging to distinguish between their different drug products, others do not. Generic drug products are more apt to be marketed in look-alike packaging than brand name drugs. Even supermarkets feature their generic line food products in the plain wrapper look-alike packaging. Therefore, it is more imperative than ever for the pharmacist to read the drug product name and dosage of each drug dispensed carefully.

Medications for eye, ear, or nose use should, as a precaution, be dispensed with the appropriate auxiliary label indicating the route of administration. Conversely, a prescription for oral antibiotic drops for a pediatric patient should be labeled for oral use, or verbal instructions to that effect should be given to the parents.

Errors in oral (telephoned) prescriptions or drug orders are particularly difficult for the pharmacist to avoid. Errors can happen in community pharmacy practice when the prescribing physician insists that directions were given (over the phone) for 1 tablet daily, and the pharmacist insists that the physician said 1 tablet, 4 times daily. If a suit arises over the matter, it is the pharmacist's word against that of the physician.

One way to minimize liability and increase accuracy in dispensing from oral prescriptions is to tape-record the telephone conversation. As a rule, a party to an oral communication may tape-record it with or without the consent of the other party or parties. An individual may lawfully tape-record his or her own telephone conversation unless the purpose is to commit a criminal or injurious act. State and federal laws prohibiting wiretaps apply to electronic interception of the telephone calls or conversations (eavesdropping) of other individuals. The principal federal law in this are is 18 U.S.C. §§2510 to 2520. This law can be interpreted by summarizing federal law 25 U.S.C. §1811, which does not prohibit a party to a telephone conversation from recording the conversation or publishing it without consent of the other party unless it is done for criminal, torturous, or injurious reasons.

In hospital practice, an oral drug chart order can result in the incorrect transcribing of the order. For example, a physician may telephone and order for his hospital patient "digoxin 0.5 mg orally every 6 hours for 2 doses." The nurse receiving the order quickly writes it down on a scratch pad and later transcribes it as "digoxin 0.5 mg 'a' q 6 hours × 2 days." An alert pharmacist will detect a possible error here in the total amount of digoxin called for in the transcribed order. In this instance, the prescribing physician should be contacted to verify or clarify the nurse's transcription of the order.

Drug strengths that differ by decimal amounts are a source of error. The problem is that the same drug is available in different strengths with a 10-fold or more spread between the lowest and the highest strength. (See *MacKay v. Crown Drug Co.*, 420 P.2nd 883 [Okla.1966]). For example, reserpine is marketed in 0.1 and 1.0 mg tablets. Another serious error occurs when *Compazine* 25 mg suppositories are dispensed on an order calling for the *Compazine* 2.5 mg suppositories. However, the manufacturer of *Compazine* now labels the foil wrappers of the 25 mg suppositories "Not for children."

A suggestion offered by Teplitsky (*Pharm Times.* 1975;41:54) is that the drug manufacturers spell out the drug strength on the label, that is, two and one half (in lieu of 2.5) or twenty five (in lieu of 25). Even so, this procedure would not correct an error in reading the prescription or drug order.

The problem can be compounded by the way physicians indicate drug strengths in their prescriptions or chart orders. For example, if a physician prescribes *Valium* in the 2.0 mg strength, the decimal point may not be noticed or be clear enough to read (if a carbon copy of the chart order is used for the dispensing copy), and the dosage may be interpreted as 20 mg. A solution was offered (*Hosp Pharm.* 1977;12:391). For instance, "8 U" should be written correctly as "8 units" because the "U" is often mistaken for a zero; "2.0 mg" should be written "2 mg" because the decimal point often is not seen; and ".5" mg should be written correctly as "0.5 mg" because the decimal point often is not seen.

Summary of Suggestions for Minimizing Dispensing Errors

(1) The potency of the medication prescribed decrees the amount of diligence that is required on the part of the pharmacist.
(2) Avoid all unnecessary distractions in the dispensing area.
(3) Indicate a lot number of the actual drug dispensed in dispensing or refilling a prescription.
(4) Applicable federal and state laws must not be violated.
(5) Ascertain the age of the individual for whom the prescription is intended.
(6) If there is any reasonable doubt as to the identity of the drug or the dosage prescribed, consult the prescriber before the drug is dispensed.
(7) Do not dispense a prescription calling for an obviously fatal dose or for a medication known to be substantially harmful to the patient.
(8) After the detection of a dispensing error, promptly take all necessary steps to rectify the error.
(9) Be certain that the patient understands the prescriber's directions and the nature of the medication prescribed.
(10) Proper technique in compounding prescriptions must be used.
(11) Labeling directions must not be ambiguous. The label must be neat and readable.
(12) Advise the patient of potential dangers involved in the drug prescribed.

PROFESSIONAL LIABILITY INSURANCE

(Editor's Note: Special thanks to Kenneth R. Baker, BS Pharm, JD, Vice President and General Counsel, Pharmacists Mutual Insurance Company, for review of this section.)

No amount of liability insurance can prevent any injury from happening or restore a damaged reputation; therefore, its purchase would seem useless. However, there are a number of good reasons for a pharmacist to purchase professional liability insurance. Professional liability insurance insures pharmacists against allegations that they failed to exercise reasonable care in the practice of their professional duties (eg, failure to counsel or dispensing the wrong medication or dosage strength).

Professional liability insurance can provide all or part of the money to pay damages for an injury caused by the error or malpractice of the pharmacist. Liability insurance also can pay for all of the legal costs of defense against a civil suit, even if the claim is without merit or is fraudulent. It can provide supplemental coverage of the medical costs for an injury, regardless of fault.

While a court may award monetary damages, which the insurance company may pay in a negligence suit, the money cannot adequately compensate for a serious injury (eg, death, disfigurement, loss of limb). However, money is the only legal atonement that the courts can procure.

The benefit that the insured individual receives from insurance is peace of mind, which is, of course, subject to all the limitations, exclusions, terms, conditions, clauses, subclasses, definitions, phrases, and disclaimers stated within the policy.

Insurance is a contract whereby the insurer agrees, in exchange for a premium, to indemnify the insured for loss, damages, liability, or other situations arising from a contingent event. There are 2 types of professional liability policies designed to protect pharmacists. Commercial policies are purchased by employers or self-employed pharmacists. They usually cover the business, pharmacy, or hospital, and should also, but do not always, protect the employed pharmacists. Commercial policies should be primary policies, meaning they are the first level of protection and respond first.

Individual pharmacists professional liability policies protect only the individual pharmacist who purchases them. Individual policies are, or should be, excess policies that respond after the commercial policy of the employer, or if, for some reason, the employer's policy does not protect the pharmacist. This is the reason individual policies generally are relatively inexpensive. Individual policies usually are "just in case" policies. This section focuses on individual pharmacists professional liability policies, except where indicated.

The employee pharmacist and the pharmacy intern should buy an individual professional liability insurance. An employee pharmacist (in community or hospital practice) should not assume that he or she is covered by the employer's commercial insurance policy. If a suit arises out of employee negligence and the employer's insurance pays the damages, or if the employer is self-insured and the employer pays the damages, the employee could be required to reimburse the employer or the employer's insurance company unless he or she is covered by the employer's policy. (See *Adams v. American Druggist Insurance*, 245 So.2d 809 [La.Ct.App. 1971] in this chapter.)

Even if the employer's professional liability insurance covers employees, the policy payment limits may be insufficient to cover a liability judgment. The current tendency is for juries to award large amounts in negligence suits, and settlements made out of court have been for increasing amounts. The employee pharmacist cannot be certain that the employer has paid the premium. An employer's policy only provides coverage for actions performed in the course of the conduct of the employer's business. Therefore, the policy will not provide coverage if the employee is moonlighting at another job. Individual pharmacist policies usually provide protection for the individual pharmacist 24 hours a day. To be certain of coverage, employee pharmacists should have their own insurance protection.

Employed pharmacists may hope, and even presume, their employer's policy protects them as well as the employer's business, but it is difficult, and perhaps even impossible to be certain. Individual professional liability policies are often referred to as excess, or "just in case" protection.

Protection by additional individual liability insurance, in all probability, does increase the chances of suit. In isolated cases, a plaintiff may not bring a defendant into a suit when the chances of recovering damages are poor because of the defendant's limited assets. However, the current trend in negligence or product liability suits is to join as a party defendant anyone who may have had responsibility for the injury. If the pharmacist does not protect himself or herself by procuring individual professional liability insurance, his or her personal assets may be exposed to the risk of a money judgment.

Extent of Coverage

The insuring agreements of most, but not all, individual professional liability policies for pharmacists are written on an "occurrence" basis. The occurrence coverage typically provides protection for damages resulting from covered acts or omissions that occur during the policy period, regardless of when claims are made. The insurance industry would prefer to limit the company's exposure beyond the policy period and often will offer policies on a "claims made" basis.

Under a "claims made" policy, the insurance carrier agrees to assume liability for any errors or omissions committed during the policy period as long as a claim is filed while the policy is in force. This provides more certainty for the insurer, particularly when it comes to calculating future reserves to be set aside for claims that are unknown when the policy is no longer in effect. For example, if a patient were injured in 1995 because of alleged negligence of an insured pharmacist, the occurrence policy in force in 1995 would be responsible for the liability claim even though the plaintiff did not notify the pharmacist of the claim until 1998. Knowing that such future claims may be made, the insurance company must set back an amount of money for these yet unknown claims. However, under a "claims made" insurance policy, if the policy is no longer in effect, the company will not be responsible for claims reported after the policy has ended. The "claims made" insurance company therefore need not reserve any money for such future claims. So long as a "claims made" policy is renewed each year claims are covered regardless of the year in which they are reported. The concern arises when the policy is not renewed.

Generally, a pharmacist shopping for professional liability insurance would prefer to purchase insurance written on an occurrence basis since it will provide longer protection. If a pharmacist purchases "claims made" insurance, the pharmacist should keep in mind the limitations and protect against future problems. Pharmacists can purchase "extended reporting" coverage. This coverage extends the time in which a claim will be covered after the policy is discontinued. Typically this coverage is available for 1- or 2-year extensions. The price for "extended reporting" varies, and may cost 1 to 2 times the annual cost of the policy itself.

When transferring from one "claims made" policy to another, the new company's policy may entice the purchaser to switch by offering to cover unreported claims occurring under the old policy as if they had occurred during the new policy period. This extension of policy terms, called "prior acts coverage" may require additional premium. A pharmacist with a "claims made" policy should not cancel or nonrenew the policy without being sure claims reported following the end of the policy period will be covered either through purchase of an extended reporting endorsement or through prior acts coverage on his new policy. One of the largest drawbacks to the "claims made" policy is the cost of ending the coverage. This cost is not a concern with an occurrence policy.

Types of Policy Clauses

Pharmacist liability policies may be written as generic policies, designed to cover many health care professions with the same form, or pharmacy specialty policies, written specifically for pharmacists. One typical generic policy for professional liability insurance contains a coverage clause similar to the one following in which the insuring company agrees:

> To pay on behalf of the insured, subject to the limits of liability, all sums which the insured shall become legally obligated to pay as damages because of injury arising out of malpractice, error, or mistake in rendering or failing to render professional services in the practice of the insured's profession, committed by or of the responsibility of the insured in the course of the insured's employment by another during the policy period, or acts or omissions of the insured as a member of a formal accreditation or similar board or committee of a hospital or professional society in the practice of the insured's profession as stated in the declarations herein.

Coverage is defined as "professional services in the practice of the insured's profession . . . ." The specific profession covered is usually entered on the "declarations" page of the policy. In the case of a pharmacist, the word "pharmacist" should be typed into the appropriate blank. Since the insurance contract does not define what is covered, it is presumed that it would include all statutorily defined acts of the particular profession, in this case pharmacy.

Pharmacy specialty policies are written specifically for pharmacists and define coverage in terms of pharmacy services. At the present time, there is only one pharmacist-specific policy commonly available. This policy defines "pharmacy services" broadly to include counseling, drug review, drug-related research, and "those acts or services necessary to perform pharmaceutical care," as well as dispensing duties. In addition, the policy includes coverage for pharmacist prescribing or collaborative practice agreements and drug administration (including immunization) "if legal in the state in which you practice." Because the practice of pharmacy has changed rapidly in recent years, the company has added to the definition of "pharmacy services" a self-expanding clause: "All other services of a professional nature usually and customarily performed by a registered pharmacist."

Both the individual specialty pharmacy policy and the individual generic policy limit coverage to specific injuries and damages. Typically liability policies cover damages caused by "bodily injury," "property damage," and "personal injury." Usually, this liability coverage is sufficient. Bodily injury covers malpractice claims alleging a patient was physically injured by an act, or failure to act, by a pharmacist. Whether this also covers emotional injury depends upon the definition in the policy of the term "bodily injury." Property damage relates to tangible property. Personal injury usually is defined as libel, slander, and unauthorized release of confidential information.

Pharmacists involved in consulting or employed as independent contractors need additional insurance. As the terms are normally used, consultants and independent contractors are self-employed and need general liability coverage in addition to professional liability coverage. Self-employed consultants also may wish to explore an errors and omissions policy covering financial loss suffered by their clients caused by the pharmacist's alleged negligence.

Other Policy Clauses of Which the Pharmacist Should Be Aware

Defense and Settlement Clauses

A typical defense and settlement clause follows:

> The Company (insurer) shall investigate occurrences covered by the Policy, negotiate the settlement of all claims made as may be deemed expedient by the Company, and defend suits for damages, even if groundless, false, or fraudulent, brought on account of such claims for damages in the name and on behalf of the insured, unless or until the Company shall elect to effect settlements thereof, and to pay in addition to the applicable limits of the Policy all expenses incurred by the company for investigation, negotiation, and defense.

In the case of *Schwamb v. Fireman's Insurance Company of New Jersey*, 363 N.E.2d 356 (1977), an insurance company refused to defend a pharmacist who was charged with illegally refilling prescriptions. The malpractice claims were based on the alleged refilling of a prescription without oral written authorization of the prescriber. Because the unauthorized refills violated a state law, the pharmacist's insurance carrier refused to defend the suit. The pharmacist filed suit to compel the insurer to defend the action, and the appellate court ruled for the pharmacist. The court stated that the insurance company could not rely on the policy exclusion for damages caused by willful violation of a penal statute. Some of the prescription refills in question had been made before the statutory ban on unauthorized refills became effective. Furthermore, the complaint contained claims of traditional negligence as well as liability for failure to warn the patient and these claims were covered by the insured's policy. The case is an example of how the courts will usually make every effort to find a basis for requiring insurance companies to defend their insured.

Some pharmacists feel it is preferable, but not always attainable, to have a malpractice insurance policy provision, which, in effect, states that settlements of claims will not be effected without the written consent of the insured. Insurance companies may desire to settle a claim even if the insured wishes to take the case to trial. With most policies, the insurance company reserves the right to settle the claim without the insured's consent.

The "consent to settle" controversy is less pronounced with pharmacy claims than with medical malpractice claims. In medical malpractice claims, the physician's judgment is most often at issue, while 80% of pharmacy malpractice claim involve mechanical errors. Even those pharmacy cases alleging intellectual errors usually center on the question of whether a pharmacist counseled or performed a drug review, not whether the pharmacist purposefully decided to include or exclude some bit of information.

Exclusion Clause

No insurance policy covers everything. Every insurance policy contains exclusions, limitations, and conditions. Below are typical exclusion clauses found in professional liability insurance policies:

- This insurance does not apply in respect to any loss based on criminal acts or on services rendered while under the influence of intoxicants or drugs.
- The company will not be liable for any claim caused by the willful violation of a penal statute or ordinance committed by the insured or any claim arising from the use of alcoholic beverages.

- This policy does not apply to damages caused by your willful violation of a regulation or a statute pertaining to the practice of pharmacy or any other willful violation of a penal statute or ordinance committed by you or with your knowledge or consent.
- This policy does not apply to any award or indemnity for fines, penalties, exemplary, or punitive damages or any other type of judgment which does not compensate for actual loss or damage sustained.
- This policy does not apply to personal injury (ie, libel, slander, and unauthorized release of confidential information) . . . if done by you or at your direction and you knew it was false . . . .
- This policy does not apply to an occurrence (ie, bodily injury or property damage) which is the result of intentional and malicious acts by you.

Generally, insurance policies do not cover illegal acts willfully performed by the pharmacist. The insurance policy excludes claims arising out of criminal acts and the insurer is not liable for claims arising from violations of law by the insured. In other words, if a negligence claim arose out of an incident in which a pharmacist dispensed a legend drug without a prescription or refilled a legend drug prescription without the prescriber's authorization, the pharmacist's insurer could raise a policy defense and refuse to represent him or her in the suit. However, the insurance company may make an exception for an emergency refill of a drug where in the pharmacist's professional judgment, lack of the drug may cause irreparable damage to the patient, such as a nitroglycerin prescription where the pharmacist cannot reach the physician for refill authority.

Limitations on Amount of Coverage

In a typical insurance policy, the monetary limits of coverage are listed in a schedule on the declarations page of the policy as, for example, $1,000,000 for each claim and $3,000,000 in aggregate. Usually, when the policy is stated in this way, it means that if there is 1 claim against the insured, the insurer's payment liability for all damages is no more than $1,000,000 on the claim; if there are 4 claims, it is no more than $1,000,000 on any 1 of the 4 but no more than $3,000,000 in total. For example, if there were 2 claims, each with a $1,250,000 judgment, the policy limitation would work out to a $2,000,000 payment total, $1,000,000 for each claim, leaving the balance of $500,000 to be paid by the pharmacist.

Policy Conditions

All insurance policies place conditions or duties on the insured in case of a claim. Typical conditions require that upon the occurrence of an accident, written notice must be given to the insurance company as soon as possible. The names and addresses of the insured and available witnesses as well as appropriate information regarding the time, place, and circumstances of the accident must be supplied. In addition, if a claim or suit is brought against the insured, every demand, notice, and summons received must be forwarded to the insurance company. The insured is generally required to cooperate with the insurance carrier and, upon request, attend hearings and trials and assist in settling the claim and in giving evidence.

Failure to give timely notice of an accident or claim covered by the policy can result in the insurance company raising a policy defense or disclaiming coverage because the insured has breached the terms of the policy. The same type of disclaimer might result if the insured fails to cooperate with the insurance company and hampers its investigation.

An insurance company may represent the insured with knowledge of a policy defense because of breach of terms or the claim being outside the limits of coverage. Usually, in such cases, the company will notify the insured that it is disclaiming coverage or reserving its rights as to policy defenses and also may require that the insured sign a nonwaiver of policy defense agreement. However, if the insured does not receive a notice, it can be assumed from the company's defense of the claim that a policy defense will not be raised at a later date.

Giving Notice of Claim

In the professional liability policy, a notice of accident or claim clause typically is worded as follows:

> Upon the occurrence of an accident written notice shall be given by or on behalf of the insured to the insurance company or its authorized agents as soon as practicable.

Often, a pharmacist is first aware that a malpractice claim has been made when he or she receives a demand letter from the claimant's lawyer or when he or she is served with the suit papers, the civil summons, and the complaint. Generally, the interpretation of a notice of claim provision in liability insurance is that trivial matters need not be reported to the insurer for policy coverage. In practice, however, the pharmacist should give written notice to the liability insurance carrier as soon as a written or oral claim or notice, demand, or threat of a claim regarding an accident or injury in the rendering of professional services or the sale of merchandise is received. When in doubt if an incident should be reported, the insurance agent should be called for advice.

Not all pharmacists' individual professional liability policies are the same. When considering purchasing a policy, the pharmacist should compare the actual policies. Cost is always a factor, but in the case of a professional liability policy, price is not the primary factor. The primary consideration should be coverage and the reputation of the insurance company.

CONTRACTUAL AGREEMENTS

Sales Transactions

The preceding portion of this section focused on that part of civil liability that is based on the legal theory of negligence (ie, an individual performs in a substandard fashion that directly results in harm to another). This section will address another branch of civil liability theory known as liability for breach of warranties involved in sales transactions.

Sales transactions are perhaps the most common form of contractual relationships existing in this country. Each day we buy numerous things from others and each of those transactions is a contract known more specifically as a sale. Because sales are so common and because legal issues related to sales arise so frequently, the drafters of the Uniform Commercial Code (UCC) have set forth detailed provisions applicable to sales transactions (see the Business Law chapter).

A sale is a contract in which title or ownership of property (personal property as opposed to real estate) is exchanged for money. A sale is a contract and, therefore, all the matters related to contracts are discussed in the Business Law section of this book. But there are some unique provisions in the UCC applicable to sales transactions that give rise to some special liability concerns for the pharmacist.

We noted that the sale is transfer of ownership of personal property in exchange for money. However, some things do not fall within the definition of a "sale":

- A contract for services (eg, one person contracts with an attorney to represent him or her).
- A contract for the lease of personal property such as a car, because ownership is not being transferred.
- Contracts for the transfer of investment securities.
- Bailment in which one gives temporary physical possession of one's goods to another (eg, when one leaves his car with a parking lot attendant).
- A gift, because, while there is transfer of ownership of personal property, it's not for an exchange of money.
- Anything related to real estate as we are using the term here.

A sale involves transfer of ownership of property, not merely the transfer of possession of that property. That is, once a sale is completed, the goods no longer belong to the seller, they belong to the purchaser.

Warranties

A warranty is an undertaking of the seller with respect to title, nature, quality, or the condition of goods he or she is selling. Warranties are generally *expressed* by a party or *implied* by the law.

Express Warranties

Express warranties are those present in the transaction because of something the seller said that induced the buyer to purchase the goods. The UCC defines express warranty this way (Section 2313):

> Express warranties by the seller are established by an affirmation of fact or a promise made to the buyer that relates to the goods and becomes a part of the basis of the bargain; by any description of the goods that is made part of the basis of the bargain; and by creation of any sample or model that becomes part of the basis of the bargain. An express warranty need not use form words such as warranty or guarantee. It is not necessary that a specific intention to make a warranty exists; however, an affirmation of merely the value of the goods or a statement of the seller's opinion or commendation of the goods does not create a warranty.

Express warranty generally relates to the ability of the product to perform. For example, in the case of *Jacobs Pharmacy Co. v. Gibson*, 159 S.E.2d 171 (Ga. 1967) the court found that there was an express warranty where "the clerk represented that a packaged remedy was the same as what the plaintiff's prescription called for, and that he is liable if the substitute product causes injury." In the Jacobs case, a physician had prescribed *Zephiran* solution 1:750 and the sales clerk told the patient that she did not need the prescription, but instead sold her a bottle of concentrated 17% *Zephiran*.

In a case involving the sale of hair dye, the court did not find an express warranty, despite certain statements made by the pharmacy clerk to the customer. In *Carpenter v. Alberto Culver Co.*, 184 N.W.2d 547 (Mich.Ct.App. 1970), a customer was trying to select a hair dye and the pharmacy clerk told her, in reference to a certain brand, that she "would get very fine results." The hair dye contained warnings that allergic reactions may occur and gave instructions for a patch test. The customer claimed to have taken the test without adverse results, but upon the use of the product, she suffered injury. She sued the manufacturer and the seller. The jury returned a verdict in favor of the pharmacy and, on appeal, the court could find no express warranty made. The following rule was issued in the appellate decision:

> In determining whether a statement of the seller is to be deemed a warranty, it is important to consider whether in the statement the seller assumes to assert a fact of which the buyer is ignorant, or merely states an opinion or judgment upon a matter of which the seller has no special knowledge and on which the buyer may be expected also to have an opinion and to exercise his judgment. Representations which merely express the seller's opinion, belief, judgment, or estimate do not constitute a warranty.

Although not involving an issue of warranty, a 1949 New York case (*Singer v. Oken*, 87 N.Y.S. 686) held that "a preparation is not 'deleterious' to human health, in the ordinary acceptation of the term, simply because one person in a multitude of those using it happens to meet with ill effects from taking it." The pharmacist sold a patient an *otc* preparation of 1% phenol in calamine lotion for use in treatment of insect bites. The customer suffered burns from use of the product and sued the pharmacy. The court ruled in favor of the pharmacy.

The pharmacist who sells a nonprescription drug may be liable for an express warranty if certain conditions are met. For example, if the customer asks for lente insulin and the pharmacist or any other employee of the pharmacy furnishes regular insulin, liability exists for violation of an express warranty that goods must conform to the description.

It is important to draw distinction between an expressed warranty and puffery or puffing, also known as seller's talk. Puffery exists when the seller makes a statement about the goods that is designed to induce the purchaser to buy but that does not relate to a specific ability of the products to perform, such as "This is our best selling cough syrup."

Implied Warranties

There are a number of implied warranties present in a sales transaction, not by virtue of anything the seller says, but which appeared as part of a sales transaction automatically (ie, the law inserts them into the transaction in order to protect the buyer). There are 4 implied warranties that are of interest to pharmacists. The implied warranties come into existence through the use of the UCC in various states. The first implied warranty is the implied warranty of fitness for a particular purpose. In this situation you have a buyer approaching a seller, describing the use to which he wishes to put the product and relying on the seller's judgment and skill in selecting the product to meet the described need. When you have this element of reliance in the sales transaction, the implied warranty of fitness for a particular purpose will be present. Such transactions are quite common in pharmacy practice, such as when a patient approaches a pharmacist, describing symptoms and asking the pharmacist to recommend therapeutic measures that will alleviate those symptoms.

The second implied warranty is the implied warranty of merchantability. Implied warranty of merchantability means that the article being sold is fit for the general or usual purpose for which it is generally used. Notice that this implied warranty does not require the product to be the best available on the market, but merely that it be fit for sale. If a product is decomposed, putrid, or subpotent, it may breach the implied warranty of merchantability.

The pharmacist selling a nonprescription drug is liable for the implied warranty of merchantability. For example, if an outdated drug is sold, the customer may have a good case against the seller for violating the implied warranty of merchantability (lack of average quality), provided that injury and causation are present.

The third implied warranty is the implied warranty of sale by sample or description. If the buyer has supplied to the seller a sample of what it is he wishes to purchase or a written description of the product desired, then the seller implicitly warrants the products he is providing will meet that implied warranty of sample or description. If they don't, a breach of the implied warranty has applied.

The last implied warranty is the implied warranty of title. By this, the seller implicitly warrants that he has title to the goods he is selling and that he can deliver good and complete ownership rights to the purchaser.

Applications to Pharmacy Practice

Over-the-Counter Products

A case involving the issue of the implied warranty of merchantability is *Davidson v. Wee*, 379 P.2d 744 (Ariz. 1963), in which use of a home permanent caused a customer's hair to fall out. The permanent wave lotion contained precautionary statements and the plaintiff claimed to have followed the directions, including taking the patch test, which gave a negative result. The court stated that:

> If the evidence is sufficient to support a finding that the application of the (home permanent) waving lotion caused the injury to the plaintiff's hair, the product necessarily was not merchantable for the general purpose for which it was sold.

The distinguishing factor in Davidson is that the cause of action was based on implied warranty rather than on negligence. Furthermore, while a home permanent may cause allergic responses, it is not expected to cause the user's hair to fall out.

An old case involving the issue of the implied warranty fitness for a particular purpose (under the Uniform Sales Act) is *Harrington v. Montgomery Drug Co.*, 111 P.2d 808 (Mont. 1941). In Harrington, a customer purchased a tube from the pharmacist to use with a douche. The pharmacist "assured her and warranted to her that it was an appliance suitable and proper for her desired use," and she relied on the assurance and warranty. The tube broke when inserted into the vagina and caused injury. The court would not allow recovery under the implied warranty of fitness for a particular purpose because both the buyer and the seller had a chance to examine the tube and discover the defect. However, under the UCC definition of implied warranty for a particular purpose, it is likely that today the court would have ruled for the plaintiff. Furthermore, she also could have claimed a violation of an express warranty, although this was not done. The pharmacist selling a nonprescription drug may be liable for implied warranty of fitness for a particular purpose if certain conditions are present. If a patient asks the pharmacist to recommend a preparation for treatment of a cough or common cold, the patient probably is relying on the pharmacist's skill and judgment, and the pharmacist, in selecting a particular cough or cold remedy, is implicitly guaranteeing it for a particular intended purpose. However, if the patient asks the nonprofessional store clerk for a cough medicine, a good argument can be made that there is no more than an implied warranty for merchantability, even in the presence of gratuitious opinions expressed by the clerk as to a particular remedy (see the discussion of *Carpenter v. Alberto Culver Co.* in this chapter). Note that the same analysis could apply if the *otc* drug product were purchased at a supermarket or other outlet where a pharmacist is not involved in the transaction.

Labeling Nonprescription Drugs

Although the pharmacist is exposed to the same liabilities as the manufacturer when nonprescription drugs are relabeled under the pharmacy's label, a number of pharmacies engage extensively in this practice. In general, the nonprescription drug product must be labeled to permit safe use by the consumer in self-medication. The minimal standard of labeling nonprescription drug products must follow verbatim the labeling regulations promulgated by federal and state agencies, but even this does not constitute adequate warning to the consumer as matter of law. (See the discussion of *Michael v. Warner/Chilcott*, 579 P.2d 183 [N.M. 1978], in the Court Cases chapter.)

In the past, if the pharmacist religiously included on the pharmacy label all of the information, including the lot number and the name of the manufacturer or distributor, that was contained on the original manufacturer's or distributor's stock package, the pharmacist was on safe ground. However, both the Michael case and *Torsiello v. Whitehall Laboratories*, 398 A.2d 132 (N.J. 1979) have changed the situation. In particular, the Michael case increased liability in the labeling area; a drugstore chain sold *Sinutab* under its own labeling as a house-brand product. The FDA regulation on labeling was cited, and the court found that the pharmacy labeling did not contain the adequate warning to the consumer that is required by law. Therefore, it is recommended that the pharmacist only sell nonprescription drugs in the manufacturer's or distributor's labeled and sealed container.

In *Michael*, the court went so far as to say that ". . . a warning merely instructing a user to consult a physician as to the product's use is, in this context, construable as no warning at all."

If a pharmacist is sued because of an injury arising out of the sale and use of nonprescription drug product, the pharmacist often has recourse against the manufacturer or distributor of the *otc* drug if it was defective when it left the source of supply or if the manufacturer or distributor was negligent in labeling the drug. Invariably, the injured plaintiff will, in the first instance, list as codefendants the retailer, distributor, manufacturer, or anyone else in the chain of distribution who has some potential liability. Of course, if the pharmacist is solely at fault because he or she breached express warranty because he or she negligently mislabeled the drug, then a recourse against the manufacturer or distributor is not possible.

Warranty and Drug Product Selection

The concept of product warranty from contract law represents an alternative theory for the plaintiff's attorney to use in a drug product selection lawsuit against the manufacturer and pharmacist. While negligence is a concept based on fault, breach of warranty arises when there is an injury as the result of failure of a product to measure up to the express or implied warranties of the manufacturer or seller. The UCC, which has been adopted by all states except Louisiana, governs the law of sales, including the sales of prescription drugs. When pharmacists select a particular generic brand or therapeutic drug product equivalent, it can be argued that they are giving either an implied warranty of general merchantability or an implied warranty of fitness for a particular purpose.

The implied warranty of merchantability requires that the goods (in our case, prescription drugs) must be fit for ordinary purposes. The product must not be outdated, must be properly labeled, must be properly stored, and must not be adulterated.

The other implied warranty is the implied warranty of fitness for a particular purpose. This warranty is created when the seller of a product knows the particular purpose for which the goods are required and the buyer relies on the seller's skill and judgment to select a suitable product. When a brand name drug is prescribed, the patient does not rely on the pharmacist's skill and judgment in the selection process, but instead is relying upon the prescribing physician. However, when the pharmacist has the authority to select a particular drug to dispense, one could make the case that the patient is relying upon the pharmacist to select a suitable product.

In *Batiste v. American Home Products*, discussed earlier, the court found no breach of warranty by the pharmacist who filled a prescription as written. In *25 American Jurisprudence 2d* it stated:

> But a druggist cannot be held liable, on the theory of breach of implied warranty, for injuries resulting from the taking of a drug furnished on a doctor's prescription directing that the drug be supplied, and which was available only to those who could present such a prescription, which was filled precisely in accordance with the directions of the prescription, from the manufacturer's original packet.

It could be argued that in filling a generic prescription, the pharmacist is the mere conduit because the physician has made the decision to prescribe generically. The issue may be eventually decided, from the implied warranty standpoint, on whether the patient, prescriber, or both should rely on the pharmacist's skill in selecting the generic drug product. If so, the pharmacist would not be a mere conduit in the chain of events. A situation that involves filling a prescription written for a brand name drug product is substantially different from that involving a prescription written for a drug by its generic or chemical name.

Removal of Warranties

If a seller wants to enter into a transaction without warranties present, how can this be done? First, in the case of a transaction where express warranties might be present, the seller controls whether there are any warranties present by what he says. If the seller makes no representation about the ability of the product to perform, there would be no express warranty present.

Implied warranties are a little more problematic. Implied warranties are present in a transaction not because of anything the seller says, but because of what the law has implicitly added to the transaction. Implied warranty of fitness for a particular purpose has the buyer or the purchaser in a very reliant position on the seller. Therefore, the law requires that if this implied warranty is to be removed from a transaction, it must be done in writing. Other specific wording is required, but there must be a written notice to the purchaser that there is no implied warranty of fitness for a particular purpose. Contrast this situation with an attempt to remove the implied warranty of merchantability from a transaction. In this case, the implied warranty may be removed orally but the specific word merchantability must be mentioned in the statement to the purchaser so that the purchaser will know that the implied warranty of merchantability is not present.

All warranties can be eliminated from a transaction by including a disclaimer such as goods are sold "as is." Sometimes the courts will nullify such disclaimers as being contrary to public policy, but ordinarily a statement such as "sold as is" will alert the purchaser sufficiently that there are no warranties being made by the seller.

Privity of Contract

Privity of contract is a relationship that exists between the parties to a transaction. If in a sales transaction we have the buyer selling a product directly to a purchaser, then it is said that these 2 parties have privity. The privity issue can be raised in a lawsuit when a third party or stranger to the buyer-seller relationship is injured by an item that has been sold. For example, the lack of privity between the seller and the party actually injured by the use of the product will be raised as a defense by the seller to attempt to avoid liability. The modern trend is for courts to extend this contract of privity to include users of foods, drugs, and other consumer items where it is foreseeable that the product will be used by someone other than the actual purchaser. For example, it is clear that a mother purchasing an *otc* fever-reducing product for use by a child is not the ultimate user even though she is the purchaser. In such a case, should the child be injured, the concept of privity would be extended to include that child in a number of states. Two cases from pharmacy involving the issue of privity are *Cos v. Laws*, 145 So.2d 703 (Miss. 1962) and *Oresman v. Searle* 321 F.Supp. 449 (D.R.I. 1971).

Notice of Breach of Warranty

If a purchaser sues on the grounds of breach by the seller of implied or express warranty, in general, the purchaser must give the seller reasonable notice of the breach prior to commencing the suit (see section 2607 of the UCC). This notice allows the seller time to make necessary arrangements and to govern his or her conduct accordingly. In *Barlow v. DeVilbiss*, 214 F.Supp. 540 (E.D.Wisc. 1963), notice given 11 months and 3 weeks after the breach was discovered was held to be untimely. In *Herman v. Smith Kline and French Laboratories*, 286 F.Supp. 694 (E.D.Wisc. 1968), a 20-year delay in giving notice after the alleged injury was judged unreasonable and barred the buyer's recovery from the seller, However, because notice must be given a reasonable time after discovery of the warranty breach, a different rule applies to latent defects. The various suits involving DES lend credence to this, since these suits have been commenced many years after the alleged injury. (See the discussion of *Lemire v. Garrard Drugs*, 291 N.W.2d 103 [Mich.Ct.App.1980].)

ADMINISTRATIVE ACTIONS

The State Board of Pharmacy

A state board of pharmacy is an administrative agency created and empowered by the state to regulate pharmacy practice and to enforce drug control laws within the state boundaries. The legislatures of the state and the federal government cannot pass all the laws necessary to regulate a profession or trade. Hence, administrative agencies were devised by the legislatures to manage professional licensure and regulation of specific situations within the profession or trade. The agency is usually composed of individuals from within the profession or industry who have the technical knowledge and experience that enables them to judge an applicant's professional ability and to determine the regulations that are necessary for professional practice. Because the board of pharmacy is responsible for protecting the public's health, many states include consumer representatives on the board.

All of the powers, functions, and limitations of any administrative agency are in the statutes that create and maintain it. The administrative agency is the child of the legislature; it can operate only in strict accordance with what power the legislature has given it. Administrative determinations are enforceable only in the manner provided by statute. If the statute has failed to provide a remedy for their enforcement, they are unenforceable.

Powers and Functions of the Board of Pharmacy

Typically, a state pharmacy board or pharmacy commission has the following functions and duties:

(1) To regulate the practice of pharmacy and administer and enforce all laws placed under its jurisdiction.

(2) To examine and investigate all applicants for registration as pharmacists or pharmacy interns, to pass upon the qualifications of applicants for reciprocal license, and to license all applicants judged to be qualified.

(3) To investigate violations of law under the pharmacy act itself or regulations issued thereunder and to institute prosecution upon advice from the attorney general, district attorney, or state prosecutor.

(4) To assist the law enforcement agencies of the state in enforcing all laws pertaining to drugs, narcotics, and pharmacy practice.

(5) To regulate drug distribution within the state and the practice of pharmacy for the protection of public health, safety, and welfare by the promulgation of rules and regulations, the violation of which constitutes grounds for refusal, suspension, or revocation of any license or permit issued by the pharmacy board.

(6) To conduct hearings or proceedings to revoke, suspend, or refuse renewal of any license or permit issued by the pharmacy board under the authority of the pharmacy act.

The powers and functions of the state board of pharmacy vary somewhat because the individual state pharmacy acts vary. In some states, the board of pharmacy shares responsibility with other drug law agencies for the enforcement of the state narcotic law or controlled substances act. In some states, the pharmacy board is authorized to execute and serve (but not issue) search warrants, arrest warrants, and administrative inspection warrants. Usually the pharmacy board is empowered to issue subpoenas, which compel witnesses to testify at board hearings.

Enforcement Powers

In most situations in which the pharmacy board has the power to institute actions, the actions instituted are civil in nature. Board powers also may include that of arrest when a felony is committed in the presence of a board enforcement officer. However, arrest warrants are issued by a magistrate or judge. In criminal prosecution cases, the board conducts the investigation and turns over the evidence to the state or county prosecutor, who then commences the action by issuing a summons and complaint or by obtaining an arrest warrant and issuing an information complaint. In criminal matters, the prosecuting attorney for the state or county maintains and controls the prosecution after it commences. The FDA and Drug Enforcement Administration (DEA) enforce the federal drug laws by investigating violations and then turning the matters over to the US Attorney's office for prosecution.

The pharmacy board also can enforce the statutes of the pharmacy act and state drug control acts and its own rules and regulations by the suspension, revocation, or withholding of a license or permit, by the imposition of a monetary penalty (if provided by law), or by seeking a court injunction, restraining order, or other court order.

A reference of the application for a court injunction as a means of enforcing a pharmacy law is the case of *State v. Red Owl Stores*, 115 N.W.2d 643 (Minn. 1962).

The pharmacy board may enforce a drug law or its own regulations when confronted with a pharmacist or pharmacy violator by simply not issuing a renewal of the pharmacist's license or pharmacy permit. The legal method to force the board to issue the license or permit is a writ of mandamus, a court order that compels a government agency to perform its duty or function under the law. (See *Thomas v. Board of Pharmacy*, 67 S.E. 925 [N.C. 1910], and *State v. Matthews*, 62 S.E. 695 [S.C. 1908].)

Pharmacy Board Disciplinary Hearings

If a licensee who is accused of a pharmacy law violation admits to the violation at a formal board hearing, the admission may be used as grounds for a separate prosecution against him or her by federal or state authorities because double jeopardy does not attach to civil proceedings. (See *Kramm v. Board of Regents of the State University of New York*, 273 N.Y.2d 413 [1966].) Similarly, a plea of guilty to a drug law violation may subject a pharmacist to a license revocation or suspension action.

When suspending, revoking, or refusing to renew a license or permit, the board gives notice and a hearing to the affected individual. The board hearing may be less formal than a judicial action, but it must satisfy constitutional requirements of due process (fair play). (See court cases *Feldman v. Board*, 160 A.2d 100 [D.C.Ct.App. 1960], and *Bengal v. Board of Pharmacy*, 279 A.2d 374 [Pa. 1971].)

A pharmacist who is faced with simultaneous board disciplinary actions and criminal prosecution for the same alleged violation legally cannot excuse his or her inaction in one matter on the basis that it might jeopardize his or her case in the other, but he or she could seek a postponement for one of the cases. (See *Rosenthall v. Board of Pharmacy*, 284 A.2d 846 [Pa. 1971]; *Hunter v. Board of Pharmacy*, 162 So.2d 524 [Fla. 1964]; *Moretti v. Board of Pharmacy*, 277 A.2d 516 [Pa. 1971]; and *Herman v. Board of Pharmacy*, 272 N.E.2d 924 [Ohio 1971].)

Challenging an Administrative Action

Appeals from an agency decision must be considered carefully because there are various presumptions entertained by the courts that favor administrative agencies such as the board of pharmacy. If these presumptions did not exist, all agency decisions would be appealed to the courts and there would be little sense in having the agency. In short, unless the board of pharmacy is grossly unfair or commits a procedural error, there are a limited number of reasons on which courts will reverse an administrative decision.

Administrative agency action may be challenged on the ground that it exceeds the agency's statutory authority or jurisdiction. The delegation of power from the state legislature is usually broad, but there is, for example, the possibility that the board of pharmacy may have mandated the requirement of continuing education or created a special class of pharmacy technicians which would exceed the board's authority as outlined in the Pharmacy Practice Act.

Another challenge of an administrative agency decision might be based upon the agency's violation of due process. When enacting rules and conducting disciplinary hearings, the board must provide the basic concepts of due process. Due process is not easily defined, but involves the intangible concepts of fairness and justice. As such, due process requires that accused pharmacists be notified of their right to a hearing, right to notice of the charges, right to counsel, and right to an opportunity to be heard. By the same token, administrative agencies also must give notice of any proposed rule changes. They must offer some sort of forum (either oral or written) in which pharmacists and others may give their views on the proposed rule. Due process further requires that most of the meetings of an administrative agency be conducted in open session. The people of the state do not yield their sovereignty to the board of pharmacy or any other administrative agency. Therefore, the people have the right to be informed and attend board of pharmacy meetings. There are certain exceptions which would permit the board to meet in private, executive session.

A third challenge against the board of pharmacy or any administrative agency would be if the decision of the board were clearly erroneous. In such a lawsuit, the plaintiffs would need to establish that there was no way the board could have reached the decision it did based upon a reasonable review of the evidence before it. Finally, the board's actions may not be arbitrary or capricious. The board may not act in an impulsive or unpredictable manner, neither can it act heavy handed and arbitrarily pass regulations adversely affecting chain-store pharmacies, hospital pharmacies, or any other facet of the profession.

The courts have divided the powers and duties of administrative agencies into discretionary and ministerial (in a sense, clerical). A discretionary function is illustrated by pharmacist licensure procedures in which the board prepares an examination to test the competence and knowledge of the applicants seeking a pharmacist license. A ministerial function involves a situation in which, if certain conditions set forth by statute are fulfilled, the board is required to act automatically. For example, in some states the board of pharmacy must issue a pharmacy permit to any applicant who fulfills the statutory requirements for equipment and payment fees. (See *Wilmington Vitamin v. Tigue*, 183 A.2d 731 [Del. 1962]; *Rayburn v. Board of Pharmacy*, 354 P.2d 423 [Okla. 1960]; *Texas Board of Pharmacy v. Martin*, 343 S. W.2d 535 [Tex. 1961].) The determination of a discretionary of ministerial duty depends on the enabling statute.

Pharmacy board regulations must relate reasonably to issues of public health and safety. Early in this discussion, it was stated that administrative agency powers are predicated entirely on the scope of the enabling statutes. Consequently, the courts closely investigate these statutes when a controversy involves a board regulation that has overtones of economic sanctions.

In a 1964 Maryland case, *Board v. Peco*, 198 A.2d 273, the court dealt with a pharmacy board regulation that specified certain physical and locational requirements for pharmacy. The court held that the regulation had no reasonable relationship to public health or safety.

If a procedure exists within the administrative agency for review or reconsideration of its own administrative action, the party aggrieved by the action should use the administrative procedure before going to court. The expertise of the administrative agency must be used to determine technical facts before the court can apply the law. Some of the various types of judicial review of administrative action are discussed below.

Declaratory Judgment

A declaratory judgment suit is a preferred method for seeking a court ruling on an administrative action before the action is enforced. However, the suit must be brought by an individual who is or would be adversely affected by the action. Declaratory judgment is a statutory remedy found in standard state administrative procedure acts or in a separate state law designated as a declaratory judgment; usually the latter provides judicial review of state statutes. In federal law, the declaratory judgment provision is in 28 U.S.C. §2201.

Collateral Attack

The collateral attack method is one that is employed by the individual who is affected by an administrative action; the individual simply ignores the action and leaves it up to the agency or board to try to enforce it. The agency or board may then institute a civil suit or criminal prosecution against the individual, who will then claim the invalidity of the administrative action as his or her defense. Obviously, collateral attack is not the preferred route when the violation of an administrative regulation is punishable as a crime pursuant to the authority of a state or federal law. Collaterial attack is often used to test the constitutionality of a criminal statute when the issue is raised as a defense to a prosecution. (See *State v. Leone*, 118 So.2d 781 [Fla. 1960].)

Suits in Equity

Suits in equity for injunctive relief sometimes are used in situations where members of the board or officers of the administrative agency are claimed to have acted unfairly, beyond their powers, or arbitrarily and capriciously. The judicial relief sought is the court's order or injunction enjoining the agency or board from enforcing its regulation or order. Equity or equitable relief is a legal system applied by the courts to effect justice when the ordinary legal remedies will not or when great injury might result unless immediate judicial action is taken.

Petitions

Petitions for **writs of certiorari, mandamus**, or **prohibition** are special legal procedures to compel or prohibit an administrative officer from acting or not acting. For example, application to a court for writ of mandamus is the usual preferred way to bring court action when a state pharmacy board fails to act on a pharmacy permit application or pharmacist license renewal. (See *Wilmington Vitamin v. Tigue*, 183 A.2d 731 [Del. 1962].)

Civil Suit against the Pharmacy Board

In a 1973 Iowa case, *VanderLinden v. Crews*, 205 N.W.2d 686 (Iowa 1973), a pharmacist brought a civil suit for damages based on a claim that he had been prosecuted maliciously by the pharmacy board. In the reported facts of the case, the secretary of the pharmacy board, who was also director of drug enforcement, arrested the pharmacist without warrant on a charge of sale of stimulant drugs without a prescription in violation of the state law. Subsequently, a grand jury indicted the pharmacist; he was tried before a jury and acquitted. He then commenced his suit for malicious prosecution. The trial court judge granted summary judgment to the defendants, dismissing the suit on the basis of judicial or governmental immunity, which protected the secretary of the board as a public officer. The pharmacist appealed the decision to the state supreme court, which reversed the trial court, sending the case back to the trial court.

The doctrine of judicial immunity protects judicial officers from civil suit when acting within their authority. The reasoning behind this doctrine is that if an individual who is aggrieved by a judge's decision could sue him or her, the judge's ability to act upon his or her own convictions would be destroyed.

The sole issue in this case is whether such judicial or governmental immunity pertains to an individual who does not occupy a judicial position. In a review of applicable cases, the state supreme court found that a number of state and federal courts had extended judicial or governmental immunity to health officers, Internal Revenue Service (IRS) agents, highway supervisors, draft board officials, superintendents of institutions, and postal inspectors. In extending the immunity, those courts balanced the need for civil redress by individuals wronged by dishonest officials and the protection of the diligent official who might make an honest mistake. However, in *VanderLinden*, the court refused to extend the immunity doctrine, stating that "extension of immunity to virtually any peace officer or law enforcement officer would result in a practical nullification of the tort of malicious prosecution . . ."

As pointed out, a number of jurisdictions would reach an opposite decision. In other words, some courts would extend governmental immunity to a pharmacy board acting within its vested authority.

Direct Judicial Review

Direct judicial review exists where a specific administrative action may be reviewed by the courts pursuant to an enabling provision in the statute that authorizes the specific administrative action or in some other section of the law. The typical example is a standard state pharmacy practice act that provides that board revocation or suspension orders or denials of license are appealable or reviewable by the court. The review powers of the court in such cases are dependent on how the statute is worded. In some states, the court can hear evidence on the matter, and in other states, the reviewing court only can act on the record of evidence made at the board or administrative level. Hence, a pharmacist appearing before a board must present the best evidence at that time or lose the opportunity to present it; on appeal or review, the pharmacist only can argue the law as it is applied to the determined facts in the case. In a few states, the pharmacy act makes no provision for judicial review of certain board actions; generally, if substantial rights are involved, this violates the spirit of due process and a court will take jurisdiction to review pursuant to any of the methods mentioned above. (See *Rayburn v. Board of Pharmacy*, 354 P.2d 423 [Okla. 1960].)

Rights of the Pharmacist

When a pharmacist is the accused in a pharmacy board disciplinary action, he or she has certain constitutional rights.

(1) **Right of Notice.** The accused has the right to be informed of the nature of the action and charges against him or her.

(2) **Right of a Hearing.** The accused has the right to be heard before an impartial board with the essentials of a fair trial according to established rules.

(3) **Right to Counsel.** The accused has the right to be assisted and represented by an attorney.

(4) **Right against Self-Incrimination.** The accused has the right not to be a witness against himself or herself (the right to remain silent).

(5) **Right to Judicial Review.** The accused has the right to have a court determine if the applicable rules of law and procedure were followed.

A few states have enacted a mandatory continuing education requirement or continuing competence requirement that is applicable to the practicing pharmacist. When a continuing education requirement is used as a prerequisite to pharmacist license renewal, the basic legal issue presented (if the requirement is contested) is whether the pharmacist's license, after being granted, is a vested property right or merely a personal privilege.

In an old California case, *Cavass v. Off et al*, 274 P. 523 (1929), a pharmacist brought a court action for writ of prohibition against the pharmacy board to prohibit its license revocation order against him. The case was eventually decided by the California Supreme Court in favor of the pharmacist. One of the byproducts of the decision was the court's rule:

> The right of a person to practice the profession for which he has prepared himself is property . . . and should not be taken from him except on clear proof that he has forfeited it, and then only in strict conformity to the statute authorizing its forfeiture.

Another California case arose some years later and involved an assistant pharmacist who tried to maintain his licensure after the state pharmacy act was amended to phase out the assistant pharmacist classification. The case, *Rosenblatt v. California Board of Pharmacy*, 158 P.2d 199 (Cal. 1945), involved the following situation: The pharmacy act allowed assistant pharmacists to renew their licenses annually and, for those with 2 years experience, to apply for the registered pharmacist exam. In 1943, the legislature revised the pharmacy act so that assistant pharmacists with 5 years actual experience immediately preceding application could be licensed automatically as registered pharmacists, but all provision for renewal of assistant pharmacist licenses was eliminated. The assistant pharmacist in question had 4 years experience and did not qualify for automatic licensure (however, he had 9 months before the effective date of the act's revision to apply for pharmacist license examination). He tendered his renewal fee; it was returned. He sought judicial action to compel the renewal, and the court ruled against him. The court held that an assistant pharmacist license is not a vested property right.

A strong dissenting opinion was expressed in *Rosenblatt* by one of the judges who disagreed with the majority's decision. He reasoned that the case law indicated that a right to practice a lawful occupation could not be taken away under the guise of regulation. In effect, the position of the dissent was that it was permissible for the legislature to act prospectively (eliminate assistant pharmacists as a future class) but it could not eliminate the classification of those already licensed (in the sense of an ex post facto law).

Current case law may support the position that a pharmacist license, once granted, is a valuable property right. In *Rosenblatt*, it must be emphasized that the court dealt with the issue of an assistant pharmacist license. In a 1972 criminal prosecution case, *Miller v. State Board*, 262 So.2d 188 (Miss. 1972), the court referred to the licensure of a professional as a "valuable property right." The deciding factor in the court cases seems to center on the type of license involved.

Continuing Education

The requirement of licensure of health professionals has existed in this country since the last century, but in the 1970s a number of states acted to require that pharmacists submit evidence of participation in continuing education as a prerequisite for renewal of their licenses to practice pharmacy. The basis for state action in requiring evidence of participation in continuing professional education is the police power of state governments. By using its power to protect the public's health, safety, and welfare, the legislature or the board of pharmacy may enact statutes or regulations requiring pharmacists to provide proof of continuing education.

When considering the argument that state action has unreasonably infringed on an individual pharmacist's rights, courts will need to weigh the purposes of the state action against the importance of the rights of the individual. For example, if a state licensing board was attempting to withhold renewal of a license because of failure to comply with mandatory continuing education requirements, the court would weigh the state's interest in ensuring that practitioners are competent against the property rights of the license holder. While the right to practice a profession is a valuable property right, no person has an absolute right to practice pharmacy or any other profession. The practitioner has only a conditional right that is subordinate to the police power of the state to protect and preserve the public health.

In order for an administrative agency, such as a board of pharmacy, to be authorized to require and enforce participation in continuing education as a condition for renewal of licensure, that authority must be assigned by the legislature. The National Association of Boards of Pharmacy (NABP) endorsed the concept of mandatory continuing education as a condition for renewal of a license in 1974. Since then, the legislatures of a number of states have enacted requirements mandating participation in continuing education as a requirement for renewal of licensure. (See NABP Survey of Pharmacy Law in the Appendix.)

There has been some litigation by pharmacists attacking the constitutionality of mandatory continuing education statutes. In *Barad v. Stadnik*, No. 68C2306, 15th Judicial Court, Palm Beach County, Florida (Dec. 3, 1969), a court found the wording of the Florida statute to be insufficiently detailed concerning the standards to be used by the board of pharmacy. The continuing education mentioned in the statute made no reference to the subject matter of pharmacy and no guidelines were provided for the board to determine what was to be accredited. The court found that there was nothing in the statute to tie the required education to the compounding and dispensing of drugs or to any other standard related to pharmacy. The statute also exempted pharmacists over 65 years of age, but the court ruled that such a provision had no reasonable basis to the protection of the public's health and was arbitrary. Continuing education statutes should provide standards that are sufficiently specific to provide license holders with an understanding of what is required for compliance.

If the legality of mandatory continuing pharmacy education is tested, the outcome might not rest so much on whether the pharmacist's license is a vested right or a personal privilege but whether it can be proven that the mandatory continuing education requirement is necessary to protect the public health and whether it can be determined to what extent a particular mandatory continuing education requirement is reasonable.

Rosinski presented an extensive critical analysis of the present mandatory continuing education situation.

> As mandatory continuing education is being enacted, it is being done on the assumption that requiring pharmacists to take a number of courses will improve their competence as practicing pharmacists. The questions remain. What courses? Any number that the pharmacist chooses? . . . Without standards the content of courses is irrelevant to practicing pharmacists' needs. It is for this very reason . . . that mandatory continuing education statutes, in themselves, are meaningless . . . the standards used to define a competent, practicing pharmacist have not been adequately formulated, therefore what he/she must do educationally cannot be decreed. (*J Am Pharm Assoc.* 1973;NS1 3:404)

STANDARDS OF THE JOINT COMMISSION ON THE ACCREDITATION OF HEALTHCARE ORGANIZATIONS

An organization known as the Joint Commission on the Accreditation of Healthcare Organizations (JCAHO) sets certain voluntary standards for hospitals. If the hospital complies (or substantially complies) with the standards, the JCAHO may give it accreditation. The standards established are not legally binding because a hospital usually may obtain state licensure regardless of whether it is accredited by the JCAHO. However, most hospitals seek the accreditation for status. Furthermore, the standards are a guide to the proper method of operating a hospital. In a suit against a hospital, the failure of compliance with the voluntary standards of the JCAHO is a factor to be considered in deciding the negligence issue (*Van Iperen v. Van Bramer*).

The JCAHO's accreditation manual for hospitals contains a pharmaceutical services section that lists 6 basic standards and the commission's interpretation of each standard. A summary of the standards and some key points in the interpretations are given below.

Standard **I** concerns the staffing of a pharmacy with competent and legally qualified personnel. A pharmacist must be available at all times on duty, on call, or as a consultant; nonpharmacist personnel only must be assigned duties that are consistent with their training and experience and not in violation of the laws and regulations specifying duties that are to be performed only by the pharmacist; clerical services must be provided; the pharmacy must be licensed as required; and if the hospital does not have a pharmacy, pharmaceutical services should be obtained from a hospital that does.

Standard **II** concerns the space and equipment in a pharmacy and the storage of drugs. Drugs for external use only must be separated in storage from drugs for internal use only; drugs must be stored in accordance with *United States Pharmacopeia* (USP) and *National Formulary* (NF) standards and otherwise be properly controlled in the hospital; provision must be made for emergency drugs on carts or in kits; the metric system must be used for all medications; and conversion charts must be made available.

Standard **III** deals with the scope of pharmaceutical services. Adequate recordkeeping systems and procedural guidelines in the preparation of pharmaceuticals must be developed; there must be participation of the pharmacy personnel in applicable patient care programs; when feasible, patient medication profiles must be maintained and reviewed for potential drug interactions; and patients must be instructed in correct drug use.

Standard **IV** involves the formulating of written policies and procedures for drug distribution within the hospital. The pharmacist must review the prescriber's inpatient drug order (or a direct copy) before the initial medication dose is dispensed, except in an emergency; there must be proper drug recall procedures, and drug defects must be reported to the USP/FDA drug defect program; and there must be initiation of proper labeling of inpatient and outpatient medications. The outpatient prescription label must contain the name, address, and phone number of the pharmacy; the date; the serial number of the drug; the full name of the patient; the drug name, strength, and amount dispensed; patient directions; the name or initials of the dispensing individual; and any required cautionary labeling.

Standard V treats drug administration policies and requires such policies to be made by the medical staff in cooperation with the pharmacy, nursing, and other departments. There must be automatic cancellation of standing orders when a patient goes to surgery; a system of drug stop orders (requiring the prescriber to reorder the drug); identification of the patient before drug administration; and the discouraged use of abbreviations in ordering drugs. Drugs must be ordered by a practitioner and must be properly labeled when given to a patient on discharge.

Section VI requires that the pharmacy department's activities be monitored and evaluated in accordance with the hospital's quality assurance program.

APHA CODE OF ETHICS

Code of Ethics for Pharmacists

Pharmacists are health professionals who assist individuals in making the best use of medications. This code, prepared and supported by pharmacists, is intended to state publicly the principles that form the fundamental basis of the roles and responsibilities of pharmacists. These principles, based on moral obligations and virtues, are established to guide pharmacists in relationships with patients, health professionals, and society.

I. *A pharmacist respects the convenantal relationship between the patient and pharmacist.*

Considering the patient-pharmacist relationship as a covenant means that a pharmacist has moral obligations in response to the gift of trust received from society. In return for this gift, a pharmacist promises to help individuals achieve optimum benefit from their medications, to be committed to their welfare, and to maintain their trust.

II. *A pharmacist promotes the good of every patient in a caring, compassionate, and confidential manner.*

A pharmacist places concern for the well-being of the patient at the center of professional practice. In doing so, a pharmacist considers needs stated by the patient as well as those defined by health science. A pharmacist is dedicated to protecting the dignity of the patient with a caring attitude and a compassionate spirit. A pharmacist focuses on serving the patient in a private and confidential manner.

III. *A pharmacist respects the autonomy and dignity of each patient.*

A pharmacist promotes the right of self-determination and recognizes individual self-worth by encouraging patients to participate in decisions about their health. A pharmacist communicates with patients in terms that are understandable. In all cases, a pharmacist respects personal and cultural differences among patients.

IV. *A pharmacist acts with honest and integrity in professional relationships.*

A pharmacist has a duty to tell the truth and to act with conviction of conscience. A pharmacist avoids discriminatory practices, behavior, or work conditions that impair professional judgment, and actions that compromise dedication to the best interests of patients.

V. *A pharmacist maintains professional competence.* A pharmacist has a duty to maintain knowledge and abilities as new medications, devices, and technologies become available and as health information advances.

VI. *A pharmacist respects the values and abilities of colleagues and other health professionals.*

When appropriate, a pharmacist asks for the consultation of colleagues or other health professionals or refers the patient. A pharmacist acknowledges that colleagues and other health professionals may differ in the beliefs and values they apply to the care of the patient.

VII. *A pharmacist serves individual, community, and societal needs.* The primary obligation of a pharmacist is to the individual patient. However, the obligations of a pharmacist may at times extend beyond the individual to the community and society. In these situations, the pharmacist recognizes the responsibilities that accompany these obligations and acts accordingly.

VIII. *A pharmacist seeks justice in the distribution of health resources.*

When health resources are allocated, a pharmacist is fair and equitable, balancing the needs of patients and society.

Approved by APhA Active and Life members, Spring 1995.

SOURCES OF ADDITIONAL INFORMATION

Abood RA. Cost containment vs quality: Who's liable when a third party makes the decision? *Leg Asp Pharm Pract.* 1987;10:3-9.

Abood RA. Physician dispensing, the FTC and state action. *Leg Asp Pharm Pract.* 1987;10:3-10.

Abood RR. Contributory negligence: The pharmacist's defense to negligence. Part I. *Leg Asp Pharm Pract.* 1979;1:1-2.

Abood RR. Contributory negligence: The pharmacist's defense to negligence. Part II. *Leg Asp Pharm Pract.* 1979;1:1-2.

Abood RR. Pharmacist dispensing: Service or sale? Applicability of strict liability. *Am Pharm.* 1980;NS20:577-581.

Almquist DD. Liability insurance for nontraditional services. *Am J Hosp Pharm.* 1992;49:2124.

Angorn RA, McCormick WC. The pharmacist as limited prescriber: The liability factor. *US Pharm.* 1986;11:30-36.

Archambault GF. Legal considerations relative to drug distribution in hospitals. *Hosp Manag.* 1968;3:30-32; 1969;4:31, 40.

Averbach A. Physician's liability for prescription drugs. *St John's Law Rev.* 1969;43:535-556.

Baker KR. Why pharmacists should document their actions. *Am Pharm.* 1991;NS31:878-881.

Baker KR, Mondt D. Risk management in pharmacy: Preventing liability claims. *Am Pharm.* 1994;NS34:60-72.

Barker KN, Valentino JG. On a political and legal foundation for clinical pharmacy practice. *J Am Pharm Assoc.* 1972;NS12:202-206, 237.

Barnett FJ. The liability for adverse drug reactions: The role of the package insert. *J Leg Med.* 1973;1:18-23, 45, 46, 47-52, 50.

Beardsley RS, Wertheimer AI. Pharmacy malpractice: Current status and trends. *J Am Pharm Assoc.* 1976;NS16:562-564.

Berns H. Pharmacists and the sword of Damocles. *Scalpel and Quill.* 1977;11:1-23.

Bernzweig EP. The pharmacist of the future: A lawyer's view. *J Am Pharm Assoc.* 1968;NS8:591, 594-597, 608.

Boatwright DE, Clark HW. Safe use of benzodiazepines and other drugs: The pharmacist's duty to counsel. *Am J Hosp Pharm.* 1991;48:1291-1296.

Brushwood DB. Admissibility of scientific testimony into evidence. *Am J Hosp Pharm.* 1994;51:683-685.

Brushwood DB. Common grounds for revoking pharmacy licenses. *US Pharm.* 1986;11:41-47.

Brushwood DB. Conscientious objection and abortifacient drugs. *Clin Therapeut.* 1993;15:204.

Brushwood DB. The duty to counsel: Reviewing a decade of litigation. *Drug Intell Clin Pharm.* 1991;25:195-203.

Brushwood DB. Government liable for failure to monitor a patient's serum gentamycin concentration in an Army hospital. *Am J Hosp Pharm.* 1992;49:1748-1750.

Brushwood DB. Grounds for revocation or suspension of a pharmacist's license. *Am Pharm.* 1982;NS22:574.

Brushwood DB. Hospital liable for allergic reaction to heparin used in injection flush. *Am J Hosp Pharm.* 1992;49:1491-1492.

Brushwood DB. Hospital liable for defect in cardiplegia solution. *Am J Hosp Pharm.* 1992;49:1174.

Brushwood DB. Hospital pharmacists' duty to question clear errors in prescriptions. *Am J Hosp Pharm.* 1994;51:2031-2033.

Brushwood DB. Hospital's independent responsibility to obtain informed consent. *Am J Hosp Pharm.* 1994;51:2176-2178.

Brushwood DB. Hospital's obligation to monitor medical services. *Am J Hosp Pharm.* 1993;50:1437-1439.

Brushwood DB. The informed intermediary doctrine and the pharmacist's duty to warn. *J Legal Med.* 1983;4:349.

Brushwood DB. Insured pharmacists' rights in settlements out of court. *US Pharm* 1983;12:18.

Brushwood DB. Liability for disparaging remarks. *US Pharm.* 1985;10:14.

Brushwood DB. Liability for dispensing to an inpatient an estrogenic drug without a patient package insert. *Am J Hosp Pharm.* 1990;47:1804.

Brushwood DB. Liability for suicide. *US Pharm.* 1984;9:25.

Brushwood DB. Liability for unauthorized prescription refills. *US Pharm.* 1988;13:29-32.

Brushwood DB. Limits to pharmacists' duty to warn. *Am J Health Syst Pharm.* 1995;52:1337-1339.

Brushwood DB. An overview of pharmacist malpractice litigation. *Pharmacy Law Annual.* 1988. Vienna, VA: American Society for Pharmacy Law; 1989:3-47.

Brushwood DB. Patient injury and attempted link with pharmacist's negligence. *Am J Hosp Pharm.* 1993;50:2382-2385.

Brushwood DB. Patient oriented practice can reduce damages in pharmacist malpractice suits. *Leg Asp Pharm Pract.* 1987;10:11.

Brushwood DB. Pharmaceutical litigation: Judicial tort reform and strict liability. *J Legal Med.* 1989;10:377.

Brushwood DB. Pharmacist liability for suicide by drug overdose. *Am J Hosp Pharm.* 1983;40:439.

Brushwood DB. The pharmacist's drug information responsibility after *McKee v. American Home Products. Food and Drug L J.* 1993;48:377.

Brushwood DB. The pharmacist's duty to warn: Toward a knowledge based model of professional responsibility. *Drake L Rev.* 1991;40:1.

Brushwood DB. Pharmacist's qualification as an expert witness on a physician's standard of care. *Am J Hosp Pharm.* 1990;47:2078.

Brushwood DB. Prison pharmacist may be liable for refusing to dispense anticonvulsants to an inmate. *Am J Hosp Pharm.* 1992;49:636-639.

Brushwood DB. Privileged information in pharmacy. *US Pharm.* 1984;9:16.

Brushwood DB. Proving causation in drug related suits. *US Pharm.* 1986;11:16.

Brushwood DB. Strict liability in tort: Appropriateness of the theory for retail pharmacists. *Food Drug Cosm L J.* 1987;42:269.

Brushwood DB, Fern F. *Clozaril* and the threat of products liability: Defensive drug distribution invites regulatory reform. *J Products Toxics Liab.* 1993;15:45.

Brushwood DB. Lively BT. Refusal to dispense a prescription: What is the law? *Am Pharm.* 1989;NS29:645.

Brushwood DB, Myers MJ. The statute of limitations. *US Pharm.* 1983;8:10.

Brushwood DB, Simonsmeier LM. Drug information for patients. *J Leg Med.* 1986;7:279.

Brushwood DB, Simonsmeier LM. Drug information for patients: Duties of the manufacturer, pharmacist, physician and hospital. *J Leg Med.* 1986;7:279.

Brushwood DB, Simonsmeier LM. Drug information for patients, part I: The manufacturer's legal duty. *Consultant Pharm.* 1988;3:149-154.

Brushwood DB, Simonsmeier LM. Drug information for patients, part II: The pharmacist's legal duty. *Consultant Pharm.* 1988;3:155-160.

Brushwood DB, Simonsmeier LM. Drug information for patients, part III: The physician's and the hospital's legal duty. *Consultant Pharm.* 1988;3:161-166.

Brushwood DB, Simonsmeier LM. *Rift v. Morgan Pharmacy*: A legal mandate for patient-oriented pharmacy practice. *Am Pharm.* 1987:NS27:232.

Cacciatore GG. Pharmacist's duty to warn. *Am J Hosp Pharm.* 1994;51:2824-2826.

Campbell NA. Legal implications for the community pharmacist distributing nonprescription drug products. *Contemp Pharm Pract.* 1981;4:216-219.

Campbell NA. Liability implications in clinical pharmacy for the community pharmacist. *US Pharm.* 1977;2:20-21, 24-25.

Campbell NA. Under-the-law liability potential for overcounter drugs. *Leg Asp Pharm Pract.* 1978-1979;1:3.

Campbell NA. Who owns the prescription? *Leg Asp Pharm Pract.* 1990;2:3.

Campbell NA, Holm AL. Shared liability for medication therapy. *US Pharm.* 1981;6:22, 24-26.

Campbell NA, Shepherd MD. Pharmacy practice definitions and their legal implications. *Am J Pharm.* 1978;150:177.

Carney JC. The pharmacist's duty to counsel. *US Pharm.* 197;12:81-88.

Cassiday JD. The prescription drug exception to the doctrine of strict liability. *Ill Bar J.* 1969;58:268-275.

Cerullo TC. Legal considerations in implementing and maintaining a total parenteral nutrition program. *US Pharm.* 1979;4:21, 23, 25, 27, 31.

Cerullo TC, Cerullo LV. Local customs: Risky defense against liability. *Leg Asp Pharm Pract.* 1979;1:3-4.

Cobb RD, Gartland FA. Liability without fault—the pharmacist's dilemma. *Pharm Manag.* 1980;152:161-163.

Coons SJ, Fink JL III. The pharmacist, the law and self-testing products. *Am Pharm.* 1989;NS29:705.

Crumley MG. Professional liability of pharmacists. *Def Law J.* 1973;22:470-489.

Davis NM. Detection and prevention of ambulatory care pharmacy dispensing errors. *Hosp Pharm.* 1990;25:18-22, 28.

Davis NM. A question: Should pharmacists make permanent entries on patients' charts? *Hosp Pharm.* 1976;11:336-338, 341, 344-345, 350.

Davis NM. Physician-pharmacist conflict over drug therapy: A pharmacy policy statement. *Hosp Pharm.* 1976;11:134-135.

DeMarco CT. The legal basis for clinical pharmacy. *Am J Hosp Pharm.* 1973;30:1067-1071.

DeMarco CT. Maximum allowable costs for medications in hospitals. *Am J Hosp Pharm.* 1975;32:1159-1160.

Emigh JF. Liability of pharmacy interns. *J Am Pharm Assoc.* 1977;NS17:387.

Enright SM. Perceived liability (with managed care). *Am J Hosp Pharm.* 1992;49:418-420.

Fern FH, Charney S. Pharmacist liability: What can you expect? *US Pharm.* 1986;11:59-67.

Fink JG. Therapeutic liabilities: The basis in law. *Drug Ther.* 1974;4:68-71.

Fink JG. Therapeutic liabilities: Drug maladministration. *Drug Ther.* 1975;5:143-144, 147-148.

Fink JG. Therapeutic liabilities: Prescription error. *Drug Ther.* 1975;5:190-191, 195-196.

Fink JL III. Antisubstitution law changes and the hospital formulary system. *Am J Hosp Pharm.* 1977;34:90-93.

Fink JL III. Child-resistant closures: Liability concerns. *US Pharm.* 1988;13:42-45.

Fink JL III. Dispensing FDA-approved drugs for non-approved uses. *US Pharm.* 1977;2:24, 26.

Fink JL III. Drug product selection and the law. *Contemp Pharm Pract.* 1979;2:128-131.

Fink JL III. The effect of prescription renewals on extending the physician-patient relationship. *Am Pharm.* 1987;NS27:746-748.

Fink JL III. Evaluating a malpractice insurance policy. *J Am Pharm Assoc.* 1977;NS17:733-734.

Fink JL III. Evaluating manufacturers' liability protection policies. *US Pharm.* 1978;3:10-14, 16.

Fink JL III. Judicial views of the pharmacist's professional status. *Drug Intell Clin Pharm.* 1979;13:30-36.

Fink JL III. The law and clinical pharmacy. *J Clin Pharmacol.* 1976;16:605-608.

Fink JL III. Legal aspects of nuclear pharmacy. In: *Selected Papers on Nuclear Pharmacy.* Washington: American Pharmaceutical Association, 1976.

Fink JL III. Legal aspects of prescription labeling. *J Cont Educ Pharm.* 1978;2:65-66.

Fink JL III. Legal issues in nonprescription drug transaction. *Pharm Manag.* 1979;151:250-253, 257.

Fink JL III. Legal issues other than negligence in drug product selection. *Tile and Till.* 1979-1980;65:20-22.

Fink JL III. Legal issues related to telephoned prescriptions. *Leg Asp Pharm Pract.* 1987;10:10-12.

Fink JL III. The legal standard of due care for pharmacists in institutional practice. *Am J Hosp Pharm.* 1980;37:1546-1549.

Fink JL III. Legality of mandatory continuing professional education. *Am J Hosp Pharm.* 1981;38:1768-1774.

Fink JL III. Liability concerns for pharmacy students and interns. *Pharm Student.* 1988;18:16-18.

Fink JL III. Liability of patient medication records. *J Am Pharm Assoc.* 1976;NS16:496-498.

Fink JL III. Liability of pharmacists serving skilled nursing facilities. *J Am Pharm Assoc.* 1977;NS17:95-96.

Fink JL III. Liability of the pharmacist as a therapeutic consultant. *Am J Hosp Pharm.* 1981;38:218-222.

Fink JL III. Mislabeling and patient liability issues for pharmacists. *Contemp Pharm Pract.* 1981;4:207-210.

Fink JL III. Ownership of prescriptions. *Leg Asp Pharm Pract.* 1987;10:1-3.

Fink JL III. Passing off: A current legal issue in marketing of pharmaceuticals. *Pharm Manag.* 1979;151:209-210.

Fink JL III. Patient package inserts and the pharmacist's responsibility. *Am J Hosp Pharm.* 1979;36:226-229.

Fink JL III. Pharmacist liability for the acts of others. *J Cont Educ Pharm.* 1978;2:60-62.

Fink JL III. The pharmacist's liability for drug interaction. *J Postgrad Pharm.* 1979;1:8-9.

Fink JL III. Privacy and confidentiality in pharmacy practice. *Leg Asp Pharm Pract.* 1981;3:1-2.

Fink JL III. Review of studies of malpractice claims based on prescribing. *Leg Asp Pharm Pract.* 1987;10:9-11.

Fink JL III. Role of JCAH standards in negligence suits. *Am J Hosp Pharm.* 1981;38:892-896.

Fink JL III. Some legal aspects of the hospital formulary system. *Am J Hosp Pharm.* 1974;31:86-90.

Fink JL III. Some legal issues presented in clinical pharmacy practice. *Drug Intell Clin Pharm.* 1976;10:444-447.

Fink JL III. Statutes of limitations. *Leg Asp Pharm Pract.* 1988;11:6-8.

Fink JL III. Subpoenas and discovery of pharmacy records. *Am Pharm.* 1987;NS27:879-882.

Fink JL III. Suicide—the pharmacist's liability. *Leg Asp Pharm Pract.* 1979;1:3-4.

Fink JL III. Therapeutic liabilities: Package insert. *Drug Ther.* 1976;6:140-143.

Fink JL III, D'Allessandro JP. Malpractice claims in community pharmacy. *Pharm Manag.* 1980;152:176-182, 184.

Fink JL III, Downs GE. Liability aspects of hypertension screening and blood pressure monitoring. *Contemp Pharm Pract.* 1978;1:43-46.

Fink JL III, Myers MJ. The legal duty to participate in continuing professional education. *Pharm Manag.* 1979;151:281-284.

Fleischer L. From pill-counting to patient care: pharmacists' standard of care in negligence law. 68 *Fordham L Rev* 165 (October 1999).

Foster TS. Drug product selection—Part 4: Selecting therapeutically equivalent products: Special cases. *Am Pharm.* 1991;NS31:825-830.

Fox LA. Good Samaritan laws. *US Pharm.* 1979;4:22-24, 56.

Fox LA. Insurance. *US Pharm.* 1980;5:12, 16, 72.

Fox LA. Medical and prescription records—patient access and confidentiality. *US Pharm.* 1979;4:15-16, 18-20.

Fraser GL, Davis TD. The pharmacist as an expert witness. *Am J Hosp Pharm.* 1990;47:2082-2085.

Haunholter JA. Negligence and the pharmacist: A consideration of some of the aspects. Part I. *Can Pharm J.* 1978;13:12-16.

Haunholter JA. Negligence and the pharmacist: A consideration of some of the aspects. Part II. *Can Pharm J.* 1978;13:57-61.

Haunholter JA. Negligence and the pharmacist: A consideration of some of the aspects. Part III. *Can Pharm J.* 1978;13:100-104.

Hayes TH. Nonapproved uses of FDA-approved drugs. JAMA. 1970;211:1705.

Hirsh HL. Therapeutic liabilities: Patient package inserts. *Drug Ther.* 1977;7:102-110.

Kaluzny EL. The doctrine of respondeat superior. *US Pharm.* 1979;4:20-22.

Kaluzny EL. Legal liability for failure to dispense or refill a prescription. *US Pharm.* 1978;3:24, 26, 27.

Kaluzny EL. Rights of the accused in pharmacy board actions. *US Pharm.* 1978;3:6-7.

Kamm RE. The liability of the pharmacist in the role of drug product selector. *Ill Pharm.* 1969;35:19-22.

Kerr WT. Professional liability of the pharmacist. *Mich Pharm.* 1972;10:22-28.

King GS. Liability for negligence of pharmacists. *Vanderbilt Law Rev.* 1959;12:695-709.

Knapp DA, Salisbury R. In offering self-medication products: Pharmacist legal and professional responsibilities. *J Am Pharm Assoc.* 1967;NS7:520-522, 541.

Liability insurance—professional protection. *J Am Pharm Assoc.* 1969;NS9:446.

Liang FZ, Greenberg RB, Hogan GF. Legal issues associated with formulary product selection when there are two or more recognized drug therapies. *Am J Hosp Pharm.* 1988;45:2372-2375.

Mandl FL, Greenberg RB. Legal implications of preparing and dispensing drugs under conditions not in a product's official labeling. *Am J Hosp Pharm.* 1976;33:814-816.

Marchitelli DJ. Liability of pharmacist who accurately fills prescription for harm resulting to user. 44 ALR 5th 393 (1996).

Mazzucca GA. Drug interactions: A new area of liability. *Leg Asp Pharm Pract.* 1979;2:1-3.

Merrill RA. Compensation for prescription drug injuries. *Va Law Rev.* 1973;59:1-120.

Metzger JP, Gardner RE. How to become a better defendant in a law suit. *US Pharm.* 1988;13:29-30, 53.

Meyer MC. Drug product selection—Part 2: Scientific basis of bioavailability and bioequivalence testing. *Am Pharm.* 1991;NS31:587-592.

Mills DH. Medicolegal responsibilities of practitioners to assure optimal therapeutical performance of drug products in patient care. *Drug Inform Bull.* 1969;3:92-95.

Mills DH. Physician responsibility for drug prescription. JAMA. 1965;192:116-119.

Misfeasance in the pharmacy: A bundle of fun, joy and affection? *Cal West Law Rev.* 1972;8:341-354.

Molzon, JA. What kinds of patient counseling are required? *Am Pharm.* 1992:NS32:234-241.

Morrell MX. Package inserts, adverse drug reactions and the physician's liability. *Rat Drug Ther.* 1975;9:1-6.

Myers MJ. Can you refuse to dispense a prescription? *Leg Asp Pharm Pract.* 1980;2:1-2.

Myers MJ, Fink JL III. Liability aspects of drug product selection. *J Am Pharm Assoc.* 1977;NS17:33-35.

Newman D. Pharmacists: The next deep pocket! Malpractice mania hits pharmacy practice. *Am Pharm.* 1978;NS18:598-605.

Parker RE, Martinez DR, Covington TR. Drug product selection—Part 1: History and legal overview. *Am Pharm.* 1991;NS31:524-540.

Parker RE, Martinez DR, Covington TR. Drug product selection—Part 3: The orange book. *Am Pharm.* 1991;NS31:655-664.

Patient package insert and pharmacist liability. *Tulsa Law J.* 1979;14:590-629.

Patterson FT. Entrapment. *J Am Pharm Assoc.* 1968;NS8:256.

Product liability for prescription drugs—the effects of generic substitution on the consumer and the pharmacist. *Syr Law Rev.* 1972;23:887.

Pumpian PA. The patient profile—legal liability. *US Pharm.* 1977;2:12-13.

Pumpian PA. Patient profile records and patient counseling. *US Pharm.* 1977;2:24-25.

Pumpian PA. Product selection—substitution. *US Pharm.* 1977;2:6-7.

Pumpian PA. Use of non-licensed personnel in the prescription department. *US Pharm.* 1977;2:22-23.

Ripepe SD. Decreasing liability potential in the hospital pharmacy. *Hosp Pharm.* 1996;31:531-535.

Rosenblum AE. Hospital pharmacy and the law. *Hosp Form Manag.* 1966;101:80, 82, 84.

Rucker NL. The effect of new clinical lab rules on your pharmacy. *Am Pharm.* 1992;NS32:541.

Salisbury R. Monitoring patient drug profiles and the legal liability of the pharmacist. *Am J Pharm Educ.* 1977;40:68-71.

Salisbury R. The pharmacist's duty to warn the patient of side effects of drugs. *J Am Pharm Assoc.* 1977;NS17:97-100.

Schmitz TM. Retail druggists' warranty of drugs. *Cleveland-Marshall Law Rev.* 1966;15:285-95.

Scholles JR. The pharmacists' legal risks in dispensing contact lens products. *Contact.* 1988;1;5-11.

Schulz RM, Brushwood DB. The pharmacist's role in patient care. *Am Pharm.* 1991;NS31:882-888.

Schwartz JI, Fink JL III. Legal issues associated with pharmacokinetic software. *Am J Hosp Pharm.* 1989;46:120-124.

Simmons JC. Pharmacy and the civil law. *J Am Pharm Assoc.* 1977;NS17:730-732.

Simonsmeier LM. Insulin sales result in injuries. *Leg Asp Pharm Pract.* 1987;10:10-12.

Simonsmeier LM. Insurance, liability and the pharmacist. *J Am Pharm Assoc.* 1976;NS16:128-132.

Simonsmeier LM. Legal responsibility for the acts of others. *Pharm Manag.* 1979;151:200-201.

Simonsmeier LM. The legal risks of peer review. *Pharm Manag.* 1980;152:7-8.

Simonsmeier LM. Legal significance of drug interactions. *Contemp Pharm Pract.* 1981;4:211-215.

Simonsmeier LM. Let the pharmacist beware: Strict liability can make you pay. *Leg Asp Pharm Pract.* 1978;1:3-4.

Simonsmeier LM. The package insert and the pharmacist's liability. *Am J Pharm.* 1977;149:82-89.

Simonsmeier LM. When are you liable for another's acts? *Leg Asp Pharm Pract.* 1981;3:1-3.

Sonnenreich MR, Mener JM Jr. State substitution laws—a lawyer's view. *US Pharm.* 1977;2:18-22.

Sonnenreich MR, Shaw DF. State substitution laws: Update on pharmacist liability. *US Pharm.* 1978;3:24, 26-29, 86.

Steeves RF. Malpractice insurance—Who? Me? *J Am Pharm Assoc.* 1966;NS6:35-36.

Steeves RF. A question of privilege. *J Am Pharm Assoc.* 1965;NS5:448, 458.

Steeves RF. Releasing prescription record information. *J Am Pharm Assoc.* 1965;NS5:329.

Steeves RF. There oughta be a law. *J Am Pharm Assoc.* 1965;NS5:383.

Steeves RF, Patterson FT. Legal responsibility of the hospital pharmacist for rational drug therapy. *Am J Hosp Pharm.* 1969;26:404-407.

Strict liability and allergic drug reactions. *Miss Law J.* 1976;47:526-543.

Susina SV. Drug product selection: More benefits than liabilities. *Leg Asp Pharm Pract.* 1979;1:2-3.

Susina SV. When drugs are used for unapproved indications. *Leg Asp Pharm Pract.* 1980;2:2-3.

Sveska KJ. Pharmacist liability. *Am J Hosp Pharm.* 1993;50:1429-1436.

Swafford WB, White BD, Hamner ME. Pharmacy malpractice: A review of indices of care. *US Pharm.* 1980;5:8-10.

Terry NP. Cyber-malpractice: Legal exposure for cybermedicine, 25. *Am J Law and Medicine* 327 (1999).

Thompson JE. Public policy protects hospital quality assurance documents from discovery in litigation. *Am J Hosp Pharm.* 1991;48:1989-1991.

Tousignaut DR. Joint commission on accreditation of hospitals' 1977 standards for pharmaceutical services. *Am J Hosp Pharm.* 1977;34:943-950.

Tozar FL, Kasik JE. The medical-legal aspects of adverse drug reactions. *Clin Pharmacol Ther.* 1967;8:637-646.

Valentino JG. An analysis of the regulatory and legal aspects of patient package inserts. *J Am Pharm Assoc.* 1977;NS17:688-691.

Valentino JG. Legal implications of USP dispensing information. *US Pharm.* 1978;3:24, 26, 28, 29, 31, 32, 76.

Valentino JG, Barker KN. On a political and legal foundation for clinical pharmacy practice. *J Am Pharm Assoc.* 1972;NS12:202, 206, 237.

Van Dusen V, Pray WS. The hospital pharmacist as an expert witness. *Hosp Pharm.* 2000;25:1296-1303.

Vivian JC. Addiction and termination. *US Pharm.* 1999;9:HS-23 (http://www.uspharmacist.com/NewLook/DisplayArticle.cfm?item_num=395).

Vivian JC. Addiction: whose fault. *US Pharm.* 1995;12:44.

Vivian JC. Admissibility of settlements. *US Pharm.* 1997;7:82.

Vivian JC. At-will employment and whistleblowing: If you were subpoenaed to testify against your employer, would you know what your rights and obligations are? *US Pharm.* 1999;8:68 (http://www.uspharmacist.com/NewLook/DisplayArticle.cfm?item_num=408).

Vivian JC. Beware the labeled indications of generic alternatives, Caveats. *J Man Care Pharm.* 1997;1:115.

Vivian JC. The caregiver's damage: A pharmacist's dispensing error causes a caregiver to unwittingly minister a highly toxic drug to a patient; is the caregiver entitled to recover damages for indirect harm? *US Pharm.* 1998;10:84 (http://www.uspharmacist.com/NewLook/DisplayArticle.cfm?item_num=193).

Vivian JC. A case of pretextual retaliatory discharge? *US Pharm.* 1999;6:75 (http://www.uspharmacist.com/NewLook/DisplayArticle.cfm?item_num=387).

Vivian JC. A case of sexual harrassment: Extreme behavior exhibited by a supervising pharmacist sounds a cautionary note about sexual harrassment. *US Pharm.* 1998;9:106 (http://www.uspharmacist.com/NewLook/DisplayArticle.cfm?item_num=193).

Vivian JC. A case of trespassers and abandoned drugs. *US Pharm.* 1998;6:74.

Vivian JC. A case study: confidentiality. *US Pharm.* 1996;9:76.

Vivian JC. Caution handling invalid scripts. *J Mich Pharm.* 1990;8:259.

Vivian JC. Compounding law invalidated. *US Pharm.* 2001;3:78 (http://www.uspharmacist.com/NewLook/DisplayArticle.cfm?item_num=684).

Vivian JC. Confidentiality of Rx records. *US Pharm.* 1996;7:106.

Vivian JC. Conspiracy to boycott. *US Pharm.* 1999;11:106 (http://www.uspharmacist.com/NewLook/DisplayArticle.cfm?item_num=449).

Vivian JC. Costly accidents. *Drug Topics.* 1991;4:76.

Vivian JC. Court fries frye. *Drug Topics.* 1993;9:57.

Vivian JC. Dealing with deceptions. *US Pharm.* 1997;8:98.

Vivian JC. Detecting prescribing errors. *US Pharm.* 2001;1:59 (http://www.uspharmacist.com/NewLook/DisplayArticle.cfm?item_num=644).

Vivian JC. Disability insurance fraud. *US Pharm.* 1997;6:91.

Vivian JC. Disclosure of prescription records. *US Pharm.* 2000;3:86 (http://www.uspharmacist.com/NewLook/DisplayArticle.cfm?item_num=490).

Vivian JC. Disease or accident. *US Pharm.* 1995;2:72.

Vivian JC. Dispensing errors: what judges decide. *US Pharm.* 1996;1:88.

Vivian JC. Dispensing interstate prescriptions: legal and ethical considerations. *Am Pharm.* 1995;11:38.

Vivian JC. Distressful errors. *Drug Topics.* 1993;3:56.

Vivian JC. Does a mistake warrant punitive damages? *US Pharm.* 1998;3:130.

Vivian JC. Dosage errors and proximate cause. *US Pharm.* 1998;12:44.

Vivian JC. Double-edged sword. *Drug Topics.* 1993;8:59.

Vivian JC. Drug error accident. *US Pharm.* 1996;8:72.

Vivian JC. E-signatures pharmacy practice. *US Pharm.* 2001;2:50 (http://www.uspharmacist.com/NewLook/DisplayArticle.cfm?item_num=665).

Vivian JC. Error: mistake or negligence? *US Pharm.* 26:12. http://www.uspharmacist.com/oldformat.asp?url=newlook/files/Phar/Law12.htm&pub_id=8&article_id=807

Vivian JC. Evolution of duties. *US Pharm.* 26:04. http://www.uspharmacist.com/oldformat.asp?url=newlook/files/Phar/ACF3DD7.cfm&pub_id=8&article_id=700

Vivian JC. Excessive refills lead to liability. *J Mich Pharm.* 1991;3:107.

Vivian JC. Expanding liability. *Drug Topics.* 1993;10:74.

Vivian JC. Expensive mistakes. *Drug Topics.* 1991;7:58.

Vivian JC. Experts and evidence. *US Pharm.* 27:03. http://www.uspharmacist.com/oldformat.asp?url=newlook/files/Phar/ACF6C8.htm&pub_id=8&article_id=856

Vivian JC. Fen-Phen and pharmacy liability. *US Pharm.* 2000;4:93 (http://www.uspharmacist.com/NewLook/DisplayArticle.cfm?item_num=509).

Vivian JC. Fiduciary duty of confidentiality. *US Pharm.* 26:05. http://www.uspharmacist.com/oldformat.asp?url=newlook/files/Phar/ACF2D07.htm&pub_id=8&article_id=717

Vivian JC. Forum shopping. *US Pharm.* 1995;6:74.

Vivian JC. Free speech limits. *US Pharm*. 1998;1:108.

Vivian JC. How to prepare for a deposition. *Am J Hosp Pharm*. 1992;49:818, 820, 822.

Vivian JC. Implications of *Bristol-Myers Squibb Co. v. Shalala* for pharmacist dispensing for off-label uses. *J Am Pharm Assoc*. 1997;NS37:2:265.

Vivian JC. Improper interchange liability. *US Pharm*. 1998;4:102.

Vivian JC. In strict confidence. *Drug Topics*. 1992;6:58.

Vivian JC. Insurance limits: a cautionary tale. *US Pharm*. 1999;5:90.

Vivian JC. Internship liability. *US Pharm*. 1998;7:98.

Vivian JC. Legal considerations: 'drugstore' or 'pharmacy'?. *US Pharm*. 2000;7:57 (http://www.uspharmacist.com/NewLook/DisplayArticle.cfm?item_num=550).

Vivian JC. Legal considerations: prescription errors. *US Pharm*. 1994;3:12.

Vivian JC. Legal proof must be carefully planned. *US Pharm*. 1997;5:106.

Vivian JC. Liability for a drug-drug interaction. *US Pharm*. 1996;6:93.

Vivian JC. Logic, common sense and science. *US Pharm*. 27:05. http://www.uspharmacist.com/oldformat.asp?url=newlook/files/Phar/ACF5D64.htm&pub_id=8&article_id=883

Vivian JC. Malpractice liability limitations. *US Pharm*. 1994;9:44.

Vivian JC. Malpractice liability and workers' compensation. *US Pharm*. 2000;1:48 (http://www.uspharmacist.com/NewLook/DisplayArticle.cfm?item_num=466).

Vivian JC. Malpractice settlements. *US Pharm*. 2003;28:01. http://www.uspharmacist.com/index.asp?show=article&page=8_1018.htm

Vivian JC. Matter of privacy. *Drug Topics*. 1992;8:70.

Vivian JC. Mistake or wanton disregard? *US Pharm*. 2000;11:85 (http://www.uspharmacist.com/NewLook/DisplayArticle.cfm?item_num=619).

Vivian JC. Multiple justice systems. *US Pharm*. 1996;12:42.

Vivian JC. Must you warn? *Drug Topics*. 1991;2:50.

Vivian JC. Necessity for expert witness. *US Pharm*. 1999;12:48 (http://www.uspharmacist.com/NewLook/DisplayArticle.cfm?item_num=455).

Vivian JC. Negligence in employee supervision. *US Pharm*. 2000;6:68 (http://www.uspharmacist.com/NewLook/DisplayArticle.cfm?item_num=535).

Vivian JC. Nonlabeled use of generics. *US Pharm*. 1996;10:82.

Vivian JC. Not your duty. *Drug Topics*. 1992;4:72.

Vivian JC. OBRA '90 and fees. *Drug Topics*. 1992;12:102.

Vivian JC. Off-label promotion approved to limited extent. *US Pharm*. 2000;5:72 (http://www.uspharmacist.com/NewLook/DisplayArticle.cfm?item_num=528).

Vivian JC. Over-use liability. *US Pharm*. 1995;4:72.

Vivian JC. Overtime pay. *US Pharm*. 1999;10:96 (http://www.uspharmacist.com/NewLook/DisplayArticle.cfm?item_num=437).

Vivian JC. Ownership of customer lists. *US Pharm*. 1998;11:96 (www.uspharmacist.com/NewLook/DisplayArticle.cfm?item_num=188).

Vivian JC. Partial duty to warn. *US Pharm*. 2000;10:48 (http://www.uspharmacist.com/NewLook/DisplayArticle.cfm?item_num=596).

Vivian JC. Patient misconduct. *US Pharm*. 1995;10:82.

Vivian JC. Pharmacy liability for patient addiction. *US Pharm*. 1994;7:87.

Vivian JC. Pharmacy malpractice. *J Mich Pharm*. 1985;9:10.

Vivian JC. Pharmacy malpractice: Crisis or crucible? *Am Pharm*. 1994;NS34:25-30.

Vivian JC. Pharmacy malpractice: New twist. *J Mich Pharm*. 1991;7:247.

Vivian JC. Pharmacy malpractice. In: Block AL, ed. *2003 Medical Malpractice Update*. New York, NY: Aspen Law and Business Publications; 2003:297-320.

Vivian JC. Prescription confidentiality. *US Pharm*. 1996;3:119.

Vivian JC. Procedure and substance. *US Pharm*. 2000;12:63 (http://www.uspharmacist.com/NewLook/DisplayArticle.cfm?item_num=637).

Vivian JC. Prosecution or persecution? *US Pharm*. 27:04. http://www.uspharmacist.com/oldformat.asp?url=newlook/files/Phar/ACF800F.htm&pub_id=8&article_id=862

Vivian JC. Proving causation without a precedent. *US Pharm.* 1998;5:102.

Vivian JC. Punitive damages. *US Pharm.* 1995;11:72.

Vivian JC. A question of pregnancy discrimination. *US Pharm.* 1999;9:84 (http://www.uspharmacist.com/ NewLook/DisplayArticle.cfm?item_num=425).

Vivian JC. Questionable justice. *US Pharm.* 27:10. http://www.uspharmacist.com/ index.asp?show=article&page=8_966.htm

Vivian JC. A review of federal controlled substances laws. *US Pharm.* 1999;9:84 (http://www.uspharmacist.com/NewLook/CE/controlled/lesson.htm).

Vivian JC. Refusal to fill. *US Pharm.* 2000;8:73 (http://www.uspharmacist.com/NewLook/ DisplayArticle.cfm?item_num=572).

Vivian JC. Rock and a hard place. *Drug Topics.* 1991;10:51.

Vivian JC. Rx (or duck)? *Drug Topics.* 1993;4:64.

Vivian JC. Safety cap liability. *Drug Topics.* 1992;1:51.

Vivian JC. Speaking of duty to warn. *J Mich Pharm.* 1991;11:394.

Vivian JC. Sports medicine and pharmacy practice liabilities. *US Pharm.* 1994;8:91.

Vivian JC. Standards of care: When a physician's judgment call overrides precautionary statements in the PDR, whose authority prevails? *US Pharm.* 1998;8:78 (http://www.uspharmacist.com/NewLook/ DisplayArticle.cfm?item_num=202).

Vivian JC. Stonewall liability. *US Pharm.* 1996;11:76.

Vivian JC. Suicide liability. *US Pharm.* 1997;12:54.

Vivian JC. Suspicion of illegal prescription activity. *US Pharm.* 1997;9:159.

Vivian JC. Tennessee waltz. *Drug Topics.* 1991;11:52.

Vivian JC. Third parties and generic substitution. *US Pharm.* 1997;10:120.

Vivian JC. Third-party liability for pharmacy fraud. *US Pharm.* 1994;11:104.

Vivian JC. Two-tiered pricing: unequal protection. *US Pharm.* 2000;9:73 (http://www.uspharmacist.com/ NewLook/DisplayArticle.cfm?item_num=585).

Vivian JC. Use as directed. *US Pharm.* 1999;4:68.

Vivian JC. Verification of controlled substance Rxs. *US Pharm.* 1999;1:49 (http://www.uspharmacist.com/ NewLook/DisplayArticle.cfm?item_num=178).

Vivian JC. What's in a name? *US Pharm.* 26:08. http://www.uspharmacist.com/ oldformat.asp?url=newlook/files/Phar/pharmlaw_080601.htm&pub_id=8&article_id=761

Vivian JC. When the same is different. *US Pharm.* 26:09. http://www.uspharmacist.com/ oldformat.asp?url=newlook/files/Phar/pharm_law1.htm&pub_id=8&article_id=776

Vivian JC. Whistleblower liability. *US Pharm.* 1994;4:52.

Vivian JC. Who is liable in a case of prolonged drug use? *US Pharm.* 1999;3:48 (http://www.uspharmacist.com/NewLook/DisplayArticle.cfm?item_num=168).

Vivian JC. Wrongful disclosure of prescription records. *US Pharm.* 1997;11:118.

Vivian JC, Brushwood DB. Monitoring prescriptions for legitimacy. *Am Pharm.* 1991;9:32.

Vivian JC, Slaughter RL. Generic drug interchange of narrow therapeutic index drugs: Clinical and legal issures for pharmacists. *J Mich Pharm.* 1997;11:24.

Weinstein BD, Brushwood DB. Reimbursement for expensive new drugs. *US Pharm.* 1991;16:64-65.

White BD, Hamner ME. Entrapment. *US Pharm.* 1981;6:17-19, 24.

White BD, Johnston PE, Hamner ME. Institutional pharmacists: Specialists with special liability. *Leg Asp Pharm Pract.* 1980;2:3-4.

Williams KG. Absence of liability in Illinois for failing to warn of a drug interaction. *Am J Hosp Pharm.* 1993;50:2095-2098.

Williams KG. Pharmacist's duty to warn of drug interactions. *Am J Hosp Pharm.* 1992;49:2787-2789.

Williams KG. Right of a defendant to refuse antipsychotic medication during a trial. *Am J Hosp Pharm.* 1993;50:1937-1939.

Witmer DR, Liang FZ. Reporting of adverse drug reactions and physician liability. *Am J Hosp Pharm.* 1992;49:538, 544.

Study Questions

CIVIL LIABILITY

(1) Which of the following would not be considered negligence?
   (a) Doing something that a reasonable person would not do.
   (b) Doing something incorrectly.
   (c) Not doing something that a reasonable person would do.
   (d) a and b
   (e) none of the above

(2) The most likely claims that pharmacists will have to face in cases involving drug product selection include which of the following?
   (a) Strict liability
   (b) Negligence
   (c) Breach of warranty
   (d) b and c
   (e) all of the above

(3) Typically, under state Medicaid systems, pharmacists are reimbursed for filling Medicaid prescriptions on the basis of:
   (a) the maximum allowable cost plus a dispensing fee.
   (b) a state-determined estimated acquisition cost.
   (c) the pharmacist's customary charge.
   (d) a, b, or c—whichever figure is lower.
   (e) a, b, or c—whichever figure is higher.

(4) Ben and Javier, who work as pharmacists at a large supermarket, are discussing liability issues. Ben says he's concerned because recently he refused to fill a prescription for a customer. Javier reassures Ben that as long as he had a "good reason," he acted within his rights. Which of the following would be considered a "good reason" in this case?
   (a) Ben thought the prescription would be harmful to the patient because of an error by the prescriber.
   (b) Ben suspected that the prescription was forged.
   (c) Ben did not have the drug in stock.
   (d) a and c
   (e) all of the above

(5) Javier also is concerned about liability—in the area of maintaining patient records. "What's my responsibility when it comes to keeping patient profiles?" he asks. "Can I refuse to keep them?" Ben explains, correctly, that:
   (a) Javier can avoid liability by simply not maintaining patient profiles.
   (b) if Javier's state requires pharmacists to maintain patient profiles, his failure to do so could constitute negligence per se.
   (c) if Javier keeps his patient profiles on his pharmacy's computer, he is relieved from liability.
   (d) b and c
   (e) none of the above

(6) A pharmacy technician is a nonlicensed individual who assists the registered pharmacist in all of the following except:

(a) drug labeling

(b) drug distribution

(c) recordkeeping

(d) drug packaging

(e) none of the above (pharmacy technicians perform all of these tasks)

(7) A mechanical error has occurred when the pharmacist dispenses:

(a) the correct drug in the wrong strength.

(b) the wrong drug in the correct strength.

(c) the correct drug in the correct strength but with the wrong directions.

(d) all of the above

(e) none of the above

(8) Ben and Javier compare notes on some unfortunate errors they have committed as pharmacists. Javier admits that he once dispensed *Isordil* 10 mg tablets for *Inderal* 10 mg tablets after misreading the prescription. This would be considered a(n):

(a) error of inexperience.

(b) error of inadvertence.

(c) labeling error.

(d) intellectual error.

(e) none of the above

(9) Ben tells Javier that he once failed to indicate the number of tablets dispensed on a vial of *Atavan*. This omission is considered a(n):

(a) error of inexperience.

(b) error of inadvertence.

(c) labeling error.

(d) intellectual error.

(e) drug product selection error.

(10) Both Ben and Javier can remember a time when they failed to recognize a problem in a prescription as written by the physician, thus potentially putting the patient at risk. In these cases, Javier and Ben committed:

(a) errors of inexperience.

(b) errors of inadvertence.

(c) labeling errors.

(d) drug product selection errors.

(e) none of the above

(11) Which of the following statements concerning the sealed container doctrine is true?

(a) This rule applies if the dispensed prescription is an unopened full bottle.

(b) This rule applies when the pharmacist neither compounds, adds, nor takes anything away from the drug product as it is prepared by the manufacturer.

(c) This rule applies if the amount dispensed is counted or poured from the manufacturer's container.

(d) a and b

(e) all of the above

(12) What doctrine or defense is crucial to the advance of clinical research trials?
  (a) Statute of limitations
  (b) Voluntary assumption of the risk
  (c) Res ipsa loquitur
  (d) Improper parties
  (e) none of the above

(13) Which of the following statements concerning statute of limitations is true?
  (a) A statute of limitations is a legislatively imposed time limit within which a lawsuit must be resolved or the plaintiff will lose the right to sue forever.
  (b) In most states, the statute of limitations for a professional negligence claim is 1 or 2 years.
  (c) The myriad of lawsuits filed by daughters of women who received DES in the 1950s and 1960s resulted in the courts shortening the statute of limitations in such cases.
  (d) a and b
  (e) b and c

(14) Res ipsa loquitur:
  (a) translated literally means "the act does not speak for itself."
  (b) sometimes is referred to in health care circles as the doctrine of informed consent.
  (c) is a legal theory of recovery that is applied in a negligence suit in which the plaintiff cannot prove the defendant's negligence but the resulting injury could have happened only as a result of the defendant's negligence.
  (d) a and c
  (e) b and c

(15) A "claims made" policy:
  (a) means that if a claim is filed while the policy is in force, the insurance carrier assumes liability for any errors or omissions committed during that policy period.
  (b) provides more certainty for the insurer.
  (c) means that a company will not be responsible for claims reported after the policy has ended.
  (d) means that claims are covered regardless of the year in which they are reported, as long as the policy is renewed each year.
  (e) all of the above

(16) Which of the following statements is true?
  (a) Generally, a pharmacist would prefer to purchase liability insurance written on an occurrence basis.
  (b) Generally, a pharmacist would prefer to purchase liability insurance written on a "claims made" basis.
  (c) Insurance written on a "claims made" basis will provide longer protection.
  (d) Typically, "extended reporting" coverage is available for extensions of 5 years.
  (e) b and c

(17) Typically, liability policies do not cover:
  (a) property damage.
  (b) bodily injury.
  (c) personal injury.
  (d) damages caused by slander.
  (e) none of the above (a, b, c, and d would all be covered)

(18) A sale is:
    (a) a contract for the transfer of investment securities.
    (b) a contract for services.
    (c) a contract in which title or ownership of property is exchanged for money.
    (d) a contract for the lease of personal property.
    (e) a and c

(19) Express warranties:
    (a) are not sufficiently established by an affirmation of fact or a promise made by the seller to the buyer that relates to the goods.
    (b) are those present in the transaction because of something the seller said that induced the buyer to purchase the goods.
    (c) generally relate to the ability of the product to perform.
    (d) b and c
    (e) all of the above

(20) A writ of mandamus is:
    (a) the withholding of a license or permit.
    (b) the legal method to force the board to issue the license or permit.
    (c) a court order that compels a government agency to perform its duty or function under the law.
    (d) a court injunction against a pharmacy.
    (e) b and c

(21) A declaratory judgment suit:
    (a) is judicial relief sought by court order or injunction enjoining the agency or board from enforcing a presumably unfair regulation or order.
    (b) is a special legal procedure to compel or prohibit an administrative officer from acting or not acting.
    (c) is a preferred method for seeking a court ruling on an administrative action before the action is enforced.
    (d) protects judicial officers from civil suits when acting within their authority.
    (e) a and c

(22) Mr. Vittitoe is an individual who is affected by an administrative action but chooses to simply ignore the action. The method Mr. Vittitoe is using is referred to as a:
    (a) petition.
    (b) collateral attack.
    (c) suit in equity.
    (d) doctrine of judicial immunity.
    (e) none of the above

(23) A suit in equity:
    (a) is judicial relief sought by court order or injunction enjoining the agency or board from enforcing a presumably unfair regulation or order.
    (b) is a special legal procedure to compel or prohibit an administrative officer from acting or not acting.
    (c) is a preferred method for seeking a court ruling on an administrative action before the action is enforced.
    (d) protects judicial officers from civil suits when acting within their authority.
    (e) exists where a specific administrative action may be reviewed by the courts pursuant to an enabling provision in the statute that authorizes the specific administrative action.

(24) _____ is the usual preferred way to bring court action when a state pharmacy board fails to act on a pharmacy permit application or pharmacist license renewal.

(a) A suit in equity

(b) The doctrine of judicial immunity

(c) A writ of mandamus

(d) A direct judicial review

(e) none of the above

(25) Which of the following statements is true?

(a) Collateral attack is the preferred route when the violation of an administrative regulation is punishable as a crime pursuant to the authority of a state or federal law.

(b) Equity or equitable relief is a legal system applied by the courts to effect justice when the ordinary legal remedies will not suffice or when great injury might result unless immediate judicial action is taken.

(c) The doctrine of judicial immunity has not been extended by state or federal courts to any individuals other than those occupying judicial positions.

(d) The purpose of the doctrine of judicial immunity is to allow individuals aggrieved by a judge's decision to sue the judge.

(e) none of the above

(26) Differentiate between the concepts of malpractice, negligence, and mistake.

(27) Can the courts be called on to establish the standards of performance in any industry or professional field? If no, why not? If yes, when might this be likely to occur?

(28) Marty is a pharmacist accused in a negligence case. He has just been informed that the prosecutor is planning to invoke statutory negligence to establish duty on Marty's part. Under what conditions can a statute be used to establish duty in a negligence case?

(29) Marty tells his colleague Birgit that he doesn't believe a statute can be used to establish a pharmacist's duty in a negligence case. Birgit disagrees and tells him, "Just think about the federal Poison Prevention Packaging Act. That's a perfect example of how a statute can be used." Use the Poison Prevention Packaging Act to argue who is right in this case. In other words, identify specific examples of how this Act might—or might not—fulfill each of the criteria required to establish duty.

(30) What is the difference between mechanical and intellectual errors? Which are more common in lawsuits against pharmacists and pharmacies?

(31) Discuss the pharmacist's duty to counsel patients, focusing in particular on the following issues: (a) Who is in the best position to know the patient's complete medical history and to decide which facts to tell the patient? (b) What should be the pharmacist's role in risk management? (c) Does risk management by the pharmacist interfere with the physician-patient relationship? Explain why or why not.

(32) Why have many courts been unwilling to recognize the pharmacist's duty to warn?

(33) What are the "Good Samaritan" laws?

(34) Differentiate between generic substitution, therapeutic alternates, and therapeutic substitution.

(35) Discuss the future of therapeutic substitution. (a) Why is it gaining popularity? (b) How might it potentially affect research-oriented pharmaceutical manufacturers? (c) What is the medical profession's response to therapeutic substitution?

(36) Describe the hospital formulary system. What does it mean for the pharmacist?

(37) Mark and Kristen, 2 pharmacy students, are studying for an upcoming exam. As they begin reviewing liability for drug product selection, Mark says he doesn't understand what the concern is in this area. "Once I'm a pharmacist," he says, "as long as I dispense from the FDA's approved drug list, I'm protected from liability." Kristen shakes her head and replies, "No, Mark, there are more variables involved than that." What is Kristen referring to? Identify variables that affect the pharmacist's liability under the drug product selection laws.

(38) Kristen decides to quiz Mark further to make sure he hasn't overlooked other areas of liability for the pharmacist. "What if a third-party drug plan requires you to substitute a drug that isn't recognized as therapeutically equivalent to the brand name product prescribed?" she asks him. "What can you do to minimize your liability in that situation? How might a particular court case—even though it didn't involve the practice of pharmacy—be used as a precedent in product selection liability cases?" Help Mark answer Kristen's questions.

(39) Mark seems fairly rattled by the level of liability faced by pharmacists. "I've heard enough about product selection liability," he says. "What's my liability if I make an error in recommending a drug or giving a patient drug information and my error allegedly results in an injury?" How should Kristen respond?

(40) Describe what is meant by direct causation.

(41) Explain the distinction between claims of strict liability and warranty in tort.

(42) Antonio's policy at his pharmacy is to keep the prescription records of family members together on one profile. Nicole, a pharmacist working for Antonio, suggests that he change this policy and keep a separate profile for each person's records. What should Antonio do? Discuss the advantages and disadvantages of having an entire family's prescription records on one profile.

(43) Before working for Antonio, Nicole was a pharmacist at a hospital where many prescriptions were dispensed in unit-dose packaging. She wonders why unit-dose packaging is not used to dispense drugs at Antonio's pharmacy. How can Antonio best explain this? Describe the unit dose system. What are some advantages and disadvantages of the system?

(44) Because Nicole has not been at the pharmacy long, Antonio occasionally monitors her work. One day as she finishes filling a prescription, he says, "You did everything right—except for one thing. You forgot to record the lot number." Why is it a good idea for the pharmacist to record the lot number of the drug dispensed on the prescription?

(45) A purchaser wishes to sue on the grounds of breach by the seller of implied or express warranty. What must be his or her first step? What is the purpose of this step?

(46) Jack, a licensee, is accused of a pharmacy law violation. What happens if he admits to the violation at a formal board hearing?

(47) If a pharmacist is faced with simultaneous board disciplinary actions and criminal prosecution for the same alleged violation, can he or she be excused for inaction in one matter on the basis that it might jeopardize his or her cause in the other?

(48) On what grounds may a pharmacy board's administrative agency action be challenged?

(49) What type of power or function is being used by the pharmacy board in each of the following situations? (a) Joanna has applied for a pharmacy license. The pharmacy board prepares an examination to test Joanna's competence and knowledge. (b) The pharmacy board issues a pharmacy permit to Alan, an applicant who has fulfilled the statutory requirements for equipment and payment fees.

(50) Suppose the pharmacy board enforces a regulation that specifies certain physical and locational requirements for Alan's pharmacy. If Alan appeals to the courts, on what grounds may he have a case?

(51) Eventually, Alan gets his pharmacy running. Unfortunately, he soon is accused in a pharmacy board disciplinary action. Identify and explain Alan's constitutional rights in this case.

(52) Despite all his problems, Alan's pharmacy stays in business long enough for him to apply for a renewal of his license to practice. After he applies, Alan receives notice from the pharmacy board that he must submit evidence of his participation in continuing professional education as a prerequisite to renewing his license. Alan believes that the board's action in this case is not legal—and that his right to practice his profession is being unreasonably threatened. Is he right? Why or why not? Discuss both sides of the argument briefly.

(53) A pharmaceutical services section appears in the JCAHO's accreditation manual for hospitals. Complete the following table to identify 6 basic standards and the commission's interpretation of each standard:

JCAHO Pharmaceutical Services Section Standards		
Standards	Identification	JCAHO Interpretation
Standard I		
Standard II		
Standard III		
Standard IV		
Standard V		
Standard VI		

(54) Match each type of implied warranty with its corresponding description. Implied warranty of merchantability _____ Implied warranty of title _____ Implied warranty of sale by sample or description _____ Implied warranty of fitness for a particular purpose _____

(a) The seller implicitly warrants that he has legal ownership to the goods he is selling and that he can deliver good and complete ownership rights to the purchaser.

(b) A patient approaches a pharmacist, describes her symptoms, and asks the pharmacist to recommend therapeutic measures that will alleviate those symptoms (relying on the pharmacist's judgment and skill).

(c) This implied warranty does not require the product to be the best available on the market but merely that it be fit for sale. This implied warranty may be breached if the product is decomposed, putrid, subpotent, or outdated.

(d) If the buyer has supplied to the seller an example or a written explanation of the product desired, then the seller implicitly guarantees that the product provided will meet that implied warranty.

Critical Thinking Activities

(1) Form teams; then, using the discussion of several court cases, prepare a presentation that contrasts how 2 cases dealt differently with the pharmacist's duty to warn. Create an in-class quiz about the cases, and have students predict answers to the questions before you give your presentation.

(2) Work in teams, with each team creating 3 scenarios that illustrate applications of 3 distinct principles of the code of ethics for pharmacists. As each scenario is presented to the entire class, all teams should participate in identifying the applicable principles in each case.

Case Study 1: An Orientation

Clark has begun working for Jan's Pharmacy. Because this is a new pharmacy and many of the recently hired staff are also new, Clark is asked to run a brief orientation on pharmacy law in his state. As the first few sessions proceed, however, Clark realizes he needs to allow more time for questions and answers: This group has a lot of good questions.

(1)   During a discussion of civil liability, Mary says, "I know a guy from pharmacy school who said that his dad once dispensed the wrong drug. Is that a civil liability issue?" "No," Ian volunteers. "A mistake like that could lead to a criminal conviction. Forget civil law." "Well," Karen says, "mistakes can happen; unless it's fatal or something, I think simple mistakes like that are a matter of license suspension. It's more an administrative issue." All three look to Clark for the answer. Who is right?

(2)   While the group is discussing negligence, Ian says, "I worry that I'll forget to do something. I don't even know for sure what!" Karen says, "The only way a pharmacist can be negligent is by doing something incorrectly. What I mean is, you can't get in trouble for something you didn't do. That would be ridiculous." Who do you agree with? Why?

(3)   As a final part of orientation, Clark has his trainees fill several prescriptions; he supervises their work and then they talk about them together afterwards. First, Mary dispenses a federal legend medication in a container without a safety closure. Clark notices that neither the prescriber nor the patient has requested a standard cap. He stops her, explaining, and then asks, "If a child were to gain access to this medication and suffer damages as a result of this cap, how might the plaintiff's attorney most easily establish duty?" "By the testimony of professional peers," Ian says. "By statutory negligence," says Mary, blushing. Who is correct?

(4)   Ian is uncomfortable with the issues surrounding drug product selection. He asks, "Can a pharmacist be made to face a claim of breach of warranty and strict liability for actual product liability?" "What do you guys think?" asks Clark. "I think 'no'," Karen says, "not if it is the product that is at fault. Then it becomes the responsibility of the manufacturer." "I'm not so sure about that," Mary says. "I think you can even incur criminal charges if a case goes bad." Is either pharmacist right? Explain.

Case Study 2: Elements of Negligence

Several pharmacists have been reported to your state's board of pharmacy for investigation of possible negligence. Your job is to weed through submissions and determine, at least initially, how likely each case is to be deemed negligence. Then you will report your initial suspicions—with rationale—to the investigator assigned to each case. Begin by listing the 4 elements of negligence; ensure that you understand what each means. Then evaluate each case below for the presence of elements of negligence.

(1)   Pierce has decided he is tired of the risks that his more experienced colleagues have run into by keeping patient profiles. "It's ridiculous!" a friend tells him over dinner one night. "I keep these meticulous files, right? And then they're used against me because I missed a potential drug-drug interaction!" This is not the first time Pierce has heard of this happening, so he decides, "If I don't even keep patient profiles, then they can't be used against me. I can't get in trouble if I don't even know." What, if any, is the flaw in Pierce's logic? Defend or debate his stance.

(2)   Trevor is charged with missing a potentially hazardous drug-drug interaction; his patient has suffered some damages as a direct result, and she sues Trevor. The plaintiff's attorney is trying to establish that Trevor should have detected this drug-drug interaction by showing that he had a duty to do this. Trevor's attorney learns that the plaintiff plans to bring in as an expert witness a pharmacist who has specialized in the study of drug-drug interactions. Should this pharmacist be allowed to testify to create the standard of expected performance for Trevor? Discuss both sides of this issue; what is an "expert witness" in a pharmacy case?

(3)   In a single evening, Irma has filled several prescriptions for *Elavil*, an antidepressant drug, in 25 mg tablets. Soon a customer presents her with a prescription for *Edecrin*, a potent diuretic, in 25 mg tablets. Glancing at it, Irma thinks it is *Elavil* once again, and that is what she dispenses. In her defense, she talks about that evening's orders and also points out that both *Elavil* and *Edecrin* are marketed by the same drug firm and are packaged in similar containers with similar labels. (a) What type of dispensing error has Irma made? (b) What aspect of negligence is she possibly guilty of?

(4)   Cal fills a prescription for a potent narcotic analgesic to a 17-year-old patient who is recovering from surgery after fracturing his wrist in a fall while skateboarding. When the young man's wrist heals, he finds that he cannot use his hand completely. His parents file suit against the manufacturer of the pain medication, claiming it has disabled their son. However, the trial establishes that the permanent damage occurred as a result of an improper setting of the broken bone. Around this same time, Cal's friend Amy dispenses *Reserpoid* 1.0 mg to a patient suffering from hypertension. This is a new medication for his patient and he finds it gives him vertigo. He even faints once, but assumes this is an expected side effect. Finally, though, he has vertigo while bike riding and falls, injuring himself. At the hospital, it is discovered that Amy has committed a dispensing error; the prescription was for *Reserpoid* 0.1 mg. Amy's attorney argues at trial that the patient should have contacted either the physician or the pharmacist when he noticed the side effects. It is ruled, in the end, that this was true, and the patient could not recover damages. Identify doctrines related to proximal cause that affect rulings in these 2 cases.

(5)   A patient leaves Oscar's pharmacy with a prescription for a skin medication. Once home, she opens the package to apply the medication and is puzzled to find that it is a semisolid in a tube. Based on her discussion with the dermatologist, she expected to receive a liquid in a bottle that she would have to shake before applying. Carefully saving the unused cream, she calls her physician in the morning and discovers Oscar is the one in error. She files a lawsuit against Oscar, alleging negligence. What are her chances of winning?

Case Study 3: Minimizing Liability

(1)   A patient comes into Garcia's pharmacy late at night, 30 minutes before closing time at 11. "Thank goodness I got here before closing time!" she puffs, out of breath. "I just got off work on the night shift, and my mother would be in big trouble without having this prescription filled tonight!" "Have a seat!" Smiling, Garcia takes the prescription from her. On close inspection, however, Garcia sees that he does not have specific information about dosage form for this drug. He calls the prescriber for the missing data, but after nearly 30 minutes, the prescriber cannot be reached. He is told the physician is out of town, but no one knows for sure how to reach him. Garcia's biggest dilemma is the fact that he can see by the nature of the prescription that this patient might suffer if administration of the drug is unduly delayed. What should Garcia do?

(2)   Ivana has discovered an error in dispensing. What should she do? Does she have to notify the patient in every case?

(3) Monika has noticed that she receives an inordinate number of telephoned prescriptions from several physicians in the community. Several times she has had to call back and verify certain information and has found that several of these original orders were either incomplete or inaccurate. What can she do to minimize liability and increase accuracy in dispensing oral prescriptions by phone?

(4) Monika's employer is pleased with the way she has handled the issue of telephoned prescriptions and asks her to create a list of strategies for minimizing dispensing errors in general. "Make it some sort of 1-page chart or list," she tells Monika, "something that can be distributed to the rest of the staff and that can be displayed easily." What kinds of points should be included in Monika's chart?

Case Study 4: Insurance Issues

(1) Jamal and Maria are both starting out as pharmacists. Both graduated at the top of their class together and have remained friends ever since. Maria mentions that she is looking for "good professional liability insurance." "What a waste," Jamal says. "What do you mean?" asks Maria. "Well, you're good. You're one of the best. Some insurance agent's going to make some money off of you!" "No," Maria says. "I need this. So do you, dummy. The question is, what type." "Type? Now they're throwing choices at you?" Jamal laughs. "This is serious," Maria says. "Listen to me." (a) Explain why Jamal should purchase professional liability insurance. (b) Describe 2 main types of professional liability insurance for pharmacists.

(2) Jamal and Maria each purchase liability policies. Maria's is much more expensive. Knowing nothing more specific about their situations, predict why Maria's is more expensive.

(3) One year later, Maria is involved in consulting and Jamal is an independent contractor. Their friend Min is also a self-employed consultant. Suggest liability insurance needs for each.

Chapter 7

Court Cases

PART I: NEGLIGENCE (MALPRACTICE), 327
Duty and Breach of Duty, 327
    Existence of a Duty, 327
    General Duty of Care, 330
    The Reasonable Person, 331
    Specific Duty of Care, 331
    Standard of Conduct (Determining the "Standard of Care"), 331
    Customary Practice, 334
    Voluntary Assumption of Duty, 334
    Advertising as the Basis of a Duty, 336
    OBRA-90 and Practice Standards, 336
    Contract Duty as a Negligence Standard of Care, 337
    Violation of Statute, 338
    Rules of Law, 338
Specific Duties for Pharmacists, 338
    Prescription Processing Errors, 338
      Factors Associated with Errors, 338
      Personnel, 338
      Environment, 339
      Systems Issues, 339
    Classes of Error, 343
      Wrong Drug, 343
      Wrong Dosage or Strength, 355
      Wrong Labeling or Directions, 359
      Wrong Route of Administration, 361
      Unauthorized Refill, 362
      Compounding Errors, 368
    Prison Services, 368
    Detection, Monitoring and Warning of Potential Problems, 372
      Duty to Warn, 372
      Refusal of Offer to Counsel, 377
      Adequate Directions for Use, 378
      Side Effects, 378
      Drug-Drug Interactions, 383
      Excessive Dosages (including refills), 393
      Contraindications, 401
      Special Knowledge of the Pharmacist, 401
      Limits on the Pharmacist's Duty to Warn, 401
      Interference with the Physician-Patient Relationship, 408
      Mandated Warnings (OBRA-90), 410
      Failure to Monitor Drug Therapy, 410
      The Duty to Detect Problems, 411
      Addiction, 412
      Drug-Disease Contraindications, 413
      Allergies, 414
      Suicide Prevention, 416
      Confidentiality, Privacy, and Privilege, 419
    Failure to Dispense Necessary Medication, 422

PART I: NEGLIGENCE (MALPRACTICE) *(cont.)*

Imputed Duty, 423
    Vicarious Liability, 423
    Servants, 426
Limitations on Duty, 427
    Trespassing, 427
    Licensees, 428
    Invitees, 428
Causation, 428
    Actual Cause, 428
    Proximate Cause, 430
    Unforeseeable Consequences, 436
    Intervening Causes, 436
Damages, 436
    General, 436
    Compensatory, 443
    Punitive, 444
    Bystander Damages, 452
    Other Forms of Recovery, 457
    Apportionment of Damages, 457
Evidence (Proof), 460
    Functions of Court and Jury, 460
    Burden of Proof and Presumptions, 461
Joint Tortfeasors, 464
    Joinder of Defendants, 464
    Defenses, 465
        Comparative and Contributory Negligence, 465
        Wrongful Conduct by Plaintiff, 468
        Immunities, 471
Malpractice Insurance, 475

PART II: STRICT LIABILITY (PRODUCTS LIABILITY), 476

    Distinction Between Negligence, Strict Liability and Products Liability, 476
    Basis of Liability, 478
    Drug Products Liability and Pharmacists, 480
        Negligent Misrepresentation, 480
        Manufacturing Defect, 482
        Warning Defect, 486
        Failure to Warn as a Products Liability Claim, 495
        Breach of Warranty, 506
        Learned Intermediary Rule, 508

PART III: PREMISES LIABILITY, 514

PART IV: INTENTIONAL TORTS, 514
    Interference With The Person, 514
    Battery and Assault, 514
    False Imprisonment, 515
    Infliction of Mental Distress, 518
    Outrageous Conduct, 519
    Defamation, 519
    Libel and Slander, 520
    Invasion of Privacy, 520
    Malicious Prosecution, 521
    Injurious Falsehood, 521
    Interference with Prospective Advantage, 522
    Defenses, 523
        Privilege, 523
        Mistake, 523
        Necessity, 523

PART V: PROCEDURAL ISSUES, 524
    General, 524
    Jurisdiction, 524
    Fraudulent Joinder, 525
    Affidavit Requirement, 530
    Statute of Limitations, 531
    Discovery, 538
    Expert Witness Testimony, 542
    Injunctions, 550
    Insurance Coverage, 550
    Successor Liability, 551
    Privileges, 551
    Evidence and Procedure, 552
    Attorney Fees, 552

PART VI: CONTRACT LAW, 553
    General, 553
    Elements, 570
    Fraud, 571
    Corporate and Individual Liability, 574
    Leases and Restrictive Covenants, 575
    Third Party Reimbursement, 576
    State Mandated Rebates, 579
    Education, 580
    Discriminatory Pricing, 581
    Promissory Notes, 582
    Any Willing Provider, 583

PART VII: ANTITRUST AND RELATED TRADE LAWS, 584
    Federal Antitrust Law, 584
    Federal Trade Commission Act, 601
    State Trade Laws, 601
    Employee Retirement Income Security Act (ERISA), 606

PART VIII: REGULATION OF THE PRACTICE OF PHARMACY, 609
State Regulation of the Practice of Pharmacy, 609
    Boards of Pharmacy, 609
    Enabling Legislation: The Practice Act, 610
    Board Membership, 610
    Powers and Duties, 611
    Immunity of Board Members, 615
    Definition of the Practice of Pharmacy, 616
    Requirements for Licensure, 619
    Disciplinary Action, 621
        Unprofessional Conduct, 621
        Conviction of a Crime, 625
        Violation of a Statute or Regulation, 629
        Disciplinary Procedures, 637
Pharmacy Practice, 660
Confidentiality, 661
Nonpharmacist Personnel, 662
Specific Areas of Regulation, 666
    Advertising, 666
    Dispensing Prescription Drugs, 674
    Record Keeping Requirements, 677
    Drug Product Selection, 679
    Poisons, 679
    Operating a Pharmacy, 679
    The Medication-Use Process, 683
        Prescribing, 683
        Dispensing, 683
        Packaging, 685
        Labeling, 685
        Drug-Drug Interactions, 685
Criminal Law, 685

PART IX: REGULATION OF DRUGS AND RELATED SUBSTANCES, 688
Federal Food, Drug and Cosmetic Act, 688
    The 1938 Act, 688
    Subsequent Amendments, 688
    Regulation of Human Drugs, 688
        Misbranding Provisions, 688
        New Drug Developments, 690
        Production of Drugs, 690
        Drug Marketing, 691
        Unlabeled Indications, 696
        Compounding, 698
        Labeling, 701
        Patient-Directed Labeling, 702
        Insulin, 704
        Generic Drug Products, 705
        Nonprescription Drugs, 706
        Dietary Supplements, 707
        Medical Devices, 709
        Patents, 710
        Trademarks, 712

PART IX: REGULATION OF DRUGS AND RELATED SUBSTANCES
  (cont.)
  Federal Food, Drug and Cosmetic Act *(cont.)*
    Regulation of Human Drugs *(cont.)*
      Personal Use Exemption, 712
  Controlled Substances, 713
    In General, 713
    Drug Enforcement Administration, 724
    Prescriptions, 726
      Record Keeping, 726
      Drug Diversion and Abuse, 728
      Corresponding Responsibility of the Pharmacist, 730
      Forged and Fraudulent Prescriptions, 732
    Inventory Requirements, 735
    Continuing Records, 739
    Inspections, 740
      The Fourth Amendment, 740
      Administrative Inspections, 745
    Penalties, 757
    Conflicts with State Laws, 759
    Use of the US Postal Service, 759

PART X: EMPLOYMENT LAW, 760
  Contractual Issues, 760
      Express Contract (Just Cause Termination), 760
      Implied Contract (At Will Termination), 761
      Overtime Pay, 764
      Whistleblowing, 765
      Public Policy Retaliation, 768
  Discrimination, 772
      Age, 772
      Disability (Americans with Disabilities Act), 773
      Equal Employment Opportunity Commissions Procedures, 778
      Gender Harassment (Sexual), 778
      Hostile Work Environment, 780
      Public Service Obligations, 782
      Race, Color, or National Origin, 784
      Religion, 790
  Independent Contractors (Tax Issues), 791
  Noncompetition Clauses, 791
  Theft From Employer, 793
  Unemployment Benefits, 793
  Unions, 794
  Workers Compensation, 794
      General Issues, 794
      Exclusive Remedy, 795

Sources of Additional Information, 796

PART I: NEGLIGENCE (MALPRACTICE)

DUTY AND BREACH OF DUTY

Existence of a Duty

McLaughlin v Hook-SupeRx Inc.
642 N.E. 2d 514 (Ind. 1994)

ISSUE: Whether a pharmacist has a duty to cease refilling prescriptions for a patient who is receiving controlled substances at an unreasonably faster rate than the rate prescribed (without receiving explicit directions from the prescribing physician).

FACTS: The plaintiff, Patrick McLaughlin, injured his back while working as a lumberjack in the state of Washington. In the course of treatment for that injury, he became addicted to propoxyphene, the active ingredient in *Darvocet* and *Darvon*. He was treated for the addiction in 1982, 1983, and 1987, but did not stop using the drug.

In 1988, the plaintiff was still experiencing pain from the injury and he began treatment with a physician in South Bend, Indiana. Over a period of months, the plaintiff obtained prescriptions for drugs containing propoxyphene from his physician. Most of these prescriptions were filled at a Hook's Pharmacy in South Bend. The prescriptions were dispensed on the basis of written prescriptions brought to the pharmacy by the plaintiff, via telephone calls to the store from the doctor's office, or as refills.

McLaughlin consumed these drugs at a rate much faster than prescribed. The pharmacy records show that dozens of prescriptions for *Darvocet* and *Darvon* were filled for the plaintiff between May 1987 and December 1988. For example, during one 60-day period in 1988, the plaintiff received 24 separate refills of propoxyphene-containing prescriptions, totaling 1072 capsules. If consumed according to the prescriptions, the number of capsules would have lasted 138 days, but instead the plaintiff consumed them in 62 days.

In late 1988, the physician apparently became aware that McLaughlin was consuming the drugs at a much faster rate than prescribed. He refused to furnish any more prescriptions. Shortly thereafter, McLaughlin's wife found her husband holding a shotgun to his head during a time of depression. He did not pull the trigger. Following treatment for drug addiction in early 1989, McLaughlin stopped taking all prescription pain medication. The plaintiff sought recovery against the pharmacy on the theory that it breached its duty of care by failing to refuse to dispense the prescriptions because the pharmacists knew or should have known that McLaughlin was consuming the drugs so frequently that it posed a threat to his health. Hook's moved for a summary judgment on the grounds that it owed no such duty or, alternatively, that the plaintiff's consumption of the drugs and his suicide attempt constituted an intervening cause of his injuries.

RULING: The Indiana Court of Appeals concluded that no duty existed and that imposition of a duty would be contrary to public policy because it would undermine the physician/patient relationship. The Court of Appeals remanded the case with instructions for the trial court to enter summary judgment in favor of Hook's. The case was transferred to the Supreme Court of Indiana, which affirmed the trial court's decision denying the pharmacy's motion for summary judgment.

REASONING: Without a legal duty, there can be no recovery in negligence. Whether the law recognizes any obligation on the part of a particular defendant to conform to a certain standard for the benefit of the plaintiff is a question of law exclusively for the court. Indi-

McLaughlin v Hook-SupeRx Inc.
642 N.E. 2d 514 (Ind. 1994)
...continued

ana courts have used a 3-part analysis to be applied when deciding whether a duty exists: (1) the relationship between the parties; (2) the foreseeability of the harm; and (3) public policy issues.

It has long been established that the existence of a duty for one to act with a certain standard of care to another arises out of the relationship between the parties. Earlier cases recognize a duty on the part of a pharmacist to follow the physician's instructions on the prescription. In this case, the court was asked to determine whether the pharmacist has a duty under certain circumstances to refrain from dispensing the prescription as written.

The relationship between the pharmacist and patient is a direct one based upon contract and is independent from the relationship between the physician and the patient. It is a matter of common expectation, as well as by statute, that pharmacists possess expertise regarding the dispensing of prescription drugs. Customer-patients rely upon pharmacists for that expertise. Upon the basis, the court concluded that the relationship between the pharmacist and patient is sufficiently close to justify imposing a duty.

The court further noted that it is well-established that a duty is imposed only where a reasonably foreseeable victim is injured by a reasonably foreseeable harm. It was not disputed here that one who consumes sufficient quantities of addictive substances may become addicted to them and that such an addiction carries with it certain reasonably foreseeable consequences. Thus, the court was satisfied that the risk of the plaintiff's addiction was foreseeable from the series of events that took place.

The court perceived three policy considerations at stake here: Preventing intentional and unintentional drug abuse, not jeopardizing the physician/patient relationship, and avoiding unnecessary health care costs.

There were several explanations for why a pharmacy patient might have a prescription for a controlled substance refilled at a rate unreasonably faster than that prescribed. For example, the customer may have developed an addiction to the drug or may have been improperly disposing of the drug. Both of these explanations give rise to a strong public policy interest in preventing intentional and unintentional drug abuse.

Indiana law provides that a pharmacist is to exercise his/her professional judgment in the best interest of the patient's health and that the pharmacist is immune from criminal prosecution or civil liability if he/she, in good faith, refuses to honor a prescription because, in his/her professional judgment, the honoring of that prescription would be contrary to the health and safety of the patient.

The court noted that the statute merely permits, but does not require, a pharmacist to decline to dispense a valid prescription. However, by empowering pharmacists to exercise a professional judgment, the statute does demonstrate that public policy concerns about proper dispensing of prescription drugs and preventing drug addiction might be paramount to policy concerns about interfering with the physician/patient relationship.

The court spent some time reviewing *Ingram v Hook's Drugs, Inc.*, 476 N.E. 2d 881 (Ind. Ct. App. 1985), which held that a pharmacist did not have to warn a patient about possible adverse reactions to *Valium*. The court, in the case at hand, agreed that the responsibility of warning patients about drug side effects lies with physicians. However, it did not find the Ingram case controlling because it did not involve the rate at which the patient was consuming drugs.

McLaughlin v Hook-SupeRx Inc.
642 N.E. 2d 514 (Ind. 1994)
...continued

"Despite Hook's lamentations to the contrary, we do not perceive that physicians and pharmacists will become adversaries if pharmacists are expected to cease refilling prescriptions where the customers are using the drugs much more rapidly than prescribed. First, as has been discussed, pharmacists currently possess that authority by statute. Second, physicians remain ultimately responsible for properly prescribing medication, and recognition of a duty on the part of pharmacists will not replace the physician's obligation to evaluate a patient's needs. We believe recognition of a legal duty will encourage pharmacists and physicians to work together in considering the best interest of their customers and patients."

The court recognized that there was concern over increased health care costs that might result from imposing new duties on pharmacists. However, a Hook's district manager testified that the company used a computerized information system that permitted pharmacists to review the prior history of a patient's prescriptions. The existence of such a system led the court to conclude that the capital investment necessary to comply with the duty had already been made.

Having recognized a duty, the court turned its attention to the standard of care to be imposed on the pharmacists. It concluded that the traditional negligence standard should apply. Pharmacists must exercise the degree of care that an ordinary, prudent pharmacist would have exercised under the same or similar circumstances. The determination of whether due care was exercised may involve such issues as the frequency with which the pharmacists dispensed prescriptions for the customer, any representations made by the customer, the pharmacist's access to historical data about the customer, and the manner in which the prescription was tendered to the pharmacist.

In imposing this standard of care, the court emphasized that dispensing prescriptions faster than prescribed is not necessarily a breach of duty. For example, it may be prudent for a pharmacist to refill a prescription at a faster rate in the first few days following surgery or in anticipation of travel. Given that cases are usually factually unique, any complete listing in the court's opinion was impossible. The court was confident that skilled pharmacists, particularly when aided by computer records, would be able to readily determine when a prescription is being refilled at an unreasonably faster rate than the rate prescribed.

The pharmacy argued that even if it was negligent in dispensing the prescriptions, the plaintiff was barred from any recovery because he caused whatever injuries he sustained. An intervening negligent act breaks the chain of causation only if the harm resulting from the intervening act could not have been reasonably foreseen by the original negligent party. Accordingly, if harm is a natural, probable, and foreseeable consequence of the negligent act, the wrongdoer may be held liable even though other independent acts occur.

Indiana decisions have held that suicide constitutes an intervening cause, if committed by one who is sane enough to realize the effect of his actions. Thus, Indiana courts have held that a pharmacist who negligently sold a poison to the underage son of an individual who used the poison to kill himself could not be held liable for that negligence because the decedent's suicide constituted an intervening cause.

The court noted that suicide constitutes an intervening cause only if it is a "voluntary" and "willful" act of the victim. Suicide induced by mental illness or involuntarily induced by a reaction to the plaintiff's drug addiction may not constitute an intervening cause. This would be an issue for the trial court to determine.

The following is a list of court cases that are related to this topic.

Jones v Walgreen Co., 265 Ill. App. 308 (1932).
Riff v Morgan, 508 A.2d 1247 (Pa. Super. 1986).
Wells v Ortho Pharmaceutical Corp., 788 F.2d 741 (11th Cir. 1986)
Dooley v Everett, et al., Docket No. 01-A-01-9005-CV-00185, Tenn. Ct. App. (1990).
Heredia v Johnson, 827 F. Supp. 1522 (D. Nev. 1993).
Fakhouri v Taylor, 248 Ill. App. 3rd 328; 618 N.E.2d 518, (Ill. App. 1993), Iv.denied, (1993)
    LEXIS 814; 187 Ill. Dec. 927.
Lasley v Shrake's Country Club Pharmacy, Inc., 1994 WL 109647 (Ariz. App. Dir. 1).
Pittman v The Upjohn Company, 1994 WL 663372 (Tenn. Nov. 28, 1994).
Evans v Rite-Aid Corp., 452 S.E.2d 9 (S.C. App. 1994), affirmed, as modified 478 S.E. 2d 846
    (1996).
Cafaralle v Brockton Oaks C.V.S. Inc., No. 94-0414A, (Mass. Super. Ct. April, 1996).
Johnson v Walgreen Co., 675 S.2d 1036 (Fla. Dist Ct. App. 1996).
Saucier v Biloxi Regional Medical Center, Slip Op. No. 97-CA-0079-SCT, March 19, 1998, 1998
    Miss. LEXIS 117.

General Duty of Care

Chiney v American Drug Stores
No WD 56895 (May 2, 2000), 2000 Mo App LEXIS 614

The patient entered a pharmacy that she had never been in before. She had a history of severe asthma and she believed she was suffering an attack when she went to the pharmacy. Her physician had prescribed an albuterol inhaler in the past. She was out of medication and did not have a prescription with her. She asked the pharmacist to provide her with an inhaler or call her doctor or the hospital to verify that the medication had been prescribed. For reasons that are not explained, the pharmacist did not make the call and he refused to provide the requested medication. As a result, the patient was taken to a hospital by ambulance. She claims that she has suffered additional breathing problems from the delay in her treatment caused by the pharmacists refusal to assist her. The defendants, the pharmacy and the pharmacist, moved to dismiss the complaint on the grounds that the pharmacist had no duty to supply prescription-only medication without a prescription and that there is no duty for a pharmacist to call a physician for a prescription when there is no current prescription on file for the patient in the pharmacy. The trial court judge agreed and entered judgment for the defendants. The patient appealed. The Missouri Court of Appeals noted the general rule that there is no legal duty to aid someone in distress unless a special relationship exists between the parties. Using these principles, the Court found that a pharmacist has no legal duty to protect the patient unless there is some established relationship that existed. At best, it could only characterize this relationship as one between a pharmacist and a potential customer. The Court also considered state and federal laws dealing with the rights and obligations of pharmacists. The state's definition of the "practice of pharmacy" includes the "dispensing of drugs pursuant to prescription orders." The Court interpreted the statute and found it does "not describe or anticipate the practice of pharmacy to include calling a doctor or hospital to see if a potential customer, who does not have a written prescription, is entitled to prescription medication when he or she requests prescription medication due to immediate need." The Court went on to observe that a pharmacist is not a medical doctor, does not prescribe or make prescription orders and dispenses drug on the directions of those who are authorized to prescribe. It also noted that the state had amended its Board of Pharmacy regulations to comply with the federal OBRA-90 statute mandating standards regarding pharmacists' consultations with patients. In part, this regulation states: "Upon receipt of a prescription drug order and following a review of the available patient information, a pharmacist or his/her designee shall personally offer to discuss matters which will enhance or optimize drug therapy with each patient or caregiver of each patient." The Court concluded that the duty to consult with a patient arises only when the pharmacist receives a prescription order. The Court affirmed dismissal of the case concluding that the pharmacist had no legal duty to the patient because she had never had a prescription filled at that pharmacy and did not present the pharmacist with a prescription.

The following is a list of court cases that are related to this topic.

Hoar v Rasmussen, 282 N.W. 652 (Wis. 1938).
Heredia v Johnson, 827 F. Supp. 1522 (D. Nev. 1993).
Lasley v Shrake's Country Club Pharmacy, Inc., 1994 WL 109647 (Ariz. App. Dir. 1).
Cafaralle v Brockton Oaks C.V.S. Inc., No. 94-0414A, (Mass. Super. Ct. April, 1996).
Evans v Rite-Aid Corp., 452 S.E.2d 9 (S.C. App. 1994), affirmed, as modified 478 S.E. 2d 846 (1996).

The Reasonable Person

The following is a list of court cases that are related to this topic.

Dooley v Everett, et al., Docket No. 01-A-01-9005-CV-00185, Tenn. Ct. App. (1990).

Specific Duty of Care

The following is a list of court cases that are related to this topic.

Riff v Morgan, 508 A.2d 1247 (Pa. Super. 1986).
France v State of New York, 506 N.Y.S.2d 254 (N.Y. Ct. Claims 1986).
Ferguson v Williams, 374 S.E. 2d 438 (N.C. App. 1988).
Brown v Southern Baptist Hospital, Slip Op. Nos. 96-CA-1990 and 96-CA-1991, La. App. 4th Cir., March 11, 1998, 1998 La. App. LEXIS 556.

Standard of Conduct (Determining the "Standard of Care")

Darling v Charleston Community Memorial Hospital
33 Ill.2d 326, 211 N.E.2d 253 (Ill. 1965)

ISSUE: Whether professional custom is conclusive on issues of professional negligence and whether a hospital may be held liable for negligence of an attending physician.

FACTS: An 18-year-old boy who had to have his leg amputated because a cast was set too tight and the circulation impaired to the extent that gangrene set in, brought suit, by his parents, against the hospital where the cast was set and against the physician who set it. The physician settled out of court for $40,000. Final judgment of the trial court was for the boy in the amount of $110,000 against the hospital. The hospital appealed the case to the Supreme Court of Illinois.

RULING: Judgment for the boy was affirmed.

REASONING: The facts in this case, as reported in the law reports, are rather extensive, but for our purposes here it may be sufficient to say that the physician who set the boy's cast

Darling v Charleston Community Memorial Hospital
33 Ill.2d 326, 2II N.E.2d 253 (Ill. 1965)
...continued

was a general practitioner and that the hospital nurses did not deviate from the standard of care in the community with reference to testing for circulation in the casted leg. Nevertheless, in this "landmark" case the court ruled, in effect, that what was done was not sufficient to the extent of being actionable negligence. In its written decision, the court stated:

> Custom is relevant in determining the standard of care because it illustrates what is feasible, it suggests a body of knowledge of which the defendant should be aware, and it warns of the possibility of far-reaching consequences if a higher standard is required-...but custom should never be conclusive...A whole calling may have unduly lagged in the adoption of new and available devices. It never may set its own tests, however persuasive be its usages. Courts must in the end say what is required; there are precautions so imperative that even their universal disregard will not excuse their omission.

With reference to hospital liability to the attending physician's actions, the court stated:

> Present-day hospitals, as their manner of operation demonstrates, do far more than furnish facilities for treatment...Certainly, the person who avails himself of 'hospital facilities' expects that the hospital will attempt to cure him, not that its nurses or their employees will act on their own responsibility.

On the basis of the evidence before it, the jury could reasonably have concluded that the nurses did not test for circulation in the legs as frequently as necessary, that skilled nurses should have promptly recognized the conditions that signaled a dangerous impairment of circulation in the plaintiff's leg, and would have known that the condition would become irreversible in a matter of hours. At that point, it became the nurses' duty to inform the attending physician, and if he failed to act, to advise hospital authorities so that appropriate action might be taken. As to consultation, there is no dispute that the hospital failed to review the physician's work or require consultation; the only issue is whether its failure to do so was negligence. On the evidence before it, the jury could reasonably have found that it was.

Lasley v Shrake's Country Club Pharmacy, Inc.
880 P.2d 1120 (Ariz. App. 1994)

ISSUE: Whether a pharmacy has a duty to warn a patient or a prescriber regarding the adverse consequences of long-term drug therapy.

FACTS: From 1960 to 1990, Dr. William Helms treated the plaintiff George Lasley with *Doriden* and codeine. Lasley had most of the prescriptions dispensed at Shrake's Country Club Pharmacy. For approximately 10 years, Shrake's mailed the allegedly addictive drugs to Lasley at his residence in another state.

The plaintiff claims that as a result of taking these drugs for an extended period of time, and in combination with each other, he required inpatient hospitalization for detoxification and psychiatric treatment for addiction.

RULING: The trial court dismissed the action and found that a pharmacist owes no legal duty to warn. The Arizona Court of Appeals reversed the decision.

Lasley v Shrake's Country Club Pharmacy, Inc.
880 P.2d 1120 (Ariz. App. 1994)
...continued

REASONING: The appellate court was called upon to determine whether the pharmacy had a duty to conform to a particular standard to protect the patient against unreasonable risks of harm. In other words, whether the relationship between the pharmacy and patient required the pharmacy to use care to avoid or prevent injury to the patient.

The trial court generally decides the question of "duty" as a matter of law. Shrake's contended that the trial court correctly ruled that the pharmacy had no duty to warn the patient or his physician of the potentially addictive nature of the drugs legitimately prescribed for Lasley. However, the appellate court concluded that the trial court's ruling confused the concept of duty with that of standard of care. Specific details of conduct do not determine whether a duty exists but instead bear on whether a defendant who owed a duty to the plaintiff breached the applicable standard of care.

In quoting from a standard legal treatise, the court noted that "duty" is a question of whether the defendant is under any obligation for the benefit of the particular plaintiff. Furthermore, in negligence cases, the duty (if it exists) is always the same—to conform to the legal standard of reasonable conduct in light of the apparent risk. What the defendant must do, or must not do, is a question of the standard of care required to satisfy the duty.

In its answer to the lawsuit, the pharmacy admitted that it owed a duty to the patient to comply with the applicable standard of care. The court agreed. Thus, the trial judge erred in finding, as a matter of law, that the pharmacy owed no duty to Lasley.

Once a court determines that a duty exists, the next question is whether the defendant breached the standard of care established pursuant to the duty. In most cases, whether the defendant's conduct met the standard of care is a question for the trier of fact. Yet, in some cases, the court may decide as a matter of law that the defendant did not breach the applicable standard and thus was not negligent. Thus, even though the trial court incorrectly granted summary judgment based on the issue of duty, if the appellate court could, as a matter of law, conclude that the pharmacy did not breach its standard of care, it could affirm the trial court's judgment in favor of the pharmacy.

The court then went on to examine the issue of standard of care. In cases involving health care providers and other professionals, the standard of care is based upon the usual conduct of other members of the defendant's profession in similar circumstances. The plaintiff must present evidence of the accepted professional conduct so the jury can measure the defendant's conduct against the applicable standard. Contrary to an ordinary negligence action where the standard of care imposed is that of a reasonably prudent person, a higher standard of care is imposed upon pharmacists and other health care providers.

In the case at hand, the plaintiffs presented an affidavit from an expert stating that the standard of care applicable to a pharmacist includes a responsibility to advise a customer of the addictive nature of a drug, to warn of the hazards of ingesting two or more drugs that adversely interact with one another, and to discuss with the physician the addictive nature of the prescribed drug and the dangers of the long-term use of the drug. The plaintiffs also presented excerpts from the APhA's Standard of Practice that describe similar standards. Based on this record, the court could not say as a matter of law that the pharmacy did not breach the standard of care for the duty owed to the patient.

The following is a list of court cases that are related to this topic.

Hoar v Rasmussen, 282 N.W. 652 (Wis. 1938).
Krueger v Knutson, 111 N.W.2d 526 (Minn. 1961).
Hand v Krakowski, 453 N.Y.S.2d 121 (N.Y. App. Div. 1982).
Riff v Morgan, 508 A.2d 1247 (Pa. Super. 1986).
Van Iperen v Van Bramer, 392 N.W.2d 480 (Iowa 1986).
France v State of New York, 506 N.Y.S.2d 254 (N.Y. Ct. Claims 1986).
Ferguson v Williams, 374 S.E. 2d 438 (N.C. App. 1988).
Ramon by and through Ramon v Farr, 770 P.2d 131 (Utah 1989).
Docken v Ciba-Geigy, 790 P. 2d 45 (Or. App. 1990).
Dooley v Everett, et al., Docket No. 01-A-01-9005-CV-00185, Tenn. Ct. App. (1990).
Pittman v Upjohn, 890 S.W.2d 425 (Tenn. App. 1994).
McLaughlin v Hook-SupeRx Inc., 642 N.E. 2d 514 (Ind. 1994).
Pittman v The Upjohn Company, 1994 WL 663372 (Tenn. Nov. 28, 1994).
Horner v Spalitto, Slip Op. No. WD 56282, July 6, 1999, 1999 Mo. App. LEXIS 925.

Customary Practice

The following is a list of court cases that are related to this topic.

Hoar v Rasmussen, 282 N.W. 652 (Wis. 1938).
Darling v Charleston Community Memorial Hospital, 33 Ill. 2d 326, 211 N.E. 2d 253 (Ill. 1965).
Pittman v The Upjohn Company, 1994 WL 663372 (Tenn. Nov. 28, 1994).

Voluntary Assumption of Duty

Baker v Arbor Drugs
544 N.W.2d 727 (Mich. App. 1996), lv. Denied, 454 Mich 853 (1997)

FACTS: A pharmacy, which heavily advertised its use of a computer system to detect danger-ous drug interactions, dispensed *Tavist-D* (a prescription-only drug at the time) to a patient who was also a long-term user of *Parnate* (an MAO inhibitor) for his depression. The patient regularly filled his *Parnate* prescriptions at the same pharmacy. The patient suffered a stroke allegedly caused by a drug-drug interaction between *Parnate* and *Tavist-D*. The patient subsequently committed suicide, leaving a note stating, among other things, that he could no longer live with the effects of the stroke. The patient's wife sued the pharmacy for negligence, fraud, and state consumer protection act violations. The trial court dismissed the case on a summary judgment motion.

HOLDING: The Michigan Appeals Court reinstated all claims based primarily on the phar-macy chain's advertising of its pharmacy computer system that claimed to alert pharma-cists when drug interactions are detected. The dispensing pharmacist testified that the patient label showed that the computer had detected an interaction, but that a pharmacy techni-cian must have overridden the alert screen. The pharmacist stated that she did not see the alert, and would not have dispensed the *Tavist-D* prescription if she had been alerted. The court distinguished a long line of "no duty to warn" precedents in the state on the basis that this pharmacy voluntarily assumed the duty to detect and prevent drug interactions. The case was remanded for trial. The Michigan Supreme Court subsequently denied the chain store's request for an appeal before trial.

Sanderson v Eckerd
Slip Op. No. 5D00955 (February 9, 2001), 2001 Fla. App. LEXIS 1246

This is an appeal from a final order dismissing Count Three of her third amended complaint with prejudice. The trial court concluded that because of the holding in *Johnson v Walgreen Co.*, 675 So. 2d 1036 (Fla. 1st DCA 1996) (a retail pharmacist has no general duty to warn a customer or his physicians of potential adverse prescription drug reaction), the voluntary assumption of duty doctrine, sometimes referred to as the voluntary undertaking doctrine, does not apply to a retail pharmacy and pharmacist dispensing prescription drugs in Florida, but that if it did, the third amended complaint would state a cause of action under that theory. The Florida Court of Appeals disagreed as to both conclusions and reversed. First, it noted that *Johnson* did not involve the voluntary undertaking theory of liability. It reasoned that although there is no case in Florida applying it to a pharmacist dispensing a prescription drug, the doctrine of voluntary assumption of a duty is well established in Florida. It also noted that the courts of other states have applied the doctrine of voluntary undertaking to pharmacists dispensing prescription drugs. See *Frye v Medicare-Glaser Corp.*, 153 Ill. 2d 26, 605 N.E.2d 557, 178 Ill. Dec. 763 (Ill. 1992) (where a pharmacist voluntarily undertakes to place computer-suggested labels on container, duty limited to extent of undertaking and not breached by attaching one correct label but not attaching the other two); *Kasin v Osco Drug Co.*, 312 Ill. App. 3d 823, 728 N.E.2d 77, 245 Ill. Dec. 346 (Ill. App. 2000) (by voluntarily undertaking to list some of a drug's side effects, a pharmacy did not assume a duty to list all possible side effects); *Baker v Arbor Drugs, Inc.*, 215 Mich. App. 198, 544 N.W.2d 727 (Mich. App. 1996) (where pharmacy implemented, used and advertised that its computer program detected harmful drug interactions, pharmacy voluntarily assumed duty to utilize its computer technology with due care); *Ferguson v Williams*, 92 N.C. App. 336, 374 S.E.2d 438 (N.C. App. 1988), appeal after remand, 399 S.E.2d 389 (N.C. App. 1991) (a pharmacist has no generalized duty to warn, but once he is alerted to the specific facts and voluntarily undertakes to advise, he must advise correctly). The appeals court concluded that there is no reason why the voluntary undertaking theory of liability could not be applied to a dispensing Florida pharmacist. The court reasoned that a Florida pharmacist is a health care professional whose standard of care is that level of care and skill which, in light of all relevant circumstances, is recognized as acceptable and appropriate to other reasonably prudent pharmacists. Having reached this conclusion, however, the appeals court went on to find that the trial judge also erred when he concluded that the third amended complaint stated a cause of action under a voluntary undertaking theory had that doctrine been applied. It is axiomatic that a complaint must allege ultimate facts establishing each and every essential element of a cause of action in order to entitle the pleader to the relief sought. It then found that the complaint omits an essential element of her cause of action. It does not allege that Appellant's decedent ingested any of the drugs prescribed. Since that is omitted entirely, there is no allegation that a drug taken by decedent, separately or in combination with one or both of the other two drugs dispensed to decedent, caused him to "become drowsy," lose control of his automobile, hit a tree, and be killed. Consequently, proximate cause, an essential allegation of a cause of action for negligence, is missing from the third amended complaint. It cannot be inferred. The court stated, in addition, that the pleading does not allege that Eckerd's pharmacist entered into performance of its alleged advertised promise that its computer system would detect and warn customers of adverse drug reactions and interactions, and that the performance was negligent as was the situation in *Baker*. The pleading does not say the pharmacist operated the computer negligently, but merely alleges that the computer "would have detected" these dangers and that Eckerd failed to warn decedent of them. Neither does the pleading allege that the decedent relied on Eckerd's advertised promise and for that reason had his prescriptions filled there. Because the court could not say with certainty that she will be unable to state a viable cause of action based on the voluntary undertaking theory, in the interests of justice, it reversed the order of dismissal and directed that an order be entered allowing her to amend at least one more time.

The following is a list of court cases that are related to this topic.

Frye v Medicare-Glaser Corporation, No. 5-90-0559, Ill App. Ct, 5th Dist. October 8, 1991.
Frye v Medicare-Glaser Corp., 1992 WL 297605 (Ill. Sup. Ct.).
Hooper v Perry Drugs, Slip Op. 178665 (Unpublished), September 20, 1996. (Mich. App).

Advertising as the Basis of a Duty

The following is a list of court cases that are related to this topic.

Baker v Arbor Drugs, 544 N.W.2d 727 (Mich. App. 1996), Iv. denied, 454 Mich 853 (1997).

OBRA-90 and Practice Standards

Pharmaceutical Society of New York Inc. v New York State Dept. of Social Services
646 N.Y.S.2d 578 (1996)

FACTS: A professional association for pharmacists brought an action against the Department of Social Services to enjoin implementation and enforcement of a patient copayment requirement for prescriptions paid by Medicaid. The program permitted the State to reduce its share of the cost of providing prescription drugs to qualified Medicaid recipients by a copayment that the provider could charge to the recipient directly. The association alleged that the copayment program is preempted by the Omnibus Budget Reconciliation Act of 1990 (OBRA), which prohibits any reduction in reimbursement payments made to providers by states otherwise in compliance with applicable federal law. The district court granted the association partial summary judgment stating that the copayment program reduced the state's reimbursement to providers and violated OBRA; however, it remanded the case to determine whether OBRA applied only to states "otherwise in compliance with applicable federal law." Before this determination was made, OBRA's prohibition expired, rendering petitioner's claim moot. Later, the state issued a directive to all participating Medicaid pharmacists that the copayment program would be implemented on September 1, 1995. The association reinstated its suit, attempting to enjoin the state's implementation and enforcement of the copayment program because it conflicted with federal law mandating that providers be reimbursed specific sums for the drugs dispensed. The court dismissed the association's petition.

HOLDING: The judgment was affirmed on appeal. The New York Supreme Court Appellate Division found that the amendments to the law the association was now contesting were intended to do nothing more than to bring the state into compliance with the federal regulations. Therefore, the copayment scheme did not violate any state law, nor was there a conflict between state and federal law.

The following is a list of court cases that are related to this topic.

Walker v Jack Eckerd Corp., 209 Ga. App. 517; 434 S.E.2d 63, (Ga. App., 1993), cert denied, Ga. S.Ct., Slip Op. No. 593C1686 (1993).

Contract Duty as a Negligence Standard of Care

Rockport Pharmacy Inc. v Digital Simplistics, Inc.
53 F.3d 195 (8th Cir. 1995)

ISSUE: Whether a breach of contract may give rise to tort liability.

FACTS: Digital Simplistics is a Kansas corporation that designs and markets various computer hardware and software to retail pharmacies. The plaintiff, Rockport Pharmacies, operates a pharmacy in Jefferson County, Missouri.

In 1985, Digital contracted to provide Rockport with a customized computer system, including hardware and software. The parties also entered into a maintenance contract. Rockport purchased the computer system to maintain pharmaceutical records, to screen for drug interaction problems, label prescriptions, and to process insurance claims. Some time after purchasing the system, the pharmacy began experiencing problems in operating it. After attempts at correcting the problems proved unsuccessful, Rockport terminated the maintenance agreement and discontinued receiving further software updates from Digital.

In 1989, Rockport filed a six-count complaint against Digital, alleging breach of contract, negligence, fraudulent misrepresentation, and breach of various warranties. Only the breach of contract and negligence claims were submitted to the jury.

RULING: The jury found for Digital on the contract claim but awarded damages of $56,000 to the plaintiff on its claim of negligence. The Court of Appeals for the 8th Circuit disagreed. It noted that the mere existence of a contract does not give rise to a duty in tort. Similarly, there is no duty to exercise reasonable care to protect against a loss that is purely economic in nature. Consequently, in determining whether a breach of contract may give rise to tort liability, the nature of the alleged injury is an essential factor that must be considered.

REASONING: The substance of Rockport's negligence claim is for the recovery of losses arising out of Digital's alleged breach of contract. Thus, the nature of Rockport's alleged injury is an essential factor in determining whether Digital can be considered to have owed Rockport a duty of reasonable care.

Missouri law prohibits a cause of action in tort where the losses are purely economic. Recovery in tort is limited to cases in which there has been personal injury or property damage. In this case, the only damage Rockport alleged was the original cost of the computer system, including the maintenance and replacement expenses. The court ruled that these constitute economic damages not recoverable under a negligence theory.

The pharmacy argued that the economic loss doctrine does not present a bar to its negligence claim because the evidence established that there was damage to property other than the computer. Specifically, the pharmacy contended that it sustained a loss of data installed in the computer system. However, the court concluded that such losses represent nothing more than commercial loss for inadequate value and consequent loss of profits.

The court further rejected the pharmacy's argument that a "computer crash" involving the loss of data can be considered a violent occurrence such as would give rise to a claim for negligence. As a general rule, a calamitous event threatening bodily harm or damage to other property is required to create a violent occurrence. A "computer crash" is a commonly used descriptive term for computer malfunction. It should not be given the literal interpretation sought by the pharmacy in order to create a "violent occurrence" for which damages in negligence might arise.

LeJeune v Trend Services
699 So.2d 95 (La.App. 1997)

Plaintiff was hurt on the job and sought worker's compensation benefits. The insurance carrier has a policy requiring the use of generics when a brand name prescription has been ordered unless the prescriber indicates "dispense as written" on the prescription. Plaintiff was not told of the exception and was "forced" to take generic drugs or pay the difference between the generic and brand name drugs. The plaintiff sued claiming, in part, that the company's policy requiring him to take generic drugs without his consent constitutes withholding of treatment. The court agreed in principle stating, "The problem with the insurer's program is that it presumes that the doctor, patient, and pharmacist are well-informed about their choices and that they are well-informed about the insurer's willingness to pay for brand name drugs under the appropriate circumstances. Additionally, the program places the duty on either the doctor, the pharmacist, the patient, or all three to adhere to the internal policy, for which there is no legal authority and which was created solely to serve the best interests of the insurer - not the employee. We find that such a program may very well constitute withholding of medical treatment upon a showing of a difference between the benefits of a generic drug vs a brand name drug." However, the court did not award the plaintiff any damages because the plaintiff did not prove that he was harmed in any way by use of the generic drugs. The court stated that plaintiff would have to show that the generic and brand name drugs were somehow different and that difference affected his treatment.

Violation of Statute

The following is a list of court cases that are related to this topic.

Peoples Service Drug Stores v Somerville, 158 A. 12 (Md. 1932)

Rules of Law

The following is a list of court cases that are related to this topic.

Jones v Walgreen Co., 265 Ill. App. 308 (1932).
Peoples Service Drug Stores v Somerville, 158 A. 12 (Md. 1932).
Hoar v Rasmussen, 282 N.W. 652 (Wis. 1938).
Arkansas State Board of Pharmacy v Whayne, 454 S.W.2d 667 (Ark. 1970).
Lemire v Garrard Drugs, 291 N.W. 2d 103 (Mich. 1980).

SPECIFIC DUTIES FOR PHARMACISTS

Prescription Processing Errors

Factors Associated with Errors

The following is a list of court cases that are related to this topic.

Harco Drugs v Holloway, 1995 Ala. LEXIS 343 (Aug. 11, 1995).
Stolfa v K-Mart Corp., 1994 WL 161095 (Mo. App. W.D.).

Personnel

The following is a list of court cases that are related to this topic.

Harco Drugs v Holloway, 1995 Ala. LEXIS 343 (Aug. 11, 1995).

Environment

The following is a list of court cases that are related to this topic.

Bookman v Ciolino, 684 So.2d 982 (La.App. 5th Cir. 1994).

Systems Issues

Bookman v Ciolino
684 So.2d 982 (La.App. 5th Cir. 1994)

ISSUE: Whether a pharmacy's workload and dispensing procedures contributed to a patient receiving the wrong medication.

FACTS: The plaintiff, Mrs. Bookman, was being treated for depression. Her psychiatrist prescribed *Restoril* and the antidepressant *Prozac*. These prescriptions were taken to C's Discount Pharmacy. The lawsuit alleges that during one of the refills, the prescriptions were erroneously switched so that the bottle labeled "*Prozac*" was actually *Restoril* and vice-versa. The plaintiff was to take one *Prozac* capsule in the morning and one or two *Restoril* capsules for sleep in the evening.

According to the plaintiff, during the following week when she took two of what she believed to be *Restoril* before bedtime, she was in fact taking two *Prozac* capsules. Mrs. Bookman claimed that as a result of the "overdose," she became increasingly disturbed and ultimately was hospitalized in a psychiatric facility for 5 weeks. She sued for damages for pain and suffering, as well as for medical expenses. The plaintiff claimed that her condition would not have deteriorated and the hospitalization would not have been necessary had the pharmacist not made the error.

During the trial, the testimony showed that Mrs. Bookman, following her receipt of the wrong prescription refills, could not sleep at all. One day, she returned from an outing and, due to her agitation, began to tear up papers and books in her apartment, feeling out of control. A friend called her psychiatrist. She was admitted to a treatment center where she remained for 5 weeks. After several weeks, the *Prozac* therapy was discontinued and the plaintiff received electroconvulsive shock therapy. She improved and was later released.

Following her release, the plaintiff's daughter found that the medications had been switched. The plaintiff denied having switched them herself.

During the time in question, three full-time pharmacists and one part-time pharmacist were employed at C's Discount Pharmacy. The pharmacy dispensed approximately 800 prescriptions per day. Based on an 8-hour day, counsel for the plaintiff contended that the average number of prescriptions filled per hour was 28.5, or one prescription every 2.1 minutes. The pharmacist who dispensed the prescriptions in question stated that he was often interrupted to answer questions or to answer the telephone, and he would need to start the dispensing process over again.

When filling a prescription, the pharmacist testified that he would first receive the computer-generated three-part label. He would read the prescription to check for accuracy. The first portion of the label is attached to the prescription; the second part of the label contains refill information and the pharmacist's name along with the name of the medication, directions, etc. The pharmacist would retrieve the medication and bring it to the counter. Then, he would check it against the prescription and the computer-generated document, count the tablets or capsules, and put them in the bottle. After stamping his name on the bottle, the contents are again checked to make sure that the medication has been correctly dispensed.

Bookman v Ciolino
684 So.2d 982 (La.App. 5th Cir. 1994)
...continued

According to the pharmacist, "there is a rule that if there is any doubt about what you're doing, then you don't do it." When dispensing more than one prescription for the same patient, both medications are pulled at the same time. However, each prescription is filled separately as outlined above. Each pharmacist is responsible for checking his own work.

The pharmacist admitted that he had made counting errors in the past and that he had also put wrong tablets in the wrong bottles. However, due to his checking procedures, this had not resulted in giving a patient the wrong medication.

Mrs. Bookman filed the lawsuit against the pharmacist who filled the prescription, the pharmacy itself, the two owners, and the pharmacy's insurance company.

RULING: The jury returned a verdict in favor of the defendants. A significant factor in the verdict was the conflicting testimony of the patient who was not able to clearly explain what had happened. The Court of Appeals of Louisiana concluded that the jury decision was reasonable based upon the record.

REASONING: Both the prescribing psychiatrist and a pharmacologist at Tulane University described the chemical effects of *Prozac* in the brain and body. Both confirmed that given the half-life of the drug, it takes approximately 3 weeks for the level of the drug to slowly decrease in the bloodstream. The physician testified that had he known of the mix-up, he would have taken the plaintiff off of the drug immediately.

A licensed pharmacist testified as an expert witness for the plaintiff. In his opinion, 2.1 minutes for dispensing a prescription "could be considered safe depending on other circumstances." To dispense prescriptions at that rate for 8 hours requires intense concentration and there is a high likelihood of making a mistake, especially if there are other interruptions. However, the expert pharmacist had no personal information about the plaintiff and gave no opinion as to the negligence of the defendants.

As to the testimony offered by the dispensing pharmacist, the court stated, "While the pharmacist did not have specific recollection of this particular event, his testimony as to his usual practices was consistent. The plaintiff presented no evidence to contradict his statements that he always double-checks his work and that he never had a complaint of having misfilled a prescription with the wrong medication. There is no reason in the record to discredit his testimony."

Harco Drugs v Holloway
669 So.2d 878 (Ala. 1995)

ISSUE: Whether the defendant pharmacy had failed to initiate sufficient institutional controls over the manner in which prescriptions were filled.

FACTS: The plaintiff, Malvina Holloway, presented a prescription for tamoxifen, a medication used to treat breast cancer, to Marry Ellis, the pharmacist at Harco Drugs. Ellis entered the prescription into the computer incorrectly and, as a result, the plaintiff's prescription was misfilled on three separate occasions.

Ellis knew that Mrs. Holloway's treating physician was an oncologist and that the drug she had incorrectly given to the patient was a heart medication (*Tambocor*). Although Ellis recognized the obvious conflict, she did not call Holloway's oncologist to confirm the prescription. A second pharmacist, who was on duty when Holloway subsequently came back to question the misfilled prescription, testified that the prescription written by the oncologist was illegible and that he would have had trouble reading it if he had been busy. He did admit that he knew Holloway's physician was an oncologist, and further agreed that being busy was no excuse for misfilling a prescription. He also admitted that the obligation for correctly dispensing a prescription is on the pharmacist. If questions arise with regard to the prescription, the pharmacist must telephone the physician and take necessary steps to see that the prescription is dispensed correctly.

One of Harco's district managers testified that misfilling a prescription could have serious consequences and that Harco had to support its pharmacists to see that this did not happen. He also testified that it was Harco's job to make certain that prescriptions were not misfilled.

The jury was informed of 233 incident reports that had been prepared by Harco employees during the 3 years preceding the incident involving Mrs. Holloway. Those reports dealt in some way with customer complaints of errors on the part of Harco employees in dispensing prescriptions. This evidence, in addition to complaints filed with the Alabama State Board of Pharmacy and lawsuits alleging that Harco employees had misfilled prescriptions, was relevant to show Harco's knowledge of the problems within its pharmacies. The court ruled that this evidence was admissible in connection with the wantonness claim.

The Supreme Court of Alabama was faced with the issue of whether the evidence was sufficient to submit the wantonness claim to the jury. In addition, the appellate court was called upon to determine whether the trial court abused its discretion in admitting evidence of incident reports prepared by Harco employees in connection with errors that had occurred in the dispensing of prescriptions. The question was also raised whether it was an error to admit evidence of complaints filed with the Alabama State Board of Pharmacy and other lawsuits that had been filed against Harco alleging the improper filling of prescriptions.

RULING: Alabama law defines "wantonness" as conduct that is carried on with a reckless or conscious disregard of the rights or safety of others. The statute provides that punitive damages may be awarded in a tort action when it is proven by clear and convincing evidence that the defendant engaged in wantonness. The jury awarded Mrs. Holloway $100,000 in compensatory damages and $150,000 in punitive damages. Mr. Holloway was awarded $5000 on his derivative claim for loss of consortium.

REASONING: Harco management had evidence of numerous incidents of incorrectly filled prescriptions; however, it failed to share this information with the stores in the Harco chain. Thus, the jury could have inferred that although the incident reports were in the possession of Harco, the drug chain did not see fit to disseminate the information to all of its

Harco Drugs v Holloway
669 So.2d 878 (Ala. 1995)
...continued

pharmacists despite undisputed evidence that a misfilled prescription could be fatal. Instead of providing this information to all of its pharmacies, a Harco representative merely encouraged its pharmacists once a year to "be careful." Given knowledge on Harco's part that misfilling a prescription could be fatal, the jury could have found that there was a reckless disregard for the safety of patients in not disseminating the information to all of the pharmacists in the Harco chain. Harco did not have clerks look at the hard copies of the prescriptions presented in order to make sure that the prescriptions were being filled correctly. They conceded that having two people, a pharmacist and a technician, looking at the prescription would reduce the chances of making a mistake in filling that prescription. However, the expense of adopting such a policy would be extreme.

The Alabama Supreme Court noted that generally the filing of a lawsuit raises no presumption as to the truthfulness of the allegations contained in the complaint. In the present case, however, the evidence of other lawsuits by Harco customers was admissible for the limited purposes of demonstrating the problems in its pharmacy departments. For these reasons, the trial court judgment and jury verdict were affirmed.

The dissenting judge believed that under the majority opinion, a business could not undertake a review of its procedures except at peril. No matter how impractical a suggestion about procedure or improvement might be, it would be liable for wantonness. The dissenting judge felt that this opinion would stifle self-review and efforts to improve a company's safety.

Harco offered testimony that the incident reports the plaintiffs relied on were generated by Harco employees and sent to the director of pharmacy operations for review. The director of pharmacy testified that he reviewed each report and counseled the pharmacist who misfilled the prescription. Occasionally, Harco transferred a pharmacist to a setting with less volume if it was believed the pharmacist could perform better in such a situation. Some pharmacists who could not adequately perform their duties were relieved. The plaintiffs offered no testimony to contradict Harco executives regarding the precautions that the drug chain took, and they offered no testimony that any other pharmacy-employed technicians to help verify a trained professional pharmacist's work for accuracy.

The plaintiffs relieved heavily on the fact that Harco management rejected the idea of implementing a policy of having technicians verify prescriptions. The plaintiffs asserted that Harco failed to implement the policy, believing that such a system would be prohibitively expensive. The director of pharmacy for Harco testified that the use of clerical employees was at the pharmacist's discretion. The dissenting judge did not agree that Harco's decision of not requiring a technician to inspect the work of a professionally trained and licensed pharmacist constitutes wantonness.

The testimony that Harco had filled between 15 and 16 million prescriptions during the 3-year period in which there were 233 incidents of misfilled prescriptions was uncontroverted. This translates into a 0.0016% chance that a prescription might be misfilled. Some of the incidents involved problems such as manufacturing errors and a customer's picking up the wrong prescription bag when their names were called. These errors would not have been caught by a technician. Given the small number of errors compared with the large number of prescriptions dispensed, the dissenting judge did not think the 233 incident reports over 3 years or the decision not to employ technicians was evidence that the company wantonly disregarded the safety of its customers.

Dunn and Ruiz v The Department of Veterans Affairs
98 F.3d 1308 (Fed. Cir. 1996)

FACTS: Two employees, a pharmacist and pharmacy technician, of The Department of Veterans Affairs Medical Center (the "VA") were fired after mistakenly labeling packages of *Mivacron*, a powerful neuromuscular blocker, as metronidazole, an antibacterial agent. Four patients who received the mislabeled drug suffered cardiac and respiratory arrest. One of the patients died. The VA discharged the employees for negligence contributing to the death and injury of these patients. The employees sought appeal of the VA's action through arbitration. The arbitrator sustained the charges finding the employees were responsible for mistakenly causing the incorrect drug to be administered to the patients. However, due to system failures, the arbitrator mitigated the penalties assessed against the pharmacy employees. The arbitrator noted the similarity in labeling between the two drugs, the proximity of storage, and that the administering nurses also failed to confirm that they had the proper drugs. The arbitrator assessed sanctions of four week suspensions without pay. The employees then filed a request for attorney's fees which the arbitrator denied.

HOLDING: On subsequent review, the U.S. Court of Appeals affirmed the arbitrator's decision stating that the arbitrator did consider the seriousness of the offense, and, while not in supervisory positions, these employees were responsible for patient care. The VA imposed greater penalties on these two employees, which the arbitrator disagreed with, but could not find that the VA's judgment was negligent or in disregard of the facts. Under those circumstances, the arbitrator did not abuse his discretion in denying the award of attorney's fees. Thus the arbitrator's decision was affirmed.

🔨 🔨 🔨

The following is a list of court cases that are related to this topic.

Baker v Arbor Drugs, 544 N.W.2d 727 (Mich. App. 1996), lv. denied, 454 Mich 853 (1997).
Cafaralle v Brockton Oaks C.V.S.. Inc., No. 94-0414A, (Mass. Super. Ct. April, 1996).
Guillory v Andrus, Nos. 96-85, 96-86, and 679 So: 2d 1004 (La. App., 1996).

Classes of Error

Wrong Drug

Hoar v Rasmussen
282 N.W. 652 (Wis. 1938)

ISSUE: Whether a pharmacist's deviation from the prescription was a violation of the standard of care, resulting in negligence.

FACTS: The civil action was brought against a pharmacist for an injury resulting to the plaintiff when the pharmacist dispensed the plaintiff's prescription with "*Cala-zine*" instead of the calamine lotion with 1% phenol as prescribed by the plaintiff's doctor. The case came to trial, but due to failure to submit certain questions to the jury, the trial judge ordered a new trial, and the defendant appealed such order to the Supreme Court of Wisconsin.

The plaintiff was suffering from a skin disorder and received a prescription from a Madison, Wisconsin, physician for "calamine lotion 1% phenol." He took the prescription to the pharmacist in his hometown of Spooner, Wisconsin. The pharmacist filled the prescription with a commercial preparation called "*Cala-zine*" which was similar to the calamine lotion with phenol but which contained a small amount of mercury. The plaintiff was allergic to

Hoar v Rasmussen
282 N.W. 652 (Wis. 1938)
...continued

mercury and eventually sustained such severe skin injury that he could not wear clothing for 2 months. The injury was sustained shortly after applying the lotion and the plaintiff's wife contacted his family physician who told her that her husband should discontinue use of the prescription. The family physician then contacted the pharmacist and asked if the prescription written by the Madison doctor contained mercury. The pharmacist answered "no" even though he knew it did. He believed it was not his duty to reveal the contents of another doctor's prescription. Eventually, it was brought to light that the prescription contained mercury.

At the trial of the case, the defendant's legal counsel produced evidence that it was customary in the area for a pharmacist to vary from the standard formula. The Wisconsin Supreme Court rejected this defense as wholly unavailable since the prescription was written by a Madison doctor from outside the area.

RULING: The court concluded that a pharmacist must exercise a high degree of care and skill and that the pharmacist had violated the standard of care required by the profession.

REASONING: In ruling in favor of the plaintiff and against the pharmacist, the court laid down the rules:

> Although the druggist may have had reason to suppose that the medicine which he supplied was just as good as what the doctor prescribed, it must be held that the risk of harm from the act of making the substitution without informing the purchaser outweighs any possible utility that the act may have had. It is even more apparent that an unreasonable risk was involved in misinforming the physician. The druggist could easily have refused to answer at all if he believed that to be his duty. Either of the druggist's acts, therefore, constituted an actionable misrepresentation.

> The circumstances of a pharmacist's or druggist's calling demand the exercise of a high degree of care and skill, such care and skill as an ordinarily prudent person would exercise under those circumstances, the highest degree of care and prudence consistent with the reasonable conduct of the business. The effect of a mistake may be swift and disastrous for injuries resulting from negligence in filling a prescription or supplying a remedy.

> In the present case, the liability is more apparent than in most, because the substitution was deliberately made under the mistaken impression that the prescription could be changed in accordance with the druggist's judgment.

While the custom or practice of pharmacists in the community under similar situations may be introduced as a possible defense to a charge of negligence, such custom or practice will not by itself defeat the negligence charge. The failure to disclose an error or substitution on a prescription only serves to aggravate the situation. It may be embarrassing for a pharmacist to bring the error to the attention of the customer and/or prescribing physician, but the timely disclosure of the error will often prevent harm to the patient and preclude any grounds for legal liability.

Boeck v Katz Drug Co.
127 P.2d 506 (Kan. 1942)

ISSUE: (1) Whether, in an action for negligence, the patient contributed to his injuries by continuing to take the drug after becoming ill and (2) whether the pharmacist should pay punitive damages.

FACTS: A 15-year-old boy commenced a suit in 1935 against a pharmacy for the negligent dispensing of a prescription for *Eserine* solution. Instead, the prescription was filled with atropine solution and caused injury to the boy's eyes. The case went to trial and judgment was in favor of the injured boy. Later, the amount was reduced by the judge to $7500. The defendant-pharmacy appealed the judgment to the Kansas Supreme Court.

It appears from the reported facts that in August of 1935, the boy received a prescription from his doctor for 1/4% *Eserine* solution. The pharmacist on duty at the defendant's pharmacy filled the prescription with atropine solution instead of *Eserine*. The boy was suffering from retinitis pigmentosa (a degenerative condition of the margin of the eye causing night blindness) and the prescription was for the treatment of his condition. The boy became nauseated from taking the prescription and he vomited quite frequently. There was a substantial change in the extent of his activities before and after the prescription therapy. Before taking the prescription, he was in Knapp's Rough Riders, drove a chariot, and was employed at Dun and Bradstreet operating a ditto machine. After being on the prescription for several weeks, he was unable to carry his former activities and at the time of trial, it was alleged that he could not see from the right or left without turning his head.

The expert medical testimony at the trial was extensive. In summation, it can be stated: The prescription was incorrectly filled with atropine instead of *Eserine*. Atropine dilates the pupil of the eye while *Eserine* contracts it; therefore, although atropine does not cause retinitis pigmentosa, it could aggravate the disease by causing dilation of the pupil. By causing the patient to vomit, it lowered the patient's vitality causing the disease to progress. There was also testimony that there were persons who were sensitive to atropine and that there was no cure for the boy's eye condition.

RULING: The court concluded that there was no evidence that the patient had contributed to his own injury by continuing to take the medication even though it did nauseate him, and that the pharmacist, who in good faith, dispenses a prescription erroneously should not be responsible for punitive damages.

REASONING: On the appeal of the case, the defendant-pharmacy corporation, through it attorneys, argued numerous reasons why the case should be reversed. It was argued that there was contributory negligence on the part of the 15-year-old boy because he continued to take the medication even after it made him sick. The Kansas Supreme Court rejected this argument and stated in its written decision:

> If he (the patient) had confidence enough to go to the doctor and to ask him to prescribe we cannot say that it was contributory negligence for him to follow the directions as to his medicine though it did nauseate him.

The defendants also argued that the boy's condition could not have been caused by the atropine. The court rejected this argument, since even though the disease was present prior to the atropine use, the atropine rendered the condition worse or aggravated it. Lastly, the defendants contended that the $15,000 damages were excessive because the issue of "punitive damages" was put to the jury. On this point, the court agreed that there was no evidence of wantonness or reckless disregard that would permit the issue of punitive damages to be before the court. The defendant's pharmacist had made four checks of the prescription

Boeck v Katz Drug Co.
127 P.2d 506 (Kan. 1942)
...continued

even though filling it incorrectly, and this showed the pharmacist's intention to guard against mistakes. The court would not hold a pharmacist who dispenses a wrong drug on prescription to be guilty of intentional wrongdoing as a matter of law.

The Kansas Supreme Court, in this case, affirmed the judgment for the injured boy, but reduced the damages further from $7500 to $5000.

Burke v Bean
363 S.W.2d 366 (Texas, 1962)

ISSUE: Whether a pharmacist is liable for a dispensing error and whether punitive damages may be assessed against a pharmacist who attempts to conceal a dispensing error.

FACTS: The plaintiff in this case was suffering from a gall bladder attack and received a prescription for *Oxacholin* tablets from his doctor. The pharmacist on duty at the defendant's pharmacy filled the prescription with *Oxsoralen* capsules. The plaintiff suffered injury from the improperly filled prescription and brought suit against the pharmacy. A jury trial resulted in a $500 actual damage award and a $2000 "punitive" damage award for the plaintiff. The defendant appealed the decision to the Civil Appeals Court of Texas.

In addition to the facts stated above, it deserves mention that *Oxacholin* is a drug used to treat gall bladder disease, whereas *Oxsoralen* is for skin depigmentation and has the side effect of inducing pain similar to that of a gall bladder attack.

When dispensing a refill of the prescription, the mistake of dispensing *Oxsoralen* in place of *Oxacholin* was discovered by the pharmacist. However, he did not inform the plaintiff or the plaintiff's physician of the error and, instead, he tried to conceal the mistake. The plaintiff first became aware of the error when he showed the medication to his physician who recognized the error and informed him that the prescription was filled with the wrong drug.

RULING: The appeals court reaffirmed judgment in favor of the plaintiff and upheld the punitive damages award, which was based in gross negligence of the pharmacist in failing to inform the patient of the error when the pharmacist discovered it.

REASONING: The court stated: "The very high degree of thoughtfulness and vigilance in the original filling of the prescription placed by law upon the druggist must also enjoin him to exercise that same vigilance and care for his customer upon discovery of a mistake to see that it is promptly rectified."

Thomsen v Rexall Drug & Chemical Co.
235 Cal.App. 2d 775 (1965)

ISSUE: Whether an erroneously dispensed prescription was the direct cause of the patient's injury.

FACTS: A pharmacy and pharmacist were both sued by a patient who developed vasculitis shortly after taking medication from an erroneously refilled prescription at the pharmacy. A jury trial resulted in a judgment in favor of the patient, and the jury awarded her $75,000 in damages. The pharmacy and pharmacist appealed the decision to a California District Court of Appeals. The appellate court reaffirmed the judgment of the $75,000 in favor of the plaintiff and against the pharmacy and pharmacist.

In the published decision of the court, it was stated that the court "...found no cases equal in medical complexity to the instant one..." The plaintiff was a 41-year-old housewife who was suffering from rheumatoid arthritis. She was being treated with cortisone (*Ataraxoid* was being prescribed) by her family physician. After being on cortisone for some time, she developed fluid retention and her doctor prescribed *Hyrodiuril*. She had the *Hyrodiuril* prescription filled at the defendant's pharmacy and received small pink tablets. Later, upon bringing the prescription container for a refill, the pharmacist on duty refilled it with large white or yellow tablets, and he reassured the plaintiff that the large white or yellow tablets were *Hyrodiuril*. Later that month, the plaintiff developed symptoms of unusual muscular tiredness/ weakness and numbness in her legs (symptomatic of vasculitis, a disease of inflammation of the small blood vessels). After hospital treatment and physical therapy, the plaintiff's condition was such that she was permanently confined to a wheelchair and no longer able to take care of herself and her family.

The medical testimony as to the cause of the plaintiff's vasculitis was complex and inconsistent. The court concluded that vasculitis was a rare disease, the exact cause of which was unknown, but it was thought that the cause was related to an allergic reaction to certain drugs, including sulfa drugs and penicillin. Some forms of the disease developed as a complication of arthritis and there was a high frequency of some types of the disease in persons on steroid therapy.

It was not determined what the "large white or yellow" tablets were that were erroneously given to the plaintiff. However, testimony was introduced that sulfa and penicillin are commonly marketed as large white tablets.

In response to a hypothetical question, the plaintiff's expert medical witness testified that "...the erroneously filled prescription would be the primary suspect as the cause of the plaintiff's vasculitis. He concluded that the plaintiff was suffering from an acute type of hypersensitivity or allergic vasculitis, caused by the reaction of her system to the erroneously refilled prescription and that this vasculitis was the cause of her nervous system disorder and the crippled condition." However, the defendant's medical witnesses testified that "the plaintiff's type of vasculitis was merely a complication of the malignant phase of her arthritis which had become quiescent," while another of the defendant's physician witnesses stated that "no drugs other than steroids had ever been implicated in the type of vasculitis that he concluded the plaintiff had..."

Counsel for the defendant pharmacy and pharmacist contended that the only testimony supporting the plaintiff's case was that of one physician, and that his testimony "at most, shows a mere possibility of causation and this is not enough since the matter remains one of pure speculation or conjecture."

RULING: The court concluded that there was support for the jury's position that the erroneously dispensed prescription was the cause of the patient's injury.

Thomsen v Rexall Drug & Chemical Co.
235 Cal.App. 2d 775 (1965)
...continued

REASONING: Faced with the dilemma that "[the plaintiff's]...condition was a complex and rare one and that there was not a great deal of medical knowledge or experience about vasculitis," the court concluded "Under these circumstances, the jury could believe the testimony of plaintiff's expert and base their finding on his conclusion that her condition was caused by allergic or hypersensitivity vasculitis brought about by the erroneously refilled prescription." In so doing, the court is rejecting the concept that her condition was the result of an arthritis complication, and choosing between the cortisone or erroneous prescription as triggering the vasculitis. The court stated "In such situations, it is recognized that neither cause can be absolved...The proper rule for such situations is that the defendant's conduct is a cause of the event as it is a material element and a substantial factor in bringing it about."

French Drug Co., Inc. v Jones
367 So.2d 431 (Miss. 1978)

ISSUE: Whether errors in the conduct of a trial of a pharmacist for negligence were such as to justify reversal of an award to the plaintiff for drug-based injuries.

FACTS: The patient in this case was suffering from insufficient blood circulation in his legs, a problem that had its origins when he sustained frostbitten legs and feet during the "Battle of the Bulge" in World War II. In June of 1974, he was hospitalized and given tests relating to the leg circulation problem. Upon his discharge, he received two prescriptions for drugs to aid in circulation. The prescriptions were taken to the defendant's pharmacy for filling. One of the prescriptions called for the drug "*Ethatab*" but was erroneously filled with the drug "*Estratab*."

The prescription error occurred June 11, 1974, and the patient continued to take the *Estratab* until the error was discovered in May of 1975 - despite the fact that the patient noticed certain changes and troubles. The patient, during this period of time, suffered continuous nausea, physical and mental fatigue, loss of memory, and had become immediately impotent, which caused certain psychological disorders. At the time of the trial, in 1976, some of the physical side effects of *Estratab* had ceased, but the impotency problem continued; the patient was still under psychiatric treatment and his relationship with his wife had deteriorated.

The case was tried before a judge and jury and the evidence was undisputed that the physician, a neurologist, had written a proper prescription which was erroneously filled by the pharmacist. The judge instructed the jury that they must return a verdict in favor of the injured plaintiff-patient on the negligence issue. In other words, the jury had no choice to make on the negligence question. However, the jury was to decide from the evidence the issues of whether or not the plaintiff-patient was guilty of contributory negligence (failure to act for his own safety as a reasonable, prudent person would act under the same or similar circumstances). The jury also was to decide the amount of damages to award the plaintiff, reduced by any percent of negligence that they might assess to him.

RULING: The Mississippi Supreme Court failed to find any fault with the above jury instructions nor did it find any other substantial error committed by the trial judge. The verdict of $135,000 was therefore affirmed.

French Drug Co., Inc. v Jones
367 So.2d 431 (Miss. 1978)
...continued

REASONING: The verdict was entirely in favor of the plaintiff-patient in the amount of $135,000. The pharmacy-defendant appealed the case to the Mississippi Supreme Court. On appeal, a number of errors were claimed to have been made by the trial judge. Nonetheless, the appellate court affirmed the jury's verdict on the grounds that the trial judge had acted correctly and the evidence supported the verdict. The high court stated that it was proper for the judge here to instruct the jury to render a verdict in favor of plaintiff on the negligence issue. The court stated:

> We agree with the authorities holding that a druggist or pharmacist is held to a high standard or degree of care in filling drug prescriptions. It is inescapable that appellant [pharmacist] did not use the required degree of care by substituting the female hormone drug for the blood circulation drug called for in appellee's [plaintiff's] prescription.

Other issues raised on the appeal dealt with the trial court judge's instructions to the jury prior to their rendering the verdict. One such instruction told to the jury was, as follows:

> ...a general customer of a pharmacy who has no special or definite knowledge concerning drugs or medicines is allowed by the law to rely upon the pharmacist who holds himself out as one having a peculiar learning and skill to fill prescriptions properly, and such a customer cannot be guilty of negligence if, having no such special knowledge of the drugs or medicine, he obeys the directions regarding the taking of the drug or medicine, which accompany the drug container received from the drug store...

However, this was not the only instruction given by the judge to enable the jury to decide the contributory negligence issue. The judge further instructed the jury as follows:

> ...if you believe from the evidence in this case that the plaintiff, after taking the *Estratab* for a period of time experienced unusual and bizarre problems, including enlargement of the breasts, tenderness of breasts, impotency, weakness, loss of hair, or other unusual symptoms, and if you further believe that the plaintiff did not use reasonable care to seek medical advice or attention regarding the aforesaid conditions, if any, and if you further believe that a reasonably prudent man would have sought medical advice or assistance upon experiencing the aforesaid problems or conditions, if any, then the plaintiff was guilty of negligence which contributed to the injuries and damages, if any, which he may have suffered...

McLean v U.S.
613 F.2d 603 (4th Cir. 1980)

ISSUE: Whether a dispensing error that results in a cardiac patient being without medication for 26 days is basis for a negligence suit.

FACTS: The plaintiff in this case was complaining of angina, extreme fatigue, and arrhythmia. His physician prescribed *Pronestyl* (an antiarrhythmic drug) and the plaintiff had the prescription filled at a U.S. Air Force Base pharmacy. The pharmacy employee (reported facts didn't indicate if the employee was a pharmacist or technician) dispensed the antibiotic

McLean v U.S.
613 F.2d 603 (4th Cir. 1980)
...continued

Prostaphlin instead of the prescribed drug. Eventually, the plaintiff had to undergo heart surgery and sued the U.S. Government under the Federal Tort Claims Act, alleging negligence in the pharmacy.

The U.S. District Court held against the plaintiff on the grounds that he failed to prove that the lack of *Pronestyl* for 26 days - the error was discovered 26 days later, and the dispensed *Pronestyl* then relieved the arrhythmia - caused damage to the heart or altered the severity of the underlying disease. Hence, the court awarded plaintiff no compensation and taxed him for court costs. He appealed to the Federal Appeals Court.

RULING: The case was reversed on this issue only, and the case went back to the lower court for its determination of the amount of damages due to the plaintiff for the 26 days of suffering.

REASONING: The appeals court, in reviewing the medical testimony, found that for the 26–day period that the plaintiff was without the *Pronestyl*, he (a) was in a potentially lethal situation, (b) was having palpitations much of the time, and (c) the palpitations caused frightening feelings and stress. For these conditions of pain, suffering, and mental anguish caused by the negligence (the negligence was conceded by the government), he should have been awarded damages (money).

Albertson's Inc. v Adams
473 So.2d 231 (Fla. App. 2 Dist. 1985)

ISSUE: Whether a physician's alleged actions rendered him jointly liable with the defendant pharmacy.

FACTS: This action arose as a result of injuries sustained by Naomi Huprich following her use of the drug *Proloid* in error for about 6 months in 1983. During a hospitalization of Mrs. Huprich, her physician discovered that the prescription had been improperly dispensed and she should have been receiving *Prolixin* to help ease the suffering associated with her cancer. Mrs. Huprich filed suit against Albertson's and the pharmacist who made the dispensing error. The complaint alleged that the improper prescription resulted in adverse physical and mental reactions leading to her hospitalization.

The defendants filed a third-party complaint against the physician. This complaint alleged that the physician, Dr. Adams, was jointly liable with the defendants because of his negligence in (1) allowing his employee to telephone a prescription order to the pharmacy instead of doing it himself to ensure its accuracy; (2) failing to monitor his patient's use of the prescription over the 6-month period; (3) failing to monitor refills of the prescription over the 6-month period; and (4) failing to supervise and review prescription telephone orders of his employees.

Dr. Adams moved for a dismissal of the third-party complaint against him by the pharmacy. He contended that his conduct in permitting an employee to telephone a prescription order fell within the accepted standard of care exercised by physicians in the community. He further argued that the complaint against him failed to state a cause of action because his alleged acts were not jointly performed with the defendants, but were separate in time and effect.

Albertson's Inc. v Adams
473 So.2d 231 (Fla. App. 2 Dist. 1985)
...continued

RULING: The trial court granted the physician's motion to dismiss the third-party complaint because the physician was, at most, a subsequent tort-feasor rather than a joint tort-feasor. The appellate court affirmed the dismissal.

REASONING: Florida law provides a right of contribution between joint wrongdoers "when two or more persons become jointly or severally liable in tort for the same injury." However, the Florida Supreme Court did not permit contribution between subsequent tort-feasors.

Joint and several liability exist when two or more wrongdoers negligently contribute to the injury of another person by their several acts, which operate concurrently, so that in effect the damages suffered are rendered inseparable. The determination of whether two parties are joint tort-feasors does not depend upon split-second timing.

The court could find no prohibition against the physician allowing an employee to telephone a prescription order to a pharmacy. However, it did not delve into this issue since it had no bearing on whether Dr. Adams and the defendants were joint tort-feasors. If Dr. Adams' office telephoned the wrong prescription, then he could not be a joint tort-feasor because he would be solely responsible in such a case. If Dr. Adams was negligent in failing to timely diagnose the negligence of the pharmacy, he would be, at most, a subsequent tort-feasor rather than a joint tort-feasor. The pharmacy was unsuccessful in establishing any claims of joint liability against the physician.

Walter v Wal-Mart
2000 Me 63, 2000 Me LEXIS 66 (April 12, 2000)

The plaintiff is an 80 year old woman who was diagnosed with a form of lymphatic cancer. Her oncologist prescribed chlorambucil (*Leukeran*). A pharmacist at the Wal-Mart pharmacy in Rockland, Maine, erroneously dispensed alkeran (*Melphalan*), another kind of chemotherapy agent that is more powerful than chorambucil and that is given in smaller doses over shorter periods of time. Because of its greater toxicity, patients on alkeran are monitored more closely than those on chlorambucil. The pharmacist that filled the prescription and did not speak with the patient, but he did provide an information sheet for alkeran when he dispensed the medication. The patient did not notice the name difference on the information sheet and assumed she had the correct medication. She took it as directed. Within 7 to 10 days she began experiencing nausea and loss of appetite. The information sheet she had been given indicated that these were common side effects with chemotherapy drugs. After three weeks of using the drug, she noticed bruises on her arms and legs and by the fourth week she developed a skin rash. The information sheet instructed patients to call their physician if bruises or rashes appear. She waited a few days before attempting to call her physician. Her physician indicated that the patient should have had a blood test 2 weeks after initiating therapy and was to have returned for a visit within 4 weeks. He also indicated that because chlorambucil is a slow-acting drug, he does not insist on blood work every 14 days, but indicates blood samples should be done periodically. The plaintiff indicated that she knew she was to have seen the doctor in 4 weeks and thought that was when she was to have had the blood work performed. In any event she had the blood samples taken on the twenty-third day after she began taking the drug and talked to the physician on the twenty-fourth day. The physician told the patient to stop taking the drug because her blood work was abnormal and scheduled an appointment 2 days later. However, she was

Walter v Wal-Mart
2000 Me 63, 2000 Me LEXIS 66 (April 12, 2000)
...continued

taken to the hospital the day she talked to the doctor after experiencing gastrointestinal bleeding. She was admitted to the hospital and had several blood transfusions over her 5–week stay. During this period she incurred infections and had a chest catheter. She was unable to eat because of bleeding gums. Because her immune system was weakened she could not have visitors come closer than 10 feet. Before this hospitalization, the plaintiff lived independently and was active. After her discharge she was weak, had to go to the hospital on a daily basis for some time and underwent several more transfusions. Her hospital bill was over $70,000. Her cancer did go into remission.

After a 2–day jury trial, the plaintiff was awarded a verdict of $550,000 against Wal-Mart. The defendant appealed, claiming the trial court erred in granting the plaintiff's motion on liability and that it should be entitled to judgment because the plaintiff failed to present any expert testimony on the standard of care by pharmacists. The defendant also claimed it was prejudiced by the remarks of plaintiff's counsel during closing arguments. The Maine Supreme Court affirmed the verdict. Reviewing the evidence, the court noted that the pharmacist admitted a mistake was made and that he gave the plaintiff the wrong drug. He also admitted that he did not follow policy on checking for errors and that he would have likely caught the mistake had he followed proper procedure. The Court noted that pharmacists have a duty to dispense the correct drug and the admission that a mistake was made constitutes proof that the duty was breached. Expert testimony is not necessary under these circumstances. As to causation, both the treating physician and Wal-Mart's own expert testified that the alkeran caused the plaintiff to become ill resulting in her hospitalization. The delay in having her blood samples drawn 23 days after receiving the wrong drug instead of at 14 days did not break the chain of causation between the error and the damages incurred by the plaintiff. At most, the delay went to the issues of mitigation of damages or comparative negligence. This court noted that the difference between mitigation and comparative negligence is "temporal" and, at least in this case, of little consequence. The jury was instructed on the mitigation doctrine and likely took the appropriate factors into account in rendering the verdict. Wal-Mart also claimed a mistrial should have been declared when, during closing arguments, plaintiff's counsel told the jury that the pharmacist appeared to have accepted his responsibility for making the error, but Wal-Mart refused to acknowledge any wrong-doing. Counsel also told the jury the plaintiff was not "sent home with the smiley face as we hear about at Wal-Mart...but with a bottle of poison...a bottle of medication that was not meant for her." Finally counsel stated that in considering the amount of damages to award, the jury should think about how much money basketball players make. The Wal-Mart attorney objected after each of the three statements and the judge admonished the jury all three times to focus on the facts. According to this Court, the instruction to ignore the lawyer's arguments cured any prejudice.

Brooks v Wal-Mart Stores
535 SE 2d 55 (August 29, 2000); 2000 NC App LEXIS 1038

Dr. Deterding, an employee of defendant Carolina Kidney Associates, P.A. (CKA), began treating the plaintiff in October 1991. On September 11, 1992, Dr. Deterding prescribed prednisone for the plaintiff's loss of kidney function. Dr. Deterding intended that the prescription reflect a dosage of eighty milligrams (80 mg) per day. The plaintiff presented the prescription to a pharmacist at Wal-Mart's Asheboro, North Carolina, store on Saturday, September 12,1992. According to the pharmacist, the prescription indicated plaintiff was to take 80 mg of prednisone 4 times per day, a daily total of 320 mg. The pharmacist claims

Brooks v Wal-Mart Stores
535 SE 2d 55 (August 29, 2000); 2000 NC App LEXIS 1038
...continued

she telephoned CKA to inquire whether 320 mg was the intended dosage, that a female answered the call, placed the pharmacist on hold, and subsequently returned and confirmed the dosage level as 320 mg. The pharmacist filled the prescription at 320 mg per day, and it was subsequently refilled at the same level on September 26, 1992, by a different pharmacist in Wal-Mart's Greenville, South Carolina, pharmacy. In later testimony, Dr. Ronald Garber, president of CKA, maintained that CKA was "never" open on Saturdays, that "no one answered the office phone] line" on Saturdays, and that an answering machine was activated on Friday afternoons that received all weekend calls and directed the caller to contact an answering service if the "call was of an urgent nature." On September 28, 1992, the plaintiff was admitted to a hospital emergency room in Greenswood, South Carolina, and diagnosed with thrush, a fungal infection of the throat. He continued ingesting 320 mg daily for 23 days until an October 5, 1992 follow-up visit with Dr. Deterding revealed plaintiff had been taking 4 times the amount of prednisone intended by Dr. Deterding. The plaintiff subsequently contracted nocardia, a bacterial infection of the lungs, and aspergillosis, a fungal infection of the brain, resulting in numerous operations and hospital stays. In a videotaped deposition taken April 24, 1998, another physician testified that the plaintiff had suffered permanent kidney failure and would "require dialysis for the rest of his life." The plaintiff sued Dr. Deterding and CKA, claiming the physician was negligent in writing the misread prescription, and Wal-Mart for negligence in dispensing the prescription.

A trial began on May 7, 1998. On May 19, 1998, the plaintiff's attorney and the attorney for Dr. Deterding and CKA informed the trial court judge that they had reached a settlement in plaintiff's favor for $10,000. Those defendants were dismissed from the case and the trial proceeded against Wal-Mart. The jury returned a verdict on May 22, 1998, finding the plaintiff was injured by the negligence of Wal-Mart and awarded plaintiff $2,500,000.00 in compensatory damages and, upon finding Wal-Mart's negligence was accompanied by aggravated conduct, awarded plaintiff $1.00 in punitive damages. The trial court entered judgment reflecting the verdict less the $10,000 paid by the settling defendants and taxing costs to Wal-Mart.

Under North Carolina law, Wal-Mart was precluded from seeking any contribution to the judgment against it from the physician or the clinic. Wal-Mart appealed, claiming, in part, that the settlement was not made in good faith and that the trial court judge should have held an evidentiary hearing on why the settlement amount was so low compared to the judgment. If successful, Wal-Mart would, at least in theory, be entitled to seek contribution from the settling defendants. The Court of Appeals rejected the claim. It noted that the judge had considered the totality of the circumstances before accepting the settlement and dismissing the other defendants. During the settlement hearing, the attorney for Dr. Deterding and CKA stated, "As the court knows, three weeks ago, [the plaintiff] made a settlement demand of $50,000.00 to my clients. We had rejected that and made a counter offer of $25,000.00, and, as the trial progressed, with the incurring of additional defense costs, my client decided not to keep the $25,000.00 there, and it went down..." The plaintiff's counsel added that he believed the case against CKA and the doctor "is a weak one, in light of the testimony that has developed. There would have been considerable costs that could have been taxed to my client, even if we win against Wal-Mart." The judge then stated: "I can say from my sitting here listening to the evidence over the last two weeks that [the plaintiff's] case as against Dr. Deterding and [CKA] has been going south all along, and I have no question in my mind that there is good reason for this renegotiation and good reason for this settlement. I'm satisfied without anything further that it's in good faith. I'm used to having officers of the court tell me the truth, and I don't think I've been told anything other than the truth here this morning. I'm just not willing to go through an exercise of hav-

Brooks v Wal-Mart Stores
535 SE 2d 55 (August 29, 2000); 2000 NC App LEXIS 1038
...continued

ing one or both of these lawyers put on the witness stand to be examined when, from all I have seen and heard in the trial of this case, I'm satisfied that this is a good faith settlement. According to the Court of Appeals, this review satisfied the trial court judge's obligation to assure the settlement was fair.

Wal-Mart also claimed that the judge committed error in allowing plaintiff's expert witness, a pharmacist from Greensboro, North Carolina, testify that the Wal-Mart pharmacist in Greenville, North Carolina, breached the applicable standard of care by filling the prednisone prescription at 320 mg per day. Wal-Mart claimed that the expert had no knowledge of or familiarity with the standards of pharmacy practice in Adams. The Court of Appeals also rejected this claims. It noted that the pharmacist testified that he received his pharmacy degree from the University of North Carolina at Chapel Hill, was currently licensed to practice pharmacy in North Carolina, and had worked in the Greensboro, North Carolina, area as a pharmacist for the past 28 years. In addition, the pharmacist was questioned by counsel for Dr. Deterding and CKA as to his familiarity with the standards of practice for pharmacists who practiced in Greenville, South Carolina, or similar communities, in September 1992. The pharmacist replied that he did.

He then went on to express the opinion that the Wal-Mart pharmacist violated the applicable standard of care by refilling plaintiff's prescription in that once the prescription was in his hands, his responsibility is no different from any pharmacist seeing that prescription for the first time. "His obligation, first and foremost, is, again, to the patient's welfare. He should know that that dose created a situation of potential harm to the patient, and the ultimate responsibility falls to him to not dispense a dose as excessive as that. On cross-examination, Wal-Mart's attorney tried to make the expert admit that he had no knowledge of how pharmacy is practiced in Greenville. The pharmacist replied, "the standard of care of a pharmacists, no matter where they are practicing, are, basically, the same, that they would not vary that much pertaining to certain areas of standard of practice. I don't think I'm unfamiliar with the standard of care in Greenville, South Carolina, because I don't feel that that standard of care is any different from any other area that a pharmacist might practice in. My opinion is that the standard of care would not be different in Greenville, South Carolina, or any other location that a pharmacist is practicing. Pharmacists attend pharmacy school and are taught standards of care and standards of practice in relation to your responsibility to the patient, and those pharmacists then go out from pharmacy school and may work in any variety of practice settings, and it doesn't matter whether that's in one state or another. The basic criteria for your standard of care is what's in the patient's best interest." As to the dosage, the pharmacist testified, "it was so excessive as to not be a gray area," and that a pharmacist should have refused to fill a prednisone prescription in that amount even if confirmed by the prescriber's office, and "there's no gray area when you get to 320 milligrams a day." The Court of Appeals concluded that the trial court correctly admitted this testimony and that it constituted sufficient evidence for the jury to find that Wal-Mart did breach its duty of care. The Court also ruled that Wal-Mart failed to preserve the rest of its objections for appeal.

The following is a list of court cases that are related to this topic.

Davis v Katz & Bestoff, Inc., 333 So. 2d 698 (La. 1976).
Reben v Ely, 705 P.2d 1360 (Ariz. Ct. App. 1985).
Fultz v Peart, 494 N.E.2d 212 (Ill. App. 5 Dist. 1986).
DeMoss Rexall Drugs v Dobson, 540 N.E. 2d 655 (Ind. App. 2 Dist. 1989).

Griffin v Phar-Mor, 1992 WL 90344 (S.D. Ala.).

Swisher-Sherman v Provident Life and Accident Insurance, No. 93-3959, Unpublished 1994 U.S. App. LEXIS 28768 (6th Cir. Oct. 13, 1994). (Table Rpt: 37F3d 1500).

Hatten v Price, 663 S.2d 351 (La. Ct. App. 1995).

Harco Drugs v Holloway, 1995 Ala. LEXIS 343 (Aug. 11, 1995).

Dunn and Ruiz v The Department of Veterans Affairs, No. 95-3732, 1996 U.S. App. LEXIS (Fed. Cir.) Dec. 11, 1996 .

Polio v Derby Center CVS, Slip Op. No. CV95-0372045, 1996 Conn. Super. LEXIS 2343, Sept. 4, 1996.

Hundley v Rite-Aid of South Carolina, No. 95-CP-46-406 (S.C. C.P. Ct., Richland, Oct. 10,1996), as reported in Pharmaceutial Litigation Reporter, p.11934, Jan., 1997.

Meeks v Shuman, Slip Op. No. 95-C-3010 (Jan. 10, 1997, US DC N. Ill.), 1997 U.S. Dist. LEXIS 179.

Wal-Mart Stores v Robbins, Slip Op. No. 2960149, Dec. 5, 1997, 1997.

Winn Dixie of Montgomery v Colburn, Slip No. 1961146, Feb. 6, 1998, Ala. S. Ct., 1998 Ala. LEXIS 48. Ala. Civ. App. LEXIS 967 and June 19, 1998, 1998 Ala. Civ. App. LEXIS 457.

Crippens v Sav On Drug Stores, Slip Op. No. 27735, July 28, 1998, S. Ct Nev., 1998 Nev. LEXIS 92.

Cackowski v Wal-Mart Stores, Slip Op. No. 1981204, January 21, 2000, S. Ct. Ala., 2000 Ala. LEXIS 22.

Nelms v Walgreen Co., Slip Op. No. 02A01805CV00137, July 7, 1999, 1999 Tenn. App. LEXIS 437.

Ellingsen v Walgreen, Slip Op. No. 98-CV-557 (JMR/FLN), December 13, 1999, U.S. D.C. MN., 1999 U.S. Dist. LEXIS 19558.

Fisher v Walgreens Louisiana, Slip Op. No. 99CA475, October 13, 1999, 1999 La. App. LEXIS 2825.

Van Hatem v K-Mart 719 N.E. 2d 212; 1999 (Ill. App. 1999).

Volner v Vantreese Discount Pharmacy, Slip Op. No. 02A01-9712-GS-00298, May 28, 1999, 1999 Tenn. App. LEXIS 337.

Burkes v Fred's Stores of Tennessee, 768 So. 2d 325 (October 3, 2000), 2000 Miss. App. LEXIS 498.

Ostrow v New London Pharmacy, Slip Op. No. 1845 (December 28, 2000), 2000 NY App. Div. LEXIS 13838.

Wrong Dosage or Strength

Lewis v DiDonna
Slip Op No 90781 (May 30, 2002), 2002 N.Y. App. Div. LEXIS 5549

In November 1997, plaintiff brought her dog of 9 years to a veterinarian and was given a prescription for an anti-inflammation drug, *Feldene*, to treat the dog's condition. The prescription was filled at defendant Eckerd's Drug Store by a licensed pharmacist. The label on the prescription bottle directed that the *Feldene* was to be administered "1 pill twice daily." Plaintiff's dog became ill and tests on the dog revealed that it had suffered renal damage due to *Feldene* toxicity. The owner discovered that the *Feldene* prescription written by the veterinarian called for 1 pill every other day and that the prescription bottle had been mislabeled. After her dog died, the autopsy revealed that the *Feldene* was a probable cause of death. The pet owner sued the pharmacist and the pharmacy regarding the mislabeling of a prescription bottle, resulting in her pet's death. The trial court denied defendants' motion to dismiss, and they appealed. The Court of Appeals held that there was no basis for treating defendants' motion to dismiss the owner's consumer fraud claim as a summary judgment motion, and the motion was properly denied because a cognizable cause of action was not flatly contradicted by documentary evidence. The owner's complaint, as supplemented by an affidavit, sufficiently alleged defendants' wanton and reckless disregard of the owner's rights to withstand the motion to dismiss her punitive damages claim. The trial court, how-

Lewis v DiDonna
Slip Op No 90781 (May 30, 2002), 2002 N.Y. App. Div. LEXIS 5549
...continued

ever, erroneously allowed the owner to introduce proof of loss of companionship regarding damages, as such a cause of action was not recognized in New York, and should not be recognized as a factor of damages. The trial court's judgment was modifed by reversing that portion which allowed the pet owner to introduce evidence of loss of companionship as to damages, and, as modified, was affirmed.

Jones v Walgreen Co.
265 Ill.App. 308 (1932)

ISSUE: Whether a pharmacist was negligent in dispensing a prescription that was an obvious overdose.

FACTS: The plaintiff presented a prescription that read "strontium salicylate 4 ounces (Wyatt), teaspoonful in water 4 times a day", signed by the prescribing physician, to defendant's clerk (graduate pharmacist) who filled the prescription with pure strontium salicylate powder made by the Parke-Davis Company. The plaintiff suffered severe injury from the effects of a gross overdose of strontium salicylate and brought suit against the pharmacy and received a $20,000 judgment. The defendant pharmacy appealed the case to the Illinois Appellate Court, which affirmed the judgment against the pharmacy and, in doing, set forth important rules of law as to the duty owed by pharmacists to their patients.

The clerk who dispensed the prescription was employed by the defendant pharmacy. He was a pharmacy graduate, 22 years old, who had passed the exam for assistant registered pharmacist before July, 1929, when the prescription was filled, but he was not licensed as a "registered pharmacist" until September, 1929.

The prescription was written for "strontium salicylate (Wyatt)." The only firm that marketed pure strontium salicylate was Parke-Davis. An effervescent strontium salicylate compound was marketed by John Wyeth & Brother, and physicians specifying a product of John Wyeth & Brother would mark "Wyeth" on the prescription. The pharmacist graduate who filled the prescription testified that "Wyatt," if slurred, sounds like "Wyeth." The usual oral dose of strontium salicylate is between 60 and 100 grains daily and that the plaintiff, by taking 4 teaspoonfuls of pure strontium salicylate received 720 grains of the drug within 16 hours - an injurious overdose.

The pharmacy graduate who dispensed the prescription was familiar with the strontium salicylate compound manufactured by Wyeth. The Wyeth preparation contained only about 5 grains of strontium salicylate per heaping teaspoonful. He was also aware that the word "Wyatt" indicated that the prescriber was specifying a particular brand, and upon consulting the "Red Book," he found no pharmaceutical brand spelled "Wyatt." He then proceeded to fill the prescription with pure strontium salicylate powder without consulting any of the registered pharmacists on duty at the pharmacy.

The expert testimony at the trial was to the effect that a physician writing "Wyatt" on the prescription meant a specific brand of strontium salicylate so that the prescription could not be filled as written without first contacting the prescriber to obtain a clarification. Pharmacists, testifying as expert witnesses at the trial, stated that when a doctor has made a mistake in a prescription, the pharmacist has no right to substitute something else.

Jones v Walgreen Co.
265 Ill.App. 308 (1932)
...continued

RULING: A pharmacist who does not consult with a physician regarding an obvious overdose may be found guilty of negligence.

REASONING: The court ruled that the injury was fully warranted in finding that the pharmacy graduate was not a competent pharmacist. Even if it could be assumed that he was competent, he was grossly negligent in filling the prescription. The dangerous nature of the drug used by him filling the prescription should have caused him to make inquiry of the prescribing physician or at least, he should have consulted with one of the other pharmacists who were on duty at the pharmacy. In the written decision on the case, the court laid down the following important rules of law:

> Finally, in applying his knowledge and exercising care and diligence, the druggist is bound to give his patrons the benefit of his best judgment; for even in pharmacy there is a class of cases in which judgment and discretion must or may be exercised. The druggist is not necessarily responsible for the results of an error of judgment which is reconcilable and consistent with the exercise of ordinary skill and care. He does not absolutely guarantee that no error shall ever be committed on the discharge of his duties. It is conceivable that there might be an error or mistake on the part of a qualified druggist which would not be held actionable negligence.

> But while, as has been seen, the legal measure of duty of druggists toward their patrons, as in all other relations of life, is properly expressed by the phrase 'ordinary care' with reference to that special and peculiar business...that while the law required of a druggist only reasonable and ordinary care in compounding prescriptions, in selling medicines, and in performing the other duties of his profession, such care with reference to him means the highest degree of prudence, thoughtfulness, and diligence, and is proportioned to the danger involved; and that a breach of such duty would be negligence rendering him liable for injuries resulting therefrom.

Hendricks v Charity Hospital of New Orleans
519 So.2d 163 (La. App. 4 Cir. 1987)

ISSUE: Whether a pharmacist should have dispensed a prescription drug without resolving the question of the proper dosage.

FACTS: The plaintiff sought medical treatment at Charity Hospital for injuries he sustained when he fell down after passing out. The treating physician learned that the plaintiff had a history of epilepsy and prescribed *Dilantin*. The prescription mistakenly called for 500 mg of the drug every 8 hours, but the physician actually intended to prescribe 500 mg daily. The plaintiff took the prescription to a pharmacy operated by the city of New Orleans, where pharmacist Leora Gonzales immediately recognized that the prescription called for an excessive dose. She sent the plaintiff back to the physician to have him reconsider the prescription because it was "enough to kill a horse."

When the plaintiff returned to the physician, he did not have the prescription, so the physician checked the hospital chart where he had written 500 mg daily. He told the plaintiff that the prescription was correct, but to have the pharmacist call if there were any more questions. After the plaintiff returned to the pharmacy, Gonzales did try to reach the physician, but without success and she finally left a message for him to call her.

Hendricks v Charity Hospital of New Orleans
519 So.2d 163 (La. App. 4 Cir. 1987)
...continued

By now, the plaintiff had become impatient and because the physician had told him that the prescription was written correctly, Gonzales agreed to dispense the prescription, putting on the label "take 5 capsules every 8 hours. NOTE: Patient should consult physician about dosage." Sometime later, the pharmacist learned from the hospital that the prescription should have called for 5 capsules daily. The plaintiff returned home and stated taking the medication as erroneously prescribed. Two days later, he was admitted to the hospital for *Dilantin* toxicity. He filed suit against the state of Louisiana, which operated the hospital and the city of New Orleans, which operated the pharmacy.

RULING: The trial court entered a judgment in favor of the plaintiff against only the state and found no fault on the part of the pharmacist. The appellate court concluded that the trial judge did not commit an error in finding that the pharmacist had not breached her duty to the plaintiff.

REASONING: It was argued that Gonzales should not have dispensed the drug until the questions of the proper dosage was cleared up. It was further claimed that she should have provided the plaintiff with a copy of the prescription when she sent him back to the physician. The plaintiff indicated that the physician was annoyed and irritated when he was questioned about the prescription, and that he quickly checked the chart and promptly sent the plaintiff back to the pharmacy with nothing more than a message for the pharmacist to call him.

The pharmacist testified that physicians typically resent questioning by pharmacists and she thought it was possible that he had prescribed the large dosage for initial use with oral instructions to the plaintiff to cut down on the dosage later. She had no knowledge that the chart showed a different dosage than the prescription. In any event, the pharmacist warned the plaintiff to contact the physician about the dosage by placing special instructions on the prescription label.

The pharmacist was quite vague about how soon after the plaintiff left the pharmacy that she found out the correct dosage was 500 mg daily. When asked if she called the plaintiff about the change in the prescription, she replied that she did not know how to contact him. The appellate court indicated that, standing alone, this testimony might support the conclusion that the pharmacist breached a duty to take some reasonable steps to locate the plaintiff and warn him of the dangerous overdose. However, the pharmacist did call the hospital and expected to hear right back, but she did not recall when she was contacted about the correct dosage. The court concluded that the pharmacist did everything required of her. "This was a close fact call, but one best made by the trial court."

Mahoney v Nebraska Methodist Hospital
560 N.W.2d 451 (Neb. 1997)

Plaintiff police officer injured her knee in 1990 after being hit by a car while providing crowd control during a riot disturbance in Omaha, Nebraska. After surgeries and other treatment to control pain caused by the injury, plaintiff began undergoing a series of sympathetic nerve block injections. The medication was prepared in the defendant hospital's pharmacy by dissolving a guanethidine pill in saline solution. The medication was injected by an anesthesiologist in an outpatient clinic. During the 13th of a 16-shot series, the plaintiff experienced severe cramping and burning at the injection site and down through her

Mahoney v Nebraska Methodist Hospital
560 N.W.2d 451 (Neb. 1997)
...continued

leg. The physician determined that the plaintiff suffered a hypertonic saline injection injury and that a pharmacist prepared the injection incorrectly. The hospital admitted liability, and the case proceeded to a jury verdict on damages only. The jury awarded plaintiff $400,000 in compensatory damages. The hospital appealed the verdict arguing procedural and evidentiary errors. The Supreme Court of Nebraska upheld the award.

The following is a list of court cases that are related to this topic.

MacKay v Crown Drug Co., 420 P.2d 883 (Okla. 1966).
Malone & Hyde, Inc. v Hobrecht, 685 S.W.2d 739 (Tex. Ct. App. 1985).
Pressler v Irvine Drugs, 215 Cal. Rptr. 807 (Cal. App. 4 Dist. 1985).
DeCordova v State of Colorado, 878 P.2d 73 (Colo. App. 1994).
Fakhouri v Taylor, 248 Ill. App. 3d 328; 618 N.E.2d 518, (Ill. App. 1993), lv. denied, (1993) LEXIS 814; 187 Ill Dec. 927.
Zuchowicz v U.S., Slip Op. No. 97-6057; 90-6099, March 20, 1998, 2nd Cir., 1998 U.S. App. LEXIS 5366.
Wainwright v Walgreen Louisiana, Slip Op. No. 99-582, December 8, 1999, 1999 La. App LEXIS 3469.
Van Hatem v K-Mart, 719 NE 2d 212; 1999 Ill. App. LEXIS 404.
Volner v Vantreese Discount Pharmacy, Slip Op. No. 02A01-9712-GS-00298, May 28, 1999, 1999 Tenn. App. LEXIS 337.

Wrong Labeling or Directions

Wimm v Jack Eckerd Corp.
3 F.3d 137 (5th Cir. 1993)

ISSUE: Whether the parents of a deceased child could amend their complaint to allege that the defendant pharmacy had falsely represented to the public that it would act as a "safety net" by warning of the dangers of prescription errors.

FACTS: Arron Speer was a normal, healthy child until he awoke one morning with severe shortness of breath. He felt very weak and could not speak above a whisper. His mother promptly took Arron to a physician who diagnosed him as having the flu and prescribed a codeine-based cough syrup.

Arron's mother went to an Eckerd pharmacy to fill the prescription for the cough syrup. The physician had prescribed a dosage of 2 teaspoons every 4 hours. However, according to the plaintiff, the label attached to the cough syrup bottle indicated that the dosage was 2 tablespoons every 4 hours.

The mother gave Arron 2 tablespoons of the cough syrup in the middle of the afternoon and again in the evening. When Arron went to bed at 10:00 p.m., his mother left the cough syrup with him and told him he could take 1 teaspoonful during the night if he needed it. When she went to Arron's room to check on him the next morning he was dead. It appeared he had taken 1 dose of the cough syrup during the night.

It was later determined that Arron suffered from viral croup, and that the condition caused the airways in his lungs to be blocked with mucus. A pathologist testified that Arron died

Wimm v Jack Eckerd Corp.
3 F.3d 137 (5th Cir. 1993)
...continued

from a lack of oxygen, resulting from airway obstruction caused by the virus. The pathologist also testified that a codeine-containing cough syrup is not an appropriate drug to prescribe for a child suffering from shortness of breath because codeine suppresses the breathing function. It also sedates the patient, making him less sensitive to air hunger.

The pharmacy chain filed a motion for summary judgment. The plaintiffs filed a motion for leave to file an amended complaint, adding two matters to the lawsuit. First, they alleged that the pharmacy negligently mislabeled the bottle of cough syrup, and thereby caused Arron's death by instructing his mother to give him an excessive dose of the medication. Secondly, the plaintiffs alleged that Eckerd, through an extensive advertising campaign, had falsely represented to the public that it would act as a safety net by warning its customers of the dangers of medications erroneously prescribed by their physicians.

RULING: The trial court denied the plaintiffs' motion for leave to amend their complaint because it found that the motion was filed in bad faith and with a dilatory motive. This lawsuit was filed roughly 20 months after the mother first stated that she learned the label on the medicine bottle was incorrect. It was not until 9 months after that, after Eckerd filed its motion for summary judgment, that the plaintiff first asserted their claim for mislabeling. The appellate court granted summary judgment in favor of the pharmacy defendant.

REASONING: The fact surrounding the deceptive advertising claims were known to the plaintiffs long before they asserted their claims. Arron's mother stated that she had been a customer of Eckerd's Drug for many years and she expected to be warned about the dangers of prescription drugs because of Eckerd's representations to her over the years. However, those representations were not made the subject of a claim in the lawsuit until approximately 33 months after Arron's death and 9 months after the lawsuit was commenced.

The appellate court noted that the plaintiffs were aware of the facts supporting their mislabeling and deceptive advertising claims before they initiated their lawsuit, but they did not present those claims until summary judgment was imminent. Consequently, the U.S. Court of Appeals for the Fifth Circuit concluded that the district court's finding of bad faith and dilatory motive was supported by the record.

The appellate court also noted that the trial court found the plaintiffs' requested amendment would have been futile because "the amount of cough syrup given to Arron had been thoroughly investigated and the determination made that he did not receive a toxic dose of the cough syrup."

The following is a list of court cases that are related to this topic.

Peoples Service Drug Stores v Somerville, 158 A. 12 (Md. 1932).
Sheils v Eckerd Corp., 560 So. 2d 361 (Fla. App 2d 1990).
Huggins v Longs Drug Stores, 1991 Cal. App LEXIS 1409 (Cal. Ct. App 5th Dist.).
Griffin v Phar-Mor, 1992 WL 90344 (S.D. Ala.).
Huggins v Longs Drug Stores California, Inc., Cal. Sup. Ct. No. 5030711 (Nov. 18, 1993).
Bookman v Ciolino, 684 So.2d 982 (La. App. 5th Cir. 1994).
Dunn and Ruiz v The Department of Veterans Affairs, No. 95-3732, 1996 U.S. App. LEXIS (Fed. Cir.) Dec. 11, 1996.
Hundley v Rite-Aid of South Carolina, No. 95-CP-46-406 (S.C. C.P. Ct., Richland, Oct. 10, 1996), as reported in Pharmaceutical Litigation Reporter, p.11934, Jan., 1997.

Griffith v Blatt, 973 P.2d 385 (Or. Ct. App. 1999).

Wrong Route of Administration

Gassen v East Jefferson General Hospital, et al
628 So.2d 256 (La.Ct.App. 1993)

ISSUE: Whether a pharmacist is legally responsible for dispensing a medication order with an incorrect route of administration.

FACTS: Following the injury to one of its patients, East Jefferson General Hospital alleged that Allied Pharmacy (which is located on the premises of the hospital) dispensed the order for "vibramycin 100 mg intramuscular (IM) two times a day" without seeking clarification from a nurse or the prescribing doctor. The hospital further claimed that the pharmacy and its insurer are liable to it on the basis of a contract between the parties for indemnity. The pharmacy answered the third-party complaint, alleging that the prescribing doctor was the informed intermediary between the pharmacy and the patient, and that it was the doctor who had the legal duty to order and administer the proper prescription.

On appeal, the pharmacy asserted that its pharmacist filled the order in the proper form, intravenously (IV), and labeled the package as such. The hospital alleged that this information was not provided to the nurse, until after the drug had been administered. In support of its motion to dismiss, Allied filed an affidavit of its director of pharmacy. The director acknowledged that the pharmacy received an order for "vibramycin 100 mg. IM BID," but the pharmacist entered the order as IV, since vibramycin injectable is manufactured only for IV use and not IM use. The pharmacist labeled the package containing the vial of vibramycin to indicate the IV administration.

The pharmacy claimed that the nursing floor received the vibramycin in the labeled package and, despite instructions that it was to be administered IV, administered it IM to the plaintiff.

Testimony on behalf of the hospital claimed that the pharmacy did not contact the doctor for clarification or communicate any change in the order to the nursing staff. An affidavit from an RN claimed that the pharmacist made the change in the medication order, but notice of the change was not available of the nursing staff until the day after the vibramycin had been administered.

RULING: Because the affidavits in this case raised questions regarding a dispute as to whether the pharmacist followed the written hospital policy dealing with the clarification of drug orders, the appellate court reversed the dismissal of the pharmacy and remanded the case for further hearings in light of this decision.

REASONING: The appellate court rejected the pharmacy's reliance upon the line of cases involving a pharmacist's duty to warn. The present case was distinguished from them because it did not involve the warning of adverse effects. Instead, the case at hand involved a prescription order, which was allegedly incorrect on its face.

The pharmacy further relied upon an earlier Louisiana case in which a plaintiff sued a physician and a pharmacy for damages caused by an excessive dose of *Dilantin*. The pharmacist recognized that the dose was excessive and sent the patient back to the physician. However, the doctor did not review the prescription again, but instead checked the plaintiff's hospital chart, which stated the proper dosage. The physician told the plaintiff that the dosage was correct, but if the pharmacist had a question, she should call him. The pharmacist did try to contact the physician again but couldn't reach him. On the patient's insis-

Gassen v East Jefferson General Hospital, et al
628 So.2d 256 (La.Ct.App. 1993)
...continued

tence, the prescription was dispensed, but the pharmacist included additional instructions on the label for the patient to check with the doctor. The pharmacist was not found liable. The case was distinguished from the one at hand by the fact that the pharmacist did try to contact the physician and did show her concern for the patient by including an additional warning on the prescription label.

The court concluded that a pharmacist has a duty to accurately dispense a prescription and to be alert for clear errors or mistakes in the prescription. The pharmacist does not, however, have a duty to question the physician's judgment as to the propriety of a prescription or to warn a patient of the hazardous side effects associated with the drug, either orally or by way of the manufacturer's package insert.

Unauthorized Refill

United States v Duggan Drug Stores, Inc.
326 F.2d 835 (1964)

ISSUE: (1) Whether the lack of bona fide prescription presented by an undercover agent may serve as a defense for a pharmacist who has dispensed refills without the prescriber's authorization and (2) whether a corporation may be found guilty when its employees have been acquitted.

FACTS: The case involved a 10-count charge against a corporation and its president and employees for refilling legend drug prescriptions without authorization as required by federal law. The case was brought against the defendants by the U.S. Attorney's office for the Southern District of Texas. A jury trial resulted in the acquittal of the president and all employees of the pharmacy corporation except one who pleaded guilty. The corporation was convicted and fined. An appeal was taken by the corporation.

Government agents presented the defendant pharmacists with what looked like valid prescriptions but were not, in fact, since no "physician-patient" relationship existed between the government agents and the prescribing physicians. After the prescriptions were initially filled, the government agents were later able to obtain refills from the defendants. However, the defendant-pharmacists did not obtain authorization from the prescribing physicians.

During the appeal, the pharmacy corporation's lawyers claimed that because the prescriptions were not bona fide in the first instance, the charge against the defendants was technically defective. It was also claimed that the jury's verdict was inconsistent because the jury found the individual persons involved to be innocent, but found the corporation guilty. Also, in the appeal, reference was made to the overzealous or aggressive tactics of the government prosecutor whose tactics were claimed to have prejudicially influenced the jury into finding at least someone guilty of something.

RULING: The lack of a bona fide prescription is not a defense since the prescription simply provides an opportunity for the violation of law. In addition, a corporation may be subject to prosecution separate from the acts of its officers or employees.

REASONING: The appellate court rejected the argument that the lack of a bona fide prescription was a defense since the prescription simply presented an opportunity for the viola-

United States v Duggan Drug Stores, Inc.
326 F.2d 835 (1964)
...continued

tion of the law. The court ruled that the inconsistency of the verdict would have no bearing in this case. Under the applicable federal law, the corporation or company itself was subject to prosecution as well as its officers and/or employees and, in fact, each could be prosecuted separately.

The court did reverse the trial court's convictions and sent the case back for retrial on the grounds that the overzealous or aggressive tactics of the government's attorney had "a probable cumulative effect on the jury that may not be disregarded as prejudicial."

After the case was sent back to the lower court for retrial, the corporation waived its right to another trial and instead pleaded nolo contendere, meaning it did not admit to the facts but it chose not to contest them. Such a plea, for purposes of imposition of sentence, is the same as a guilty plea. However, because the defendant, while taking the punishment, is not admitting to the facts charged, the conviction cannot be used as conclusive evidence of the facts charged in a future state prosecution, civil suit, or administrative agency disciplinary action.

Stafford v Nipp
502 So.2d 702 (Ala. 1987)

ISSUE: Whether a pharmacy refilled a prescription without authorization and whether the pharmacist failed to adequately instruct the patient as to the use of the drug.

FACTS: The plaintiff suffered a stroke in December of 1980, which she alleged was caused by her prolonged use of *Ovulen-21*, which had originally been prescribed for her by Dr. Nevill in October 1971. The plaintiff claimed that the oral contraceptive had been dispensed and subsequently refilled on a monthly basis by a pharmacist, William Nipp, until the day before the plaintiff's stroke. The physician agreed that he did prescribe *Ovulen-21* for the plaintiff, but claimed that he only issued a 6-month supply. While the plaintiff continued to see Dr. Nevill for other medical problems, she did not seek further consultation with regard to the birth control pills.

Pharmacist Nipp testified that he would not have refilled the prescription without authorization, but he no longer had the original prescription since he only kept his prescription records for 2 or 3 years. The pharmacist claimed he did not remember the plaintiff coming to his pharmacy on a monthly basis from 1971 to 1980.

RULING: The trial court granted summary judgment in favor of both physician and pharmacist. On appeal, the Supreme Court of Alabama determined that there was a genuine issue of fact regarding liability. It reversed the trial court's dismissal of the plaintiff's claim against the pharmacist for breach of warranty and it also reversed the judgment in favor of the physician and returned the matter to the trial court for further deliberation.

REASONING: The Supreme Court of Alabama reasoned that if the jury believed the pharmacist would not have refilled the prescription without authorization, there was a genuine issue as to whether the physician was liable for prescribing the drug for an extended period of time. By the same token, although the pharmacist denied that he would have dispensed the medication over nine years without authorization, the physician stated that he did not

Stafford v Nipp
502 So.2d 702 (Ala. 1987)
...continued

prescribe the oral contraceptive for longer than a 6-month period of time. Thus, there was again another question of fact for the trial court and the case should not have been summarily dismissed.

The court also found that there was a factual question as to whether the pharmacist failed to warn the plaintiff concerning the taking of *Ovulen-21* for a long period of time without authority from the physician and without periodic physical examinations. The court held that the manufacturer's package insert warnings so not, as a matter of law, shield the pharmacist from liability when the pharmacist continues to fill the prescription without authorization from the physician.

Bickowicz v Sterling Drug, Inc.
557 N.Y.S.2d 551 (App. Div. 1990)

ISSUE: Whether a drug manufacturer and a pharmacy that illegally refilled prescriptions were liable for the plaintiff's injuries resulting from her addiction to a prescription drug.

FACTS: The physician began administering *Talwin* to the plaintiff in 1968 as treatment for her migraine headaches. Injections were administered at the physician's office or at the hospital. When the plaintiff informed the physician in 1973 of a lengthy trip to Florida, the physician wrote prescriptions for *Talwin*, *Dramamine*, and disposable syringes. She also instructed the plaintiff's husband on how to administer the injections.

Allegedly, the prescription for *Talwin* was not refillable. Yet, the plaintiff, from 1973 through 1981, obtained many refills from Nedco Pharmacy through its respective owners, even though the physician stopped treating the plaintiff in 1975. By 1980, the plaintiff was allegedly injecting the drug every hour. She was admitted to the hospital in 1980 for an unrelated problem, at which time she realized she was addicted to *Talwin*, and her neurologist then discussed the problem with a psychiatrist.

As part of the treatment plan, the psychiatrist prescribed decreasing doses of *Talwin* over the period of the plaintiff's hospitalization. Upon her discharge from the hospital, the plaintiff told the psychiatrist of another impending trip and he gave her a prescription for injectable *Talwin* that would reportedly last until the plaintiff's trip ended. This prescription was also allegedly nonrefillable. Nonetheless, the plaintiff managed to obtain repeated refills from this prescription and from her original 1973 prescription until she was admitted to a detoxification unit in 1981. As a result of the repeated injections of *Talwin* in the leg and thigh area over the years, the plaintiff suffered serious and permanent damage to those areas.

RULING: The pharmacy and the defendant physicians settled with the plaintiff for a collective sum of $400,000. The case proceeded to the jury, which awarded the plaintiff $650,000 and apportioned liability as follows: 65% liability to the pharmacy and its various owners, 18% to the plaintiff, and 17% to the defendant manufacturers. (Note: The settlement between the pharmacy and the plaintiff does not serve as a legal precedent. The appeal focused on the manufacturer's liability.) The appellate court concluded that, because of the pharmacists' intervening acts of illegally refilling the prescription, the case should be remanded for a new trial to consider the manufacturer's liability.

Bickowicz v Sterling Drug, Inc.
557 N.Y.S.2d 551 (App. Div. 1990)
...continued

REASONING: The defendant manufacturers argued that in light of the evidence concerning the intentional and/or culpable conduct of the plaintiff and the pharmacists at Nedco, a jury charge on the law governing superseding causes was warranted on behalf of the manufacturers. The appellate court cited the basic premise that a defendant's negligence must be a substantial cause of the injury, and any break in the connection between the defendant's negligence and a plaintiff's injury may affect the liability of the defendant. However, if the intervening act is a natural, normal, and foreseeable consequence of the situation created by the defendant, the defendant will continue to be liable. More importantly, when the intervening act is intentional or criminal in nature, the liability of the tort-feasor (the manufacturer in this case) will usually be severed unless the intentional intervention was reasonably foreseeable.

There was evidence produced at the trial that all of the pharmacists at Nedco Pharmacy illegally and improperly refilled the prescriptions for *Talwin* in quantities beyond that called for in the prescription, illegally sold syringes to the plaintiff, and failed to properly label the vials of *Talwin* and maintain proper records. There was also evidence concerning the conduct of the later owners of the pharmacy from which the jury could conclude that the owners were criminally responsible for improperly refilling the 1980 prescription for *Talwin*.

Similarly, regarding the plaintiff herself, there was sufficient evidence of her own intentional conduct to justify an inference that her actions exceeded mere contributory negligence and could be considered an intervening force that would absolve the defendant manufacturers from any alleged liability.

Although the plaintiff maintained that she did not obtain *Talwin* illegally, she readily admitted that she not only continued to refill the 1973 prescription long after she returned from the trip, but that she took the drug in ways she knew she was not supposed to. She further admitted that she simultaneously refilled two separate prescriptions for *Talwin* at two different pharmacies without the knowledge of either the pharmacists or the prescribing physicians. Additionally, the plaintiff testified that she may have lied to the pharmacist or may have made up excuses that were not true in order to obtain additional amounts of *Talwin*.

Clair v Paris Road Drugs, Inc.
573 So. 2d 1219 (La. App. 1991)

ISSUE: Whether a pharmacy and its insurance carrier were liable for damages resulting from a patient's drug addiction that she claimed was caused by the defendant's negligence in illegally dispensing prescriptions.

FACTS: The plaintiff was treated, during the 1980s for nervousness and weight reduction and was prescribed *Valium*, *Doriden*, *Ativan*, and *Noludar*. Most were prescribed without refills.

Clair had her prescriptions dispensed by Paris Road Drugs during this time. During the latter part of 1983, the pharmacy was sold to Larry Renz who advertised for a pharmacist. Ron Meisler applied. During the job interview with Renz, Meisler disclosed that he had previously been suspended by the Louisiana State Board of Pharmacy for drug shortages. In spite of his background, he was hired.

Clair v Paris Road Drugs, Inc.
573 So. 2d 1219 (La. App. 1991)
...continued

Shortly after he began employment, Meisler informed the plaintiff that whatever medication she wanted he would refill for her if she brought in the empty bottles. Clair accepted Meisler's offer. Over the next two years she became increasingly addicted until she could not function. Without the drugs she experienced severe withdrawals, consisting of bladder and bowel dysfunction, vomiting, and seizures.

In 1985, her 10-year-old daughter ran away from home because of Clair's addiction. She also lost temporary custody of her son. During her last seizure, she remained in the Charity Hospital's emergency room for 3 days before she was conscious and sufficiently coherent to sign herself into a drug detoxification unit. She was eventually discharged from detox and she has remained drug free.

RULING: The jury found the plaintiff 50% negligent and the various defendants 50% negligent. The jury awarded the plaintiff $3000 for past and future medical costs and $4000 for past and future physical pain and suffering. The appellate court concluded that the jury was wrong in not apportioning a greater share of fault to the pharmacist. It therefore reapportioned the plaintiff's fault to 35% with the defendants being 65% responsible.

REASONING: The prescribing physicians testified that they did not authorize most of the prescriptions that the plaintiff took over a number of years. A Board of Pharmacy inspector testified that an audit of Paris Road Drugs, during the time Meisler was in charge, indicated shortages of *Valium* and *Percodan*.

The plaintiff testified, at great length, about the many tragedies in her life. She spoke about the deaths of her sister and brother and described how she fatally stabbed her abusive husband in self defense. The plaintiff claimed that these traumatic events greatly affected her emotional ability. As a result she turned to tranquilizers, pain medications, and sleeping pills. She further testified that prior to Meisler's employment, the previous pharmacist had been very strict and warned her to be careful about the addictive nature of the drugs and refused to refill the prescriptions without authorization.

Clair testified that most of the time she was physically unable to purchase the drugs herself and sent her boyfriend to buy them. She claimed that Meisler was well aware of her condition because on one occasion she went into the drugstore and could hardly stand up. When Clair informed her physician that the pharmacy was refilling the drugs without a prescription, her physician asked her why she did not report this to the authorities. Clair stated that she had no willpower. "Why would I report him? He was giving me this medication. Without it I was very sick."

The plaintiff contended that the comparative fault principles of Louisiana law should not be applied in this case. Her own fault, she contended, should not be considered because it was so outweighed by the high degree of care owed by the pharmacist. In particular, the plaintiff argued that the pharmacist's high duty of care extends to the protection of the "helpless" patient.

The record was clear that Clair voluntarily engaged in the activity that contributed to her own addiction by requesting refills of medications clearly marked "no refills." She also ignored the early warnings of the first pharmacist that the drugs she was taking were highly addictive. By her own admission, she was able to withdraw from her addiction within a matter of days after being confined to the detox unit.

Clair v Paris Road Drugs, Inc.
573 So. 2d 1219 (La. App. 1991)
...continued

Balanced against these facts, the court weighted the duty of care owed by the pharmacist. He knew that he was illegally dispensing harmful drugs and it became increasingly clear that the plaintiff had become addicted. At that point in time, Meisler's position was far superior to that of the plaintiff, and the jury was wrong in not apportioning a greater share of fault to the pharmacist.

Bailey v Johnson
48 F.3d 965 (6th Cir. 1995)

FACTS: A pharmacy repeatedly filled an oral methotrexate prescription for severe psoriasis treatment based on the fact that the prescription was entered into the pharmacy computer system as "refillable". The prescribing physician gave no authorization for, nor knew of, the refills. The otherwise healthy 77-year-old patient later died from a massive infection. An autopsy revealed a "preleukemic condition," allegedly enhanced by the drug's effects. The patient's wife filed a malpractice suit in federal district court with jurisdiction premised on the claim that a prescription-only drug was dispensed without a valid prescription in violation of the federal Food, Drug & Cosmetic Act (the "FDCA").

HOLDING: In this case of "first impression," the Sixth Circuit held that the FDCA does not create a private cause of action against a "druggist." The case was dismissed for lack of federal jurisdiction.

Austermiller v Dosick
Slip Op No L-01-1223 (December 31, 2001), 2001 Ohio App. LEXIS 5964

Following hospitalization in 1994, a physician released the decedent with instructions that he should take daily doses of *Coumadin*. The doctor ordered a follow-up examination to monitor the effects of the drug. It was uncontested that the decedent failed to attend his follow-up appointment or again consult with the doctor. What is disputed is an allegation that during the next 18 months, the physician, or someone in the physician's office, telephoned refill prescriptions for *Coumadin* to the patient's pharmacy. The last of these refills was for a 1-year supply. It was dated March 11, 1996, and was phoned into a Bowling Green, Ohio, pharmacy. On December 20, 1996, the patient transferred this prescription to the Napoleon, Ohio, branch of the same pharmacy chain. In doing so, the Napoleon pharmacist erroneously recorded the date of the prescription as the date of the transfer. This resulted in the Napoleon pharmacy continuing to refill the *Coumadin* prescription beyond the anniversary date upon which the prescription would have ordinarily expired. The patient received *Coumadin* refills on April 22, 1997, and August 14, 1997. On September 19, 1997, the patient died from internal bleeding. Following a settlement with the pharmacy, the matter proceeded to a jury trial solely against the physician. At trial, the autopsy report set the cause of death as "gastrointestinal exsanguination" and listed "long-term *Coumadin* use" among significant conditions relating to death. The patient's medical expert testified that it was his opinion that the patient died of "uncontrolled bleeding secondary to *Coumadin* toxicity." The expert also testified that a physician who continues to prescribe *Coumadin* without appropriate monitoring "departs from accepted standards of care." The executor of the plaintiff's estate brought a medical negligence suit against the doctor and the pharmacy that

Austermiller v Dosick
Slip Op No L-01-1223 (December 31, 2001), 2001 Ohio App. LEXIS 5964
...continued

filled the decedent's prescription. Following a settlement with the pharmacy, the matter proceeded to a jury trial solely against the doctor. At the conclusion of the evidence, appellee moved for a directed verdict, contending that the nonparty pharmacy was guilty of negligence per se when it continued to refill the *Coumadin* prescription beyond the 1 year period allowed by the Ohio Administrative Code. Since the estate's own medical expert testified that it was the *Coumadin* taken "in the weeks before" that caused the patient's death, physician argued the pharmacy's negligence constituted an intervening and superseding cause which absolved the physician of liability. The trial court granted the physician's motion, directing a verdict against appellant and dismissing the jury. The appellate court found that the doctor premised his motion for a directed verdict on the pharmacy's per se negligence and the "admission" of the executor's expert witness that death was caused by the drug taken in the weeks before the death. Further, the appellate court found that the issue was whether the pharmacy's negligence was new and independent of the doctor's alleged negligence. Pursuant to standing precedent, this was a question of fact. The judgment of the trial court was reversed and remanded.

The following is a list of court cases that are related to this topic.

United States v Carlisle, 234 F. 2d 196 (1956).
Arenstein v California State Board of Pharmacy, 71 Cal. Rptr. 357 (1968).
Speer v United States, 512 F. Supp. 670 (N.D. Tex 1981).
Riff v Morgan, 508 A.2d 1247 (Pa.Super. 1986).
Mutual Benefit Insurance v Haver, 725 A.2d 743 (Pa. 1999).

Compounding Errors

The following is a list of court cases that are related to this topic.

Schroeder v Cox Medical Center, 1991 WL 241055 (Mo. App. Ct.).
Malon v Hueseman, WD 53338, April 8, 1997, 1997 Mo. App. LEXIS 565.
Mohoney v Nebraska Methodist Hospital, 251 Neb. 841: 560 N.W. 2d 451 (S. Ct., 1997).
Brown v Southern Baptist Hospital, Slip Op. Nos. 96-CA-1990 and 96-CA-1991, La. App. 4th
    Cir., March 11, 1998, 1998 La. App. LEXIS 556.

Prison Services

France v State of New York
506 N.Y.S.2d 254 (Ct. Claims 1986)

ISSUE: Whether a pharmacist who failed to refill a prescription for a patient was liable for negligence.

FACTS: The plaintiff, Earl France, was an inmate at the Eastern New York Correctional Facility. Mr. France was diagnosed as having atopic dermatitis as a result of an unbalanced oil content, a nervous condition, and a vitamin deficiency. This condition caused his skin to dry, crack, and scale. His skin was very itchy and he was uncomfortable as a result of the condition. The inmate's physician prescribed an ointment consisting of *Eucerin* and hydrocortisone to relieve his discomfort.

France v State of New York
506 N.Y.S.2d 254 (Ct. Claims 1986)
...continued

The inmate alleged that the pharmacist employed by the correctional facility did not refill his prescription for a 1-month time period. It was claimed that the pharmacist refused to prepare the ointment and, thus, the inmate was without any medication for a 30-day time period. As a result, the plaintiff suffered discomfort, and he was unable to relieve any of his pain without the ointment.

RULING: The court found that the pharmacist was negligent in failing to dispense the prescription and awarded the inmate $450 for the discomfort he endured as a result of not receiving his medication.

REASONING: The failure of a pharmacist to exercise the standard of care required of him or her constitutes negligence, which renders the pharmacist liable for damages that are the proximate result of the negligence. The legal measure of the duty of pharmacists toward their patients is ordinary care. The rule of ordinary care as applied to the profession of pharmacy means the highest practical degree of prudence, thoughtfulness, and vigilance.

It was the pharmacist's responsibility to compound and dispense the salve as prescribed by the inmate's physician. The plaintiff, as an inmate, was confined to the prison and was not at liberty to take his business to another pharmacy. By failing to provide the inmate with the medication for 1 month, the pharmacist did not meet the required level of care. Thus, he was negligent. The state failed to present any evidence explaining why the pharmacist refused to dispense the prescription. As an employee of the state of New York, the state was answerable in damages for the pharmacist's negligence.

Johnson v Hay
931 F.2d 456 (8th Cir. 1991)

ISSUE: Whether a pharmacist who refused to fill a prescription for an antiseizure medication for a prison inmate violated the inmate's Eighth Amendment rights.

FACTS: E. L. Johnson was transferred from a county jail to the Missouri Department of Corrections where he was examined by a prison physician. Although Johnson's medical records were not forwarded with him, he told the physician that he suffered from seizures and he had been taking *Dilantin* and phenobarbital. The physician noted this in the medical records and wrote prescriptions for these drugs.

Several years later, another prison doctor issued Johnson a 30-day prescription for the same two medications. These prescriptions expired thirty days later on June 4, 1986. On July 3, 1986 yet another physician issued another prescription for *Dilantin* and on July 18, another prison physician issued a 30-day prescription for phenobarbital and *Dilantin*. On August 4, Johnson was issued prescriptions for a 6-month supply of both drugs.

Pharmacist Bill Hay refused to fill the July 18 or August 4 prescriptions. Johnson suffered a seizure on approximately July 21 and another one about a week later. The pharmacist stated that he did not fill these prescriptions based on his determination that the seizure medications were not appropriate. He made this determination based upon his review of Johnson's medical records and discussions with the physician. Hay also talked to Johnson's housing supervisor. No one indicated that they had observed Johnson having a seizure during the period of time when he would have been without medication.

Johnson v Hay
931 F.2d 456 (8th Cir. 1991)
...continued

The pharmacist further stated that he did not fill the prescriptions because he found certain discrepancies in the prescriptions and numerous inconsistencies in the inmate's version of his medical history. In particular, he noted that there was an overlap in the timing of some of the prescriptions. When a 6-month prescription is written, the institution's policy was to actually distribute the drug on a daily basis.

Hay could find no diagnosis of Johnson's seizure disorder, only a statement that he claimed to have such a problem. However, the inmate was later able to obtain the statement of a physician who had examined him in the county jail. This physician had determined that Johnson suffered from seizure activity.

RULING: The court was not convinced that the pharmacist acted as a reasonable pharmacist in denying the medication and the case was returned to a jury for a hearing on whether the pharmacist acted with deliberate indifference to the prisoner's medical needs.

REASONING: In determining whether the pharmacist was protected by qualified immunity, the court had to decide the legal question of whether the conduct of which the inmate complained violated clearly established law.

The pharmacist claimed that his refusal to dispense the prescriptions did not violate Johnson's clearly established rights. He claimed that at the time he withheld Johnson's medicines, the law governing his conduct was not clearly established and that a reasonable pharmacist could have believed that he was not violating Johnson's constitutional rights in refusing to fill the prescriptions. The pharmacist pointed to the lack of any case law that had interpreted a prison pharmacist's constitutional responsibility as support of his argument that the law governing his conduct was not clearly established. (Note: to show that the law is "clearly established," a plaintiff must make a particular showing that a reasonable official would understand that what he is doing violated a plaintiff's rights.)

However, the court concluded that at the time Hay withheld Johnson's seizure medication, the law governing his conduct was clearly established. In an earlier case, the U.S. Supreme Court held that "deliberate indifference to serious medical needs of prisoners constitutes the unnecessary and wanton infliction of pain...proscribed the Eighth Amendment." There was no doubt Hay intentionally, not inadvertently, refused to dispense Johnson's prescriptions and that this conduct amounted to intentional interference with the treatment prescribed by his attending physicians.

The pharmacist claimed that his refusal to fill the prescriptions was medically justified and objectively reasonable in view of the information available to him. For support, he pointed out that (1) Johnson's available medical records did not contain any documentation or diagnosis of a seizure disorder; (2) he believed Johnson was receiving *Dilantin* pursuant to the July 3 prescription; (3) Johnson had not sought renewal of his May 5 prescription until July 3 and had been without medication for about 30 days without suffering a seizure; (4) Johnson had a long history of drug-seeking behavior; (5) security problems in the prison warranted the pharmacist's delay in filling the prescriptions; and (6) that Hay's legal and ethical responsibilities prevented him from filling the prescriptions.

The court was not convinced that Hay acted as a reasonable pharmacist. He did not personally examine Johnson or request a prison doctor to examine the inmate to determine the appropriateness of the medication orders. Neither did he advise any doctor that he intended to withhold Johnson's medications, nor did he try to contact the original diagnosing phy-

Johnson v Hay
931 F.2d 456 (8th Cir. 1991)
...continued

sician. While Hay claimed that he relied on the advice of an attorney in refusing to dispense the prescription, the court noted that his reliance was actually on an article published by an attorney in a professional medical journal. The article discussed a pharmacist's responsibility for dispensing controlled substances. Hay's reliance on this article did not establish that he acted reasonably in withholding the inmate's medications.

Meeks v Shuman
Slip Op. No. 95-C-3010 (Jan. 10, 1997, US ir N. Ill.), 1997 U.S. Dist. LEXIS 179

been pre prisoner of the Illinois Department of Corrections, where he is serving a 45-year d murder. He suffers coronary artery disease and hypertension and has purchases its medications only including Cardizem. The pharmacy from which the prison plaintiff claims that his rights were violated when he was denied access to prescribed medication. The trial court dismissed the claim because "substituting medication does not rise to the level of a constitutional violation." The judge accepted the affidavits of three Department of Corrections physicians who opined that substituting a 170 mg dose of *Dilacor* for the 300 mg dose of *Cardizem* that was prescribed would not constitute a health risk to the plaintiff and concluded, "The medicine (administered by the prison), although not the name brand prescribed, was the generic substitute for the prescribed drug and did not compromise his health."

Walls v Hollarnd
198 F.3d 248 (6th Cir. 1999)

A federal prisoner sued the warden, a prison physician, an administrator, a corrections officer, and the prison pharmacist both as individuals and in their official positions. He charged that after his hand was amputated following an accident while at work in the prison he has been deprived of necessary medical care for treatment of his injuries. Insofar as the claim against the pharmacist, the prisoner claimed that he was deprived of prescribed medications and that his medications were confiscated from his prison cell. The pharmacist is a commissioned officer in the Public Health Service. As such, the only remedy that the prisoner could pursue against the pharmacist was under the Federal Tort Claims Act. This act prevents lawsuits against officers in their individual capacities. It also provides immunity from lawsuits by prisoners. The court also determined that the prisoner could seek compensation from the prison under the Inmate Accident Compensation Act, 18 USC §4126 but that he had failed to state a claim against the prison system. The Court of Appeals affirmed the trial court's judgment.

The following is a list of court cases that are related to this topic.

Bowers v Milwaukee County Jail Medical Staff, Slip Op No 02–1259 (October 23, 2002), 7th Cir, 2002 U.S. App. LEXIS 24244.

Detection, Monitoring, and Warning of Potential Problems

Duty to Warn

Krueger v Knutson
111 N.W.2d 526 (Minn. 1961)

ISSUE: Whether a pharmacist has a duty to warn of the dangerous explosive properties of a chemical purchased in the pharmacy.

FACTS: Terry Krueger and several of the boys from his high school formed a rocket club and proceeded to experiment in making rockets. The boys needed a mixture of potassium chlorate, sulfur, and charcoal to make the fuel, and they purchased these chemicals at the defendant's pharmacy. The boys told the pharmacist that they were working with rockets, but there was no indication he gave any warning concerning the explosive properties of the chemicals. The record indicated that the pharmacist knew the chemicals used to be explosive if combined with certain other ingredients.

The evidence showed that the plaintiff did not know the properties of potassium chlorate except that he believed, when mixed with sulfur and charcoal, the mixture would "burn" if a match was applied to it. All of the boys assumed that a fuse would have to be attached and a match applied before there could be an explosion. However, a rocket exploded while being tamped with the chemical mixture and the plaintiff's left hand was seriously injured.

In the lawsuit by the plaintiff and his parents against the pharmacist, it was contended that the standard of care of a pharmacist in dispensing potassium chlorate, sulfur, and charcoal would be to have proper labeling and to sell it only to competent persons and not to minors, who are sometimes irresponsible. The plaintiffs further contended that if the pharmacist did sell these chemicals to 16-year-olds, he should caution them on the use of combinations of the chemicals. Since the pharmacist knew these chemicals were to be used as a rocket fuel mixture, the standard of care would require the pharmacist to caution the boys very highly about the danger involved. The plaintiff testified that the pharmacist placed the potassium chlorate in a paper bag. The pharmacist denied any knowledge of selling potassium chlorate to the boys.

RULING: The Minnesota Supreme Court upheld a jury verdict of $5000 in damages to the plaintiff and $1300 in damages to his father for the pharmacist's failure to exercise due care in warning the plaintiff.

REASONING: The court cited *Fuhs v Barber*, 36 P.2d 962 "it has been held that where the druggist knows that a drug, harmless in itself, is to be mixed with, or used in conjunction with, another which would then have an injurious effect, of which the purchaser has no knowledge, he should advise the purchaser of it, and a failure to do so would make him liable for the consequences."

The court could not find any clear evidence of contributory negligence on the part of Terry or his father. The appellate court noted that the jury was at liberty to accept either the plaintiff's version or the pharmacist's version. The jury apparently gave more credence to the testimony of the plaintiffs.

The plaintiffs also appealed alleging that $5000 in damages was so insufficient as to appear to have been given under the influence of prejudice. The evidence showed that the explosion resulted in severe injury to the plaintiff's left hand. After all the treatment was complete, the evidence still showed the plaintiff suffering a 90% disability of the hand and 81%

Krueger v Knutson
111 N.W.2d 526 (Minn. 1961)
...continued

impairment of his arm as a result of this injury. However, the court would not set aside the jury verdict simply because it might be inadequate. The court stated that age-old rule that whether to grant a new trial on grounds of excessive or inadequate damages rests almost wholly in the sound discretion of the trial court. The trial court decision will not be disturbed on appeal except if there is evidence of clear abuse of discretion.

Kasin v Osco Drugs
No 2-99-0356 (April 12, 2000), 200 Ill App LEXIS 242

The plaintiff sought treatment from a physician for a swollen ankle. The doctor prescribed *Daypro*. With the exception of treatment for flu symptoms 3 months earlier, the plaintiff had been healthy and had not seen a physician for over 25 years. The plaintiff had the prescription filled at a local Osco Drugs and was given an information sheet that listed common side effects. There was no oral consultation with a pharmacist. On the tenth day after initiating therapy the plaintiff noticed that his stools were black and complained that he had no energy. He collapsed later that day and was admitted to a hospital through an emergency room where he was diagnosed with three ulcers and renal failure. While in the hospital, he learned for the first time that he was born with only one kidney, which was now failing. After being on dialysis for 7 months, he underwent kidney transplant surgery with a kidney donated by his brother. He sued, claiming that the pharmacy voluntarily undertook a duty to warn him about complications associated with use of the drug by giving him the information sheet and that the information was incomplete because it did not list renal failure among the known side effects. In other words, he claimed that by voluntarily undertaking the duty to warn of some side effects, the pharmacy was obligated to warn of all side effects. Osco moved for summary judgment claiming that it was protected from liability under the learned intermediary doctrine. The trial court dismissed the case and the plaintiff appealed. Under the authority of *Frye v Medicare-Glaser*, 153 Ill 2d 26; 605 NE 2d 557 (1992), the Illinois Court of Appeals affirmed dismissal. It ruled that while the learned intermediary doctrine does not necessarily protect a pharmacy that voluntarily undertakes the duty to warn, the pharmacy is only liable to the extent of its undertaking. Here the pharmacy only undertook to warn of common side effects and there was no question that it those warnings were accurate. The pharmacy did not make an effort to warn about renal failure and could not be held liable for not doing so. This Court feared that any other ruling would deter Illinois pharmacists from giving consumers any information. Using the policy announced in Frye, This court believes that patients should rely primarily on their physicians, not pharmacists for drug information.

Pettus v Wal-Mart
No 03-99-00700-CV (August 10, 2000), 2000 Tex App LEXIS 5282

Cameron Pettus was 12 years old in 1991 when he was diagnosed with attention deficit hyperactivity disorder (ADHD). His physician prescribed desipramine, an antidepressant. The FDA has not approved this drug for use in ADHD and the labeling indicates the drug should not be used in children. The child's mother initially had the prescription filled at a Walgreen pharmacy. The mother testified that no one in the pharmacy ever talked to her or gave her any literature about the drug. Two months after initiating the drug, the child com-

Pettus v Wal-Mart
No 03-99-00700-CV (August 10, 2000), 2000 Tex App LEXIS 5282
...continued

plained of chest and groin pain. He was diagnosed as suffering musculoskeletal pain related
to playing sports. He continued to suffer chest pains and was admitted to a hospital in September 1991. He was diagnosed with pleurisy and the physician told the mother that the condition would clear up on its own. The physician was told that the child was taking
desipramine, but he did not attribute the chest pains to the drug. In August 1992, the mother
had the prescription transferred to a Wal-Mart store because it was less expensive. She had
the prescription refilled three more times at Wal-Mart up until February 1993. In July 1993
the child complained again of chest pains. He was taken to a hospital and diagnosed as being
dehydrated. Over the next few days his condition became more severe. He was admitted
to a hospital on July 23, 1993, and had a lymph node surgically removed. After surgery, he
became extremely agitated and told his mother he felt like he was dying. His condition
deteriorated until he slipped into a coma. He died on August 2, 1993. An autopsy revealed
that he died of hypereosinophilic syndrome involving the heart, lungs, liver, and central
nervous system as a result of taking desipramine.

The mother sued several physicians, the drug manufacturer, Walgreen and Wal-Mart. All
of the parties except Wal-Mart settled with the mother prior to trial. The complaint against
Wal-Mart claimed the pharmacy failed to properly warn about the hazards associated with
the drug. The parties agreed that no Wal-Mart pharmacist ever talked to the mother about
the drug and that the manufacturer's insert was not given to the mother. The pharmacist
who refilled the prescription in October 1992 testified that the computer generated a label
and an information sheet that is customarily attached to the bag in which the medication is placed before it is picked up. The pharmacist testified that she worked 10 hour shifts
at the time and that she filled approximately 150 prescriptions per day. She did not recall
ever talking to the child's mother. The mother testified that she never received an information sheet from the pharmacy. After a 3–day trial, a jury returned a verdict of nearly $3 mil-
lion. The verdict apportioned 60% of the responsibility on the prescribing physician and
approximately 15% each against Wal-Mart and Walgreen. Approximately 10% was attributed to the comparative negligence of the plaintiffs. After setoffs, a verdict in the amount of
$843,250 plus costs and attorney fees was entered against Wal-Mart.

Wal-Mart appealed claiming there is no duty on the part of Texas pharmacists to warn about
drug effects because that duty rests with the prescribing physician. The Texas Court of
Appeals agreed and vacated the verdict. In doing so, the Court examined several cases from
around the country as well as other academic writings addressing the pharmacist's duty to
warn. It noted that in the cases where courts have imposed such a duty there were other factors, such as known contraindications or improprieties on the face of the prescription, that
should have lead the pharmacist to take additional action beyond merely filling the prescription accurately. The plaintiff claimed that both OBRA-90 and the Texas statutes and
regulations implementing OBRA-90 require pharmacists to communicate risks of drug use to
patients. The Court read those statutes and rules as mandating the pharmacist to use professional judgment as to what information should be communicated and not as mandating
any particular communication be undertaken. The court stated that Texas laws recognize
that pharmacists are trusted professionals with varied and important responsibilities. Nevertheless, imposing a duty to warn on pharmacists would potentially interfere with the
patient-physician relationship. Given that the physician knows more about the patient's condition, it is not appropriate to have a pharmacist question the physician's prescribing practices as a matter of law. The Court acknowledged that the role of pharmacists has changed
in the past decades from a mere dispenser of drugs to a vital professional in the care of
patients. It also noted that pharmacies have advanced computer systems that can detect
and analyze drug interactions and other problems in seconds. Despite this, the Court stated

Pettus v Wal-Mart
No 03-99-00700-CV (August 10, 2000), 2000 Tex App LEXIS 5282
...continued

that the learned intermediary doctrine requires no generalized duty to warn be imposed on pharmacists. It emphasized that pharmacists certainly may warn about drug problems, but was limiting its holding to not mandating warnings absent some other special condition.

As to the claim that the manufacturer's labeling, warning against the use of the drug in children, could give rise to a duty to warn by the pharmacist, the Court questioned whether there was any evidence that Cameron Pettus was a child when Wal-Mart "sold" the medication for his use. The Court noted that Cameron was 12 when he first started taking the drug and that he was 13 by the time Wal-Mart first dispensed it for him. Cameron was 14 when Wal-Mart last sold the drug on his behalf. The Court also noted that the labeling draws a clear distinction between non-use of the drug in children and an adolescent dose beginning at 25 mg. The only evidence the Court could find in the transcript was a brief mention by plaintiff's pharmacy expert, James O'Donnell, that Cameron was an adolescent when Wal-Mart dispensed the drug. Based on the lack of unequivocal testimony that Cameron was a child, the Court could not conclude that the labeling created a question of a clear or obvious problem that would give rise to a duty by a pharmacist when dispensing this drug to a 13-year–old.

Cottam v CVS Pharmacy
436 Mass. 316, 764, N.E.2d 814 (Mass. 2002).

The patient brought negligence action against a pharmacy alleging that pharmacy failed to warn him about prescription antidepressant drug's potential side effect of priapism, which could cause permanent impotence if not immediately treated. The Superior Court jury found the pharmacy to be 51% negligent and the pharmacy appealed. The Supreme Judicial Court affirmed. In March 1994, the patient was admitted to a hospital to receive treatment for depression. His psychiatrist prescribed trazodone to him and instructed him to continue taking the drug after he was released from the hospital. In May 1994, CVS Pharmacies implemented a computer system designed to provide customers with information about risks and side effects of prescription drugs. This system could produce either a short form or a longer more inclusive form of risks and side effects for prescription drugs. It was the CVS Pharmacies' policy to distribute the long form when first filling a customer's prescription. On August 16, 1994, the patient had his prescription filled at a CVS Pharmacy. The parties dispute whether the short or long form was provided to the patient regarding side effects, but the pharmacist admitted that she did not orally warn the patient of priapism as a potential side effect. In addition, the manufacturer's warning was not given to the patient although it was not CVS Pharmacies' policy to distribute these warnings. Finally, CVS Pharmacy did not list priapism as a side effect, but listed it only as one of numerous adverse reactions for which a causal connection had not been confirmed or refuted. The psychiatrist did testify that he had warned the patient of priapism as a potential side effect before prescribing the medication. The patient first took a dose of the trazodone at night before he went to bed and awoke the next morning with an erection that persisted throughout the day and that became uncomfortable that evening. He decided not to contact his physician and to wait until his scheduled appointment the next day and took another dose of trazodone before going to bed that evening. On August 18, 1994, the patient attended his appointment with his primary care physician and was sent immediately to a urologist who diagnosed the condition as priapism and scheduled him for emergency surgery. The surgery left the patient permanently impotent. The patient waited approximately 30 hours before seeking treatment for this condition and ideally should have waited only 6. He claimed that he would

Cottam v CVS Pharmacy
436 Mass. 316, 764, N.E.2d 814 (Mass. 2002).
...continued

have sought medical attention immediately if he had been warned that priapism was a potential and serious side effect of trazodone. The Supreme Judicial Court found that although a pharmacy generally has no duty to warn its customers of the side effects of prescription drugs, CVS Pharmacy voluntarily assumed a duty to provide the information, advice or warnings to the patient. The judge affirmed the decision of the jury. In so holding that a pharmacy generally has no duty to warn its customers of the side effects of prescription drugs, the Court extended the learned intermediary doctrine to pharmacies. The Court's rationale for extending this doctrine to pharmacies was based on its finding that "the physician is the appropriate person to perform the duty of warning a patient of the possibility of side effects of prescription drugs." The Court went on to discuss cases in which a duty was imposed on pharmacies with specific knowledge of an increased danger to a customer and distinguished these cases from its holding by stating, "where the pharmacist has no specific knowledge of an increased danger to a particular customer, the pharmacist has no duty to warn that customer of potential side effects." This statement by the Court basically operates as a limitation on its holding. The implication of this limitation is to place a duty on the pharmacy if it specifically knows that there is an increased danger to a past patient. Despite the holding that pharmacies do not have any general duty to warn, the Court held that a pharmacy can voluntarily assume a duty not otherwise imposed on it. The Court explained that one who voluntarily assumes a duty must perform that duty with due care. The scope of the voluntarily assumed duty "is a fact-specific inquiry based on the totality of the pharmacy's communications with the patient and the patient's reasonable understanding, based on those communications, of what the pharmacy has undertaken to provide." Applying this rule, the Court distinguished between the situations where a pharmacy's communication was a single label warning of only one side effect (did not voluntarily assume duty to warn) and one where a pharmacy provides a detailed listing of warnings (did voluntarily assume duty to warn). The difference between the two situations that the Court found to be persuasive was that, in the first, the pharmacy only undertook a duty to warn correctly as to that specific side effect and did not undertake a duty to warn of all potential side effects. In the second situation, the Court found that where the information provided could be reasonably understood by the patient as a complete list of side effects, then it is appropriate to impose the duty to warn as to all potential side effects. The Court in this case rejected the pharmacy's argument that the plaintiff had to prove the scope and breach of its duty by expert testimony. The Court found that the issue presented in this case was the adequacy of the warning and not the technical performance of the pharmacist. Therefore, the Court found that the determination as to the adequacy of the CVS Pharmacy's warning and whether a reasonable person would have been misled is a commonsense determination regarding the understanding of the reasonably prudent person and is properly left to a jury without expert testimony. Two additional points are worth mentioning. First, the CVS Pharmacy attempted to argue that because the patient failed to heed health warnings on cigarette packages, he would have failed to heed the warning of the Pharmacy with regard to the potential side effect of priapism. This was an apparent attempt to argue that the Pharmacy was not the proximate cause of the injury to the patient. However, the Court rejected this argument emphasizing the difference between people who fail to heed the warning regarding cigarettes because they are addicted to the cigarettes and the suggestion that the same individuals would fail to heed a warning regarding the potential side effects of a prescription drug. Second, the CVS Pharmacy argued that evidence of a settlement between the psychiatrist and the Customer was improper evidence of a settlement used to prove liability and that it should have been excluded. However, the Court found that evidence of the settlement was admissible because it was offered to show that the psychiatrist might be biased against the Customer.

The following is a list of court cases that are related to this topic.

Fuhs v Barber, 36 P. 2d 962 (Kan. 1934).
Holbrook v Rose, 458 S.W.2d 155 (Ky. 1970).
Hand v Krakowski, 453 N.Y.S.2d 121 (N.Y. App. Div. 1982).
Kinney v Hutchinson, 449 So.2d 696 (La. Ct. App. 1984).
Pysz v Henry's Drug Store, 457 So.2d 561 (Fla. Dist. Ct. App. 1984).
Ingram v Hook's Drugs, Inc., 476 N.E.2d 881 (Ind. Ct. App. 1985).
Jones v Irwin, 602 F. Supp. 399 (S.D. Ill. 1985).
Kirk v Michael Reese Hospital, 483 N.E.2d 906 (Ill. App. 1 Dist. 1985).
Raynor v Richardson-Merrell, Inc., 643 F. Supp. 238 (D.D.C. 1986).
Riff v Morgan, 508 A.2d 1247 (Pa. Super. 1986).
Steele v Organon, Inc., 43 Wash. App. 230 (1986).
Van Iperen v Van Bramer, 392 N.W.2d 480 (Iowa 1986).
Docken v Ciba-Geigy, 739 P.2d 591 (Ore. Ct. App. 1987).
Kirk v Michael Reese Hospital and Medical Center, 513 N.E.2d 387 (Ill. 1987).
Stafford v Nipp, 502 So.2d 702 (Ala. 1987).
Ferguson v Williams, 374 S.E.2d 438 (N.C. App. 1988).
Dooley v Everett, et al., Docket No. 01-A-01-9005-CV-00185, Tenn. Ct. App. (1990).
Nichols v Central Merchandise, Inc., 817 P.2d 1131 (Kan. App. 1991).
Vollendorf v U.S., 1991 WL 256188 (9th Cir. Wash).
Heredia v Johnson, 827 F. Supp. 1522 (D. Nev. 1993).
Gassen v East Jefferson General Hospital, et al, 1993 La. App. LEXIS 3985.
Walker v Jack Eckerd Corp., 209 Ga. App 517; 434 S.E.2d 63, (Ga. App., 1993), cert denied, Ga. S. Ct., Slip Op No. 593C1686 (1993).
Wimm v Jack Eckerd Corp., 1993 App. LEXIS 25102 (U.S. Ct. App. 5th cir.).
Lasley v Shrake's Country Club Pharmacy, Inc., 1994 WL 109647 (Ariz. App. Dir. 1).
McLaughlin v Hook - SupeRx Inc., 642 N.E. 2d 514 (Ind. 1994).
Pittman v The Upjohn Company, 1994 WL 663372 (Tenn. Nov. 28, 1994).
Baker v Arbor Drugs, 544 N.W.2d 727 (Mich. App. 1996), Iv. denied, 454 Mich 853 (1997).
Cafaralle v Brockton Oaks C.V.S. Inc., No. 94-0414A, (Mass. Super. Ct. April, 1996).
Hooper v Perry Drugs, Slip Op. 178665 (Unpublished), September 20, 1996. (Mich. App.).
Johnson v Walgreen Co., 675 S.2d 1036 (Fla. Dist Ct. App. 1996).
Kohl v American Home Products, Slip Op. No. 99-3085, December 29, 1999, U.S.D.C. Ark., 1999 U.S. Dist. LEXIS 20242.
Gayle Moore v Wyeth-Ayerst Laboratories, Slip Op No CCB-02-2691 (November 14, 2002, Decided), USDC MD, 2002 U.S. Dist. LEXIS 22213.
Moore v Memorial Hospital of Gulfport, Slip Op No 2000-CA-01976 (Sept. 5, 2002), 2002 WL 2027353.

Refusal of Offer to Counsel

Hooper v Thrifty Payless
Slip Op No C037465 (December 17, 2002), 2002 Cal. App. LEXIS 11715

The patient admitted that he refused the pharmacy's offer to counsel him about a new prescription for trazodone because he knew it was just a "sleeping pill" and that such medications could be purchased from a grocery store. The pharmacy also produced evidence that the patient signed a statement that he refused counseling. Several days after taking the drug at bedtime, he awoke with an erection that did not subside. The condition, priapism, is a known adverse reaction that occurs in approximately 1% of males taking the drug. The condition could lead to irreversible effects if not treated within 6 hours. The pharmacy's written handout typically given to patients when the medication is dispensed contains a warning about the condition and advises patients to seek immediate medical care if the condition develops. There was a dispute at trial over whether the patient ever received this

Hooper v Thrifty Payless
Slip Op No C037465 (December 17, 2002), 2002 Cal. App. LEXIS 11715
...continued

handout. The psychiatrist who prescribed the drug testified that he also warned the patient about this possible condition. The trial court granted the pharmacy's motion for summary judgment on the grounds that the California statute that normally mandates counseling contains a waiver clause that does not require consultation when the patient refuses it. The Court of Appeals affirmed the judgment.

Adequate Directions for Use

The following is a list of court cases that are related to this topic.

Kinney v Hutchinson, 449 So.2d 696 (La. Ct. App. 1984).
Stafford v Nipp, 502 So.2d 702 (Ala. 1987).

Side Effects

Ingram v Hook's Drugs, Inc.
476 N.E.2d 881 (Ind. Ct. App. 1985)

ISSUE: Whether a pharmacist had a duty to provide a patient with warnings regarding the possible adverse reactions or side effects associated with the use of *Valium*.

FACTS: The plaintiff in this case, Ronald Ingram, received a prescription for *Valium* from his physician. His wife took the prescription to a Hook's pharmacy in Fort Wayne, Indiana, to have it filled. The pharmacist dispensed the prescription exactly as ordered by the physician. The medication received by Mr. Ingram was the correct drug, in a proper strength and unadulterated. The prescription label contained all of the instructions and warnings for use that were ordered by the physician. The pharmacist did not provide Mr. Ingram with any warnings, either verbally or in writing, concerning the possible adverse reactions or side effects associated with *Valium*.

Ten days after receiving the prescription, Ingram fell off a ladder while at work and fractured his leg. He alleged that this accident was directly due to the *Valium* and that the pharmacist failed to warn him of the side effects associated with the drug, including dizziness, drowsiness, and syncope. He further claimed that the pharmacist failed to advise him to avoid working near machinery and that he failed to add any of these warnings to the prescription label. The treating physician was not named as a defendant. The trial court granted the defendant pharmacy's motion for summary judgment. The plaintiff appealed.

RULING: The court concluded that the duty to warn of hazards associated with prescription drugs is part of the physician-patient relationship and the pharmacy had no duty to warn the patient of the hazards associated with the use of *Valium*.

REASONING: In Indiana, the tort of negligence is comprised of three elements: (1) a duty on the part of the defendant in relation to the plaintiff; (2) failure on the part of the defendant to conform its conduct to the requisite standard of care required by the relationship; and (3) an injury to the plaintiff resulting from that failure. The plaintiff contended that the question of duty on the part of the pharmacist to warn patients is a mixed question of law and fact and, therefore, summary judgment was inappropriate by the trial court. How-

Ingram v Hook's Drugs, Inc.
476 N.E.2d 881 (Ind. Ct. App. 1985)
...continued

ever, the Indiana Court of Appeals disagreed. It noted that Indiana case law holds that "the duty to exercise care for the safety of another arises as a matter of law out of some relationship existing between the parties, and *it is the province of the court to determine whether such a relationship gives rise to such duty.*" Consequently, the trial court was correct in granting summary judgment if it found Hook's pharmacist owed no duty to Mr. Ingram.

The plaintiff introduced Indiana statutes, which defined the "practice of pharmacy" to include the responsibility for "advising as necessary, as to the contents, therapeutic values, hazards, and appropriate manner of use of drugs or devices." The plaintiff contended that this language created a mandatory duty on the part of the pharmacist to include his own warnings on the label of a prescription container. The defendants argued that this statutory language required advising only "as necessary." Hook's further contended that the Indiana Board of Pharmacy had specifically regulated what warnings should be placed on the label of a prescription drug. In addition to containing the name and address of the pharmacy, prescription number, physician name, etc., the regulations required that the "directions for use of the drug *as contained in the prescription*" be placed on the label. The defendant argued that this regulation clearly places the duty to warn on the physician who prescribed the drug and prohibits the pharmacist from including his own warnings.

In the court's examination of the Indiana statutes, it could find no evidence of a mandatory duty on the part of the pharmacist to warn a patient of all possible hazards associated with a drug. The pharmacy regulations required a pharmacist to only include directions for use as contained in the prescription. While the court could not accept Hook's conclusion that this regulation prohibited pharmacists from including their own warnings, the court did conclude that a pharmacist does not have a statutory duty to warn patients of all hazards associated with a prescription drug.

Next, the court turned to examine the case law in other jurisdictions to determine if such a duty existed. The court found that other jurisdictions have overwhelmingly held that a pharmacist does not have a duty to warn the patient of all the hazards associated with prescription drugs. Quoting *Reyes v Wyeth Laboratories, Inc.*:

> The reasons for this rule should be obvious. Where a product is available only on prescription or through the services of a physician, the physician acts as a "learned intermediary" between the manufacturer or seller and the patient. It is his duty to inform himself of the qualities and characteristics of those products which he prescribes for or administers to or uses on his patients, and to exercise an independent judgment, taking into account his knowledge of the patient as well as the product. The patient is expected to and, it can be presumed does, place primary reliance upon that judgment. The physician decides what facts should be told to the patient...

In *McLeod v W.S. Merrell Co.*, an action was brought against a drug manufacturer and the retail pharmacists for injuries allegedly resulting from taking "Mer/29," a drug prescribed by the plaintiff's physician to control body cholesterol. The plaintiff sued the pharmacists, contending they breached an implied warranty of fitness. The lower courts had dismissed the plaintiff's complaint against the retail pharmacists and the Supreme Court of Florida affirmed.

> In the instant case, the commodity, "Mer/29" was not available to the general public in the sense that it could be purchased by any customer who entered the store and paid the price. Actually, it was available only to a very limited segment of the public who had previously been seen by their personal physician and who presented their

Ingram v Hook's Drugs, Inc.
476 N.E.2d 881 (Ind. Ct. App. 1985)
...continued

doctor's prescription directing that the drug be supplied. Obviously, the patient-purchaser did not rely upon the judgment of the retail druggist in assuming that the drug would be fit for its intended purpose. This confidence had been placed in the physician who prescribed the remedy. Supposedly he, in turn, placed his reliance on the representations of the manufacturer.

Similarly, in *Batiste v American Home Products Corp.*, the plaintiff brought a negligence and strict liability action against the manufacturer, prescribing physician, and retail pharmacist for the prescription and sale of an oral contraceptive. The trial court dismissed the cause of action against the retail pharmacist. In affirming the dismissal, the court stated:

> Here plaintiff alleges that she had consulted a physician, obtained a prescription and carried it to defendant Pike's Drug Store, Inc., to be filled. The prescription was filled as directed. There is no allegation that the product was other than it was supposed to be. There is no allegation that the druggist did any compounding or added to or took from the product as prepared and contained in the sealed container, or that the druggist did anything to change the prescription given him, or that the drug delivered to plaintiff was in any way different than the drug prescribed by plaintiff's physician, or contained any foreign material. Certainly defendant is not qualified or licensed to advise plaintiff with respect to the best oral contraceptive for her to use to prevent pregnancy. Defendant is not a physician.

A third case, holding that a pharmacist has no duty to warn a customer having a prescription filled, is found in *Kinney v Hutchinson*. Here, the plaintiff was shot by someone under the influence of alcohol and *Preludin*, a prescription drug obtained at the defendant pharmacy. He sued the pharmacy, claiming it negligently failed to warn of the hazards of *Preludin*. The Louisiana Court of Appeals affirmed summary judgment, holding that the pharmacist had no knowledge that the person would use the drug in connection with alcohol, and that no duty exists to warn every customer of every potential hazard.

Finally, in *Bichler v Willing*, the court held that a pharmacist had no duty to warn a customer of the dangers associated with taking DES during pregnancy. In discussing the relationship between a prescription drug customer and a pharmacist, the court stated:

> When a consumer asks a druggist to fill a prescription, thus enabling him to obtain a drug which is not otherwise available to the public, he does not rely on the druggist's judgment as to whether that particular drug is inherently fit for its intended purpose but rather he places that confidence and reliance in the physician who prescribed the remedy.

Based upon all of these authorities, the court concluded that the duty to warn of hazards associated with prescription drugs is part of the physician-patient relationship, which has the benefits of medical history and extensive medical examination. "It is not present, however, in the context of a pharmacist filling a prescription for a retail customer. The injection of a third party in the form of a pharmacist into the physician-patient relationship could undercut the effectiveness of the ongoing medical treatment."

During the trial, the Ingrams introduced several pages from the *U.S.P. Dispensing Information*. This publication contained approximately 20 to 25 instructions and cautionary statements suggested for the patient who was taking *Valium*. The plaintiff's position, the court noted, would require a pharmacist filling a prescription for *Valium* to give the entire list of side

Ingram v Hook's Drugs, Inc.
476 N.E.2d 881 (Ind. Ct. App. 1985)
...continued

effects and cautionary statements. "Such voluminous warnings would only confuse the normal customer and be of dubious value. This matter is better handled by the treating physician."

Van Iperen v Van Bramer
392 N.W.2d 480 (Iowa 1986)

ISSUE: Whether a hospital was liable for failing to have formal drug monitoring procedures established through its hospital pharmacy.

FACTS: The plaintiff, John van Iperen, had suffered for many years from Crohn's disease. The disease had resulted in the removal of all of his large intestines and much of his small intestines. Only 5 inches of his intestines remained attached to his rectal cavity. This segment was not connected to any other body organ and was sutured closed on the anterior end.

The plaintiff was admitted to St. Luke's Regional Medical Center in Sioux City, Iowa, when an infection developed in the area where this segment pressed against the bladder wall. At the time of his hospitalization, the plaintiff was attended by Dr. van Bramer, a specialist in internal medicine and Dr. Oei, who was certified in nephrology. While several treatment alternatives were discussed, the two physicians elected to forego surgery and engage in a rectal flush program.

Dr. Oei prepared a solution of 1 g *Neomycin* and 1 g *Kanamycin* with 50 mL saline solution. The prescribed rectal flush solution was administered 2 or 3 times daily. The plaintiff was discharged from the hospital several weeks later and was directed to continue application of the rectal flush solution at home twice daily.

The plaintiff was subsequently hospitalized 3 times during 1981 for dehydration and an electrolyte imbalance caused by the small amount of surface area remaining in his gastrointestinal tract. During the last hospitalization, the plaintiff complained of ringing in his ears. Dr. van Bramer believed this was due to the dehydration and electrolyte imbalance. However, by the next hospitalization the plaintiff had lost much of his hearing and the *Neomycin* and *Kanamycin* were discontinued. By the time of the trial, the plaintiff was unable to hear sound levels below the intensity of a chain saw. While both physicians were aware of the potential side effects of the drugs, the evidence indicated that Dr. van Bramer did not inform the plaintiff of these prior to initiation of the rectal flush. Dr. Oei testified that he had advised the plaintiff of potential side effects to the kidney and of possible hearing loss and that he obtained the plaintiff's informed consent to proceed with the therapy.

RULING: The district court directed a verdict in favor of the hospital. The case was submitted to the jury against the two physicians on the theories of (1) failure to obtain informed consent prior to initiation of drug therapy, and (2) administration and prescribing of drugs in a manner not in accordance with accepted medical practice. The jury found that neither physician was negligent. The plaintiff appealed, contending that the trial court erred in (1) not determining that the jury's verdict on the informed consent claim was against the great weight of evidence, and (2) directing a verdict in favor of the hospital.

REASONING: Much of the appeal focused on the issue of informed consent. The plaintiff argued that he was entitled to the warning of potential adverse consequences from the drug

Van Iperen v Van Bramer
392 N.W.2d 480 (Iowa 1986)
...continued

therapy at the time he was consulting with Dr. van Bramer on whether to elect a surgical solution to his problem. The appellate court concluded that the jury could have found that a division of the responsibility regarding informed consent was unavoidable in view of the fact that Dr. Oei was in charge of the selection of drugs. The jury rejected the plaintiff's claim that he had not been informed of side effects prior to initiation of therapy.

The plaintiff further argued that the trial court made an error by directing a verdict in favor of the hospital. The plaintiff based his argument on the accreditation standards of the Joint Commission on the Accreditation of Hospitals (JCAH) which require that within the limits of available resources, a hospital should provide drug monitoring services through its pharmacy. These services are to include:

> (1) The maintenance of a medication record or drug profile for each patient, which is based on available drug history and current therapy and includes the name, age, and weight of the patient, the current diagnosis(es), the current drug therapy, any drug allergies or sensitivities, and other pertinent information relating to the patient's drug regimen...

> (2) A review of the patient's drug regimen for any potential interactions, interferences or incompatibilities, prior to dispensing drugs to the patient. Such irregularities must be resolved promptly with the prescribing practitioner, and when appropriate, with notification of the nursing service and administration.

The plaintiff argued that the hospital's procedures were not in accordance with the above standards because it had no formal procedures for implementing the responsibilities of the hospital pharmacy to make independent evaluations of proposed drug therapy and communicating such recommendations to patients and physicians.

The Supreme Court of Iowa did not believe the accreditation standards nor this case's evidence were sufficiently clear to generate a jury question on the claim made against the defendant hospital and its pharmacy. The trial court directed a verdict in favor of the hospital.

Martin v Hacker
550 N.Y.S.2d 130 (App. Div. 1989)

ISSUE: Whether a drug distributor was liable for failure to warn of a drug's side effects.

FACTS: The plaintiff sought to recover damages for the death of her husband from a self-inflicted gunshot wound to the head. The complaint alleged that the suicide was the direct result of severe depression induced by certain drugs that her husband was taking for hypertension. The defendant, Interstate Drug Exchange, was the distributor of at least one of the drugs, reserpine, which it allegedly sold to the defendant, Fays Drug Company, which dispensed the product to the decedent pursuant to a prescription written by the physician, who is also a defendant in this action. The complaint alleged that the distributor breached its duty to warn of the drug's side effects.

RULING: The court dismissed the complaint against the distributor because it was not the manufacturer of the drug and, therefore, had no duty to warn of possible side effects.

Martin v Hacker
550 N.Y.S.2d 130 (App. Div. 1989)
...continued

REASONING: It was conceded that the distributor did not manufacture the drug but merely passed the product along to the pharmacy in the same packaging that the drug was in when it was delivered to the distributor. The only evidence that the distributor represented the drug as its own product was contained in the label placed upon the packaging by the manufacturer. The front of the label contained Interstate's logo along with the name of the drug. The side panel described Interstate as the distributor and stated "this is a bulk package- ...manufactured by Richlyn Laboratories."

Interstate took delivery of the drug from the manufacturer in sealed bulk containers and shipped the drug to retail pharmacies in the same packaging. Retailers would order the drug from a catalog or by phone, using the name of the drug or its product number. There was nothing in the record to suggest any party other than the manufacturer and the pharmacy was even aware of Interstate's involvement in the distribution of the drug.

The following is a list of court cases that are related to this topic.

Krug v Sterling Drug, Inc., 416 S.W.2d 143 (Mo. 1967).
Stevens v Parke, Davis & Company, 207 Cal. Rptr. 45, 507 P.2d 653 (Cal. 1973).
Kinney v Hutchinson, 449 So.2d 696 (La. Ct. App. 1984).
Pysz v Henry's Drug Store, 457 So.2d 561 (Fla. Dist. Ct. App. 1984).
Raynor v Richardson-Merrell, Inc., 643 F. Supp. 238 (D.D.C. 1986).
Makripodis v Merrell Dow Pharmaceuticals, Inc., 523 A.2d 374 (Pa. Super. 1987).
Stebbins v Concord Wrigley Drugs, Inc. et al., Docket No. 88734 (Mich. Ct. App. 1987).
Leesley v West, 518 N.E.2d 758 (Ill. App. 2 Dist. 1988).
McKee v American Home Products, No. 53941-3 (Wash. Sup. Ct. Nov. 30, 1989).
Docken v Ciba-Geigy, 790 P.2d 45 (Or. App. 1990).
Nichols v Central Merchandise, Inc., 817 P.2d 1131 (Kan. App. 1991).
Frye v Medicare-Glaser Corp., 1992 WL 297605 (Ill. Sup. Ct.).
Gassen v East Jefferson General Hospital, et al, 1993 La. App. LEXIS 3985.
Walker v Jack Eckerd Corp., 209 Ga. App. 517; 434 S.E.2d 63, (Ga. App., 1993), cert denied, Ga. S.Ct., Slip Op. No. 593C1686 (1993).
Lasley v Shrake's Country Club Pharmacy, Inc., 1994 WL 109647 (Ariz. App. Dir. 1).
Pittman v Upjohn, 890 S.W.2d 425 (Tenn. App. 1994).
Pittman v The Upjohn Company, 1994 WL 663372 (Tenn. Nov. 28, 1994).
Johnson v Walgreen Co., 675 S.2d 1036 (Fla. Dist Ct. App. 1996).

Drug-Drug Interactions

Fuhs v Barber
36 P.2d 962 (Kan. 1934)

ISSUE: Whether a pharmacist has a legal duty to effectively warn a patient about a potential drug-drug interaction.

FACTS: A housewife was suffering from poison ivy contact dermatitis and she consulted a physician who prescribed sugar of lead (lead acetate). A pharmacist supplied the medication and she used it but upon returning to the pharmacy for a refill of the prescription, the pharmacist remarked that he had a remedy that was better than sugar of lead. The patient was induced to use the substitute remedy, which was an ointment consisting of sulfur, oil of win-

Fuhs v Barber
36 P.2d 962 (Kan. 1934)
...continued

tergreen, *Vaseline*, and lanolin. The pharmacist warned the patient not to use the ointment concomitantly with the sugar of lead as the two did not work well together. But he did not tell the patient why. Later, the patient returned to the pharmacy and complained about a black spot on her skin where the ointment was applied. The pharmacist sold her more ointment and told her to continue using it as the preparation would remove the black spot. The black spot became worse and after using two and a half jars of the ointment, the patient consulted doctors in Kansas City. After extensive medical treatment, most of the black spots were removed but some remaining areas could not be cleared without skin grafting at great expense and of doubtful success. The patient sued the pharmacist for negligence.

RULING: A jury trial resulted in a verdict in favor of the patient and against the pharmacist for $1000. The pharmacist's attorneys asked for a new trial, claiming that sufficient evidence was presented to show that the patient may have used the sugar of lead after being told not to by the pharmacist. If such were the case, the patient-plaintiff's contributory negligence may have been the cause of the injury. Since the issue of possible contributory negligence on the part of the plaintiff was not submitted for the jury's consideration, the Kansas Supreme Court sent the case back for retrial.

REASONING: While the plaintiff's contributory negligence, if the jury found such, may have been the intervening causative factor in her injury, the court had no doubt that the pharmacist had acted negligently in the situation. The court stated:

> The defendant was a registered pharmacist, who was selling drugs and compounding medicines, and the general rule is that they are required to use great care in the sales made. He did not explain to her when he made the sale that sugar of lead could not be used or that is must be thoroughly washed out of the flesh before applying the defendant's remedy with sulphur in it. The reaction should have been and was well known to the defendant that it would cause blackness of the skin and that the reaction was inevitable. According to her testimony, he sold it to her without telling her of the effect...

Further on in the court's written opinion, it is stated:

> The defendant did not exercise the care required of him in the sale of the skin cure. He knew the effect of the combination of the articles and she did not.

Kinney v Hutchinson
449 So. 2d 696 (La. Ct. App. 1984)

ISSUE: Whether a pharmacist has a duty to inform a patient of the possible adverse effects and dangers of prescribed drug in combination with other substances.

FACTS: Larry Kinney, the plaintiff, was shot in the throat by Wanda Hutchinson, a total stranger, at the "Everybody's Here Too Lounge." It was alleged that Hutchinson was under the influence of a combination of the drug *Preludin* and alcohol when the shooting occurred. Kinney brought suit against Hutchinson, the manufacturer of *Preludin*, and the Walgreen's Company.

Kinney v Hutchinson
449 So. 2d 696 (La. Ct. App. 1984)
...continued

The plaintiff's complaint alleged that the *Preludin* prescription had been dispensed by a Walgreen's pharmacist who "failed to adequately disclose, warn or inform Hutchinson of the proper use of said drug; and failed to warn, disclose or inform her of possible adverse effects and dangers of said drug in combination with others..." Walgreen's admitted that the pharmacist did not warn Hutchinson of the effects of mixing alcohol and *Preludin*, but they further alleged that the pharmacist was under no duty to warn customers of the effects of this combination of drugs. Walgreen's moved for and was granted summary judgment. The plaintiff appealed.

RULING: The court held that there was not duty to warn on the part of the pharmacist of the dangers associated with a combination of *Preludin* and alcohol.

REASONING: The court concluded that the burden to warn of a prescription drug's adverse effects is placed upon the prescribing physician. When the manufacturer has informed the prescribing physician of the risks and benefits of a drug, the manufacturer is relieved of a duty to warn since the physician is the informed intermediary between the manufacturer and the patient.

In a separate action, the manufacturer of *Preludin*, Boehringer Ingelheim, also was granted a motion for summary judgment. The package insert for *Preludin* included a warning that the drug was related chemically and pharmacologically to the amphetamines. The warnings also listed the manifestations of chronic intoxication with such drugs, including "personality changes." The insert stated that "the most severe manifestation of chronic intoxication is psychosis, often clinically indistinguishable from schizophrenia." The manufacturer alleged that it had complied with all of the regulations of the FDA regarding the manufacture and marketing of the drug. It was further alleged that the company had been advised by the FDA as to the specific warnings to be included in the package insert.

The plaintiff claimed that the manufacturer was negligent in failing to give adequate warnings of the risks inherent in the use of *Preludin*. However, the court found that the plaintiff had not shown any connection between Hutchinson's taking *Preludin* and his gun shot wounds. Hutchinson stated in her deposition that she did not remember anything about the episode except taking a *Preludin* in the afternoon, going to the bar with friends, and having some drinks. She was hospitalized in a psychiatric ward for an unspecified period of time afterward.

Again, the court concluded that the decision to use the drug rests with the physician and the patient, not with the manufacturer or with the pharmacist. While there was no specific warning as to the adverse results from using alcohol with *Preludin*, the plaintiff had not submitted any evidence suggesting possible adverse effects from the combination. The court concluded that the warnings as issued by the manufacturer were sufficient to put the physician on notice that *Preludin* carried the possibility of psychosis under normal dosage. The motion dismissing the manufacturer from the lawsuit was affirmed. *Kinney v Hutchinson*, 468 So.2d 714 (La. App.5 Cir. 1985).

Frye v Medicare-Glaser Corp.
605 N.E.2d 557 (Ill. 1992)

ISSUE: Whether a pharmacist who failed to inform a patient about the dangers of taking a drug with alcohol was guilty of negligence.

FACTS: The patient had been prescribed *Fiorinal* following knee surgery. Evelyn Nightengale, the dispensing pharmacist, affixed two labels to the prescription container. One of the labels warned "May cause drowsiness" and the other federally required label cautioned against the transfer of the prescription drug to another person. The physician's prescription did not instruct or suggest that any warning label should be placed on the prescription container. Several days later the patient was found dead in his home, allegedly as a result of consuming alcohol with the *Fiorinal*.

(Note: During the pharmacist's testimony, she stated that she did not warn about the use of *Fiorinal* with alcohol because she did not want her patients to believe that she thought they drank alcohol. The pharmacist further testified that she had been "chewed out" in the past for placing such labels on containers because it offended so many people.)

RULING: The trial court dismissed the lawsuit, but the appellate court reversed that decision by holding that even if the pharmacist did not have a duty to warn the decedent of the dangerous side effects of the drug, once she voluntarily assumed the responsibility to warn of the drowsiness she needed to provide complete warnings including a caution to avoid the use of alcohol (see *Frye v Medicare-Glaser Corporation*, No. 5-90-0559, Ill App. Ct, 5th Dist. October 8, 1991). However, the Illinois Supreme Court ruled that the pharmacist had no duty to warn, and that it was the prescribing physician's responsibility to convey the appropriate warnings.

REASONING: The Illinois Supreme Court concluded that it did not believe that a genuine issue of material fact existed as to whether the pharmacy and its pharmacist performed their voluntary undertaking negligently. Pursuant to the voluntary undertaking theory of liability, one who gratuitously or for consideration renders services to another is subject to liability for bodily harm caused to the other by one's failure to exercise due care.

In this case, the plaintiff argued that the extent of the defendant's undertaking was to warn the decedent of all potential dangers involving *Fiorinal*. The court believed that this was an overly broad interpretation. It contended that if the court were to hold that by choosing to place the drowsiness warning on the prescription container, the defendants were assuming the duty to warn the decedent of all of the drug's side effects, that in the future pharmacists would refrain from placing any warning labels on prescription containers. Thus, consumers would be deprived of any warnings that might be beneficial.

Moreover, the court believed that requiring the pharmacist to warn a patient of all potential side effects would be difficult from a practical standpoint. It noted that there were a wide variety of additional warnings that might be given beyond the three included in the pharmacist's computer software. The court contended that the drowsiness warning was accurate and it did not accept the plaintiff's argument that the pharmacist misled the patient into believing that drowsiness was the only side effect of *Fiorinal*. In the court's opinion, consumers should look primarily to their prescribing physician to convey the appropriate warnings regarding drugs.

(Note: a number of professional associations filed "friend-of-the-court" briefs. The Illinois Trial Lawyers Association claimed that a pharmacist should have a duty to properly warn under special circumstances such as when she voluntarily assumes the duty to warn. The Illinois Pharmacist Association urged the court to impose upon the pharmacy profession the same duty as that owed by other professionals practicing their professions, and the National

Frye v Medicare-Glaser Corp.
605 N.E.2d 557 (Ill. 1992)
...continued

Association of Boards of Pharmacy claimed that a pharmacist has an affirmative duty to warn a patient of potential drug interactions and possible side effects of drugs.

Kirk v Michael Reese Hospital
483 N.E.2d 906 (Ill. Ct. App. 1985)

ISSUE: Whether a hospital and its physicians have a duty to warn a patient, prior to discharge, that the drugs he has been given may impair his mental and physical abilities.

FACTS: A passenger injured in a car accident sued a hospital, two psychiatrists, and two drug companies for failing to warn the driver about adverse consequences of taking *Prolixin* and *Thorazine* with alcohol. Michael Reese Hospital personnel had injected the patient with *Prolixin* and gave him *Thorazine* for oral consumption. Following his dismissal from the hospital that same day, the patient consumed an alcoholic beverage and drove his automobile with the plaintiff as a passenger. It was alleged that these two drugs diminished the patient's mental and physical abilities, which caused him to lose control of the automobile and hit a tree. The plaintiff suffered severe and permanent injuries in the accident.

The plaintiff alleged that the drug manufacturers had failed to provide adequate warnings of the adverse effects of their drugs and that the physicians and hospital failed to warn the patient prior to his discharge that the drugs would impair his mental and physical abilities. The defendants argued that they should be dismissed from the case because they owed no duty to the plaintiff.

RULING: The court held that each defendant owed a duty to warn, which extended to the plaintiff and other members of the general public. The dissenting judge argued that extending a duty to warn to such a remote party as the passenger would unduly burden the health care industry.

REASONING: The court first had to deal with the foreseeability of the plaintiff's injury. The court stated that it was not essential that the defendants should have foreseen the precise hazard that would result. "A duty may exist to one who is unknown and remote in time and place." The court concluded that the event that occurred was sufficiently foreseeable for the physicians, hospital, and drug manufacturers to have known that their failure to adequately warn of the adverse effects of the drug would result in injury to the plaintiff or to other members of the general public.

The defendants argued that the patient's consumption of alcohol and his negligent driving constituted superseding, intervening causes of the accident. These actions, they claimed, broke the causal relationship between any original wrong and the injury. However, the court determined that the patient's consumption of alcohol and the plaintiff's presence in the automobile were all within the realm of foreseeability and these actions did not break the causal connection of the defendant's failure to warn.

The physicians in the hospital also argued that they should not owe a duty to an injured party who is merely a member of the general public and not their patient. They contended that the imposition of a duty to a nonpatient would unjustly render them liable to an undetermined group of people. The drug manufacturers argued that their duty to warn the medi-

Kirk v Michael Reese Hospital
483 N.E.2d 906 (Ill. Ct. App. 1985)
...continued

cal profession did not cover third parties who do not use the drugs. The court did not find the defendants' arguments persuasive and did not believe the imposition of a legal duty to warn was an undue burden on the defendants. The court noted that the duty involved in this case simply required a warning, not control or prevention. This duty to warn would arise only if the defendants know or should have known of the adverse effects of a drug. The court emphasized that legal causation, as well as breach of duty, must still be proven. The liability of the defendants must still be substantiated by their peers.

The hospital argued that it could not be liable for the negligence in this case because the administration of drugs was a medical question entirely within the discretion of the treating physicians. The physicians were neither employed nor controlled by the hospital. However, the court concluded that the negligence action against the hospital involved the hospital's negligence for failure to warn rather than a claim that the medical treatment itself was improper. "Plainly, hospitals do far more than merely furnish an edifice for treatment. Rather, they regularly employ on a salaried basis, a staff of physicians, nurses, pharmacists...the cost for these personnel are factored into the amount the patients are charged by the hospital. It follows that hospitals must assume certain responsibilities for the care and treatment of their patients." The court concluded that before a patient is discharged from the hospital, the hospital has a duty to warn the patient of the adverse effects of drugs that were administered in the hospital. If the hospital knows, or should have known, that the drugs would impair the patient's physical or mental abilities or would be potentially dangerous in combination with other foods, beverages, or drugs, then it must provide a warning.

Dooley v Everett, et al.
805 S.W.2d 380 (Tenn. App. 1990)

ISSUE: Whether a pharmacist has a duty to warn a patient or a physician of the potential interaction between two prescription drugs.

FACTS: The plaintiff, a three-year-old child, was prescribed theophylline when hospitalized for pneumonia in June 1985. Early in 1986, the physician confirmed the diagnosis of asthma and again prescribed theophylline.

A Revco pharmacy dispensed the theophylline prescriptions on various occasions in 1987. The dosage was increased by the physician to 200 mg three times a day. In December 1987, the physician also prescribed erythromycin, 400 mg four times a day for 10 days. The prescription was also dispensed by the Revco Pharmacy. Shortly thereafter, the child suffered cerebral seizures as a result of the toxic levels of theophylline in his blood.

The package insert for erythromycin provided in part:

> Recent data from studies of erythromycin reveal that its use in patients who are receiving high doses of theophylline may be associated with an increase of serum theophylline levels and potential theophylline toxicity. In case of theophylline toxicity and/or elevated serum theophylline levels, the dose of theophylline should be reduced while the patient is receiving concomitant erythromycin therapy.

The pharmacist at Revco did not warn or explain the potential for interaction between the two drugs to the plaintiffs, nor did the pharmacy alert the physician of the potential inter-

Dooley v Everett, et al.
805 S.W.2d 380 (Tenn. App. 1990)
...continued

action. It was established that the pharmacist dispensing the prescription did *not* know that the combination of drugs posed a risk of serious injury to the child.

The plaintiffs presented expert testimony by a pharmacist (B.S. Pharm., PharmD.) who was the owner of a community pharmacy. He testified that the accepted standard of care of professional practice that existed in Tennessee included that "pharmacies maintain a patient profile system, which should be reviewed by the pharmacist prior to filling a new prescription," including a determination of whether a drug interacts with any other drug currently ordered for the patient. He further testified:

> The standard of care also required the pharmacist alerted to the interaction to call the erythromycin prescriber, alert him or her to the potential interaction, and/or advise the patient or patient's representative of the potential interaction and encourage him or her to (1) have his or her serum theophylline levels monitored and/or (2) be alert for side effects of theohylline toxicity. It is difficult to articulate what the standard of care requires of a pharmacist without knowing the exact circumstances under which the prescription for *Ery-Ped* was presented but, regardless of the circumstances, the pharmacist is required to alert the patient or patient's representative to the potential interaction.

The pharmacist expert also testified that there exists, and did exist at the time of the injury, computer technology, which was available to the pharmacist to identify drug interactions in general and the erythromycin and theophylline interaction in particular.

RULING: The Tennessee Court of Appeals reversed the trial court decision, which had held that a pharmacist has no duty to warn.

REASONING: On appeal, the court carefully examined the legal duty required of a pharmacist in such a situation. It noted that the establishment of a legal duty requires a finding on whether the defendant is under any obligation for the benefit of a particular plaintiff. It noted that a duty rests on everyone to use due care under the circumstances, and negligence constitutes a failure to do what a reasonable and prudent person would do under the given circumstances.

Professionals are judged according to the standard of care required by their profession. The court refused to debate the question whether the practice of pharmacy was a profession. It noted that the Tennessee Pharmacy Practice Act provided that "the practice of pharmacy is declared a professional practice affecting the public health, safety, and welfare." The court concluded that the pharmacist is a professional who has a duty to his patients to exercise the standard of care required by the profession of pharmacy in the same or similar communities as the community in which he practices his profession.

The fact that a pharmacy owes its patients a duty of due care in dispensing prescription drugs was without question. The defendant pharmacy argued that the duty to warn of potential drug interactions is not a part of its duty. The plaintiffs introduced expert proof disputing this assertion. Therefore, whether the duty to warn of potential drug interactions is included within the pharmacist's duty to patients was a disputed issue of fact, which prevented the granting of summary judgment. The case was returned to the trial court.

Frye v Medicare-Glaser Corporation
579 N.E.2d 1255 (III. App. 1991); reversed by 605 N.E.2d 557 (III. 1992)

ISSUE: Whether a pharmacy can be held liable for damages to a consumer if the pharmacist undertakes to warn the consumer of the dangerous side effects of a prescription drug, but does so in an incomplete manner.

FACTS: Corina Frye, administrator of the estate of Stephen Frye, filed a complaint against Dr. John Barrow, M.D., for medical malpractice alleging that the physician failed to warn the decedent of the dangerous effect of taking *Fiorinal* in conjunction with alcohol.

The plaintiff also sued the Medicare-Glaser Corporation, the pharmacy that dispensed the prescription, and Evelyn Nightengale, the licensed pharmacist who dispensed the medication. The plaintiff alleged that although the defendant pharmacist had no duty to warn of the dangerous side effects of the drug, once she undertook the duty to warn and did so negligently, she was responsible for the death of Stephen Frye.

The decedent had arthroscopic surgery on his knee which was performed by Dr. Barrow. The physician prescribed *Fiorinal* following the surgery. Barrow did not include any directions or instructions in the prescription regarding the placement of any label on the prescription container or the provision of any warning that alcohol should not be consumed when taking the drug.

During her deposition, Nightengale testified that in preparing a label for a prescription, patient information is typed into the pharmacy's computer and the label is printed out. In this case, Nightengale filled the prescription and labeled the container using the label generated by the computer.

Nightengale further testified that in addition to printing the label, the computer is programmed to print a separate document that lists warnings that might be applied to the patient's prescription container. When asked what standard warnings would be provided by the computer software when the drug *Fiorinal* is typed in, Nightengale answered "drowsiness...alcohol and...impairing ability to drive." She explained that these warnings may be given as three separate cautionary labels or may be combined into one. In this case, the pharmacist attached two labels to the back of the prescription container. One label read "May cause DROWSINESS." The second label read "CAUTION: Federal law prohibits the transfer of this drug to persons other than the patient to whom it was prescribed."

Nightengale testified that the label that warned about the effects of alcohol when used in combination with the drug *Fiorinal* said something to the effect that alcohol may intensify the action of the drug. The decision whether or not to place any of the suggested warnings on the container is left to the discretion of the pharmacist. Nightengale testified that she did not use the warning label about the possible interaction of the drug with alcohol because she believed people might be offended to think that she believed they drank.

RULING: The Illinois Appellate Court overturned the trial court decision and ruled that a plaintiff may maintain an action against a pharmacist who voluntarily assumes a duty to warn of a drug's adverse reactions, but does so in an incomplete manner.

REASONING: The defendants contended that they could not be held liable because the law imposes no duty upon a pharmacy or its pharmacists to warn consumers of the dangers of taking prescription drugs in combination with other drugs or to warn of the dangerous side effects of prescription drugs. The defendants cited the case of *Kirk v Michael Reese Hospital* in which the Illinois State Supreme Court applied the "learned intermediary" doctrine which holds that the manufacturers of prescription drugs have a duty to warn prescribing

Frye v Medicare-Glaser Corporation
579 N.E.2d 1255 (Ill. App. 1991); reversed by 605 N.E.2d 557 (Ill. 1992)
...continued

physicians of the dangerous propensities of the drug. The physicians, in turn, using their medical reasoning, have a duty to convey the warnings to their patients.

In the Illinois case of *Eldridge v Eli Lilly & Co.*, the Illinois courts reasoned that a prescription that is excessive for one patient may be entirely reasonable for another. Therefore, to impose a duty to warn would require the pharmacist to learn the customer's condition and monitor his drug use, which would cause the pharmacist to interject himself into the physician-patient relationship and "the practice of medicine without a license."

Based on these previous decisions, the court concluded, in this case, that under the learned intermediary doctrine, the defendant pharmacy and pharmacist were under no initial duty to provide warnings regarding *Fiorinal* to the deceased. However, the plaintiff framed her claims on the theory that the defendants negligently performed the voluntary undertaking of warning the deceased.

The Restatement (Second) of Torts provides that "one who undertakes, gratuitously or for consideration, to render services to another which he should recognize as necessary for the protection of the other's person or things, is subject to liability to the other (a) if his failure to exercise such care increases the risk of harm, or (b) if the harm is suffered because of the other's reliance upon the undertaking."

The plaintiff did not contend that the warning given was inaccurate because one of the side effects of *Fiorinal* is drowsiness. However, the court concluded that a consumer who receives a warning from a pharmacist is entitled to rely upon the accuracy and completeness of that warning. A consumer who receives no warnings from a pharmacist must consult his physician to obtain additional information.

The defendants in this case had no initial duty to protect the plaintiff but voluntarily assumed the duty by placing a warning on the drug. Having undertaken a responsibility to warn the patient, the defendants assumed the duty to do so in a reasonable manner.

Hooper v Perry Drugs
Slip Op. 178665 (Unpublished), September 20, 1996. (Mich. App)

FACTS: In 1992, a physician issued prescriptions for *Seldane* and erythromycin, which were dispensed to the patient by the defendant pharmacy without warnings of known drug-drug interactions. The patient died from a myocardial infarction secondary to coronary thrombosis. In 1990, the manufacturer of *Seldane* issued a warning to health care practitioners that use of this drug with drugs in the same category as erythromycin "should be approached with caution" out of concern for cardiac complications. Five weeks after the prescriptions were dispensed to the patient, the manufacturer issued a press release indicating the *Seldane* and erythromycin are contraindicated due to the possibility of life-threatening cardiac arrhythmia's.

HOLDING: The Court of Appeals distinguished the *Baker v Arbor Drugs* case on the basis the pharmacy there had voluntarily assumed a duty to warn because of the advertising claims. In this case the pharmacy did not claim it would check for drug-drug interactions, therefore the pharmacy could not be held liable for failing to warn when it had no such duty in

Hooper v Perry Drugs
Slip Op. 178665 (Unpublished), September 20, 1996. (Mich. App)
...continued

the first place. The court also indicated the manufacturer's 1990 warning letter was not specific and did not prohibit concurrent use of these drugs. The case was dismissed.

⚖   ⚖   ⚖

Johnson v Walgreen Co.
675 So.2d 1036 (Fla. Dist Ct. App. 1996)

FACTS: A patient with numerous health problems, treated by different physicians who prescribed different medications, took *otc Benadryl* on the advice of the pharmacist at the pharmacy where he regularly filled all of his prescriptions. The patient subsequently died from
multiple drug toxicity due to prescription drug interactions. At no time did the pharmacist advise the customer, or any of his physicians, of the potential lethal effects of combining all of his prescribed medications or of the side effects of *Benadryl*. The customer's wife
filed suit claiming the pharmacy breached its duty of care by failing to consult the husband's
prescribing physicians regarding the potential drug interactions, failing to warn her husband of the potential harmful effects of combining the prescribed drugs, and recommending
inappropriate *otc* medication. The trial court dismissed the case on the ground that a pharmacist's sole duty is to accurately and properly fill all lawful prescriptions presented.

HOLDING: The Florida Appellate Court recognized that while there are good policy reasons for imposing liability under circumstances as in this case, Florida law imposes no duty to
warn on pharmacists. A Board of Pharmacy rule requiring consultation with patients and
warnings when needed only created an ability for the Board to sanction pharmacists. The rule
does not create a malpractice duty or create a private cause of action.

⚖   ⚖   ⚖

Silves v King
970 P.2d 790 (Wash. Ct. App. 1999)

Silves went to the emergency room at St. Joseph Hospital complaining of a sore and swollen toe. Silves was concerned that he might be experiencing a blood clot; he had a problem with blood clotting and at the time was taking heparin, an anticoagulant. At the
emergency room, Dr. King examined Silves, diagnosed gouty arthritis, and prescribed indomethacin, a nonsteroidal, anti-inflammatory drug. According to the *Physician's Desk Reference* (*PDR*), indomethacin is indicated for the treatment of gouty arthritis. The *PDR* does
not indicate that indomethacin should not be used by a patient who is taking heparin. It
does, however, advise caution when prescribing indomethacin to a patient with coagulation
defects. A licensed pharmacist on staff at St. Joseph Hospital filled Silves' prescription. The
pharmacist did not recall filling the prescription, but testified that had she known the patient
was taking heparin. Her standard practice would have been to call the prescribing doctor
to make sure the doctor was aware of that fact before filling the prescription. Because there
are no absolute contraindications to giving indomethacin to a patient taking heparin, the
pharmacist would have filled the prescription had Dr. King indicated she knew Silves was taking heparin and nevertheless wanted him to have the indomethacin. For several days, Silves
took both heparin and indomethacin, then suffered a pulmonary hemorrhage. Silves filed
a medical malpractice action against Dr. King for prescribing indomethacin, and against the
hospital for the alleged negligence of the pharmacist for her failure to warn him of possible harmful drug interactions and to discuss the prescription with Dr. King. The trial court

Silves v King
970 P.2d 790 (Wash. Ct. App. 1999)
...continued

entered summary judgment in favor of the hospital on Silves' claim alleging negligence by the pharmacist, and a jury returned a verdict in favor of Dr. King. Silves appealed and contended that summary judgment in favor of the hospital and pharmacist was improper. Silves alleged that the hospital pharmacist was negligent for failing to warn him of potential drug interaction and contraindications between heparin and indomethacin. The court of appeals held that summary judgment was proper because the pharmacist did not have a duty to warn Silves under the circumstances. A pharmacist has a duty to accurately fill a prescription and to be alert for clear errors or mistakes in the prescription. The pharmacist does not, however, have a duty to question a judgment made by the physician as to the propriety of a prescription or to warn customers of the hazardous side effects associated with a drug. Requiring a pharmacist to warn of potential risks associated with a drug would interject the pharmacist into the physician-patient relationship and interfere with ongoing treatment. In this case, the *PDR* recommended using caution when prescribing indomethacin to a patient with coagulation defects, but there are no absolute contraindications to prescribing indomethacin to a patient who is taking heparin. Because there was no clear error or mistake in Silves' prescription for indomethacin, the pharmacist was under no duty to warn Silves. The court of appeals also held that the pharmacist had no duty to question Dr. King's judgment and because indomethacin would have been prescribed and dispensed in any event, the pharmacist's failure to consult Dr. King could not have been the proximate cause of Silves' injuries. Therefore, the court of appeals upheld summary judgment.

The following is a list of court cases that are related to this topic.

Kirk v Michael Reese Hospital and Medical Center, 513 N.E.2d 387 (Ill. 1987).
Baker v Arbor Drugs, 544 N.W.2d 727 (Mich. App. 1996), lv. denied, 454 Mich 853 (1997).
Guillory v Andrus, Nos. 96-85, 96-86, and 679 So: 2d 1004 (La. App., 1996).
Perkins v K-Mart Corp., Slip Op. No. 96-535313CL, Sept. 28, 1999 (Mich. Ct. App., Unpublished).

Excessive Dosages (including refills)

Jones v Irvin
602 F.Supp. 399 (S.D. Ill. 1985)

ISSUE: Whether a pharmacist, who correctly fills a prescription, is negligent for failing to warn the patient, or notify the physician, that a drug is being prescribed in dangerous amounts.

FACTS: The plaintiffs brought this lawsuit seeking to recover damages for personal injuries and loss of consortium allegedly sustained as the result of the plaintiff, Carole Jones', consumption of an excessive amount of the drug *Placidyl*. Mrs. Jones and her husband filed the action against the physician who prescribed the drug and against the K-Mart Corporation whose pharmacist dispensed the drug. The plaintiffs alleged that the defendant K-Mart was negligent because it knew or should have known that *Placidyl* is a drug of abuse, that the drug was being prescribed in massive amounts, and that K-Mart should have notified either the plaintiff or the physician prescribing the drug that something was wrong.

K-Mart moved for dismissal of the complaint, arguing that its pharmacist owed no duty to warn the plaintiff or her physician of any dangers. The trial court granted K-Mart's motion.

Jones v Irvin
602 F.Supp. 399 (S.D. Ill. 1985)
...continued

RULING: The court concluded that the pharmacist has no duty to warn the patient or notify the physician that a drug is being prescribed in dangerous amounts, that the patient is being overmedicated, or that the various drugs could cause adverse reactions to the patient.

REASONING: The federal court had to rely on Illinois law to resolve the issue. The court could find only one Illinois decision defining the duty that a pharmacist owes to a patient. In *Jones v Walgreen Company*, 265 Ill. App. 308 (1932), the court stated that "while the law requires of a druggist only reasonable and ordinary care in compounding prescriptions, in selling medicines, and in performing the other duties of his profession, such care with reference to him means the highest degree of prudence, thoughtfulness, and diligence and is proportionate to the danger involved; and that a breach of such duty would be negligence rendering him liable for injuries resulting therefrom." Using the standard of the Jones decision, the court, in this case, held that a pharmacist's legal duty goes further than merely dispensing the right drug. However, the Jones case dealt with a situation in which the pharmacist filled a prescription with the wrong product. Because the factual pattern was not the same, the decision was not controlling the case-at-hand.

The court examined a long line of other cases and concluded that the overwhelming majority of recent state cases stand for the proposition that the pharmacist has no duty to warn. The only recent case found upholding a pharmacist's duty to warn was *Hand v Krakowski*, 453 N.Y.S.2d 121 (1982), where a New York court concluded that a pharmacist was potentially liable for failure to warn a patient of the possible side effects of taking a prescribed drug with alcohol when it was shown that the pharmacist knew that the patient was an alcoholic, and that the drug in question was contraindicated for alcoholics.

Based upon the analysis of all these cases and the general policy concerns, the court concluded that the pharmacist has no duty to warn the patient or notify the physician that a drug is being prescribed in dangerous amounts or that the patient is being overmedicated. The court felt that this is the duty of the prescribing physician. The court stated that the physician has a duty to know the characteristics of the drug he is prescribing, to elicit from the patient what other drugs the patient is taking, to properly prescribe various combinations of drugs, to warn the patient of any dangers associated with taking the drug, to monitor the patient's dependence on the drug, and to tell the patient when and how to take the drug. Further, the court held that it is the duty of the patient to notify the physician of the other drugs the patient is taking.

Finally, it is the duty of the drug manufacturer to notify the physician of any adverse effects or other precautions that must be taken in administering the drug. Placing these duties to warn on the pharmacist would only serve to compel the pharmacist to second-guess every prescription a physician ordered in an attempt to escape liability. The court emphasized in its decision that its holding was a narrow one. It stated that a pharmacist still owes the patient the highest degree of prudence, thoughtfulness, and diligence.

Riff v Morgan Pharmacy
508 A.2d 1247 (Pa. Super. Ct. 1986)

ISSUE: Whether a pharmacist has a duty to warn a patient of the maximum dosage for *Cafergot* suppositories or if this responsibility rests solely on the prescriber.

FACTS: The plaintiff, Patricia Riff, experienced a severe migraine headache. She contacted her physician and received a prescription for *Cafergot* suppositories, which was filled at Morgan Pharmacy. The written instructions read "Insert one in the rectum every four hours for headache." There were no refills indicated. The pharmacist typed the physician's instructions on the prescription label and did not issue any additional instructions or warnings.

That evening, Mrs. Riff used three or four suppositories before obtaining relief. Three months later, she suffered a second severe migraine. Over the next several days, she used the remaining suppositories from her original prescription and had it refilled at Morgan Pharmacy. This migraine lasted almost 4 days, during which the plaintiff used 15 to 17 suppositories - 1 every 4 hours as instructed. This was repeated 4 months later when the pharmacy again refilled the prescription.

Shortly thereafter, Mrs. Riff had discomfort in her right foot. A hospital examination determined the cause as toxic effects of a *Cafergot* overdose. Physicians initially told the plaintiff she was likely to die. That opinion was later revised, and she was told that her leg would probably have to be amputated. Amputation became unnecessary, but Mrs. Riff's foot suffered permanent damage, tends to drag, and is in constant discomfort.

The Riffs brought suit against Morgan Pharmacy and the prescribing physician. The physician testified that he knew *Cafergot* is dangerous and that he should have indicated maximum dosage. He also said that he did not authorize refills and had no knowledge of Mrs. Riff's refills. The maximum *Cafergot* dosage specified in medical literature is 2 suppositories per attack; the user should not take over 5 in 1 week.

RULING: The jury awarded $170,000 in damages and returned a verdict of 35% fault against the physician and 65% fault against the pharmacist. The jury's verdict was upheld on appeal.

REASONING: The defendant pharmacy argued that it was the physician's duty to determine the number of suppositories to be used by the plaintiff. The pharmacy's function was simply to supply the medication. The court found this statement "quite illustrative of the appellant's disregard for the professional duty owed the plaintiff by the defendant pharmacy. The appellant would seem to argue that a pharmacy is no more than a warehouse for drugs and that a pharmacist has no more responsibility than a shipping clerk who must dutifully and *unquestioningly* obey the written orders of omniscient physicians. Such is not the case."

The court reviewed the pharmacists' training, internship requirements, and comprehensive licensure examination. The court stated "a pharmacist is a professional. In the performance of his professional duties, he will be held to the standard of care, skill and intelligence, which ordinarily characterizes the profession. In judging this degree of skill, consideration will be made of the advanced state of the profession at the time of the injury."

The pharmacy argued that it was not the cause of the plaintiff's injuries because she relied solely upon the physician's instructions. However, the court found sufficient evidence that Morgan Pharmacy breached its duty of care by failing to warn the patient or notify the physician of the prescription's obvious inadequacies. But for this negligence, the injuries would not have occurred. In affirming the judgment, the court made a powerful statement regarding responsibilities of the pharmacist:

Riff v Morgan Pharmacy
508 A.2d 1247 (Pa. Super. Ct. 1986)
...continued

Expert testimony established that the 'reasonable pharmacist' has an affirmative duty to read the prescription and to be aware of patent inadequacies in the instructions as to maximum safe dosage of known toxic drugs and medicines. Morgan Pharmacy's pharmacists failed in that duty.

Fallibility is a condition of the human existence. Doctors, like other mortals, will from time to time err through ignorance or inadvertence. An error in the practice of medicine can be fatal; and so it is reasonable that the medical community including physicians, pharmacists, anesthesiologists, nurses and support staff have established professional standards that require vigilance not only with respect to primary function, but also regarding the acts and omissions of the other professionals and support personnel in the health care team. Each has an affirmative duty to be, to a limited extent, his brother's keeper.

It is not for this court to delineate the precise bounds of a medical professional's responsibilities. It is for the medical community to determine what degree of vigilance is required in this respect. They are in the best position to balance the interests and prescribe a standard of conduct which is consistent with the best interests of the patient.

In the instant case, the testimony of the medical experts, both physicians' and pharmacists', fell below the level of reasonable conduct in the practice of pharmacy. The jury heard the evidence and found that Morgan Pharmacy was not only negligent but more negligent than Dr. Stack.

Walker v Jack Eckerd Corp.
434 S.E.2d 63, (Ga.App., 1993), cert denied, Ga. S.Ct. (1993)

ISSUE: May a pharmacy be found liable for malpractice for excessive refills and failing to warn a patient about known risks associated with a drug?

FACTS: A physician prescribed *Blephamide* for plaintiff on two different occasions. The plaintiff claims that both the prescriptions contained "PRN" refill instructions. State law permits a "PRN" prescription to be refilled as needed over a lengthy time period, usually not to exceed 1 year. The physician denied that he issued either prescription as "PRN" or otherwise refillable. In any event, the defendant pharmacy dispensed this drug under one of the prescription numbers 15 times to the plaintiff in less than 1 year. The package insert issued to pharmacies with the drug warned that prolonged use could result in glaucoma. Plaintiff subsequently was diagnosed with glaucoma, which allegedly was caused by excessive *Blephamide* use.

HOLDING: The trial court granted the pharmacy's motion for summary judgment. On appeal, a majority of the panel of judges reviewing the case upheld the trial court judgment. One judge wrote a dissenting opinion.

REASONING: The plaintiff claimed that the trial court erred in holding there was no breach of a legally recognized duty on the part of the pharmacy to either warn the patient about excessive use of the drug or to refuse to refill the prescriptions. There is no state law expressly

Walker v Jack Eckerd Corp.
434 S.E.2d 63, (Ga.App., 1993), cert denied, Ga. S.Ct. (1993)
...continued

imposing a pharmacist's duty to warn or to refuse to fill prescriptions when provided with manufacturers' literature warning of potential adverse effects if certain drug dosages are exceeded. However, both parties identified the two conflicting lines of authority in other states pertaining to the common-law duty of pharmacists regarding the warning of patients and the refusal to fill prescriptions.

The court was aware that effective January 1, 1993, the Georgia State Board of Pharmacy imposed certain new drug review and patient counseling rules on pharmacists (Rules of Ga. State Board of Pharmacy, §§480-31-.01.) However, this does not alter the legislature's intent prior to these rules to except certain prescription drugs from various labeling and warning requirements. Accordingly, this case is not intended to serve as controlling precedent for cases involving pharmacists' duties arising after January 1, 1993.

The trial court was correct in granting the pharmacy's motion for partial summary judgment. The majority opinion states, "At best there existed but a shadowy semblance of an issue as to Eckerd's liability. Summary judgment law does not require the movant to show that no issue of fact remains but only that no genuine issue of material fact remains; and while there may be some shadowy semblance of an issue, the case may nevertheless be decided as a matter of law where the evidence shows clearly and palpably that the jury could reasonably draw but one conclusion."

The dissenting judge agreed with the majority that, under the common law, a pharmacist has no duty to warn a patient about all possible adverse effects incident to the use of properly prescribed medications and that a pharmacist has no duty to provide patients with manufacturers' inserts containing drug warnings or contraindiactions of use or to advise the patient of such warnings. He was of the opinion, however, that a pharmacist is and should be more than a mere warehouse for drugs or a shipping clerk who must dutifully and unquestioningly obey the written orders of omniscient physicians. He would hold that a pharmacist has a duty to notify the prescribing physician of "obvious inadequacies appearing on the face of the prescription which create a substantial risk of serious harm to the plaintiff" and question a prescription which is erroneous or which is irregular on its face. This duty would protect the patient and the physician from physician errors that the patient could not detect but that would be readily apparent to a properly trained pharmacist. If this limited duty were to be applied to the facts of this case, a material question of fact remains for jury resolution concerning whether dispensing the drug *Blephamide* "PRN" constitutes such a patent or obvious error that the pharmacist should have contacted the prescribing physician before repeatedly dispensing the medication.

Cafaralle v Brockton Oaks C.V.S. Inc.
No. 94-0414A, (Mass. Super. Ct. April, 1996)

FACTS: The patient, a long-time asthma sufferer, filled a prescription for a *Proventil* inhaler and other medications at a pharmacy, which maintained an in-store computer to track patient medication profiles. The pharmacy's computer system included a warning prompt that alerted the pharmacist if a customer refilled a prescription at a rate faster than prescribed. The pharmacy refilled the patient's *Proventil* prescription three times more frequently than the standard practice or recommended use in one year's time. The patient subsequently died from acute respiratory failure associated with severe asthma. The patient's parents sued the pharmacy for negligently filling the prescriptions for an asthmatic teenager at a rate faster than prescribed.

Cafaralle v Brockton Oaks C.V.S. Inc.
No. 94-0414A, (Mass. Super. Ct. April, 1996)
...continued

HOLDING: The Massachusetts Superior Court denied the pharmacy's motion for summary judgment, rejecting the argument that its only duty is to accurately fill prescriptions. The Court stated that the pharmacy had a duty to exercise reasonable care in dispensing medication, therefore, a jury could conclude that it had failed to warn the physician or parents of overuse and, therefore, breached its duty. Further, a jury could find that the pharmacy knew of the teenager's overuse based on its computer system and that the pharmacist should have known the dangers associated with the overuse of inhalers. The court also found that the alleged unfair trade practice's count (ie, the pharmacy's overriding the computer warning system for insurance payment purposes) may have been an unfair practice that created dangerous conditions that could potentially injure customers. Accordingly, the case was remanded for trial.

Zuchowicz v U.S.
140 F.3d 381 (2nd Cir. 1998)

ISSUE: May a physician and a pharmacy be held liable for injuries sustained by a patient as a result of taking an excessive dose of a drug when there is no apparent reason for the injuries other than the use of the drug?

FACTS: In February 1989, after visiting her physician, the patient presented a prescription for *Danocrine* to the pharmacy. The prescription label instructed the patient to take 1600 mg/day. This is double the normal dose of 800 mg/day. The opinion does not indicate whether the physician erroneously prescribed the 1600 mg dose or the pharmacy made a mistake and filled the prescription with a higher-than-intended dose. The patient took the excessive dosage for approximately 5 weeks, and then took the 800 mg/day dose for approximately 9 more weeks. While taking the medication, she experienced abnormal weight gain, bloating, edema, hot flashes, night sweats, a racing heart, chest pains, dizziness, headaches, acne, and fatigue. In late May 1989, she saw a different physician who discontinued the medication. Over the summer, she continued to experience severe fatigue and chest tightness. She also experienced shortness of breath and pain. In October 1989, she was diagnosed with primary pulmonary hypertension (PPH). While waiting for a lung transplant as part of her treatment plan, she became pregnant. This made her ineligible for the transplant. She gave birth to a son in November 1989, and died 1 month later.

LAWSUIT: The husband brought a wrongful death lawsuit against the Navy. The prescribing physician was a Navy officer and the pharmacy is located on a Naval base. The patient was married to a Naval officer and entitled to spousal benefits offered by the Navy. The suit was brought against the Navy under the Federal Tort Claims Act, 28 USC §§1346(b). The Navy base is located in Groton, Connecticut, and therefore, Connecticut malpractice law controls. Because the only defendant was the Navy, the plaintiff did not have to establish whether the prescriber or the pharmacy made the error that resulted in the excessive dose. (Editor's Note: Although it was not stated in the court's written

HOLDING: After a trial before a federal judge (without a jury), the plaintiff (the estate of the patient as represented by her husband) was awarded $1,034,236. The judgment was upheld on appeal.

REASONING: The difficulty in establishing causation in this case lies in the fact that there are apparently no other cases of PPH associated with the use of *Danocrine*. Absent prece-

Zuchowicz v U.S.
140 F.3d 381 (2nd Cir. 1998)
...continued

dence and scientific data supporting the plaintiff's claim of the causal link, the only other avenue of proof available is to rule out any other causal connection between the disease and the drug. In an attempt to meet the requisite burden of proof, at trial the plaintiff relied on the expert witness testimony of a pulmonary disease physician and a pharmacologist who specializes in vascular tissue drugs. The pulmonary care physician testified that the relationship between the onset of the disease and the time at which the overdose occurred suggested a logical relationship between the two events. He also indicated that he use a "differential etiology" method of ruling out other possible causes of the disease. Using this method, the physician was able to conclude that the patient did not suffer secondary pulmonary hypertension and that no other drugs the patient had previously used caused PPH. He was not, however, able to rule out every other possible cause of PPH. He noted that prior to the overdose, the patient was a healthy and active young woman with no history of cardiovascular problems and that symptoms of PPH began shortly after she started taking the drug. He also testified that the onset of symptoms with other drugs known to cause PPH follow a similar sequence of events. The pharmacologist also concluded that the patient suffered from *Danocrine*-induced PPH. His opinion was based on the analysis of hormonal shifts experienced by the patient and study of the literature that indicates that these kinds of hormonal changes cause endothelial dysfunction and an imbalance of vasoconstrictor effects leading to PPH.

In its appeal, the defendant did not deny the wrongful conduct of either the physician or the pharmacy in giving the patient an excessive dose of the drug. Nor did it dispute the plaintiff's injuries. Instead, it claimed that there was no basis to conclude that the excessive dose caused the PPH. In rejecting this argument, the Court of Appeals noted that there has been a fairly recent change in the way that courts are to review the value and admission into evidence of scientific data. Under the older notions of fairness, courts could admit only scientific data or theory that has been "generally accepted by the scientific community." The more contemporary standard requires judges to act as a "gatekeeper" by making a "preliminary assessment of whether the reasoning or methodology underlying the testimony is scientifically valid and of whether that reasoning or methodology properly can be applied to the facts in issue." Using the newer standard, the trial court judge acted properly in admitting the expert testimony. In analyzing the evidence, the Court of Appeals took care to point out that this case is not just about the negligent prescribing or dispensing of a drug that allegedly caused plaintiff's injuries where no such injury has ever before been linked to the drug. Rather, this is a case about the negligent prescribing or dispensing of an overdose of the drug. In other words, exposure to *Danocrine* is not the issue. Instead, the issue is whether exposure to the overdose caused the injury and ultimate death of the patient.

In considering this issue, the court characterized the relationship between the FDA's procedures for approving a new drug at specified dose levels and the whole concept of causation in malpractice cases. The court states:

> The reason the FDA does not approve the prescription of new drugs at doses above those for which extensive tests have been performed, is because all drugs involve risks of untoward side effects in those who take them. Moreover, it is often true that the higher the dose, the greater the likelihood of negative effects. At the approved doses, the benefits of the particular drug have presumably been deemed worth the risks it entails. At greater-than-approved dosages, not only do the risks of tragic side effects (known and unknown) increase, but there is no basis on the testing that has been performed to suppose that the drug's benefits outweigh these increased risks. See generally 21 U.S.C. §§355(d) (indicating that the FDA should refuse to approve a new

Zuchowicz v U.S.
140 F.3d 381 (2nd Cir. 1998)
...continued

drug unless the clinical tests show that the drug is safe and effective for use under the conditions "prescribed, recommended, or suggested in the proposed labeling.") It follows that when a negative side effect is demonstrated to be the result of a drug, and the drug was wrongly prescribed in an unapproved and excessive dosage (ie, a strong causal link has been shown), the plaintiff who is injured has generally shown enough to permit the finder of fact to conclude that the excessive dosage was a substantial factor in producing the harm. Using this approach, the court emphasized that the expert witness testimony regarding the timing of the patient's illness, relative to when she took the overdose, is sufficient evidence of causation.

Horner v Spalitto
1 S.W.3d 519 (Mo. App. 1999)

The pharmacist, filled two prescriptions for the plaintiff, Horner. One of the prescriptions prescribed a strong hypnotic drug, three times the strength of a normal dose. Concerned about the strength of the prescription, Pharmacist Spalitto telephoned the physicians office, but was assured by the office that the prescription was "okay." Six days after the filling, Horner died of an apparent drug overdose. Horner's family sued Spalitto for wrongful death allegedly caused by Spalitto's negligent filling of the prescriptions. The trial court granted Spalitto summary judgment, finding that his only duty was to fill prescriptions accurately. The court of appeals reversed, finding that pharmacists have functions and duties beyond merely filling and dispensing drugs according to physician prescriptions. Relegating a pharmacist to the role of order-filler fails to fully appreciate the role of a pharmacist. Rather, the court of appeals held that the appropriate duty for a pharmacist was to act as a reasonably careful and prudent pharmacist would to minimize the risk that a reasonably prudent pharmacist would foresee. The court of appeals found that there was insufficient evidence on the record to determine whether Spalitto had acted as a reasonably careful and prudent pharmacist. Therefore, the court of appeals reversed the trial court's summary judgment and remanded the case for trial.

Payne v Galen Hospital
4 S.W.3d 312 (Tex. App. 1999)

Payne was a nurse at Galen Hospital when she injured her back assisting a patient. Payne received treatment from an independent (not employed by the hospital) physician who prescribed *Toradol* for her back pain. *Toradol* is labeled to be used for only limited duration and not in the management of chronic pain. Payne obtained her prescriptions and refills at the hospital pharmacy. She took *Toradol* for 4 1/2 months and then experienced a severe reaction to the prolonged use. Payne is now a chronic pain patient, totally and permanently disabled, and confined to a wheelchair for the rest of her life. Payne asserted that the hospital pharmacists were grossly negligent because they never warned her that *Toradol* was for acute use only. Payne received worker's compensation benefits for her initial injury and her reaction to *Toradol*. Payne sued the hospital and its pharmacist for negligence. The trial court granted Galen Hospital summary judgment on the grounds that the exclusive remedy provision of the worker's compensation act barred Payne's claims for negligence. Payne appealed and contended that her reaction to the *Toradol* was an independent injury that did

Payne v Galen Hospital
4 S.W.3d 312 (Tex. App. 1999)
...continued

not occur during the course and scope of her employment. Recovery under the worker's compensation act is intended to be an employee's sole remedy for work-related injuries. The question before the court of appeals was whether the second injury from the reaction to *Toradol* was a work-related injury. The court of appeals found that Payne's reaction to *Toradol* was an extension of her back injury, occurring in the probable sequence of events and arising from the actual compensable injury. Therefore, the court of appeals held that Payne's second injury, suffered during treatment of a job-related injury, was work related for purposes of the worker's compensation exclusive remedy. The court of appeals affirmed summary judgment for Galen Hospital.

The following is a list of court cases that are related to this topic.

Speer v United States, 512 F. Supp. 670 (N.D. Tex 1981).
Steele v Organon, Inc., 43 Wash. App. 230 (1986).
DeCordova v State of Colorado, 878 P.2d 73 (Colo. App. 1994).
Fakhouri v Taylor, 248 Ill. App. 3d 328; 618 N.E.2d 518, (Ill. App. 1993), Iv.denied, (1993) LEXIS 814; 187 Ill. Dec. 927.

Contraindications

The following is a list of court cases that are related to this topic.

Ferguson v Williams, 374 S.E.2d 438 (N.C. App. 1988).
Guillory v Andrus, Nos. 96-85, 96-86, and 679 So.2d 1004 (La. App., 1996).
Hooper v Perry Drugs, Slip Op. 178665 (Unpublished), September 20, 1996. (Mich. App).

Special Knowledge of the Pharmacist

The following is a list of court cases that are related to this topic.

Fuhs v Barber, 36 P.2d 962 (Kan. 1934).
Krueger v Knutson, 111 N.W.2d 526 (Minn. 1961).
Griffin v Phar-Mor, 1992 WL 90344 (S.D. Ala.).

Limits on the Pharmacist's Duty to Warn

Stebbins v Concord Wrigley Drugs, Inc. et al.
416 N.W.2d 381 (Mich. App. 1987)

ISSUE: Whether the plaintiff who was injured by a motorist who was taking an antidepressant drug may collect from a pharmacy that failed to warn the motorist of the side effects or hazards of the prescription mediation.

FACTS: The plaintiff, Bonnie Stebbins, was seriously injured when her automobile was struck by a car driven by Joseph Zagone. Zagone was under the treatment of a psychiatrist and he had received prescriptions for the antidepressant drug, *Tofranil*, which were dispensed at Concord Discount Drugs. After eating breakfast at a local restaurant, Zagone ran a red light and hit the plaintiff's automobile. He remembered very little about the accident. While he was included as a defendant in the lawsuit, the plaintiff eventually settled with Zagone. The lawsuit proceeded against the physician, pharmacy, and pharmacist.

Stebbins v Concord Wrigley Drugs, Inc. et al.
416 N.W.2d 381 (Mich. App. 1987)
...continued

The plaintiff alleged that the physician failed to warn Zagone of the side effects of *Tofranil* and failed to warn him not to drive while using the drug. Similar allegations were also made with regard to the defendant pharmacy. It was alleged that *Tofranil* caused psychological and physical impairments in Zagone's driving ability which resulted in the collision.

The pharmacy claimed that it had no duty to warn patients of the side effects or hazards of prescription drugs. The physician also asked to be dismissed from the lawsuit because he claimed he had warned Zagone of the side effects, including the increased hazard in operating a motor vehicle. It was also argued that the dosage that was prescribed was to be taken at night and could not have caused Zagone's alleged drowsiness the next morning.

RULING: The trial court granted the pharmacy's motion for summary judgment because the pharmacist had no duty to warn the patient of side effects but that such duty remained with the physician. The court also granted the physician's motion for summary judgment because it concluded he had given the warning. More importantly, any effect the drug might have had on Zagone the following morning was pure speculation. The Michigan Court of Appeals agreed with the trial court decision that a pharmacist has no duty to warn a patient of possible side effects when the prescription is proper on its face and when neither the physician nor the manufacturer has required that any warning be given to the patient by the pharmacist. (NOTE: The court did leave open the possibility of considering a pharmacist's duty to warn under a proper fact pattern such as those situations in which the pharmacist knows of a particular patient's unique problems or where a pharmacist fills two incompatible prescriptions.)

REASONING: The appellate court found that Zagone's prescription required him to take a 75 mg capsule of *Tofranil* at bedtime and there was confusion as to whether he took any on the date of the accident. Zagone had been taking the drug for some time and he had never complained of drowsiness or other side effects even when the physician prescribed twice the dosage he was taking at the time of the accident. A pharmacologist testified that *Tofranil* taken as prescribed or even twice the prescribed dosage would not have affected Zagone's ability to drive the next morning.

It was agreed that the *Physician's Desk Reference* required a warning to be given to patients taking *Tofranil* that there might be some impairment of mental and/or physical abilities when operating an automobile or machinery. However, there was a genuine dispute as to whether the physician had appropriately warned Zagone. Yet, it was still necessary for the plaintiff to show a causal connection between the physician's alleged failure to warn and the accident. All of the evidence submitted suggested that Zagone would not experience the potential side effects at the prescribed dosage on the following morning. The court ruled that the plaintiff had failed to carry her burden of showing that Zagone's use of *Tofranil* proximately caused the accident regardless of whether or not the physician gave any warning.

The court found that an even more fundamental difficulty existed in the plaintiff's case against the pharmacy because it concluded that the pharmacy had no duty to warn Zagone of the potential side effects of *Tofranil*. The court stated the general rule in Michigan that a pharmacist is held to a very high standard of care in dispensing prescriptions, but that pharmacists are generally not held liable for failing to warn when correctly filling prescriptions. The court cited a long string of cases that indicated that it is the physician's responsibility to monitor the patient's drug therapy and provide appropriate warnings. Only two exceptions to the general rule were noted. The court elected not to follow *Hand v Krakowski* because the plaintiff was a known alcoholic in that case. It also declined to follow the

Stebbins v Concord Wrigley Drugs, Inc. et al.
416 N.W.2d 381 (Mich. App. 1987)
...continued

precedent in *Riff v Morgan Pharmacy* because the pharmacist in that case had exceeded the accepted maximum dose and refilled the prescription without authorization. While those courts determined that pharmacists may have a responsibility to provide a warning, similar fact patterns were not alleged in this case and the court elected not to follow these two precedents.

Adkins v Mong et al.
Docket No. 90217 (Mich. Ct. App. 1988)

ISSUE: Whether a pharmacy has a legal duty to monitor a patient's prescriptions issued by a licensed physician and to intervene to warn the patient.

FACTS: The plaintiff filed this action against various physicians and pharmacies alleging that as a result of their negligence, he became addicted to *Seconal, Valium, Tandearil, Nembutal,* and *Gantanol.* This particular appeal was based upon the defendant Motor City Prescription Center's request for a motion for summary judgment.

The plaintiff alleged that Motor City Prescription Center breached its statutory and common law duties by (1) failing to maintain accurate patient profile cards, (2) failing to maintain accurate prescription records, (3) failing to identify over-prescribing by physicians, (4) failing to independently determine that the plaintiff was a drug abuser, (5) failing to communicate with other area pharmacies regarding the plaintiff's status as a drug abuser, and (6) dispensing the plaintiff's prescriptions for highly abused substances. The briefs filed in this case referred to 116 prescriptions filled by the defendant pharmacy for the plaintiff over a period of 6 years. There was no dispute that each of the prescriptions had been written by a licensed physician.

RULING: The trial court rejected the defendant's argument that a pharmacy owes no legal duty to its patients to monitor prescriptions issued by licensed physicians because facts might develop that would support such a claim. However, following previous precedents, the Michigan Court of Appeals overturned the trial court decision and dismissed the pharmacy from the lawsuit because it found no legal duty on the part of a pharmacist to monitor prescriptions and provide warnings to the patient.

REASONING: The Michigan Court of Appeals noted that it had recently decided the case of *Stebbins v Concord Wrigley Drugs* in which it concluded that "a pharmacist has no duty to warn the patient of possible side effects of a prescribed medication where the prescription is proper on its face and neither physician or the manufacturer has required that any warning be given to the patient by the pharmacist." As the court explained in Stebbins, a pharmacist owes a very high standard of care in properly dispensing lawful prescriptions, but that generally a pharmacist will not be held liable for correctly filling a prescription issued by a prescriber.

The plaintiff argued that the pharmacy owed him the additional duty of maintaining detailed prescription records and a corresponding duty to identify addicted patients and their over-prescribing physicians, either independently or through the combined efforts of other local pharmacies. The plaintiff argued that a pharmacist who identifies the addicted customer as a patient of an over-prescribing physician would then be obligated to (1) refuse to fill the pre-

Adkins v Mong et al.
Docket No. 90217 (Mich. Ct. App. 1988)
...continued

scriptions, (2) warn the customer, or (3) notify the physician. The court noted that other jurisdictions that have been presented with this same theory of liability have overwhelmingly rejected it in favor of the more limited duty described in Stebbins.

In making its decision, the court referred to the case of *Pysz v Henry's Drug Store* in which a Florida court refused to require a pharmacist to warn a patient of the addictive properties of *Quaalude* which he had been taking for a period of 9 years. The Florida court held that it is the physician who owes the duty to the patient to monitor prescription drug usage. The court further cited *Jones v Irvin*, a federal district court decision that concluded that pharmacists should not be placed in the position of having to second-guess every prescription in an attempt to avoid tort liability to their patients. Also noted was the case of *Eldridge v Lilly* in which an Illinois appellate court rejected the theory that pharmacists owe their patients a duty to act as a "safety supervisor" reviewing the propriety of prescriptions issued by a patient's treating physician.

The court also rejected the plaintiff's reliance for authority upon the standards of practice adopted by the American Pharmaceutical Association in 1979 and upon other articles published in professional journals. The court was "not persuaded by these nonlegal authorities, particularly in light of the cases cited above."

McKee v American Home Products
782 P.2d 1045 (Wash. 1989)

ISSUE: Whether a pharmacist was negligent for dispensing a drug for an extended period of time without warning the patient of the adverse effects and whether the pharmacist was negligent in failing to give the patient the manufacturer's package insert.

FACTS: From 1974 through 1984, Elaine McKee received a prescription for *Plegine*, an appetite supressant, from her family physician to control an ostensible weight problem. The labeling for the drug warned that it is indicated in the management of obesity only as a short-term adjunct. The potential for dependency and abuse were also discussed in the package labeling. McKee's prescriptions for 100 tablets were dispensed in the manufacturer's container, but the pharmacy removed the package insert and placed its own label on the bottle. In 1985, McKee brought action against the prescriber, the drug manufacturer, and the pharmacist, seeking damages for physical and psychological injuries allegedly due to addiction to the drug.

RULING: The trial court ruled that the pharmacists who had filled the prescriptions had no duty to warn the plaintiff of the adverse side effects of the long-term administration of the drug. The Washington Supreme Court affirmed the lower court decision.

REASONING: The only evidence offered by McKee concerning the pharmacist's standard of care was an affidavit of an Arizona physician. The court noted that the standard must be established by the testimony of experts who practice in the same field. Thus, the defendant pharmacists were entitled to summary judgment because there were no genuine issues of fact. Yet, because of the importance surrounding the issue of the pharmacist's duty to warn and a public interest therein, the court proceeded to further examine this question.

McKee v American Home Products
782 P.2d 1045 (Wash. 1989)
...continued

The court eventually adhered to the traditional philosophy that it is the physician who is in the best position to decide when to use a drug and how and when to inform the patient regarding risks and benefits pertaining to durg therapy. The court concluded that neither the manufacturer nor the pharmacist has the medical education or knowledge of the medical history of the patient which would justify the judicial imposition of a duty to intrude into the physician-patient relationship.

The statutes and regulations of the state of Washington include provisions for pharmacists to monitor drug therapy, advise of therapeutic values, and provide information regarding the use of prescription drugs. The court concluded the regulation requiring pharmacists to orally explain a prescription's directions for use did not create a mandatory duty on all pharmacists to warn customers of *all* dangers associated with a drug. The court interpreted the regulaiton to only include nonjudgmental information, but not that information affecting a decision to take or continue using a drug. The court believed that pharmacists should have a duty to be alert for errors in a prescription such as lethal dosages, inadequate instructions, known contraindications, or incompatible prescriptions, but the alleged negligence in this case involved the exercise of a physician's judgment in determining whether *Plegine* was an appropriate drug and what length of time the plaintiff could safely use it. "If the legislature intended pharmacists to be liable for failure to warn, the Legislature could have so provided."

The court also declined to impose a duty on pharmacists to provide patients with a package insert because this would place an unknown burden on them. Pharmacists would have the economic and logistic burden of copying the insert as well as developing a storage, filing, and retrieving system to ensure the current insert is dispensed with the proper drug. Furthermore, the court felt that the package insert would confuse or frighten the patient. "A requirement that consumers receive the manufacturer's insert abrogates the learned intermediary doctrine and could impact not only pharmacist's liability, but that of manufacturers and physicians as well."

The court noted that its holding was narrow. The pharmacist still has a duty to accurately fill a prescription and to be alert for clear errors or mistakes in a prescription. The pharmacist does not, however, have a duty to question a judgment made by a physician as to the propriety of a prescription or to warn customers of the hazardous side effects associated with a drug, either orally or by way of a manufacturer's package insert.

The four dissenting judges noted that for 10 years the pharmacists in this case removed labeling from the prescription container, which would have warned the plaintiff that the medication she was receiving was not necessary or endangering her health. The failure was repeated not over a few weeks or a few months, but for 10 years. The dissent questioned, "Isn't knowing that *Plegine*, an amphetamine, should be prescribed only several weeks rather than 10 years within the definition of the majority's concern for obvious lethal dosages?"

Nichols v Central Merchandise, Inc.
817 P.2d 1131 (Kan. App. 1991)

ISSUE: Whether a pharmacist owed a duty to warn a pregnant customer of the potential side effects of a drug prescribed by her physician.

FACTS: During the first trimester of her pregnancy, Juanita Nichols developed a urinary tract infection. Her physician, aware of her pregnancy, prescribed *Gantanol*, which was dispensed by a pharmacist at Super D Drugs. Dixie Wilson, the dispensing pharmacist, knew that the package insert for *Gantanol* warned that the use of sulfonamides in pregnancy had not been established. She further knew or suspected that Nichols was pregnant, but the pharmacist did not consult with the prescribing physician regarding the advisability of the drug. She also did not inform Nichols of the warning statement contained in the package insert. Nichols' child was later born without hands or feet.

RULING: The drug manufacturer and prescribing physician settled out of court. The trial court granted a summary judgment in favor of the pharmacy that was upheld by the appellate court.

REASONING: Pharmacy regulations of the state of Kansas define a pharmacist's duties to include "initiating oral patient consultation of new prescriptions as a matter of routine to encourage proper patient drug utilization and administration." The pharmacist attached warning labels to the prescription container instructing the patient to drink lots of water and to avoid sunlight. The court seemingly concluded that these warning labels would satisfy the requirements of encouraging proper utilization and administration of a drug.

In its review of the issues, the court dismissed the application of a 1934 Kansas case that suggested that a pharmacist has a duty to warn of a possible drug interaction. This early case involved a pharmacist who recommended and compounded an ointment by his own invention. In sharp contrast to the present case, the *Gantanol* dispensed to Nichols was not manufactured by the pharmacist nor did the pharmacist recommend its use.

Instead, the court noted that manufacturers of prescription drugs have a duty to warn of dangerous side effects, but that this duty is satisfied when the prescribing physician is informed of the drug's inherent risks. It is the physician who must determine what facts should be told to the patient. Thus, the pharmacist has no legal duty to warn the patient of potential consequences from the use of a prescribed drug. The court emphasized that *Gantanol* was not contraindicated for use during early pregnancy, but that the package insert merely stated its effect on a fetus had not been determined.

Citing previous case law, the court determined it would be both illogical and unreasonable to impose a greater duty on the pharmacist dispensing the drug than on the manufacturer of the drug. The court also cited the McKee decision by the Washington Supreme Court, which concludes "the pharmacist still has a duty to accurately fill a prescription and to be alert for clear errors or mistakes in the prescription. The pharmacist does not, however, have a duty to question a judgment made by the physician as to the propriety of a prescription or to warn customers of the hazardous side effects associated with a drug, either orally or by way of the manufacturer's package insert."

Pittman v Upjohn
890 S.W.2d 425 (Tenn. 1994)

ISSUE: Whether a drug manufacturer, the prescribing physician, and the dispensing pharmacist owed a duty to warn an unauthorized user of a prescription medication about the potential side effects.

FACTS: Mrs. Richards, the plaintiff's grandmother, was diagnosed as having adult onset diabetes and her physician prescribed *Micronase*. Mrs. Richards had the prescription filled at the Portland Prescription Shop in Portland, Tennessee. The pharmacy dispensed the drug to Mrs. Richards in a nonchildproof container as requested by Mrs. Richards because of her advanced age and poor eyesight.

Instructions for taking the medication were placed on the label, as was a warning to keep all medicines out of the reach of children. The pharmacy did not relay any other warnings about the *Micronase*. Mrs. Richards kept the prescription container on the top of her refrigerator. She also kept her high blood pressure medication and a bottle of aspirin in the same place.

Mrs. Richards' adult grandson, Donald Pittman, Jr., was staying with her when he told her that he was not feeling well and thought he was coming down with the flu. Mrs. Richards told him that there was some aspirin in a bottle on the top of the refrigerator and he could take some if he needed them. She watched as he took the aspirin bottle down but did not watch to see if he actually took any aspirin. The two of them sat in the living room for a short while. Pittman said he was feeling better and Mrs. Richards went to bed. The conversation with his grandmother was the last one Pittman was known to have had with anyone.

At some point of time during the middle of the night, Mrs. Richards got up and found Pittman lying in the middle of the living room floor. She was able to awaken him, but he could not get up by himself. He indicated that he could not move his feet. With his help, Mrs. Richards was able to get her grandson on the couch where he promptly went back to sleep. Pittman became progressively worse over the next 3 days, developing a fever and refusing food. Both his mother and grandmother were concerned about his health, but neither called a doctor at this point.

Pittman was taken to the hospital when he became comatose. It was concluded that he was suffering from hypoglycemia and that he had sustained permanent brain damage necessitating institutionalization. Mrs. Richards discovered that 6 *Micronase* tablets were missing, but she initially thought that the pharmacy might have put too few in the bottle.

RULING: The court ruled that the defendants could not have foreseen that an unauthorized user would consume the medications and granted summary judgment in their favor.

REASONING: The court noted the proposition that pharmaceutical manufacturers are required, as a general rule, to only warn the prescribing physician who acts as a learned intermediary between the manufacturer and the consumer. Thus, the court concluded that Upjohn had no duty to warn Pittman, who was an unauthorized user of the *Micronase*. The court stated that the pharmacy owed a duty to Mrs. Richards as it did to all of its prescription drug customers, to refrain from negligently doing an act that would injure her. Thus, the pharmacist had a duty to act with due ordinary care and diligence in compounding and dispensing the prescription medication. The plaintiffs failed to convince the court that the normal standard of care required the pharmacy to also provide a duty to warn noncustomers. The court ruled that the defendants could not have foreseen that an adult houseguest of Mrs. Richards would take a prescription medication clearly belonging to someone else and

Pittman v Upjohn
890 S.W.2d 425 (Tenn. 1994)
...continued

ingest several tablets without the knowledge and permission of the owner. Because the plaintiff was not within the general field of danger that could have reasonably been foreseen by the defendants, summary judgment was appropriate for all of them.

A dissenting judge pointed out that the plaintiffs had submitted evidence from other pharmacies showing that a warning not to share prescriptions with others is an arguable standard of care generally adhered to by pharmacists. In the dissent's opinion, this created a question of fact for the jury to decide.

The following is a list of court cases that are related to this topic.

Kinney v Hutchinson, 449 So.2d 696 (La. Ct. App. 1984).
Pysz v Henry's Drug Store, 457 So.2d 561 (Fla. Dist. Ct. App. 1984).
Ingram v Hook's Drugs, Inc., 476 N.E. 2d 881 (Ind. Ct. App. 1985).
Jones v Irvin, 602 F. Supp. 399 (S.D. Ill. 1985).
Raynor v Richardson-Merrell, Inc., 643 F. Supp. 238 (D.D.C. 1986).
Makripodis v Merrell Dow Pharmaceuticals, Inc., 523 A.2d 374 (Pa. Super.1987).
Leesley v West, 518 N.E.2d 758 (Ill. App. 2 Dist. 1988).
Hofherr v Dart Industries, Inc., 853 F.2d 259 (4th Cir. 1988).
Docken v Ciba-Geigy, 790 P. 2d 45 (Or. App. 1990).
Laws v Johnson, 1990 WL 97851 (Tenn. App.).
Frye v Medicare-Glaser Corp., 1992 WL 297605 (Ill. Sup. Ct.).
Fakhouri v Taylor, 248 Ill. App. 3d 328; 618 N.E.2d 518, (Ill. App. 1993), Iv.denied, (1993) LEXIS 814; 187 Ill. Dec. 927.
Gassen v East Jefferson General Hospital, et al, 1993 La. App. LEXIS 3985.
Walker v Jack Eckerd Corp., 209 Ga. App. 517; 434 S.E.2d 63, (Ga. App., 1993), cert denied, Ga. S. Ct., Slip Op. No. 593C1686 (1993).
Baker v Arbor Drugs, 544 N.W.2d 727 (Mich. App. 1996), Iv. Denied, 454 Mich 853 (1997).
Hooper v Perry Drugs, Slip Op. 178665 (Unpublished), September 20, 1996. (Mich. App).
Johnson v Walgreen Co., 675 S.2d 1036 (Fla. Dist Ct. App. 1996).

Interference with the Physician-Patient Relationship

Makripodis v Merrell Dow Pharmaceuticals, Inc.
523 A.2d 374 (Pa. Super. Ct. 1987)

ISSUE: Whether a pharmacy which correctly dispenses a prescribed drug is liable for breach of warranty or strict liability when the use of the drug by a pregnant woman allegedly results in congenital abnormalities.

FACTS: The plaintiff, Dolly Makripodis, used *Bendectin* during her pregnancy for the treatment of nausea. Her son was born with certain congenital abnormalities, allegedly a result of the ingestion of the drug. The Makripodis family filed suit against Merrell Dow Pharmaceuticals which manufactured the product and Rite Aid Corporation whose pharmacy dispensed the drug. The plaintiffs alleged that the pharmacy had (1) breached an implied warranty of merchantability because the drug was unsafe for ordinary use and that it was (2) strictly liable in tort because *Bendectin* was a defective product, unreasonably dangerous to the user without proper warnings.

Makripodis v Merrell Dow Pharmaceuticals, Inc.
523 A.2d 374 (Pa. Super. Ct. 1987)
...continued

RULING: The trial court judge granted the pharmacy corporation a motion to dismiss it from the lawsuit. The appellate court affirmed the lower court decision holding that a pharmacy that dispenses the correct drug, labeled in accordance with the physician's prescription, is not guilty of breach of warranty and does not have an independent duty to warn the patient of the risks associated with the drug.

REASONING: The plaintiffs argued that there is an implied warranty whenever goods are sold by a person who is a merchant. The pharmacy countered by arguing that the dominant role of the pharmacist is the performance of a service rather than the sale of a product and thus, no warranties arise as an incident of the sale or a prescription drug. The court concluded that the very nature of prescription drugs precludes imposition of a warranty of fitness for ordinary purposes since the individual for whom they are prescribed is a unique person who must be examined by a physician. A pharmacist who dispenses a prescription drug only warrants (1) that he has compounded the drug with due care, (2) that the drug is the strength and quantity prescribed, (3) that he has used the proper methods in the compounding process, (4) that the drug is pure and unadulterated, and (5) that he has labeled the drug in accordance with the physician's prescription.

The plaintiffs also contended that the failure of the pharmacy to warn Mrs. Makripodis of the teratogenic potential of the drug caused the product to be unreasonably dangerous. They sought to impose an independent duty to warn the patient of all the possible adverse consequences associated with the drug. The court concluded that such a duty would be greater than that imposed upon the drug manufacturer who is required to provide such warnings only to the prescribing physician. Pharmacists would, in most instances, be unfamiliar with the medical history and condition of the patient. A requirement to provide warnings would intrude upon the doctor-patient relationship. "We believe that to impose such a duty upon retail pharmacists would be unwise and would ill serve the interests of the consuming public."

Fakhouri v Taylor
618 N.E.2d 518 (Ill.App. 1993)

ISSUE: May a pharmacy be held liable for failing to warn a patient of risks known to be associated with a prescribed drug?

FACTS: The patient allegedly died from taking an overdose of imipramine, which a physician prescribed for treatment of a psychiatric condition.

LAWSUIT: The estate of the patient sued the pharmacy and pharmacists who dispensed the drug for wrongful death. The physician who prescribed the drug was also sued, but that part of the litigation is not relevant here. The complaint alleged that the pharmacy and pharmacists (collectively defendants) had been negligent in filling prescriptions for quantities of imipramine beyond those normally prescribed. It also claimed liability because the defendants failed to warn either the physician or the patient that the prescriptions were for an excessive and unsafe quantity. The trial court judge dismissed the claims. On appeal, the plaintiff sought to have the court impose on pharmacists a duty to warn their customers of prescribed medication doses in excess of the manufacturer's recommended limits.

HOLDING: The Court of Appeals affirmed the order of the trial court dismissing the case against these defendants.

Fakhouri v Taylor
618 N.E.2d 518 (Ill.App. 1993)
...continued

REASONING: The plaintiff argued that the Illinois Pharmacy Act (225 ILCS 85/1 et seq.) indicates that "a pharmacist has independent duties to his or her patients," and that this statute supports the imposition of the duty to warn on the pharmacist. The Court of Appeals rejected this argument stating, "The legislature was not concerned with making pharmacists perform a safety check on physician's prescriptions." The statute does not dictate that any warnings must be given to the customer, either orally or as part of the labeling requirement. In contrast, this court believes that the statute's purpose is to regulate the legal storage and distribution of prescription drugs and to promulgate standards within which pharmacies and pharmacists would operate.

In the opinion of the court, the determination of which medication should be utilized in any given case requires an individualized medical judgment that only the patient's physician can provide. The physician presumably knows the patient's current condition, as well as the patient's complete medical history. Imposition of a duty to warn on the pharmacist would place the pharmacist in the middle of the doctor-patient relationship without the benefit of having the physician's knowledge of the patient. Accordingly, it would be illogical and unreasonable to impose such a duty on the pharmacist who properly fills a prescription.

The following is a list of court cases that are related to this topic.

Nevada State Board of Pharmacy v Garrigus & Block, 496 P.2d 748 (Nev. 1972).
McKee v American Home Products, No. 53941-3 (Wash. Sup. Ct. Nov. 30, 1989).
Gassen v East Jefferson General Hospital, et al, 1993 La. App. LEXIS 3985.
Heredia v Johnson, 827 F.Supp. 1522 (D. Nev. 1993).

Mandated Warnings (OBRA-90)

The following is a list of court cases that are related to this topic.

Walker v Jack Eckerd Corp., 209 Ga. App. 517; 434 S.E.2d 63, (Ga. App., 1993), cert denied, Ga. S. Ct., Slip Op. No. 593C1686 (1993).

Failure to Monitor Drug Therapy

Georgia Osteopathic Hospital v O'Neal
403 S.E.2d 235 (Ga. App. 1991)

ISSUE: Whether a hospital pharmacy had a duty to monitor a patient's medications to prevent him from "going berserk."

FACTS: The children of George O'Neal brought a wrongful death action against the Georgia Osteopathic Hospital after their father was killed by police when he "went berserk" and began attacking people with a knife at the hospital. One of the allegations against the hospital was that its pharmacy was negligent for failing to monitor the decedent's medication for possible adverse reactions.

The decedent was originally admitted to the hospital where it was determined he was suffering from neurovascular and muscle-contraction headaches. He later exhibited symptoms of hypertension and there was concern that he might be a candidate for a stroke. During the

Georgia Osteopathic Hospital v O'Neal
403 S.E.2d 235 (Ga. App. 1991)
...continued

course of therapy, he received numerous central nervous system depressants including *Tigan*, *Nubain*, *Flexeril*, *Indocin*, *Halcion*, *Robaxin*, *Dalmane*, *Soma*, and *Haldol*. It was claimed that the coadministration of these pharmaceutical products precipitated an anticholinergic drug reaction, which ultimately caused the plaintiff to "go berserk."

During this course of therapy, the hospital records indicated that the nursing staff was concerned about the decedent's constant confusion and unusual behavior. The neurologist concluded that the patient was suffering from a "confusional state secondary to medication effect." All of the prior medications, except *Haldol*, were discontinued.

During the next nursing shift, the decedent grabbed a knife and charged a nurse who was examining him. Although she escaped uninjured, the decedent ultimately stabbed and wounded another nurse, a security guard, and himself before the police arrived and shot him to death in the hallway.

RULING: The jury returned a verdict in favor of the plaintiffs in the amount of $550,000. The hospital appealed and the case was reversed by the Appellate Court, which refused to place any liability on the hospital for failure to monitor the decedent's medications for possible adverse interactions.

REASONING: All of the drugs being administered to the decedent had been prescribed by his attending physicians. There was no suggestion that the pharmacy made any mistake in filling these prescriptions. The court ruled that the pharmacy staff was in no position to second-guess the medical judgment of the decedent's physicians as to what drugs were appropriate for him.

While an expert for the plaintiffs testified that the hospital pharmacy had a duty to monitor these medications for potential interactions, he offered no opinion as to which, if any, of the various prescriptions should have been objected to by the pharmacy.

The following is a list of court cases that are related to this topic.

Adkins v Mong et al, Docket No. 90217 (Mich. Ct. App. 1988).
McKee v American Home Products, No. 53941-3 (Wash. Sup. Ct. Nov. 30, 1989).
Cafaralle v Brockton Oaks C.V.S., Inc., No. 94-0414A, (Mass. Super. Ct. April, 1996).

The Duty to Detect Problems

The following is a list of court cases that are related to this topic.

Jones v Walgreen Co., 265 Ill. App. 308 (1932).
Moskowitz v Board of Regents of Univ. of N.Y., 380 N.Y. S.2d 107 (1976).
Bichler v Willing, 397 N.Y.S.2d 57 (1977).
Speer v United States, 512 F. Supp. 670 (N.D. Tex 1981).
E.R. Squibb & Sons, Inc. v Cox, 477 So.2d 963 (Ala. 1985).
Hendricks v Charity Hospital of New Orleans, 519 So.2d 163 (La. App. 4 Cir. 1987).
Wimm v Jack Eckerd Corp., 1993 App. LEXIS 25102 (U.S. Ct. App. 5th cir.).
McLaughlin v Hook - SupeRx Inc., 642 N.E.2d 514 (Ind. 1994).
Orzel v Scott Drug, 1995 Mich. LEXIS 1481 (No. 98506, August 15, 1995).
Cafaralle v Brockton Oaks C.V.S., Inc., No. 94-0414A, (Mass. Super. Ct. April, 1996).

Addiction

Pysz v Henry's Drug Store
457 So.2d 561 (Fla. Dist. Ct. App. 1984)

ISSUE: (1) Whether a licensed pharmacist has a duty not only to properly fill a prescription, but also to warn the patient of the dangerous properties of a prescription drug and (2) whether a licensed pharmacist who has actual or constructive knowledge of a patient's dependency and addiction to a prescription drug has a duty to warn the patient's treating physician of this fact.

FACTS: The patient in this lawsuit brought an action against a pharmacist alleging that the pharmacist's failure to warn him of the addictive properties of *Quaaludes* constituted negligence. Also named as defendants in the lawsuit were the physician and two manufacturers. The patient further alleged that the pharmacist committed a negligent act when he filled the *Quaalude* prescriptions for more than 9 years because the pharmacist knew, or should have known, that the use of this drug over an extended period of time would subject the patient to physical and psychological dependence and addiction. Finally, the patient alleged that the pharmacist knew that the plaintiff had become addicted to *Quaalude* and was negligent because he failed to inform the plaintiff's physician. The trial court dismissed the patient's complaint against the pharmacist and held that there was no duty to warn the patient that he would become physically and psychologically dependent upon the drugs.

RULING: The appellate court agreed that the pharmacist had no duty to warn the customer of the dangerous properties of the prescription drug, nor was there a duty to warn the patient's physician of this fact.

REASONING: The court found that the patient had not only alleged that the prescribing physician knew of the type and amount of drugs prescribed over the 9 years, but the patient also claimed that he personally knew he was addicted to the drug. Under these circumstances, the court could not view the pharmacist's failure to warn the patient, or to notify the physician, as a failure to exercise due care. In reaching this conclusion, the appellate court cited the Supreme Court of Florida in *McLeod v W.S. Merrell Company*:

> The right of the consumer can be preserved, and the responsibilities of the retail prescription druggist can be imposed, under the concept that a druggist who sells a prescription warrants that (1) he will compound the drug prescribed; (2) he has used due and proper care in filling the prescription (failure of which might also give rise to an action in negligence); (3) the proper methods were used in the compounding process; (4) the drug has not been infected with some adulterating foreign substance.

The plaintiff sought to distinguish the McLeod case on the basis that the case at hand was an action for negligence rather than warranty. The plaintiff further cited numerous out-of-state cases in support of his position. However, the court held they were all distinguishable from the facts alleged in the complaint. In two of the cases that the plaintiff cited, the pharmacist improperly filled the prescriptions by giving the customers the wrong drugs. Such an action clearly constituted a breach of duty giving rise to an action for negligence. In four of the other cases cited by the plaintiff, the pharmacist sold poisons or explosive chemicals without giving any warnings. None of the cases cited by the plaintiff concerned a pharmacist who properly filled a lawful prescription.

The plaintiff suggested to the court that the profession of pharmacy had changed drastically in the past 20 years. Therefore, he urged the court to take a new look at the duty of a pharmacist to either warn the customer of the dangerous properties of a drug prescribed by a licensed physician or, in the alternative, to notify the physician of the dangerous proper-

Pysz v Henry's Drug Store
457 So.2d 561 (Fla. Dist. Ct. App. 1984)
...continued

ties and the effect that they were having on the patient. The plaintiff argued that the pharmacist has greater knowledge of the properties than does the physician. The court noted that although this may be true in some instances, it is the physician who has the duty to understand the properties of the drug that he is prescribing and to properly monitor the patient. Therefore, the court affirmed the dismissal of the plaintiff's complaint. However, the court limited its decision to the facts of the case, since it recognized that a factual situation could exist, which would support an action for negligence against a pharmacist who has lawfully filled a prescription issued by a licensed physician.

The following is a list of court cases that are related to this topic.

Adkins v Mong et al, Docket No. 90217 (Mich. Ct. App. 1988).
Clair v Paris Road Drugs, Inc., 573 So. 2d 1219 (La. App. 1991).
Lasley v Shrake's Country Club Pharmacy, Inc., 1994 WL 109647 (Ariz. App. Dir. 1).
McLaughlin v Hook - SupeRx Inc., 642 N.E. 2d 514 (Ind. 1994).
Orzel v Scott Drug, 1995 Mich. LEXIS 1481 (No. 98506, August 15, 1995).

Drug-Disease Contraindications

Hand v Krakowski
453 N.Y.S.2d 121 (N.Y. App. Div. 1982)

ISSUE: Whether a pharmacist had a duty to warn a known alcoholic of the possible dangers involved with taking certain psychotropic drugs.

FACTS: The lawsuit was brought by the executrix of the estate of a known alcoholic. For over 6 years, the employees of the defendant's pharmacy had dispensed certain psychotropic drugs to a patient pursuant to signed prescriptions issued by her physicians. It was undisputed that the pharmacist knew that the patient was an alcoholic during this peril. The patient died at age 55. During the 10-month period preceding her death, the pharmacy issued 728 units of psychotropic drugs, even though it was known that such opiates were contraindicated with the use of alcohol. The autopsy report stated that the cause of death was pancreatitis associated with a severe degree of cirrhosis.

The pharmacy moved for summary judgment of dismissing the complaint, and the motion was granted. The executrix of the estate appealed.

RULING: The court found that the pharmacist may have had a duty to warn the decedent of the grave dangers involved and to inquire of the prescribing physicians if such drugs should not be discontinued. The summary judgment was reversed.

REASONING: The court reviewed the standard of care required of a pharmacist. This standard of care was described as "ordinary care in the conduct of his business. The rule of ordinary care as applied to the business of a druggist means the highest practical degree of prudence, thoughtfulness, and vigilance commensurate with the dangers involved and the consequences that may attend inattention." The court concluded that to dispense the psychotropic drugs to a known alcoholic constituted a breach of the pharmacist's duty of ordinary care in that it knowingly ignored the danger and consequences of ingestion by an alcoholic of prescription drugs commonly recognized to be contraindicated. Yet, the court was

Hand v Krakowski
453 N.Y.S.2d 121 (N.Y. App. Div. 1982)
...continued

not willing to exclude the possibility that the defendant physicians and pharmacists might be able to justify the use of the prescribed drugs in this case. Therefore, the trial court should not have dismissed the action on the motion for summary judgment, but should have proceeded to take testimony to resolve the issue of whether the pharmacist breached the standard of care required.

The following is a list of court cases that are related to this topic.

Jeans v Caraway, 649 S.2d 1141 (La. Ct. App. 1995).

Allergies

Ferguson v Williams
374 S.E.2d 438 (N.C. App. 1988)

ISSUE: Whether a pharmacist who is alerted to specific facts regarding a patient and undertakes to advise the patient has a duty to advise correctly.

FACTS: The lawsuit was initiated by the plaintiff who, as administratrix of her husband's estate, is seeking damages for wrongful death. The lawsuit was originally instituted against the physician, dispensing pharmacist, and pharmacy.

In her complaint, the plaintiff alleged that the physician prescribed *Indocin* to the decedent who had the prescription filled by the defendant pharmacist at Bobbitt's Pharmacy. The next day the decedent took one of the capsules that caused him to have an anaphylactic reaction resulting in his death.

The plaintiff alleged that the physician was negligent in prescribing the drug. The plaintiff further claimed that prior to having the prescription dispensed, the decedent informed the pharmacist that he was allergic to aspirin, *Percodan*, and penicillin. It was further alleged that the decedent sought out and relied upon the skill, judgment, and expertise of the pharmacist with respect to the safety of taking *Indocin*, given the fact that it interacted with the decedent's medical condition. It also was claimed that the decedent was advised by the pharmacist that it was safe to take the drug *Indocin* even though the medical literature specified that the use of the drug was contraindicated in people who suffer aspirin allergies or sensitivities.

RULING: The plaintiff voluntarily dismissed her action against the physician. The trial court entered an order dismissing the pharmacist and pharmacy as defendants because of the plaintiff's failure to state a claim upon which relief could be granted. The North Carolina Court of Appeals reversed, holding that the complaint did state a claim.

REASONING: A complaint should not be dismissed for insufficient grounds unless it appears that the plaintiff was entitled to no relief under any facts that could be proved in support of the claim. It was noted that the North Carolina courts had previously stated that "people trust not merely their health but their lives to the knowledge, care, and skill of druggists, and in many cases, a slight want of care is liable to prove fatal to someone."

Ferguson v Williams
374 S.E.2d 438 (N.C. App. 1988)
...continued

The court also noted that the standard of care required of a pharmacist was "that ordinary care, in reference to the business of a druggist, that must be held to signify the highest practical degree of care consistent with the reasonable conduct of the business."

In this case, the plaintiff alleged that *Indocin* is contraindicated in patients who suffer from an aspirin allergy, such as the decedent. She alleged that the decedent told the pharmacist that he was allergic to aspirin and certain other drugs. The decedent sought out and was relying upon the skill, judgment, and expertise of the pharmacist with respect to the safety of taking the drug *Indocin*, given the fact that he suffered the aspirin sensitivity. The plaintiff further alleged that her husband had been advised by the pharmacist that it was safe to take the drug.

Even though there was no allegation that the product dispensed was other than it was supposed to be, the complaint alleged that the decedent had asked for and was given advice by the pharmacist. Subsequently, the decedent relied upon that advice in taking the drug. While a pharmacist has only a duty to act with ordinary care and diligence, this duty, like all others, expands and contracts with the circumstances. Here, it was alleged that the pharmacist undertook to dispense not only drugs, but also advice. Under previous North Carolina case law, a pharmacist has no duty to advise absent knowledge of the circumstances, but once the pharmacist is alerted to the specific facts and he or she undertakes to advise a customer, the pharmacist then has a duty to advise correctly. The Court therefore concluded that the trial court erred in dismissing the complaint.

Happel v Wal-Mart Stores
766 N.E.2d 1118 (Ill. 2002)

The plaintiffs sued Wal-Mart Stores for the alleged negligence of its pharmacy personnel in dispensing *Toradol*. Wal-Mart was aware that the patient was allergic to aspirin and ibuprofen and also knew that the medication prescribed by her physician was contraindicated for a person with those allergies. A Wal-Mart pharmacy manager testified that it was the pharmacy's policy and procedure to ask customers about their known allergies. Such information is used to check for known contraindications prior to dispensing medication. The central issue in the case concerned the existence of a duty, ie, whether Wal-Mart and the patient stood in such a relationship to each other that the law imposed upon Wal-Mart an obligation of reasonable conduct for the benefit of the patient. In determining whether a duty existed, the court looked at several factors, including: 1) the reasonable foreseeability that the defendant's conduct may injure another; 2) the likelihood of an injury occurring; 3) the magnitude of the burden of guarding against such injury; and 4) the consequences of placing that burden on the defendant. Given the superior knowledge on the part of Wal-Mart, and particularly given the nature of the knowledge, ie, that *Toradol* was contraindicated for individuals with the allergies of the patient, the court found that it was reasonably foreseeable that a failure to convey this knowledge might result in injury to her, and that the likelihood of injury to her was great. The court then held that the burden on Wal-Mart of imposing this duty is minimal, because all that is required is that the pharmacist provide the information to the patient or telephone the physician and inform him or her of the contraindication. Wal-Mart contended that imposing such a duty would have a "chilling effect" on pharmacies and their customers. The court disagreed and found that by accepting Wal-Mart's argument, the court would be sanctioning the status quo, and the status quo was unacceptable. By asking customers about their drug allergies, the court deter-

Happel v Wal-Mart Stores
766 N.E.2d 1118 (Ill. 2002)
...continued

mined that Wal-Mart was engendering reliance that the pharmacy would take steps to ensure that the customer would not receive a drug to which the customer was allergic. Accordingly, the court concluded that in this case, any negative consequences of recognizing a duty to warn were far outweighed by the substantial reasons favoring such a duty. The final point of contention involved whether the learned intermediary doctrine, under which the prescribing physician has the primary responsibility to warn of drug interactions and side effects, exempted pharmacists and pharmacies from giving warnings to patients. While the doctrine may be applied to justify not imposing a duty to warn on pharmacists, the reasons supporting such an application did not apply in this case. The court found that the doctrine did not relieve the pharmacy's duty to warn because: 1) the pharmacy already had knowledge it needed in order to give an effective warning; and 2) such duty did not involve monitoring customer's drug usage, or intruding into the doctor-patient relationship. The court concluded that a narrow duty to warn exists where a pharmacy has patient-specific information about drug allergies, and knows that the drug being prescribed is contraindicated for the individual patient. In such instances, a pharmacy has a duty to warn either the prescribing physician or the patient of the potential danger. Because Wal-Mart did not satisfy this duty, the appellate court's decision to reverse the granting of Wal-Mart's motion for summary judgment was affirmed.

Suicide Prevention

Speer v United States
512 F.Supp. 670 (N.D. Tex. 1981)

ISSUE: Whether the U.S. Veterans Administration (VA) and its pharmacists were responsible for the death of a patient due to a suicide with a drug overdose.

FACTS: The decedent, Jerry Speer, had suffered from a recurring history of depression and serious psychiatric problems, along with the abuse of alcohol and drugs. He was diagnosed by a VA psychiatrist as a "paranoid schizophrenic." It was concluded that he should respond to adequate doses of antidepressant and antischizophrenic medications. They physician prescribed *Etrafon* along with weekly therapy sessions. Speer attended the group therapy sessions, but he continued to take the *Etrafon* in increasing numbers and higher dosage levels. He accelerated his daily dosage from 3 tablets a day to 12 tablets a day. Both his wife and employer perceived changes in his personal grooming and work habits. His wife became so concerned that she contacted the chief of staff of the VA Hospital as well as a U.S. Senator. She received assurances that the treatment of her husband indicated no problems. She was convinced that her husband was abusing the *Etrafon*, along with alcohol, and she destroyed some of the medication to prevent her husband from using it. However, the psychiatrist refused to remove Speer from the *Etrafon* treatment.

One morning, Speer called his wife at work and told her that he had taken 2 bottles of *Etrafon* tablets. He was still conscious when his wife and the ambulance arrived. On admission to the hospital, Speer indicated that he had been taking 12 *Etrafon* tablets a day in addition to self-prescribed *Dexedrine*, and that he had consumed 400 to 500 *Etrafon* tablets that morning. While in the hospital, he suffered a cardiac arrest and died. The cause of death was attributed to complications from an *Etrafon* overdose.

Speer v United States
512 F.Supp. 670 (N.D. Tex. 1981)
...continued

The evidence indicated that when the VA pharmacy dispensed a prescription, the pharmacist had a computerized information packet that included patient information, instructions on drug use, address labels, data on authorized refills, and the patient's history of such refills. Each pharmacist was responsible for reviewing these documents to ensure that prescriptions were dispensed in the correct amounts and at the proper intervals. The VA system failed to perform these functions because Speer was able to obtain refills beyond those authorized by the psychiatrist. The computerized prescription system at the VA was structured to cancel earlier prescriptions when a physician wrote new prescriptions for the same drug and the same patient. However, Speer was allowed to receive refills of old prescriptions for *Etrafon* and then, a few days later, receive a new prescription for 150 additional tablets. There also was evidence that the VA pharmacist failed to notice that an earlier prescription of 360 tables was being filled by mail when he filled a walk-in prescription for 240 tablets. The frequency of refills and the large amount of tablets involved should have alerted the pharmacist that a problem existed.

RULING: The pharmacists' negligence in failing to monitor the prescription refills was not the proximate or direct cause of Speer's death, so the VA and its pharmacists were not legally responsible.

REASONING: The court concluded that the conduct and omissions of the VA pharmacy constituted a breach of the standard of care, which pharmacists are required to meet. However, there was no showing that, under the circumstances, the pharmacists should have foreseen that Speer intended to use the tablets to commit suicide. The act of the decedent in voluntarily ingesting the drug, with knowledge of its effects, amounted to a new and intervening cause and thus insulated the effect of the pharmacists' negligence.

Guillory v Andrus
679 So.2d 1004 (La. App., 1996)

FACTS: A patient with a history of numerous ailments was prescribed *Pamelor*, an antidepressant, after a hospitalization for chest pains. The patient discontinued the medication on his own and two years later reported symptoms of depression for which he was prescribed *Limbitrol*, an antidepressant that also treats nervousness. The patient subsequently committed suicide and his spouse brought this action against the prescribing physician and the dispensing pharmacy alleging negligence and overmedication. During her deposition, the spouse stated that she believed her husband was overmedicated, but other than *Halcion*, *Xanax*, and *Lortab*, she did not know what medications he had been taking or what other physicians had treated her husband. The lawsuit alleged negligence against the pharmacy for dispensing medications that produced profound depression and suicidal thinking and for failing to discuss possible medication interactions with the various prescribing physicians, and warn the patient regarding contraindicated medication. The trial court granted the defendant's requests for dismissal of the charges.

HOLDING: On appeal, the plaintiff argued that the trial court should not have considered the defendant's expert witnesses' affidavits, which stated that they had reviewed the pharmacy's records, kept in the regular course of business, including a computer program printout, which cross-checked the drugs her husband had been taking and indicated that none were contraindicated. The Court of Appeals affirmed the summary judgments for the physi-

Guillory v Andrus
679 So.2d 1004 (La. App., 1996)
...continued

cian and pharmacy. The Appellate Court noted plaintiff's testimony where she stated that she did not know what drugs her husband was taking or who was prescribing drugs for him.

Kirk v Porter Drug Store
Slip Op. No. 96-1196-JTM, October 3, 1997, U.S. Dist. Kan., 1997 US Dist LEXIS 15639

ISSUE: May the divorced husband of a patient who commits suicide by taking an overdose of a prescribed drug recover damages from the pharmacy that dispensed the drug?

FACTS: The patient suffered from a manic-depressive condition for several years. The couple saw her physician in October 1994 and advised him that they were divorcing. While visiting relatives out of state in December 1994, she was hospitalized for a bipolar affective disorder. Her discharge medications consisted of *Tegretol, Klonopin, Mellaril,* and *Trilafon*. When she returned home, her husband arranged for an apartment for her. The husband and the couple's children remained in the nearby family home. The patient started to run low on medication and contacted her physician to ask for refill authorization. She told the receptionist that she wanted the prescriptions called into a pharmacy near the new apartment. Apparently, she never had prescriptions filled at this pharmacy before this date. When she went to the pharmacy, she was told that the prescriptions had not been called in. Nevertheless, the pharmacist gave her a small supply of each drug because he knew that abrupt withdrawal could be harmful. A few days later the patient and her husband returned to the pharmacy but the prescriptions had still not been called in. The pharmacist claimed he called the physician's office and talked to a woman that he thought to be a receptionist. After he requested the prescription authorization, the woman put him on hold for a few minutes and returned to communicate the prescription information. The pharmacist dispensed a 30-day supply of the medications. The husband went to the patient's apartment on Christmas Day to bring her home for the holiday. When she did not answer the door, the husband let himself in and found his wife unconscious. She died from an intentional overdose of *Trilafon* obtained from the pharmacy a few days earlier. They physician denied that he authorized the prescriptions and claimed he would not prescribe a 30-day quantity of *Trilafon* because the patient was suicidal.

HOLDING: The federal trial court, applying Kansas law, refused the defendant pharmacy's motion to dismiss and scheduled the case for a jury trial.

REASONING: The pharmacy sought dismissal of the lawsuit on the basis that suicide is not foreseeable under Kansas law. The court disagreed, noting that the monograph for *Etrafon* in the *Physician's Desk Reference* warns against dispensing large quantities of the drug to suicidal patients. One of the active ingredients in *Etrafon* is the same active ingredient in *Trilafon*. According to the court, this warning meant the pharmacist knew or should have known that suicide might result under the circumstances. Given the dispute as to whether the physician authorized the prescriptions, the court stated that the pharmacist could not defer judgment on the quantity of the drug dispensed to the prescriber.

The following is a list of court cases that are related to this topic.

Martin v Hacker, 550 N.Y.S.2d 130 (A.D. 3 Dept. 1989)

Confidentiality, Privacy, and Privilege

Anonymous v CVS
188 Misc. 2d 616; 728 N.Y.S.2d 333; 2001 N.Y. Misc. LEXIS 227 (March 1, 2001)

A patient brought a class action lawsuit on behalf of himself and other similarly situated patients against an independent pharmacy and the pharmacist owner along with a corporate chain pharmacy for violating patient confidentiality after the independent pharmacy was sold to the chain without prior notice to the patient. The patient had been diagnosed with Human Immunodeficiency Virus and Acquired Immune Deficiency Syndrome in 1989. He claimed that he selected the independent pharmacy based on his expectation of privacy. Now that the records are online and in the hands of the chain, the records may be accessed by thousands of employees and third parties. The court held that the practice of intentionally declining withholding notice of a transfer of prescription information from patients in order to increase the value of that information is deceptive. The court noted that this practice prevents the patient from exercising his right to take action to prevent or minimize the disclosure of his medical information.

Anonymous v CVS Corp.
Slip Op No 665N (April 4, 2002) N.Y. App. Div.

This case was decided by the New York Supreme Court, Appellate Division. The two-paragraph decision upholds a ruling by Judge Charles E. Ramos, of the New York Supreme Court, who certified a class in the case in 2001. The New York Supreme Court is the state's trial-level court. The plaintiffs alleged that their consent was not obtained before their prescription information was transferred under CVS's "File Buy Program," in which the plaintiffs said CVS required purchased drug stores not to tell customers in advance that they were closing their doors, or to inform customers that their prescription information was being transferred to CVS. The plaintiff class alleged that CVS engaged in a deceptive business practice and/or breach of a fiduciary duty or implied contract in violation of their right to confidentiality of their medical or prescription information, and claimed that CVS acquired the customer files of hundreds of independent pharmacies in 1998 alone under the "File Buy Program." In a novel ruling, the trial court judge held that pharmacies may owe a fiduciary duty of confidentiality with respect to prescription records.

Murphy v Mounts
No. 444227-98 (March 12, 2000), 2000 Wash. App. LEXIS 419

Plaintiff, a former county sheriff, filed suit in both federal and state courts against Albertson's alleging that a pharmacist-employee disclosed confidential health information about him without permission in violation of a state statute. RCW 70.02.020. The statute provides that a health care provider may disclose information if it is reasonably believed that disclosure may minimize the risk of imminent danger to the patient or any other individual. RCW 70.02.050(1)(d). The pharmacist communicated her concerns about plaintiff's use of prescription narcotics to authorities operating an investigative task force in that county. After an investigation, criminal charges were filed against the plaintiff. Those charges were dismissed after the evidence was suppressed. The federal case against Albertson's was dismissed after the district court judge found that the pharmacist acted reasonably in making the disclosure and did not violate the state statute. The judge noted that no cases had been found anywhere imposing civil liability on a pharmacist for disclosing prescription drug infor-

Murphy v Mounts
No. 444227-98 (March 12, 2000), 2000 Wash. App. LEXIS 419
...continued

mation to law enforcement authorities. After the federal judgment was entered, the defendants sought summary judgment in the state court action on the basis res judicata and collateral estoppel. The state trial court denied the motion and an appeal followed. The Washington state Court of Appeals reversed the trial court ruling and dismissed the case. The appeals court determined that the plaintiff had a full and fair opportunity to litigate the same issues pending in the state action during the federal lawsuit. Therefore the state action is barred.

Nefris v DeStefano
697 N.Y.S.2d 108 (N.Y. App. 1999)

The plaintiff was injured in an auto accident in which her car was hit by the defendant's. During discovery, the defendant admitted that she had taken *Navane* and *Cogentin* in a 24 hour period before the accident for treatment of her "nerves." The plaintiff sought to discover the name of the prescribing physician and the pharmacy records where the defendant purchased the medication. The trial court determined that these records are subject to a patient-physician privilege and are therefore not subject to discovery requests. The appellate court disagreed. The records were sought to show that the defendant's medical or physical condition is in controversy. The plaintiff's testimony that she was taking the drugs for nerves makes her psychiatric condition relevant and allows the plaintiff to show that the drugs may have impaired her driving ability. The court held that the name of the treating physician is not privileged in any event. It also noted that the pharmacy records are not privileged and may be disclosed as to the quantities of drugs dispensed over a 6-month period prior to the accident.

Hannigan v Sundby Pharmacy
224 Wis 2d 910; 593 N.W. 2d 52, Wis App 1999

In an underlying lawsuit, the pharmacy patient sued his employer for personal injuries. During the course of discovery in that lawsuit, the patient signed medical release forms authorizing his physicians to disclose his medical records to attorneys for the employer. There was never any authorization for disclosure of pharmacy records. The employer's attorneys did, however, subpoena the pharmacy's records and supposedly supplied a medical release form authorizing the disclosure. The pharmacy provided the requested records. After the patient found out about this disclosure, he went to the pharmacy and asked to see the release form. The pharmacy was not able to provide a copy of the release even though a state statute requires that a copy be kept whenever records are disclosed. The patient sued the pharmacy in small claims court for unauthorized disclosure of his prescription records in violation of a state statute that provides for monetary damages when records are knowingly and willfully disclosed without authorization. The patient sought $5,000 in actual and exemplary damages. The trial court dismissed the claims because there was no evidence that the pharmacist knew he was supposed to retain a copy of the record release request or that he knowingly or willfully disclosed records without authorization. The Wisconsin Court of Appeals reversed on the basis that ignorance of the law is no excuse. As licensed health care professionals, pharmacists may be constructively presumed to know the law and to know

Hannigan v Sundby Pharmacy
224 Wis 2d 910; 593 N.W. 2d 52, Wis App 1999
...continued

that disclosure of prescription records without specific authorization could be harmful. The
case was remanded for further proceedings.

Shiffrin v IV Services of America
53 Conn App 129; 729 A 2d 784 (1999)

The state's Commissioner of Consumer Protection Services served an investigative demand
on the defendant pharmacy seeking information and documents about its business practices in conjunction with an investigation that the pharmacy violated the state's Unfair Trade
Practices Act by billing customers for medical devices and services after representing to
them that insurance coverage would pay, and by unfairly and deceptively inflating prices on
prescription medications. The investigative demand specifically sought the names of all customers and billing records over a certain period. The pharmacy objected on the grounds of
pharmacy-patient privilege and sought a protective order against disclosure. The trial court
denied the protective order and ordered the pharmacy to provide the information and documentation with the exception of any indication of patients' physical or mental condition.
The state statute on point provides that pharmacists are not required to disclose "information concerning the nature of pharmaceutical services rendered to a patient" without the
patient's consent. The Court of Appeals affirmed the lower court ruling. It noted that pharmacists do not enjoy a general privilege and that the statute in question only protects
against disclosure of treatment records. This limited privilege does not protect against disclosure of billing information.

Washburn v Rite Aid
695 A.2d 495 (R.I. 1997)

In an underlying action, plaintiff sued her husband for divorce. During discovery in that case,
the husband's attorney subpoenaed the pharmacy records of the wife without informing the
wife or her attorney about the subpoena. The subpoena commanded the pharmacy to bring
its records to a court hearing on a specified date. Without giving notice to or obtaining consent from the plaintiff, the pharmacy mailed the records directly to the husband's attorney. The wife found out about the disclosure just before the hearing began when her husband
threatened to disclose the pharmacy record and reveal her drug-taking habits. She then sued
the pharmacy for invasion of a statutorily recognized right of privacy and breach of the
state's Confidentiality of Health Care Information Act. The Rhode Island Supreme Court
reversed dismissal of the claims finding that while the pharmacy is not a health care provider (dispensing prescription medicines on the order of a health care provider is not providing health care services) by definition, it is still subject to the Act's prohibition against
disclosure of confidential health care records by a third party. Because neither party contested the point, the court assumed that prescriptions are confidential records subject to privilege. The court also reinstated plaintiff's claim for compensatory and exemplary damages
under the Privacy Act. The Court was particularly critical of the pharmacy's legal department in ignoring the orderly judicial procedure associated with the disclosure of confidential information subject to subpoena.

Evans v Rite-Aid Corp.
452 S.E.2d 9 (S.C. App. 1994), affirmed, as modified 478 S.E. 2d 846 (S.C. 1996)

FACTS: A pharmacy employee falsely told others in the community that a prescription drug obtained by the patient was used to treat venereal disease. Three years later, the patient filed a lawsuit against the pharmacy for breach of confidentiality and negligent supervision. The complaint claimed that the pharmacy failed to ensure the accuracy of disclosures by its employees and "outrage" as a result of the false disclosure. The South Carolina trial court dismissed the breach of confidentiality claims because pharmacists have no duty of confidentiality with respect to dispensed medication. Further, the pharmacy cannot be held liable for disclosures by its employees. The other counts were dismissed as being untimely under the State's two-year statute of limitation claims for defamation.

HOLDING: Dismissal was affirmed at the Court of Appeals level on the basis that the State recognizes no statutory or common law privilege between patients and pharmacists and there is no corresponding right of confidentiality between the parties. The South Carolina Court of Appeals agreed that the other claims were nothing more than an artful attempt to avoid the two-year statute of limitations for defamation. The Supreme Court also affirmed dismissal but modified the opinion of the Court of Appeals to make clear that pharmacists do owe a duty of due care and may be sued for negligence in a properly pled and timely filed complaint.

Suarez v Plarard
663 N.E.2d 1039 (Ill. App. 1996)

FACTS: A pharmacy customer shared confidential information with a pharmacist in connection with filling her prescription for drugs used to treat her mental health disorder. During a subsequent chance meeting at a public tavern between the customer and the pharmacist, the pharmacist discussed the confidential information in the presence of other persons causing the customer embarrassment. The customer sued, alleging the pharmacist had a duty not to disclose confidential information under the Illinois Mental Health and Developmental Disabilities Confidentiality Act (the "Act").

HOLDING: The circuit court dismissed the case. The judgment was upheld on appeal. The appellate court found that the Act was intended to apply to persons entering into a therapeutic relationship. The Court held that a "therapeutic relationship" could not be expanded to include a pharmacist's routine dispensing of drugs, even if this included discussing a customer's medical condition and treatment.

Failure to Dispense Necessary Medication

The following is a list of court cases that are related to this topic.

France v State of New York, 506 N.Y.S.2d 254 (N.Y. Ct. Claims 1986).
Johnson v Hay, 931 F.2d 456 (8th Cir. 1991).
LeJeune v Trend Services, Slip Op 96-550 (June 4, 1997, La. App.), 1997 La. App LEXIS 1541.
Meeks v Shuman, Slip Op. No. 95-C-3010 (Jan. 10, 1997, US DC N. Ill.), 1997 U.S. Dist. LEXIS 179.
Winn Dixie of Montgomery v Colburn, Slip No. 1961146, Feb. 6, 1998, Ala. S. Ct., 1998 Ala. LEXIS 48.

IMPUTED DUTY

Vicarious Liability

Vollendorf v U.S.
951 F.2d 215 (9th Cir. 1991)

ISSUE: Whether the U.S. government was responsible for a Army member's negligence in permitting an infant child to have access to prescription medications.

FACTS: When Nicole was 19 months old, she ingested chloroquine, which had been prescribed for her grandfather by an Army physician at Madigan Army Medical Center. Nicole's grandfather was a helicopter pilot who had a recent tour of duty in Honduras. Because Honduras is an endemic malarial area, the Army requires that its personnel serving there take chloroquine, a malarial prophylactic prescription drug.

Because Nicole's grandfather disliked childproof prescription containers, he stored the medication on the kitchen counter of his home without securing the bottle top. On two earlier occasions, Nicole had gained access to her grandfather's tablets when she was placed on the kitchen counter. Both times, the tablets were taken from Nicole and she was removed from the countertop. In spite of his knowledge that Nicole had been attracted in the past to his medication, the grandfather continued to store his prescriptions on the countertop without securing the childproof bottle top.

When Nicole's grandparents went on vacation, she and her parents "housesat." One day, Nicole's mother placed her on the countertop while she was washing dishes. The mother heard tablets spilling and looked to see Nicole with an open prescription container in her hand. Her mother noticed that Nicole had something in her mouth and removed part of a tablet. She took the bottle from the child, believing that she had averted an accident. Ten minutes later, Nicole began to show signs of distress prompting her mother to call the local hospital. Emergency crews arrived to find Nicole unconscious. The resuscitation efforts continued for about an hour.

At the hospital, it was determined that Nicole had suffered permanent brain damage resulting in substantial cognitive and communicative impairment. The package labeling for chloroquine notes that it is especially toxic to young children.

RULING: The Federal District Court earlier held that the prescribing Army physician and dispensing Army pharmacist had breached a duty to warn, which resulted in the child's injury. The trial court also held that the Army was vicariously liable for the grandfather's negligent handling of his medication. This decision was confirmed on appeal.

REASONING: The government contended that the grandfather's duty to Nicole, as a licensee on his premises, was to refrain from willfully injuring her. To buttress its contention, the government cited a 1986 Washington case that recognized the common law distinction between invitees and licensees. However, the court noted that the government overlooked another case that replaced the willful conduct standard toward licensees with a duty to exercise reasonable care where there is a known dangerous condition that the owner can reasonably anticipate the licensee will not discover.

The court found that the grandfather knew that he was leaving a prescription drug in a place accessible to a young child and failed to make the conditions safe by storing the medicine in an inaccessible place.

The government further contended that, as a matter of law the grandfather's conduct was not within the scope of his employment with the Army because (a) his use of the drug was

Vollendorf v U.S.
951 F.2d 215 (9th Cir. 1991)
...continued

for his personal benefit, and (b) his storage of the drug was not sufficiently related to his employment. The court stated that the test is whether the employee was engaged in the performance of duties required of him by his contract of employment or by the specific direction of his employer. The evidence showed that the grandfather was under orders to take chloroquine. Government regulations required him to take the drug and Army commanders had the authority to direct such disease control measures.

The government argued strongly that the grandfather took the drug for his own personal benefit. However, under Washington law, the employer is vicariously liable for the conduct of the employee even if the predominant motive of the employee was to benefit himself or a third party.

Next, the government argued that the grandfather's storage of the drug was dictated by personal convenience, not governmental interest, and therefore his conduct in that regard was not within the scope of his employment. The court noted that the critical question was whether the Army should have expected that the grandfather would ignore the warning "Keep out of the reach of children" that was plainly printed on the label.

Expert testimony by the plaintiff's witness concluded that people do not respond to a generic warning such as this one...and that it was quite common for people to place unsecured medication on kitchen counters. It was claimed that such warnings are not taken seriously enough. Thus, the court concluded that an award of damages to Nicole and her family was appropriate and that the grandfather's conduct at home in leaving the drug accessible was within the authorized scope of his employment with the army.

Brown v Southern Baptist Hospital
715 So.2d 423 (La.App. 1998)

ISSUE: Who is responsible for a patient's injuries when a pharmacy student commits an act of malpractice while doing a school-sponsored externship rotation in a hospital?

FACTS: Mr. Brown, the plaintiff, was admitted to the hospital in June 1989 for treatment of a severe infection of his finger caused by an injury at work. At the time of the accident, an animal hospital employed him as a veterinarian technician earning $4.90 per hour. While the plaintiff was in the hospital, a pharmacy student was doing her school-arranged externship in the hospital's pharmacy. On June 30, 1989, the student, working under the supervision of a hospital pharmacist, allegedly prepared a compound of *Bunnell's Irrigation Solution* pursuant to a prescription for Mr. Brown. The solution was dripped into the gauze of the dressing on his infected finger for 10 hours. Mr. Brown complained to the nurses that he felt a burning sensation in his hand, but his complaints went unheeded. On July 1, when the bandages were removed, it was discovered that he suffered third-degree burns to the infected finger, his hand, wrist, and forearm. As a result of the burns, Mr. Brown underwent six surgeries including the amputation of his finger and several skin grafts.

The formula for *Bunnell's Solution* calls for 0.49% glacial acetic acid in sterile water and glycerin. A chemical analysis of the solution administered to Mr. Brown showed it contained 47% glacial acetic acid. The student testified that she made two *Bunnell's Solution* mixtures and that one mixture was prepared under the supervision of the pharmacist while she

Brown v Southern Baptist Hospital
715 So.2d 423 (La.App. 1998)
...continued

mixed the other alone. The student did not know which of the two preparations was used for this patient. However, the student claimed that she put her own initials on the bottles that she prepared alone. The label on the bottle administered to the patient only indicated the pharmacist's initials. The pharmacist admitted that she was supervising the intern for the purpose of preventing formulation errors, yet there were times the pharmacist could not see the student's actions because the pharmacist was talking on the phone.

The hospital and the pharmacy school at the university where the student was enrolled had a written contract governing the externship program. The agreement required that the hospital name a preceptor to oversee the training of pharmacy interns rotating through its pharmacy and provided that the preceptor "shall have a nonsalaried adjunct clinical instructor appointment to the extramural faculty of the university." Part of the externship program requires that the students purchase a malpractice insurance policy to cover any errors that might occur while participating in the program. The insurance policy stated that in addition to the student, it would also cover "faculty members of the school or university" sponsoring the externship program but limited this additional coverage to "claims arising out of the supervision/instruction of the student" insured by the policy.

LAWSUIT: Mr. Brown sued the student individually, the university she attended, the insurance company that issued the student's malpractice policy, and the hospital. The hospital filed a claim against the student's insurance carrier claiming that it should be reimbursed for the student's negligence in case the hospital was found liable. The worker's compensation insurance company for the animal hospital that employed the patient at the time of the accident also sued the student for the damages it paid to the patient as a result of the work-related injury.

At the conclusion of the trial, the jury returned a verdict in favor of the patient against the hospital for $1,009,344. Although the jury found the student was negligent in her preparation of the solution, it determined that her negligence was not the proximate cause of the patient's injuries. Accordingly, no liability was assessed against the student or the university. Finally, no damages were awarded on the hospital's claim against the student's insurance company. In other words, the hospital was found liable for the entire judgment.

HOLDING: The Court of Appeals affirmed the trial court's judgment but reduced the jury's damage award by a significant amount to $463,807. The higher court determined that several aspects of the award were duplicative and excessive in light of the evidence presented during the trial. Furthermore, the state has a statutory cap on medical malpractice awards of $100,000 that will be the hospital's responsibility to pay. The remainder of the award will be paid by a state fund established to make up the difference between the health care provider's capped damages and the judgment.

REASONING: The hospital argued that it was held to a higher standard of care in determining the responsibility of its pharmacist for supervising the student than permitted under state law. The hospital claimed its supervising pharmacist should not have been obligated to "maintain constant surveillance" of the student unless there was some notice or indication of possible trouble. The Court of Appeals noted, however, that the degree of supervision required by a proctor or teacher depends on the risk and type of duty the student performed. In this case, the pharmacist was monitoring a student in a hospital who was mixing drugs to be administered to patients. Therefore, according to the court, it was proper to find that the pharmacist's duty to supervise was much higher than that of an ordinary schoolteacher.

Brown v Southern Baptist Hospital
715 So.2d 423 (La.App. 1998)
...continued

The hospital also claimed that the student's malpractice insurance carrier should be liable for the judgment against the hospital because its supervising pharmacist was acting as a preceptor for the student and that the pharmacist, under the terms of the policy, is an adjunct professor at the university. However, at the trial, the externship director of the pharmacy school testified that he was the faculty member who supervised the student's practicum in the course that constituted the externship. He also stated that he did not know the hospital's pharmacist and that she was not an adjunct faculty member. Therefore, according to the court, there was no error in finding that the pharmacist's occasional supervision of the student did not make her a "faculty member" within the meaning of the insurance policy.

It was also argued that the university should have been held liable because the externship director had a duty, under the contract between the university and the hospital, to visit the hospital at regular intervals to monitor the progress of students. The director happened to be visiting the hospital on the day of the incident. According to the claim, if he was there to monitor the student's progress but did not prevent the student's negligence, then he and the university, as his employer, should be liable. The court stated that even if this were true, the jury's finding that the student's negligence was not the cause of the injuries makes the argument meaningless.

On that point, an argument was also made that the jury committed an error in finding the student's negligence was not the legal cause of the patient's injuries. The court rejected this claim noting that state law requires the initials of the "person actually and personally" compounding a prescription to appear on the medication label. In this case, the pharmacist's initials appeared on the medication label administered to the patient. Therefore, the jury may have believed that the pharmacist actually prepared the defective solution, or that the student prepared the defective solution, but that the pharmacist was negligent in her supervision because she was on the phone for at least part of the time. Either way, the student's negligence in preparing the solution did not have to translate into being a cause of the patient's injury.

The following is a list of court cases that are related to this topic.

United States v Duggan Drug Stores, Inc., 326 F.2d 835 (1964).
Darling v Charleston Community Memorial Hospital, 33 Ill. 2d 326, 211 N.E. 2d 253 (Ill. 1965).
Randle v California State Board of Pharmacy, 49 Cal. Rptr. 485 (1966).
United States v Siler Drug Store Company, 376 F.2d 89 (1967).
Arenstein v California State Board of Pharmacy, 71 Cal. Rptr. 357 (1968).
Duensing v Huscher, 431 S.W.2d 169 (Mo. 1968).

Servants

The following is a list of court cases that are related to this topic.

Randle v California State Board of Pharmacy, 49 Cal. Rptr. 485 (1966).

LIMITATIONS ON DUTY

Trespassing

Saucier v Biloxi Regional Medical Center
708 So.2d 423 (Miss. 1998)

ISSUE: May a teenager who enters an abandoned hospital and finds discarded drugs recover damages for injuries sustained after using those drugs?

FACTS: In mid-1993, three teenage boys (all approximately 16 years old) decided to enter an abandoned hospital in the city of Biloxi for the purpose of finding a place to smoke marijuana and "see the ghosts that purportedly lived in the morgue." The boys entered the facility through a broken window, smoked their marijuana, and wrote their names on a wall with spray paint. They estimated that they were in the building for 20 minutes. The next evening, they returned to the hospital and discovered a large amount of drugs in the hospital's pharmacy. Finding a box, the boys filled it with various bottles of capsules and tablets. They went to the home of one of the boys and used the family's *Physician's Desk Reference* to identify as many pills as they could. They made a determination of which kind would give them a high, divided those drugs evenly, and threw out the rest. Each boy ingested some of the drugs during this process. Two days later, one of the boy's father came home from work to find his son unconscious in the bathtub. The boy was taken to the hospital where blood and urine samples determined that he had taken amphetamines and barbiturates in addition to marijuana. While recovering, the boy told his parents that he obtained the drugs from the abandoned hospital. They did not believe this story could be true so they went to the abandoned hospital and discovered a huge stockpile of drugs, just as their son had described. The parents called the police the next morning, and after investigating, the police confirmed the presence of the drugs. The parents and the police also found syringes, hypodermic needles, and other medical equipment strewn throughout the hospital.

LAWSUIT: On behalf of their son, the parents sued the city because it had taken ownership of the facility. Also named as a defendant was the pharmacist who was the director of the pharmacy in the hospital at the time it closed. The complaint alleged that the drugs had been carelessly and negligently left in the building and that the defendants knew or should have known that the drugs had been left in an unsecured building. The complaint also claimed that these acts were the product of gross or willful and wanton negligence and constituted a willful and wanton disregard for the safety of others. The defendants denied liability on the basis that the injured boy was a trespasser and their only duty was to not intentionally or wantonly harm him.

HOLDING: The trial court judge agreed and dismissed the case. In doing so, the judge found that the 16-year-old knew the hospital was closed and that he did not have the owner's permission to enter the building. This made him a trespasser who voluntarily removed the drugs from the building. Further, he voluntarily consumed the drugs off the premises for the purpose of getting high. The State Supreme Court upheld the judgment.

REASONING: The parents claimed the court had applied the wrong standard of care that the defendants owed to their son. Instead of being an ordinary trespasser, the parents claimed that the boy was an "invitee" on the property, and as such, the defendants owed him a duty to exercise ordinary and reasonable care as opposed to the much lower duty of avoiding intentional or wanton harm. The parents contended that by failing to keep teenagers from entering into the hospital and because the police knew teenagers and other children frequently crawled through broken windows and barricaded doors that had been vandalized, the hospital owners were implicitly asking people, as invitees, to use the abandoned facility. The

Saucier v Biloxi Regional Medical Center
708 So.2d 423 (Miss. 1998)
...continued

Supreme Court noted, however, that the plaintiffs' claim that other children were known to go into the hospital was based solely on the son's statement that this was a well-known fact around town and had been going on for 3 or 4 years. There was no evidence of personal knowledge or sworn affidavits to support this claim. Further there was no evidence to support the claim that neighbors of the hospital frequently called the police to complain about children entering the facility. The police, who accompanied the parents in searching the hospital after the drugs were discovered, allegedly implied that they had frequent complaints about the building. This allegation was also unsupported by any evidence. The allegations against the former pharmacy director were dismissed because the primary claim was that the defendants knew that children were frequenting the building after it had been abandoned. The pharmacy director could not possibly be liable under this claim, because she was not employed there once the hospital closed. As such, the pharmacist had no duty to secure the abandoned building. As to liability claimed for leaving the drugs in the abandoned building in the first place, the Supreme Court simply noted that the Board of Pharmacy had absolved the pharmacist from any negligence after it fully investigated the situation.

EDITOR'S NOTE: Unfortunately, there is no description of how or why the drugs were left behind anywhere in the decision.

Licensees

The following is a list of court cases that are related to this topic.

Vollendorf v U.S., 1991 WL 256188 (9th Cir. Wash.)

Invitees

The following is a list of court cases that are related to this topic.

Saucier v Biloxi Regional Medical Center, Slip Op. No. 97-CA-0079-SCT, March 19, 1998, 1998 Miss. LEXIS 117.

CAUSATION

Actual Cause

Holbrook v Rose
458 S.W.2d 155 (Ky. 1970)

ISSUE: Whether the evidence introduced at trial in this case was sufficient to establish causation.

FACTS: A man was informed that his family should be treated for worms, and he asked a pharmacist for a medicine for such. The pharmacist sold him an *otc* drug called *Jayne's PW Vermifuge*. The adult preparation and the pediatric preparation were both purchased. The pediatric preparation was labeled by the manufacturer with the following warning: "CAUTION — Tablets must be swallowed WHOLE — not chewed or crushed. Examine the mouth thoroughly to make sure children do not hide tablets under the tongue or in the

Holbrook v Rose
458 S.W.2d 155 (Ky. 1970)
...continued

cheeks." The preparations were sold by the pharmacist in the manufacturer's labeled containers. The tablets were coated (probably enteric coated) so that the drug would be released
in the intestinal tract, as the active therapeutic ingredient of the *PW Vermifuge* was hexyl-
resorcinol, a drug which causes superficial erosion of the mucous membranes of the mouth
and gastric irritation of the stomach.

The father read the instructions on the vermifuge aloud to his family and the 3-year-old member of the family was given 3 tablets of the pediatric preparation in accordance with the
labeled dosage directions. The child was told not to chew the tablets but she did nevertheless. Later the same day, she complained of discomfort in the mouth and her lips became
sore but otherwise she acted much as usual. On the next day, the child began to vomit. On
the day following, she was acutely ill and was taken to a hospital. She died the next day
of respiratory failure preceded by convulsions. A toxicology report showed that another drug
called *Darvon* was found in the child's stomach and a trace amount or resorcinol was found
in the child's kidneys. But neither drug was present in quantities, which the toxicologist
believed would be sufficient to cause death, and the cause of death could not be determined
by the toxicologist.

The child's father, as administrator of her estate, sued the pharmacist and the drug firm that
marketed the vermifuge. At a jury trial, the plaintiff based his action on alternative theories of liability — negligence (improper preparation of product or failure to adequately warn);
breach of warranty (failure to conform to a particular purpose); strict liability (an unreasonably dangerous product because of inherent danger or inadequate warning); and violation of poison state law. As to the last assertion, it was claimed that the Kentucky poison sale
law, KRS 217.400, required warnings and antidote information, which the product did not
have on its label. At the trial, the court did not allow the case against the pharmacist to
go to the jury because of the plaintiff's failure to prove his case against the pharmacist. But
the jury was allowed to make a finding on the case against the manufacturer, and a verdict of $15,400 was returned in the plaintiff's favor. The court granted judgment to the defen-
dant-manufacturer despite the jury's verdict. The plaintiff received nothing.

RULING: On appeal, the Kentucky Court of Appeals sustained the trial court's ruling.

REASONING: The appellate court reasoned that regardless of the plaintiff's alternative claims
for recovery, the issue of causation or whether the vermifuge caused the death must be established by the evidence to a degree of "probability" or that it was "more likely than not" that
the drug caused the death. Despite some conflict in the medical testimony at trial, no medical witness could testify that the drug taken in the dosage the plaintiff said it was taken could
have caused the death...either alone or in combination with the other drug (*Darvon*).

The following is a list of court cases that are related to this topic.

Thomsen v Rexall Drug & Chemical Co., 45 Cal. Rptr. 642 (1965).
Zuchowicz v U.S., Slip Op. No. 97-6057; 90-6099, March 20, 1998, 2nd Cir., 1998 U.S. App.
    LEXIS 5366.

Proximate Cause

Peoples Service Drug Stores v Somerville
158 A.12 (Md. 1932)

ISSUE: Whether a pharmacist's failure to consult a physician regarding a dosage was the direct cause of the patient's injuries.

FACTS: A lawsuit was brought against a pharmacist for dispensing a compounded prescription for 1/4 grain strychnine capsules of which the patient took one capsule every 2 hours for 3 doses and was injured. The prescription was correctly dispensed as written by the physician. The suit was commenced on the theory that the pharmacist should either have refused to dispense the prescription or should have inquired of the prescriber before dispensing. The trial court gave judgment in favor of the patient-plaintiff and against the pharmacist-defendant.

The prescription was accurately dispensed as written, and the pharmacist made no inquiry to the prescriber as to the nature of the prescription or use. Even if the pharmacist had inquired, the physician may well have not changed the prescription since it was a usual dose. The pharmacist did not label the prescription container with either the words "poison" or "strychnine" because Maryland law made exceptions from such labeling for poisons dispensed in normal quantities on prescription. Medical testimony presented at the trial conflicted substantially as to the fatal dose of strychnine; some doctors said it was 1 1/2 grains; one doctor said 1/2 grain was fatal; another doctor said a case existed where 15 grains was not fatal; doctors and pharmacists testifying for the plaintiff stated that 1/30 grain was the usual prescribed dose of strychnine, but one expert witness said 1/20 grain of strychnine had been known to kill.

RULING: The pharmacist's actions in correctly dispensing the prescription were not the direct cause of the patient's injuries.

REASONING: The injured person in this case asserted that the pharmacist-defendant had violated the Maryland statutes regulating sales of poisons by failing to inquire of either the patient or the physician the purpose of the strychnine prescription.

The Maryland Supreme Court rejected this assertion stating:

> The violation of a statute will not support an action for damages on account of the injury sustained, unless such violation is the proximate cause of injury.

There was no proof that the pharmacist's actions were the direct cause of the plaintiff's injuries, and the judgment against the pharmacist was reversed.

The court did not decide if the Maryland poison statutes were in fact violated, since there was no evidence that such alleged violation was the proximate cause of injury. As pointed out previously, the poison statutes carried an exception as to poisons dispensed in normal amounts or doses on prescription. Although the court was not put to the test of a specific determination of the proximate cause of the plaintiff's injury, the facts of the case indicate that it was the prescription as written by the physician that caused the injury. Even in this respect, a jury could have concluded from the conflicting medical testimony that the prescription was not on its face negligent. The plaintiff chose to sue the pharmacist rather than the physician, and his argument against the pharmacist was that he should have refused to dispense the prescription or inquired of the physician as to the merits of the dose. The court, in its ruling, noted that the pharmacist could have refused to dispense the prescription but, under the facts of this case, he was not obligated to refuse and an inquiry to the physician would have been futile.

Peoples Service Drug Stores v Somerville
158 A.12 (Md. 1932)
...continued

Commenting on the issue of under what circumstances should a pharmacist set up his judgment against that of a physician, the court put forth the following rules:

> If a druggist is negligent in filling a prescription, he cannot escape liability because
> the doctor who wrote the prescription is also liable. But it does not follow because a
> physician in a given case is liable that the druggist that filled the prescription is also
> liable.

> It would be a dangerous principle to establish that a druggist cannot safely fill a pre-
> scription merely because it is out of the ordinary. If that were done, many patients
> might die from being denied unusual remedies in extreme cases.

> Of course this does not mean that the pharmacist can safely fill prescriptions calling
> for doses that are obviously fatal; or that where the doses prescribed appear to be
> unusual the prescription can be safely filled without inquiry of the physician to make
> sure there has been no error.

Wells v Ortho Pharmaceutical Corp.
788 F.2d 741 (11th Cir. 1986)

ISSUE: Whether the manufacturer of a contraceptive spermicide (1) was responsible for the
birth defects of a child born to the plaintiff who had used the product several months before
and after conception and (2) failed to warn the plaintiff that an increased risk of birth
defects accompanied the use of its product.

FACTS: The plaintiff, Mary Maihafer, was a 32-year-old college instructor who had no family history of birth defects. Gary Wells, the father of the injured child, also had no family
history of birth defects. In July 1980, Ms. Maihafer obtained a prescription for a diaphragm
and also received a sample tube of *Ortho-Gynol* contraceptive jelly ("the product").

A nurse instructed the plaintiff on the proper use of the diaphragm and the spermicidal jelly,
and Ms. Maihafer testified that she read the directions that accompanied the product. The
spermicidal jelly was available *otc* and, in 1980, contained only a warning that the product might cause irritation of the female or male genitalia, was not 100% effective, and should
be kept out of the reach of children.

Plaintiffs allege that Ms. Maihafer used the diaphragm and contraceptive jelly in accordance with the instructions every time she had sex with Gary Wells from the time the diaphragm was prescribed until mid-November 1980. Ms. Maihafer missed her menstrual period
around November 1, 1980, and later discovered she had become pregnant in October.

On July 1, 1981, Ms. Maihafer gave birth to plaintiff Katie Wells, who was born with a cleft
lip, an abnormal formation of her right hand, the complete lack of a left arm, and only partial development of the left shoulder. She also suffered from damage to her right optic
nerve which left her almost 90% blind in her right eye.

The plaintiffs filed this action alleging that the spermicide's active ingredient, a nonionic surfactant that works to break down sperm cell membranes, caused the birth defects by either

Wells v Ortho Pharmaceutical Corp.
788 F.2d 741 (11th Cir. 1986)
...continued

injury to the sperm, injury to an unfertilized egg, injury to the fertilized egg, or injury to the developing fetus. The plaintiffs alleged that the defendant manufacturer knew, or should have known, of certain studies that were available to the scientific community linking the use of spermicides to birth defects in the children of mothers who used the products around the time of conception. They further alleged that this knowledge imposed a duty on the manufacturer to warn health professionals and prospective users of the risk by placing a warning on the product.

The defendant vehemently denied any association between the use of its product and birth defects. It noted that since 1950, it had sold the product in its present form to millions of women. The manufacturer argued that at the time of Katie Wells' conception, no published reports had concluded that spermicides caused birth defects.

RULING: The U.S. District Court concluded that the plaintiffs had proven to a reasonable degree of medical certainty that the birth defects of Katie Wells' left arm and shoulder and her right hand were proximately caused by Ortho's product, but found otherwise with respect to her cleft lip and right optic nerve defect. The District Court also found that Ortho Pharmaceuticals knew, or should have known, that its product might cause birth defects. Damages were awarded exceeding $5.1 million. The U.S. Court of Appeals for the Eleventh Circuit affirmed the District Court decision with some modification of damages to $4,700,000.

REASONING: The District Court decision (615 F.Supp. 262) contains an extensive review of the expert testimony regarding causation and duty to warn. The manufacturer further complained that despite the inconclusive nature of the scientific and medical studies introduced at trial, the District Court erroneously held that the plaintiffs carried their burden of proof regarding causation.

The appellate court rejected the defendant's arguments and concluded that the plaintiffs presented well-qualified experts who testified at length concerning causation. These experts relied upon their particular areas of expertise, their personal examination of the child, and the medical and scientific studies relative to causation to conclude that the spermicide caused Katie Wells' birth defects. Several epidemiological studies were presented that indicated an association between spermicide use and deleterious effects on the fetus. In facing the battle of experts, the District Court was forced to make credibility determinations to decide the victor. Citing from another case, the court recognized that a cause-effect relationship need not be clearly established by animal or epidemiological studies before a doctor can testify that, in his opinion, such a relationship exists. The court noted a distinction between legal sufficiency and scientific certainty. While the medical community might require more research and evidence before conclusively resolving the question, the trial court judge found sufficient evidence of causation in a legal sense and that finding was not clearly erroneous.

The manufacturer next argued that the District Court misinterpreted Georgia law on the duty to warn and that the court failed to consider two FDA review panels' determinations that no warning was necessary for nonionic surfactant spermicides. It is interesting to note that at the trial, a college of pharmacy dean forcefully stated that the warning on the label of the product was insufficient. He testified that "as soon as the first study is done and any information that is provided...gives the hint that there is a possibility of a drug causing birth defects, the label should be changed to include a warning." This expert noted that the manufacturer should have provided a warning when results of several studies were produced

Wells v Ortho Pharmaceutical Corp.
788 F.2d 741 (11th Cir. 1986)
...continued

in the mid-1970s. While one of these studies was not published, the court concluded that the research studies were available to the manufacturer through several means. Thus, the defendant had actual or constructive knowledge that the product might cause birth defects. The trial court agreed with the expert's testimony that the defendant should have given such warning no later than 1977 when there was a "hint" that the product caused birth defects.

The appellate court also found that the trial court was not required to accept the FDA reports as conclusive. "An FDA determination that a warning is not necessary may be sufficient for federal regulatory purposes but still not sufficient for state tort law purposes." As the court previously stated "compliance with regulatory standards may be admissible on the issue of care, but does not require a jury to find a defendant's conduct reasonable."

January v Peace
738 S.W.2d 355 (Tex. App. 1987)

ISSUE: Whether a pharmacist and drug wholesaler were negligent in providing a customer with a poison which he subsequently used to kill his wife.

FACTS: Billy Jack Peace, a licensed pharmacist and owner of Peace Drug Store in Canton, Texas, received a telephone call on Nov. 5, 1982, from Murry January who requested some strychnine for the purpose of killing wolves. January told Peace that wolves had been attacking his cattle while they were calving. Peace advised January that he did not stock strychnine but January could contact area farm and ranch stores to procure the product.

Later the same day, January called Peace back and reported he had been unable to purchase the strychnine. Peace concluded that January wanted the strychnine "immediately" to prevent further loss of livestock. In order to accommodate his customer, Peace called Behren's Drug at their Tyler, Texas, wholesale warehouse and arranged for January to go to the warehouse and pick up a quantity of the poison. The poison was delivered to January in person, but charged to the account of a pharmacy owned by Peace.

Peace stated in his affidavit that at no time did he ever have an idea that January was going to use the strychnine to harm or kill his wife. There were no circumstances, inferences, statements or any other actions that would have led Peace to believe that January would use the strychnine for that reason. The division manager of the wholesaler also testified that he had no reason to even discuss January's professed need for the strychnine.

The plaintiffs alleged in their petition that January used the strychnine, which he obtained from the wholesaler after contacting the pharmacy, to kill his wife. It was further alleged that the defendants assisted January in obtaining the strychnine contrary to federal and state law and were guilty of negligence per se, which was the direct and proximate cause of the death of January's wife.

RULING: The trial court granted summary judgment in favor of the pharmacist and drug wholesaler. The appellate court ruled that even if the pharmacist and drug wholesaler were negligent in providing the customer with the poison, they did not proximately cause the wife's death and were not liable to the wife's survivors.

January v Peace
738 S.W.2d 355 (Tex. App. 1987)
...continued

REASONING: The court noted the long-standing rule that an act must be the proximate cause of injuries in order to constitute negligence or negligence per se. The negligent act must be a substantial factor in bringing about the injury and without which no harm would have been incurred. The act must also be foreseeable. Foreseeability is satisfied by showing that a person of ordinary intelligence should have anticipated the danger to others by his negligent act.

The evidence showed that neither Peace nor the drug wholesaler had knowledge of any facts even remotely suggesting that January had any motive to injure or murder his wife. In fact, January had informed Peace that wolves were killing his cows and that he wanted the strychnine to use on the wolves. There was no evidence that the defendant's acts (even if in violation of the law) were the proximate cause of the death of January's wife.

Jeans v Caraway
649 S.2d 1141 (La. Ct. App. 1995)

FACTS: A pharmacist was engaged in a 30-year business of "concocting his own medicines" using what he believed were *otc* drugs. The mixtures were sold under his own label. On the advice of friends, a patient asked the pharmacist for a product to treat headaches and sinus problems. The pharmacist asked about the patient's general health, but not about the patient's high blood pressure. The pharmacist did not explain that the 3 products he sold the patient were contraindicated for hypertension patients. The patient purchased and used one mixture containing phenylpropanolamine (PPA) 50 mg, pheniramine 25 mg, pyfilamine 25 mg, and an undisclosed strength of ibuprofen. During a visit to his allergist, the patient's blood pressure was recorded at 170/108. The patient did not tell the allergist about the medicine supplied by the pharmacist. Six days after the allergist appointment, the patient was hospitalized for a hypertensive crisis with his blood pressure recorded as high as 270/150. The patient suffered permanent brain damage. In a lawsuit against the pharmacist, the trial court found in favor of the pharmacist stating that the pharmacist's negligence (arguably selling prescription PPA as an *otc* drug, and improper drug labeling) was not the proximate cause of the patient's injury. Although the treating physician indicated that he would not prescribe PPA for this patient, other expert witnesses indicated that it would be highly unusual for PPA 50 mg to cause a hypertensive crisis of the magnitude suffered. Evidence showed that the patient had taken PPA and similar drugs in the past without any significant effect on his blood pressure.

HOLDING: The Louisiana Appellate Court upheld the verdict based on the jury's ability to weigh and resolve the conflicting expert testimony on causation.

Pietrzyk v River Oaks Sav-Mor Pharmacy
Wayne County Cir Ct No. 98-833287-NM (February 14, 2000), 14 Mich Layers Weekly 877

This jury verdict report filed by the plaintiff's attorney states that an 82-year-old woman suffering from hypothyroidism was given *Lanoxin* instead of the prescribed *Synthroid*. She took the wrong medicine for 92 days before becoming dizzy, falling and hitting her head. Eight days later she was hospitalized with hallucinations and diagnosed with traumatic brain injury

Pietrzyk v River Oaks Sav-Mor Pharmacy
Wayne County Cir Ct No. 98-833287-NM (February 14, 2000), 14 Mich Layers Weekly 877
...continued

caused by her fall. The pharmacy admitted that it dispensed the wrong medication, but denied that this error was the proximate cause of the plaintiff's fall and subsequent injuries. Two physicians testified that there was a direct correlation between the medication error and the plaintiff's injuries. The jury returned a verdict for the plaintiff for $340,000. According to this report, the jury recognized that prior to this incident the plaintiff had led an exceptionally active lifestyle for her age. The highest settlement offer prior to trial was $100,000.

Ostrow v New London Pharmacy
Slip Op. No. 1845 (December 28, 2000), 2000 NY App. Div. LEXIS 13838

Plaintiff alleged that her ulcerative colitis was worsened by her ingestion of the drug sulfadiazine, which defendant pharmacy mistakenly dispensed to her instead of sulfasalazine, the drug her physician had actually prescribed. On the day prior to trial, defense counsel disclosed for the first time that the pharmacy's experts would testify that plaintiff's injuries were likely caused by steroid medications plaintiff had also been taking at the relevant time, and the court denied plaintiff's motion to preclude such testimony. The jury found that although the pharmacy had negligently dispensed the wrong drug, such negligence had not proximately caused the injuries of which plaintiff complained. Plaintiff's motion to set aside the verdict on the ground that the defense had failed to give notice of its experts' opinion that plaintiff's use of steroids had caused her injuries, as required by N.Y. C.P.L.R. 3101(d) (1) (i), was denied by the trial court. Judgment affirmed because the trial court's decision to permit the expert testimony questioned was not abuse of its discretion. The fact that plaintiff was using powerful drugs other than the one dispensed raised the question of whether the effects of which she complained could have been caused thereby.

The following is a list of court cases that are related to this topic.

Stevens v Parke, Davis & Company, 207 Cal. Rptr. 45, 507 P.2d 653 (Cal. 1973).
Timm v Upjohn Co., 624 F.2d 536 (5th Cir. 1980).
Speer v United States, 512 F. Supp. 670 (N.D. Tex 1981).
E.R. Squibb & Sons, Inc. v Cox, 477 So.2d 963 (Ala. 1985).
Stebbins v Concord Wrigley Drugs, Inc., et al., Docket No. 88734 (Mich. Ct. App. 1987).
Quinn v Memorial Medical Center, 764 S.W.2d 915 (Tex. App. - Corpus Christi 1989).
Holbrook v Rose, 458 S.W. 2d 155 (Ky. 1970).
Brown v Southern Baptist Hospital, Slip Op. Nos. 96-CA-1990 and 96-CA-1991, La. App. 4th Cir., March 11, 1998, 1998 La. App. LEXIS 556.
Clodgo v Kroger Pharmacy, Slip Op. No. 98AP-569, Mar. 18, 1999, 1999 Ohio App. LEXIS 1246.
Van Hatem v K-Mart, 719 NE 2d 212; 1999 Ill. App. LEXIS 404.
Espinosa v US, Slip Op No 00 C 3435 (November 29, 2001), USD Ill., 2001 US Dist. LEXIS 19478.
Trach v Fellin and Thrift Drugs, Slip Op No 1921 EDA 2000 (January 18, 2002), 2002 Pa. Super 11; 2002 Pa. Super LEXIS 11.

Unforeseeable Consequences

The following is a list of court cases that are related to this topic.

January v Peace, 738 S.W.2d 355 (Tex. App.-Tyler 1987).
Pittman v The Upjohn Company, 1994 WL 663372 (Tenn. Nov. 28, 1994).

Intervening Causes

The following is a list of court cases that are related to this topic.

Fuhs v Barber, 36 P. 2d 962 (Kan. 1934).
Speer v United States, 512 F. Supp. 670 (N.D. Tex. 1981).
Kirk v Michael Reese Hospital, 483 N.E.2d 906 (Ill. App. 1 Dist. 1985).
Bickowicz v Sterling Drug, Inc., 557 N.Y. S.2d 551 (A.D. 3 Dept. 1990).
McLaughlin v Hook-SupeRx Inc., 642 N.E. 2d 514 (Ind. 1994).
Hatten v Price, 663 S.2d 351 (La. Ct. App. 1995).
Austermiller v Dosick, Slip Op No L-01-1223 (December 31, 2001), 2001 Ohio App. LEXIS 5964.

DAMAGES

General

Malone & Hyde, Inc. v Hobrecht
685 S.W.2d 739 (Tex. Ct. App. 1985)

ISSUE: Whether a pharmacy is liable for damages to the widow and children of a patient who received the wrong syringes for the injection of insulin.

FACTS: The decedent, Roland Hobrecht, was a 66-year-old advertising executive who was married and had three children. Hobrecht had been seeing his family physician for a long time because of his diabetes. In August, 1980, Hobrecht was admitted to the Park North General Hospital for aggravation of his diabetes. Although Hobrecht's diabetes had previously been controlled by oral medications, the physician, Dr. Pomerantz, decided to start him on injectable insulin. Dr. Pomerantz wrote a prescription for NPH insulin, insulin syringes and 5/8 x 26–gauge needles.

In order to save time, Dr. Pomerantz telephoned the prescription to the pharmacist at Sommer's Drug Store in San Antonio, Texas, where the Hobrechts routinely had their prescriptions filled. The pharmacist on duty mistakenly dispensed the prescription with non-insulin syringes. These syringes were 25 gauge with total capacity of 3 ccs and did not have the "units" marked on the barrel for the insulin. Hobrecht's prescription required him to inject 25 units of NPH insulin daily. As a result of receiving the wrong syringes, Hobrecht injected himself with approximately 6 times his prescribed dosage of insulin on 2 consecutive days. He was readmitted to the hospital and died approximately 30 days later. The Hobrecht family filed a lawsuit against the pharmacy.

RULING: The appellate court upheld the $250,000 verdict to the widow for the pecuniary loss associated with the death of her husband and $250,000 for loss of consortium. The jury verdict awarding damages to two of the children was upheld, but the awarded damages to the other son for pecuniary loss was contrary to the evidence. The estate was also awarded $250,000 for damages for physical pain and suffering as well as $20,000 for medical expenses and $3000 for funeral and burial expenses.

Malone & Hyde, Inc. v Hobrecht
685 S.W.2d 739 (Tex. Ct. App. 1985)
...continued

REASONING: The pharmacy joined the physician as a third party defendant alleging that Dr. Pomerantz failed to properly instruct Hobrecht in how to administer the insulin. The pharmacy also alleged that the Hobrechts were negligent in failing to adhere to the instructions of the physician and also alleged that the hospital employees failed to properly instruct the family in the proper administration of insulin. The jury exonerated the Hobrechts of contributory negligence and neither the physician nor the hospital employees were found to be negligent.

The pharmacy, on appeal, presented a number of contentions suggesting that the jury verdict should be overturned. First, the pharmacy argued that the $250,000 in damages for physical pain and mental anguish was excessive and not supported by the evidence. During the 30 days that Hobrecht was hospitalized, he developed congestive heart failure and had severe damage to his kidneys which eventually led to dialysis. The pharmacy advanced the untenable notion that the decedent suffered no physical pain or mental anguish during this time period because there was no evidence that he ever told anyone that he was experiencing pain. Yet, by the pharmacy's own admission, following the initial overdose, the decedent became tired, confused, and had difficulty moving; his appetite disappeared and he began to make gasping noises; he broke out in a sweat and his eyes began bugging out; confusion set in followed by disorientation, lethargy, sleepiness, slurred speech, and loss of ability to speak. The court noted that conscious pain and suffering may be inferred from circumstantial evidence and did not have to be based upon an express statement from the decedent. It became a duty of the jury, as a matter of discretion, to weigh the pain and anguish and then to convert it into a monetary award.

The pharmacy also contended that the $250,000 in pecuniary damages was excessive. The jury had been instructed to take into account the care, maintenance, support, services, advice, counsel, and other contributions that Mr. Hobrecht would have provided to his wife during his lifetime had he lived. The pharmacy argued that Hobrecht was making only around $20,000 a year and had a life expectancy of 8 to 10 years. The pharmacy felt that additional evidence of future earning capacity or a probable increase in earnings was necessary to support such a large jury verdict. The court held that such an argument ignored services and contributions provided by Mr. Hobrecht not related to earnings from employment. The records showed that the decedent and his wife were very close and spent considerable time playing bridge and traveling to various race tracks. Mrs. Hobrecht had always looked to her husband for counsel and protection, and following his death she seemed lost and disoriented. Often times, it is extremely difficult to determine the pecuniary value of a spouse aside from the actual monetary contributions made to the marriage. The law vests the jury with considerable discretion and latitude in drawing upon their own knowledge and experience in reaching such a conclusion. A review of the record convinced the court that the jury's award was supported by sufficient evidence.

The pharmacy also argued with the award of pecuniary damages to the Hobrecht children. The pharmacy particularly took issue with the award of damages to one of the sons. Although the loss of his father was tragic, there was no evidence that there was any pecuniary loss. The other son did periodically borrow money from his father and relied upon his advice on how to resolve certain financial matters. The daughter testified that her father had helped her with medical expenses for one of her children and the evidence suggested that she depended heavily upon her father for financial assistance in coping with such expenses. The court concluded that the evidence supported the jury verdict for two of the children, but the award of damages to the other son for pecuniary loss was contrary to the evidence.

The pharmacy next argued against the $25,000 award for loss of consortium for the period prior to the death of the deceased. The pharmacy argued that $25,000 for a 30-day period

Malone & Hyde, Inc. v Hobrecht
685 S.W.2d 739 (Tex. Ct. App. 1985)
...continued

translated into an award of $800 per day. The evidence showed that the Hobrechts were a very close family, but the $25,000 award was not in keeping with the evidence. Although the jury may consider many subjective factors when awarding loss of consortium, the court determined that the award should be reduced to $2,500. In a rather lengthy decision, the court went on to consider other issues of contention by the pharmacy, but generally concluded that the jury verdicts and decisions were correct.

Reben v Ely
705 P.2d 1360 (Ariz. Ct. App. 1985)

ISSUE: Whether the University of Arizona Poison and Drug Information Center and several other defendants were responsible for the injuries suffered by a 10-year-old patient who was administered a dose of cocaine, mistakenly thought to be *Tylenol*.

FACTS: During an office visit to George B. Ely, MD, a nurse accidentally administered a 10% cocaine solution instead of acetaminophen to the 10-year-old plaintiff. The cocaine solution was colored red and stored in a bottle labeled "Red Solution" to decrease the chances of pilferage. A local pharmacy had supplied the solution as labeled at the request of the physician. As soon as the nurse realized the mistake, she informed the physician who called the pharmacy. The pharmacist referred the physician to the University of Arizona Poison and Drug Information Center.

Pharmacist Susan Moss, who had worked at the center for 2 years, answered the physician's call. According to Moss' testimony, the physician asked whether there was a specific antidote for cocaine. Moss relied that there was none. Moss contended at the trial that she described the life-threatening nature of cocaine ingestion and the importance of carefully monitoring the patient's status. She instructed the physician to call the poison center again, if necessary, and she told him that she would call him back for follow-up information. Upon completing the call, Moss alerted the poison center's medical director, who indicated he was available for further help if necessary. About 20 minutes later, Moss called the physician back, but he was unavailable.

The plaintiff suffered seizures in the physician's office. About 40 minutes after the ingestion, the physician transported the plaintiff to the hospital across the street where the child was determined to have experienced cardiopulmonary arrest. He was resuscitated, but lapsed into a coma for 2 weeks. Brain damage resulted, and the plaintiff will require continuous nursing care for life.

The jury awarded the child and his parents a total of $6.5 million. Of this, the physician and nurse were assessed $2.2 million, which was the ceiling on their liability insurance. The local pharmacy agreed to pay $650,000 in an out-of-court settlement reached early in the trial. The state of Arizona was liable for the remaining $3.6 million.

There was conflicting testimony from expert witnesses regarding the standard of care in poison centers. One expert testified that the center operated below the standard of practice because the physician was not offered a consultation by the medical director of the center. Another expert testified that the center clearly provided a level of care superior to many poison centers. The trial court judge instructed the jury that the center could be found neg-

Reben v Ely
705 P.2d 1360 (Ariz. Ct. App. 1985)
...continued

ligent if it failed to perform the responsibilities of a "health care provider." The issue was whether the poison center simply provided information and consultation services to physicians with the physician being ultimately responsible for making the final decision, or if the center itself had the responsibilities of a health care provider.

Another issue on appeal was whether the parents should be awarded damages for the loss of consortium of their child. Many states permit one spouse to recover damages for the loss of affection and company of the other spouse, but under Arizona law it was not clear whether individuals could recover such damages for the loss of love and affection of a child. The parents were specifically awarded $1.5 million for loss of consortium.

RULING: The jury award to the parents for loss of consortium of their son was affirmed.

REASONING: The Arizona Court of Appeals noted that only a handful of other states recognized a cause of action for loss of filial consortium. The court said that recognizing a claim for loss of filial consortium due to negligence was a function for the courts, rather than the legislature. The court reviewed the recovery under the Arizona wrongful death statute and concluded that recovery for the loss of companionship of the injured child should be allowed in negligence actions that do not result in the death of the victim. The trial court verdict was affirmed.

Baas v Hoye
766 F.2d 1190 (8th Cir. 1985)

ISSUE: Whether a pharmacy that violated a consumer products safety rule by dispensing a prescription drug in a nonchild-resistant container was (1) guilty of negligence for a child's death and (2) was guilty of negligent infliction of emotional distress on the child's father.

FACTS: The plaintiffs, Julie and Ricky Baas, had a prescription for *Tedral SA* on file at the Hoye Super Rexall Drugstore in Estherville, Iowa. In July 1981, Robert Young, a pharmacist employed at the pharmacy, filled a prescription for 50 *Tedral SA* tablets in a nonchild-resistant container. About one month later, the father again returned to the pharmacy, handed another pharmacist the nonchild-resistant container and requested a refill. Without asking any questions regarding the type of container the father desired, the second pharmacist refilled the prescription in a nonchild-resistant container. Shortly thereafter, the plaintiff's daughter ingested a number of the *Tedral* SA tablets contained in the prescription bottle. Medical efforts to save the child's life were unsuccessful, and she died in September 1981.

The plaintiffs filed a 3-count complaint in federal district court requesting (1) compensatory and punitive damages for the wrongful death of their child, (2) damages for loss of companionship and services of the child, and (3) damages for negligent infliction of emotional distress.

The facts as reported indicate that the father did not actually observe his daughter ingesting the *Tedral* SA tablets because he was sleeping at the time. He was not aware of what was happening until the mother started screaming. The father sat on the edge of the bed while his wife took the child into the bathroom to attempt to induce her to vomit. Because he

Baas v Hoye
766 F.2d 1190 (8th Cir. 1985)
...continued

was ill, the father went back to bed and remained there for approximately 2 hours until a decision was made to take the child to the physician's office.

RULING: The jury determined that both pharmacists had violated a consumer products safety rule by dispensing the prescription drug in a nonchild-resistant package. The jury awarded $30,000 compensatory damages and $100,000 in punitive damages for the wrongful death of the child. The jury also awarded $60,000 for the loss of companionship and services of the child. The father was awarded $15,000 for the negligent infliction of emotional distress. Because the parents also had been negligent in allowing the child access to the drug, the court reduced the damages to $15,000 each under the 2 claims. The trial court also eliminated the father's claim for negligent infliction of emotional distress. The trial court's decision was affirmed on appeal.

REASONING: On appeal, the pharmacists contended that recovery by the plaintiffs was improper because they had not violated a consumer products safety rule. The pharmacists claimed that the drug they dispensed was not required by federal law to be dispensed only pursuant to a prescription. To support their argument, they pointed out that *Tedral SA* is the brand name of a product that contains the ingredients theophylline, ephedrine, and phenobarbital. They argued that other products containing the same 3 ingredients are available without a prescription. Thus, they contended that the product was available without a prescription, and they did not need to dispense it in a child-resistant package.

The U.S. Court of Appeals disagreed with the pharmacists' argument. The court found that *Tedral SA* was listed as a prescription drug under federal law. The mere fact that other products containing different percentages of the same ingredients could be obtained without a prescription was of no consequence.

The pharmacists argued that they were unaware of any requirement that prescription drugs be dispensed in child-resistant packaging. They believed that use of such packaging was simply "recommended." The court concluded that a jury could reasonably find that, as experienced pharmacists, they were aware of the consumer products safety rule requiring prescription drugs to be dispensed in child-resistant packaging.

The pharmacists also contended that the father had requested a nonchild-resistant container for the *Tedral SA* prescription and that federal law exempts pharmacists from liability in such circumstances. The statute authorizes the use of noncomplying packages "when requested by the purchaser." While one could infer that the father wanted the prescription filled in a nonchild-resistant container when he handed the package to the pharmacist, another reasonable inference was that the father simply wanted a refill. The court ruled that the jury was correct in determining that the father had not specifically requested a nonchild-resistant container.

The plaintiffs contended that the trial court committed an error when it denied the father his claim for negligent infliction of emotional distress. Under Iowa law, "there must be a sensory and contemporaneous observance of the accident, as contrasted with the learning of the accident from others after its occurrence" before one is entitled to damages for emotional distress. A recovery for negligent infliction of emotional distress is intended to compensate the plaintiffs for the emotional trauma caused by their visceral participation in the event. Because the father did not actually observe his daughter ingesting the tablets, the court determined that he should not be awarded such damages.

Pressler v Irvine Drugs
169 Cal.App.3d 1244 (1985)

ISSUE: (1) Whether a pharmacy was negligent in selling the wrong insulin to a customer and (2) whether it was permissible for the court to reduce the award of noneconomic damages pursuant to a California tort reform statute.

FACTS: The plaintiff, Michael Pressler, had been a diabetic since age 13. In September 1979, he requested his usual semilente insulin from a clerk at the pharmacy counter of Danber Drugs. The clerk replied that there was no prescription waiting for Mr. Semi Lente. The plaintiff informed the clerk that semilente was the product he wanted to purchase and not his name. The clerk spoke to the pharmacist and was told to "give him some lente."

Without noticing that he was given lente insulin rather than semilente, the plaintiff injected the drug for several days. He experienced episodes of disorientation, and he fell asleep for approximately 15 hours. Upon awakening, he was confused and disoriented, and called his girlfriend to find out what time it was. He apparently told her he had discovered he was using lente rather than semilente insulin.

The plaintiff spent the following afternoon at his girlfriend's apartment. At 2 a.m., she was awakened by his heavy breathing and noticed that he was losing body fluids and had become rigid. She called paramedics who injected him with glucose and transported him to the hospital for treatment. Despite returning to the correct insulin, he continued to suffer hypoglycemic attacks. His family began to notice changes in his physical abilities, mental attitude, memory, awareness of his diabetic condition, and his sexual habits. It was reported that the plaintiff, an expert skier, went out of control on an intermediate run in Sun Valley. He took no evasive action whatever and shot over the edge of the run and crashed into a tree. Pressler filed a negligence action against the pharmacy and the pharmacist. The defendants raised the issue of contributory negligence against the plaintiff.

RULING: The jury returned a verdict of no negligence on the part of the plaintiff. It also found that the pharmacist was absolved of liability because there was no evidence that he was the particular pharmacist on duty when the wrong insulin was sold. The jury returned a verdict of $425,000 against the pharmacy that included: $25,000, medical costs; $75,000, loss of earnings; and $325,000, general damages. The judge reduced the award of general damages by $75,000 pursuant to a California statute which placed a $250,000 ceiling on noneconomic losses in lawsuits against health care providers based upon professional negligence.

REASONING: The appellate court confirmed that the pharmacy had been negligent in selling the wrong insulin. It also concluded, without explanation, that the plaintiff had not been contributorily negligent.

The primary issue on appeal centered on the reduction of the damages for noneconomic losses. The plaintiff argued that the defense attorney had never followed the proper procedures set forth in the statute limiting noneconomic awards and thus waived any right to reduction of the general damages. The evidence showed that the attorney for the pharmacy requested the court's guidance on how the issue should be presented to the jury. The trial court was cautious and exhibited concern about whether the section in question was constitutional and acknowledged that the issue was under consideration by the California Supreme Court.

The appellate court concluded that the pharmacy clearly stated its desire to avail itself of the protection of the statute and did not waive its right to the section's required reduction. In light of the uncertainty of the law at the time, the trial court was understandably hesitant to require more of the jury than might be necessary. The plaintiff argued that the court

Pressler v Irvine Drugs
169 Cal.App.3d 1244 (1985)
...continued

had no authority to require the jury to render a breakdown of damages once it had returned a general verdict. While it is generally an error to require special questions after the return of a verdict, under the unique circumstances of this case, the court concluded that the judgment must be affirmed. If the trial court did commit an error, it did so with the acquiescence, if not the invitation, of the attorneys for both parties. (Note: The constitutionality of the statute requiring limits on non-economic losses was upheld by the California Supreme Court while this case was being appealed).

Hatten v Price
663 So.2d 351 (La. Ct. App. 1995)

FACTS: A pharmacy erroneously filled a prescription for *Lasix* with *Inderal* for a 76-year-old patient with a complex medical history. Shortly thereafter, she was hospitalized for treatment of congestive heart failure. The dispensing error was found and corrected. Approximately one month later, she was admitted to the hospital for treatment of obstructive pulmonary disease, and later placed in a nursing home at her adult children's insistence. In answer to the patient's complaint for malpractice, the pharmacy admitted liability, but claimed that damages should be limited to those associated with the first hospitalization. The trial court judge, without a jury, found the pharmacy liable for both hospital admissions and the nursing home placement. He awarded $875,000 to the patient and her children.

HOLDING: The Louisiana Court of Appeals examined the medical records and physician testimony in great detail, emphasizing the patient's preexisting medical problems. The court reduced the verdict to $56,000, agreeing with the pharmacy that it should not be liable for preexisting health problems that continued after the effects of the dispensing error were treated and resolved.

Wainwright v Walgreen Louisiana
No. 99-582 (December 8, 1999), 1999 La. App LEXIS 3469

The pharmacy admitted that it misfilled a prescription written for an 8-year-old child for 5 mg liquid *Prozac* with the 20 mg strength. The child was being treated for post-traumatic stress disorder arising out of a kitchen fire in his home a few months earlier. The father first administered a dose to the child on a Saturday morning. Within an hour, the child became agitated, abusive and belligerent. He cried and was anxious for several hours. On Sunday morning, the father gave the boy another dose of the medicine and he again exhibited such bizarre behavior that the parents could not dress him to attend church. While the father and his daughters were at church, the son became so agitated that he attempted to poke his mother with a fireplace poker. While she and another daughter attempted to hold the boy down, he picked up his mother and catapulted her over his head. The parents suspected the *Prozac* may be source of their son's behavioral difficulties and called the pharmacy that day. A manager looked on the computer screen, but not at the actual prescription. The pharmacist told the parents that the psychiatrist had ordered the 20 mg strength. The father took the boy to work with him on Monday morning, but he became so enraged that the father had the mother pick the boy up to take him home. That afternoon, the parents, in consultation with the prescriber, learned about the pharmacy error. The boy was

Wainwright v Walgreen Louisiana
No. 99-582 (December 8, 1999), 1999 La. App LEXIS 3469
...continued

admitted to the hospital for observation and treatment of the overdose. After being released and upon return to school, the boy's performance on tests plunged and he has had trouble learning even basic skills. After a jury trial, a verdict of $1,500 was entered for medical expenses, but nothing for general damages to cover physical or mental suffering. The parents appealed, claiming the medical damages were inadequate and that the jury erred in not awarding any pain or suffering award. The Court of Appeals amended the damage award, finding that the evidence clearly showed $7,372 in actual medical expenses. Although there does not appear to be any basis expressed in the opinion, the Court of Appeals also awarded $40,000 in general damages. A dissenting judge would have awarded only $2,500 for this "regrettable but minor episode."

Wainwright v Fontenot
Slip Op. No. 00C0492 (October 17, 2000), 2000 La. LEXIS 2727

The plaintiffs brought suit against a pharmacist and a pharmacy alleging that defendants' negligence in filling a prescription for an antidepressant for plaintiff child led to a worsened emotional state, and increasingly combative and aggressive behavior. On appeal, at issue was whether the jury erred as a matter of law when it declined to award general damages after finding defendants at fault for plaintiff child's injuries and awarding special damages for plaintiffs' medical expenses. The Supreme Court, in reversing the lower appellate court, found that there was no inconsistency in the awards made by the jury. The jury apparently did not believe that pain and suffering resulted from the injury that the defendants caused. It did believe that medical and incidental expenses were incurred as a result of the injury, and it awarded damages for those claims. The jury made its determinations, and it was not for the court, absent evidence of unfairness, mistake, partiality, prejudice, corruption, exorbitance, excessiveness, or a result that was offensive to the conscience and judgment of the court, to disturb them. The Court of Appeals was reversed. There was no inconsistency in the jury verdict in awarding damages to plaintiffs for medical expenses, but in refusing to award general damages.

The following is a list of court cases that are related to this topic.

Kollenberg v Ramirez, 339 NW.2d 176 (Mich. App. 1983).
Fultz v Peart, 494 N.E.2d 212 (Ill. App. 5 Dist. 1986).
LeJeune v Trend Services, Slip Op 96-550 (June 4, 1997, La. App.), 1997 La. App. LEXIS 1541.
Cackowski v Wal-Mart Stores, No 1981204 (January 21, 2000), SCt Ala, 2000 Ala. LEXIS 22.

Compensatory

Missouri ex rel Nixon v Stallknecht
No. 99CV212429, October 25, 1999, Jackson County Cir. Ct., Mo., (reported in Health Law Digest)

A pharmacist owned and operated 6 pharmacies in Texas and 2 internet sites. Without ever seeing a prescriber, users of the sites could order a prescription-only drug, sign a waiver of liability, pay a fee and, upon approval of a Texas physician who issued a prescription, obtain the drug. Missouri charged the pharmacist with practicing pharmacy in Missouri without

Missouri ex rel Nixon v Stallknecht
No. 99CV212429, October 25, 1999, Jackson County Cir. Ct., Mo., (reported in Health Law Digest)
...continued

a state-issued license after drugs purchased from the Web sites were shipped to Missouri residents. The Circuit Court entered a permanent injunction prohibiting the pharmacist from shipping drugs into Missouri without first obtaining the required licenses. The injunction also ordered the pharmacist to prominently post on all of his Web sites that the services were not available to Missouri residents. The court also ordered the pharmacist to refund all monies paid to the pharmacy by Missouri residents from the time the lawsuit was filed until the injunction took effect.

The following is a list of court cases that are related to this topic.

McLean v U.S., 613 F.2d 603 (5th Cir. 1980).
Hundley v Rite-Aid of South Carolina, No. 95-CP-46-406 (S.C. C.P. Ct., Richland, Oct. 10, 1996), as reported in *Pharmaceutical Litigation Reporter*, p.11934, Jan., 1997.
Mohoney v Nebraska Methodist Hospital, 251 Neb. 841: 560 N.W.2d 451 (S. Ct., 1997).
Hannigan v Sundby Pharmacy, 224 Wis. 2d 910; 593 N.W.2d 52 (Wis. App. 1999).
Payne v Galen Hospital, Slip Op. No. 01-97-00087-CV, Aug. 26, 1999, 1999 Tex. App. LEXIS 6367.

Punitive

Schroeder v Cox Medical Center
833 S.W.2d 441 (Mo.App. 1992)

ISSUE: Whether a hospital was liable for punitive damages when its pharmacist improperly compounded a dextrose solution that led to a patient's death.

FACTS: During an operation, the decedent's heart was stopped by a surgeon to permit arterial grafting. A cardioplegic solution was administered to the patient to protect the heart from damages while it was stopped. The solution had been prepared in the Medical Center's pharmacy by Glenda Adams, a pharmacist. When preparing the solution, Adams used a machine called a compounder, which was manufactured by Baxter-Travenol, a nonparty. A compounder is a type of pump used to measure and mix fluids. There was evidence that the compounder malfunctioned while Adams was preparing the solution, although she was unaware of the malfunction.

After the physician completed the bypass, he attempted to restart the decedent's heart, but was unable to do so. At the physician's request, the cardioplegic solution was tested immediately. The laboratory results showed that the solution did not contain the proper amount of dextrose, which caused the decedent's death.

RULING: The jury returned a verdict in favor of the plaintiff for compensatory damages of $92,453. The jury also returned a verdict assessing punitive damage "for aggravating circumstances" of $400,000. The jury verdict was upheld on appeal.

REASONING: In reviewing the evidence, the court decided that the negligent conduct upon which the punitive damage award was based included the failure of the pharmacist to observe the compounding of the cardioplegic solution. The recipe for the solution had been provided by the surgeon since the product was not available from commercial sources.

Schroeder v Cox Medical Center
833 S.W.2d 441 (Mo.App. 1992)
...continued

The testimony centered on the fact that, while there was an alarm on the compounder to alert the pharmacist of an improper mixing, the alarm never went off. The manufacturer's manual for the device included a warning, however, that compounding should be monitored at the beginning of a cycle and at certain intervals thereafter. It was not disputed that the pharmacist did not observe the process; in addition, there was testimony that the solution was not end-tested to ensure that the proper ingredients were included. The pharmacist testified that she had prepared the surgeon's recipe more than 150 times before she prepared the fatal solution. She further stated that the containers of water and dextrose solution were hung by someone else earlier in the day and that she simply started the compounder and turned away to do some other work. She stated that if it had been the policy of the pharmacy to watch the machine, she would have done so. She noted that if she had looked at the machine for just an instant during the dextrose cycle and seen that the machine was not turning, however, she would have known something was wrong...but still she contended that the machine should have sounded an alarm.

The pharmacy director testified that he did not require his pharmacist to observe the operation of the compounder like the manual required, but that the Medial Center now has a policy for the pharmacist to observe the compounder at least periodically during the cycle.

Expert witnesses testified that the pharmacy department was negligent because it failed to use ordinary care by not having adequate controls in the preparation of compounded solutions. The machine was designed to allow visual inspection, and it was alleged that pharmacists should not walk away from it during the preparation of solutions.

The Medical Center argued that the evidence was insufficient to support the $400,000 punitive award because the manufacturer's representative told the pharmacy employees that the compounder was extremely safe and reliable and it did not have to be watched constantly. The Medial Center claimed it had no knowledge that the compounder could malfunction without activating any of its alarms. In addition, the expert witnesses did not identify any hospital that required its pharmacists to watch a compounder while it was operating.

The court concluded that the evidence was sufficient to support an award for punitive damages. Ordinarily, punitive damages are not recoverable in actions for negligence because negligence, a mere omission of the duty to exercise due care, is the antithesis of willful or intentional conduct. An act of omission may manifest such reckless indifference to the rights of others, however, that the law will imply that an injury resulting from it was intentionally inflicted.

The solution was compounded for the specific purpose of using it to protect a human heart from damage while it was stopped. The potential of harm arising from miscompounding could not have been greater.

Winn Dixie of Montgomery v Colburn
709 So.2d 1222 (Ala. 1998)

ISSUE: May a pharmacy be held liable for compensatory and punitive damages when a pharmacist makes an improper generic interchange and the patient experiences an allergic reaction to an ingredient in the substituted drug?

Winn Dixie of Montgomery v Colburn
709 So.2d 1222 (Ala. 1998)
...continued

FACTS: The patient saw a physician for treatment of migraine headaches. Because she reported a history of allergic reactions to codeine, the physician prescribed *Sedapap* tablets (acetaminophen and butalbital, Mayrand). The prescription was signed over a line that indicated "product selection permitted," which, under state law, permits a pharmacist to dispense the generic equivalent of the prescribed brand name drug. The pharmacy where the patient went to have the prescription filled did not have *Sedapap* in stock. The pharmacist testified at trial that he looked in the store's computer drug profile and learned that *Fiorinal #3* is the same as *Sedapap*. In reality, however, these products are not generic equivalents. *Fiorinal #3* contains butalbital, aspirin, caffeine, and codeine. Within minutes of taking the substituted drug, the patient went into anaphylactic shock. She experienced chest tightness, her eyes watered, and her throat began to close to the extent that she could not speak and could barely breath. She indicated that she was terrified and thought she was going to die. Her husband put her into their car and began driving to a nearby hospital. But her condition deteriorated on the way, and the husband stopped to call an ambulance to meet them halfway because he thought they would not make it to the emergency room in time. When they met the ambulance, the patient was given intravenous epinephrine and *Benadryl*. Additional medications were administered in the emergency room to counteract the codeine allergy. She was allowed to return home that evening but continued to experience side effects including a severe headache. At trial, she testified that she is still afraid to take any prescription drugs. She also produced medical evidence that she would have died from the reaction had it not been for the swift action of her husband. An incident report completed by the pharmacist after the fact indicated that he substituted *Fiorinal #3* for *Sedapap* because it was the "closest formula" and that he felt certain that the physician would permit the substitution. The patient, however, submitted evidence that the pharmacist had called the physician's office and that the physician had her associate tell the pharmacist that the substitution was not permitted. Evidence also showed that the pharmacy did not correct its computer database showing *Sedapap* and *Fiorinal #3* to be generic equivalents for some time after it was made aware of the error.

HOLDING: On her claims against the pharmacy and pharmacist for wanton misconduct (which allow for punitive damages under state law) and negligence (permitting recovery for "compensatory" or actual and emotional damages), the jury awarded a general verdict of $130,000. The general verdict form, which both parties agreed to use, did not differentiate between punitive and compensatory damages. The Supreme Court of Alabama upheld the liability portion of the judgment against the defendants but remanded the damages award back to the trial court judge for findings as to whether the jury award is reasonable. The court's opinion suggests several reasons as to why the trial court judge should uphold the original judgment.

REASONING: The defendants appealed, claiming that the patient had not suffered any permanent injuries and that the damages award is excessive relative to the actual injuries. The Supreme Court of Alabama rejected these arguments. The court noted the evidence that the pharmacist had ignored the instruction from the physician's office to not substitute *Fiorinal #3* for *Sedapap*. This would support a finding of the pharmacist's reckless disregard for the patient's safety. Furthermore, the pharmacy's erroneous listing of the two drugs as generic equivalents in its computer database would support a finding of negligence. More telling, however, is the fact that the pharmacy did nothing to correct the computer error until well after it was discovered. This, noted the court, could increase the risk of harm to other patients and is sufficiently "reprehensible" to support a large punitive damages award. The court also indicated that the jury award of $130,000 is appropriate in light of the natural terror experienced by the patient who thought she was in jeopardy of imminent death.

Wal-Mart Stores v Robbins
707 So.2d 284 (Ala.Civ.App. 1997)

ISSUE: May a court award punitive damages against a pharmacy that erroneously types the strength of a drug into the computer and mistakenly refills the drug several times without checking the original prescription?

FACTS: In January 1993, a physician wrote a prescription for thyroid 1 grain to be taken by the patient once daily. He prescribed 100 tablets and 4 refills, intending that the patient have a 1-year supply of the medication. At the local pharmacy, the pharmacist misread the dose and dispensed 3 grain tablets. The erroneous dose was typed into the computer prescription database that was used to generate refills on 4 occasions over the following year until April 1994, when the mistake was detected. The patient had a preexisting history of depression for many years, including a hospitalization for depression and anxiety in 1992 (prior to the thyroid prescription error). While taking the excessive dose of thyroid, her symptoms were significantly worse. In 1995, after she stopped taking the excessive dose of thyroid, she was again hospitalized with a diagnosis of major depression with psychotic features. On admittance, she was considered suicidal and possibly even homicidal.

LAWSUIT: She filed a lawsuit claiming the pharmacy and pharmacist were negligent in filling the prescription with the wrong dose of the prescribed drug. The case was tried before a jury in May 1996. The pharmacist testified that the original prescription is kept in the pharmacy and is available for review at any time if she or any other pharmacist had any questions. She stated that she did not review the original prescription after it was initially dispensed because she did not have any questions. Instead, she used information from the computer screen to dispense the refills. After taking this testimony, the plaintiff's attorney asked the trial court judge for permission to amend the original complaint to allege the pharmacist was negligent and wanton for each refill that was dispensed. Over the objections of the defendants, the amendment was granted. The jury returned a verdict of $10,000 in actual damages and $190,000 in punitive damages.

HOLDING: After remanding the case back to the trial court for a determination as to whether the punitive damages were excessive or not, the Court of Appeals reaffirmed the verdict.

REASONING: The evidence showed that during the period when the pharmacy had filled her prescriptions, the pharmacy also misfilled prescriptions for 3 other patients, yielding a total of 14 prescription errors. This evidence was sufficient to permit the jury to award substantial punitive damages.

Cackowski v Wal-Mart Stores
No. 1981204 (January 21, 2000), SCt Ala, 2000 Ala. LEXIS 22

The plaintiff entered a weight-loss treatment program in 1995 and was given prescriptions for *Verelan* (antihypertensive), *Profast* and *Pondamin* (commonly called the fen/phen diet). At the pharmacy she agreed to have the prescriptions filled with generic drugs. The pharmacist misread the *Pondamin* prescription, thinking it called for prednisone and dispensed *Deltasone*. The pharmacist testified that because it was during the cold and flu season it would not be unusual for a doctor to prescribe a steroid, which often causes weight gain, along with a diet drug. The plaintiff took the steroid along with the other drugs for a 30-day period. When she returned to the pharmacy for refills, all of the prescriptions were correctly filled. Within days after this, she began to experience blurred vision and lethargy. After consult-

Cackowski v Wal-Mart Stores
No. 1981204 (January 21, 2000), SCt Ala, 2000 Ala. LEXIS 22
...continued

ing with her physician, the pharmacy error was detected. She claims to have suffered several physical and mental ailments as a result of the mistake. She sued the pharmacy and the pharmacist for negligence and wantonness. A claim of wanton disregard for the plaintiff's well-being would, if proven, entitle the plaintiff to seek punitive damages. The pharmacy's expert witnesses contradicted the plaintiff's experts as to causation and the extent of damages suffered. A state statute requires that malpractice claims against "health care providers" be proven by substantial evidence. The trial court judge ruled that pharmacists are health care providers and therefore come within the substantial evidence mandate. The judge ruled that the plaintiff had failed to submit substantial evidence that the pharmacy or pharmacist had acted with wanton disregard and dismissed the claims. The plaintiff voluntarily dismissed the pharmacist. After a jury trial against the pharmacy on the negligence claim, the jury returned a verdict in favor of the pharmacy. The plaintiffs appealed to the state's Supreme Court. This court upheld the finding that a pharmacist is a health care provider because the dispensing of drugs is an integral part of health care services. The court also upheld dismissal of the wantonness claim. The pharmacist's mistake in reading the prescription does not rise to the level of reckless disregard necessary to sustain a wantonness claim. The jury verdict on the negligence claim against the pharmacy was reversed because the jury instructions on the burden of proof were confusing.

Nelms v Walgreen Co.
Slip Op. No. 02A01805CV00137, July 7, 1999, 1999 Tenn. App. LEXIS 437

Nelms appealed a trial court's decision to deny his request for punitive damages. The pharmacist filled Nelms' prescription for *Paxil*, a drug commonly used to treat depression. Two weeks later, Nelms returned to Walgreens to have the prescription refilled. This time the pills looked different than in the first prescription. Nelms returned to Walgreens and questioned the pharmacist. The pharmacist discovered that the first prescription contained *Tagamet* instead of *Paxil*. The pharmacist on duty made a mistake in filling Nelms' original prescription. Nelms suffered a low platelet count and minor injuries. As a result, Nelms sued Walgreens alleging negligent filling of the *Paxil* prescription. Nelms sought compensatory and punitive damages. The trial court awarded $25,000 in compensatory damages but denied Nelms' request for punitive damages. On appeal, Nelms alleged that a Walgreens pharmacy technician filled and dispensed the *Paxil* prescription without obtaining the approval of a pharmacist on duty. Nelms contended that he was entitled to an award of punitive damages. The court of appeals disagreed, noting that courts award punitive damages only in the most egregious cases, ie, cases of intentional, fraudulent, malicious, or reckless conduct. The court of appeals concluded that Nelms failed to present clear and convincing evidence that Walgreens engaged in fraudulent conduct with respect to filling Nelms' prescription. The court of appeals found that although a pharmacy technician might have filled Nelms' prescription without authorization, there was an equal possibility that a pharmacist filled the prescription and failed to make the proper recording. The court of appeals held that while the evidence clearly supported a claim of ordinary negligence, the evidence did not support a finding that Walgreens engaged in reckless conduct such as to constitute a gross deviation from the required standard of care. Therefore, the court of appeals affirmed the denial of punitive damages

Hundley v Rite-Aid of South Carolina
No 3126 (February 28, 2000), SC App, 2000 S C App LEXIS 34

A physician diagnosed a 7 year-old child with attention deficit hyperactivity disorder and pre-scribed *Ritalin* on February 20, 1995. The child's mother took the prescription to the local Rite-Aid pharmacy. The pharmacist on duty was nearing the end of a 12 hour work day in a 60 hour work week. He worked this schedule on a weekly basis without the assistance of any other pharmacists. He was 65 years old and his wife had died just 1 month earlier. After he filled the prescription, the mother took the medication home. The next morning she gave her daughter the first tablet. She also took several tablets to the child's school and asked the officials there to administer 1 tablet each day at 11:30 AM. Doing as instructed, the child received a second tablet at the specified time. The child suffered a seizure at 2:30 PM. She was taken to a hospital by ambulance, where she was diagnosed as suffering from a hypoglycemic coma. It was discovered that the pharmacist filled the prescription *Glynase* 6 mg tablets instead of the prescribed *Ritalin*. This is a high dose of *Glynase* even for an adult. *Glynase* is not approved for use in children at any dose. While the child was in the coma, her blood sugar level fell so severely that she experienced significant damage to the brain cells in the cerebral cortex. Although apparently healthy before this incident, her intelligence quotient dropped 30 points to an average of 69. She has been diagnosed with permanent mental retardation that will require constant medical supervision.

The parents sued the pharmacist individually and his employer, Rite-Aid. They sought com-pensation for the child's own actual damages and well as their pain and suffering. Prior to the trial, held in October 1996, the parents amended the complaint to allege that the phar-macy was negligent in the hiring, retention and supervising of the pharmacist. Rite-Aid aggressively defended against discovery attempts by plaintiffs. It initially claimed that com-puter data and other records required under state law could not be located or retrieved. The pharmacy denied that any *Glynase* 6 mg was dispensed from this particular store for a 3-month period preceding this incident. After refusing to produce other evidence at scheduled times, the trial court judge ordered the pharmacy comply with discovery requests. The pharmacy again refused to cooperate and claimed this time that the original prescription for *Ritalin* had disappeared. Displaying an obvious level of disgust for what he considered dilatory behav-ior, the judge ordered that the next answers be certified by a senior corporate officer.

Amazingly, the missing computer records were located. Contrary to prior sworn testimony, the records showed that *Glynase* had been dispensed from the store on the same day that the prescription for *Ritalin* was presented. These computer records showed that the pharmacist filled a *Glynase* prescription for exactly the number of tablets that the mother picked up when she thought the medication was *Ritalin*. Although several prescriptions were produced for the day in question, the original *Ritalin* and *Glynase* prescriptions were, according to the Court, "mysteriously missing." These revelations occurred just 8 weeks before trial. Dur-ing this same time frame, the plaintiffs gave notice that they wanted to take the deposi-tions of five employees of the pharmacy, including its treasurer. On the date scheduled for the depositions, without any prior notice, the pharmacy informed attorneys for the plaintiffs that no witnesses would be attending. The excuse was that most of the witnesses no longer worked for the corporation and the treasurer refused to travel from the headquarters in Pennsylvania to South Carolina. The pharmacy continued to disobey discovery orders. It never answered any questions about the relationship between the South Carolina corpora-tion that owned the particular store and the parent corporation. It also failed to answer any questions about its financial conditions. The trial court judge ruled during a motion just before trial that the pharmacy's "conduct in this matter was intentional and in bad faith." The judge found that this behavior cost the plaintiffs unnecessary delay and expense. He ordered the pharmacy to pay $40,000 in pretrial attorney fees and a fine of $10,000 pay-able to the Court. He also ruled that he would instruct the jury to disregard the pharmacy's ability to pay any punitive damages if they found punitive damages in order because the pharmacy would not respond to questions about its financial affairs. At the conclusion of the

Hundley v Rite-Aid of South Carolina
No 3126 (February 28, 2000), SC App, 2000 S C App LEXIS 34
...continued

trial, the jury returned a verdict against the pharmacist individually and against the pharmacy for $5 million in actual damages for the child and $20,000 for her parents. In addition, it returned a punitive damages verdict against the pharmacy, but not the pharmacist, in the amount of $10 million for the child and $1 million for the parents. Both the pharmacist and the pharmacy appealed. (At the time of this writing, the verdict together with interest, attorney fees and discovery sanctions is now valued at over $24 million).

The entire verdict was upheld by the South Carolina Court of Appeals. While several issues were addressed, the most significant to pharmacists and pharmacy owners centers on the question of the pharmacist's competence and the pharmacy's lack of corrective action. The defendants claimed that the punitive damages awards should be reversed because there was no clear and convincing evidence of gross negligence in the misfiling of the *Ritalin* prescription. The Court of Appeals noted that this argument misses the point because the allegation was made that the pharmacy was grossly negligent in the retention and supervision of the pharmacist. The Court stated that the pharmacy required or allowed the 65 year old pharmacist to work 12 hour days and 60 hour weeks just 1 month after he suffered the tragic loss of his wife. The pharmacy did not make any other pharmacists available to relieve the pharmacist. The pharmacist had a history of misfiling other prescriptions, but the corporation did nothing about it. The pharmacist was known not to keep up with required record-keeping activities and he had been cited by the state for violating various regulations. A memo in his personnel file indicated that a supervisor took 14 hours to clean up the pharmacy where this pharmacist worked. The memo also indicates that the supervisor found many other violations including multiple bottles of the same drug open and medication vials on the counters without caps. The Court noted that the pharmacy has no policies or procedures designed to ensure the competencies of its pharmacists. Evidence showed that the pharmacy believes a pharmacist is fit to work as long as the state pharmacist license is maintained. The pharmacy has no policies, procedures, manuals or directives dealing with the storage or handling of medications or the filling and labeling of prescriptions. Instead, these matters are left up to the discretion of the individual pharmacist. These factors, stated the Court, are all ample evidence for the jury to conclude that the pharmacy was reckless in its retention and supervision of the pharmacist.

Cross Reference: See Ex Parte Rite-Aid in the Discovery section, infra, with regard to discovery issues in the negligent retention and supervision of a pharmacist.

🔨 🔨 🔨

McClure v Walgreen
No 100/98-1821 (July 8, 2000), SCt Iowa, 2000 Iowa Sup LEXIS 125

Plaintiff was diagnosed with pancreatic cancer in 1995. She underwent radical surgery to remove her stomach, parts of her small intestine and her pancreas. In 1997, after undergoing further surgery, her physician prescribed fluorouracil chemotherapy and radiation. Upon release from this hospitalization, she had prescriptions for *Diflucan*, *Kytril* and *Pepcid* taken to the defendant pharmacy. The prescription for *Pepcid* 20 mg was erroneously filled with *Paxil* 20 mg. The normal starting dose for *Paxil* is 10 mg. She consumed the *Paxil* as directed, twice daily, for approximately 1 month. During this time she exhibited increased irritability, weakness, confusion and inattention to hygiene. Approximately 2 weeks after the prescription was erroneously filled, and without knowing about the error, her physician prescribed *Zoloft* to address the signs of depression displayed by the patient. However, within 5 days, the doctor stopped the *Zoloft* because the patient presented with very low blood pres-

McClure v Walgreen
No 100/98-1821 (July 8, 2000), SCt Iowa, 2000 Iowa Sup LEXIS 125
...continued

sure. A few days later, she got up to go to the bathroom when she fell, causing her to frac-
ture her leg and foot. Testimony indicated that her loss of equilibrium was due to the *Paxil*.
She was admitted to a nursing home. Her daughter brought all of her medications from home
and the nurses continued to administer them, including the *Paxil*. The error was discovered by a nurse 5 days after admission to the nursing home. Her physician discontinued the
Paxil immediately upon learning of the error. When her daughter told the pharmacy about
the mistake, the pharmacy indicated that it would fill out an incident report. No one at the
pharmacy discussed any of the side effects associated with *Paxil* or the dangers of abrupt
withdrawal. Ten days after the error was discovered, the patient was to be released from the
nursing home. However, she fell causing injuries to her head, back and pelvis. Testimony
indicated this fall was caused by abrupt withdrawal of the *Paxil*. She sued both the pharmacy and the pharmacist. The jury returned a general damages verdict of $100,000 against
both defendants and $150,000 in punitive damages against Walgreen only. Walgreen appealed
the punitive damage award claiming there was insufficient evidence to submit the claim to
the jury. Walgreen asserted that this was a simple mistake, not willful and wanton disregard for another's safety. It also disputed the jury instructions on punitive damages and challenged evidentiary rulings allowing the submission of incidence reports and licensee
disciplinary proceedings associated with this incident. The Court found that there was
enough evidence to submit the punitive damages question to the jury. The pharmacist who
made the error was on duty alone during the noon rush hour when the mistake occurred.
The pharmacist admitted that she had asked for extra technicians to help her during busy
times. The evidence showed that during a preceding three year period, 34 mistakes of a
similar nature occurred at this pharmacy. All involved dispensing the wrong drug with the
same first alphabetical letter as the prescribed drug. The Supreme Court of Iowa concluded
that the jury could have reasoned from this evidence that Walgreen knew it had a problem
and did not take adequate steps to correct it. The Court stated that Walgreen's conduct was
"particularly egregious" because it failed to warn the plaintiff or her physicians about the
adverse consequences of using *Paxil* or dangers associated with its abrupt withdrawal. Walgreen knew of the error 12 days before the plaintiff fell in the nursing home, yet, in violation of its own written policy manual, neglected to tell the plaintiff, her family or her
physicians what signs or symptoms should be watched for. A jury could have concluded that
warnings of this type could have prevented the last fall. Failing to take action after it
learned of the error could be taken as evidence of obvious indifference in support of the punitive damage award. Therefore the trial court did not err in submitting the punitive damages question to the jury. There was also no error in the jury instruction that indicated
"punitive damages are intended to punish the defendant ... and protect the public by deter-
ring the defendant and others from doing such wrong in the future. Nor did the trial court
err in admitting evidence of Walgreen's financial worth for purposes of calculating the punitive damage award. Likewise, the trial court correctly admitted the reports of 34 other incidents involving misfilled prescriptions as evidence of the existence of a dangerous condition.
The fact that 30 of the incidents did not involve the pharmacist that misfilled this prescription is not relevant to the claim for punitive damages against Walgreen; these incident
reports are evidence that Walgreen knew there was a problem at this pharmacy and did not
take any corrective action. The trial court did commit reversible error in admitting evidence regarding the Board of Pharmacy investigation and administrative proceedings about
this incident. The trial court erroneously admitted a stipulation and consent order agreed
to by the state and Walgreen. The consent order specifically stated that the parties entered
into it for the purpose of settling the charges without hearing and that Walgreen did not
admit the charges were true or that it was guilty of any wrongdoing. The charges in the Board
of Pharmacy complaint "convey an atmosphere of criminality" against Walgreen and did
carry the threat of criminal penalties. This evidence was not probative and its admission

McClure v Walgreen
No 100/98-1821 (July 8, 2000), SCt Iowa, 2000 Iowa Sup LEXIS 125
...continued

caused harm to Walgreen's rights. For this reason, the Supreme Court of Iowa remanded the case for retrial only on the issue of punitive damages against Walgreen. The compensatory damages award against both the pharmacist and Walgreen were affirmed. One judge dissented finding there was insufficient evidence of willful misconduct on the part of Walgreen to submit the issue of punitive damages to a jury. This judge reasoned that Walgreen justifiably relied on the plaintiff's treating physician to render appropriate care after the error was discovered. This judge noted the fact that the pharmacy took no action when it learned of the mistake may be "egregious conduct" but believed the lack of action does not amount to willful or wanton misconduct where the pharmacy could reasonably assume that the physician would take whatever steps were necessary to protect the patient.

The following is a list of court cases that are related to this topic.

Boeck v Katz Drug Co., 127 P.2d 506 (Kan. 1942).
Burke v Bean, 363 S.W.2d 366 (Texas, 1962).
Orzel v Scott Drug Company, 537 N.W. 2d 208 (Mich. 1995).

Bystander Damages

Huggins v Longs Drug Stores
11 Cal.App. 4th 550 (1992), depublished by 845 P.2d 1085 (Cal. 1993)

ISSUE: Whether the parents of a child have the right to sue a pharmacist for negligent infliction of emotional distress when the pharmacist negligently dispenses a prescription resulting in an overdose to the child.

FACTS: The plaintiff's pediatrician prescribed *Ceclor* for an ear infection in their 2-month-old-child. One day after administering the first dose, the mother arrived home and noticed that the child was "out of it," was unresponsive and appeared to be in a very deep sleep. Later that day, the plaintiffs received a call from the child's grandmother, who had learned that there had been a dispensing error and that the child had received an overdose. The wife called her husband, leaving word of the mistake, and quickly took the child back to the pediatrician.

The child's legal action was resolved by arbitration, but the parents sued the defendant pharmacy for the negligent infliction of emotional distress. The mother's deposition stated that she observed her child's lethargy and suspected the medication caused it. The pharmacist's mistake had caused her to make her own son ill when she administered the medication, and that this shocked and grieved her. She stated that she still worries about the future effects of the overdose. The father's declaration showed that his distress occurred after he learned that his son had received an overdose.

The dispensing pharmacist stated that the dosage should have been 1/2 teaspoon or 2 1/2 cc's rather than 2 1/2 teaspoons on the prescription label.

RULING: The trial court dismissed the lawsuit, concluding that the parents could not recover under a theory of negligent infliction of emotional distress because there was no contemporaneous connection between the negligent act and the injury. The appellate court reversed the trial court's summary judgment in favor of the pharmacy. The case was returned to the

Huggins v Longs Drug Stores
11 Cal.App. 4th 550 (1992), depublished by 845 P.2d 1085 (Cal. 1993)
...continued

trial court to determine whether the pharmacist knew or should have known that the medication was going to be administered to an infant according to his instructions.

REASONING: The appellate court considered two theories to determine whether the parents were entitled to recover damages for the negligent infliction of emotional distress. It was noted that this area of law has undergone significant development in the past 25 years. Among the guidelines established by the California courts in previous cases was whether or not the shock resulted from a direct emotional impact from the sensory and contemporaneous observance of the accident, as contrasted with learning of the accident from others after its occurrence.

In the present case, the depositions showed that the parents did not suffer emotional distress until they learned of the overdose from third parties. The mother stated that she suspected or thought it might have been medication that caused the child to be drowsy or sleepy. The court noted that while it may be inferred that the mother thought the medication was a factor in the child's drowsiness, there was no known basis for such an inference.

The court noted that the plaintiff must show a contemporaneous awareness of the connection between negligent conduct and the resulting injury or else the case could not be distinguished from any standard medical malpractice case in which the injury is witnessed by the plaintiff, but the plaintiff does not see or comprehend the actual injury-causing event. In this case, it was abundantly clear that the facts did not support the parents' contemporaneous bystander claims.

As an alternative theory, the parents asked for recovery for negligent infliction of emotional distress because they were the direct victims of the act. Previous California case law relied on forseeability that serious emotional distress might result. Damages are recoverable when they result from the breach of duty owed the plaintiff and which arises out of the relationship between the two parties. The distinction between bystander and direct victim cases is found in the source of the duty owed by the defendant to the plaintiff. The parents here contend that the pharmacist, by providing the drug and dosage, assumed a duty to them because he knew or should have known they would have to administer the prescription to their infant son and would do so in accordance with the directions on the prescription label.

The court agreed. The action of the pharmacist in providing the incorrect dosage, which under the circumstances made it necessary for the parents to administer the medication, would constitute negligence directed at the caregiver. The court found that it would be ludicrous to argue that a 2-month-old infant could either take the medication without help or could comprehend the misdirection of the dosage labeling. Therefore, under the circumstances, the negligent giving of instructions to the parents was by its very nature, directed at the parents rather than the infant and gave rise to a cause of action for negligent infliction of emotional distress. The parent's injuries were not merely derivative of the child's injuries, but flow from their role as participants in this treatment.

Huggins v Longs Drug Stores California, Inc.
862 P.2d 148 (Cal. 1993)

ISSUE: Whether a pharmacy is guilty of the negligent infliction of emotional distress to the parents of a child who had been given the wrong prescription medication.

FACTS: Barbie Huggins took her 2-month-old son to a physician for treatment for an ear infection. The physician prescribed *Ceclor*, to be administered every 8 hours in 2.5 cc doses. Mrs. Huggins had the prescription filled at Longs Drug Store, but the pharmacist mistakenly dispensed the prescription with directions for administering the medication in doses of 2 1/2 teaspoonfuls (5 times the amount prescribed by the physician). The infant was administered doses of this excessive amount every 8 hours by either his mother or by daycare personnel.

That same day, Mrs. Huggins noticed that the child was lethargic and unresponsive. Soon thereafter, she received a telephone call from her mother reporting that another pharmacy, to which the prescription had been transferred, had discovered the dosage error. Mrs. Huggins allegedly became shocked, grieved, worried, and emotionally distressed. The father became similarly distressed when he was summoned home from work and told of the mistake.

RULING: The California Court of Appeals concluded that a pharmacist automatically assumes a duty of care toward a patient's caregivers simply by dispensing a prescription with actual or constructive knowledge that the patient is an infant or is otherwise helpless. The California Supreme Court overruled this decision.

REASONING: The Supreme Court noted that pharmacy is a dynamic patient-oriented health service and that pharmacists spend substantial amounts of time advising patients about the proper use of a prescribed drug. However, it contended that none of these duties impose any legal responsibility upon pharmacists for the emotional well-being of a patient's parents, even if the pharmacist knows the patient is an infant. The imposition of regulations requiring pharmacists to provide oral consultation about prescription drugs has nothing to do with an agent's personal welfare. The purpose is simply to assure that the pharmacist's advice is put to good use for the benefit of the patient. The plaintiffs sought to differentiate their claims by stressing that they were emotionally distressed, not merely by observation of the injury, but by their roles as the "unwitting agents of destruction." The court noted that the same comments would apply to practically all outpatient care of an infant. If a child is seriously injured by erroneous medical treatment caused by professional negligence, the parent is practically certain to suffer correspondingly serious emotional distress. The court could not agree that such involvement would warrant its establishing a new legal right of recovery for intangible injury.

In reversing the Court of Appeals decision, the Supreme Court held that the duty the lower court would impose on pharmacists would inevitably enlarge the potential liabilities of practically all providers of medical goods and services obtained by parents solely for the treatment of their children, or by other caregivers solely for the treatment of dependent family members. All of those providers, unlike the providers of care to competent adult patients, would be exposed to new claims of emotional distress allegedly incurred in administering the prescribed medication or treatment of the patient. That expansion of potential liability not only would increase medical malpractice insurance costs, but also would tend to inject undesirable self-protective reservations impairing the provision of optimal care to the patient.

Because the parents were not the patients to whom the pharmacy dispensed the prescribed medication, the court held that they could not recover as direct victims of the defendant's negligence.

Polio v Derby Center CVS
Slip Op. No. CV95-0372045, 1996 Conn. Super. LEXIS 2343, Sept. 4, 1996

In the course of treating their child's medical condition, the parents learned that the medication contained in the child's prescription vial was not the medication that had been prescribed. The parents returned to the pharmacy where the prescription had been filled and asked the pharmacist to identify it. The pharmacist refused to provide any information or render any other assistance even after being shown convincing evidence that a mistake occurred. The parents filed a lawsuit on behalf of their son seeking damages for his injuries. The parents also sought recovery for their own emotional distress and monies they spent in treating their son's illness. The defendant pharmacy sought dismissal of the parents' claims, alleging that they did not meet the state law requirements for bystander liability or for recovery of personal expenditures. In addressing the conditions that must be met to recover under this theory, the court suggested that the parents' observation of their child's trauma following receipt of a wrong drug is not the kind of sudden accident that bystander liability is meant to address. If this is true, the parents' theory of recovery against the pharmacist would have to fail. The court did not, however, dismiss the parents' claims. Instead, it closely reviewed that complaint and concluded that the parents were not even claiming recovery under a bystander theory of liability. Instead, the complaint set forth a cause of action for intentional or unintentional infliction of emotional distress for events that occurred after the dispensing error was made. In other words, this claim is not for distress caused by witnessing the child's injuries. Rather, it is for distress caused by the pharmacist's refusal to respond to requests for help after the mistake was discovered. In specific, this claim focused on the pharmacist's failure to identify the drug wrongly dispensed when asked or otherwise help the parents in their attempts to discover what had happened. Under the circumstances presented, the court determined that it would be improper to dismiss the parents' emotional distress claims. The court reached the same conclusion with respect to the parents' claims for out-of-pocket expenditures on the child's care.

Crippens v Sav On Drug Stores
961 P.2d 761 (Nev. 1998)

ISSUE: May a close relative and caregiver of a patient recover damages from a pharmacist who commits malpractice that harms the patient?

FACTS: In this case, the plaintiff is the daughter and the primary caregiver of the patient. She claims damages in her own right for having witnessed her mother's adverse effects from the administration of prescription medication that the defendant pharmacy negligently dispensed. The plaintiff obtained her mother's medication from a pharmacist who filled the prescription with the wrong drug. After administering the drug to her mother over a period of time, the plaintiff saw her mother become incoherent, experience hypoglycemic shock, and become permanently disabled.

HOLDING: A majority number of the judges sitting on the State Supreme Court voted to reverse the summary judgment that had been entered by the trial court in favor of the pharmacy. The case is remanded back for a trial on the plaintiff's claims. One dissenting judge voted to uphold the judgment of dismissal.

REASONING: In the vast majority of cases, the only parties allowed to recover damages from a negligent defendant are those who have either been directly harmed or those who are representing the injured party. People who experience indirect harm usually are not allowed to sue. A fairly narrow exception is made under the doctrine of "bystander liability." A

Crippens v Sav On Drug Stores
961 P.2d 761 (Nev. 1998)
...continued

bystander is someone who witnesses another person become injured. Sometimes bystanders sue defendants for the emotional harm they suffer from witnessing the injury suffered by the other person. However, in order to be successful, the bystander plaintiff must be closely related to the victim of an accident, be located near the scene of the accident, and suffer a shock resulting from direct emotional impact stemming from the sensory and contemporaneous observance of the accident. According to the majority view, it is not the precise position of the plaintiff or what the plaintiff saw that determines the bystander's right to recover damages. Instead, the overall circumstances must be examined to determine whether the harm to the plaintiff was reasonably foreseeable. Under the law of the state where this case was tried, foreseeability is the cornerstone test for negligent infliction of emotional distress.

In this case, a daughter purchased prescription medication for her mother. The daughter then initiated and continued administration until her mother was rendered comatose. The majority opinion states that "because of the pharmacist's negligence, the daughter poisoned her mother." Therefore, it is legally foreseeable that the drug would significantly harm the actual patient and that a close relative would continue administration until the ultimate catastrophic effect was realized.

It should be noted that the majority opinion does not mean that the plaintiff will automatically be successful at trial. She will still have to prove her damages and that the emotional distress that she did suffer was caused by the pharmacist's negligence. The jury will determine those issues. It is also noteworthy that the court considered and rejected the plaintiff's claim that she is entitled to recover under a state statute, NRS 639.266, that requires pharmacists to "communicate" certain data relating to the use of dispensed drugs. The court noted that this statute is intended to protect users of drugs and does not relate directly or indirectly to other persons who might observe the adverse effects of a negligently dispensed drug. In this case the plaintiff's claim for emotional distress does not relate to the manner in which the drug was administered, but rather, to the negligent dispensing of the wrong drug.

One judge wrote a dissenting opinion that stands in stark contrast to that of the majority. This judge's view of the bystander liability doctrine is probably more in line with most of the other states that have considered these questions. The judge wrote that a daughter's witnessing of the slowly emerging, not accidental effects, of wrongly prescribed medication should not be the basis for a negligently inflicted emotional distress tort action. This judge would find that the elements of bystander liability are not present because there was no "contemporaneous observance" of an "accident." The plaintiff cannot properly be described as a "bystander," nor can it be said that she suffered a "shock" which resulted from a "direct emotional impact." The judge's dissenting opinion follows:

> Allowing those who are emotionally impacted by the physical injuries of others to recover for their emotional distress under ordinary negligence principles alone would encourage an unwarranted proliferation of this special kind of tort litigation. Reliance on foreseeability of injury alone in finding a duty, and thus a right to recover, is not adequate when the damages sought are for an intangible injury. In order to avoid limitless liability out of all proportion to the degree of a defendant's negligence, and against which it is impossible to insure without imposing unacceptable costs on those among whom the risk is spread, the right to recover for negligently caused emotional distress must be limited. Although it is probably safe to say that none of the elements of this tort (other than the close relationship of the mother and daughter) can

Crippens v Sav On Drug Stores
961 P.2d 761 (Nev. 1998)
...continued

be said to be present here, the negligently treated mother was not the victim of an "accident." Most of these kinds of cases truly do involve an "accident" (for example, cases in which mothers witness serious injuries being inflicted on their children, thus suffering a "direct emotional impact" and "shock" in the "observance" of the accident). This pattern does not fit the plaintiff's case. An "accident" means an unexpected or unforeseen event happening suddenly and violently, with or without human fault, and producing at the time objective symptoms of an injury. There was no "accident" here: Ms. Crippens did not observe an accident, and she did not suffer a "shock" from observing an accident. It cannot be argued that the mother's progressive mental deterioration can be called an "accident." Certainly, the mother's failing condition did not occur "suddenly and violently," and the negligent acts (dispensing the wrong drug) did not cause at the time objective symptoms of an injury. The glove just does not fit. This is clearly not a case of negligently inflicted emotional injury: The trial judge was correct in granting summary judgment to Sav On.

The following is a list of court cases that are related to this topic.

Hundley v Rite-Aid of South Carolina, No. 95-CP-46-406 (S.C. C.P. Ct., Richland, Oct. 10, 1996), as reported in *Pharmaceutical Litigation Reporter*, p. 11934, Jan., 1997.

Other Forms of Recovery

The following is a list of court cases that are related to this topic.

Krug v Sterling Drug, Inc., 416 S.W.2d 143 (Mo. 1967).
DeCordova v State of Colorado, 878 P.2d 73 (Colo. App. 1994).
Dunn and Ruiz v The Department of Veterans Affairs, No. 95-3732, 1996 U.S. App. LEXIS (Fed. Cir.) Dec. 11, 1996

Apportionment of Damages

Brown v Glaxo
Slip Op. No. 99CA1531 (November 15, 2000), 2000 La. App. LEXIS 2942

Plaintiffs sued for damages to Mrs. Brown caused by her use of the drug *Imitrex*. By the time of trial, the remaining named defendants were Mrs. Brown's doctor and the drug manufacturer. Glaxo asserted that Mr. Brown, Mrs. Brown, and Dr. Girod were at fault. In this adequacy of warning case, the jury found that the warning was inadequate and held in favor of plaintiffs. Glaxo appealed. For the relief of migraine headaches, Dr. Girod prescribed *Imitrex* injections for his patient, Mrs. Brown, in April 1993. Before the drug was prescribed, Mrs. Brown had been seen by a cardiologist in 1992. He determined that she had no coronary artery disease. Mrs. Brown's husband, the chief pharmacist at a Baton Rouge pharmacy, filled the *Imitrex* prescription. Dr. Girod and Mr. Brown both received information or "details" on *Imitrex* from a Glaxo salesman. During the presentation, the salesman reviewed promotional materials. He also provided his customers with the package insert for doctors and the consumer information insert. The *Imitrex* injections provided significant relief for Mrs. Brown's headaches. However, by September 1993, Mrs. Brown noted that the chest pains she often experienced after taking *Imitrex* were increasing in severity. She had also begun vomiting after taking the *Imitrex*. In a journal entry dated September 25, 1993, Mrs. Brown

Brown v Glaxo
Slip Op. No. 99CA1531 (November 15, 2000), 2000 La. App. LEXIS 2942
...continued

wrote that she was "getting scared of *Imitrex* for first time ever." In the spring of 1994, Mrs. Brown reported a more severe reaction from *Imitrex* to her husband. He suggested that she tell her doctor. In February 1994, a woman in Kansas City, Missouri, died from a cardiac arrest shortly after taking *Imitrex*. This incident occurred in the prescribing physician's office. Soon afterward, Glaxo became aware that the death was *Imitrex*-related. However, Glaxo did not issue a new warning, or alert doctors to an actual drug *Imitrex*-related death until August 1994. On August 30, 1994, prior to the receipt of the new Glaxo warning in Baton Rouge, Mrs. Brown had a severe reaction shortly after taking an *Imitrex* injection. The paramedic on the scene recorded the chief problem as cardiac arrest secondary to anaphylaxis. She was taken by ambulance to a local hospital where she remained in a vegetative state until her death on June 20, 1996. Dr. Girod opined that the *Imitrex* caused the following medical problems: Her cardiac arrest, her brain damage from lack of oxygen, and her ultimate death. The jury found that the *Imitrex* was unreasonably dangerous from a reasonably anticipated use of the product; as of August 30, 1994, the warning was inadequate; the inadequate warning was the cause of the damages; Dr. Girod was not negligent or liable; Mrs. Brown was negligent, but not liable because her negligence did not cause "her adverse event of August 30, 1994"; and Mr. Brown was also negligent, but not liable because his negligence was not a cause of the "adverse event." One hundred percent of the fault was attributed to Glaxo. The jury awarded damages to plaintiffs, which included $650,000 for Mrs. Brown's loss of enjoyment of life. Other damages were also awarded to Mr. Brown for medical expenses and the loss of his wife, and to the Browns' son for his mental anguish and the loss of his mother. On appeal, the verdict was affirmed in part and reversed in part. The Court of Appeals agreed that the jury properly concluded that Glaxo should be held liable because its local representative induced both the husband-pharmacist and treating physician to not take the written warnings seriously. However, The Court found that the jury was manifestly wrong in determining the patient's failure to inform her physician about her chest pains was not a contributing cause of her death. The Court of Appeals, without any discussion, reduced the verdict by 30% to account for the patient's comparative negligence.

Fultz v Peart
494 N.E.2d 212 (Ill. App. 5 Dist. 1986)

ISSUE: Whether a pharmacy and a physician were jointly liable to a diabetic patient who alleged that the pharmacy negligently dispensed the wrong medication and that the physician provided substandard medical care.

FACTS: The plaintiff, Eugene Fultz, was a diabetic whose disease had been under control for a number of years with the use of 5 *Dymelor* tablets a day. In June 1980, the plaintiff's wife went to Marco Pharmacy to obtain a refill of her husband's *Dymelor* prescription. Unfortunately, the pharmacist mistakenly dispensed *Aldomet* tablets which the court noted were "a slightly different color, shape and size from *Dymelor* tablets." Fultz ingested the medication dispensed to him, and he unknowingly was not producing sufficient insulin to maintain control of his diabetes. He was further receiving an *Aldomet* dosage greater than the maximum recommended dosage for an individual suffering from high blood pressure.

One day later Fultz began experiencing chills, shakes, drowsiness and a decrease in appetite. When Fultz contacted his physician, he was informed that the doctor was on vacation and he was referred to another doctor in the clinic. During the office visit, Fultz's blood

Fultz v Peart
494 N.E.2d 212 (Ill. App. 5 Dist. 1986)
...continued

pressure was 100/60 which was low for a man of his age, but still within the normal range. He also had a very fast pulse rate and high blood sugar. The physician diagnosed the plaintiff as suffering from diabetes out of control with a fever of unknown origin. Neither the physician nor Fultz was aware that the plaintiff was receiving the wrong medication.

Fultz was admitted to the hospital where additional tests were performed. Shortly thereafter, the plaintiff's wife realized the development of his symptoms coincided with the recent refill of his *Dymelor* prescription. She further recalled that her husband mentioned that the tablets were a slightly different shape from his previous prescription. Suspecting the possibility of a medication error, she took some of the tablets to the hospital where the physician identified them as *Aldomet* and not *Dymelor*. A week later, Fultz suffered a stroke resulting in permanent loss of function to his right side.

Fultz brought suit against both the pharmacy and the physician claiming that the negligently filled prescription and substandard medical care were the proximate cause of his stroke. He alleged that, if the defendant pharmacy had properly refilled the prescription, he would not have suffered the stroke and that if the defendant physician had properly treated him with IV fluids, he would not have suffered the stroke either.

RULING: The jury found both of the defendants guilty of negligence and assessed damages of $1,689,641 against the defendant pharmacy. This verdict was reduced by 15% for contributory negligence on the part of the plaintiff. An additional $1,689,641 was assessed against the defendant physician and clinic. The appellate court concluded that the jury really intended to establish one joint and several damage award in the amount of $1,689,641. The pharmacy settled out of court for $330,000 and thus, the physician was entitled to have the judgment against him reduced by the amount paid by the pharmacy.

REASONING: There was little question about negligence on the part of the pharmacy and thus, it agreed to settle with the plaintiff for $330,000 prior to the appeal. A board-certified toxicologist testified for Fultz that the physician failed to meet the standard of care in providing treatment to a diabetic presenting the plaintiff's symptomatology. It was claimed that the plaintiff was dehydrated as a result of taking the *Aldomet*. The prolonged period of dehydration resulted in a reduction of blood volume which in combination with the lowered blood pressure caused clotting of blood vessels in the brain, resulting in the stroke. The physician-toxicologist testified that if IV fluids had been administered to replace lost fluids, the stroke probably would not have occurred.

After presenting a number of defenses, the physician's final contention was that the jury erred in entering identical judgments against both the pharmacy and the physician and clinic. The defendants argued that they were joint tortfeasors and therefore a joint and several judgment should have been entered. The physician argued that because the pharmacy had already settled for $330,000, he was entitled to have judgment against him reduced by that amount.

The plaintiff countered that the defendants were not joint tortfeasors, but concurrent tortfeasors and that each owed a separate amount. The plaintiff claimed that he suffered separate and distinct injuries and that recovery from each defendant did not constitute a double recovery for the single injury. However, the court noted that the plaintiff premised his arguments on the fact that the defendants were jointly responsible. The jury was never instructed to apportion the damages between the defendants based on any degree of fault. While a person injured through another's negligence can recover for both the original injury and any

Fultz v Peart
494 N.E.2d 212 (Ill. App. 5 Dist. 1986)
...continued

aggravation of that injury caused by a treating physician's negligence, the court concluded that the jury intended to establish one joint and several damage award in the amount of $1,689,641.

The following is a list of court cases that are related to this topic.

Clair v Paris Road Drugs, Inc., 573 So. 2d 1219 (La. App. 1991)

EVIDENCE (PROOF)

Functions of Court and Jury

Van Hatem v K-Mart
719 N.E. 2d 212 (Ill. App. 1999)

At the time of his death in 1995, the patient was 76 years old and had been taking several medications including *Coumadin*. This drug was initially prescribed in 1991 to prevent phlebitis. By the middle of 1994, the patient was on a regimen of *Coumadin* 2 mg to be taken one tablet daily for 2 days and 2 tablets for one day and then to be repeated. The prescription was filled and refilled at the same pharmacy for several years. In June, 1995, while the patient and his wife were vacationing in Michigan, the patient noted that he had passed blood in his urine. He returned home that evening and his wife noticed splatters of blood on the front of the toilet after the patient had gone to the bathroom. The patient made plans to see his doctor about his "prostate" the next day. The patient also complained to his wife that he was having a severe migraine headache. The next morning his wife found him unconscious and bleeding from his mouth and nose. He was taken to the hospital and admitted. While he was still hospitalized, the wife went home and looked in the *Coumadin* prescription vial and noticed the number "5" on the tablets even though the label indicated that it should contain the 2 mg strength. The patient's daughter, a registered nurse, looked in a *Physician's Desk Reference* and confirmed that the "5" on the tablets meant that they were 5 mg *Coumadin*. The patient died the next day. The family put the vial with the remaining tablets in a safe. After they retained an attorney, he put the vial in a safe deposit box at a bank. Prior to the trial, the pharmacy sought to exclude the prescription bottle and the tablets because there was no proof that those tablets were placed in the bottle by the pharmacy. The request was denied. A pharmacist testified at trial that the pharmacy had misfilled the prescription with the wrong strength and that this violated the applicable standard of care. A physician testified that the higher than prescribed dose of the drug caused the patient's death. The pharmacy's experts disputed those opinions. After the close of evidence, the pharmacy's attorney moved for a mistrial because a local television station aired a news story during the trial featuring the patient's wife discussing the patient's death as being caused by a misfilled prescription. The judge asked the jurors if any had seen the story and determined that the four who had were not biased as a result. The motion was denied and the jury returned a verdict for the patient's estate in the amount of $900,000; the verdict was reduced by 10% as a result of finding that the patient was comparatively negligent in not noticing that the 5 mg tablets looked different from the 2 mg strength. The pharmacy appealed. The judgment was reversed and the case remanded for a new trial. The Court of Appeals found the news story and the timing of its broadcast so prejudicial as to prevent the pharmacy from having a fair trial. As to the argument that the prescription bottle and its contents should not be admitted because there was no proof that the patient, his wife

Van Hatem v K-Mart
719 N.E. 2d 212 (Ill. App. 1999)
...continued

or someone else might have put the 5 mg tablets in the vial labeled 2 mg, the court found no support and ruled that the evidence was properly admitted.

Volner v Vantreese Discount Pharmacy
Slip Op. No. 02A01-9712-GS-00298, May 28, 1999, 1999 Tenn. App. LEXIS 337

The plaintiff had a long history of lupus erythematosus. On December 22, 1992, her physician prescribed prednisone 5 mg. She took the prescription to her pharmacy where it was filled with prednisone 10 mg. She took the 10 mg tablets for four days. She began to experience a severe headache, was admitted to a hospital and diagnosed with a stroke. As a result, she suffered partial blindness. She sued the pharmacy and the pharmacist for malpractice. During the closing arguments of a jury trial, the attorney for the pharmacy noted that there was no evidence that the erroneous dose of the prednisone caused the plaintiff's optic damage. He went on to state that the plaintiff's attorney, "with all his resources and all his camera equipment and all his electronic stuff would have a videotape in here running showing you this lady has a problem with her face . . . It's a lawyer trying to sell you something just like through the years (they) have sold juries on McDonald's coffee spills, on using dynamite to unclog a toilet and the guy that lit the dynamite got hurt. It's lawyers who sell the cases where you use hedge trimmers to try to cut your grass and you cut your toe. But you know what that has caused? That's caused drug manufacturers to put in their warnings every conceivable thing on earth ..." At this point, the plaintiff's attorney objected because there had been no evidence introduced concerning the manufacturer's product insert or warnings associated with the drug. The trial court judge sustained the objection and ordered the jury to disregard the statement about package inserts. The judge instructed the jury, "What lawyers say are not evidence. The evidence has come to you in the form of testimony. And the lawyers, we give them a great deal of latitude in making jury arguments. Some people may think we give them too much, but I feel like I have great confidence in jurors, and I think that jurors know how to receive this, and we like to give lawyers latitude and let them go at it." The jury returned a verdict in favor of the pharmacy and pharmacist. The plaintiff asked the judge to grant a new trial because of the alleged prejudice during closing arguments. The motion was denied and the plaintiff appealed. The judgment was affirmed on appeal. No prejudice was found because closing arguments do not constitute reversal error unless there is some egregious statement that taints the minds of the jury. No prejudice of this type could be found and any error that did occur was corrected by the judge's instructions to the jury to ignore the lawyers.

The following is a list of court cases that are related to this topic.

Nichols v Kaiser Foundation Health Plan of the Mid-Atlantic States, Slip Op. No. 981388 (April 16, 1999), S. Ct. Va., 1999 Va. LEXIS 65.

Burden of Proof and Presumptions

Bloching v Albertson's
934 P.2d 17 (Idaho 1997)

The events central to this case occurred in 1992. The marketing and availability of the medications at issue are very different today. The patient is a diabetic who used beef insulin to

Bloching v Albertson's
934 P.2d 17 (Idaho 1997)
...continued

control the disease. He had a history of experiencing a seizure approximately every four to six weeks caused by hypoglycemic reactions to the insulin. He sent his girlfriend to the pharmacy to pick up a supply of the medication, but the pharmacy was out of stock. The pharmacist allegedly told the woman that a blend of beef and pork insulin could be used as a direct substitute for beef insulin. She called the patient at his home to ask him whether she should purchase the blended insulin. During this conversation, the patient claimed he heard the pharmacist indicate that the blend could be used as a substitute. Based on this representation, the patient told her to purchase the product recommended by the pharmacist. After using the beef-pork insulin, the patient's seizures became more violent and frequent, occurring almost daily. He discontinued using the blended insulin after one week but continued to experience the extreme and frequent seizures. The patient filed a complaint against the pharmacy claiming that it was responsible for his continuing seizures and permanent injuries. The treating physician indicated during his deposition that while it was possible that the switch in insulin products could have caused permanent injury, he believed within a reasonable degree of medical probability that the beef-pork insulin blend had absolutely nothing to do with the patient's seizures. Another physician, acting on behalf of the pharmacy, signed an affidavit that also offered the opinion that the switch in insulin products was not causally related to the more violent and frequent seizures suffered by the patient. In answer to written interrogatories, the patient indicated that he based his belief that the pharmacy was the cause of his injuries on the statement of the treating physician that the insulin switch was a possible causal link to his increased seizure activity. Based on the deposition and affidavit of the physicians, the pharmacy asked the trial court judge to dismiss the complaint premised on the idea that there was no credible evidence that it was responsible for the patient's condition. The patient opposed the pharmacy's motion to dismiss using his interrogatory answers and the possible link to his injuries identified by the treating physician. After considering only the evidence that would be admissible at trial, the judge agreed with the pharmacy and granted the request for summary judgment. The Idaho Supreme Court upheld the judgment on appeal.

State v Dutton Drugs, Inc.
209 N.E.2d 597 (Ohio 1965)

ISSUE: (1) Whether the defendant was "entrapped" into the sale of a prescription drug by an undercover agent, (2) whether the state of Ohio had met its burden of proof of the sale of a prescription drug and (3) whether the defendant had to prove he was a pharmacist.

FACTS: Ohio authorities brought a criminal action against the president of a pharmacy corporation and against him as an individual for (1) selling *Seconal* on a prescription when he was not a registered pharmacist and (2) operating a pharmacy without having a registered pharmacist in the employ of said pharmacy. It was claimed that both acts were in violation of Ohio law (Sec. 4729.28 and 4729.27, respectively), and the defendant was convicted on both charges. The defendant, for the pharmacy corporation and as an individual, appealed both convictions to the Ohio Supreme Court.

On the appeal of the case, the defendant's attorney claimed that his convictions should be reversed because (1) he was entrapped into the sale by the state narcotic agent, (2) that the state's charges against him merely referred to an item as "*Seconal*" and that no evidence as to its pharmacological nature was offered to the jury at the time of trial and (3) the court put the burden on the defendant to prove that he was a pharmacist when the burden should have been on the state to prove he was not.

State v Dutton Drugs, Inc.
209 N.E.2d 597 (Ohio 1965)
...continued

RULING: The Ohio Supreme Court ruled (1) that the defendant had not been "entrapped", (2) that the state had not met its burden of proof of the sale of the drug and (3) the defendant did not need to prove that he was a pharmacist, but rather the burden was on the state to prove he was not.

REASONING: The Ohio Supreme Court rejected the "entrapment" claim, putting it to test of "whether the defendant was induced by the investigation to violate the law, or was he merely presented with the opportunity to do so?" On cross-examination, at the trial, the defendant admitted that he pleaded guilty to a similar charge in 1961. Hence, the Ohio Supreme Court concluded that: "Such an admission negates entrapment in the instant case." The defendant's former conviction for the same offense showed his predisposition to committing the crime when presented with an opportunity.

However, the Ohio Supreme Court did accept the defendant's contentions regarding the lack of convicting evidence since the jury was not instructed as to the medical use of *Seconal*. The defendant was charged with unlawfully selling a drug, but no evidence was introduced by the state to prove that *Seconal* was a drug. The high court commented that the jury could not assume to be educated in law and medicine and the failure of the trial court to instruct the jury on the intended use of *Seconal* was in error.

The Ohio Supreme court also concluded that placing the burden upon the defendant to prove that he was a pharmacist was also in error. The Ohio Supreme Court, though it was loath to do so, reversed both of the convictions against the defendant. In so doing the court stated:

> On a criminal charge, it is incumbent upon the state to establish by evidence beyond a reasonable doubt each essential element of the crime charged and as specified in the statute...Nothing can destroy government more quickly than its failure to observe it own laws, or worse its disregard of the charter of its own existence...Even those guilty of the most heinous offenses are entitles to a fair trial. Under the circumstances...we believe defendant did not receive a fair trial. Whatever the degree of guilt may be of those charged with a crime, they are entitled to be tried by the standards which the Legislature and Supreme Court have prescribed.

Ramon by and through Ramon v Farr
770 P.2d 131 (Utah 1989)

ISSUE: Whether the recommendations contained in a manufacturer's package insert are "prima facie" evidence of the standard of care.

FACTS: Mrs. Ramon based her negligence claim on the fact that her physician injected her in the cervical region with the anesthetic, *Marcaine*, approximately 1 hour before her son's birth. Following birth, the infant began to show symptoms of serious problems and when he was transferred to an intensive care unit, he suffered grand mal seizures. It was agreed that the infant had permanent physical and mental defects.

Both the package insert and the 1980 edition of the *Physician's Desk Reference* (PDR) stated "until further clinical evidence is gained, paracervical block with *Marcaine* is not recom-

Ramon by and through Ramon v Farr
770 P.2d 131 (Utah 1989)
...continued

mended." The plaintiffs argued that the mere introduction into evidence of the package insert or the *PDR* shifts the burden of proof on the standard of care to the defendant physician.

In response, the physician urged the court to hold that the package insert is only some evidence that the jury can take into account in determining the standard of care. He further contended that the plaintiff in a medical malpractice action usually bears the burden of introducing evidence on the standard of care in the form of expert testimony.

RULING: The trial court refused to give a jury instruction that would have made the recommendation included in the manufacturer's package insert "prima facie" evidence of the standard of care. The appellate court agreed and affirmed the decision in favor of the physician.

REASONING: The court recognized that the various jurisdictions are split on whether the recommendations contained in a package insert should serve as "prima facie" evidence of the standard of care. While some courts have made such a determination, the Utah Supreme Court, in this case, decided that the better rule is that manufacturers' inserts do not by themselves establish the standard of care. Instead, a manufacturer's recommendation is some evidence that the finder of fact may consider along with expert testimony on the standard of care.

Although package inserts provide useful information, the court indicated that they are not designed to establish a standard of medical practice. In making such a determination, the court noted the following statements from an article "Drug Labeling as a Standard for Medical Practice:"

> Differences between the package insert and accepted medical practice represent the difference between the rigorous proof a regulatory agency must demand and the clinical judgment of a physician based on his training, experience and skill as related to the needs of his individual patient. One cannot be taken as a standard for the other. *J Legal Med* 22 (Jan 1976).

The following is a list of court cases that are related to this topic.

Young v Board of Pharmacy, 462 P.2d 139 (N.M. 1969).
Holbrook v Rose, 458 S.W. 2d 155 (Ky. 1970).
Rite Aid Corp. v Board of Pharmacy of the State of New Jersey, 421 F. Supp. 1161 (D.N.J. 1974).
French Drug Co., Inc. v Jones, 367 So. 2d 431 (Miss. 1978).
United States v Bycer, 593 F.2d 549 (3rd Cir. 1979).
Docken v Ciba-Geigy, 790 P. 2d 45 (Or. App. 1990).

JOINT TORTFEASORS

Joinder of Defendants

The following is a list of court cases that are related to this topic.

Piedmont Pharmacy, Inc. v Patmore, 240 S.E.2d 888 (Ct. App. Ga. 1977).
Albertson's Inc. v Adams, 473 So.2d 231 (Fla. App. 2 Dist. 1985).

Defenses

Comparative and Contributory Negligence

Murdock v Walker
43 Ill. App. Ct. 590 (1892)

ISSUE: Whether a physician who negligently writes a prescription may claim that the pharmacist's negligence in dispensing such prescription caused the injury

FACTS: The parents of a baby who died from an overdose of opium brought suit against the prescribing physician. The physician wrote a prescription for the child, one of the ingredients of which was written as "opii pulv." Although the reported facts of this case do not indicate such with clarity, it appears that doctor meant to write for "opii camph," or camphorated tincture of opium (paregoric) but instead wrote for "opii pulv," and tincture of opium (laudanum) was dispensed on the prescription.

The trial court ruled in favor of the plaintiff and against the physician. The physician appealed the case and claimed that the intervening negligence of the pharmacist, in failing to have the prescription clarified by contacting the prescriber, should relieve the physician of liability.

RULING: The concurrent negligence of both the physician and the pharmacist was responsible for the injury.

REASONING: The appellate court rejected the physician's claim and affirmed the judgment against him. The court ruled that, at most, the negligence of the pharmacist concurred with that of the doctor in producing the injurious result. Thus, in this particular fact situation, the negligence of the negligent party was not available as a liability defense to the other negligent party.

MacKay v Crown Drug Co.
420 P.2d 883 (Okla. 1966)

ISSUE: Whether a patient who continued to suffer drowsiness from an incorrectly dispensed prescription was guilty of contributory negligence.

FACTS: In the case, the plaintiff brought a civil suit against a pharmacy for injuries resulting from the incorrect dispensing of a prescription. The case was tried before a jury who found that the plaintiff's own contributory negligence, as a matter of law, barred his recovery of damages from the defendant even though the evidence established that the prescription was incorrectly filled. The plaintiff appealed the case to the Supreme Court of Oklahoma.

On July 27, 1962, the plaintiff received a prescription for 0.1 mg of *Reserpoid* (a brand of reserpine) from his physician. He took the prescription to the defendant's pharmacy, but the pharmacist on duty inadvertently filled the prescription with 1 mg of *Reserpoid*. The plaintiff took the medication in a dosage regimen of two tablets daily. While taking the medication as prescribed, the plaintiff became drowsy and would fall asleep at work. On Aug. 17, 1962, the plaintiff fell asleep at work and injured his hand. On Aug. 22, 1962, he returned to the pharmacy for a refill of the prescription. The pharmacist on duty at the time dis-

MacKay v Crown Drug Co.
420 P.2d 883 (Okla. 1966)
...continued

covered that the prescription had originally been incorrectly filled. At the trial of the case, the plaintiff's doctor testified that if the patient took 1 mg of *Reserpoid* twice daily instead of 0.1 mg, he would quite likely become drowsy and confused. The pharmacist who originally filled the prescription testified that a prescription for 1 mg of *Reserpoid* was not unusual, but that such an amount might cause a patient to become dizzy.

RULING: The court concluded that the patient was guilty of contributory negligence because, after having experienced drowsiness from the drug, he continued to use the product and risk injury.

REASONING: At the trial, the evidence established that the prescription was incorrectly filled. However, the attorney representing the pharmacy contended that the plaintiff was guilty of "contributory negligence" in that, after having experienced drowsiness from taking the drug, he continued to use it and expose himself to the risk of falling when drowsy. The jury found that the plaintiff was guilty of contributory negligence, and under Oklahoma law such a finding barred recovery from the defendant.

The Oklahoma Supreme Court, in upholding the trial court's ruling in favor of the defendant, stated:

> The weight of authority is that contributory negligence on the part of one who sustains an injury from the use of drugs or medicine is a proper defense in a suit filed against the druggist.

Davis v Katz & Bestoff, Inc.
333 So.2d 698 (La. 1976)

ISSUE: Whether a patient who was still somewhat incoherent following oral surgery was guilty of contributory negligence for taking medication labeled for someone else.

FACTS: A customer brought suit against a pharmacy and its insurer for damages resulting from the ill effects sustained when she ingested a prescription prepared and labeled for another person, but mistakenly placed by the pharmacy's employee in a bag labeled with plaintiff's name.

The pharmacy-defendant did not dispute its negligence, but it claimed that the plaintiff's failure to read the patient's name on the prescription label before ingesting the medication as contributory negligence so as to bar recover. The trial court judge awarded the plaintiff $4500 in damages and the defendant claimed the amount was excessive. The trial court's judgment was appealed. On appeal, the judgment was affirmed.

At the trial of the case, the defendant's version of the facts differed from the plaintiff's. The defendant claimed that both the prescription container label and the label on the bag were that of a person other than the plaintiff. On the other hand, the plaintiff claimed that upon picking up her prescription at the pharmacy, she noticed her name on the bag as well as the doctor's name. A pharmacist employed by the defendant testified that although safety measures were used to prevent a mix-up, a possibility existed in which medication for one person could be placed in the bag of another.

Davis v Katz & Bestoff, Inc.
333 So.2d 698 (La. 1976)
...continued

The plaintiff had undergone oral surgery and *Percodan* was prescribed, but the drug she received was *Meticorten*. The plaintiff took the *Meticorten* for 3 days until her niece noticed that the container was labeled with another person's name. Medical testimony at trial indicated that the plaintiff suffered weakness, nausea and hypertension as complications brought on by the *Meticorten*. In addition, and bearing on the issue of contributory negligence, was testimony showing the plaintiff was dizzy, feeling ill and incoherent for several days following the oral surgery.

RULING: The court concluded that, given the patient's condition, she was not contributorily negligent for failing to inspect the prescription container label when the prescription bag in which the container had been placed bore her name.

REASONING: On the contributory negligence issue, the appellate court held that a duty exists on the part of the purchaser of a prescription, as follows:

> ...to inspect the label of the prescription container when the bag in which the container was placed bears the name of the person for whom the prescription is intended.

However, in this instance, the patient's postoperative state caused the court to hold that, "we cannot conclude that after once having observed her name on the prescription bag, plaintiff was contributorily negligent for failing to make a further inspection of the prescription container label."

On the issue of excessive damages, the court concluded that $4500 in damages was high considering the ill effects but not to the extent that it would change the amount. The case was affirmed in favor of the plaintiff.

Machin v Walgreen
Slip Op No 3D01-3432 (November 27, 2002), 27 Fla. L. Weekly D 2564; 2002 Fla. App. LEXIS 17562

A mother took her 3-month-old daughter to her pediatrician for treatment of a mouth ailment. The pediatrician diagnosed the girl as having thrush, a common yeast infection, for which he prescribed nystatin, an antifungal oral suspension. She took the prescrition to Walgreen pharmacy to be filled. The Walgreen pharmacist incorrectly dispensed *Triotann*, the generic substitute not for nystatin, but for the antihistamine-decongestant *Rynatan*. Along with the *Triotann* dispensed to the mother, the Walgreen's pharmacist provided her with a data sheet advising that she was receiving *Triotann* and that it is a generic substitute for *Rynatan*. Nowhere on the data sheet (or the medicine container) did there appear the name nystatin. The mother gave the erroneously dispensed medicine to her daughter without first assuring – by reading the data sheet or having it read for her (she does not read or speak English, a fact which this court says does not dilute or negate any duty she has toward her daughter) – that the actually dispensed medicine was the one her pediatrician prescribed. The daughter stopped eating and developed sleep problems. The thrush worsened. When this was reported to the pediatrician, he discovered that the Walgreen pharmacist had dispensed the wrong medication. Removed from the wrong medication and properly treated, the daughter's thrush infection disappeared quickly, but she continued to experience a lack of appetite and sleeping disorders for months thereafter. At trial, Walgreen contended that the

Machin v Walgreen
Slip Op No 3D01-3432 (November 27, 2002), 27 Fla. L. Weekly D 2564; 2002 Fla. App.
LEXIS 17562
...continued

mother was negligent by paying no attention to the data sheet, an examination of which
would have quickly informed her that the prescription was not what the doctor ordered. The
mother testified that she trusted her pediatrician and the pharmacy and therefore had no
duty to do anything to assure that she was feeding her child the correct medicine. The jury
found the mother comparatively negligent to the extent of 45% fault for her daughter's condition. The trial court denied her motion for directed verdict and entered judgment accordingly. On the mother's appeal, the courts stated "the obvious": that parents have a constant
and continuous duty as ordinary, prudent persons to watch over, supervise, and protect
their children who are too young to exercise judgment to care for themselves. Persons chargeable with a duty of care and caution toward children must take the precautions which are
available to them. Here, the mother was in the position to assure that the dispensed medication was that prescribed by the pediatrician. She was handed a document, Walgreen's
data sheet, containing the information that would have informed her that the medicine dispensed was not the right one. The name nystatin was not to be found on the data sheet,
whereas the name *Rynatan* and its generic, *Triotann*, were. The principal purpose of such data
sheets is to inform the purchaser which medicine is being placed in his or her hands so that
the purchaser can be assured that the prescription has been filled properly. The mother
also claimed that she was not negligent because she was not aware of the name of the medicine prescribed by the pediatrician. This does not relieve her from her parental duty. It was
incumbent upon her to take the simple steps of inquiring of the pediatrician the name of
the prescribed medicine, checking the data sheet and the container of the actually dispensed
medicine, then contacting her pediatrician when she discovered (as she would have done)
the discrepancy. The trial court's judgment was affirmed.

The following is a list of court cases that are related to this topic.

Fuhs v Barber, 36 P. 2d 962 (Kan. 1934).
Boeck v Katz Drug Co., 127 P.2d 506 (Kan. 1942).
Krueger v Knutson, 111 N.W.2d 526 (Minn. 1961).
French Drug Co., Inc. v Jones, 367 So. 2d 431 (Miss. 1978).
Malone & Hyde, Inc. v Hobrecht, 685 S.W.2d 739 (Tex. Ct. App. 1985).
Bickowicz v Sterling Drug, Inc., 557 N.Y.S.2d 551 (A.D. 3 Dept. 1990).
Clair v Paris Road Drugs, Inc., 573 So. 2d 1219 (La. App. 1991).
Orzel v Scott Drug, 537 N.W. 2d 208 (Mich. 1995) 1995 Mich. LEXIS 1481 (No. 98506, August
     15, 1995).

Wrongful Conduct by Plaintiff

Orzel v Scott Drug
537 N.W.2d 208 (Mich. 1995)

ISSUE: Whether plaintiffs can maintain a tort action when their asserted injuries arise out
of illegal conduct on their own part.

FACTS: The plaintiff, John Orzel, and his relatives filed this suit in 1983 against several
defendants, claiming that each defendant negligently supplied *Desoxyn* to him. In his complaint, the plaintiff asserted that the negligence of the dispensing pharmacy caused him to
become physically and psychologically addicted to *Desoxyn*. Further, he argued that said
addiction resulted in auditory and visual hallucinations and mental illness, including para-

Orzel v Scott Drug
537 N.W.2d 208 (Mich. 1995)
...continued

noid schizophrenia. As a result of mental derangement and illness, the plaintiff sustained pain, suffering and disability, including the loss of earning capacity. The plaintiff contended that these injuries are not only permanent in nature, but have caused relatives to experience a loss of companionship.

When the trial finally commenced in 1988, the dispensing pharmacy, Scott Drug, was the only remaining defendant. The plaintiffs alleged that the defendant pharmacy had breached its common law and statutory duties when it dispensed *Desoxyn* prescriptions to him without asking for identification and without allowing an adequate interval between prescriptions. The evidence also showed that the plaintiff presented the pharmacy with prescriptions for *Desoxyn* that had been written for persons with names other than "John Orzel." Further, while the prescriptions were for a one month's supply, the pharmacy, on several occasions, filled more than one prescription within the same month.

In his deposition, Orzel stated that sometime in 1979 he began to use *Desoxyn* purchased from his co-workers at General Motors. By 1980, he was taking one or two tablets a day; by 1981 he had increased his intake to three to five tablets a day; later that year he began to hear voices, experience hallucinations and suffer from paranoid delusions. By June 1981, he was consuming eight to ten tablets a day, and in July 1981, he was forced to take medical leave from his job.

The plaintiff testified that he knew his purchase and use of *Desoxyn* was illegal. He further contended that by July 1981, he was no longer taking the drug voluntarily, that he was suffering from amphetamine psychosis to the point of being rendered legally insane and was not able to conform his conduct to the requirements of law.

In August 1981, John Orzel started going to the Figure Eight Weight Loss Clinic one to three times a week. There he would misrepresent to physicians that he desired to lose weight and the physicians would write *Desoxyn* prescriptions for "weight control." It was uncontested that he never wanted or needed to lose weight and that the only reason he went to the clinic was to obtain *Desoxyn*.

The defendant pharmacy filled the *Desoxyn* prescriptions for the plaintiff. Each one presented had been signed by a licensed physician and was for a medically acceptable one month's supply of 30 tablets. In the meantime, the plaintiff continued to obtain *Desoxyn* from other sources and, at his peak, was using between ten to fifteen tablets a day. He entered a mental hospital in 1982, but resumed his use of controlled substances shortly after his discharge.

The psychiatrist who examined the plaintiff testified that he suffered from amphetamine psychosis. Although the plaintiff was genetically predisposed to schizophrenia, it was the opinion of the physician that the large doses of *Desoxyn* had caused its onset.

RULING: The jury found the pharmacy negligent and assessed the plaintiff's damages at $3.8 million. The jury further found the plaintiff to be 50% comparatively negligent and the verdict was reduced to $1.9 million. The pharmacy moved for judgment notwithstanding the verdict, and the trial court judge granted the motion on the basis that the plaintiff's illegal acts barred his claim.

The Michigan Court of Appeals reversed the trial court in an unpublished opinion. The majority of the court opined that the plaintiff's illegal conduct should not operate to bar his

Orzel v Scott Drug
537 N.W.2d 208 (Mich. 1995)
...continued

claim. The plaintiff's illegal conduct would normally bar recovery, but the Court of Appeals would not apply such a bar in this case. The evidence showed that the plaintiff was insane at the time he committed his illegal acts and was thus unaccountable for them. The defendant pharmacy appealed to the Michigan Supreme Court which reversed the Court of Appeals decision and reinstated the trial court's judgment overturning the jury verdict.

REASONING: The common law holds that when a plaintiff's action is based, in whole or in part, on his own illegal conduct, he is barred from such a lawsuit. If a defendant has participated equally in illegal conduct, the law will not generally provide relief to either party. By making relief available for wrongdoers, courts in effect would condone and encourage illegal conduct. Secondly, some wrongdoers would be able to receive a profit or compensation as a result of their illegal acts. Additionally, the public would see the legal system as a mockery of justice should it allow wrongdoers to shift the responsibility for their illegal acts to other parties.

The mere fact that a plaintiff engaged in illegal conduct at the time of his injury does not mean that his claim is automatically barred under the principle described above. The plaintiff's conduct must be prohibited under a penal or criminal statute. In contrast, where a plaintiff's illegal conduct only amounts to a violation of a safety statute such as traffic speed law, the act, while illegal, does not rise to the level of serious misconduct sufficient to bar a cause of action.

In examining the facts in this case, the court held that the plaintiff's illegal conduct is of the type that warrants application of the common law principle. By his own admissions, the plaintiff repeatedly violated several provisions of the Controlled Substances Act when he obtained and possessed the *Desoxyn* without a valid prescription.

Another important limitation under the wrongful conduct principle involves causation. For the principle to apply, there must be a sufficient causal nexus between the plaintiff's illegal conduct and the plaintiff's asserted injuries. The fact that a person has been guilty of a wrong in one particular instance does not cause him to forfeit his right to legal protection in regard to other situations.

In the case at hand, the plaintiffs did not dispute that the illegal conduct of John Orzel at the time he dealt with the defendant was the proximate cause of his asserted injuries. However, the plaintiffs argued that his illegal conduct cannot be considered because he was insane at the time. In view of all the facts in this case, the court did not find it necessary to decide whether John Orzel was legally insane so as not to be held criminally responsible for his actions. Even assuming that Orzel did at some point become legally insane, the court was still able to conclude that his illegal acts, committed while he was sane, directly caused his damages.

The court noted that the plaintiff decided to escalate his purchase and use of *Desoxyn* while he was sane. The escalation continued quickly over the next several months to the point that he became addicted to the drug and suffered hallucinations. The chronology of the plaintiff's use of *Desoxyn* while he was sane made it clear that his illegal use during that time was the direct, immediate and proximate cause of his addiction, his hallucinations and his mental illness. The plaintiff's initial consumption of *Desoxyn* while he was sane could not be characterized as a separate transaction from his subsequent use while he was insane. Consequently, any injuries that were the direct result of his drug use while he was insane were foreseeable consequences when he was sane.

Orzel v Scott Drug
537 N.W.2d 208 (Mich. 1995)
...continued

Even though a plaintiff is engaged in serious illegal conduct and such conduct has directly caused his injuries, a plaintiff may still seek recovery against a defendant if the defendant's culpability is greater than the plaintiff's. It is undisputed that both the plaintiff and the defendant pharmacy engaged in wrongful conduct. John Orzel's conduct was wrongful because he repeatedly did the following: (1) Made misrepresentations to doctors in order to obtain prescriptions for *Desoxyn*; (2) presented prescriptions to be filled when they were written for persons with other names and (3) purchased and used *Desoxyn* that he obtained pursuant to false prescriptions. The defendant filled many *Desoxyn* prescriptions for the plaintiff and when they did, their conduct was also wrongful. The pharmacy dispensed *Desoxyn* prescriptions for the plaintiff without first confirming his identity, it filled the prescriptions too frequently and for arguably illegitimate purposes.

In comparing the plaintiff's wrongful conduct with the pharmacy's wrongful conduct, the court concluded that the two wrongdoers are equally at fault. Both parties played pivotal rolls in making the illegal acts possible and the court could not say that one party was more guilty than the other. Thus, the court ruled that the plaintiff's claim is barred based upon his illegal conduct.

The following is a list of court cases that are related to this topic.

Fuhs v Barber, 36 P. 2d 962 (Kan. 1934).

Immunities

Quinn v Memorial Medical Center
764 S.W.2d 915 (Tex. App. 1989)

ISSUE: (1) Whether a county hospital pharmacy, which sold a drug to a physician who subsequently used it to induce an abortion in his girlfriend was immune from a lawsuit from the girlfriend and (2) whether the action of the pharmacist was the direct cause of the plaintiff's injuries.

FACTS: The plaintiff, Venetia Quinn, was dating Dr. Julio De Pena, a physician who was serving his residency at Memorial Medical Center in Nueces County, Texas, when she allegedly became pregnant with De Pena's child. The physician telephoned John Villarreal, the pharmacist on duty in the medical center, and told Villarreal that he was working in the emergency room. The physician inquired as to the availability of prostin E-2, a hormone used to induce abortions. The pharmacist informed the physician that the pharmacy did have the drug in stock.

De Pena went to the pharmacy and wrote a prescription to obtain the drug, but he failed to write a patient's name on the prescription. The pharmacist called this to the physician's attention, but De Pena told him to use De Pena's name and he would "settle up later." The physician was charged for the hormone.

De Pena drove to the plaintiff's apartment and administered the drug, which resulted in an abortion. However, the following day the plaintiff was taken to another hospital because of hemorrhaging, and a dilation and curettage had to be performed to remove remaining products of conception.

Quinn v Memorial Medical Center
764 S.W.2d 915 (Tex. App. 1989)
...continued

De Pena was authorized as a resident to write prescriptions to be dispensed at the medical center pharmacy. However, his contract with the medical center and his institutional permit restricted him to practicing medicine only inside the hospital because he was a physician in the transitional residency program. De Pena was neither authorized nor granted permission to take any drug from the medical center for use on or by other persons or to perform any medical care or treatment outside the hospital.

RULING: The plaintiff sued the medical center and hospital district for damages. The trial court granted the defendants' motion for summary judgment. On appeal, the plaintiff argued that the trial court erred in granting the motion for summary judgment because a material issue of fact existed concerning whether the hospital pharmacy's alleged negligence in dispensing the drug caused her injuries. The appellate court reversed the trial court decision and the case was remanded for reconsideration.

REASONING: The hospital argued that because it was a political subdivision of the state of Texas, it was not liable for damages unless the negligent or wrongful act fell outside its protection of governmental immunity. Texas law provides for a waiver of immunity in three general areas: (1) damages resulting from the use of publicly owned vehicles; (2) injuries caused by a condition or use of tangible personal property; and (3) injuries caused by condition or use of real property.

The court concluded that the dispensing of a drug by a hospital pharmacy is a use of tangible personal property and fell outside the protection of governmental immunity. The hospital argued that it did not waive its immunity because the drug was used by an off-duty employee outside the hospital premises after possession and control by the hospital had ceased. However, the court concluded that under the facts of this case, the actual negligent acts took place when the pharmacy did, in fact, possess and control the hormone.

The court next had to determine whether the defendants' alleged negligence in dispensing the prescription was the proximate cause of the plaintiff's injuries. It noted that the hormone was not available at all pharmacies, but was normally only stocked by hospital pharmacies. Further, the physician's practice of medicine was limited to the hospital setting, and he testified that he did not believe he was going to get the drug. Therefore, a fact issue existed concerning whether, but for the defendants' alleged negligent act of dispensing the hormone, the physician would not have administered the hormone and the plaintiff would not have been injured.

It was also contended that the pharmacist should have foreseen that an injury such as this one may have occurred when a male physician in a residency program was prescribing a female hormone for either himself or an undisclosed person. The standard procedure would have been to write the patient's name on the prescription. The pharmacist never asked the physician if the hormone was for a hospital patient and never inquired as to why he needed it. Thus, an issue of fact existed concerning whether the defendants should have anticipated that the failure to take reasonable precautions in dispensing this hormone could have resulted in its wrongful use and danger to others.

DeCordova v State of Colorado
878 P.2d 73 (Colo. App. 1994)

ISSUE: Whether the University of Colorado Health Sciences Center, its School of Pharmacy and other public entities were liable for damages allegedly attributable to drug overdoses caused by error of the university hospital's pharmacy.

FACTS: In 1982, the plaintiff's daughter was born at the defendant University of Colorado Health Sciences Center. Because of a risk of neonatal infection, the attending physicians ordered that the infant receive a specified dosage of an intravenous antibiotic every 12 hours.

The prescribed antibiotic was known to be ototoxic, and the drug's toxicity increases with elevated and repeated dosages over time and can result in permanent hearing impairment. Due to an error in the hospital pharmacy, the infant received approximately five times the prescribed dosage. Exactly how many overdoses of the medication received by the infant before the error was discovered was contested at trial.

In 1987, the child was diagnosed as having moderately severe sensorineural hearing loss bilaterally. The condition worsened over the next several years. In 1989, the child, through her mother as conservator, filed a complaint against the defendants alleging that the overdose she had received was the cause of her hearing loss. Prior to trial, the plaintiff made two offers of settlement which were rejected by the defendants.

RULING: After presentation of all of the evidence, the trial court ruled that, as a matter of law, the defendants were negligent and submitted to the jury the issues of causation and damages. In a special verdict, the jury found that the child had incurred injuries and that the defendant's negligence was the cause of those injuries, and it awarded damages of $295,000.

The trial reduced the judgment to $150,000, the maximum amount recoverable pursuant to Colorado statutes (particularly, the Governmental Immunity Act). The plaintiff then sought actual costs of over $46,000 that had been incurred after the defendant's rejection of her settlement offers. She argued that she was entitled to the additional recovery because the judgment entered was greater than her rejected offers of settlement. The trial court concluded that the statute limited the government's total liability to $150,000, inclusive of actual costs and interest. The plaintiff appealed. The judgment was affirmed on appeal.

REASONING: The Colorado Governmental Immunity Act was enacted in 1971 in response to the Supreme Court of Colorado's abrogation of sovereign immunity. In the same statute, the state legislature reinstated immunity from tort liability for public entities in some circumstances and established recovery limits, declaring that "unlimited liability could disrupt or make prohibitively expensive the provision of essential public services and functions."

In the statute in question, the maximum amount that could be recovered in any single occurrence, whether from one or more public entities and public employees, was the sum of $150,000 for any injury to one person in any single occurrence.

In 1990, the Colorado legislature expanded the availability of cost recovery in civil cases in order to discourage the filing of unnecessary litigation and encourage the timely resolution of disputes. The 1990 statute reads that "notwithstanding any other statute to the contrary... if the plaintiff makes an offer of settlement which is rejected by the defendant and the plaintiff recovers a final judgment in excess of the amount offered, then the plaintiff shall be awarded actual costs accruing after the offer of settlement to be paid by the defendant."

In the case at hand, the Colorado Court of Appeals was called upon to interpret this statutory meaning, in light of the Governmental Immunity Act. The court's primary task was

DeCordova v State of Colorado
878 P.2d 73 (Colo. App. 1994)
...continued

to provide a statutory construction that would render the enactments effective in accomplishing the purposes for which they were adopted. The court concluded that nothing in the Governmental Immunity Act prohibits the "awarding" of actual costs to a plaintiff, but rather places a limit on the total recovery that a single plaintiff may receive from the government. For example, had the jury returned a verdict for $100,000, the plaintiff would have been entitled to recover from the government the full amount of damages and all of the actual costs awarded. Thus, the plaintiff may recover from the government, in addition to an award for damages, actual costs but only to the extent that the total recovery does not exceed $150,000.

The defendants asserted, on appeal, that it was reversible error for the trial court to enter a directed verdict by finding that, as a matter of law, they were negligent.

It was not contested that the hospital pharmacy made an error in dispensing the prescription. As a result, the child received at least one overdose of approximately five times the level of medication prescribed.

The plaintiff presented evidence, through an expert on acceptable standards of pharmacy practice, that the pharmacist is responsible for accurately filling a prescription and for insuring that the dosage corresponds reasonably for the dosage range for a given patient. The expert further testified that the error committed here was avoidable and fell below minimal acceptable standards of pharmacy practice.

The defendants did not present any witness to controvert the plaintiff's expert. Nor did they offer any evidence that would establish either a lower standard of care or evidence that the conduct in question was within the applicable standard of care. The Court of Appeals could find no error in the trial court's decision to grant the plaintiff's motion for a directed verdict on the single issue of negligence.

There was no evidence in the record from which it could be inferred that a reasonably careful pharmacist would make the kind of error that occurred here. The undisputed evidence established that the standard of care owed by the hospital pharmacy is clearly defined and was breached in this case. However, the defendants argued that because it can be predicted that a certain percentage of errors will occur in filling pharmacy orders, and because not all errors are negligence, the jury could have reasonably inferred that the mistake was the type of calculation error that was not due to negligence, but rather to a statistical error rate that cannot be eliminated. The court concluded that such an argument is disingenuous.

Some negligence in the course of human endeavors is predictable. The mere fact that a certain percentage of errors will predictably occur provides no basis to infer that an error on a particular occasion was free of negligence. "To err is human, to forgive is divine. To be responsible for injuries caused by undisputed negligence is the law of this state." The trial court judgment was affirmed.

The following is a list of court cases that are related to this topic.

Walls v Holland, Slip Op. No. 98-6506, October 19, 1999 (6th Cir.), 1999 U.S. App. LEXIS 26588.
Mark v Williams, 724 P.2d 428 (Wash. App. 1986).

MALPRACTICE INSURANCE

Allstate Insurance Company v Chicago Insurance Company
676 S.2d 271 (Miss. 1996)

FACTS: A pharmacist was sued by the estate of a former patient in a wrongful death lawsuit that claimed the pharmacist was professionally negligent. The pharmacist sought coverage from one or both of the two insurance companies that covered damages claims against the pharmacy. One company insured the pharmacist professionally while the other company insured the business. Both policies contained excess or "other insurance" clauses which conflicted. The Circuit Court granted declaratory judgment ordering one of the insurers to bear the defense costs and potential liability for the claim. That insurer appealed.

HOLDING: The Mississippi Supreme Court ruled that clauses in both of the policies were mutually repugnant and must be disregarded. The Court reversed the lower court decision and remanded the case for determination of the prorated responsibilities of each parties, stating that both parties were to pay one-half of all costs.

Mutual Benefit Insurance v Haver
725 A.2d 743 (Pa. 1999)

The issue in this case was whether an insurance carrier has a duty to defend and possibly indemnify an insured pharmacist. John and Candice Macko filed a complaint against pharmacist Haver seeking recovery for damages allegedly sustained by Candice Macko as a result of Haver's distribution of medications without any prescription. The complaint alleged that Haver dispensed codeine, *Demerol*, barbiturates, sedative hypnotics, sleeping pills, *Valium*, and *Percocet* to Macko without a prescription. The complaint also alleged that Haver ignored requests by Macko's family, physician and psychologist to not provide her with any further medications. Haver submitted Macko's complaint to his insurance carrier, Mutual Benefit Insurance Company. Mutual Benefit contended that it did not have to defend or indemnify Haver because the insurance policy did not cover injuries as a consequence of Haver's "willful harm" or "knowing endangerment." Mutual Benefit asserted that Macko's injuries were the result of Haver's knowing endangerment of dispensing controlled substances without a prescription. A trial judge held that Mutual Benefit was obligated to defend and indemnify Haver for any damages assessed pursuant to the Macko's complaint. The Pennsylvania Supreme Court reversed that decision and held that the insurance carrier had neither the duty to defend nor indemnify. The supreme court found that the allegations of Macko's complaint constituted knowing endangerment as a matter of law, and therefore the knowing endangerment exclusion of the insurance policy prevents Mutual Benefit from having to defend or indemnify. Two justices wrote in a concurring opinion that Haver's guilty plea to federal criminal charges of knowingly, intentionally, and unlawfully distributing controlled substances supported the finding of knowing endangerment.

PART II: STRICT LIABILITY (PRODUCTS LIABILITY)

Distinction Between Negligence, Strict Liability and Products Liability

Mink v University of Chicago, et al
460 F.Supp. 713 (N.D. Ill. 1978)

ISSUE: While a number of legal issues were involved, the court here only decided the threshold question of whether the plaintiffs have a cause of action against the defendants. The actual merits of the case or final outcome was not decided at this point. The plaintiffs framed their case on 3 separate counts, or claims. The court ruled they had a cause of action only on count #1 and on that score would be entitled to their "day in court." Without going into detail, it is enough to state here that counts' #2 and #3 were dismissed because plaintiffs failed to state in the complaint what specific "abnormalities" they themselves suffered from the DES. The court did indicate that they could amend their complaint (if they had evidence of such injuries).

FACTS: This case is different from the usual patient suit against a pharmaceutical manufacturer and physician prescriber for drug product injury. The typical suit against the drug maker is in strict liability and negligence for failure to warn of a known danger or that a defective drug was marketed. The typical claim against the physician is for negligence in prescribing and failing to warn. In the case here, the plaintiff-patients were part of a university experiment, and they were not told of the drug treatment. Therefore, they claim a legal cause of action for "battery" based on their lack of consent to administration of the drug. Further, after the cancer risks of the drug therapy became medically known, it is claimed the notification on the part of the university was insufficient and on the part of the drug maker, nonexistent as to the plaintiff-patients.

Note: As stated in *Hill v E.R. Squibb and Sons*, the general rule is that the drug maker's duty to adequately warn as to dangers inherent in prescription drugs runs only to the physician, not to the patient or public (see *Torsiello v Whitehall Laboratories, etc*). But, on a state-by-state basis, the courts differ on this rule. Perhaps, the key word is "adequate" in relation to the warning to the physician.

The reported facts may be summarized as follows: The plaintiffs are representing themselves and 1000 other women who were part of a general medical experiment conducted by defendants, a university hospital and a drug manufacturer. The experiment took place between 1950 and 1952 and entailed the administration of diethylstilbestrol ("DES") as prenatal care. The experiment was part of a "double-blind" study to determine if DES would prevent miscarriages. The women involved in this suit were not told they were part of an experiment or that DES was being given to them. The relationship between DES therapy and cancer became medically known in 1971 and the university notified the plaintiffs in 1975 and 1976. The notification was of the use of DES in pregnant women and the possibility of genital abnormalities in their offspring. The notice told the plaintiffs to contact their sons and daughters for medical examination.

Claim #1 was based on action for battery. In the usual legal sense, a battery claim is predicated on the "unauthorized touching of the person by another"; the touching may be even harmless, but offensive, and the victim has a right of action which includes recovery for any mental disturbance inflicted. The essence of the "battery" here was the administration of the DES. This act provided the physical contact, claimed by the plaintiffs to be without consent. However, the defendants claimed that when the plaintiffs entered the university hospital, the general consent to treatment signed by them was "consent" to the DES treatment.

Mink v University of Chicago, et al
460 F.Supp. 713 (N.D. Ill. 1978)
...continued

But, the court indicated that this was a question for a jury to decide, and, on the surface, the complaint stated a cause of action in battery against both defendants.

RULING: As previously stated, the court acknowledged that plaintiffs had stated a cause of action in battery against both defendants and the case was then returned to the trial stage for further proceedings on that issue.

REASONING: The importance of this case is in what the court stated as to the duty to notify of the risks of DES therapy. The court stated as follows:

> We agree that both defendants had a duty to notify the plaintiff patients of the risks inherent in DES treatment when they became aware, or should have become aware, of the relationship between DES and cancer...The university's duty to notify is simply an extension of duty of physicians to warn their patients of the risks inherent in treatment...The fact the knowledge of the risk was obtained after the patient was treated does not alter the obligation...Defendant Lilly has a continuing obligation as a manufacturer of drugs to warn of risks inherent in its drugs...A claim based on a drug manufacturer's failure to warn may be premised on strict liability or negligence...The breach, if any, thus occurred when the defendant Lilly learned, or should have learned, of the connection between DES and cancer, and failed to issue a warning revealing that risk. (citations and parts of quotation omitted)

It should be mentioned that the university did issue a warning in 1975 and 1976 to the patients treated with DES, but the plaintiff-patients claimed the notification was insufficient because of its delay and because it failed to advise of the precautions that should be taken by DES patients.

Altieri v CVS Pharmacy
Slip Op No X06CV020171626S (December 13, 2002), 2002 Conn. Super. LEXIS 4041

The decedent presented a prescription for opium tincture camphorated to a CVS Pharmacy on June 14, 2001. Instead of properly filling the prescription, the defendants allegedly misfilled the prescription with opium tincture, which contains a substantially higher concentration of morphine than opium tincture camphorated. The decedent died on June 15, 2001. The patient's estate filed a 12-count amended complaint against, among others, defendants, a pharmacy corporation, a pharmaceutical staff employer, and a pharmacist employer. The estate administrator's amended complaint named, among others as defendants, the pharmacy corporation, the pharmaceutical staff employer, and the pharmacist employer. It alleged that they acted negligently, that they acted recklessly, that they violated the Connecticut Unfair Trade Practices Act, *Conn. Gen. Stat. §42–110a* et seq. (CUTPA), and that the pharmaceutical staff employer violated the Connecticut Products Liability Act, *Conn. Gen. Stat. §52-572m* et seq. The defendants moved to strike the counts alleging recklessness, CUTPA violations, and the alleged violation of the product liability statute. The Court of Appeals determined that the recklessness claims against the respective corporate defendants do not merely repeat the negligence allegations. The recklessness counts differ from the negligence counts by their inclusion of the allegation that there are numerous instances of prior misfilled prescriptions. If the plaintiff were to demonstrate numerous misfilled prescriptions of which the defendants had prior knowledge, and deaths resulting from such mis-

Altieri v CVS Pharmacy
Slip Op No X06CV020171626S (December 13, 2002), 2002 Conn. Super. LEXIS 4041
...continued

filled prescriptions, then such conduct could meet the legal standard of reckless conduct. As to the strict liability claim, the court finds the act of filling a prescription is a service and therefore is not subject to the products liability act. The Court held that CUTPA claims against health providers are limited to the entrepreneurial or business aspect of the provision of services, aside from medical competence. In this case, the CUTPA claims did not implicate the required "entrepreneurial aspects" of the business of pharmacies.

The following is a list of court cases that are related to this topic.

Perez v Wyeth Laboratories, Inc., 734 A.2d 1245 (N.J. 1999).
Rivera v Wyeth-Ayerst Laboratories, Slip Op No G-00-345 (November 7, 2000), USDC Tx., 2000 U.S. Dist. LEXIS 17143.
Washington v Bayer, Slip Op No 02–0856R (May 16, 2002), USDC La. 2002 U.S. Dist. LEXIS 9153.

Basis of Liability

Elsroth v Johnson & Johnson
700 F.Supp. 151 (S.D.N.Y. 1988)

ISSUE: Whether the manufacturer and retailer of an *otc* drug that had been tampered with by an unknown third person were liable to the estate of a woman who died after ingesting the product.

FACTS: In September of 1982, this country was faced with a series of homicides in Chicago stemming from cyanide tampering of *Extra-Strength Tylenol* capsules. In response to those tragedies, the pharmaceutical industry, in concert with the federal government, moved to protect consumers from the perils by requiring tamper-resistant packaging applicable to most *otc* drugs. FDA regulations define a "tamper-resistant package" as one having an indicator or barrier to entry which, if breached or missing, can reasonably be expected to provide visible evidence to consumers that tampering has occurred (21 CFR Section 211.132[g][1987]). Following the issuance of this rule, the makers of *Tylenol* marketed the product in packaging with a foil seal glued to the mouth of the container or bottle, a "shrink seal" around the neck and cap of the container, and a sealed box. In 1986, after a considerable period of market losses, *Tylenol* regained its dominant position in the market for *otc* pain relievers. It is against this backdrop that the present case took place.

On February 4, 1986, Harriet Notarnicola purchased a box of *Extra-Strength Tylenol* capsules from a grocery store owned by the Great Atlantic & Pacific Tea Co. Mrs. Notarnicola testified that the package did not appear out of the ordinary in any way. The decedent, Diane Elsroth, was visiting her boyfriend, the son of Mrs. Notarnicola. When Elsroth complained of a headache, the son went to the kitchen, opened the box and took out two capsules. The son testified that he noticed nothing unusual about the packaging and that the flaps of the box were glued shut. Furthermore, the foil seal had not been broken.

A short time after ingesting the capsules, Ms. Elsroth retired, mentioning that she was not feeling will. Her dead body was found the next day. The medical examiner concluded that the *Tylenol* capsules she had ingested were contaminated by a lethal dose of cyanide. The murder remains unsolved. The most likely scenario appears to suggest that an unknown third

Elsroth v Johnson & Johnson
700 F.Supp. 151 (S.D.N.Y. 1988)
...continued

party purchased or stole the product from the grocery store, breached the packaging, and placed cyanide inside several of the gelatin capsules. The individual replaced the now contaminated capsules in the container and somehow was able to reseal the container and box in such a way that the tampering was not readily detectable. Ms. Elsroth's estate brought this action against the grocery store chain and McNeil Consumer Products, a division of Johnson & Johnson. The plaintiff sought $1 million in compensatory damages and $92 million in punitive damages along with $500,000 for medical, funeral and other expenses.

RULING: The federal district court granted the defendant's motion for summary judgment.

REASONING: The plaintiff contended that as a result of the Chicago tampering cases in 1982, the retailer was on notice that *Tylenol* could be the target of tampering. The court's decision began with the well-traveled proposition that negligence conditioned on the existence of a legal duty. While the retailer-patron relationship triggers the existence of certain duties, the court concluded that preventing acts of tampering by an unknown third party did not fall within this legal responsibility. This was particularly true in this case where the evidence suggested that the tampering took place off the premises with the contaminated product being returned to the store's shelves by the wrongdoer. There was simply no feasible way in which the retailer could have prevented the kind of tampering that occurred here. The court was not willing to impose a duty to place such a product "behind-the-counter" despite the fact that the same brand of drug had been tampered with three years earlier.

The plaintiff next argued strict products liability claims. However, the court noted that strict liability is not absolute liability. The plaintiff's claims, if adopted, would create absolute liability by rendering retailers guarantors of the products they sell. While the tampering obviously caused the product to be in an unreasonably dangerous condition when it left the retailer's shelf, that condition could not be attributed to the retailer on a product defect theory. It was attributable solely to the criminal intervention of a third party. The court could find no common law duty which required drug manufacturers to design their products in such a way as to anticipate and frustrate criminal tampering. While manufacturers are under a duty to warn of dangers that may be associated with the normal and lawful use of their products, there is no duty to warn that a product may be susceptible to criminal misuse.

The following is a list of court cases that are related to this topic.

Anderson v International Industries, Slip Op No 2000-CA-2554 (November 14, 2001) 2001 La. App. LEXIS 2709.

DRUG PRODUCTS LIABILITY AND PHARMACISTS

Negligent Misrepresentation

Foster v American Home Products Corp.
29 F.3d 165 (4th Cir. 1994)

ISSUE: The issue presented at trial and on appeal was whether the manufacturer of a brand name prescription drug could be held liable on a negligent misrepresentation theory for a death caused by another company's generically equivalent drug.

FACTS: In 1988, the Fosters' physician prescribed *Phenergan* syrup for their infant twins Brandy and Bradley who were suffering from colic. The pharmacy substituted promethazine syrup, a generic equivalent of *Phenergan*, manufactured and sold by My-K Laboratories, Inc.

The Foster twins were given the generic promethazine several times over the next several days. One morning, 6-week-old Brandy was found dead in her crib. The autopsy report attributed her death to Sudden Infant Death Syndrome (SIDS). A pediatrician from the Maryland SIDS Center opined that Brandy's death was caused by promethazine.

The Fosters brought suit in the Maryland court system against Wyeth and Barre-National Corporation. At the time of filing suit, the Fosters believed that Barre-National had manufactured the generic promethazine that their daughter was given. Wyeth removed the case to the federal court system on grounds of diversity of citizenship. The District Court granted Barre-National summary judgment when it was determined that My-K Laboratories had manufactured the drug actually dispensed. The Fosters then brought suit against My-K, but agreed to a dismissal with prejudice for reasons not stated in the record.

The Fosters' complaint against Wyeth included 4 counts: (1) negligence - wrongful death; (2) negligence - survivorship; (3) strict liability; and (4) breach of warranty. Wyeth moved for summary judgment on all counts arguing that it could not be liable for Brandy's death because it did not manufacture the promethazine that was dispensed.

RULING: The trial court allowed the Fosters' negligent misrepresentation action to proceed because it was viewed as distinct from the plaintiff's product liability claims. The U.S. Court of Appeals did not see any validity in this distinction. Although actions for negligent misrepresentation arise in many contexts other than product liability, in this case the allegations of negligent misrepresentation were seen as an effort to recover for damages caused by a product without meeting the requirements the law imposes in product liability actions. Maryland law requires a plaintiff seeking to recover for an injury by a product to demonstrate that the defendant actually manufactured the product at issue. The Fosters were attempting to hold Wyeth liable for injuries caused by another manufacturer's product, which would be rejected under Maryland law.

REASONING: The trial court granted Wyeth summary judgment on the negligence, strict liability and breach of warranty counts because Wyeth did not manufacture the drug at issue. However, the trial court allowed the negligent misrepresentation claim to stand.

The court stated that it was assuming that Wyeth was promoting the use of promethazine in general, as opposed to only its own product, *Phenergan*. The court further stated that if Wyeth made a false representation concerning the safety of promethazine for use in infants and the prescribing physician relied on the representation in prescribing the drug for Brandy Foster, then Wyeth may be liable for harm caused to Brandy as a result of the ingestion of the drug, even if it was not Wyeth's product.

Foster v American Home Products Corp.
29 F.3d 165 (4th Cir. 1994)
...continued

The Food, Drug and Cosmetic Act requires that manufacturers obtain regulatory approval for drugs prior to marketing them. For drugs that have never been marketed before, the approval process requires submission of a new drug application (NDA) which mandates costly and time-consuming studies of the drug's safety and efficacy. With the enactment of the Drug Price Competition and Patent Term Restoration Act of 1984, generic drugs can now gain approval pursuant to an abbreviated new drug application (ANDA) which permits the applicant to provide data demonstrating that the generic drug is the same as a previously approved drug in terms of its use, active ingredients, method of administration, dosage, strength and bioequivalence... all of this in lieu of studies necessary for an initial NDA.

Thus, a generic manufacturer is not required to perform safety and effectiveness studies if it can prove its drug is equivalent to a previously approved drug. Manufacturers of generic drugs may alter a drug's labeling "to add or strengthen a contraindication, warning, precaution or adverse reaction or to delete false, misleading or unsupported indications for use or claims for effectiveness" without prior FDA approval.

For economic reasons, generic manufacturers accept without question the studies performed by brand name drug companies and simply copy verbatim the brand name drug's package labeling. Unless a physician affirmatively indicates that a prescription is to be dispensed as written, most states permit a pharmacist to substitute a lower-priced generic equivalent of the name brand drug actually prescribed.

In a rather ingenious argument, the plaintiffs contended that because generic drugs are required by federal law to be equivalent to their brand name counterparts, any representations Wyeth makes when advertising *Phenergan* also apply to generic promethazine. The plaintiffs further argued that brand name manufacturers know that generic companies rely on their studies and duplicate their labeling and that if the brand name manufacturer does not issue a warning, it will simply not be made.

As part of their argument, the plaintiffs stated that they will be unable to recover from a generic manufacturer on a negligent misrepresentation theory because the generic manufacturer did not formulate any of the representations it made regarding its product, but simply duplicated the brand name manufacturer's representations. The court would not accept this assertion. When a generic manufacturer adopts brand name manufacturer's warnings and representations without independent investigation, it does so at the risk that such warnings may be flawed.

Following the court's logic, a manufacturer of generic products is responsible for the accuracy of labels placed on its products. Although generic manufacturers must include the same labeling information as the brand name drug, they are also permitted to add or strengthen warnings and delete misleading statements in the labeling, even without prior FDA approval. The statutory scheme governing premarket approval for drugs simply does not provide evidence that Congress intended to insulate generic drug manufacturers from liability for misrepresentations made regarding their products.

The court also rejected the contention that a brand name manufacturer's statements regarding its drug can serve as the basis for liability for injuries caused by another manufacturer's drug. Brand name advertising benefits generic competitors because generics are generally sold as substitutes; the more a brand name drug is prescribed, the more potential sales exist for its generic equivalents. There is no legal precedent for using a brand name manufacturer's statements about its own product as a basis for liability for injuries caused by anoth-

Foster v American Home Products Corp.
29 F.3d 165 (4th Cir. 1994)
...continued

er's products, over whose production the brand name manufacturer has no control. This would be especially unfair when the generic manufacturer reaps the benefits of the brand name manufacturer's statements by copying its labels and riding on the coattails of its advertising.

The court also concluded that the plaintiffs' negligent misrepresentation action should fail because Wyeth was under no duty of care to the Fosters. To impose a duty in the circumstances of this case would stretch the concept of foreseeability too far. There was no relationship between the parties to this case since Brandy was injured by a product that Wyeth did not manufacture. Because Wyeth has no duty to the users of other manufacturers' products, a negligent misrepresentation action cannot be maintained based on the facts of this case.

The following is a list of court cases that are related to this topic.

Raynor v Richardson-Merrell, Inc., 643 F. Supp. 238 (D.D.C. 1986).

Manufacturing Defect

Murphy v E.R. Squibb & Sons, Inc.
202 Cal.Rptr. 802 (Ct. App. 1984)

ISSUE: Whether a pharmacy can be held strictly liable in tort for injuries caused by a drug that was allegedly defectively designed.

FACTS: In 1976, Christine Murphy filed a complaint for injuries against Exclusive Prescription Pharmacy Corporation (hereafter referred to as pharmacy) and E. R. Squibb & Sons Company for injuries allegedly resulting from her mother's ingestion of the drug, diethylstilbestrol (DES). Murphy alleged that her prenatal exposure to the drug DES caused her cancer, and she proceeded on the theory that the drug was defectively designed and that pursuant to California law, the drug's retailer and one of the drug's known manufacturers (Squibb) were both strictly liable in tort for her injuries.

The trial was set for February 2, 1982, but on February 3, prior to the selection of a jury, the court granted the pharmacy's motion for judgment on the pleadings. On the following day, the plaintiff and defendant Squibb went to the trial on the issue of product identification. After receiving conflicting evidence as to the identification of the drug taken by the plaintiff's mother, the jury determined (11 to 1) that the DES purchased by the plaintiff's mother was not manufactured by Squibb. The plaintiff appealed the jury verdict and the court's order dismissing the pharmacy.

RULING: The legal theory of strict liability does not apply to pharmacists who dispense a drug that was allegedly defectively designed.

REASONING: The plaintiff's main argument against the pharmacy was that the retailer as well as the manufacturer of a defective product may be held strictly accountable in tort for injuries caused by said product. The court found that such reasoning had no basis under existing California law. The crux of the issue was whether the pharmacy performed a service, sold a product, or both. The significance of such a determination was that where the pri-

Murphy v E.R. Squibb & Sons, Inc.
202 Cal.Rptr. 802 (Ct. App. 1984)
...continued

mary objective of a transaction was to obtain or perform a service, rather than the sale of a product, the doctrine of strict liability did not apply. As a corollary, it was fundamental that persons providing services for others must satisfy only a duty of reasonable care and could not be held responsible for injury in the absence of negligence or intentional misconduct.

The court stated that "Undeniable suppliers of a product, pharmacists have also been resolutely declared by our Legislature to be service-performing professionals. This fact, in and of itself, would seem to be determinative of the issue at hand. However, the problem is far more complex due to the pharmacists' obvious duality of function." The plaintiff acknowledged pharmacy as a profession, but insisted that merchandising is the pharmacist's primary function. The plaintiff contended that "each party responsible for bringing a product to the consumer gains a financial benefit from the ultimate sale of that product, thereby giving rise to a modern theory of 'risk-spreading,' which forms the basis of California products liability law."

Essentially, the plaintiff advocated that a long line of California cases (well familiar to law students) sets the standard that all merchandisers of products to the public are potentially accountable under strict liability theories, without regard to whether or not they also provide a service.

In response, the court noted that claims against pharmacists for the sale of defective drugs, based upon the doctrine of strict liability, had been met with unequivocal rejection in other jurisdictions. The court reviewed the *McLeod*, *Batiste*, and *Bichler* cases that all rejected strict liability claims against pharmacists. The plaintiff challenged the cases as being non-reflective of California law.

Mindful of the plaintiff's criticisms of previous case authority, the court made a powerful statement regarding the profession of pharmacy. The court found it impossible to ignore certain policy considerations regarding the service performed by pharmacists. Doctors and dentists provide a service, and pharmacists provide a service too and should be exempt from strict liability claims of the type discussed in this case. Citing previous case law, the court stated that

> "The services of experts are sought because of their special skill. They have a duty to exercise the ordinary skill and competence of members of their profession, and a failure to discharge that duty will subject them to liability for negligence. Those who hire such persons are not justified in expecting infallibility, but can expect only reasonable care and competence. They purchase service, not insurance."

Thus, the court concluded that the purchasers of a service cannot expect perfection as one might expect from a product.

The appellate court was appreciative of the fact that providing a service often entails providing a product. The court reviewed a long line of judicial decisions that attempted to exempt the providers of a service from strict liability. These cases illustrated a reluctance by the courts to extend strict liability to individuals offering medical treatment or services. The court found that although the shadow of commercialism was endemic to pharmacy, the profession still performed a service that was far greater than its business aspects and thus exempted the profession from strict liability.

Murphy v E.R. Squibb & Sons, Inc.
202 Cal.Rptr. 802 (Ct. App. 1984)
...continued

The court made the following statements:

> "Prescription drugs are chemicals which pose a real danger to life and health. Consequently, only persons with special training are allowed to prescribe and handle them. For the same reason, the sale of drugs is highly regulated which in turn creates an entirely different chain of merchandising than the that ordinarily encountered with other products...Both the doctor and the patient place great trust in the professional abilities of the pharmacist to deliver not only the exact formula, but also the exact amount of the drug to the patient as prescribed. Further, it is the pharmacist's obligation to have specialized knowledge in the area of toxicology, being able to recognize various contraindications for drugs prescribed, inclusive of numerous potentially dangerous drug interactions. Hence, the skill of the pharmacist directly safeguards the patient and is perhaps inextricably coupled with the prescriber's treatment of same. Either as a service provider himself, or as an intermediary, necessary in the treatment offered by a licensed drug prescriber, a pharmacist's learned abilities feature far more prominently than his commercial pursuits in determining his liability."

Thus, the court rejected any application of strict liability to the pharmacy in connection with the sale of the DES. The court went on to affirm the trial court decision exonerating Squibb of any liability because of the plaintiff's failure to prove that Squibb manufactured the product ingested by the plaintiff's mother.

This case was upheld by the California Supreme Court in a 4 to 3 decision. Rejecting arguments that the practice of pharmacy has fallen to the level of a common retail enterprise comparable to a hardware store, a sharply divided court refused to expand the liability of pharmacists. In his opinion for the court, Justice Mosk wrote "it is pure hyperbole to suggest, as does the plaintiff, that the role of the pharmacist is similar to that of a clerk in an ordinary retail store." The plaintiff's lawyers argued that modern day pharmacists simply fill bottles and sell the drugs, but attorneys for the pharmacy countered that pharmacists are highly trained professionals, who provide services such as advising patients about proper drug usage and detecting possible harmful drug interactions. The judge wrote that if strict liability were extended to pharmacists, they might refuse to dispense drugs that present even a remote risk of harm.

🔨 🔨 🔨

Welkener v Kirkwood Drug Store Co.
734 S.W.2d 233 (Mo. App. 1987)

ISSUE: Whether the pharmacy that sold a pair of crutches may obtain indemnity from the manufacturer for a jury verdict in favor of a consumer who was injured when the crutches broke.

FACTS: The plaintiff, a 39-year-old man weighing 265 pounds, was injured on the job when he attempted to unload a heavy bag of flour. He fell on his leg and injured his left knee. Hospital personnel placed a bandage on the knee and advised him to contact an orthopedic physician and "rent a set of crutches." The plaintiff left the hospital and went to the Kirkwood Drug Store where a salesperson attempted to fit a pair of crutches to his height. After reconstructive knee surgery, the plaintiff spent a period of time at home convalescing.

Welkener v Kirkwood Drug Store Co.
734 S.W.2d 233 (Mo. App. 1987)
...continued

One evening while trying to negotiate the stairway to his basement bedroom, the left crutch fell apart and the plaintiff fell down the flight of steps. He broke his wrist and his forearm was also injured. He spent several weeks in the hospital and suffered a substantial amount of lost wages.

The crutches were made, designed and distributed by the Pioneer Company. The crutches were made about 20 years prior to the lawsuit.

The plaintiff brought a products liability lawsuit against Kirkwood Drug Store for the injuries sustained while using the crutches. Kirkwood then filed a third party claim against Pioneer for indemnity or contribution.

RULING: The jury returned a verdict in favor of the plaintiff for $255,000 and also awarded the plaintiff's wife $10,000 for loss of consortium. The court then found in favor of Kirkwood Drug Store against Pioneer for the same amount based upon the pharmacy's indemnity claim.

REASONING: Missouri has adopted the doctrine of strict liability that one who sells a product in a defective condition, unreasonably dangerous to the user, is subject to liability for injury caused by the defect. All parties in the chain of distribution of a product, including manufacturers, sellers, wholesalers or other middlemen come within the umbrella of the rule.

Generally, the seller-retailer who neither knows nor has reason to know that a product manufactured by another is defective has no duty to test or inspect the product. However, if the defect is such that a reasonably prudent seller should have discovered it before selling the product, the seller may be held liable for injuries caused by the defect. The law generally places final responsibility upon the party primarily responsible for the defective product, in most instances, its manufacturer.

The Missouri Court of Appeals agreed that the seller, who is lower in the chain of distribution, who sells a product without actual or constructive knowledge of a defect and who has no duty to inspect, is entitled to indemnity against one higher in the chain of distribution, such as the manufacturer.

The following is a list of court cases that are related to this topic.

Holbrook v Rose, 458 S.W. 2d 155 (Ky. 1970).
Michael v Warner-Chilcott, 91 N.M. 561, 579 P. 2d 183 (1978).
Coyle v Richardson-Merrell, Inc., 538 A.2d 1379 (Pa. Super. 1988).
Ross Laboratories v Theis, 725 P.2d 1076 (Alaska 1986).
Pilet v Ciba-Geigy, No. 96-021 Section: E/2, 1996 U.S. Dist. LEXIS 2344 (E.D. La. Feb. 29, 1996).

Warning Defect

Kaspirowitz v Schering Corp.
175 A.2d 658 (N.J. 1961)

ISSUE: Whether sale of a federal legend drug without a prescription constitutes negligence and whether labeled warnings provided by the manufacturer were adequate.

FACTS: Plaintiff entered the defendant's pharmacy and asked the pharmacist for "something for dandruff." The pharmacist sold him *Sebizon*, a legend drug preparation made by Schering Corporation for the treatment of dandruff; the sale was *otc* and without prescription. The plaintiff observed the warning legend on the label of the container "Caution: Federal law prohibits dispensing without prescription." Upon inquiring of the pharmacist about the warning, the plaintiff received the reply from the pharmacist: "That was all right...nothing to worry about." The plaintiff used the *Sebizon* on his scalp and developed a severe case of contact dermatitis, which expert medical testimony attributed to the use of *Sebizon*.

The plaintiff sued the pharmacist, claiming the pharmacist was negligent in selling the drug in violation of federal law and also that the pharmacist violated the implied warranty of fitness for a particular purpose, and sued the manufacturer, claiming the manufacturer (1) was negligent in failing to warn the public of the dangers inherent to the use of *Sebizon*; (2) breached an express warranty that the product was safe; and (3) violated an implied warranty of merchantability. In essence, the plaintiff's claim against Schering was that it should have labeled the container "Federal Law prohibits use without prescription" instead of the "Federal Law prohibits dispensing without prescription;" the latter phrase applying caution only to the pharmacist and not the public as claimed by the plaintiff.

In the suit against the pharmacist, a settlement was reached out of court and the suit dropped. (Although the reported facts do not state the circumstances or terms of the settlement, presumably, the pharmacist or his insurance company paid the plaintiff monetary damages but did not admit liability.)

RULING: The trial court dismissed the suit against Schering and the plaintiff appealed. The Appellate Division of the Superior Court of New Jersey affirmed the dismissal.

REASONING: The New Jersey court ruled that this was not a case brought on a charge of defective product, but rather a claim of inadequate warning to the public and such a claim was not proved since, in fact, the product was to be dispensed by prescription only and the manufacturer correctly labeled it so in accordance with federal law.

Krug v Sterling Drug, Inc.
416 S.W.2d 143 (Mo. 1967)

ISSUE: Whether a pharmaceutical manufacturer has a legal duty to warn the medical profession in a timely fashion of product side effects and whether a pharmacist has an obligation to alert prescribers or patients of potential side effects.

FACTS: A person who suffered irreversible eye damage as a side effect of chloroquine drug treatment sued the pharmaceutical manufacturer and the pharmacy that dispensed the drug to her on her doctor(s) prescriptions. The trial court ruled in favor of the patient and against the drug firm, awarding the patient $125,000 damages; the court ruled in favor of the pharmacy acquitting it of liability to the patient. The drug company appealed the ruling against

Krug v Sterling Drug, Inc.
416 S.W.2d 143 (Mo. 1967)
...continued

it, and the pharmacy filed a cross-complaint against the drug company asking the drug company to reimburse it for the $5,753 it spent in defending itself in the lawsuit.

Basically, the plaintiff's (patient's) claim against the pharmaceutical firm was that it failed to give timely and adequate warning to the medical profession of certain side effects of the drug chloroquine (trade names, Aralen, Triquin, and Plaquenil), all produced by 2 drug firms which actually are one and the same company. The plaintiff was on chloroquine from about 1953 until 1961 or 1962. In the original package insert material, the drug firm noted among the side effects of the drug "blurred vision" but noted that this disappeared on reduction of dose or discontinuance of the drug. Irreversible eye damage as a side effect of chloroquine was first reported in a 1959 issue of the English medical journal *Lancet*.

Reports of such in American medical journals began appearing in 1961; the drug firm's first effective warning to physicians appeared in 1963.

RULING: The appellate court reaffirmed the trial court's $125,000 judgment against the drug firm.

REASONING: The action was based on the negligence of the drug firm in failing to give adequate warnings of the side effect to the medical profession. In this respect, the court stated:

> [W]here the drug is a prescription drug, the manufacturer has a duty to properly warn the doctor of the dangers involved.

> But significant here as far as _____ is concerned is the fact medical journals, of which [it] was bound to have knowledge...warned of the hazardous side effects of chloroquine and even then the appellant [drug firm] did not change its literature timely and adequately to warn the profession.

With reference to the pharmacy's cross-complaint against the drug firm for reimbursement of attorney fees spent by the pharmacy in defense of the suit, the appellate court ruled that the drug firm was not liable for reimbursement of these fees. The argument presented on the appeal, by the attorneys representing the pharmacy was, in effect, that the plaintiff was injured by the fault of the drug firm and, in turn, the drug firm's fault exposed the pharmacy to the suit; hence, the drug firm should pay the pharmacy's costs in its defense. However, and this is the point made by the appellate court, the plaintiff in her complaint alleged that the pharmacy was negligent in its own right in that it (1) failed to inform itself by literature or by any other means of the dangerous qualities of said drug...(2) and it failed to warn the medical profession or the public through advertisement or in any manner of the danger of the further use of said products. As it so happened, the trial court directed verdict in favor of the pharmacy, thereby absolving it from liability, but the appellate court refused to allow attorney fee reimbursements on the grounds that the accusation against the pharmacy was "primary" in nature.

Michael v Warner-Chilcott
579 P. 2d 183 (N.M. 1978)

ISSUE: Whether cautionary labeling on an *otc* sinus medication was sufficient to bar a suit against the manufacturer for alleged adverse effects.

FACTS: This rather interesting court case may open a whole series of law suits against the manufacturers of nonprescription or *otc* drugs.

The plaintiff-consumer in this case brought suit for kidney damage claimed to have occurred to him because of the use of a nonprescription sinus relief drug product, *Sinutab*, and its chain store in-house counterpart called *Sinus Congestion Tablets*. The plaintiff sued the manufacturers and sellers of these drug products including the pharmacy drug chain and the drug wholesaler. The plaintiff predicated his claims against these numerous defendants associated with the production, distribution or sale of *Sinutab* and *Sinus Congestion Tablets*, in strict liability and negligence in that:

(a) The products were defectively designed (in that their risks outweighed their benefits), and
(b) The warnings provided were inadequate.

At the trial of the case, some of the defendants moved (asked) the judge for summary judgment in their favor. The trial court judge refused to grant the defendant's request for summary judgment. At this point in the trial, the defendants had the right to, and did, appeal the judge's ruling to an appellate court, in this case the New Mexico Court of Appeals.

The appeals court affirmed the trial judge's refusal to grant summary judgment (dismissal) for the defendants and in so doing put forth certain rules of law applicable to the marketing of nonprescription or *otc* drugs. By its ruling, the appeals court, in effect, sent the case back to the trial court for trial of the factual issues raised by the plaintiff in his suit.

The reported facts of the case are as follows: The plaintiff-consumer had been suffering from sinus congestion since 1952. He took a variety of medicines for the condition and, in 1965, his physician prescribed *Sinutab* by a prescription with directions to take 4 tablets daily. When the plaintiff-consumer found out he could buy this drug without the prescription, he threw it away and purchased the *Sinutabs otc*. He read the labeling on the *Sinutab* container as to dosage but did not recall reading the warning about possible kidney damage. He took the *Sinutabs* at 4 tablets daily from 1965 on, and continued to see his physician intermittently until 1970.

In 1979, the plaintiff went to a certain chain-store pharmacy and was told by a cashier that the in-house brand, called *Sinus Congestion Tablets*, contained the same ingredients as *Sinutab* and was cheaper. The plaintiff compared the ingredients and, finding them to be identical, purchased the *Sinus Congestion Tablets*. The front panel of the box contained the name of the product and ingredients. The left side label contained the dosage. The right side label contained the following "WARNING" in small lettering, as follows:

> This medication may damage the kidneys when used in large amounts or for a long period of time. Do not take more than the recommended dosage, nor take regularly for longer than 10 days without consulting your physician. Keep this and all medications out of the reach of children. In case of accidental overdose, contact a physician immediately.

Again, the plaintiff-consumer's claims against the defendants can be summarized as (1) a claim of failure to adequately warn the plaintiff, as an ordinary consumer, of the danger that long-term ingestion of the product will cause permanent, severe, life-shortening kidney dis-

Michael v Warner-Chilcott
579 P. 2d 183 (N.M. 1978)
...continued

ease, and (2) a claim of strict liability on the part of the defendants, irrespective of any warnings provided [that is to say that the product itself was defective].

RULING: The appeals court then affirmed the trial court judge's ruling, which denied summary judgment (dismissal) for defendants - in effect, sending the case back to the trial court for full trial.

REASONING: The majority of the judges on the appeals court addressed themselves solely to the issue of whether the label warning was adequate. As a defense, the defendants claimed that the plaintiff had seriously abused the use of the product by taking it beyond 10 days without consulting a physician. The court answered this point by indicating that if this was, in fact, true, it would be contributory negligence on the part of the plaintiff but it does not bear on the issue of the labeling adequacy.

Defendants also raised the defense that "The warning on the label was adopted verbatim from the warning promulgated by the FDA in 1964. The regulation is still in effect, 21 C.F.R. Sec. 201.309 (1977)." The court answered this argument by citing cases that held that the Federal Act does not purport to change the common-law duty to warn that, "Statutes and regulations of these agencies [federal/state drug control agencies] merely set minimum standards."

The appeals court then looked at the labeling itself and found that a genuine issue existed on the adequacy of the warning because of the following factors: The warning stated that this medication *may* damage the kidneys, it did not apprise the consumer that it *will* damage the kidneys...when used in *large* amounts (emphasis added). Further, the court said the term "large" was vague and indefinite to the consumer. The labeling also did not state that "phenacetin" was a dangerous drug and the warning lettering was so small it might require a consumer to use a magnifying glass in order to read it.

Note: One of the appellate court judges, while concurring in the decision of the other judges, wrote a specially concurring opinion. In it, he stated that the plaintiff-consumer's real issue of fact was "with regard to the claim of 'defective design,' or risks that outweigh benefits so far that no warning could provide adequate protection for the consumer." The plaintiff was able to present some medical testimony to the trial court, even though the court did not complete the trial because of the defendants' motion for summary judgment in their favor, the court's denial of the motion and the defendants' subsequent appeal. A nephrologist testified that he was of the medical opinion that "...products containing phenacetin or acetamenophen [sic] are unreasonably dangerous for over-the-counter sales not controlled by physicians' prescription because any beneficial effect they may have is outweighed by the danger of their use without control by a qualified physician." The physician further stated "...No laymen could be expected to medically evaluate the seriousness or the risk of kidney damage, even with specific data."

Hill v E.R. Squibb & Sons
592 P.2d 1383 (Mont. 1979)

ISSUE: Adequacy of warnings contained in a package insert.

FACTS: The plaintiffs, husband-patient and his wife, sued a drug manufacturer and the pre-scribing physician for side effects suffered by the husband as a result of steroid therapy. The plaintiffs claimed that the drug maker marketed a defective steroid product and that the pre-scribing physician failed to advise of the risks of steroid treatment and failed to properly monitor it. The plaintiffs lost their case at the trial court level and, on appeal, the Supreme Court of Montana affirmed the decision in favor of defendants.

A brief summary of the reported facts of the case are as follows: The plaintiff was an auto mechanic who suffered from contact dermatitis precipitated by several substances, mostly petro chemicals. His physician treated him with ACTH injections (to stimulate natural body production of cortisone, an anti-inflammatory hormone), steroid (cortisone-like) creams, and steroid oral drugs. From 1965 to 1970, the physician gave the plaintiff-patient injections of a steroid called *Kenalog-40*; this was in addition to the other steroid therapy. Eventually, the plaintiff sought treatment at the Billings Clinic where the steroid therapy was tapered off, but his dermatitis worsened to the point of disability and loss of job. He later developed cataracts and osteoporosis (loss of calcium in bones), which are characteristic side effects of steroid therapy. In 1974, he and his wife sued the defendants.

The plaintiffs lost their case against the drug manufacturer. The court held as follows.

RULING: As a general rule, the duty of a drug manufacturer to warn of the dangers inher-ent in a prescription drug is satisfied if adequate warning is given to the physician who pre-scribed it.

Therefore, the appellate court affirmed the trial court judge's directed verdict in favor of the drug manufacturer and the jury's verdict in favor of the prescribing physician.

REASONING: The plaintiffs were unable to produce any medical expert testimony at trial to show that the package insert was inadequate in its warning of dangers in use of the ste-roid [*Kenalog-40*]. On the negligence issue, the jury rendered a verdict in the physician's favor. The testimony in the case indicated that while the doctor did not warn the patient about specific side effects, he did tell the patient several times that steroid treatment was danger-ous and that the patient-auto mechanic should get a different job. The plaintiff tried other employment but failed due to lack of alternative skills. There was further testimony that the plaintiff's condition was severe and the decision on long-term steroid therapy was judgmen-tal on the part of the physician.

Note: Several court cases have held that if the warning on a prescription drug to the physi-cian was inadequate (ie, incomplete, misleading, inaccurate), the drug maker would be liable to the patient-consumer if the inadequate warning contributed to patient's injury, even though the prescribing doctor's presence is characterized as a "learned intermediary." The reader's attention is directed to the cases of *Hamilton v Hardy*, 549 P. 2d 1099 (Colo. 1976) and *Givens v Lederle*, 556 F. 2d 1341 (5th Cir. 1977)

Timm v Upjohn Co.
624 F.2d 536 (5th Cir. 1980)

ISSUE: Whether warnings in the labeling of a drug product were adequate regarding potential adverse effects.

FACTS: On review by a Federal Court of Appeals, the judgment of the trial court (Federal District Court) on a jury verdict that found a drug maker causally negligent in its marketing of *Cleocin* (clindamycin) was affirmed. The jury had set damages suffered by the injured plaintiff at $195,000 and $115,000 for her husband's damages.

The reported facts of the case are that the plaintiff consulted her physician for relief from sinusitis and he prescribed *Cleocin*. She used the *Cleocin* as directed and, shortly after discontinuing its use, she developed severe pseudomembranous colitis or chronic ulceration in the colon. She did not have colitis prior to use of *Cleocin*. She and her husband did not sue the prescribing doctor, but brought this action against the drug manufacturer, claiming negligence in its marketing of the drug. The jury found such negligence and that the negligence was a proximate cause of plaintiff's injuries; the causation issue was not disputed on the appeal. Plaintiff's colitis worsened to toxic megacolon; her colon had to be removed and she suffered two additional surgeries as a result thereof.

A number of trial court errors were claimed by the drug manufacturer on appeal, but the main gist of its argument was that warnings contained in the *Cleocin* package insert and published in the *Physician's Desk Reference* (*PDR*) adequately warned the medical profession about the possibility of acute colitis and that the prescribing physician was aware that colitis and even colectomy could result from *Cleocin* therapy. The appeals court disagreed.

The warning that appeared in the *PDR*, with reference to *Cleocin*, was as follows:

> WARNINGS
>
> The following reactions have been reported with the use of clindamycin. CASES OF SEVERE AND PERSISTENT DIARRHEA HAVE BEEN REPORTED AND HAVE AT TIMES NECESSITATED DISCONTINUANCE OF THE DRUG. THIS DIARRHEA HAS BEEN OCCASIONALLY ASSOCIATED WITH BLOOD AND MUCUS IN THE STOOLS AND HAS AT TIMES RESULTED IN ACUTE COLITIS.

RULING: The labeling warnings were inadequate.

REASONING: The court in its written decision felt that the testimony of the prescribing doctor's awareness of *Cleocin*'s potentially dangerous side effects was not unequivocal, and at best confused. At one point in the doctor's testimony at trial, he said he relied on the package insert and *PDR* to give him full and complete information as to the side effects of *Cleocin*. At another point, he said in response to a hypothetical question (a question that assumes certain facts but the expert opinion expressed is pertinent only if the assumed facts are true) that had he known of the types of adverse reactions (ulcerative colitis, toxic megacolon, fatalities and 10% incidence of pseudomembranous colitis), he probably would not have prescribed *Cleocin* for the plaintiff. The doctor then stated he first became aware that colectomy could result from using *Cleocin* when the plaintiff's lawyer informed him of her condition.

The court in arriving at its decision reviewed the various prior cases on drug product liability and restated their rulings. Prior cases held that the drug maker had no obligation to warn a consumer of a [prescription only drug] as long as the prescribing physician has been

Timm v Upjohn Co.
624 F.2d 536 (5th Cir. 1980)
...continued

adequately warned of any potentially adverse side effects...the prescribing physician acts as a "learned intermediary" between drug manufacturer and consumer, since the doctor is in the best position to weigh the benefits to risks of a particular drug therapy.

The appeals court upheld the trial court's verdict in favor of the plaintiff; in so doing, it found a rational basis for the jury's verdict on the evidence of the drug maker's inadequate warning to the prescribing doctor.

E.R. Squibb & Sons, Inc. v Cox
477 So.2d 963 (Ala. 1985)

ISSUE: (1) Whether the defendant manufacturer was negligent in the packaging and labeling of its insulin products and (2) whether the pharmacist was negligent in failing to detect an insulin mispackaging.

FACTS: In 1981 Squibb's line of insulin preparations included its regular U-100 insulin which was undiluted and clear in appearance. Squibb also marketed a modified insulin, cloudy in appearance, known as NPH U-100 insulin. Both kinds of insulin were packaged in boxes of the same size and color. The external labeling and the package inserts of the insulin were also substantially identical, but a letter indicated the kind of insulin contained in the box (eg, "N" or "R").

The plaintiff, Royce Cox, was a diagnosed diabetic and had always taken NPH insulin. The plaintiff went to Moody's Pharmacy and requested the "N" insulin as he always did. He assumed he had been given the right product, took it home, placed it in his refrigerator and never read the insulin box or package insert. However, prior to using the insulin he noticed that it was clear rather than cloudy in appearance.

According to the plaintiff's testimony, he took the insulin back to Moody's Pharmacy and explained his concern. The plaintiff claimed that Moody told him the product was clear because Squibb was in the process of removing impurities from its insulin preparations. Pharmacist Moody's testimony varied from that of the plaintiff. Moody admitted that he told the plaintiff that Squibb was in the process of removing impurities from its insulin, but he asked the plaintiff to come to the pharmacy so he could look at the product. The pharmacist testified that the plaintiff never came into the store.

At any rate, it was undisputed that the plaintiff began to take the clear regular insulin from a bottle that was so labeled. Four days later, the plaintiff complained to his brother-in-law that he was nauseous and not feeling well. He had also not eaten in several days. He was taken to the hospital emergency room where doctors diagnosed hypoglycemia caused by the use of the incorrect insulin. The plaintiff suffered permanent brain damage, memory loss and a personality change.

RULING: The jury returned a $300,000 verdict against both the manufacturer and the pharmacist. Both Moody and Squibb appealed, but the pharmacist entered into a settlement agreement with the plaintiff prior to the completion of the appeal. The Supreme Court of Alabama ruled that a plaintiff who does not read an allegedly inadequate warning cannot maintain a negligent failure to warn lawsuit unless the nature of the alleged inadequacy pre-

E.R. Squibb & Sons, Inc. v Cox
477 So.2d 963 (Ala. 1985)
...continued

vents him from reading it. It was determined that the trial court erred in overruling Squibb's motion for a directed verdict. The jury verdict was reversed.

REASONING: During the appeal, Squibb alleged numerous errors in the conduct of the trial court. In reviewing the record, the Supreme Court of Alabama agreed that the trial was replete with errors, but the only issue that needed to be addressed on appeal was whether the plaintiff had made a *prima facie* case of negligent mispackaging or negligent failure to give adequate warning.

The court noted that the plaintiff had no direct proof of Squibb's mispackaging since he had thrown the box and the package insert away. The plaintiff argued that the defendant pharmacist's deposition provided evidence of Squibb's mispackaging. In his deposition, the pharmacist testified that he personally sold NPH insulin to the plaintiff in July, 1981. However, the court found that reliance on such testimony was misplaced because the plaintiff admitted that he purchased the insulin in question in August, 1981.

The plaintiff also alleged that defendant Squibb negligently failed to provide adequate warning of the consequences of taking regular insulin instead of NPH insulin. However, the evidence was undisputed that the plaintiff did not read any of the instructions or warnings that Squibb provided with its regular insulin. The court noted that even if the warning accompanying the insulin had notified the users that inappropriate use could cause permanent brain damage, it would not have made any difference or prevented the injury because the plaintiff would not have read it. Thus, the presumed or alleged inadequacy of Squibb's warning did not proximately cause the plaintiff's injury.

Raynor v Richardson-Merrell, Inc.
643 F.Supp. 238 (D.D.C. 1986)

ISSUE: (1) Whether the manufacturer of the drug *Bendectin* was responsible for the birth defects of the infant plaintiff and (2) whether the pharmacy that dispensed the prescription failed to warn the mother of the drug's danger and was strictly liable for selling a defective and unreasonably dangerous drug.

FACTS: The plaintiff, Veronica Griffin, ingested *Bendectin* during her pregnancy in 1979 and subsequently gave birth to the infant plaintiff Donald Raynor, Jr., who had severely malformed limbs. The plaintiffs alleged that *Bendectin* caused the birth defects and accused the manufacturer of fraud and misrepresentation, breach of implied warranty, breach of express warranty, strict liability in tort, violation of the food and drug disclosure laws and negligence. The plaintiffs also sought damages from the Standard Drug Company, which dispensed the prescriptions. Merrell developed *Bendectin* as an anti-nauseant between 1953 and 1956. The manufacturer did not test *Bendectin* for possible teratogenicity until 1961 after the thalidomide disaster. These published studies did not reveal any teratogenicity.

In 1963, the manufacturer published a study comparing the pregnancy outcomes of over 2000 women who had ingested *Bendectin* with over 2000 women who bore children at the same time but had not taken the drug. This study showed no statistically significant difference between the two groups in terms of congenital defects. The plaintiffs contended that these studies were severely discredited, but nothing in the record supported their position.

Raynor v Richardson-Merrell, Inc.
643 F.Supp. 238 (D.D.C. 1986)
...continued

RULING: The court concluded that the plaintiffs had not presented facts of sufficient degree to create a genuine dispute and ruled that the manufacturer was entitled to judgment as a matter of law. The plaintiffs' claims against Standard Drug Company were also dismissed.

REASONING: The court found that there was no evidence that prior to November 1979 the manufacturer knew or believed that *Bendectin* caused birth defects. While there was some suggestion that the manufacturer was aware of the drug's possible teratogenicity, the plaintiffs did not produce any evidence indicating the company misrepresented or ignored this evidence in its testing and marketing of the drug. No convincing evidence was presented of any false representation on the part of the manufacturer. The FDA Commissioner testified that *Bendectin* would have remained on the market as a pregnancy anti-nauseant, even if the additional data that the plaintiffs alleged existed would have been submitted to the agency.

The court noted that in previous litigation against the manufacturer, a 1985 lawsuit involving more than 800 consolidated actions brought by over 1100 plaintiff children ended in a unanimous jury verdict in favor of the manufacturer on the issue of causation.

The plaintiffs also sought to recover against the pharmacy based upon its failure to advise the mother of *Bendectin's* adverse effects and that it contained proven teratogens. The court was unwilling to impose a duty to warn on pharmacies, reasoning that such a duty would, in effect, require a pharmacy to substitute its judgment for that of the prescribing physician.

The plaintiffs' strict liability claims were also rejected by the court. While the District of Columbia holds a seller liable for marketing a defective and unreasonably dangerous product, it has adopted an important exception to the rule for products such as drugs that are unavoidably unsafe. If a drug is accompanied by adequate warnings of the risks involved, it is neither defective nor unreasonably unsafe. The court concluded that a patient relies upon her physician, not her pharmacist, to warn her of the risks associated with prescription drugs during pregnancy.

The following is a list of court cases that are related to this topic.

Heredia v Johnson, 827 F.Supp. 1522 (D. Nev. 1993).
Holbrook v Rose, 458 S.W. 2d 155 (Ky. 1970).
Stevens v Parke, Davis & Company, 207 Cal. Rptr. 45, 507 P.2d 653 (Cal. 1973).
Torsiello v Whitehall Laboratories, Etc., 165 N.J. Super. 311, 398 A. 2d 132 (1979).
Wells v Ortho Pharmaceutical Corp., 788 F.2d 741 (11th Cir. 1986).
Pittman v The Upjohn Company, 1994 WL 663372 (Tenn. Nov. 28, 1994).
Hooper v Perry Drugs, Slip Op. 178665 (Unpublished), September 20, 1996. (Mich. App).
Wright v Abbott Laboratories, No. 97-1333-JTM, Aug. 16, 1999, 1999 U.S.Dist. Kan. LEXIS 13531.

Failure to Warn as a Products Liability Claim

Bichler v Willing
397 N.Y.S.2d 57 (1977)

ISSUE: Whether the injured patient in this case may sustain a suit against a pharmacist on theories of negligence, breach of express warranty, breach of implied warranty or strict products liability.

FACTS: A minor and her father sued a pharmacist and others for injuries allegedly occasioned because of the use of a prescription drug, diethylstilbestrol (DES), dispensed by the pharmacist pursuant to a prescription. In 1953, while plaintiff's mother was pregnant with her, the drug diethylstilbestrol was prescribed for the mother by a physician, and dispensed by the pharmacist. Some time later, the plaintiff allegedly suffered severe and permanent injuries because of the drug. Several suits were commenced and this one involved the pharmacist as defendant. The pharmacist's attorney claimed that the plaintiff had no legal cause of action against the pharmacist and the suit should be dismissed as it applied to him. A lower court refused to do this, and the case was appealed to a higher court.

The plaintiff based her suit against the pharmacist on four theories: Negligence, breach of express warranty, breach of implied warranty and strict products liability.

RULING: The appellate court found that, in the instant case, none of these claims applied to the pharmacist's conduct.

REASONING: As to the negligence charge, the court found the pharmacist had filled the prescription precisely as he was directed. The plaintiff, however, claimed the pharmacist should have tested the drug for latent defects. The court disagreed, stating,

> And, in view of the absence of any showing of difference between the DES chosen by the druggist and other available brands, his choice of the particular brand of DES cannot be classified as negligence.

As to the claim of breach of expressed warranties, the court found that the pharmacist made no oral or written warranty of the drug's safety or side effects, or that he even generally commented on its use. The court found no basis for the express warranty claims.

As to the implied warranty claim of fitness (for a particular purpose) and merchantability, the court found none here. Prior cases held that implied warranties were conditioned on the buyer's reliance on the skill and judgment of the seller. But, as to drugs dispensed on prescription, the court stated:

> ...when a consumer asks a druggist to fill a prescription thus enabling him to obtain a drug which is not otherwise available to the public, he does not rely on the druggist's judgment as to whether that particular drug is inherently fit for its intended purpose but rather he places that confidence in the physician who prescribed the remedy.

As to strict liability claim, the court found the trial record unclear as to whether or not at the time of the sale there was any recognized risk that called for a warning. The court then stated:

> A seller of drugs is only required to give a warning if he has knowledge of the dangerous ingredient or side effect, or if by the application of reasonable, developed, human skill and foresight he should have such knowledge. (Comment j to Restatement, Second, Torts, 402A). But this does not mean a retail pharmacist, like the appellant,

Bichler v Willing
397 N.Y.S.2d 57 (1977)
...continued

> is under any obligation to independently test the drug's chemical structure for side effects or other possible risks...once floated on the market, many articles...defy detection of defect...

The court dismissed plaintiff's action as it applied to the pharmacist. But, one judge of the appellate court panel dissented in part with the court's ruling. The basis of his dissent was that the pharmacist failed to show that he did not have actual knowledge of the potential risks of DES or that he could not, at the time, have attained the knowledge by exercise of reasonable human skill.

Chambers v G.D. Searle & Co.
567 F.2d 269 (4th Cir. 1977)

ISSUE: Whether a manufacturer of oral contraceptives should be held liable for a stroke suffered by a patient while using the product.

FACTS: A woman taking an oral contraceptive suffered a stroke and sued the drug manufacturer. She alleged that the cerebral thrombosis was a result of taking the oral contraceptive and the manufacturer was liable on grounds of fraud, implied warranty, strict liability and negligence. The court ruled in favor of the drug manufacturer.

The court found that the evidence presented was insufficient for the jury to return a verdict for the plaintiff on any one of the four theories of liability.

RULING: The court directed a verdict in favor of the defendant. On appeal, the appeals court sustained the verdict in favor of the drug company.

REASONING: On the negligence issue, the court stated:

> We are not persuaded that the evidence was sufficient to permit the jury to determine whether Searle was negligent in not pursuing medical research to determine the possible consequences from taking the oral contraceptive, or in failing to discover those consequences, or in the adequacy of the warnings given to physicians in the light of the medical knowledge at the time, or in overpromotion of sales of the product.

Bristol-Myers Co. v Gonzales
561 S.W.2d 801 (Tex. 1978)

ISSUE: Whether a manufacturer of drugs will be held liable if it knew or should have known about a danger associated with use of the product but failed to communicate that.

FACTS: A hospital patient became deaf because of excessive administration, by tablets, injections and irrigation, of *Kantrex* (kanamycin) and Upjohn's neomycin. The patient sued the drug manufacturer and the physician who prescribed the drugs. The doctor's insurance carrier made a settlement agreement before trial with the plaintiff whereby $100,000 was

Bristol-Myers Co. v Gonzales
561 S.W.2d 801 (Tex. 1978)
...continued

advanced to him to be repaid out of any recovery against the drug company. The fact of this settlement was excluded from the evidence by the trial judge. The jury returned an $800,000 verdict for plaintiff (later reduced, as excessive, to $400,000 by the judge). The case was appealed by the drug maker and the appeals court sent the case back for retrial on the grounds that the settlement agreement should have been told to the jury.

RULING: This case is important because of an important rule reiterated by the court. On appeal, the issue of liability of one of the drug companies was discussed and the evidence showed that the drug company officials knew of the ototoxic effects of *Kantrex* but failed at the time to give adequate warnings. At the time the physician used *Kantrex* on the plaintiff, the FDA-approved package insert for *Kantrex* failed to adequately warn of the ototoxic dangers of the drug. But even prior to this, officials at the drug company knew; that is, they knew this long before the inadequacy of the warning became known to the government and required a change in the package insert.

REASONING: The court fashioned out of this case the following rule: If a manufacturer knows or should know of potential harm to a user because of the nature of its product, the manufacturer is required to give an adequate warning of such dangers.

Docken v Ciba-Geigy
739 P.2d 591 (Ore.Ct.App. 1987)

ISSUE: Whether the manufacturer, prescribing physician or dispensing pharmacist owed a duty of care to warn someone for whom the drug was not prescribed.

FACTS: In 1979, Dr. Carey prescribed *Tofranil* for the plaintiff's son, Tim. The drug, manufactured by Geigy Pharmaceuticals, was dispensed by a Kaiser Foundation hospital pharmacy. In August of 1983, the plaintiff's other son, Terry, ingested several of the *Tofranil* tablets hoping that they would remedy a problem he had that was similar to that of his brother, Tim. Unfortunately, Terry died as a result of ingesting the drug. The prescribing physician, dispensing pharmacy and manufacturer were all named as defendants.

The plaintiff used a strict product liability theory alleging that the drug was dangerous and defective because of inadequate labeling, particularly (1) in failing to label the *Tofranil* in a manner adequate to ensure its safe use, (2) in failing to warn that *Tofranil* must be taken and administered with extreme caution and under conditions supervised by a doctor because of the potentially fatal effect of excessive dosage, (3) in failing to warn that *Tofranil* must be disposed of properly after use because of the potentially fatal effect of excessive dosage, (4) in failing to warn that *Tofranil* must be stored out of reach or access by children, (5) in failing to warn that *Tofranil* does not quickly leave a person's body, resulting in a potentially fatal buildup when the drug is taken over a short period of time, and (6) in failing to warn that excessive dosage of *Tofranil* may result in death, particularly to children. The complaint further alleged that the defendants were negligent by failing to warn of the dangers listed above.

RULING: The trial court dismissed both the negligence claim and the strict product liability claim against all three defendants, but the Oregon Court of Appeals reversed and remanded to the trial court to consider negligence claim of failure to warn on the part of all of the defendants and the manufacturer was required to face strict product liability claims.

Docken v Ciba-Geigy
739 P.2d 591 (Ore.Ct.App. 1987)
...continued

REASONING: The court noted that the plaintiff must establish a particular legal duty arising from a status, relationship, statute or some other legal source. If the plaintiff's injury falls outside the foreseeable risk of the alleged negligent conduct, then the defense would argue that there was no legal duty to provide a warning. The defendants contended that a person who does not have the status of a patient (such as Terry) could not recover damages, but they failed to point out any legal foundation for that position. Essentially, the defendants argued that the harm Terry suffered by using a drug prescribed for his brother was not a foreseeable risk. Yet, the court would not state as a matter of law that the harm was not foreseeable or that the complaint failed to allege facts from which a jury could find the defendants negligent. Thus, the appellate court concluded that the trial court erred in dismissing the negligence claim against the defendants.

Because the plaintiff failed to allege that the physician and Kaiser Foundation were in the business of selling drugs, the plaintiff's complaint was missing an important element and failed to state a cause of action based on strict product liability. Thus, the manufacturer was the only defendant left to face strict liability claims.

Geigy argued that strict liability was not intended to cover situations such as were alleged in the complaint. The manufacturer contended that Terry was not a "user or consumer" under strict liability principles. However, the user of a product as contemplated in product liability law includes a broad potential class of plaintiffs. It is not necessary that the user or consumer have acquired the product directly from the seller. Thus, the court ruled that the plaintiff had stated a strict product liability claim against the manufacturer.

Ross Laboratories v Theis
725 P.2d 1076 (Alaska 1986)

ISSUE: (1) Whether a pharmacy that stocked a glucose solution in its baby section was strictly liable for an injury to an infant and (2) whether the manufacturer also was liable in tort for the injuries and for misbranding the product.

FACTS: The plaintiff, Jan Theis, brought this action on behalf of her infant daughter. Theis fed *Polycose* to her daughter, who subsequently became severely dehydrated. The product, manufactured by Ross Laboratories, is a solution consisting of glucose and water that is dangerous to infants if not sufficiently diluted. Theis contended that Ross and Pay 'N Save, the retailer that placed *Polycose* on its shelf, were liable for the infant's injuries.

RULING: The trial court ruled that Pay 'N Save and Ross Laboratories were liable on the basis of strict products liability. It further concluded that Ross was liable under the doctrine of negligence per se for violating Alaska statutes and that the pharmacy was not entitled to indemnity from the manufacturer. The appellate court affirmed the decision, but remanded the issue of whether Pay 'N Save was entitled to indemnity from the manufacturer back to the trial court.

REASONING: Under Alaska law, manufacturers and retainers are strictly liable in tort for personal injuries caused by defects in products they make or sell. "A product is defective, if the use of the product in a manner that is reasonably foreseeable by the defendant involves a substantial danger that would not be readily recognized by the ordinary user of the product and manufacturer fails to give adequate warning of such danger."

Ross Laboratories v Theis
725 P.2d 1076 (Alaska 1986)
...continued

During the appeal, both the retailer and manufacturer argued that there was a genuine issue of fact as to whether it was reasonably foreseeable that *Polycose* would be fed to infants. However, the court noted that the solution was sold in a nipple-ready bottle. Ross marketed many products for consumption by infants in the same type bottle. The *Polycose* label contained no warning that the product was dangerous if it was not sufficiently diluted.

The court ruled that the nipple-ready bottle, taken together with the similarity in name, label and contents of other baby products, required the manufacturer to foresee that some consumers would mistakenly believe that *Polycose* was a product to be fed to infants. Ross argued that the pharmacy mishandled the product by stocking it on the baby products shelves instead of in the adult dietary section. It was alleged that this was the cause of the injury and that the manufacturer did not put a defective product on the market.

The court rejected these arguments because it was foreseeable that a product package in a container that looks like a baby bottle and was similar to other such products would confuse people into thinking that it was, in fact, a baby product. A duty to foresee required the manufacturer to place a warning on the product to protect consumers against mistakes by Pay 'N Save or other merchants. "The safety of infants should not test on the stocking wisdom of the retailer."

The Alaska Food, Drug and Cosmetic Act prohibits the manufacture or sale of drugs that are misbranded. A substance is misbranded unless it bears "adequate" directions and warnings. The issue in this case was not the adequacy of any warnings since no warning was given. The issue was whether a warning against infant use was required. The court concluded that it was.

The manufacturer argued that *Polycose* is not a drug since it is not intended for use in the diagnosis, cure, mitigation, treatment or prevention of disease. Ross contended that the product is a food supplement and the fact that it is given to people who are ill or injured does not mean that it is a drug. The court did not agree with this argument and found that the company's training manual showed that the manufacturer intended the product to be used for the treatment of numerous diseases.

The court noted that the general rule is that a retailer who is liable on a theory of strict liability may obtain indemnity from a manufacturer, provided that the retailer is not negligent. However, the Alaska Supreme Court concluded that even if Pay 'N Save did not act negligently, it was liable under Alaska misbranding statutes which the court claimed applied equally to the manufacturer and retailer.

Kirk v Michael Reese Hospital and Medical Center
513 N.E.2d 387 (Ill. 1987)

ISSUE: Whether a hospital, psychiatrist and two pharmaceutical manufacturers were liable to a third party for failing to warn a discharged patient about driving after taken *Prolixin* and *Thorazine* with alcohol.

FACTS: The plaintiff was injured while riding as a passenger in a car driven by Daniel McCarthy. McCarthy had been a psychiatric patient at Michael Reese Hospital. Hospital person-

Kirk v Michael Reese Hospital and Medical Center
513 N.E.2d 387 (Ill. 1987)
...continued

nel injected McCarthy with *Prolixin* and gave him *Thorazine* orally. Following his dismissal from the hospital that day, he consumed an alcoholic beverage and drove his automobile with the plaintiff as a passenger. The car left the roadway and struck a tree resulting in the plaintiff's injuries.

RULING: An intermediate appellate court determined that a duty may exist to one who is unknown and remote in time and place. Thus, the injury to the passenger was sufficiently foreseeable for the hospital and the other defendants to have known that their failure to provide a warning could result in an injury to the plaintiff or to other members of the general public. However, the Illinois Supreme Court reversed the appellate court decision because the plaintiff failed to establish the existence of a legal duty.

REASONING: The court recognized that a legal duty may extend to those outside the purchasing chain of the product. However, this protection extends only to conduct that is reasonably foreseeable. The court concluded that the defendant manufacturers could not have reasonably foreseen that their drugs would be dispensed without warnings by the physicians at the hospital, that the patient would be discharged from the hospital, drink alcohol, drive a car, lose control of the car, hit a tree and injure the passenger on the same day. "Strict liability is not the equivalent of absolute liability. There are restrictions imposed upon it."

The plaintiff claimed that the hospital had an independent duty to warn and that this duty extended to third parties. The plaintiff argued that a third party with no patient/hospital or patient/physician relationship should be allowed to bring a cause of action for failure to warn. Again, the court concluded that this injury could not be considered reasonably foreseeable on the part of the hospital and there was no legal duty to warn.

The court found that holding the hospital responsible for all of the harmful acts committed by patients who had been released would be an unreasonable burden on the institution. The court observed that the Illinois legislature had already taken actions to try to reduce the burden on the health professions as the result of the perceived medical malpractice crisis.

While the physicians acknowledged that they had a duty to warn the patient about the adverse effects of taking a prescription drug, this duty did not extend to unknown non-patients in the general public. The court agreed and concluded that the plaintiff did not fall into the class of people to whom a duty of care was owed by the defendant psychiatrists.

Coyle v Richardson - Merrell, Inc.
538 A.2d 1379 (Pa. Super. 1988)

ISSUE: Whether a pharmacy may be held strictly liable in a products liability action as the supplier of a prescription drug.

FACTS: The plaintiffs' son was born with badly deformed limbs due to ingestion of the drug *Bendectin* by his mother during the early part of her pregnancy. The *Bendectin* was prescribed by Mrs. Coyle's physician to relieve her nausea and vomiting associated with pregnancy. The plaintiffs filed their lawsuit against Merrell Dow Pharmaceuticals, the manufacturer of the drug, and Bonnet Lane Pharmacy, the supplier of the drug. The claim

Coyle v Richardson - Merrell, Inc.
538 A.2d 1379 (Pa. Super. 1988)
...continued

against Bonnet Lane Pharmacy was based upon strict liability. The manufacturer claimed that the plaintiffs included the pharmacy as a defendant to fraudulently defeat diversity jurisdiction in federal court.

RULING: The state court granted summary judgment to the pharmacy, holding that pharmacists are not strictly liable for damages that occur as the result of ingestion of a prescription drug.

REASONING: The court based its decision upon the Makripodis case which had facts exactly on point. In that case, a child with congenital abnormalities was born to a mother who had taken *Bendectin* during her pregnancy. Merrell Dow was sued along with the Rite-Aid Corporation, the pharmacy that supplied the drug to the mother. The court found that a pharmacy was not strictly liable for failure to warn of any teratogenic potential.

The plaintiffs in this case argued that *Bendectin* was unsafe and inherently defective for use by pregnant women. However, the court noted from its conclusion in the Makripodis case that it could "perceive no benefit to be derived from the imposition of strict liability upon the pharmacist who properly dispenses a prescription drug upon the prescription of a duly licensed physician." It was concluded, therefore, that a pharmacist could not be held strictly liable as a supplier in the chain of distribution of a prescription drug.

Hofherr v Dart Industries, Inc.
853 F.2d 259 (4th Cir. 1988)

ISSUE: Whether the franchiser of a retail pharmacy was responsible to warn physicians and franchisees of the danger of diethylstilbestrol (DES).

FACTS: The plaintiffs, Jean and Robert Hofherr, instituted this product liability action against Dart Industries and Eli Lilly & Co. for injuries suffered by Mrs. Hofherr as a result of her mother's ingestion of DES while pregnant. The plaintiff's mother took the drug while pregnant in 1959 as a precaution to prevent a possible miscarriage. The plaintiff was diagnosed, 23 years later, as suffering from permanent gynecological injuries allegedly as a result of her prenatal exposure to DES, which resulted in her infertility.

The plaintiff's mother testified that she purchased the DES tablets from Tennant's Professional Pharmacy in Baltimore, MD. Tennant's was a locally and independently owned franchise of the Rexall Drug Co. (which has since changed its name to Dart Industries). There was no corporate reorganization and thus there was no issue of whether Dart was liable for acts committed while it operated under the Rexall name. The individual pharmacy was not named as a defendant in the lawsuit.

The plaintiff's mother testified that she remembered the DES tablets to be shiny, red, hard-coated tablets, a little smaller than an aspirin tablet. While Rexall did produce DES in 1959, it was uncontroverted that Rexall did not produce DES in a red tablet form. There was no record of the pharmacy purchasing DES or any prescription drug from Rexall. Thus, it was undisputed that the drug was actually manufactured by a pharmaceutical company other than Rexall.

Hofherr v Dart Industries, Inc.
853 F.2d 259 (4th Cir. 1988)
...continued

The plaintiffs contended that the pharmacy was either an express or apparent agent of Rexall, which made Rexall responsible for the pharmacy's sale of the drug. In addition, the plaintiffs argued that since Rexall was a manufacturer of DES, it had a non-delegable duty to warn its franchisees of the potential dangers of DES irrespective of whether the franchisees were agents of Rexall. The plaintiff's theory of recovery was that since the pharmacy sold the DES to the plaintiff's mother and if the pharmacy was Rexall's agent, then Rexall had a duty to warn physicians and franchisees of the dangers of the drug, even if Rexall had not manufactured the drug in question.

RULING: The court ruled that Rexall was not responsible for the pharmacy's activities and had no duty to warn the customer of the franchisee pharmacy.

REASONING: Three elements needed to be proved under Maryland law in order to establish an express agency. First, the agent must be subject to the principal's right of control. Second, the agent must have the duty to act for the benefit of the principal. Third, the agent must hold the power to alter the legal relationships of the principal. In this case, the franchise contract was little more than an agreement for the pharmacy to sell Rexall products at retail. The contract did give Rexall some leverage to revoke the franchise for contract violation.

However, there was no evidence of control by Rexall over the pharmacy's marketing of prescription drugs of other manufacturers. In addition, there was no evidence indicating that Rexall could or did exercise any control over the day-to-day operation of the pharmacy. Thus, there was no evidence for the jury to conclude that Rexall controlled the pharmacy's activity sufficiently to create an express agency relationship.

The court concluded that any obligation of Rexall to warn of the dangers of the drug extended not to the consumer or the franchisee, but rather to the physician that prescribed it. The court noted that prescription drugs are purchased from a pharmacist only on the prescription of a physician. "A pharmacist or manufacturer who advised a patient not to take a drug prescribed by a physician might easily cause death or serious injury and we think the practice of medicine by pharmacists and pharmaceutical manufacturers is not a field in which we should even encourage them to engage, much less require it, as the plaintiffs would have."

Coyle v Richardson-Merrell, Inc.
584 A.2d 1383 (Pa. 1991)

ISSUE: Whether a pharmacy should be subject to liability as a supplier of drugs under the principle of strict liability, sometimes termed "liability without fault."

FACTS: William and Marie Coyle brought this action against Richardson-Merrell, Inc. (now Marion-Merrell Dow Pharmaceuticals) and the pharmacist owners of Bonnet Lane Pharmacy alleging that *Bendectin* manufactured and supplied by the defendants caused their son to be born with malformed limbs.

RULING: The court declined to extend the rule of strict supplier liability to pharmacies.

Coyle v Richardson-Merrell, Inc.
584 A.2d 1383 (Pa. 1991)
...continued

REASONING: The court reviewed earlier Pennsylvania decisions that also involved the concept of strict liability of a pharmacy that had dispensed *Bendectin*. In these previous cases, the courts had determined that the drug manufacturer must provide adequate and proper warnings to the prescribing physician. The courts noted that it would be incongruous to impose on pharmacists a greater duty to warn patients than is imposed on drug manufacturers.

In the cited cases, the previous courts held that "a retail is not required to provide to the patient-consumer such warnings as are required to be provided to physicians by the manufacturers on prescription drugs." The plaintiffs argued that these earlier cases were wrongly decided and should be overruled.

The concept of strict liability is set forth in the Restatement (Second) of Torts, Section 402A that provides that "one who sells any product in a defective condition unreasonably dangerous to the user or consumer is subject to liability for physical harm...."

The courts of Pennsylvania have concluded that the principle of strict liability is applicable to sellers of products as well as manufacturers. The plaintiffs contended that the rule of strict supplier liability provides no exception for pharmacists, who they characterized as simply suppliers of prescription drugs. However, the court noted that it has the power, and indeed the obligation, to refuse to apply a rule where there is not reasoning to support it.

The court notes that unlike the marketing system for most other products, the distribution system for prescription drugs is highly restricted. Pharmacists, as suppliers, do not freely choose which products they will make available to consumers. Patients, as consumers, do not freely choose which prescription product to buy. Physicians exercising sound medical judgment act as intermediaries in the chain of distribution and preempt the exercise of discretion by supplier-pharmacist. The court recognized this as a real distinction that required a different rule.

The court could find no solid reason for imposing on pharmacists the duty to supply information about the risks of drugs that have already been prescribed. Such a rule, in the court's opinion, would have the effect of undermining the physician-patient relationship.

Heredia v Johnson
827 F.Supp. 1522 (D.Nev. 1993)

ISSUE: Whether a pharmacy is guilty for failure to warn under both strict products liability law and negligence law.

FACTS: The plaintiff, Joaquin Heredia, received medical treatment from the Ruby Mountain Medical Clinic in Elko, Nevada, after suffering from pain and numbness in his left ear. The attending physician at the clinic diagnosed Mr. Heredia's condition as acute severe left otitis media with bullous myringitis. Three medications were prescribed. The plaintiff took the three prescriptions to a Payless Drug Store where they were filled by the pharmacist on duty.

The plaintiff claims that he carefully took all of the medications as directed on the label. However, he contends that one of the medications, *Pediotic Otic Suspension* was not prop-

Heredia v Johnson
827 F.Supp. 1522 (D.Nev. 1993)
...continued

erly labeled in that it did not contain a warning that use or administration of the drug should be discontinued and the prescribing physician contacted in case of symptoms of tympanic membrane rupture. The plaintiff contends that due to the defective and unreasonably dangerous manner in which the drug was dispensed without appropriate labeling and warnings, he suffers from severe and permanent injuries including brain damage.

RULING: The pharmacy's motion to dismiss was denied.

REASONING: The plaintiff claimed that the *Pediotic Otic Suspension* was in a "defective condition," which rendered it "unreasonably dangerous" when it left the control of Payless and delivered to the plaintiff. Strict tort liability may be imposed upon sellers and those in a chain of distribution, as well as manufacturers, for their role in placing a defective product into the stream of commerce. To the extent that the plaintiff bases his strict liability claims against Payless on the pharmacy's role in the chain of distribution, the claim is valid.

For purposes of strict liability, the allegation is not directed at the conduct of the pharmacist, but rather the nature of the product as it made its way through the stream of commerce. The Nevada courts have recognized that strict liability may be imposed even though the product is faultlessly made if it is unreasonably dangerous to place the product in the hands of the user without suitable and adequate warnings concerning safe and proper use. A failure to warn may constitute a product defect.

The federal district court hearing this action could not find that the Nevada Supreme Court would hold that the strict liability doctrine does not apply to the defendant simply because the transaction in question was the sale of a prescription drug. In addition, evidence before the court indicated that this prescription drug is packaged in a box which included written information containing an express warning, "this product should be used in care in cases of perforated ear drum."

The plaintiff further claimed that Payless, acting through its employees and agents, committed acts and/or omissions of negligence that included failing to properly label the prescription container. The court stated that it is not for the pharmacists to second guess a licensed physician unless in such circumstances that would be obviously fatal. In addition, the court noted that the pharmacist clearly does not have a greater duty than the physician nor is the pharmacist the insurer of the safety of the drug. However, it was clear to the court that the attending pharmacist owes some duty to the persons for whom he or she is filling prescriptions.

While a general duty to warn has been held to be inappropriate in some jurisdictions, generally a pharmacist has a duty to exercise due care in dispensing prescriptions. At a minimum, a pharmacist must be held to a duty to fill prescriptions as prescribed and to properly label them.

Strickland v Brown Morris Pharmacy
Slip Op. No. 96-815 C/W 96-823 §L, Sept. 18, 1997, (U.S. Dist. E. La.), 1997 US Dist. LEXIS 14693

ISSUE: May a pharmacist be held strictly liable under a products liability theory for damages sustained by a patient after purchasing the drug from the pharmacy?

FACTS: After using *Primatene Mist* purchased from the defendant pharmacy, the 33-year-old patient suffered a seizure, heart failure, and died. The cause of death was listed as status asthmaticus.

LAWSUIT: A products liability suit was commenced against Whitehall Laboratories as the manufacturer and the pharmacy as seller of the drug. The pharmacy sought summary judgment. Louisiana's Products Liability Act imposes liability, in part, on the seller of a product who exercises control over the quality of a product that causes injury. La. RS 9:2800.53(1)(b). Whitehall also sought summary judgment.

HOLDING: The court dismissed the case against the pharmacy but permitted the case against Whitehall to proceed for trial.

REASONING: The plaintiffs offered no evidence to show that the pharmacy exercised any kind of control over the quality of the *Primatene Mist* that it sold to the patient. The state's Products Liability Act does permit liability to be imposed when a seller knows or should know that a defective product has a dangerous characteristic. Plaintiffs produced a handful of newspaper articles from around the country that expressed concern about the safety of *Primatene Mist* and its main ingredient, ephedrine. Some of the articles noted that other states restrict the sale of ephedrine. The Court held that plaintiffs failed to show that the pharmacy was aware of these warnings and that at least one article reported that the FDA concluded that "it is vital to offer these (ephedrine) products for asthmatics." According to the court, no jury could find the pharmacy liable on these facts. The court denied Whitehall's motion to dismiss and concluded that there were questions of fact to be decided under the state statute.

In re: *Propulsid* Products Liability Litigation
2002 WL 1446714 (E.D. La. 2002)

Consumers brought a state court products liability action against manufacturers of *Propulsid* as well as certain pharmacies that allegedly sold *Propulsid* to consumers. The court held that the pharmacy in the motion to dismiss could not be deemed a "manufacturer" under the Louisiana Products Liability Act ("LPLA") because the pharmacy neither made the product nor did it have any input into the design of the product. Further, it did not have any control over either the construction or quality of the product. Thus, it did not meet the statutory definition of "manufacturer" for the purposes of a products liability claim under Louisiana law. The plaintiffs' claim based on negligent and intentional misrepresentation did, however, survive the Federal Rule of Civil Procedure 12(b)(6) ("Rule 12(b)(6)") motion to dismiss. The plaintiffs alleged that the pharmacies affirmatively misrepresented the side effects of the drug by acting as independent advisors to the prescribing physicians and offering objective professional opinions and advice concerning the possible side effects of *Propulsid*. The plaintiffs also claimed that the pharmacies misrepresented to the plaintiffs themselves the possible side effects of the drug. Because the court is required to assume the truth of the allegations for Rule 12(b)(6) motions to dismiss, it determined that the pharmacies may have voluntarily assumed a duty of care which would not ordinarily be imposed.

In re: *Propulsid* Products Liability Litigation
2002 WL 1446714 (E.D. La. 2002)
...continued

A claim construed as one in "redhibition" also survived the Rule 12(b)(6) motion to dismiss. Article 2545 of the Louisiana Civil Code provides that a "seller who knows that the thing he sells has a defect but omits to declare it, or a seller who declares that the thing has a quality that he knows it does not have, is liable to the buyer for the return of the price with interest from the time it was paid, for the reimbursement of the reasonable expenses occasioned by the sale and those incurred for the preservation of the thing, and also for damages and reasonable attorney fees." La. Civ. Code Ann. art. 2545. Article 2520 defines a "redhibitory" defect as one that, among other things, "renders the thing useless, or its use so inconvenient that it must be presumed that a buyer would not have bought the thing had he known of the defect. The existence of such a defect gives a buyer the right to obtain rescission of the sale." Insofar as the plaintiffs had alleged that the defendants knew of the defect, the court found that the plaintiffs had stated a claim in "redhibition" under which they may seek damages. Accordingly, the motion to dismiss was denied for the claims asserted against the pharmacies that were based on alleged affirmative misrepresentations and "redhibition" and granted for the claim based on liability under the LPLA.

The following is a list of court cases that are related to this topic.

McLeod v Richardson-Merrell, Inc., 174 So. 2d 736, May 5, 1965 (Fla. S. Ct., 1965).
Holbrook v Rose, 458 S.W. 2d 155 (Ky. 1970).
Michael v Warner-Chilcott, 91 N.M. 561, 579 P. 2d 183 (1978).
Raynor v Richardson-Merrell, Inc., 643 F. Supp. 238 (D.D.C. 1986).
Makripodis v Merrell Dow Pharmaceuticals, Inc., 523 A.2d 374 (Pa.Super.1987).
Leesley v West, 518 N.E.2d 758 (Ill. App. 2 Dist. 1988).
Martin v Hacker, 550 N.Y.S.2d 130 (A.D. 3 Dept. 1989).
Foster v American Home Products Corp., 29 F.3d 165 (4th Cr. 1994).

Breach of Warranty

McLeod v Richardson-Merrell, Inc.
174 So. 2d 736 (Fla. 1965)

ISSUE: Whether a pharmacist who properly fills a prescription is liable to an injured patient for breach of an implied warranty of fitness or merchantability.

FACTS: The plaintiff's physician prescribed a drug for controlling body cholesterol. The manufacturer sold the drug to the pharmacy defendants, International Pharmacies, Inc. and James Drug Shop, Inc., for resale only on prescriptions of medical doctors. These pharmacy defendants filled the prescriptions for the plaintiff strictly in accordance with instructions of the doctor. It was stipulated that the manufacturer had prepared the drug and that the pharmacy defendants had received the drugs in the original sealed packets. The parties all agreed that the drugs were sold to the plaintiff in the original unbroken containers without alterations by the pharmacy. There was no dispute that the plaintiff's personal physician prescribed for the plaintiff.

LAWSUIT: The complaint charged the three defendants, the manufacturer, and the two pharmacies with breaches of implied warranties of (1) reasonable fitness for the intended purpose, (2) merchantability, and (3) wholesomeness or reasonable fitness for human consumption. Plaintiff claimed that although intended as a remedial control of cholesterol,

McLeod v Richardson-Merrell, Inc.
174 So. 2d 736 (Fla. 1965)
...continued

the drug actually exposed the user to a grave risk of harm when used in ordinary doses. Allegedly, the drug causes severe side effects, such as the formation of cataracts and other eye damage. There was no warning by any of the pharmacies suggesting a possible inherent danger in the use of the drug.

HOLDING: These allegations were dismissed as to the pharmacies. The trial judge held the view that a pharmacy does not warrant the inherent fitness of drugs it sells on prescription. The Court of Appeals affirmed the action of the circuit judge.

REASONING: An implied warranty of fitness for a particular purpose is conditioned upon the buyer's reliance on the skill and judgment of the seller to supply a commodity suitable for the intended purpose. Therefore, in order to be merchantable, the goods must be fit for ordinary uses for which such goods are sold. In this case, the drug was not available to the general public in the sense that any customer who entered the store and paid the price could purchase it. It was available only to a limited segment of the public who had previously been seen by their personal physicians and who presented their doctor's prescription to a pharmacy directing that the drug be dispensed. The patient did not rely upon the judgment of the pharmacist in assuming that the drug would be fit for its intended purpose. This confidence was placed in the physician who prescribed the remedy. The physician in turn had placed his reliance on the representations of the manufacturer. In effect, the plaintiff seeks to impose upon pharmacists an absolute, strict liability without fault tort. While the claim is presented as an alleged breach of implied warranties, the real theory is strict liability. The effect of the application of this concept would be to convert the pharmacists into insurers of the safety of the manufactured drug. The concept of strict liability without fault should not be applied to the pharmacists under these facts. The rights of the consumer can be preserved, and the responsibilities of the pharmacist can be imposed, under the concept that a pharmacist who sells a prescription warrants that (1) he will compound the drug prescribed, (2) that he has used due and proper care in filling the prescription (failure of which might also give rise to an action in negligence), (3) that the proper methods were used in the compounding process, and (4) that the drug has not been infected with some adulterating foreign substance.

Pilet v Ciba-Geigy
No. 96-021 Section: E/2, 1996 U.S. Dist. LEXIS 2344 (E.D. La. Feb. 29, 1996)

FACTS: A patient on *Tegretol* experienced a seizure while driving, resulting in an accident causing physical and property damages. He later learned of an alleged defect and product recall of *Tegretol* in a letter from the dispensing pharmacy. The suit filed against the manufacturer and pharmacy under the State's product liability statute claimed ordinary negligence alleging that the slow drug dissolution reduced the effectiveness of the drug and caused the seizure. The trial court granted the defendant's motion for summary judgment. The court dismissed the products liability claim against the pharmacy because the pharmacy did not meet the statutory definition of a "manufacturer" (even though it did put its label on the dispensing vial) and because it did not act as the "seller" of the product, altering or affecting its design.

HOLDING: The Louisiana court also dismissed negligence claims as the plaintiff produced no evidence showing that the pharmacy knew or should have known of the product defect at the time of its sale.

The following is a list of court cases that are related to this topic.

Holbrook v Rose, 458 S.W. 2d 155 (Ky. 1970).
Stevens v Parke, Davis & Company, 207 Cal. Rptr. 45, 507 P.2d 653 (Cal.1973).
Bichler v Willing, 397 N.Y.S. 2d 57 (1977).
Raynor v Richardson-Merrell, Inc., 643 F. Supp. 238 (D.D.C. 1986).
Makripodis v Merrell Dow Pharmaceuticals, Inc., 523 A.2d 374 (Pa.Super.1987).
Sheils v Eckerd Corp. 560 So. 2d 361 (Fla. App 2d 1990).
Foster v American Home Products Corp., 29 F.3d 165 (4th Cr. 1994).

Learned Intermediary Rule

Leesley v West
518 N.E.2d 758 (Ill. App. 1988)

ISSUE: Whether the manufacturer of a prescription drug owed a duty to directly warn the patients of the drug's side effects and whether a pharmacy had a duty to convey to its patients any relevant warning given to it by the manufacturer.

FACTS: The plaintiff, Sylvia Leesley, filed suit against Dr. James West, Pfizer and Villa Park Pharmacy for damages resulting from severe GI bleeding caused by the prescription drug, *Feldene*. The drug was prescribed for the plaintiff to treat her osteoarthritis. Peptic ulcers and GI bleeding are known, but infrequent, side effects of *Feldene*. The plaintiff did not allege that Pfizer failed to adequately disclose the drug's potential hazards, but that the pharmacy and Pfizer failed to directly warn the plaintiff. Villa Park Pharmacy and Pfizer filed a motion for summary judgment claiming that the pharmacy and drug manufacturer had no duty to directly warn the consumer about the potential hazards of a prescription drug.

RULING: The Illinois appellate court concluded that a pharmaceutical manufacturer does not have a duty to directly warn prescription drug consumers of known side effects and a pharmacy does not have a duty to convey to its patients any relevant warnings given to it by the manufacturer.

REASONING: The court reviewed the "learned intermediary" doctrine as described by the Illinois Supreme Court in *Kirk v Michael Reese Hospital*, which concluded that because of the complexity of prescription drugs, manufacturers have a duty to warn only prescribing physicians of the inherent dangers. The Kirk court stated that drug manufacturers have a variety of available methods to communicate warnings to the medical profession. That court concluded that "the doctor, functioning as a learned intermediary between the prescription drug manufacturer and the patient, decides which available drug best fits the patient's needs and chooses which facts from the various warnings should be conveyed to the patient, and the extent of disclosure is a matter of medical judgment." Following the reasoning of the Kirk case, the court concluded that Pfizer had no duty to directly warn consumers of the potential side effects of *Feldene*.

The court next turned to the issue of the pharmacist's responsibility to convey to his patients any relevant warnings given to him by the manufacturer. Villa Park Pharmacy received the *Feldene* in a bulk container to which Pfizer had attached a package insert describing the drug's potential hazards. The pharmacy did not convey any of that information to the plaintiff nor was it instructed to do so by Dr. West.

The plaintiff filed both negligence and strict liability claims against the pharmacy. The court concluded that where the manufacturer gives the required warnings to the prescribing physician, the drug is not an unreasonably dangerous product and strict liability does not apply to the manufacturer. Before the court could apply the strict liability doctrine to the phar-

Leesley v West
518 N.E.2d 758 (Ill. App. 1988)
...continued

macy, it would have to conclude that the product somehow became unreasonably danger-ous in the pharmacy's hands in order to hold that the pharmacy was required to provide every patient whose prescription was filled from the bulk container with a copy of the informa-tion contained in the single package insert. The court ruled that such a conclusion would obviously be unreasonable.

A similar conclusion was reached with respect to the negligence claim. No Illinois court had yet decided whether a pharmacist has an independent duty to warn his or her patients of known, potential hazards of prescription drugs. A federal district court in the case of *Jones v Irvin* held that placing on the pharmacist a duty to warn would "compel the pharma-cist to second guess every prescription a doctor orders in an attempt to escape liability."

It was also concluded that requiring the pharmacy to convey the warnings it received from the manufacturer to its customers would be very burdensome. The court was not willing to impose the burden on pharmacists of providing cautionary information directly to the con-sumers because this might mean that they would bear additional costs of reproducing the package insert. It noted that the pharmacy would face the oppressive burden of retaining and cataloging every document and warning it received in order to be certain that each warn-ing was distributed with the appropriate drug. The court found that placing this burden on pharmacists was simply inconsistent with the exemption afforded to manufacturers by the learned intermediary doctrine. "We do not conclude by this decision that warnings beyond those given by the physician are harmful or are to be discouraged. We simply decline to subject pharmacists to liability for failure to give warnings which the physician has not requested. We believe that this position is most consistent with this State's legislative policy against expanding the liability risks of health professionals."

Laws v Johnson
799 S.W.2d 249 (Tenn. App. 1990)

ISSUE: Whether a pharmacist may be liable for negligence for not providing a package insert when dispensing a prescription medication.

FACTS: The plaintiff was prescribed *Timoptic* for the treatment of glaucoma. He took the pre-scription to the defendant, Johnson City Eye and Ear Pharmacy, to be dispensed.

Timoptic, manufactured by Merck, is a liquid eye drop medication packaged in a small card-board box along with a package insert. The package insert includes two full pages of "extremely fine print detailing in technical and scientific terminology which, for the most part, could be interpreted and comprehended only by persons skilled in the medical, pharm-aceutical or chemical fields." It includes information on the clinical pharmacology of the drug, contraindications, warnings, precautions, drug interactions, and a wide variety of other information.

The prescription was first dispensed in 1979. From then until June of 1985, each time the plaintiff had his prescription filled, the pharmacist removed (prior to dispensing) the printed package insert from the cardboard box containing the medication. After 6 years, the plain-tiff inadvertently received a prescription in which the printed inserts had not been removed. After reading the information, the plaintiff went back to the pharmacy and inquired as to

Laws v Johnson
799 S.W.2d 249 (Tenn. App. 1990)
...continued

why the package inserts were not included with his previous prescriptions. Because the plaintiff had earlier suffered a heart attack, he asked his physician if using *Timoptic* could have been a contributing factor. The physician informed him that very rarely did the drug cause heart problems and he advised the plaintiff to continue using the medication.

In 1986, the plaintiff filed a lawsuit against the physician, the manufacturer, and the pharmacy for medical malpractice. Specifically, the complaint alleged that the five pharmacists employed by the defendant pharmacy were negligent for dispensing the product over 7 years because they removed the package insert from the manufacturer's container prior to dispensing the product.

The plaintiff contended that this negligence was the proximate cause of his heart problems. It was further alleged that the pharmacist had violated Tennessee law, which required all prescriptions to be filled in strict conformity with the directions of the prescribing physician. The plaintiff argued that removing the package insert from the cardboard box prior to sale was not in compliance with the law since the physician did not direct the pharmacists to take the manufacturer's package insert out of the box.

RULING: The trial court granted the defendant pharmacists' motion for the summary judgment. The appellate court affirmed.

REASONING: The court found the affidavit of one of the pharmacist-defendants to be pertinent: "Package inserts are designed for the purpose of the manufacturers' conveying to the prescribing physician the benefits and risks, etc., of the use of the drug. Package inserts, therefore, are commonly removed by the filling pharmacist simply because the inserts as above stated, are designed for the use of the prescribing physician, and not the patient. The inserts contain a mass of technical information, including the basic molecules, chemical composition of the drug and other highly technical information that a lay person is incapable of understanding, and this often results in complete confusion on the part of the patient and may result in the patient discontinuing the medication as prescribed by the physician."

The physician also provided an affidavit that he continuously prescribed *Timoptic* for the control of the plaintiff's severe chronic open angle glaucoma. The physician stated that he was familiar with the information contained in the package insert and that without treatment with the drug, the plaintiff would have lost his vision in both eyes. The only other alternative was surgery, which also had the risk of causing loss of sight.

When a product is available only by prescription or through the services of a physician, the physician acts as the learned intermediary between the manufacturer and the patient. The court would not quarrel with the general proposition that where prescription drugs are concerned, the manufacturer's duty to warn is limited to an obligation to advise the prescribing physician of any potential dangers that may result from the drug's use.

The plaintiff argued that he was entitled to receive information from the package insert that provided warnings about certain cardiovascular effects, such as possible cardiac failure and worsening of arterial insufficiency. The court notes that the issue raised is not whether the information should be disclosed at all, but instead who was in a better position to disclose the risks. The court had little trouble imagining situations of total disclosure by a manufacturer to a consumer that would not be in the patient's best interest.

The plaintiff further argued that because pharmacists must fill prescriptions in strict conformity with the directions of the prescriber, the prescription for *Timoptic* had to be dispensed

Laws v Johnson
799 S.W.2d 249 (Tenn. App. 1990)
...continued

in the sealed box with the package insert. Yet, the plaintiff cited no authority to support
his argument. The pharmacists claimed to have dispensed the drug in accordance with the
physician's order, and there was nothing in the record to refute this.

Griffith v Blatt
334 Or. 456, 51 P.3d 1256 (Or. 2002)

The patient visited her physician seeking treatment for a skin condition. The doctor gave
her a prescription for 2 oz. of *Lindane* 1% lotion, and instructed the pharmacist to fill the prescription and to type "as directed" on the label. A pharmacist filled the prescription as
directed by the doctor. The patient applied the lotion over her entire body once a day for
5 or 6 days until she had used the entire bottle. After each application, she did not shower for
the next 24 hours. Properly used, *Lindane* lotion should be applied no more than 2 times,
and should be washed off within 12 hours after any application. Within a week or two after
beginning to use the *Lindane* lotion, the patient began to suffer medical problems, including convulsions, dizziness, weight loss, hair loss, sleep disturbance, and precognitive dysfunction. She consulted with another physician who diagnosed her symptoms as central nervous
system toxicity due to overexposure to *Lindane* lotion. The patient sued the manufacturer
and dispensing pharmacist for product liability and negligence. The trial court granted the
defendants' summary judgment and Griffith appealed. The court of appeals held that the
product liability claim against the manufacturer was barred by the 2-year statute of limitations. As to the defendant pharmacist, the court of appeals applied the "learned intermediary" doctrine and dismissed the patient's strict liability claim. Under the "learned
intermediary" doctrine, the duty of a drug manufacturer is to warn the doctor, rather than
the patient. No Oregon appellate decision had addressed the application of the "learned intermediary" doctrine to claims arising from a pharmacist's failure to warn of the risks associated with a prescription drug. If drug manufacturers only have to warn physicians, not
patients, then it is unreasonable to impose a duty on pharmacists to warn individual patients.
The court of appeals held that application of the "learned intermediary" doctrine to pharmacists was consistent with Oregon law, and therefore affirmed the trial court's dismissal of
the patient's strict liability claim against the defendant pharmacist. The court of appeals
also affirmed the dismissal of the patient's negligent failure to warn claim because she failed
to offer expert testimony as to the standard of care for pharmacists for warning of dangers
of a prescription drug. The Oregon Supreme Court affirmed the Court of Appeal's determination that the claim against the manufacturer was untimely, but reversed the decision of
the Court of Appeals that the "learned intermediary" doctrine applied to strict liability claims
under Oregon law. Therefore, the Oregon Supreme Court remanded the case to the trial
court for further proceedings. The Oregon Supreme Court found that the Court of Appeals
had erred in disposing of plaintiff's claim against the manufacturer on preservation grounds.
The Court explained that the limitations period in the relevant Oregon statute [ORS
30.905(2)], "commences when the plaintiff's injury occurs, whether or not the plaintiff has
discovered the injury at that time." The court concluded that because the plaintiff had filed
her product liability claim against the manufacturer more than 2 years after the date that the
injury occurred, the claim was time barred. Therefore, the Court held that the trial court
did not err in granting summary judgment to the manufacturer on that claim. The Court
affirmed the decision of the Court of Appeals granting summary judgment in favor of the
pharmacist on plaintiff's negligence claim because the plaintiff had presented no argument
against that conclusion.

Perez v Wyeth Laboratories, Inc.
734 A.2d 1245 (N.J. 1999)

This case concerns the *Norplant* contraceptive. Wyeth, the *Norplant* manufacturer, began a massive nation-wide advertising campaign directed at women rather than their physicians. A group of women filed suit complaining of injuries from using *Norplant*, and that Wyeth failed to adequately warn about *Norplant*'s side effects. The issue in this case was whether the "learned intermediary" doctrine applied to relieve pharmaceutical manufacturers of a duty to warn the ultimate users of a prescription drug, so long as it supplied physicians with information of the drug's dangers. The trial court held that the learned intermediary doctrine applied, granted Wyeth summary judgment, and the court of appeals affirmed. The New Jersey Supreme Court reversed and held that the learned intermediary doctrine did not apply to the direct marketing of drugs to consumers. Had Wyeth simply supplied physicians with information about *Norplant* and not advertised directly to patients, then the learned intermediary doctrine would have applied and Wyeth would have had no independent duty to warn patients. The supreme court concluded, however, that prescription drug manufacturers who market their products directly to consumers should be subject to claims by consumers if the advertising fails to provide adequate warnings of dangers. The supreme court found that neither the manufacturer nor the physician should be relieved of their respective duties to warn patients. Therefore, manufacturers may seek contribution, indemnity, or exoneration because of the physician's deficient role in prescribing a drug. The New Jersey Supreme Court, therefore, held that direct marketing of drugs to consumers generates a corresponding duty requiring manufacturers to warn of defects in the products.

Wright v Abbott Laboratories
62 F.Supp.2d 1186 (D.Kan. 1999)

Wright claimed personal injuries due to allegedly inadequate warnings by Abbott Laboratories. Shortly after Wright's birth, he went limp and required resuscitation. Wright's doctor prescribed normal saline (0.9%) to raise Wright's blood pressure levels. A nurse removed a vial of saline from a medication cart to administer to Wright. The nurse, however, incorrectly selected a 14.6% solution instead of the 0.9% solution. The package label and insert on the vial that the nurse selected clearly identified the solution as 14.6% and cautioned that the solution must be diluted for IV use. As a result of injecting the concentrated saline solution, Wright incurred severe and permanent physical injuries. Wright alleged that Abbott Labs, as a drug manufacturer, had a duty not only to provide adequate warnings, but also to warn learned intermediaries and skilled health care professionals of the dangers of ignoring the adequate warnings. The court held that the warnings given by Abbott Labs were adequate, that medical practitioners were aware of the risk, and any additional warnings by Abbott Labs would not have prevented the injury to Wright. Therefore, the court granted Abbott Labs summary judgment.

Moore v Memorial Hospital of Gulfport
Slip Op No 2000-CA-01976 (Sept. 5, 2002), 2002 WL 2027353

The parents of a minor child brought a negligence action against a pharmacy that dispensed the drug *Diovan* to the mother during her pregnancy with the child. Four days after the child's birth, the child suffered from kidney failure and needed a kidney transplant. The parents sued the pharmacy for its negligence in filling a prescription for *Diovan*, a medication that was contraindicated for pregnant women. The parents alleged that the *Diovan*

Moore v Memorial Hospital of Gulfport
Slip Op No 2000-CA-01976 (Sept. 5, 2002), 2002 WL 2027353
...continued

caused their child's kidney failure and other physical ailments. The pharmacy countered by asserting that it accurately filled the *Diovan* prescription in accordance with the prescription written by the physician, and that under the learned intermediary doctrine, it was under no duty to advise the patient of the possible side effects of *Diovan* or second guess the appropriateness of the medication. The trial court agreed with the pharmacy and granted it summary judgment. On appeal the Supreme Court of Mississippi affirmed the trial court's holding by applying the learned intermediary doctrine. The court stated that the "cornerstone of the learned intermediary doctrine is the ability of the physician to intervene between the drug and the patient, and to make an informed decision as to the course of treatment based on the physician's knowledge of the drug as well as the propensities of the patient." The court further stated that under this doctrine, it is the physician, and not the pharmacist, who is best situated to know the propensities of the drug and the needs of the patient. The court therefore found that the Winn-Dixie had no legal duty to warn the patient of the hazards of taking *Diovan*. The court, however, set forth the following two exceptions to the learned intermediary doctrine which could have placed a duty on the pharmacy to warn the patient: 1) if the patient had informed the pharmacy of health problems which contradicted her use of the *Diovan*; and/or 2) if the pharmacy had filled the *Diovan* prescription in quantities inconsistent with the recommended dosage guidelines. The court, however, found that these exceptions were inapplicable, because there was no evidence that the pharmacy either knew of the pregnancy when filling the prescription or improperly filled the prescription. Finally, the parents of the child asserted that the pharmacy negligently violated the State of Mississippi Board of Pharmacy's internal regulations. The court disagreed and stated that while a violation of the Board of Pharmacy's internal regulations may serve as evidence of negligence, such violation did not create a separate legal duty of care on the pharmacy.

The following is a list of court cases that are related to this topic.

Hill v E.R. Squibb & Sons, 592 P. 2d 1383 (Mont. 1979).
Torsiello v Whitehall Laboratories, Etc., 165 N.J. Super. 311, 398 A. 2d 132 (1979).
Frye v Medicare-Glaser Corporation, No. 5-90-0559, Ill App. Ct, 5th Dist. October 8, 1991.
Pittman v The Upjohn Company, 1994 WL 663372 (Tenn. Nov. 28, 1994).
Gennock v Warner-Lambert, 208 F. Supp.2d 1156 (D. Nev. 2002).

PART III: PREMISES LIABILITY

Premises Liability

The following is a list of court cases that are related to this topic.

Rodgers v Hook-SupeRx Inc., 562 N.E. 2d 358 (Ill. App. 4 Dist. 1990).

PART IV: INTENTIONAL TORTS

Interference With The Person

The following is a list of court cases that are related to this topic.

Bales v Wal-Mart Stores, Slip Op. Nos. 97-3029, 97-3030 and 97-3032, May 7, 1998, 8th Cir., 1998 I.S. App. LEXIS 9008.

Battery and Assault

Rodgers v Hook-SupeRx Inc.
562 N.E.2d 358 (Ill. App. 1990)

ISSUE: Whether a pharmacy was negligent for the injuries incurred when one of its customers was attacked in its parking lot.

FACTS: Mary Rodgers brought a negligence action against Hook Drugs as a result of an April 1986 robbery outside Hook's store in Danville, Illinois. The plaintiff entered the pharmacy to make a purchase, and when leaving, she exited through the front entrance onto a private sidewalk that surrounded a portion of the front of the store. The plaintiff was confronted by two men who took her purse and knocked her to the ground.

The plaintiff alleged that the defendant pharmacy chain had a duty to protect her from the criminal attacks by third persons, which the defendant knew or should have known were reasonably likely to occur. It was further alleged that the defendant should have had knowledge that the attack was likely since the two men had earlier been inside the store harassing a customer. It was also rumored that two months prior to this incident, a similar robbery had occurred in the area. The plaintiff further alleged that the defendant was negligent in failing to provide adequate lighting.

RULING: The court granted the defendant's motion for summary judgment, concluding that the attack by a third party was not reasonably foreseeable.

REASONING: The Appellate Court of Illinois noted that generally there is no duty to protect another against the criminal attacks of third persons. However, the owner or occupier of land owes a duty to those who come on his premises to reasonably guard against attacks of third parties when such attacks are reasonably foreseeable. The issue in this case was whether the attack upon the plaintiff was reasonably foreseeable.

The store cashier testified that while the plaintiff was in the store, two men entered and began to verbally harass a young female customer. The cashier asked the two men to leave the store and they promptly responded. Several minutes later, the plaintiff came through the checkout line. After she left the store, the cashier heard war whoops and saw the two men jumping up in the air outside. The plaintiff then came in and said she had just been mugged in the parking lot.

Rodgers v Hook-SupeRx Inc.
562 N.E.2d 358 (Ill. App. 1990)
...continued

The pharmacist, who was also the assistant manager, stated that it was store policy of Hooks to ask troublemakers to leave the premises. He also stated that the front lighting around the building was operating that evening, because he had checked it as part of his routine schedule.

The court concluded that the attack upon the plaintiff by a third party was not reasonably foreseeable. The allegations regarding a previous purse snatching and the actions of the two men while in the store were insufficient to make the attack foreseeable. There was a factual dispute between the plaintiff and the defendant regarding the exterior lighting, but the court concluded that the lighting did not appear to be the cause of, or a factor in, the criminal attack.

False Imprisonment

Taylor v Johnson
Slip Op. No. 00-1660 (April 18, 2001), 2001 La. App. LEXIS 820

On Saturday, January 16, 1988, Ginger Taylor, complaining of pain associated with an abscessed tooth, called Dr. B. C. Hollier, an oral surgeon, to obtain a prescription for pain medication at about three o'clock in the afternoon. Dr. Hollier called Jim Hill, a pharmacist at Wal-Mart, and ordered a prescription for *Darvon Compound 65*, a Class IV narcotic. After Jim Hill took down the information and filled the prescription, he decided to verify the prescription with Dr. Hollier. Jim Hill said he was suspicious because the phone connection was not clear when he spoke with Dr. Hollier. It did not sound as if Dr. Hollier had pronounced his own name correctly. He attempted to reach Dr. Hollier twice with no success. Finally, he spoke to Dr. Hollier's answering service and discovered Dr. Hollier was not on call that weekend. Mr. Hill spoke to Dr. Hollier's partner, Dr. Marks, who was on call and who told him it was unlikely Dr. Hollier called in the prescription. Dr. Marks explained to Mr. Hill their office had a policy that only the on-call dentist would phone in prescriptions. This increased Mr. Hill's suspicions. He ultimately decided to call a policeman whose responsibilities included investigating prescription fraud. When Ms. Taylor arrived at Wal-Mart to pick up her prescription, the pharmacy clerk told her it would be a few more minutes and asked her to wait. Ms. Taylor waited a short time and checked again to see if the prescription was ready. Again she was told it would be a few minutes. While waiting, Ms. Taylor moved freely around the store. She did some shopping. At no time did Mr. Hill or any employee of Wal-Mart attempt to physically detain her. At no time was she told he could not leave the store. Upon being contacted, a policeman immediately went to the Wal-Mart pharmacy. Upon arrival, Mr. Hill explained to the policeman why he was suspicious of Ms. Taylor. He identified her for the trooper. After identifying her, he continued with his duties at the pharmacy and had no further contact with Ms. Taylor. The trooper conducted the investigation and made all the decisions from that point forward. He ultimately placed Ms. Taylor under arrest, handcuffed her, and took her outside. Deputies from the Rapides Parish Sheriff's office transported her to jail. She was booked. Later that evening, a Rapides Parish Sheriff's deputy contacted Dr. Hollier, who verified the prescription. Ms. Taylor was released.

She sued both the pharmacist and the pharmacy as well as others in the police department that are not part of this decision. Following a bench trial, the defendants were found 75%

Taylor v Johnson
Slip Op. No. 00-1660 (April 18, 2001), 2001 La. App. LEXIS 820
...continued

at fault on a total judgment of $40,000. Before trial, the parties stipulated damages would not exceed $20,000 so the judgment was only enforceable up to that amount. The defendants argued the trial court erred in assessing any liability on their part. Although the trial judge did not explicitly state the legal theory upon which he based the award, the award suggested several possible theories upon which it is based, including false imprisonment and intentional or negligent infliction of emotional distress.

The appellate court stated an essential element of the tort of false imprisonment is detention of the person. It found the record void of any evidence that Mr. Hill or any other Wal-Mart employee detained Ms. Taylor, restricted her movement in the store, advised her she could not leave, or caused her to be arrested. Ms. Taylor did other shopping while she waited. She testified that at one point she had grown so tired of waiting she nearly left the store. Therefore, false imprisonment is not a valid theory of recovery in this case as it pertains to Mr. Hill and Wal-Mart. It also found that the tort of intentional infliction of emotional distress inapplicable in the matter because essential elements were not present. Mr. Hill's conduct could in no way be categorized as "outrageous." In fact, the trial court made a finding of fact that his actions were "logical." This theory is inapplicable. The court also found that because the pharmacist's actions were "logical," the negligence claim must also fail. When faced with the situation and facts he had before him at that time, especially in light of his conversation with Dr. Hollier's partner, Mr. Hill acted logically by calling the authorities to report a call-in prescription that appeared suspicious. Having found the pharmacist's actions were "logical," however, it follows that his actions were also "reasonable." Because the appeals court found neither James Hill nor any other Wal-Mart employee negligent, the plaintiff cannot recover damages for any injuries alleged from James Hill or Wal-Mart based on a negligence theory. Judgment reversed.

Jack Eckerd Corp. v Smith
558 So.2d 1060 (Fla. 1990)

ISSUE: Whether a pharmacy was guilty of malicious prosecution and false imprisonment when they interrogated and prosecuted a suspected shoplifter.

FACTS: Delores Smith went to a Jacksonville, Florida, Eckerd store to pick up two prescriptions. Because of her husband's insurance, Smith was only required to pay $1 on each prescription. According to Smith, she offered to pay the clerk at the pharmacy counter, but was told she needed to pay at the front of the store. Smith picked up a few more items and returned to the front counter. She testified that she laid all of her items, including the prescription bag, on the counter. The cashier rang up the items and asked for $11.18. According to Smith, the cashier put the household items in a small bag and Smith put the prescriptions in her purse. Smith attempted to leave the store and an alarm went off. The alarm system in the store is activated by a tag on each piece of merchandise, which is normally deactivated upon receipt of payment.

Smith returned to the cashier in an attempt to determine what had caused the alarm to go off. They determined that the household items were accounted for and were somewhat perplexed when the assistant manager joined them. At this point, Smith took the prescription bag from her purse commenting that perhaps the medicine was the problem. According to Smith, she paid the cashier $2 for the medicine in the presence of the assistant manager.

Jack Eckerd Corp. v Smith
558 So.2d 1060 (Fla. 1990)
...continued

The assistant manager disputed this. He asked Smith to accompany him to his office. Shortly thereafter, a police officer arrived. Smith became upset and started crying. Based upon the facts that the officer learned from the assistant manager, he determined that there was probable cause to arrest. He did not take Smith to jail to book her, but instead gave her notice to appear.

The assistant manager testified that he didn't actually see the cashier ringing up Smith's purchases or even become aware of Smith until the alarm sounded and Smith returned to the cashier. He had no knowledge of whether or not Smith put her prescriptions on the counter for the cashier to ring up. He made up his mind to call the police after Smith removed the unpaid-for prescriptions from her purse where they had been concealed, and after talking to the pharmacy clerk and learning that Smith had been told to pay for the prescriptions at the front counter. He admitted that it would have been good practice to talk to the cashier and the suspect, but he commented that they never offered any explanation to him of the incident. He indicated that he followed Eckerd's policy to call the police and report the incident because there had been "concealment" of the prescription in Smith's purse.

RULING: The jury returned a verdict awarding the plaintiff $25,000 in compensatory damages. They further awarded punitive damages of $100,000. The appellate court reversed the award of punitive damages.

REASONING: Legal malice, which may be implied or inferred from an absence of probable cause, must be proved in order to recover compensatory damages in a malicious prosecution action. Such proof of legal malice may be sufficient for recovery of punitive damages if it encompasses a showing of wanton disregard of the plaintiff's rights. This requires evidence of excessive and reckless disregard of the plaintiff's rights.

The court concluded that it appeared from the evidence that the defendant was liable to the plaintiff for causing humiliation, indignity, and mental suffering resulting from the defendant's wrongful interference with her peaceful security of person and reputation. However, in the court's opinion the wrong done was the result of an honest, but mistaken suspicion on the part of the assistant manager. "Had the defendant's employees stripped the plaintiff of her clothing in an effort to find articles supposed to have been stolen, or beat her in an effort to make her confess her alleged guilt, or purported some other similar atrocious and excessive act of violence toward the plaintiff, the situation would have been different." It was not shown that the act was deliberately done on the account of any malicious intent by the assistant manager.

Smith argued that Eckerd should have conducted a more thorough investigation before calling a law enforcement officer and that the failure to do so justified the award of punitive damages. However, It was the court's view that the brief investigation, which established that Smith was leaving the store with concealed merchandise and the prompt call to the police officer, was an honest, but mistaken effort to comply with the law which gives a merchant immunity from prosecution for false imprisonment if he acts with probable cause and calls law enforcement officials immediately after taking a shoplifting suspect into custody.

The following is a list of court cases that are related to this topic.

Southwest Drug Stores of Mississippi, Inc. v Garner, 195 So.2d 837 (Miss. 1967).

Infliction of Mental Distress

Gorden, et al v Frost, et al
388 S.E.2d 362 (Ga. App. 1989)

ISSUE: Whether a pharmacist who accused a patient of fraudulently obtaining a prescription drug is liable for intentional infliction of emotional distress.

FACTS: The plaintiff, Gail Gorden, awoke one night with a migraine headache and decided to take some prescribed *Fiorinal* #3 with codeine. She had requested refills for the prescriptions by telephoning the pharmacy where she indicated she was on a first name basis with the pharmacists. She also believed that the pharmacists recognized her voice on the phone because they would refer to her by her first name when she called.

In this particular instance, an assistant or intern pharmacist answered the telephone. Mrs. Gorden stated "I am calling to renew a prescription for Gail Gorden." The intern asked if the prescription was refillable, but Mrs. Gorden responded that she did not know. After a number of other questions, Mrs. Gorden was asked to supply the physician's DEA number. The intern informed the plaintiff that they could not fill the prescription without the DEA number. Pharmacist Frost took over the telephone call and reiterated that they could not fill the prescription without the DEA number.

Apparently believing that the caller requesting *Fiorinal* was a representative from the physician's office, Frost returned the call to inquire about the prescription when she learned that no one had authorized the prescription. Apparently, pharmacist Frost commented to a fellow worker that she thought Gorden was a hypochondriac and that Gorden was attempting to fraudulently acquire the prescription. Frost called the DEA and shortly thereafter, a police officer arrived and arrested Gorden when she came to the pharmacy to pick up the prescription.

RULING: The jury awarded Mrs. Gorden $200,000 on her claims for emotional distress and her husband was awarded $20,000 on his loss of consortium claim, but the trial court granted the pharmacist's motion notwithstanding the verdict. The appellate court overturned the trial court's decision and reinstated the jury verdict.

REASONING: The court noted that the pharmacist did not inquire as to whether or not the physician would have authorized the prescription, did not check the store computer to review the status of the prescription and did not call the plaintiff to attempt to clarify the situation. It was reported that the physician did not believe that the plaintiff abused prescription medications, and probably would have authorized the refill.

The tort of intentional infliction of emotional distress occurs when the defendant's actions are so insulting as to humiliate, embarrass, or frighten the plaintiff. The court noted that there was a relationship of professional trust between Mrs. Gorden and pharmacist Frost. Frost was in a position of control over the plaintiff's health and welfare to the extent of properly dispensing prescriptions. Frost's position allowed her access to computerized documentation of the plaintiff's medication. There was additional information that Frost perceived that Mrs. Gorden had emotional problems and that the quality of her medications indicated hypochondriac behavior.

In the context of the relationship of trust between a patient and a pharmacist, the evidence of Frost's previously expressed opinions about the plaintiff and the pharmacist's lim-

Gorden, et al v Frost, et al
388 S.E.2d 362 (Ga. App. 1989)
...continued

ited investigation, the court concluded that there was sufficient evidence to support the jury's determination that the defendant had intentionally inflicted emotional distress upon the plaintiff.

The following is a list of court cases that are related to this topic.

Huggins v Longs Drug Stores, 1991 Cal. App LEXIS 1409 (Cal. Ct. App 5th Dist.).
Huggins v Longs Drug Stores California, Inc., Cal. Sup. Ct. No. 5030711 (Nov. 18, 1993).
Shepard's Pharmacy v Stop and Shop, 640 N.E.2d 1112 (Mass. App. 1994).

Outrageous Conduct

The following is a list of court cases that are related to this topic.

Harco Drugs v Holloway, 1995 Ala. LEXIS 343 (Aug. 11, 1995).
Winn Dixie of Montgomery v Colburn, Slip No. 1961146, Feb. 6, 1998, Ala. S. Ct., 1998 Ala. LEXIS 48.
Petrarca v Phar-Mor, Slip Op No (Accelerated case) 2000-T-0121 (September 21, 2001), 2001 Ohio App. LEXIS 4293.

Defamation

Southwest Drug Stores of Mississippi, Inc. v Garner
195 So.2d 837 (Miss. 1967)

ISSUE: Whether the customer of a pharmacy had been defamed and falsely arrested when the store manager accused her of stealing a bar of cosmetic soap.

FACTS: Mrs. Garner and her sister stopped at the Southwest Drug Store in Laurel, Mississippi to purchase cosmetic soap. The women went into the drug store, leaving their father who was ill in the car in the parking lot in front of the building. While at the cosmetic counter, the store manger approached Mrs. Garner and asked if he could be of assistance. Mrs. Garner told the manager that she wanted a bar of *Lowila* soap. He replied that he would have one of the clerks assist her.

A sales lady assisted Mrs. Garner with the purchase of her soap. She received a sales ticket and the soap was placed in a small paper bag. Mrs. Garner was concerned about her father and left the store to check on him. The store manager saw Mrs. Garner leaving the premises. He hurried after Mrs. Garner yelling, "Hey, wait here! You stole a bar of soap!" A number of people were close by and heard the manager's accusations. The store manager did not touch Mrs. Garner or her belongings, but he did demand that she return to the store. Once back in the drug store, the cashier stated that Mrs. Garner had paid for the soap. Mrs. Garner was embarrassed and began to cry. The manager denied that he accused her of stealing the soap. Mrs. Garner brought an action against the pharmacy and the manager for slander and unlawful detention. She recovered a judgment of $8000.

RULING: The court upheld the $8000 jury verdict against the pharmacy and the store manager for defamation and false imprisonment.

Southwest Drug Stores of Mississippi, Inc. v Garner
195 So.2d 837 (Miss. 1967)
...continued

REASONING: The defendants argued that they had a qualified privilege to investigate suspected shoplifting based on a Mississippi statute that protected merchants when they acted in good faith and with reasonable grounds. The court held that the defendants lost their statutory privilege by the manner in which it was exercised. The jury found that the plaintiff had been falsely accused of stealing, and that this was done in a rude and loud voice in the presence of other people. The manager was also careless and negligent in his method of determining whether Mrs. Garner had paid for a bar of soap. If the manager had asked the cashier whether the plaintiff had paid for a bar of soap, he would have found that she had.

The jury also found that the actions of the store manager showed that he did not care whether the words he spoke were true or not. Thus, the jury found that he maliciously spoke the words in a reckless manner without knowing or caring whether they were true. While the jury verdict was large considering the fact pattern, the appellate court would not overturn it.

The following is a list of court cases that are related to this topic.

Kollenberg v Ramirez, 339 N.W.2d 176 (Mich. App. 1983).
Evans v Rite-Aid Corp., 452 S.E.2d 9 (S.C. App. 1994), affirmed, as modified 478 S.E. 2d 846 (1996).

Libel and Slander

The following is a list of court cases that are related to this topic.

Kollenberg v Ramirez, 339 N.W.2d 176 (Mich. App. 1983).

Invasion of Privacy

Doe v Southeastern Pennsylvania Transportation Authority (SEPTA)
72 F.3d 1133 (3rd Cir. 1995)

FACTS: A self-insured public bus transportation agency obtained pharmacy prescription claims data including employee names and prescribed drugs as method of monitoring the prescription drug benefit program for fraud and abuse. Human resource and staff physicians learned from this data that the plaintiff is HIV positive. No employment action was taken as a result of his HIV status. The employee sued his employer for violation of his constitutional right of privacy. The jury awarded him $125,000 in compensatory damages.

HOLDING: Reversed on appeal. Although pharmacy and medical records are within the constitutionally protected right of privacy against disclosure of personal information, a publicly funded employer has a legitimate interest in obtaining prescription data from pharmacies to assure that the benefit is being properly utilized. As the employer did not misuse the confidential information, the employee suffered no compensible damages.

The following is a list of court cases that are related to this topic.

Shepard's Pharmacy v Stop and Shop, 640 N.E.2d 1112 (Mass. App. 1994).

Malicious Prosecution

The following is a list of court cases that are related to this topic.

Kollenberg v Ramirez, 339 N.W.2d 176 (Mich. App. 1983).
Jack Eckerd Corp. v Smith, 558 So. 2d 1060 (Fla. 1990).

Injurious Falsehood

Kollenberg v Ramirez
339 N.W.2d 176 (Mich. App. 1983)

ISSUE: Whether a pharmacist had been defamed by a physician's remarks to a patient about an alleged dispensing error.

FACTS: Eugene Kollenberg, the plaintiff, was a licensed pharmacist and the owner and operator of Garden City Medical Center Prescriptions in Garden City, Michigan. On May 24, 1977, a regular customer of the pharmacy, Ronald Semmel, brought two prescriptions to the plaintiff to fill. The prescriptions had been written by Dr. Jamie Ramirez. Kollenberg believed that one prescription was for an extremely high dosage. He telephone Dr. Ramirez to inform the physician of the possible error. Ramirez allegedly answered the telephone inquiry by ordering the pharmacist to fill the prescription as written. The plaintiff did so.

Upon taking the prescribed medication, Mr. Semmel suffered a severe reaction that resulted in his hospitalization. During Semmel's hospital stay, the physician allegedly told Semmel that the reaction was caused by the pharmacist's error in dispensing the prescription. As a result of this information, Semmel filed a lawsuit against pharmacist Kollenberg. Semmel voluntarily dismissed his lawsuit against the pharmacist without any settlement.

Following the dismissal of Mr. Semmel's law suite, Kollenberg filed this action against Dr. Ramirez with a 3 count complaint alleging malpractice, malicious prosecution and libel and slander. On March 13, 1981, the trial court granted summary judgment in favor of Dr. Ramirez on the malpractice claim. On April 2, 1981, the plaintiff filed an amended complaint against Dr. Ramirez alleging negligence by the physician arising from his intentional communication of a false statement to Mr. Semmel. The physician argued that the plaintiff's amended complaint was actually a reiteration of the defamation claim that the plaintiff had originally alleged. As such, the defendant argued that the claim should have been dismissed because it was barred by the running of the 1-year statute of limitation for defamation actions.

RULING: Although the law varies from state to state, the Michigan court concluded that the plaintiff was correct in arguing that the 3-year period of limitation applied to this tort. The court found that the pharmacist did sufficiently allege the elements of injurious falsehood in his amended complaint. While the plaintiff was not entitled to general personal damages for injuries to his reputation, he was entitled to damages resulting from his defense of the lawsuit by Mr. Semmel and to the loss of earnings that he suffered because he was unable to be gainfully employed for a period of several years.

REASONING: The issue of this case is confused because the plaintiff alleged elements of defamation, injurious falsehood, and negligence. While the time limit within which to institute the action had run for some of the claims, the court concluded that the pharmacist should have some remedy for the intentional act of which he complained, particularly since the act resulted in a cost to the pharmacist for defending the lawsuit by Mr. Semmel. Injurious falsehood typically involves derogatory or disparaging communications regarding the title to property or the quality of property. The gist of the tort is some interference with an economically advantageous relationship that results in a pecuniary loss rather than an action that directly affects the property.

Kollenberg v Ramirez
339 N.W.2d 176 (Mich. App. 1983)
...continued

An individual who publishes a false statement harmful to the interest of another is subject to liability if (1) he intends the publication to result in harm, or should recognize that it is likely to do so, and (2) he knows that the statement is false or acts in reckless disregard of its truth. The statement made by Dr. Ramirez resulted in both damages to Kollenberg's reputation and to his pecuniary interest. Thus, the torts of injurious falsehood and defamation overlapped. When 2 torts overlap, the plaintiff may bring suit for both torts as long as damages are not duplicated.

The following is a list of court cases that are related to this topic.

Evans v Rite-Aid Corp., 452 S.E.2d 9 (S.C. App. 1994), affirmed, as modified 478 S.E. 2d 846 (1996).

Interference with Prospective Advantage

Shepard's Pharmacy v Stop and Shop
640 N.E.2d 1112 (Mass. App. 1994)

FACTS: A pharmacist negotiated the sale of his pharmacy to a chain. A few days before the scheduled closing, a second chain made the pharmacist a substantially higher offer. The pharmacist refused to sell to the first chain. However, an advertisement announcing the sale to the first chain appeared in a local newspaper with a picture of the pharmacist and a statement that he would stay on as the new manager. As a result of the ad, the second chain learned of the pending sale and withdrew its offer. Suit was brought against the first chain for unfair and deceptive business practices, economic coercion in announcing the sale before being completed, interference with business opportunities, emotional distress, and invasion of privacy for publishing his picture without permission. The jury awarded $750 for tortious interference with the pharmacist's customers, but denied interference between the pharmacist and the second chain. The judge awarded the pharmacist $750,000 for invasion of privacy and doubled the amount under State law, finding the conduct was willful. Nearly $57,000 in attorney's fees was also awarded.

HOLDING: The judgment was reversed on appeal because the evidence did not support a finding that the first buyer's conduct "attained a level of rascality that would raise an eyebrow of someone injured in the rough and tumble world of commerce."

DEFENSES

Privilege

The following is a list of court cases that are related to this topic.

Rodgers v Hook-SupeRx Inc., 562 N.E. 2d 358 (Ill. App. 4 Dist. 1990).

Mistake

The following is a list of court cases that are related to this topic.

Jack Eckerd Corp. v Smith, 558 So. 2d 1060 (Fla. 1990).

Necessity

The following is a list of court cases that are related to this topic.

Doe v Southeastern Pennsylvania Transportation Authority (SEPTA), 72 F.3d 1133 (3rd Cir. 1995).

PART V: PROCEDURAL ISSUES

General

Sciolino v US
Slip Op. No. 98-CV-0450E(M) (March 16, 2001), USDC WDNY, 2001 U.S. Dist. LEXIS 2811

Plaintiff filed an administrative claim, under the Federal Torts Claim Act (FTCA), 28 U.S.C. §§2671-2680, listing both her husband and herself as claimants, with the Department of Veterans Affairs, alleging that the agency's pharmacy had improperly filled a prescription, causing plaintiff's husband to overdose. Plaintiff further alleged that her husband developed complications and remained unconscious. Plaintiff later filed the present action alleging negligence on the part of the pharmacy, as well as a derivative claim. Defendant sought to discover the specific acts that constituted malpractice. Plaintiff replied that defendant's agents failed to properly diagnose, treat, and care for her husband in regard to the overdose. The court denied defendant's motion to dismiss the medical malpractice claim raised during discovery. The statement in plaintiff's administrative claim about "complications" reasonably raised the malpractice claim. Further, plaintiff's derivative claim was properly asserted in the administrative claim. The agency had sufficient notice of plaintiff's derivative claim under the FTCA. Plaintiff's total claim was limited, however, to the $5,000,000 originally claimed.

The following is a list of court cases that are related to this topic.

Wimm v Jack Eckerd Corp., 1993 App. LEXIS 25102 (U.S. Ct. App. 5th Cir.).
Malon v Hueseman, WD 53338, April 8, 1997, 1997 Mo. App. LEXIS 565.
Maryland Pharmacists Association v Office of the Attorney General, Slip Op. No. 1444 (May 30, 1997, Md. Ct. Special App.), 1997 Md, App. 95.

Jurisdiction

Bumgarner v Carlisle Medical
809 F.Supp. 461 (S.D.Miss. 1993)

ISSUE: Whether the Mississippi courts had jurisdiction over an Alabama pharmacist.

FACTS: The plaintiff in this action alleges that Carlisle Medical, Inc., an Alabama corporation that distributes prescription medications by mail, delivered incorrect medication to the plaintiff at his residence in Natchez, Mississippi. As a result of the plaintiff's ingestion of these medications, he suffered physical and mental injuries and became violent and abusive toward his wife and children.

Carlisle answered the plaintiff's complaint, and also filed a third-party complaint against James Crump, the licensed pharmacist who dispensed the prescription. Carlisle alleged that if the patient's allegations should be proved, then Crump should be held liable for any judgment against Carlisle. In effect, the pharmacy sought to bring the Alabama pharmacist into the lawsuit that was filed in federal court in the state of Mississippi.

RULING: The court held it would be unfair to have a dispute between an Alabama pharmacy and its pharmacist resolved by a Mississippi court.

REASONING: Due process requires that a nonresident defendant must have purposefully established "minimum contacts with the state in which the lawsuit is filed." The minimum contact inquiry focuses on the relationship between the nonresident defendant, the state in which the action is filed, and the litigation.

Bumgarner v Carlisle Medical
809 F.Supp. 461 (S.D.Miss. 1993)
...continued

The pharmacy alleged, in its action for indemnification from Crump, that the pharmacist personally addressed and shipped the plaintiff's medication to him in Mississippi. Crump denies this allegation and states that a shipping clerk performed these duties. The pharmacy presented an affidavit of a former coworker of Crump's, in which it stated that Crump filed an average of 22 prescriptions per week for customers living in Mississippi.

However, the pharmacy failed to show any evidence suggesting that Crump knew that any of these customers, let alone the plaintiff in action, actually lived in Mississippi. Because the pharmacy failed to establish the existence of sufficient contacts between Crump and the state of Mississippi, the court granted Crump's motion to dismiss for lack of personal jurisdiction.

The following is a list of court cases that are related to this topic.

Bailey v Johnson, 48 F.3d 965 (6th Cir. 1995).
Barbuto v Medicine Shoppe International, 166 F.Supp.2d 341 (W.D. Penn. 2001)
Kennedy v Lubar, 273 F.3d 1293 (10th Cir. 2001)

Fraudulent Joinder

Crain v Eckerd Corp.
Slip Op. No. 96-3485, August 21, 1997, D.C. La., 1997 U.S. Dist. LEXIS 13113

ISSUE: May a pharmacist-employee of a corporation be held personally liable in a malpractice claim for purposes of establishing jurisdiction in a state court and defeating diversity jurisdiction in a federal court?

FACTS: The plaintiffs claim that a pharmacist of Eckerd Drugs in Bogalusa, Louisiana, incorrectly labeled a prescription issued by the child's treating physician. The amount on the label directed the mother to administer an excessive amount of *Ventolin* to her son, which allegedly caused the child and his family to suffer damages. The plaintiffs, who are Louisiana residents, filed a suit in the state's district court naming as defendants Eckerd Corporation (hereinafter "Eckerd"), a corporate citizen of Florida, and the pharmacist, who is also a resident of Louisiana. Eckerd sought to have the case tried in the federal court sitting in Louisiana by filing a "Notice of Removal."

HOLDING: The federal court refused to assume jurisdiction over the state law claims and sent the case back to the state court where it was originally filed.

REASONING: Eckerd argued that the case should be remanded because 1) diversity is not destroyed in that the pharmacist defendant was fraudulently joined and 2) plaintiffs' state law claims are preempted by federal law. As far as the diversity issue is concerned, a federal court can only assume jurisdiction over a state law claim if diversity of citizenship between the plaintiffs and defendants is complete. That means that none of the parties are citizens of the same state. Since the pharmacist defendant is from Louisiana, she would defeat subject matter jurisdiction based on diversity because plaintiffs are also from Louisiana. Eckerd argued that under the doctrine of respondeat superior, it is solely liable for damages caused by its pharmacist-employee. However, the court was persuaded by plaintiffs' argument that the 4 elements needed to impose liability on an individual, when the duty breached arises

Crain v Eckerd Corp.
Slip Op. No. 96-3485, August 21, 1997, D.C. La., 1997 U.S. Dist. LEXIS 13113
...continued

solely because of the employment relationship, are satisfied. Those elements are: 1) The employer must owe a duty of care to the customer; 2) this duty must be delegated by the employer to the particular employee; 3) the employee must breach this duty through his own personal fault; and 4) personal liability cannot be imposed on the employee simply because of his general administrative responsibility, but instead the employee must have a personal duty to the plaintiff that was not delegated to another employee.

As for the first element, Eckerd clearly has a duty of care to its customers. Under the second element, simple logic dictates that Eckerd hires their pharmacists with the instructions to be careful and diligent in their work. In addition, the drugstore chain must hire only those pharmacists who are licensed. Element 3 is met as the pharmacist was the individual personally filling the prescription. Furthermore, Louisiana law allows for pharmacists to be found personally liable for negligence in filling prescriptions. Regarding the fourth requirement, a pharmacist is not merely fulfilling an administrative function, but is acting as a licensed professional. Filling prescriptions cannot be delegated to the store manager or cashier. Because these 4 elements that circumvent the doctrine of respondeat superior are met, the court found that the pharmacist was not fraudulently joined, and therefore, diversity does not exist as a basis for subject matter jurisdiction.

The court also determined that federal status does not preempt state law. Eckerd failed to show any explicit preemptive language regarding prescription drugs within the Food, Drug and Cosmetic Act. Therefore, to determine if a federal statute implicitly overrides state law, it is necessary to see if state law is an actual conflict with federal law or if the scope of the federal statute indicates that Congress intended the legislation to occupy a field exclusively. No such conflict exists between the state laws and the Food, Drug and Cosmetic Act governing a pharmacist's negligent labeling. OBRA-90 responsibilities do not apply to this situation because the statute pertains to a drug review of the prescription by the pharmacist with a customer who is eligible for medical assistance programs under the Social Security program.

Aucoin v Vicknair
Slip Op. No. 97-1885, August 29, 1997, D. C. La., 1997 U.S. Dist. LEXIS 13381

ISSUE: May a pharmacist-employee of a corporation be held personally liable in a malpractice claim for purposes of establishing jurisdiction in a state court and defeating diversity jurisdiction in a federal court?

FACTS: The plaintiff claimed that she suffered damages as a result of the pharmacist-defendant's negligence in filling her prescription. The complaint states that her treating physician issued the prescription and instructed the pharmacist to direct the plaintiff to take 1 to 2 tablets of *Prozac* a day. However, the label directed her to take 3 tablets of *Prozac* 4 times a day. The Eckerd Corporation ("Eckerd") employed the pharmacist. It is undisputed that the plaintiff and the pharmacist are both citizens of the state of Louisiana. Eckerd is a Florida corporation with its principal place of business located in Florida. Eckerd attempted to have the case heard in the federal court sitting in Louisiana. In order to do so, it claimed that the state court should not be allowed to retain the case because the pharmacist was fraudulently named as the defendant solely to defeat federal diversity jurisdiction. Eckerd also claimed the plaintiff's claims are preempted by federal law under specific provisions of the

Aucoin v Vicknair
Slip Op. No. 97-1885, August 29, 1997, D. C. La., 1997 U.S. Dist. LEXIS 13381
...continued

Food, Drug and Cosmetic Act, 21 U.S.C. 301, et seq., and the Pharmaceutical Access and Prudent Purchasing Act of 1990 within the Omnibus Budget Reconciliation Act, 42 U.S.C. §1396R-8.

HOLDING: The federal district court refused to assume jurisdiction over the state law claims, thereby defeating Eckerd's attempt to remove the case from the state court.

REASONING: The issue of fraudulent joinder is determined by whether the plaintiff has any possibility of establishing a valid claim against the pharmacist-defendant under state law. Eckerd argued that the pharmacist, as an employee of Eckerd, cannot be held individually liable for his actions performed in the scope of his employment. Eckerd asserted that liability, if any, rests with Eckerd through the doctrine of respondeat superior. However, under Louisiana law, an employee can be held individually liable for injuries to third parties under certain circumstances. Employees have a general duty to exercise due care to avoid injuries to third persons. Individual liability may be imposed upon an employee when the duty breached arises solely because of the employment relationship. A pharmacist has a personal duty to his or her customers. A pharmacist has a duty to fill a prescription correctly and to warn the patient or to notify the prescribing physician of an excessive dosage or of obvious inadequacies on the face of the prescription that create a substantial risk of harm to the patient. Accordingly, the court determined that the pharmacist was properly named and that diversity is incomplete. Therefore, the federal court has no authority to hear the case on this ground.

Eckerd also argued that federal law preempted the state law claims asserted by the plaintiff. The Court found this argument to be completely meritless. The Food, Drug, and Cosmetic Act does not explicitly or implicitly preempt state law claims.

EDITOR'S NOTE: It is common for large corporations that are incorporated in and have a principal place of business outside the state in which the lawsuit has been filed to try and have the case "removed" to a federal court. Many defense attorneys pursue this strategy on the belief that the corporation will obtain a more favorable trial in federal court as opposed to a state court, where the organization may be portrayed as a "foreign corporation."

Kohl v American Home Products
78 F.Supp.2d 885 (W.D.Ark. 1999)

Plaintiff, a resident of Arkansas, sued 3 manufacturers of drugs for products liability used in what was popularly known as the Fen/Phen diet after she contracted valvular heart disease. She also sued the Arkansas incorporated pharmacy where the prescriptions were filled for negligence in failing to warn her against using the combination of these drugs. The manufacturers removed the case to federal court on the basis of diversity of citizenship. The manufacturers claimed that the pharmacy was named for the sole purpose of defeating diversity as a means to avoid removal. The propriety of removal depends on whether the pharmacy could be held liable under Arkansas law for failing to warn. If yes, removal would be improper and jurisdiction should remain in the state court. If not, then the pharmacy should be dismissed and there would be complete diversity between the parties giving the federal court jurisdiction. The question of whether a pharmacist in Arkansas could be held liable for breaching a duty to warn has not been addressed by any prior decision of the Arkan-

Kohl v American Home Products
78 F.Supp.2d 885 (W.D.Ark. 1999)
...continued

sas courts. The federal district judge hearing the case considered precedence from several other states along with academic writings on the subject and noted that there are arguments going both ways. He concluded that the Arkansas courts would hold that a pharmacist has duties that go beyond just accurately filling a prescription and that pharmacists could be held liable for failing to warn. However, he also found that pharmacy malpractice cases are subject to the state's 2-year statute of limitations as opposed to the 3-year limitation period for ordinary negligence. Because the plaintiff had not filed the case until after the 2-year period had elapsed, her claim would be barred. Accordingly, dismissal of the pharmacy was required and removal was proper.

In re: *Rezulin* Products Liability Litigation
Slip Op. No. MDL No. 1348, Master File 00 Civ. 2843 (LAK) (February 28, 2001), USDC SD NY, 2001 U.S. Dist. LEXIS 2008

This multidistrict litigation involves 16 actions that were considered together. They each sought recovery for personal injuries allegedly resulting from the use of the prescription diabetes medication, *Rezulin*, formerly manufactured by defendants. Each of the 16 originally was commenced in a state court and removed by defendants on the basis of diversity of citizenship. Plaintiffs moved to remand on the ground that subject matter jurisdiction was lacking. Plaintiff's chief claim was that these actions were removed improperly because there was at least one defendant in each — usually a pharmacy or an employee of one of the defendant pharmaceutical companies — that was a citizen of the same state as a plaintiff, thus destroying the complete diversity of citizenship essential to the exercise of removal jurisdiction. The court found joinder of the sales representatives to have been improper. There was no reasonable possibility that plaintiffs alleged legally sufficient claims for relief against the defendant's sales representatives for failure to warn, fraudulent or negligent misrepresentation, or breach of warranty, the sales representatives were joined improperly in the 16 actions. The affidavits stated that the sales representative had no dealings with plaintiffs and did not make any statements to the general public or participate in any advertising or promotion to the general public concerning *Rezulin*, thus there was no reasonable factual basis for the claims against them.

Gayle Moore v Wyeth-Ayerst Laboratories
Slip Op No CCB-02–2691 (November 14, 2002, Decided), USDC MD, 2002 U.S. Dist. LEXIS 22213

Several patients who took diet drugs sued the pharmaceutical manufacturers and dispensing pharmacies in state court for injuries suffered as a result of taking the medication. The company removed the case to federal district court. The patients moved to remand. The manufacturer moved to defer consideration of the motion to remand and for a stay of pretrial proceedings pending transfer to the pending Multidistrict Litigation involving these product liability cases. The pharmaceutical company alleged that removal to federal court was proper because the patients fraudulently joined a pharmacy as a defendant. The company alleged that there was no cause of action against the pharmacy. The trial court concluded that the instant case appeared to be within the scope of the Multidistrict Litigation and that the court handling those cases transferee had already ruled on a number of motions to remand involving state law claims against pharmacies. Those cases required that court to determine

Gayle Moore v Wyeth-Ayerst Laboratories
Slip Op No CCB-02–2691 (November 14, 2002, Decided), USDC MD, 2002 U.S. Dist. LEXIS 22213
...continued

the scope of the learned intermediary doctrine as applied to a pharmacy, which was the same issue presented in the instant case. The Maryland district court indicated that there was no case against the pharmacy given that a pharmacist generally should not "second-guess" a doctor's prescription under Maryland law.

Alexis v GlaxoSmithKline
Slip Op No 02-059 SECTION: E/1 (May 17, 2002), USDC La., 2002 U.S. Dist. LEXIS 9654

This is a personal injury/products liability case involving the prescription drug *Lotronex*, marketed to treat irritable bowel syndrome (IBS). *Lotronex* was first introduced to the U.S. market in February 2000, and was withdrawn from the market in November 2000, based on extremely serious and fairly common side effects. The plaintiffs' claim the manufacturers knew of the dangers associated with the use of the drug and deliberately concealed the results of their clinical studies from even the FDA, or at least, underreported the known adverse effects. The plaintiffs sued a pharmaceutical company, pharmacies, and physicians in a state court claiming injuries allegedly suffered due to using *Lotronex*. Defendants removed the action to federal court based on diversity of citizenship, asserting that the resident physicians were fraudulently joined and that no cause of action existed with regard to the resident pharmacy. Plaintiffs moved to remand the action. The court first held that the suit against the defendant doctors stated a potentially viable claim against the physicians in state court and thus survived defendants' allegation of fraudulent joinder. As to the pharmacists, the court concluded that, at best, Louisiana law is "unsettled." The plaintiffs claimed that Louisiana courts have gradually enlarged the legal duties of a pharmacist under varying factual scenarios. In addition to the traditional duty to accurately fill the prescription as written, on a case by case basis, given the particular facts of each case, Louisiana courts have found a duty to warn of inadequacies apparent on the face of the prescription, and to intervene if excessive doses are prescribed referring to *Glassen v East Jefferson Gen. Hosp.*, 628 So.2d 256 (La. App. 5th Cir. 1993). (See Part I, Wrong Route of Administration.) The plaintiffs allege that in August 2000, the FDA required GlaxoSmithKline to provide a "Medication Guide," written especially for patients and containing FDA approved information detailing *Lotronex* side effects and that the pharmacists were required to distribute with products that the FDA had determined pose a serious risk to consumers and patients. Although clearly not certain, it is plausible that a Louisiana court may find that under the particular facts of the case, the pharmacies had a duty to at least inform the patients to whom they dispensed *Lotronex* of the information provided to the pharmacy in the Medication Guide. Given the ambiguities in Louisiana law at this point in time, and at this preliminary stage of the litigation, the court cannot say with certainty no plaintiff in this matter has a cause of action against any of the pharmacy defendants. Therefore, the plaintiffs' motion to remand back to a state court was granted.

Gennock v Warner-Lambert
208 F. Supp.2d 1156 (D. Nev. 2002)

On January 31, 2002, the plaintiff, a Nevada citizen, filed a lawsuit in a Nevada state court against the following defendants: 1) Pfizer, a Delaware corporation with its principal place of business in New York; 2) Warner-Lambert, a Delaware corporation with its principal place of business in New Jersey; 3) Sav-On, an Illinois corporation with its principal place of business in Idaho; and 4) Chang, a Nevada citizen. On March 15, 2002, the defendants collectively removed the case to the federal district court of Nevada. The plaintiff challenged the defendants' removal by asserting that such removal was ineffective because: 1) the Notice of Removal was not timely filed; and 2) all defendants did not join the Notice of Removal as required by federal statute. The court first ruled that the defendants sufficiently filed their Notice of Removal in a timely manner. The court determined that the defendants had until March 25, 2002, within which to file their Notice of Removal and that all of the defendants correctly joined and filed the Notice of Removal by March 15, 2002. Thus, the court held that the Notice of Removal was timely and effective as to all defendants. Second, the court analyzed whether the defendants properly removed the case to the federal court pursuant to diversity jurisdiction. Under federal law, diversity jurisdiction exists only where the plaintiff is a citizen of a different state than each of the defendants. The defendants argued that Chang, a pharmacist, was fraudulently named solely to defeat diversity jurisdiction. The defendants asserted that under the learned intermediary doctrine, the plaintiff could not bring an action against Chang as a pharmacist. The court explained that a "learned intermediary" was a medical expert "such as a prescribing physician, whose task is to weigh the benefits of any medication against possible dangers and to make 'an individualized medical judgment bottomed on a knowledge of both patient and palliative'." The court reasoned that if the learned intermediary doctrine applied in Nevada, then Chang could not be held strictly liable for filling a lawful prescription in the state and would therefore be dismissed as a defendant. Having reviewed Nevada case law, the court concluded that the learned intermediary doctrine was *not* law in Nevada and that a pharmacist, at a minimum, must be held to a duty to correctly fill prescriptions as prescribed and properly label such filled prescriptions. Thus, the court found that it was proper for the plaintiff to include Chang in the complaint, and therefore, no diversity of citizenship existed because the plaintiff and Chang were both Nevada citizens. The court granted the plaintiff's motion to remand the case back to the Nevada state court.

The following is a list of court cases that are related to this topic.

Humes v Eckerd Corporation, 2002 WL 2022958 (Pa. Super. Ct. 2002).
In re: Rezulin Products Liability Litigation, 168 F. Supp.2d 136 (S.D.N.Y. 2001).

Affidavit Requirement

Ellingsen v Walgreen
78 F.Supp.2d 965 (D.Minn. 1999)

The plaintiff presented a prescription to the pharmacy for quinidine that had been prescribed to treat a heart condition. The pharmacy admitted that it erroneously supplied quinine. The plaintiff used the quinine for approximately 1 month when she began to experience hearing and vision problems. By the end of the month, she suffered psychotic episodes resulting in a six-day admission to a psychiatric hospital. It was during this admission that the mistake was discovered and corrected. Her condition improved. She filed a pharmacy malpractice claim in the state court. It was removed to federal court based on diversity of citizenship. During discovery, the plaintiff indicated that her treating physician and one other

Ellingsen v Walgreen
78 F.Supp.2d 965 (D.Minn. 1999)
...continued

medical doctor would testify that her injuries were caused by the misfilled prescription. A controlling state statute requires that medical experts for a party supply a signed affidavit verifying the nature of the expected testimony. The pharmacy moved to dismiss the claim because the plaintiff did not produce the necessary affidavits. The court initially denied the motion. However, on reconsideration, the court dismissed the case. The plaintiff admitted that the affidavits were not timely filed but claimed no expert was necessary because any juror could determine that a pharmacist is negligent in misfilling a prescription even without an expert. The court acknowledged that a juror could determine that the standard of care owed by a pharmacist was violated without an expert, but that an expert would still be needed to establish causation and damages.

Statute of Limitations

Piedmont Pharmacy, Inc. v Patmore
240 S.E.2d 888 (Ct. App. Ga. 1977)

ISSUE: Whether the addition of a pharmacy as a defendant in a lawsuit was barred by the statute of limitations.

FACTS: The plaintiff brought a lawsuit in 1974, some 6 months after an eye ailment was diagnosed as steroid-induced glaucoma. The plaintiff believed the disease was caused by a prescription drug that she had used for 3 years. She filed suit against two physicians, a pharmacy, a pharmacist, and later applied to the court for permission to add Piedmont Pharmacy as another defendant. Piedmont filed an objection, alleging that the action against it was barred by the statute of limitations. Piedmont had last filled the plaintiff's prescription in 1971; this lawsuit was filed in 1974, and Piedmont was added as a defendant in July 1975.

Georgia law provided that personal injury actions must be brought within 2 years after the cause of action accrued. Piedmont insisted that the time period began when the prescription was dispensed to the plaintiff in February 1971. By Piedmont's analysis, it was too late after February 1973 to bring a suit against it. However, the plaintiff insisted that the doctrine of "continuing tort" tolled the statute of limitations until October 1973 when she discovered the condition of her eyes and the cause of that condition.

RULING: The Court of Appeals of Georgia permitted the addition of Piedmont Pharmacy as a defendant because the statute did not begin to run until the patient had knowledge of the existence of the injury.

REASONING: The pharmacy argued that the plaintiff knew, or should have known, of her injury prior to July 1973. The plaintiff went to an ophthalmologist in January 1972 because she was having problems with her eyes. This conduct, the pharmacy asserted, showed that the plaintiff was aware of her injury and recognized that the medication was connected with the injury. However, the plaintiff pointed out that the ophthalmologist, after examining her eyes, indicated that her problems were correctable by a change of contact lenses. He never told her to discontinue the use of the medication. It was not until a thorough examination by another physician revealed no physiological reasons for her trouble that a third eye doctor was consulted. He diagnosed steroid-induced glaucoma. This examination took place

Piedmont Pharmacy, Inc. v Patmore
240 S.E.2d 888 (Ct. App. Ga. 1977)
...continued

in October 1973, less than 2 years before the plaintiff amended her complaint to add Piedmont Pharmacy as a defendant.

Steele v Organon, Inc.
716 P.2d 920 (Wash.App. 1986)

ISSUE: Whether the statute of limitations should begin to run when the plaintiff is aware of some injury even if she does not know the full extent of the injuries until 7 years later.

FACTS: Doris Steele was hospitalized under the care of Dr. Welty for severe migraine headaches. Upon discharge, Dr. Welty prescribed *Wigraine*, and Mrs. Steele had the prescription filled at a Skaggs Drug Center. The directions on the prescription read "Take two tablets at onset of headache. Repeat every half to one hour for three doses." Mrs. Steele began taking 8 tablets a day for her headaches when needed. Neither the pharmacist nor the physician warned her that she should not exceed 10 to 12 tablets per week because of the nature of the drug. After approximately 3 weeks, Mrs. Steele experienced loss of sensation in her arms and legs and was again hospitalized, this time with ergot poisoning. She was treated by two heart specialists and released after symptoms subsided. Several months later, she returned to the heart specialist complaining of tingling in her hands and feet, which was diagnosed as Raynaud's syndrome.

Mrs. Steele sought advice from an attorney as to whether she had a cause of action for damages resulting from the overdose. The attorney then exchanged correspondence with the two heart specialists who were of the opinion that "it is highly improbable that there would be any relationship between this episode and her present symptoms." The only damages at this time appeared to be limited to the first hospitalization. Because insurance had covered most of the expenses associated with the hospitalization, Mrs. Steele and her attorney decided that the cost of the lawsuit could exceed the amount of recovery.

Over 8 years later, Mrs. Steele suffered a heart attack and re-entered the hospital for bypass surgery. While hospitalized, she suffered a stroke. During her hospitalization, Mrs. Steele overheard a neurologist and another physician discussing the 1973 overdose episode in relation to her stroke. After her discharge, she consulted another physician who advised her that the heart attack and stroke were both related to the *Wigraine* overdose.

In December 1982, a lawsuit was filed against Dr. Welty, Skaggs Drug Centers, and the manufacturer of *Wigraine*. The manufacturer was dismissed and the physician and pharmacy moved for summary judgment, contending that the statute of limitations had run.

RULING: The court granted the defendants' motion to dismiss the case because the time period to file the lawsuit had expired. Mrs. Steele was aware of all of the elements of her cause of action more than 7 years prior to the commencement of the lawsuit and it was now too late to initiate a legal action.

REASONING: It was undisputed that in April 1977 neither Mrs. Steele's doctor nor the pharmacy, both of whom owed her a duty of care, had warned of the need to limit her intake of *Wigraine*, which resulted in the overdose. Mrs. Steele argued that she did not have any damages until 1981 when she suffered the heart attack. However, the court disagreed. The

Steele v Organon, Inc.
716 P.2d 920 (Wash.App. 1986)
...continued

statute of limitations begins to run when the plaintiff is aware of some injury even if he or she does not know the full extent of the injuries. Although Mrs. Steele may have considered the amount of her damages small in 1973, evidence was clear that she was aware of some injury. Mrs. Steele exceeded the 3-year statute of limitation in filing her lawsuit. Dismissal was affirmed.

The dissenting judges equated Mrs. Steele's case to the occupational disease cases such as those involving asbestos. The dissent alleged that her exposure to the drug led to some immediately apparent problems, but also to other problems that did not manifest themselves until much later.

Koderick v Snyder Bros. Drug, Inc.
413 N.W.2d 856 (Minn. App. 1987)

ISSUE: (1) Which statute of limitation applied to a corporate pharmacy defendant in the negligent dispensing of prescription drugs and (2) when does a cause of action accrue for the negligent sale of a narcotic drug?

FACTS: Joyce Koderick consulted Dr. Janna Peake for jaw pain. Dr. Peake prescribed *Talwin* injectable. Koderick had her prescription dispensed at Snyder Brothers Drug. Dr. Peake continued to prescribe the injectable *Talwin* for the relief of pain over the next 8 years. All the prescriptions were filled at the Snyder pharmacy.

Eight years after initiating the drug therapy, Koderick was hospitalized for ulcerated sores on her legs. Dr. Peake discontinued the *Talwin* and began prescribing *Elavil* as a mood-altering drug and *Dolophine* as a pain reliever. The last prescription of *Talwin* was filled in November of 1983. In June of 1986, Koderick served Snyder with a summons and complaint alleging that she suffered personal injuries as a result of the pharmacy's negligent sale of *Talwin*.

RULING: The court granted summary judgment in favor of the pharmacy since the 2-year statute of limitations applied. The time period for filing the lawsuit began when the plaintiff was hospitalized for injuries caused by the drug.

REASONING: Minnesota law requires that all actions against physicians, dentists, and other health care professionals be filed within 2 years of a negligent act. It was clear that pharmacists are included as health care professionals under Minnesota law, but the plaintiff argued that she was not suing the individual pharmacist, but was suing the corporate employer. The plaintiff claimed that the Snyder Brothers Drug Corporation was negligent not only in the actual dispensing of the drug, but in the maintenance of conditions under which the pharmacists worked, the record keeping procedures of the business, and the lack of guidance and control. The plaintiff claimed that these acts of negligence were independent of any acts of the pharmacist, and therefore, the case was controlled by a 6-year general statute of limitations for injuries.

The complaint against Snyder alleged failure to use reasonable care in selling *Talwin* to the plaintiff. Any potential liability arising from such a claim would be based upon the theory of respondeat superior. Thus, the corporation stands in the shoes of its agent and a statute

Koderick v Snyder Bros. Drug, Inc.
413 N.W.2d 856 (Minn. App. 1987)
...continued

that bars a claim against the employee will also bar a claim against the employer. There were no facts introduced to support independent acts of negligence on behalf of the pharmacy corporation.

As a general rule, a cause of action accrues when the accident occurs. However, in a case such as this, there was no specific date of injury. The trial court found that the plaintiff knew, or should have known, of her injuries no later than the date when she was hospitalized. In fact, the plaintiff retained legal counsel and started a lawsuit against the physician at least 6 or 7 months prior to the expiration of the 2-year statute of limitation.

The plaintiff argued that she continued to receive drugs from the Snyder pharmacy even after the last *Talwin* prescription was dispensed. She argued that the statute of limitations should not begin until the termination of treatment. However, the court was unwilling to apply this rule to pharmacists since they do not treat patients, but dispense prescriptions. The pharmacist may have no idea as to what the patient was being treated for or when the course of treatment ends. The course of treatment with *Talwin* ended when the last prescription was dispensed in November of 1983. The lawsuit needed to be filed within 2 years from the discovery of the injury.

Sheils v Eckerd Corp.
560 So.2d 361 (Fla. App 2d 1990)

ISSUE: Whether a statute of limitations applying to products liability should apply to a case involving a pharmacist's professional negligence.

FACTS: The parents of Timothy Sheils challenged a summary judgment that held that their lawsuit was barred by a Florida statute that presented a 2-year time period for professional malpractice.

Timothy's mother presented a pharmacist at a Jack Eckerd Pharmacy in Lakeland, Florida, with a prescription for *Dimetapp*. The directions called for 1/2 teaspoonful of *Dimetapp* 4 times/day. When the pharmacist prepared the label, the directions were erroneously transcribed to call for 2 teaspoonsful 4 times/day. The dosage error was not discovered until the plaintiffs returned the container to the pharmacy for a refill. The plaintiffs filed a lawsuit seeking compensatory damages for the injury to Timothy based on strict product liability, negligence, and breach of warranty. They also requested punitive damages.

The plaintiffs argued that they brought their cause of action as a product liability case, which, under Florida law, has a 4-year statute of limitations.

RULING: Both the trial court and appellate court agreed with the defendants that the 2-year professional malpractice statute of limitations should apply. Thus, the plaintiffs' lawsuit was barred.

REASONING: The court agreed with the defendants that the 2-year professional malpractice statute of limitations should apply. It was not disputed that the pharmacist is a "professional" within the meaning of the professional malpractice statute of limitations. However, the plaintiffs forcibly argued that they chose to sue the corporate pharmacy, rather than its

Sheils v Eckerd Corp.
560 So.2d 361 (Fla. App 2d 1990)
...continued

pharmacist, and to structure their complaint around a cause of action based on strict liability arising out of the sale of a defectively labeled product, rather than an action for professional malpractice. The court was not persuaded. It was concluded that, but for the negligence of the pharmacist, there would have been no error in the prescribed dosage and the plaintiffs would have had no cause of action under any theory.

Florida has generally favored liberality in its construction of statutes of limitations: "Florida cases hold that when two statutes limit the time in which an action may be brought, both apply, and the dilatory litigant is caught by whichever runs first."

The court also noted that it has repeatedly followed the general rule that a more specific statute covering a particular subject controls over another statute covering the same subject in more general terms. It was concluded that the professional malpractice statute was more specific and that the general products liability limitation did not apply.

Griffin v Phar-Mor
790 F.Supp. 1115 (S.D.Ala. 1992)

ISSUE: Whether a pharmacy that makes a dispensing error is guilty of fraud and misrepresentation so as to extend the statute of limitations.

FACTS: Mrs. Griffin was taking *Micronase* for her blood sugar, but the pharmacist mistakenly dispensed *Maxzide*. However, the label on the prescription container indicated that it contained *Micronase*. Not realizing that the medicine she was taking was not prescribed medication, Mrs. Griffin unwittingly ingested 4 of the *Maxzide* tablets a day. She became lethargic and unable to perform her daily functions. She later wondered if she had been given the wrong medication and she called the pharmacy. The defendants checked their records and discovered that indeed she was given the wrong medication and they informed the plaintiff of that. Mrs. Griffin filed her lawsuit too late unless she could show fraud.

Alabama law states that misrepresentation of the fact made willfully to deceive, or recklessly without knowledge, or if made by mistake and acted on by the opposite party, constitutes legal fraud. Any suppression of a material fact that the party is under obligation to communicate constitutes fraud. The obligation to communicate may arise from the confidential relationship of the parties.

The plaintiffs alleged that the defendants negligently or recklessly misrepresented the contents of the medicine bottle they dispensed by indicating on the label of the bottle that it contained *Micronase* instead of *Maxzide*. There was a misrepresentation (the mislabeling) of a material fact (that the prescription was misfilled) that was relied upon by the plaintiff (she took the medicine thinking it was *Micronase*), and the plaintiff was injured by her reliance (her blood sugar rose dramatically and she became lethargic and unable to function).

RULING: After reviewing the pharmacist/patient relationship, the court concluded that the pharmacy's failure to disclose the dispensing error was a fraudulent concealment of information and that the statute of limitations should be extended to give the plaintiff her day in court.

Griffin v Phar-Mor
790 F.Supp. 1115 (S.D.Ala. 1992)
...continued

REASONING: The defendant argued and the magistrate seemed to accept the argument that the only fraud that will toll the statute of limitations is intentional fraud. The U.S. District Court could find no support for such a position. According to the plaintiff's allegations, the defendant pharmacy at least had constructive knowledge of the facts allegedly concealed. The mislabeling was the reason that Mrs. Griffin did not learn of the accrual of her cause of action. The defendant's failure to communicate to Mrs. Griffin the fact that she received the wrong medication was a suppression of material fact.

The court stated that the relationship between a pharmacist and a client is one in which the client places extreme trust in the pharmacist. The patient trusts the pharmacist to decipher the physician's handwriting and to dispense the prescription in accordance with the physician's orders. A patient is compelled to trust a pharmacist because the patient cannot legally have the prescription dispensed by a nonpharmacist.

The court found that the relationship of trust is reinforced by the esoteric nature of the pharmacist's profession. The court reviewed the pharmacist's training and the requirements that a pharmacist pass an examination administered by the Alabama Board of Pharmacy. It noted that pharmacists possess important specialized knowledge that is possessed by few nonpharmacists, and it is this specialized knowledge that puts patients in the position of having to put complete trust and confidence in a pharmacist's skill.

In the court's opinion, a person needs to know the type of medicine he or she is taking so that the person can know what activities to avoid while taking the medication. The court also noted the statutory duty of a pharmacist to convey the contents of prescription medicine on the label of the container. After reviewing the facts and circumstances, including the fact the special relationship between pharmacists and their patients, the court concluded that the defendant pharmacy was under a duty to disclose to the plaintiffs the fact that Mrs. Griffin received the wrong medicine (before she called and asked).

Fisher v Walgreens Louisiana
746 So.2d 161 (La.App. 1999)

The plaintiff had used *Topicort Cream* over several years to treat her dry skin on her hands caused by diabetes mellitus. Her physician gave her a new prescription on January 7, 1997, and she took it to her pharmacy to be filled on that day. When she opened the package while still in the pharmacy, she noticed that the tube was red and white. In the past, the tube was always blue and white. She asked a clerk in the pharmacy about the discrepancy and was told it was the same cream. The plaintiff testified that when she applied it, she could tell it was not the same because it was greasier. That evening she began feeling ill. Her hand was itching and she noticed her skin breaking out in red spots. The next morning her hands were swollen, red and looked infected. She went to her physician and discovered that she had been given something other than what was prescribed. (The court's opinion does not disclose what was actually dispensed.) She filed suit against the pharmacy on January 12, 1998. The pharmacy moved to dismiss the complaint because it was filed more than one year after the error was committed. The state has a 1-year statute of limitations for malpractice claims. In opposition to the motion, the plaintiff argued that she did not discover the error until January 11, 1997. January 11, 1998 was a Sunday so she could not file the complaint until Monday, January 12, 1998. The court held that the evidence showed that she

Fisher v Walgreens Louisiana
746 So.2d 161 (La.App. 1999)
...continued

knew something was wrong on January 9, 1997, the day the medication was dispensed. Actual knowledge of the error, not knowledge of which product was dispensed, sets the limitation period running according to this court. Therefore, dismissal of the complaint as being untimely filed was proper.

Kohl v American Home Products
No 99-3085, December 29, 1999, USDC Ark, 1999 U.S. Dist. LEXIS 20242

This case is summarized under the Malpractice, Fraudulent Joinder section. It was ultimately decided that the plaintiff's malpractice action had to be dismissed because the claim was filed after the 2-year limitations period established for malpractice cases had expired.

Robinson v Williamson
No A00A0250 (July 11, 2000), 2000 Ga App LEXIS 895

A complaint was filed in February 1997, against an individual pharmacist and Revco claiming that the pharmacist dispensed the wrong drug to a patient in August 1994 causing the patient to suffer a stroke. The trial court dismissed the complaint, finding that it had been filed after the running of the applicable 2-year statute of limitations for malpractice claims. On appeal, the plaintiffs contended that the limitations period did not apply to the patient, their mother, because she was not medically competent at the time of the dispensing error. The Court of Appeals disagreed, finding that nothing in the statute exempts a legal guardian from filing a timely complaint. Plaintiffs also claimed that the limitations period did not apply to their claims for product liability or breach of warranty. The Court held that where a pharmacist repackages a product pursuant to a prescription, the pharmacist is acting as a product seller and not a manufacturer and is therefore not subject to the products liability statutes. It also held that claims for breach of warranty against a pharmacy or pharmacist are essentially claims for medical malpractice and, therefore, subject to the medical malpractice statute of limitations.

The following is a list of court cases that are related to this topic.

Evans v Rite-Aid Corp., 452 S.E.2d 9 (S.C. App. 1994), affirmed, as modified 478 S.E. 2d 846 (1996).
Kollenberg v Ramirez, 339 N.W.2d 176 (Mich. App. 1983).
Kohl v American Home Products, Slip Op. No. 99-3085, December 29, 1999, U.S.D.C. Ark., 1999 U.S. Dist. LEXIS 20242.
Holmes v Van Lee, Slip Op No 35,021-CA (September 28, 2001), 2001 La. App. LEXIS 2040.
Kroger Co. v Estate of Hinders, 773 N.E.2d 303 (Ind. Ct. App. 2002).

Discovery

DeMoss Rexall Drugs v Dobson
540 N.E.2d 655 (Ind.App. 1989)

ISSUE: Whether certain recorded statements taken from representatives of a pharmacy and from a pharmacist by their insurance carrier are discoverable by the plaintiffs in a lawsuit against the pharmacy.

FACTS: The plaintiffs, Barbara and James Dobson, alleged in their complaint that Barbara went to DeMoss Rexall Drugs to have a prescription for *Synthroid* filled, but the pharmacist dispensed *Catapres* instead. Dobson began experiencing pain and numbness about the jaw and face, consulted a dentist and discovered that her thyroid level was low. An examination of the medication remaining in the bottle revealed the pharmacy's error.

The pharmacy reported the claim to its insurer, Farm Bureau insurance, on Friday, September 25, 1987. The following Monday a claims representative from Farm Bureau conferred with a supervisor by telephone advising that the company had a potentially difficult claim coming into the office. The representative recalled a claim involving Barbara Dobson 4 or 5 years earlier and knew that James Dobson had pursued a claim against his employer.

Two weeks later, the claims representative obtained the recorded statements, which are the subject of this litigation. Among other things, the claims representative noted in his report that the claim "will probably end up being a tuffy;" according to the pharmacist, Dobson should have noticed the difference in her tablets by shape, size, and color; that the claims representative had this same claimant about 4 or 5 years ago with big problems; and that the claimant's husband also had a huge claim against his employer.

RULING: The court ruled that the statements obtained by the defendant's insurance company were not work products prepared in anticipation of litigation and were not privileged communications and were discoverable by the plaintiffs.

REASONING: Indiana courts have repeatedly and consistently left to the legislature the determination of whether a particular interest is of sufficient importance to society to justify the protection afforded privileged communications. The court recognized that evidenciary privileges frustrate the fact-finding process by foreclosing the consideration of relevant and material information. All privileges are statutory in nature in Indiana and their creation is solely the prerogative of the legislature.

While there may be policy considerations favoring an inclusionary rule for communications between insured and insurer, the court left the determination of this public policy question to the legislature. Thus, statements made by representatives of the insured pharmacy to the insurer's claims representative concerning the misfiling of prescriptions were not protected as privileged communications and could be discovered by the plaintiff.

The court next turned its attention to the meaning of the phrase "prepared in anticipation of litigation," which, under trial court rules, provides protection for work products. The difficulty posed in the insurance industry context was discovering documents prepared by an insurer in anticipation of litigation versus those prepared in the routine course of the business. There is a point after the filing of a claim when an insurance investigation shifts from mere claim evaluation to anticipation of litigation.

The U.S. Supreme Court formulated the work products doctrine to insure the fullest possible knowledge of the issues and facts involved in the case without sacrificing the "wits" of attorneys preparing for litigation. The doctrine identifies materials created or collected by

DeMoss Rexall Drugs v Dobson
540 N.E.2d 655 (Ind.App. 1989)
...continued

an attorney on behalf of a client containing facts that are privileged from disclosure to opposing counsel by drawing a line at the point that the attorney's purpose becomes one of preparation for litigation. Facts in these materials become discoverable only upon showing need
and unavailability, but facts within the attorney's possession obtained under circumstances
other than in anticipation of litigation are freely discoverable. An attorney's mental
impressions, conclusions, opinions, or legal theories remain protected.

The pharmacy defendant argued that all documents prepared by insurers should be immune
from discovery. The court concluded that a document generated or obtained by an insurer
is entitled to protection from discovery if the document can fairly be said to have been prepared or obtained because of the prospect of litigation and not because it was a part of the
company's regular operating procedure.

Farm Bureau obtained statements from the pharmacist less than two weeks after having been
informed of the claim. There had only been internal discussions about the claim and
research about the effects of the medication allegedly dispensed. There was no indication
that Farm Bureau had decided to refuse to pay the claim. The logical inference from the evidence was that the statements were taken for purposes of exploring the validity of the claim
and to enable the insurance company to make an initial determination of its position with
respect to the claim. The pharmacy alleged that the court ignored Farm Bureau's contention that, given Dobsons' claims history, the matter would likely end up in litigation. The
pharmacy also expressed concern that the mix-up in medication may have caused the plaintiff to develop multiple sclerosis, which also surely would result in litigation.

The court did not dispute the pharmacy's assertion that insurance people can sometimes recognize a claim that will result in litigation merely by being advised of the general claim and
the parties involved. The work product doctrine demands more than just a recognition
that a claim will eventually lead to litigation. There is a requirement of evidence that the
insurer is actively working on the premise that the claim will lead to litigation and has
obtained the statements for that purpose. Such was not the case herein. The trial court's ruling in favor of discovery was affirmed.

Stolfa v Ely
875 S.W.2d 579 (Mo.App. 1994)

ISSUE: Whether a pharmacy could be compelled to produce records of previous lawsuits.

FACTS: The plaintiffs in this action allege that they are parents of twin daughters who died
at birth in 1990. They claim that the negligence of K-Mart and its pharmacist, in mistakenly dispensing a medication when the mother was 25 weeks pregnant, caused the premature birth and death of the two infants.

The plaintiffs argued that the pharmacist was negligent in furnishing *Ritalin* instead of *Rito-
drine*, the actual prescribed medication. The plaintiffs also argued that K-Mart was negligent in failing to establish and maintain proper protocol and procedures to ensure that
appropriate drugs were dispensed to consumers. Therefore, they sought to discover from
K-Mart information about other, earlier lawsuits involving allegations of professional liability pertaining to prescription errors in the pharmacy. The plaintiffs also requested information about the training of K-Mart's pharmacy staff.

Stolfa v Ely
875 S.W.2d 579 (Mo.App. 1994)
...continued

RULING: The court ordered the pharmacy corporation to produce the records even if inconvenient to the pharmacy.

REASONING: K-Mart offered three arguments for its position that it ought not be required to disclose the information sought by the plaintiffs. The defendants stated that the discovery sought by the plaintiffs was not relevant and was not reasonably calculated to lead to the discovery of admissible evidence. Furthermore, the defendant claimed that the discovery sought by the plaintiffs invaded the attorney/client and work product privilege. Lastly, it was alleged that an order compelling K-Mart to respond to the discovery request would impose an extraordinary and unreasonable burden on the pharmacy.

The plaintiffs in this case made their claims, not only for the negligence of K-Mart's pharmacist, for which K-Mart would be vicariously liable under the respondeat superior doctrine, but also alleged K-Mart's corporate negligence in its protocols and procedures, which according to the plaintiff's allegations, were inadequate to prevent the kind of error that occurred here. To prove that K-Mart's procedures were inadequate, the court ruled that it would be relevant that other claims that had been made against K-Mart be produced as part of the discovery process.

In this case, the plaintiffs limited their request to a period of 3 years preceding the incident in question. K-Mart has a computer database that identified 120 claims involving pharmacy professional liability actions. However, the files are unindexed and are stored in boxes in a warehouse. K-Mart claimed that it would be a prodigious task to locate and produce the 120 files. The court was not particularly sympathetic. The court ruled that it was K-Mart's decision to store the files without a convenient system of retrieval and that the absence of indexing was not the plaintiff's problem. The need for discovery by the plaintiffs outweighed the inconvenience to K-Mart in supplying it.

Finally, the court recognized that certain items sought to be discovered might be protected by the attorney-client privilege, but that fact did not defeat the discovery request. Any such privileged materials could be protected by the court's order upon K-Mart's motion.

Amikar v Drugs for Less
No 97-CA-01493-SCT (August 17, 2000), SCt Miss, 2000 Miss LEXIS 192

The plaintiff claims that between October 1992 and April 1993 a pharmacist misfilled his prescriptions, dispensing antidepressants instead of the prescribed antihypertensive and heart medications. As a result, the plaintiff has suffered from increased blood pressure, causing a stroke and leaving him permanently disabled. After a trial, a jury returned verdicts against the plaintiff in favor of both the pharmacy and the pharmacist. The plaintiff filed motions for JNOV, a new trial and discovery sanctions. Plaintiff claims that the defendants intentionally caused him to believe that its insurance limits were only $1 million, when in reality the amount was over $30 million. The discrepancy was found during an in-camera review of files by the trial judge. Plaintiff also claims prejudice because the defendants did not produce evidence of prior claims for negligent misfilling of prescriptions until the fourth day of trial despite repeated orders from the judge to make the documents available during discovery. The trial judge granted the motion for a new trial based on the clear and continuous discovery abuses by the defendants and their counsel. They had documents known to be

Amikar v Drugs for Less
No 97-CA-01493-SCT (August 17, 2000), SCt Miss, 2000 Miss LEXIS 192
...continued

relevant, but refused to produce them and displayed a cavalier attitude toward the court when ordered on several occasions to produce the documents by stating that "Drugs for Less is in the business of producing sales and not producing discovery." The motion for JNOV was granted against the pharmacy only for its clear role in misleading the plaintiff and the court on the amount of insurance coverage. As a result, a judgment on liability was entered against the pharmacy and a new trial ordered on the issue of damages only. Discovery sanctions of over $50,000 were also ordered paid to the plaintiff. Before the new trial could be held, the trial judge retired and a new judge was assigned. On defendant's motions for reconsideration, the judge ordered a new trial against the pharmacy, but did not enter an order of liability against the pharmacy. This judge also affirmed the jury verdict in favor of the pharmacist. The plaintiff appealed, claiming that the original trial judge's orders should control. The Mississippi Supreme Court agreed and the original post-trial orders were reinstated.

Ex Parte Rite-Aid of Alabama In Re: Deal v Rite-Aid of Alabama
No 1981998 (April 7, 2000), 2000 Ala LEXIS 136

A patient died after a Rite-Aid pharmacy allegedly dispensed 100 mg tablets of *Lopressor* instead of the 50 mg dosage prescribed. Plaintiffs sued, claiming the pharmacy was negligent in dispensing the wrong dose and in failing to properly train and supervise the pharmacist who made the error. During discovery, plaintiffs requested Rite-Aid to furnish incident reports about other patients who received the wrong medication. Rite-Aid objected on the grounds that it is a "health care provider" exempted from furnishing discovery as to any other acts or omissions under Alabama law. § 6-5-542(1) Ala. Code 1975. The trial court ruled that Rite-Aid is not a "health care provider" under § 6-5-481(8) and ordered the incident reports be produced. Rite-Aid appealed. The Supreme Court of Alabama noted that it had just decided, in Cackowski (See Punitive Damages Section, supra) that a pharmacist is a health care provider. Based on that decision, this Court held that Rite-Aid is also a health care provider and therefore exempt from having to produce the incident reports of other acts and omissions as requested. One judge dissented, noting that the discovery rule in question only exempts a defendant from producing evidence of acts or omissions not specifically pled in the complaint. In the original complaint, plaintiffs sued Rite-Aid for negligently filling the prescription. An amended complaint added a claim for negligent training and supervision of the pharmacist who committed the error. The amended complaint also stated the plaintiffs have the information and belief that Rite-Aid has a history of misfilling prescriptions resulting in overdosing of numerous patients. This judge would rule that the incident reports sought by plaintiffs are not for "pattern and practice" evidence, but specifically tailored to show willfulness and wantonness in causing the death of the grandmother. In other words, the evidence is sought to show the "systematic failure" of the pharmacy to provide procedures to minimize the risk of harmful acts leading to the death of patients and by understaffing and hiring under-qualified, under-trained and unsupervised persons to operate the pharmacies.

Mableton Parkway CVS, Inc. v Salter
561 S.E.2d 478 (Ga. Ct. App. 2002)

The patient brought a lawsuit against a pharmacy business ("CVS"), seeking damages that allegedly resulted from the misfilling of a prescription. The trial court held that where a court has ordered a defendant corporation to designate a witness to respond to inquiries in certain areas known to the corporation, the designated witness' lack of knowledge in those areas justifies a finding of contempt against the corporation itself. According to the facts, the designated representative for the pharmacy could not give the most elementary information regarding: 1) CVS's involvement in other suits, including whether CVS had filed an answer; 2) what CVS's position was; 3) what CVS pharmacists were involved; 4) what the current status of the case was; 5) whether an incident report had been filed; or 6) who at CVS could answer such questions. In addition, the designated representative could not identify the nature of the allegations in 6 of the 25 lawsuits and could not even confirm whether the list of 25 suits was complete. Based upon the facts enumerated, the appellate court found that CVS clearly did not obey the trial court's discovery order. In holding that the trial court's discretion is particularly broad when dealing with a party's failure to obey a discovery order, the appellate court determined that the evidence presented in the case supported an order directing that CVS pay the patient's attorney fees for filing the contempt motion. The appellate court did, however, find that the trial court abused its discretion by compelling CVS to disclose the amounts it had paid in settling similar tort cases in Georgia. The plaintiff never sought this information in the lower court, and because he was unable to articulate how the information would be relevant to the case on appeal, such information was found to be outside the scope of relevance in the discovery of the case. Accordingly, the ordering of the disclosure of settlement amounts was reversed and the remainder of the order was affirmed.

The following is a list of court cases that are related to this topic.

Nefaris v DeStefano, Slip Op. 98-10295 (Oct. 18, 1999), SCt., NY App, 1999 NY App. Div LEXIS 10434.

Expert Witness Testimony

Young v Key Pharmaceuticals
770 P.2d 182 (Wash. 1989)

ISSUE: Whether a pharmacist is competent to testify as an expert regarding the standard of care that a physician must meet when prescribing medications.

FACTS: The plaintiff, a child who was being treated for an acute asthma condition, was prescribed theophylline, which has an optimal therapeutic range between 10 and 20 mcg/mL. Blood levels under 10 mcg/mL are not sufficient to treat asthma, while levels over 20 mcg/mL are toxic. The child was first prescribed *Elixophyllin*, but the medication required the child's mother to get up in the middle of the night to administer 1 of the doses.

The medication was changed to *Theo-Dur*, which required fewer doses per day to achieve the proper blood level. The child received 200 mg of *Theo-Dur* twice daily, but this was later changed by an allergy clinic to 300 mg twice daily. The child began to have seizures and was taken to the hospital for emergency treatment, where it was discovered that his theophylline level was 68 mcg/mL, which resulted in permanent brain damage and rendered him mentally incompetent.

Young v Key Pharmaceuticals
770 P.2d 182 (Wash. 1989)
...continued

The physician's affidavit presumed that the daily dose of 400 mg was continued throughout the child's therapy. It was claimed that this was consistent with reasonably prudent allergy and immunology practices. However, the plaintiff submitted the affidavit of a pharmacist who pointed out that the allergy clinic increased the therapy to 600 mg/day just prior to the child's seizure. The pharmacist stated that according to the professional literature, the maximum dosage for a 3-year-old child is 400 mg/day.

RULING: The court concluded that a pharmacist is not competent to testify on the physician's standard of care for treatment using medications.

REASONING: The court noted that the pharmacist who provided the expert testimony had reviewed the child's medical records. The Washington courts have rejected the rule that non-physicians are per se disqualified from testifying as experts in medical malpractice actions. However, the courts in the state of Washington have never adopted a rule that would allow a non-physician to testify as an expert regarding the proper standard of care for a physician practicing a medical specialty. "Such a role would severely degrade the administration of justice in medical malpractice actions."

While non-expert testimony is sometimes admissible for matters such as observation of health, disease, or injury, the court would not permit testimony regarding proper dosages of medications as an area in which non-physicians were competent to testify. "Although a pharmacist may be more familiar with the names of medication, the literature, and perhaps the usual practice of physicians prescribing certain medications than other non-physicians, a pharmacist is not competent to testify on the physician's standard of care or treatment using medication."

The dissenting judges argued that the practice of the pharmacy in the state of Washington included by statute "the monitoring of drug therapy and the advising of therapeutic values, hazards, and uses of drugs." The dissent concluded that the pharmacist's affidavit raised a question as to whether the health care defendant's monitoring of the child's theophylline levels breached the standard of care.

Docken v Ciba-Geigy
790 P.2d 45 (Or. App. 1990)

ISSUE: Whether expert testimony was required to establish the standard of care of a pharmacist to independently warn of the hazards of a drug.

FACTS: The plaintiff in this case is the personal representative of the estate of her deceased son, Terry. In November of 1979, a Kaiser Foundation Health Plan pharmacy dispensed a prescription for imipramine for the plaintiff's older son, Tim, according to the physician's instructions. The defendant dispensed the brand name *Tofranil*, manufactured by the defendant Ciba-Geigy. In August of 1983, Terry swallowed several tablets of his brother's prescription and died. The plaintiff filed this wrongful death action.

In the first appeal of this case, the court ruled that a drug manufacturer, pharmacy, or prescribing physician could be held liable for harm to anyone other than the person for whom the drug was prescribed if injury results from the other person's taking the drug (*Docken v*

Docken v Ciba-Geigy
790 P.2d 45 (Or. App. 1990)
...continued

Ciba Geigy, 739 P. 2d 591 [1987]). The court held that there is liability if the harm suffered from the other person's taking the drug is a foreseeable risk. The court concluded that it could not say, as a matter of law, that the harm suffered by Terry was not foreseeable. It was further determined that the complaint by the plaintiff alleged facts from which the jury could find the defendants negligent.

RULING: The court ruled that the plaintiff failed to provide expert testimony as to the standard of care for a pharmacist to warn of the dangers associated with the use of prescription drugs. The pharmacy's motion for a directed verdict was granted.

REASONING: The Kaiser HMO argued that whether or not the plaintiff was correct that the trial court gave erroneous instructions, the appellate court should confirm the lower court decision because the plaintiff provided no evidence of one of the elements of her cause of action. Kaiser contended the plaintiff did not establish a breach of the standard of care on the part of the HMO. Thus, the case should not have gone to the jury.

The plaintiff countered by claiming that the jury could determine without the aid of experts that a prescription drug is dangerous and requires a pharmacist to independently warn of its hazards, regardless of the instructions of the prescribing physician or any statutory requirements to warn. There was no warning by the defendant's pharmacist. With this evidence, the plaintiff argued that the jury could find that a duty to warn existed and was breached.

The defendant argued that expert testimony is required to prove the community standard of care for a pharmacist and that the plaintiff provided no evidence that the community standard was not met. Because no expert testified that the standard of care in the professional community required a pharmacist to warn of the hazards of this prescription drug, the defendant contended that no breach of due care could be found even if the warning were lacking.

No Oregon appellate court has decided the standard of care for a pharmacist in a negligence action. Yet other Oregon law concludes that in most cases of negligence against professional persons, expert testimony is required to establish what the reasonable practice is in the community. Without such expert testimony, a plaintiff cannot prove negligence. The reason for this rule is that what is reasonable conduct for a professional person is ordinarily not within the knowledge of the usual jury. Nonetheless, the court noted that in some situations the breach of a standard of care is within the knowledge and experience of laypersons and expert testimony would not be required. One such example would be surgeons operating without sterilization of their instruments.

The court further noted that most jurisdictions have not found any common law duty of pharmacists to independently warn of the hazard of drugs prescribed by physicians, preferring to leave decisions about warning requirements to legislatures and the prescribing physicians. It noted that most courts expressed concern that pharmacists not be expected to second-guess physicians.

Considering the complex relationship between a physician, a patient, and a pharmacist, the court concluded that an expert must testify as to the standard of care in the community for warning of the dangers of a prescription drug before a jury could determine that such a standard was breached. The only expert evidence consisted of testimony that it was standard practice for the pharmacy to use a label to warn that an overdose of imipramine was potentially fatal. There was conflicting evidence about whether that warning was given in this case.

Docken v Ciba-Geigy
790 P.2d 45 (Or. App. 1990)
...continued

The testimony describing the defendant pharmacy's usual practice only referred to the practice of one facility in a large city, Portland. The defendant's practice may have reflected care in excess of the standard of care in the community and, if so, the failure to follow that practice would not be evidence of breach of due care.

Note: The court refused to comment on the standard of care in other circumstances, such as when a pharmacist sells a nonprescription substance or when a pharmacist has personal knowledge of the customer's medical condition.

Nichols v Kaiser Foundation Health Plan of the Mid-Atlantic States
514 S.E.2d 608 (Va. 1999)

ISSUE: In a malpractice case against a pharmacy, is the injured patient required to produce expert witness testimony to support the claim that injuries incurred were caused by a drug that was admittedly dispensed to the patient in error?

FACTS: The patient suffered from severe respiratory distress for several years. Her physician prescribed *Medrol* to treat the condition in August 1993. She had the prescription filled at the defendant pharmacy. She continued to use the drug under the physician's care and obtain refills from the pharmacy until April 1995. At that point in time, the pharmacy negligently dispensed dexamethasone, a steroid that is 5 times more potent than *Medrol* when used at comparable doses. The next day, the patient was seen by her physician and was diagnosed as suffering from Cushing's syndrome. The defendant health care organization that owns the pharmacy also employs the physician. Over the next 21 days, the patient consumed 183 tablets of dexamethasone, averaging 9 tablets/day. During this time she experienced extremely high blood glucose levels and was diagnosed with sugar diabetes. As soon as the medication error was detected and corrected, the diabetes symptoms began to subside. Her physician recorded in the patient's chart that she suffered from dexamethasone-induced hypergylcemia.

LAWSUIT: The patient sued the defendant for malpractice. The pharmacy admitted that it dispensed the wrong drug. At trial, the patient's personal physician testified as to the contents of the medical chart. He did not offer expert witness testimony for the plaintiff or render an opinion, other than those contained in the chart, as to the cause of the patient's injuries as a result of the drug error. The patient and her son testified about the extent of injuries she suffered after taking the wrong medication. She did not produce any evidence showing that the pharmacy breached the duty of care owed to a patient when it dispenses the wrong drug, nor did she offer any further evidence showing that the consumption of the wrong drug caused her damages. The defendant asked the court to dismiss the case because the patient did not satisfy her responsibilities to show that any duty had been breached or that the breach of duty was the proximate cause of the injuries claimed. The trial court judge ruled that no expert testimony is needed to establish that a pharmacy breaches its duty when it dispenses the wrong drug because an average juror could make that conclusion without the aid of an expert. The jury returned a verdict of $75,000 in favor of the patient. The trial court judge set aside the verdict and ruled in favor of the defendant. He reasoned that the patient had failed to establish a causal link between her injuries and use of the wrong drug.

Nichols v Kaiser Foundation Health Plan of the Mid-Atlantic States
514 S.E.2d 608 (Va. 1999)
...continued

HOLDING: The Virginia Supreme Court reversed the trial court judgment and reinstated the jury's verdict.

REASONING: The Supreme Court believed that the jury could conclude that a causal link was established between the patient's use of dexamethasone and the injuries she complained about from the testimony of the personal physician and the medical records that were presented. Further, the testimony of the patient and her son established the nature of the injuries for which she sought compensation. This combination of medical opinion and lay testimony was sufficient to permit the jury to decide the case. No additional formal expert witness testimony was required.

A. Clodgo v Kroger Pharmacy
Slip Op. No. 98AP-569, Mar. 18, 1999, 1999 Ohio App. LEXIS 1246

Clodgo saw a physician for treatment of an infection. The physician wrote two prescriptions to treat her infection, nitrofurantoin and *Pyridium*. Clodgo was to take 1 capsule of nitrofurantoin 4 times/day for a period of 10 days. She was to take 1 capsule of *Pyridium* 4 times/day for a period of 5 days. A Kroger pharmacist filled the prescriptions for Clodgo. Clodgo took 1 capsule of each drug around noon, and over the next 3 or 4 hours she took several more nitrofurantoin capsules, speculating that she took 4 nitrofurantoin capsules between the time she received them and 4:00 that afternoon. She also took 1 more *Pyridium* capsule around 4:00 that afternoon. After taking the drugs, Clodgo began to experience nausea, lightheadedness, dizziness, and vomiting. Around 4:00 that afternoon, she called Kroger because she was concerned about the amount of pills she was taking. Clodgo talked to the Kroger pharmacist, who told her that the instructions on the nitrofurantoin bottle were incorrect. Instead of the dosages the physician had prescribed, the instructions on the bottle said "take 1 capsule by mouth for 4 days until finished." Clodgo's symptoms nonetheless remained for another day or two, but then subsided as did the infection. As a result of the symptoms, she missed two days of work. Clodgo filed a complaint against Kroger and its pharmacist, alleging claims of negligence and negligent supervision. The trial court granted summary judgment for Kroger and the pharmacist, finding no negligence in dispensing *Pyridium*, as the instructions on that bottle matched that prescription. The trial court also found that Clodgo offered no expert medical testimony to refute her physician's testimony that the symptoms Clodgo suffered were side effects that would normally occur with nitrofurantoin. Clodgo appealed on the grounds that the trial court alleged error in refusing to consider the affidavit of Clodgo's pharmacist expert, Jolliffe. The court of appeals held that excluding Jolliffe's report was not an error because the report did not mention any knowledge, skill, experience, training, or education regarding the subject matter to prove Jolliffe's expertise, nor did the report state that Jolliffe was sworn when she signed the report. Without the report, Clodgo failed to present any expert medical testimony to establish a disputed material fact regarding the proximate cause of her alleged injuries. Therefore, the court of appeals affirmed the judgment of the trial court.

In Re: Diet Drugs Products Liability Litigation
MDL Docket 1203 (June 28, 2000), USDC Pa, 2000 US Dist LEXIS 9661 (Order No 1351)

This is a products liability class action lawsuit for damages against the manufacturers of the weight loss drugs phentermine, fenfluramine and dexfenfluramine (often called the fen/phen diet). In this opinion, the trial court considered the motions of two defendants to exclude the expert witness testimony of two individuals, Dr. Maher, a pharmacologist and Dr. Wellman, a behavioral psychologist. The essence of their opinion is that fenfluramine and phentermine act synergistically to increase cardiovascular toxicity than when using fenfluramine alone. After analyzing the proffered testimony and these individual's qualifications (neither of whom are medical physicians), the Court ruled that the testimony is not based on scientific knowledge, but more on personal opinion. Their opinions are not shared by the scientific community and are not based on epidemiological studies.

In Re: Diet Drugs Products Liability Litigation
MDL Docket 1203 (June 20, 2000), USDC Pa, 2000 US Dist LEXIS 9037 (Order No 1332)

This is the same litigation described in the case above. In this opinion, the court considers the motions of American Home Products (AHP) to exclude plaintiff's expert witnesses, Dr. Avorn and Dr. Rubin, both medical doctors and pharmacoepidemiologists and pharmacoeconomists, on the issues of health risks and benefits associated with fenfluramine (*Pondimin*) and dexfenfluramine (*Redux*). After examining the expert's qualifications and the proffered testimony, the Court will allow some opinions, but limit others. Specifically, the witnesses are barred from testifying on the corporate intent of AHP in marketing its drugs. However, the Court will allow the physicians to testify about the labeling on the drugs and as to the validity of medical and scientific facts stated on that labeling.

Burkes v Fred's Stores of Tennessee
768 So. 2d 325 (October 3, 2000), 2000 Miss. App. LEXIS 498

In August 1996, suffering from leg cramps, the plaintiff consulted her physician. He prescribed quinine sulfate. The plaintiff took her prescription to the defendant-pharmacy located in Lexington, Mississippi. According to the complaint, the pharmacist mistakenly filled the prescription with quinidine. The pharmacy denies it dispensed the wrong drug even though the label states that the contents of the pharmacy vial are quinidine. The pharmacy only admitted that the pharmacist "mistakenly mislabeled the medicine dispensed to the plaintiff as quinidine sulfate instead of quinine sulfate." The pharmacist refused to admit that he dispensed quinidine instead of quinine. In fact, he never indicated what he dispensed, limiting the admission only to mislabeling the vial. In any event, the plaintiff did not notice the difference in the drug names. Not knowing that she had the wrong drug, the plaintiff took her medication as directed on the label for two weeks. She began suffering severe stomach cramps and was admitted to a hospital in Jackson with gastritis. During her stay, the error was discovered. Her blood levels showed that she had consumed toxic amounts of quinidine. She was discharged a few days later with a diagnosis on her chart of "adverse drug reaction to quinidine." She filed a lawsuit in the Mississippi state court on December 4, 1996. Discovery commenced and on March 24, 1997, the plaintiff answered interrogatories from the defendants that identified two pharmacists who would serve as her expert witnesses. The answer did not indicate the basis of the experts' opinions or what their ultimate opinions would be. On April 15, 1997, the defendants "removed" the lawsuit from the state court system to the federal district court sitting in Mississippi. Upon the filing of the motion to

Burkes v Fred's Stores of Tennessee
768 So. 2d 325 (October 3, 2000), 2000 Miss. App. LEXIS 498
...continued

remove the case, discovery ceased. The federal district court determined on December 12, 1997, that jurisdiction was proper in the state court, and remanded it back to the court where the complaint was originally filed. On January 8, 1998, the defendants filed a Motion for Summary Judgment or, in the alternative, to compel more discovery. On April 21, 1998, the state court judge entered an order extending discovery until August 15, 1998. An order was also entered to compel the plaintiff to name expert witnesses and describe their expected testimony by June 22, 1998. The plaintiff did not respond to that order and the case was dismissed on August 24, 1998. In a final order entered May 3, 1999, the trial court judge refused to reinstate the case because the plaintiff "failed to properly designate expert witnesses." The plaintiff appealed.

The defendants argued that dismissal was proper because the plaintiff could not prevail unless she was able to show by expert testimony that the pharmacist was negligent in filling her prescription and that the injuries suffered by Burkes were proximately caused by his negligence. The defendants reasoned that since discovery had been concluded without the plaintiff's answer to their interrogatory stating the opinion that her experts would give, she could not meet her burden at trial. The plaintiff countered that she did in fact timely name expert witnesses, but that she could not describe the bases for their opinions because the pharmacist had repeatedly refused to appear for scheduled depositions. The Court of Appeals noted that when summary judgment was entered, the only real issue was whether the pharmacist had in fact misfilled the plaintiff's prescription. The medical records showed without contradiction that upon admission to the hospital she had an abnormally high serum quinidine level and that she suffered acute gastritis that was quinidine-induced. The pharmacist also admitted that the medicine prescribed was quinine sulfate but was mislabeled as quinidine sulfate. Whether it was mislabeled or was in fact quinidine sulfate was a genuine issue of material fact. Under these circumstances, according to this Court, the plaintiff need not present expert testimony to prove that misfilling a prescription is negligence. Further, her medical records showed that her problems were caused by ingestion of quinidine. The Court found that the trial court judge abused his discretion and ordered the case be reinstated.

Ruiz v Walgreen
Slip Op No 14-00-01255-CV (June 6, 2002), 79 S.W.3d 235, 2002 Tex. App. LEXIS 4144

The patient presented a prescription for "*Magsal*" to a Walgreen pharmacist to be filled. However, he misfilled the prescription with "*Nizoral*." After examining the medication at the pharmacy, the patient told the pharmacist she thought he had made a mistake – that the prescription had been improperly filled. The pharmacist assured her that he had not made a mistake, explaining that the drug looked different because it was a generic substitute. Later that evening, when Manuela opened the medication at home, she again became concerned and telephoned the pharmacist. He encouraged the patient to take the medication, explaining again that it only appeared to be the wrong medication because it was a generic substitute. The patient did as told and took the medication and subsequently refilled the prescription. During the time Manuela was taking the medication, she felt weak and nauseous. She also vomited and experienced dry heaves. Ultimately, due to these symptoms, Manuela was hospitalized for 3 days. The patient's family physician and the consulting physician determined that her condition was caused by an overdose of the incorrectly filled prescription, *Nizoral*. The pharmacist later admitted to Manuela that he had misfilled the prescription. The patient and her family gave notice of their claims to Walgreen "pursuant

Ruiz v Walgreen
Slip Op No 14-00-01255-CV (June 6, 2002), 79 S.W.3d 235, 2002 Tex. App. LEXIS 4144
...continued

to the provisions of Art. 4590i § 4.01(d) of the Medical Liability and Insurance Improvement Act." The plaintiffs then filed suit against Walgreen. Their second amended petition
alleges the following in the alternative that: (1) "negligent acts and omissions," ie, the
pharmacist failed to read the prescription correctly and failed to verify the correct prescription; (2) "breach of express and implied warranties"; and (3) "breach of contract." The petition also alleged that these "negligent acts and omissions" caused the patient to become
seriously ill and suffer "extensive, debilitating and life-threatening injuries which severely
diminished her enjoyment of life and her life expectancy." Finally, the petition alleged that
"prior to the incident...[the patient] was not suffering from any of the symptoms that resulted
from the incorrect filling of the prescription that was also an overdose." However, the
plaintiffs did not file an expert report as required by the Act, and Walgreen filed a motion
to dismiss for the failure to do so. After an initial dismissal and reinstatement, the plaintiffs again failed to file an expert report, and, after a second motion to dismiss, the trial court
dismissed the case with prejudice. The plaintiffs appealed. On appeal, the plaintiffs asserted
two reasons why an expert report was not required: (1) The MLIIA is not intended to govern any other area of the Texas legal system or tort law, and accordingly their causes of action
for breach of warranty and deceptive trade practices are governed by the common law or
the Deceptive Trade Practices Act ("DTPA"), which do not require an expert report; and (2)
if the MLIIA does apply to their case, the case is excepted from the expert report requirement because *res ipsa loquitur* (the thing speaks for itself) applies to the pharmacist's negligence and no expert is needed. The Court of Appeal determined that the complaint does
not allege what implied warranties were made, much less what express warranties were made.
In fact, other than the mention of the word "warranty" in the pleading in which they set
out their causes of action, "warranty" appears nowhere in the petition, nor is there any mention of a promise or guarantee. Likewise, the DTPA is never mentioned and there are no
allegations that the pharmacist's actions violated particular sections of the DTPA, nor does
the petition contain any language from the DTPA (such as alleging that Walgreen represented that the goods or services had characteristics, uses, or benefits that they did not have).
The Court could not find any DTPA allegations and held the complaint is nothing more
than a straightforward medical malpractice claim. In short, this case involves no separate
fraudulent act and no separate tort. This is a medical malpractice case in its purest form.
It derives from the pharmacist's alleged negligent actions that were inextricably related to his
professional duty of dispensing medication. The plaintiffs also argue that, even if the Act
applies, an expert report is unnecessary because this is a matter "plainly within the common knowledge of laymen." They point out that they invoked the doctrine of *res ipsa loquitur* and that the doctrine is incorporated into the Act in article 4590i, section 7.01. That
section limits application of the doctrine to "those cases to which it has been applied by
the appellate courts of this state as of the effective date of this subchapter." Further, the doctrine applies only when the nature of the alleged malpractice and injuries are plainly within
the common knowledge of laymen, requiring no expert testimony. According to this Court,
the plaintiffs did not point to any pre-1977 cases applying the doctrine to substitution of a
prescribed medication, and do not explain how laymen would know that substitution in
this case was improper. Even assuming that an expert is not necessary to testify that it is unacceptable for a pharmacist to give a patient a different medication than the one prescribed,
they would still be required to prove by expert testimony that they were injured, and that
the pharmacist's negligence proximately caused their injuries. In addition, because they are
also claiming that the pharmacist gave the patient too great a dosage of *Nizoral*, they would
need an expert to testify that the amount was an overdose and that the overdose caused
Manuela's injuries. Therefore, the judgment of the trial court was affirmed.

The following is a list of court cases that are related to this topic.

Bloching v Albertson's, Slip No. 22858 (March 13, 1997), 1997 id. LEXIS 35 (Idaho Sup. Ct.).
Thomsen v Rexall Drug & Chemical Co., 45 Cal. Rptr. 642 (1965).
Agbogun v State of Texas, 756 S.W.2nd 1 (Tex. Ct. App. 1988).
Guillory v Andrus, Nos. 96-85, 96-86, and 679 So: 2d 1004 (La. App., 1996).
Jeans v Caraway, 649 S.2d 1141 (La. Ct. App. 1995).
Zuchowicz v U.S., Slip Op. No. 97-6057; 90-6099, March 20, 1998, 2nd Cir., 1998 U.S. App.
    LEXIS 5366.
New York v Czarnowski, 702 N.Y.S. 2d 398 (App.Div. 2000).
Ellingsen v Walgreen, 78 F.Supp.2d 965 (D.Minn. 1999).
Higgins v Thrifty Payless, Slip Op No B141142 (January 16, 2002), 2002 Cal. App. LEXIS 529.

Injunctions

National Association of Chain Drug Stores v Thompson
Slip Op No 01-1554, September 6, 2001

This opinion is an order granting an injunction against the Bush administration's plan to introduce a discount "Medicare Prescription Card" program. The program has been originally introduced as Social Security regulations published in the Federal Register on July 18, 2001. Several national pharmacy groups immediately joined together in litigation to stop the program that would cause the pharmacy community to shoulder the burden of absorbing the discounts it mandated. The Court determined that the government violated the Administrative Procedures Act and acted without any legal authority to adopt the program in the first place. The injunction was premised on the fact that the plaintiff pharmacies showed a substantial likelihood that they would succeed on the merits of their claim and that the pharmacies would suffer irreparable damage if the injunction were not granted.

Insurance Coverage

Swisher-Sherman v Provident Life and Accident Insurance
No. 93-3959, Unpublished 1994 U.S. App. LEXIS 28768 (6th Cir. Oct. 13, 1994).
(Table Rpt: 37F3d 1500)

FACTS: A pharmacy dispensed *Tenormin* instead of prescribed *Lanoxin* and the patient died. The wrongful death case against the pharmacy concluded in favor of the patient's spouse. She then sought accidental death benefits under the decedent's insurance policy. Coverage was denied based on a contract clause excluding loss directly or indirectly from medical or surgical treatment of a disease. The bad faith lawsuit claimed that the pharmacist's negligence in dispensing the wrong drug was a superseding act to the treatment of any medical condition and, therefore, a covered "accident."

HOLDING: The trial court dismissed the claim. The Appellate Court affirmed, stating that every act of malpractice is an "accident," as bad outcomes are not intended results of treatment. Further, all medical mishaps occur during treatment and the pharmacist is an integral part of medical treatment. The Court concluded that the contract clause at issue clearly excludes coverage for all medical mishaps, accidental or not.

The following is a list of court cases that are related to this topic.

Allstate Insurance Company v Chicago Insurance Company, 676 S.2d 271 (Miss. 1996).
Brown v Southern Baptist Hospital, Slip Op. Nos. 96-CA-1990 and 96-CA-1991, La. App. 4th Cir., March 11, 1998, 1998 La. App. LEXIS 556.
Harrow v Prudential Insurance Company of America, 76 F.Supp.2d 558 (D.N.J. 1999).

Successor Liability

Lemire v Garrard Drugs
291 N.W.2d 103 (Mich. 1980)

ISSUE: Whether a pharmacy owner should be liable for injuries due to DES dispensed by the prior owner of the pharmacy when the medication was dispensed as requested.

FACTS: The plaintiff brought suit against the pharmacy owner, claiming that liability for the plaintiff's cervical cancer stemmed from the fact that the pharmacy owner's predecessor pharmacy had sold [dispensed] diethylstilbestrol (DES) to the Plaintiff's mother for use during pregnancy.

The reported facts are that the plaintiff developed cervical cancer; that DES produces a cancerous condition of the cervix of the female offspring of women who use DES during pregnancy. It was claimed that sometime in 1954 or 1955 when the plaintiff's mother was pregnant, the predecessor of the defendant pharmacy had sold DES to the plaintiff's mother (the reported facts showed that if DES was indeed sold, it was pursuant to prescription). The defendant-pharmacy owner had taken over the business of the pharmacy that allegedly dispensed the DES.

As to the issue of breach of warranty of fitness for a particular purpose and breach of implied warranties of merchantability, the court denied these claims on the basis that the pharmacy-owner defendant had not directly sold the DES, nor did he assume the former pharmacy owner's liability (if any). Further, the original pharmacy had no liability because it simply filled the doctor's prescription.

RULING: The trial court dismissed the complaint against the pharmacy and the plaintiff appealed the dismissal. The Court of Appeals of Michigan, where the case arose, affirmed the dismissal.

REASONING: To restate the rule, the court stated:

> It appears, as a general rule, that druggists [pharmacists] are not liable for correctly filling a prescription.

Privileges

The following is a list of court cases that are related to this topic.

DeMoss Rexall Drugs v Dobson, 540 N.E. 2d 655 (Ind. App. 2 Dist. 1989).
Evans v Rite-Aid Corp., 452 S.E.2d 9 (S.C. App. 1994), affirmed, as modified 478 S.E 2d 846 (1996).
Nefaris v DeStefano, Slip Op. No. 98-10295 (Oct. 18, 1999), 1999 NY App. Div. LEXIS 10434.

Evidence and Procedure

The following is a list of court cases that are related to this topic.

Burkes v Fred's Stores of Tennessee, 768 So 2d 325 (October 3, 2000), 2000 Miss App LEXIS 498.

Attorney Fees

Dempsey v Pease
Slip Op Nos 222894 and 225065, December 4, 2001, 2001 Mich. App. LEXIS 273

A nurse allegedly injected a patient admitted to a hospital with an exceptionally high dose of *Prolixin*, causing him to suffer permanent impotence. The hospital, its staff, and the nurse all denied liability and claimed that there was no scientific evidence linking an overdose of the drug to permanent impotence. A jury trial resulted in a verdict against the defendants in the amount of $200,000. The trial judge also awarded an additional amount of $150,000 in attorney fees based on an hourly rate of $200. On appeal, the court reduced the jury award by $100,000 because of duplication in the damages claims. However, it let stand the attorney fees based on a finding that the case was complex and involved countless hours of preparation made necessary by the defendants' attempts to fight the claims.

PART VI: CONTRACT LAW

General

Beharry v Mascara
516 A.2d 872 (Pa. Cmwlth. Ct. 1986)

ISSUE: Whether a county controller had the right to refuse to pay a pharmacist for services rendered without a formal contract.

FACTS: For some time, William Duvall was the licensed pharmacist in charge of the Washington County Medical Center under contract with the county. On December 14, 1984, Duvall requested and received a leave of absence. Philip Sollon, also a pharmacist, was appointed by the county commissioners to take his place. On January 24, 1985, the county commissioners executed a contract under which Sollon agreed to perform the services of a vendor and consultant pharmacist effective January 1, 1985.

Beharry, the county controller, refused to honor Sollon's bills for services from December 14, 1984, to January 24, 1985. The county commissioners brought an action to compel payment and also filed a simultaneous action for emergency relief.

The controller contended that the contract under which the pharmacist operated was invalid because its terms were unclear and ambiguous; that no standard was set for prices charged for the drugs; and that no written contract for the period was ever made.

RULING: The court ruled that the county commissioners had the responsibility to manage the affairs of the municipality and that the contract was lawfully entered into under a situation of an emergency nature. The controller was ordered to pay the pharmacist for his services.

REASONING: The court found that the county medical center was operated as a governmental agency. The medical director would prescribe drugs that the pharmacist would then dispense as needed. The pharmacist would send a statement to the staff of the center who would review the bill and forward them to the county controller for payment. The court found that no advertising or bidding was employed by the commissioners to obtain the services of the pharmacist in this case. However, the county code stated that no bidding was required in contracts involving services of members of the medical or legal profession, architects, engineers, certified public accountants, or other professional services.

The records clearly showed that the duties of the pharmacist in this situation included examining patient charts, submitting reports, and participating in the formulating of policies and procedures for the Center. Dispensing drugs and consulting in formulating policies required the expertise of a professional and clearly came within the terms of the county code, which did not require bidding in contracts involving personal services and the advise of a professional expert. The controller failed to comply with county procedures. The court noted that the controller was not an overlord of the other county officers.

Gaston Drugs, Inc. v Metropolitan Life Insurance Co.
653 F.Supp. 1104 (S.D. Ohio 1986)

ISSUE: Whether the audit by a prescription drug insurance company of participating pharmacies constituted a contractual violation and an invasion of the patient's privacy.

FACTS: General Motors and other employers retained the services of Metropolitan Life Insurance Co. to administer a prescription drug plan for their workers. The program reimbursed participating pharmacies for prescriptions with the patient paying a small co-payment or deductible. In order to participate in the program, pharmacies executed a non-negotiable contract with the insurance company with the pharmacies being reimbursed according to schedules approved by the various employers. Reimbursement was usually based on acquisition cost, which meant the actual cost of a covered drug including trade and volume discounts and other allowances. The agreements also provided that Metropolitan had the right to review business records and prescriptions of participating pharmacies.

Two different pharmacy owners joined as plaintiffs in this action. Both of these pharmacies admitted that they did not indicate actual acquisition costs on the insurance forms, but instead submitted claims based upon Average Wholesale Price (AWP). After one plaintiff was audited, he received a bill from the insurance company seeking $8,000 in overpayments. The second plaintiff was asked to repay $77,000 in alleged overpayments. Metropolitan threatened termination of the agreement unless the plaintiffs reimbursed the company.

RULING: The court ruled that the pharmacy owners had violated the terms of the contract by over-reporting the acquisition costs and that the proposed audit did not constitute a violation of the patients' privacy.

REASONING: Ohio statutes prohibited the inspection of prescription records except by law enforcement officers and employees of the state board of pharmacy. However, the court noted that the plaintiffs completed a "Universal Claim Form" for each prescription filled under the provider agreements. This claim form included the patient's name, the pharmacy name, the prescription number, the national drug code numbers for the drugs provided, and the quantity of drugs. The plaintiffs failed to show that any prescription information sought by the insurance company in its audits had not already been revealed by the pharmacies on the claim forms. In addition, the court noted that each of the patients signed a release on the form that "authorized release of all information pertaining to this claim to the plan administrator...and the employer."

The plaintiffs argued that the insurance company's audits and threats to terminate were violations of their rights under the contract. The court found that on the face of the contract, its provisions appeared to give the defendant insurance company the power to engage in precisely the type of conduct that the plaintiffs claimed was unlawful. The court found that "average wholesale price" and "acquisition cost" could not reasonably be construed as consistent. Testimony at the hearing plainly showed that the average wholesale price was not determined by the price that a particular pharmacy paid a particular drug company for a specific quantity of the drug. The contract between the insurance company and the pharmacies provided that it could be modified only in writing signed by both parties. The plaintiffs were unable to show any commercial practices by the defendant insurance company amounting to a waiver of the "acquisition cost" terms of the contract.

Alderman Drugs v Metropolitan Life Insurance Co.
515 N.E.2d 689 (Ill.App. 1987)

ISSUE: Whether a third party insurance company that terminated pharmacies from participating in its prescription drug plan when they rejected amendments to the provider agreement was guilty of breach of contract.

FACTS: This lawsuit was brought on behalf of a number of pharmacies which were "participating providers" under agreements with Metropolitan Life Insurance Co. The contractual arrangement, referred to as the MediMET program, was designed to service the health insurance and prescription drug needs of certain major companies and their employees who belonged to Metropolitan's group health insurance plans.

Under the program, employees of General Motors of North American Rockwell are entitled to purchase prescription drugs for a deductible or co-payment fee from participating pharmacies. The pharmacy would then bill Metropolitan for the actual cost of the drugs plus a dispensing fee minus the employee's co-payment. To become a participating provider under the MediMET plan, a pharmacy must execute a provider agreement with the insurance company. Two paragraphs in the contract were at issue in this case, one of which involved the termination of the contract. The other contract term in dispute provided that the agreement could not be amended except upon the mutual, written agreement of the parties.

While relations between Metropolitan and the pharmacies were amicable at the start, a dispute arose in 1977 when amendments to the contract increased the employee co-payments from $2 to $3 and increased the maximum allowable dosage for a number of drugs from 100 to 200 doses. Also, a new employer was proposed to be covered in the contract. This litigation arose after certain pharmacies were terminated from the program when they refused to accept these amendments. The plaintiffs objected to the increase in dosage because of the reduction in their profits since a customer would come into their pharmacy less often for refills. The pharmacies also felt that the larger dosage was not pharmaceutically appropriate because the drugs would remain on the patient's shelf for over 6 months.

According to the plaintiffs, Metropolitan failed to disclose to them that they would be terminated if they refused to accept the unilateral amendments. Since the pharmacies were financially dependent upon the covered customers they served, many pharmacies accepted these amendments without question. Those who did not were subject to termination, which they contended was in violation of the agreement that gave them the right to accept or reject amendments. The plaintiffs further testified that they had increased paper work because of these changes and that the claims were not always paid within the 30-day period provided in the contract.

In response, Metropolitan denied having a policy of termination upon a pharmacy's refusal to accept amendments. The insurance company argued that the changes were necessary because of the collective bargaining agreements between the unions and covered employers and that both Metropolitan and the pharmacies were free at any time to terminate the contract upon 30 days notice. The company also argued that since the agreement expressly allowed for a pharmacist's professional judgment in deciding the dosage to dispense, an increase in the maximum dosage of a drug was not a directive to dispense that amount.

RULING: The trial court found in favor of Metropolitan, noting that the pharmacies had voluntarily entered into the program to stay competitive. The court held that the contract expressly and unambiguously allowed for mutual termination at will. The court entered a judgment in favor of the insurance company. The appellate court affirmed the trial court decision.

REASONING: The plaintiffs contended that two doctrines should bar Metropolitan from terminating participants who rejected amendments to the plan: (1) The covenant of good faith

Alderman Drugs v Metropolitan Life Insurance Co.
515 N.E.2d 689 (Ill.App. 1987)
...continued

and fair dealing; (2) equitable estoppel. Essentially, the plaintiffs asserted that the duty of good faith and fair dealing is a covenant implied in every contract and should operate as a limitation on Metropolitan's right to terminate the provider agreement.

The court found that the contract provision was not ambiguous and was a good example of a perfectly acceptable contractual provision. It noted that terminable at will contracts permit termination for any reason, good cause or not, or for no cause at all. If a contract does not have a specified duration, it will be considered to be terminable at the will of either party.

The parties to this contract explicitly intended to provide for termination without the need to itemize specific reasons or causes. Because of the changing nature of the collective bargaining agreements, the termination at will clause was considered essential. The fact that Metropolitan could not prevent the schedules from changing upon the collective bargaining negotiations of covered employer and employees, there was simply no other plan in existence for MediMET customers to take advantage of since the old schedules would become obsolete. Furthermore, some of the plaintiffs had accepted the increases in their dispensing fees without signing a formal modification document. The court ruled that a party could not repudiate a contract after accepting modification by their actions.

The court concluded that the plaintiffs had not sustained their burden of proving that their inability to reject unilateral amendments to the contract was a violation of good faith and fair dealing. The court also could find no evidence that Metropolitan made untrue statements or omissions of material fact that were intended to knowingly mislead the pharmacies. The plaintiffs contended that Metropolitan had a secret policy of terminating providers who rejected amendments to the agreement. They argued that the plaintiffs relied to their detriment on Metropolitan's representation as to the increases in dispensing fees, increased business opportunities, prompt reimbursement, limited dosages and the mutual acceptance of proposed amendments. While Metropolitan's marketing plan persuaded the pharmacies to join the MediMET program, there was no evidence that the insurance company misled them as to any of these representations.

R.T. Cornell Pharmacy, Inc. v Guzzo
522 N.Y.S.2d 725 (App.Div. 1987)

ISSUE: Whether a pharmacy that purchased a computer system based upon a salesman's representations was entitled to the return of the full purchase price when the system failed to perform as proposed.

FACTS: Cornell Pharmacy purchased a computer package including both hardware and software for the processing of prescriptions. Pursuant to the written contract, the pharmacy retained the option to cancel the contract within 120 days after installation if "the system failed to perform as proposed." The contract contained no definition of the phrase "as proposed." The salesman who negotiated the contract on behalf of the defendant computer company made certain oral representations that all third-party prescription plans would be programmed into the system. It was undisputed that such a program was not, in fact, preprogrammed.

The computer company claimed that the salesman may have stated that the program could be included, but only after the necessary customer information was obtained from the pharmacy's records. However, the salesman was not produced as a witness.

R.T. Cornell Pharmacy, Inc. v Guzzo
522 N.Y.S.2d 725 (App.Div. 1987)
...continued

RULING: The jury returned a verdict in the pharmacy's favor for the full purchase price, and the appellate court affirmed the verdict.

REASONING: The trial court included a "missing witness" charge in its instructions to the jury. Such a charge may be given where the uncalled witness bears information on a material issue and would be expected to provide testimony in favor of the opposing party. The pharmacy's claim depended entirely on what representations the salesman made as to the performance of the computer system. The salesman was a material witness who, as the defendant's sales representative, could reasonably be expected to testify favorably on the defendant's behalf. Thus, it was incumbent upon the defendant computer company to demonstrate that the salesman was no longer under its control or was otherwise unavailable.

The defendant company simply testified that the salesman no longer maintained any business relationship with the company. However, the fact that the salesman was no longer an employee or agent did not preclude a finding of control as a matter of law. The court noted that there was no explanation as to whether the defendant's relationship with the salesman had changed in such a manner that the witness might prove hostile or uncooperative. The company simply indicated that it attempted to obtain the salesman's presence at the trial, but was informed that he would be out of town for 3 or 4 days. The attempt to locate the salesman was clearly less than diligent. The trial court properly instructed the jury that the unfavorable inference could be drawn from the failure to call the salesman as a witness.

Empire State Pharmaceutical Society, Inc. v Perales
672 F.Supp. 146 (S.D.N.Y. 1987)

ISSUE: Whether a State Pharmacy Association's lawsuit against a Medicaid program was ripe for adjudication when no member of the Association had been denied enrollment or threatened with denial.

FACTS: The Empire State Pharmaceutical Society (Society) is an association whose members include registered pharmacies and licensed pharmacists, most of whom are enrolled in the New York State Medicaid Program as "providers" of Medicaid coverage. The Society and one of its individual members who joined as a plaintiff alleged that they had been deprived of their right to due process under the Fourteenth Amendment by the enactment of a New York law that prescribed new procedures for enrollment and continuation of providers in the Medicaid program. Parties wishing to participate in the program were required, under the new regulations, to submit an application. They were also subject to an investigation. The New York State Department of Social Services could also elect not to contract with a prospective provider who had been sanctioned by another governmental agency or who had engaged in activities that created an undue risk to the Medicaid program. Providers enrolled in the program prior to the enactment of the new regulations were also required to re-enroll within 60 days of receiving notice from the Department to do so. If the provider failed to submit an application, that provider was automatically terminated from the program. The plaintiffs pointed out that prior to the adoption of the new regulations, providers would not be terminated without cause and an opportunity for a hearing. The plaintiffs argued that continued participation in the program was a property interest, protected by the due process clause of the Fourteenth Amendment and that the new regulations stripped provider of their right to prior notice and a hearing.

Empire State Pharmaceutical Society, Inc. v Perales
672 F.Supp. 146 (S.D.N.Y. 1987)
...continued

RULING: The court concluded that the complaint by the Society should be dismissed because no member had been denied enrollment or threatened with denial. Thus, the action was not ripe for adjudication.

REASONING: Courts have traditionally been reluctant to grant declaratory judgment unless the rights of the interested parties are ripe for judicial resolution. There was no evidence in this case that the "taking" that the plaintiffs feared was imminent or even probable. The plaintiffs merely asserted that the Department might deny their application for re-enrollment or might terminate them once they are enrolled. However, this was too hypothetical and speculative to warrant judicial intervention. Since the plaintiffs sought a present court determination of a possible future controversy, this suit was not ripe for adjudication. If the regulations were applied as the plaintiffs feared, the court would have a concrete record upon which to base an informed decision. The plaintiffs were not presented with any hardship in this case since all they had to do was submit an application for re-enrollment, which imposed little or no cost to them.

Thatcher's Drugs v Consolidated Supermarkets
571 A.2d 490 (Pa. Super. 1990)

ISSUE: Whether a shopping center tenant who was promised by another tenant not to open a competing pharmacy could succeed in a lawsuit based upon an alleged violation of an oral agreement between the parties.

FACTS: The plaintiff, Ronald Zukin, was president and sole stockholder of Thatcher's Drugs. Zukin entered into a 10-year lease agreement with Enal Construction Company to locate his retail pharmacy business in a shopping center complex. The plaintiff shared a common wall with Shop-Rite Supermarket, a franchise operated by the defendant.

Sometime in 1976, Thatcher's Drugs began selling "drinks and milk." Thereafter, Zukin noticed a sign in Shop-Rite's window: "Coming Soon - A Shop-Rite Pharmacy." When Zukin contacted Shop-Rite to complain, he was referred to the vice president of the supermarket's parent company. The discussion between Zukin and the vice president was one in which the latter stated, "We don't want you in the dairy business. Get out of the dairy business and we won't open a pharmacy." The sign stayed in the window until Zukin removed his refrigerator case from the pharmacy.

When the 10-year lease expired in 1983, Zukin contacted and informed the landlord of his desire to renew the lease for an equal term. He was told there were problems because Shop-Rite wanted to open a pharmacy. Zukin began to search for a new site, and did find space within three blocks of his existing store. He executed a new lease and drew a check to pay the rent at the new site. However, he remained in contact with his former landlord to advise him that he was still interested in remaining at the old location.

As a result of his conversation with his original landlord, Zukin received a new lease increasing the rent and requiring that he occupy additional space in the shopping center. Before agreeing to the terms of the new lease, Zukin contacted the vice president of the supermarket corporation. Zukin informed the supermarket executive that (1) he had been offered a new lease, (2) he had a lease at another location for 10 years, and (3) he wanted some assur-

Thatcher's Drugs v Consolidated Supermarkets
571 A.2d 490 (Pa. Super. 1990)
...continued

ances that Shop-Rite was not going to open a pharmacy. According to Zukin, the executive's direct words were, "We don't hurt the little guys. We have no desire to want to hurt you and we have no intention of opening a pharmacy." Thereafter, Zukin contacted the shopping center landlord to renew his lease, and advised his realtor that he would not be moving to the new location.

A year later, Zukin advertised "soda drinks and soda business." Shop-Rite reacted by placing its own sign reading "Shop-Rite Pharmacy coming soon." As before, the supermarket chain indicated to Zukin they wanted him out of the "soda" business before they would remove the "pharmacy" sign. The end result was that both parties removed the offending signs from the respective windows.

Thereafter, Zukin learned that Shop-Rite acquired additional space in the shopping center to open a retail pharmacy in direct competition with Thatcher's Drugs. Efforts to dissuade the shopping center to discard the pharmacy idea proved fruitless, even though Zukin pointed out that his lease prohibited the landlord from renting any store within the premises for use as a drugstore or pharmacy or for the sale of medical equipment or prosthetic supplies. However, this restriction did not apply to any portion of the shopping center presently used as a supermarket or department store.

RULING: Both the trial court and appellate court permanently prohibited the defendant from operating a competing retail prescription pharmacy in the shipping center.

REASONING: One of the issues on appeal was whether, in the absence of a writing signed by the parties, the Statute of Frauds precluded the court from restricting the supermarket chain from operating a pharmacy.

The purpose of the Statue of Frauds is to prevent the enforcement of unfounded fraudulent claims by requiring certain contracts pertaining to interests in real estate to be supported by written evidence.

There was no dispute that the defendant's oral promise not to open a pharmacy on its leased premises did not meet the requirements of the Statute of Frauds. However, an oral promise or representation that certain land will be used in a particular way, although otherwise unenforceable, is enforceable to the extent necessary to protect expenditures made in reliance upon the promise.

The appellate court was not willing to permit the defendant to profit from its remarks and leave the plaintiff without any recourse. This was based upon a finding that the defendant had made a promise not to compete and this induced the plaintiff to terminate a lease agreement that would have afforded an alternate store site within three blocks of his present location.

The doctrine of equitable estoppel prevents one from doing an act differently from the manner in which another was induced by word or deed to expect. The essential elements of this doctrine are inducement and justifiable reliance on that inducement. Zukin was induced to renew his lease with the owner of the shopping center based upon Shop-Rite's statement that they did not intend to open a pharmacy. The trial court indicated that it found Zukin to be credible, but that the vice president of Shop-Rite was not credible when he denied making such a statement.

Thatcher's Drugs v Consolidated Supermarkets
571 A.2d 490 (Pa. Super. 1990)
...continued

The court ruled that there was no reason to change the trial court's order prohibiting the defendant from opening a pharmacy adjacent to the supermarket in competition with the plaintiff during the 10-year term of the Shop-Rite's representative that a competing pharmacy would not be opened in the shopping center.

Lubman v Insurance Commissioner of Maryland
585 A.2d 269 (Md. App. 1991)

ISSUE: Whether the modification of a third party payor contract pertaining to prescription dispensing fees was fair and reasonable.

FACTS: In May, 1989, Blue Cross submitted a contract to the Insurance Commissioner that would amend the formula for reimbursing independent pharmacies that participate in Blue Cross's prescription drug program. The proposed contract provided that participating pharmacies would be reimbursed for the average wholesale price of the pharmaceutical product or ingredient, plus a dispensing fee of $3.30 for each prescription filled, less a provider discount of 30 cents per claim to be returned to MMS.

The Commissioner held a hearing in which testimony was received from 5 independent pharmacies and an expert in pharmacy management. Pharmacist Ronald Lubman testified that he would lose between $2500 and $3200 in profit under the proposed contract as compared with the old contract. The plaintiff's expert witness, D.C. Huffman, testified that a dispensing fee of $5.36 plus the cost of the drug should be paid to pharmacists to enable them to meet expenses and receive any equitable return on investment. Huffman also testified that the cost to dispense prescription drugs has followed the consumer price index. He stated that if the consumer price index were applied to the $3.30 dispensing fee established in 1983, the dispensing fee would have risen to $4.20 by 1989.

David Banta, Director of Pharmacy Relations for Blue Cross, testified that under the existing contract the actual acquisition cost of a drug is difficult to determine, but the average wholesale price is a published figure and easily determined. Therefore, while the existing contract called for the payment of actual acquisition costs, Blue Cross has reimbursed pharmacists for the average wholesale price, or for the submitted charges, whichever is less.

Banta explained that what a pharmacist makes when reimbursed by Blue Cross consists of 2 elements. The first element is the dispensing fee, which is designed to cover overhead. The second element is the difference between the actual acquisition cost and the average wholesale price. He stated that high volume pharmacies, with great purchasing power, are able to obtain pharmaceutical products at the best price. This maximizes the difference between the actual acquisition cost and the average wholesale price.

Banta stated that as the cost of prescription drugs has risen, coupled with inflationary increases in the average wholesale price, the total dollar amount of difference between the actual acquisition cost and the average wholesale price has increased. This provides pharmacists a greater return on investment and a hedge against inflation. He further testified that the funds generated by the provider discount would be used by MMS to create a pharmacy advisory committee, patient education projects, drug utilization review, and other changes designed to reduce costs and enhance the quality of care provided to patients. He

Lubman v Insurance Commissioner of Maryland
585 A.2d 269 (Md. App. 1991)
...continued

also stated that the provider discounts sought by Blue Cross from chain pharmacies were significantly larger than those sought from independent pharmacies.

The hearing officer concluded that a dispensing fee of $3.30 less the provider discount of 30 cents was not fair, but the proposed contract would be reasonable if the discount was reduced to 15 cents per claim.

RULING: It was concluded that the Insurance Commissioner erred in modifying the dispensing fee contract.

REASONING: The Commissioner presumed that the 1983 contract was just, fair, equitable, and adequate. He then adjusted the 1983 dispensing fee using the consumer price index. He calculated the additional income to pharmacists by using the average wholesale price rather than the actual acquisition cost. The Commissioner concluded that a reimbursement formula of the average wholesale price plus a $3.30 dispensing fee, less a 15 cent provider discount was comparable to the 1983 contract.

The court concluded that while this method may seem reasonable at first blush, there was a fatal flaw. There was no evidence in the record that the original 1983 contract met the requirements of fairness.

Blue Cross argued that because the contract had been in use since 1983, the contract must have been approved by the Commissioner. The court found that this argument assumed too much. The required procedures may well have been circumvented in 1983 and it was unreasonable to assume that the contract had been approved when the record was devoid of such proof.

The court sent the case back to the Commissioner for further consideration. The court also suggested that the Commissioner might want to decide whether Blue Cross could own a for-profit subsidiary, which would be funded by revenues from the not-for-profit corporation. Also to be considered was whether the provider discount was an illegal kickback or rebate and whether the proposed contract was discriminatory with respect to independent pharmacies.

The plaintiffs pointed out that the revenue created from the provider discount would be paid to an unregulated for-profit subsidiary of Blue Cross. The court asked the Commissioner to consider whether this revenue would be used for a proper purpose and whether this reimbursement scheme was ripe for abuse. On the one hand, the activities of the for-profit subsidiary may indeed have the altruistic purpose of benefiting all Blue Cross subscribers. However, without regulation, the Commissioner may be unable to ensure that this revenue is utilized in a legal and appropriate manner.

The court was also concerned that because the provider discount would be paid to a for-profit subsidiary, this revenue might not be taken into account in other rate-making cases. Thus, the Commissioner might not be aware of Blue Cross's true financial situation in determining reimbursement rates for other healthcare providers or premium rates for subscribers. Essentially, subscribers could be forced to pay higher premiums needlessly when Blue Cross, in fact, had sufficient funds to provide health care without an increase in premiums.

Sullivan's Wholesale Drug Company v Faryl's Pharmacy, et al.
1991 WL 95952 (Ill. App.)

ISSUE: Whether the defendant pharmacies and nursing home were engaged in an illegal kick-back scheme involving the sale of drugs to nursing home residents.

FACTS: Maurice Sullivan, a registered pharmacist, operated a retail pharmacy in Hillsboro, Illinois. Sullivan provided pharmacy services to the residents of an area nursing home, many of whom were customers of Sullivan's Drug before they entered the facility. Sullivan continued to serve these patients even though there were numerous changes in the nursing home's ownership.

The nursing home was acquired by Health Group Care (one of the defendants) in 1982. Under his agreement with the owners, Sullivan billed patients individually, just as if they were customers of his retail pharmacy. Sullivan assumed full responsibility for collecting the amounts due.

In the spring of 1983, Health Group Care advised Sullivan that it intended to amend the terms of the agreement. The new agreement provided that Sullivan's would retain responsibility for billing Medicaid patients, but that Medicare and private patients would be billed directly by the nursing home. The nursing home would then forward payment to Sullivan's. Sullivan's would not be entitled to the full amount of the patient billings; however, because the contract authorized the nursing home to deduct 15% of the total account billed and keep that amount for itself.

Sullivan believed that this proposed 15% deduction was, in effect, a kick-back that the nursing home sought to exact in exchange for granting the pharmacy exclusive access to the business generated by the home's Medicaid patients. The pharmacy protested that such kick-backs were illegal, unethical, and immoral and it refused to sign the agreement.

The nursing home informed Sullivan that it intended to find a different pharmacy provider. The nursing home administrator explained to Sullivan that "we have to generate money in any way we can." Sullivan was terminated as the consultant pharmacist for the nursing home and was informed that his company would no longer serve as the primary pharmaceutical provider. Patents were now required to use Faryl's pharmacy, which agreed to the alleged 15% kickback scheme.

RULING: The trial court entered summary judgment in favor of the defendants, but the appellate court concluded that punitive damages based upon violations of the Illinois Consumer Fraud Act should be reconsidered by the trial court.

REASONING: The defendants attempted to justify the 15% deduction on the grounds that it was common practice among other nursing homes and represented reasonable compensation for the expenses occurred for labor, materials, and management time on the nursing home. The evidence also showed that the rebate was intended to help offset the risk of bad debt and to compensate the nursing home for various services it provided to the pharmacies, including ordering, storing, and accounting for drugs. The plaintiff countered that these claimed services were in fact illusory. The plaintiff argued that the 15% rebate had no relation to the actual cost of services and risks that the nursing home assumed. The nursing home had simply incorporated the pharmacy's statement into its billing to the nursing home residents. The only real savings to the pharmacy was that it no longer had to prepare and pay to have the individual bills mailed. In addition, the plaintiff was able to show that the risk of non-payment was low. Furthermore, the evidence established that when the new system went into effect, the pharmacy charges to the nursing home's residents increased. When patients complained, the nursing home administrator issued a letter in which she

Sullivan's Wholesale Drug Company v Faryl's Pharmacy, et al.
1991 WL 95952 (Ill. App.)
...continued

indicated that the change had been made due to circumstances beyond the home's control. The court found that the method of billing now gave the patients the impression that they were being billed by the nursing home for exactly what the pharmacy was charging for medication. In actuality, the residents were being charged 15% more than the drugs cost. (Note: the nursing home contract eventually went to another pharmacy that offered similar terms under similar terms to other nursing homes and even permitted some to retain up to 25% of the gross pharmacy billings.) To establish a cause of action for tortuous interference with a business relationship, the plaintiff must prove (1) the existence of a valid business relationship, (2) the defendant's knowledge of that relationship, and (3) intentional interference by the defendant that causes the breach or termination of the relationship. In this case, the court could find no evidence that either of the pharmacy defendants induced or caused the residents of the nursing home or the nursing home itself to sever the business relationships they had with the plaintiff. The defendant pharmacies merely agreed to take over the business after Sullivan's contract was terminated. The defendants further argued that they could not be held liable since they did not engage in any deceptive practice. A trial court could certainly conclude, however, that the 15% discrepancy in billing was patently deceptive. The defendants argued that the pharmacy contract was available for all of the residents to review if they made such a request. The court was not persuaded and it rejected the defendants' attempt to place the burden on the residents. The court did not believe that patients would ever have thought to check with the government agencies charged with enforcing Medicare and Medicaid rules or to check with their private insurers regarding the charges for their medication.

Pittman v Mast Advertising, Inc.
619 So.2d 1377 (Ala. 1993)

ISSUE: Whether a pharmacist, who is president of a corporation that is wholly owned by his wife, can maintain legal action for negligent failure of an advertising company to include the corporation in the local telephone directory.

FACTS: In 1990, Jim and Mary Pittman formed a corporation to operate a pharmacy in Bayou La Batre, Alabama. The Pittmans serve as directors and officers of Modern Drug, Inc., but Mrs. Pittman is the sole stockholder. Mr. Pittman works for the pharmacy as a pharmacist, and he supervises the daily operations of the business.

As part of the operation of the business, Mr. Pittman entered into a written agreement with the Mast Advertising Publishing Company for an advertisement in the 1991 Bayou La Batre telephone directory. Mr Pittman paid for the advertisement on behalf of Modern Drug.

When published, the 1991 telephone directory contained no listing or advertisement for Modern Drug. Consequently, the corporation and Mr. Pittman sued Mast Advertising. In the complaint, Modern Drug alleged breach of contract and Mr. Pittman alleged negligent failure to perform the contract, and he sought damages for "severe inconvenience, anxiety, pain and suffering, and mental anguish."

RULING: The court concluded that, as a general rule, an individual stockholder, officer, or employee of a corporation does not have an independent right to sue to recover damages based on claims that derived from the corporation.

Pittman v Mast Advertising, Inc.
619 So.2d 1377 (Ala. 1993)
...continued

REASONING: In support of his argument that the summary judgment was improper, Pittman relied on an earlier Alabama case in which the court held that two periodontists who paid for listings in a telephone directory could recover damages for mental anguish in a negligence action against the telephone company and the agency that had solicited the listing when one of their names was omitted. In so holding, the Alabama Supreme Court noted "The rule which seems to have emerged from the decisions in the United States is that there will be liability in tort whenever misperformance [of a bargaining transaction] involves forseeable, unreasonable risk of harm to the interest of the plaintiff or where there would be liability for performance without the contract. More simply stated, we must determine whether there is a legal duty sufficient to support an action for negligence: (1) The nature of the defendant's activity; (2) the relationship between the parties; and (3) the type of injury or harm threatened."

In the case involving the periodontists, the court noted that despite complaints from the plaintiff's verification of information by the defendant directory company, the error was not corrected in any of three subsequent directories. At the time the periodontists opened their office, a listing in the Yellow Pages was the only permanent form of advertising permitted by the State Board of Dental Examiners. Thus, the court concluded that the imposition of tort liability was appropriate even though the relationship between the parties was primarily contractual because the defendants, knowing that the plaintiffs depended on a listing as their only form of advertisement, performed the contract in such a negligent manner that the name of one of the plaintiffs was omitted four times in succession.

Based on the evidence presented, the court concluded that this case is distinguishable from that of the periodontist. This case involved only one omission from the directory. Also, although the Pittmans had recently bought Modern Drug from the previous owner, it was not a new business which, arguably, would at least initially be dependent upon advertising. Unlike previous cases, there was no evidence presented indicating that Modern Drug depended on the telephone directory listing as it exclusive, or even its main, form of advertising.

The court held that these distinctions are significant because they demonstrate that in the previous cases, mental anguish and other contractual damages were reasonably forseeable and that the defendants in the previous case had duties independent of the contracts. In contrast, the allegations in this case were based solely on the failure to publish an advertisement. The fact that the defendant did not do so did not make it reasonably forseeable that Mr. Pittman would suffer the injury or harm he alleged. Therefore, Mast Advertising did not have a duty independent of its agreement with Modern Drug.

Dantonio, et al v Fontana, et al
636 So.2d 218 (La. 1994)

ISSUE: Whether the seller of a pharmacy could prohibit the purchaser from using the seller's family name of the pharmacy following the sale.

FACTS: Felix Ciolino, a licensed pharmacist for over 40 years, opened the Ciolino Pharmacy in Metairie, Louisiana, in 1974. In 1977, he and his wife sold the business to several pharmacists, one of whom had worked for him. The sale included the moveables and property of the pharmacy, including fixtures and prescription files, as well as the business goodwill.

Dantonio, et al v Fontana, et al
636 So.2d 218 (La. 1994)
...continued

The sales agreement provided that "the purchasers shall have the right to use the business name of Ciolino Pharmacy for the conduct of their business, including the right to use same on any signs, prescriptions, labels or any form of advertising until such time that vendor gives to purchaser 6 months prior advance notice to cease and desist with the use of said business name. Should purchaser use the said business name after notice to cease and desist has been given, the purchasers agree to pay vendors, as liquidated damages, the sum of $100 per day for as long as such violation shall continue, in addition to reasonable attorney's fees."

The buyers thereafter made use of the name "Ciolino Pharmacy," but as early as 1982 the name used in their full-page newspaper advertisements was "Ciolino B&B Pharmacy." Ten years after the sale, the Ciolinos gave the buyers a 6-month notice to cease using the name Ciolino Pharmacy. In the meantime, Felix Ciolino had formed a corporation named "Ciolino Pharmacy, Inc." and had registered Ciolino Pharmacy as a trade name. Shortly after giving notice to the purchasers to cease using the name, he placed a sign advertising "Ciolino Pharmacy opening soon" on a building on Veterans Boulevard in Metairie.

The pharmacist-purchasers then sued to enjoin the Ciolinos from using the Ciolino Pharmacy name. The Ciolinos asked for a declaratory judgment arguing that the contract gave the buyers only a non-exclusive right to use the name, and that the right would terminate 6 months after notice. The Ciolinos also asked for liquidated damages of $100 for every day the purchasers used the name.

RULING: The District Court preliminarily enjoined the Ciolinos from using their family name. A month later, Ciolino and his pharmacist son opened "C's Discount Pharmacy." Below the name of the pharmacy, in much smaller letters, the sign stated "Felix Ciolino -- Pharmacist -- Steven Ciolino." The purchasers' claim for contempt against the Ciolinos for so using their own name was dismissed by the District Court. The Supreme Court of Louisiana overturned the lower court decision.

REASONING: The trial court judge stated that to allow the seller of a business an indefinite period to reclaim a name after the buyer's work had made that name into a commercially identifiable name would fly in the face of equitable dealings. Accordingly, the judge ruled that the business name "Ciolino Pharmacy" was included in the goodwill that was sold in 1977 along with the sale of the inventory, equipment, and furnishings. He further ruled that the contract's limitation on the use of the seller's name was totally void and inconsistent with the sale. He refused to enjoin the purchasers from using the name, but quite the reverse, he enjoined the Ciolinos from using their own name for their new pharmacy.

The Supreme Court of Louisiana, in its review of the case, noted that the sale of a professional business and name that uses the seller's own name must be expressed to be effective. To prohibit a professional person from using his or her own name in professional practice is a restraint of trade unless expressly agreed to.

The court then turned its attention to the intent of the parties in drafting the sales contract. It noted that parties are free to contract for any object that is lawful. When the words of a contract are clear and explicit and lead to no absurd consequences, no further interpretation may be made in search of the party's intent. Notwithstanding that some might infer that the sale of business goodwill ought to include sale of the family business name, one could not reasonably so interpret this contract. It was important for the court to review the other contract clauses that granted only a limited use of the business name, and also penalized the buyers for use of the name after notice to cease and desist.

Dantonio, et al v Fontana, et al
636 So.2d 218 (La. 1994)
...continued

The lower court's invalidation of the name clause of the contract could not be reconciled with the bedrock principle that parties are free to contract for any object that is lawful. Even if the sale of business goodwill would ordinarily convey the business name, parties nevertheless have the freedom to contract for a sale including goodwill, but expressly exclude the business name. This principle is not diminished by the fact that the price of the contract was too high not to include the name (note: there was evidence that $827,851 of the $1,350,000 sales price was attributable to goodwill). A contract selling goodwill, but allowing the use of the business name for 6 months, is equally within the parties' freedom to contract.

The court did not believe that the contract language led to any absurd consequences. It gave the buyers 6 months to use the name and to gradually change to the use of their own name. It also afforded a minimum period of time for the buyers to use up the stock of printed material and to wean their patrons, acquired largely from the 30,000 prescriptions on file, from the old to the new name and the new owners.

Thus, the Supreme Court of Louisiana reversed the lower court's decision and issued an injunction against the purchasers from using the name Ciolino Pharmacy. The Ciolinos abandoned their claim for liquidated damages. Their attorney stated that they were not in court for money, but simply wanted their name back. Even where a geographic or descriptive trade name has acquired a "secondary meaning" identifying it with a particular business (as the buyers here alleged, but did not prove), one must prove fraud to enjoin another's use of their own name. Without a non-competition clause, the buyers could not prevent the Ciolinos from competing in a similar business, even shortly thereafter and in the immediate vicinity. Any non-competition contract that is unlimited as to time and place is void.

Rite Aid of Ohio, Inc. v Marc's Variety Store, Inc.
638 N.E.2d 1056 (Ohio Ct. App. 1994)

ISSUE: Whether a health and beauty aid store could be prevented from operating in a shopping center that had provided an exclusive lease to a pharmacy chain. The case turns on whether or not the variety store operates as a "drug store" in violation of the pharmacy's exclusive use provision, even though the variety store does not offer prescription drugs.

FACTS: Rite Aid of Ohio operates a 9600 square foot store with a pharmacy at the Brookgate Shopping Center in Brook Park, Ohio, under a 1981 lease. The lease gave Marshall Drug, Rite Aid's predecessor, the right to operate a "retail drug and variety store" on the premises. The lease listed the items that Rite Aid could sell: "Proprietary and ethical drugs, health and beauty aids, sundries, tobacco products and smoking supplies, liquor, beer, and wine, school supplies, housewares, small electrical appliances, toys, recreation equipment, cameras..."

The lease went on to grant Rite Aid "the exclusive privilege for the operation of a Drug Store in the shopping center." At the time Rite Aid's predecessor entered into the lease, the anchor tenant in the shopping center was Zayre's, a general merchandise store selling every item listed above except prescription drugs. Another tenant was a grocery store which also sold said items but not prescription drugs. Both of these stores or their successors still operate at the present time.

Rite Aid of Ohio, Inc. v Marc's Variety Store, Inc.
638 N.E.2d 1056 (Ohio Ct. App. 1994)
...continued

Rite Aid has never claimed that Zayre's or the grocery store were drug stores or violated its exclusive use privilege, even though they offered the same items as Rite Aid except prescription drugs.

In November 1990, the general merchandise store went out of business. The 45,000 square feet of anchor space remained unoccupied until October 1992, when the defendant opened Marc's Variety Store. Because the shopping center had been without an anchor tenant for nearly 2 years, there was a deleterious effect on the general success of the shopping center and the business tenants during that time.

Total sales at Rite Aid's store consisted of 90% pharmacy and health and beauty aid items and 10% food and general merchandise items. The Marc's store does not have a pharmacy. Accordingly, it does not call itself a drug store. The allocation of space within the store is 45% devoted to general merchandise, 27% to food and 14% to health and beauty aids.

On the day before the grand opening of Marc's, Rite Aid filed a complaint against Marc's and the shopping center management, seeking preliminary and permanent injunctive relief, which would prohibit Marc's from operating a drug store in the shopping center. The temporary restraining order was denied, but expedited discovery was allowed.

In order to obtain the relief it sought, Rite Aid had to establish each of the following elements: (1) the defendants committed a wrongful act, (2) the plaintiff has no adequate remedy at law, (3) the harm to the plaintiff if the injunction does not issue clearly outweighs the harm which the injunction would do to the defendants, and (4) the public interest will be served by granting the injunction.

Rite Aid did not attempt to define in its brief to the court the term "drug store." Rite Aid contended that the term has a broad meaning, but it did not distinguish Marc's from Zayre's or the grocery store which operated in the shopping center without objection when Rite Aid assumed its lease. One of the practical difficulties for Rite Aid at trial was to construct a definition of "drug store" which was broad enough to include Marc's, while at the same time excluding the other grocery and general merchandise stores in the shopping center. Eventually, Rite Aid's district supervisor was forced to acknowledge that what makes Rite Aid a drug store is the very thing that distinguishes it from Marc's.

The defendants argued if "drug store" could not be clearly defined, it would remove any limit on the scope of the lease's exclusive use clause. Such a construction would enable Rite Aid to exclude from the shopping center any store that would compete with it in the sale of any of its product categories, thereby threatening the shopping center's management from leasing the anchor space.

RULING: The appellate court concluded that the trial court was correct in relying upon the statutory definition in Ohio law to support its conclusion that Marc's was not operating a drug store because it did not have a pharmacy. Rite Aid's request for injuctive relief was denied.

REASONING: Drug stores have been regulated by statute in Ohio for many years. A drug store must be under the management or control of a legally registered pharmacist, otherwise, it may not call itself a drug store. The trial court also found that Ohio's statutory definition of a drug store, as containing a pharmacy or offering prescription drugs, was consistent with the common meaning of the word as contained in 17 dictionary definitions.

Rite Aid of Ohio, Inc. v Marc's Variety Store, Inc.
638 N.E.2d 1056 (Ohio Ct. App. 1994)
...continued

Rite Aid argued that dictionaries should not be considered because they do not identify the party's intent. However, the courts are bound to construe contract language based on the ordinary, everyday meaning of words. The court of appeals concluded that the dictionary authorities referenced displayed ample support for the trial court's conclusion that Marc's is not a "drug store" because it does not have a pharmacy. The court of appeals further found that the authorities relied upon by Rite Aid simply stand for the unremarkable proposition that drug stores may sell items other than prescription drugs.

Rite Aid next claimed that the lease should be interpreted in light of the surrounding circumstances to give effect to the intent of the parties (ie, to preserve Rite Aid from direct competition). However, the history of the relationship did not support this argument. When the original lease was assumed in 1981, two other stores were already selling all of the products which Rite Aid's predecessor was permitted to sell, except for prescription drugs. It was also undisputed that when Rite Aid assumed the lease, the stores were still selling all of the same products. Rite Aid did not object to this fact.

Rite Aid's acquiescence to those stores' operation was evidence that it did not view the exclusive provision as protection against competition in the sale of non-pharmacy items. Rite Aid further asserted that Marc's was a "drug chain." Rite Aid cited the 1981 issue of a trade publication called "Chain Drug Review," which placed Marc's on a list of drug chains. However, the lease did not grant Rite Aid the exclusive privilege to operate a store which is a part of a "drug chain," but only the exclusive privilege to offer a "drug store."

There was also substantial evidence introduced that in terms of sales dollars, floor space and advertising, Marc's heavily emphasizes groceries and general merchandise, which only account for 10% of Rite Aid's sales.

The trial court found that Rite Aid had not proved that it would be harmed if the injunction was not granted, but granting the injunction would cause substantial harm to the defendants, innocent third parties, and the public. Granting the injunctive relief requested by Rite Aid would shut down the anchor tenant of a major shopping center, putting 125 people out of work and reducing traffic for the other tenants. Indeed, if Rite Aid were given the power to exclude retailers which sell some combination of food, general merchandise, and health and beauty aids, regardless of whether they have a pharmacy, the pool of potential tenants for this anchor space would be severely limited and the harm to the shopping center would be substantial.

While the Rite Aid store manager claimed that sales fell approximately 25% immediately after Marc's opened, he later acknowledged that the store's sales fell by a similar percentage during this same time in each of the two previous years. This suggests that the decline was a seasonal phenomenon rather than the impact of the opening of Marc's. There was also evidence to support the trial court's finding that Rite Aid and every other tenant in the shopping center would suffer from the lack of an anchor tenant. Rite Aid's request for injunctive relief was denied.

Preferred Rx v American Prescription Plan
46 F.3d 535 (6th Cir. 1995)

FACTS: In exchange for a $25 membership fee and an assignment of benefits agreement with plaintiff, defendant mail order pharmacy waived patient's "co-pay." Plaintiff and defendant entered into an exclusive dealing contract whereby defendant billed plaintiff for each prescription at the average wholesale price (AWP) and plaintiff billed the patients' insurance company at its retail price, approximately 30% to 40% higher than the AWP. After deducting the co-pay, the insurance companies paid plaintiff. Plaintiff brought a breach of contract and fraud suit when he learned that the defendant did business with other benefits administrators and competed against plaintiff for customers. A jury awarded $1.12 million in compensatory damages and $1 million in punitive damages. Approximately $61,000 was awarded on a counterclaim against plaintiff.

HOLDING: In all major respects, the verdict was affirmed on appeal.

Pennsylvania Pharmacists Assoc. v Pennsylvania Dep't of Pub. Welfare
733 A.2d 666 (Pa. Commw. Ct. 1999)

Pennsylvania Pharmacists Association ("PPA") is a non-profit corporation representing over 440 pharmacists who own and operate independent pharmacies and over 1000 pharmacists employed there. Those pharmacies entered into agreements with the Department of Public Welfare ("DPW") to participate in the Medical Assistance Program. PPA petitioned for a declaration that all outpatient pharmacy rates implemented under a managed-care program known as "Health Choices" were implemented in violation of the law and the agreements were therefore, a nullity. DPW secured a waiver from certain provisions of Title XIX to implement Health Choices in five counties. PPA complained that DPW's method of implementing the Health Choices program permitted pharmacy benefits managers to systematically decrease outpatient pharmacy benefit rates to unreasonably low levels. PPA alleged that 229 of 448 independent pharmacies participating in Health Choices closed since its inception and that 35% of the 960 retail pharmacies originally participating in the plan have dropped out. PPA alleged that the rates were set below the cost of acquisition and of dispensing the drugs and resulted in a situation inconsistent with efficiency, economy, and quality of care. DPW first objected that the PPA failed to state a cause of action because no state or federal statute confers a right to a certain minimum payment. PPA responded that the DPW was still required to assure rates that were sufficient to enlist enough providers so that care and services were available at least to the same extent that they are available to the general population. The court agreed with PPA. DPW also alleged that PPA had no enforceable right to challenge DPW's administration of the health choices waiver. DPW asserted that Petitioners' sole remedies were to cease participation in the Health Choices program or to petition HCFA for review of their concerns. The court disagreed and concluded that PPA had a private right of action to enforce Section 1396a(a)(30)(A). Finally, DPW asserted that the court did not have jurisdiction because PPA failed to exhaust the available and adequate administrative remedies. PPA contended that exhaustion of administrative remedies was not required because the case did not require agency expertise and any proceeding before DPW would be futile. The court sustained DPW's objection and held that it did not have jurisdiction because PPA did not exhaust its administrative remedies. The court therefore dismissed the case without prejudice.

Harrow v Prudential Insurance Company of America
76 F.Supp.2d 558 (D.N.J. 1999)

Plaintiff filed a class action lawsuit in May 1998 for wrongful denial of insurance benefits in violation of ERISA after the insurance company denied coverage for his *Viagra* prescription following a diagnosis by his physician of impotence. (The original plaintiff died before a hearing on the claim could commence and he was replaced by his wife as administrator of his estate.) The plaintiff had to pay for his prescription in cash. The defendant moved to dismiss the claim on the basis that the plaintiff failed to exhaust administrative remedies. The plaintiff called the insurance company after the pharmacy informed him that Prudential denied coverage for the medication. He was told that the drug was not covered because it was new but that he should keep his receipt in case the company ever approved it. In June 1998, Prudential made a public statement that the drug would not be covered. During a deposition, a representative from the insurance company stated that *Viagra* claims would not be granted even after an internal appeal. The plaintiff opposed dismissal of the claim on the grounds that the administrative appeals process within Prudential would be futile. The trial court judge dismissed the case finding that the plaintiff had not exhausted administrative remedies. The mere allegation that an internal appeal would be futile does not meet the requirement that futility must be shown by clear and convincing evidence. The one telephone call made to the company to find out why the claim was initially denied does not constitute an internal complaint. The subsequent statement that Prudential would not cover the drug does not indicate that an appeal would be futile when there is no evidence that anyone ever tried to appeal denial of the claim.

The following is a list of court cases that are related to this topic.

Hofherr v Dart Industries, Inc., 853 F.2d 259 (4th Cir. 1988).
Albertson's Inc. v Florida Department of Professional Regulation, 1995 WL 405278 (Fla. App. 1 Dist., July 1, 1995).
Rockport Pharmacy Inc. v Digital Simplistics, Inc., 53 F.3d 195 (8th Cir. 1995).
Massachusetts v Stop and Shop Cos., Inc., No. 96-0104-8 (Mass. Sup. Ct., Jan. 5, 1996).
Texas Pharmacy Assn. v Prudential Life Insurance Co. of America, Slip Op. No. 95-50807 (Feb. 14, 1997 5th Cir.), 1997 U.S. App. LEXIS 2723.
Mutual Benefit Insurance v Haver, 725 A.2d 743 (Pa. 1999). Merck-Medco Managed Care v Rite Aid, Slip Op. No. 98-2847, Sept. 7, 1999,1999 U.S. App. LEXIS 21487 (4th Cir.).
Cecchanecchio v Continental Casualty, Slip Op No 00-4925 (November 15, 2001), USDC Pa., 2001 US Dist. LEXIS 18704.
Powers v Powers, Slip Op No E2001-0018-COA-R3-CV (November 29, 2001), 2001 Tenn. App. LEXIS 872.

Elements

Reliable Refuse & Recycling v Glastonbury Towne Pharmacy
Slip Op. No. CV 96556691. (Supr. Ct. Con., Feb. 11, 1997), 1997 Conn. Super. LEXIS 373

Plaintiff entered into a contract with the defendant pharmacy in November 1992 to remove its garbage for a period of 3 years at the rate of $390.88 per month. In February 1993, plaintiff reduced its price to $250.88 per month and again dropped the price to $150 per month in April 1995. The pharmacy paid the amount invoiced each month and, at the end of the 3-year term, elected not to renew the contract. Plaintiff sued the pharmacy claiming it should be entitled to the full amount due under the original agreement because it had an expectation that the contract would be renewed and that it had lowered its price for garbage hauling for that reason. It claimed that the price reductions were not supported by

Reliable Refuse & Recycling v Glastonbury Towne Pharmacy
Slip Op. No. CV 96556691. (Supr. Ct. Con., Feb. 11, 1997), 1997 Conn. Super. LEXIS 373
...continued

consideration and therefore the difference between the amount it billed and that called for
in the contract is due and owing. The court dismissed the claims because plaintiff unilaterally reduced the monthly payment amount when it became aware that the pharmacy was
considering someone else to handle its garbage. Plaintiff wanted to keep the pharmacy's
business because its location was an important and visible stop, which helped with plaintiff's advertising. The court concluded that plaintiff should not be paid the amount stated in
the original contract because it unilaterally reduced its price for its own benefit.

Fraud

RNH, Inc. v Beatty
571 So.2d 1039 (Ala.1990)

ISSUE: Whether a pharmacist who sold his pharmacy and later relocated to another downtown pharmacy could be guilty of fraud and misrepresentation.

FACTS: The evidence showed that prior to 1986, Billy Beatty worked as a pharmacist for
Price Drug Company. After 10 years, Beatty became a stockholder in Price Drug. In December of 1986, Beatty purchased City Drug, a competing pharmacy in downtown Montgomery. He retained his stock in Price Drug Company while he operated the competing pharmacy.

When the owner of Price Drug Company died, RNH, Inc., sought to acquire all of the stock
of Price Drug Company including that held by Beatty. A memorandum of understanding
was executed by the shareholders of Price Drug Company and a 91-page stock purchase agreement was presented to Beatty's attorney. His attorney advised Beatty that as the owner of
another pharmacy he could not sign the contract because of the "non-solicitation" clause and
the "preservation of organization" clause. Eventually Beatty signed the contract when he
was told that it meant he could not directly solicit customers by standing in front of Price
Drug.

The clauses of the stock purchase agreement that were in question provided that the sellers
agreed not to solicit the customers of Price Drug in any area within a 50-miles radius of
Montgomery County for a period of 5 years. Furthermore, it was agreed that the sellers would
not solicit any employee of Price Drug to leave his or her employment relationship for 5
years. The sellers further agreed to exercise their reasonable best efforts to preserve the good
will of the suppliers, customers, and others having a business relationship with Price Drug
so that they would continue to do business with the company.

At some point after the sale of Price Drug, Beatty moved City Drug to another building in
downtown Montgomery several blocks from its original location. Beatty said that his move
was made because the original City Drug building was deteriorating and that his landlord had
refused to make the premises suitable. RNH claimed this was a breach of the sales agreement.

RULING: The court ruled that there was no fraud and misrepresentation because the plaintiff and his attorney knew at the time the agreement was drafted and signed that the defendant was operating a pharmacy in direct competition with them.

RNH, Inc. v Beatty
571 So.2d 1039 (Ala.1990)
...continued

REASONING: The plaintiff contended that the new City Drug was larger than the old store and consequently, in the plaintiff's opinion, violated the agreement. However, the plaintiff testified that Beatty had not solicited customers, nor had he harmed the goodwill of Price Drug.

The court concluded that it was clear that Beatty did not violate the terms of the agreement. At the time the agreement was signed, the plaintiff was aware that Beatty had been in direct competition with Price Drug Company for 2 years and that he planned to remain in competition. Although this was of some concern to the plaintiff and his attorney, this concern was never conveyed to Beatty, and Beatty never agreed not to change his location.

The plaintiffs further contended that Beatty knew before he signed the contract that he would move City Drug. It was therefore argued that Beatty had a duty to disclose his plan to them. However, the court concluded that Beatty had no duty to disclose. The record showed clearly that the parties were knowledgeable businessmen dealing at arm's length and acting upon the advise of competent attorneys. When the agreement was negotiated and signed both sides inquired as to the competition aspect of the contract.

Massachusetts v Stop and Shop Cos., Inc.
No. 96-0104-8 (Mass. Sup. Ct., Jan. 5, 1996)

A Massachusetts-based supermarket chain agreed to pay more than $1 million to settle charges that the chain's pharmacy operations overcharged Medicaid programs in Massachusetts, Connecticut, and Rhode Island. The defendants agreed to reimburse the three States for their share of certain pharmaceutical promotional programs, to offer consumer-oriented wellness programs, and to institute a strict compliance program to prevent future occurrences. The charges against the defendants were brought by Attorneys General in the three States following a year-long investigation of the chain's pharmacy practices by the Massachusetts Medicaid Fraud Control Unit. The main issues of the dispute were certain promotional programs that offered repeat purchasers a set amount off the price of their eleventh prescription refill. The State officials charged that the defendants failed to offer the same discounts to State Medicaid programs and other incentive programs offered through the government. Additionally, the State examined a gift certificate program under which consumers were given certificates of up to $15 for filling new prescriptions with the defendant. Investigators alleged that some Medicaid consumers received cash after making small purchases with the gift certificate, yet the defendant still billed Medicaid for the prescriptions using improper codes. They also failed to properly retain prescription documentation required by law and billed for Medicaid prescriptions ordered but never picked up by Medicaid customers.

Zwerin v Maccabees Mutual Life Ins. Co.
111 F.3d 140 (10th Cir. 1997)

The pharmacist owned an independent community pharmacy n California. The pharmacy did quite well for several years. However, profits in the store eroded significantly between 1981 and 1983 and the pharmacy was robbed five times between 1978 and 1983. In 1984, the pharmacist moved to Palm Springs, a two-hour commute from the store. In 1982, he pur-

Zwerin v Maccabees Mutual Life Ins. Co.
111 F.3d 140 (10th Cir. 1997)
...continued

chased one disability insurance policy from Maccabees and two from Northwestern. In early 1983 he purchased six life insurance policies from Northwestern. The pharmacist filed his first disability claim with Northwestern in January 1985, very soon after the incontestability period kicked in. The claim indicated that he could not work as a pharmacist because he could not stand because of a blocked artery. The claim was supported by a medical opinion from a physician indicating that the pharmacist could not stand for prolonged periods. The pharmacist filed similar claims with Maccabees. Both companies began paying disability benefits in 1985, and the pharmacist collected up to $10,000 per month until the benefits were cut off by the companies in 1993. Northwestern also waived the premiums on the life insurance policies during this period. In October 1985, one of the insurers had the pharmacist examined by its own physician who concluded that the pharmacist was not disabled. Over the next several months, the pharmacist was examined by two more insurance company physicians who found no evidence of vascular disease or disability. After this, the pharmacist's own physician changed the diagnosis to a torn ligament, back injuries from being kicked while the pharmacy was robbed and paranoia about future robberies. The physician then indicated that the disability would last indefinitely. The pharmacist stated that he could not walk more than two blocks at a time, that it was difficult for him to drive, that he could not stand for more than 20 minutes, and could not tolerate lifting any weight. Two more insurance company physicians examined the pharmacist and concluded that there was no disability. The pharmacist moved to Wyoming in November 1991 and found a new physician, this time a well-known orthopedic surgeon, who rendered an opinion in September 1992 indicating that the patient remained totally disabled because of post-traumatic stress syndrome. The physician changed his opinion, however, after the insurance companies showed him surveillance videos with the pharmacist engaged in strenuous physical activities. By September 1993, both companies terminated benefits. The pharmacist sued both companies in federal district court claiming that they terminated his benefits in "bad faith." Northwestern filed a countersuit against the pharmacist claiming that he had committed fraud in obtaining the disability benefits. During trial, the pharmacist admitted that he had filled out the majority of the physician statements supporting his disability and that the physicians just signed the reports. He admitted that he engaged in hiking, horseback riding, tennis, football, walking, and jogging while claiming to be disabled. His ex-wife testified that the pharmacist did not moderate any of these activities after he filed for disability and that he kept a cane in the closet to use if an investigator came to the door. She indicated that the pharmacist never complained of pain or discomfort. The pharmacist's son testified that his father would not play basketball with him if he thought anyone was watching. The jury verdict went against the pharmacist and in favor of Northwestern's restitution claims. The verdict against the pharmacist was $971,299, and the judge added pre-judgment interest and fees that increased the judgment to $1,349,067. The jury verdict was upheld on appeal.

United Healthcare Insurance Co. and AARP v Advance PCS
Slip Op No 02-1790 (November 1, 2002), 8th Cir., 2002 US App. LEXIS 22707

When an insurance company recently began to administer the American Association of Retired Persons' (AARP) pharmacy services, it terminated the Prescription Drug Manager's (PBM's) services and sent AARP program participants new cards and code numbers. The PBM continued to process claims that involved the old code numbers it assigned to AARP participants without notifying them. The insurance company and AARP sued a PBM alleging violations of the Minnesota Deceptive Trade Practices Act, MSA § 325D.43 et seq. Based

United Healthcare Insurance Co. and AARP v Advance PCS
Slip Op No 02-1790 (November 1, 2002), 8th Cir., 2002 US App. LEXIS 22707
...continued

on affidavits alone, the US District Court for the District of Minnesota preliminarily enjoined the PBM from processing certain drug discount claims. The PBM appealed. The appellate court found that the district court did not clearly err in finding that an adverse drug reaction as a result of divergent prescription information held by the PBM and the insurance company constituted a threat of irreparable harm in the AARP's potential loss of reputation and goodwill among its customers. Because the PBM's processing of AARP participants' claims using old code numbers without their consent was likely to deceive them into believing that they received AARP services, the district court did not err when if found that the AARP and the insurance company were likely to succeed on the merits of their "passing off" claim under the Minnesota law. Thus, the grant of the preliminary injunction was upheld.

The following is a list of court cases that are related to this topic.

Greenwald v LeMon, No. 2000-00853 (November 6, 2000), 2000 NY App LEXIS 11182.

Corporate and Individual Liability

Thrift Drug v Universal Prescription Administrators
131 F.3d 95 (2nd Cir. 1997)

ISSUE: May the sole shareholder of a corporation engaged in providing prescription drug benefits be held personally liable for corporate debts owed to a pharmacy?

FACTS: Universal Prescription Administrators (UPA) is a corporation owned in whole by a single shareholder. As a prescription benefits administrator, UPA enters into contracts with pharmacies to dispense prescription drugs to eligible recipients and send the bill to UPA. The plaintiff pharmacy and UPA entered into an agreement in 1980. Due to a cash flow problem in 1991, UPA failed to pay the plaintiff's invoices. The pharmacy terminated the agreement and sued UPA for breach of contract.

HOLDING: The trial court entered a summary judgment for the pharmacy in the amount of $59,472. After a bench trial, the judge ruled that the pharmacy could "pierce the corporate veil" of UPA and collect the judgment from the assets of UPA's sole shareholder. The liability portion of the judgment was upheld on appeal. The order allowing the pharmacy to collect damages from the individual shareholder was reversed and remanded back to the trial court for further proceedings.

REASONING: On appeal, the defendants claimed ERISA preempted the breach of contract claim brought under state law because the prescription claims are actually benefits of ERISA-sponsored plans. The Court of Appeals rejected this argument, finding that the pharmacy sought reimbursement for products it dispensed under a valid contract. Defendants also claimed that the amount of the judgment was in error because not all of plaintiff's claims were submitted within the 30-day time limit required by the agreement. The Court of Appeals also rejected this claim because the district court judge was well within his discretion to calculate the amount of damages. Finally, defendants objected to the ruling allowing the pharmacy to seek payment from the shareholder instead of the corporation. Under New York law, an individual shareholder may be held liable for corporate liabilities when the individual exercises complete domination over the corporation and uses the corpora-

Thrift Drug v Universal Prescription Administrators
131 F.3d 95 (2nd Cir. 1997)
...continued

tion to commit a fraud or some other wrongful act to the harm of the plaintiff. The Court of Appeals found that while the individual shareholder did exercise complete domination over UPA, there was no finding that he did so to defraud the pharmacy or to cause it to suffer the damages at hand. Accordingly, the Court of Appeals reversed this part of the ruling.

Leases and Restrictive Covenants

Providence Square v GDF
No 99-1246 (May 3, 2000), 4th Cir, 2000 US App LEXIS 8631

A pharmacy negotiated a lease with a landlord, Providence Square Associates in 1977 for space to operate a drugstore as an anchor tenant in a shopping center. The lease also indicated that a national chain food store would be another anchor tenant. The drugstore lease also provided that no other drugstore operations would be permitted in the shopping center. This exclusivity clause lists specific liquidated damages to be paid by the landlord in the event of a breach. Rite-Aid assumed the lease from the prior drugstore. In 1996, the original supermarket left the shopping center and a new food store, Hannaford, negotiated a new lease with Providence Square. The new lease provided that Hannaford was prohibited from operating a pharmacy in the shopping center to the extent that the Rite-Aid lease foreclosed it from doing so. Nevertheless, Hannaford began remodeling the supermarket space and began constructing a pharmacy area within it. Rite-Aid heard rumors about this and requested Providence Square to take action to prevent Hannaford from operating its pharmacy. Providence Square unsuccessfully attempted to negotiate an indemnification agreement with Hannaford to hold Providence Square harmless from any damages sought by Rite-Aid for breach of its lease. Hannaford opened its "Food and Drug Superstore" with a full service pharmacy in June 1998. Four months after opening, the Hannaford pharmacy was averaging approximately $31,000 in monthly sales, which represented 2.3% of the total supermarket sales for that period. Rite-Aid's pharmacy volume declined at approximately the same amount during this time. In lawsuits involving all three parties, the federal district court judge ruled that Hannaford was not violating Rite-Aid's lease by operating a pharmacy within the supermarket. That Court also ruled that the 2.3% of business representing Hannaford's pharmacy income was incidental to the supermarket operations. Hannaford argued that the Rite-Aid lease prohibits operation of any other "drugstore" within the shopping center and that Hannaford is a supermarket that has a "pharmacy" located within it. The Court of Appeals reversed, noting there is no practical distinction between a "pharmacy" and a "drugstore." The Court indicated that it must be guided by the substance of the operation, not its label. The Court of Appeals also ruled that the district court erred by focusing on the percentage of pharmacy income generated by Hannaford compared to its overall income. Instead the focus should have been on the fact that $30,000 per month is not incidental from any perspective especially considering that the Rite-Aid store generated a total of approximately $55,000 per month after Hannaford opened.

The following is a list of court cases that are related to this topic.

Eckerd v Corners Group, 786 So, 2d 588 (Fla. App., 2001).
Eckerd v Zaremba Land Development, (Slip Op. No. 5D00-3389, August 3, 2001 Fla. App. LEXIS 10926.

Third Party Reimbursement

American Society of Consultant Pharmacists v Patla
Slip Op. No. 00 C 7821 (February 27, 2001), USDC ND Ill., 2001 US Dist. LEXIS 2061

Plaintiffs were providers of pharmacy services to Medicaid recipients in long-term care facilities. Plaintiffs were reimbursed by defendant department of public aid. Pursuant to an emergency rule, defendant department implemented a new reimbursement formula that reduced the rate the state would reimburse the pharmacies. Plaintiffs sued, claiming that, under the new formula, such rates of reimbursement were unreasonably low and would result in pharmacies going out of business. Defendants moved to dismiss the lawsuit on Eleventh Amendment immunity grounds. The court held (1) plaintiffs' Medicaid Act claim against defendant department was barred under the Eleventh Amendment; (2) plaintiffs' Medicaid Act claim against defendant director was not barred, and (3) plaintiffs' state law claim under the Illinois Public Aid Code was barred by the Eleventh Amendment since this claim would require determinations of state law regarding decisions by state officials that were a matter of comity better left to the state courts.

American Society of Consultant Pharmacists v Garner
Slip Op. No. 00 C 7821 (August 8, 2001), USDC ND Ill., 2001 US Dist. LEXIS 11798

This is the same case as above denying a motion for injunctive relief. The court determined that while pharmacies had a right of action to assert that the state's newly adopted reimbursement formula for brand name, generic, and OTC drugs violated federal Medicaid law requiring the reimbursement to be "reasonable" *42 U.S.C. § 1396a(a)30(A)*, the pharmacies failed to establish a likelihood of prevailing on that claim sufficient to support a preliminary injunction. The court stated new rates must stand or fall on whether access to pharmacies and pharmacy services is actually diminished because a number of pharmacies will not accept unreasonable reimbursement. The pharmacies could not prove a violation merely by predicting a diminished level of access and quality of care.

Pennsylvania Pharmacists Association v Houston
283 F.3d 531 (3d Cir. 2002), USDC E Penn, 2000 US Dist LEXIS 7807

The PPA brought suit against the state's Public Welfare Department, claiming that the Department had set pharmacy reimbursement rates for a Medicaid managed care program it operates in violation of federal laws. The claim alleged that the pharmacy outpatient reimbursement rates were set below the cost of the acquisition and dispensing drugs to eligible Medicaid patients. The district court considered several relevant factors including the number of pharmacies participating in the plan and the ability of Medicaid patients to access pharmacy services. The court concluded there is no right under the Social Security Act for providers to be reimbursed for costs to be reasonable or adequate. Recognizing that while independent pharmacies are finding it difficult to maintain any level of profits, the Court also considered that the state has difficulties in providing Medicaid benefits to eligible

Pennsylvania Pharmacists Association v Houston
283 F.3d 531 (3d Cir. 2002), USDC E Penn, 2000 US Dist LEXIS 7807
...continued

patients with its limited economic resources. The court ruled against the PPA and entered judgment for the defendants.

Wal-Mart Stores v Knickrehm
No 4:00CV00359GTE (June 7, 2000), USDC E Ark, 2000 US Dist LEXIS 8070

Wal-Mart and Walgreens sought an injunction from the federal district court to prevent implementation by the Arkansas Medicaid program of a two-tier reimbursement scheme scheduled to go into effect in April 2000. The plan would reimburse "chain" pharmacies at AWP minus 17.3% plus a dispensing fee of $5.51 for each Medicaid prescription. It would pay "independent" pharmacies at the rate of AWP less 10.5% plus a dispensing fee of $5.51. Approximately 75% of the state's pharmacies are independents. The controlling law, 42 USC §1396a(a)(30)(A) requires that reimbursement rates must be set to assure that payments to providers are efficient, economic, result in quality care and will assure reasonable access to health care for patients. The state had relied on surveys done in other states with two-tier pricing schemes to determine the acquisition cost rates. It also asserted, without any actual evidence, that it is common knowledge that the chains obtain "secret" rebates from manufacturers that lower actual acquisition costs. The Court determined that the state had not considered the relevant factors in setting the cost determinations and that it had violated federal law by relying on data from other states in determining its own reimbursement rates. The Court granted the injunction and ordered that the state reimburse chain pharmacies at the same level it pays independent pharmacies.

Walgreen v Hood
Slip Op No 01-30314 (December 20, 2001), 5th Cir., 2001 US App. LEXIS 26929

The pharmacy appealed a judgment of the federal trial court denying its motion for a preliminary injunction barring the Department of Health and Hospitals from using tiered Medicaid pharmacy reimbursement rates to calculate payments to pharmacies serving Louisiana Medicaid recipients allegedly in violation of 42 USC§ 30(A) requiring the reimbursement rate to be "reasonable." The trial court determined that there was no substantial likelihood that the pharmacy would prevail on the merits because it did not have to remedy violations of that statute. The appeals court affirmed the trial court on that ground because the pharmacy is not an intended beneficiary of the statute. The statute does not create an entitlement for individual providers to a particular level of payment because it does not directly address those providers.

Jones v Howell
(Miss. 2002), 2002 WL 1381050

A taxpayer brought this lawsuit against a pharmacist and a member of the Mississippi House of Representatives. The taxpayer alleged that the pharmacist had a conflict of interest in violation of the Mississippi Constitution because the pharmacist had participated in the Leg-

Jones v Howell
(Miss. 2002), 2002 WL 1381050
...continued

islature's appropriation of funds to the Mississippi Division of Medicaid and also received Medicaid funds as a pharmacist. Another legislator-pharmacist intervened as a party-defendant and the Mississippi Ethics Commission was joined as a plaintiff by court order. The chancellor found constitutional violations and enjoined the legislators' further receipt of Medicaid funds. On appeal, the Mississippi supreme court noted that the issue was the proper interpretation of Article 4, Section 109 of the Mississippi Constitution. The court reviewed the statutory language and the purpose of Section 109, ie, to instill public confidence in the integrity of government and to remove any temptation to invade its proscription. The court found that the legislators' interest in Medicaid appropriations was so remote as to remove them from the purpose of Section 109. Specifically, the court accepted the legislators' argument that no decision they could make in voting on a Medicaid appropriation bill would affect the amount of reimbursements they receive. They could not negotiate a contract with the state for a better or different price to charge because the rates for prescription drugs were fixed by law. Additionally, the individual Medicaid recipients were entitled to choose to purchase drugs from any pharmacy before the state was obligated to pay the provider, and the legislators have absolutely no control over this individual consumer choice. The court also reviewed the provider participation agreements, finding them to be a means of providing financial aid to the needy, and not the type of contracts contemplated by Section 109. The court noted that the legislators' salaries were not linked to or based upon the amount of Medicaid reimbursements their pharmacies received. Although a true conflict of interest would exist if the legislators had used their position in the Legislature to gain special privileges that were not available to all others in their class, that was not the case here, as they received no special preference over other pharmacists in the field. Because the legislators were not in a position to advance the rights and benefits for themselves beyond those provided to other members in their professional class, the court held that the legislators were not in violation of Section 109 and were not required to reimburse the state for funds accepted during their roles as Medicaid providers through their pharmacies' participation in the Medicaid program.

National Association of Chain Drug Stores (NACDS) v Thompson
Slip Op No 01-1554 (PLF) (November 8, 2001) USDC DC, 2001 US Dist. 18411
(affirming the preliminary injunction preventing implementation of the Bush administration's plan to adopt a Medicare Discount Prescription Drug Card plan).

EDITOR'S NOTE

On January 29, 2003, the US District Court for the District of Columbia granted the request for an injunction made by the NACDS and the National Community Pharmacists Association (NCPA) regarding the administration's Medicare-endorsed PBM (pharmacy benefit manager) prescription discount card initiative. The trial court judge issued an oral opinion from the bench enjoining the administration's second attempt at instituting a Medicare-endorsed PBM prescription drug discount card program. The original suit was filed in response to the original proposal and alleged lack of legislative authority on the part of the administration, violations of the Administrative Procedures Act and the Federal Advisory Committee Act, and an unlawful delegation of regulatory power to a private consortium by the administration in designing the plan.

The following is a list of court cases that are related to this topic.

Indiana Family and Social Services Administration v Walgreen, Slip Op No 49S00-0112-CV-647
(May 28, 2002) S Ct IN, 2002 Ind. LEXIS 460.

State Mandated Rebates

Pharmaceutical Research and Manufacturers of America (PhRMA) v Michigan Department of Community Health
Slip Op No 238862 (December 13, 2002), 2002 Mich. App. LEXIS 1994

The department responsible for administering the Medicaid program in Michigan announced
plans to implement a new requirement that manufacturers of certain drugs agree to provide "supplemental rebates" to the state for drugs dispensed to eligible recipients. If the manufacturers of the affected drugs do not agree to pay the rebates, providers would have to
obtain "preauthorization" from the state before the drugs would be paid for. PhRMA moved
for and obtained a preliminary injunction to prevent implementation of the program on the
grounds that it was unconstitutional and not authorized under the federal statutes governing Medicaid. The state appealed. The Court of Appeals found that there were no prohibitions in federal law preventing states from seeking additional rebates from manufacturers.
It also determined that the preauthorization scheme did not violate the separation of powers doctrine in the US Constitution. Accordingly, the Court of Appeals reversed the
injunction and allowed the state program to be implemented.

Pharmaceutical Research and Manufacturers of America (PhRMA) v Thompson
Slip Op No 02-5110 (December 24, 2002), 313 F.3d 600 (DC App.); 2002 U.S. App. LEXIS 27252

PhRMA challenged a Medicaid demonstration project administered by the State of Maine
in conjunction with the federal Medicaid program. However, unlike the federal arrangement, Maine's program offered low-income citizens not eligible for Medicaid a discount on
prescription drugs. The US District Court for the District of Columbia rejected the association's challenge and granted summary judgment for the Secretary. The Court of Appeals
found that Maine's initial version of the disputed demonstration program was explicitly pat-
terned after Vermont's program. After a court decision finding Vermont's program unlawful,
Maine modified its program, adding a 2% state contribution to the manufacturer rebates to
avoid the fate of Vermont's program. 42 U.S.C.S. §1315(a) of the Social Security Act
required the Department of Health and Human Services to approve all Medicaid demonstration projects. All parties agreed that the Secretary had never formally considered or endorsed
Maine's revised program that included the 2% contribution. Therefore, the revised program was not properly before the court for review. To the extent that the modified Maine program purported to be different from the flawed Vermont program, it had yet to be considered
or approved by the federal government. The only program from Maine that the Secretary had endorsed was one identical to the Vermont program that had been found unlawful. Therefore, the judgment of the district court was reversed, and judgment was entered for
PhRMA.

The following is a list of court cases that are related to this topic.

American Society of Consultant Pharmacists v Concannon, 214 F.Supp. 2d 23 (D. Me. 2002).

Education

Basile v Albany College of Pharmacy
No. 87744 (January 11, 2001), 2001 NY App Div LEXIS 288.

Two fourth year pharmacy students were found guilty by a College honors committee of cheating on examinations in various courses over a 2-year period as charged by various professors. As a result, they were expelled from the college. A third student was also found to be involved in cheating and given a failing grade in a single course. The evidence in support of the charges consisted of compilations by various professors showing that petitioners gave the same incorrect answers to multiple choice examinations. There were two anonymous notes, one of which claimed that two of the students requested information concerning the contents of exams and the second questioning whether the same two students were cheating. In addition, there were similar answers to questions which required calculations, although each student utilized different calculations uncorrelated to the answer arrived at. The students filed suit to reverse the College's action. The trial court dismissed the claims and the students appealed. The Appeals Court reversed, holding that the College's determinations that the students cheated on various examinations had no rational basis. The determinations were based solely on a statistical compilation, which was based upon false assumptions. The other allegations of cheating were either hearsay anonymous notes or based on sheer speculation.

Richmond v Fowlkes
228 F. 3d 845 (8th Cir, October 2, 2000), 2000 US App LEXIS 24822

The plaintiff enrolled in the University of Arkansas College of Pharmacy in 1993 and successfully completed five semesters in an eight semester curriculum. In evaluating academic progression, the College utilizes "non-cognitive evaluations," reports submitted by a professor about a student's performance in a course in areas such as preparedness, maturity in interpersonal relations, timeliness, and various other attributes of professionalism considered "non-cognitive," but relevant to the academic development of future pharmacists. A professor makes an evaluation of each student's non-cognitive performance, but a report is filed only for those students who perform exceptionally and for those who perform inadequately. A student may be dismissed by the College for receiving two negative non-cognitive evaluations. During the spring semester of the plaintiff's third year, two of his professors submitted negative non-cognitive evaluations for his behavior, which included the failure of basic examinations, sleeping in and lack of preparation for class, and inappropriate commentary during class. The student was given a chance to respond and gave assurances that his behavior would not be repeated. The student was put on probation and informed that another negative evaluation would result in dismissal. In June of 1996, university police officers reported to a College administrator that the student had been drinking, playing loud music, and yelling in the hallway of his residence hall. The administrator referred the student to a committee that deals with addiction problems, but did not report the incident to the committee that had placed the student on probation. Subsequently, in the fall of 1996, the student successfully completed the four clinical rotation courses of his seventh semester in the program. During his final rotation he fell behind in his work, was late or did not report for work several times. He was warned by his supervisor that the behavior would result in dismissal from the rotation and a negative evaluation would be given if repeated. His erratic behavior continued and the supervisor dismissed him from the rotation and informed the College of this action. The College notified the student that it would hold a hearing on his situation. The student appeared at the hearing and the College outlined a course of remedial action necessary to complete to avoid dismissal from the program. The student was asked

Richmond v Fowlkes
228 F. 3d 845 (8th Cir, October 2, 2000), 2000 US App LEXIS 24822
...continued

to sign the action plan, but failed to do so by the date indicated. He was then dismissed from the college. He sued, claiming violation of due process and equal protection. The trial court dismissed the claims and the student appealed. The Court of Appeals affirmed finding that the College conducted fair hearing and awarded him all of the consideration and due process necessary. The College was careful and deliberate in reviewing the circumstances and gave the student several opportunities for remedial correction of his problems.

Discriminatory Pricing

Witt v Aetna US Healthcare
No 00-31-B-C (September 14, 2000), USDC ME, 2000 US Dist LEXIS 13264

Plaintiffs are two independent pharmacies who provide pharmacy services to defendant-Aetna's insureds pursuant to Pharmacy Services Agreements. Defendant Express Scripts, Inc. (ESI) and Aetna entered into an agreement in 1996 providing ESI an exclusive right to provide mail-order pharmacy services to Aetna's insureds. Patients who use the ESI service pay lower co-payments and are able to get larger quantities of medications than at the plaintiff pharmacies. Other pharmacies located in rural parts of Maine are also paid higher dispensing fees than plaintiffs. After complaints by the pharmacists, the Maine Insurance Bureau concluded that Aetna's arrangement with ESI violated the state's Third Party Prescription Program Act, 32 MRSA §§13771-13777 in that local pharmacies are not able to dispense medications on the same terms available to mail-order pharmacies. Aetna and the Insurance Bureau entered into a Consent Agreement to resolve the findings. The plaintiffs filed this civil lawsuit. Aetna moved to have it dismissed. In this Opinion a magistrate recommends that the district court judge dismiss the claims for violations of the Maine Insurance Code and the Third Party Prescription Program Act. This recommendation is premised on the conclusion that those statutes do not give plaintiffs a private cause of action. The magistrate, however, recommends against dismissal of the remaining counts for violation of the state's Deceptive Trade Practice Act, fraudulent misrepresentation, and interference with a business expectancy or advantageous relationship. The magistrate found the allegations in each of these counts to be plead with sufficient detail and clarity as to state a cause of action.

Langford v Rite-Aid of Alabama
231 F. 3d 1308 (11th Cir, 2000)

Several plaintiffs who were regular uninsured customers of defendant pharmacy appealed an order of the federal trial court in Alabama dismissing their claims under the Racketeer Influenced and Corrupt Organizations Act, 18 U.S.C. § 1961 et seq., alleging that the pharmacy violated federal mail and wire fraud statutes, 18 U.S.C. §§ 1341, 1343 by charging them higher prices for medication than it charged its insured customers, and failing to disclose that fact. Plaintiffs claimed that Rite-Aid maintained a policy of charging the uninsured higher prices for prescription medication, and failed to disclose this fact to its uninsured consumers. Rite-Aid allegedly implemented this policy in three ways: (a) through an online computer network that would automatically increase the price of prescription drugs once the operator noted that the customer was uninsured, (b) through managerial and staff train-

Langford v Rite-Aid of Alabama
231 F. 3d 1308 (11th Cir, 2000)
...continued

ing policies that ensured that employees would know to increase the retail price for uninsured consumers, and (c) through Rite-Aid's intensive monitoring of the extent to which its
individual pharmacies participated in "up-charging" individual consumers through the online
computer system. Plaintiffs charged that this pricing policy and its implementation were
little more than fraudulent attempts to prey upon the vulnerabilities of uninsured consumers. The trial court determined that the pharmacy had no affirmative duty to disclose its
pricing practices, and that silence in the absence of a duty to speak could not constitute fraud.
The trial court relied almost exclusively upon state common law in coming to its conclusion. Dismissal was affirmed by the Court of Appeals, because the plaintiffs failed to show that
the pharmacy had a duty to disclose its pricing scheme, and, therefore, could not show that
defendants committed the predicate acts of mail fraud and wire fraud. The Court stated
that consumers have the appropriate incentives to obtain information about acceptable cost
of consumer goods, and to make purchases from the retailer who most closely matches that
price. Retailers are not expected to disclose information about their pricing schemes because
consumers are best able to gather pricing information and put it to its highest and best use. If
uninsured consumers were somehow less able to shop around and identify attractive drug
prices than were other consumers, the situation may have demanded that Rite-Aid make certain disclosures to them. However, uninsured consumers are just as capable of seeking and
using information as are others. In fact, because the uninsured are shouldering the entire cost
of their prescription drug needs, they have even more powerful incentives than insured consumers do to actively obtain information about retail drug prices. Rite-Aid's failure to disclose its pricing practices seems less an element of a fraudulent scheme than a powerful
argument for uninsured consumers to seek another pharmacy that makes some effort to retain
their business. As to the relationship between a pharmacist and a patient, the Court noted:

> It is true that pharmacists and their patients share an intimate bond, and that rela-
> tionship gives rise to certain duties on the part of the pharmacist. However, plaintiffs
> have been unable to identify a case or persuasive authority holding that pharma-
> cists have a duty to disclose their parent company's pricing structure with regard to pre-
> scription drugs. Pharmacists owe duties to their patients ranging from diligence in
> recommending medication to confidentiality in maintaining patient's records; how-
> ever, nothing in their professional code of conduct suggests, even obliquely, that phar-
> macists violate that duty by not disclosing the pricing policies of their pharmacy.
> Nothing in the record suggests that Rite-Aid's pharmacists breached their code of con-
> duct in any way, and we decline to infer the duty to disclose plaintiffs seek in this
> case.

Promissory Notes

Greenwald v LeMon
No. 2000-00853 (November 6, 2000), 2000 NY App LEXIS 11182

The plaintiffs sold a pharmacy to the defendant. The written contract set forth a purchase
price of $350,000. The defendant paid $10,000 in cash and executed two promissory notes
in the sums of $170,000 at the closing to constitute the purchase price. He also executed two
promissory notes in the sums of $50,000 to the plaintiffs in exchange for covenants not to
compete. The security agreement executed in connection with the sale indicated that
there was a "total indebtedness in the amount of $440,000.00 with interest," listing the four

Greenwald v LeMon
No. 2000-00853 (November 6, 2000), 2000 NY App LEXIS 11182
...continued

promissory notes. The promissory notes were signed in the presence of counsel and witnessed by a notary public. After the closing, outside the presence of counsel, the defendant executed two additional notes in which he promised to pay each plaintiff an additional sum of $137,500. These notes consisted of a single handwritten sheet and were not witnessed by a notary public. The defendant made payments on the six notes from August 1997 through October 1998. His records consisted of typewritten amortization schedules for the two notes of $170,000 and the two notes of $50,000, reflecting the payment date, beginning balance, payment amount, principal reduction, interest paid, and ending balance. The second record was a handwritten schedule of cash payments made to the plaintiffs on the two notes of $137,500 executed after the closing. At their depositions, both the plaintiffs testified that they did not report the cash payments on their income tax returns. The plaintiffs commenced this action to recover on the six promissory notes and moved for summary judgment. The defendants opposed the motion, arguing that the two notes executed after the closing were void for lack of consideration and as against public policy since the amount reflected in the closing documents was $450,000. In reply, the plaintiffs submitted an affidavit stating that "the actual price was $725,000.00, as agreed, with $450,000.00 reflected in the attorney drawn legal documents and $275,000 in the 'under the table' notes." The trial court granted summary judgment to the plaintiffs on the issue of liability and set the matter down for an inquest on the issue of damages. On appeal, that decision was reversed. The Court noted that the evidence indicates that the sale of the pharmacy may have been structured to avoid the payment of income taxes. The documents drafted by the attorneys did not reflect the alleged full purchase price of the business, since the two notes at issue were executed "under the table" after the closing. The Court noted that while agreements providing for the evasion of tax payments are not per se unenforceable, the defense of illegality should be resolved.

Any Willing Provider

Reeves-Sain Medical v Blue Cross Blue Shield of Tennessee
No. M2000-00182-COA-R3-CV (October 10, 2000), Tenn App.

A state statute, Tennessee Code Ann. § 56-7-2359, prevents a health insurance issuer from excluding any licensed pharmacy or pharmacist from its list of participating providers if the pharmacy or pharmacist agrees to the terms and conditions offered to other participating providers. The trial court held that the statute also required Blue Cross Blue Shield of Tennessee to include all licensed pharmacies or pharmacists in their list of home infusion therapy providers and that the only condition the insurer could impose was a pharmacist's license and held the defendant in contempt for a technical violation of its rulings. The Court of Appeals reversed. After examining the "any willing provider" statute, the Court determined that it did not extend to home infusion services. In doing so, the court noted that, "a license to practice pharmacy does not empower pharmacists to inject drugs into a patient. A pharmacy license covers the pharmaceutical component of home infusion therapy, but by its terms it does not cover the non-pharmaceutical component. Therefore, the statute does not prevent the defendant from imposing additional requirements on the non-pharmaceutical component of home infusion therapy."

PART VII: ANTITRUST AND RELATED TRADE LAWS

Federal Antitrust Law

Abbott Laboratories, et al v Portland Retail Druggists Association
425 U.S. 1 (1976)

ISSUE: Whether drugs purchased at referential prices may be dispensed by nonprofit hospitals in competition with community pharmacies.

FACTS: A pharmaceutical association, on behalf of some 60 community pharmacies, brought suit in federal court against 12 pharmaceutical manufacturers, charging them with violating the Robinson-Patman Price Discrimination Act. It was claimed that the drug makers violated Sec. 13(a) of Title 15 of the U.S. Code when they sold drugs to nonprofit hospital pharmacies at lower prices than those charged to their retail pharmacy customers. Section 13(a) makes it unlawful for one engaged in commerce to "discriminate in price between different purchases of like commodities when among other things, the effect of such discrimination may be substantially to lessen competition." The association sought treble damages and an injunction (court order) prohibiting the alleged price discrimination.

As a defense, the drug makers claimed that the Federal Nonprofit Institutions Act of 1938 (52 Stat 446) modified the Robinson-Patman Act by adding Sec. 13(c), which exempted the purchases of their supplies for their own use by schools...hospitals and charitable institutions not operated for profit. Consequently, the issue in this case was the interpretation put on the words "for their own use."

On one hand, it was argued that the section 13(c) exemption, "for their own use," encompassed a broad variety of uses, including the dispensing of drugs by the hospital pharmacy for: Hospital inpatient treatment, employee or student prescriptions, take-home prescriptions for discharged patients, staff physician drug purchases, and the so-called occasional "walk-in" customer prescriptions. The federal District Court (trial court) went along with this view and summarily dismissed the complaint. But on appeal, a Federal Appeals court overruled the trial court and gave a restrictive meaning to the term "for their own use." The appeals court ruling held that the 13(c) exemption applied only to drugs dispensed for hospital inpatient treatment and emergency patient treatment.

RULING: On further appeal, the U.S. Supreme court overruled the Federal Appeals Court and sent the case back to the trial court for a new determination in accord with certain guidelines issued in the Supreme Court decision.

REASONING: In making its decision, the Supreme Court held that not all of the nonprofit hospital's purchases were exempt from the Robinson-Patman Act. Instead, the test was that only those purchases by the hospitals "for their own use" were exempt and the term meant "...what may reasonably be regarded as use by the hospital in the sense that such use is a part of and promotes the hospital's intended institutional operation in the care of persons who are its patients."

Therefore, a drug supplier could sell drugs to nonprofit hospital pharmacies at a lower price and not violate the antitrust law if the drugs are dispensed in the following situations:

    (1) To the inpatient for use in his treatment at the hospital;
    (2) To the patient admitted to the hospital's emergency facility for use in the patient's treatment there;
    (3) To the outpatient for personal use on the hospital premises;
    (4) To the inpatient, outpatient, or emergency facility patient upon discharge and for his personal use away from the premises provided the "take-home prescrip-

Abbott Laboratories, et al v Portland Retail Druggists Association
425 U.S. 1 (1976)
...continued

        tion" is intended for a limited and reasonable time, as a continuation of, or supplemental to, the treatment administered at the hospital;

      (5) To hospital employee or student for personal use, or for use of his dependent;

      (6) To staff physician for his personal use, or for use of his dependents.

Not covered within the 13(c) exemption are drugs dispensed by hospital pharmacies in the following situations: (1) to refill the prescription of the discharged inpatient, outpatient or emergency facility patient; (2) to fill the prescription of the walk-in patient who has no present connection with the hospital or its pharmacy (except the occasional emergency prescription); and sales of drugs to physicians for their private practice or for use by nondependents.

In the written opinion, the court indicated that a drug supplier could avoid antitrust liability by a reasonable and noncollusive reliance on the proper certification by the nonprofit hospital customer as to its dispensation of the products purchased from the supplier.

The court further indicated two ways the hospital pharmacy could comply with the certification. It could choose not to dispense drugs in any way outside the exemptions of Sec. 13(c), or it could establish recordkeeping procedures and segregate the nonexempt use from the exempt use and appropriately account for such to the drug supplier.

Group Life & Health Insurance Co., et al v Royal Drug Company, et al
440 U.S. 205 (1979)

ISSUE: In this court case, the U.S. Supreme Court dealt only with the threshold question of whether third party prescription payment agreements (called herein by the court as "pharmacy agreements") are exempt from the federal antitrust laws under the exemption granted by Sec. 2(b) of the McCarran-Ferguson Act, which granted an exemption to the "business of insurance."

FACTS: The background information on this case is that Blue Shield offered its policyholders a prescription payment plan whereby participating pharmacies in Texas accepted a "pharmacy agreement" from Blue Shield and policyholders would then pay on $2 for each prescription filled at the participating pharmacies. Blue Shield would reimburse the participating pharmacies their actual acquisition cost for the drugs dispensed on the prescriptions. If the policyholder took his/her prescription to a nonparticipating pharmacy, the insured would pay the pharmacy the full price charged by it for the prescription and Blue Shield would reimburse the policyholder for 75% of the difference between that price and $2.

The dispute arose from the fact that only pharmacies for which the #2 markup (price paid by policyholder to participating pharmacy) was profitable could, from a business standpoint, participate in the plan. The nonparticipating pharmacies were, in effect, not participating because they couldn't do so profitably on a $2 over acquisition cost markup. These pharmacies would have Blue Shield pay them their actual and customary charge per prescription (less the $2 paid by the customer) — if Blue Shield wanted their participation.

Consequently, some of the pharmacies in Texas joined the Blue Shield pharmacy agreement and some did not. Those that did participate would then be most likely discriminated upon by the Blue Shield policyholder since he/she would have paid full price for the pre-

Group Life & Health Insurance Co., et al v Royal Drug Company, et al
440 U.S. 205 (1979)
...continued

scription at the nonparticipating pharmacy and would then have taken steps to try to collect at least 75% of the difference between full price and $2. The nonparticipating pharmacies then claimed the net result would be "price-fixing" and an anticompetitive scheme against them in violation of the Sherman Act.

The mathematics of the situation are important to fully understand this case. For example: If the usual and customary charge for a certain prescription is $10 among both participating and nonparticipating pharmacies and the acquisition cost is $8, the insured pays the participating pharmacy $2 and the nonparticipating pharmacy $10 for the same prescription. The participating pharmacy is then reimbursed $8 acquisition cost from Blue Shield. The nonparticipating pharmacy has received its full $10 customary charge from the insured customer. The insured customer must then, in this latter instance, apply to blue Shield for the 75% reimbursement - in this case $6 (the difference between $10 and $2 fee). The prescription has then cost the insured $2 more at the nonparticipating pharmacy. But if the acquisition cost for the participating pharmacy is $5 instead of $8, it would receive $5 from Blue Shield and $2 from the customer or $7 total. The nonparticipating pharmacy might still charge $10 for the prescription, making a $5 profit if its acquisition cost was also only $5 instead of $8.

RULING: By the narrow 5 to 4 vote, the court held that such pharmacy agreements were not exempt as "business of insurance."

The court did not decide the issue of whether such pharmacy agreements are illegal under the antitrust laws since that question was not before the court. The U.S. Attorney General's office, in a brief filed in this case, was of the opinion that the pharmacy agreements probably do not violate the antitrust laws.

REASONING: As to the legal issues involved, the majority of the court wrote a rather lengthy decision, which is summarized here by saying that the exempt "business of insurance" was underwriting or spreading the risks but, instead, the pharmacy agreements were for goods and services and between the insurance company and a third party rather than between the insured and the insurance company. The pharmacy agreements are actually agreements to "reduce the insurer's costs" and while this is the "business of insurance companies," it is not, in the viewpoint of the court's majority, the "business of insurance." Hence, it is not exempt from the antitrust laws. The case was then sent back to the Federal District Court for trial on the actual issue of whether the pharmacy agreement here violated the federal antitrust laws.

Note: The four court dissenting justices wrote a separate opinion in which it was written as follows: [Not law, just opinion.]

> ...fixed provider agreements are the "business of insurance." Such agreements themselves perform an important insurance function. It may be true, as the court (majority of the court) contends, that conventional notions of insurance focus on the underwriting of risk. But they also include efforts to reduce the unpredictable aspects of the risks assumed. Traditional plans achieve this end by setting ceilings on cash payments or utilizing large deductibles...A fixed-price provider agreement attempts to reach the same result by contracting in advance for a price rather than agreeing to pay as the market fluctuates...

The pharmacy agreement then controls the "variable" of the markup at a set $2 fee. The other unknown variable is the acquisition cost, which may still fluctuate. In a footnote (#19)

Group Life & Health Insurance Co., et al v Royal Drug Company, et al
440 U.S. 205 (1979)
...continued

of the dissenting opinion, the minority justices indicated that, if Blue Cross set acquisition costs as well as markup, "In that event they (pharmacies) might not even meet the cost of their own outlays."

Federal Prescription Service, Inc. v American Pharmaceutical Association
663 F.2d 253 (D.C. Cir. 1981)

ISSUE: Whether the American Pharmaceutical Association (APhA) was in violation of the Sherman Antitrust Act because of its activities in opposition to mail order pharmacy.

FACTS: Federal Prescription Service, an Iowa-based mail order pharmacy, brought suit against the American Pharmaceutical Association (APhA), along with a number of other alleged co-conspirators for establishing anticompetitive policies that restrained Federal's interstate sales of prescription drugs by mail. The U.S. District Court for the District of Columbia found that the APhA had participated in an unlawful conspiracy with the Iowa Board of Pharmacy Examiners to harm Federal Prescription service through a series of governmental actions aimed at Federal's mail order pharmacy practice in Iowa. The case was appealed to the U.S. Court of Appeals for the District of Columbia.

RULING: The lower court decision against the APhA was reversed. While the evidence may have supported a conclusion that the APhA engaged in a number of activities violative of the spirit of the antitrust laws, those activities did not contribute materially to Federal's injury, or appear to have harmed Federal only through the intervention of governmental action, which is not subject to antitrust laws.

REASONING: The American Pharmaceutical Association had, for some time, campaigned against the distribution of prescription drugs by mail because the pharmacist-patient relationship did not exist in such situations and thus threatened public safety. The APhA sought to persuade governmental agencies, other trade groups and national journals that mail order dispensing of prescription drugs was harmful to the public health, and it urged other associations to adopt resolutions calling on physicians to discourage use of mail order prescription service, except in rural areas.

The U.S. Court of Appeals noted that the Sherman Act was to regulate only "business activity," not "political activity." Even the direct infliction of harm on a competitor is not subject to the Sherman Act so long as it is the incidental effect of a publicity campaign to influence governmental action. The lobbying of the APhA and the other organizations was found to be a genuine attempt to secure governmental action with regard to mail order pharmacies, and, thus, was an exception to the antitrust laws. The APhA could not be held liable for "damages resulting from its genuine and legitimate attempts to secure governmental action, whether through financing lawsuits, lobbying legislators or petitioning administrative bodies."

The Court of Appeals found that the activities of the APhA and the other co-conspirators were too remote to cause the damages alleged by Federal. Federal claimed that some of the co-conspirators colluded together to present forged prescriptions to the mail order house to see if the company would fill them, and thus expenses were incurred by Federal to guard against forgeries. However, the court found these claims too speculative. The court further held that Federal's decline in gross sales could not be directly attributed to the activities

Federal Prescription Service, Inc. v American Pharmaceutical Association
663 F.2d 253 (D.C. Cir. 1981)
...continued

of the APhA, but the competition from other mail order pharmacies and aggressive merchandising by chain store pharmacies had an effect.

Jefferson County Pharmaceutical Association v Abbott Laboratories, et al
460 U.S. 150 (1983)

ISSUE: Whether the restrictions on uses of drugs purchased at preferential prices, as established by the Supreme Court in the Portland case, applied to governmental hospitals.

FACTS: Based on the partial success of the pharmacy owners in the Portland case, a group of pharmacy owners in Birmingham, Alabama, filed suit against a group of pharmaceutical manufacturers to contest their practice of selling at preferential prices to governmental institutions, most notably hospitals. It was alleged that the drugs were being resold by the hospitals in competition with the community pharmacies.

The U.S. District Court ruled that the sales to governmental hospitals were "beyond the intended reach of the Robinson-Patman Price Discrimination Act." Following dismissal of the suit at this trial court level, the pharmacy association appealed to the U.S. Court of Appeals, where the dismissal was upheld.

The association then appealed to the U.S. Supreme Court.

RULING: Sales to governmental hospitals are not exempt from application of the Robinson-Patman Act.

REASONING: The reasoning used by the court was highly technical and based on the original legislative intent when the Robinson-Patman Act and the Nonprofit Institutions Act were enacted. However, it is important to note that the issue decided was quite narrow and the outcome of the decision was that the association could proceed with its suit, which had originally been dismissed by the trial court.

Mario DeModena, dba Sixth Avenue Pharmacy, et al v
Kaiser Foundation Health Plan, Inc., et al
743 F.2d 1388 (9th Cir. 1984)

ISSUE: Whether the Portland case categories of permissible uses for drugs purchased at preferential prices apply to nonprofit health maintenance organizations (HMOs).

FACTS: A group of community pharmacy owners filed suit against an HMO, alleging that the constraints on use of drugs purchased at preferential prices under the Portland decision applied to the activities of a nonprofit HMO. At the trial court, summary judgment was entered for the defendant HMO and the pharmacy owners appealed to the U.S. Court of appeals for the Ninth Circuit.

**Mario DeModena, dba Sixth Avenue Pharmacy, et al v
Kaiser Foundation Health Plan, Inc., et al**
743 F.2d 1388 (9th Cir. 1984)
...continued

RULING: Nonprofit HMOs may use pharmaceuticals purchased at preferential prices for uses consistent with the basic institutional function of the HMO and are not constrained by the Portland categories.

REASONING: The court viewed the Kaiser HMO and the Kaiser hospitals as one organization and the purpose of the entire structure as broadly conceived so that nearly all uses of drugs purchased at special prices fall within the phrase "own use."

It should be noted that a request to appeal to the U.S. Supreme Court was denied [53 U.S.L.W. 3587 (U.S. Feb 19, 1985)].

Memorial Hospital/Adair County v Heckler
539 F.Supp. 434 (D.D.C. 1986)

ISSUE: Whether a hospital whose total operational costs are unexceptional is entitled to reimbursement under the Medicare Act for the extraordinary expenses of a costly state-of-the-art pharmacy.

FACTS: Memorial Hospital is a 50-bed, nonprofit hospital in rural Oklahoma. In 1977, Memorial opened a new facility and contracted with Hospital Pharmacies, Inc. (HPI) for the latter to provide pharmacy services. HPI is the nation's largest pharmacy contractor. It was noted by the court that HPI offers more sophisticated services than traditional in-house hospital pharmacies usually do.

Blue Cross of Oklahoma, which served as Medicare's fiscal intermediary, conducted an audit of the hospital and disallowed reimbursement of approximately $80,000 during 1979 and 1980 because the pharmacy's costs were substantially out of line with similar hospitals in the same geographic area. The audit found that Memorial's pharmacy costs were approximately 45% higher than those of the most expensive peer group provider. The Department of Health and Human Services (HHS) also disallowed the $80,000 on the same grounds. HHS alleged that Memorial had not been a prudent buyer of pharmacy services when it engaged HPI as its pharmacy contractor.

RULING: The federal court concluded that the facts were sufficient to constitute substantial evidence in support of the HHS determination that Memorial acted imprudently in purchasing pharmacy services. For this reason, the court concluded that the agency's decision to deny reimbursement was rational and supported by substantial evidence.

REASONING: In reviewing the Medicare Act of 1965, the court found that hospital expenses do not have to be identical to those of similar institutions, but the law provides that they must not be substantially out of line. HHS regulations require that a hospital be reimbursed only if it is a prudent buyer of goods and services. A hospital which fails to shop wisely may have its extravagance penalized by reductions in its allowable costs.

The hospital contended that the use by the auditors of a cost-per-patient-day analysis was arbitrary and capricious. Memorial maintained that the audit should have measured pharmacy output in patient care units, which is more flexible than cost-per-patient-day reviews. A professor of pharmacy who testified for the hospital found Memorial's pharmacy costs to be average when calculated as a cost per unit of work.

Memorial Hospital/Adair County v Heckler
539 F.Supp. 434 (D.D.C. 1986)
...continued

However, the court concluded that the cost-per-patient-day was a rational basis for comparison of hospital costs. The American Hospital Association employed such an analysis when comparing operating costs of hospitals in this country. In addition, Medicare regulations specifically required participating hospitals to keep their records in the form of "patient days." The court was not willing to simply set aside the agency's interpretation because another interpretation may possibly be better, so long as the agency's interpretation was within a reasonable range.

The HHS regulations would not permit a hospital to decide for itself to upgrade pharmacy services and then expect Medicare reimbursements to pay for a portion of the increased costs regardless of how much Medicare patients might benefit. The court found that it was reasonable to conclude that Congress did not intend hospitals to be able to look to Medicare reimbursement to defray the costs of their improvements indirectly without some relationship to the purposes of the Medicare Act.

The court also found that Memorial had not been a prudent buyer of pharmacy services. The court concluded that the hospital acted hastily and unwisely in contracting with HPI. The hospital seriously considered only HPI as an alternative source of pharmacy services after its existing pharmacy was disapproved during a Medicare certification inspection two weeks before it was to open. Memorial contended that it had to act quickly to remedy the deficiency, so it never advertised for other pharmacy services or contacted the state pharmacy association to seek applicants for employment. The hospital's accountant simply made a quick, mental estimate of HPI's cost to Memorial which the administrator very quickly presented to the hospital board for approval. Thus, the hospital did not show that HPI was the only available source of pharmacy services and was not justified in engaging the contract pharmacy.

Key Enterprises of Delaware v Venice Hospital
703 F.Supp. 1513 (M.D. Fla. 1989)

ISSUE: Whether a hospital that encouraged home health nurses to refer patients to a durable medical equipment supplier jointly owned by the hospital violated antitrust laws by unreasonably excluding competition.

FACTS: The case involves the marketing of durable medical equipment to home users in Venice, FL. The DME included such items as prosthetic devices, hospital beds, oxygen, wheelchairs, ostomy supplies, etc. DME suppliers depend upon referrals from many sources (eg, hospitals, nursing homes, home health agencies, physicians, physical therapists).

The plaintiff, Venice Convalescent Aids Medical Supply (VCA) is one of several DME suppliers in Venice, FL. The defendant is a DME supplier jointly owned by the Venice hospital, a nonprofit corporation, and the Sammett Corporation. When the hospital began investigating the home medical and supply business, it purchased from Sammett a 50% interest in Sammett's durable medical equipment business.

Before the joint venture, it was common practice in the Venice DME market for home health nurses to choose the DME vendor who would supply patients discharged from the hospital with their medical equipment and supply needs. The plaintiff concentrated its sales efforts

Key Enterprises of Delaware v Venice Hospital
703 F.Supp. 1513 (M.D. Fla. 1989)
...continued

on the home health nurses and consequently received most of its business from the home health agencies. However, after the joint venture was created, the hospital instituted a new policy encouraging the nurses to select the joint venture as the DME supplier. If a patient, home health nurse, or physician made a request for a particular DME vendor, the request would be honored. However, in the absence of such a choice, referrals of all DME business were made to the joint venture.

RULING: After a 2-week trial, the jury found that the defendants had violated the Sherman Act by conspiring to monopolize the Venice DME market. It concluded the hospital had used its monopoly power to gain an unfair advantage in the DME market and that the defendants tortiously interfered with the plaintiff's business relationship with the home health agencies. The jury awarded $760,983 in damages, which was trebled on the antitrust counts to $2,282,949. The defendants asked the court for a judgment not withstanding the verdict. The appellate court reversed the jury's verdict, finding no evidence of coercion or unfair competition.

REASONING: Antitrust liability under the Sherman Act requires a finding that the defendants engaged in unreasonably restrictive, exclusionary or coercive conduct that caused injury to competition. The issue was whether the evidence was sufficient to support a finding of prohibited antitrust behavior.

The court found that the defendant's behavior was not, as a matter of law, coercive. There was no evidence that the defendants required the home health nurses to refer patients to the joint venture or the home health agency would face a cut-off in patient referral from the hospital. Testimony was presented that the defendants encouraged the nurses to make such referrals, but it never reached the level of a mandatory requirement.

In addition, the evidence did not establish that the home health nurses lost their autonomy to choose whichever DME supplier they wished. At best, some felt subjectively pressured to recommend the venture. Moreover, the testimony of nurses who chose the joint venture indicated that their choice was not made because the defendants forced them to do so, but because they thought it was beneficial to the home health agency.

Finally, there was no evidence presented that any of the defendants ever attempted to retaliate or enforce their policy in the face of noncompliance. Even if the hospital vigorously encouraged the nurses to order their DME equipment from its joint venture supplier, the hospital respected their choice and did not penalize anyone. Thus, there was simply no coercive or restricted link — no evidence of threats of loss of autonomy — between the fact that the hospital established a policy encouraging the nurses to select the joint venture and the fact that some, though not all, did so. Without such a link, the inference of coercion was unreasonable as a matter of law.

Behavior that restricts or inhibits a consumer's freedom to choose is indicative of unreasonably exclusionary conduct. Throughout the case, the plaintiff focused the inquiry on the effect the joint venture had on the nurses' ability to choose a DME vendor. The court noted that the home health nurses are not the consumers of DME; the patients are. It was uncontradicted that the patient always had the freedom to choose any DME vendor desired and that this freedom was not restricted. The stark fact was that the hospital and the joint venture never excluded or restricted patients, nurses or physicians from choosing any DME supplier.

Key Enterprises of Delaware v Venice Hospital
703 F.Supp. 1513 (M.D. Fla. 1989)
...continued

The plaintiff complained of being excluded from only one source of referrals — those from the hospital. It still could compete for DME patients from other sources, including walk-ins, nursing homes, physical therapists and physicians. There was, in fact, evidence that the hospital offered all of its patients a brochure, printed at the hospital's expense, listing all of the local DME suppliers, including the plaintiff. The court noted that this gratuitous gesture went beyond the defendant's obligation to the plaintiffs. The underlying policy and purpose of the antitrust laws is to protect competition, not competitors. Therefore, liability under the laws results only when competition, rather than any specific competitor, was injured by the joint venture, competition as a whole was not. Consumers did not complain about the joint venture, suppliers were not excluded from the market, prices actually dropped and market concentration actually diminished. The evidence did not support a finding that the defendant's behavior was coercive or unreasonably exclusionary or that competition was injured.

Arkansas Hospital Association v Arkansas State Board of Pharmacy
763 S.W.2d 73 (Ark. 1989)

ISSUE: Whether nonprofit hospitals were entitled, under Arkansas law, to hold retail pharmacy permits.

FACTS: The statutes of the state of Arkansas distinguish between nonprofit and for-profit hospitals by allowing for-profit hospitals to hold retail pharmacy permits, but not allowing nonprofit hospitals to do so unless they were "grandfathered." A group of nonprofit hospitals and a trade association filed suit against the Arkansas State Board of Pharmacy in an effort to prevent enforcement of the statute. The plaintiffs argued that the statute violated their right to equal protection. The plaintiffs further contended that the legislature should have only made the retail sale of pharmaceuticals purchased at the discount nonprofit rate unlawful rather than broadly eliminating retail sales by nonprofit hospitals.

RULING: The Arkansas Supreme Court ruled that a rational basis existed for the legislation and it upheld the statute.

REASONING: The court stated that its function was to decide whether there was a fully rational basis between the legislation and state objectives and to make sure that the statute was not the product of arbitrary and capricious government purposes. The court concluded that a rational basis did exist — the prevention of drug diversion which was defined as a diversion of drugs from one wholesale submarket to another with a resulting loss of control over the drugs.

The court reviewed the report of Congressman Dingell, who was instrumental in having federal laws enacted to prevent drug diversion. Dingell's subcommittee report discussed the existence and operation of the drug diversion market and how it prevents effective control over the true source of drugs. The report states that pharmaceuticals that have been mislabeled, misbranded, improperly shipped, are expired, or are counterfeits, are injected into the national distribution system for ultimate sale to consumers. The report further states that nonprofit hospitals buy at below-average wholesale price under a special exemption to federal antitrust laws. "These nonprofit institutions that buy in excess of their legitimate needs and then resell the excess are a significant and growing source of diverted merchandise."

Arkansas Hospital Association v Arkansas State Board of Pharmacy
763 S.W.2d 73 (Ark. 1989)
...continued

The court noted that the Arkansas legislature may have been aware of the diversion market and decided to limit its operation. While nonprofit hospitals could not rationally be prevented from buying authorized drugs for their own in-house use, they could be prevented from selling drugs at retail to someone who has no connection with the hospital. This would eliminate the possibility of a nonprofit hospital purchasing drugs at a discount for its own use, and then diverting those drugs to its retail pharmacy.

Key Enterprises v Venice Hospital
919 F.2d 1550 (11th Cir. 1990)

ISSUE: Whether a hospital that encouraged home health nurses to refer patients to durable medical equipment supplier jointly owned by the hospital violated antitrust laws by unreasonably excluding competition.

FACTS: The facts of this case are set forth in the lower court decision reported previously.

RULING: A jury awarded the plaintiff $761,000 in damages, which was trebled on the antitrust counts to $2,283,000. A federal district court overturned the jury verdict, but the court in this appellate decision reinstated the jury verdict.

REASONING: As with any antitrust lawsuit, this case turns on whether certain acts committed by the defendants were anticompetitive. The court noted that patients are very susceptible to recommendations made by anyone who appears to be knowledgeable on a subject. The hospital was able to easily channel patient choice by limiting the patient's exposure to the competition in the DME market. The court could find no justification of efficiency for the hospital's behavior. The hospital's refusal to allow other DME vendors access was just one of several identifiable anticompetitive acts, which, when viewed together, supported the jury's findings that the defendant's actions impaired competition in an unnecessarily restrictive way.

The trial court noted that the plaintiff failed to show that the patients as consumers suffered any injury. However, the appellate court stated that the channeling of patient choice is sufficient to show injury to consumers. Antitrust laws do not require the consumer to suffer some sort of monetary damage before a defendant's anticompetitive conduct is actionable. Thus, a court must consider the effect on competition and not simply the effect on the ultimate consumer. Competition was injured because there was no effective means by which competing DME vendors could reach those patients who require medical equipment when discharged from the hospital.

The plaintiff claimed that the defendants entered into reciprocal agreement with one or more home health agencies whereby the home health care nurses would continue to have access to patients prior to discharge in exchange for the nurses' preferentially referring their patients to the hospital's DME supplier. Reciprocal dealing arrangements exist when two parties face each other as both buyer and seller. The court found that the arrangement between the defendants and the home health agencies had sufficient elements of a reciprocal "tying" arrangement, which could unreasonably restrain trade.

The appellate court had no difficulty concluding the plaintiff presented sufficient evidence to support the jury's finding that a reciprocal arrangement existed between the hospital

Key Enterprises v Venice Hospital
919 F.2d 1550 (11th Cir. 1990)
...continued

and at least one home health care agency. While only one of the home health care nurses admitted she felt pressured, all of the nurses stated that they were aware that the hospital was considering an exclusive arrangement with one of the home health agencies. They also indicated that the services of the plaintiff were superior to the hospital's supplier in quality, but none of them wanted to jeopardize the negotiations of the hospital with their agency.

The plaintiff's superiority in services did not change, yet the nurses started recommending the defendant in lieu of the plaintiff. While no individual piece of the evidence presented was sufficient to support the jury's finding, when viewed as a whole the evidence reasonably supported the inference that, because of a possible threat to their job security and in response to the hospital's solicitations, the home health care nurses preferentially recommended the defendant over other competing DME vendors.

Albertsons' Inc. v Florida Department of Professional Regulation
658 So.2d 134 (Fla.App. 1995)

ISSUE: Whether the State of Florida can sustain a challenge to a statute limiting access to certain "independent pharmacies" as a part of the state's health care and insurance reform.

FACTS: The provision at issue is as follows:

Notwithstanding any provision of this act to the contrary, if an accountable health partnership has entered into a contract with providers or facilities licensed or permitted under Chapter 465 for the purpose of providing prescribed medicine services, an individual may use an independent pharmacy which is not a party to the contract, if such independent pharmacy selected agrees to provide the service at a rate equal to or less than the rate set forth in the contract negotiated by the accountable health partnership with parties to the contract and such independent pharmacy meets all of the qualifications for participation in the accountable health partnership. ...For the purpose of this subsection, the term "independent pharmacy" means a pharmacy facility which is not part of a group of affiliated pharmacy facilities which are under common ownership directly or indirectly any interest in any facilities licensed under another state's laws for the purpose of providing prescribed medicine services, and the term "pharmacy facility" means a pharmacy facility which is permitted by the Board of Pharmacy in accordance with Chapter 465.

The plaintiffs in this action are chain drug stores that provide pharmacy services in the state of Florida. With one exception, all of the plaintiffs operate more than 12 pharmacies in the state.

The plaintiffs argued that the Florida statute in question violates the Commerce Clause and the Equal Protection Clause of the U.S. Constitution. They claimed that this section illegally limits access to certain Florida-based companies defined as independent pharmacies by barring (1) all pharmacies licensed under another state's law and (2) all pharmacies with more than 12 Florida stores.

RULING: The trial court struck down the provision relating to pharmacies licensed in another state as violating the Commerce Clause and severed that language from the stat-

Albertsons' Inc. v Florida Department of Professional Regulation
658 So.2d 134 (Fla.App. 1995)
...continued

utc. However, the trial court did uphold the remainder of the statute. The Florida appellate court found no error in the trial court's determination.

REASONING: In enacting the above law, the Florida Legislature found that the current health care system within the state does not provide access to affordable health care for all persons. Health insurance costs for small- and medium-sized businesses and their employees has spiraled. The legislature also found that rural and other medically underserved areas have too few health care resources. Managed care and group purchasing options are not widely available to small group purchasers.

It was the intent of the Florida Legislature that a structured health care competition model, known as managed competition, be implemented throughout the state to improve the efficiency of the health care markets. This model was to promote the pooling of purchaser and consumer buying power, ensure informed cost-conscious consumer choice of a managed care plan, reward providers for high-quality economical care, increase access to care for uninsured persons and control the rate of inflation in health care costs. Under the Act, Community Health Purchasing Alliances (CHPAs) are to be established and are responsible for assisting members in securing the highest quality of health care at the lowest possible price. These CHPAs are located in each of the 11 health service planning districts established by the legislature.

One of the ways to achieve the legislative goal of economical high quality health care is through the use of managed care systems or techniques. Such techniques include contracts with selected health care providers. Pursuant to the statute, partnerships may be created by health care providers, health maintenance organizations and health insurers for the purpose of providing health care services to the alliance members. One of the legislative criteria for such alliances includes the ability to assure enrollees adequate access to providers of health care, including geographic availability and adequate numbers and types of services.

It is generally conceded that if it were not for the independent pharmacy exemption, the small independent pharmacy would have great difficulty in providing services to alliance members because of certain provisions in the statute. Chain drug stores would be the only pharmacy companies in a position to compete for contracts with the various health alliance partnerships to provide services to members. The purpose of the "independent pharmacy" exemption is to allow these smaller pharmacies to continue to provide services to alliance members under the new statutory framework.

During the lawsuit, the state of Florida presented two potential rationales to justify the independent pharmacy exemption. First, the state argued that the independent pharmacy exemption promotes access to affordable and geographically accessible health care. The state also argued that the independent pharmacy exemption protects small businesses. The plaintiffs alleged that the definition of "independent pharmacies," which excludes any pharmacy that has more than 12 facilities in the state, violates the Commerce Clause of the U.S. Constitution. The court concluded that the numerical limitation does not indirectly violate the Commerce Clause.

Citing previous Supreme Court cases, the court noted that, "where a statute regulates evenhandedly to effectuate a legitimate local public interest, and its effects on interstate commerce are only incidental, it will be upheld unless the burden imposed on such commerce is clearly excessive in relation to the putative local benefits. If a legitimate local purpose is found, then the question becomes one of degree and the extent of the burden that will be tol-

Albertsons' Inc. v Florida Department of Professional Regulation
658 So.2d 134 (Fla.App. 1995)
...continued

erated will, of course, depend on the nature of the local interest involved and on whether it could be promoted as well with a lesser impact on interstate activities."

In the instant case, the court found that the challenged statute regulates evenhandedly with only incidental effects on interstate commerce. The numerical limitation operates to exclude both intrastate and interstate pharmacy companies that operate more than 12 facilities in Florida. One of the plaintiffs, Kash N' Karry, which is an intrastate pharmacy corporation, is a case in point. Because Kash N' Karry operates more than 12 affiliated pharmacy facilities in Florida, it does not fall within the independent pharmacy exemption, even though it operates solely within the state. Likewise, 10 of the other 11 plaintiffs do not meet the numerical limitation necessary to benefit from the independent pharmacy exemption.

The court found that the statute serves a legitimate local purpose of promoting access to health care services in the state. First, there is the problem of affordable health care and health care insurance. Second, there is the problem of geographical access in rural and under-served areas.

The numerical limitation on the independent pharmacy exemption is completely consistent with regard to the problem of affordable health care and insurance. The statute provides that the various health care alliances established under the law will contract with various health care providers (including pharmacies) to provide health care services within an alliance area.

The goal of the statute is to obtain health care services at the lowest possible cost. This is done through contracts with selected health care providers. It logically follows that a guarantee with a health care provider such as a chain pharmacy, would offer the majority of health care services within an alliance district. In turn, the contract would operate as an incentive to the health care organization to provide the services at the lowest possible price. In contrast, if many pharmacies offer services without a contract but match a contract price, there is little incentive for a chain store to bid fiercely for the opportunity to provide health care services.

In the instant case, the legislature has drawn a line in defining the independent pharmacy exemption so that only approximately 10% of the pharmacies operating within the state would benefit from the exemption. The other 90% (including both intrastate and interstate pharmacy corporations) are beyond the scope of the exemption and must obtain a contract to provide services to the alliance members.

The court found that the numerical limitation contained in the independent pharmacy exemption is logically related to the legislative goal of access to affordable health care. Furthermore, the extent that the legislation allows independent pharmacies located in rural and underserved populations to provide pharmacy services even though they have no contract with a health alliance district, augments pharmacy services in areas in which the legislature has found them to be lacking. The court also supported the protection of small business as a legitimate local purpose. Thus, the court concluded that the burden imposed upon interstate commerce is not clearly excessive in relation to the local benefits.

The dissenting judge noted that there are some 1,950 pharmacies in the state of Florida. Of this total, 239 were operated by 45 companies that did not do business outside the state. On the interstate side of the pharmacy store ledger, 18 companies operated 1,775 of Florida's pharmacies. Thus, almost 9 out of 10 pharmacy stores in the state were operated by inter-

Albertsons' Inc. v Florida Department of Professional Regulation
658 So.2d 134 (Fla.App. 1995)
...continued

state pharmacy companies. While all of these pharmacies are free to compete for contracts under Florida's new health care plan, the owners of 9 out of 10 Florida pharmacies deny the opportunity to compete by agreeing to provide prescriptions at a "rate equal to or less than" what is set forth in the negotiated contracts.

The majority of the court determined that some burden imposed on intrastate commerce could justify any burden on interstate commerce. The dissenting judge believed that the issue was whether interstate and intrastate businesses were treated equally under the statute. He concluded that they were not.

The numerical cap imposed by the state eliminates 98.7% of all interstate competition from the "equal to/less than" prescription medicine market. Of the 2000 pharmacies in Florida, only 183 qualify for the designation of "independent pharmacy." The judge viewed this as hardly the type of even-handed application required by case law. Considerations of economic protectionism of Florida-based pharmacy companies aside, the dissenting judge believed that the statute discriminated among and between interstate operations based upon their contacts with Florida's economy. Thus, the burden on interstate commerce was impermissible and struck down.

In re: Brand Name Prescription Drugs Antitrust Litigation
No. 94 C 897, Jan. 19, 1999, 1999 U.S. Dist. LEXIS 550 (N.D. Ill.)

Pharmacists joined in a national class-action lawsuit to allege a price-fixing conspiracy in violation of the Sherman Antitrust Act. The pharmacists claimed that the manufacturers and wholesalers of brand name prescription drugs unlawfully conspired to maintain a structure of differential pricing that imposed the highest prices on retail pharmacies, while other "favored" buyers like hospitals, health maintenance organizations (HMOs), and mail-order pharmacies were given lower, more competitive prices. The defendants countered that the denial of discounts to the retail pharmacists was based on individual decisions and justified by market considerations. Defendants also claimed that they extended discounts to favored buyers based on the ability of those buyers to "move market shares." According to defendants, hospitals and HMOs create "formularies," which are restrictive lists of drugs from which the hospital or HMO limits their physicians' ability to prescribe to patients. Defendants asserted that the favored buyers use formularies to negotiate discounts or rebates from the manufacturers. By threatening to exclude a manufacturer's product from their formularies, favored buyers possess the market power to negotiate discounts on brand name drugs. The defendants also asserted that retail pharmacies do not have that same market power to exclude brand name prescription drugs from their respective markets. The pharmacists asserted that they did possess the power to move market share, and it was only the existence of an industry-wide conspiracy among the defendants that excluded the plaintiffs from the brand name prescription drug discounts. The plaintiffs presented live fact witnesses to attempt to prove the existence of the defendants' alleged price-fixing conspiracy. The district court determined that the plaintiffs' evidence only established that defendants refused to offer discounts to resale pharmacies because those pharmacies lacked the market power of hospitals and HMOs. The court found that evidence to be incompatible with the plaintiffs' theory of an antitrust conspiracy. The Plaintiffs also presented evidence showing that during National Wholesale Druggists' Association (NWDA) meetings, the manufacturers and wholesalers had an opportunity to gather and discuss the emergence of retail buyer groups and engage in co-conspirator discussions. Based on its review of the evidence presented, the

In re: Brand Name Prescription Drugs Antitrust Litigation
No. 94 C 897, Jan. 19, 1999, 1999 U.S. Dist. LEXIS 550 (N.D. Ill.)
...continued

court, however, determined that it was not probable that the defendants ever joined or became members of any conspiracy. The court found no evidence of an industry-wide conspiracy to deny retail pharmacies discounts on brand name prescription drugs. The court held that no reasonable juror could reach a verdict in favor of the plaintiffs; therefore, the court granted judgment as a matter of law to the defendants.

K. Hefner, Inc. v Caremark, Inc.
918 P.2d 595, (Idaho 1996)

FACTS: The owners and operators of independent pharmacies throughout Idaho filed a complaint against Blue Cross of Idaho (BCI), a large provider of health care insurance, and Caremark, Inc., which administers BCI's prescription drug reimbursement plan under a contract. Caremark contracted with the pharmacies offering a drug reimbursement plan that reimburses the pharmacies for the drugs at rates set by BCI. The plaintiffs alleged that the reimbursement scheme requires participating pharmacies to sell many drugs "below cost" in violation of the Idaho Unfair Sales Act. Since the plan constitutes a contract, combination, or conspiracy in restraint of trade, it allegedly violates the state antitrust law. The Idaho trial court dismissed the case and awarded attorneys' fees to BCI.

HOLDING: The Idaho Supreme Court found that nonparticipating pharmacies may pursue charges that the plan constitutes an unreasonable restraint of trade by requiring participating pharmacies to agree to be paid at below cost rates for many drugs. The court found that the BCI reimbursement scheme had the effect of restraining trade, reducing competition in pharmacy trade, and unfairly diverting trade from the plaintiffs and other pharmacists who did not enter into the arrangement. Accordingly, it reversed the lower court's dismissal of the complaint.

Lee v United Church Homes
686 N.E.2d 288 (Ohio App. 1996)

Mrs. Lee was admitted to a nursing home operated by the defendant in April 1994. The nursing home had an agreement with Westhaven Pharmacy, a large provider of nursing home pharmacy services and also a named defendant in the case. The contract provided that the nursing home would use Westhaven as a vendor of prescription medications "whenever possible." However, in accordance with Ohio law, the nursing home was obligated to provide residents with a choice in picking their own pharmacy provider. The contract provided that the nursing home and its residents "reserve the right to purchase and obtain prescription medications and supplies from other sources, in accordance with all (nursing home) policies regarding purchases from an outside pharmacy." The home required each resident, upon admission, to sign a Pharmacy Services Agreement specifying the pharmacy of choice. While the vast majority of residents did obtain pharmaceuticals from Westhaven, at least eight individuals used other pharmacies. Mrs. Lee was assisted by her brother when she was admitted to the nursing home. The brother met with the nursing home personnel and signed the necessary paperwork to have his sister admitted. In a sworn statement, the brother indicated that he was informed that Westhaven was the only pharmacy approved by the nursing home and that the admission of his sister to the home was conditioned upon his

Lee v United Church Homes
686 N.E.2d 288 (Ohio App. 1996)
...continued

agreement to use Westhaven. He also indicated that when he was given the Pharmacy Services agreement to sign, the part where patients are to indicate the pharmacy of choice was already filled in with Westhaven's name. Plaintiff sued the nursing home and Westhaven for antitrust and violations of the freedom of choice provision in the state act. The trial court granted the summary judgment motions of both the nursing home and Westhaven and ordered that the complaint be dismissed. On appeal, the court held that dismissal of the antitrust allegations against the defendants was proper. On the state claim, the court of appeals upheld dismissal against Westhaven because there was no evidence that Westhaven or any of its employees ever had any contact with the residents or their representatives. With respect to the nursing home, the court of appeals made the opposite decision. There was enough evidence to go to a jury on the question of whether residents really had freedom to choose any pharmacy they liked.

Texas Pharmacy Assn. v Prudential Life Insurance Co. of America
105 F.3d 1035 (5th Cir. 1997)

Texas amended its 1991 "any willing provider" statute in 1995 prohibiting any health insurance policy or managed care plan from prohibiting or limiting a beneficiary's use of the pharmacy of his or her own choosing and denying a pharmacy's or pharmacist's right to participate in a pharmacy benefit program so long as the pharmacy or pharmacist consents to accepting the terms of the program as offered to all other pharmacies and pharmacists. The amendment made the law applicable to all employer-purchased pharmacy benefit programs. Prior to the amendment, Prudential established a "closed" network of pharmacies from which beneficiaries could have prescriptions filled. The Texas Pharmacists Association and several pharmacies brought suit against Prudential for violation of the Texas statute. The Fifth Circuit Court of Appeals held that the statute is unconstitutional because it violates federal ERISA laws. ERISA exempts self-funded employer health benefit plans from most state insurance laws. Because the amendment to the Texas statute broadened coverage to include application to self-funded benefit plans, it conflicts with the ERISA exemption.

In re: Warfarin Sodium Antitrust Litigation
Slip Op. No. MDL 98-1232-SLR, Dec. 7, 1998, 1998, U.S. Dist. LEXIS 19555 (D. Del. 98)

After Barr Laboratories was thwarted in its attempts to introduce generic warfarin sodium into the market, it sued DuPont Merck, in connection with the sale and marketing of *Coumadin*, the brand name of warfarin sodium, an anticoagulant agent. A class of 1.8 million users of *Coumadin* also sued defendant. Barr Laboratories and the patients alleged that DuPont Merck engaged in unlawful monopolization in violation of the Sherman Antitrust Act, and commercial misrepresentation in violation of the Lanham Act. DuPont Merck filed a motion to dismiss both cases. Both plaintiffs alleged that DuPont Merck tried to protect its market share for *Coumadin* by attacking the generic warfarin sodium, thereby increasing costs to enter the market and drive up consumer prices. Plaintiffs alleged that DuPont Merck petitioned the FDA to postpone approval for generic warfarin sodium products pending the adoption of stricter bioequivalence standards, petitioned the U.S. Pharmacopeia (USP) to adopt *Coumadin*'s uniformity specifications as the USP standard for all

In re: Warfarin Sodium Antitrust Litigation
Slip Op. No. MDL 98-1232-SLR, Dec. 7, 1998, 1998, U.S. Dist. LEXIS 19555 (D. Del. 98)
...continued

warfarin sodium drugs, and allegedly issued communications that *Coumadin* was safer and
more effective than the plaintiff's warfarin sodium tablets. Also, DuPont Merck allegedly
entered into anticompetitive rebate incentives with pharmacy benefit managers, retail
pharmacies, and pharmaceutical wholesalers to preserve its monopoly in the oral anticoagulant market. Plaintiffs asserted that DuPont Merck's action amounted to predatory conduct or the willful acquisition of monopoly power. For purposes of this decision, the claims
of Barr and the patients were consolidated. The district court dismissed the plaintiffs' claim
with respect to DuPont Merck's petition to the FDA and USP under a doctrine of immunity for petitions to government entities. The district court refused to dismiss the plaintiffs' antitrust claims based on DuPont Merck's allegedly false and misleading statements to
the general public and health care community, and DuPont Merck's use of rebate incentives to pharmacies in an effort to restrain trade in the market. The district court also refused
to dismiss the plaintiffs' claims under the Lanham Act because DuPont Merck's allegedly
false and misleading commercial speech does not enjoy First Amendment protection. On the
other hand, the court dismissed the class action plaintiffs' claims because the class plaintiffs lacked antitrust standing. The district court found that the class plaintiffs purchased
DuPont Merck's *Coumadin* from intermediaries such as drug stores and managed care companies, rather than from DuPont Merck. The district court concluded that insurance companies most likely absorbed the increased cost of *Coumadin*, so any injuries the class plaintiffs
suffered were too remote to justify antitrust standing. The remaining issues in the Barr complaint are subject to ongoing discovery and further litigation. Editors Note: The parties
settled this lawsuit in January 2000 before trial.

Drug Emporium v Blue Cross of Western New York
No 99-CV-579C (June 28, 2000), USDC W NY, 2000 US Dist LEXIS 9139

Defendants Blue Cross and Rite-Aid entered into an exclusive pharmacy services network
for eligible HMO and PPO members. Drug Emporium sued, claiming the contract violates
federal and state antitrust and other laws. The district found that contract is not a per se
violation of the Sherman Act but is, instead, subject to a rule of reason analysis. The court
withheld a decision on this claim pending further proceedings. On the state claims that
Blue Cross and Rite-Aid tortuously interfered with Drug Emporium's previous business
arrangement with Blue Cross, the Court found in favor of Blue Cross, but declined to dismiss the claims against Rite-Aid. It reasoned that Blue Cross can choose who to do business with and that there is no obligation to include any particular pharmacy in the network.
However, the Court ruled that Rite-Aid may have used unlawful economic pressure, as
opposed to mere persuasion, on Blue Cross to cause it to terminate pre-existing contracts with
Drug Emporium and use Rite-Aid as the exclusive pharmacy provider.

The following is a list of court cases that are related to this topic.

Blue Cross v Commonwealth, 176 S.E. 2d 439 (Va. 1970).
Cafaralle v Brockton Oaks C.V.S.. Inc., No. 94-0414A, (Mass. Super. Ct. April, 1996).
Massachusetts v Stop and Shop Cos., Inc., No. 96-0104-8 (Mass. Sup. Ct., Jan. 5, 1996).

The Federal Trade Commission Act

The following is a list of court cases that are related to this topic.

Patterson Drug Co. v Kingery, 305 F. Supp. 821 (W.D.Va. 1969)

State Trade Laws

Blue Cross v Commonwealth
176 S.E.2d 439 (Va. 1970)

ISSUE: Whether a prepaid prescription drug insurance program wherein pharmacies are reimbursed on the basis of cost-of-drug plus a uniform professional fee violates antitrust laws.

FACTS: The State Corporation Commission of the Commonwealth of Virginia disapproved a Blue Cross prepaid prescription payment plan on the basis that (1) it violated a particular Virginia statute pertaining to prepaid hospital service plans, and (2) that it violated both Virginia and federal antitrust laws. Blue Cross appealed the Commission's ruling to the Virginia Supreme Court. In a lengthy and complex written opinion, the court upheld the Commission's action but only on the grounds of an antitrust violation.

From the published facts of the case, it can be said that the Blue Cross system of Virginia was, in effect, an intermediary payment agent, for 55 hospitals and a number of doctors who had made contracts with consumer subscribers to provide prepaid hospital services.

In our case facts, the Blue Cross Board of Directors decided to add a prepaid prescription feature to the Blue Cross plan. The drug payment coverage would be an added endorsement to the plan and it would obligate the plan to pay 100% of the charge for drugs furnished subscribers by pharmacists who contracted with Blue Cross to furnish such drugs and 75% of the prescription charge by pharmacists who did not contract with Blue Cross. Payment would be made directly to the contracting pharmacists or at Blue Cross' option directly to the non-contracting pharmacist or to the subscriber.

Next, Blue Cross unilaterally decided that the cost of the medication plus a $1.85-per-prescription professional fee would be an acceptable amount to pay the contracting pharmacists. Blue Cross approached the Virginia Pharmaceutical Association and obtained membership approval of the plan in principle. Blue Cross submitted the plan to the Bureau of Insurance within the State Corporation Commission and obtained initial approval from the Bureau. In one year of operation, 82% of the pharmacies in Virginia contracted with Blue Cross to furnish drugs on out-of-hospital prescriptions to Blue Cross subscribers at the cost-plus-$1.85 price. Then, one pharmacist complained about the plan to the State Corporation Commission and, after a public hearing, the Commission disapproved the plan which was previously approved by its Bureau.

The Sherman Act (15 USC § 1) makes illegal every contract, combination, or conspiracy in restraint of trade or commerce. The term "combination" as used in the Sherman Act, was defined by the courts as "...a combination for the purpose and with the effect of raising, depressing, fixing, pegging, or stabilizing the price of a commodity in interstate or foreign commerce is illegal per se." (Citing *US v Socony-Vacuum*, 310 US 150) [Note: Federal antitrust law enters into our case on the premise that the drugs used in filling the prescriptions flow in interstate commerce.]

Counsel for Blue Cross contended that, because Blue Cross unilaterally came up with the cost-plus-$1.85 figure, there was no combination or conspiracy violating the Sherman Act. The attorneys for the State Commission argued that each pharmacist signing the Blue

                                                  Pharmacy Law Digest

Blue Cross v Commonwealth
176 S.E.2d 439 (Va. 1970)
...continued

Cross contract had reason to believe his contract was not an isolated contract; he was, in effect, acting in concert with other pharmacists who were all signing a contract with the same price terms and who must have known that the success of the plan depended on many pharmacists agreeing to the identical contract. The fact that Blue Cross solicited the approval of the Virginia Pharmaceutical Association supported the inference that Blue Cross intended to deal with the pharmacist as a group.

RULING: The Virginia Appeals Court accepted the Commission's interpretation of the matter, ruling in favor of the Commission and against Blue Cross.

REASONING: The court stated:

> The evidence in this case shows a combination of competing pharmacists formed for the purpose and with the effect of stabilizing the price of drugs. The Blue Cross drug plan therefore involves illegal price fixing under the Sherman Act.

The Virginia Court also ruled that the Blue Cross prescription prepayment plan also violated the state antitrust law for the same reasons it violated the federal Sherman Act. As an incidental point in the case, the State Corporation Commission in its hearing findings apparently decided that pharmacists who signed Blue Cross contracts committed acts of unprofessional conduct, in that they indirectly advertised their charges for prescription drugs in violation of Sec. 54-426.1(4) of the Virginia Annotated Code of 1968. However, the court ruled that its affirmance of the Commission's ruling did not include the Commission's decision on unprofessional conduct aspect, the reason being that the State Board of Pharmacy's authority pre-empted the Commission's with respect to pharmacist licensure matters.

Pharmaceutical Society v Abrams
522 N.Y.S.2d 298 (A.D. 3 Dept. 1987)

ISSUE: Whether the practice of pharmacy is a profession and is thus exempt from the state's antitrust laws.

FACTS: The Attorney General of the State of New York issued a subpoena *duces tecum* to the Pharmaceutical Society of the State of New York, seeking information regarding an investigation the state was conducting concerning a proposed prescription drug plan for state employees and retirees. The Pharmaceutical Society moved to quash the subpoena.

In an effort to oppose the Pharmaceutical Society's motion, the State of New York submitted an affidavit stating that the proposed prescription drug plan included incentives for the use of generic drugs and an optional method of acquiring drugs by mail. It also included a dispensing fee to be paid to pharmacies to cover costs other than the drug itself, as well as a provision to reimburse pharmacies for drugs at a percentage discount from average wholesale price. Many pharmacists and pharmacies not only declined to enroll in the plan, but also took part in lobbying activities to register their disapproval of the plan. As a result of low enrollment and opposition to the plan, the reimbursement rate was increased. This resulted in increasing the cost of the prescription drug program to the State of New York by approximately $6,000,000.

Pharmaceutical Society v Abrams
522 N.Y.S.2d 298 (A.D. 3 Dept. 1987)
...continued

Based on these events, the state began an investigation and issued the subpoena in question. The Attorney General argued that there was the possibility that there had been a violation of the state's antitrust laws. The Pharmaceutical Society's application to quash the subpoena was based on its assertion that pharmacy is a profession, and therefore, is exempt from investigations conducted pursuant to state antitrust laws.

RULING: The trial court denied the Society's motion to quash the subpoena because it concluded that pharmacy was not a profession under New York antitrust laws. Even though the appellate court affirmed the denial of the Society's motion to quash the subpoena, it concluded that pharmacy was a profession, but that the pharmaceutical association did not retain the antitrust exemption because it was composed of both members and nonmembers of the profession.

REASONING: In support of its argument that pharmacy is a profession and is therefore exempt from the state's antitrust laws, the Pharmaceutical Society relied on a case in which the New York courts found that the legal profession was not a business or trade, and was exempt from the proscription of the state's antitrust law. In another case, the state ruled that physicians were also professional since the court could discern no basis for distinguishing between the legal profession and the medical profession. Therefore, the medical profession was also entitled to an exemption from state antitrust restrictions.

The Attorney General, while conceding that pharmacists are licensed professionals, argued that the two cases cited by the petitioner did not stand for the proposition that all professionals are exempt from state antitrust provisions. In support of his position, the Attorney General relied upon the case of *Matter of Westchester County Pharmaceutical Society v Abrams* (515 N.Y.S. 2d 971), wherein the court rejected the argument that pharmacy was exempt from antitrust laws. The Westchester case distinguished previous case law by concluding that, unlike physicians and lawyers, pharmacists do not primarily provide services, but instead sell goods. In the case at hand, the court disagreed.

Contrary to the Westchester decision, the court concluded that the dispensing of pharmaceuticals and advising of patients with respect to prescription drugs is professional in nature rather than commercial. This is true even though a portion of the services rendered include the dispensing of medicines. The court also rejected the state's argument that the word "professional" was a word of art and intended to be used only for lawyers.

Instead, the court opined that pharmacists are highly regulated, and that the state could revoke or suspend a pharmacist's or pharmacy's license. In addition, pharmacy was regulated almost identically to medicine. In fact, the statutory guidelines for pharmacy were much more extensive than they were for the profession of medicine.

The court noted that a profession "...is distinguished by the requirements of extensive formal training and learning, admission to practice by a qualifying licensure, a code of ethics imposing standards... beyond those that prevail or are tolerated in the marketplace, a system for discipline...a duty to subordinate financial reward to social responsibility, and...an obligation on its members...to conduct themselves as members of a learned, disciplined, and honorable occupation." Therefore, the court concluded that pharmacists should be found exempt from the provision of state antitrust laws.

However, despite this conclusion that individual pharmacists are professionals and exempt from antitrust provisions, the court found otherwise with respect to the status of the petition-

Pharmaceutical Society v Abrams
522 N.Y.S.2d 298 (A.D. 3 Dept. 1987)
...continued

ing Pharmaceutical Society. The court noted that, from the point of view of the employer for whom the pharmacist works, the sale of drugs is a trade or commerce. Business organizations subject to antitrust laws cannot escape liability by cloaking their actions with participation of exempt individuals. Since the pharmaceutical association was composed of both members and nonmembers of the profession, it should not be found exempt from antitrust laws.

Wal-Mart Stores v American Drugs
891 S.W.2d 30 (Ark. 1995)

The Arkansas Supreme Court reversed lower court rulings in favor of independent pharmacies that held that the chain store's pattern and practice of selling health and beauty items and prescription drugs below cost does not violate the State Unfair Practices Act absent evidence that the conduct is intended to injure or destroy competition. According to the court, the statutory prohibition against predatory pricing does not bar "loss leader" sales in highly competitive marketplaces.

Maryland Pharmacists Association v Office of the Attorney General
694 A.2d 492 (Md.App. 1997)

During the National Association of Retail Druggists 1991 Annual Convention held in Baltimore, Maryland, an exhibit entitled "Hallmark Hall of Shame" was displayed to make attendees aware that Hallmark Card Company endorsed mail-order prescription benefit plans for its employees while using independent pharmacies as the centerpiece of its greeting card marketing program. The Maryland Attorney General's Office (AGO) began an investigation into whether pharmacists might "care enough to boycott the best" and sent the Maryland Pharmacists Association a Civil Investigatory Demand (CID) letter August 1993 requesting documents concerning the "Hall of Shame" exhibit. The association turned over the requested documents and denied any involvement with the exhibit. Extensive communications concerning the investigation were exchanged between the parties with the AGO refusing to disclose the status of the investigation. Finally, in February 1996, the AGO returned the association's documents without further explanation as to whether the investigation was continuing or closed. The association assumed it was closed and filed suit to recover its costs of cooperating with the CID. The trial court dismissed the claim because the association's costs were not incurred during a "contested case," as required by the state statute that permits recovery of CID expenses. The dismissal was upheld on appeal because the AGO never opened a contested case. Instead, said the Maryland Court of Appeals, the AGO merely conducted a lengthy investigation.

Merck-Medco Managed Care v Rite Aid
201 F.3d 436 (4th Cir. 1999)

Maryland awarded Medco a contract to manage the prescription drug benefits program for state employees and retirees. Under the terms of the award, Medco was required to assemble an extensive state-wide network of pharmacies that would agree to fill prescriptions at a steeply discounted rate. Two weeks before the benefits plan was scheduled to begin, Maryland became concerned about Medco's ability to put together a satisfactory network in time. Because Medco failed to assemble a satisfactory network, Maryland terminated Medco's contract and awarded it to Medco's competitors. Medco sued these competitors (the defendants — Rite Aid and four other retail pharmacies) under the Sherman Antitrust Act alleging that they jointly agreed to sabotage Medco by boycotting its pharmacy network. Collectively, the defendants own or represent approximately 50% of the retail pharmacies in Maryland. The district court granted defendants' summary judgment because Medco presented insufficient evidence to support its allegation of conspiracy to violate the antitrust laws. Medco appealed, and the Fourth Circuit affirmed summary judgment against Medco because Medco did not produce evidence tending to exclude independent action by the defendants. Medco cited circumstantial evidence of a conspiracy including, among other things, the defendants' adverse reaction to the Maryland plan and conversations between high level officers within the defendants' companies. However, the Fourth Circuit concluded that all of the evidence viewed together did not create a reasonable inference of conspiracy, and therefore affirmed the decision of the district court.

Park Medical Pharmacy v San Diego Orthopedic Associates Medical Group
Slip Op No D038051 (June 11, 2002), 2002 Cal. App. LEXIS 4225

A pharmacy sued a medical group for dispensing drugs in violation of the *Cal. Bus. & Prof. Code § 4170* and for unlawfully operating a retail pharmacy. The physicians of the medical group individually dispensed drugs on a for-profit basis to their worker's compensation patients after informing the patients that they could get a prescription that could be filled anywhere. The pharmacy also alleged that the medical group interfered with its business by diverting patients away from the pharmacy and included causes of action for violations of unfair business practices. The appellate court found that: (1) under the provisions of *Cal. Bus. & Prof. Code § 4170*, the medical group was entitled to dispense drugs on a for-profit basis to their patients as a part of their treatment, (2) maintaining a separate room to hold the drugs was not a "pharmacy" because the drugs were not for sale to the public, and (3) the legislative intent was to prohibit physicians from having a store where they sold drugs to the general public, and to limit physicians to dispensing drugs to their own patients for the condition for which the patient was seeking treatment. The trial court granted summary judgment in favor of the medical group. The judgment was upheld on appeal.

The following is a list of court cases that are related to this topic.

Pennsylvania Pharmacists Assoc. v Pennsylvania Dep't of Pub. Welfare, 733 A.2d 666 (Pa. Commw. Ct. 1999).
American Society of Consultant Pharmacists v Concannon, 214 F. Supp. 2d 23 (D. Me. 2002).
Walgreen Co. v Hood, 275 F. 3d 475 (5th Cir. 2001).

Employee Retirement Income Security Act (ERISA)

Express Scripts v Wenzel
Slip Op. No. 00-2788 (August 22, 2001), 8th Cir., 2001 U.S. App. LEXIS 18824

In 1997, Missouri amended its insurance laws to include "any willing provider" language allowing HMO beneficiaries the option to use local retail pharmacies for prescriptions instead of mail order pharmacies exclusively as required by some HMOs before the law was changed. Prior to that change, some Missouri HMOs provided incentives to enrollees to fill maintenance prescriptions to treat a medical condition for a period of greater than 30 days at mail service pharmacies, rather than at local retail pharmacies. Prior to the enactment of the Missouri statutes, an HMO could limit the quantity enrollees could obtain from retail pharmacies to a 30 day supply while allowing them to obtain up to a 90 day supply from a mail service pharmacy. An HMO also could charge enrollees a higher copayment to fill a maintenance prescription at a retail pharmacy than at a mail order pharmacy. Such a mail service pharmacy provider would give discounts to the HMO in return for the benefit of becoming the preferred provider of maintenance prescriptions and the exclusive provider in the network of 90 day prescriptions. The plaintiff, a mail order pharmacy challenged the legislation claiming it is preempted by the Employee's Retirement Income Security Act of 1974 (ERISA). The lower court found in favor of the state. The judgment was upheld on appeal. The 8th Circuit found that the challenged provisions fall within ERISA's savings clause. It found that the Missouri statutes do not fall within the scope of ERISA preemption because they do not "relate to " employee benefit plans. The court reasoned that the statutes do not act "immediately and exclusively" on such plans, but only indirectly, and that the existence of ERISA plans is not essential to their operation. It also concluded that the statutes were saved from ERISA preemption because they regulate HMOs which are in the business of insurance.

Vaughn v CVS Revco
Slip Op. No. COA00-159 (July 3, 2001), 2001 NC App. LEXIS 534

Pharmacist-employee sued employer for anticipatory breach of contract and unfair and deceptive trade practices. The trial court found that the employee's claims were preempted by ERISA 29 U.S.C. §§1001-1461. When the pharmacist was rehired by the employer's predecessor, it was agreed that he would retain his original tenure date for purposes of the benefits plan. The employer purchased the predecessor and the pharmacist was advised that his tenure date would be changed to the date he was rehired. The complaint made no reference to an ERISA plan or that the benefit he sought was connected to an ERISA plan. The appeals court found that the benefits at issue did not threaten ERISA's objectives or interfere with the purposes of ERISA's preemption provision to protect the interests of participants in employee benefit plans or provide a nationally uniform administration of such plans. They did not mandate an employee benefit structure of administration, seek to bind a plan administrator to particular choices, or preclude uniform administrative practice, thereby functioning as a regulation of an ERISA plan. The claims were not an alternate enforcement mechanism for obtaining ERISA plan benefits. They were directed against the employer for an anticipated breach of a promise to provide pension benefits based on an agreed date of hire. They only tangentially involved the benefit plan itself. Therefore, the trial court's judgment was reversed.

American Drug Stores v Harvard Pilgrim Health Care
973 F.Supp. 60 (D.Mass. 1997)

Plaintiff brought suit against an insurance company and a pharmacy benefits manager for violation of Massachusetts' "Any Willing Provider" law after plaintiff had been refused participation rights in the "closed" provider network. The statute requires prescription benefit plans to allow any pharmacy willing to abide by contract terms participation rights on the same basis as other "preferred" pharmacies already in the plan's network. Defendants sought dismissal claiming the state law is preempted by the federal ERISA statutes governing employee benefit plans. The court analyzed several earlier cases involving "any willing provider" status, including the very recently decided Texas case (see the following case) and noted that the majority of those cases, interpreting Supreme Court opinions, strike down such laws because they affect employee benefit plans. The judge in this case distinguished those earlier opinions because two recent Supreme Court cases hold that Congress had no intention of preempting state laws regulating insurance just because those laws might "relate to" an employee benefit plan. Based on these decisions, the judge applied a "common sense" approach and determined that the state act is "saved" from preemption because it is intended to regulate insurance business.

New York State Teamsters Council Health and Hospital Fund v Centrus Pharmacy Solutions
Slip Op No 02-CV-0560 (December 10, 2002), USDC NY, 2002 U.S. Dist. LEXIS 24461

The parties entered into a prescription drug services agreement where the provider supplied prescription drugs to plan participants. Under the agreement, the provider received a set amount for each claim it processed. The provider recommended to the trustees a preferred formulary program, where the participant co-payment would be half that for other drugs. In implementing the program, the provider mistakenly collected only the reduced co-payment for all drugs, and sought reimbursement of the amount that the provider should have charged but didn't. The Teamster Union, through its trustees sued the prescription drug provider for (1) breach of fiduciary duty under the Employee Retirement Income Security Act of 1974 (ERISA), 29 U.S.C.S. § 1001 et seq., (2) engaging in a prohibited transaction with the plan in violation of 29 U.S.C.S. § 1106(a) of ERISA, and (3) breach of contract. The provider moved to dismiss under Fed. R. Civ. P. 12(b)(6) for failure to state a claim. The court found that the provider was not a fiduciary under ERISA. The plan bore ultimate responsibility for all decisions and the provider only carried out its ministerial obligations under the parties' agreement, subject to the plan's control. The provider merely took in plan monies and distributed them to the pharmacies to pay for the participants' prescription drugs. The provider's billing the plan for reimbursement did not violate 29 U.S.C.S. § 1106(a)(1)(D) of ERISA. The provider received a flat rate for every claim it processed regardless of whether it collected a reduced or full co-payment. It received no excess compensation.

Alves v Harvard Pilgrim Health Care
204 F. Supp. 2d 198 (D. Mass. 2002)

The plaintiffs in the case were members of a health care benefit plan that was offered by Harvard Pilgrim Health Care (HPHC) and was subject to ERISA. They brought this proposed class action, claiming that Harvard's decision to charge co-payments in excess of costs, their failure to disclose material information pertaining to the prescription drug costs, and

Alves v Harvard Pilgrim Health Care
204 F. Supp. 2d 198 (D. Mass. 2002)
...continued

their disclosure of misleading information violated the terms of the plans and constituted a breach of fiduciary duty under ERISA and federal common law. The court initially addressed the issue of standing, finding that plaintiffs had standing to bring claims against co-defendants that were wholly owned affiliates of HPHC, in which plaintiffs were participants and the co-payment plan provisions were substantially the same, stating that a single resolution of the dispute would be expeditious. The court also addressed issues of standing related to which statutory claims could be brought by plaintiffs based on their membership status at the time the suit was filed. The court then turned to plaintiffs' claims that the defendants had breached the terms of their contract with members in violation of ERISA. The court noted that the Plan defines the terms of the policy and what plaintiffs are due, and that the court had authority to review ERISA claims because the benefit plan did not confer upon the administrator discretionary authority to construe the terms of the plan. Because the contract provisions of the plans specified the required co-payment amounts, without making exceptions for cases where the fee exceeds the insurer's true cost, the provisions should be given their natural meaning. Thus, defendants did not breach the contract terms by charging members a co-payment that may exceed its own per-unit cost because of discounting arrangements with prescription drug providers. Then the court addressed plaintiffs' claims that the defendants had breached their fiduciary obligations in collecting co-payments in excess of the actual cost and in failing to disclose that practice. The court acknowledged that an employer's decisions regarding the content of a benefits plan are not themselves fiduciary acts, and that an ERISA fiduciary is not restricted from pursuing reasonable business behavior. The court then stated that there could be no breach of fiduciary duty where an ERISA plan is implemented according to its written, nondiscretionary terms. The court then pointed out that the named plaintiffs actually came out ahead in the co-payment plan, paying less in co-payments than the actual costs of the prescriptions. The court concluded that the defendants did not breach their fiduciary duties by charging a flat co-payment amount, even though the policy could disadvantage some beneficiaries some of the time. The court also addressed the plaintiffs' argument that defendants made affirmative misrepresentations to plan beneficiaries about co-payments because the receipts dispensed at the in-house pharmacies listed the "retail value" of the prescription medication without disclosing defendants' actual costs. The court found that the receipt actually did provide a comparison between the co-payment and the retail value, even though it did not provide the wholesale price as well, and was not an affirmative representation. Further, the court discussed plaintiffs' contention that defendants were affirmatively required to disclose that the co-payment would exceed defendants cost for some medications. The court noted that there was no statutory or regulatory requirement to disclose plan costs, and found no breach of fiduciary duty for failure to disclose such costs. Finally, the court dismissed plaintiffs' allegations of self-dealing, finding that there was no evidence that any defendant sought personal gain or advantage from the co-payment provisions, and that using discounting arrangements to reduce their net cost of providing prescription drug benefits did not constitute self-dealing. Thus, the court granted the defendants' motion for summary judgment.

PART VIII: REGULATION OF THE PRACTICE OF PHARMACY

STATE REGULATION OF THE PRACTICE OF PHARMACY

Boards of Pharmacy

State Board of Pharmacy v Weinstein
514 N.E.2d 1143 (Ohio Com. Pl 1987)

ISSUE: Whether a pharmacist who successfully appealed a finding of violation of state pharmacy laws was entitled to attorney fees.

FACTS: Woodrow Weinstein was a registered pharmacist for Elmwood Place Pharmacy. Weinstein received notice of a hearing from the Ohio State Board of Pharmacy declaring that Elmwood Place Pharmacy had received and sold misbranded drugs. After a hearing, the Ohio State Board of Pharmacy issued an order declaring the conduct of Weinstein to constitute gross immorality and dishonesty in the practice of pharmacy. Weinstein's license was suspended for 1 year and he received a $4,000 penalty.

RULING: Weinstein appealed the Board of Pharmacy decision, and the Court of Common Pleas found the board's order not to be supported by reliable, probative and substantial evidence. The court found the record to include conjectural evidence which consisted entirely of self-serving statements. Based on these findings, the court reversed the Board of Pharmacy's order and granted Weinstein's motion for attorney fees.

REASONING: Ohio statutes provide that an individual whose net worth does not exceed $1 million and who prevails as a party to an appeal involving the state, is entitled to compensation for attorney fees incurred by him in connection with such an appeal. After considering the entire record, the appellate court concluded that the Board of Pharmacy failed to meet its burden of proving that it was substantially justified in initiating this controversy.

The record below disclosed only conjectural evidence, which consisted entirely of self-serving statements. The state had to prove that it was substantially probable that evidence in its possession would lead to a finding of a legal violation committed by Weinstein. The state also had to be substantially convinced that, considering the totality of the evidence, reasonable minds could find the alleged violator guilty by a preponderance of the evidence. There was no reliable evidence supporting the Board of Pharmacy's ruling that the pharmacy purchased misbranded drugs and dispensed such drugs to patients.

The court granted Weinstein an award of attorney's fees in the amount of $3,371. The court found that this award was clearly reasonable. Attorneys who are specialized in administrative appeals are entitled to at least $100 per hour as a reasonable rate of attorney's fees. Weinstein's counsel's request for 35.25 hours of legal work was found to be reasonable as documented.

The following is a list of court cases that are related to this topic.

Rite Aid Corp. v Board of Pharmacy of the State of New Jersey, 421 F. Supp. 1161 (D.N.J. 1974).
Malon v Hueseman, WD 53338, April 8, 1997, 1997 Mo. App. LEXIS 565.

Enabling Legislation: The Practice Act

The following is a list of court cases that are related to this topic.

Morris v Commonwealth of Pennsylvania, Dept. of State, 537 A.2d 93 (Pa. Cmwlth. 1988).
Brown v Commonwealth of Pennsylvania, 506 A.2d 913 (Pa. Cmwlth. 1989).

Board Membership

Rite Aid Corp. v Board of Pharmacy of the State of New Jersey
421 F.Supp. 1161 (D.N.J. 1974)

ISSUE: Whether a state statute which permits pharmacists to be regulated by a board composed primarily of their competitors is constitutional.

FACTS: The New Jersey Board of Pharmacy was composed of five licensed pharmacists and one public member. At the time the lawsuit was filed, all of the pharmacist board members were the owners of independent retail pharmacies. Based upon letters of complaint and an investigation, the board concluded that a Rite Aid pharmacy had filled and refilled prescriptions without authorization. Rite Aid was the largest pharmacy chain store system in the state of New Jersey. The hearing officer, appointed to hear the charges against Rite Aid and its pharmacists, recommended that the pharmacy permit of the particular store be suspended for 30 days. The Board of Pharmacy adopted the hearing officer's report, but it increased the suspension to 90 days followed by a probationary period of 2 years.

In its complaint against the board, Rite Aid alleged that the statute discriminated against chain store pharmacies because the pharmacists employed in such establishments could not be chosen to serve as members of the Board of Pharmacy. This allegation was predicated on the statutory requirement that board members be "engaged in conducting a pharmacy," which was interpreted to mean that the board member must be the owner of a pharmacy. Thus, Rite Aid argued that the board members were necessarily biased and could be neither impartial in their regulatory functions nor in adjudicating alleged violations by other nonboard member pharmacists.

RULING: The court concluded that the New Jersey Pharmacy Act did not create a situation of probable bias in the regulation of pharmacists and that mere theoretical competition alone was not a sufficient basis for conclusion of bias.

REASONING: The court emphasized that Rite Aid had failed to factually establish a record to satisfy the burden of proof. To make its case, the plaintiff should have proven that by "the reason of intrinsic competitive nature of the practice of pharmacy, any independent pharmacist (no matter how small or large his own establishment, no matter where it is located vis-à-vis a Rite Aid store or any other chain or multi-independent pharmacy, no matter the relevant trade practice or customs) would be so economically affected by the establishment of a Rite Aid or other chain store anywhere in New Jersey that he could not be impartial in deciding the outcome of a proceeding involving Rite Aid." No such proof was offered. The majority of the court concluded that the chain store posed no greater financial threat to an independent pharmacy than the financial threat posed by another competing independent. In addition, the majority stated that Rite Aid's share of the New Jersey pharmacy volume was so small that pharmacy board members were unlikely to be prejudiced against it.

Powers and Duties

Kansas State Board of Pharmacy v Wilson
657 P.2d 83 (Kan.1983)

ISSUE: Whether the state of Kansas, within its police power, could prohibit the use of the title "Farmacy" in an establishment which did not have a licensed pharmacist on duty.

FACTS: The defendant, Larry Wilson, operated a health food store in Wichita, Kansas under the name of "Nature's Farmacy." Wilson obtained from the state of Kansas a trademark consisting of those words, and his letterhead stationery contained a mortar and pestle symbol. Wilson's business included the sale of health foods and vitamins, but he did not sell prescriptions or over-the-counter drugs. Wilson described himself as a naturopathic physician.

Wilson applied to the Kansas State Board of Pharmacy for a retail dealer's permit, but the board rejected his application because the word "Farmacy" was prohibited by a Kansas statute which held that the use of any words similar to "pharmacy" could not be used by businesses which were not licensed pharmacies. Wilson continued to operate his business using the name "Nature's Farmacy" and this action resulted.

The definition of a pharmacy found in a Kansas Pharmacy Act included any place (1) where drugs were offered for sale, or (2) which had displayed upon it the words "pharmacy," "apothecary," "druggist" or (3) where the characteristic symbols of pharmacy were exhibited. The defendant argued that the state had no right to regulate his business so as to deprive him of his property without due process of law.

RULING: The court concluded that it was clearly within the police power of the state of Kansas to regulate pharmacies and drugs and to see that the public was protected from fraud and deception. Thus, the defendant was prohibited from continuing to use the name "Farmacy" without a licensed pharmacist on duty.

REASONING: The court found that although the defendant contended that his word "Farmacy" was derived from the word "Farm" and connoted agricultural products, it was phonetically indistinguishable from "pharmacy." An individual hearing a radio commercial for the defendant's business would assume that he sold prescription drugs. Furthermore, the defendant's letterheads used the mortar and pestle symbol which were characteristic of a pharmacy.

The court concluded, "pharmacists are highly skilled professionals, tested, licensed and regulated by the state for the protection of the public. The public expects that pharmacies, or drug stores, will be staffed or controlled by such professional persons. To permit the defendant, by his trade name advertising, to confuse or mislead the public into believing his health food store enjoys the same professional reputation as does a pharmacy has great potential for public mischief and is properly subject to the state police power."

Missouri Hospital Association v Department of Consumer Affairs
731 S.W.2d 262 (Mo. App. 1987)

ISSUE: Whether the Missouri Board of Pharmacy had the authority to enact rules and regulations regarding in-hospital dispensing of drugs.

FACTS: The Missouri State Board of Pharmacy, represented by the Department of Consumer Affairs, is responsible for the administration and enforcement of statutes, rules, and regulations pertaining to the licensure and regulation of pharmacists and pharmacies within the state of Missouri. In April 1984, the Board filed a rule requiring hospital pharmacies that provide in-house dispensing of drugs to hold a permit issued by the Board of Pharmacy. In August, the Board filed additional rules regarding pharmacists-in-charge and electronic data processing, which also related to hospital pharmacies.

The Missouri Hospital Association and seven individual hospitals filed a suit challenging the validity of these regulations. The plaintiffs contended that the rules promulgated by the Board to regulate in-hospital dispensing of drugs, staffing practices, and data processing were beyond the jurisdiction and authority of the Board.

RULING: The trial court entered summary judgment in favor of the plaintiffs. The court found that the defendant Board of Pharmacy exceeded the jurisdiction and authority granted to it by the legislature. The Missouri Court of Appeals affirmed the trial court judgment declaring the regulations enacted by the Board of Pharmacy to be void.

REASONING: The appellate court reiterated the basic concept that rules are void if they are beyond the scope of the legislative authority conferred upon the state agency or if they attempt to extend or modify the statutes. Therefore, the court was required to examine the statutes governing pharmacies to determine the validity of the regulations. The Missouri statutes defined a "pharmacy" to be any place conducted for the "purpose of compounding and dispensing or retailing any drug, medicine, chemical or poison..." It was apparent to the court that the statute was designed to regulate pharmacies that dispense drugs to the general public. Nowhere in the statutes was there a reference to hospital pharmacy services. There were, however, several references to retail operations where there is direct contact between the pharmacist and consumer.

The statutes further referred to the posting of the pharmacy permit and also limited what business name could be used to designate a pharmacy. The court noted that, obviously, in a hospital setting patients would seldom see that part of the hospital where the drugs are stored. The court did not believe that the requirements of a pharmacy permit could apply to emergency crash carts or to a nursing station. It further noted that a separate statute specifically provided for the regulation of hospitals, including pharmaceutical services. Under these other statutes, hospital pharmaceutical services were regulated by the Missouri Department of Social Services which required that hospital pharmacy services be directed by a registered pharmacist who was responsible to a hospital administrative officer. Thus, it was determined that another agency was already regulating hospital pharmacies and that the Board had no authority to do so.

The defendant Board of Pharmacy argued that its statutes required at least one member of the Board be a hospital pharmacist or employed in a nursing home. The court rejected the argument that this requirement indicated a legislative intent that the Board of Pharmacy also had jurisdiction to regulate hospitals. The Board of Pharmacy did license all pharmacists whether employed in hospitals or in retail, but this did not give the Board the right to require hospital pharmacies to hold a permit issued by the Board.

Newcomb Sales v New Jersey Board of Pharmacy
526 A.2d 1122 (N.J. Super. Ct.App.Div. 1987)

ISSUE: Whether the New Jersey State Board of Pharmacy had the right to deny a hospital a permit to operate a retail pharmacy on the premises.

FACTS: New Jersey statutes mandate the issuance of a pharmacy permit upon a showing that the pharmacy will be operated by a registered pharmacist in conformance with the laws of that state. When presented with an application from a New Jersey hospital to operate a retail pharmacy on the ground floor of the hospital, the board denied the application. The board set forth six reasons for its denial, all of which were directly related to the proposed location of the pharmacy within the hospital: (1) the location would result in an unfair advantage for the pharmacy business of outpatients and discharge patients and would serve as a detriment to their freedom of choice; (2) there would be a potential for inventory leakage from the hospital's institutional pharmacy to the retail pharmacy; (3) there would be the potential for steering patients to the retail pharmacy; (4) the hospital's institutional pharmacy had been found guilty of four pharmacy violations in 1980; (5) there would be the potential for assigning employees from the tax exempt hospital to work in the retail pharmacy; and (6) the general public might be unaware of the location of the pharmacy within the hospital, which would interfere with the pharmacy's statutory requirement of rendering "complete service to the community."

RULING: The court reversed the pharmacy board's decision to deny the retail pharmacy permit to the hospital.

REASONING: The court found that none of the board of pharmacy's reasons established a failure to comply with the statutory standards for granting pharmacy permits. In fact, the decision to deny the pharmacy permit was contrary to the advice given to the board of pharmacy by the attorney general who served as its legal advisor. During the appeal by the hospital, the board's attorney general appointed special counsel to represent the board of pharmacy and he, in turn, intervened to urge a reversal of the board's decision.

The court concluded that the location of the pharmacy within the hospital would in no way endanger the public health or safety. "The possibility of violations envisioned by the board rested upon groundless speculation." Outpatients and discharge patients would be free to have their prescriptions filled elsewhere or at the proposed pharmacy. The fact that the hospital's institutional pharmacy was reprimanded in 1980 in no way suggested that a retail pharmacy on the premises, run by a distinct corporate entity, would be prone to the same violations.

New Mexico Pharmaceutical Association v State of New Mexico
738 P.2d 1318 (N.M. 1987)

ISSUE: Whether a medical board could enact a rule permitting physicians' assistants to dispense legend drugs when there was a statutory prohibition to the contrary.

FACTS: The New Mexico Board of Medical Examiners enacted a rule that permitted physicians' assistants (in certain circumstances) to dispense dangerous drugs. The supervising physician was permitted under the rule to delegate to his or her assistant the authority to dispense a 48-hour supply of a specified pre-packaged or unit-dose drug if the patient was located more than 12 miles from the nearest pharmacy open at the time of dispensing. The rule excluded the dispensing of controlled substances.

New Mexico Pharmaceutical Association v State of New Mexico
738 P.2d 1318 (N.M. 1987)
...continued

The New Mexico Pharmaceutical Association filed this action against the State of New Mexico and its Board of Medical Examiners seeking a declaration that the rule was void, invalid, and contrary to law.

RULING: The District Court upheld the Board's action, ruling that the Board acted within the scope of its authority and not contrary to law. The Supreme Court of New Mexico reversed the District Court decision and held that the Board's rule was contrary to law because New Mexico statutes expressly prohibited physicians' assistants from dispensing dangerous drugs.

REASONING: New Mexico statutes provided that the licensing of the practice of medicine shall not apply to:

> "any act, task or function performed by a physician's assistant at the direction of and under the supervision of a licensed physician when:
>
> (1) Such assistant is certified by and annually registered with the Board as one qualified by training or experience to function as an assistant to a physician;
> (2) such act, task or function is performed at the direction of and under the supervision of a licensed physician in accordance with rules and regulations promulgated by the board; and
> (3) the services of the physician's assistant are limited to assisting the physician in the particular fields for which the assistant has been trained, certified and registered; provided that *this subsection* shall not limit or prevent any physician from delegating to a *qualified person* any acts, tasks or functions which are otherwise permitted by law or established by custom *except the dispensing of dangerous drugs.* [Emphasis added.]"

While the Board had been authorized by the legislature to adopt reasonable rules and regulations, it had no power to adopt a rule or regulation that was not in harmony with the statutory authority. The Board contended its rule allowing physicians' assistants to dispense dangerous drugs was not inconsistent with the statutory prohibition. It argued that the "qualified persons" mentioned in subsection (3) above did not include physicians' assistants.

The court resorted to the basic rule of statutory construction and interpretation that the entire statute as a whole should be read so that each provision may be considered in relation to every other part. The entire statute cited above governs physicians' assistants. The court ruled that when the legislature used the term "qualified person" in the final clause of the subsection, it meant a physician's assistant. The Board's interpretation of its statutory authority was clearly wrong. It acted outside its scope of authority and contrary to law when it promulgated the rule.

The following is a list of court cases that are related to this topic.

In the Matter of Heller, 374 A.2d 1191 (N.J. 1977).
Sutton v Ohio State Bd. of Pharmacy, 2002 WL 819059 (Ohio Ct. App. 2002).

Immunity of Board Members

Mark v Williams
724 P.2d 428 (Wash. App. 1986)

ISSUE: Whether a pharmacist was entitled to damages from a pharmacy board investigator and the executive secretary of the Board of Pharmacy for a search of his pharmacy and the seizure of items pursuant to an overly broad administrative inspection warrant.

FACTS: On January 3, 1983, the manager of AMFAC Drug, a wholesaler, notified a diversion investigator for the Drug Enforcement Administration that Mark's Westside Prescriptions, Inc., was purchasing unusually large quantities of *Valium*. Several days later, the DEA advised the Washington State Board of Pharmacy of the purchases and the two agencies began a joint investigation. They found that from January 1, 1983 to January 24, 1983, Mark had purchased 17,500 tablets of *Valium*. During a normal administrative review of Mark's pharmacy records, the investigator found prescriptions accounting for approximately 200 tablets of the drug.

On January 31, 1983, a surveillance post, using video tapes and photographs was established in a motel across the street from the pharmacy. The surveillance disclosed suspicious activity which usually began 2 hours after the wholesaler delivered *Valium* to the pharmacy. Richard Morrison, an investigator for the Board of Pharmacy, applied for an Administrative Inspection Warrant from a Seattle district court judge. The application for the warrant requested the seizure of "all controlled substances at the premises, samples of amber plastic vials and paper bags, all records pertaining to the acquisition and distribution of controlled substances."

On the same day that the warrant was issued, the investigator arrested three customers leaving Mark's pharmacy with unlabeled vials of *Valium*. Twenty minutes later, Morrison served the warrant on Mark. Mark was arrested and the investigators then inventoried and seized the drugs and records pursuant to the warrant. Mark was repeatedly asked if he wished to stay at the pharmacy to allow the inventory or if he wished to go for processing and complete the audit later. Mark indicated that he wished to stay. The inventory and seizure concluded at 1:30 a.m. on the following morning. Seventy controlled substances were audited with 111,585 unaccounted dosage units.

On March 24, 1983, Mark was charged with five violations of the Uniform Controlled Substances Act. Mark filed a motion to suppress the evidence and the trial court found that the administrative inspection warrant was invalid because its scope was too broad, the affidavit in support of the warrant was deficient, and the additional information provided in support of the warrant was not summarized in writing.

Therefore, the trial court concluded that the items at the pharmacy had been seized illegally and suppressed them as evidence. Despite this ruling, Mark was convicted of four violations.

Five months later, Mark filed a complaint against Morrison and Donald Williams, the Executive Secretary of the Washington State Board of Pharmacy for a violation of his civil rights, abuse of process, intentional infliction of mental distress, defamation, and invasion of privacy. The complaint alleged that Mark was damaged in excess of $523,000. Mark also filed a lawsuit in Federal District Court seeking damages against the Washington investigator and executive secretary and also from the DEA. The federal court granted the defendants' motion for summary judgment, finding that the defendants had a qualified immunity from liability. Williams and Morrison filed a motion for summary judgment in the state action as well. The state trial court entered an order granting the motion and dismissed Mark's complaint with prejudice.

Mark v Williams
724 P.2d 428 (Wash. App. 1986)
...continued

RULING: The trial court held, and the Washington Court of Appeals affirmed, that the Board of Pharmacy investigator and executive secretary enjoyed qualified immunity from civil rights claims arising out of an overly broad administrative search warrant and that this immunity provided a complete defense to constitutional tort law claims.

REASONING: Using civil rights allegations, the plaintiff must allege that (1) the conduct complained of was committed by a person acting under color of state law and (2) that this conduct deprived the plaintiff of rights or privileges secured by the United States Constitution or laws. The court found that there was no question that the search and seizure were carried out pursuant to state action. The court also accepted the trial court's ruling that the administrative inspection warrant was invalid and that the items were seized in violation of the Fourth Amendment. However, the court went on to note that the investigator and executive secretary enjoyed a qualified immunity against liability for their actions. "Government officials performing discretionary functions generally are shielded from liability for civil damages insofar as their conduct does not violate clearly established statutory or constitutional rights of which a reasonable person would have known."

The court concluded that the statutory language was very broad, and it was reasonable for the investigator to believe that the warrant was validly issued. The statute required that the warrant be served during normal business hours. Mark argued that because his pharmacy closed at 6 p.m. and the warrant was served at 6:20 p.m., the investigators acted unreasonably. The court found that under the circumstances it was not unreasonable to serve the warrant at approximately 6:20 p.m., especially when two customers were arrested immediately before the warrant was served.

Mark also claimed that the defendants committed the tort of "abuse of process" but the court found there was no evidence that the defendants had an ulterior purpose. There was also no evidence that they improperly used the legal proceedings to accomplish a purpose for which they were not designed. "It would be strange indeed if after conducting an administrative investigation in which evidence of criminal activity was obtained, criminal charges could not be filed."

Definition of the Practice of Pharmacy

DePanfilis v Pennsylvania State Board of Pharmacy
551 A.2d 344 (Pa. Cmwlth. Ct. 1988)

ISSUE: Whether a pharmacist's conviction for Medicaid fraud, in connection with billing a state welfare department for brand name drugs when generic drugs were dispensed, was a crime concerning the "practice of pharmacy" for purposes of suspension of a license to practice pharmacy.

FACTS: In September 1985, pharmacist Michael DePanfilis was charged with 34 counts of Medicaid fraud. He later pled guilty to 11 counts of Medicaid fraud in the Commonwealth of Pennsylvania. DePanfilis was billing the Department of Welfare for name brand prescription drugs when, in fact, generic drugs were dispensed. Based upon his guilty plea in the criminal action, the Board of Pharmacy issued an administrative complaint directing the pharmacist to appear at a board hearing to show cause why his license should not be suspended or revoked based upon his guilty plea to Medicaid fraud charges.

DePanfilis v Pennsylvania State Board of Pharmacy
551 A.2d 344 (Pa. Cmwlth. Ct. 1988)
...continued

The pharmacist denied that his conduct constituted an offense in connection with the practice of pharmacy. At the hearing, the Board's prosecutor introduced a copy of the criminal information which had been filed against the pharmacist in the court action. The pharmacist objected, but to no avail.

RULING: The Board found that the pharmacist's guilty pleas to Medicaid fraud constituted offenses in connection with the practice of pharmacy. Consequently, the Board suspended the pharmacist's license for two years and assessed a $750 civil penalty against him. The court affirmed the Board's decision.

REASONING: The issues raised by the pharmacist in his appeal were whether his guilty pleas to 11 counts of Medicaid fraud constituted an offense committed in the practice of pharmacy and whether the Board abused its discretion by permitting the introduction of the criminal information in the Board's hearing.

The pharmacist contended that his violation of state law did not constitute an offense committed in the practice of pharmacy since the legislature did not include fraud or misrepresentation in welfare billing within the definition of "the practice of pharmacy." Thus, the pharmacist argued that the Board incorrectly charged him with a crime in connection with the practice of pharmacy rather than simply charging him with a crime involving moral turpitude.

However, the court noted that it had consistently held that fraud in the practice of a health profession was not limited to conduct that directly affected the care of patients, but instead encompassed all aspects of professional conduct. The definition of the "practice of pharmacy" contained in state law clearly encompassed within its meaning the dispensing of drugs and the maintenance of proper records. The court found that the acts to which the petitioner pled guilty, ie, billing the Department of Welfare for brand name prescriptions and actually dispensing generic products, unequivocally fell within the practice of pharmacy. Thus, because the pharmacist pled guilty to 11 felony counts of offenses committed in the practice of pharmacy, the Board's penalty of suspending his license was not in error.

The pharmacist further argued that allowing the admission of the criminal information in the Board hearing unduly prejudiced him and unfairly tainted the Board's determination. However, an administrative agency is not typically bound by the technical rules of evidence when conducting an administrative hearing. Accordingly, agencies may receive all evidence that is relevant and has reasonable probative value. The criminal information was introduced for the limited purpose of establishing a foundation for the admission of the order of the trial court in the criminal case. The court could find nothing within the Board's decision to suggest that it based its final order upon all of the 34 counts with which the pharmacist was originally charged rather than the 11 counts to which he pled guilty. Because the Board's decision was based solely upon the pharmacist's guilty pleas to 11 felony counts, the court concluded that the admission of the criminal information constituted a harmless error.

Walgreen v Selcke
595 N.E.2d 89 (Ill.App. 1992)

ISSUE: Whether a pharmacy that utilized technicians was guilty in letting two unlicensed employees engage in the practice of pharmacy.

FACTS: The lawsuit was initiated when the Walgreen pharmacy in Oak Lawn, Illinois was visited by an inspector from the Department of Professional Regulation. At that time, the pharmacist in charge was not present, but another pharmacist was on duty. A pharmacy technician was working, but his license had expired. The other employee in the pharmacy area was unlicensed. The inspector determined that the two employees were unlawfully engaged in the practice of pharmacy.

The unlicensed employee testified that she began working for Walgreen as a cashier and that she also cleaned shelves, sold vitamins and other *otc* drugs. On the night of the inspection, the unlicensed employee was ringing sales on the cash register, cleaning the pharmacy area, and answering the telephone. When someone wanted a refill, she would write the name, prescription number, and telephone number on a pad of paper and give it to a person at the computer terminal. She did not receive new prescriptions, compound prescriptions, package medication in containers, interpret the label directions on the prescriptions, or advise about medication. She did not receive her pharmacy technician license until a month after the inspection.

The pharmacy technician who had failed to renew his license testified that he had been working for Walgreen for several years as a technician. He testified that his duties were to put prescription information into the computer and occasionally to take drugs from the shelf to be counted. When he received a telephone call, he would put the prescription number into the computer.

The pharmacy technician had sent in his renewal fee and application two months before it expired. Upon inquiry as to the non-receipt of his license, he was informed that the Department was backed up and that he should "keep going." He inquired several months later, but was informed his application had not been received. He never received a renewal form as requested. Almost a year later, he was informed that the Department had lost his license and a new renewal from would be sent.

RULING: The Illinois Board of Pharmacy recommended that the pharmacy be found to have illegally allowed unlicensed persons to engage in the practice of pharmacy and that its license should be placed on probation. The court reversed the Board's decision.

REASONING: The uncontested facts in the case revealed that the two employees each rang up cash register sales of prescription drug products. They took payment for items sealed in packages and handed the packages to customers. They gave no directions, advice, or explanations concerning the products to the customers. At all times, a registered pharmacist was present. In addition, the pharmacy technician entered refill information into the computer. Products were also retrieved off the shelves for the pharmacists.

Ringing up a sale on a cash register is no more dispensing of pharmaceuticals than a delivery boy taking money from a customer at the latter's home in payment of a prescription. The court ruled this was simply a business transaction. Nor does the fact that the cash register is located at the pharmacy counter permit the legal conclusion that the salesperson recording the sale is engaged in the practice of pharmacy.

Entering refill information by pressing computer keys in order to transcribe the information from a written to an electronic vehicle is no more the practice of pharmacy than allow-

Walgreen v Selcke
595 N.E.2d 89 (Ill.App. 1992)
...continued

ing an unlicensed employee to write on a pad of paper prescription refill information as received over the telephone (the latter conduct was admitted by the Department to be appropriate under Illinois law).

The court also ruled that merely retrieving a container of a pharmaceutical product from the shelf at the request of the pharmacist who was compounding or dispensing a prescription does not fall within the exercise of the practice of pharmacy. It calls for no interpretation, skill, or knowledge of medicine or drugs. The pharmacist chooses and describes the desired ingredients and determines from his or her own knowledge whether what has been brought by the employee correctly corresponds with the product prescribed. Simply fetching the product requested cannot place the employee within the practice of pharmacy anymore than a law clerk bringing law books from a library at a lawyer's request can be deemed to be the practice of law.

The court found that the Illinois Pharmacy Practice Act is designed to ensure that only professionally qualified individuals engage in pharmacy practice. It also noted that the statute emphasizes the performance of acts requiring professional study and training in the science of pharmacy rather than the business aspects of the practice of pharmacy. The Department's arguments simply were not convincing and the case against Walgreen was dismissed.

The following is a list of court cases that are related to this topic.

Arkansas State Board of Pharmacy v Whayne, 454 S.W.2d 667 (Ark. 1970).
Nevada State Board of Pharmacy v Garrigus & Block, 496 P.2d 748 (Nev. 1972).
Ye Olde Apothecary v McClellan, 253 S.E. 2d 545 (W. Va. 1979).
Ingram v Hook's Drugs, Inc., 476 N.E.2d 881 (Ind. Ct. App. 1985).
Sheffield v State of New York, 571 N.Y. Supp 2d 350 (1991).
Borchardt v Department of Commerce, 218 Mich. App. 367, (1996).

Requirements for Licensure

Gumbhir v Kansas State Board of Pharmacy
618 P.2d 837 (Kan. 1980)

ISSUE: Whether an individual who graduated from a foreign school of pharmacy, but who had attained advanced training in pharmacy in the United States, is eligible for a reciprocal license to practice pharmacy.

FACTS: The plaintiff received a bachelor's degree in pharmacy from Punjab University in India. He later received a Master of Science in Pharmacy degree from the University of Minnesota and a PhD in Pharmacy Administration from Ohio State University. The plaintiff was licensed as a pharmacist by examination in the state of Ohio, and subsequently registered by reciprocity as a licensed pharmacist in the state of Missouri. The plaintiff, who is a professor of pharmacy at the University of Missouri-Kansas City, also manages and is part owner of a pharmacy located in Overland Park, Kansas. He applied to the Kansas State Board of Pharmacy for licensure either by examination or by reciprocity. He contended that his master's and doctorate degrees from American universities qualified him for registration by examination, and that his licenses to practice pharmacy in the states of Missouri and Ohio qualified him for reciprocal registration.

Gumbhir v Kansas State Board of Pharmacy
618 P.2d 837 (Kan. 1980)
...continued

The Kansas Board of Pharmacy countered that Kansas law required that the individual have a pharmacy degree from a university accredited by the American Council on Pharmaceutical Education (ACPE). The ACPE does not accredit foreign or graduate schools such as those from which the plaintiff had graduated. Therefore, the board of pharmacy denied the plaintiff's application.

RULING: The court ruled that the decision of the Kansas Board of Pharmacy to deny the plaintiff's application for registration was not arbitrary or capricious, nor was it unconstitutional.

REASONING: The plaintiff argued that this Kansas statute should be interpreted to require graduation from a school or college that had a pharmaceutical program accredited by the ACPE, and that it made no difference whether the degree awarded was a bachelor's degree, a master's degree, or a doctorate degree. The court held that postgraduate study is specialized and "does not involve the broad range of skills which all general practitioners of the profession should possess." In examining the plaintiff's postgraduate record, it found that only 4 of the 28 classes listed on his resume were included under "pharmacy and pharmacology." The remaining classes the plaintiff had taken in graduate school fell under the categories of business and pharmacy administration.

The court concluded that the Kansas law required that an applicant for licensure be a graduate of an accredited program, and graduate programs do not come within the language of the statute. While the court recognized there was merit in the fact that the plaintiff possessed both a master's and doctorate degree in pharmacy areas, he still had not complied with the requirement of the statute. An Attorney General's opinion advised the registration and that the Board did not have the discretion to determine whether the plaintiff nonetheless possessed the qualifications of a graduate of an accredited program.

The plaintiff's final assertion was that the Kansas statute unlawfully delegated legislative power to a private organization (ie, the ACPE). The statute read "every applicant shall be a graduate of a school or college of pharmacy or department of a university accredited by the American Council on Pharmaceutical Education *and recognized and approved by the board*..." The court concluded that this was a delegation of authority to the board, not to the ACPE. The Board of Pharmacy could rely upon the standards established by the ACPE to aid in the determination of an applicant's educational background prior to licensure.

The following is a list of court cases that are related to this topic.

Missouri ex rel Nixon v Stallknecht, No. 99CV212429, October 25, 1999, Jackson County Cir. Ct., Mo., (reported in *Health Law Digest*)

Disciplinary Action

Unprofessional Conduct

Nevada State Board of Pharmacy v Garrigus & Block
496 P.2d 748 (Nev. 1972)

ISSUE: Whether two pharmacists who unknowingly dispensed large quantities of controlled substances to a drug dependent individual could have their licenses revoked for unprofessional conduct.

FACTS: Pharmacists Garrigus and Block were employed at a pharmacy in a large shopping center in Las Vegas, Nevada. Between April 6, 1970 and August 22, 1970, pharmacist Block dispensed, pursuant to prescription orders, a total of 5800 *Numorphan* tablets on 33 occasions to Larry Chapmen. Pharmacist Garrigus also dispensed 3450 of the tablets to Chapmen on 19 separate occasions. In addition to the *Numorphan* prescriptions, Chapmen purchased 580 hypodermic syringes from the pharmacists between June and August 1970. The *Numorphan* prescriptions were dispensed on the order of a Dr. Hulse. The two pharmacists were concerned about the large amount of the narcotic being dispensed, and the uncontroverted testimony indicated that they verified the authenticity of the prescriptions by calling the physician's office. The pharmacists were informed that Mr. Chapmen suffered from terminal cancer and required significant amounts of the pain reliever. However, it was later learned that Chapmen was a "cheat and an addict" and was using several names and addresses to acquire narcotics. These facts were unknown to the defendant pharmacists. After an investigation and hearing by the Nevada Board of Pharmacy, the two pharmacists' licenses were revoked under a provision of Nevada law, which allows the board to suspend or revoke the license of a pharmacist who is guilty of "unprofessional conduct or conduct contrary to the public interest..."

RULING: Due process requires that unprofessional conduct be defined so the defendants know that they have violated the law. Pharmacists Garrigus and Block did not breach professional standards because such guidelines did not exist. The revocation of their licenses was overturned.

REASONING: There was no evidence submitted that the Nevada Board of Pharmacy had established standards of professional conduct. Unprofessional conduct must be clearly defined so that an individual knows what is expected of him. The Board of Pharmacy rules did not define what amounts of drugs are medically and pharmaceutically excessive, and there was no evidence in the record that the amount of *Numorphan* sold to Chapmen was excessive under the circumstances. The Supreme Court of Nevada held that "it would be a dangerous principle to establish that a druggist cannot safely fill a prescription merely because it is out of the ordinary. If that were done, many patients might die from being denied unusual remedies in extreme cases." The appellate court recognized that there were no guidelines as to when a pharmacist should set his judgment up against that of a physician. "It is not for the pharmacist to second-guess a licensed physician unless in such circumstances that would be obviously fatal." Because the pharmacists had made several inquiries as to the situation, the court felt that they had discharged their duty.

In the Matter of Heller
374 A.2d 1191 (N.J. 1977)

ISSUE: The Board's action was appealed to the New Jersey Supreme Court where the two basic issues raised were: (1) Was the revocation of the pharmacist's license for "grossly unprofessional conduct" valid? (2) Was the civil penalty of $50,472 a valid exercise of the Board's powers?

The attorneys for the pharmacist contended that he had violated no specific statute or board regulation and the conduct complained of was particularly defined as "grossly unprofessional conduct" under the applicable statute. The Pharmacy Act in §45:14-12(a)-(f) of the New Jersey Statutes Annotated listed six types of conduct constituting "grossly unprofessional conduct." But the sale of exempt narcotics for non-medical use was not among the six. (Note: The board had statutory power to revoke a license of a pharmacist convicted of violating any state or U.S. drug law relating to narcotic drugs. Further, N.J. S.A. 24:21-15(c) prohibited the sale of a Schedule V drug (exempt narcotic) for a non-medical purpose. But the pharmacist had not been convicted of violating 24:12-15(c) or any other narcotic drug law. Hence, the Board chose to proceed against him on the principle that his conduct constituted "grossly unprofessional conduct.")

FACTS: This case involves an appeal from an order of the New Jersey Board of Pharmacy revoking a pharmacist's professional license and his pharmacy permit, and assessing him a civil penalty of $50,472. These actions stem from charges of "grossly unprofessional conduct" in that the pharmacist sold some 18,000 bottles of codeine base cough syrup in a 17-month period, selling the bottles at retail for $8 each.

The summarized facts of the case are: The pharmacist was the pharmacist in charge and major shareholder in a corporate-held pharmacy. The store, in a declining area, had a drop of 5,000 in the prescription volume from 1971 to 1974. Between May 1973 and October 1974, the pharmacist sold 18,766 bottles (4 oz) of a Schedule V codeine-base cough remedy. The pharmacist had scrupulously maintained his "exempt narcotic" records, made all such sales personally and meticulously recorded them. He would not sell to a given customer more frequently than once every 48 hours. But he did sell the preparations for $8 a bottle (wholesale cost about $1.20 to $1.75 per bottle) while the usual retail price was $1.69 to $3. Many of his customers stated that they bought from him because "it was hard to get and not many other people sold it." At the time of the Board's determinations, the pharmacist had not been convicted of violating any law or regulation pertaining to sale of Schedule V controlled substances (exempt narcotics), nor any other pharmacy law.

Nonetheless, the Board, after notice and hearing, determined that the pharmacist had "pandered to those intending an illicit and non-medical use of the medications, had realized unconscionable profits therefrom, and consequently had been guilty of grossly unprofessional conduct." The Board revoked both the personal license and store permit of the pharmacist and assessed him a "civil penalty" of $50,472 based on what the Board had determined to be "excess profit."

RULING: The New Jersey Supreme Court ruled that the list of acts constituting unprofessional conduct was not exclusive.

REASONING: The court stated, "This need for special identification does not exist in respect to conduct inherently wrong and obviously 'unprofessional.'" The court buttressed its position by a lengthy discussion of case law including a New Jersey case holding that "...misconduct against a police officer need not be predicated upon the violation of any particular regulation or rule."

As to the civil penalty issue, they found that the enabling statute only permitted the Board to assess a per diem penalty, and, consequently, the Board did not follow the law. As another

In the Matter of Heller
374 A.2d 1191 (N.J. 1977)
...continued

reason for setting aside the civil penalty, the court found that the Board's complaint against the pharmacist failed to notify him of its intent to impose such a penalty. Citing 407 U.S. 80, 92, the court stated:

> Parties whose rights are to be affected are entitled to be heard; and in order that they enjoy that right, they must first be notified.

Since both the statute was not followed (N.J. S.A. 45:14-37 & 38) and procedural due process violated, the civil penalty was vacated. The license revocation and the pharmacy store permit revocation were affirmed.

Six of the seven supreme court justices ruled as indicated above and one justice dissented. The dissenting justice disagreed only with the aspect of the decision dealing with the pharmacist's professional license revocation. In his judgment, the list of proscribed acts of 'unprofessional conduct' was exclusive. He felt the legislature intended the term "grossly unprofessional conduct" to be limited and restricted to the activities particularized. Citing *Boller Beverages, Inc. v Davis*, 183 A.2d 64, he stated, "Fair process does not sanction license revocation on ad hoc basis absent statutory underpinning."

However, it was the majority of the court whose ruling decided the fate of the pharmacist in this case.

Vermont & 110th Medical Arts Pharmacy v Board of Pharmacy of the State of California
125 Cal.App.3d 19 (1981)

ISSUE: Whether a pharmacist's failure to verify the validity of prescriptions may result in the revocation of a license to practice pharmacy.

FACTS: The Vermont & 110th Medical Arts Pharmacy dispensed, over a 45-day period, 10,000 prescriptions written by a small number of physicians for controlled substances. These prescriptions provided 748,000 dosage units of four controlled substances which are popular in the illicit market. On one day, the pharmacy filled 247 prescriptions written by one person (an unlicensed practitioner) for controlled substances. This unlicensed individual issued 4000 prescriptions during the 45-day period of time, and all of these prescriptions were filled by the pharmacy under investigation.

Large numbers of prescriptions for controlled substances were filled in consecutively numbered batches for the same person, but often with many different addresses. The names of many of the patients were highly questionable, such as "Wells Fargo," "Fairlane Ford," "Henry Ford," "Glen Ford," "Pearl Harbor," "Johnny Cash" and many others. Many of the addresses were nonexistent. Some of the pharmacy's clients received *Ritalin* and *Tuinal* from the same physician on the same day. These antagonist prescriptions were honored without being questioned.

Some of the pharmacists employed by the pharmacy had questioned the propriety of the dispensing practices, but the pharmacy owner made no change in pharmacy procedures. The Board of Pharmacy of the state of California concluded that the pharmacists should have

Vermont & 110th Medical Arts Pharmacy v Board of Pharmacy of the State of California
125 Cal.App.3d 19 (1981)
...continued

been on notice of the suspicious nature of the prescriptions they were filling, and that there could be no reasonable probability that the prescriptions were for a legitimate medical purpose. The Board of Pharmacy revoked the license of the pharmacy and the pharmacists based upon California law which prohibits unprofessional conduct. The defendants contended that the board of pharmacy's action was invalid because the Board had never set forth the duties of pharmacists in such circumstances, and that they were not aware of what factors should cause them to question the *actual* validity of a *facially* valid prescription.

RULING: The court upheld the revocation of the pharmacists' licenses for unprofessional conduct.

REASONING: The court held that the statutory scheme under California law clearly called upon pharmacists to use their common sense and professional judgment when dispensing prescriptions. The ambiguities in the prescriptions and the sheer volume of the controlled substances prescribed by a single practitioner for a small number of persons should have provided a signal to the pharmacists to refuse to dispense the prescriptions. The court concluded that, "Society cannot tolerate the presence of individuals within professions who abdicate their professional responsibility and permit themselves to be used as a conduit by which these controlled substances reach the illicit market and become that force of evil to which we allude. More importantly, such prostitutors of their profession will not be heard to explain their dereliction by the juvenile-like complaint, 'Nobody told me it was wrong.' A true professional does not have to be told such things."

Swartz v New York State Department of Education
522 N.Y.S.2d 727 (App.Div. 1987)

ISSUE: Whether a hearing panel was entitled to consider prior disciplinary actions against a pharmacist when imposing a penalty following a routine inspection which revealed that conditions in the pharmacy were dangerous to the public and in violation of the licensing agency's rules.

FACTS: A routine inspection of the pharmacy owned by the plaintiff revealed numerous unlabeled or misbranded drugs as well as medications whose expiration dates had passed. The plaintiff was charged with unprofessional conduct, gross negligence, and gross incompetence. At the hearing, the plaintiff admitted that there were problems with his pharmacy inventory that were caused by his "faulty housekeeping."

The licensing agency sought to introduce evidence that the plaintiff's license had been suspended in 1966 when he pleaded guilty to welfare fraud and in 1978 when he pleaded guilty to giving a controlled substance to an undercover police officer in return for sexual favors. The administrative officer excluded this evidence, stating that it would be considered only if the plaintiff were found guilty.

The hearing panel unanimously found the pharmacist guilty of unprofessional conduct. The panel took "a very serious view of the petitioner's misconduct including his history of disciplinary actions in the past" and recommended that his license be revoked. Consequently, the Commissioner of Education issued an order revoking the pharmacist's license. The pharmacist appealed. He did not dispute that there was sufficient evidence to uphold the

Swartz v New York State Department of Education
522 N.Y.S.2d 727 (App.Div. 1987)
...continued

licensing agency's determination that he was guilty of the charges filed against him. Instead, he argued that he was not notified that his prior disciplinary actions would be considered in determining the penalty to be imposed. He also argued that the infractions that were over 10 years old should be excluded from consideration.

RULING: The appellate court held that the hearing panel was entitled to consider prior disciplinary actions against the pharmacist when imposing a penalty. The court affirmed the revocation of the pharmacist's license for unprofessional conduct.

REASONING: The court reasoned that the pharmacist had been duly warned that his prior disciplinary actions would be considered if he were found guilty. While the remoteness of prior infractions should, as a matter of fairness, be weighed when considering the imposition of a penalty, there is no specific line as to what is so remote that it should not be considered. The court held that the hearing panel was justified in considering the 1966 and 1978 actions.

The court also concluded that the revocation of the pharmacist's license was not an excessive penalty. The pharmacy contained misbranded drugs, vials with quantities of drugs that exceeded the amount specified on the label, and outdated drugs. These conditions were potentially dangerous to the public and were in violation of the licensing agency's rules. The pharmacist's prior record should have heightened his awareness of the necessity to strictly comply with the agency's regulations. Tolerance of repeated disregard of pertinent rules would undermine public confidence in the regulated profession of pharmacy.

The following is a list of court cases that are related to this topic.

McKaba v Board of Regents of the State of New York, 294 N.Y.S.2d 382 (1968).
Fountain v Oelshelgel, 415 P.2d 316 (Ariz. 1969).
Patterson Drug Co. v Kingery, 305 F. Supp. 821 (W.D. Va. 1969).
Young v Board of Pharmacy, 462 P.2d 139 (N.M. 1969).
Blue Cross v Commonwealth, 176 S.E. 2d 439 (Va. 1970).
Jay v Board of Regents of Univ. of N.Y., 376 N.Y.S.2d 664 (N.Y. App. Div. 1975).
Shermack v Board of Regents of the State University System, 407 N.Y.S. 2d 926 (1978).
Duckworth v State Board of Pharmacy, 583 So. 2d 200 (Miss. 1991).
Sheffield v State of New York, 571 N.Y. Supp 2d 350 (1991).
Tadrus v Missouri Board of Pharmacy, 849 S.W. 2d 2224 (1993).

Conviction of a Crime

Morris v Commonwealth of Pennsylvania, Dept. of State
537 A.2d 93 (Pa. Cmwlth. Ct. 1988)

ISSUE: Whether the suspension of a pharmacist's license for 10 years was valid since his narcotic convictions were committed prior to the enactment of the statute requiring such a suspension.

FACTS: The plaintiff held a license to practice pharmacy in the Commonwealth of Pennsylvania. Criminal charges were filed against the plaintiff for unlawfully dispensing *Dilaudid* and *Tussionex* in violation of Pennsylvania drug laws. The plaintiff entered a plea of no contest and the trial court imposed a criminal sentence of five years and a $50,000 fine.

Morris v Commonwealth of Pennsylvania, Dept. of State
537 A.2d 93 (Pa. Cmwlth. Ct. 1988)
...continued

The Pennsylvania State Board of Pharmacy sent the plaintiff a "Notice of Automatic Suspension" which informed him that his license to practice pharmacy was automatically suspended and that he could apply for reinstatement only after a period of 10 years had elapsed. The suspension was based upon a change in the Pennsylvania Pharmacy Act which required that licenses be automatically suspended for at least 10 years upon the conviction of a felony related to a violation of drug laws. Conviction included an admission of guilt or plea of no contest.

Legal counsel for the plaintiff requested a hearing before the Board of Pharmacy, but was informed that no hearing would be held. Prior to changes in the Pennsylvania Pharmacy Act, the board was required to hold a hearing before suspending a pharmacist's license and it also had the discretion to suspend the license for a lesser period of time.

RULING: The suspension of the pharmacist's license for 10 years due to his conviction of felonies under drug laws was affirmed.

REASONING: A statute does not operate retrospectively merely because some of the facts or conditions upon which its application depends came into existence prior to its enactment. The pharmacist's commission of the felonies was merely an antecedent act which put a chain of events into motion. In this case, the plaintiff was convicted of felonies after the effective changes in the Pharmacy Act. Application of the Pharmacy Act to the facts of this case simply involved a prospective operation of the statute.

The plaintiff also contended that due process required that he be provided with a hearing at which he would have the opportunity to provide evidence that would mitigate against the imposition of a 10 year suspension. However, under the Pharmacy Act, as amended, the Board of Pharmacy did not have the discretion to impose sanctions for less than 10 years on persons who had been convicted of felonies under the state's drug laws.

Brown v Commonwealth of Pennsylvania
506 A.2d 913 (Pa. Cmwlth. Ct. 1989)

ISSUE: Whether a pharmacist's property rights in a license to practice the profession could be adversely affected by the retroactive application of a statute.

FACTS: Desmond Brown was licensed to practice pharmacy until December 16, 1985, at which time his license was automatically suspended by the Board of Pharmacy following the pharmacist's conviction of five felony counts under the Pennsylvania Drug Acts. The Board's suspension was based upon the Pharmacy Act of that state, which provides for the automatic suspension of a license following such convictions.

Several days after the Board issued its notice of suspension, the state legislature amended the Pharmacy Act by adding a section that stated that anyone whose license was suspended because of a felony conviction could apply for reinstatement after a period of at least 10 years had elapsed from the date of conviction. This law became effective 12 days after Brown received his notice of suspension.

RULING: In October of 1988, Brown filed a petition for reinstatement of his license. The Board denied the petition based upon the new law and further notified Brown that the law

Brown v Commonwealth of Pennsylvania
506 A.2d 913 (Pa. Cmwlth. Ct. 1989)
...continued

prohibited the Board from even considering an application for reinstatement until 10 years after the date of his conviction. The Appellate Court reversed the Board of Pharmacy and ordered that the pharmacist be given a hearing on his petition for reinstatement.

REASONING: The court noted that the holder of a valid professional license has a property interest in such a license. "The right to practice a profession, once acquired, does constitute a property right in the license." Even though Brown's license was not revoked, but suspended, he still possessed a property right entitled to due process protection.

The court then was faced with the issue of whether the Board's reliance on the new law was a retroactive application since Brown's conviction and suspension preceded the effective date of the law. The Board argued that the fact that Brown applied for reinstatement after the effective date of the legislation made his petition subject to the new law, while pharmacist Brown maintained that the date of his suspension was the critical date and that the new law should not apply.

A statute is not to be construed retroactive unless it is clearly so intended by the legislature. Retrospective laws will be deemed reasonable when they do not impair or disturb any vested right, but only cure defects in proceedings. Thus, retroactive application of legislation is not constitutionally objectionable when a statutory amendment involves a mere procedural change.

Prior to the enactment of the 10 year limitation, the Pharmacy Act was silent as to the length of any suspension for a drug-related conviction. The Board interpreted this silence to mean that the pharmacist had no right to a hearing for reinstatement. In fact, the Board argued that when the new law became effective, the pharmacist gained a substantive right to petition for reinstatement. The court noted that this argument was inconsistent. If the pharmacist had a substantive right under the new law to petition for reinstatement after 10 years, it did not logically follow that he enjoyed no rights under the prior legislation which allowed pharmacists to petition for a rehearing at any time.

Because the new provision of the Pharmacy Act impaired the pharmacist's right to petition the Board for revival or reinstatement of his license, the court found that its retroactive application was unconstitutional.

U.S. v Stone
110 F.3d 65 (6th Cir. 1997)

An independent community pharmacist established a fictitious company to buy prescription drugs from an individual at prices significantly cheaper than available through traditional channels. That company then sold the drugs to the pharmacy at a significant markup. The pharmacist claimed that the individual who sold him the drugs indicated they came from the inventory of liquidated pharmacies. The pharmacist failed to report any income from the fictitious company. After being charged as a co-conspirator with the individual who sold him the drugs, the pharmacist pled guilty to theft and misapplication of drugs from a local hospital that received federal funding, and tax evasion. He was sentenced to 21 months of imprisonment and was ordered, along with the co-conspirator, to make restitution payments to the hospital in the amount of $554,447.48. He has 3 years from the date of his release

U.S. v Stone
110 F.3d 65 (6th Cir. 1997)
...continued

from prison to make restitution. The pharmacist claimed that by making him jointly and severally liable with his co-conspirator to make full restitution to the hospital, the judge failed
to take into account his relative culpability and therefore abused the discretion permitted to the courts by the *Victim and Witness Protection Act*, 18 USC §3663. This law sets forth
factors that judges may consider in deciding whether an offender would be required to repay
the victim of a crime and, if so, the amount of restitution required and the conditions
under which it must be paid. "Relative culpability" or blameworthiness is a consideration that
some courts use when two or more defendants are involved in criminal activities and one
is more responsible for the victim's losses than the other. The Sixth Circuit Court of Appeals
noted that the trial judge made a statement just prior to sentencing that he saw little difference in the relative culpability of the parties. The pharmacist also claimed that the trial
judge failed to take into account the pharmacist's ability to repay the hospital. The Court
disagreed. The pre-sentence report showed that the pharmacist had a net worth of $417,171,
that his spouse is employed and that his only dependent is a 16-year-old son. The trial court
judge noted that while the pharmacist lost his license, he should be able to eventually
repay the debt. In addition, the judge waived a criminal fine and costs of incarceration that
could have been imposed under the law because the pharmacist would not be able to pay
these costs and still make restitution.

Iowa v Carter
618 NW 2d 374 (October 11, 2000), 2000 Iows Sup LEXIS 203

The defendant applied to the Iowa Board of Pharmacy for registration as a pharmacy technician in December 1997. She completed and submitted a form application provided by
the Board. The two-page application form required her to disclose various background information, including whether she had ever been charged or convicted of a crime other than
a traffic violation involving a fine of less than $100. The application also required a signa-
ture. Immediately above the signature line, the form provided "I certify to the Iowa Board
of Pharmacy Examiners that the information I have provided on this registration application is true and correct." The application indicated she had never been charged or convicted of a crime. She signed her name to the application in the space provided immediately
below the certification. The application was not notarized or otherwise verified. The application contained false information because she had been convicted and sentenced to a
term of incarceration not to exceed 10 years for the felony crime of possession of cocaine with
the intent to deliver. This conviction occurred in 1989. The State subsequently charged her
with perjury for failing to reveal the felony offense on the application. Prior to trial, she
moved to dismiss the charge, claiming she did not commit perjury as a matter of law because
the certification on the application did not constitute an oath or affirmation essential to
the commission of perjury. The trial court agreed and dismissed the charge. The state
appealed. The Iowa Supreme Court affirmed finding that the state perjury statute requires
that false statements be made under oath. Further, at common law, the crime of perjury could
only occur in the course of a judicial proceeding while a person was under oath or affirmation. Because those requirements were not satisfied, the defendant did not commit statutory perjury.

New York v Czarnowski
702 N.Y.S.2d 398 (App.Div. 2000)

On January 8, 1998, while searching for a missing hairclip behind a refrigerator, the supervising pharmacist and another employee found an unlabeled vial containing white pills. The supervising pharmacist determined that the tablets were a generic form of *Vicodin*. After reporting the incident to her own supervisor, the pharmacist returned the medication to stock. The defendant, a pharmacy intern employed in the pharmacy admitted later in the day that he had taken the tablets and that he had intended to give them to his father who was suffering from back pain. The pharmacist called the local police. The defendant was indicted on possession of a controlled substance. He moved to dismiss the indictment because there was no chemical analysis proving that the drug he was accused of taking was a controlled substance. The motion was denied and he was convicted after a jury trial. On appeal, the defendant also claimed that the testimony of the supervising pharmacist was not competent on the identity of the generic *Vicodin* because she relied on manufacturer inserts and reference journals to identify the drug and the inserts and journals were not put into evidence. The court rejected these arguments. The statute that requires a chemical analysis of alleged controlled substances only applies to drugs seized by a police agency. Here, the police did not take custody of the drugs. The pharmacist is competent to testify as to her opinion on the identity and quantity of the drugs hidden behind the refrigerator based on her training and experience.

The following is a list of court cases that are related to this topic.

Schwartz v Florida Board of Pharmacy, 302 So.2d 423 (Fla. Dist. Ct. App. 1974).
Intrieri v Commonwealth, 296 A.2d 927 (Pa. 1979).
Brown v Idaho State Board of Pharmacy, 746 P.2d 1006 (Idaho App. 1987).
DePanfilis v Pennsylvania State Board of Pharmacy, 551 A.2d 344 (Pa. Cmwlth. 1988).
Cooper v Missouri State Board of Pharmacy, 774 S.W.2d 501 (Mo. App. 1989).

Violation of a Statute or Regulation

Randle v California State Board of Pharmacy
49 Cal.Rptr. 485 (1966)

ISSUE: Whether a pharmacist may have his license revoked for dispensing prescriptions that had been authorized by an office nurse while the physician was out of town.

FACTS: The California Board of Pharmacy brought a disciplinary action against a California pharmacist and his wife who was the operator of the pharmacy in which her husband was employed. The Board of Pharmacy filed a complaint charging the pharmacist and his wife with four violations of California state law and a fifth charge was made against the husband alone. The pharmacy board, upon a hearing in the matter, found all five counts to be true and thereby revoked the pharmacist's license to practice in California and revoked his wife's permit to operate the pharmacy. A review of the board's actions was made by a superior court which, upon its independent judgment of the evidence, decided that four of the five counts were true and upheld the license revocations. The pharmacist and his wife appealed to a California District Court of Appeals.

The charges against the pharmacist and his wife, as operator of the pharmacy, were as follows: Charge #2 was that the defendants sold 6072 (4 oz) bottles of terpin hydrate with codeine and 1614 (2 oz) bottles of the same and 3259 (4 oz) bottles of cerodine and 1005 (2 oz) bottles of the same without recording the sales as required by the California Health

Randle v California State Board of Pharmacy
49 Cal.Rptr. 485 (1966)
...continued

and Safety Code. Charges #3 and #4 against the defendants were that they sold 1260 *Methedrine* ampules (*Methedrine* is an amphetamine) without first obtaining a valid prescription.

Upon testimony before the pharmacy board, the pharmacist was asked, in reference to the unrecorded exempt narcotic sales: "Did you neglect to enter some in the book?" His answer: "I'm quite sure I did." For practical purposes, his admission to unrecorded sales ended the issue then. With reference to the *Methedrine* ampules, the issue is more complex. It seems that a certain routine procedure was followed in the pharmacy in specific regard to 21 prescriptions, each for 60 *Methedrine* ampules. A customer would bring in a receipt for payment of $7.50 for an office visit to a certain physician. Then, the pharmacist or one of the other employed pharmacists would phone the physician's office and his office nurse would approve the sale of 60 *Methedrine* ampules to the customer. The pharmacist handling the transaction then made out a prescription for the 60 *Methedrine* and signed the doctor's name to it. During each of the 21 transactions, the doctor was out of town and this fact was known to the pharmacist(s). The testimony of the pharmacist was that "Well, I assumed the nurse had authorization to do so or she wouldn't have done it."

RULING: The court ruled that prescriptions that are authorized by an office nurse while the physician is out of town are invalid and a pharmacist's license may be revoked for dispensing such prescriptions.

REASONING: The appellate court in upholding the Board of Pharmacy and the superior court's rulings stated:

> It is obvious that the 21 prescriptions under which 1260 ampules in question were sold were not valid prescriptions and that, therefore, the finding that such ampules were sold "without first having obtained a prescription" therefore is supported by substantial evidence.
>
> The interrelated fourth count charges forgery, in that Dr. _____'s name was signed as the prescriber on these 21 prescriptions without authorization from him to do so. The overwhelming circumstantial evidence supports this charge...

As to the charges against the pharmacist's wife as operator of the pharmacy, the court upheld these even though there was no evidence that she had actual knowledge of the misconduct. Her liability for these was, as the appeals court pointed out, based on the doctrine of *respondeat superior*.

The legal doctrine of *respondeat superior* means, in literal translation that "The master is liable for the acts of his servants." Its practical application is that if a licensee operates his profession through employees, he is liable for the criminal or negligent acts committed within the scope of such license even though he may not authorize such misconduct or, in some instances, not even know about it.

Arenstein v California State Board of Pharmacy
71 Cal.Rptr. 357 (1968)

ISSUE: (1) Whether a pharmacist's guilty plea in federal court could be used by a board of pharmacy as evidence in a state proceeding, and (2) whether a corporation may be held liable for the criminal acts of employees.

FACTS: The California State Board of Pharmacy brought a disciplinary action against two pharmacists and a pharmacy, operating as a corporation, for refilling legend drug prescriptions without having or obtaining refill authorization as required by §4229 of the California State Business and Professional Code. After a hearing on the matter, the pharmacy board suspended the pharmacy license and the pharmacists' individual licenses for a fixed period of time. The pharmacy and pharmacists appealed the Board's suspension to the California Superior Court, and the court eventually sustained the suspension. A further appeal was taken to the California Court of Appeals.

The pharmacist-defendant was operating his pharmacy under the corporate form of ownership. He and his employee pharmacist both pleaded guilty in the United States District Court to charges of refilling prescriptions for *Dexedrine* and *Equanil* without refill authorization in violation of 21 U.S.C. 353(b)(1)(B). Upon accepting their pleas of guilty, the federal judge imposed sentence on each of the pharmacists of 4 years probation and fined the pharmacy $900.

Sometime later, the California State Board of Pharmacy instigated a disciplinary proceeding against the pharmacists and the pharmacy. The Board based its proceeding under §4357 of the California state law as it existed at that time. In finding against the pharmacists, the California pharmacy board used the certified copies of the pharmacists' federal court convictions as convincing proof that the pharmacists also violated §4229 of the California law when they filled the prescriptions for *Dexedrine* and *Equanil*.

However, at a board hearing, the pharmacists were given an opportunity to be heard; among other claims, the pharmacists argued that they were innocent of the illegal refill charges and that their pleas in federal court were made on the advice of their attorneys. The accused pharmacists offered no testimony of any prescribing physician to back up their claims that the refills were authorized.

RULING: (1) A pharmacist's plea of guilty in federal court could be used as evidence in a state proceeding arising out of the same incident, and (2) a corporation may be held liable for the criminal acts of its employees acting within the scope of employment.

REASONING: The California Court of Appeals sustained the Superior Court's decision and also reaffirmed the California State Board of Pharmacy's disciplinary action. One of the main issues presented to the court was, in simplified terms: Could a plea of guilty in federal court be used as convicting evidence in a state proceeding arising out of the same incident? The court answered the question by stating:

> ...that when he pleaded guilty to the offense charged in Count I he admitted committing the specific act alleged therein contrary to provisions of 21 U.S.C. 353(b)1; and that the specific act by which he committed the federal violation of misbranding as alleged in Count I contains all of the elements of a violation of §4229, Business and Professional Code, as charged in the administrative accusation. Thus, _____ and _____ each by his guilty plea admitted refilling the same prescription for the same person on the same date for the same drug without authorization from the prescriber as charged in paragraphs III and IV of the administrative accusation.

632   *Pharmacy Law Digest*

Arenstein v California State Board of Pharmacy
71 Cal.Rptr. 357 (1968)
...continued

> A plea of guilty means guilty 'as charged' in the information, and by it all averments
> of facts are admitted...The effect is the same as if the defendant had been tried before
> a jury and had been found guilty upon evidence covering all the material facts.

As to the pharmacy board's action against the pharmacy corporation for violations by the corporation's employees, the court stated:

> If a licensee elects to operate his business through employees, he must be responsible
> to the licensing authority for their conduct in the exercising of his license and he
> is responsible for the acts of his agents or employees done in the course of his busi-
> ness in the operation of the license.

In this case, the court speaks of a corporate licensee being liable for the criminal acts of its
employees committed in the course of the operation of its license. It should be noted that
the broad language of the court's rule does not limit such liability to only licensees operating under the corporate form of ownership but is equally applicable to any licensee who
operates through employees—thus it would apply to a pharmacy operated as a partnership
or sole proprietorship.

Arkansas State Board of Pharmacy v Patrick
423 S.W.2d 265 (Ark. 1968)

ISSUE: (1) Whether a pharmacist who fills an unauthorized prescription presented by an
undercover agent may use "entrapment" as a defense, and (2) whether the pharmacist, who
permits a clerk to fill the container and type the prescription label, may have his license
revoked for aiding and abetting the unlicensed practice of pharmacy.

FACTS: This case involved a license revocation proceeding against a pharmacist who was
charged, and found guilty of willfully violating the Arkansas pharmacy laws. After due notice
and a hearing, the Arkansas Board of Pharmacy permanently revoked the license of the
pharmacist (who apparently had a 28-year unblemished record prior to the revocation) upon
finding that he willfully violated two separate sections of the state pharmacy laws. The pharmacist appealed his case to the Circuit Court of Union County, Arkansas, and the circuit court reversed the pharmacy board's decision. However, the pharmacy board appealed
the circuit court reversal to the Arkansas Supreme Court which, in turn, reversed the circuit court's ruling, but reduced the punishment against the pharmacist (defendant) to a
license suspension for 1 year.

A special investigator of the Arkansas Board of Pharmacy had a prescription container prepared with a Walgreen drugstore label containing the following: The name of a fictitious
person, the words "*Enovid E,*" a prescription number, and the name of a bona fide doctor in
the community. The inspector, posing as a customer, took the *Enovid E* container to the
defendant's pharmacy and asked the defendant, who was the pharmacist on duty at the time,
to refill the container. The defendant then sold the inspector another container of 20 *Enovid
E* tablets but labeled it with the label of defendant's pharmacy and his prescription number 185622. (At the trial of the case, the inspector testified that he was to contact every pharmacy in the area in the same manner.) A prescription blank was prepared in the defendant's
pharmacy for the *Enovid E* dispensed and the doctor's name was signed to it along with the

Arkansas State Board of Pharmacy v Patrick
423 S.W.2d 265 (Ark. 1968)
...continued

signature of the defendant. Arkansas law required that the pharmacist dispensing a drug on prescription must sign his name, "as dispensing pharmacist" on the prescription.

At trial, the defendant testified that he didn't recall whether he actually filled the prescription (written by someone in the pharmacy but signed by defendant as dispensing pharmacist) and "If I did, I probably tried to call Dr. _____. If I don't try to call them on these situations we call them later and get their OK because _____ and _____ are particular about their prescriptions."... There was no doubt as to what it was and knowing Dr. _____ and knowing that he gives them for a year at a time I wouldn't hesitate to fill it."

Two months later, the pharmacy board inspector again went to defendant's pharmacy taking with him the container given to him by the defendant. This time a Mrs. _____ was employed in the pharmacy and waited on the inspector; Mrs. _____ was not a pharmacist. According to the inspector's testimony, Mrs. _____, the nonpharmacist, filled the container or at least she typed the label for it and placed the label on it. At any rate, another prescription blank was written for it at the pharmacy and the defendant-pharmacist signed the prescription as the dispensing pharmacist. At trial, the defendant denied that he had knowledge of the act performed by Mrs. _____, the nonpharmacist. The pharmacy board charged the defendant-pharmacist that he "directly aided or abetted the practice of pharmacy by a person not authorized to practice pharmacy by the Arkansas State Board of Pharmacy" in violation of §71-1040(5) of the state statutes.

At the trial, the pharmacist raised the defense of "entrapment" in answer to the illegal drug dispensing charge. In answer to the charge of aiding and abetting a nonpharmacist in the practice of pharmacy, the defendant raised the issue that putting a printed label on a prescription container does not, in itself, constitute the practice of pharmacy.

RULING: (1) Because the undercover agent did no more than present an opportunity for violation of the law, the pharmacist could not allege entrapment as a defense, and (2) the pharmacist's license was suspended for a 1-year period of time for aiding and abetting the practice of pharmacy by an unlicensed person.

REASONING: The Arkansas Supreme Court, in review of both issues, rejected them as defenses to the facts of the cases. In defining "entrapment" as a defense or excusing factor, the Arkansas Supreme court (quoting from *Sherman v U.S.*, 356 U.S. 369) stated:

> However, the fact that government agents 'merely afford opportunities or facilities for commission of the offense does not' constitute entrapment. Entrapment occurs only when the criminal conduct was the 'product of the creative activity' of the law enforcement officials. The records show that the agents did no more than present an opportunity for the violation of the Act by the sale of a prescribed drug without the necessary refill authorization (quoted from another case).

With reference to the issue of aiding a nonpharmacist to practice pharmacy, the Arkansas Supreme Court, in effect, ruled that because the defendant had signed the prescription, as the dispensing pharmacist, he made it possible for the clerk to illegally dispense the drug and to practice pharmacy without a license. The court in its written memorandum stated:

> There are hundreds of drugs on the market at this time, and an erroneous set of directions could well result in the impairment of a customer's health. It is true that there is a difference between the act performed by Mrs. _____ and the compounding or mix-

Arkansas State Board of Pharmacy v Patrick
423 S.W.2d 265 (Ark. 1968)
...continued

ing of a preparation called for by a prescription. Nonetheless, we think the public welfare demands that the dispensing of drugs, including the giving of prescriptions, be
performed only by an authorized pharmacist.

Because of the good record of the pharmacist and the distinction drawn by the court between
illegally dispensing *Enovid E* and illegally dispensing a narcotic or barbiturate drug, the court
reduced the punishment from permanent license revocation to a 1-year license suspension. One judge on the Arkansas Supreme Court (while concurring with the majority on the
nature of the offenses) believed that the issue of punishment should be returned and left
to the Board of Pharmacy for reconsideration. This particular judge felt that, as a practical
matter, the 1-year suspension of the defendant's license was not too damaging since he was
now practicing in Louisiana (he had a Louisiana license) and there was no Louisiana law that
would authorize suspension of a reciprocal pharmacist license for a conviction in another
state.

Sloman v Iowa Board of Pharmacy Examiners
440 N.W.2d 609 (Iowa 1989)

ISSUE: Whether a pharmacist who sold large amounts of Schedule V cough syrups violated
Iowa law by selling these preparations without a legitimate medical purpose.

FACTS: David Sloman was the sole proprietor of Medicap Pharmacy in Cedar Rapids, Iowa.
In June of 1986, an audit by an investigator of the Board of Pharmacy revealed that Sloman had made a total of 802 sales of Schedule V narcotic cough syrups between October
1983 and June 1986 and that 514 sales had been made to 10 individuals. These sales had
been made after Sloman was advised by an investigator that they were questionable because
there did not appear to be any legitimate medical purpose.

The Board did not find any evidence that Sloman had violated its rule against multiple sales
of Schedule V preparations within a 48-hour time frame. There was also no evidence that
any of Sloman's records had been altered. However, based upon the frequency and number of
sales, the Board concluded that Sloman had violated Iowa law. Because this was his second offense regarding sales of Schedule V cough preparation, it was concluded he should have
realized that indiscriminate selling of such products would be taken seriously by the Board.
In addition, it was concluded that he did not use good professional judgment when he routinely sold these cough syrups without regard to whether his customers were using them for
legitimate medical purposes.

RULING: The Board of Pharmacy suspended Sloman's license to practice pharmacy for 1
year and placed him on probation for 5 years. The District Court concluded that the phrase
"medical purpose" in Iowa law was unconstitutionally vague. In addition, the trial court
determined there was no substantial evidence that Sloman's sales were for other than medical purposes. The Iowa Supreme Court overturned the lower court decision by concluding
that the phrase "medical purpose" provided a sufficiently clear practice guide for law abid-
ing behavior for a person of ordinary intelligence.

REASONING: The court noted that a statue will violate due process and be unconstitutionally vague if it does not give a person of ordinary intelligence a reasonable opportunity to

Sloman v Iowa Board of Pharmacy Examiners
440 N.W.2d 609 (Iowa 1989)
...continued

know what is prohibited. The court rejected Sloman's challenge since the statute was clearly intended to grant the Board of Pharmacy contradiction of state or federal law.

In the similar case of the *United States v Hayes*, 595 F.2d 258 (1979), a pharmacist appealed his conviction of distributing controlled substances that were not issued for a "legitimate medical purpose." In the *Hayes* case, the court rejected the pharmacist's contention that, because he was not a physician, he did not have any reasonable means of determining whether a prescription was valid. The volume of prescriptions filled by the pharmacist, for a single individual as well as the prices he charged, supported the jury's conclusion that the pharmacist knew that the prescriptions were not issued for a legitimate medical purpose. The facts of a case can show how a pharmacist may know that prescriptions are not issued for a legitimate medical purpose without his needing to know anything about medical science.

The evidence showed that Sloman sold a large amount of codeine-containing cough syrups to a limited number of people for more than 2 years. Expert testimony suggested that these preparations would be most appropriate for short-term suppression of coughs rather than the treatment of a chronic, persistent cough. The medical danger presented by the use of these preparations is that suppression of a cough for a long period of time could worsen the underlying condition.

One of the reasons for requiring that a pharmacist not dispense Schedule V preparations for other than a medical purpose is to place the responsibility for preventing abuse and psychological dependence upon the trained professional instead of upon the unknowing layperson. The Board concluded that Sloman abdicated this responsibility by indiscriminately selling these preparations to the same people over and over.

Ohio State Board of Pharmacy v Poppe
549 N.E.2d 541 (Ohio App. 1988)

ISSUE: Whether a pharmacist who purchased a dangerous drug from someone other than a registered wholesale distributor and received prescription drugs in plastic bags with handwritten labels violated Ohio pharmacy laws.

FACTS: Pharmacist C. David Poppe operated a Medicine Shop in Ohio. The evidence showed that Tri-State Pharmaceuticals was a wholesale distributor of dangerous drugs and that Rudy Smith was a salesperson and shipping clerk for the wholesaler. As a salesman, Smith made sales calls upon defendant Poppe. In addition to his legitimate sales activities, Smith simultaneously operated an illegal venture in which he repackaged pharmaceuticals that had been returned in damaged containers and then resold them without an invoice for cash. Poppe also received prescription drugs in plastic bags and/or prescription vials with handwritten labels.

RULING: The Ohio State Board of Pharmacy suspended Poppe's license for 24 months and imposed a $28,000 fine. It later suspended 18 months and $23,000 of the fine based on Poppe's performance of certain conditions. The Ohio Appellate Court affirmed in part and reversed in part.

Ohio State Board of Pharmacy v Poppe
549 N.E.2d 541 (Ohio App. 1988)
...continued

REASONING: The Board of Pharmacy found that Poppe violated Ohio law because he purchased repackaged drugs from Smith while Smith was not acting as an authorized representative of the wholesaler. It was claimed that Poppe should have known when Smith wore a coat and tie he was working for the wholesaler and when he wore warehouse clothing he was not. The court concluded that the Board of Pharmacy took too narrow a view of the evidence because the statutory definition of a "wholesale distributor of dangerous drugs" included any agents or employees that a distributor authorized to engage in dangerous drug sales, but the statute did not limit such agents' authority to sales occurring within the scope of their employment. Thus, a salesman for a wholesale distributor of drugs fell within the statutory definition even when he was acting outside the course of his employment and selling repackaged pharmaceutical products that had been returned to his employer.

None of the allegedly misbranded prescription drugs in plastic bags were produced at the hearing. The court thought it would be speculative to assume from the prescription bottles that were in evidence on how the prescription containers that were not in evidence were labeled. Thus, there was no reliable and substantial evidence of a misbranded drug.

On appeal, the pharmacist argued that his license could be revoked or suspended only if the Board found him guilty of *willfully* violating provisions of the law. A willful tort involves the element of malice or ill will and cannot be shown by proving a simple violation of a statute unaccompanied by the intent or purpose to do injury. While the pharmacist's purchase of the inadequately labeled drugs was a violation of the statute, there was no evidence to elevate his culpability to "willful" misconduct. Thus, part of the charges were reversed; the $28,000 fine was also reversed and set aside.

The following is a list of court cases that are related to this topic.

State v Reardon, 219 A.2d 767 (R.I. 1966).
McKaba v Board of Regents of the State of New York, 294 N.Y. S.2d 382 (1968).
Pennsylvania State Board of Pharmacy v Pastor, 213 Pa. Super. 227, 247 A.2d 651 (Pa. 1968).
Fountain v Oelshelgel, 415 P.2d 316 (Ariz. 1969).
Schwartz v Florida Board of Pharmacy, 302 So.2d 423 (Fla. Dist. Ct. App. 1974).
Simon v Missouri State Board of Pharmacy, 570 S.W. 2d 334 (Mo. 1978).
White v North Carolina Board of Pharmacy, 241 S.E. 2d 730 (N.C. 1978).
Miller v Department of Registration and Education, 387 N.E. 2d 300 (Ill. 1979).
State Board of Pharmacy v Weinstein, 514 N.E.2d. 1143 (Ohio Com. Pl. 1987).
In the Matter of CVS Pharmacy, 561 A.2d 1160 (N.J. 1989).
Cooper v Missouri State Board of Pharmacy, 774 S.W. 2d 501 (Mo. App. 1989).
Tadrus v Missouri Board of Pharmacy, 849 S.W. 2d 2224 (1993).
Sender v Department of Professional Regulation, 635 N.E. 2d 849 (Ill. App. 1994).
Arkansas State Board of Pharmacy v Fenwick, No. CA 95-904, 1996 Ark. App. LEXIS 603, (Ark. App. Oct. 2, 1996).
Borchardt v Department of Commerce, 218 Mich. App. 367, (1996).
Ohio v Hutton, 2002 Ohio 742; 2002 Ohio App. LEXIS 753 (Feb 22, 2002), Appeal Not Accepted for Review, 95 Ohio St. 3d 1487; 2002 Ohio 2625; 769 N.E.2d 403; 2002 Ohio LEXIS 1476, June 12, 2002.

Disciplinary Procedures

Blazy v Ohio State Board of Pharmacy
Slip Op. Nos. 01AP-210 and 01AP-273 (August 7, 2001), 2001 Ohio App. LEXIS 3465

The pharmacy board, after a full hearing, suspended appellant pharmacist's license for 30 years following charges of drug theft. The board denied the pharmacist's subsequent request to take the pharmacy examination. The Franklin County Court of Common Pleas (Ohio) dismissed the appeal of as untimely, pursuant to *Ohio Rev. Code Ann. § 119.12*. The pharmacist appealed. The board's order specifically held that the pharmacist could not apply to the board for issuance of a new license for 30 years. Three years later, upon the request to take the pharmacy examination, the board informed the pharmacist by letter that he could not take the examination due the previous order. The pharmacist claimed that his appeal was from the letter, not the suspension order. The appellate court held that the letter was informative, not an order issued by the board. There could be no collateral attack upon the order by the legal fiction of attempting to convert a letter explaining the reason for his ineligibility to take the pharmacy examination as another order of the board. Therefore, as the pharmacist did not file his appeal within the required time period, under § 119.12, the trial court did not have jurisdiction to entertain the matter or to order the board to prepare a transcript. The judgment of the trial court was affirmed.

Fountain v Oelshelgel
415 P.2d 316 (Ariz. 1969)

ISSUE: Whether the term "gross immorality" as used in the Arizona statutes was so vague as to be unconstitutional in the revocation of a pharmacist's license for dispensing legend drugs without a prescription.

FACTS: The Arizona State Board of Pharmacy brought a disciplinary action against a pharmacist who was licensed to practice pharmacy in Arizona and who also had a license to practice pharmacy in Texas. The basis for the board's action was the pharmacist had committed "gross immorality" within the meaning of §32-1927 of the Revised Arizona Statutes in that the pharmacist had been convicted by a United States District Court in Texas on three charges of violating the Federal Food, Drug, and Cosmetic Act. The conviction was for violations committed by the pharmacist while he was practicing pharmacy in Texas. Before a Board of Pharmacy hearing was held, the pharmacist petitioned an Arizona Supreme Court for an order prohibiting the board from proceeding in the matter. The Superior Court judge granted the pharmacist's petition and the Board of Pharmacy appealed the Superior Court's order to the Supreme Court of Arizona.

The pharmacist had been convicted in federal court in Texas in 1962 for refilling a prescription for chlorothiazide (trade names - *Hydrodiuril, Esidrix*, etc) without refill authorization; for selling glutethimide (trade name - *Doriden*, etc) without a prescription, and for selling meprobamate (trade names - *Equanil, Miltown*) without a prescription, all in violation of federal law. At first, the Arizona Board of Pharmacy in its complaint (filed 1966) claimed that the pharmacist, in violating the federal law, also violated §32-1964 and 32-1965 of Arizona law. Later, the Board of Pharmacy admitted that since the violations occurred in Texas, such violations were outside the jurisdiction of Arizona in that they could not be considered violations of Arizona statutes. However, the board claimed the violations, evidenced by the conviction, were sufficient grounds for the state board to investigate the morality of the pharmacist and revoke or suspend his Arizona pharmacist's license if he was found to be guilty of gross immorality.

Fountain v Oelshelgel
415 P.2d 316 (Ariz. 1969)
...continued

Section 32-1927 of the Arizona Revised Statutes listed four grounds for revocation or suspension of a pharmacist's license and among such was "3. The registrant is found by the board to be guilty of gross immorality."

RULING: The court upheld the constitutionality of the term "gross immorality" and ruled that the Board of Pharmacy could proceed with a formal hearing against the accused pharmacist, if it so desired.

REASONING: While upholding the constitutionality of the term "gross immorality" as used in the Arizona statute and, while also ruling that the board's complaint satisfied the due process requirements, the high court stated:

> Even though the hearings are informal, [referring to Board of Pharmacy disciplinary hearings] this does not mean that the State Board can ignore the due process requirements of a punitive character since the agency can prohibit a person from practicing his profession. It appears in this case that the State Pharmacy Board is the accuser, a party to the proceedings, and ultimately makes the decision on the safeguards to be taken to protect the rights of the accused. It is for this reason that the courts are very strict in determining that the accused have proper notice of the proceedings, and adequate knowledge of the allegations against him so that he may prepare his defense.

The Arizona Supreme Court in its ruling reversed the judgment of the Superior Court for Maricopa County, Arizona, and permitted the Board of Pharmacy to proceed with a formal hearing against the accused pharmacist, if the board so desired.

Schwartz v Florida Board of Pharmacy
302 So.2d 423 (Fla. Dist. Ct. App. 1974)

ISSUE: Whether a Board of Pharmacy hearing for the revocation of a pharmacist's license must occur after the criminal action for the same charges.

FACTS: The case involved a writ of certiorari to the District Court of Appeals of Florida to review an order of the Board of Pharmacy revoking the license of a pharmacist. The pharmacist was charged by a complaint of the board with violating §465-101(1)(e) and 465.18(2)(c) of the Florida statutes by delivering drugs without a prescription. At the same time, the pharmacist was being prosecuted in Circuit Court for violating §893.13 Florida statutes by selling methaqualone and a barbiturate without a prescription. The board hearing on its charges against the pharmacist was scheduled for December 12, 1973, and the court trial was set for December 3, 1973. Both the board complaint and criminal charges were based on the same occurrence — sale or delivery of the drugs without a prescription. However, the criminal trial was subsequently rescheduled for January, and the pharmacist could not get his board hearing reset so it could be after the trial. At the board hearing, the pharmacist was represented by counsel. Although the witnesses for the board were cross-examined by the pharmacist's attorney, no testimony was offered in opposition or rebuttal to the board's evidence (the board had the burden of proof and, of course, the accused pharmacist had the constitutional right of silence if he chose). The board found the pharmacist guilty on two charges and revoked his license.

Schwartz v Florida Board of Pharmacy
302 So.2d 423 (Fla. Dist. Ct. App. 1974)
...continued

RULING: The court ruled that the Board of Pharmacy could hold a revocation hearing prior to the conclusion of the criminal action.

REASONING: On appeal, the pharmacist contended as follows: (1) The refusal of the board to continue, or postpone, the hearing until after his trial violated due process, and (2) the revocation of his license was arbitrarily and unreasonably harsh and excessive.

The appeals court somewhat *summarily* dismissed the two contentions. As to the first contention, the court stated that the board had a duty to proceed "...as rapidly as possible... Delay could result in serious harm to the public at large as during such period a pharmacist could continue to perpetrate the prohibited acts." As to the second issue, the court answered it by indicating that the court record contained competent substantial evidence to support the findings and judgment of the board.

Jay v Board of Regents of Univ. of N.Y.
376 N.Y.S.2d 664 (N.Y. App. Div. 1975)

ISSUE: Whether the records of a drug wholesaler may be introduced into a Board of Pharmacy hearing to show a pharmacist's failure to keep accurate records of the sale of controlled substances.

FACTS: A pharmacist had his license suspended for 6 months and his pharmacy permit suspended for 2 weeks, followed by a 24-week suspension that was with probation. The suspensions arose out of a charge against the pharmacist of unprofessional conduct (violation of §6804(1) (h) of New York Education Law, now renumbered as §6509(9) of the law) in that he failed to keep accurate records reflecting the receipt and sale of *Protussin AC*, an exempt narcotic at the time. It was claimed that the pharmacist's records from August 13, 1970, to December 10, 1970, showed one sale of *Protussin AC* and the purchase of 168 bottles of same from the wholesaler, but the wholesaler's records showed the sale of 4500 bottles of *Protussin AC* to the pharmacist during this period.

The State Board of Pharmacy conducted a hearing at which the records of both the pharmacy and the drug wholesaler were introduced as evidence, and testimony of the pharmacy inspectors was heard. The pharmacy board found that the pharmacist had violated the law. The board then made its recommendations to the Board of Regents who, in turn, gave the recommendations to the New York Commissioner of Education. The Commissioner issued the license suspension orders which were subsequently appealed to the New York Supreme Court, Appellate Division.

RULING: The records of a drug wholesaler may be introduced under the "business records" exception to the hearsay rule.

REASONING: On appeal, the pharmacist, through counsel, argued that the records of the drug wholesaler should not have been admitted in evidence at the hearing because the records were "hearsay." (That is to say that the wholesaler's records [invoices] were written statements made outside of court and offered in court as evidence without an opportunity to question the person(s) who made the records.) The court found the argument without merit since the wholesaler's records were "business records" kept in the usual course of

Jay v Board of Regents of Univ. of N.Y.
376 N.Y.S.2d 664 (N.Y. App. Div. 1975)
...continued

business and admissible, as a hearsay exception, under New York rules of evidence. Further, testimony at the hearing by a pharmacy inspector and the pharmacist's wife showed the *Protussin AC* sales contrary to what the pharmacy drug records demonstrated.

Also raised on appeal was the claim that the punishment inflicted was "so disproportionate to the offense, in light of all the circumstances, as to be shocking to one's sense of fairness." The court's reply may be simply stated that in the court's view it was not so. The suspensions were affirmed and the appeal petition dismissed.

Young v Texas State Board of Pharmacy
519 S.W.2d 680 (Tex. Civ. App. 1975)

ISSUE: Whether a pharmacist may have his pharmacist's license and pharmacy license revoked because he permitted his wife to dispense legend drugs without a prescription.

FACTS: A pharmacist-owner brought an appeal to the Civil Appeals Court of Texas from a District Court decision, which upheld the Board of Pharmacy's order revoking the pharmacist's license and canceling his pharmacy permit. The board's order was based on testimony (uncontested) that the pharmacist violated §4542a 12(b), (c) and (f) of the Texas Pharmacy Act. The appeals court held for the board and against the pharmacist.

An agent of the Texas Department of Public Safety had "shopped" the pharmacy and on a few occasions it was claimed that the pharmacist sold penicillin tablets without a prescription. It was also alleged by the agent that the wife of the pharmacist sold the agent two 4 oz bottles of *Protussin AC* (a Schedule V controlled substance) and that on certain dates the pharmacist himself sold more than one bottle of *Protussin AC* or *Robitussin AC*. All of these acts were in violation of the Texas Controlled Substances law which required (1) the sales of nonprescription Schedule V drugs to be made by a registered pharmacist only, and (2) no more than a 4 ounce bottle could be sold without a a prescription to a customer in a 48-hour time period.

The wife of the pharmacist was not a pharmacist, and her unlawful sale of the *Protussin AC* was the main factor in which the case turned. The defendant-pharmacist was accused by the board of violating article 4542a, 12(b), (c) and (f) of which §12 states:

> The State Board of Pharmacy may in its discretion refuse to issue a license to any applicant, and may cancel, revoke or suspend the operation of any license granted by it for any of the following reasons:

> (f) That said licensee, directly or indirectly, aids or abets in the practice of pharmacy any person not duly licensed to practice under this Act; provided further, that said licensee is responsible for the legal operation of the pharmacy, dispensary, prescription laboratory or apothecary shop as long as his name appears on the permit issued for the operation of such establishments.

At the board hearing on the matter, the pharmacist did not testify. At the trial in district court, when the agent testified that the pharmacist-owner's wife sold him the *Protussin AC* in quantities of more than 4 oz in 48 hours, there was no testimony to the contrary. In fact,

Young v Texas State Board of Pharmacy
519 S.W.2d 680 (Tex. Civ. App. 1975)
...continued

the reported facts indicate that the wife of the pharmacist was not even present at the trial. On appeal, the gist of the pharmacist's position was not that the evidence was insufficient to support the charges but only that it was insufficient under the applicable statute. The pharmacist argued that Section 12, and sub-section (f) "do not prescribe offenses or 'violations' of the act — only 'reasons' for canceling, revoking or suspending a pharmacist's license." His contention, further, was that the charges against him may be violations under some other law but not under the act (ie, the Pharmacy Practice Act).

RULING: The pharmacist was responsible for the acts of his wife in his pharmacy as long as his name appeared on the pharmacy permit. His license could be revoked for aiding and abetting an unlicensed person in the practice of pharmacy.

REASONING: The court disagreed with the pharmacist's contentions that he had not violated Texas law. The Texas Pharmacy Practice Act authorized the revocation of a pharmacist's license for impermissible conduct which, in this case, was the sale of penicillin tablets without a prescription and the aiding and abetting of his wife in the unlawful practice of pharmacy.

The Texas statutes had been specifically amended to provide that the pharmacist whose name appeared on the pharmacy permit was responsible for the operation of the pharmacy. As a professional man engaged in a field of endeavor affecting the public health and well-being, he was charged *in law* with knowledge that the specific facts set out in the agent's affidavit constituted impermissible conduct authorizing the revocation of his licenses. The statutory language was clear — the pharmacist was responsible for the acts of his wife in his pharmacy so long as his name appeared on the pharmacy permit.

Burley v U.S. Drug Enforcement Administration
443 F.Supp. 619 (D. Tenn. 1977)

ISSUE: Whether a grant of immunity from prosecution in a federal proceeding prohibits the DEA from transferring information about the testifying pharmacist to the state board of pharmacy and the board taking action based on that information.

FACTS: A pharmacist had his store inspected by the DEA pursuant to inspection warrants; the DEA removed prescriptions, drug order forms, and drug invoices from the store (later returned but subpoenaed by the Federal Grand Jury). The grand jury investigation resulted in indictments for conspiracy and illegal distribution of drugs against a certain doctor and an indictment against the pharmacist as co-conspirator. But later the pharmacist testified at the doctor's trial as the government's witness and was granted an immunity for anything he said at the trial. The immunity consisted of a promise of no future criminal prosecution for any transactions involved in the DEA investigation.

However, the DEA mailed copies of its investigative reports to the Tennessee Board of Pharmacy and the board initiated a civil procedure against the accused pharmacist. Attorneys for the pharmacist went into federal district court seeking an order prohibiting the DEA from testifying or furnishing documents at the board hearing. The argument made to the court was that immunity previously granted was applicable to the state disciplinary action.

Burley v U.S. Drug Enforcement Administration
443 F.Supp. 619 (D. Tenn. 1977)
...continued

RULING: The injunction sought was denied and the board was, therefore, free to use the DEA reports at its hearing.

REASONING: The court agreed that the rule was "...well settled that testimony given after immunity has been granted or information directly or indirectly derived therefrom may not be used against the witness in any criminal proceeding." It ruled here that the board's action was a civil matter. Under §63-1020(d) of the Tennessee Code Annotated, the powers of the Board of Pharmacy were limited to revocation/suspension of a license or permit, or assessment of a civil penalty of no more than $500. It was also claimed by the pharmacist that disclosure of the DEA investigation to the board violated the Federal Privacy Act (5 U.S.C. §522a), which prohibits disclosure of information between government agencies except in certain instances. One of the exceptions under the act was disclosure of a "routine" nature and the court fond the DEA reports were of such "routine" nature.

Hofmeister v Department of Registration and Education
379 N.E.2d 383 (Ill. App. Ct. 1978)

ISSUE: Whether a pharmacist who is found guilty of practicing pharmacy with an unlicensed person should have his license suspended for "gross immorality."

FACTS: The Illinois Board of Pharmacy filed a complaint against Ronald Hofmeister alleging that he had engaged in the practice of pharmacy with Timothy Orr, an unlicensed person. At the Board hearing, Orr testified that he was a licensed pharmacist in the State of Iowa but was not licensed to practice pharmacy in Illinois until December, 1972. Yet, Orr was actively engaged in the practice of pharmacy in Illinois at a Medicine Shoppe Pharmacy in September, 1972. Orr testified that on four different occasions he informed the plaintiff that he was unlicensed in Illinois, but Hofmeister informed Orr that the pharmacy would process his reciprocity papers and that Orr could practice pharmacy without a license during such processing.

Hofmeister testified that he did not interview or have any part in the decision to hire Orr. Hofmeister claimed that he was sent by the company to train Orr to run the Peoria Medicine Shoppe Pharmacy. Hofmeister denied having any conversations with Orr regarding reciprocity and claimed he had no specific knowledge that Orr was unlicensed in Illinois. Hofmeister never asked Orr for his certificate, although he was aware of the regulation that a pharmacist must display his certificate of registration.

The Board of Pharmacy found Hofmeister guilty as charged and recommended that his license be suspended for six months. At a second hearing in front of the Board of Pharmacy, the Chairman of the Board of Directors of the Medicine Shoppe, Inc., accepted the ultimate responsibility for the incident and testified that it was not within Hofmeister's normal duties to train such personnel. However, the Board continued to recommend that Hofmeister's license be suspended for six months. The Illinois trial court affirmed the decision of the Board of Pharmacy, and Hofmeister appealed. On appeal Hofmeister contended that the decision to suspend his license was contrary to the weight of the evidence.

Hofmeister v Department of Registration and Education
379 N.E.2d 383 (Ill. App. Ct. 1978)
...continued

RULING: The findings of the Board of Pharmacy on the questions of fact were given a great deal of credence. The court ruled that the Board's findings should not be set aside unless they were against the manifest weight of evidence. The previous decision to suspend Hofmeister's license was affirmed.

REASONING: The Illinois Pharmacy Act provides that an individual's license to practice pharmacy may be suspended if the person is guilty of gross immorality. Rules and regulations promulgated by the Board of Pharmacy defined gross immorality as "any act or practice hostile to the public health, safety and welfare..." An additional rule by the Board stated that a license holder shall be considered guilty of gross immorality when he or she is associated with any pharmacy that permits an authorized person to engage in the practice of pharmacy.

The court ruled that "gross immorality" may be measured by the standards of the profession, and the agency's interpretation should be relied upon. Hofmeister argued that his conduct was not in violation of the Board's rules and regulations since he did not have the authority to hire or fire Orr. The court recognized that the record supported the pharmacist's contention because his role as training supervisor in the Peoria store was temporary and was not part of his normal duties. Relying on an earlier case, the court held that a registered pharmacist who has been placed in charge of a pharmacy becomes personally liable if he permits an unlicensed person to dispense drugs. While it was not within Hofmeister's normal duties to train and supervise new personnel, he was the registered pharmacist in charge of the Medicine Shoppe. The court found it unlikely that he had ever asked Orr for his certificate. The record indicated that Hofmeister displayed his own license in the pharmacy and did not remove it when he left the store. He only removed it after Orr received his Illinois license. The court found that the pharmacist's failure to remove his own license from display raised the inference that he did so to cover for Orr's lack of a license.

Shermack v Board of Regents of the State University System
407 N.Y.S.2d 926 (1978)

ISSUE: Whether alleged violations of state drug control laws constituted sufficient basis for revocation of a pharmacist's license to practice.

FACTS: This case involves a court review of the determination of the New York Commission of Education revoking a pharmacist's license. After being investigated by the pharmacy board, the pharmacist was charged with several counts of fraudulent and unprofessional practice in violation of subparts (2) and (9) of §6509 of the New York Education Law. A Hearing Panel of the Committee on Professional Conduct of the State Board of Pharmacy found the pharmacist guilty by substantial legal evidence of the following:

(1) Selling certain prescription drugs (ie, penicillin, tetracycline, *Valium* and *Ovral-21*) without prescription;
(2) failing to keep adequate records and suffering inventory shortages of certain controlled substances; and
(3) maintaining an outdoor electric sign reading: "CUT-RATE PRESCRIPTIONS."

The hearing panel recommended a six-month license suspension, but the Regents' Review Committee, while adopting the panel's findings of fact, went further and recommended

Shermack v Board of Regents of the State University System
407 N.Y.S.2d 926 (1978)
...continued

revocation of the pharmacist's license to practice pharmacy. The Board of Regents then adopted the hearing panel's findings and imposed the recommendation of the review committee — revocation of license.

RULING: The revocation order was affirmed.

REASONING: On seeking court review of the revocation, the pharmacist, through counsel, argued that the fact finding was inadequate and that the penalty imposed was unduly harsh. With respect to the finding of selling prescription drugs without a prescription, the pharmacist claimed that on four of the five occasions in question, he had obtained an oral prescription from a physician. However, the court accepted the hearing panel's findings that the pharmacist "dispensed, without a prescription, (the particular prescription drug) in an unlabeled container." Further, under New York controlled substances law, *Valium*, like other Schedules III and IV drugs, required [in New York] a written prescription except in the limited instance of an emergency oral prescription reduced to writing for a limited supply with a written prescription received within 72 hours.

On the issue of the recordkeeping/inventory shortage, the pharmacist's defense was that these defects were the result of robberies. However, the hearing panel's findings stated "(he) failed to maintain proper records required in a pharmacy in that the daily ledger failed to contain pharmacist's initials."

On the issue of the "CUT-RATE PRESCRIPTION" sign, it was contended the restriction in New York law against such type of pharmacy advertising violated the First Amendment. While the reviewing court agreed that accurate advertising of prescription drug pricing was protected by the First Amendment, the type of advertising regulated here does not advertise particular prices.

Finally, the court summarily decided that the revocation of license to practice "is not shocking to one's sense of fairness, and therefore, should not be upset" (citing as precedent the case of *Matter of Martin v Nyquist*, 389 N.Y.S. 2d 179).

Simon v Missouri State Board of Pharmacy
570 S.W.2d 334 (Mo. 1978)

ISSUE: Whether entry of a plea of *nolo contendere* can serve as basis for suspension of a pharmacist's license to practice under Missouri law.

FACTS: This case involved a pharmacist who pleaded *nolo contendere* to a criminal charge of distribution of controlled substances in violation of federal law. The federal court imposed sentence under 18 U.S. Code §3651 which allows for probation on judgment of conviction of any [federal] offense not punishable by death or life imprisonment. The punishment given was a $5000 fine and five years probation with payment of the fine as condition of the probation.

Thereafter, the State Board of Pharmacy brought a license revocation/suspension action against the pharmacist on the basis that he had been convicted of a felony within the meaning of the term in §338.055.3 of the Revised Statutes of Missouri (1975). After conduct-

Simon v Missouri State Board of Pharmacy
570 S.W.2d 334 (Mo. 1978)
...continued

ing a hearing, the board suspended the pharmacist's license for two years. He appealed the suspension to a Missouri circuit court which reversed the suspension. The Board of Pharmacy then appealed the reversal to the Missouri Court of Appeals.

RULING: The Court of Appeals affirmed the circuit court's order reversing the suspension of license.

REASONING: This case turns on a rather unique situation in Missouri. In a 1944 case, *Meyer v Missouri Real Estate Commission*, the court held that a suspended sentence on a *nolo contendere* plea to the federal charge is not a conviction under Missouri law. In *Meyer*, the court stated:

> [w]here sentence is suspended, and so the direct consequences of fine and imprisonment are suspended or postponed temporarily or indefinitely, so, also, the indirect consequences are likewise postponed.

On appeal, it was argued by the board that the *Meyer* decision was unsound, since the states are bound by the federal practice that suspension of imposition of sentence on a *nolo contendere* plea is still viewed as a conviction. However, the Missouri court held here that "federal law determines federal definition, the values of a local statute flow from the definitions which accord with the public policy of the state law — in this case, that a suspension of imposition of sentence does not result in a criminal conviction."

White v North Carolina Board of Pharmacy
241 S.E.2d 730 (N.C. 1978)

ISSUE: Whether conviction of a violation of federal controlled substances recordkeeping requirements can serve as basis for revocation of a license to practice pharmacy.

FACTS: Following an administrative hearing, the state pharmacy board revoked the license of a pharmacist on the grounds that he had willfully failed to comply with both state and federal law governing the practice of pharmacy. Prior to the state board action, the pharmacist had been audited by the DEA. On one audit, he could not account for 3,178 tablets of morphine sulfate with atropine and, on the other audit, he was unable to account for 76 morphine tablets. Subsequently, the pharmacist pleaded guilty in federal court to "knowingly and unlawfully" refusing to keep an accurate record of morphine sulfate. He received a 1-year jail sentence which was suspended in lieu of 5 years probation.

RULING: The court sustained the revocation.

REASONING: The pharmacist appealed the conviction and claimed, on appeal, that the board allowed "hearsay evidence" and "opinion" at the hearing over his objections. The court agreed that North Carolina law required the administrative hearing to be conducted by accepted rules of evidence — the exclusion of incompetent, irrelevant, immaterial, unduly repetitious, and hearsay evidence. But, the evidence that supported the board's decision was (1) the audits conducted by the DEA, heard without objection, and (2) the facts of the guilty plea in federal court. The latter was admitted into evidence upon a stipulation (agreement) between board and counsel for the pharmacist. By pleading guilty in federal court

White v North Carolina Board of Pharmacy
241 S.E.2d 730 (N.C. 1978)
...continued

to the recordkeeping violation [21 U.S.C. §827(a)(3)], the pharmacist also violated his state law (G.S.-90-104 which required the pharmacist to keep and maintain recordkeeping in conformance with the federal law). This was sufficient to show that he "(willfully) failed to comply with the laws governing the practice of pharmacy and the distribution of drugs," a ground for license revocation under G.S. §90-65(a)(7) of North Carolina law.

Intrieri v Commonwealth
296 A.2d 927 (Pa. 1979)

ISSUE: Whether a revocation of a pharmacy license is appropriate punishment for a pharmacist who pleaded guilty to three misdemeanors and one felony related to drugs.

FACTS: In this case, a pharmacist pleaded guilty to four violations of the Pennsylvania Drug Act, three of which were misdemeanors and one a felony. The pharmacist was sentenced by the court to one year in prison, immediately paroled, and given 5 years probation plus a $2500 fine and ordered to pay the costs of the prosecution. Later, the Board of Pharmacy revoked his pharmacy license and he appealed the revocation order to the court, claiming the magnitude of the punishment was disproportionate to the severity of the offense.

RULING: The court found one of the violations of the conviction under the Drug Act to be a felony. While, under the holding in the *Duda* case, the board had power to revoke for a single felony violation, they would not have the obligation to do so. "Their discretion would certainly be reviewable by this court." Because the claim of the pharmacist was based solely on the excessiveness of the punishment in relation to the severity of the offense, the court sent the matter back to the board, "out of fairness and justice to him."

Miller v Department of Registration and Education
387 N.E.2d 300 (Ill. 1979)

ISSUE: Whether a conviction of a federal misdemeanor offense to which pharmacists pleaded guilty could constitute the basis for the revocation of their licenses under an Illinois law prohibiting acts of "gross immorality."

FACTS: Three Illinois pharmacists had their licenses to practice pharmacy revoked after the Illinois Department of Registration and Education (representing the Board of Pharmacy) made a determination that they were guilty of "gross immorality." The revocations were premised upon federal convictions following the entry of guilty pleas by the three pharmacists to the federal misdemeanor offense of offering and making a kickback or bribe in connection with the furnishing of drugs and pharmaceutical services for which payment was made out of federal funds. At the hearings for the pharmacists' license revocation, certified copies of the federal convictions were introduced, over the objection of counsel, as evidence. In each case, the Board of Pharmacy found that the conviction of such an offense constituted "gross immorality" within the meaning of the Illinois Pharmacy Practice Act.

While offering and making kickbacks or bribes to nursing homes was a misdemeanor under federal law, the Illinois Pharmacy Practice Act contained no express provisions for revoca-

Miller v Department of Registration and Education
387 N.E.2d 300 (Ill. 1979)
...continued

tion of licenses for the commission of misdemeanors or for the payment of bribes or kickbacks. Thus, the revocation of the licenses had to be based upon the general ground of "gross immorality."

RULING: A misdemeanor conviction for the payment of kickbacks or bribes is not "gross immorality" for the purposes of pharmacists' license revocations under Illinois law.

REASONING: The principal concern of the Illinois Pharmacy Practice Act is with the protection of the public health, safety, and welfare. The law was designed to assure that only those who possess the requisite professional qualifications were licensed to practice pharmacy in the state of Illinois. The court found that the term "practice of the profession of pharmacy," as used in the statute, emphasized the performance of acts requiring professional study and training in the science of pharmacy rather than the business aspects of the practice of pharmacy.

The court held that the payment of kickbacks or bribes was not concerned with the exercise of the professional skill of a pharmacist such as was defined in the statute. In the court's opinion, the actions of the pharmacists did not endanger the public health, safety and welfare of the people of Illinois. It should be noted that subsequent to the commission of the acts which led to the pharmacists' federal convictions, the Illinois Pharmacy Act was amended to include fee splitting as a ground for license revocation. This amendment was a further indication that such conduct was not included in the general term "gross immorality" and could not constitute a basis for the revocation of the pharmacists' licenses.

Brown v Idaho State Board of Pharmacy
746 P.2d 1006 (Idaho App. 1987)

ISSUE: Whether a board of pharmacy could revoke a pharmacist's license when there was evidence that the pharmacist engaged in the illegal use of marijuana and participated in the sale and delivery of a misbranded drug.

FACTS: The executive secretary of the Idaho Board of Pharmacy lodged a complaint against pharmacist Jack Brown alleging that (1) Brown had been convicted of possession of drug paraphernalia; (2) Brown admitted using marijuana; (3) Brown had delivered a controlled substance in violation of Idaho statutes; and (4) Brown had sold and delivered a misbranded drug.

During the Board hearing, a certified copy of a judgment of conviction for possession of drug paraphernalia was admitted into evidence. The hearing officer also admitted into evidence a taped interview between a Board investigator and Brown during which Brown admitted that he used marijuana approximately twice a week. However, during the hearing, Brown testified that his actual use of marijuana was more sporadic and that he was no longer using it. Based on the evidence, the hearing officer concluded that Brown was a "habitual" user of marijuana. However, it was determined that Brown had not delivered a controlled substance and no action was taken on this allegation. Finally, based on conflicting evidence, the hearing officer found that Brown had sold and delivered a misbranded drug. The hearing officer concluded that the Board had grounds to take disciplinary action against Brown's pharmacist license but not against his controlled substances registration.

Brown v Idaho State Board of Pharmacy
746 P.2d 1006 (Idaho App. 1987)
...continued

RULING: The Board of Pharmacy adopted the hearing officer's findings and conclusions and revoked Brown's pharmacist license. The district court affirmed the Board's decision and the revocation was upheld on appeal.

REASONING: On appeal, Brown asserted that (1) the Board erred in finding that he had pleaded guilty to possession of drug paraphernalia and in not allowing him to collaterally attack the conviction; (2) the Board erred in finding that he habitually used marijuana; (3) the Board erred in finding that he sold and delivered a misbranded drug; and (4) the Board's decision to revoke his license was arbitrary and capricious.

Brown argued that he pleaded guilty to the charge of possession of drug paraphernalia without being advised of his right to counsel and without being advised of the consequences of his plea. Therefore, he maintained that the judgment of conviction should have been inadmissible in the Board hearing. However, the court noted that the sole purpose of the Board's action was to determine the qualification and fitness of Brown to practice pharmacy. The legislature had determined that the conviction of a felony or any violation of the state's drug laws was sufficient grounds for discipline. The Board was ill-equipped to consider whether a criminal action was valid, and the agency must be allowed to rely upon the conclusive effect of a conviction. The administrative hearing was not the proper forum for challenging the validity of the criminal conviction. If Brown wished to challenge the conviction, he could have asked the Board to stay its proceedings while he petitioned the district court to set aside the conviction.

Based upon Brown's statement that he used marijuana approximately twice a week, the Board determined that he was a "habitual" user of the drug. Brown mentioned that one-fourth ounce of marijuana would supply his need for a considerable period of time. The Board distinguished between "being addicted" and "being habituated" to a substance. Being habituated to a controlled substance means that a person, out of a desire and not out of compulsion, has repeatedly used a controlled substance. Brown's admission revealed that he had a desire to use marijuana approximately twice a week. Such repeated use indicated the process of forming a habit or routine and the Board's conclusion that he was "a habitual user" was not erroneous.

Evidence was also presented that the pharmacist had sold and delivered an over-the-counter drug in an unmarked container, which was in violation of Idaho statutes which prohibited the sale or delivery of a misbranded drug. Based on all of these charges, the court concluded that the Board had ample factual grounds for disciplining Brown. The Board was faced with facts indicating that Brown was engaged in the illegal use of a controlled substance and in selling and delivering a misbranded drug. These actions reflected that Brown was unfit and unqualified for the practice of pharmacy. The Board's decision was not arbitrary or capricious.

State v Heath
513 So.2d 493 (La. App. 1987)

ISSUE: Whether there was sufficient evidence to convict a pharmacist of Medicaid fraud when generic drugs were dispensed, but the pharmacist billed for the more expensive brand name product.

FACTS: The defendant, Thomas Heath, owned and operated Heath's Drugs in Rayville, Louisiana. He also owned 40% of another pharmacy in Mangham, Louisiana. Both pharmacies were participants in the state of Louisiana's Medicaid program. Each pharmacy had a separate provider contract and number.

In August of 1982, David Harrison, a licensed pharmacist and former employee of the defendant, contacted the Medicaid Fraud Unit of the Louisiana Attorney General's office and reported irregularities in the dispensing of prescriptions at both pharmacies. These irregularities primarily involved the substitution of generic drugs for brand name drugs for Medicaid recipients.

As a result of this report, an investigation was initiated. The Medicaid Fraud Unit sent letters to Medicaid recipients in the general area of the pharmacy and asked them to bring all of their prescription drugs to the welfare office on a specific date. This process revealed that some of the prescription vials issued by the pharmacies contained generic drugs while the labels indicated that they should contain brand name drugs. The investigation which followed uncovered evidence that the pharmacies had submitted claims for reimbursement that listed higher priced brand name medications rather than the less expensive generic drugs actually dispensed. The defendant was charged with 13 counts of Medicaid fraud.

RULING: The jury found the pharmacist guilty of four of the 13 counts of Medicaid fraud. The appellate court affirmed the conviction.

REASONING: An expert in pharmacology testified that each of the products contained in the bottles obtained from Medicaid recipients was, in fact, a generic drug and not the drug for which the state had been billed. The drugs and prescription containers were compared to the claim forms filed by the pharmacist to receive reimbursement. This evidence also showed that the state had been billed for brand name drugs when generic drugs had actually been dispensed.

The pharmacist explained that existence of generic drugs in the brand name bottles on the shelves of his pharmacies was a procedure employed to save space. He also responded that he was not aware of the state requirement that the name of the pharmacist who dispensed the prescription be placed on the label. He further testified that he could not say whether he had dispensed any of the prescriptions at issue. It should also be noted that Mr. Heath did not sign any of the forms submitted for reimbursement. Through his testimony, the defendant attempted to contradict the state's evidence that he knowingly and intentionally submitted the false information to obtain greater compensation than that to which he was entitled.

The former employee, who initiated the investigation, testified that he was instructed by Mr. Heath to "check out" Medicaid customers with respect to such characteristics as age and intelligence to determine if a customer was a likely candidate for substitution of generic drugs. He further testified that the national drug code numbers on the prescriptions were changed to reflect a smaller package size than that originally ordered in order to take advantage of the higher per unit price.

Another pharmacist, who worked in Heath's pharmacies, testified that she had unknowingly dispensed prescriptions from brand name containers which contained generic drugs.

State v Heath
513 So.2d 493 (La. App. 1987)
...continued

After she discovered this fact, she complained to Mr. Heath. He informed her not to worry about it because he would take full responsibility. He conceded to her that he knew this course of action was "not right."

One Medicaid recipient testifies that she received her prescriptions at a number of pharmacies and that, on many occasions, she mixed the same medication obtained from different pharmacies in the same bottle for the sake of convenience. The court noted that while it seemed highly likely that generic drugs were intentionally substituted for this recipient's prescriptions, it could not support the defendant's conviction on this count since the recipient admitted to mixing drugs from different pharmacies. However, the totality of the evidence in the other cases supported the defendant's conviction. The evidence demonstrated that on each of these counts the state was billed for more expensive brand name drugs and paid for those drugs when in fact generic drugs were actually dispensed. The testimony of Heath's pharmacists revealed that he initiated and participated in the scheme of substitution in order to receive greater compensation than he was entitled.

State of Nebraska v Hinze
441 N.W.2d 593 (Neb. 1989)

ISSUE: Whether a pharmacist should be held in criminal contempt for violating an injunction prohibiting him from engaging in the practice of medicine without a license.

FACTS: Pharmacist John Hinze was permanently enjoined from engaging in the practice of medicine without a license by the state of Nebraska. This injunction was the result of Hinze's having established a "clinic" at which he diagnosed and treated individuals' ailments. Hinze was specifically enjoined from (1) publicly professing to be a physician, (2) prescribing and furnishing medicine for any disease or ailment or treating someone by surgery, (3) holding himself out to be qualified in the diagnosis or treatment of disease, (4) suggesting, recommending, or prescribing any treatment for physical or mental ailments, (5) maintaining an office for the examination and treatment of disease, and (6) attaching to his name any word or abbreviation indicating that he is engaged in the treatment or diagnosis of disease.

Several months after the court order, an investigator with the Nebraska Department of Health attended the seminar conducted by the defendant at a Lutheran church in Hastings, Nebraska. Approximately 50 people paid $45 each to attend the seminar. The defendant introduced himself as "Dr. John Hinze" and informed the gathering that he would be providing information with regard to homeopathic and naturopathic remedies. He did not explain that he uses the title "doctor" because he holds a doctorate degree in pharmacy from the University of Tennessee and a degree in naturopathy from a Canadian college.

One woman in the audience told Hinze that her son had been run over by a car and was experiencing seizures. Hinze advised her that her child should be given arnica and also suggested that silica could be applied to the scars that the child had received. Another woman asked Hinze about dark circles under her children's eyes. He explained that such circles are often associated with poor digestion and allergies. He suggested that the woman give her children fennel, anise, and gentian to help digest proteins. A third woman stated that she had children who were infested with pinworms. The defendant suggested that carrots, pumpkin seed, and gentian be used to treat the pinworms.

State of Nebraska v Hinze
441 N.W.2d 593 (Neb. 1989)
...continued

A number of other complaints were also presented to the defendant to which he responded by suggesting natural remedies. Also attending the seminar was a business partner of the defendant. It was his purpose to sell herbs and vitamins and take orders for the remedies suggested for the participant's ailments.

RULING: The pharmacist was fined $500 and sentenced to 60 days in jail. The Supreme Court of Nebraska affirmed the lower court decision.

REASONING: Hinze argued that the contempt order infringed upon his freedom of speech. The court found his claim to be without merit. There is no vested right to practice medicine but rather it is a conditional right subject to the police power of the state to protect and preserve the public health. Many courts have ruled that a state's compelling interest in regulating the health and welfare of its citizens outweighs any incidental infringement of free speech of individuals who are not licensed to practice medicine. In the exercise of its police power, the state of Nebraska has chosen not to recognize naturopathy as a legitimate branch of medicine. Until the Legislature of Nebraska reverses that position, Hinze was enjoined from practicing naturopathy in its various forms.

Hinze also argued that his doctorate in pharmacology gave him the right to use the title "doctor." Many courts when faced with this issue had noted that the very use of the title "doctor" to the average public person implies a particular skill or knowledge. The evidence established that the defendant was not acting as a pharmacist but as a practitioner of the healing arts. He referred to himself as "doctor" in order to lead members of the audience to believe that he was qualified to diagnose and treat physical ailments.

Cooper v Missouri State Board of Pharmacy
774 S.W.2d 501 (Mo. App. 1989)

ISSUE: Whether a pharmacist who sold sample packets of drugs labeled "not for sale" and committed acts of Medicaid fraud should have his license suspended.

FACTS: The case began when a complaint was received by the Missouri Board of Pharmacy from a consumer who alleged that a label on a packet of birth control pills purchased in one of Eugene Cooper's pharmacies had been painted over with silver paint. The paint hid an inscription that stated that the tablets were samples, not to be sold.

A Board investigator later went to Cooper's pharmacy and found sample packets of birth control pills on which the "not for sale" inscription had been painted over; the tablets were not in their original manufacturer's containers and they did not have a lot number or a proper NDC number. The word "sample" had been scraped off of some drugs.

Evidence was also introduced at a Board hearing that Cooper had pleaded guilty in federal court to charges of mail fraud. Cooper admitted that he used the Postal Service to submit fraudulent billings to Medicaid, and he had overcharged Medicaid for drugs. Cooper purchased medications in large quantities at discounted prices but billed Medicaid as if he had purchased the prescription drugs in small quantities at a higher price.

Cooper v Missouri State Board of Pharmacy
774 S.W.2d 501 (Mo. App. 1989)
...continued

The relevant statutory provisions in this case pertain to (1) fraud, misrepresentation, or dishonesty in performance of duties, (2) violation of any professional trust or competence, and (3) violation of drug laws or regulations in the state of Missouri, any other state or the federal government.

RULING: The Board of Pharmacy suspended Cooper's license for one year with five years of probation. The court upheld the suspension.

REASONING: It was found that Cooper had purchased drugs in packages that did not contain lot numbers and which were not in original packages. This constituted "misbranding" of drugs in violation of federal law. It was also found that some of the drugs Cooper sold had been altered by scraping off the word "sample," and this alteration affected the strength and purity of the drugs making them "adulterated." It was further determined that Cooper was subject to discipline for violation of professional trust by submitting fraudulent billings to the state Medicaid program.

Cooper's submission of false claims to the Medicaid program supported the Board's finding of a violation of professional trust. Missouri law provided that upon finding any statutory violation, the Board of Pharmacy could place a pharmacist on probation or suspend or revoke his license. The court ruled that there was no need to detail the sufficiency of evidence to support the other charges, but that Cooper's admission of mail fraud violations and filing fraudulent claims with Medicaid was enough to uphold the Board's decision to suspend his license.

Duckworth v State Board of Pharmacy
583 So.2d 200 (Miss. 1991)

ISSUE: Whether a pharmacist was denied due process when representatives of the Board of Pharmacy implied that the charges against him were not serious.

FACTS: During a routine inspection of Booneville Discount Drugs, agents of the Mississippi Board of Pharmacy discovered evidence of unprofessional conduct by its pharmacist-owner, Joseph Duckworth. The Board issued a complaint that charged that Duckworth possessed and sold drugs that had been diverted from the purpose for which they were distributed. These drugs were professional samples that were plainly marked "not to be sold." The pharmacist admitted using alcohol to remove these words prior to sale.

The complaint against Duckworth also charged that he failed to maintain all drugs in the manufacturer's original containers. Thus, the expiration date and control lot numbers were not readily available. The pharmacist claimed that he "knew in his head" the expiration date of all the improperly stored drugs. Incredulous, a pharmacy board member asked him if he was that good. Unchastened, he replied "yes."

Among the improperly stored drugs were over 1000 drug patches for various disorders, over 25,000 tablets of a number of pharmaceutical products, and an odd assortment of inhalers. The pharmacist attended the hearing without an attorney and admitted to all the charges against him.

Duckworth v State Board of Pharmacy
583 So.2d 200 (Miss. 1991)
...continued

The pharmacist testified that the pharmacy board inspector delivered the complaint and notice of hearing. He stated that "When Grantham presented me, I suppose — I guess it was this document. I asked Mr. Grantham if I need to take an attorney with me, and he said, 'That's your choice. You may just want to go down and talk to them, though'."

RULING: The board revoked the pharmacist's license and the revocation was upheld by the court.

REASONING: The pharmacist's first argument, on appeal, was that the board precluded effective judicial review by failing to make specific findings of fact or failing to articulate reasons to support its decision. Most legal authorities hold that it is better form for a fact-finding administrative agency to make a specific finding of fact on which to base an award or to reject a claim. This makes it much easier for the reviewing court to consider the evidence in the record and avoids any conclusion that the administrative agency was arbitrary and capricious.

In this case there was no conflicting evidence and no real reason to make any findings of fact. The pharmacist admitted to all of the charges against him. The agency's failure to make findings of fact, standing alone, was not cause for reversal.

The pharmacist's real contention, on appeal, was that he was denied due process when the Board's agent implied that the charges against him were not serious in nature. This caused the pharmacist to believe that he did not need an attorney and deprived him of his right to counsel.

Certainly the right to retain counsel is part of the procedural due process guaranteed to defendants in cases such as this. The court noted that while administrative agencies rarely actively undertake to deny the right of defendants to legal counsel, they sometimes seek to discourage individuals from securing legal representation. This practice has led to the passage of statutes in some states that require that the notice of hearing clearly indicate the existence of the right to retain counsel.

In this case the facts showed that the pharmacist received written notice that clearly highlighted his right to retain counsel. The notice also stated that the charges, if proved, could result in suspension or revocation of his pharmacy license. His claim that the agent's implied statements coerced him into not retaining counsel was really an attempt to reconsider his decision not to retain counsel in the first place.

Riddle v Mississippi Board of Pharmacy
592 So.2d 37 (Miss. 1991)

ISSUE: Whether a pharmacist was denied his right to an attorney during a Board of Pharmacy hearing to revoke his license.

FACTS: Stanley Riddle was the pharmacist-owner of the Medicine Shoppe in Tupelo Mississippi. In June 1988, agents from the Mississippi State Board of Pharmacy investigated Riddle's drug dispensing activities and found that over a 17-month period, the pharmacist (a) dispensed a controlled substance without a prescription on 192 occasions; (b) dispensed leg-

Riddle v Mississippi Board of Pharmacy
592 So.2d 37 (Miss. 1991)
...continued

end drugs without a valid prescription on 45 occasions, and (c) refilled prescriptions at greater frequency than allowed on 107 occasions.

The investigating agents found that most of the prescriptions under scrutiny were telephone prescriptions with a physician reportedly calling the pharmacy and authorizing the prescription. Agents reviewed the files of patients who seemed to be receiving large amounts of prescription drugs. They recorded in painstaking detail the physician's name, the type of drug, the date, and quantity dispensed and then personally called the physician whom the pharmacy's records reflected as authorizing the prescriptions.

In July 1988, the Mississippi State Board of Pharmacy issued a 31 page formal complaint setting forth each of the occasions on which it appeared that Riddle had dispensed a drug or controlled substance without proper authority. The complaint was served on Riddle and advised him to appear before the Board for an administrative hearing. The complaint further instructed the pharmacist that the charges, if proven ... "could result in the suspension or revocation of your license to practice pharmacy."

RULING: The Mississippi Board of Pharmacy revoked the pharmacist's license. The decision was affirmed by both the trial court and the Mississippi Supreme Court.

REASONING: The court noted that its responsibility in reviewing administrative board decisions is to see whether a fair-minded fact finder might have found the evidence clear and convincing and, if so, the courts will not disturb the Board's judgment.

The documents produced before the Board overwhelmingly supported the charges. They identified by date, prescription number, drug, patient name, and physician each of the violations that occurred. These prescription documents were augmented by affidavits of the prescribers.

The court could find nothing in the record suggesting that the Board had been arbitrary and capricious in its decision against Riddle. Instead, the evidence showed that the physicians had not authorized the 344 challenged "prescriptions." The fact that a physician's records may not show a telephoned prescription on isolated occasions may suggest an error in the physician's office, but whether the court had hundreds of "non-records," the inference was too powerful to ignore.

Riddle's procedural complaint was that he was without counsel before the Board and that he had not made an effective waiver of counsel. The court pointed out that the notice Riddle received in July, 1988 advised him that he may appear with or without counsel. In addition, at the onset of the hearing, counsel for the Board advised Riddle of his right, but he again insisted that he come before the Board and present his own case. Under these circumstances, the court found that Riddle was advised that he had a right to have counsel assist him and that he effectively waived that right.

Riddle further complained that he did not have the right to question the physicians who submitted their affidavits. Again, the court noted that a month before the hearing, Riddle was given the details of the charges against him and was advised that he had the right to call witnesses or to have subpoenas issued. Riddle was found to have effectively waived his right to cross-examine the witnesses. While in retrospect, Riddle feels he may have faired better at the hearing had he taken advantage of some of the rights noted above, the court found that this is always the case when a party waives his rights and things do not turn out so well.

Riddle v Mississippi Board of Pharmacy
592 So.2d 37 (Miss. 1991)
...continued

According to the court, "Suffice it to say that we do not credit such 20-20 hindsight as grounds for reversal."

Tadrus v Missouri Board of Pharmacy
849 S.W.2d 2224 (1993)

ISSUE: Whether a pharmacist was denied due process of law by the Board of Pharmacy's failure to promulgate guidelines or standards which would have informed him of what actions would subject him to discipline.

FACTS: The defendant, Salim Tadrus, was a licensed pharmacist and the owner of three pharmacies called Sam's Prescription Shop. The complaint against the defendant grew out of inspections by the Missouri State Board of Pharmacy. Based on its authority to discipline license holders for: (1) incompetency, misconduct, negligence, fraud, and misrepresentation; (2) violation of the regulations of the Board of Pharmacy; and (3) violation of any drug laws of the state of Missouri or the federal government, the Board ordered suspension and probation of the pharmacist's and pharmacies' licenses.

The defendant complained about the finding that he had violated Missouri law by failing to have on hand the current revision of the United States Pharmacopeia (U.S.P.) and the National Formulary (N.F.) during the 1985 inspection of the pharmacy. The law required a pharmacy to keep on file these two reference books... including their latest decennial revision.

During the inspection, the inspector found that the pharmacy had on hand a 1980 edition of the U.S.P., but this was not the latest revision. A new revision of the two books (not published in a single volume) had become available in October 1984. The cover of the newest revision announced that it was "official from January 1, 1985."

The defendant claimed that he was in compliance with the statute by having the 1980 edition. While it was not the latest revision, the defendant argued that he was in compliance by having the "latest decennial revision," since his edition was less than 10 years old. When the statute was enacted, the U.S.P. was revised every decade but was then changed to five-year intervals so there is no longer a "decennial revision" of the reference. The court was faced with a statute which, if read literally, did not make any sense.

During the Board inspection, it was also found that the license of one of the pharmacists working there was not displayed on the premises, as required by law. As the pharmacist-in-charge, the defendant was responsible to see that the licenses of all pharmacists employed were conspicuously displayed in the pharmacy. The failure to display the pharmacist's license was chargeable to the defendant.

The court also found that the defendant did not comply with the recordkeeping regulations with respect to prescription refills. When records are kept on computer, the regulation requires a daily printout of refill information. This printout is to be verified, dated and signed by the dispensing pharmacist. There was evidence that the defendant failed to verify some of the daily printouts. Some of the refill entries on the daily printouts were not accurate when checked against the original prescriptions. These inaccuracies were evidence of the defendant's failure to verify the records.

Tadrus v Missouri Board of Pharmacy
849 S.W.2d 2224 (1993)
...continued

Missouri law requires the prescription label to contain, among other information, the exact name and dosage of the drug dispensed. The Board found that the defendant had violated this statute by failing to show the exact name of the generic drug dispensed. The computer-generated label showed on one line "Generic for Colace." The next line stated "100 DSS 100 MG." DSS is the chemical name for the generic version of *Colace*.

RULING: The Board of Pharmacy suspended the pharmacist's license for 3 months followed by a 5-year probation and placed the pharmacy on probation for 5 years as well. The trial court affirmed the decision of the Board of Pharmacy. The appellate court concluded that the Board's disciplinary action was not excessive, arbitrary or capricious, except that it did reverse the Board's finding with respect to the alleged label infraction.

REASONING: The court concluded that it was impossible to define and categorize all of the acts which might constitute unprofessional conduct or gross negligence. The crucial aspect is that the legislature established minimal guidelines to govern disciplinary actions. Every infraction found by the Board of Pharmacy at Sam's Prescription Shop was a violation of a statute or regulation in effect at the time of the inspections. The defendant could hardly assert that he was unaware of the regulations and statutes governing the conduct of licensed pharmacists at the time of inspections.

The court ruled that the plain intent of the legislature was to require pharmacies to have on hand the latest revision of the U.S.P. Therefore, the court read the statute as if the word decennial had not been there. Under this interpretation, the pharmacy was found not to be in compliance with Missouri law.

The pharmacy's failure to display the license of one of its pharmacists and its failure to keep accurate refill records were clearly in violation of state regulations.

The court concluded that DSS would be the accepted chemical designation of the product in the alleged labeling infraction. The ordinary patient would understand DSS as well as he or she would understand the generic name of the drug. To understand either, the patient would have to consult a reference book or an expert. The court found that the use of an accurate, unambiguous abbreviation satisfied the requirement of the statute. The requirement of "exact" labeling did not necessarily mean full and unabbreviated.

Sender v Department of Professional Regulation
635 N.E.2d 849 (Ill. App. 1994)

ISSUE: Whether two pharmacists whose licenses were suspended after an audit of their pharmacy showed that 38,000 tablets of controlled substances were missing from the pharmacy's inventory were too harshly disciplined by the Board of Pharmacy, particularly when one pharmacist was disciplined simply because he held stock in the corporation that owned the pharmacy.

FACTS: Dennis Sender and Sheldon Weiner were both licensed pharmacists and each owned 50% of the shares of the corporation which owned Sure Save Drugs. Following an audit of the pharmacy, the Illinois Department of Professional Regulation filed a complaint against the pharmacy and the pharmacists, alleging violations of the Controlled Substances Act and the Illinois Pharmacy Practice Act.

Sender v Department of Professional Regulation
635 N.E.2d 849 (Ill. App. 1994)
...continued

At the hearing, neither pharmacist disputed the audit. Instead, they contended that an employee had stolen the drugs. They also claimed that once the theft had been discovered, the employee had been fired. However, there was no audit of the inventory after the discharge of the employee.

The hearing officer concluded that Wiener failed in his duty as pharmacist-in-charge by the mere fact that such substantial shortages had occurred. There was no evidence presented that either of the pharmacists had diverted any of the controlled substances. The hearing officer also concluded that, given the years of professional experience of both pharmacists (Weiner, 32 years; Sender, 25 years), it was incomprehensible that they should not conduct or request an audit after the alleged theft. This was particularly true since the overall security of the pharmacy and the controlled substances area was so lacking.

RULING: The Board of Pharmacy suspended Wiener's license for a minimum of 5 years and ordered him to pay a $2,000 fine. The Board suspended Sender's pharmacist license for 3 years and ordered him to pay a $1,500 fine. The appellate court vacated the fine and suspension imposed on Wiener and remanded his case for reconsideration. The court reversed the findings as to Sender and vacated his fine and suspension.

REASONING: Illinois statutes provide that the operations of the pharmacy are the responsibility of the pharmacist-in-charge and that the establishment and maintenance of security provisions are the dual responsibility of the pharmacist-in-charge and the owner of the pharmacy. The Department interpreted the term "owner" to include Sender because he owned 50% of the parent corporation.

The appellate court disagreed. The owner of Sure Save Drugs was a corporation, not Sender. A corporation is a distinct legal entity and a shareholder is not the owner of the corporate property. Sender did not own controlling shares. Thus, the Department erred when it found Sender was an owner of the pharmacy based solely on his status as a 50% shareholder of the corporation.

The court went on to note that Sender was not the pharmacist-in-charge. He was a staff pharmacist who worked part-time at the pharmacy. He did not order the prescription drugs, nor was he responsible for the shortage. While Sender did dispense prescriptions, his primary responsibilities were ordering cigarettes, sundries, and *otc* drugs. Because there was no evidence that Sender was responsible for maintaining the records or inventory of the prescription drugs at the pharmacy, the court was not willing to extend the statute to a person who is a part-time pharmacist and who is not responsible for keeping records or maintaining inventories.

Finally, Weiner argued that his suspension of 5 years and fine of $2,000 were an abuse of discretion. The court noted that the hearing officer recommended that Weiner's license be suspended for a minimum of 30 months, but the Department had doubled the sanction and added a monetary fine without explanation. Weiner had admitted that his employee had stolen the prescription drugs, and there was evidence that he had hired a private investigator when he first learned of the theft. When the investigator verified that the employee had stolen the prescription drugs, Weiner had fired the employee. Weiner had been practicing pharmacy for more than 32 years. He had never before been disciplined. The court found the penalty imposed on him was overly harsh and arbitrary.

Borchardt v Department of Commerce
218 Mich.App. 367 (1996)

FACTS: The Michigan State Board of Pharmacy (the "Board") suspended a pharmacist's controlled substance license and his license to practice pharmacy for a period of six months and assessed a $5,000 fine. The Board cited the pharmacist's activities involving the sale of drugs between two other pharmacists, one in Illinois and the other in Michigan, as grounds for the disciplinary action, stating that in these actions, the pharmacist functioned as a wholesale distributor without a license. The pharmacist appealed to the Michigan Circuit Court. The court found that the Board was within its authority to sanction the petitioner, as pharmacists are not allowed to engage in wholesaling activities without a license. Further, as a wholesale distributor, the pharmacist failed to maintain complete records of his supply and distribution of drugs to the Michigan-based pharmacist, thus violating another statute. The court disagreed with the Circuit Court's finding that a pharmacist's license allowed him to act as the middleman between two other pharmacists for the sale of drugs. The statutory definition of the practice of a pharmacy does not include the actions as defined in the statutory definition of a wholesale distributor.

HOLDING: The Circuit court action was reversed and the Board's order was reinstated.

Malon v Hueseman
942 S.W.2d 424 (Mo.App. 1997)

The Missouri Board of Pharmacy charged the pharmacist with illegal compounding in 1990 and informed her that it would not renew her pharmacy permit. The Administrative Hearing Commission (AHC) ordered a permit reinstated. The Board then filed a 16-count complaint claiming that the pharmacist compounded drugs from bulk chemicals and made dispensing errors or illegal substitutions that endangered her patients. In March 1991, the AHC dismissed the board's complaint finding in favor of the pharmacist even though it did find some irregularities in her compounding procedures. The board then filed another complaint alleging nearly the same misconduct. This time, however, the pharmacist agreed to settle the claims, allegedly because successfully defending the first two cases had drained her of funds. The agreement stated that the pharmacist admitted filling prescriptions from bulk chemicals and substituted drugs other than those prescribed for settlement purposes only. The AHC entered a Consent Order in October 1991 accepting the terms of the agreement and placing the pharmacist on probation for 5 years. In May 1995, the board issued a new complaint claiming that the pharmacist violated the terms of her probation by incorrectly filling prescriptions and making illegal substitutions. The board and the pharmacist entered into a second settlement agreement where the pharmacist admitted, for settlement purposes but not as an admission of liability, that she did incorrectly fill prescriptions for an individual identified as "Patient 1" as well as several other patients. At approximately the same time, the individual who was identified as "Patient 1" filed a malpractice case in a civil court alleging that the pharmacist dispensed prednisone instead of the *Eldepryl* (selegiline) that had been prescribed. The complaint included a claim for punitive damages based on an allegation that the pharmacist repeatedly demonstrated willful, wanton, and malicious conduct in making dispensing and substitution errors. As evidence, the plaintiff attached the 1991 and 1995 settlement agreements and AHC findings. The pharmacist asked the trial court judge to exclude the settlement agreements and AHC findings on the basis that those documents were not relevant to the malpractice claims. The judge refused, ruling that portions of the settlement agreements dealing with misfilled prescriptions could be read to the jury. He reasoned that the fact that the pharmacist had admitted to misfilling prescriptions prevented her from now denying these facts and that the jury could properly weigh the value of those admissions in determining whether she had committed the alleged mal-

Malon v Hueseman
942 S.W.2d 424 (Mo.App. 1997)
...continued

practice. The pharmacist filed a request for a "writ of prohibition" with the state court of appeals asking the trial court's evidentiary ruling be reversed before proceeding with the trial. After examining the facts, the court of appeals granted the pharmacist's request and reversed the trial court's ruling. The court recognized that if the settlements were permitted into evidence in this case, few licensed professionals would ever accept settlement proposals in the future.

Sunscript Pharmacy v North Carolina Board of Pharmacy
Slip Op No COA00-1089, December 4, 2001, 2001 N.C. App. LEXIS 1172

An investigation by the North Carolina Board of Pharmacy concluded that a pharmacist formerly employed by the pharmacy had committed several dispensing errors within a few weeks. One of the errors was a cause of the death of an institutionalized long-term care patient. As a result, the Board suspended the pharmacist's license and the license of the pharmacy for 7 days. The primary issue on appeal was whether the trial court erred when it held that the board did not have the authority to discipline a pharmacy permit holder for the negligence of one of its pharmacists who was also licensed by the board. The trial court determined that if the legislature had intended for the board to have such disciplinary authority it would have expressly granted it. The court of appeals disagreed with the trial court finding that N.C. Gen. Stat. §90-85.38(b) provided that the board could suspend, revoke, or refuse to grant or renew any permit for the same conduct for which a licensed pharmacist might be disciplined. The court of appeals held that in light of the purpose of the North Carolina Pharmacy Practice Act to insure minimum standards of competency and to protect the public health, safety, and welfare, the legislature intended for the board to have authority to discipline a permit holder for the conduct of one of its licensed pharmacists. Therefore, the court of appeals reversed the decision of the trial court and remanded the case for further proceedings.

The following is a list of court cases that are related to this topic.

Randle v California State Board of Pharmacy, 49 Cal. Rptr. 485 (1966).
Arenstein v California State Board of Pharmacy, 71 Cal. Rptr. 357 (1968)
Arkansas State Board of Pharmacy v Patrick, 423 S.W.2d 265 (Ark. 1968)
Pennsylvania State Board of Pharmacy v Pastor, 213 Pa. Super. 227, 247 A.2d 651 (Pa. 1968)
Arkansas State Board of Pharmacy v Whayne, 454 S.W.2d 667 (Ark. 1970)
Vermont & 110th Medical Arts Pharmacy v Board of Pharmacy of the State of California, 59716 (Cal. App. 2d, Oct. 29, 1981)
State Board of Pharmacy v Weinstein, 514 N.E.2d. 1143 (Ohio Com. Pl. 1987)
Swartz v New York State Department of Education, 522 N.Y.S.2d 727 (A.D. 3 Dept. 1987)
Morris v Commonwealth of Pennsylvania, Dept. of State, 537 A.2d 93 (Pa. Cmwlth. 1988)
DePanfilis v Pennsylvania State Board of Pharmacy, 551 A.2d 344 (Pa. Cmwlth. 1988)
Sloman v Iowa Board of Pharmacy Examiners, No. 88-709, Sup. Ct. Iowa (May 17, 1989)
Ohio State Board of Pharmacy v Poppe, 549 N.E. 2d 541 (Ohio App. 1988)
Brown v Commonwealth of Pennsylvania, 506 A.2d 913 (Pa. Cmwlth. 1989)
Walgreen v Dept. of Professional Regulation, Ill. Ct. App. May 26, 1992
Arkansas State Board of Pharmacy v Fenwick, No. CA 95-904, 1996 Ark. App. LEXIS 603, (Ark. App. Oct. 2, 1996)

PHARMACY PRACTICE

Missouri ex rel Nixon v Stallknecht
No. 99CV212429, October 25, 1999, Jackson County Cir. Ct., Mo., (reported in *Health Law Digest*)

In this case, a pharmacist owned and operated six pharmacies in Texas and two internet sites. Without ever seeing a prescriber, users of the sites could order a prescription-only drug, sign a waiver of liability, pay a fee and, upon approval of a Texas physician who issued a prescription, obtain the drug. Missouri charged the pharmacist with practicing pharmacy in Missouri without a state-issued license after drugs purchased from the web sites were shipped to Missouri residents. The Circuit Court entered a permanent injunction prohibiting the pharmacist from shipping drugs into Missouri without first obtaining the required licenses. The injunction also ordered the pharmacist to prominently post on all of his web sites that the services were not available to Missouri residents. The court also ordered the pharmacist to refund all monies paid to the pharmacy by Missouri residents from the time the lawsuit was filed until the injunction took effect.

Hegner Pharmacy v Borough of Beaver
Slip Op No 1361 CD 2001 (November 13, 2001), 2001 Pa. Comw. LEXIS 845

Since 1960, Beaver, Pennsylvania, has had a Mercantile License Tax set at the rate of 1½ mills for each dollar of retail sales in "goods, wares and merchandise." In 1979 the town enacted a Business Privilege Tax at the rate of 5½ mills on the gross receipts of businesses. The term "business" means "the carrying on or exercising whether for gain or for profit or otherwise within the Borough, any trade or business... [or] any profession..." However, the ordinance also provides that the Business Privilege Tax "shall not include that portion of any business which is subject to the Borough of Beaver mercantile tax." The retail pharmacy located in Beaver since 1997 sells prescription and nonprescription medications as well as other sundries. In 1997 and 1998, the pharmacy paid Mercantile taxes but no Business Privilege taxes. In 1998, Beaver determined that the pharmacy is a profession subject to the Business Privilege Tax and it filed a notice of assessment for underpayment of taxes on the gross business receipts for the first 2 years of operation. The pharmacy sued, claiming it was exempt from the Business Privilege Tax because it paid Mercantile taxes. Beaver replied that because pharmacy is a profession, the pharmacy is subject to taxation on the entire receipts for the corporation under the Business Privilege ordinance. The Court of Appeals concluded that the pharmacy is exempt from the Business Privilege Tax and reversed the lower court ruling to the contrary. It noted that whether pharmacy is a profession or a business is irrelevant because those are popular, not legal terms. The proper focus is whether there is a sales transaction between the pharmacy and the customer making the transaction subject to the Mercantile Tax. Because the distribution of prescription medication and devices constitutes the sale of goods and is properly taxed pursuant to the Mercantile Tax, the gross receipts from those sales are excluded from taxation under the Business Privilege Tax Ordinance.

In re: Misha Tereschouk
Slip Op No 01-1112 (April 4, 2001), Fed. Cir. 2001 U.S. App. LEXIS 5640

Petitioner filed an application to patent a method for automatically distributing drugs to the holder of pre-encoded portable medical data carrier. The application claims methods for automatically distributing drugs to the holder of a pre-encoded portable medical data carrier. The claims recite methods in which a doctor encodes a patient's prescription onto an

In re: Misha Tereschouk
Slip Op No 01-1112 (April 4, 2001), Fed. Cir. 2001 U.S. App. LEXIS 5640
...continued

updateable portable medical data carrier, such as a credit-card sized integrated circuit card. The data carrier includes identification data, prescription data, and financial data. During the encoding process, the prescription is safety-checked for items such as contraindications, maximum approved dosages, and adverse drug interactions. After the safety check, the data carrier is given to the patient. The patient may then present the data carrier to a drug-dispensing machine. The drug dispensing machine verifies the patient's identification by means similar to the manner in which a bank ATM card might be validated, such as a memorized code or the patient's physical features (fingerprint, voice, etc). After identity verification, an optional safety check may be performed similar to the check performed when the prescription was encoded. The drug-dispensing machine then delivers the prescribed drugs to the patient. The data carrier is re-encoded to reflect the dispensing transaction and then is returned to the patient. The US Patent and Trademark Office's Board of Patent Appeals and Interferences (board), rejected all of petitioner's patent claims in his application on the grounds of obviousness under 35 U.S.C.S. § 103. Petitioner appealed, but judgment of the board was affirmed because the purported elimination of supervision was not a patentable distinction from the prior art. Substantial evidence supported the board's finding that petitioner's purported privacy advantage was illusory. Furthermore, the fact that the prior art recognized the legal requirement for a licensed professional to participate in drug dispensing did not mean that the elimination of the pharmacist's participation constituted a patentable novelty. Judgment was affirmed.

The following is a list of court cases that are related to this topic.

Nevada State Board of Pharmacy v Garrigus & Block, 496 P. 2d 748 (Nev. 1972)
Mutual Benefit Insurance v Haver, 725 A.2d 743 (Pa. 1999).

CONFIDENTIALITY

Evans v Rite-Aid Corp.
452 S.E.2d 9 (S.C. App. 1994), affirmed, as modified 478 S.E 2d 846 (S.C. 1996)

FACTS: A pharmacy employee falsely told others in the community that a prescription drug obtained by the patient was used to treat venereal disease. Three years later, the patient filed a lawsuit against the pharmacy for breach of confidentiality and negligent supervision. The complaint claimed that the pharmacy failed to ensure the accuracy of disclosures by its employees and "outrage" as a result of the false disclosure. The South Carolina trial court dismissed the breach of confidentiality claims because pharmacists have no duty of confidentiality with respect to dispensed medication. Further, the pharmacy cannot be held liable for disclosures by its employees. The other counts were dismissed as being untimely under the State's two-year statute of limitation claims for defamation.

HOLDING: Dismissal was affirmed at the Court of Appeals level on the basis that the State recognizes no statutory or common law privilege between patients and pharmacists and there is no corresponding right of confidentiality between the parties. The South Carolina Court of Appeals agreed that the other claims were nothing more than an artful attempt to avoid the two-year statute of limitations for defamation. The Supreme Court also affirmed dismissal but modified the opinion of the Court of Appeals to make clear that pharmacists do owe a duty of due care and may be sued for negligence in a properly pled and timely filed complaint.

Suarez v Plarard
663 N.E.2d 1039 (Ill. App. 1996)

FACTS: A pharmacy customer shared confidential information with a pharmacist in connection with filling her prescription for drugs used to treat her mental health disorder. During a subsequent chance meeting at a public tavern between the customer and the pharmacist, the pharmacist discussed the confidential information in the presence of other persons causing the customer embarrassment. The customer sued, alleging the pharmacist had a duty not to disclose confidential information under the Illinois Mental Health and Developmental Disabilities Confidentiality Act (the "Act").

HOLDING: The circuit court dismissed the case. The judgment was upheld on appeal. The appellate court found that the Act was intended to apply to persons entering into a therapeutic relationship. The Court held that a "therapeutic relationship" could not be expanded to include a pharmacist's routine dispensing of drugs, even if this included discussing a customer's medical condition and treatment.

Washburn v Rite Aid
695 A.2d 495 (R.I. 1997)

In an underlying action, plaintiff sued her husband for divorce. During discovery in that case, the husband's attorney subpoenaed the pharmacy records of the wife without informing the wife or her attorney about the subpoena. The subpoena commanded the pharmacy to bring its records to a court hearing on a specified date. Without giving notice to or obtaining consent from the plaintiff, the pharmacy mailed the records directly to the husband's attorney. The wife found out about the disclosure just before the hearing began when her husband threatened to disclose the pharmacy record and reveal her drug-taking habits. She then sued the pharmacy for invasion of a statutorily recognized right of privacy and breach of the state's Confidentiality of Health Care Information Act. The Rhode Island Supreme Court reversed dismissal of the claims finding that while the pharmacy is not a health care provider (dispensing prescription medicines on the order of a health care provider is not providing health care services) by definition, it is still subject to the Act's prohibition against disclosure of confidential health care records by a third party. Because neither party contested the point, the court assumed that prescriptions are confidential records subject to privilege. The court also reinstated plaintiff's claim for compensatory and exemplary damages under the Privacy Act. The Court was particularly critical of the pharmacy's legal department in ignoring the orderly judicial procedure associated with the disclosure of confidential information subject to subpoena.

The following is a list of court cases that are related to this topic.

Hannigan v Sundby Pharmacy, 224 Wis. 2d 910; 593 NW 2d 52 (Wis. App. 1999).
Nefris v DeStefano, Slip Op. No. 98-10295 (Oct. 18, 1999), 1999 NY App. Div. LEXIS 10434.
Shiffrin v IV Services of America, 53 Conn. App. 129; 729 A. 2d 784 (1999)

NONPHARMACIST PERSONNEL

Duensing v Huscher
431 S.W.2d 169 (Mo. 1968)

ISSUE: Whether a pharmacist could be held liable for the actual and punitive damages associated with the negligence of a nonpharmacist employee in dispensing a prescription.

Duensing v Huscher
431 S.W.2d 169 (Mo. 1968)
...continued

FACTS: This is a civil lawsuit against a pharmacy and its employee for injuries resulting to a 2 1/2-year-old child who received *Seconal* suppositories instead of aspirin suppositories prescribed by the doctor. The parents of the child brought suit for $25,000 actual damages and asked for $100,000 more as "punitive damages."

The case was tried before a jury who found in favor of the parents and awarded them damages of $22,000 against the pharmacy and $10,000 punitive damages against the pharmacy and against the employee. The case was appealed to the Missouri Supreme Court which, while upholding the trial court's ruling in favor of the plaintiffs, reduced the punitive damages to $2500 against each defendant. The $22,000 actual damages were left intact.

The child became ill on July 27, 1965 and the child's parents consulted a physician who gave the child a penicillin injection. Later that day, the child's condition failed to improve and the physician was consulted again. This time, the doctor phoned in a prescription to the defendant's pharmacy. The pharmacy employee who received the telephone prescription was not a registered pharmacist, nor was a registered pharmacist on duty in the pharmacy at the time. Nonetheless, the nonpharmacist employee filled the prescription. The testimony at the trial of the case (although conflicting in some respects) tended to show that the prescription phoned in by the doctor was for 2 grain aspirin suppositories, but the prescription was filled with 2 grain *Seconal* suppositories.

The child's mother obtained the prescription, and after inserting several suppositories in accordance with the directions of the doctor, it became apparent the child's condition was worse instead of better. The child was then hospitalized and after extensive medical treatment recovered from an overdose of barbiturates. An independent laboratory analysis showed that the prescription contained barbiturate suppositories.

At the trial, the plaintiff's parent's attorney contended that there were signs in the pharmacy indicating that a registered pharmacist was on duty and that such signs carried the defendant-employee's name in such fashion as to indicate that he was a pharmacist, all in violation of Missouri law. It was also contended that the defendant-employee himself violated Missouri law when he filled the prescription while not being a pharmacist nor filling it under the supervision of a registered pharmacist. (§338.010 of the Missouri Pharmacy Act permitted a nonpharmacist employee to fill prescriptions under the supervision of a registered pharmacist.) The accepted facts of the case showed that the owner of the pharmacy was a registered pharmacist and the father of the employee-defendant, but that he (the owner) was not present when the prescription was filled.

RULING: The court found that the pharmacy was responsible for the acts of its employees and that punitive damages, as well as actual damages, might be awarded because of the deception on the part of the nonpharmacist employee in dispensing the prescription.

REASONING: The Missouri Supreme Court ruled in favor of the plaintiff's parents, and in its published opinion stated:

> In the case before us defendant _____ well knew he was not a registered pharmacist and had no authority to fill prescriptions unless supervised by a registered pharmacist. Further, when no registered pharmacist was on duty the law required the display of a sign informing the public of that fact...We rule that under the law and evidence plaintiff was entitled to actual damages and also punitive damages.

Arkansas State Board of Pharmacy v Whayne
454 S.W.2d 667 (Ark.1970)

ISSUE: Whether a pharmacist who permits a clerk to place a prescription label on an empty container is aiding and abetting the practice of pharmacy by a person not authorized to practice pharmacy.

FACTS: Two pharmacists had their licenses revoked by the Arkansas Board of Pharmacy on the grounds that they violated §72-1040(5)(1969 revisions) of the Annotated Statutes of Arkansas, in that they "aided and abetted the practice of pharmacy by a person not authorized to practice pharmacy..." The pharmacists had their license revocations reviewed by a court and the court reversed and dismissed the charges against the pharmacists. The Arkansas State Board of Pharmacy appealed the reversal to the Arkansas Supreme Court, and the state supreme court upheld the reversal and dismissal.

The pharmacists, in this case, had in their employ a nonpharmacist clerk who assisted them in the prescription department. Although there was some inconsistency as to what functions the clerk did or did not do (each side to the case claiming differently), the Arkansas Supreme Court, for the purposes of the decision, treated the evidence to show the following:

> ...with respect to refill prescriptions, the clerk "does affix or place in the container the prescription labels before the prescription is filled by the druggist."

> ...the clerk "does go back into the medicine department and brings forth the bulk drug and sets it on the label prior to the filling of the container by the druggist."

> ...One of the pharmacists testified that the clerk "interprets the directions on the prescriptions and types them on the labels." The same pharmacist also testified, however, that the pharmacist took the telephoned prescriptions.

RULING: The court determined that placing a prescription label on an empty container is a mechanical function and does not constitute the practice of pharmacy.

REASONING: The Arkansas Supreme Court in affirming the lower court's reversal of the revocations, stated the following rule:

> "It appears to us that the affixing of a label to an empty container for the proposed use by a licensed pharmacist is not subject to the same construction (referring to the case of *Arkansas Board of Pharmacy v Patrick*, in which a clerk placed a label on a filled prescription container). In the latter case, the clerk performs only a mechanical function and needs no knowledge whatever of the nature of the drugs involved or their effect upon a patient."

State v Austin
228 S.E.2d 507 (N.C. Ct. App. 1976)

ISSUE: Whether a nonpharmacist who violates the state pharmacy act by dispensing a prescription in absence of a pharmacist also violates the state Controlled Substances Act if the drug involved is a controlled substance.

FACTS: In this case, a nonpharmacist drug store owner was convicted of violating the state CSA law and his employee-pharmacist was convicted of aiding and abetting him in the

State v Austin
228 S.E.2d 507 (N.C. Ct. App. 1976)
...continued

violations. The North Carolina Court of Appeals ordered a new trial in the case against the store owner and vacated completely the convictions of the employee-pharmacist.

Article 4 of G. S. Chapter 90-71 of the North Carolina Pharmacy Act prohibits a nonpharmacist from dispensing or selling at retail any drug or pharmaceutical preparation — upon prescription or otherwise — except as an aide to and under the immediate supervision of a licensed pharmacist or assistant pharmacist. In other words, the nonpharmacist (whether a nonpharmacist owner or manager, or a technician, clerk, aide or other) could legally sell or dispense drugs at retail, but only as an aide to and under the immediate supervision of a licensed pharmacist.

A state enforcement agent presented a prescription for *Phenaphen* with codeine (*Phenaphen* #3), a Schedule III controlled substance, to a certain nonpharmacist pharmacy owner and asked him to fill the prescription. The store owner replied that he couldn't, but that the pharmacist would be in later, the prescription was left for filling. On another occasion, a different undercover agent came into the pharmacy and asked for a refill of the same *Phenaphen* #3 prescription. This time, the nonpharmacist store owner proceeded to refill the prescription even though the pharmacist was not on duty.

A second refill of the prescription was obtained by the agent from the store owner. On January 9, 1975, the same agent then delivered a prescription for *Seconal*, a Schedule II controlled substance, to the store owner who then filled it. On all these occasions, the employee-pharmacist was not on duty.

Subsequently, the nonpharmacist store owner was charged with the criminal offense of selling or delivering a controlled substance in violation of the state CSA law (§95(a)(1) of G.S. 90. The employed pharmacist was charged with aiding and abetting the owner because it was claimed by the state authorities that he furnished false and fraudulent information in making the notations on the prescriptions as required by law (ie, the initials of pharmacist filling the prescription and date of dispensing it).

RULING: When a nonpharmacist violated state law by dispensing a prescription in the absence of the pharmacist, he has also violated the state Controlled Substances Act if the drug involved is a controlled substance.

REASONING: Since the *Phenaphen* #3 and the *Seconal* were dispensed pursuant to prescriptions (though the case does not indicate if the *Phenaphen* #3 prescription was refilled pursuant to refill authorization from the doctor), the essence of the case against the nonpharmacist owner was that he violated the state pharmacy act in dispensing drugs in the absence of a pharmacist or assistant pharmacist. If the nonpharmacist owner had no lawful authority to dispense the controlled drugs in absence of the pharmacist, he sold the drugs in violation of the Controlled Substances Act. The court's holding may be summarized as follows:

> We hold, therefore, that when a drug is old under circumstances which render the sale unlawful under the [pharmacy practice act] there is also a violation of [the state Controlled Substances Act] if, as in the present case, the drug involved is a controlled substance.

Because of procedural errors committed by the state prosecutor, the decision against the nonpharmacist was vacated and his case sent back to the trial court for retrial. All the charges

State v Austin
228 S.E.2d 507 (N.C. Ct. App. 1976)
...continued

against the employee-pharmacist were vacated...the state's handwriting expert witness did not positively identify the entries on the prescription. Further, there was no evidence at the trial to show that the employee-pharmacist was physically present or did anything to assist or encourage the nonpharmacist store owner in filling the prescriptions for controlled substances.

The following is a list of court cases that are related to this topic.

Arkansas State Board of Pharmacy v Patrick, 423 S.W.2d 265 (Ark. 1968)
Young v Texas State Board of Pharmacy, 519 S.W.2d 680 (Tex. Civ. App. 1975)
Hofmeister v Department of Registration and Education, 379 N.E. 2d 383 (Ill. App. Ct. 1978)
Walgreen v Dept. of Professional Regulation, Ill. Ct. App. May 26, 1992

SPECIFIC AREAS OF REGULATION

Advertising

Pennsylvania State Board of Pharmacy v Pastor
247 A.2d 651 (Pa. 1968)

ISSUE: Whether a state legislature may prohibit prescription drug price advertising.

FACTS: The Pennsylvania State Board of Pharmacy brought a disciplinary action against a Pennsylvania pharmacist who placed an advertisement in a local newspaper advertising certain drugs with the retail prices for each. As a result of the advertisement, the board revoked the license of the pharmacist on the grounds that he had advertised, to the public, the price of dangerous drugs in violation of §8(11) of the state pharmacy act. The pharmacist appealed the revocation action to the Commonwealth Court, which modified the revocation by changing it to a 6-month suspension. The pharmacist then appealed the suspension ruling to the Pennsylvania Superior Court.

In his appeal, the pharmacist contended that §8(11) of the state pharmacy act was unconstitutional in that it deprived him of his property right to conduct his business and such was done "without due process of law."

RULING: The majority of the judges of the Pennsylvania high court disagreed with the pharmacist's contentions and instead, in effect, upheld the constitutionality of the law prohibiting dangerous drug advertising by name and price. However, one justice of the Pennsylvania Superior Court disagreed with the majority's ruling and wrote a dissenting opinion on the case in which he alluded to the theory that the law in question was not to prevent the unwarranted dispensing of drugs, nor did advertising make drugs more available for use; "rather, the statute solely tends to stifle price competition and, therefore, of necessity, serves to deny information as to drug pricing to the needy."

As stated previously, the majority opinion prevailed and the suspension was upheld.

Florida Board of Pharmacy v Webb's City, Inc.
219 So.2d 681 (Fla. 1969)

ISSUE: Whether a state legislature may prohibit prescription drug price advertising.

FACTS: The issue of the validity of a new Florida law purporting to prohibit pharmacists from advertising the sale or use of drugs was brought before a Florida court for determination. The court ruled that only that portion of the law, which prohibited advertising of any drugs that required a prescription, was invalid. The decision was appealed by the State Board of Pharmacy to the Florida Supreme Court.

The pertinent parts of the law are as follows: (certain parts omitted)

(2) No pharmacist, owner or employee of a retail drug establishment shall use any communication media to promote or advertise the use or sale of any of the following:

   (a) narcotics;
   (b) central nervous system stimulants;
   (c) tranquilizers;
   (d) barbiturates;
   (e) other hypnotic and somnifacient drugs;
   (f) any drugs which require a prescription

Only the last section, Section (f), was in issue in this case.

RULING: The Florida Supreme Court upheld the lower court's decision, which invalidated section (2)(f) only.

Patterson Drug Co. v Kingery
305 F.Supp. 821 (W.D.Va. 1969)

ISSUE: Whether a state legislature may prohibit prescription drug price advertising.

FACTS: A retail chain corporation and one of its employed pharmacists sought a federal injunction (court order) from the United States District Court for the Western District of Virginia by which such injunction would restrain the Virginia State Board of Pharmacy from enforcing a Virginia state law relating to "unprofessional conduct" of pharmacists. The injunction was sought under 28 U.S.C. §2281 of the federal law.

The Virginia pharmacy statute in question was §54-426.1 (as amended in 1968) and the portions of issue were: Any pharmacist shall be guilty of unprofessional conduct who...

   (3) issues, publishes, broadcasts by radio or otherwise, or distributes...advertising matter in which grossly improbable or extravagant statements are made about his professional service, which have a tendency to deceive or defraud the public, contrary to the public health and welfare; or

   (4) issues, publishes, advertises, or promotes directly or indirectly, in any manner whatsoever, any amount, price, fee, premium, discount, rebate, or credit terms for professional services or for drugs containing narcotics or for any drugs, which may be dispensed only by prescription.

What appears to have happened in this court case, is that the Virginia board of Pharmacy (utilizing the above sections) forbade the drug chain from advertising as a "Discount Drug

Patterson Drug Co. v Kingery
305 F.Supp. 821 (W.D.Va. 1969)
...continued

Chain" and forbade the drug chain from giving prescription discounts to senior citizens as part of a prescription discount plan, and, in the enforcement of its prohibitions, the Board of Pharmacy threatened to revoke the licenses of any pharmacists who were employed at any chain drugstore that so advertised or gave discounts.

The result was that the drug chain discontinued the discounts and discount advertising, but in its federal court action it claimed the board's enforcement caused it to lose business and, as such, the Virginia statute violates the First Amendment guarantee of free speech, the "due process and equal protection clauses" of the 14th U.S. Constitutional Amendment and that the statute [illegally] imposes a burden on interstate commerce and [illegally] regulates matters that are the subject of exclusive federal regulation.

RULING: The federal court dismissed the argument that the Virginia statute interfered with interstate commerce (there was no interference here since the Virginia law only sought to regulate a public health area within the state); the federal court also dismissed the argument that the Virginia law illegally intruded upon an area of exclusive federal regulation of advertising under the Federal Trade Commission Act and Communications Act. (There was no illegal intrusion here since the Virginia statute was not in conflict with the federal law and the subject of advertising was not one requiring exclusive federal regulation; federal regulation of a subject is exclusive or "preempts the field" only if there is a need for a national uniformity of law — such was not needed here.)

As to the First Amendment freedom of speech violation claim, the federal court held that the "regulation of commercial advertising does not intrude upon First Amendment rights of free speech." Likewise, the court found that a Virginia statute, §54-399(a) (as amended in 1967), designated the practice of pharmacy as a profession, and hence, that statute was valid and the state could validly classify and regulate pharmacy as a professional practice. Such a ruling by the federal court is significant because, in reference to the Fourteenth Amendment "due process" clause, the court stated, in reference to the "price discount" prohibitions of the "unprofessional conduct" Virginia statute, as follows:

> ...even if the statute fixes prices, it is nevertheless valid. We accept the major premise...prescription drugs are so intimately related to the public health that the state can fix prices at which they are sold without violating the due process clauses of the Fourteenth Amendment...

However, the court went on to rule that while the basic premises of a state statute fixing prescription prices is valid, the particular Virginia statute here did not determine any maximum or minimum prescription prices nor did the Board of Pharmacy or any other state agency determine the retail price of prescription drugs. Hence, the price the statute seeks to preserve is so vague and uncertain that an offending pharmacist is denied due process of law.

The court ruled further:

> ...The evidence discloses no adverse effect on the public health, safety, or welfare by the issuance of discounts to doctors, nurses, institutions, elderly persons, and employees. And the evidence fails to establish whether a discounted price is either more or less than the retail price charged by other pharmacists in the state. Because of these deficiencies in the proof, revocation of a pharmacist's license on the ground that he has sold prescription drugs to a class or classes of customers at less than he sells to others would be arbitrary and capricious.

Patterson Drug Co. v Kingery
305 F.Supp. 821 (W.D.Va. 1969)
...continued

> Even though the price fixing functions [§(3) & (4) of 54-426.1] are invalid, it is pos-
> sible to leave intact the other definitions of unprofessional conduct...We, therefore,
> find it unnecessary to hold that the entire statute is unconstitutional.

Virginia Citizens Consumer Council, Inc. v State Board of Pharmacy
373 F.Supp. 684 (D.Va. 1974)

ISSUE: The claim here is that freedom of the reader to have the publication available to
him (in this case the prescription drug prices) is essentially the same as freedom of the press
or the publisher to publish. The court framed the controversy for decision as:

> ...whether the State may legally exclude from publication prescription drug prices not
> otherwise fairly available to those consumers who vitally need the drugs, but who,
> because of disability, illness or poverty, can only afford the very lowest price.

FACTS: The case involved a suit brought in federal court for a declaratory judgment invali-
dating a state law and for a federal injunction order to prevent the state from enforcing the
law. A Virginia law made it unprofessional conduct for any pharmacist to advertise the price
of prescription-only drugs, and a consumer's group sought to have such law invalidated and
obtain a court injunction that would prevent the pharmacy board from enforcing the law.
The consumer's group claimed the law "precluded them from information as to where prescription drugs may be bought at the least expense." Further, they claimed that "there are
costly disparities in the amounts charged (for prescription drugs); that a material part of elderly persons' income is laid out on medicine; that at many times the medicine prescribed
is vital to their well-being; and that their finances may control where they can procure des-
perately needed drugs."

The consumer's group claimed the Virginia law was a substantial infringement of the privileges of freedom of speech under the First Amendment of the United States Constitution.

RULING: The court ruled in favor of the consumer's group and made the following statements in its published case opinion, as follows:

> The right-to-know is the foundation of the First Amendment; it is the theme of this
> suit. Consumers are denied this right by the Virginia statute. It is on this premise
> that we grant the plaintiffs the injunction and declaration they ask.

> Why the customer is refused this knowledge is not convincingly explained by the State
> Board of Pharmacy and its members. Enforcement of the ban gives no succor to pub-
> lic health; on the contrary, access by the infirm or poor to the price of prescrip-
> tion drugs would be for their good. This information "serves as a tool to educate rather
> than deceive." (citing) *Maryland Board of Pharmacy v Sav-A-Lot, Inc.* 3111 A.2d 242
> (Md. 1973).

Virginia Citizens Consumer Council, Inc. v State Board of Pharmacy
373 F.Supp. 684 (D.Va. 1974)
...continued

Further, the court stated:

> The belief that price advertising will inflate the market for the drugs is wholly untenable, since the medicine is controlled by prescriptions of physicians and so the sale of the drugs is not even at the druggists' will.

Note: For additional case studies on the topic of prescription drug advertising the reader can consult: *Osco Drug v Wis Pharmacy Examining Board*, 214 N.W. 2d 47 (Wis. 1974); *Urowsky v Board of Regents of U. Of N.Y.* 349 N.Y.S. 2d 600 (1973); and *Revco v N.C. Board of Phcy*, 204 S.E. 2d 38 (N.C. 1974). These cases are not discussed in this book but are available at the law libraries.

Virginia State Board of Pharmacy, et al v
Virginia Citizens Consumer Council, Inc., et al
425 U.S. 748 (1976)

ISSUE: Whether a state legislature may prohibit prescription drug price advertising.

FACTS: The case of *Virginia Citizens Consumer Council, Inc. v State Board of Pharmacy* was directly appealed to the United States Supreme Court by the Virginia pharmacy board.

RULING: The U.S. Supreme Court affirmed the lower court's decision and, thereby, rendered void the part of the Virginia statute prohibiting prescription drug price advertising.

REASONING: In a lengthy decision, the U.S. Supreme Court generally followed the reasoning of the lower Federal District Court in that the price advertising prohibition violated the First Amendment constitutional right of "freedom of speech;" more specifically in this instance, the right of the advertiser to advertise prescription drug prices and the right of the prescription drug consumer to receive the advertised information. Basically, the Supreme Court only reconsidered the matter in light of two arguments. One was that the First Amendment protections did not apply to "commercial speech," and the other was that prescription drug advertising would undermine the high professional standards of the pharmacist.

In its decision, the court admitted that earlier court decisions gave some credence to the theory that the First Amendment freedom of speech did not apply to purely commercial advertising, but the court indicated that in light of current decisions "...speech does not lose its First Amendment protection because money is spent to project it, as in a paid advertisement of one form or another (citations omitted)." Even though the state could regulate commercial speech as to time, place, and manner or as to truthfulness, this was not the case here because Virginia law singled out a particular kind of information and sought to prevent its dissemination completely.

In attempting to justify the prescription drug advertising ban, the pharmacy board argued, "Price advertising...will place in jeopardy the pharmacist's expertise and, with it, the customer's health." In support of this premise, it was pointed out by the appellants that aggressive price competition will result from unlimited advertising, make it impossible for pharmacists to supply professional services in compounding, handling, and dispensing drugs, and further, that advertising drug prices may not result in lower prices since someone even-

Virginia State Board of Pharmacy, et al v Virginia Citizens Consumer Council, Inc., et al
425 U.S. 748 (1976)
...continued

tually must bear the cost of the advertising expense. They also argued that advertising will, in effect, make professional practice of drug monitoring impossible, because the patient will shop various pharmacies to get the lowest price. Finally, it was argued that price advertising will damage the image of the pharmacist reducing it to that of "a mere retailer."

The Supreme Court dealt with these arguments (categorized by the court as "...highly paternalistic approach") by stating that:

> The advertising ban doses not directly affect professional standards one way or the other. It affects them only through the reactions it is assumed people will have to the free flow of drug price information. There is no claim that the advertising ban in any way prevents the cutting of corners by the pharmacist who is so inclined. That pharmacist is likely to cut corners in any event.

Further:

> Virginia is free to require whatever professional standards it wishes of its pharmacists; it may subsidize them or protect them from competition in other ways (citation omitted). But it may not do so by keeping the public in ignorance of the entirely lawful terms that competing pharmacists are offering.

Consequently, the majority of the justices of the Supreme Court affirmed the District Court decision.

Justice Rehnquist disagreed with the majority of the court and wrote a dissenting opinion in which he noted that while the Virginia statute prohibited the pharmacist from advertising drug prices, it did not preclude a consumer group from gathering price data and publishing on its own. He further indicated the general advertising of drugs might create promotion of drug use for every ill, real or imaginary, against the interest of the public welfare.

In the Matter of CVS Pharmacy
541 A.2d 242 (N.J.Super.Ct.App.Div. 1988)

ISSUE: Whether New Jersey pharmacies could be prohibited, by law, from offering discounts, rebates, and coupons in connection with the sale of prescription medications.

FACTS: In March of 1985, CVS Pharmacy distributed mail circulars advertising 30-day supplies of all prescriptions for a flat price of $3. The pharmacist-in-charge was accused of violating New Jersey law, which provided a $500 penalty for the "advertisements of discounts to persons under 62 years of age" (ie, the distribution of premiums or rebates of any kind in connection with the sale of drugs and medications).

At a Board of Pharmacy hearing, the pharmacist-manager testified that he was responsible for the CVS Pharmacy in question during the week of the $3 prescription offering. He testified that the decision to run the advertisement was not made by him, but by corporate officials. He also stated that $3 was not the customary price for most prescriptions, and in fact, this price was less than the pharmacy's acquisition costs.

In the Matter of CVS Pharmacy
541 A.2d 242 (N.J.Super.Ct.App.Div. 1988)
...continued

RULING: The New Jersey Board of Pharmacy found the pharmacist-manager to be guilty of violating New Jersey law prohibiting the advertisement of discounts for prescription drugs. This decision was reversed by the Appellate Division of the New Jersey Superior Court, which ruled that all New Jersey pharmacies may offer discount prices along with rebates and coupons. In so ruling, the court held that New Jersey law that prohibited the advertisement of such discounts was unconstitutional.

REASONING: First, the court noted that CVS was using its pharmacist-in-charge as "the vehicle for making an assault upon the constitutionality of New Jersey statutes." The court noted its distaste for risking penal sanctions rather than testing a statute under declaratory judgment options. Undoubtedly, the parent corporation would pay the fine or penalty imposed against the pharmacist-in-charge, as well as providing him with legal services, but there was little that CVS could do for the pharmacist to ameliorate the professional blemish that would result from a suspension or revocation of his license.

The state argued that the prohibition against rebates and premiums discouraged patients from shopping around from one pharmacy to another for the best prescription price. It was contended that this would help keep the patient anchored to one pharmacy and promote greater opportunities to monitor patients' prescription purchases, thereby lessening the potential for drug interactions. The court questioned the validity of a statute that purported to perpetuate a "marriage between customer and pharmacist."

Even if the statute contained a valid public purpose, the court ruled that the public was not well served by a statute that prohibited the distribution of discounts or rebates, but permitted trading stamps. As the court noted, enough trading stamps or similar devices could be provided to the consumer as to make the sale of the prescription drug a virtual gift. The court was more concerned with the consequences of a statute that only prohibited the advertising of discounts and rebates to any person under 62 years of age. If the statutory intention of the law was to provide effective monitoring of a patient's prescriptions, that purpose was thwarted by a provision that exempted from the discount ban a significant group of the population who were over the age of 62 — a group that is in great need of protection against the danger of receiving antagonistic prescription medications. The court noted that the older the person becomes, the more likely the need for prescription drugs and the need for protection from adverse consequences.

The court could simply not accept the state's premise that the prohibition against rebates would lessen drug interactions because patients would be discouraged from going from pharmacy to pharmacy. It further noted that the problem of prescription monitoring had already effectively been dealt with by other New Jersey statutes that required patient profile record systems.

In the Matter of CVS Pharmacy
561 A.2d 1160 (N.J. 1989)

ISSUE: Whether a New Jersey statute subjecting pharmacists to a penalty for offering discounts or rebates in connection with the sale of prescription drugs was constitutional. (Note: This is an appeal of the previous case.

In the Matter of CVS Pharmacy
561 A.2d 1160 (N.J. 1989)
...continued

FACTS: Consumer Value Stores (CVS), a chain of retail pharmacies operating in New Jersey distributed mail circulars advertising a one-week, $3 price for the vast majority of its prescription drugs. The advertised price was less than the regular price for most of the drugs, and in many instances, the price was less than the cost to CVS.

New Jersey statute provides that it is "grossly unprofessional conduct" for a pharmacist to offer discounts or rebates on the sale of drugs or medications. However, the statute exempted trading stamps and similar devices and further provided that discounts, premiums, and rebates may be provided in connection with the sale of medications to any person 62 years of age or older.

Based upon the statute, the Board of Pharmacy issued a letter to Timothy Brophy, the chief pharmacist of the CVS drug store in Wayne, New Jersey, charging him with a violation of the statute.

RULING: After an administrative hearing, the Board of Pharmacy found Brophy guilty and fined him $500. The case was appealed into the court system where it was ruled that the statute was unconstitutional and was not reasonably related to the promotion of the public interest. The Supreme Court of New Jersey reversed the lower court decision and reinstated the fine imposed by the Board of Pharmacy.

REASONING: The New Jersey Supreme Court noted that as local pharmacies and large chains have battled in the marketplace, the Legislature and the Board of Pharmacy have sought to maintain the quality of pharmaceutical services through such requirements that pharmacists keep patient profiles. The Board believed that the legislative purpose behind the New Jersey patient profile requirement would be defeated by practices that encouraged customers to buy drugs at whatever pharmacy happens to be selling them at the cheapest price that week. The Board maintained that the statute prevented price wars that could reduce the number of pharmacies and adversely affect pharmaceutical services and professional standards. It further contended that the Legislature could recognize that for senior citizens, cost is often the major concern, but for the general populations, the Legislature could decide patient monitoring is the dominant consideration.

The court noted that the statute need not be the best or only method of achieving the legislative purpose. The court could not conclude that the restriction on discounts or rebates was an irrational response to the goal of patient monitoring. The court also found that the exemption for senior citizens was a reasonable legislative response to the economic pressure on the elderly. The court concluded that the statute was rationally related to the legislative goals of monitoring patients' drug therapy and protecting the public's health, safety, and welfare.

The following is a list of court cases that are related to this topic.

Knoll Pharmaceutical v Sherman, 57 F.Supp. 2d 615 (N.D. Ill. 1999).
Washington Legal Foundation v Henney, 56 F. Supp. 2d 81 (D.D.C. 1999), vacated, Slip Op.
   No 99-5304, February 11, 2000 (DC App.), 2000 US App LEXIS 1816
Western States Medical Center v Shalala, Slip Op. No. 98-01650, Sept. 16, 1999, 1999 U.S. Dist.
   Nev. LEXIS 16515.
Zeneca. v Eli Lilly, Slip Op. No. 99 Civ. 1452 (JGK), July 19, 1999, 1999 U.S. Dist. LEXIS
   10852 (S.D.N.Y.),.

Dispensing Prescription Drugs

United States v Siler Drug Store Company
376 F.2d 89 (6th Cir. 1967)

ISSUE: Whether the president of a pharmacy corporation can be held criminally liable for the illegal sale of legend drugs by corporation employees.

FACTS: A corporation called the Siler Drug Store Company, its president, and a certain employee of the drug store corporation were found guilty of 8 to 10 counts of selling legend drugs without prescription in violation of §353(b)(1) and 331 (k) of the Federal Food, Drug and Cosmetic Act. The federal trial court imposed a $500 fine on each count against the corporation. The corporation president (herinafter referred to as the "pharmacy owner") and his employee were each sentenced to 1 year in prison on each count with the sentences to be served concurrently (meaning only 1 year in prison total).

Although the trial testimony of the defendants and the testimony of the government agents were conflicting on certain key points, the following events appeared to have taken place. The drugstore owner testified that a man (later identified as a federal agent) represented himself to be a physician and sought to obtain a tranquilizer, which the man said would be used for his grandmother. The pharmacy owner obtained a prescription blank signed by the agent who signed it as "Mr. Robert Engel." The printed letters "M.D." appeared on the blank below the agent's signature. At the trial, the agent denied that he posed as a physician, and, although admitting that he signed the prescription blank, he testified that he was not familiar with prescription blanks and didn't notice the "M.D." letters printed on the form.

Later, a group of federal agents entered the pharmacy and informed the owner that they had evidence that he illegally dispensed drugs. The owner's reply was that one of the agents "had posed as a doctor." Subsequently, the prescription blank in question was produced for the agents to view at that time. However, the pharmacy owner, in reference to the prescription blank, told agents, "Boys, don't mark up or mutilate this in any way or you won't make it to the front door. Don't do it boys." The owner had a revolver in the prescription counter drawer where he kept it for protection against holdups. Later, upon trial of the case, the federal prosecutor emphasized the pharmacy owner's threat against the agents. The threat may have been a significant factor in the judge's imposition of a prison sentence.

RULING: The corporation president and the corporation employee were each sentenced to 1 year in prison and a $5000 fine was levied against the corporation.

REASONING: The Court of Appeals pointed out that if the government agent had not signed the prescription blank, the probability is that the pharmacy owner would not have filled it, and, accordingly, there would have occurred no threat when the agents took the prescription form in their hands to examine it. However, the appellate court also mentioned that there may have been other considerations weighing on the trial judge in causing him to impose the prison sentence.

Although somewhat critical of the government's method of executing the illegal drug sale, the appellate court affirmed the trial court's sentence and conviction. In its written decision, the court stated: "Under the rule in the *Dotterweich* case (320 U.S. 277),...even though he might have had no consciousness of any wrongdoing by the clerk and might have known nothing whatever of his actions, the corporation president was subject to liability for such wrongdoing, including the comparatively heavy penalty of imprisonment for a year and the payment of a $5000 fine levied against his company..."

This case is important from two aspects: First, it reiterates the rule that a corporation or company is liable for the criminal acts of its employees committed within the scope of employ-

United States v Siler Drug Store Company
376 F.2d 89 (6th Cir. 1967)
...continued

ment, and second, although not specifically discussed above, the defense of entrapment might have existed in this case were it not for the fact that there were 10 counts against the corporation and 8 counts against the employee. A defense of entrapment exists when it can be proven that the defendant would not have committed the crime but for the investigating officer's trickery or temptation. However, it can be shown that the defendant committed similar crimes before or that more than one isolated incident is involved, then a predisposition of the defendant towards committing the crime negates the defense that he was "trapped" into it.

Ye Olde Apothecary v McClellan
253 S.E.2d 545 (W.Va. 1979)

ISSUE: Whether a physician may dispense medications to patients of other practitioners.

In this particular case, the evidence indicated that the physician had sold legend drugs to nonpatients who presented containers either labeled with the name of the drug or which contained a tablet or 2 of the medication...the physician testified that drugs may be given out at his office especially to people where there is danger to their lives and away from home.

FACTS: A certain physician dispensed drugs to his own patients but, in addition, sold drugs to people not his patients who had prescriptions for the drugs from other sources. A pharmacy sought an injunction or court order prohibiting the doctor from any "selling" of drugs and a lower court granted the injunction.

At first glance, it would seem an odd situation for a physician to sell drugs on prescriptions written by others since this issue was decided 77 years ago on *Commonwealth v Hovious*, 66 S.W. 3 (Ky. 1902) where the court held "the physician might sell drugs to his own patients but not fill prescriptions sent to him by others."

However, this court case had an unusual twist to it, because it involved a Board of Pharmacy rule defining "sale" in rather broad and all-encompassing terms. The West Virginia Pharmacy Practice Act was like that of other states in that §30-5-9 of the Code prohibited the retail sale of poisonous, deleterious, or habit-forming drugs by any person other than a registered pharmacist. It further prohibited any person not a pharmacist from conducting a pharmacy for the purpose of "retailing, compounding or dispensing medicines, poisons, or narcotic drugs..."

§30-5-21 contained the typical exclusion for a doctor dispensing to his/her own patients. It excluded from the above prohibitions, the medical practitioner "...in compounding of his own prescriptions, or to prevent him from supplying to his patients such medicine as he may deem proper, if such supply is not made as a sale. [court's own emphasis]"

The West Virginia State Board of Pharmacy gratuitously defined the term "sale" as used in the State Code via a regulation defining sales as the "...supply of drugs and medicines for any consideration whether charged separately or incorporated with other charges for professional services." Further the term "sale" was defined to include "...providing of patients with quantities of drugs beyond those for immediate administration."

Obviously, the board rule was an attempt to curtail *any* doctor dispensing beyond the initial or stat emergency dose. However, the so-called test case here involved a physician whose

Ye Olde Apothecary v McClellan
253 S.E.2d 545 (W.Va. 1979)
...continued

dispensing operation was more akin to running a pharmacy, because he sold or dispensed drugs prescribed by other physicians to persons who were not his patients.

RULING: The doctor appealed the case to the West Virginia Supreme Court of Appeals; the injunction was affirmed but modified.

REASONING: The Court of Appeals looked at the situation as it would apply to a physician dispensing in general. If the pharmacy board rule defining sale was accepted, the doctor would be limited to dispensing drugs to his/her patients either (1) as a "gift" without charge (directly or indirectly), (2) by use of sample drugs given free to the patient, or (3) limited to the stat dose only — leaving the patient to possible suffering or danger until a pharmacist could be found to fill a prescription. The court concluded that this was not the legislative intent; the board's rule was too much of an overreach.

Instead, the court held that the legislature intended the term "sale" to mean "retail sale" and the act "guarantees those to pharmacists, and a physician cannot sell at retail." In citing the *Hovious* case, the court reiterated the rule, but in the following terms, as follows:

> ...that [the law] purports to allow a physician to supply his patients with drugs but not sell them to the patients, to hold that physicians may supply drugs to their own patients but not fill prescriptions written by other physicians; nor sell at retail such drugs as they supply to their own patients. They may make reasonable charges for their services, including any medications they supply, they may dispense amounts of drugs as they deem sufficient to the patient's course of treatment.

Further Notation: In *U.S. v Moore*, 423 U.S. 122 (1975), the U.S. Supreme Court made it quite clear that a physician registered under Federal CSA law was not exempt from prosecution by his mere registration when his dispensing activities fell outside the usual course of professional practice. The key issue was the prescribing of controlled substances without "adequate physical examinations or none at all."

In a Michigan case, *People v Berg*, 272 N.W. 2d 167 (1978), a licensed osteopathic physician was found guilty of violating the state controlled substances law where he "sold" amphetamines to an undercover agent without performing any physical examination or obtaining a medical history. If we compare this situation with the one described in *McClellan*, it is easy to see where the physician's sale of drugs to nonpatients could expose him to grave criminal liability under the CSA law if the drugs sold were Schedule II, III, or IV controlled substances.

The following is a list of court cases that are related to this topic.

Kaspirowitz v Schering Corp., 175 A.2d 658 (N.J. 1961)
Arenstein v California State Board of Pharmacy, 71 Cal. Rptr. 357 (1968)
Duensing v Huscher, 431 S.W.2d 169 (Mo. 1968)
Fountain v Oelshelgel, 415 P.2d 316 (Ariz. 1969)
Young v Board of Pharmacy, 462 P.2d 139 (N.M. 1969)
Olson v State of Florida, 287 So.2d 313 (Fla. 1973)
McLean v State, 527 S.W.2d 76 (Tenn. 1975)
United States v Enserro, 401 F. Supp. 460 (1975)
Young v Texas State Board of Pharmacy, 519 S.W.2d 680 (Tex. Civ. App. 1975)

Norman Bridge Drug Co. v Banner Bartles, Jr., DEA, et al., 529 F.2d 822 (5th Cir. 1976)
State v Austin, 228 S.E.2d 507 (N.C. Ct. App. 1976)
Shermack v Board of Regents of the State University System, 407 N.Y.S. 2d 926 (1978)
New Mexico Pharmaceutical Association v State of New Mexico, 738 P.2d 1318 (N.M. 1987)
Agbogun v State of Texas, 756 S.W.2nd 1 (Tex. Ct. App. 1988)
Riddle v Mississippi Board of Pharmacy, 1991 WL 161411 (Miss. Sup. Ct.)
Drennan v Commuoft Health Investment, 905 S.W.2d 811 (Tx. Ct. App. 1995)
State v Dutton Drugs, Inc., 209 N.E.2d 597 (Ohio 1965)
Arkansas State Board of Pharmacy v Patrick, 423 S.W.2d 265 (Ark. 1968)

Record Keeping Requirements

Young v Board of Pharmacy
462 P.2d 139 (N.M. 1969)

ISSUE: (1) Whether a Board of Pharmacy's decision to revoke a license must be supported by substantial evidence and (2) whether a pharmacist's failure to maintain accurate drug records was "unprofessional conduct."

FACTS: The New Mexico Pharmacy Board, after due notice and hearing, revoked the license of a pharmacist upon the board's finding that he sold dangerous (legend) drugs without a prescription and that he conducted himself in an "unprofessional" manner by not keeping adequate records and inventory of depressant and stimulant drugs as required by law. The pharmacist appealed the revocation order to a New Mexico State District Court, which reversed or set aside the order. The pharmacy board appealed the reversal to the New Mexico Supreme Court.

An undercover agent approached the defendant pharmacist and asked him for some penicillin. The defendant sold him some tablets in an unmarked and unlabeled container. The agent took the container to a deputy sheriff who placed identifying marks on it and mailed it to the FDA for analysis. The FDA subsequently returned the tablets by mail to the deputy sheriff with a letter stating that the tablets were penicillin.

On a separate occasion, a board inspector asked the defendant for the pharmacy's depressant and stimulant drug records and received from the defendant invoices for drugs received and prescriptions for drugs dispensed. An inventory of 96 depressant and stimulant drugs was taken. The inventory, when compared with receipt and disposition records, showed a shortage for some drugs and a surplus for others.

At the board hearing, the attorney representing the pharmacist-defendant objected to the introduction of the container of tablets on the ground that the board produced no witnesses who could account for the period of time from when the deputy mailed the container until when he received it back. The attorney asserted that witnesses must be presented to account for the continuous possession of the container. An objection was also raised by defense counsel to the introduction of the FDA letter into evidence on grounds it was "hearsay," because the author of the letter was not available at the hearing for cross-examination by defense counsel.

The objected-to evidence was admitted into the hearing and formed the basis of the board's finding and conclusions. However, defense counsel's timely objection saved the issue for litigation upon judicial review.

In the appeal of the case, the pharmacy board contended that in administrative hearings, "boards may admit any evidence and may give 'probative effect' to evidence that is a kind commonly relied on by reasonably prudent men in the conduct of serious affairs" (from §67-26-1 et seq of New Mexico Annotated Statutes, Uniform Licensing Act).

Young v Board of Pharmacy
462 P.2d 139 (N.M. 1969)
...continued

The board claimed that at administrative hearings the "rules of evidence" are not as strictly applied and any evidence that tends to prove a relevant point may be admitted and given effect.

RULING: The court ruled that (1) "incompetent evidence" alone will not legally support a pharmacist's revocation of license, and (2) the failure to keep accurate drug records did not constitute "unprofessional conduct" on the part of the pharmacist.

REASONING: While the state supreme court agreed in principle with the board's argument, the court pointed out that "incompetent evidence" alone will not legally support an administrative finding. It must be supported by at least a residuum of competent evidence. The court stated:

> ...in administrative adjudications where a person's livelihood (a property right) is at stake, any action depriving him of that property must be based upon such substantial evidence as would support a verdict in a court of law.

> ...while the evidence in question here was admissible and entitled to "probative effect," it was not of that quality, certainty, and credibility, standing alone, to support findings....We cannot escape the conclusion that there was a failure to establish the nature of the pills sold.

The court also reviewed the charge that inaccurate drug records constituted "unprofessional conduct" on the part of the defendant. Again, the court's ruling on this point was also that the board's finding was arbitrary. The court stated:

> ...we fail to see why accurate recordkeeping should be a test of a man's professional character. This is particularly true when there is no showing that the shortcomings did not result from some improper or unlawful reason or purpose, as distinguished from negligence...

The New Mexico Supreme Court's ruling in the case was in favor of the pharmacist-defendant.

The following is a list of court cases that are related to this topic.

State v Reardon, 219 A.2d 767 (R.I. 1966)McKaba v Board of Regents of the State of New York, 294 N.Y. S.2d 382 (1968)
State v Williams, 171 N.W.2d 521 (Iowa 1969)
Tadrus v Missouri Board of Pharmacy, 849 S.W. 2d 2224 (1993)
Borchardt v Department of Commerce, 218 Mich. App. 367, (1996)
Drennan v Commuoft Health Investment, 905 S.W.2d 811 (Tx. Ct. App. 1995)
Massachusetts v Stop and Shop Cos., Inc., No. 96-0104-8 (Mass. Sup. Ct., Jan. 5, 1996)

Drug Product Selection

Rhone-Poulenc Rorer Pharmaceuticals v Marion Merrell Dow
93 F.3d 511 (8th Cir. 1996)

Rhone-Poulenc Rorer Pharmaceuticals (RPR) brought suit against Marion Merrell Dow (MMD) for false advertising with respect to the competing forms of diltiazem (referred to by the court as "a miracle drug for the treatment of hypertension and angina"). MMD filed a countersuit claiming that RPR had also engaged in false advertising. The district court agreed with both claims finding that both parties had misled the public in claims of product superiority. No damages were awarded and RPR was ordered to undertake corrective advertising to counter the effects of its false advertising to pharmacists, physicians, and hospitals concerning the "food effect" on use of the competing products. The federal Court of Appeals for the Eighth Circuit vacated that portion of the order, because it did not believe sufficient evidence existed to conclude that RPR had mislead its intended audience. The court made interesting observations concerning pharmacists' ability and obligations to "substitute generic equivalents." It noted that RPR's *Dilacor XR* is rated as a "BD" drug compared to MMD's *Cardizem*, meaning, under FDA regulations, that the two drugs are "not necessarily bioequivalent." The court characterized the significance of this classification as, "Pharmacists may freely substitute among AB drugs, but only a prescribing physician may substitute one BD drug for another." (The court used *Dorland's Medical Dictionary* to define and explain the significance of bioequivalency). This classification, according to the court, set the battle ground for RPR to convince doctors, pharmacists, and hospitals that its lower cost product is bioequivalent to the MMD product and for MMD to convince the same audience that it is not appropriate to substitute these products.

The following is a list of court cases that are related to this topic.

LeJeune v Trend Services, Slip Op 96-550 (June 4, 1997, La. App.), 1997 La. App LEXIS 1541.

Poisons

The following is a list of court cases that are related to this topic.

Peoples Service Drug Stores v Somerville, 158 A. 12 (Md. 1932)
Krueger v Knutson, 111 N.W.2d 526 (Minn. 1961)
January v Peace, 738 S.W.2d 355 (Tex. App.-Tyler 1987)

Operating a Pharmacy

North Dakota Board of Pharmacy v Snyder's Drug Stores, Inc.
414 U.S. 156 (1973)

ISSUE: Whether a state legislature may restrict ownership of pharmacies to pharmacists or a corporation with a majority of the stock held by pharmacists.

FACTS: The North Dakota legislature enacted a law (§43-15-35(5)) that provided to the effect that an applicant for a new pharmacy permit (or a renewal permit) had to be "a registered pharmacist in good standing" or "a corporation or association, the majority stock in which is owned by registered pharmacists in good standing, actively and regularly employed in and responsible for the management, supervision and operations of such pharmacy."

The restrictive provision did not apply to any holder of a pharmacy permit on July 1, 1963, if such permittee was otherwise qualified to conduct a pharmacy (the exception made in

North Dakota Board of Pharmacy v Snyder's Drug Stores, Inc.
414 U.S. 156 (1973)
...continued

the law for persons owning pharmacies prior to the effective date of the law is referred to as the "Grandfather clause," and its purpose is to preserve the property rights of such persons since they have a substantial investment already made in their business). Also exempted were hospital pharmacies.

An application for a new pharmacy permit was denied by the North Dakota State Pharmacy Board to Snyder's Drug Stores, Inc. (the common stock of which was owned by Red Owl Stores), because it was not shown that stockholders were pharmacists in good standing. Snyder's Drug Stores appealed the denial to the state district court and obtained a favorable ruling. The North Dakota pharmacy board appealed the district court decision to the North Dakota Supreme Court; the state supreme court also ruled in favor of Snyder's and declared the state statute unconstitutional by relying on the U.S. Supreme Court's ruling in *Liggett v Baldridge*, 278 U.S. 105 (1928).

The case was further appealed to the United States Supreme Court. Two issues were presented on the appeal; one a jurisdictional, or legal procedural issue and the other an issue of constitutional law — whether or not the state pharmacy ownership law was valid. The North Dakota Supreme Court predicated its ruling on the decision in *Liggett v Baldrige*.

RULING: The U.S. Supreme Court in the present case did not go into the merits of the North Dakota statute, but simply reversed the North Dakota Supreme Court and specifically overruled its own decision in the *Liggett* case. In the words of the court, "*Liggett*, decided in 1928, belongs in that vintage of decisions which exalted substantive due process by striking down state legislation, which the majority of the court deemed unwise."

REASONING: In overruling *Liggett*, the court is returning to what it calls an "earlier constitutional principle" stated:

> ...states have power to legislate against what are found to be injurious practices in their internal commercial and business affairs, so long as their laws do not run afoul of some specific federal constitutional prohibition, or of some valid federal law.

Snyder's Drug Stores, Inc. v North Dakota Board of Pharmacy
219 N.W.2d 140 (N.D. 1974)

ISSUE: Whether the North Dakota pharmacist-only ownership law was reasonably related to the public health so that it would withstand attack.

FACTS: Freed from the prohibitive mandate of the *Liggett* case, the North Dakota Supreme Court dealt squarely with the issue of the validity of the state pharmacy ownership law under the federal and state constitutions. In summary, it was now argued to the court that the pharmacist-only pharmacy ownership law was not reasonable or related to the public health since it added nothing to the already close control of pharmacies by federal and state laws. Further, it was argued that the law created a limited privileged class (or classes) that received preferential treatment in violation of the North Dakota constitution, which prohibited the state legislature from conferring special benefits upon small groups. The argument on this point was that restricting drug store ownership to pharmacists denied it to almost all others, and that the exemption made for pharmacies owned on July 1, 1973, and

Snyder's Drug Stores, Inc. v North Dakota Board of Pharmacy
219 N.W.2d 140 (N.D. 1974)
...continued

for hospital pharmacies was a special privilege not available to others. Another argument was that the ownership law violated the U.S. Constitution commerce clause (Art. I, Sec. 8, Clause 3) in that it interfered with interstate commerce. The issue here is that the law would exclude from North Dakota pharmacies owned by (out-of-state) nonpharmacist corporations. In other words, out-of-state nonpharmacist firms couldn't open up new pharmacies in North Dakota.

RULING: The North Dakota Supreme Court upheld the pharmacist-only pharmacy ownership law despite the challenges to it. In brief, the court's decision was a matter of weighing "Snyder's right to do business and the right of the public to be protected from abuse that could result from the improper dispensation of drugs..." The court chose the public's health interest over the interest of a merchant.

REASONING: With reference to the issue of whether the ownership requirement added anything to the existent federal/state pharmacy regulation, the court listed seven possible reasons for the pharmacist-only ownership of pharmacies. In summary, these were: (1) Pharmacists (by professional/ethical standards) are concerned with the quantity/quality of drugs in stock and a drug not in stock poses a threat to the individual who needs it. Hence, decisions made in this regard by nonpharmacist owners could be detrimental to public health; (2) supervision of hired pharmacists by pharmacist-owners would be in the best interest of public health; (3) responsibility for improper action could be pinpointed when supervision is in pharmacist-owners; (4) the dignity of a profession is enhanced by prohibiting the practitioner from subordinating himself to untrained supervisors; (5) if control and management are placed in laymen unacquainted with pharmaceutical service, the risk is that social accountability will be subordinated to the profit motive; (6) the term "pharmacy" is identified with the health professions and more than a mere means of making a profit. He who holds the purse strings controls the policy, and (7) doctor-owned pharmacies with built-in conflict of interest problems could be restricted.

With reference to the issue of validity of the ownership law under the "equal protection" test of state and federal constitutions, the court's holding was to the effect that it did not mean that the state legislation was prevented from adopting a particular classification — even though the classification was discriminatory (but not arbitrary). What would be prohibited is an invidious discrimination, an evil or unjust discrimination. The exemption made in the law for pharmacies operating on July 1, 1963, was approved by the court as not violative of equal protection since in the court's words "...most corrective legislation necessitates a Grandfather Clause..." (reform may be taken one step at a time; preventive legislation need not enact a perfect cure). Similarly, the exemption made for hospital pharmacies was concluded by the court to be a justified sacrifice of some control because of the emergency of providing immediate and continuous pharmaceutical service to a limited clientele (hospital patients).

Finally, the court disposed of the contention that the ownership law violated the commerce clause of the federal constitution by interfering with interstate commerce. The court's viewpoint here was that only statutes that created economic barriers without justification would be unconstitutional while the ownership law was justified as protective of the public health and welfare.

In re Appeal of Morgan
742 A.2d 101 (N.H. 1999)

Morgan, a pharmacist, appealed a disciplinary order by the New Hampshire Board of Pharmacy imposing a fine and prohibiting him from serving as a pharmacist-in-charge. During a compliancy inspection, the inspector observed inaccurate and disorganized records. After an audit, the Board charged Morgan with failing to maintain accurate and complete controlled drug records, dispensing controlled drugs in unlawful quantities, and dispensing incorrect medication. In a hearing before the Board, the Board found sufficient evidence to sustain the charges relating to record keeping and data entry, but found insufficient evidence to prove willful misconduct in dispensing controlled substances. The Board imposed a fine and restricted Morgan's pharmacist license to preclude him from serving as a pharmacist-in-charge. Morgan challenged the legality of the Board's order. Morgan charged that the audit constituted an illegal administrative search. New Hampshire has an administrative search exception and therefore did not require a warrant to conduct the audit. Morgan contended that there was no evidence that he personally failed to keep correct records. The supreme court held that his status as pharmacist-in-charge imposed heightened responsibilities, so he could not escape his duty by denying personal involvement. Finally, Morgan alleged that the sanction imposed was disproportionate to the offense and violation. The supreme court found that his suspension as pharmacist-in-charge did not prevent him from practicing pharmacy, and that Morgan could petition the Board to lift the restriction upon showing his capability of assuming the duties of a pharmacist in charge. Therefore, the supreme court affirmed the findings and sanctions imposed by the Board of Pharmacy.

National Pharmacies v Feliciano
No 99-1803 (August 2, 2000), 1st Cir, 2000 US App 18541

National Pharmacies obtained a contract with Blue Cross of Puerto Rico to provide prescription drugs to its members through mail-order pharmacy services from a pharmacy not located in Puerto Rico. The Department of Health issued letters to the parties advising them the Puerto Rico laws forbid the use of mail-order pharmacies in 1994. National Pharmacies sought injunctive relief, claiming the Pharmacy Act violates the commerce clause and the first amendment to the Constitution. The district court rejected the Department's argument that pharmacy is a profession and therefore not subject to the commerce clause. The District Court also found that regulations applied to discriminate against out-state organizations run afoul of the commerce clause and the first amendment. The District Court also held that parts of the Pharmacy Act requiring patients to obtain prescriptions from a local pharmacy do not apply to out-of-state pharmacies. The Court of Appeals affirmed the lower court's orders. It went through a history of the development of mail-order pharmacy and how several other states have dealt with the issues raised by this practice.

Walgreen v Feliciano
No 00-1227 (HL) (June 21, 2000), USDC PR, 2000 US Dist LEXIS 8778

The Secretary of the Department of Health for Puerto Rico denied a Certificate of Necessity and Convenience to Walgreen, thereby preventing it from opening and operating any pharmacies. Walgreen sued, claiming that the statutes and regulations have been applied to unconstitutionally discriminate against out-of-state parties. An association of independent pharmacies sought permission to intervene as defendants. The court found that the

Walgreen v Feliciano
No 00-1227 (HL) (June 21, 2000), USDC PR, 2000 US Dist LEXIS 8778
...continued

association does not have standing to intervene because it could not show any legal harm it or its members would suffer no matter how the underlying case is determined.

The following is a list of court cases that are related to this topic.

United States v Ralph Clayton Robinson, 707 F.2d 811 (4th Cir. 1983)
Newcomb Sales v New Jersey Board of Pharmacy, 526 A.2d 1122 (N.J. Super. A.D. 1987)

The Medication-Use Process

Prescribing

The following is a list of court cases that are related to this topic.

Drennan v Commuoft Health Investment, 905 S.W.2d 811 (Tx. Ct. App. 1995)

Dispensing

Sheffield v State of New York
571 N.Y.S.2d 350 (1991)

ISSUE: Whether a hospital and its head pharmacist could be disciplined for permitting nurses to prepare, compound, and mix IV solutions.

FACTS: Genesee Hospital and Stanley Zack, the hospital's head pharmacist, were found guilty of misconduct in the practice of pharmacy because they permitted persons without pharmacy licenses (in this case nurses) to measure, weigh, compound, mix, and dispense ingredients in the preparation of hyperalimentation and intravenous solutions, an activity reserved to pharmacists.

Sandra Sheffield and Mary Kay Schroeder, nurses who worked for the hospital, were also charged with unprofessional misconduct in the practice of nursing by practicing beyond its scope in that they participated in the preparation of these solutions. They were reprimanded and placed on probation for 18 months to ensure their completion of a course of instruction in the legal aspects of nursing.

RULING: The hospital was censured, reprimanded, and fined $1,000 under each specification while the pharmacist was censured, reprimanded, and fined $250 under each specification.

REASONING: The petitioners contended that the determinations of professional misconduct were based on arbitrary and capricious interpretations of vague regulatory provisions. They argued that the statutory law failed to define "dispensing of drugs" and that the Nurse Practice Act failed to prohibit the conduct for which they were disciplined. They contended that the nursing practice in question had been going on at the hospital for more than 25 years and that since 1988, Health Department regulations explicitly permitted not only nurses, but licensed practical nurses under the supervision of a nurse, to prepare intravenous solutions, including those ultimately administered to patients by other nurses.

Sheffield v State of New York
571 N.Y.S.2d 350 (1991)
...continued

It was noted by the Court that the use of intravenous drugs has undergone substantial changes and has been in a state of flux for a considerable period of time. It was not disputed that the nurses could prepare intravenous solutions, prescribed by a physician, for patients to whom they personally administered the IV solutions.

However, the state contended that nurses cannot prepare such solutions for administration by other nurses in that the latter practice constitutes a dispensing of drugs, an activity reserved for pharmacists. The State also argued that while the law permits practical nurses with special training to perform certain IV therapy procedures, this regulation only authorizes them to do what nurses may legally do, but that this does not include practicing pharmacy.

The State's determination of guilt must be based upon a preponderance of evidence. When reviewing the facts, a court may not substitute its judgment for that of the administrative body. The Court noted that the legal definition of the practice of pharmacy in the state of New York only permitted pharmacists to prepare or compound drugs.

It concluded that the unrefuted facts established that the hospital and pharmacist improperly delegated the responsibility of preparing and compounding drugs and mixing IV solutions to unlicensed persons, namely the nurses at the hospital. It was further established that the nurses acted outside the scope of nursing.

Drennan v Commuoft Health Investment
905 S.W.2d 811 (Tx. Ct. App. 1995)

FACTS: A scoliosis patient was hospitalized for back surgery to be performed under a physician's order for a "general anesthetic." Following long-standing standard procedures, a registered nurse-anesthetist selected and administered the drugs to be used during surgery. A private pharmacy under contract with the hospital supplied the "floor stock" medications that were routinely used in surgical procedures. The records showed that the nurse anesthetist and pharmacist followed all record keeping procedures in accounting for this medication use. During surgery, the patient developed a cardiac arrhythmia and suffered neurological damage. Claims against the pharmacy and pharmacist for per se negligence in dispensing drugs to a nurse-anesthetist without specific orders from a licensed prescriber were premised, in part, on an expert opinion to the effect that pharmacists violate the standard of care when dispensing under these circumstances.

HOLDING: The Texas Court of Appeals dismissed the plaintiff's pharmacy and pharmacist claims finding that the physician has authority under the State health code to delegate prescribing and administering drugs to qualified individuals. Texas Board of Pharmacy rules also permit the "floor stock" procedures that were followed in this case.

The following is a list of court cases that are related to this topic.

Arkansas State Board of Pharmacy v Patrick, 423 S.W.2d 265 (Ark. 1968)
Ye Olde Apothecary v McClellan, 253 S.E. 2d 545 (W.Va. 1979)

Packaging

The following is a list of court cases that are related to this topic.

Baas v Hoye, 766 F.2d 1190 (8th Cir. 1985)

Labeling

The following is a list of court cases that are related to this topic.

Agbogun v State of Texas, 756 S.W.2nd 1 (Tex. Ct. App. 1988)
Tadrus v Missouri Board of Pharmacy, 849 S.W. 2d 2224 (1993)

Drug-Drug Interactions

The following is a list of court cases that are related to this topic.

Johnson v Walgreen Co., 675 S.2d 1036 (Fla. Dist Ct. App. 1996)

CRIMINAL LAW

U.S. v Kim
298 F. 3d 746 (9th Cir. 2002)

Two pharmacists were charged with possessing and/or distributing pseudoephedrine, knowing it would be used to manufacture the controlled substance methamphetamine. In separate cases, each pharmacist successfully moved to dismiss the indictment and vacate the judgment. The federal prosecutors appealed both decisions. On appeal, the issue was whether an indictment of a licensed pharmacist for illegal distribution of a named drug must contain an allegation that the pharmacist knew that the drug would be used to manufacture a drug outside the scope of his authority as a licensed pharmacist. The defendants argued that the government appeals were not timely. Under the Federal Rule of Appellate Procedure, the appellate court determined that the appeals were made within the required time period. The court held that the indictments of both defendants sufficiently set forth the elements of the crimes for which they were accused and reversed the lower courts' decisions for dismissal.

US v Travia
180 F. Supp. 2d 115 (D.C. Nov. 29, 2001)

The individuals who sell nitrous oxide-filled baloons in the parking lots of arenas hosting rock concerts violate FDA regulation by selling misbranded drugs, according to the US District Court for the District of Columbia. The laughing gas merchants' defense that the Food Drug and Cosmetic Act is vague and does not apply to non-professionals did not persuade the judge. He determined that the intended use of the "unlabeled" balloons determines whether these articles are drugs. The fact that the defendants did not label or advertise their products did not defeat application of the definition of a drug under the Act. The judge determined that the environment provides the necessary evidence of an intent to sell mind-altering articles without a prescription, thereby rendering the laughing gas balloons to be deemed misbranded drugs.

Healthscript v State
770 N.E. 2d 810 (Ind. 2002)

Healthscript, Inc. is a licensed pharmacy authorized to provide health-related services under Indiana's Medicaid program. Between November 1995 and June 1997, Healthscript submitted claims to and was paid by Medicaid for deliveries of sterile water to a long-term care facility. In 1998, the state of Indiana charged Healthscript with the crime of "Medicaid Fraud" in violation of state law on the theory that it overcharged Medicaid for the sterile water delivered to the long-term care facility. Healthscript filed a motion to dismiss, arguing that it could not be charged under the statute cited for the acts that Indiana had alleged. The trial court rejected Healthscript's motion to dismiss. The court of appeals then reversed, granting the motion to dismiss, and the prosecutors appealed to the Indiana Supreme Court. The issue on appeal was whether the criminal statute cited was sufficiently definite to put defendant on notice that its alleged conduct was prohibited. The Supreme Court examined the language of the criminal statute, which provided that a person who knowingly or intentionally files a Medicaid claim in violation of Indiana code §12-15 commits Medicaid fraud. Section 12–15 is a statute that requires Medicaid providers to comply with the statutes and rules governing the program. A Medicaid regulation in effect at the time that Healthscript submitted its claims stated that providers could not be paid more than their "usual and customary charge" to private non-Medicaid customers. The prosecutors' theory was that Healthscript did not comply with the regulation, as it overcharged the Medicaid program; this in turn violated §12–15 because it did not abide by its agreement to comply with the rules governing Medicaid. The Supreme Court reviewed the criminal statute to determine whether it gave fair warning that the conduct was prohibited. Because the criminal statute cross-referenced an entire article of the Indiana Code, of which only a portion applied to Medicaid provider, it did not provide "fair warning" and "sufficient definiteness" that due process was required for criminal statutes. Thus, the court held that the general reference to §12-15 was too vague in defining the conduct to be prohibited to meet the requirements of due process. The case was remanded to the trial court with directions to dismiss the charge without prejudice.

State v Hutton
Slip Op No 742 (Feb. 22, 2002), (Ohio App.) WL 252380

The pharmacist owned a Toledo pharmacy that dispensed large quantities of "exempt substances," defined as medical preparations containing a defined amount of otherwise controlled substances — narcotics, such as certain cough syrups that contain a small amount of codeine. Exempt substances may be sold by a pharmacist without a prescription. However, Ohio statutes prohibit pharmacists from selling more than one exempt preparation to an individual in less than a 48-hour period. Also, the Ohio State Board of Pharmacy promulgated regulations requiring a pharmacist to make the purchaser provide identification, including proof that he or she is over the age of 18, before dispensing exempt substances. The pharmacy must also maintain a bound record book of exempt sales that include the names and addresses of the purchasers, the type and quantity of the substances sold, and the date and initials of the dispensing pharmacist. Pharmacy Board agents inspected the pharmacy and seized the exempt substances books dating back 4 years. The agents analyzed the books and discovered what they believed to be excessive sales of exempt substances to certain individuals as well as other sales in violation of the 48-hour restriction. The Pharmacy Board took administrative action against the pharmacist's license and caused criminal proceedings to be instituted. The pharmacist was originally charged with 80 counts of drug trafficking and 20 counts of violating the 48-hour restriction. Although several counts were eventually withdrawn or dismissed, he was ultimately tried and convicted of the remaining 38 drug trafficking counts and acquitted on the 48-hour violations. The pharmacist appealed, arguing

State v Hutton
Slip Op No 742 (Feb. 22, 2002), (Ohio App.) WL 252380
...continued

that his conviction must be vacated because the exempt preparations at issue were specifically exempted from the drug abuse and trafficking laws. The appellate court reviewed the criminal statute and the exempt preparation statutes. The court determined that the statutes indicated that the legislature intended to exempt pharmacists from criminal culpability and specifically take exempt substances sold by pharmacists out of the specter of criminal prosecution. The court also held that, because all crimes in Ohio are statutory, the pharmacist would have had to violate a statute, not merely regulations that governed the pharmacy profession, to be convicted of drug trafficking. Because Hutton's conviction was based in part on the element that Hutton violated a regulation, the conviction had to be vacated.

PART IX: REGULATION OF DRUGS AND RELATED SUBSTANCES

FEDERAL FOOD, DRUG AND COSMETIC ACT

The Federal Food, Drug and Cosmetic Act of 1938

The following is a list of court cases that are related to this topic.

United States v Carlisle, 234 F.2d 196 (1956)
United States v Siler Drug Store Company, 376 F.2d 89 (1967)
United States v Stanack Sales Co., 387 F.2d 849 (3d. Cir. 1968)
Daley v Weinberger, 400 F. Supp. 1288 (1975)
Bailey v Johnson, 48 F.3d 965 (6th Cir. 1995)
Bristol-Myers Squibb Co. v Shalala, 91 F.3d 1493 (D.C. Cir. 1996)

Subsequent Amendments

The following is a list of court cases that are related to this topic.

United States v Carlisle, 234 F.2d 196 (1956)

Regulation of Human Drugs

Misbranding Provisions

United States v Carlisle
234 F.2d 196 (1956)

ISSUE: Whether the federal government could legally charge a pharmacist with violating federal law pertaining to misbranding because he refilled a legend drug prescription without first obtaining the authorization of the prescriber.

FACTS: A pharmacist, doing business as a sole proprietor of a pharmacy, was charged by federal authorities with violating, on three separate occasions, 21 U.S.C.A. 331(k), otherwise known as §301(k), 331(k) of the Federal Food, Drug and Cosmetic Act, as amended, in that the defendant pharmacist refilled prescriptions for *Seconal* and pentobarbital without the authorization of the prescriber, as required by 21 U.S.C.A. 353(b)(1), otherwise known as §503(b), 353(b)(1) of the Federal Food, Drug and Cosmetic Act.

The pharmacist-defendant, on February 11, 1953, and on another date, refilled a prescription for *Seconal* without first obtaining the authorization of the prescriber, and on another date refilled a prescription for pentobarbital without authorization of the prescriber.

Before the proceeding reached trial, the attorney for the pharmacist made a motion to the court to dismiss the charges on the grounds that they failed to state facts sufficient to charge an offense of the particular federal law. The judge granted the motion, in part and dismissed three of the six charges against the defendant. The government appealed the dismissal.

RULING: The court determined that Congress has prohibited the refilling of a prescription without authorization of the prescriber and that a pharmacist may face charges for "misbranding" in such circumstances.

REASONING: The federal government charged that a pharmacist who refilled a legend drug prescription without authorization violated §353(b)(1) of the federal law and such pharma-

United States v Carlisle
234 F.2d 196 (1956)
...continued

cist also violated §331(k) of federal law since "dispensing a drug contrary to the provisions of 353(b)(1) was an act of misbranding the drug."

This becomes important because §353(b)(1) of the federal law did not in itself, provide a direct penalty, and hence, if a penalty was to be imposed, it had to be obtained from some other section of the law.

> §353(b)(1) states "A drug intended for use by man which ...Shall be dispensed only (i) upon a written prescription of a practitioner licensed by law to administer such drug, or (ii) upon oral prescription of such practitioner which is reduced promptly to writing and filled by the pharmacist, or (iii) by refilling any such written or oral prescription if such refilling is authorized by the prescriber either in the original prescription or by oral order which is reduced promptly to writing and filled by the pharmacist. The act of dispensing a drug contrary to the provisions of this paragraph shall be deemed to be an act which results in the drug being misbranded while held for sale."

> §331 reads, "The following acts and the causing thereof are hereby prohibited: (k) The alteration, mutilation, destruction, obliteration, or removal of the whole or any part of the labeling of, or the doing of any other act with respect to, a food, drug, device, or cosmetic, if such act is done while such article is held for sale (whether or not the first sale) after shipment in interstate commerce and results in such article being adulterated or misbranded."

Counsel for the pharmacist-defendant argued that both sections 353(b)(1) and 331(k) were unconstitutional in that they gave meaning to the word "misbranding" which is contrary to the usual dictionary meaning. Counsel further contended that to say in §331(k), "or the doing of any other act with respect to, a food, drug...and results in such article being misbranded or adulterated," is to produce such vagueness in the particular sections of the law as to deprive the defendant of due process in failing to give him notice of the offense charged.

The appellate court did not accept defendant's contention. Instead, it reversed the lower court's decision on the dismissal. Hence, the case was, in effect, reinstated and sent back to the lower court for further proceedings against the pharmacist. The appellate court in its written decision stated:

> ...it is an unduly awkward way to go about charging an offense to have to rely upon three separate sections to make it out. While at first blush this seems to be so, upon analysis and understanding [,] it clearly enough appears: That, as to drugs of the habit forming group, Congress has prohibited the refilling of a prescription thereof without authorization of the issuing physician; and that, instead of fixing the penalty for this act by directly setting it out in the section carrying the prohibition, it has declared the act of so refilling to be the same as misbranding and subject to the same penalty.

🔨 🔨 🔨

The following is a list of court cases that are related to this topic.

United States v Evers, 453 F. Supp. 1141 (D. Ala. 1978)

New Drug Developments

The following is a list of court cases that are related to this topic.

Bristol-Myers Squibb Co. v Shalala, 91 F.3d 1493 (D.C. Cir. 1996)

Production of Drugs

Knoll Pharmaceutical v Sherman
57 F.Supp.2d 615 (N.D. Ill. 1999)

FACTS: Knoll manufactures *Meridia*, a prescription weight-loss aid, and developed a nation-wide, direct-to-consumer advertising campaign. Once Knoll received FDA approval for its *Meridia* ads, Knoll launched a massive advertising campaign in newspapers, magazines, on cable and local television, and on its web site. The Illinois Controlled Substances Act (ICSA) prohibits advertising controlled substances by name to the public. The Illinois Department of Professional Regulation (IDPR) is the state agency empowered to enforce the advertising ban and has the power to suspend or revoke a provider's license to distribute pharmaceuticals in Illinois. Knoll contended that the ICSA ban on advertising violated the First Amendment protection for commercial speech. Also, Knoll contended that the ban on advertising would, in effect, ban its *Meridia* ads outside Illinois in violation of the Commerce Clause. The district court agreed with Knoll that the ICSA created unconstitutional restrictions on commercial speech. The district court analyzed the ICSA under the Supreme Court's Central Hudson test for commercial speech regulation. The district court found that Knoll's ads for *Meridia* concerned lawful activity and were not misleading. Although Illinois had a substantial interest in suppressing drug abuse and illegal trafficking, the district court held that the advertising ban did not directly advance that interest. There was no evidence that advertising *Meridia* by name had any effect on drug abuse. Moreover, the district court found the Illinois ban to be more extensive than necessary to advance Illinois' interest. The district court also found that Knoll could not black out its *Meridia* ads only in Illinois. To comply with the ICSA ban on advertising, Knoll would have had to cancel its entire *Meridia* advertising campaign nationwide. Therefore, the district court held that the ICSA was unconstitutional as applied, because it regulated markets outside Illinois in violation of the Commerce Clause. The district court therefore enjoined IDPR from enforcing the ICSA against Knoll's *Meridia* ads.

KV Pharmaceutical v Missouri St Bd of Pharmacy
No WD 56948 (March 7, 2000), 2000 Mo App LEXIS 318

The plaintiff is an FDA-registered wholesale drug distributor licensed to do business by the Missouri State Board of Pharmacy. In 1992, it manufactured and shipped two lots of erythromycin ethylsuccinate (EES) oral suspension that did not meet assay standards. KV failed to report the discrepancy to the FDA. Because the expiration date on the labels could not be substantiated, the drugs were deemed misbranded under federal law. KV eventually recalled the two lots and stopped making EES later that same year. In 1995, KV pleaded guilty to federal charges of introducing misbranded drugs into interstate commerce and agreed to a four-year probation and payment of $600,000 in fines and costs. A plant inspection of the facility and records resulted in a report that found KV in compliance with the current good manufacturing practice regulations. In 1996, the Missouri Board of Pharmacy filed a complaint under state law against KV based on the same facts underlying the federal action. In 1998, the Board issued a final order placing KV's distributor license on probation for 3 years. KV appealed to the state circuit court, which affirmed the Board's order. KV appealed to the Court of Appeals, claiming that the state statute under which it was charged does

KV Pharmaceutical v Missouri St Bd of Pharmacy
No WD 56948 (March 7, 2000), 2000 Mo App LEXIS 318
...continued

not give the Board authority to sanction KV. The statute requires a finding of fraud, dishonesty, violence, or lack of moral turpitude. The Court determined that none of the federal charges involved any of these elements and there was no other evidence on which KV could be sanctioned under the state statute. Therefore the lower court's order was reversed.

The following is a list of court cases that are related to this topic.

Bristol-Myers Squibb Co. v Shalala, 91 F.3d 1493 (D.C. Cir. 1996)

Drug Marketing

Stevens v Parke, Davis & Company
507 P.2d 653 (Cal. 1973)

ISSUE: Whether warnings about potential adverse reactions to drug therapy can be negated by the manufacturer's promotional activities and whether such warnings may be viewed as merely minimal.

FACTS: A 38-year-old housewife and mother of three children was suffering from a chronic lung disorder that caused susceptibility to lung infections. She wanted to improve her condition and she consulted a physician who diagnosed her condition as stemming from an anatomical disorder that he believed could be helped by surgery. The housewife had the surgery done in September of 1964 and her physician prescribed *Chloromycetin* (chloramphenicol) post-op as a precaution against post-surgery infection. Some months later, a second physician found her to have aplastic anemia and in 1965 she died of pneumonia. The second doctor's opinion was that her death was caused by the *Chloromycetin* — the pneumonia death was due to the inability of the patient's bone marrow to produce sufficient white blood cells to overcome the infection. The patient's husband sued the pharmaceutical firm that made and marketed *Chloromycetin*, and he also sued the doctor who prescribed it for his wife. The suit against both the drug company and the doctor was based on causes of action in implied warranty, strict liability, and negligence. The negligence of the drug firm was alleged as failure to warn of the aplastic anemia side effect; the overpromotion of the drug nullifying the package labeling warning. The negligence of the prescribing doctor was alleged in that he prescribed the drug where he shouldn't have and against medical practice.

A jury trial verdict was $400,000 in favor of the plaintiff and against the doctor and drug firm. The verdict was given on the negligence claim only. The trial court judge, however, reduced the damage award to $64,673.43, because he believed that the jury acted out of prejudice and passion in determining the high amount.

RULING: Both the drug firm and plaintiff appealed the case. The appellate court ruled in favor of the plaintiff (reinstating the $400,000 award) and against the drug firm. The doctor did not appeal the verdict against him.

REASONING: On appeal, the drug firm claimed to the effect that it was not negligent in providing the warning labeling on *Chloromycetin* as it had followed the FDA regulations. Besides, even if the warning were "watered down" by its overpromotion of the drug, the physician's negligence in prescribing it was an intervening factor — the proximate cause of the injury.

Stevens v Parke, Davis & Company
507 P.2d 653 (Cal. 1973)
...continued

The evidence introduced at the trial showed that the drug firm had labeled the product as required by the FDA regulations, but it had promoted the drug to the medical profession by direct and subliminal advertising, some of which carried the blood dyscrasia warning and some of which didn't. Salespeople would call on doctors and not mention the warning, or the "give away" rulers or calendars would carry the name of the drug thereon but not the warning. Hence, the court concluded that the pharmaceutical firm had "overpromoted" the drug so as to induce physicians to prescribe it where they shouldn't prescribe it. The court stated, as follows:

> ...mere compliance with regulations or directives as to warnings, such as those issued by the United States Food and Drug Administration here, may not be sufficient to immunize the manufacturer or supplier of the drug from liability. The warnings required by such agencies may only be minimal in nature and when the manufacturer or supplier knows or has reason to know of greater dangers not included in the warning, its duty to warn may not be fulfilled...an adequate warning to the profession may be eroded or even nullified by overpromotion of the drug through a vigorous sales program which may have the effect of persuading the prescribing doctor to disregard the warnings given.

The court further reasoned that the extensive promotion of the drug was such that the drug firm could foresee that the patient's doctor would negligently prescribe the drug. Hence, the doctor's negligence was not intervening; it was a direct result of the drug firm's negligence — overpromotion of the drug.

Regarding the issue of the $400,000 damage award which was reduced by the trial court judge, the appellate court reinstated the $400,000, because the trial court did not specifically identify what in the trial might have prejudiced the jury's verdict. The higher court reviewed the trial court's proceedings and did not find where the jury was so prejudiced as to overstate the damages. There were some references by plaintiff's counsel in his opening statement to the court and jury in which he referred to *Chloromycetin* as "a toxin" and "a poison." He also made references to the dollar sales of the drug made by its manufacturer. But the court did not find such statements so prejudicial to a fair decision as to be misconduct of counsel. The trial court judge had instructed the jury not to consider the statements of the attorneys as evidence.

Zeneca. v Eli Lilly
Slip Op. No. 99 Civ. 1452 (JGK), July 19, 1999, 1999 U.S. Dist. LEXIS 10852 (S.D.N.Y.)

Zeneca manufactures a breast cancer drug tamoxifen citrate ("tamoxifen"), marketed under the name *Nolvadex*. Tamoxifen has been approved by the FDA for the reduction of the incidence of breast cancer. Eli Lilly manufactures and sells the drug raloxifene hydrochloride marketed under the name *Evista*. *Evista* has been approved by the FDA for the prevention of osteoporosis in postmenopausal women. Zeneca alleged that Eli Lilly made three false claims about *Evista*: (1) that *Evista* has been proven to reduce the risk of breast cancer, (2) that *Evista* is comparable or superior to tamoxifen for the prevention of breast cancer, and (3) that *Evista* has been indicated or approved by the FDA for the prevention of breast cancer. Zeneca sued Eli Lilly, alleging false or misleading representations, unfair competition and deceptive trade practices under the Lanham Act and New York state law. The court found abundant evidence that Eli Lilly's representatives systematically made claims that

Zeneca. v Eli Lilly

Slip Op. No. 99 Civ. 1452 (JGK), July 19, 1999, 1999 U.S. Dist. LEXIS 10852 (S.D.N.Y.)
...continued

Evista had been proven to reduce the risk of breast cancer and that *Evista* had been proven comparable or superior to tamoxifen for the reduction of the risk of breast cancer. The court found that data from Eli Lilly's research trial was insufficient to support its claims, thus making its claims for proof false. The court, however, found insufficient evidence to conclude that Eli Lilly communicated that *Evista* was approved or indicated by the FDA for the reduction of the risk of breast cancer. The court also concluded that Eli Lilly's claims that *Evista* had been proven to reduce the risk of breast cancer and that *Evista* was comparable or superior to tamoxifen were false. Therefore, the court preliminarily enjoined Eli Lilly from stating in its advertisement or promotional materials that *Evista* had been proven to reduce the risk of breast cancer or that *Evista* had been proven comparable or superior to tamoxifen.

Novartis v FTC
No 99-1315 (August 18, 2000), Ct App DC, 2000 US App LEXIS 20940

The FTC issued a cease and desist order to Novartis after finding its advertisements for *Doan's Pills* to be deceptive because they contained unsubstantiated claims of superior efficacy as a treatment for back pain. The order also would require Novartis to place a corrective disclaimer of superiority on future ads. *Doan's* products have been on the market for over 90 years. When Ciba-Geigy, the predecessor of Novartis, acquired the *Doan's* product line in 1987, it began an aggressive ad campaign to renew interests in the *otc* medications. Many of the ads stated that *Doan's* has been particularly effective for relieving back pain and that it contains an ingredient not found in other analgesics. After reviewing the legal elements of "deception," the Court affirmed the FTC orders.

Warner-Lambert v Shalala
No 99-5048 (February 11, 2000), US Ct App DC, 2000US App LEXIS 18125

"When is a pill a capsule rather than a tablet?" Thus begins the Court of Appeals opinion in a case involving a challenge by Warner-Lambert to the FDA's approval of a generic form of phenytoin by Mylan. The formulation used by Mylan inserts a tablet formed base inside a capsule. Warner-Lambert's brand name phenytoin, *Dilantin*, is formulated as a powder contained in a capsule. Warner-Lambert maintains that the products are not "therapeutically equivalent" and that the FDA should not have granted Mylan's abbreviated new drug application. The FDA regulations provide that therapeutic equivalence means pharmaceutical equivalence, which in turn means identical dosage form (21 CFR § 320.1(c). The USP defines a capsule as a "solid dosage form in which the drug is enclosed in a hard or soft soluble container of shell. Warner-Lambert did not claim that this definition on its face rendered the products pharmaceutically different, rather, it relied on the written opinions of two USP Committee members. The argument went that the FDA acted capriciously by "classifying Mylan's capsule-shaped tablet in a gelatin shell as a capsule while classifying gelatin-coated capsule-shaped tablets as tablets," The FDA countered that it historically makes dosage form equivalence determinations based on a drugs' physical appearance and how it is administered. In this case, both products are administered orally and both look like a capsule shell with internal contents. This Court sided with the FDA, concluding that, absent any evidence of therapeutic inequivalence, there really isn't much difference between a capsule and a tablet anyway.

Washington Legal Foundation v Henney
No 95-5302 (February 11, 2000), USCt App DC, 2000 US App. LEXIS 1816

In 1996 and 1997, the FDA produced 3 guidelines that discuss when enforcement action could be taken against a manufacturer that engages in prohibited conduct concerning off-label promotional activities. One guideline deals with the conditions under which a manufacturer might distribute scientific articles written by independent authors that discuss off-label uses. Another deals with distribution of textbooks dealing with the same issue. The third addresses conditions under which a manufacturer might support continuing medical education programs or seminars (CME) in which speakers discuss off-label uses. Soon afterwards, the Washington Legal Foundation (WLF), a non-profit public interest law and policy center sued the FDA, seeking an injunction against enforcement of the guidelines on the theory that they violated the free speech rights of a manufacturer to disseminate information about a drug just because the information was not approved by the government. The anomaly, according to this argument, is that anyone else could say anything they wanted to about the drug, but the manufacturer was restricted to saying only what was approved by the FDA. The manufacturer could not even tell a practitioner that additional information about a drug is available. In a lengthy and detailed analysis, the district court agreed with the WLF and enjoined the FDA from enforcing the guidelines (*WLF v Friedman*, 13 F. Supp. 2d 51 (DCDC, 1998) (WLF-1)). The Order specifically prohibits the FDA from restricting the ability of a drug manufacturer to disseminate to health care practitioners articles published in bona fide peer-reviewed professional journals and reference textbooks published independent of the manufacturer where the article or text refers to off-label uses of a drug. The Order also prohibits the FDA from restricting the ability of a manufacturer to suggest content or speakers and provide support for independent continuing education programs or other symposiums.

Shortly after this decision was filed, the Food and Drug Administration Modernization Act of 1997, Pub. L. No 105-115, 111 Stat 2296 (FDAMA), an amendment to the FD&CA, became effective. FDAMA contains provisions regarding dissemination of written articles and texts discussing off-label uses similar to the FDA guidelines discussed in WLF-1. Because of the timing of the Court's decision in WLF-1 and the effective date of FDAMA, there was some confusion, at least in the minds of FDA officials, as to the effect on the Court's injunction. All parties agreed that the FDAMA statutes superceded the FDA guidelines on these issues. FDAMA does not address this subject matter of a manufacturer's support for CE programs. The FDA contended that the injunction should not apply to the FDAMA provisions. In a subsequent decision, the Court held that that the underlying policies embodied in the FDA guidelines are unconstitutional and the injunction continued (*WLF v Friedman*, 36 F. Supp. 2d 16 (DCDC 1999)(WLF-2)). The Court asked the parties to provide additional briefings on whether the FDAMA provisions are also unconstitutional. This resulted in a third decision explicitly holding the FDAMA provisions in question are unconstitutional (WLF v Henney, 56 F. Supp. 2d 81 (DCDC 1999)(WLF-3)). The injunction was amended to include a prohibition against enforcement of the FDAMA restrictions on dissemination of off-label materials. The injunction against enforcement of the continuing education guidelines also continued. By the time of this third go-round, the judge displayed his disgust with the FDA's arrogance in trying to limit the effects of his rulings. He wrote that the government's argument that the case did not involve "speech" is nothing more than "preposterous." He went on to state that the requirement that a manufacturer seek a supplemental new drug application to amend the labeling of a drug before disseminating off-label information amounts to "constitutional blackmail — comply with the statute or sacrifice your First Amendment rights." He concluded that the FDA's position could not withstand judicial scrutiny.

The FDA appealed these ruling to the Court of Appeals for the District of Columbia. The higher Court seemed no less flabbergasted with the antilogy of arguments advanced by the FDA. The Court noted that the FDA took inconsistent positions regarding the intent of FDAMA and the guidelines. At times the FDA agreed with the WLF that FDAMA does

Washington Legal Foundation v Henney
No 95-5302 (February 11, 2000), USCt App DC, 2000 US App. LEXIS 1816
...continued

indeed limit free speech, but the limitations are constitutional. Under this position, the FDA would have authority to prosecute a manufacturer that violates the FDAMA provisions or the continuing education guidelines. At other times, the FDA argued that the statute and guidelines establish a "safe harbor." The FDA asserted that statutes ensured that certain forms of conduct cannot be used against a manufacturer in a misbranding enforcement action. This later position would seem to be an abandonment of earlier arguments where the FDA claimed authority to prosecute a manufacturer who violated any of the FDA's guidelines or FDAMA provisions. By the time the case came to oral argument, the FDA firmly embraced the "safe harbor" theory and when pressed, admitted that "neither FDAMA nor the CME Guidance independently authorizes the FDA to prohibit or sanction speech." The Court of Appeals opinion further characterizes the FDA's new attitude:

> Were a pharmaceutical company to send out reprints of an article devoted to its drug's off-label uses to thousands of physicians tomorrow, the government agreed — indeed stipulated — that the agency would draw no independent prosecutorial authority from FDAMA to buttress any enforcement proceeding. And the FDA offers a similar view of the CME Guidance: If a drug manufacturer wishes to suggest content to a CME program provider in a manner that runs afoul of all the Guidance's twelve "factors" that, by itself, is not a violation of law. Although the FDA retains the prerogative to use both types of arguably promotional conduct as evidence in a misbranding or "intended use" enforcement action, the agency insists that nothing in either of the provisions challenged in this case provides the FDA with independent authority to regulate manufacturer speech. (citations omitted)

The U.S. Court of Appeals held that the there is no constitutional argument and dismissed the case. Because of the last minute flip-flop by the FDA concerning its own prosecutorial authority, the series of opinions and accompanying injunctions should cause significant doubt about just how far manufacturers may go in promoting off-label uses without running afoul of the FD&CA's "misbranding" prohibitions.

Bober v Glaxo Wellcome
Slip Op. No. 99-3440 (April 5, 2001), 7th Cir., 2001 US App. LEXIS 5992

The plaintiff alleged violations of the Illinois Consumer Fraud and Deceptive Business Practices Act where he was given a prescription for *Zantac 150*, which was more than twice as expensive per tablet than *Zantac 75*, which did not require a prescription. When he called defendant manufacturer and marketers' hot line, he was told he could not take two 75s instead of one 150 without his doctor's authorization. The appellate court determined that, while the two dosages were not different drugs, they had been approved separately for different medical uses, and defendants were limited in how they could recommend usage based on Food and Drug Administration approvals. Because § 10b(1) of the Illinois Consumer Fraud and Deceptive Business Practices Act, 815 Ill. Comp. Stat. 505/10b(1), excluded from liability actions specifically authorized by laws administered by any regulatory body or offices acting under statutory authority of Illinois or the United States, defendants were protected from liability for any consumer misrepresentation concerning the distinctions between the 75 and 150 products. The judgment of the trial court was upheld because the allegedly misleading statements fell within the boundaries established by federal law and state case law, and were entitled to protection under the state consumer fraud statute.

The following is a list of court cases that are related to this topic.

Foster v American Home Products Corp., 29 F.3d 165 (4th Cir. 1994)
Bristol-Myers Squibb Co. v Shalala, 91 F.3d 1493 (D.C. Cir. 1996)
Rhone-Poulenc Rorer Pharmaceuticals v Marion Merrell Dow, 93 F.3d 511 (8th Cir. 1996).
Pearson v Shalala, Slip Op. No. 98-5043, United States Court of Appeals for the District of
    Columbia, January 15, 1999.
Perez v Wyeth Laboratories, Inc., 734 A.2d 1245 (N.J. 1999).

Unlabeled Indications

United States v Evers
453 F.Supp. 1141 (D. Ala. 1978)

ISSUE: The basis of this FDA case against a physician was that he used a drug for a use not approved in the package insert. The package insert, or labeling of EDTA, is in the treatment of lead poisoning and in the treatment of certain other heavy metal poisoning.

FACTS: The FDA instigated an action against a physician claiming he misbranded or mislabeled a drug in violation of the Federal Food, Drug and Cosmetic Act. The federal government brought the action in Federal District Court and sought a court order enjoining or preventing the physician from using calcium disodium versenate (commonly called calcium EDTA or EDTA) in the treatment of arteriosclerosis and other cardiovascular problems.

The physician's defense rested on the proposition that as a physician he had the right to use a drug for a disease or weakness in a patient in any manner that is not contraindicated on the [FDA-approved] package insert. [The drug calcium EDTA is neither indicated nor contraindicated on the package insert for treatment of arteriosclerosis.] The physician also claimed, as a defense, that he was "not using the drug for other than treatment of metal poisoning, its recommended use."

The manner in which the EDTA was used by the physician may be briefly described as follows: EDTA is medically used by a process called "chelation." It involves intravenous injection in the patient of chemicals which tend to react with the harmful metals that accumulate in and deter blood passage. The reaction causes the harmful metals to dissolve and pass out of the body via the kidney. The risk involved in the process is that dissolved substances may pass too rapidly through the kidneys and cause kidney failure and death to the patient.

In the reported fact of the case, the physician testified that in treating metal toxicity, he found that chelation with calcium EDTA had proven effective to aid not only the heavy metal poisoning, "but also, the arteriosclerosis." He explained that the metal content of the blockage in the arteries was neutralized by the chelating agent and passed out of the blood, and that the calcium deposit remaining in the blood vessels, having lost its mineral structural balance, tended to disintegrate and pass out through the kidneys along with other undesirable elements. Although he achieved success with EDTA, the physician stated he is "now of the opinion that no chelating agent is necessary for arteriosclerosis as the treatment may be accomplished through intravenous injections of mineral sand vitamins without a chelating agent."

RULING: The court ruled in the physician's favor and dismissed the government's suit against him.

REASONING: As to the various schools of medical thought on treatment of arteriosclerosis, the court indicated that it was aware from the medical testimony that persons suffering from advanced cases "...may expect an early disabling resulting from stroke, hypertension,

United States v Evers
453 F.Supp. 1141 (D. Ala. 1978)
...continued

heart failure or other related diseases or cardiovascular problems." The primary school of medical thought was that chelation therapy is not a proper treatment for the disease, because it is dangerous and may cause renal failure and death. However, several physicians testified to success in chelation therapy for treatment of cardiovascular problems, and one doctor indicated it to be the preferred treatment in at least one European country. The defendant-physician's position was that chelation therapy was the best treatment for even the more advanced stages of cardiovascular disease and that, "the risks and the wear and tear on the patient are less than those associated with bypass surgery."

In discussing the medical issues, the court indicated that if chelation therapy was used, the alternative treatment for arteriosclerosis, bypass surgery, might be delayed to the extent that the patient might lose his/her life when proper action might have saved it. The government, and most experts, agree that calcium is not the cause of, nor is it universally associated with, the development of arteriosclerosis, and that there is no known method of removing calcium from the arterial wall. On the other hand, physicians following the defendant-physician's chelation method "have found it successful even though they do not profess to have conducted any controlled clinical evaluation thereof such as ordinarily required [by the FDA] for approval of a new drug."

Turning to the legal arguments in the case, the court stated:

> 37 Fed. Reg. 16053-05 provides that a physician is not required to file an investigational new drug plan before prescribing an approved drug for nonapproved use but that the Food and Drug Administration does have duties when it appears that the unapproved use of an approved new drug becomes widespread or endangers the public's health...When a manufacturer or anyone in the chain of distribution suggests to a patient that an approved drug may properly be used for unapproved use..., that action constitutes a violation of the act and is punishable accordingly as misbranding of the drug.

But the court stated further, as follows:

> ...once a drug is in a local pharmacy, after interstate shipment, a physician may, as part of the practice of medicine, lawfully prescribe a different dosage for his patients or may vary the conditions of use from those approved in the package insert, without informing or obtaining approval of the Food and Drug Administration.

> Congress did not intend the Food and Drug Administration to interfere with medical practice as between the physician and patient. Congress recognized a patient's right to seek civil damages in the courts if there should be evidence of malpractice, and declined to provide any legislative restrictions upon the medical practice.

The court then indicated the reasoning for allowing the physician to use an approved drug for uses not in the package insert: "New uses for drugs are often discovered, reported in medical journals and at medical meetings, and subsequently may be widely used by the medical profession."

However, the package insert is useful because "[its] most important educational value derives from the fact that it is a well-reviewed, authoritative document." However, the FDA does not permit amendment of the drug package insert unless the manufacturer takes the required steps and the manufacturer may not be commercially interested in following the necessary

United States v Evers
453 F.Supp. 1141 (D. Ala. 1978)
...continued

steps to obtain FDA approval for the new uses. "When physicians go beyond the directions given in the package insert it does not mean they are acting illegally or unethically...[But] obviously the physician's failures are also subject to the ever increasing possibilities of malpractice suits in current times."

The following is a list of court cases that are related to this topic.

Bristol-Myers Squibb Co. v Shalala, 91 F.3d 1493 (D.C. Cir. 1996)

Compounding

Professionals and Patients for Customized Care v Shalala
56 F.3d 592, (5th Cir., 1995)

ISSUE: Is the Food and Drug Administration (FDA) required to promulgate a Compliance Policy Guide (CPG) as a formal rule under the Administrative Procedures Act (APA)?

FACTS: In 1992, the FDA promulgated CPG 7132.16 to address what the agency perceived to be a burgeoning problem in the pharmaceutical industry: The manufacture of drugs by establishments with retail pharmacy licenses. Pharmacies have long engaged in the practice of traditional compounding, the process whereby a pharmacist combines ingredients pursuant to a physician's prescription to create a medication for an individual patient. This type of compounding is commonly used to prepare medications that are not commercially available, such as diluted doses for children and altered forms of medications for easier consumption. Soon after CPG 7132.16 was issued, the FDA notified some of the organization's members that their activities were more consistent with drug manufacturing than with traditional compounding, and that they and their products were thus subject to the regulations applicable to drug manufacturers.

LAWSUIT: The plaintiff (P2C2), an organization comprised of individuals and entities engaged in the practice of pharmacy, contends that the Food and Drug Administration (FDA) Compliance Policy Guide 7132.16 (CPG 7132.16) is a substantive rule and is subject to the APA's formal rulemaking requirement that a period of time be permitted for public notice and comment before the policy can become effective. Given that this procedure was not valid, P2C2 claimed the CPG was invalid.

HOLDING: The district court dismissed the claim on appeal; the Court of Appeals found no reversible error and affirmed the trial court's judgment.

REASONING: State law primarily regulates pharmacies that practice traditional compounding, and the drugs that they compound are exempt from many federal misbranding provisions. Drug manufacturers and their products, however, are subject to rigorous federal oversight. By the 1990s, the FDA had become aware that many establishments with retail pharmacy licenses were purchasing large quantities of bulk drug substances, combining those substances into specific drug products before ever receiving any valid prescriptions, and then marketing those drug products to practitioners and patients. The FDA suspected that establishments engaged in this large-scale speculative "compounding" were doing so to circumvent the drug, adulteration, and misbranding provisions of the Food, Drug, and Cosmetic Act that regulate the manufacture of drugs.

Professionals and Patients for Customized Care v Shalala
56 F.3d 592, (5th Cir., 1995)
...continued

To address this perceived problem, the FDA issued CPG 7132.16 in an effort to establish its policy. (The Policy is reproduced in the Regulation of Pharmaceuticals chapter). This CPG identifies nine factors that the FDA instructs its field office investigators to consider in determining whether to initiate an enforcement action against a pharmacy suspected of manufacturing without the proper authorization. The guideline also explains that the "list of factors is not intended to be exhaustive and other factors may be appropriate for consideration in a particular case." There is no dispute that the FDA issued CPG 7132.16 without complying with APA notice and comment procedures as the agency considered CPG 7132.16 to be for internal guidance. The FDA explains that CPG 7132.16 was intended to be used within the agency, primarily by FDA district offices, as an aid in identifying those pharmacies that manufacture drugs under the guise of traditional compounding.

There was no dispute that CPG 7132.16 is a "rule," and its promulgation constituted "rulemaking" under the APA. But the APA exempts from notice and comment procedures "interpretative rules, general statements of policy, (and) rules of agency organization, procedure, or practice." In contrast, if a rule is "substantive," the exemption is inapplicable, and the full notice and comment requirements must be followed. If CPG 7132.16 were a substantive rule, it would be unlawful, for it was promulgated without the requisite notice and comment. The pivotal issue, therefore, is whether CPG 7132.16 is a substantive rule.

In analyzing whether an agency's pronouncement is a statement of policy or a substantive rule, the starting point is "the agency's characterization of the rule." It is undisputed that the FDA has consistently classified the instant rule as a statement of policy. The rule is self-described as "policy," and it was promulgated as a "compliance policy guide." In addition, the FDA has steadfastly insisted that CPG 7132.16 was intended to propound policy. Further, the FDA chose to promulgate the information contained in this rule in the form of a compliance policy guide, which FDA regulations classify as an "advisory opinion." A touchstone of a substantive rule is that it establishes a binding norm.

P2C2 argued that CPG 7132.16 establishes a binding norm, as it imposes significant new obligations on compounding pharmacists. Most of these obligations are manifested in the nine "factors," which, according to P2C2, are tantamount to binding norms. The district court found that the nine factors merely provide guidance to help FDA agents distinguish traditional compounding from drug manufacturing, and that the factors are not finally determinative of whether a particular pharmacy is violating the Act. According to the court, enforcement actions are brought only for violations of the Act, and CPG 7132.16 merely restates a long-standing FDA position regarding the traditional practice of pharmacy; it does not represent a change in FDA policy and does not have a significant effect on pharmacy practice or traditional compounding.

The Court concluded that CPG 7132.16 affords an opportunity for individualized determinations. It expressly provides that the list of nine factors is not intended to be exhaustive. It recognizes that "other factors may be appropriate for consideration in a particular case" and states that even if the factors are present, the FDA retains discretion whether to bring an enforcement action. The rule does not contain specifications of precise quantities or limits that, once exceeded, trigger a mandatory FDA response. The factors provide, for example, that only the compounding or distributing of "inordinate amounts" of drugs is impermissible, but nowhere does the rule further define "inordinate amounts." As such, CPG 7132.16 leaves to the sound discretion of the FDA the determination when a particular quantity has exceeded the amount considered to be within the bounds of traditional compounding.

Thompson v Western States Medical Center
2002 US LEXIS 3035; 70 U.S.L.W. 4275, April 30, 2002

Several pharmacies sued the federal government, alleging that the ban on advertising compounded drugs set out in 21 USCS § 353a (§ 503A of the Act) violated the pharmacies' free speech rights. The statute was an amendment to the Food, Drug and Cosmetic Act (FDCA) that was part of the Food and Drug Administration Modernization Act of 1997 (FDAMA). Drug compounding is an activity that pharmacists have traditionally engaged in. During the 1990s, the Food and Drug Administration (FDA) instituted several actions against pharmacies that regularly engaged in compounding services, claiming that the pharmacies were actually manufacturing new drugs without a manufacturer's license and without the benefit of going through the standard New Drug Application (NDA) premarket approval process as required by the FDCA. In order to ensure that pharmacists would be permitted to compound drugs in an appropriate manner, Congress added the FDAMA statute that exempts "compounded drugs" from the NDA process. However, the statute permits compounding only so long as pharmacies abide by several restrictions, including that the prescription be "unsolicited" and that the providers "not advertise or promote the compounding of any particular drug, class of drug, or type of drug." A group of licensed pharmacies that specialize in compounding drugs sought to enjoin enforcement of the advertising and solicitation provisions, arguing that they violate the First Amendment's free speech guarantee. The FDA, in defense, claimed that since drugs were compounded for use by individuals for whom commercially available medications were not suitable, the advertising of compounded drugs constituted an attempt to attract a large-scale market. The government maintained that prohibiting such advertising would ensure that large-scale manufacturing of compounded drugs would be precluded unless the drugs were subjected to the NDA premarket approval process to protect the public health and safety. The district court judge who heard the case held that the advertising ban is an unconstitutional restriction on commercial speech. The United States Court of Appeals for the Ninth Circuit upheld the district court's finding that the entire statute in question is unconstitutional. By a margin of 5–4, the majority of the United States Supreme Court affirmed the Court of Appeals. The majority reasoned that even if it were assumed that the ban directly advanced the government's interest, the government failed to demonstrate that the restrictions on the pharmacies' commercial speech were not more extensive than necessary to serve those interests. The majority noted that there are non-speech-related means to achieve the government's goal, such as regulating large-scale manufacturing, prohibiting wholesale sales, or limiting manufacturing to prescriptions received. The majority also read the ban as prohibiting the pharmacies' beneficial speech such as advising physicians concerning available compounded drugs for special medical needs.

EDITOR'S NOTE

Within days of the *Thompson* Decision by the Supreme Court, the Food and Drug Administration (FDA) "re-issued" a Compliance Policy Guidance (Guidance) (CPG Ch. 4 § 460.200 (May 2002) to give the FDA and pharmacists notice of what factors will be taken into account to determine whether the pharmacy is engaged in legal compounding as opposed to unlawful manufacturing of drugs under the guise of compounding. It is noteworthy that the Guidance was published as FDA policy without any advance public notice or comment period. The irony of that action is that it was the original 1992 Guidance on compounding issued by the FDA (CPG Ch. 4 § 7132.16 [March 1992] renumbered to § 460.200) that underlies the compounding case discussed at the beginning of this subchapter. The facts surrounding that case created such a furor that Congress had to step in and adopt the compounding statute in FDAMA — the section that the Supreme Court just days earlier had held unconstitutional. Taking these developments into account, it should be clear the pharmacies may advertise compounding services but still not "manufacture" large quantities of drugs under the guise of compounding. For a much more detailed explanation, see the article

Thompson v Western States Medical Center
2002 US LEXIS 3035; 70 U.S.L.W. 4275, April 30, 2002
...continued

online addressing this subject at http://www.uspharmacist.com/index.asp?page=ce/2654/default.htm.

The following is a list of court cases that are related to this topic.

Sheffield v State of New York, 571 N.Y. Supp.2d 350 (1991)
Jeans v Caraway, 649 S.2d 1141 (La. Ct. App. 1995)

Labeling

Ramirez v Plough, Inc.
863 P.2d 167 (Cal. 1993)

ISSUE: Whether the manufacturer of an *otc* children's aspirin must provide warnings in Spanish.

FACTS: Jorge Ramirez, a minor, sued Plough alleging that he contracted Reye syndrome as a result of ingesting *St. Joseph Aspirin for Children* that was manufactured and distributed by the defendant. When he was less than 4 months old, the plaintiff exhibited symptoms of a cold or similar upper respiratory tract infection. To relieve these symptoms, the plaintiff's mother gave him the aspirin product in question.

Although the product label stated that the dosage for a child under 2 years old was "as directed by doctor," the plaintiff's mother did not consult a physician before using the product. She gave him 3 of the tablets over a 2-day period. She then took the infant to a hospital where the physician advised her to administer *Dimetapp* or *Pedialyte* (nonprescription medications that do not contain aspirin), but she disregarded the advice and continued to treat the child with *St. Joseph Aspirin for Children*. The plaintiff thereafter developed Reye syndrome, resulting in severe neurological damage including cortical blindness, spastic quadriplegia, and mental retardation.

First described by the Australian pathologist Douglas Reye in 1963, the syndrome occurs in children and teenagers during or while recovering from mild respiratory tract infections, flu, chicken pox, or other viral illness. The disease is characterized by severe vomiting and irritability or lethargy which may progress to delirium and coma.

The disease is fatal in 20 to 30 percent of the cases with many of the survivors sustaining permanent brain damage. While the cause of Reye syndrome is unknown, or at least uncertain, studies have shown an association between ingestion of aspirin during viral illness and the subsequent development of the syndrome. These studies prompted the FDA to propose a labeling requirement for aspirin products warning of the dangers of Reye syndrome.

Even before the federal regulation became mandatory, packages of *St. Joseph Aspirin for Children* displayed this warning: "Warning: Reye syndrome is a rare but serious disease which can follow flu or chicken pox in children and teenagers. While the cause of Reye syndrome is unknown, some reports claim aspirin may increase the risk of developing this disease. Consult a doctor before use in children or teenagers with flu or chicken pox." The package insert also included the statement: "REYE SYNDROME IS SERIOUS SO EARLY DETECTION AND TREATMENT ARE VITAL."

Ramirez v Plough, Inc.
863 P.2d 167 (Cal. 1993)
...continued

The defendant's aspirin product printed the above warning only in English. The plaintiff's mother, who was born in Mexico, was literate only in Spanish. She was unable to read any of the warnings on the aspirin label and package insert, but she did not ask anyone to translate the information in Spanish even though other members of her household could have done so.

RULING: The court rejected the plaintiff's attempt to require *otc* drug manufacturers to provide warnings in Spanish.

REASONING: FDA regulations specify both the subject matter of required warnings and the actual words to be used. For example, aspirin products must contain warnings for use by pregnant or nursing women. It must also carry a warning to keep the product out of the reach of children. The FDA has stated that it encourages the preparation of labeling to meet the needs of non-English speaking populations so long as the labeling fully complies with agency regulations. However, the controlling regulation requires only that manufacturers provide full English labeling for all nonprescription drugs except those distributed solely in the commonwealth of Puerto Rico or in a territory where the predominant language is one other than English. California law parallels the federal law on these points.

Existing statutes demonstrate that the legislature is able and willing to define the circumstances in which foreign language communication should be mandated. Since the statutes in question expressly require that package warnings on nonprescription drugs be in English, the court inferred that the legislature had deliberately chosen not to require that manufacturers also include warnings in foreign languages. Presumably, the FDA had concluded that despite the obvious advantages of multilingual package warnings, the associated problems and costs are such that, at present, warnings should only be mandated in English.

The following is a list of court cases that are related to this topic.

Stevens v Parke, Davis & Company, 207 Cal. Rptr. 45, 507 P.2d 653 (Cal. 1973)
E.R. Squibb & Sons, Inc. v Cox, 477 So.2d 963 (Ala. 1985)
Bristol-Myers Squibb Co. v Shalala, 91 F.3d 1493 (D.C. Cir. 1996)
Pearson v Shalala, Slip Op. No. 98-5043, United States Court of Appeals for the District of Columbia, January 15, 1999.

Patient-Directed Labeling

Torsiello v Whitehall Laboratories, Etc.
398 A.2d 132 (N.J. Super.Ct.App.Div. 1979)

ISSUE: The principal issue of this case was whether the label warning (see quote of warning) was adequate to the consumer as a matter of law.

FACTS: The reported facts of this case were that the plaintiff-consumer took about eight *Anacin* tablets a day for 14 months for relief of arthritis pain. He then suffered gastrointestinal hemorrhage which was ultimately diagnosed as gastrointestinal bleeding secondary to aspirin gastritis. The plaintiff sued the manufacturer of *Anacin,* claiming that the warning on the label failed to give "adequate warning of this inherent danger of prolonged use of the product." The plaintiff produced a medical specialist at the trial who was steadfast in his opin-

Torsiello v Whitehall Laboratories, Etc.
398 A.2d 132 (N.J. Super.Ct.App.Div. 1979)
...continued

ion that the aspirin component of *Anacin* caused the gastrointestinal hemorrhage. The judge of the trial court dismissed the case without submitting it to the jury for a verdict, and the plaintiff appealed the dismissal. The appellate court reversed the dismissal and sent the case back to the trial court for a new trial.

A more detailed look of the facts of the case and the rulings of law made by the appellate court in its reversal and demand for new trial are as follows:

The plaintiff, on the way to work, fell and injured a preexisting osteoarthritis condition. He consulted the factory physician on his arrival at work and was given medical treatment which did not relieve his pain. A couple of months later, he purchased a bottle of *Anacin* after hearing TV commercials extolling it as affording relief of arthritic pain. He read the label on the bottle which recommended dosage not exceeding eight tablets per day. The label also warned as follow:

> CAUTION — If pain persists for more than 10 days, or redness is present, or in arthritic or rheumatic conditions affecting children under 12 years of age, consult a physician immediately.

The plaintiff-consumer received noticeable relief from the *Anacin* and again consulted the factory physician asking him if he could continue to use the *Anacin*. The physician told him that the aspirin component of *Anacin* was having the analgesic effect and if it worked for him he could continue to take it. The plaintiff-consumer continued to see the physician for about 13 visits over a 7-week period and frequently asked and obtained reassurance from the physician as to the *Anacin* usage. Following discharge from the physician's care, he continued taking the *Anacin*. He claimed to have done so on reliance of the label directions, assuming that no danger was inherent in the use of product so long as he did not exceed the recommended daily dosage. Fourteen months after he stared on the *Anacin* therapy, he suffered the gastrointestinal hemorrhage for which he brought suit against the maker of *Anacin*.

RULING: On those grounds, the appellate court reversed the lower court's dismissal and sent the case back for new trial.

REASONING: To arrive at a rule applicable to this case, the appellate court had to review the law applicable to the duty of the seller to warn the consumer of dangers or potential dangers of the product sold. A general rule is that the seller is not required to warn as to products or ingredients in them, which are only dangerous, or potentially so, when consumed in excessive quantity, or over a long period of time, when the danger, or potential danger, is generally known and recognized. A common example of this type of product is alcoholic beverages.

The next questions to answer were such as: What is the duty to warn the consumer as to drug products, and, in particular, as to *otc* or nonprescription drugs? And, is the inherent danger of prolonged aspirin usage generally known and recognized by the consumer?

As to the prescription-only or legend drugs versus the over-the-counter or nonprescription drugs, the court stated the general rule as follows:

> The emphasis of the doctrine (that a manufacturer's duty is to warn the attending physician and not the lay public) is carefully limited to prescription drugs...An entirely different rule would be applicable in connection with drugs sold over the counter to anyone who asks for them.

Torsiello v Whitehall Laboratories, Etc.
398 A.2d 132 (N.J. Super.Ct.App.Div. 1979)
...continued

The court stated further:

> Thus, we perceive the rule applicable to over the counter drugs as requiring the con-
> sumer to be adequately warned by manufacturer of all known specific and appre-
> ciable inherent product dangers so that he can protect himself from the risks of use
> whether or not he consults a physician, and this is precisely because he is likely to use
> an over the counter product based on his own judgment, molded by advertising, and
> without ever consulting a physician at all...

The court's rationale for the distinction between rules applicable to prescription drugs versus nonprescription drugs is that, in the case of the prescription drugs, the physician is the
"learned intermediary" between drug maker and consumer. The physician must be sufficiently
warned so that the prescriber can make an intelligent choice of treatment based on the
"benefit to risk" principal. On the other hand, the consumer is encouraged by the *otc* drug
industry to "self-prescribe." The court stated:

> He [the consumer] must, therefore, also be given such information by the manufac-
> turer as will permit him to self-prescribe with a minimum of risk. Thus, a warn-
> ing merely instructing a user to consult a physician as to the product's use is in this
> context, construable as no warning at all.

In the instant case, the *Anacin* label warning merely told the consumer to consult a physician if pain persists for more than ten days or if redness is present. This warning fell far
short of a warning of inherent danger in the use of the drug over a period past 10 days. The
court said the *Anacin* label warning as such "...could readily have been found by a jury to
be inadequate."

As to the intervening situation of the plaintiff-consumer consultation with his physician
and the physician's reassurance, the court indicated that a manufacturer could anticipate that
a physician might generally approve aspirin therapy without realizing that the patient
intends to use the product indefinitely after discharge from therapy.

The following is a list of court cases that are related to this topic.

Pearson v Shalala, Slip Op. No. 98-5043, United States Court of Appeals for the District of
    Columbia, January 15, 1999.

Insulin

The following is a list of court cases that are related to this topic.

Malone & Hyde, Inc. v Hobrecht, 685 S.W.2d 739 (Tex. Ct. App. 1985)
Pressler v Irvine Drugs, 215 Cal. Rptr. 807 (Cal. App. 4 Dist. 1985)
E.R. Squibb & Sons, Inc. v Cox, 477 So.2d 963 (Ala. 1985)

Generic Drug Products

Agbogun v State of Texas
756 S.W.2d 1 (Tex. Ct. App. 1988)

ISSUE: Whether a pharmacist who substitutes the generic version of a drug in a bottle labeled with the brand name is guilty of a deceptive business practice.

FACTS: The pharmacist claimed that he substituted metronidazole for the prescribed brand name product, *Flagyl*, only after seeking and receiving the physician's approval. The pharmacist contended that he did not type the prescription label, but that this task was performed by one of the technicians. He testified that he picked up the label and affixed it to the container in which he had previously placed a generic product and then handed it to the technician for delivery to the patient. He claimed that he told the technician that the product was a substitute for *Flagyl*. The technician responded that she would "handle this." (Note: the physician's testimony was not sought in this case.)

The technician testified that she did not type the label that was introduced into evidence, even though it was standard procedure for the technicians to type labels. She stated that she did not know who had typed the label and that the pharmacist did not tell her that he was substituting a generic product. The jury heard testimony that when a generic drug is substituted for a brand name product, the generic name must appear on the prescription container label.

The offense of deceptive business practice requires that the person charged "intentionally, knowingly, recklessly or with criminal negligence, represents that a commodity or service is of a particular style, grade, or model if it is of another."

RULING: The jury assessed a punishment against the pharmacist of a 30-day jail sentence, probation for one year, and a $100 fine. The appellate court affirmed.

REASONING: The court concluded that the jury had sufficient evidence to justify its findings, as the pharmacist had not proved that he had a reasonable, but mistaken, belief that he had the physician's permission to dispense the prescription with the generic drug and then label the container with the brand name.

The pharmacist further contended that the trial court erred in allowing the state's expert witness to infer that the pharmacist had violated the "pharmacy law" of the state of Texas. The state's witness was a licensed pharmacist with 36 years of experience and was employed by the state as a consultant pharmacist. While it would have been improper for the trial court to allow any opinion evidence as to the pharmacist's guilt or innocence, this did not happen. The expert's testimony did not constitute opinion testimony as to the guilt of the pharmacist, but instead pertained to the procedures commonly followed in the pharmacy profession, eg, that a bottle containing a generic drug must be labeled with the name of the generic and not the name of the brand name product.

The pharmacist also argued that, as a black man, he is a member of a protected racial group. He contended that the state excluded all blacks from the jury by peremptory challenge solely because they were black and for no other reason. The prosecutor testified that she did strike two black women from the jury, but that this was done based upon the amount of eye contact and the amount of agreement and affirmative nods they showed when discussing the case with the defense. It was also shown that one black person had been struck from the jury panel by the defense itself. The court concluded that there was no finding of purposeful racial discrimination in the selection of the jury.

Bristol-Myers Squibb Co. v Shalala
91 F.3d 1493 (D.C. Cir. 1996)

FACTS: The plaintiff, a Drug manufacturer, sued the Food and Drug Administration (FDA) challenging a regulation that allows the filing of an abbreviated new drug application (ANDA) to approve a generic version of a previously approved drug. Under this regulation, the labeling of the generic drug does not need to include all of the indications that are required on the label of the listed drug. The suit claimed that the ANDA approval is unlawful under the federal Food, Drug & Cosmetic Act (the FDCA), because it fails to protect the manufacturer of the listed drug from competition by generic manufacturers. The U.S. District Court for the District of Columbia dismissed the case due to the drug manufacturer's lack of standing. The drug manufacturer appealed.

HOLDING: The Court of Appeals affirmed the dismissal but for different reasons. The Appellate Court held that the FDCA did not intend to give listed drug manufacturers continued protection from generic manufacturers every time a new indication was added to the label of an approved drug. The FDA may approve an ANDA for new generic drugs even though labels will not show all indications of the listed drug.

The following is a list of court cases that are related to this topic.

Foster v American Home Products Corp., 29 F.3d 165 (4th Cir. 1994)
Rhone-Poulenc Rorer Pharmaceuticals v Marion Merrell Dow, 93 F. 3d 511 (8th Cir. 1996).

Nonprescription Drugs

Carey v Population Services International
97 S.Ct. 2010 (1977)

ISSUE: Whether, under New York law, it was a crime (1) for any person to sell or distribute contraceptives to minors under the age of 16; (2) for anyone other than a licensed pharmacist to distribute contraceptives to persons over 16; and (3) for anyone, including licensed pharmacists, to advertise or display contraceptives.

FACTS: New York statutes prohibited the sale of nonprescription contraceptives to minors under the age of 16, prohibited the advertising and display of contraceptives, and permitted sales of these items to adults by licensed pharmacists only. The plaintiffs challenging these statutes included a population planning group, physicians, and a coordinator of an anti-venereal disease group. The defendants included the regulatory agency for pharmacies in the state of New York.

RULING: The United States Supreme Court held that the New York statutes were unconstitutional.

REASONING: The defendants argued that the prohibition of the sale or distribution of contraceptives to minors under the age of 16 was a legitimate exercise of the state's police power to promote morality and discourage promiscuity. The lower courts had agreed that sexual intercourse by minors is of legitimate concern to the state, but there was no evidence that teenage premarital sexual activity increases in proportion to the availability of contraceptives ([see 398 F. Supp.321] [1975]). The Supreme Court recognized that the state restrictions inhibiting privacy rights of minors are valid only if they serve any significant state interest that is not present in the case of an adult. Because New York law permitted males to marry at the age of 16 and females at the age of 14, the court felt that such conflict-

Carey v Population Services International
97 S.Ct. 2010 (1977)
...continued

ing policies indicated that it "was not constitutionally permissible to discourage getting married, but it was constitutionally permissible to discourage sexual intercourse." Such conflicting policies could not continue. It was further noted that unwanted pregnancies and venereal disease were less likely to occur if contraceptives were used.

The defendants argued that the sale or distribution of nonprescription contraceptives should be limited to licensed pharmacists, because this permitted purchasers to receive professional advice from the pharmacists as to the quality and use of the products. However, the court noted that "nothing in the record suggests that pharmacists are particularly qualified to give advice on the merits of different nonmedical contraceptives, where such advice is more necessary to the purchaser of contraceptive products and to consumers of other nonprescription items...Limiting the distribution of nonprescription contraceptives to licensed pharmacists clearly imposes a significant burden on the right of individuals to use contraceptives if they choose to do so." Therefore, the court could find no compelling reason for the state's restriction on the sale of nonprescription contraceptives.

The final provision under attack was the absolute ban on any advertisement or display of contraceptives. The plaintiffs argued that this was in violation of the First Amendment. In response, the defendants argued that the speech in issue was commercial in nature, and therefore lacking in First Amendment protection. The lower court found, and the U.S. Supreme Court agreed, that there was an element of "public interest" advertising mixed in with the commercial ads. Because of the concern over unwanted pregnancies and the fight against venereal disease, protection was extended to this type of advertising. The court held that the absolute prohibition of any advertisement or display of contraceptives was unconstitutional, but the states were allowed to regulate against obscene advertisements.

Justice Rehnquist dissented by claiming that the drafters of the constitution would roll over in their graves if they knew that "their efforts had enshrined the right of commercial vendors of contraceptives to peddle them to unmarried minors through such means as window displays and vending machines located in the men's room of truck stops, notwithstanding the considered judgment of the New York Legislature to the contrary."

The following is a list of court cases that are related to this topic.

Michael v Warner-Chilcott, 91 N.M. 561, 579 P. 2d 183 (1978)
Torsiello v Whitehall Laboratories, Etc., 165 N.J. Super. 311, 398 A. 2d 132 (1979)
Ramirez v Plough, Inc., 1993 WL 503508 (Sup. Ct. Cal.)

Dietary Supplements

Pearson v Shalala
164 F.3d 650 (D.C. Cir. 1999)

ISSUE: Is the FDA requiring the manufacturer of a dietary supplement to obtain FDA approval before advertising a beneficial relationship to a disease or health-related condition and use of the supplement constitutionally valid?

FACTS: Plaintiffs, distributors of dietary supplements, asked the FDA to approve four separate health claims on the labels of various supplements that they market. They sought approval of claims that:

Pearson v Shalala
164 F.3d 650 (D.C. Cir. 1999)
...continued

(1) Consumption of antioxidant vitamins may reduce the risk of certain cancers;
(2) consumption of fiber may reduce the risk of colorectal cancer;
(3) consumption of omega-3 fatty acids may reduce the risk of coronary heart disease; and
(4) 0.8 mg of folic acid in a dietary supplement is more effective in reducing the risk of neural tube defects than a lower amount in foods in common form.

Under 21 CFR §101.14(c) (1998), the FDA will approve claims of this type only when there is "significant scientific agreement" that the claims are approved by the evidence. The quoted term is not defined in statute or rule. The FDA rejected the plaintiffs' claims because the evidence was inconclusive. Plaintiffs sued the FDA in federal district court claiming that various statutes and rules are constitutionally invalid as applied to the facts of the case. One of the primary allegations is that the term "significant scientific agreement" is so vague that it fails to provide any context for plaintiffs to know what standard they must meet before the claims would be approved.

HOLDING: The district court rejected the constitutional and statutory challenges. The Court of Appeals reversed and remanded the case back to the district court with instructions that the case be sent back to the FDA for further consideration in light of the holding that the regulations used to deny the claims are invalid.

REASONING: The standard embodied in 21 CFR §101.14 violates the First Amendment to the Constitution because it precludes approval of less well-supported claims accompanied by appropriate disclaimers and because it is impermissibly vague. The FDA has not described how it determines whether any scientific agreement over evidence supporting a health claim is significant. As long as the health claims are not false or misleading, the FDA cannot seek to bar the claims under regulations that do not provide clear standards.

Pharmanex, Inc. v Shalala
35 F.Supp. 1341 (D. Utah 1999)

Pharmanex sought judicial review of an administrative decision issued by the FDA. In that decision, the FDA ruled that *Cholestin*, a product marketed by Pharmanex, was a drug rather than a dietary supplement. *Cholestin* is a capsule consisting solely of milled red yeast rice, a traditional food that has been eaten and valued for its health benefits in China for centuries. *Cholestin* contains HMG-CoA reductase inhibitors, which reduce cholesterol levels. One HMG-CoA inhibitor is mevinolin, a natural substance that the FDA has determined is chemically indistinguishable from lovastatin. Lovastatin is a synthetic substance which is the active ingredient in the prescription drug *Mevacor*. The issue in the case was whether *Cholestin* was a "dietary supplement" as defined by the FDA. The definition in 21 U.S.C. §321(ff)(3)(B) of "dietary supplement" excludes "an article that is approved as a new drug." Under the FDA's interpretation of §321(ff)(3)(B), a component of a purported dietary supplement may be "an article that is approved as a new drug" any time the FDA determines that the manufacturer intends to market and manufacture that component. The FDA reasoned that lovastatin was an article that was approved as a new drug in 1987. Because *Cholestin* was manufactured and marketed with a great emphasis on its lovastatin content, *Cholestin* should be equated with lovastatin. Therefore, the FDA excluded *Cholestin* from the category of "dietary supplements," because it was not marketed as a dietary

Pharmanex, Inc. v Shalala
35 F.Supp. 1341 (D. Utah 1999)
...continued

supplement before lovastatin was approved as a drug. Pharmanex asserted that the only kind of article that is "approved as a new drug" is a finished drug product. According to Pharmanex, §321(ff)(3)(B) cannot apply to either lovastatin or *Cholestin* because neither has been approved as a finished drug product. The district court found a pervasive body of regulatory and judicial authority establishing that "article approved as a new drug" refers only to finished drug products. Thus, the district court found that *Cholestin* fit within the definition of "dietary supplement" in Section §(ff)(3)(B). Therefore, the district court granted Pharmanex's motion to set aside and hold unlawful the FDA's decision that *Cholestin* is a drug and not a dietary supplement.

Medical Devices

Georgia State Board of Dispensing Opticians v Dunaway Drug Stores
378 S.E.2d 115 (Ga. 1989)

ISSUE: Whether a pharmacy that accepted prescriptions from licensed optometrists, which were subsequently dispensed by a contact lens supplier, was engaged in the unlicensed practice of opticianry.

FACTS: The customers of Dunaway Drug Stores placed their orders for contact lenses with a pharmacy employee. Each of these customers provided the employee with a prescription from an optometrist or licensed physician in the state of Georgia. The pharmacy employee then consulted a price list and forwarded the prescription and order to the store's contact lens supplier which was located in the state of Ohio.

The supplier's employees were opticians licensed in Ohio working under the supervision of an Ohio optometrist. The company provided lenses according to the prescriptions as interpreted by the optician and supervising optometrist at the company. The product was sent back to the pharmacy in the manufacturer's sealed container. The pharmacy employees then delivered the lenses in the manufacturer's sealed container to the customer.

RULING: The Georgia State Board of Dispensing Opticians filed a complaint against the pharmacy for engaging in the unlicensed practice of dispensing opticianry in violation of state law. The court granted summary judgment in favor of the pharmacy.

REASONING: The court noted that the literature accompanying each of the filled prescriptions advised the customer to return to the prescribing optometrist or physician if there were any problems. The court ruled that the pharmacy was merely a conduit, and its activities did not fall under any of the prohibitions in Georgia law regulating the practice of dispensing opticians.

The following is a list of court cases that are related to this topic.

Key Enterprises of Delaware v Venice Hospital, 703 F. Supp. 1513 (M.D. Fla. 1989)

Patents

In Re: Misha Tereschouk
Slip Op. No. 01-1112 (April 4, 2001), Fed. Cir., 2001 US App. LEXIS 5640

Petitioner filed an application to patent a method for automatically distributing drugs to the holder of pre-encoded portable medical data carrier. The application claims methods for automatically distributing drugs to the holder of a pre-encoded portable medical data carrier. The claims recite methods in which a doctor encodes a patient's prescription onto an updatable portable medical data carrier, such as a credit card-sized integrated circuit card. The data carrier includes identification data, prescription data, and financial data. During the encoding process, the prescription is safety-checked for items such as contraindications, maximum approved dosages, and adverse drug interactions. After the safety check, the data carrier is given to the patient. The patient may then present the data carrier to a drug-dispensing machine. The drug-dispensing machine verifies the patient's identification by means similar to the manner in which a bank ATM card might be validated, such as a memorized code or the patient's physical features (fingerprint, voice, etc.). After identity verification, an optional safety check may be performed similar to the check performed when the prescription was encoded. The drug-dispensing machine then delivers the prescribed drugs to the patient. The data carrier is re-encoded to reflect the dispensing transaction and then is returned to the patient. The United States Patent and Trademark Office's Board of Patent Appeals and Interferences (board) rejected all of petitioner's patent claims in his application on the ground of obviousness under 35 U.S.C. § 103. Petitioner appealed, but judgment of the board was affirmed because the purported elimination of supervision was not a patentable distinction from the prior art. Substantial evidence supported the board's finding that petitioner's purported privacy advantage was illusory. Furthermore, the fact that the prior art recognized the legal requirement for a licensed professional to participate in drug dispensing did not mean that the elimination of the pharmacist's participation constituted a patentable novelty. Judgment was affirmed.

Watson Pharmaceuticals v Henney
Slip Op. No. 00-3516 (January 18, 2001), USDC MY, 2001 U.S. Dist. LEXIS 2477

Plaintiff filed suit, aiming to obtain a mandatory injunction ordering the de-listing of a patent. Before the court were plaintiff's motion for injunctive relief and defendants' motions for summary judgment. The court found that the action was, at base, a quest for judicial review of a federal agency's final decision. The court found that the Food and Drug Administration (FDA), in deciding to make an Orange Book listing, was not acting as a patent tribunal. In making its decision to list a patent, it was entirely appropriate and reasonable for the FDA to rely on the patentee's declaration as to coverage, and to let the patent infringement issues play out in other proper arenas. The court determined that it was not the business of the FDA, or of the court in an Administrative Procedure Act, 5 U.S.C. § 706 review, to adjudicate the merits of the scope and/or validity of the claims covered by a patent. Since the FDA's action under attack was not unreasonable, arbitrary, or capricious, but was, rather, a reasonable exercise of its statutory and regulatory powers, the court determined that the federal defendants were entitled to summary judgment on the merits, and no injunction would issue.

In re Omeprazole Patent Litigation
Slip Op. No. MDL Docket No. 1291 (BSJ) (May 31, 2001), USDC SD NY, 2001 US Dist. LEXIS 7103

Plaintiff corporation brought an action against defendant corporations, pursuant to 35 U.S.C. § 271(c)(2)(A), alleging defendant's products for which they were seeking approval would induce and contribute to the infringement of its patent. Defendants moved for summary judgment of noninfringement, claiming that plaintiff's patent was invalid as anticipated by prior art, or that their patents would not infringe plaintiff's patent. The court granted summary judgment for defendants, holding that defendants' products did not infringe plaintiff's patent. The court concluded that the patent claims, specification, and prosecution history demonstrated that plaintiff's patent did not cover defendants' products, and that any claim by plaintiff that its patent covered defendants' products was anticipated by prior art. Summary judgment of noninfringement was granted for defendant corporations.

Glaxo Group v Apotex
130 F Supp. 2d 1006, USDC ND Ill, 2001 US Dist. LEXIS 4270 (February 23, 2001)

Defendant drug company argued that although it was developing a generic form of plaintiff's patented product, it had no immediate plan to bring it to market before the patent expired. Plaintiff sought a declaration adjudicating that defendant would infringe the patent by its threatened acts of manufacture, importation and sale of products and ordering that the effective date of any approval of defendant's generic, to preclude use earlier than the expiration date of the patent. Defendant moved to dismiss the declaratory claim pursuant to Fed. R. Civ. P. 12(b)(1), for lack of a justiciable controversy, but the court found its activities and the existing market for the product significant enough to make infringement an actionable threat, and the controversy a concrete one pitting adverse legal interests against each other. Defendant's motion to dismiss was denied because defendant was engaged in meaningful preparation of activity directed toward making, selling, or using the infringing product, and an actual controversy existed, the court exercised its discretion to take jurisdiction over the action.

Mylan Pharmaceuticals v Henney
94 F Supp. 2d 36, DCDC, 2000 US Dist. LEXIS 6157 (March 31, 2000)

Plaintiff pharmaceutical manufacturers sued under the Federal Food, Drug, and Cosmetic Act (FDCA), 21 U.S.C. § 301 et seq., and the Administrative Procedure Act, 5 U.S.C. § 706, asserting the Food and Drug Administration (FDA) acted arbitrarily and capriciously in granting the request of the manufacturer of the generic drug tamoxifen, exclusively licensed by the patent owner to market the drug, to stay approval of tamoxifen drugs other than the manufacturer's own. The effect was that plaintiffs could not market their generic version of tamoxifen until the patent expired in 2002. Plaintiffs maintained the decision violated the FDCA and ran contrary to the agency's own regulations. The court granted plaintiffs' declaratory relief and vacated the FDA's stay of approval to the extent it violated Title 21 U.S.C. § 355(j)(5)(B), remanding to the FDA for its permissible interpretation of the governing statute and regulations. Mylan's and Pharmachemie's motions for injunctive relief denied. Their claims for declaratory relief granted. FDA's March Letter vacated to the extent it violates the plain meaning and purpose of Title 21 U.S.C. §355(j)(5)(B). Parties' remaining claims to the FDA for its permissible interpretation of the governing statute and regulation remanded.

Trademarks

Eli Lilly & Company v Natural Answers
Slip Op. No. 00-1375 (November 21, 2000), 7th Cir., 2000 US App. LEXIS 29547

Plaintiff alleged defendant's product, HERBROZAC's similarity to plaintiff's PROZACthorn
was indicative of a likelihood of confusion. The district court agreed and enjoined defendants from further use of the HERBROZAC name. Defendants contended on appeal that consumers were unlikely to be confused by the HERBROZAC name. The appellate court
affirmed the district court's preliminary injunction finding inter alia that the strong similarity of the marks and the similarity of the two products' mood altering functions would lead
consumers to believe the two marks designated similar products. The court of appeals added
that the "causes dilution" element of 11 U.S.C. § 1125(c)(1) could be satisfied by evidence of a mere likelihood of dilution, and that plaintiff had demonstrated a likelihood of
dilution where its PROZACthorn mark had achieved substantial renown and was substantially
similar to defendant's HERBROZAC mark. Accordingly, the district court's holding that
plaintiff had shown a likelihood of success in proving a likelihood of dilution was affirmed.

Personal Use Exemption

U.S. v Haas
171 F.3d 259 (5th Cir. 1999)

ISSUE: May an individual import drugs from Mexico to a pharmacy in the United States
without declaring the drugs to any customs authority and thereby avoid FDA regulations governing importation of drugs?

FACTS: The defendant operated a mail-order pharmacy business that claimed it could supply pharmaceuticals at lower than average wholesale prices because it took advantage of
international trade agreements. Orders for drugs were received from United States customers at a San Antonio, Texas, pharmacy. These orders were transmitted to a pharmacy in
Mexico. The Mexican pharmacy obtained its inventory of drugs from suppliers that are not
registered with the FDA. In the beginning of the operation, prescriptions were filled at the
Mexican pharmacy and mailed directly to customers in the United States. Later on, employees of the operation would bring the drugs from the Mexican pharmacy to the Texas pharmacy in their cars. The drugs were never declared to customs officials at the border as is
required by law.

Well before any criminal charges were brought against the defendant, he met with customs
officials to discuss the legality of his operation. The defendant was told that he could not
take advantage of any personal exemptions in the FDA or customs laws that allow individuals to import small amounts of certain drugs from foreign countries for personal use. He was
also told that his operation was commercial in nature and that he would have to comply with both the FDA and customs laws governing importation of drugs. Soon after these
meetings, the FDA began to confiscate drugs it intercepted in the mail sent from the Mexican pharmacy. It was at this time that the defendant began having the drugs transported by
car to the San Antonio pharmacy. The FDA sent the defendant two warning letters informing him that the drugs he was importing could not be marketed in the United States.
Although he quit advertising his service in the United States after these letters were received,
he continued to fill prescription drug orders for United States customers. He was arrested
and charged with several counts of importing misbranded drugs. Following a trial, the defendant was convicted by a jury on all counts.

HOLDING: The Court of Appeals upheld the conviction ruling that there was sufficient evidence to conclude that the defendant knowingly violated the law.

U.S. v Haas
171 F.3d 259 (5th Cir. 1999)
...continued

REASONING: After the defendant's initial meetings with customs officials and the FDA, he could not rationally believe that the personal exemption for importation of drugs from companies properly registered with the FDA to do business in the United States, 21 CFR §207.40, could apply to his commercial operation. He was warned that he was in violation of the law on several occasions. After receiving warning letters and having his drug orders confiscated from the mail, he changed his methods and had cars transport unregistered drugs into the country. He never took steps to comply with the law before his arrest. This was sufficient for the jury to infer that the defendant knowingly broke the law.

Wright v Texas
981 S.W.2d 197 (Tex. Crim.App. 1998)

Wright, a United States citizen, crossed the border for a shopping trip in Mexico. She saw a physician there who gave her prescriptions for an appetite suppressant and a tranquilizer. Wright had the prescription filled at a Mexican pharmacy, declared her purchases to U.S. Customs officials, and crossed the border back into Texas. While driving, Wright was stopped by a sheriff, arrested, and charged with possession of controlled substances. A jury found Wright guilty and the trial court judge assessed the minimum punishment, imprisonment for two years, probated. The Texas Court of Appeals reversed, finding that Wright had a viable defense to prosecution because her controlled substances were obtained pursuant to a valid foreign prescription and brought into the country in accordance with federal law. The state asked for discretionary review of the Court of Appeals' decision. The Texas Court of Criminal Appeals agreed that Wright had a defense to prosecution but under a different analysis. The Court of Criminal Appeals considered the "ultimate user" exemption to prosecution. That exemption provides that a person may lawfully possess a controlled substance when it is lawfully obtained in accordance with state or federal law for the person's own use. The Court of Criminal Appeals recognized that federal law allows possession of a controlled substance obtained pursuant to a valid prescription from a physician licensed in the United States or any other jurisdiction. Such controlled substances may be imported for personal medical use so long as they are imported in accordance with regulations promulgated by the DEA. Therefore, the Court of Criminal Appeals remanded the case to trial court for consideration of whether Wright followed the correct procedures for bringing controlled substances prescribed for personal medical use into the United States.

CONTROLLED SUBSTANCES

In General

State v Rasmussen
213 N.W.2d 661 (Iowa 1973)

ISSUE: Whether the state of Iowa could, under its law, require all nonresident physicians to register in that state before a pharmacist could dispense a controlled substance prescription written by the nonresident physician.

State v Rasmussen
213 N.W.2d 661 (Iowa 1973)
...continued

FACTS: This case resulted when the state pharmacy board sought a permanent injunction enjoining a certain Iowa pharmacy from dispensing prescriptions written by nonresident physicians not licensed by Iowa authorities. The Iowa Uniform Controlled Substances Act was enacted in 1973 and was basically the same Uniform Act as drafted by the Conference of Commissioners on Uniform State Laws in August of 1970. The term "practitioner" in the Uniform Act meant, "A physician, dentist, veterinarian, scientific investigator, registered or otherwise permitted to distribute, dispense, conduct research with respect to or to administer a controlled substance...in this state." The term "in this state" meant the state of Iowa.

There was no question that physicians residing in Iowa had to be registered with Iowa authorities in order for Iowa pharmacists to legally dispense their prescriptions. (Section 204.302 of the Iowa Uniform Controlled Substances Act exempts certain foreign physicians, medical interns, military and public health service officials from registration. See Iowa Administrative Code §620-8.11(204)(1) to (3).) The issue was whether the Iowa act required out-of-state physicians to register in Iowa before they could prescribe drugs to Iowa residents. The argument advanced by the state was it could not be certain the physicians who were registered by other states were competent to prescribe drugs which were dispensed by Iowa pharmacies and that an Iowa pharmacist could not always be sure the out-of-state prescriber was, in fact, registered under the Federal CSA.

RULING: Once a physician is registered under the Federal Controlled Substances Act, an Iowa pharmacist could dispense prescriptions for controlled substances from such a nonresident physician.

REASONING: The court answered the argument of the state by stating:

> To require all nonresident physicians to register in Iowa would be in practical effect negating the operation of the Federal Act in this state.

Further, the court concluded that such a situation would place the Iowa act in positive conflict with the federal act and contravene both the supremacy and commerce clauses of the U.S. Constitution. In the latter instance, the state's proposed interpretation of the Iowa statute would give effect to a law to insulate in-state business against interstate competition and such a local benefit statute would be unconstitutional as placing an undue burden on interstate commerce.

In addition, the court considered the purposes of the Federal CSA in controlling drug abuse through national registration supplemented by the states. The federal interest clearly outweighed any local interest Iowa might have in requiring out-of-state physicians to register in Iowa. The court ruled in favor of the defendants and against the state. The rule stated is as follows:

> ...practitioners registered under the Federal Controlled Substances Act, although not registered in Iowa, and not resident in this state, are governed solely by the federal act, and ...prescriptions emanating from out-of-state may be filled by duly authorized Iowa pharmacies.

McLean v State
527 S.W.2d 76 (Tenn. 1975)

ISSUE: Whether a pharmacist who is charged under an inapplicable statute may be convicted of a violation of the Controlled Substances Act.

FACTS: A pharmacist was convicted on two charges of selling a legend drug, *Valium*, without a prescription in violation of the Tennessee Code Annotated (T.C.A.) §52-1204. He received punishments of a $500 fine and 11 months, 29 days in the county jail. He was simultaneously indicted, tried and convicted of selling a controlled substance, a barbiturate derivative in Schedule III, in violation of T.C.A. §52-1432(a). The punishment imposed was a $1000 fine and 3 years in the state penitentiary. All sentences were ordered to run consecutively.

The pharmacist appealed his convictions to a Court of Criminal Appeals where one of the convictions under T.C.A. §12-1204 was dismissed, but the other convictions were affirmed. The case was further appealed to the Tennessee Supreme Court.

The testimony at trial was at times sharply conflicting and the principal witness for the prosecution was a police informer who, himself, had been convicted a number of times on different charges. Evidence offered by the prosecution showed that on October 23, 1972, the pharmacist sold *Valium* without a prescription to the police informer. The informer claimed other sales were made on different occasions and police officers testified to observing the sales and identifying the pharmacist involved. Similar testimony was offered to show the sale of a controlled substance on November 2, 1972. Although the charges were heatedly denied by the pharmacist, the determination of the facts was a matter for the jury, and the jury found the pharmacist guilty.

The main issue presented on the appeal, however, was that indictment for the controlled substances sale was under an inapplicable statute, T.C.A. 2-1432, per se forbids, except as authorized by other portions of the Controlled Substances Act, any person to manufacture, sell or possess controlled substances, etc. It is the statute under which a member of the general public is indicted if he traffics in controlled substances. Other sections of Tennessee controlled substances law apply specifically to "registrants." For instance, §5201435(a) expressly makes it unlawful for any person who is subject to §52-1424 through 52-1431 (in effect "registrants") to distribute or dispense a controlled substance in violation of §52-1431 (insofar as here pertinent, selling a controlled substance without a prescription from a practitioner). The penalty in §52-1435 is a felony of not less than 2 years or more than 10 years imprisonment or a fine of not more than $20,000, or both. On the other hand, the penalty for a §52-1432 violation is imprisonment of not less that 3 years nor more than 8 years and a fine of up to $10,000.

RULING: The court ruled that the pharmacist could not be charged with one crime and convicted of another.

The court concluded that the pharmacist should have been indicted and tried under §52-1431 with its penalty §52-1435, since these sections deal specifically with pharmacists and other registrants. Therefore, the conviction under §52-1432 could not stand. The court's reasoning was that §52-1432 prohibitions against the sale, possession, distribution and manufacture of controlled substances by the public at large were modified or qualified by the term "except as authorized" by other code sections. What was meant was that specific authorization for possession and dispensing was granted to pharmacists and other registrants under the conditions and penalties of such other sections of the code. To interpret §52-1432 by making the general prohibitions applicable to the pharmacists and other registrants would, in the words of the court, create "uncertainties and ambiguities of an undesirable nature." The conviction under §52-1204 was affirmed but the conviction under §52-1432(a) was dismissed.

McLean v State
527 S.W.2d 76 (Tenn. 1975)
...continued

If the pharmacist-defendant in this case had been charged under T.C.A. §52-1431, his conviction would have been upheld. The court indicated the evidence was clearly sufficient to sustain the conviction under §52-1431. The state argued that the error was really as to the degree of punishment and a (revised) charge should be retried on the punishment aspect rather than dismissed. The court disagreed. Although in criminal case a person may be convicted of a lesser included offense of the crime charged, this was not the case here. The penalties for §52-1431 and 52-1432 varied to the extent that in the former the fine was higher, while in the latter the minimal imprisonment was more. The general rule is that a person cannot be charged with one crime and convicted of another.

Roe, et al v Ingraham
403 F.Supp. 931 (S.D.N.Y. 175)

ISSUE: Whether a state statute requiring submission of a copy of all Schedule II prescriptions to a state office was constitutional or whether it invades the patient's right of privacy.

FACTS: Plaintiffs sought a federal court order permanently enjoining the State of New York from computerizing or instant recall the names of recipients of prescribed Schedule II controlled substances. New York (like several other states) has a state controlled substances law that requires a doctor when prescribing a Schedule II drug to use a triplicate prescription form furnished him by the state. The physician keeps one copy of the prescription; the original and the other copy are given to the patient, who presents them to a pharmacist for filling. The pharmacist keeps the original and sends the copy to the New York Bureau of Controlled Substances, Licensing and Evaluation (BCSLE) in Albany, New York. A similar triplicate prescription form is proscribed by the state for the physician who dispenses Schedule II drugs rather than prescribe them; in the former situation, a copy of the original and the original are sent to BCSLE in Albany. BCSLE then computerizes the information on approximately 100,000 prescription copies sent to it each month. Among the information computerized: The patient's name and address as found on the prescription. BCSLE's purpose in securing the information is to identify who, without using an alias name, goes from doctor to doctor to obtain Schedule II drugs, or to identify persons securing more than a 30-day supply in any single month. It was testified at a hearing that in a 20-month period, only one unresolved incident in this category had been unearthed by the computerized system.

The main thrust of plaintiff's argument against the "system" described above was that furnishing the name and address of patients receiving Schedule II drugs unconstitutionally interfered with rights of privacy guaranteed by the 14th Amendment to the U.S. Constitution; it was an unwarranted intrusion in the doctor-patient confidential relationship. The court agreed.

Plaintiffs, husband and wife, expressed concern as parents, that their children being treated with *Ritalin* for hyperkinesias will be stigmatized because the state will have a long file on them in a narcotics and dangerous drug context. Another patient testified that when she learned her name was reported to Albany, she stopped taking the medication prescribed for her migraine headaches. A cancer patient testified he had his *Percodan* prescription filled out of state when he learned his name would (otherwise) go to Albany. Physicians testified that patient reaction was shock, fear, and concern upon learning their names would be sent to Albany.

Roe, et al v Ingraham
403 F.Supp. 931 (S.D.N.Y. 175)
...continued

RULING: Accordingly, the U.S. District Court held, "...so much of the New York Health Law as requires reporting to state authorities in Albany the names and addresses of patients who receive Schedule II drugs as medication prescribed by duly licensed physicians is an unconstitutional interference with the plaintiff's rights of privacy guaranteed under the Fourteenth Amendment." Judgment was entered for plaintiffs.

REASONING: Speaking on the right of privacy and how it applied to the doctor-patient relationship, the federal court stated:

> The concept of privacy is an affirmation of the importance of certain aspects of the individual and his desired freedom from needless outside interference...It is apparent (therefore) that the right of privacy is constitutionally protected. It is the when and how which create the problem...Justice Douglas has described the expectation of privacy in the doctor-patient relationship as having been exceeded only by that expectation in the relationship of a penitent to his priest...

> An individual's physical ills and disabilities, the medication he takes, the frequency of his medical consultation are among the most sensitive of personal and psychological sensibilities. One does not normally expect to be required to have to reveal to a government source, at least in our society, these facts of one's life. Indeed, generally one is wont to feel that his is nobody's business but his doctor's and his pharmacist's.

> ...A name on a prescription in the files of one of many thousands of pharmacists in the state of New York is entirely different from one's name on a form in Albany which is transferred to computerized records and stored for instant retrieval.

Whalen v Roe
429 U.S. 589 (1977)

ISSUE: Whether a state statute requiring submission of a copy of all Schedule II prescriptions to a state office was constitutional or does it invade the patient's right to privacy.

FACTS: The *Roe* case was appealed to the U.S. Supreme Court, which reversed the decision of the Federal District Court. In Roe v Ingraham, the District court declared a New York drug control law unconstitutional to the extent it required the reporting and computerized filing by the state of the names of patients receiving Schedule II drugs pursuant to a triplicate prescription system. The District court had based its ruling on finding the patient identification aspect of the New York statute violated the constitutionally protected right or "zone" of privacy and that the state did not demonstrate the necessity for the patient identification requirement. If there was no necessity for the patient identification requirement, it was, as the District Court saw it, an unreasonable interference with an individual's right of personal liberty protected by the Constitution.

RULING: The U.S. Supreme Court did not agree with the Federal District Court.

REASONING: One of the important facts disclosed in the District Court trial is that in the 20-month period of computerized patient identification data, the data were only used in two

Whalen v Roe
429 U.S. 589 (1977)
...continued

investigations. (Note: This fact probably led the District Court into concluding the patient identification aspect unnecessary.) However, the Supreme Court looked at the matter differently. It reasoned that the patient identification requirement might aid in the enforcement of laws designed to minimize drug misuse and the requirement "could reasonably be expected to have a deterrent effect on potential violators."

Further, the court stated its position that individual states were free to "experiment" with possible solutions to problems of vital local concern. And, if the experiment resulted in a foolish expenditure of funds, it was for the state legislature [not the Supreme Court] to terminate the unwise experiment. The necessity [or non-necessity] was indicated by the court as not being a sufficient reason for holding the patient identification requirement unconstitutional. In other words, if a state law has some effect on individual liberty or privacy, the Supreme court will not find it unconstitutional simply because the court believes that the state law is unnecessary.

Next, the court addressed itself to the more crucial issue of whether or not the patient identification requirement substantially interfered with the so-called constitutional right of privacy...the individual's interest here in "avoiding disclosure of personal matters." The court, when looking at the reality of health care procedures, concluded that the New York statute did not pose a grievous threat to nondisclosure of private information. The court pointed out that "...many unpleasant invasions of privacy...are associated with health care...disclosures of private medical information to doctors, to hospital personnel, to insurance companies, and to public health agencies are often an essential part of modern medical practice even when the disclosure may reflect unfavorably on the character of the patient."

Further, the court noted that in the New York statute and its implementing administrative procedures, there was a concern with, a protection of, the individual's interest in privacy. Public disclosure of the patient's identity was prohibited; computer tapes containing the data were kept locked; the data receiving room was protected by a locked wire fence and alarm system, and only a limited number of authorized state employees had access to the data.

An issue raised in the District Court trial was that some persons might decline to have their doctor prescribe Schedule II drugs because of concern that their names would be fed to the computerized file. The Supreme Court dismissed this argument on the basis that if 100,000 prescriptions per month were issued for these drugs, clearly the public was then not being deprived of access to the drugs.

Summarizing the court's ruling, it can be said that neither the immediate nor threatened impact of the New York statute's patient identification requirement was sufficient to constitute an invasion of any right or liberty protected by the 14th Amendment. However, the court was careful not to make its ruling too broad. In fact, the court decision stated therein that, "We therefore need not, and do not, decide any question which might be presented by the unwarranted disclosure of accumulated private data — whether intentional or unintentional — or by a system that did not contain comparable security provisions."

Chesteen v State
365 So.2d 102 (Ala. 1978)

ISSUE: Although the audit records were under subpoena at trial, they were not introduced by the state into the evidence. Instead, the *Ionamin* shortage was simply testified to by the investigator, as a witness. On the appeal of the case, the issue was raised that the conviction rested on circumstantial evidence. Another issue raised was that the defendant-pharmacist was convicted under the felony section of the CSA law and, as a pharmacist, he could only be convicted of violating the provisions of the CSA law applicable to unlawful activities of registrants [§258(48)(a)(1) as applied to §258(46)(c)].

FACTS: A pharmacist was convicted on a jury verdict of guilty of the charge of violating Title 22, §258(47) (1973 Cumulative Supplement) of the Alabama Uniform Controlled Substances Act. The conviction stemmed from a charge of selling *Ionamin* (phentermine) in violation of the state controlled substances law. The jury assessed a $15,000 fine, but the court added an additional punishment of 7 years imprisonment in the state penitentiary.

The reported facts of the case are summarized as follows: A certain individual was under surveillance by the county sheriff's investigators and was apprehended upon leaving defendant's pharmacy carrying a white paper bag. It contained two large bottles of *Ionamin-30*, each with 400 capsules.

Defendant was then investigated by the Diversion Investigation Unit of the Alabama Bureau of Investigation and an audit was done at the pharmacy of *Ionamin* 15 mg and 30 mg capsules. On comparing the pharmacy inventory records, purchase records, distribution records and the *Ionamin* in stock, a shortage of 17,608 *Ionamin-30* capsules was found. The pharmacist, after first being given his Miranda rights (warning), was asked if he could explain the shortage; he replied "I can't."

At the trial of the case, a number of pharmacist witnesses came forward and testified to the defendant-pharmacist's reputation for truth and veracity as being good. However, these same pharmacists testified, in one instance, that no more than 1000 or 1200 *Ionamin* were prescribed in a drugstore per year, and, in another instance, no more than 7000 *Ionamin-30* were sold in a year. One pharmacist-witness stated, "He would never have reason to buy 22,000 of these pills in a year. Nor did he ever keep 4000 *Ionamins* in stock at a time."

RULING: The appeals court affirmed the conviction.

REASONING: The appeals court answered the first issue by stating that the records were voluminous and the testimony of the audit finding accomplished the same purpose. Although the court did not state so in its written opinion of the case, the records were subpoenaed and the pharmacist would have introduced them into evidence if the records could prove his defense. As to the issue of the pharmacist's status as such under CSA law, his status did not provide him an absolute defense to a charge of distributing controlled drugs in violation of the CSA law [trafficking controlled substances]. The existence of prescriptions to account for all the missing *Ionamin* would have been a defense, but it was not upon the state to prove the defendant had such prescriptions. In addition, there was evidence that the pharmacy had not been robbed or burglarized during the period in question.

United States v Ralph Clayton Robinson
707 F.2d 811 (4th Cir. 1983)

ISSUE: Whether the owner of a pharmacy is a "registrant" within the meaning of the Controlled Substance Act.

FACTS: Defendant was the owner of a pharmacy in the state of North Carolina. The pharmacy was authorized to dispense controlled substances under North Carolina law and defendant-owner filed an application with the DEA for renewal of the pharmacy's registration to handle controlled substances. Robinson was charged and convicted in federal district court for the Western District of North Carolina for violating recordkeeping requirements of the federal Controlled Substances Act.

RULING: The 4th Circuit of Appeals upheld defendant's conviction and affirmed the judgment of the district court.

REASONING: The owner of a pharmacy is a "registrant" within the meaning of 21 U.S. Code 827 (a)(3). The court held that "...although there are no reported cases defining 'registrant,' the plain language of the statute shows a Congressional intent to hold the owner of a drug store accountable under the circumstances present in this case."

United States v Jack Edgar Burns
816 F.2d 1354 (9th Cir. 1987)

ISSUE: Whether the Drug Enforcement Administration (DEA) is authorized under the Controlled Substances Act to reclassify methamphetamine from a Schedule III to a Schedule II controlled substance.

FACTS: Defendant challenged the statutory authority of the U.S. Attorney General to delegate to the DEA authority to reclassify controlled substances from one schedule to another. The district court convicted defendant on a criminal charge of distribution of methamphetamine.

RULING: The judgment of conviction was affirmed by the 9th Circuit Court of Appeals.

REASONING: The DEA is authorized under the CSA to reclassify methamphetamine from Schedule III to Schedule II. The delegation of authority in 28 Code of Federal Regulations 0.100 to DEA from the attorney general was a proper exercise of the power conferred under 21 U.S. Code 871(a). This section of the statute authorizes the attorney general to delegate any of his functions to any officer or employee of the U.S. Department of Justice. The delegation was therefore proper and constitutional.

United States v James David Daniel
813 F.2d 661 (5th Cir. 1987)

ISSUE: Whether Congressional delegation of authority to reclassify controlled substances granted to the Drug Enforcement Administration was an unconstitutional delegation of lawmaking authority.

United States v James David Daniel
813 F.2d 661 (5th Cir. 1987)
...continued

FACTS: Defendant was charged with a criminal violation of the Controlled Substances Act and alleged a denial of his due process rights because the DEA had reclassified amphetamine from a Schedule III to a Schedule II substance. Defendant contended that the reclassification was not valid because the DEA's doing so was an unconstitutional delegation of lawmaking authority by Congress. Defendant further alleged that Congress' amending Schedule II in 1984 to clarify the definition of coca leaves implicitly repealed the reclassification of amphetamine as a Schedule II controlled substance.

RULING: The district court convicted the defendant, and the defendant appealed. The 5th Circuit Court of Appeals affirmed the conviction.

REASONING: Reclassification of amphetamine from a Schedule III to a Schedule II controlled substance in 1971 was not an unconstitutional delegation of lawmaking authority, even though it resulted in a change in criminal penalties. The delegation of classification authority did not violate the defendant's due process rights because prescribed conduct remained unchanged following reclassification. Neither did Congress' amending Schedule II in 1984 to clarify the definition of coca leaves implicitly repeal the reclassification.

State v Collier
581 N.E.2d 525 (Ohio 1991)

ISSUE: Whether a member of the public can be held legally responsible for failing to keep a controlled substance in its original prescription container.

FACTS: While executing a search warrant pertaining to an illegal drug transaction involving crack cocaine, a Hamilton, Ohio, police officer noticed one of the occupants in the house run to an upstairs bedroom. The defendant was found hiding face down in a closet. She was searched at the scene and six white tablets were found loose in her change purse. These tablets were later identified as *Ritalin*.

Upon questioning, the defendant stated that the tablets were prescribed for her 15-year-old son, but no prescription container was found. The defendant testified that the *Ritalin* tablets were not in the original prescription container because she feared being robbed. The defendant alleged that she left the original container with her mother who would bring the required daily dosage to the defendant for administration to her son.

RULING: The defendant was convicted of illegal possession of *Ritalin* and the statute requiring the controlled substances be kept in the original container was upheld.

REASONING: The court noted that the defendant must show that, upon examining the statute, an individual of ordinary intelligence would not understand what she is required to do under the law. To escape responsibility, the defendant must prove, beyond a reasonable doubt, that the statute was so unclear that she could not reasonably understand that it prohibited acts in which she engaged.

The court could find little room for speculation as to the meaning of the statute that stated that "no person shall knowingly obtain, possess, or use a controlled substance...unless it was obtained pursuant to a prescription issued by a practitioner, and the drug is in the original

State v Collier
581 N.E.2d 525 (Ohio 1991)
...continued

container in which it was dispensed to such a person." Thus, an ordinary person is provided with adequate notice and fair warning as to the standard of conduct required by the statute.

Further, the mere fact many people store prescription drugs in containers other than the original prescription container does not trigger the application of the void-for-vagueness doctrine since there is no constitutionally protected right to obtain, possess, or use a controlled substance. The defendant's claim that the statute was so broad as to impinge on constitutionally protected freedoms was not successful because no constitutional rights were at issue.

The three dissenting justices noted that the statute provides no standards by which an ordinary person or law enforcement officer could determine when a person taking a controlled substance is engaging in conduct the legislature intended to criminalize. Literally interpreting the statute would mean that a person violates the law when emptying prescription drugs from the bottle into his or her hand before swallowing them, or when carrying medication in a coin purse or pillbox.

The dissenting justices felt that the definition of criminal conduct was not well defined in the statute and was instead left to the prosecutor and jury. "Police officers, prosecutors, and courts can then determine that the Tonie Colliers (ie, the defendant) of our society are in violation of the law, while excusing junior executives who embark on business junkets carrying a pill case containing sleeping pills, muscle relaxants, and tranquilizers along with their *Maalox* and *Nuprins*. Enforcement depends upon who the defendant is and where the defendant is found rather than on the conduct of the defendant."

United States v ALN Corporation d/b/a Gilbert Pharmacy
1993 WL 40283 (D. Conn.)

ISSUE: Whether a pharmacist acted in good faith when he dispensed 66 prescriptions for controlled substances to the prescriber.

FACTS: The pharmacist-defendant, Michael Gemma, purchased Gilbert Pharmacy in March 1991. In November of that year, a drug control agent for the state of Connecticut visited the pharmacy in order to perform a routine audit. During the visit, the inspector asked Gemma if he had filled any prescriptions for individuals whose doctor picked up the prescriptions rather than the patients themselves. Gemma responded that he had filled prescriptions for a number of individuals and had given them to their physician, Dr. Fox. When the pharmacist asked the inspector if it was an acceptable practice to give prescription drugs to the attending physician and not to the patients themselves, the inspector responded that under appropriate circumstances it could be acceptable.

Several months later, another agent visited the pharmacy and took sworn statements from Gemma attesting that the physician had picked up numerous prescriptions for Schedule II controlled substances for a variety of patients. During the last visit, Gemma asked the inspector if he should continue filling Dr. Fox's prescriptions. The agent responded that the pharmacist would have to use his own professional judgment in making that determination.

During this timeframe, Dr. Fox personally presented 66 prescriptions for Schedule II controlled substances in the names of persons other than himself. Gemma filled all these pre-

United States v ALN Corporation d/b/a Gilbert Pharmacy
1993 WL 40283 (D. Conn.)
...continued

scriptions and Fox paid the pharmacist personally by means of a check or credit card rather than a form of payment linked to the named recipient of the prescription.

RULING: The court concluded that the pharmacist may have acted in reasonable reliance upon the representation of the physician and the previous pharmacy owner. It was improper to award summary judgment in favor of the government.

REASONING: The court noted that the Controlled Substances Act states that to avoid criminal liability for the distribution of a controlled substance, a medical practitioner must act in the good faith belief that his distribution is for a legitimate medical purpose and in accordance with the usual course of generally accepted medical practice. The "good faith" definition is governed by an objective standard of reasonableness.

The government argued that Gemma should have known that these prescriptions were being used for an unacceptable medical purpose and that he failed to make even a minimal inquiry. In a sworn statement, the pharmacist claimed that he discussed this matter with both Fox and the prior owner of the pharmacy. Gemma testified that both informed him that Fox's area of specialty was pain management and that his patients were not compliant when it came to proper dosages and usages of prescriptions. According to Gemma, he was led to believe that Fox wanted to ensure that the medication was properly administered since his patients were addicted and therefore required close attention.

The government appeared to suggest that no rational juror could possibly rule in favor of the pharmacist by emphasizing that (1) the pharmacist was not an authority in pain management, (2) most of the named recipients of the prescriptions lived far from either the physician or the pharmacy, (3) Fox personally paid for the prescriptions, and (4) the case involved a series of 66 related transactions over a 9-month period of time. The court noted that the proper medical practice in such situations is a question of fact, not law. There clearly was a disputed question of fact in this case, and it was not the court's responsibility to resolve this dispute at the summary judgment phase.

The following is a list of court cases that are related to this topic.

United States v Carlisle, 234 F. 2d 196 (1956)
1962 Ford Thunderbird v Div. of Narcotic Control, 198 N.E.2d 155 (Ill. App. Ct. 1964)
United States v Anile, 352 F. Supp. 14 (N.D. W. Va. 1973)
Young v Texas State Board of Pharmacy, 519 S.W.2d 680 (Tex. Civ. App. 1975)
Norman Bridge Drug Co. v Banner Bartles, Jr., DEA, et al., 529 F.2d 822 (5th Cir. 1976)
State v Austin, 228 S.E.2d 507 (N.C. Ct. App. 1976)
In the Matter of Heller, 374 A.2d 1191 (N.J. 1977)
Mark v Williams, 724 P.2d 428 (Wash. App. 1986)
United States v William Spain, 855 F.2d 1426 (10th Cir. 1987)
Sloman v Iowa Board of Pharmacy Examiners, No. 88-709, Sup. Ct. Iowa (May 17, 1989)
United States v Green Drugs, 905 F. 2d (3rd Cir. 1990)
U.S. v Hughes, 895 F.2d 1135 (6th Cir 1990)
Orzel v Scott Drug Company, 537 N. W. 2nd 208 (Mich. 1995)
Rothenberg v Double D Drug, Slip Op. No. 96-8316 (March 26, 1997 US DC E. Pa.), 1997 U.S. Dist. LEXIS 3851.

Drug Enforcement Administration

Norman Bridge Drug Co. v Banner
529 F.2d 822 (5th Cir. 1976)

ISSUE: Whether the Drug Enforcement Administration's refusal to obey a court restraining order should result in a contempt of court decision and a monetary fine for the DEA agents.

FACTS: The unusual aspect of this case is best illustrated by the words of the U.S. Court of Appeals, Fifth Circuit, when the court stated: "We are thus confronted with the odd spectacle of persons charged with enforcement of the law refusing, themselves, to obey a specific court order."

On May 3, 1974, the president-pharmacist of a corporately operated pharmacy pleaded guilty in federal court to a single illegal sale of 100 *Didrex* tablets without a prescription. The pharmacist was convicted upon his guilty plea and was fined and served a brief prison term. Prior to the May 3, 1974, guilty plea, the DEA conducted an accountability audit of the pharmacy and supposedly found large and excessive overages and shortages of controlled substances. Sometime before November 11, 1974, the president-pharmacist of the corporate pharmacy was back working in the store — though there was evidence that he had personally stopped filling prescriptions after June 1974.

On November 11, 1974, the DEA issued certain administrative decisions to (1) order immediate (without notice) suspension of the pharmacy's DEA registration on grounds that "there is an imminent danger to the public health or safety," and (2) instigate a proceeding to revoke the DEA registration of the pharmacy under 21 U.S.C. 824(d) or §304(d) of Federal Controlled Substances Act. In support of its own suspension order, the DEA made its own findings and alleged therein, in addition to the pharmacist's prior conviction, that: The pharmacy failed to take the initial May 1, 1971, controlled substances inventory; it failed to take the biennial inventory; it failed to maintain records as required by 221 CFR 1306.04(d)(1), 21 CFR 1304.21(a) and 21 CFR 1305.09(e); and that some prescriptions were filled or refilled at the pharmacy in violation of certain procedures in the DEA regulations.

On November 11, 1974, the DEA served its order, giving notice of the DEA registration revocation proceedings, and, in the middle of the business day, simultaneously seized the pharmacy's controlled substances inventory. As the agents worked, customers entered the pharmacy, freely witnessing the seizure. The DEA claimed the immediate drug seizure was necessary because of "imminent public danger." The seizure was pursuant to 21 USC 824(f) or §304(f) of Public Law 91-513. While the DEA agents were packing up the controlled drugs, the pharmacist contacted his lawyer, who immediately drafted a complaint against the DEA agents and the DEA and served the complaint on the agents while they were still in the store. The complaint sought an immediate court restraining order which would require the DEA to return possession of the drugs to the pharmacy. At 5:30 pm on the same day, a Federal District Judge telephoned the U.S. Attorney and told him that he (the Judge) was inclined to issue the temporary restraining order. On November 12, 1974, the order was, in fact, issued by the court.

However, on advice from the U.S. Attorney, the DEA failed to immediately respond to the order and kept the seized drugs. The drugs were returned by the DEA on November 19, 1974, but only after a panel of federal judges declined to lift the restraining order. The DEA agents and the DEA were subsequently made party to a contempt of court proceeding. The DEA asserted, as a defense, a claim that the restraining order did not comply with the usual procedures and did not comport with the usual standard. (Technically speaking, federal procedure required that the court order contain a recital that [1] petitioner (pharmacy)

Norman Bridge Drug Co. v Banner
529 F.2d 822 (5th Cir. 1976)
...continued

would probably prevail in the suit; [2] that the restraining order would not disserve the public interest, and [3] the injury to the pharmacy would outweigh any injuries suffered by DEA. The judge had omitted all such words of art.)

RULING: The court found the DEA agents in contempt of court for their disobedience to the restraining order and ordered the DEA agents to pay the $500 fine as restitution to the pharmacy. The pharmacy was given 1 month to dispose of its controlled substances in a lawful and regular manner.

REASONING: The reasoning of the Court of Appeals in affirming can be summarized as follows: (a) The DEA's disobedience to the District court's restraining order was not the proper method of testing its validity. The DEA could have asked (and eventually did) for a quick judicial determination of the validity of the order, and (b) The unlawful drug sale by the pharmacist in April 1974, and the claimed discrepancies in drug accountability had occurred some 6 to 7 months prior to the drug seizure — obviously, the time lag precluded the existence of such an "imminent public danger" prerequisite needed for a without-notice immediate drug seizure.

In a somewhat separate, but related proceeding, a 3-day court hearing was conducted by an administrative law judge whose function was to make recommendations to the DEA on whether the DEA registration of the pharmacy should be revoked or suspended. After the hearing, the administrative judge recommended that the DEA registration be neither revoked nor suspended. However, the DEA Acting Administrator went ahead and revoked the registration with a proviso that the pharmacy could make new application for it in 6 months. The DEA could legally do this since the administrative law judge's recommendation was not binding on the agency.

As a result, the Federal Court of Appeals vacated the District Court's temporary restraining order and the pharmacy was given 31 days to dispose of its controlled substances in a lawful and regular manner — presumably by sale to another registrant or return for credit to the supplier. As stated previously, the DEA agents were jointly ordered to pay the $500 fine to the pharmacy.

United States v William Spain
855 F.2d 1426 (10th Cir. 1987)

ISSUE: Whether the DEA has authority under 21 U.S. Code 811(h) to temporarily schedule a drug as a controlled substance.

FACTS: Defendant challenged the statutory authority of the U.S. Attorney General to delegate to the DEA authority to temporarily schedule drugs in Schedule 1. The DEA temporarily placed MDMA under schedule pursuant to 21 U.S. Code 811(h), which permits the attorney general to temporarily schedule drugs to avoid an imminent hazard to the public safety. Defendant was convicted of a criminal charge for distribution of a Schedule I controlled substance and appealed the judgment.

RULING: The 10th Circuit Court of Appeals reversed the judgment of the district court and the defendant's conviction.

United States v William Spain
855 F.2d 1426 (10th Cir. 1987)
...continued

REASONING: The 1973 delegation of authority from the attorney general to the DEA (28 Code of Federal Regulations 0.100) to schedule drugs under the Controlled Substances Act did not apply to temporary scheduling. Under the temporary scheduling provision of 21 U.S. Code 811(h), the attorney general alone is delegated authority and may temporarily schedule drugs in Schedule I only to avoid an imminent hazard to the public safety.

Bzdzuich v Drug Enforcement Administration
76 F.3d 738 (6th Cir. 1996)

FACTS: A pharmacist pled guilty to racketeering involving a controlled substance, and relinquished his license. Several years later, the state's Board of Pharmacy reinstated his license provided that he practice under supervision for six months. In accordance with a 1991 amendment to a DEA regulation, 21 CFR §1301.76, the pharmacy-employer sought a waiver of a prohibition against employment of anyone who has been convicted of a controlled substance crime in a pharmacy where controlled substances are dispensed. The DEA denied the waiver request several times. The affected pharmacist and pharmacy employer sued the DEA to obtain a waiver. The Federal District Court dismissed the lawsuit.

HOLDING: The decision was upheld on appeal. The court stated that the pharmacist had no standing because the regulation only applies to DEA registrants wishing to employ convicted felons. The court rejected the pharmacy's due process claims finding that the DEA is not required to grant waivers or hold hearings on waiver requests and that pharmacies do not have the right to employ any state licensed pharmacist of their choosing when that pharmacist has a history of controlled substance felonies.

The following is a list of court cases that are related to this topic.

United States v Anile, 352 F. Supp. 14 (N.D. W. Va. 1973)
Burley v U.S. Drug Enforcement Administration, 443 F. Supp. 619 (D.Tenn. 1977)
United States v Harold Donald Henry, 727 F.2d 1373 (5th Cir. 1984)
United States v Jack Edgar Burns, 816 F.2d 1354 (9th Cir. 1987)
United States v James David Daniel, 813 F.2d 661 (5th Cir. 1987)

Prescriptions

Record Keeping

United States v Green Drugs
905 F.2d (3rd Cir. 1990)

ISSUE: Whether a violation of the record keeping provisions of the Controlled Substances Act may be punished by a fine when the drug shortages are due to human error without any intent to violate the statute.

FACTS: In October of 1986, the Drug Enforcement Administration, acting pursuant to an administrative inspection warrant, conducted an audit of Green Drugs and its owner, Ray-

United States v Green Drugs
905 F.2d (3rd Cir. 1990)
...continued

mond Kauffman, a registered pharmacist. This Philadelphia retail pharmacy attracted the DEA's attention because it was one of the state's largest purchasers of several Schedule II substances. The investigation showed that the pharmacy's receipt records accounted for more drugs than its dispensing records and inventory indicated. Specifically, the investigators found shortages of 4798 *Percodan* tablets, 1902 *Percocet* tablets, and 2753 *Preludin* tablets.

The government commenced this civil action alleging that the defendant's failure to keep complete and accurate records violated the record keeping provisions of the Controlled Substances Act (CSA). The government sought a $25,000 civil penalty for each count.

The defendants challenged the government's computation of shortages, contending that the deficiencies were minor considering the large quantity of drugs processed by the pharmacy. It was the defendant's contention that any shortages were due to human error and "inadvertent mistake." The defendants further argued that, as a matter of law, they could not be held liable because the record keeping provision did not provide for strict liability.

RULING: The federal trial court assessed a $6000 fine, which was upheld by the appellate court.

REASONING: Every registrant under the Controlled Substances Act engaged in the manufacture, distribution, or dispensing of controlled substances is required to make a complete and accurate record of all stocks on hand. Failure to maintain the requisite records subjects the offender to civil or penal penalties, depending on whether the act was committed knowingly. "Inadvertent" mistakes due to sloppy record keeping subject pharmacies and owners to fines while "knowing" violations subject them to criminal sanctions of imprisonment, fines, or both.

The court in this case looked to the legislative history of the governing law to determine if Congress intended strict regulation. On initial scrutiny, the record keeping provisions of the Controlled Substances Act appeared to fall within the expanding regulatory area involving activities affecting public health, safety, and welfare where it need not be shown that the alleged offender committed a willful violation. The court also reviewed previous case law supporting such a contention.

The legislative history revealed Congressional concern to reduce the diversion of drugs from legitimate course of commerce into illegal channels. Congress sought measures to monitor the drug transactions of registrants, who, because they have the greatest access to controlled substances, also have the greatest opportunity for diversion.

Senator Griffin, in speaking for strict record keeping requirements in the law, stated that "drug accountability audits will not deal in approximations but rather in very precise figures." The reading of the statutory text and legislative history made it clear that Congress intended strict compliance with the record keeping provisions. Thus, strict liability could attach for civil violations of the law.

The defendants argued that the court's position would allow the government to hold virtually any pharmacy liable for the most minor infraction even where the greatest care had been exercised and good faith demonstrated. It was noted that these factors could be considered as part of the broad discretion possessed by the court in assessing fines. In any event, the shortages of tablets in the present case were not deemed insignificant. The Congressional mandate providing for strict accountability of the drug inventory caused the court to uphold the civil penalties against the pharmacy.

The following is a list of court cases that are related to this topic.

Randle v California State Board of Pharmacy, 49 Cal. Rptr. 485 (1966)
State v Reardon, 219 A.2d 767 (R. I. 1966)
McKaba v Board of Regents of the State of New York, 294 N.Y. S.2d 382 (1968)
State v Williams, 171 N.W.2d 521 (Iowa 1969)
United States v Greenberg, 334 F. Supp. 364 (W.D. Pa. 1971)
Jay v Board of Regents of Univ. of N.Y., 376 N.Y. S.2d 664 (N.Y. App. Div. 1975)
United States v Enserro, 401 F. Supp. 460 (1975)
Moskowitz v Board of Regents of Univ. of N.Y., 380 N.Y. S. 2d 107 (1976)
Norman Bridge Drug Co. v Banner Bartles, Jr., DEA, et al., 529 F.2d 822 (5th Cir. 1976)
Shermack v Board of Regents of the State University System, 407 N.Y.S. 2d 926 (1978)
White v North Carolina Board of Pharmacy, 241 S.E. 2d 730 (N.C. 1978)
United States v Bycer, 593 F.2d 549 (3rd Cir. 1979)
United States v Poulin, 926 F.2d 246 (D. Mass. 1996)

Drug Diversion and Abuse

Bill Lloyd Drug
64 Fed.Reg. 1823 (1999)

The Deputy Administrator of the DEA revoked Bill Lloyd Drug's Certificate of Registration. In termination proceedings before an Administrative Law Judge, Bill Lloyd failed to file a pre-hearing statement, and therefore waived his right to a hearing. The DEA initiated an investigation of Bill Lloyd following receipt of information that individuals were getting controlled substances from Bill Lloyd without a prescription. DEA investigators conducted an audit and discovered significant shortages and overages. Physicians told investigators that they had not authorized prescriptions attributed to them. Individuals also told DEA investigators that Bill Lloyd would sell them controlled substances for $1 to $3 per pill, or trade controlled substances for things of value. The Deputy Administrator of the DEA found that the shortages and overages revealed that Bill Lloyd Drug did not keep complete and accurate account of its controlled substances. Bill Lloyd was also actively involved in the diversion of controlled substances into the illicit market. Therefore, the Deputy Administrator concluded that continued registration would be inconsistent with the public interest and thereby revoked Bill Lloyd Drug's DEA Certificate of Registration.

Daniel Family Pharmacy
64 Fed.Reg. 5314 (1999)

The Deputy Administrator of the DEA ordered that Daniel Family Pharmacy's Certificate of Registration be continued subject to certain conditions. George Daniel is the owner and managing pharmacist of Daniel Family Pharmacy. In 1991, Daniel's delivery person injured his back and was given a prescription for *Vicodin* (hydrocodone) by his treating physician. When the prescription ran out, Daniel gave his employee a refill of *Vicodin* without a prescription believing that his physician would authorize the refill. Thereafter, the physician told Daniel not to give the employee any more *Vicodin*. A month later, the employee persuaded Daniel to give him more *Vicodin*, and threatened Daniel that he would go to the authorities if Daniel did not give him the drug. In January 1993, the employee, now cooperating with law enforcement officials, twice persuaded Daniel to give him *Vicodin* without a prescription. Daniel was arrested and pled guilty to two felony counts of distributing hydrocodone. Daniel then learned that the employee and another pharmacy technician engaged in a pattern of stealing controlled substances from the pharmacy. A subsequent DEA audit showed considerable shortages of controlled substances. The DEA brought an action to revoke

Daniel Family Pharmacy
64 Fed.Reg. 5314 (1999)
...continued

Daniel's Certificate of Registration. An Administrative Law Judge (ALJ) concluded that the government made a prima facie case for revoking the registration, however, the ALJ recommended that Daniel nonetheless be permitted to remain registered. Although Daniel engaged in egregious conduct, the ALJ found that Daniel was genuinely remorseful and for the last six years had acted in a responsible manner and maintained his DEA registration. Also, as Daniel's pharmacy was the only one in the area that performed prescription compounding, it would not have been in the public interest to revoke Daniel's registration. The Deputy Administrator of the DEA agreed with the ALJ's finding, and continued Daniel's registration subject to a 3-year period of audits and inspections.

Pettigrew Rexall Drugs
64 Fed.Reg. 8855 (1999)

This was a proceeding to revoke the DEA Certificate of Registration for Pettigrew Rexall Drugs. A DEA investigation revealed that between 1987 and 1991, Pettigrew filled an extraordinarily large number of oral prescriptions for controlled substances. Pettigrew's records indicated that many of the oral prescriptions did not contain all of the required information, were refilled more than five times, were refilled in an amount exceeding the original prescription, and were refilled even though the original prescription did not authorize a refill. Physicians denied authorizing many of the prescriptions. An Administrative Law Judge (ALJ) recommended that Pettigrew's Certificate of Registration be revoked. The ALJ found that Pettigrew dispensed controlled substances without physician authorization on numerous occasions. In light of Pettigrew's failure to show remorse for his actions, the ALJ concluded that Pettigrew's misconduct was likely to recur. In appealing before the Deputy Administrator of the DEA, Pettigrew pointed out that there were no allegations of any wrongdoing since 1991, that patients were in medical need for the controlled substances he dispensed to them, and that revoking his registration would harm the public interest. The Deputy Administrator agreed with the ALJ that the government made a prima facie case for revocation of Pettigrew's registration. The Deputy Administrator also expressed great concern over Pettigrew's failure to acknowledge or accept responsibility for wrongdoing. The Deputy Administrator, however, found revocation of registration to be inconsistent with the public interest because Pettigrew was one of only two pharmacies in a poor, medically underserved community. Therefore, the Deputy Administrator decided to continue Pettigrew's Certificate of Registration subject to Pettigrew's completion of a training course regarding the proper handling of controlled substances and submitting to random, unannounced inspections by the DEA.

The following is a list of court cases that are related to this topic.

State v Dutton Drugs, Inc., 209 N.E.2d 597 (Ohio 1965)
Randle v California State Board of Pharmacy, 49 Cal. Rptr. 485 (1966)
McKaba v Board of Regents of the State of New York, 294 N.Y. S.2d 382 (1968)
Moskowitz v Board of Regents of Univ. of N.Y., 380 N.Y. S. 2d 107 (1976)
Norman Bridge Drug Co. v Banner Bartles, Jr., DEA, et al., 529 F.2d 822 (5th Cir. 1976)
United States v Goldfine, 538 F. 2d 815 (9th Cir., 1976)
United States v Schiffman, 572 F. 2d 1137 (5th Cir., 1978)
United States v Bycer, 593 F.2d 549 (3rd Cir. 1979)

Brown v Idaho State Board of Pharmacy, 746 P.2d 1006 (Idaho App. 1987)
United States v Nechy, 827 F.2d 1161 (7th Cir. 1987)
U.S. v Hughes, 895 F.2d 1135 (6th Cir 1990)
Clair v Paris Road Drugs, Inc., 573 So. 2d 1219 (La. App. 1991)
U.S. v Russell, Slip Op. No. 96-2128, March 19, 1998, 6th Cir., 1998 U.S. App. LEXIS 5775.
Mutual Benefit Insurance v Haver, 725 A.2d 743 (Pa. 1999).

Corresponding Responsibility of the Pharmacist

United States v Harold Donald Henry
727 F.2d 1373 (5th Cir. 1984)

ISSUE: Whether the DEA regulation, which provides that a pharmacist may not fill an order purporting to be a prescription if it is known that the prescribing practitioner issued it outside the usual course or professional practice, violated constitutional due process.

FACTS: Defendant-pharmacist dispensed controlled substances at frequent intervals to a paid government informant and an undercover police agent. He was convicted on 11 counts of dispensing controlled substances for improper purposes by a federal district court in Texas. Defendant contended his convictions should be reversed on the grounds the regulation was irrational because a pharmacist cannot determine whether a controlled substance was properly prescribed, and must rely on the judgment of the physician.

RULING: The judgment of conviction was affirmed by the 5th Circuit Court of Appeals.

REASONING: The regulation placing a corresponding responsibility upon pharmacists who fill prescriptions does not place an undue burden on the pharmacist. Henry often dispensed the prescriptions under extremely dubious circumstances. The prescriptions were brought in at frequent intervals by the same individual, who also mentioned plans to share the prescriptions with others. These facts provided a basis for the pharmacist to believe the prescriptions were invalid despite their verification by the prescribing physician, and supported the jury's conclusion that Henry knew the drugs he dispensed were to be used for recreational, not medical purposes.

U.S. v Hughes
895 F.2d 1135 (6th Cir 1990)

ISSUE: Whether a pharmacist has a duty to determine the medical necessity of prescriptions ordered by a licensed physician.

FACTS: The Hubble Medical Clinic was located in Detroit, Michigan. The clinic's patients were drug addicts who came to obtain Schedule III drugs. Under the clinic's policies, four tubes of blood were drawn from each new patient. Patients who refused to give blood were denied prescriptions for controlled substances. The controlled substance prescriptions were telephoned to a cooperating pharmacy.

The policy of taking blood from every new patient was necessary for the clinic to make a profit. The comprehensive blood test allowed the lab to bill Medicaid and Blue Cross for the most money.

The clinic obtained the services of a "doctor of record" for $500 cash per week. However, he did not meaningfully supervise the medical practice of the clinic. Instead, he directed the physician's assistant to provide patients with controlled substances of their choice.

U.S. v Hughes
895 F.2d 1135 (6th Cir 1990)
...continued

The cooperating pharmacy agreed to receive controlled substance prescriptions from the clinic, as per the agreement. Schedule II drugs were not prescribed since they might alert government investigators of the scam. The pharmacy kicked back a portion of each prescription to the clinic for rent, but it never actually occupied any space. The pharmacist working at the pharmacy knowingly filled controlled substance prescriptions from the clinic, which he knew were outside the scope of legitimate medical practice.

RULING: The court ruled that a pharmacist who knowingly fills a prescription not issued in the usual course of professional treatment is criminally liable. The physician, pharmacy owner and dispensing pharmacist were sentenced to 3 years in prison. In addition, fines and terms of parole were imposed.

REASONING: The pharmacist alleged that he had no duty to determine the medical necessity of prescriptions ordered by a licensed physician. It was therefore claimed to be an error to hold the pharmacist criminally liable for dispensing controlled substances outside the course of legitimate medical practice.

The government's pharmacy expert, past president of the Michigan Pharmacist Association and an adjunct professor in the College of Pharmacy at Wayne State University, testified that it would not be within the usual course of pharmacy practice to meet with non-medical personnel and establish quotas of *Tylenol with Codeine* to be dispensed each day. The dosage prescribed is determined by the patient's needs and therefore would not be known in advance. He further testified that it would be highly unusual in the course of pharmacy practice to dispense over 20,000 dosage units of *Tylenol with Codeine* in a 30-day period.

The government presented evidence, including taped conversations between the clinic owner and the dispensing pharmacist. Over 90% of the patients from the clinic received *Tylenol #3*. Consistent with the good faith practice of pharmacy, the dispensing pharmacist recognized the problems with the clinic prescriptions and initially refused to fill them. However, the pharmacist agreed to dispense the prescriptions "if you don't tell anybody."

The court relied on the sections of the Controlled Substances Act, which provide that pharmacists may not dispense prescriptions that are not issued for a legitimate medical purpose. 21 C.F.R. 1306.04 provides that "an order purporting to be a prescription issued not in the usual course of professional treatment or in legitimate and authorized research is not a prescription within the meaning of the Act and the person knowingly filling such a purported prescription, as well as the person issuing it, shall be subject to the penalties provided."

Arkansas State Board of Pharmacy v Fenwick
No. CA 95-904, 1996 Ark. App. LEXIS 603, (Ark. App. Oct. 2, 1996)

FACTS: Father and son pharmacists, practicing together, were charged with dispensing anabolic steroids in violation of state and federal law. The Arkansas State Board of Pharmacy (the "Board") found that the pharmacists dispensed the steroids knowing they were not prescribed for treatment of disease, but for weight gain and body building purposes. The Board imposed a fine of $2,000, a 60-day suspension of their licenses to practice pharmacy, and probation for one year. The father sought reconsideration and his suspension was decreased to 30 days, but the fine was unchanged. He subsequently appealed to the Arkansas Circuit Court, which reversed and dismissed.

Arkansas State Board of Pharmacy v Fenwick
No. CA 95-904, 1996 Ark. App. LEXIS 603, (Ark. App. Oct. 2, 1996)
...continued

HOLDING: On appeal, the Court of Appeals sustained the Board and reversed the Circuit Court. The Appellate Court found that the Board circulated numerous bulletins informing pharmacists that anabolic steroids had been reclassified as Schedule III Controlled Substances by the Drug Enforcement Administration (DEA), that steroid abuse was prevalent and that steroids were being illegally used among athletes and bodybuilders. The evidence showed that the pharmacists filled 381 prescriptions for some 35 patients, far more than any other area pharmacy. The prescribing physician, in his license suspension hearing before the Arkansas State Medical Board, testified that the prescribed steroids were strictly for body building purposes. The pharmacists testified that they repeatedly contacted the prescribing physician to clarify that he meant to prescribe steroids and that patients came to their pharmacy because of their competitive pricing. They also testified that upon DEA investigation, they stopped filling prescriptions for steroids. The court found that the pharmacists had ample warning that steroids should not be used for weight gain or body building, and that the Board's finding that this was a prohibition of the pharmacist's license was correct. The suspensions and fines were upheld.

The following is a list of court cases that are related to this topic.

Moskowitz v Board of Regents of Univ. of N.Y., 380 N.Y.S.2d 107 (1976)
State v Poleyeff, 1993 Ohio App. LEXIS 2483
U.S. v Russell, Slip Op. No. 96-2128, March 19, 1998, 6th Cir., 1998 U.S. App. LEXIS 5775

Forged and Fraudulent Prescriptions

Moskowitz v Board of Regents of Univ. of N.Y.
380 N.Y. S. 2d 107 (1976)

ISSUE: Whether a pharmacist has a duty to investigate, based upon certain factors, prescriptions that are valid on their face, but in actuality, are forged.

FACTS: The New York Commissioner of Education suspended the license of a pharmacist for 1 year and suspended his pharmacy permit for 1 year with execution thereof stayed. (The 1–year suspension would be postponed pending the outcome of a probation period.) The suspensions resulted from charges against the pharmacist and the pharmacy for failure to maintain proper narcotic drug records and for filling 39 forged prescriptions for narcotic drugs not in "good faith."

RULING: Under New York law, the pharmacist has a detailed duty to inquire into the "good faith" validity of a prescription prior to dispensing.

REASONING: The pharmacist and the pharmacy corporation appealed the suspension orders to a New York appellate court, where it was argued that shortages of narcotics (discovered on audit) were the result of a burglary rather than diversion. It was further argued that certain other shortages and overages in drug supplies were de minimis (minimal) and, therefore, should not constitute violations. The burglary was not reported to the Commission as required by law, nor did the records contain a list of the narcotic drugs stolen, again as required by New York law. Thus, the burglary excuse was not a valid defense to the failure to keep accurate narcotic records. The court ruled that "...there is a valid public purpose

Moskowitz v Board of Regents of Univ. of N.Y.
380 N.Y. S. 2d 107 (1976)
...continued

to the requirement that precise records of dangerous drugs be kept,...no violation, regardless of how 'minor', should be tolerated. At best, the degree of the violation is a matter to be taken into consideration in assessing the penalty..."

As to the forged prescriptions, the defendants claimed the prescriptions were regular on their face; therefore, no duty arose to further inquire into their validity. The court answered the claim by citing New York law, which imposed a detailed duty upon the pharmacist to inquire into the bona fide (good faith) nature of a prescription and satisfy himself as to its validity before filling it. The court called attention to particular factors in this case that might have alerted a diligent pharmacist:

(a) Issuance of a prescription on the form of a New Jersey physician to a Manhattan resident that was attempted to be filled in a Bronx pharmacy;

(b) one or more customers returned repeatedly to fill prescriptions for narcotic or stimulant/depressant drugs when such customers had previously received prescriptions for identical drugs, the supply of which could not be been exhausted if taken as directed in the prescriptions;

(c) certain prescriptions required that they be filled in containers that appeared to be improper in size relative to the quantity of the drug prescribed; and

(d) large quantities of *Dolophine* (methadone) were prescribed in certain instances.

Other arguments made to the court were ineffective to persuade the court against confirming the Commissioner's determinations and dismissing the appeal.

State v Poleyeff
1993 Ohio App. LEXIS 2483

ISSUE: Whether a pharmacist who dispensed a small volume of amphetamine prescriptions for weight loss knowingly violated controlled substance statutes.

FACTS: The defendant in this case had been a licensed pharmacist since 1949. He worked part-time to supplement his retirement income. The owner of the pharmacy in which the defendant was employed was one of the co-defendants.

Over the course of two years, the defendant filled 36 prescriptions for *Desoxyn* prescribed by the third co-defendant, a physician, for weight loss. The state of Ohio argued that these prescriptions were not written for a legitimate medical purpose. Fifteen different patients presented these prescriptions to the defendant over a 2-year period of time. One of the patients filled four prescriptions, four patients filled three prescriptions, and ten different patients each filled two *Desoxyn* prescriptions.

RULING: The defendant was indicted and found guilty on 72 counts of selling (dispensing) a false or forged prescription and for selling or offering to sell a controlled substance for other than a legitimate purpose. The defendant appealed, and the conviction was overturned.

REASONING: The defendant argued that there was no evidence to support his conviction of unlawfully selling controlled substances or filling forged prescriptions. He contended that there was no basis for concluding that he had any reason to believe that the prescriptions he dispensed, in the ordinary course of his practice, were not for legitimate medical purposes.

State v Poleyeff
1993 Ohio App. LEXIS 2483
...continued

The court noted that the offenses require a willful violation of the statute. The issue presented to the court was whether the state of Ohio presented sufficient evidence to prove beyond a reasonable doubt that the defendant had the requisite state of mind.

The state presented numerous expert witnesses to testify that very few physicians prescribe *Desoxyn* to treat obesity because of its potential for abuse and its questionable value to aid in weight loss. The experts testified that prescribing *Desoxyn* for more than 6 to 8 weeks fell below the minimum standards for medical professionals. The experts also testified as to the "corresponding responsibility" of a pharmacist to dispense prescriptions only in the course of legitimate medical treatment.

The state further argued that the following facts supported the conviction: (1) all of the prescriptions written by the physician were filled at the pharmacy in question; (2) the defendant filled the prescriptions past a period of 6 to 8 weeks, contradicting warnings in the package insert; (3) the volume of patients over a 2-year period of time; (4) there was no sign of weight loss in patients; and (5) the defendant filled prescriptions for both *Desoxyn* and depressants simultaneously.

The Court of Appeals of Ohio was unwilling to find that this conduct was so egregious as to constitute a violation of either of the charged offenses. The fact that the defendant dispensed prescriptions for patients beyond the 6- to 8-week time frame recommended by the *Desoxyn* package insert did not support the state's case. The court also was not impressed by the volume of patients over the 2-year period. Fifteen patients was not enough volume to put the defendant on notice of any pattern of wrongdoing. The low volume also argued against finding that the defendant violated any corresponding duty to decide whether the customer appeared to need *Desoxyn*.

U.S. v Russell
142 F.3d 438 (6th Cir.)

ISSUE: May a pharmacist be found guilty of conspiracy to distribute controlled substances without valid prescriptions where controlled substances are dispensed on the authority of prescriptions issued by a physician?

FACTS: A 7-year undercover investigation by the DEA showed that between 80% and 93% of the pharmacist's patients came from the physician who prescribed almost exactly the same drugs for all of his patients. New prescriptions for a 30-day supply of controlled and noncontrolled drugs were issued every time the patients saw the physician. The pharmacist, in the vast majority of cases, only filled the controlled substances.

HOLDING: The pharmacist was convicted in a jury trial of conspiring with a physician and his office manager to distribute controlled substances without valid prescriptions. The Court of Appeals upheld the conviction and sentencing, finding the evidence supported the conspiracy charges.

REASONING: The combinations and large quantities of the drugs prescribed by the physician were considered dangerous and addictive, especially over the long periods of time that were involved. Most area pharmacists would not fill the physician's prescriptions because of

U.S. v Russell
142 F.3d 438 (6th Cir.)
...continued

the danger of the combinations prescribed, because the patients were often troublesome and unruly, and because many patients appeared to be under the influence of drugs. The defendant-pharmacist ignored these "red flags" and did nothing to stop the patients who overtly sold the prescription drugs on the street in front of the pharmacy. The pharmacist regularly spoke to the office assistant about steering patients into his small pharmacy and supplied the physician with blank prescription drug pads.

The following is a list of court cases that are related to this topic.

Vermont & 110th Medical Arts Pharmacy v Board of Pharmacy of the State of California, 59716 (Cal. App. 2d, Oct. 29, 1981)
Commonwealth v Slaton, 556 A.2d 1343 (Pa. Super. 1989)
U.S. v Hughes, 895 F.2d 1135 (6th Cir 1990)United States v Poulin, 926 F.Supp. 246 (D. Mass. 1996)

Inventory Requirements

State v Reardon
219 A.2d 767 (R.I. 1966)

ISSUE: Whether a pharmacist's statement to an inspector so prejudiced the jury that a new trial should be granted.

FACTS: A Rhode Island pharmacist was charged, by state authorities, with violating §21-29-3 of the state statutes of 1956 in that he failed to keep and maintain records on the acquisition and disposition of barbiturates and amphetamines. The Rhode Island law required the pharmacist to keep and retain for 2 years his purchase invoices, and prescriptions or other disposition records, as such related to barbiturates and CNS stimulants. The failure to do so was a violation of the state statutes, which would subject the violator to prosecution and penalty if convicted.

Upon an investigation of a drug wholesaler's file of duplicate invoices, state authorities found that a certain pharmacist purchased some 4000 *Seconal* capsules from the wholesaler as evidenced by seven invoices covering the purchases. When the pharmacist was investigated by state inspectors, he only produced two of the original invoices covering such purchases, and, worse yet, could only account for 1100 *Seconals* via his prescription records. Later, at the trial of the case, the pharmacist was able to produce a total of six invoices, but could not produce the seventh invoice and was thereby convicted of failing to keep or retain such original invoices as records required to be preserved under the Rhode Island statutes. Also, certain statements made by the pharmacist to the state inspector were presented to the jury over the objection of the pharmacist's attorney. The statements tended to incriminate (self-convict) the pharmacist.

On the appeal of the case, the pharmacist's lawyer argued that the fact that the drug wholesaler had seven duplicate invoices covering a total sale of 4000 *Seconal* to the pharmacist was not, standing alone, evidence that the pharmacist actually received seven of the original invoices. Absent some evidence showing that the pharmacist did, in fact, receive all seven invoices, the case against him should have been dismissed upon the defendant's motion to have a verdict directed in his favor. There was evidence that the usual practice of the

State v Reardon
219 A.2d 767 (R.I. 1966)
...continued

wholesaler was to execute invoices in duplicate, sending the original along with the merchandise and keeping the duplicate. The appellate court held that from such evidence, it could be reasonably inferred that the pharmacist received the invoice. The court in its reported decision stated:

> It is settled that on motion for a directed verdict in a criminal case the court must view the evidence in the light most favorable to the state and to draw therefrom such reasonable inferences as support the state's contentions. (Citation omitted.)

Another argument made to the appellate court by counsel for the defendant-pharmacist was that, over his objection, certain prejudicial (tending to influence by emotion rather than fact) testimony was allowed to be heard by the jury. The state inspector, while on the witness stand, was asked if anything was said while he was taking an inventory of the *Seconal* in the defendant's pharmacy. The inspector answered: "I asked why he could only produce records that would account for approximately, either dispensing or having on hand, 1100 sodium *Seconals*, and the fact that he only purchased 1000 for the year, when he had the records to show that he had purchased 4000 sodium *Seconals*, and that he was approximately 2900 sodium *Seconals* short that he could not account for, and he answered that he could not keep track of all the pills in this particular store, and that all he would have to do to make up the shortage was to go down the street and buy a couple of bottles; and that we should come around more often and remind him when he is short of pills."

RULING: The pharmacist's statement tended to incriminate himself and prejudice the jury so that a new trial should be granted.

REASONING: Upon examination of the statement, the court was presented with, on one hand, the statement's value to the case because it, along with other evidence, tended to establish that a shortage of *Seconal* existed if the purchase invoices were balanced against the inventory plus disposition records. On the other hand, the pharmacist's reply to the inspector's question implied that he (the pharmacist) only had to go down the street and buy a couple of bottles of pills to make up the shortage, and, hence, the jury could conclude that the pharmacist was dealing in an illegal drug traffic trade, an offense for which he was not being charged.

The appellate court, in a lengthy discussion of rules of evidence, finally concluded that the statement so prejudiced the jury that the defendant should have a new trial. In its reported discussion of the case, the high court stated:

> ...the nature of the statement attributed to the defendant by the inspector was clearly of such a character as to divert the jury from the question of determining his guilt under the indictment returned to the grand jury. We cannot say in such circumstances that the jury was not prejudiced and that in the interest of justice a new trial is not warranted.

United States v Bycer
593 F.2d 549 (3rd Cir. 1979)

ISSUE: Whether a conviction for illegal drug distribution can be based solely on inventory shortages and whether conviction for improper recordkeeping can be based solely on inventory shortages.

FACTS: This case involved an appeal from the U.S. District Court's convictions of a pharmacist on seven separate counts of illegal controlled drug distribution (violating 21 U.S. Code §841(1)(a), a high penalty section) and one count of violating 21 U.S. Code §827(a)(3), failure to maintain complete and accurate records of controlled substances. The Federal Appeals Court overturned the seven convictions of violating §841(1)(a) and ordered the District Court to enter judgments of acquittal on these. The improper recordkeeping conviction was upheld.

The convictions of illegal drug distribution predicated solely on inventory shortages were overturned here in light of two important factors: (a) the pharmacist involved, though manager of the pharmacy, had non-exclusive possession of the controlled drugs (other employed pharmacists had access to the narcotic drawer) and (b) there was no evidence to establish illegal drug distribution.

The reported facts of the case are as follows: The pharmacist-manager was in charge of the pharmacy from May 3, 1975, to May 25, 1977; over that period of time, an audit showed a discrepancy of 100,000 tablets of controlled drugs and 400 grams of cocaine. The audit consisted of calculating the drugs received and subtracting from it the amount in inventory and the amount accounted for by prescriptions. Adjustments to the audit were made to take into account two separate burglaries within the period in question. Also reported was the fact that six other pharmacists were employed during this time period (none of whom were called at trial as witnesses) and these pharmacists had access to the narcotic drawer at times when the accused pharmacist-manager was not present.

In addition, other reported facts were significant. The pharmacist-manager's father, former manager of the pharmacy, was suffering from a prolonged fatal illness and the evidence indicated this had an unsettling effect on the pharmacist; it may have contributed to the gap in the pharmacy's records. Another very important factor was that a DEA undercover agent-informer had "shopped" the pharmacy on two occasions in an effort to buy illegal drugs from the pharmacist-manager, and on each occasion the agent was rebuffed by the pharmacist. On the second such attempt, the pharmacist-manager called the police. Hence, the prosecution's case rested mainly on the inference that the inventory shortage established illegal drug distribution. Other arguments advanced by the prosecution were: That the pharmacist was in possession of the drugs [though, non-exclusive]; that the drugs offered a potential for financial gain because of their "street value," and that none of the other six pharmacists was discharged by the manager for drug theft. (However, no evidence was introduced to show that any of the other pharmacists were involved in drug stealing.)

RULING: Conviction for illegal drug distribution was vacated but conviction for improper recordkeeping was upheld.

REASONING: The court characterized the prosecution's position as simply suspicion — therefore, insufficient evidence. The court stated, as follows:

> We are all too aware of the seriousness of the illegal drug traffic problem and the difficulty of prosecution in many cases. But we are not willing to abandon the protection designed to aid the innocent — requiring proof beyond a reasonable doubt not simply suspicion — to sustain a conviction. Since there is insufficient evidence to justify the convictions on Counts 1 through 7, they must be vacated.

United States v Bycer
593 F.2d 549 (3rd Cir. 1979)
...continued

In reference to the specific facts of the case and effect of circumstantial evidence, the court clarified the law in the area of drug accountability shortages. The court stated:

> Inferences from established facts are accepted methods of proof when no direct evidence is available. It is essential, however, that there be a logical and convincing connection between the facts established and the conclusion inferred. We find that correlation lacking in this case where inferences of illegal drug distribution were drawn from a pharmacist's inability to reconcile his inventory of controlled substances with records of shipments to his store. Since there was no other evidence to establish the prosecution's case on distribution, we vacate those convictions...

United States v Poulin
926 F.Supp. 246 (D. Mass. 1996)

FACTS: This civil action was brought against two pharmacies and their owner-proprietor for violations of the Comprehensive Drug Abuse Prevention and Control Act (the "Act"). On a regulatory inspection, large quantities of Schedule II drugs were found to be missing (possibly stolen) from both pharmacies owned by the defendant, a pharmacist. The pharmacist claimed that he kept the drugs in an unlocked wooden cabinet in paper bags, because they were out of date. The pharmacist also failed to maintain a biennial inventory or order forms containing the number of controlled substances received or the date received as required by statute. The pharmacist was also cited for filling a total of six invalid prescriptions, and for not providing effective controls and procedures to guard against theft and diversion of controlled substances.

HOLDING: At a bench trial, the Federal District Court found the owner-proprietor personally liable for all violations, stating that he failed to keep biennial inventories, failed to keep and complete accurate records of Schedule II controlled substances, was liable for filling invalid prescriptions, and failed to provide adequate security. The defendant was fined $50,000 for the violations.

The following is a list of court cases that are related to this topic.

Randle v California State Board of Pharmacy, 49 Cal. Rptr. 485 (1966)
McKaba v Board of Regents of the State of New York, 294 N.Y. S.2d 382 (1968)
United States v Greenberg, 334 F. Supp. 364 (W.D. Pa. 1971)
Jay v Board of Regents of Univ. of N.Y., 376 N.Y. S.2d 664 (N.Y. App. Div. 1975)
United States v Enserro, 401 F. Supp. 460 (1975)
Moskowitz v Board of Regents of Univ. of N.Y., 380 N.Y. S. 2d 107 (1976)
Norman Bridge Drug Co. v Banner Bartles, Jr., DEA, et al., 529 F.2d 822 (5th Cir. 1976)
Shermack v Board of Regents of the State University System, 407 N.Y.S. 2d 926 (1978)
White v North Carolina Board of Pharmacy, 241 S.E. 2d 730 (N.C. 1978)
United States v Green Drugs, 905 F. 2d (3rd Cir. 1990)
Sender v Department of Professional Regulation, 635 N.E. 2d 849 (Ill. App. 1994)

Continuing Records

State v Williams
171 N.W.2d 521 (Iowa 1969)

ISSUE: Whether a pharmacist should be sentenced to 2 years in the state penitentiary for violating the recordkeeping provisions of the laws governing the sale of *otc* narcotics.

FACTS: In January of 1967, two Iowa State Pharmacy Board inspectors visited the pharmacist's pharmacy and told him that they were there to conduct an "audit or survey" of the Class X narcotics. The inspectors asked for the invoices and exempt registry book covering the period from July 1, 1966, to Dec. 31, 1966. They also announced that they would inventory the Class X drugs on hand in the pharmacy. The defendant, without objection, produced an exempt registry record showing recorded sales of 1961 4 oz bottles of *Robutussin* AC and no recorded sales of Elixir Terpin Hydrate with codeine. The defendant produced, as a record of receipt, invoices showing purchase of 2328 bottles of *Robitussin* AC and 66 bottles of Elixir Terpin Hydrate with codeine for the 6-month audit period. The invoices produced were from only one drug wholesaler. The pharmacist produced no other invoices or retail sales records. As a follow-up on the audit, the inspectors checked with the drug wholesalers and found at one wholesaler several invoice copies showing an additional 546 bottles of *Robitussin* AC sold to the defendant. At another drug wholesaler, they found 29 invoices showing a total of 1392 bottles of *Robitussin* AC sold to the defendant. In both instances, the defendant had not produced such invoices for the pharmacy inspection/audit. The inspectors submitted a report to the Board and the result was a prosecution commenced against the pharmacist for violating recordkeeping requirements of the State Narcotic Act.

The defendant-pharmacist's contention at the trial court level and on appeal of the case was that "he was not required to keep records regarding his purchase and sale of the narcotic preparations, *Robitussin* AC and Elixir Terpin Hydrate with codeine." The prosecution's position was that "prescriptions are not required for these items but that is the extent of the exemption in the law." The determination of the issue depended on the interpretation of §204.8(5) of the Iowa statutes, which read "except as otherwise provided, this chapter shall not apply to the administering, dispensing or selling of any preparation not more than one grain (64.8 mg) of codeine...per one avoirdupois ounce...when such pharmaceutical preparations are administered, dispensed or sold by persons under conditions prescribed by the board." The court also relied on the interpretation of §204.9, which read in part, "In every case the record of narcotic drugs received shall show the date of receipt, the name and address of person from whom received...The record of all narcotic drugs sold...shall show-...name and address of person...to whom sold...The keeping of a record required or under the federal narcotic laws containing substantially the same information as is specified by this chapter, shall constitute compliance with this section, except that every such record shall contain a detailed list of narcotic drugs lost, destroyed or stolen..." In essence, the defendant was contending that §204.8(5) provided an exemption of Class X narcotics from the entire chapter, and, hence, §204.9 was inapplicable. It should be mentioned here, that the pharmacy board had made no rules regulating exempt narcotic sales or recording such sales.

RULING: The pharmacist was sentenced to 2 years imprisonment in the Iowa State penitentiary upon his conviction for violating §204.9 of the Iowa statutes, relating to receipt and disposition records of narcotic drugs. The Iowa Supreme Court upheld the trial court's imposition of the 2-year imprisonment and $2000 fine.

REASONING: The court ruled that the recordkeeping requirements of §204.9 did, in fact, apply to exempt narcotics of the Class X type, namely the *Robitussin* AC and Elixir Terpin Hydrate with codeine purchased and sold by the defendant. The court based its decision on the premise that cases in other jurisdictions held that the Uniform Narcotic Act exempted

State v Williams
171 N.W.2d 521 (Iowa 1969)
...continued

certain drugs from the prescription requirements, but did not exempt them from the record-keeping. When §204.8(5) is read observantly, it reads "Except as otherwise provided, this chapter shall not apply to the administering, dispensing or selling of any preparation containing not more than one grain of codeine..." Likewise, when §204.9 is read, in such manner, it reads "In every case the record of narcotic drugs...shall show..." Also, there was no mention in §204.8(5) as to the exemption from application of the "Chapter" with reference to "record-keeping"; §204.9 by placing the words "all" or "every" in connection with the words "narcotic drugs" could only mean that the recordkeeping requirements applied to narcotic drugs whether such were of the exempt Class X type or nonexempt type. The court reasoned this to be so since it was undisputed that *Robitussin* AC and Elixir Terpin Hydrate with codeine were narcotic drugs as the term "narcotic drugs" was defined in the law. With interest, the court mentioned that the defendant knew and understood that records of exempt narcotic sales were required because, without protest or objection, he handed over an exempt narcotic registry showing 1961 recorded sales.

The following is a list of court cases that are related to this topic.

Randle v California State Board of Pharmacy, 49 Cal. Rptr. 485 (1966)
State v Reardon, 219 A.2d 767 (R.I. 1966)
McKaba v Board of Regents of the State of New York, 294 N.Y. S.2d 382 (1968)
United States v Greenberg, 334 F. Supp. 364 (W.D. Pa. 1971)
Jay v Board of Regents of Univ. of N.Y., 376 N.Y. S.2d 664 (N.Y. App. Div. 1975)
United States v Enserro, 401 F. Supp. 460 (1975)
Moskowitz v Board of Regents of Univ. of N.Y., 380 N.Y. S. 2d 107 (1976)
Norman Bridge Drug Co. v Banner Bartles, Jr., DEA, et al., 529 F.2d 822 (5th Cir. 1976)
Shermack v Board of Regents of the State University System, 407 N.Y.S. 2d 926 (1978)
White v North Carolina Board of Pharmacy, 241 S.E. 2d 730 (N.C. 1978)
United States v Bycer, 593 F.2d 549 (3rd Cir. 1979)
United States v Green Drugs, 905 F. 2d (3rd Cir. 1990)
Sender v Department of Professional Regulation, 635 N.E. 2d 849 (Ill. App. 1994)
United States v Poulin, 926 F.2d 246 (D. Mass. 1996)

Inspections

The Fourth Amendment

McKaba v Board of Regents of the State of New York
294 N.Y.S.2d 382 (1968)

ISSUE: Whether a pharmacist's consent to a search of narcotic records negates the requirement of a search warrant.

FACTS: The New York State Board of Pharmacy brought a disciplinary action against a New York pharmacist and accused him of unprofessional conduct in that (1) he failed to maintain narcotic records as required by the New York State Public Health Law; (2) he dispensed narcotic exempt preparations not in good faith; (3) he failed to give access to inspectors of the Narcotic Bureau to records required to be kept by him; (4) he violated the New York State Education Law (a state law regulating the practice of pharmacy); and (5) he had been

McKaba v Board of Regents of the State of New York
294 N.Y.S.2d 382 (1968)
...continued

convicted of violating such law. The Board of Pharmacy found the pharmacist guilty of all charges and suspended his pharmacist's license for 3 months. On review, the Committee on Discipline of the New York Board of Regents accepted the Board's findings and recommended acceptance by the Regents with suspension increased to 6 months. The Board of Regents accepted the recommendation. The pharmacist appealed to the Appellate Division of the New York Supreme Court.

On appeal, the pharmacist contended that, although the narcotic bureau inspector had a right to examine his purchase and sales records, the inspector could not take an inventory of the drugs without first presenting a search warrant or securing permission from him (the pharmacist). In the reported discussion of the case, the appellate court reflected on the testimony given by the pharmacist at the Board of Pharmacy hearing. At the hearing, the pharmacist was recorded to have said to the narcotic inspector:

> I said, 'Go right ahead, do what you want.' I would leave them in the store for five or ten minutes in the prescription department. I have nothing to hide, absolutely nothing.

RULING: The pharmacist's consent to the search and failure to object to the evidence negated the requirement of a search warrant.

REASONING: The New York appellate court ruled that the statement by the pharmacist granted the inspectors permission to examine his records and inventory his narcotic drugs. A further point in this case was that the pharmacist was, at all stages of the hearings, represented by his lawyer and no objection was made by him or by his attorney to the introduction of the inventory exhibits or statements made to the inspector. Hence, the court ruled that failure of the defendant to make a timely objection to the admission of such evidence resulted in his loss of the right to raise constitutional objections to the admissibility of the evidence when the case was appealed.

The court stated:

> Assuming that upon proper objection the evidence as to the interviews and statements would be inadmissible, there still remains ample evidence with regard to the inspection of petitioner's records or purchases and sales of narcotic drugs to sustain the suspension. In accepting his license, the petitioner accepted the incident obligation of keeping the required records and permitting the inspection. The dangers and hazards of narcotics to health and public safety are known to all. Such records are non-privileged records required by statute to be kept for proper regulation and protection of the general public and their inspection without a search warrant was constitutionally valid.

There are two factors present in this case which preclude the assertion of the constitutional right against an illegal search. First, the pharmacist did not challenge the constitutionality of the statute which opened narcotic sale and purchase records to inspection; secondly, he only objected to the inventory inspection at the appellate stage of the case. At that point, the objection was too late. Hence, the court did not have to decide the issue of whether the taking of the inventory was constitutionally legal. Likewise, the court did not have to decide if the statute permitting inspection of sale and disposition records required a search warrant since the pharmacist said the records were open to inspection.

Olson v State of Florida
287 So.2d 313 (Fla. 1973)

ISSUE: Whether the search of a pharmacy's prescription and business records was constitutional without a warrant.

FACTS: A criminal action was commenced against a pharmacist for dispensing a barbiturate without first being furnished a prescription as required by §465.18(2)(c) of the Florida Drug Abuse Act.

It was charged that the pharmacist feloniously delivered or caused to be delivered amobarbital and methamphetamine in violation of the Florida Drug Abuse Act. The pharmacist claimed that a warrantless search and seizure was made of his pharmacy and that certain prescriptions from his business records were obtained by state authorities acting pursuant to the broad inspection powers of §465.131 of the Florida Pharmacy Act. The pharmacist sought a court order suppressing the evidence as being illegally obtained in absence of a search warrant. The first court of record granted the suppression order; but on appeal by the state the State District Court reversed the order. The pharmacist then appealed the case to the Supreme Court of Florida. The claim made on appeal is that inspection powers under §465.131 only apply to enforcement of provisions of the Pharmacy Act and do not extend to enforcement of the state drug abuse law.

RULING: As a general rule, the search of a pharmacy, just as the search of a private home, requires a search warrant.

REASONING: The court's decision was premised on the general legal principle that criminal laws and enforcement procedures must be strictly construed. Hence, an inspection provision of a statute could not be used to permit a warrantless search and seizure in the aid of enforcing another state statute (unless the legislature clearly was fit to indicate such). Thus, the court held for the pharmacist and stated as follows:

> Fair and equal treatment of citizens requires that owners and operators of business establishments be accorded the full protection of the Fourth and Fifth Amendments to the United States Constitution against harassment and intrusion of government agents and self-incrimination from their own papers and effects, except in those exceptional situations where the public welfare demands different treatment for them and only then when the exceptions are made plainly in the governing statutes.

There was one dissenting opinion expressed by a Florida justice who did not go along with the courts' majority. His position was that "Knowing of the reservation for state inspection, each licensed pharmacist agrees to all reasonable drug inspections by the state when licensed and waives the right to object when he is weighed in the balance and found wanting."

United States v Enserro
401 F.Supp. 460 (S.D.N.Y. 1975)

ISSUE: Whether a search by the Drug Enforcement Administration required a warrant in the absence of the defendant's consent.

FACTS: In 1974, a pharmacist-owner was indicted in a Federal District Court in New York and charged with distributing Schedule II controlled substances without proper written

United States v Enserro
401 F.Supp. 460 (S.D.N.Y. 1975)
...continued

orders and with failing to maintain required reports and records. Lawyers representing the defendant-pharmacist filed a motion asking the court to suppress the drugs seized by the DEA as a result of its inspection of the pharmacy. Essentially, the claims made by the defendant were that the DEA pharmacy inspection was without legally effective consent; without an administrative inspection warrant; and violative of the applicable federal statute and the Fourth Amendment. The federal court ruled in favor of the pharmacist and suppressed the evidence obtained as a result of the inspection.

From the reported facts of the case, it appears that DEA agents received a complaint from a local police department that illegal drug distributions were taking place at the defendant's pharmacy. DEA agents then came to the pharmacy during business hours. The defendant-owner was not present, but the agents presented a "Notice of Inspection" (DEA Form 82) to the pharmacist on duty.

The agents told him, "...he (the pharmacist) would face criminal penalties under Title 21 of the United States Code unless he signed a consent permitting the inspection." Faced with this threat, the pharmacist signed the consent and permitted inspection. The agents made a drug inventory and found the pharmacy had more cocaine HCl than it should have, based on order forms and physical count. Later, when the pharmacist-owner arrived, he stated that he had removed some drugs from a hospital pharmacy of which he was in charge to his own pharmacy for purposes of destruction.

During the trial, the government agreed that, "...there was no legally effective consent given pursuant to §880(c)(1). The representations made by the agent at that time were clearly erroneous and a search by consent was not justified." (If the consent was not valid, then the inspection was illegal unless an inspection warrant was issued or the situation was one where neither consent nor warrant was constitutionally required.)

RULING: The court ruled that if the consent was not valid, an administrative inspection warrant was required under the circumstances of the case.

REASONING: The government's position in court was that 221 U.S.C. §880(c)(5) of the Comprehensive Drug Abuse Prevention and Control Act, provided circumstances where a warrant was not required for inspection. Next, the government argued that the United States Supreme Court in *U.S. v Biswell*, 406 U.S. 311, eliminated the need for an inspection warrant.

The Federal District Court found the government's theory was without merit. *Biswell* was concerned with the Gun Control Act of 1968, 18 U.S.C. Sec., 923(g), while the situation here was under 21 U.S.C. §880 wherein, "Congress laid out an elaborate scheme of applying for a warrant before the search may be conducted with certain exceptions not applicable here." Further, the Court stated: "Although Congress, if it desired, could have given the drug agents the authority given to Treasury agents under *Biswell*, it decided not to." The defendant's motions to suppress evidence gathered during the inspection and statements made by the defendant at the time were granted.

Stone v City of Stow et al
593 N.E.2d 294 (Sup. Ct. Ohio 1992)

ISSUE: Whether governmental authorities could conduct administrative searches of pharmacy records without a search warrant.

FACTS: The defendants were various cities in the state of Ohio that had established a system to collect and analyze prescription drug records in regard to the possible diversion of controlled substances from legitimate channels, either by patients obtaining multiple prescriptions of the same drug from multiple physicians or excessive doses of the same drug being dispensed in multiple pharmacies within the six-community area.

One of the plaintiffs was a pharmacist who operates six pharmacies, some of which are located in the six-community area involved in the inspection program. Prescription records of this pharmacy were regularly inspected by city police, but no warrant had ever been issued to conduct such inspections.

The data were obtained by having both uniformed and nonuniformed police enter pharmacies and record the names of patients receiving certain controlled substances. The collected data were then entered by each community onto computer floppy disks. The police officers conducted the inspection program without warrants in accordance with applicable Ohio statutes and regulations. Ohio law authorizes the collection of individual prescription data without a warrant by police officers and employees of the Board of Pharmacy. It is these statutes and regulations that the plaintiffs contend are unconstitutional.

RULING: The Ohio Supreme Court concluded that since pharmacy is a pervasively regulated profession, a pharmacist has a reduced expectation of privacy in the prescription records he or she keeps. Therefore, an administrative search warrant was not required.

REASONING: The plaintiffs argued that such warrantless searches violate their right of privacy and the prohibition against unreasonable searches and seizures set forth in the U.S. and Ohio Constitutions. The court noted that there are at least two separate kinds of privacy rights. One type is the individual's interest in avoiding disclosure of personal matters, while the other right protects an individual's independence in making important personal decisions in confidence.

The court stated that the types of disclosure involved in this case were not meaningfully distinguishable from a host of other unpleasant invasions of privacy that are associated with any facet of health care. The court further noted that security measures were implemented to protect prohibited public disclosure, that the statute and regulation expressly prohibited public disclosure, and that willful violation of the nondisclosure provisions had been made a crime.

The court disagreed with the plaintiff's argument that the system of collecting data had too few limits on the improper use of the information and that too many employees at the police departments had access to this very personal information. While there was the possibility of unauthorized disclosure, the threat itself was insufficient to invalidate the system.

The next issue the court faced was whether the statutory and administrative provisions at issue violated the prohibitions against unreasonable searches and seizures found in the U.S. and Ohio Constitutions. In general, the Fourth Amendment provides a right for persons to be secure in their homes, papers, and effects against unreasonable searches and seizures. In order for a party to succeed in challenging a search on Fourth Amendment grounds, it must be established that the challenging party had an expectation of privacy and society must be prepared to recognize that expectation to be reasonable.

Klingenstein v State of Maryland
624 A.2d 532 (Md. 1993)

ISSUE: Whether the search of a pharmacist's home for evidence of violations of the Controlled Substances Act was constitutionally valid.

FACTS: Defendant Klingenstein's pharmacy was located in Greenbelt, Maryland. He lived in College Park, Maryland. On October 12, 1990, a trooper of the Maryland State Police obtained a warrant to search the pharmacy (the business warrant) and later that day another trooper obtained a warrant to search the home (the home warrant). It was later determined that the business warrant was proper, but the home warrant raised questions as to the constitutionality of its issuance.

It was determined at the hearing that the police officers serving the warrant were accompanied by Jack Freedman, a pharmacist and an auditor with the Drug Control Division of the State Department of Health. It was not disputed that Freedman expressed his intention to have Klingenstein's pharmacist license suspended and, to that end, instructed the officers to seize all drugs listed in Schedule II of the Controlled Substances Act. The officers did so.

The judge noted that although the officer who applied for the warrant was careful to specify particular drugs, he instead relied upon the direction of Mr. Freedman. The state conceded that some of the items seized from the home were beyond the terms of the warrant.

RULING: The trial court suppressed all of the evidence since the search was conducted without regard to the limits of the search warrant. The appellate court concluded that the tainted information in the warrant did not necessarily render the warrant unconstitutional.

REASONING: Absent some sort of flagrant disregard, the appropriate rule, in the court's eyes, was that where officers seize some items outside the scope of a valid warrant, this by itself will not effect the admissibility of the other items seized at the same time which do fall within the warrant. It was noted that the issue presented in this case had not been definitively answered by the U.S. Supreme Court. After reviewing the decisions of the federal courts and state appellate courts, it was concluded that it appears to be universally recognized that, under the Fourth Amendment, the exclusionary rule does not act to suppress evidence seized within the scope of a warrant simply because the evidence outside the scope of a warrant was unlawfully seized. In other words, the general rule is that only those items that were unconstitutionally seized are to be suppressed; those that were constitutionally seized may stand.

The following is a list of court cases that are related to this topic.

United States v Anile, 352 F. Supp. 14 (N.D. W. Va. 1973)
United States v Pugh, 417 F. Supp. 1019 (W.D. Mich. 1976)
Mark v Williams, 724 P.2d 428 (Wash. App. 1986)

Administrative Inspections

United States v Stanack Sales Co.
387 F.2d 849 (3d. Cir. 1968)

ISSUE: (1) Whether an inspector of the Food and Drug Administration is required to obtain a subpoena to inspect records relating to the receipt and distribution of drugs and (2) whether permission to inspect the premises constituted a waiver of the defendant's constitutional right to demand such subpoena.

United States v Stanack Sales Co.
387 F.2d 849 (3d. Cir. 1968)
...continued

FACTS: The defendants operated a family corporation in the drug repacking business. On November 19, 1964, an FDA inspector appeared at the premises to make a "routine" inspection as authorized by federal drug law. The government agent presented his credentials and written notice of his intent to inspect the "factory warehouse...and all pertinent equipment, finished and unfinished materials and labeling therin." Permission to inspect was granted by one of the defendants (the company salesman). While inspecting the plant, the FDA agent suspected that the company might be guilty of misbranding prescription drugs and, therefore, asked to inspect company records relating to receipt and distribution of drugs. The company salesman told the agent that such records were part of the financial records and that the inspector had no authority to see them. On November 23, an FDA agent again requested to inspect receipt and distribution records, and the request was refused by company management. The government prosecuted the company and the persons refusing inspection and conviction was obtained.

The defendant corporation, its secretary-treasurer and its salesman were all convicted of violating 21 U.S.C. 331 (f) by refusing to allow FDA inspectors to make an inspection as authorized by 21 U.S.C. 374 (Section 704 of the Federal Food, Drug, and Cosmetic Act). The defendants appealed their convictions to the United States Court of Appeals for the Third Circuit

RULING: The conviction of the corporation and its officers for failing to permit an inspection by the Food and Drug Administration was overturned.

REASONING: The Federal Court of Appeals, in vacating the lower federal court's convictions of the defendants, cited the rulings in the cases of *Camara v Municipal Court*, 387 U.S. 523, and *See v City of Seattle*, 387 U.S. 541, in which it was, respectively, stated:

> "...a homeowner could refuse to permit a search of his premises pursuant to an administrative regulator code unless the administrative inspector first procured a search warrant and that the homeowner could not be prosecuted for such refusal."

> "The [administrative] agency has the right to conduct all reasonable inspections of such documents [corporate books and records] which are contemplated by statute, but it must delimit the confines of a search by designating the needed documents in a formal subpoena. In addition, while a demand to inspect may be issued by the agency, in the form of an administrative subpoena, it may not be made and enforced by the inspector in the field, and the subpoenaed party may obtain judicial review of the reasonableness of the demand prior to suffering penalties for refusing to comply."

In the instant case, the court, in effect, decided that the government agent did not proceed with a "carefully delimited subpoena" and that the initial inspection permission did not act as a waiver of the defendant's constitutional right to demand such subpoena.

United States v Greenberg
334 F.Supp. 364 (W.D. Pa. 1971)

ISSUE: Whether the search of a pharmacy may be ruled illegal because of a lack of probable cause under the Controlled Substances Act.

FACTS: On June 1, 1971, a Pennsylvania pharmacy was visited by a BNDD (now DEA) agent who presented an Administrative Inspection Warrant issued by a federal magistrate pursuant to 21 USC 880 or §510(d) of the Federal Comprehensive Drug Abuse Prevention and Control Act of 1970. An inspection of the pharmacy was conducted, and on June 4, 1971, the operator of the pharmacy was arrested on charges of violating the recordkeeping requirements of the CSA law (violating 21 USC 82(a)(5) or §402(a)(5) of the Act). At the same time, the inventory stock of certain controlled substances was seized pursuant to the forfeiture provisions of the Act.

The pharmacy operator-defendant later sought a federal court ruling to suppress the evidence obtained by the government and for the return of the seized drugs. Essentially, the claim made was that the inspection warrant was issued illegally; that is, without probable cause as required in the law. The defendant also claimed that the drugs seized were outside the scope of the inspection warrant. The Federal District Court held for the government and denied the defendant's motions for suppression of the evidence and return of the drugs.

RULING: The court ruled that the mere passage of time since the last inspection would support the probable cause portion of the Controlled Substances Act and would justify an administrative inspection.

REASONING: First, the court pointed out that as to inspection warrants, the standard of probable cause which will make the issuance of such inspection warrant lawful is defined in the CSA. The Act states that such "probable cause" is "a valid public interest in the effective enforcement of the subchapter (21 U.S.C.A. §801-886) or regulations thereunder sufficient to justify administrative inspections of the area..."

Secondly, the court made the observation that "The statutory scheme envisioned by the Act (Controlled Substances Act) is one of control through recordkeeping." The court reasoned that while, in the usual "probable cause" situation, supporting the issuance of a warrant is one of belief that a crime has been committed and the premises sought to be inspected contain the fruit of the crime, the situation with the inspection warrant under the CSA law is different. The court stated: "...we believe that in absence of any evidence of the commission of some violation of the Act, a valid public interest in the enforcement of the Act could still be shown. For instance, there is a valid public interest in insuring compliance with the recordkeeping requirements of the Act. To this end it would seem entirely proper to conduct an inspection of a particular premise simply because a substantial period of time had passed since the last inspection. In the instant case no inspection had ever been made of the premise in question."

Moreover, in Greenberg, the BNDD was prompted to inspect the pharmacy because of extraordinary quantity purchases of certain controlled drugs. In fact, the BNDD agent, in applying for the inspection warrant, made the alleged fact of such purchases known in his supporting affidavit. This created a "suspicion" of the type that the court held could support issuance of the inspection warrant.

United States v Anile
352 F.Supp. 14 (N.D. W. Va. 1973)

ISSUE: Whether a pharmacist's consent to an administrative inspection by the DEA given in mere acquiescence to authority is valid to support an inspection without a search warrant.

FACTS: On June 3, 1970, three special agents of the BNDD (now DEA) paid a visit to a pharmacy in West Virginia. The agents identified themselves to the pharmacy owner and presented a written notice of inspection. In the reported court opinion, the court indicated that whether the agents advised the pharmacy owner that it was a routine inspection or an in-depth compliance investigation was not clearly established. The court stated in regard to the reported facts:

> When the defendant asked, 'Do I have a choice?' or words to that effect, the agents replied that he did not. Thereupon, the agents began an inspection which carried over to the next day. On both days the agents removed and took with them drugs, prescriptions, records and other related material.

On July 15, 1970, the agents returned and presented an inspection notice to the employee pharmacist who was on duty and the agents conducted a second inspection. On August 26, 1970, the pharmacy owner (now defendant) was arrested as a result of discrepancies in his narcotic records. At no time were the inspections conducted pursuant to a search warrant and the defendant was first advised of his constitutional rights by the government agents after the first inspection. (Note: In the *Anile* case, the administrative inspection was under provisions of the old DACA law [former 21 USC 30a(d)] which did not have any provisions for administrative inspection warrants. The federal Controlled Substance act was passed in 1970, while the *Anile* matter had started, and it affected the government's prosecution of the defendant in that he was charged with a felony violation of former 26 USC 7237 on November 30, 1970, and that section of the law was repealed in October 1970. Hence, the government had to go back to its original charge of a misdemeanor in willfully failing to keep the required records under the law. The original charge was made prior to October 27, 1970; the Federal CSA law was signed on that day and "saved" any prosecutions made under the old law prior to the date, but of more significance here, the federal court took cognizance of the Federal Controlled Substance Act in arriving at its decision in Anile.)

The pharmacy-owner, now defendant, through his attorney, asked the Federal District Court to suppress the evidence seized by the government and to return all of it to him on grounds that the inspections were illegal as being made in absence of a search warrant and without consent. The Federal District Court agreed with the defendant to the extent of granting his motion to suppress the evidence, and it returned the evidence to him.

RULING: The mere acquiescence to authority is not consent, and a search warrant should have been obtained.

The court noted that the inspections were not routine but prompted by complaints and, hence, the possibility of a criminal prosecution was great in the minds of the investigators. The court stated that "Under the facts here, a search warrant obviously should have been obtained prior to the agents' first entry upon defendant's place of business."

Further, the court considered the prior decision in *U.S. v Greenberg* and also another case of *U.S. v Thriftimart*, 429 F. 2d 1006; as well as the U.S. Supreme Court case of *U.S. v Biswell*. The court then repeated some of the rules of those cases, as follows:

> The standards that apply to administrative inspections are not, by their very nature, the same that apply to criminal searches and seizures...Regardless of the type of search conducted, however, it is well settled that an individual may waive any rights...

United States v Anile
352 F.Supp. 14 (N.D. W. Va. 1973)
...continued

Then, quoting from *Biswell*, the court states, "In the context of a regulatory inspection system of business premises which is carefully limited in time, place and scope, the legality of the search depends not on consent but on the authority of a valid statute."

> The court recognizes that on many occasions it can be successfully argued that suspicion does not convert an administrative investigation into a traditional criminal investigation. The problem is, of course, one of degree. The prime consideration must be the protection of recognized basic individual rights, and these individual rights should not be affected by mere labels, particularly where the substance of the matter under investigation is not consistent with the label that is attached to it.

The court concluded that: "Having not been fully advised of the circumstances of his rights, defendant's consent was not valid. Mere acquiescence to authority is not consent."

Daley v Weinberger
400 F.Supp. 1288 (1975)

ISSUE: Whether a physician could obtain a court order prohibiting the Food and Drug Administration from making an inspection of her office.

FACTS: The case involves a physician who brought a court action aimed at preventing an FDA inspection of her office. The action was started before any such inspection was ever made, and was brought under a federal declaratory judgment law, 28 U.S.C. §1331 and 1337.

It appears from the reported facts of the case that the physician used various cortisone and hormone drug preparations in her treatment of rheumatoid arthritis. The FDA believed that the physician may have been distributing a drug called *Liefcort*, a foreign preparation containing prednisone, testosterone, and estradiol. *Liefcort* was not FDA-approved and its shipment in interstate commerce would violate federal law unless shipment was pursuant to authority of an FDA-approved NDA or IND. On two occasions, FDA agents visited the physician's office, interrogated her nurse, and served a Notice of Inspection pursuant to provisions of §704(a) of the Federal Food, Drug and Cosmetic Act (21 U.S.C. §374(a)). The inspection notice did not specify the purpose of the proposed inspection or what the FDA expected to find on the premises. However, the FDA agents merely served the notice and no inspection was in fact conducted.

The physician-plaintiff sought a federal court order prohibiting the FDA from making any inspection of her office. In turn, the FDA asked the court to dismiss the physician's complaint on grounds that the law gave the FDA power to inspect a physician's office and, therefore, no real controversy was before the court. The court agreed and dismissed the complaint.

RULING: The court ruled that the FDA has the authority to enter and inspect a physician's office at reasonable times and if the physician wanted to test the proposed FDA inspection, she could do so by refusing inspection.

REASONING: The court's ruling was that the physician's complaint was premature since §374 of the Food, Drug and Cosmetic Act "simply and unequivocally authorized FDA to

Daley v Weinberger
400 F.Supp. 1288 (1975)
...continued

enter and inspect certain specified premises at reasonable times." Further, the court indicated that if the physician wanted to test the proposed FDA inspection, she could do so by refusing inspection. The burden would then shift to the FDA. The FDA could pursue the matter by (1) seeking a court order prohibiting the physician from refusing FDA entry and inspection (reference - see §302 and 301(f) of the Food, Drug and Cosmetic Act) or (2) The FDA could institute criminal proceedings against the physician for her inspection refusal (see §303(a) of the Food, Drug and Cosmetic Act or 21 U.S.C. §333 (a)). In either event, the physician would have her day in court and the opportunity to test the legality of the inspection. However, as was so appropriately pointed out by the plaintiff-physician, "She should not be required to test the legality of the FDA's right to inspect her office in a criminal proceeding, on pain of conviction should she lose." The court answered that issue by indicating that the fear of prosecution here was unlikely. The court stated a general rule, as follows:

> ...in construing statutes providing criminal penalties for individuals who refuse to honor administrative summonses, the courts have held in parallel situations that good faith noncompliance is not subject to prosecution. See *Reisman v Caplin*, 375 U.S. 444, 446-49, 84 S.Ct. 508, 11 L.Ed. 2d 459 (1964) (good faith refusal to honor an Internal Revenue Service summons would be a defense to a prosecution under 26 U.S. C. §7210)...

Note: The situation of administrative inspection of business premises is still very much where it was left in *See v Seattle*, 387 U.S. 541 (1967); that is, "to be resolved on a case-by-case basis." What is said in this case regarding the noncompliance with a Notice of Inspection does not apply to the noncompliance with an administrative inspection warrant issued under the Federal Controlled Substances Act. The DEA regulations indicate that a person subject to the CSA law may refuse inspection pursuant to a Notice of Inspection (DEA Form 82), but refusing inspection or interfering with it in the face of a court-issued administrative inspection warrant could result in an arrest. (See DEA regulation 1316.12.)

🔨 🔨 🔨

United States v Goldfine
538 F.2d 815 (9th Cir., 1976)

ISSUE: Whether an administrative inspection warrant is sufficient basis for collection of evidence of commission of a crime or whether a criminal search warrant is required.

FACTS: Two pharmacists, who are brothers, were convicted of violations. One brother, who was owner of one pharmacy and part owner of another, was convicted of a nine-count indictment and received concurrent sentences of 1 to 5 years in jail plus a $45,000 fine. The other brother, an employee pharmacist, received concurrent sentences of 1 to 3 years without fine on a five-count conviction.

Both brothers were involved in a pharmacy operation whereby out-of-state purchases of controlled drugs were made, paid for by money orders purchased with cash, and no records kept showing the orders, receipt, or disposition of the drugs. The pharmacy also made other purchases of controlled drugs, paid by check, with records maintained as to acquisition and disposition. However, the drugs purchased out-of-state were sold to addicts for exorbitant profits.

United States v Goldfine
538 F.2d 815 (9th Cir., 1976)
...continued

The convictions were obtained upon evidence obtained by a DEA drug audit of the pharmacy pursuant to an inspection warrant issued under 21 U.S.C. §880(b) and (d) [under §510(b) and (d) of the Act.] In appealing the convictions, the pharmacist brothers contended, through their attorneys, that "the audit was not an administrative inspection, but, in truth, was a search for evidence of a crime and that a showing under traditional standards of probable cause to suppose that evidence of crime was present, and seizing was necessary, in order to support the warrant." Note: The contention here is if the DEA has cause to suppose a violation was committed, it should get a search warrant and not use an inspection warrant as a substitute.

RULING: The court did not accept the above contention. To do so would exempt every pharmacist suspected of violating the CSA law from the administrative inspection procedure, and the court would not allow such a result.

REASONING: The court indicated that if evidence of commission of a crime is sought, which evidence could not be disclosed by an administrative inspection, then, a search warrant specifying such evidence would be required. But in the instant case, the DEA obtained evidence of a crime from an inspection conducted under an administrative inspection warrant, the application for which merely specified that the registrant's establishment had not previously been inspected. In the court's view, this was sufficient for sustaining the inspection warrant as proper.

In the course of the DEA investigation, one of the pharmacists, after receiving the Miranda warnings, was asked by the DEA if he had made out-of-state purchases. The DEA knew he had. He stated that he had not. The false reply resulted in a conviction for violating 19 U.S.C.§ 1001, which prohibits anyone from knowingly and willfully falsifying or covering up a material fact in any matter within the jurisdiction of any department or agency of the United States. On the appeal of the conviction, the majority of the appeals court affirmed the conviction. One judge, however, disagreed with the majority on this issue because the DEA had not relied on the false statement. The dissenting judge wrote a lengthy opinion in which he indicated that the purpose of said §1001 was to prevent willful submission of false statements to federal agencies inducing action or reliance thereon, but here there was no such reliance on the false statement.

United States v Pugh
417 F.Supp. 1019 (W.D. Mich. 1976)

ISSUE: Whether consent to administrative inspection and audit constitutes consent to seize physical evidence.

FACTS: This case involves a seizure of prescriptions by the DEA after inspection of a pharmacy pursuant to a Notice of Inspection (see §510[c][1]) of the Act or 21 U.S.C. §880[c][1] and regulation 1316.08[b]). The inspection was made on the basis of the alleged consent of the pharmacist to the inspection (audit and seizure) and on the premise that this was a case in which a warrant (search warrant or inspection warrant) was not "constitutionally required." The pharmacist sought to have the seized evidence suppressed on the grounds that the search and seizure violated his Fourth Amendment rights. The court agreed.

United States v Pugh
417 F.Supp. 1019 (W.D. Mich. 1976)
...continued

RULING: Seizure of physical evidence pursuant to consent in this case was impermissible. A warrant should have been obtained.

REASONING: The court found that while consent to an audit was present, the consent to the seizure of prescriptions was not. This case was directly in line with the *Enserro* case. Further, the court found that since an inspection warrant was easy for the DEA to obtain, there was no excuse for not obtaining one. The court suppressed the evidence seized; that is, the prescriptions could not be used as evidence against the pharmacist.

United States v Schiffman
572 F.2d 1137 (5th Cir., 1978)

ISSUE: Whether evidence found pursuant to a warrantless administrative inspection of a pharmacy may be used for conviction of a federal offense.

FACTS: A pharmacist was convicted in federal court in a nonjury trial for conspiracy to possess and distribute controlled drugs and distribution of same, and for furnishing false information in records required by law to be kept...in violation of §401(a)(1) (or 21 U.S.C. §841[a][1]) and §403(a)(4) of the controlled Substances Act (or 21 U.S.C. §843[a][4]). The pharmacist appealed the conviction; the conviction was affirmed by the U.S. Court of Appeals, Fifth Circuit.

A summary of the reported facts leading up to the conviction: Sometime in 1976, Florida police arrested a man for illegal sale of controlled drugs and the police found bottles of *Tuinal* in the suspect's apartment. The *Tuinal* bottles contained the manufacturer's labeling and the police contacted the DEA. The latter was able to trace the manufacturer's distribution of the *Tuinal* (a Schedule II substance) to one of two pharmacies in the area. The DEA then contacted the Florida Board of Pharmacy to aid in the investigation and a board inspector conducted an inspection of one pharmacist's store. The board inspector found that large amounts of drugs could not be accounted for. The state inspector then informed the DEA of this finding. Note: Under Florida law, a warrantless inspection of a pharmacy under §465-131 of the Florida statutes precludes the state from using the fruits of the inspection in a subsequent criminal prosecution - based on *Olson v State*, 287 So. 2d 313.

Since the Florida board could not use the evidence obtained on the inspection, the information was furnished to the DEA which conducted its own inspection under an administrative inspection warrant issued under 21 U.S.C. §880(d) (or Section 510[d] of the Controlled Substances Act).

The DEA inspection showed that the pharmacist could not account for 90% of his drug purchases.

The pharmacist sought a reversal of his conviction on the sole ground that the evidence obtained on the DEA inspection should have been suppressed — that is to say, the claim is the inspection warrant was invalid and, hence, the evidence obtained from the inspection is inadmissible in court. The pharmacist claimed that the inspection warrant was issued on the strength of the information supplied to the DEA by the Florida state inspector — which information was statutorily prohibited from use in Florida state courts.

United States v Schiffman
572 F.2d 1137 (5th Cir., 1978)
...continued

RULING: In answering the pharmacist's claim, the Federal Appeals Court did not address itself to the issue stated but, instead, held that there were enough other facts to support the "probable cause" requirement for a valid issuance of an administrative inspection warrant.

REASONING: In its decision, the court made the following rules of law. First, it indicated that an administrative inspection warrant under 21 U.S.C. §880(d) may issue only on "probable cause." However, the act defines such "probable cause" differently from Fourth Amendment type of "probable cause" required for search warrants. "Probable cause" in the context of the CSA law means:

> ...a valid public interest in the effective enforcement of this subchapter of regulations thereunder sufficient to justify administrative inspections of the area, premises, building, or conveyance, or contents thereof, in the circumstance specified in the application for the warrant.

Further the court states:

> The precise question is whether large purchases of controlled drugs by a registered retail pharmacy alone create such a valid public interest. We hold that they do.

> ...a potential registrant is put on notice that, as a condition of engaging in the manufacture or distribution of drugs, he subjects himself to the regulatory system imposed by the Act including administrative inspections by the DEA as authorized by §880.

> ...several courts have held that there is a 'valid public interest' in ensuring compliance with the recordkeeping requirements of the Act, and that a warrant may be issued simply because a substantial period time has passed since the last inspection. (citations omitted)

In the instant case, the drugstore was registered to dispense controlled substances and had never previously been inspected (or at least never been previously inspected by the DEA). In light of its positions as stated above, the court easily sustained the conviction.

Weyerhauser Co v Marshall
452 F.Supp. 1375 (E.D. Wisc. 1978)

ISSUE: Whether the information provided by the Occupational Safety and Health Administration (OSHA) to the federal magistrate in this case was sufficient to support granting an administrative inspection warrant.

FACTS: This is a case involving inspection under OSHA, 28 U.S.C. §657(a). Compliance inspectors came to inspect a manufacturing plant pursuant to a complaint being filed with OSHA that the conditions at the plant threatened physical injury to employees. Inspection was initially refused, and OSHA then obtained a federal inspection warrant issued by a magistrate.

In the face of the inspection warrant, the employer yielded to entry and inspection but only "under protest." The inspection took place on three separate days and resulted in cita-

Weyerhauser Co v Marshall
452 F.Supp. 1375 (E.D. Wisc. 1978)
...continued

tions for violations. The employer went to U.S. District Court on motions for (1) an injunction against OSHA enforcing its citations; (2) an order quashing the inspection warrants and suppressing the evidence obtained thereunder; a declaration that its Fourth and Fifth Amendment rights had been violated and that §8(a) of the OSHA law is unconstitutional; (3) the return of all evidence seized on the search; and (4) for certain other relief.

OSHA counterclaimed with a motion to dismiss the defendant's motion(s) on the basis that the defendant did not exhaust its administrative remedies before seeking the aid of the court. Citing a number of supporting cases, the court held that an administrative inspection warrant may be challenged in district court without first exhausting administrative remedies. As to the other issues presented by the defendant's motions, the crucial test was whether the inspection warrant was valid.

RULING: The court granted the employer's motions to quash the inspection warrant and to suppress the evidence seized. The court also gave the employer a permanent injunction, or relief, from the OSHA citations against him in connection with alleged violations disclosed by the inspection.

REASONING: Whether the warrant was valid depended on whether it was supported by "probable cause." The application for the warrant sought to demonstrate probable cause on the basis of "an existing violation on the premises (as evidenced by the employee complaint) and on the basis of an 'inspection program designed to assure compliance with the act'."

As to the issue that the employee complaint was (per se) "probable cause" to support issuance of the inspection warrant, the court found fault with OSHA's argument. In its warrant application, OSHA merely recited existence of the complaint without detailing the nature of alleged violations. The federal magistrate was then presented with less information to satisfy himself that probable cause existed to believe a violation was committed than OSHA, who had the benefit of the full complaint. The court stated:

> ...if the warrant procedure is to be anything more than a rubber stamp proceeding, the defendants [OSHA] must be required to do more than read the statute to the magistrate. Yet, the defendant's compliance officer's application did little more here...the nature of the alleged violation was not described in any form.

Another "probable cause" for the issuance of the inspection warrant was the claim in the application that "inspection is to assure compliance with the act." But the court ruled that this did not satisfy the "neutral criteria" in the guidelines of the U.S. Supreme Court's decision in *Marshall v Barlow's Inc.* — that is, "reasonable legislative or administrative standards for conducting an inspection with respect to a particular establishment."

Another issue in the case was whether §8(a) of the OSHA law was constitutional. This issue was now decided in the *Barlow* case, where the court held warrantless inspections under §8(a) unconstitutional but permissible if conducted with a *proper* warrant. (Again, the inspection warrant in the instant case was improper for lack of acceptable, "probable cause.")

All other arguments failing, OHSA then claimed the inspection was with consent since the employer eventually allowed entry and inspection. But the court found otherwise since upon seeing the inspection warrant, the employer allowed inspection but only "under protest."

Weyerhauser Co v Marshall
452 F.Supp. 1375 (E.D. Wisc. 1978)
...continued

The court also indicated that a search conducted upon a warrant cannot later be justified on consent if the warrant turns out to be invalid (citing *Bumper v North Carolina*, 391 U.S. 543).

Hosto v Brickell
577 S.W.2d 401 (Ark. 1979)

ISSUE: Whether an audit of pharmacy records may be conducted without an administrative inspection warrant, a criminal search warrant or consent of the pharmacist and whether the proceeds of the audit may be used in a proceeding against the pharmacist.

FACTS: An Arkansas pharmacist had his license suspended as result of charges stemming from a drug accountability audit conducted by the Division of Drug Control. The audit was conducted without a search warrant or administrative inspection warrant and without consent of the pharmacist. The pharmacist appealed the suspension order to the circuit court, which reversed it and dismissed the charges against him on the basis that the inspection was without warrant or consent and, thus, in excess of the agency's statutory authority. On appeal by the state, the Arkansas Supreme Court reversed the circuit court and remanded the case back for further proceedings.

The reported facts of the case are sparse. When the inspectors arrived at the pharmacy, the pharmacist asked them their purpose and if they had a search warrant. They responded that they did not need a search warrant. The pharmacist answered "there was not much he could do" and tried to contact his attorney. A comprehensive audit of the pharmacy prescription records was conducted over a 2-day period. The court found that he did not consent to the inspection but his actions were "...an acquiescence to an assertion of lawful authority under the circumstances shown to exist." However, the real issue, the court felt, was the propriety of the audit without a warrant.

RULING: Here the court held that a warrant was not constitutionally required.

REASONING: The court stated as follows:

> In a business where there is a legitimate public interest and close regulation, such as the distribution of drugs, procedure for issuance of a warrant prior to an administration is not constitutionally required.

The court cited as authority, *U.S. v Biswell*, 406 U.S. 311 (1972) and *State v Albuquerque Publishing Company*, 571 P.2d 117 (1977).

Upon a review of the applicable Arkansas statutes regulating pharmacy practice, the court noted that §82-2626 provided for administrative inspection warrants "when constitutionally required." Other statutes of the state relating to narcotic drugs required the pharmacist to retain narcotic prescriptions on file and have such readily accessible for inspection by officers engaged in the enforcement of the narcotic laws. The court concluded that "Inspection is clearly crucial to the regulatory scheme. Unannounced inspections without a warrant are crucial to a proper enforcement of the applicable laws through effective inspection...The

Hosto v Brickell
577 S.W.2d 401 (Ark. 1979)
...continued

inspection of records in this case was not such that the prior issuance of a warrant was constitutionally required."

United States v Nechy
827 F.2d 1161 (7th Cir. 1987)

ISSUE: Whether evidence obtained under an administrative inspection warrant may be used
in a criminal prosecution.

FACTS: The defendant-pharmacist was charged in federal district court (Eastern District,
Wis.) of possessing with intent to distribute and distributing a controlled substance and aiding and abetting the distribution of controlled substances. A DEA compliance investigator obtained an administrative inspection warrant under 21 U.S. Code 880 on the basis of
the investigator's affidavit that the pharmacy was registered with DEA, had never been
inspected before, and was buying pentazocine in suspiciously large quantities. Defendant's
motion for suppression of the evidence was denied and the pharmacist was convicted as
charged.

RULING: The court of appeals affirmed defendant's conviction and judgment of the district
court.

REASONING: The administrative search of the pharmacy was objectively reasonable and
the investigator's motive behind the administrative search, even if it was to gather evidence
for a criminal prosecution, was immaterial.

The court also held that participation of local police officers in the search did not require
the seized evidence to be suppressed, and the variance between the indictment and the government's proof that the defendant engaged in "dispersing" rather than "distributing" controlled substances was harmless.

Ohio v Desper
Slip Op No JE 30 (December 20, 2002), 2002 Ohio 7176; 2002 Ohio App. LEXIS 6963.

An agent of the Ohio State Board of Pharmacy was assigned to administratively inspect the
prescription records of pharmacies. He found inconsistencies with regard to the prescriptions written by oxycodone. He obtained the pharmaceutical records of 1000 to 1500 citizens. The number was then lowered to 10 by consulting a pharmacist on the Board. The agent
then contacted 3 physicians who wrote the prescriptions to those patients. The owner of
the pharmacy was also a patient of the 3 physicians. Each of them told the agent that they
issued prescriptions for controlled substances to the pharmacist and were unaware that he
was seeing other physicians. The pharmacist was indicted for obtaining controlled substances
prescriptions by fraud. At his criminal trial, the pharmacist sought to suppress all of the
statements given by the physicians without his consent. The trial Court ordered the suppression of all evidence seized without a search warrant from defendant's pharmacies, and the
suppression of all statements given by defendant's physicians without his consent. The state

Ohio v Desper
Slip Op No JE 30 (December 20, 2002), 2002 Ohio 7176; 2002 Ohio App. LEXIS 6963.
...continued

appealed on the issues of whether obtaining pharmaceutical records without a search warrant violates the Fourteenth Amendment of the Constitution and whether the questionnaires given to pharmacists' physicians by an agent from the State Board of Pharmacy constituted a communication protected by the physician-patient privilege. The appellate court held the trial court erred in finding *Ohio Rev. Code Ann. § § 3719.13, .27* and *Ohio Admin. Code §4729-5-29* unconstitutional. In the warrantless search at issue, the discovery of evidence of penal violations was incidental to the administrative search, and not its objective, since the purpose behind the search was to monitor controlled substance dispensing. Since the physician-patient privilege was not a constitutional privacy right, the trial court incorrectly suppressed the evidence based upon that reason. The questionnaires did not violate defendant's physician-patient privilege because lies were not communications as defined by the statute. The judgment of the trial court was reversed and the matter was remanded for further proceedings.

The following is a list of court cases that are related to this topic.

Mark v Williams, 724 P.2d 428 (Wash. App. 1986)
United States v Enserro, 401 F. Suppl 460 (1975)

Penalties

1962 Ford Thunderbird v Div. of Narcotic Control
198 N.E.2d 155 (Ill. App. Ct. 1964)

ISSUE: Whether the defendant's automobile may be confiscated when she unlawfully possessed narcotics pursuant to a prescription that had been post-dated.

FACTS: The defendant was arrested, by virtue of an arrest warrant, and in the process of the arrest was found to possess six vials of *Dolophine*. The *Dolophine* was obtained from a pharmacy, pursuant to prescriptions signed by a physician who had "post-dated" or dated the prescriptions later than the day on which they were signed. The prescriptions had been filled after the physician had died. The Illinois Division of Narcotic Control, pursuant to a hearing, found that the defendant's automobile was, as a "matter of law" used in the unlawful transportation of narcotics, and, thereby, the Narcotic Division confiscated the car. The Illinois Uniform Narcotic Act provided for confiscation of the vehicle. The Narcotic Division's confiscation was based on a finding that the Division's administrative rule regarding the dating of narcotic prescriptions had been violated by the defendant and, therefore, the defendant unlawfully possessed the narcotics. The defendant appealed the confiscation to an Illinois court which set aside the confiscation. The Narcotic Division then appealed the case to the Illinois Appellate Court.

It appears from the reported facts of the case that the defendant and her husband had both received prescriptions for *Dolophine* from their physician who would write out several prescriptions at a time but would postdate them to dates when he believed his patients would require them.

On the appeal of the case, the Narcotic Division contended that such prescriptions were void (even if the doctor had not died) since rule 5 of the Division's regulations provided "All prescriptions for narcotic drugs...shall be signed and dated by the practitioners...as of the

1962 Ford Thunderbird v Div. of Narcotic Control
198 N.E.2d 155 (Ill. App. Ct. 1964)
...continued

day on which issued." It was argued by the Division that the Illinois Narcotic Act required that "A pharmacist, in good faith, may sell and dispense narcotic drugs to any person upon a written prescription of a physician...dated and signed by the person prescribing on the day when issued..." The Illinois Uniform Narcotic Act further limited narcotic prescribing to "only in such quantity and for such length of times as are reasonably necessary."

RULING: The Illinois court set aside the confiscation of the automobile based upon its interpretation of state law regarding post-date prescription.

REASONING: The Illinois Appellate Court affirmed the lower court's decision to set aside the confiscation of the car, but in its written memorandum, the court stated:

> "...a physician may prescribe narcotic drugs, in good faith, to a patient when the patient is suffering from a disease or ailment, in quantity, and for a time reasonably necessary **so long as he dates the prescription on the date they may be required for such length of time.** The pharmacist is authorized to sell and dispense such prescriptions **only on the dates they bear.**" (Emphasis added.)

At the time of this Illinois case, the court's ruling was at odds with the Federal Narcotics Act (the Harrison Narcotic Act) as it existed at that time. The former federal narcotic law, §4705(c)(2)(A) required prescriptions for Class A narcotics to be dated as of the date signed. There was no prohibition in the federal law then, or now, which would prohibit a pharmacist from filling such prescriptions, in good faith, even if dated and written a few days or weeks before the time presented for refilling. While this Illinois case appears to permit (pre-dating) post-dating of narcotic prescriptions, the ruling conflicts with the federal regulation then in effect which required dating of narcotic prescriptions as of the date of issue or signature.

The current law on the matter of dating prescriptions for controlled substances is that the prescription must be dated as of, and signed on, the date when issued...see DEA Reg. 1306.05. Consequently, this Illinois court rule is still in conflict with the federal rule. The pharmacist should not fill prescriptions for controlled substances where the date is not the date of issuance. However, there is no prohibition in the federal law for the pharmacist to insert the date of issuance...where such date is known to the pharmacist and the prescriber merely inserted the wrong date through inadvertence or ignorance of the law. But, again, the matter of "good faith" in filling the controlled substance prescription enters the picture and, where the prescriber's post-dating indicates his bad faith in issuance of the prescription, the pharmacist should not fill it.

The following is a list of court cases that are related to this topic.

State v Poleyeff, 1993 Ohio App. LEXIS 2483
United States v Poulin, 926 F.2d 246 (D. Mass. 1996)

Conflicts with State Laws

United States v Oakland Cannabis Buyers' Co.
190 F 3d 1109 (9th Cir 1999), modified, Nos 99-15838, 99-15844 and 99-15879 (May 10, 1999), 2000 US App LEXIS 9963, application for stay granted, No 00A145 (Aug 29, 2000), US SCt, 2000 US LEXIS 4832

The Oakland Cannabis Buyers' Cooperative ("OCBC") appealed a preliminary injunction to stop the distribution of cannabis in the wake of California's Initiative (Proposition 215) supporting the medical use of marijuana. The district court held that distribution of marijuana by cannabis clubs, including OCBC likely violated the Comprehensive Drug Abuse Prevention and Control Act of 1970, 21 U.S.C. § 841(a)(1). OCBC appealed an order denying its motion to modify the injunction to permit cannabis distribution to persons having a doctor's certificate stating that marijuana is a medical necessity for them. OCBC asked the district court to modify the injunction to allow cannabis distribution to patients who certify that: (1) the patient suffers from a serious medical condition; (2) if the patient does not have access to cannabis, the patient will suffer imminent harm; (3) cannabis is necessary for the treatment of the patient's medical condition; and (4) there is no legal alternative to cannabis for the effective treatment of the patient's medical condition. The district court denied OCBC's motion, stating that it lacked the power to make the modification because to do so would force the district court to ignore federal law. The 9th Circuit initially reversed, holding that the district court was not asked to ignore federal law, rather to take into account a legally cognizable defense. The 9th Circuit found that the district court failed to analyze OCBC's evidence of a class of people with serious medical conditions for whom the use of cannabis is necessary to treat their conditions and for whom there is no legal alternative to cannabis. Therefore, 9th Circuit reversed the order denying modification and remanded with instructions for the district court to reconsider OCBC's request for a modification to allow cannabis distribution to seriously ill individuals who need marijuana for medical purposes. In a later opinion, the Court of Appeals instructed the district court to consider the Fifth Amendment Rights of the claimants. The Supreme Court granted an emergency request from the U.S. Justice Department for injunctive relief preventing a California clinic from distributing marijuana to patients for medicinal use. The emergency stay does not end the case, which is still under review in the 9th Circuit.

Use of the US Postal Service

The following is a list of court cases that are related to this topic.

Cooper v Missouri State Board of Pharmacy, 774 S.W. 2d 501 (Mo. App. 1989)

PART X: EMPLOYMENT LAW

CONTRACTUAL ISSUES

Express Contract (Just Cause Termination)

Brannan v Wyeth Laboratories, Inc.
526 So.2d 1101 (La. 1988)

ISSUE: Whether a pharmaceutical manufacturer was liable for breach of employment contract, defamation, and wrongful denial of stock option rights in a lawsuit by one of its sales representatives.

FACTS: The plaintiff, Edwin Brannan, began work for Wyeth Laboratories in September, 1964. Eighteen years later, he was terminated for falsifying physician call reports. He testified that he was concerned about job security when he first interviewed with Wyeth. It was made clear to him that he was applying for a permanent position and that he would be able to keep the job as long as he performed satisfactorily.

The plaintiff also claimed that Wyeth had a policy not to terminate without a reasonable just cause. If there was a problem with his job performance, he would be placed on probation and given an appropriate length of time in which to correct it. The plaintiff relied upon these statements, along with some signed documents, to show that he had an oral employment contract for a definite term — until he reached retirement age. Most of the documents upon which the plaintiff relied were standard forms that referred to the employee reaching normal retirement age.

In 1979, the plaintiff was placed on a performance improvement program in order to increase his number of daily calls on physicians. His average did not change after the performance improvement program. While the plaintiff received raises each year, they were not the highest raises given because they were tied to his sales. While the plaintiff showed an increase in sales over the years of his employment, it was claimed this was partially due to new products and increased prices.

Several physicians complained about attempts to place orders with the plaintiff. It was further alleged that he did not call upon the physicians on a regular basis. Wyeth conducted a two-day surveillance of the plaintiff and also visited a number of physicians in the plaintiff's territory in Louisiana. This investigation resulted in the plaintiff's termination for falsifying physician call reports. The plaintiff was given the option of resigning, but he refused.

RULING: The trial court awarded the plaintiff damages of $300,000 for breach of the employment contract, $250,000 for defamation, and $40,000 for denial of stock option rights. The appellate court reversed the trial court's judgment.

REASONING: Louisiana law holds that an employment contract for life or for an indefinite term is terminable at the will of either party. The Louisiana courts have previously stated that an employee is never assumed to engage in his services permanently, thereby cutting him off from all chances of improving his condition.

The oral contract of employment was terminable at will. In addition, the pharmaceutical company had established just cause for termination. There was considerable evidence by independent witnesses confirming that there had been complaints from physicians about the plaintiff not calling on them regularly. In light of the evidence, even if there had been a contract, which could have run until the plaintiff's retirement, the defendant had just cause to terminate the plaintiff's employment.

Brannan v Wyeth Laboratories, Inc.
526 So.2d 1101 (La. 1988)
...continued

The plaintiff also alleged that Wyeth employees defamed him by saying that he was, "...terminated for arriving late at work, leaving work early, and falsifying company records." The plaintiff alleged that these statements were false and made without substantiation and with malice, and resulted in damage to his reputation. The court concluded that there was ample evidence to find that the statements actually made were true and therefore were not defamatory.

Wyeth's stock option plan provided that terminated employees were entitled to exercise the option within 90 days of termination. However, the exercise of the option was not permitted if the employee was fired for "gross misconduct" or if the employee voluntarily resigned. Although the plaintiff's actions amounted to misconduct, and justified the termination of his employment, the court did not find that his conduct amounted to "gross misconduct" such that he should be denied the stock option rights which he sought to exercise.

Implied Contract (At Will Termination)

Diberardinis-Mason v Superfresh
No 99-3410 (April 14, 2000), USDC E PA, 2000 US Dist LEXIS 4787

The plaintiff was hired as a pharmacist to work in an A & P Supermarket pharmacy in the Philadelphia area after being interviewed in February 1997. On her application, she indicated that she was leaving her current employment because there was no chance for advancement. In reality, she was fired after it was discovered that there was a shortage of several controlled substances, including the weight-loss drug, phentermine, in the pharmacy that she managed. (Her claims against the prior employer for sex discrimination were settled before the current action.) After completing her training period, several other employees began complaining about the pharmacist's performance. She was transferred to another pharmacy, but complaints about her behavior continued. She also dispensed the wrong medication on at least one occasion. During a meeting to address the problems, allegations were made that several tablets of phentermine were missing. She abruptly left the meeting and was terminated. After suit was filed for wrongful termination, the defendant moved for summary judgment on the grounds that the pharmacist was an at-will employee who could be terminated for any reason under Pennsylvania law. The only exception is when termination results in a violation of a clear public policy. The pharmacist claimed she was fired because she engaged in union organizing activities with her prior employer and she was cooperating with state officials investigating dispensing irregularities in her pharmacies. The Court disagreed, finding that there is no affirmative duty on the part of pharmacists to report suspicious behavior to the authorities. As to her claim involving union organizing activities, her remedy would be available under NLRA regulations and not state civil liabilities. The Court further reasoned that the defendant has ample legitimate reasons to fire the pharmacist because she had lied on her application, she dispensed the wrong medication and there was evidence of phentermine missing from the inventory she was responsible for.

Peiper v Modern Pharmacy Consultants, Inc.
1992 WL 366936 (Ohio App. 11th Dist.)

ISSUE: Whether a pharmacist who was discharged from employment, after quitting a previous job and moving over 1,000 miles, could sue for breach of promise.

FACTS: Brian Peiper, the plaintiff in this action, is a pharmacist who responded to a job advertisement in the Cleveland Plain Dealer. At the time, pharmacist Peiper was employed in Boca Raton, Florida. The plaintiff wrote a letter to the defendant, Modern Pharmacy Consultants, expressing an interest in the position of pharmacy purchasing specialist, which was being advertised. The plaintiff also submitted his resume and, in his cover letter, expressed his desire to return to the Cleveland area.

Two weeks later, Peiper was invited to visit Cleveland for an interview. He interviewed with the president of Modern Pharmacy Consultants and also toured the defendant's facility and met with his eventual supervisor.

Three days after an interview, the plaintiff called the defendant. A position as a consultant pharmacist was offered, not as a purchasing specialist (the job for which the plaintiff applied). Peiper's salary was $45,000 per year with insurance and vacation benefits. The plaintiff informed the defendant that he would sell his Florida home after his daughter's school term ended and would move to Cleveland to start the job shortly thereafter. The defendant agreed to this plan.

In response to the plaintiff's request, the defendant offered the plaintiff $1,000 for moving expenses. At no time was the plaintiff offered employment for a guaranteed period of time. The plaintiff eventually sold his home in Florida and purchased a house in the Cleveland area. The bank required a verification of employment form to be completed. On this form the defendant responded that the plaintiff's "probability of continued employment was very good."

When the plaintiff asked the defendant's general manager whether he was subject to a probationary period, the plaintiff was informed that "you are a professional, and you are not subject to a probationary period." The general manager later denied making this exact statement, but he did say that he told the plaintiff that the 90-day evaluation was not a formal "sit-down" evaluation.

The plaintiff worked for the defendant from July 24 to October 31. He was terminated thereafter and was told he was not a team player. The plaintiff was also told that he did not pass his probationary period. The plaintiff claimed that he would never have resigned his job in Florida, sold his house there, and moved his family, if he had known he was subject to a probationary period and could be discharged without cause.

Immediately following his termination, the plaintiff was hired as a full-time pharmacist at a local discount retail pharmacy. He received $48,000 a year and became obligated to remain for at least one year.

RULING: The court found that none of the representations by the defendant were promises to the pharmacist that he would be employed for any specific period of time. The pharmacist's case was dismissed.

REASONING: The presumption in Ohio employment law is that employment contracts are terminable at will by either party. There is, however, a promissory estoppel exception to an employer's unfettered right to discharge an employee-at-will. The test for determining whether the promissory estoppel exception is applicable in a given instance is whether the

Peiper v Modern Pharmacy Consultants, Inc.
1992 WL 366936 (Ohio App. 11th Dist.)
...continued

employer should have reasonably expected its representation to be relied upon by its employees, and if so, whether the expected action was detrimental to the employee.

Standing alone, praise of job performance and a discussion of future career development and benefits will not modify the employment-at-will relationship. The plaintiff must demonstrate detrimental reliance on specific promises of job security in order to create an exception. Under this test, the plaintiff's attempt to establish promissory estoppel failed. The plaintiff did not come forth with evidence of a specific promise by the defendant that he would not be terminated except "for cause." Instead, the plaintiff identified the bank verification form on which the defendant indicated the plaintiff's probability of continued employment was "very good." In addition, it was alleged that the general manager told him that he was not subject to a probationary period.

The defendant's statement to the bank was solicited by the plaintiff prior to the commencement of his employment. Certainly the defendant's expression of the probability of the plaintiff's continued employment was accurate, given the fact that the plaintiff was about to be given work. Similarly, the defendant's general manager did not represent to the plaintiff that the employment was for any period of time. Instead the general manager's statement dealt with the review procedures engaged in by the defendant. Taken on its face, the statement made by the general manager was viewed by the court as a neutral one.

Of equal importance in this case was the failure by the plaintiff to demonstrate detrimental reliance. While the plaintiff points to moving expenses and other costs, the court notes that one month after his termination, the plaintiff obtained employment which paid him $3,000 more annually, and since that time he has received a $2,500 raise. In addition, the plaintiff admitted that he was seeking employment that would return him to the Cleveland area.

Urfer v St. Vincent Medical Center
Slip Op. No. L-00-1046 (October 27, 2000), 2000 Ohio App. LEXIS 4971

The pharmacist worked for defendant hospital for 21 years until he was terminated by defendant after he received a poor performance evaluation. The pharmacist sued for breach of contract and fraud. The hospital sought summary judgment. After plaintiff withdrew his claim for fraud, the trial court granted summary judgment. The appellate court affirmed. The plaintiff was an employee at-will. The pharmacist signed a statement acknowledging his understanding of his status as an at-will employee. He failed to present any evidence to support an implication that the hospital had contractually agreed to deal with him honestly and fairly. The appeals court determined that the trial court did not err when it failed to recognize a public policy exception to the employment-at-will doctrine because the pharmacist failed to set forth a cause of action for wrongful discharge in violation of public policy.

Roberson v Wal-Mart Stores
(Ariz. Ct. of Appeals, April 23, 2002)

The plaintiff worked for Wal-Mart as a pharmacist. Wal-Mart had an employee handbook that contained a number of at-will disclaimers. It also contained a "performance coaching" policy. The performance coaching policy included four progressive steps: 1) coach and counsel, 2) verbal reminder, 3) written reminder, and 4) a decision-making day. The decision-making day was a day off with pay given to an employee so the employee could decide if he or she wanted to continue working for Wal-Mart. On January 25, 1993, the pharmacist got into an argument with his assistant store manager in front of several customers. The next day, his coach met with him and delivered a written improvement plan that he asked the pharmacist to sign. He refused and the coach fired him without giving him a decision-making day. The trial court concluded that in doing so, the pharmacist's coach violated the performance coaching procedures. Applying Arizona common law, a majority of the three-member panel on the Court of Appeals held that the disclaimers given to the pharmacist in his employee handbook and other employment documents concerning the at-will nature of his employment were adequate to prevent any reasonable expectation that his employment was anything other than at-will. These disclaimers were found in the pharmacist's employment application, in the handbook itself, and in his manager's bonus plan. Additionally, the performance coaching policy itself stated that employees were not entitled to "any disciplinary procedures." One judge on the Court of Appeals dissented arguing that although the majority had articulated a reasonable rule of law, he believed the matter was a question of fact that was properly submitted to the jury. The dissenting judge also pointed to Wal-Mart's consistent application of its performance coaching process and testimony from Wal-Mart witnesses that the process had always been followed. He noted that the pharmacist also testified that he relied upon the performance coaching process. This evidence, according to the dissenting judge, was adequate to support the jury's verdict.

Overtime Pay

Caperci v Rite Aid
Slip Op No C.A. NO. 95-12720-RCL (August 18, 1998), USDC MA, 43 F. Supp. 2d 83; 1998 U.S. Dist. LEXIS 21498

Twenty-one pharmacists who are presently or formerly employed by Rite Aid brought suit under the Fair Labor Standards Act ("FLSA"), 29 U.S.C. § 201 et seq., alleging the employer failed to pay them overtime compensation in accordance with the requirements of 29 U.S.C. § 207(a), which requires, with certain exceptions that employer pay overtime at the rate of one-and-a-half times the employee's regular rate for hours worked by employee in excess of 40 during any week. Rite Aid concedes that plaintiffs and the thousands of other pharmacists employed by its subsidiaries are not paid overtime in accordance with the FLSA, but it claims that they are not entitled to it because they are covered by the exemption for salaried professionals. The pharmacists agree that they are professionals, but they deny that they are salaried. Therefore, the only dispute is whether the pharmacists are salaried within the meaning of applicable law. Rite Aid moved for summary judgment on the ground that pharmacists are salaried and are therefore exempt from the FLSA's overtime requirements. Under the applicable law, an employee is considered to be paid "on a salary basis" if under his employment agreement he regularly receives each pay period on a weekly, or less frequent basis, a predetermined amount constituting all or part of his compensation, which amount is not subject to reduction because of variations in the quality or quantity of the work performed. Subject to certain exceptions, the employee must receive his full salary for any week in which he performs any work without regard to the number of days

Caperci v Rite Aid

Slip Op No C.A. NO. 95-12720-RCL (August 18, 1998), USDC MA, 43 F. Supp. 2d 83;
1998 U.S. Dist. LEXIS 21498
...continued

or hours worked. On the other hand, an employee will not be considered to be "on a salary basis" if deductions from his predetermined compensation are made for absences occasioned by the employer or by the operating requirement of the business. In this case there is evidence that to assure that at least one pharmacist will be on site during each hour that a Rite Aid pharmacy is open, Rite Aid will typically staff each pharmacy with two pharmacists. When Rite Aid hires a pharmacist, it assigns to him or her a schedule of hours he or she will be expected to work. Taking into account the number of hours scheduled and other factors, such as Rite Aid's needs and the pharmacist's level of experience, a regular, weekly salary is established. Thereafter, Rite Aid carefully monitors the number of hours the pharmacist actually works. If the pharmacist works more hours than he or she was scheduled to work in a week, Rite Aid will customarily pay the pharmacist overtime compensation for the additional hours (although not necessarily at the rate of time and one-half and not necessarily for all hours in excess of 40, if the pharmacist's regular workweek happens to be longer than 40 hours). If the pharmacist must take a partial day absence for personal reasons, Rite Aid will often require the pharmacist to account for the time by requiring that he or she 1) swap hours with another pharmacist who agrees to cover for him or her, 2) pay back the hours by working additional hours on another occasion, or 3) take a charge against accrued vacation pay, based on a rate equal to the pharmacist's regular weekly salary divided by the pharmacist's regular number of hours. For a number of reasons, a pharmacist's regular weekly pay can change from time to time. For example, the regular weekly pay can change if the pharmacist receives a raise based on increased experience or tenure with Rite Aid; if the pharmacist relocates to a different store with different hours of operation; or if Rite Aid and the pharmacist agree to increase or decrease the pharmacist's regular number of hours at the store to which he or she is assigned. The latter can occur either because the pharmacist simply decides that he or she wants to work longer or shorter hours (and Rite Aid concurs) or because the local manager unilaterally decides to change the regular hours of store operation (such as by deciding to close at 9:00 p.m. instead of remaining open until 11:00 p.m.). In each instance, Rite Aid is apt to change the pharmacist's regular weekly pay and to do so, in the case of a raise, based upon a higher imputed hourly rate of pay, or, in the case of a change in the pharmacist's regular number of hours, in direct proportion to the change in hours. Once the new weekly amount of pay is set, however, the pharmacist's gross weekly pay is never reduced below the agreed upon amount. There is no evidence in the summary judgment record that Rite Aid ever took a deduction from, offered or threatened to take a deduction from, or would even have entertained a pharmacist's request to take a deduction from a paycheck as a means of accounting for a pharmacist's partial day absence. Rite Aid may have charged partial day absences to paid leave, but as a matter of law such practice does not defeat plaintiffs' exempt status. For these reasons, the judge concluded that the pharmacists are salaried professionals and granted Rite Aid's motion for summary judgment.

Whistleblowing

Liberatore v Melville
168 F.3d 1326 (D.C.Cir. 1999)

ISSUE: May a pharmacist maintain an action for wrongful discharge against a former employer when he is terminated after threatening to report the employer to the FDA for dispensing adulterated drugs?

Liberatore v Melville
168 F.3d 1326 (D.C.Cir. 1999)
...continued

FACTS: The pharmacist was the manager of the pharmacy department in a retail store in the District of Columbia. In January 1993, the corporate owner of the pharmacy remodeled the store and located the pharmacy department in a glass-enclosed area that protruded beyond the exterior wall of the building housing the store. Soon thereafter, the pharmacist and other pharmacy employees began to notice that there was inadequate temperature control in the pharmacy and that certain drugs were being adversely affected. The pharmacist brought this condition to the attention of his immediate supervisor. He also reported the situation to the next higher supervisor. The temperature in the pharmacy kept rising into the spring and early summer of that year. The pharmacist continued to express his concerns to upper-level management including his observation that the high temperatures were adulterating some drugs. While the management told the pharmacist that they were working on the problem, no action was taken.

In July 1993, the pharmacist contacted an area vice president of CVS and told him that he had a neighbor who is "the number three guy in the FDA" and wondered what the FDA would think about a "7-month delay in a drugstore that can't control the temperature of the pharmacy." That evening, management removed $250,000 of pharmacy inventory from the store and marked it for reclamation and eventual destruction. The pharmacist's immediate supervisor told the pharmacist that an audit showed that some drugs were missing from the inventory. The company and the local police conducted an investigation. On the day the police questioned the pharmacist, he was fired. He was told that he was not terminated because of the drug loss investigation, but because his pharmacist's license had lapsed. Management claimed it learned of the license problem during the inventory investigation.

LAWSUIT: The pharmacist sued the corporation for wrongful discharge claiming that his termination was in retaliation to his threat to report his employer's conduct in creating an environment where drugs were becoming adulterated. He also claimed that the employer's stated reason for the discharge, that his pharmacist license had lapsed, was a mere pretext advanced to cover the employer's real motives. He asserted that the corporation had several other pharmacists in its employ that had lapsed licenses and none of them were ever fired. He also claimed that his immediate supervisor had known about the lapse for several months and was not concerned.

HOLDING: The Circuit Court of Appeals reversed the trial court's grant of summary judgment for the employer and reinstated the pharmacist's claims.

REASONING: In most employment situations, an "at-will" employee may be terminated for any reason or no reason at all. Most jurisdictions, however, have created a "public policy" exception that allows former employees to sue for wrongful discharge if the employer violated some kind of "public policy" in firing the employee. In the District of Columbia, prior cases had limited application of the public policy to situations where the employee is fired after refusing to violate a law. In this case, there were no allegations that the pharmacist was forced to violate any law or risk termination; therefore, the trial court dismissed the pharmacist's lawsuit. The judge reasoned that because the pharmacist continued to voluntarily dispense the drugs in question, he did not present his employer with an outright refusal to violate any specific law. The Court of Appeals, however, interpreted the public policy exception in a broader context. It stated that an employee may maintain a wrongful discharge lawsuit in circumstances other than an outright refusal to violate a law as long as the employer's alleged violation of the law is based on a statute or regulation that embodies a clear public policy issue. The higher court concluded that the Food and Drug Administration regulations governing drug storage conditions do embrace a public policy concern. The regu-

Liberatore v Melville
168 F.3d 1326 (D.C.Cir. 1999)
...continued

lations require the storage of drug products under appropriate conditions of temperature, humidity, and light so that the identity, strength, quality, and purity of the drugs are not affected (21 CFR §211.142[b]). Where failure to comply with these regulations results in adulterated drugs, the violator may be punished by fines, imprisonment, or both (21 CFR §201.1[b]). These laws are designed to protect the public policy exception to the at-will employment doctrine. As such, the pharmacist should have the opportunity to pursue his claims against his former employer.

Liberatore v CVS New York
Slip Op. No. 94-1422 (RWR) (September 5, 2001), DCDC, 2001 US Dist. LEXIS 14097

EDITOR'S NOTE

This opinion is an appeal from a judgment for the plaintiff. An earlier decision entitled *Liberatore v Melville*, reported at 168 F.3d 1326 (summarized above) involving the same parties is an appeal from summary judgment for the defendant that was reversed based on a public policy exception to the at-will doctrine.

A pharmacist employed from 1980 through July 1993 sued CVS alleging that it had wrongfully terminated him because he had threatened to inform the Food and Drug Administration ("FDA") that his CVS store kept prescription drugs at improper temperatures in violation of certain controlled temperature requirements. On the same day that he made his whistleblowing threat, the director of professional and government relations at CVS decided to conduct a drug reclamation process, whereby the store's drug stocks were returned to their respective manufacturers as defective. Although the pharmacist normally would have directed such a reclamation, in this instance, a district manager was ordered to direct the reclamation and not to tell the pharmacist about it to avoid a public relations concern. In a separate incident, CVS initiated an investigation into the district manager's claim that drugs had been missing from this pharmacy for over a month. The district manager produced a written theft form only after the pharmacist made the whistleblowing threat. After the trial in this case, the jury returned a verdict in plaintiff's favor for $1,312,426, consisting of $1.1 million for emotional distress damages and $212,426 for lost earnings. The appeals court held that there was just barely sufficient evidence for a reasonable jury to have found in plaintiff's favor. Therefore, defendant's motion for judgment as a matter of law, or for a new trial, was denied. However, because the jury's emotional distress damage award was excessive, defendant's motion for remittitur (reduction of the judgment) was granted.

The following is a list of court cases that are related to this topic.

Kalman v Grand Union Company. 443 A.2d 728 (N.J. Super.Ct.App.Div. 1982)

Public Policy Retaliation

Dillard v Armed Forces Retirement Home
Slip Op. No. 00-3257 (October 6, 2000), US App. Fed. Cir. 2000 US App. LEXIS 25024

The pharmacist was employed with the United States Navy at the Armed Forces Retirement Home. He was terminated from service following allegations that he was absent without leave, failed to follow leave procedures, allowed his pharmacy license to expire, and verbally abused a patient. He appealed to the Merit Systems Protection Board, who affirmed the rulings of an administrative law judge that the termination was proper. The pharmacist sued in court. The trial court found the Board did not err in failing to find that an alleged understaffing of the pharmacy justified his conduct. The Administrative Law Judge (ALJ) repeatedly articulated that his findings were based, at least in part, on admissions by the pharmacist contraindicating this claim. The ALJ also explained that he simply found the testimony and evidence produced by the agency more credible than that proffered by the pharmacist. Therefore, the court affirmed the Board's decision.

Flores v American Pharmaceutical Services, Inc.
994 P.2d 455 (Colo.App. 1999)

Flores brought an action against American Pharmaceutical Services for wrongful termination of employment in violation of public policy. Flores was a computer system support coordinator for American Pharmaceutical. In March 1996, Flores overheard a conversation at the pharmacy. American Pharmaceutical's area sales manager told a pharmacy technician to bill a certain prescription to American Pharmaceutical's health insurance provider and stated that the insurance company "will never know they are paying for a cancer drug for a dog." The next day, Flores overheard another conversation between the pharmacy technician and a staff pharmacist. The staff pharmacist explained to the pharmacy technician that what he was asked to do was illegal and that the staff pharmacist would have no part in it. The staff pharmacist asked Flores to obtain information about the prescription. After acquiring the information, Flores contacted a supervisor and informed him of the incidents. In June 1996, Flores was terminated, purportedly for inappropriate use of the computer system and accessing confidential information. Flores brought suit for a wrongful discharge in violation of public policy. The public policy exception to the at-will employment doctrine is grounded on the principal that an employer should be prohibited from discharging an employee for reasons that contravene substantial and widely accepted public policies. The court found that American Pharmaceutical's business decision to retaliate against Flores for exposing suspected insurance fraud was against public policy. Therefore, the court held that the American Pharmaceutical's retaliatory discharge of Flores was against public policy and constituted a wrongful termination.

Kalman v Grand Union Company
443 A.2d 728 (N.J. Super.Ct.App.Div. 1982)

ISSUE: Whether a pharmacist was wrongfully discharged from employment for complying with public policy as set forth in statutes, administrative regulations, or professional codes of ethics.

FACTS: The plaintiff pharmacist had been employed by the defendant for approximately 8 years. The pharmacist was in charge of the defendant's pharmacy located in Paramus, New

Kalman v Grand Union Company
443 A.2d 728 (N.J. Super.Ct.App.Div. 1982)
...continued

Jersey. The pharmacy portion of the establishment was not separated by a partition from the other parts of the mercantile establishment, and it was not capable of being secured. Therefore, the entire store was licensed as a pharmacy.

In June of 1978, the store's supervisor advised the pharmacist that the pharmacy would close on July 4, 1978, although the rest of the store would be open for business as usual. The pharmacist objected because he felt that state regulations required the pharmacy to be open as long as the store was open and his own license could be suspended or revoked. The supervisor responded by saying that "no one would know." After some objection, the supervisor did finally agree to check with the New Jersey Board of Pharmacy regarding state regulations. He subsequently notified the pharmacist that the board had given its permission to close the pharmacy on July 4. Apparently disbelieving his supervisor, the pharmacist telephoned the board and learned that, to the contrary, the pharmacy was required to be open as long as the store was open. The pharmacy was kept open on July 4, but another pharmacist was on duty. When the plaintiff reported to work on July 5, he was discharged with no reasons being offered. The pharmacist filed this lawsuit against his employer alleging that he was discharged solely for attempting to comply with the state regulations and his own professional code of ethics.

RULING: The court held that the state statutes and the pharmacist's code of ethics were an expression of public policy and were designed to protect the public from dangers associated with the sale of drugs by unqualified persons. The appellate court reversed the trial court's summary judgment in favor of the employer. (Note: The case was returned to the trial court for a new trial consistent with the appellate court's holdings. However, the matter was settled in open court before the new trial was concluded. The settlement amount was not to be revealed by either party, but best information is that the settlement was satisfactory from the standpoint of the pharmacist.)

REASONING: While the general rule under the common law is that employees may be discharged "at will," many states have recognized the need to protect employees, who are not parties to collective bargaining agreements or other contracts, when they are wrongfully discharged by their employer. A common law cause of action has been found to exist for those who are employed at will and are discharged for reasons that violate public policy. The case that has attracted the most attention in this area is *Pierce v Ortho Pharmaceutical Corporation*, 417 A.2d 505 (N.J. Sup. Ct., 1980). Pierce was a physician employed as a research director for a major pharmaceutical manufacturer. She alleged that she was forced to resign when she was removed from a project involving research on a drug containing saccharin. Pierce was concerned about the possible carcinogenic effects of saccharin and refused to continue the research project. In her lawsuit, she grounded her objections upon certain clauses of the Hippocratic Oath. The New Jersey Supreme Court acknowledged that the traditional rule allowing the termination "at will" of employees without cause might, in certain cases, need to yield to public policy. The court would need to distinguish between public policy considerations and the employee's own values. The burden is upon the employee to identify a clear mandate of public policy that might bar his discharge.

In the case at hand, the trial court reasoned that the administrative regulations and the pharmacist's code of ethics were not clear expressions of public policy to qualify under the exception recognized in the Pierce case. The question the court was forced to address was whether the rules regulating the practice of pharmacy qualified as a clear mandate of public policy or if they were designed only to serve the interest of the pharmacy profession. The court stated that the pharmacist argued persuasively that the requirement that the pharmacy area be

Kalman v Grand Union Company
443 A.2d 728 (N.J. Super.Ct.App.Div. 1982)
...continued

open and attended by a pharmacist whenever the premises were open was, indeed, an expression of public policy. An unsecured, unsupervised pharmacy counter created a risk that potentially dangerous substances would be dispensed by unqualified persons or stolen. The purpose of requiring that pharmacists be present is to protect the public from the dangers associated with the sale of drugs by unqualified persons. Thus, the pharmacist was correct when he alleged that he was vindicating a clear mandate of public policy when he reported the employer's plan to the board of pharmacy.

The pharmacist also alleged that the Code of Ethics of the American Pharmaceutical Association was an additional source of public policy prohibiting the employer's actions. Under the code, a pharmacist has the duty "...to expose without fear or favor, illegal or unethical conduct in the profession." The court held that this ethical obligation was not designed to serve only the interest of the pharmacy profession, but also to serve the interest of the public as a whole.

Loomstein v Medicare Pharmacies, Inc.
750 S.W.2d 106 (Mo. App. 1988)

ISSUE: Whether a pharmacy corporation that discharged a pharmacist after 7 years of employment is legally responsible for retaliatory discharge and breach of contract.

FACTS: Pharmacist Jack Loomstein brought this lawsuit when he was discharged by Medicare Pharmacies, Inc. from his position as pharmacist and manager after 7 years of employment. Loomstein presented three incidents in which Medicare Pharmacies allegedly demanded that he violate the law and then fired him because of his refusal to do so.

The first incident involved a prescription written by a physician for twice the amount of the proper dosage of a drug. Loomstein contended that Medicare requested that he deliver the original prescription back to the physician, which was in violation of state law. Loomstein also questioned the authenticity of the signature on another prescription; Loomstein testified that he thought the doctor had not told the truth. The third incident involved a dispute between Loomstein and his supervisor regarding the dispensing of generic drugs according to a negative formulary.

The record was filled with testimony that Loomstein had difficulties relating to his superiors. It was also indicated that he had a condescending manner and was sarcastic and rude to the customers. A state board of pharmacy inspector also had a "run in" with Loomstein. The inspector informed Loomstein's supervisor that he had taken "all the guff" that he could from Loomstein, and that he expected some corrective action be taken. The supervisor contacted the vice-president of Medicare and recommended that Loomstein be terminated. The vice-president agreed.

RULING: The jury returned a verdict in favor of Loomstein, awarding him $1.00 in damages on his breach of contract theory, $1.00 in damages on his wrongful discharge theory and $700,000 in punitive damages. The trial court granted the defendant's motion for a new trial. The appellate court reversed the jury verdict.

REASONING: In order to prevail on his claim for retaliatory discharge, Loomstein had to prove that Medicare Pharmacies discharged him because he refused to violate the law, or

Loomstein v Medicare Pharmacies, Inc.
750 S.W.2d 106 (Mo. App. 1988)
...continued

some other clear mandate of public policy as expressed in the Constitution, statutes and regulations. In other words, Loomstein had to present evidence to establish a causal connection between his discharge and his alleged refusal to violate the law.

The court noted that Loomstein testified that the incident regarding the physician who prescribed the overdose occurred 8 weeks before his termination. The court was not convinced that the three incidents, standing alone, provided the evidence required to make a case for retaliatory discharge. After the second incident, even assuming that Medicare did demand that Loomstein dispense the prescription, he would not have violated the law because the physician testified that his signature was genuine. The third incident involving the negative formulary also did not serve as a basis for the retaliatory discharge. The record indicated that the negative formulary did not answer the question of whether the pharmacist should discontinue dispensing a particular manufacturer's drug when the list changed in the middle of a patient's course of treatment. Loomstein failed to present evidence that the pharmacy demanded that he dispense a prescription that would be in violation of the formulary.

Loomstein claimed that the pharmacy handbook and its policies and procedures and fringe benefit plans made up a contractual obligation between the plaintiff and the pharmacy. Loomstein argued that the pharmacy failed to give him verbal and/or written warning, thereby violating the terms of the employee handbook. Yet, the evidence showed that Loomstein had been verbally reprimanded for speaking rudely to a customer. In addition, there was a written employment report stating that "...if Jack Loomstein had one more complaint of this type..." his services would no longer be needed. Thus, the company complied with the provisions contained in the employee handbook. Loomstein did receive his 14 days' severance pay in compliance with the company policy. Therefore, the pharmacy did not breach its employment contract.

Rothenberg v Double D Drug
Slip Op. No. 96-8316 (March 26, 1997 US DC E. Pa.), 1997 U.S. Dist. LEXIS 3851

FACTS: The plaintiff pharmacist began working for the defendant pharmacy in April 1995 until August 1995 during which time he claimed to have witnessed and been ordered to participate in several violations of state and federal law, including the dispensing of controlled substances to addicted individuals and billing irregularities. The FDA closed the pharmacy in August 1995, and the plaintiff agreed to cooperate in the investigation. He brought suit for violations of the Racketeer Influenced and Corrupt Organizations Act claiming the defendants conspired to violate various laws causing plaintiff lost employment opportunities. In essence, he claimed he was hired as a pharmacist exclusively to give legitimacy to the illegal activities of the defendants. The defendants moved for and were granted summary judgment by the district court because the plaintiff did not claim any of the alleged legal violations were directed at him. Plaintiff was given additional time to file an amended complaint.

Wilson v State of Washington
929 P.2d 448 (Wash.App. 1996)

The plaintiff pharmacist claimed the Western State Hospital management wrongfully removed him as director of the pharmacy department in retaliation for his critique of personnel management policies and attempts to undermine management of his department as he tried to bring the pharmacy into compliance with JCAHO accreditation requirements. The critiques were contained in a "White Paper" publicized by plaintiff in response to critiques about the plaintiff's staffing orders, a union grievance by the pharmacy technicians and alleged gender discrimination against a female pharmacist. The plaintiff refused to follow procedures set forth in the grievance resolution process and was removed as director and reassigned to another pharmacy. A jury awarded the plaintiff $900,000 on his claim that the hospital violated his constitutional right to free speech. The Washington Court of Appeals reversed, holding that the hospital's interest in proper personnel management outweighs the minor public safety concerns contained in plaintiff's comments.

The following is a list of court cases that are related to this topic.

McMellon v Safeway Stores, 945 F.Supp. 1402 (D. Or. 1996)

DISCRIMINATION

Age

Perkins v K-Mart Corp.
Slip Op. No. 96-535313CL, Sept. 28, 1999 (Mich. Ct. App., Unpublished)

Perkins, a pharmacy manager, sued for age discrimination after his termination from employment at K-Mart for making a prescription dispensing error that harmed a patient. It was alleged that he dispensed *Seldane* and erythromycin together for the same patient and ignored a computer warning of a drug-drug interaction. During discovery, Perkins requested all incident reports, prescription override reports, and prescription logs for his younger replacement. K-Mart objected that the requested information was confidential as it involved disclosure of patient names and medication use. K-Mart sought summary judgment. Perkins asked the court to compel K-Mart's discovery. Perkins claimed that his requested information would have shown that his younger replacement was subject to a similar number of incident reports, and establish a pretext for age discrimination. The trial court judge agreed that the discovery would cause a breach of confidentiality and granted K-Mart's request for dismissal. The court of appeals held that the trial court erred in dismissing Perkins' age discrimination claim before ruling on his motion to compel discovery. Because Perkins was denied evidence that could have established that K-Mart's proffered reason for termination was false, the trial court did not evaluate whether K-Mart's proffered reason for termination was just a pretext for age discrimination. On remand, the trial court ordered that the discovery sought by the plaintiff be allowed. The discovery showed that the younger replacement pharmacist had not engaged in any errors of the magnitude committed by the plaintiff. The trial court judge therefore dismissed the claim again.

Disability (Americans with Disabilities Act)

Olson v Alick's Drugs
Slip Op. No. 00-1887 (November 1, 2000), 7th Cir., 2000 US App. LEXIS 27993

A pharmacist-employee brought an action against former employer alleging disability discrimination. The district court dismissed the action under Fed. R. Civ. P. 16(f), holding that following his attorney's withdrawal, the pharmacist's failure to appear at the pretrial conference constituted misconduct. The district court subsequently denied the pharmacist's motion to reconsider, holding that he failed to show excusable neglect. The appeals court vacated and remanded holding that the district court abused its discretion in dismissing the action for misconduct because the pharmacist had only a single incident of late arrival (10 minutes) in the history of the case and that the pharmacist failed to receive a direct and explicit warning of the possible consequences of his failure to appear after his counsel had withdrawn. In addition, no prior continuances of the trial date had been requested, and the district court failed to consider the likely merits of the pharmacist's claims before dismissing the case.

Roth v Lutheran General Hospital, et al
57 F.3d 1446 (7th Cir. 1995)

ISSUE: Whether a hospital and various members of its resident selection committee discriminated against the plaintiff in their selection process because of his eye disability and retaliated against him (a pharmacist-attorney-physician) for exercising his rights to obtain legal redress under the Americans with Disabilities Act (ADA).

FACTS: Plaintiff Stephen Roth was diagnosed as legally blind in his right eye when he was 12 years old. Despite his visual condition, Roth earned a degree in Pharmacy in 1979 from the University of Illinois and later became a licensed pharmacist. He then entered DePaul Law School as a full-time student, working 15 to 35 hours per week as a pharmacist while going to school. While in law school, Roth experienced eye strain and was fitted with a contact lens that improved the visual acuity in his right eye. According to Roth, during the years following this adjustment, he perceived no problems with his vision and functioned very well, both as a registered pharmacist and as an attorney.

Roth worked as a consultant and as a prosecutor/medical attorney for the Illinois Department of Professional Regulation. He was also employed as a faculty lecturer at the University of Illinois.

In 1989, Roth was admitted to the University of Illinois at Chicago Medical School. In his medical school application, he referred to his visual condition as a "former" problem, stating that the condition no longer confronted him and that it had been cured.

In his first quarter at medical school, Roth experienced eye strain and had some difficulty using a binocular microscope. He was examined by an ophthalmologist who concluded that Roth's visual condition was congenital. According to the physician who examined Roth, any laboratory tests requiring fine perception of depth would be difficult for Roth. However, he noted that Roth had adapted well to daily activities and should have the visual capacity to function in most medical specialties.

Based upon the physician's recommendation, the medical school made several accommodations for Roth. These included modifying his laboratory examinations and relieving him

Roth v Lutheran General Hospital, et al
57 F.3d 1446 (7th Cir. 1995)
...continued

from night call and surgical procedures which required him to look downward for prolonged periods of time. He was also allowed to select hospital clerkship sites that had lighter
duty schedules. In spite of his eye problem, Roth continued to serve as a defense attorney/
consultant during medical school. He also continued to be gainfully employed as a pharmacist and published several law-related articles during medical school. He later denied under
oath that he had worked as a pharmacist during medical school and also claimed not to be
directly responsible for one of the articles listed in his resume.

In 1992, Roth filed a complaint alleging that he received a below average grade in an obstet-
rics/gynecology clerkship program as a result of discrimination. The United States Department of Education found that Roth was disabled under the Rehabilitation Act and the ADA,
and that Roth's grade in the clerkship was likely to have been tainted by bias. The medical school eventually re-evaluated Roth's grade and gave him a passing score.

Roth also filed other discrimination complaints against the medical school relating to his failure to gain admission to an honor society, denial of his application for an independent study
program, a negative evaluation in a surgery clerkship, and other alleged discriminatory
conduct. None of those claims resulted in a finding of discrimination.

While in medical school, Roth participated in three clerkships at Lutheran General Hospital and did not request any accommodation during those clerkships. The supervising physician felt that Roth did a good job and would be a strong candidate for the residency
program. Roth was encouraged to apply to the hospital's residency program.

In his application, Roth stated that, although he was born with strabismus, he no longer considered this an obstacle because he had been fitted with a contact lens which corrected his
visual acuity. He was invited for an interview and was told that "things look very positive." During this interview, he told the director of the residency program about his eye problems and that he could be dysfunctional if he were to work more than an 8- to 10-hour shift.
Roth asked that he be excused from the hospital's alleged requirement that a resident be
on call for 36 hours at a time, three times a week. The director asked Roth whether he had
discussed his disability with other directors of pediatric residency programs at other hospitals. Roth responded that he had. When Roth referred to the various disability laws, the
director asked Roth to explain them. When the physician asked Roth what he would do if
he did not secure a residency position, Roth responded that he would have no alternative but to pursue legal action.

At the conclusion of the interview, the director advised Roth not to discuss his visual impairment or need for accommodation with any of the other interviewers. He stated that he
would check with the administration concerning accommodating Roth, such as adding an
extra residency position to accommodate his inability to take night calls.

Roth received mixed ratings in his further interviews for the residency program. He was rated
superior in education, experience, and research but apparently came across as insolent and
arrogant.

Sometime after the interview, the director spoke to a hospital administrator who agreed to
accommodate Roth if he should become a resident. In the past, the hospital had provided a full-time interpreter for a deaf resident in the family practice department. Thereafter, the program director prepared a preliminary ranking wherein Roth was number 49 out
of 60 applicants. The committee decided not to rank Roth at all. Up to this point, no mem-

Roth v Lutheran General Hospital, et al
57 F.3d 1446 (7th Cir. 1995)
...continued

ber of the resident selection committee (other than the director) was aware of Roth's condition. He did not reveal Roth's alleged disability until after the committee had made its decision. In spite of being informed that Roth might pursue legal action against the hospital, the committee remained firm in the decision not to rank him.

The director later informed the hospital administrator of the committee's decision and expressed his concerns about Roth not being ranked because of his performance in one interview. The administrator suggested that the selection committee be reconvened to reconsider Roth's application. The administrator indicated that if Roth were ranked, he would probably match with the hospital (in light of the hospital's prior history of being unable to fill its quota of pediatric residents through the matching system). The second review committee ultimately ranked Dr. Roth at the bottom of its list.

Roth did not match with the hospital, missing it by 2 positions. He did not attempt to obtain any of the 260 pediatric residency positions still available after the match. Thereafter, he commenced discrimination actions against Lutheran General Hospital and sought a preliminary injunction for immediate admission to the program pending the outcome of the litigation.

RULING: The trial court found that Roth failed to establish that he was an individual with a disability within the meaning of the statutes. It concluded that his impairment did not rise to the level of substantially limiting one or more of the major life activities. The court also noted that Roth was less than credible with regard to his physical limitations. It appeared to the court that Roth had attempted over a 10-year period to utilize the impairment to his benefit. The appellate court affirmed the lower court decision.

REASONING: The United States Court of Appeals concluded that the trial court did not abuse its discretion in finding that Roth had failed to establish some likelihood of success on the merits of this case. To succeed in his claims, he needed to establish that he was "disabled" within the meaning of the statutes. An individual is "disabled" if there is a physical or mental impairment which substantially limits one or more of the major life activities. These include such functions as caring for oneself, performing manual tasks, walking, seeing, hearing, speaking, learning, and working. While Roth's impairment may have affected his major life activities, he failed to establish that the impairment rose to the level of a disability. The court noted that the record did not establish that each and every pediatric residency program required 36-hour calls or long shifts. In fact, part-time residency programs were permitted under accreditation guidelines.

Drawing an analogy to employment cases, the inability to perform either a particular job or narrow range of jobs for an employer is not a disability. Therefore, the court could not say that an inability to fulfill long shifts necessarily proved that Roth was disabled within the meaning of the Acts. More importantly, no objective medical findings supported the plaintiff's assertion that he is significantly restricted by his visual impairment, rendering him incapable of performing night calls.

The court noted that Roth was able to successfully complete both his pharmacy and law degrees without any accommodation. Although Roth argued that medical study is more demanding than law school or pharmacy school, he went to law school full-time while being employed as a pharmacist for up to 35 hours a week.

The District Court determined that Roth was not a credible witness, and he was substantially impeached during his hearing. Statements in his affidavit that he was the only gradu-

Roth v Lutheran General Hospital, et al
57 F.3d 1446 (7th Cir. 1995)
...continued

ate in his class not to have been matched with a residency program were found to be untrue. Additionally, on cross-examination he denied certain aspects of his resume, which had been submitted along with his application to the residency program.

Significantly, Roth had repeatedly presented that his visual condition was a "former" problem in his medical school and residency program applications. His application to the residency program stated that his visual condition no longer confronted him, but he informed the director at the first interview that he would not be able to work for more than 8 to 10 hours at a time. The appellate court agreed with the trial court that when it was beneficial and opportune to disclose his alleged disability, Roth would do so, and would then advise that the failure to accommodate him would violate disability laws.

The court also paid attention to the fact that some of Roth's interviewers did not support his admission to the program because of his apparent personality shortcomings. One could very well conclude that the committee's initial decision not to rank Roth was motivated by its concern about his attitude, maturation and questionable personality traits rather than by any alleged prejudice on the part of the program. The court concluded that "Roth has failed utterly to rebut the hospital's valid, nondiscriminatory reasons of his character flaws, and thus, he has failed to meet the threshold burden of demonstrating some likelihood of success on his discrimination claim."

The Rehabilitation Act and the Americans with Disabilities Act are important pieces of legislation that seek to integrate disabled individuals into the economic and social mainstream, and to insure that the truly disabled will not face discrimination because of stereotypes or insurmountable impairments. However, there is a clear, bright line of demarcation between extending the statutory protection to a truly disabled individual and allowing an individual with marginal impairment to use disability laws as bargaining chips to gain a competitive advantage. The District Court's evaluation that Dr. Roth fell on the wrong side of the line is well supported in the record. There was no abuse of discretion.

Thalos v Dillon Companies
86 F Supp 2d 1079 (March 8, 2000), USDC CO, 2000 US Dist LEXIS 2773

The pharmacist-plaintiff, who suffers from cerebral palsy, sought part-time employment in a King Soers pharmacy in Denver. After being interviewed in person, she was denied employment. Up until that time she had been employed in a hospital pharmacy. She is married and has three sons. In addition to her pharmacy degree, she also has an undergraduate degree in journalism, and a masters degree in counseling. Her disease causes her to walk with a "scissors gait," causes tremors and unsteadiness, and affects her speech. During her interview with King Soers, she admitted that she did not count pills as fast as some pharmacists, but that she learns quickly and is able to perform the tasks of any pharmacist. She did not ask for any accommodation for her disease. The agent for King Soers told her she was not being hired because the defendant cannot accommodate her handicap. The plaintiff sued, claiming violations of the ADA. The court ruled that the pharmacist had not demonstrated that she is "disabled" under the ADA because she is not substantially limited in the major life activity of performing tasks. She can swim, ride bikes and has piloted a plane. Her difficulties in walking do not constitute a substantial impairment. She is able to care for three boys and lives in a two-story home with the master bedroom on the second floor. She cleans her house, does laundry, cooks, and shops for groceries. In the hospital, she regularly climbed

Thalos v Dillon Companies
86 F Supp 2d 1079 (March 8, 2000), USDC CO, 2000 US Dist LEXIS 2773
...continued

the stairs because it was faster than waiting for the elevators. Her speech impediment is not sufficient to constitute an impairment. She gave two days of deposition testimony without difficulty and has addressed the assembly at a National Pharmaceutical Council convention. The judge concluded that the plaintiff is a commendable person who has succeeded in accommodating her impairment to achieve many personal and professional successes. The Court did not dismiss the case, however, because he found that evidence had been presented that the pharmacist was "regarded as having a disability" by the defendant. The fact that the defendant's interviewers expressed concern over her handicap and her ability to communicate with customers is sufficient to create a question of fact as to whether the defendant considered her to be disabled in violation of the ADA.

Orr v Wal-Mart Stores
297 F. 3d 720 (8th Cir. 2002)

A pharmacist employed by Wal-Mart was a diabetic. To control his diabetes, he used a glucometer to monitor his blood glucose levels, took insulin (injected 3 times daily), and ate a special diet within 30 minutes of taking insulin. He controlled his diabetes to the best of his ability, but when his diabetes was not well-controlled, he suffered from vision impairment, low energy, lack of concentration and mental awareness, lack of physical strength and coordination, slurred speech, difficulties typing and reading, and slowed performance. He was hired as a full-time pharmacist at a Wal-Mart store in Nebraska. The store was a single-pharmacist facility and he was the only pharmacist on duty during his workday. Before accepting the position, he informed his District Manager (DM) that he was an insulin-dependent diabetic and the DM authorized the pharmacist to take a lunch break and mid-day breaks during his 10-hour work shift. There is a question whether the pharmacist was authorized to close the pharmacy to take an uninterrupted 30-minute lunch break, but that was his routine. The DM that hired the pharmacist was replaced by a new DM who informed the pharmacist that Wal-Mart policy required the pharmacy to remain open during store hours and instructed him not to close the pharmacy during his lunch break. The pharmacist did not comply with newly announced Wal-Mart policy and continued to close the pharmacy for an uninterrupted 30-minute lunch break. The pharmacist was given a written warning advising him that further noncompliance would result in his termination. He responded to the written warning, initially agreeing to abide by the policy. Shortly thereafter, the pharmacist requested that the new DM rescind the written warning based on the pharmacist's understanding and agreement with the former DM related to his lunch breaks. The pharmacist wrote letters expressing his concern that not having an uninterrupted lunch break could adversely affect the control of his diabetes. The new DM refused to rescind the warning and indicated that the pharmacist was permitted to control his diabetes by bringing food into the pharmacy, having access to a refrigerator, and eating or snacking in the pharmacy. The pharmacist wrote more letters requesting that his warning be rescinded and informing the new DM that he would resume his noon lunch breaks away from the pharmacy. The new DM then terminated the pharmacist. The pharmacist sued Wal-Mart, alleging violations of the Americans with Disabilities Act (ADA) and the Nebraska Fair Employment Practices Act (NFEPA). The district court granted summary judgment for Wal-Mart and the pharmacist appealed. The issue on appeal was whether the district court erred in finding that the pharmacist was not disabled within the meaning of the ADA. Under the ADA, a disability is defined as "a physical or mental impairment that substantially limits one or more of the major life activities of such individual." The court noted that the United States Supreme Court has held that a diabetic is not *per se* disabled but must dem-

Orr v Wal-Mart Stores
297 F. 3d 720 (8th Cir. 2002)
...continued

onstrate that his condition substantially limits one or more major life activities. If the physical or mental impairment is corrected by medication or other measures, the person does not have an impairment that presently substantially limits a major life activity. The pharmacist claimed that his disability substantially affected his ability to see, speak, read, and walk, and that it would not be unreasonable to expect that his diabetes *will* significantly disrupt his lifestyle. He also claimed that, if he failed to properly monitor and treat his diabetes, he *could* experience adverse symptoms that *would* substantially limit the major life activity of working. However, because the pharmacist failed to present evidence explaining how his diabetes substantially affected his major life activities and because the court could not consider the future effects of his diabetes, the court found that he was not disabled under the ADA or the NFEPA.

Equal Employment Opportunity Commission Procedures

Park v Howard University
71 F.3d 904 (D.C. Cir. 1995)

FACTS: A foreign-born female minority pharmacy professor at a university applied for an administrative position that was awarded to a Caucasian U.S. born male. She filed a discrimination claim with the state employment agency and later filed with the Federal Equal Employment Opportunity Commission (EEOC). The state complaint contained a "hostile work environment" claim that was attached to the EEOC complaint. The EEOC complaint itself did not contain any hostile work environment issues. Following normal procedures, the EEOC declined to pursue the case, and plaintiff filed a federal complaint nearly identical to the one filed with the EEOC. An amended count of the complaint added a "sexual harassment" claim. The trial court judge dismissed the discrimination claims, finding that the applicant was better qualified but awarded her $150,000 on the sexual harassment claim.

HOLDING: The Court of Appeals reversed on procedural grounds stating that the plaintiff failed to exhaust her administrative remedies because she failed to specifically include the hostile work environment claim in the EEOC complaint.

Gender Harassment (Sexual)

Moman v Gregerson's Foods, Inc.
570 So.2d 1215 (Ala. 1990)

ISSUE: Whether a pharmacy could be found liable for damages for sexual harassment of a pharmacy technician.

FACTS: In February 1985, Sonia Moman was hired by Gregerson's Foods to work as a part-time cashier in its store in Gadsden, Alabama. Shortly thereafter, Moman was seriously injured in an automobile accident and had to take a 6-week leave of absence. Upon returning to work, the plaintiff discovered that she could no longer endure the long hours of standing required by her job as a cashier and, at her request, was transferred to the store pharmacy.

Moman v Gregerson's Foods, Inc.
570 So.2d 1215 (Ala. 1990)
...continued

In October 1986, Rohit Patel began working as a relief pharmacist in the store and later became a full-time employee. Moman testified that her work hours often coincided with those of Patel. During the times they worked together, the plaintiff alleged that the pharmacist engaged in physical and verbal sexual harassment of her.

Among other things, the plaintiff alleged that Patel made inquiries into her personal life, told dirty jokes, used very foul language, touched her in a sexual way, and told her that he would take care of her if she would "treat him right." The plaintiff testified that she never complained to anyone other than Patel because she was afraid no one would believe her.

When the hours of all the pharmacy assistants at the store were cut to 20 hours a week, Moman quit her job. She filed for unemployment compensation benefits but was denied when it was held that she left Gregerson's without good cause connected with work. Moman appealed the agency's decision and a hearing was held. The Alabama Department of Industrial Relations found that Moman had "quit work due to sexual harassment and mistreatment which included sexual advances, suggestive remarks, vulgarities, and physical abuse." The Department held that the plaintiff was entitled to receive unemployment compensation benefits.

RULING: Because there was no evidence that anyone in the pharmacy corporation's management had reason to know of the pharmacist's alleged sexual harassment towards the plaintiff, the court found no basis to hold the pharmacy liable for damages for sexual harassment.

REASONING: The court noted that for Gregerson's to be liable for its pharmacist's misconduct, the employee pharmacist must have been acting within the scope of his employment or the employer must have ratified, confirmed, or adopted the unauthorized wrongful conduct of the employee.

The plaintiff argued that Gregerson's ratified Patel's alleged misconduct in two ways. First, it was noted that two other female employees had complained about Patel's using foul language and telling dirty jokes, but Gregerson's had done nothing about it. Secondly, Gregerson's had not appealed the Department of Industrial Relation's decision that granted unemployment compensation based on sexual harassment. The plaintiff argued that this was a ratification or confirmation of the misconduct.

The court reviewed an earlier Alabama case in which four employees had complained of incidents of sexual harassment. However, their complaints to their employer were made both orally and in writing on numerous occasions. Despite the complaints, the alleged conduct continued. The Alabama Supreme Court held that the employer's failure to stop the alleged behavior, despite numerous complaints, raised an issue of fact as to whether the employer had ratified such conduct.

However, in the case at hand, although there was evidence that two other employees had complained to a company official, their complaints were limited to Patel's use of foul language towards customers. There was no evidence that anyone in the corporation's management had reason to know of Patel's alleged misconduct toward Moman. In fact, Moman stated that because she was afraid no one would believe her, she complained only to Patel himself. Without knowledge of the alleged misconduct, the employer cannot be found to have ratified the conduct.

Moman v Gregerson's Foods, Inc.
570 So.2d 1215 (Ala. 1990)
...continued

The court further concluded that the failure of the employer to appeal the Department of Industrial Relations decision in no way suggested liability. The court noted that the purpose and design of the statutes pertaining to unemployment compensation are totally unrelated to the requirements of proving liability for sexual harassment in the workplace.

Mowery v Rite Aid
40 Fed. Appx. 926, 2002 WL 1608342 (6th Cir. 2002)

The female pharmacist was employed by Rite Aid Corporation. She brought a suit against Rite Aid alleging that she was paid less than comparable male employees in violation of the Equal Pay Act. The district court concluded that the pharmacist had stated a prima facie case, but only when her co-worker at the one store was used as the comparable male employee. The district court concluded that she had not produced any evidence to contradict Rite Aid's assertion that the salary differences among stores in different locations were attributable to the fact that the duties and responsibilities of pharmacists varied depending upon location. The district court also found that Rite Aid had an affirmative defense that the salary differential between the female pharmacist and the male counterpart was based on a factor other than sex, as the male pharmacist had negotiated his salary as part of the buy-out of his store. The court of appeals disagreed with the district court's determination that Rite Aid's other pharmacists could not be used as comparable employees. Rite Aid acknowledged that pharmacists in all of its stores share the same primary duties of filling prescriptions and serving customers and agreed that the "essential job duties" of pharmacists are the same regardless of location. Rite Aid's evidence concerning the primary differences among stores related not to the nature of the position, but to the intensity of the workload and type of clientele. Additionally, Rite Aid failed to explain how these potential differences impact its wage determinations. The court concluded that Mowery had raised a dispute of material fact concerning whether pharmacists in Rite Aid's other stores perform substantially equal work by identifying male pharmacists in other stores who are paid more, by pointing out that the highest paid male pharmacists are not employed in urban areas, and by obtaining Rite Aid's acknowlegement that the essential duties of all pharmacists are the same. The court of appeals reversed and remanded the case to the district court to resolve the factual dispute.

The following is a list of court cases that are related to this topic.

Mummert v Vencor, 21 Fed. Appx. 710, (9th Cir. 2001) 2001 WL 1345999

Hostile Work Environment

Bales v Wal-Mart Stores
143 F.3d 1103 (8th Cir. 1998)

ISSUE: Is a corporate-employer responsible for damages suffered by an employee who has been subjected to a hostile work environment created by a pharmacist-employee?

FACTS: The 22-year-old female plaintiff began working as a clerk in the pharmacy department of the defendant's Boone, Iowa, store in January 1994. Her employment terminated

Bales v Wal-Mart Stores
143 F.3d 1103 (8th Cir. 1998)
...continued

in November 1995. A male pharmacist in his mid-40s was in charge of the pharmacy during this time. In September 1994, the plaintiff called in sick. The next day she called again and said she could not come to work for personal reasons. The pharmacist insisted on knowing the reasons, but the plaintiff refused to discuss the situation and hung up. The pharmacist called her at home several times and threatened to fire her if she did not discuss the nature of her problems. She told the pharmacist to fire her because she was not going to talk to him or anyone else about the problem and again hung up the phone. The pharmacist called back one more time, and the plaintiff related that she had a fight with her boyfriend over his infidelity with a prostitute. Some time later, the plaintiff had another fight with her boyfriend and moved to a motel. The next morning she was visibly upset and the pharmacist asked why. When she told him she was now living in a motel, the pharmacist said this was a good time for him to leave his wife and he would probably see her at the motel. On several occasions, the pharmacist mentioned to the plaintiff his dissatisfaction with his wife and related stories about his affairs with other women.

The plaintiff often heard the pharmacist talking aloud to himself and when asked about it, he would say he was having conversations with the plaintiff "in his head." He called her at home and told her he was dreaming of her in a sexy red dress. Another time he called her at home and said he dreamed about her in a blue swimsuit. He referred to the plaintiff and all of his female employees as "honey," "hon," or "dear." The pharmacist "regularly annoyed" the plaintiff by pulling her hair and twisting or tugging her smock.

In the summer of 1994, the pharmacy held a demonstration on how to properly use an inhaler. The pharmacist made crude jokes about the similarities between use of the inhaler and oral sex. There were several other examples of sexual innuendo and bantering by the pharmacist. The plaintiff indicated that she was not allowed to do functions or tasks she enjoyed unless she participated in this behavior. Whenever she resisted or told the pharmacist to stop, he would assign her to less desirable jobs.

Just prior to her termination, the plaintiff had some professional photographs taken of herself. The studio did a "makeover" of the plaintiff with her hair styled, makeup applied, and different clothes selected. The photos showed her in several different poses and attire, including one with a "low-cut black dress that shows a lot of skin." She showed the proofs to several coworkers at the store, including the pharmacist. She selected a modest picture showing her wearing a jacket to have made into walled-size photos and gave them to some of the employees. After the pharmacist obtained one of the photos, he drove to Des Moines where the studio is located and ordered several more poses. He told the studio that he was the plaintiff's boyfriend in order to obtain the photographs. On April 4, 1995, while at work, the pharmacist told the plaintiff that he bought the photos. This event was characterized as the proverbial "last straw."

The next day, the plaintiff complained to an assistant manager who took the complaint to the store manager. The pharmacy district manager was called, and he took statements from the plaintiff, the pharmacist, and several other pharmacy personnel. The plaintiff stated that she could no longer work for the pharmacist. The pharmacist declined an invitation to move to a different store. The plaintiff was assigned to a different department. Later, the pharmacist was reprimanded for his inappropriate behavior. Nevertheless, the plaintiff claimed that the pharmacist continued to harass her by stalking her, wandering through her department for no reason, and driving past her house. Eventually she asked to be transferred to another store. In October 1995, she began working in the Ames, Iowa, store. However, because of scheduling problems and the distance from home, she quit in November 1995. The

Bales v Wal-Mart Stores
143 F.3d 1103 (8th Cir. 1998)
...continued

plaintiff brought suit against the pharmacist and the corporation for "quid pro quo" and hostile work environment sexual discrimination. She also claimed that she was "constructively discharged" because the harassment was so bad that she was forced to quit.

After a 4-day trial, the jury found in favor of the defendants on the quid pro quo and constructive discharge claims. On the issue of hostile work environment, however, the jury found in favor of the plaintiff and awarded her $28,000 against the pharmacist and $1.00 against the corporation. The trial court judge ruled that the pharmacist was liable only as an employee and shifted responsibility from him to the corporation.

HOLDING: The Court of Appeals affirmed the judgment entered by the trial court.

REASONING: The contested issue was whether the pharmacist's conduct was "unwelcome." The pharmacist claimed that his conduct was welcome, because he and the plaintiff exchanged gifts and she gave him a photograph of herself, showed him photos of herself in suggestive poses, and treated him like a friend. The court concluded that none of the plaintiff's behavior suggested an invitation to engage in sexual discourse, including the pharmacist's purchase, under false pretenses, of photos from the studio that took the pictures. Moreover, the plaintiff complained on many occasions when the pharmacist called her "honey" or "dear," touched her smock, or pulled her hair. The pharmacist even admitted that the plaintiff complained about his behavior four or five times.

The defendant corporation claimed that the "few" incidents mentioned by plaintiff were not based on sex. The court stated that this "half-hearted" defense "verges on the frivolous" and was "disingenuous" because there was no evidence to suggest that the pharmacist treated any male employees the way he treated the plaintiff. The court also dismissed the argument that these incidents were not severe enough to alter the conditions of plaintiff's work environment. The court determined that the pharmacist engaged in a clear pattern of offensive conversation and behavior that created a hostile work environment based on sexual discrimination. The court also affirmed the ruling that the corporation is liable for the damages caused by the pharmacist. The reasoning being that the pharmacist, as an employee of the corporation, is its agent and that the discrimination could not have occurred except by way of his employment.

Public Service Obligations

Mace v Charleston Area Medical Center
442 S.E.2d 624 (W.Va. 1992)

ISSUE: Whether a hospital breached an employment contract and retaliated against a pharmacy technician who joined the National Guard.

FACTS: Robert Mace began working as a pharmacy technician in January, 1981. In 1985, Mace informed his employers that he had joined the National Guard and would have to report for active duty on August 1, 1985. The Medical Center's personnel director informed Mace that his job would be posted if he was gone for more than 30 days. According to Mace, his wife spoke with management employees at the Medical Center during his 13-week basic

Mace v Charleston Area Medical Center
442 S.E.2d 624 (W.Va. 1992)
...continued

training and told them that his position was protected by federal law while he was serving in the National Guard. Nevertheless, while he was away, Mace's position as a pharmacy technician was eliminated.

Following his 13 weeks of active duty, Mace applied for reemployment at the Medical Center. He was informed that he could be placed in another position of like status, seniority, and pay until he could be returned to the position of pharmacy technician. Mace refused to accept a position as a nursing attendant and insisted on having his former job back. The United States Department of Labor interceded on Mace's behalf, and he was reinstated to his original position after another employee was transferred out of a pharmacy technician position. However, Mace's efforts to collect back pay continued for over a year.

In July 1986, Mace injured his back while on his annual active duty training with the National Guard. During this time off, he began to take several prescribed medications for back pain. When he returned to work at the hospital, he refused to obey an order to take a drug cart up to the next floor. He reported to the Medical Center's employee health division and complained of back pain and was sent home early that day.

Mace was asked to submit to a drug screen or face termination. During the trial, he explained that he was tempted to go ahead and submit to the screen because he had a family to support, but he felt he was being singled out and punished by the Medical Center for asserting his rights under the Veteran's Reemployment Rights Act and for pursuing his ongoing claim for back pay. Mace then submitted a letter of resignation but several days later contested his "resignation."

Pursuant to hospital policy, Mace appealed his dismissal to a grievance committee. The committee recommended that he be reinstated after a two-week suspension and that the hospital establish a clear written statement of its drug testing policy. The committee also asked for a thorough investigation of Mace's allegations against the pharmacy. However, hospital management chose not to follow the grievance committee's recommendations that Mace be reinstated.

RULING: A jury awarded the technician $55,000 in damages for lost wages, $50,000 for emotional distress, and $125,000 in punitive damages. The appellate court affirmed the jury's conclusion that the hospital was guilty of retaliatory discharge. The damage award for lost wages and emotional distress was upheld, but the appellate court reversed the award of punitive damages.

REASONING: Mace alleged that the Medical Center actually discharged him because he exercised his rights under the Veteran's Reemployment Rights Act, and thus his firing was against public policy. The Medical Center maintained that he was discharged for valid nondiscriminatory reasons unrelated to his actions for seeking redress because he joined the National Guard. First, the Medical Center maintained that the evidence was undisputed that they had probable cause and reasonable suspicion that (1) Mace was using drugs and (2) he was insubordinate at work. Thus it was the hospital's contention that he would have been discharged even in absence of his exercise of rights under federal laws.

The rule that an employer has an absolute right to discharge an "at will" employee must be tempered by the principle that where the employer's motivation for the discharge is to contravene some substantial public policy principle, then the employer may be liable to the employee for damages. The hospital's motivation in this case was clearly a question of fact to be resolved by the jury.

Mace v Charleston Area Medical Center
442 S.E.2d 624 (W.Va. 1992)
...continued

While the facts did not lead to simple resolution, the court found there was sufficient evidence to support the jury's verdict against the hospital on the issue of retaliatory discharge. Perhaps most damaging to the Medical Center's case was its refusal to follow its own grievance committee's recommendation that Mace be reinstated following a two-week suspension. In addition, the fact that the jury awarded punitive damages was a strong indication that it believed Mace's firing was unjust.

Race, Color, or National Origin

Anaeme v Lovelace Health Systems
202 F.3d 281 (10th Cir. 1999)

The plaintiff, a pharmacist of Nigerian origin, claimed that he tried to secure employment with the defendant hospital several times in 1995. He alleged that the New Mexico hospital refused to interview or hire him because of his race, color, and national origin. The district court dismissed the claim because the plaintiff failed to produce sufficient evidence of discrimination. The judgment was affirmed on appeal. The court found no evidence that the plaintiff even applied for seven of the nine positions he claims to have sought. As to the two positions that he actually applied for, the plaintiff did not produce enough evidence to overcome the legitimate non-discriminatory reasons that the hospital advanced for not hiring the plaintiff. One of those jobs was given to an internal candidate who had preference based on longevity. The personal director stated that she would not have interviewed the plaintiff for the other position because his sporadic employment history, 10 different positions in a 5-year period, would not qualify him for consideration.

Bell v Supermarkets General Corp.
1993 U.S. Dist. LEXIS 14967

ISSUE: Whether a pharmacist was discharged as a result of sex and race discrimination and also in retaliation for her filing three Equal Employment Opportunity Commission (EEOC) claims against the pharmacy corporation.

FACTS: Pathmark hired Bell as a staff pharmacist in 1987. Two years later, she filed a charge of discrimination with the EEOC alleging that Pathmark had discriminated against her both racially and sexually. Neither Bell's charge nor the record in this case, however, sets forth the specific facts of the alleged discrimination.

In 1991, Pathmark transferred Bell to another one of its pharmacies. It claimed that the transfer was the result of "adverse customer complaints." Bell responded to her transfer by filing a second charge of discrimination with the EEOC, alleging that the transfer was the result of further race and sex discrimination and that Pathmark orchestrated the transfer in retaliation for her filing the previous EEOC charge.

In August of 1991, the EEOC issued a brief determination in which it concluded that the evidence obtained during its investigation did not establish that Pathmark had engaged in dis-

Bell v Supermarkets General Corp.
1993 U.S. Dist. LEXIS 14967
...continued

crimination. In October of 1991, Pathmark discharged Bell from her position as a staff pharmacist. According to Pathmark, Bell was fired because she had been insubordinate and had used abusive language with her supervisor. Subsequently, Bell filed a third EEOC charge claiming that she had been discharged in retaliation for her previous discrimination complaints to the EEOC.

In March of 1992, the EEOC issued a second determination that addressed the claims in Bell's second and third complaints with the agency. The Commission once again concluded that there was insufficient evidence for it to pursue her claims, and it advised Bell that she could file a private lawsuit within 90 days.

After Bell's termination, her union brought her discharge to arbitration pursuant to its collective bargaining agreement with Pathmark. An arbitration hearing was held and the arbitrator issued an opinion in which he found that Bell had been discharged because she "unreasonably failed to fill a prescription in a timely fashion, without a sufficiently good reason and that she may have used abusive language with her supervisor." The arbitrator also found, however, that the confrontational behavior of Bell's supervisor exacerbated the situation. In light of these findings, the union arbitrator ultimately concluded that Pathmark's punishment of Bell had been harsher than was necessary and he directed that Pathmark reinstate Bell and convert her discharge into a six-month suspension without pay.

In the meantime, Bell had also filed a claim for unemployment compensation benefits. The Pennsylvania agency responsible for these benefits concluded that Bell was ineligible for benefits because she had been discharged from Pathmark's employment for "willful misconduct."

Finally, Bell appealed to the Pennsylvania Commonwealth Court, which affirmed the state's denial of unemployment compensation benefits. The court further described the factual situation leading to Bell's discharge. Her supervisor had directed her to fill a prescription containing the notation "WSB." Although Bell did not know the meaning of the notation, her supervisor instructed her that the abbreviation stood for "water soluble base" and that *Aquaphor* was an appropriate substitute. Nevertheless, Bell, having no personal knowledge of the meaning of WSB, refused to fill the prescription. The next morning, Davis called the prescribing physician, who informed him that *Aquaphor* was, in fact, an acceptable substitute. When Bell arrived at work, Davis ordered her to fill the prescription using *Aquaphor*. Bell once again refused and used abusive and profane language. The court agreed that the plaintiff's conduct leading to her discharge constituted insubordination that amounted to willful misconduct and it affirmed the denial of benefits.

RULING: Because the pharmacist only stated her beliefs as to the discriminatory actions and provided no evidence, the court granted the pharmacy's motion for summary judgment.

REASONING: To establish a prima facia case of race or sex discrimination under Title VII, Bell must show that (1) she belongs to a protected class, (2) she is qualified for the position from which she was discharged, and (3) other employees were treated more favorably. It was undisputed that the plaintiff satisfied the first element of her case because she is a member of two protected classes, African-Americans and women. The court also presumed that she was qualified for the position from which she was discharged because she held her pharmacist's position for four years. To make out a case of discrimination, Bell must produce evidence such that a reasonable jury could find that other employees were treated more favorably. Furthermore, if she is to prove retaliatory discharge, she must also show that there was some link between her protected activity and the discharge.

Bell v Supermarkets General Corp.
1993 U.S. Dist. LEXIS 14967
...continued

Bell claimed that her supervisor sexually harassed her prior to her discharge by making sexual advances and engaging her in explicit sexual conversations. She further contended that the supervisor became angry with Bell when she resisted his advances and his anger led him to treat her differently than he treated other employees. More importantly, Bell claimed that other Caucasian and male employees had both disobeyed their supervisors' instructions and used abusive language with their supervisors and yet Pathmark had not disciplined them.

Aside from these bald allegations, however, Bell put forth no evidence in support of her assertion that other employees were treated differently than she. The exhibits which Bell attached to her complaint included a letter from Bell's union to Pathmark, the arbitrator's opinion, Pathmark's employment manual, and the union's contract with Pathmark. None of these provided evidence suggesting that Pathmark treated other employees differently than it treated Bell.

Hazra v National RxServices, Inc.
746 F.Supp. 733 (S.D. Ohio 1990)

ISSUE: Whether a mail-order pharmacy was guilty of discrimination after terminating a pharmacist who made six dispensing errors over a six-month period of time.

FACTS: Pharmacist Joganandra Hazra was originally from India and is of the Asian race. Hazra was born in 1935 and was over age 40 when this alleged cause of action arose. The plaintiff complained that National Rx Services, a mail-order pharmacy, unlawfully discriminated against him based on his national origin, race, and age when they terminated his employment in October 1987.

Hazra began employment with the defendant in 1983 when he was hired as a junior pharmacist, an unlicensed pharmacy position. He later transferred to the company's facility in Ohio and registered as a pharmacy intern in order to become a licensed pharmacist. The employer agreed to act as a preceptor so that Hazra later could become registered. Hazra was later employed as a registered pharmacist with the defendant in 1985. He admitted that there was no discrimination when he was hired for the position.

Hazra's position called for him to take prescription containers off a conveyor belt and compare the dispensed prescription with its label to determine if it had been filled properly. The job carried with it the standard responsibilities of any registered pharmacist licensed by the state of Ohio. In the plaintiff's own deposition, he noted that a registered pharmacist has the responsibility of ensuring that the label on a prescription bottle correctly identifies the dispensed drug, and that the pharmacist is held strictly accountable if the wrong drug or the wrong strength of a drug is dispensed to the patient.

The defendant instituted a disciplinary policy for registered pharmacists who committed dispensing errors. Corrective action was to be taken when a registered pharmacist dispensed a prescription that resulted in a patient receiving the wrong drug, the wrong strength, the wrong dosage or form of drug, or its equivalent generic form when the brand name of the drug was prescribed.

Depending upon the situation, the company would employ the following corrective measures: Counseling, warnings, probation, and termination. As a general rule, a staff pharma-

Hazra v National RxServices, Inc.
746 F.Supp. 733 (S.D. Ohio 1990)
...continued

cist is warned and placed on probation if he or she commits three significant dispensing errors within a three-month period. The policy further provides that any dispensing error during the probationary period can result in termination.

In 1987, Hazra dispensed a drug which was double the strength prescribed by the physician. His supervisor met with him and discussed the importance of accuracy and allegedly informed Hazra to slow his pace if it would aid in improving accuracy. A month later, Hazra dispensed *Depakote* 500 mg when 250 mg was prescribed. He was again cautioned. A few days later, Hazra was again reprimanded for erroneously dispensing a sublingual form of a drug rather than the prescribed oral dosage. The plaintiff was placed on probation and informed that any additional mistakes in the next 60 days would result in his termination.

Less than 30 days later, the plaintiff committed an additional dispensing error. He admitted that he could have been discharged but instead was permitted another chance. Hazra was placed on 90 days probation and was again informed that any additional errors would result in termination. In October 1987, Hazra committed two additional dispensing errors when he dispensed the wrong drug. The defendant contended that the termination of Hazra's employment was based upon these six separate errors.

Hazra argues that while he may have committed the above-referenced errors, based on the total number of prescription errors, and the total number of prescriptions he filled, his error rate was below that of the company's average for all pharmacists. The plaintiff obtained the defendant's error rate from an article printed in the October 1987 issue of U.S. Pharmacist entitled "What Do Mail-Order Rxs Really Mean for Pharmacy?" Based upon these statistics, the plaintiff concluded that the defendant must have discriminated against him based either on his age, race, nationality, or a combination of these factors because his error rate was below the company's average.

RULING: While the plaintiff was a member of a protected class, there was no evidence that he suffered discriminatory action. The defendant's motion for summary judgment was granted.

REASONING: The court noted that age discrimination cases are decided on a case-by-case basis, with the plaintiff having the burden of proving by the preponderance of the evidence a prima facie case of discrimination. If the plaintiff succeeds in proving the prima facie case, the burden shifts to the defendant to articulate some legitimate, nondiscriminatory reason for the employee's rejection.

To show a prima facie case of discrimination, the plaintiff must show (1) that he is a member of a protected class, (2) that he qualified for the position and performed as required, (3) that despite his qualifications and performance, he was terminated, and (4) that the defendant placed a person outside the protected class in the position.

The court found that the plaintiff failed to meet his initial burden of establishing a case of discrimination. While the plaintiff is a member of a protected class, there were serious questions as to whether his performance was that expected of him in light of his numerous errors. The plaintiff admitted the errors, but instead focused on his supposed rate of error as compared with the entire company. However, the plaintiff did not place the error rate found in the magazine article into context for use in this matter. Instead, the plaintiff asked the court to accept the number quoted as being reliable and relevant, and to draw from it a serious inference of race, nationality or age discrimination. The court found that this was merely hypothecation and speculation.

Hazra v National RxServices, Inc.
746 F.Supp. 733 (S.D. Ohio 1990)
...continued

The court noted that it was readily apparent that the defendant instituted a very strict policy in an attempt to lower the error rate of prescriptions being dispensed. There was no evidence provided suggesting that the policy was applied disparately. The plaintiff admitted that he could not name another person who had made more errors who had not been terminated. Therefore, there appears to have been equal application of the policies to all employees of the defendant.

Thomas v Rite Aid Corporation
1994 U.S. Dist. LEXIS 15600 (E.D. Penn., Nov. 1, 1994)

ISSUE: Whether the defendant pharmacy discriminated against the plaintiff on account of her race in violation of federal law, and further, whether the union breached its duty of fair representation of her as a union member.

FACTS: Julie Thomas is an African-American who was employed as a part-time pharmacy cashier by Rite Aid in two of their Pennsylvania stores. Her primary responsibility was to make pharmacy deliveries. She was also a member of the local union, which was the exclusive bargaining unit for those employees covered by the collective bargaining agreement.

In April 1992, the plaintiff left the pharmacy to make deliveries. The manager of the store saw the plaintiff leave with two bags of potato chips. He asked the pharmacy manager and a cashier whether the plaintiff had paid for them. Both replied in the negative. Relying on this information, the store manager and the pharmacy manager checked the plaintiff's bag when she returned from making deliveries. They found potato chips and several greeting cards. When asked about the items, the plaintiff showed the store manager the receipt for the potato chips and told him that she had no receipt for the greeting cards but that she had received them on credit at the other Rite Aid store for which she made deliveries.

It was later learned that the plaintiff had not bought any greeting cards on credit at the other Rite Aid store. After being informed of her discharge, the plaintiff contacted a representative for the local union who handled employee grievances. She told him that she had previously purchased a tube of lip balm on credit with the permission of the pharmacist at a Rite Aid store. This was later confirmed. The union also contacted a pharmacy cashier who stated that she had written down the greeting cards as being purchased on credit. The union representative did not ask any further questions at that time.

At the grievance hearing, the cashier admitted that she had written the cards down on her own initiative after having seen the plaintiff take the cards and not because the plaintiff had asked to purchase the cards on credit. The Rite Aid division supervisor offered to allow the plaintiff to resign instead of being discharged and to give her a good reference for future jobs, and further, not to oppose her receipt of unemployment benefits. The plaintiff rejected this offer because she was already receiving unemployment benefits.

Another grievance hearing was held, but the plaintiff interrupted the meeting several times and eventually walked out because she felt that the other people were lying. The union attorney was asked to provide his legal opinion about the case. He concluded that there was no likelihood of success and arbitration would be an inappropriate use of union resources.

RULING: Summary judgment was granted in favor of the defendants.

Thomas v Rite Aid Corporation
1994 U.S. Dist. LEXIS 15600 (E.D. Penn., Nov. 1, 1994)
...continued

REASONING: The plaintiff charged that both defendants discriminated against her on account of her race in violation of federal law. A plaintiff who alleges disparate treatment may prove this in one of two ways, either (1) by producing direct evidence of discriminatory treatment or (2) by producing circumstantial evidence that would allow a reasonable fact-finder to infer discrimination.

In order to establish a case of discriminatory discharge against Rite Aid, the plaintiff needed to produce evidence that would allow a reasonable fact-finder to conclude (1) that she was a member of a protected class; (2) that she was qualified for the job from which she was discharged; (3) that she was discharged; and (4) that her position remained open and her employers sought other applicants to fill it. It was undisputed that the plaintiff was African-American, that she was qualified for her job as a pharmacy cashier, that she was discharged, and that her position was filled subsequent to her dismissal.

The court found that Rite Aid had met its burden of producing non-discriminatory evidence as reason for discharging the plaintiff. Thereafter, the plaintiff must present evidence that would allow the fact-finder to determine that the stated non-discriminatory reason was merely a pretext for discrimination.

The plaintiff noted that there was a factual dispute over whether she took the cards without telling anyone or whether she received permission to purchase the cards on credit. The plaintiff also noted that a white pharmacist had given her permission to purchase a tube of lip balm on credit, and he only received a written reprimand for his behavior with no suspension or lost pay.

The fact that Rite Aid chose to believe the pharmacy cashier instead of the plaintiff was insufficient to undermine the pharmacy's stated reason for the discharge. With regard to the discipline of the white pharmacist, the court found that the difference in the level of discipline received is readily explainable without resorting to discriminatory reasons. He gave permission to the plaintiff to purchase an item on credit; he did not allow her to take it without ever paying for it.

The plaintiff failed to produce any evidence that similarly situated white individuals who filed grievances were treated differently by the union. In fact, the union was able to point to numerous white employees whose grievances were not pursued to arbitration.

The plaintiff further claimed that in deciding not to pursue her grievance to arbitration, the union breached its duty of good faith to her as a union member. In order for there to be such a breach, a union's conduct toward a member must be arbitrary, discriminatory, or in bad faith. Individual union members do not have an absolute right to force their unions to take all of their grievances to arbitration.

The court noted that the union did pursue her grievance in a number of ways. It investigated the plaintiff's allegations and scheduled two grievance hearings with Rite Aid. The second highest officer in the union, an African-American, became involved in the case and obtained a written opinion from the union's attorney not to pursue arbitration.

Williams v Advocate Health and Hospitals
No. 98 C 6869, December 20, 1999, U.S.D.C. Ill., 1999 U.S. Dist. LEXIS 19660

The plaintiff, an African-American was employed as a staff pharmacist at the defendant's hospital from February 8, 1996, until November 15, 1998, when she voluntarily resigned after filing this lawsuit. During her first year of employment, the pharmacy supervisor received complaints from co-workers that the plaintiff was not doing her fair share of the work and spent too much time on the phone. In early 1998, during a performance evaluation review, the supervisor and another pharmacist met with the plaintiff to discuss these and other work related complaints. As a result, the plaintiff was reassigned from the night shift to the day shift so that the supervisor could "watch" her. After this, the plaintiff made numerous dispensing errors. The supervisor ordered her not to engage in activities such as diabetic counseling until she learned how to do her job. The plaintiff complained to the Human Resources Department that she was being harassed and discriminated against. The Director of Pharmacy investigated, and concluded that the plaintiff was treated fairly. Another performance evaluation later in the year described severe problems with the plaintiff's ability to perform job functions. She then applied for and was denied a promotion to a supervisory position. She filed this lawsuit, resigned her position, and took a higher paying job at K-Mart. The trial court judge found that none of the evidence produced by the plaintiff showed that she was treated unfairly or subjected to discrimination, noting that an unpleasant environment is not unlawful.

The following is a list of court cases that are related to this topic.

Farooqui v Cook County, No 99-2222 (August 25, 2000), US App (7th Cir), 2000 US App LEXIS 22407.

Daigle v Thomas, Slip Op No. 2002 CA 0184 (December 20, 2002), 2002 La. App. LEXIS 3989.

Nwagbologu v Regents of the Univ. of New Mexico, 33 Fed. Appx. 449, (10th Cir. 2002), 2002 WL 532430.

Religion

Farooqui v Cook County
No 99-2222 (August 25, 2000), US App (7th Cir), 2000 US App LEXIS 22407

The plaintiff-pharmacist was fired from his position as a supervisor in the defendant-hospital's outpatient pharmacy. He claims that he was the subject of discrimination based on national origin and his religion. The plaintiff is a Muslim and native of India. A jury returned a verdict in favor of the defendant. The plaintiff appealed, claiming the district court made several procedural errors during the trial. He claims he should have been able to introduce derogatory remarks made about him over 18 months prior to his initial performance review. Both the district and appellate courts found that stray workplace comments made long in advance of any adverse employment decisions do not implicate discrimination unless there is a causal nexus. The plaintiff could not show any evidence linking the earlier remarks to his termination. He also claimed that he should have been able to introduce evidence about other Indians and Muslims who also asked to be transferred out of his department because of discrimination. The Court of Appeals held that the District Court did not abuse its discretion to bar this testimony because it was not probative to his own claims of discrimination. The upper Court also ruled that it was proper to limit questions on the reasons that the plaintiff's supervisor had been suspended because the questions did not relate to the supervisor's character for truthfulness or untruthfulness.

INDEPENDENT CONTRACTORS (TAX ISSUES)

Kaib's Roving R.Ph. Agency, Inc. v Employment Department
984 P.2d 886 (Or.App.1999)

Kaib's provided a service to match licensed pharmacists interested in filling temporary vacancies with Oregon pharmacies in need of temporary relief services. Two state agencies, the Department of Revenue and the Employment Department, audited Kaib's to determine whether its pharmacists were properly classified as independent contractors. If the pharmacists were independent contractors, then Kaib's did not have to pay employment taxes on those pharmacists. On the other hand, if the pharmacists were not independent contractors but were considered to be employees of Kaib's, then employment taxes would be assessed against Kaib's. In 1991, a Department of Revenue officer determined that Kaib's pharmacists were independent contractors. The Employment Department, however, determined that Kaib's pharmacists were not independent contractors. Thus, the Employment Department assessed employment taxes against Kaib's, and Kaib's appealed. Kaib's contended that the Employment Department was bound by the Department of Revenue's earlier determination that the pharmacists were independent contractors. The court referred to precedent establishing that the state legislature intended uniformity and consistency among state agencies when determining independent contractor status. Kaib's argued that the mandate for consistency and uniformity precluded the Employment Department from making a finding different from the Department of Revenue. The Employment Department contended, however, that its determination was made in a different year and that working relationships change over time, so it should be able to make its own determination. The court held that the Employment Department must consider the Department of Revenue's earlier determination of independent contractor status. Therefore, the court reversed the assessment of employment taxes and remanded the case for reconsideration of the independent contractor status in light of the Department of Revenue decision.

NONCOMPETITION CLAUSES

Slijepcevich v Caremark
No. 95 C 7286, 1996 U.S. Dist. LEXIS 110 (N.D. Ill. Jan. 8, 1996)

FACTS: A pharmacist was employed in a mail-order pharmacy under a written contract that prohibited his employment with a competitor for one year after termination from the defendant pharmacy if the competitive employment could involve disclosure of confidential information or trade secrets. He quit and took a job with a competing mail-order pharmacy. The former employer sought to bar the new employment in court, claiming that everything the pharmacist knew about mail-order pharmacy was learned in the course of his prior work.

HOLDING: The Federal District Court in Illinois dismissed the claims noting that there was no allegation that the pharmacist took files, stole customers, or used any secret information. The Court concluded that the non-competitive clause was overly broad and would not be interpreted to prevent gainful employment in a competitive marketplace absent evidence of an actual breach of its prohibitions.

George v Brewer
797 A. 2d 920 (Mo. Ct. App. 2001)

The plaintiff-pharmacist sold a pharmacy business to the defendants and agreed to a non-compete clause that had a spatial restriction and a time restriction of 10 years after the date of closing. The plaintiff then filed a declaratory judgment asking the trial court to determine whether or not the time restriction contained in the contract was reasonable and ought to be enforced, or if the trial court ought to limit the covenant to some other reasonable time restriction. The defendant-purchasers subsequently filed a motion to dismiss, which was granted. The pharmacist appealed. The appellate court noted that for any action under the state's Declaratory Judgment Act to be proper, there must be a justifiable controversy. It determined that the plaintiff's petition did not plead facts supporting his claim of an actual controversy with the defendants. Based upon this fact, the Court of Appeals determined that plaintiff was merely seeking an advisory opinion on a speculative or hypothetical situation that may or may not come to pass. Accordingly, the defendant's motion to dismiss was affirmed.

OVERTIME PAY

Danesh v Rite Aid Corp.
39 F.Supp.2d 7 (D.D.C. 1999)

Danesh, a pharmacist, brought an action under the Fair Labor Standards Act for overtime pay earned while an employee of the defendant. Danesh had an employment contract for annual salary of $52,000 paid at $2,000 bi-weekly per 80 hours worked. Danesh's paychecks were subject to deductions for tardiness. Danesh claimed that he was entitled to one and one-half times his regular pay for overtime hours. Under the Fair Labor Standards Act, employees who work more than 40 hours per a 7-day week are entitled to overtime pay at one and one-half times regular pay. Executive, administrative, and professional employees are exempt from the overtime pay provision. Federal regulations define an exempt "professional" as an employee doing work requiring advanced knowledge acquired by specialized intellectual instruction and study, and being compensated for services on a salary or fee basis. The district court found that Danesh was not paid on a salary basis because his pay was subject to reductions on an hourly basis for tardiness or absences from work. Therefore, the district court granted Danesh summary judgment and awarded Danesh his unpaid overtime compensation as well as liquidated damages provided under the Fair Labor Standards Act.

In re Wal-Mart Stores, Inc.
58 F.Supp.2d 1219 (D. Colo. 1999)

The plaintiffs were full-time pharmacists employed by Wal-Mart. Plaintiffs did not receive overtime compensation for hours worked over 40 hours per week and asserted that they were entitled to overtime compensation. Wal-Mart argued that the plaintiffs were within the professional exemption to the Fair Labor Standards Act and therefore not eligible for overtime compensation. Whether the plaintiffs were entitled to overtime compensation hinged on whether they were salaried employees as defined by Fair Labor Standards Act regulations. The court found that the plaintiffs' base hours fluctuated for Wal-Mart's convenience and to reduce store hours in times of slow business. The district court held that the flexibility and convenience regarding plaintiffs' salaries demonstrated that the plaintiffs were

In re Wal-Mart Stores, Inc.
58 F.Supp.2d 1219 (D. Colo. 1999)
...continued

hourly employees and not salaried employees. Therefore, the district court granted plaintiffs' summary judgment and held that Wal-Mart violated the Fair Labor Standards Act.

The following is a list of court cases that are related to this topic.

Caperci v Rite Aid, 43 F. Supp. 2d 83; 1998 U.S. Dist. LEXIS 21498.

THEFT FROM EMPLOYER

Gewirtz v Commissioner of Labor
714 NYS 2d 586; 2000 NY App. Div. LEXIS 10788, October 26, 2000

The pharmacist was dischanrged from his employment as a drug store pharmacist after an investigation revealed that he had filled several hundred dollars worth of prescriptions for a store security guard without ringing them through the cash register, charging the co-payment, or billing the insurance company. He appealed a decision ruling that he was disqualified from receiving unemployment insurance benefits due to his termination for misconduct. The court affirmed. Although the pharmacist claimed that he could not process the prescriptions because the computer was down, he failed to follow his employer's procedures for dispensing prescriptions during computer downtime. The pharmacist's exculpatory explanation for his conduct created a credibility issue which could be freely resolved against him. Substantial evidence supported the decision. The decision was affirmed.

In Re: Gewirtz
714 NYS 2d 586 (October, 26, 2000); 2000 NY App Div LEXIS 10788

The plaintiff was discharged from his employment as a retail pharmacist after an investigation revealed that he had filled several hundred dollars worth of prescriptions for a store security guard without ringing them through the cash register, charging the co-payment, or billing the insurance company. He applied for unemployment insurance benefits which was denied on the grounds that he was disqualified due to his termination for misconduct. The court affirmed. Although the pharmacist claimed that he could not process the prescriptions because the computer was down, he failed to follow his employer's procedures for dispensing prescriptions during computer downtime. Substantial evidence supported the decision. The court stated that his exculpatory explanation for his conduct created a credibility issue which could be freely resolved against him.

UNEMPLOYMENT BENEFITS

Park v Employment Security Department of the State of Washington
Slip Op. No. 46316-1-I (February 20, 2001), 2001 Wash. App. LEXIS 317

The pharmacist-employee accepted the promotion to manager knowing that it involved 12-hour shifts with no overlapping shifts of additional pharmacists. She experienced back

Park v Employment Security Department of the State of Washington
Slip Op. No. 46316-1-I (February 20, 2001), 2001 Wash. App. LEXIS 317
...continued

pain, blurry vision, and depression, but did not consult a physician. She declined a transfer to return to her former position. She then voluntarily quit her job because of stress induced by long shifts and low staffing levels. She applied for unemployment but the Employment Security Department denied her benefits. She asked the appellate court to remand to for consideration of new evidence, and contended that substantial evidence did not support the conclusion that she did not quit for good cause. The appellate court declined to remand because generalized problems pervasive in the industry were not evidence of specific conditions at the store where the pharmacist worked that would have constituted good cause to quit. Further, the appellate court found that substantial evidence supported the decision, and it was not arbitrary and capricious because the stresses involved in the pharmacist's position were usual and customary in the industry and she knew the conditions of her employment before she accepted it.

The following is a list of court cases that are related to this topic.

Gewirtz v Commissioner of Labor, 714 N.Y.S. 2d 586; 2000 N.Y. App. Div. LEXIS 10788.

UNIONS

The following is a list of court cases that are related to this topic.

Thomas v Rite Aid Corporation, 1994 U.S. Dist. LEXIS 15600 (E.D. Penn., Nov. 1, 1994)

WORKERS COMPENSATION

General Issues

McMellon v Safeway Stores
945 F.Supp 1402 (D.Or. 1996)

FACTS: The plaintiff was a pharmacy technician who noticed that the pharmacy manager and pharmacist regularly dispensed several different outdated prescription drugs. The pharmacy corporation had a procedure in place for removing outdated drugs from the pharmacy, but the pharmacist appeared to intentionally disregard the policy. The technician's attempts to comply with the policy were regularly thwarted by the pharmacist. When she removed over $9,000 of outdated drugs from the shelves, he became angry and threatened to reduce her hours from full-time to part-time. Over a period of several months, the technician complained to the store manager and the corporation's director of pharmacy operations. After they spoke to the pharmacist, he called the technician and stated that he was going to "get her for this." She filled a worker's compensation complaint for undue stress on June 17, 1994 and, a few days later, called the Oregon Board of Pharmacy to complain about the pharmacist. The Board found the pharmacist in violation of its regulations against dispensing expired drugs. In July 1994, the corporation notified the technician that it had made a change in the management of the store and invited her to return to work. The notice indicated that the corporation would assume she did not want to keep her employment if she did not respond within 10 days. She did not respond and was terminated in April 1995.

HOLDING: On motion for summary judgment, her claim for constructive and wrongful discharge was found to be meritorious. The several months that lapsed between the time she

McMellon v Safeway Stores
945 F.Supp 1402 (D.Or. 1996)
...continued

first complained about the pharmacist and the corporation's non-action on those complaints until after the Board of Pharmacy ruling are evidence of intolerable working conditions that could support a claim of constructive discharge.

The following is a list of court cases that are related to this topic.

Anderson v International Industries, Slip Op No 2000-CA-2554 (November 14, 2001) 2001 La. App. LEXIS 2709.

Exclusive Remedy

Erwin v Methodist Hospital
No. 03A01-9811-CV-0039, October 18, 1999, 1999 Tenn. App. LEXIS 708

The hospital had a contract with a pharmacy corporation to have pharmacy services provided within the hospital. An employee of the pharmacy was hurt while on the job inside the hospital. She tripped over electrical wires that were left on a hallway corridor during some remodeling. She was transporting medications from the pharmacy to a nursing station at the time. The plaintiff sought and received worker's compensation benefits from the pharmacy employer. She also brought a negligence lawsuit against the hospital. The hospital sought dismissal of the complaint on the basis that the plaintiff's exclusive remedy is in worker's compensation benefits. A state statute provides that "principal contractors" are not liable in negligence when a subcontractor's employees are hurt on the job and entitled to worker's compensation benefits. The trial court dismissed the complaint. That decision was affirmed on appeal. Several factors are taken into account in determining the relationship between service contractors. In the case, the pharmacy corporation had an exclusive right to provide service within the hospital. The pharmacy, not the hospital, had total control over the injured employee's employment relationship including her compensation, scheduling, and termination.

Payne v Galen Hospital
No. 99-1011 (August 24, 2000), 2000 Tex. LEXIS 87

Payne was a nurse at Galen Hospital when she injured her back assisting a patient. Payne received treatment from an independent (not employed by the hospital) physician who prescribed *Toradol* for her back pain. *Toradol* is labeled to be used for only limited duration and not in the management of chronic pain. Payne obtained her prescriptions and refills at the hospital pharmacy. She took *Toradol* for four and one-half months and then experienced a severe reaction to the prolonged use. Payne is now a chronic pain patient, is totally and permanently disabled, and is confined to a wheelchair for the rest of her life. Payne asserted that the hospital pharmacists were grossly negligent because they never warned her that *Toradol* was for acute use only. Payne received worker's compensation benefits for her initial injury and her reaction to *Toradol*. Payne sued the hospital and its pharmacist for negligence. The trial court granted Galen Hospital summary judgment on the grounds that the exclusive remedy provision of the worker's compensation act barred Payne's claims for negligence. Payne appealed and contended that her reaction to the *Toradol* was an indepen-

Payne v Galen Hospital
No. 99-1011 (August 24, 2000), 2000 Tex. LEXIS 87
...continued

dent injury that did not occur during the course and scope of her employment. Recovery under the worker's compensation act is intended to be an employee's sole remedy for work-related injuries. The question before the court of appeals was whether the second injury from the reaction to *Toradol* was a work-related injury. In its original decision, the Court reversed judgment for the hospital. On re-hearing, the Court of Appeals withdrew its opinion and affirmed summary judgment for the hospital. In the later opinion, the Court found that Payne's reaction to *Toradol* was an extension of her back injury, occurring in the probable sequence of events and arising from the actual compensable injury. Therefore, Payne's second injury, suffered during treatment of a job-related injury, was work-related for purposes of the worker's compensation exclusive remedy. The Supreme Court of Texas also affirmed.

SOURCES OF ADDITIONAL INFORMATION

Fleischer, Lauren. Note: From Pill-Counting to Patient Care: Pharmacists' Standard of Care in Negligence Law, 68 *Fordham L Rev* 165 (October, 1999).

Terry, Nicolas P. Cyber-Malpractice: Legal Exposure for Cybermedicine, 25 *Am J Law and Medicine* 327 (1999).

Vivian JC. Can advancing technologies edge out the pharmacist? *US Pharm.* 26:06. http://www.uspharmacist.com/oldformat.asp?url=newlook/files/Phar/ACF15FE.htm&pub_id=8&article_id=734

Vivian JC. State prescription benefit programs. *US Pharm.* 26:07. http://www.uspharmacist.com/oldformat.asp?url=newlook/files/Phar/ACF234C.htm&pub_id=8&article_id=745

Vivian JC. Whistleblowing damages. *US Pharm.* 26:11. http://www.uspharmacist.com/oldformat.asp?url=newlook/files/Phar/Law11.htm&pub_id=8&article_id=801

Vivian JC. Lower fees, less service and Medicaid. *US Pharm.* 26:10. http://www.uspharmacist.com/oldformat.asp?url=newlook/files/Phar/ACF2D98.htm&pub_id=8&article_id=786

Vivian JC. Definitions in disability. *US Pharm.* 27:12. http://www.uspharmacist.com/index.asp?show=article&page=8_1011.htm

Appendix

Glossary of Terms, 799

State Boards of Pharmacy, 807

State Laws Affecting Pharmacy Practice, 813

National Association of Boards of Pharmacy
    Survey of Pharmacy Law Tables, 815

Answer Key
    Regulation of Pharmaceuticals, 901
    Controlled Substances, 908
    Pharmacy Inspection, 911
    Business Law, 913
    Civil Liability, 919

Glossary of Terms

A

Abrogate. To repeal or annul a law

Acknowledgment. An admission; the statement of a notary that the individual who signed a legal paper did so freely

Acquittal. A judicial determination of the innocence of an accused individual

Act. An action carried out purposefully; an exercise of power with legal consequences

Ad hoc. Relating to a specific intention (an ad hoc committee is a special committee)

Adjudication. A judicial decision or "determination" in a legal cause or controversy; applies to both the pronouncement of a judgment and the judgment itself

Administrative agency. A subdivision of the government that is charged with administering particular legislation

Affiant. An individual who swears to an affidavit

Affidavit. A written statement sworn to under oath

Agency. Relationship where one party represents another party by the latter's legal authority

Agent. An individual who is authorized to act for a principal

Allegation. A statement of what a party to a legal action expects to prove

Allege. To declare or claim

Amendment. A change in an existing law or a proposed bill by modifying or deleting some part of it, or adding to it

Amicus curiae. (Friend of the court) An individual who is not a party to a case but who is allowed by the court to file a written argument concerning the matter

Annul. To render invalid by legal authority; to nullify or cancel

Answer. The pleading by the defendant in response to the plaintiff's complaint

Appellant. An individual who appeals the decision of a lower court to a higher (appellate) court

Appellate court. A court that has power to review, affirm, reverse, or modify the judgment of another court

Appellee. A party to an appealed lawsuit who did not initiate the appeal

Arraignment. The point in a criminal proceeding at which the defendant is read the detailed charges against him or her and is asked to enter a plea

Arrest. To apprehend, detain, or hold an individual to answer for a criminal charge or accusation

Assault. A willful attempt to inflict bodily harm on another person

Assign. To transfer the interests of one party to another party, as in a lease; to appoint or designate for a specific purpose. For example, a Medicare enrollee may assign to a physician the right to be reimbursed for care, rather than the payment coming to the patient who would then pay the physician

Assignment. The transfer of property

Attachment. A court order directing a law officer to seize a particular property

Attest. To affirm the truth of or bear witness to; to authenticate

Averment. A statement of alleged facts; an allegation

B

Bad Debt. A debt that cannot be collected

Bankruptcy. The inability to pay bills when due; a formal adjudication of a court declaring an individual insolvent

Battery. The unlawful beating or use of force against an individual

Bill. A draft of a law presented to a legislature for enactment; in commercial law, a written statement of the terms of a contract (also a general name for any item of indebtedness)

Bind over. To hold for trial

Bona fide. In good faith

Bond. A written obligation guaranteeing payment by the signatory upon a specific occurrence (eg, bail bond)

Breach. A violation of a law or legal duty; a failure to obey the terms of a contract

Brief. A written argument of counsel that is submitted to the court

Burglary. The act of breaking into a building (esp. a private residence or office) with the intent of stealing someone else's property.

C

Capital. Property or assets; the property or money that is given to a corporation or partnership in exchange for stock or partnership interest; describing a crime punishable by death

Case Law. Law based on the combined results of other similar cases; law of a certain subject as formed by the adjudged cases therein

Caveat. (Latin) A warning to a person to beware or use caution

Caveat Emptor. (Latin) "Let the buyer beware," a maxim stating that a purchaser must judge for himself or herself the quality of what he/she buys in the absence of a warranty

Certiorari. (Latin) The writ of a higher court issued to a lower court requiring it to produce certain records

Change of Venue. The transferring of a lawsuit begun in one place to another place for trial

Chattel. Personal property (as opposed to real property)

Citation. An official summons to appear

Civil liberties. Those liberties that are free from governmental restrains

Class Action. A type of lawsuit where one or more people act on behalf of a larger group sharing a common interest in the matter

Code. A systematic statement of a body of law, given legislative authority

Codicil. An addition or modification to a will

Commercial Paper. A negotiable instrument for the payment of money, ie, a promissory note, bank check, etc.

Common law. The old law of England and early America as based on custom and upheld by court decisions; an enforceable part of United States law with the exception of those portions that have been abolished or modified by legislation

Complaint. In a civil action, the initial demand or claim by the plaintiff; in a criminal action, the initial written document charging an individual with a crime

Concurring opinion. An opinion that agrees with that of the majority but possibly for reasons that differ from those of the majority

Confidential information. Information that may not be divulged

Consent. Voluntary agreement

Contempt of court. Disobedience of a court order; an act that obstructs or embarrasses the court and for which the court can impose a penalty

Contingent Fee. A legal arrangement granting compensation to an attorney in the event of a successful case (usually a percentage of the actual amount recovered by the client in a lawsuit)

Contract. A written or oral agreement between two or more parties to do or not do a certain thing

Controlled substances. Drugs and substances that are subject to the controls of the Federal Comprehensive Drug Abuse Prevention and Control Act of 1970 (Public Law 91-513) and usually having a potential for abuse and physical and psychological dependence

Copyright. An exclusive right given by law to the author, originator, or owner of a literary or artistic work to reproduce, publish, and sell that work

Counsel. Attorney, lawyer

Counterclaim. A claim filed by the defendant against the plaintiff

Covenant. A written agreement or promise between two or more parties, usually under seal, for a certain action to be carried out

Cross-complaint. A document wherein the defendant sets up a claim or an allegation against the plaintiff

Cross-examination. To question through the use of leading questions, which are usually intended to test the accuracy of previous testimony

D

Damages. Monetary compensation for a loss or injury

DEA. Drug Enforcement Administration

Deed. A written instrument transferring the title to or an interest in landed property

De Facto. (Latin) In fact, in actuality

Defamation. Making false or malicious and injurious statements either orally (slander) or in writing (libel)

Default. The failure to perform a legal duty

Defendant. In a civil or criminal proceeding, the individual against whom the action is brought

Demurrer. A defense to the plaintiff's complaint in which the defendant admits to the plaintiff's alleged facts but denies that they are legally sufficient to support the claim

Deponent. One who attests to the truth of certain facts or provides evidence; a witness

Deposition. Testimony taken down, in writing, under oath and outside of court

Directed verdict. A decision by a trial judge that the evidence presented clearly favors one party and that the trial need not proceed

Discovery. The pretrial activities through which the attorney for one party learns important evidence held by the opposing party

Dissenting opinion. An opinion that disagrees with that of the majority

Domicile. For legal purposes, an individual's permanent home

Due Process of Law. The carrying out of legal proceedings according to established rules and principles; a guarantee of judicial fairness

Duress. Coercing or forcing another person to do something against his or her will

Duty. Legal or moral responsibility; mandatory obligation

E

Eleemosynary. Related to or supported by charity

Enacting Clause. The section at the beginning of a statute identifying the legal authority by which it was enacted

Enjoin. To prohibit; to require something of a person by authoritative order

Entrapment. A situation in which a law officer, for the purposes of prosecution, lures an individual into committing a crime

Equity. Justice; the fundamentals by which justice may be obtained in cases in which ordinary forms of law seem to be insufficient

Escrow. Deposit of money or papers with a third party to hold pending the fulfillment of a condition or transaction

Et al. And others, abbreviation for "et alia" meaning "and friends"

Et seq. And following, abbreviation for "et sequliae" meaning "and following"

Evidence. That which is used to ascertain the truth of a matter legally

Ex parte. A term used in legal proceedings that describes the point of view of only one party to the controversy; a partisan viewpoint

Execution. Completion of an act; carrying out a judgment

Execution sale. The enforcement of a money judgment by a sheriff's sale of the debtor's property or the debtor's interest in property

Expert witness. An individual with special training, knowledge, or skill who testifies at trial as an authority

Express warranty. An affirmation of fact made by a seller to a buyer regarding the goods that were purchased; any description of the goods which is then made part of the basis of the transaction

F

FDA. Food and Drug Administration

Federal question. A legal issue involving the United States Constitution or a federal statute

Federal Register. The daily publication of the federal government, which informs the public of rules, regulations, and other legal documents. It includes proposed changes of governmental agencies to which any citizen or group can respond before the change or regulation is made official

Felony. A serious crime punishable under federal law by death or imprisonment for 1 year or longer

Fiduciary. A trustee; a person responsible, by his or her undertaking, for acting for another's benefit in matters relating to such undertaking

Foreclosure. A legal proceeding that forces the sale of property to pay the debt owed by the mortgagor to the mortgagee

Forgery. The illegal copying or altering of another's writing without his or her authority and with intent to defraud

Fraud. Intentional deception or distortion of truth for the purpose of inducing another to give up something valuable or surrender a legal right; false representation

G

Garnishment. A legal device used by a creditor to attach the wages or assets of a debtor to satisfy a debt

Grand jury. A jury that determines whether sufficient evidence exists to indicate that an individual has committed a crime

Grandfather Clause. A provision in a new law that creates an exemption based on previously existing circumstances

H

Habeas corpus (writ of). A procedure to obtain a decision on the legality of an individual's custody; it tests the procedure used to imprison an individual, not his or her guilt or innocence

Hearsay. Secondhand information; evidence that derives its validity both from the witness on the stand and from the veracity of another individual

Held. Decided, ruled

Heir. One named in a will or designated by statute to inherit property when there is no will

HEW. Health, Education, and Welfare; former name of the Department of Health and Human Services

Holding. The ruling in a lawsuit, particularly on appeal; a statement of the application of law to the facts of the case and the resultant ruling

I

In Camera. (Latin) In private; in the judge's chambers

In Personam. (Latin) Against a person, with intent to impose an obligation or liability

In Rem. (Latin) Against a *thing* (ie, property) rather than a person

Incarcerate. To imprison

Incriminate. To disclose involvement in a crime; self-incrimination is self-disclosure of involvement in a crime

Indictment. The written accusation of a grand jury charging an individual with a crime; if differs from a criminal complaint in that a grand jury, rather than a magistrate, determines if evidence is sufficient to charge an individual with a crime

Inference. The drawing of a conclusion from other proved or admitted facts

Informed Consent. A legal requirement that a patient be told by the physician the nature of a medical procedure and its potential risks and benefits, so that the patient may make an informed decision whether to undergo the procedure

Injunction. A court order mandating that an individual do or refrain from doing a certain thing

Interrogatories. Part of discovery consisting of lists of questions submitted by one party to the other party to answer before trial

Ipso Facto. By the mere fact; by the nature of the case

J

Judgment. A decision of a court

Judiciary. The branch of government given the judicial power (ie, the system of courts), or the power to interpret and apply the law

Jurisdiction. The power or authority to interpret and apply the law; the limits within which authority may be exercised

Jurisprudence. The philosophy or science of law

L

Landmark Case. A precedent-setting case, usually one that marks a turning point in a matter of great importance

Lease. A written agreement between a landlord and tenant, specifying the rights and responsibilities of each

Legal Duty. Responsibility as required by law

Legal representative. An executor or an administrator

Legend drug. A drug, which by federal law, must bear the inscription, "Caution: Federal law prohibits dispensing without prescription;" prescription drug and dangerous drug are synonymous terms, with limited exceptions as indicated in the text

Lessee. The tenant or renter under a lease

Levy. A seizure of property by law or by force to satisfy a judgment

Liability. Responsibility; an obligation arising from an act or from a failure to act

Liability insurance. A contractual agreement in which a second party assumes responsibility against loss in return for the payment of premiums

Libel. To defame by writing or any form of representation; a compliant in an admirality procedure

License. Lawful permission to perform a certain activity for a limited period of time

Licentiate. A licensed individual

Lien. A claim against property for the payment of a debt

Limited. (Ltd.) Synonymous with incorporated; united in a legal corporation

Litigate. To carry out a lawsuit

Litigation. A lawsuit

M

Malfeasance. The doing of an unlawful or wrong thing

Malice. Intent to cause harm or injury

Malpractice. Failure to meet a professional standard of care that results in harm to another

Mens rea. Criminal intent; a guilty or wrongful purpose

Miranda Rule. The legal requirement that the law enforcement officials give certain information to anyone taken into custody before the evidence obtained during questioning is acceptable. The information consists of four basic statements: 1. The person has a right to remain silent. 2. Any statement he/she does make may be used as evidence against him/her. 3. He/she has a right to an attorney. 4. If he/she can't afford an attorney, one will be appointed for him/her.

Misdemeanor. A crime that is less serious than a felony, usually punishable by fine, imprisonment for less than 1 year, or both

Misfeasance. An incidence of doing a lawful thing in an illegal or improper way

Mitigate. To reduce or diminish; alleviate

Moot. Undecided; open to question. Moot point means one not settled by judicial decisions

Mortgage. A transaction in which money is borrowed by an individual on his or her property; the title and possession of the property remain with the mortgagor (debtor), the lien rights remain with the mortgagee (lender)

N

Negligence. Failure to exercise due care; carelessness, inadvertence; negligence is considered gross when the careless conduct is reckless or intentional

Negligence per se. Negligence that involves no questionable issue because the duty of the defendant toward the plaintiff has been violated by the defendant to the injury of the plaintiff, negligence that occurs through breach of a standard of conduct imposed legally

Nolo Contendre. (Latin) A plea in a criminal case meaning "I will not contest it"; has the effect of pleading guilty

Nonfeasance. Failure to do what should be done; neglect of duty

Notary public. A public official empowered to administer oaths and certify documents

Null and Void. Having no legal force, invalid; voidable

O

Oath. A solemn affirmation of the truth of one's own words

Opinion. The reason given for the judgment of a court, in contrast to the decision, which is the judgment itself

Ordinance. An enactment of a municipal government; certain legislative regulations sometimes are referred to as ordinances

Over the counter (OTC) drug. Drug that can be sold legally without a prescription; nonprescription drug, patent medicine, and proprietary medicine are synonymous

P

Per curiam. The legal opinion of the entire court in contrast to the opinion of any of the individual judges

Perjury. To lie willfully and knowingly while under oath

Petit Jury. Regular jury for a civil or criminal trial, usually of no more than 12 members

Plaintiff. One who starts a lawsuit; the initial complaining party in a legal action

Police power. The authority of government to enact and enforce laws relating to public health, safety, and welfare

Power of Attorney. Written statement which authorizes one person to act as agent or attorney for another

Preamble. Introductory clause in a statute or legal document explaining the reasons for its enactment and its goals

Precedent. A previous case or court ruling which serves as an example for similar questions of law or other cases later on

Preliminary hearing. In a criminal case, the first examination of an accused individual before a judge or magistrate to determine if the individual should be held or released

Presumption. A conclusion drawn from the circumstances

Prima facie case. A case in which there is cause to warrant submission of the evidence to a jury

Pro Bono Publico. (Latin) For the public good

Pro rata. In proportion according to the liability, share, or interest of each concerned individual

Promulgate. To publish; to officially announce a law after its enactment

Proximate. Imminent, nearest; that immediately preceding or following

Punitive Damages. Damages awarded to a plaintiff in excess of simple compensation, intended to punish the defendant for serious wrong

Q

Quash. To void a legal process

Quid pro quo. An even exchange, literally "this for that"

R

Reasonable Care. Due care; what a reasonable person would do in the same or similar circumstances

Rebut. To offer evidence against or to oppose legal charges

Registrant. A person registered or enrolled in order to secure a right or privilege legally granted upon such registration

Regulation. A rule or order having the force of law and issued by government authority

Regulatory agency. A subdivision of the government that is charged with regulating activities in a particular field (eg, the Food and Drug Administration [FDA] regulates drugs)

Release. In a lawsuit or a claim, the giving up of a legal right against the defendant or against the party responsible for paying compensation for an injury; in criminal law, the setting free of an imprisoned individual

Remand. To send back

Repeal. To annul or abolish a previous law by enacting a new statute declaring that the former law will be revoked

Replevin. A legal proceeding to recover possession of goods

Res gestae. All circumstances that form a litigated issue

Res ipsa loquitor. A legal doctrine that states that the defendant is negligent because the injury caused to the plaintiff was under the control of the defendant and, in absence of negligence, could not have happened

Res judicata. The matter in controversy that has already been decided by the court and that is not subject again to litigation by the same parties

Respondeat superior. (Let the master answer) a doctrine that makes the employer liable for certain acts of the employees

Restraining Order. A preliminary legal order that the court may issue to keep a situation unchanged or prevent a defendant from doing a certain threatened act, pending decision upon application for an injunction

Rider. An attachment modifying or appending an insurance policy, a legislative bill, or any written document

S

Seal. A mark, symbol, or inscription that is stamped or impressed on paper

Sine qua non. An indispensible thing

Slander. Injuring another's reputation by uttering false and malicious statements about him or her

Stare decisis. A doctrine in which fundamentals laid down in previous decisions are followed unless they contradict the principles of justice

Statute. A written law enacted by the legislative branch of government

Statute of limitations. A time limit imposed by the legislature within which a lawsuit must be filed or the right to do so is lost

Stipulation. An agreement settling a controversy or a point in conflict; in reference to an ordinance violation, a written confession of guilt by the individual charged with the violation

Subpoena. A court order commanding an individual to appear in court or be penalized

Subpoena ad Testificandum. (Latin) A written order of the court commanding a person to appear as a witness to testify

Subpoena duces tecum. A subpoena that orders a witness to bring a particular document or item to court

Subrogate. To substitute (eg, the payment of a claim by an insurance company substitutes for the insured collecting from the responsible party)

Substantive Law. The part of law which establishes, defines, and regulates rights and obligations

Suit. In civil court, a proceeding undertaken by an individual against another to seek a remedy or damages for a wrongdoing

Summons. A legal notice ordering an individual to appear in court

Surety. One who insures the debt or obligation of another in the same contract by which the original debtor becomes liable

Suspension. A temporary delay or interruption; the temporary removal or cessation of a privilege (as in one's profession, such as pharmacy)

T

Testimony. Oral evidence introduced at a trial

Tort. A civil wrong usually arising out of a breach of duty

Tortfeasor. One who commits a tort

Trade Secret. Any information, process, or formula used in one's business to gain an advantage over competitors who may not have that information

Trademark. A design, symbol, motto, name, or mark by which the source of a product or service can be identified

Trial court. A court in which a case is first heard (as distinguished from an appellate court)

U

Ultra vires. Exceeding the powers granted to an authority or legal agency

Unprofessional Conduct. Conduct considered unbecoming or unethical according to the code of that profession; breach of duty

V
Valid. Legally justifiable; legally enforceable
Venue. A specific geographical location in which a case is heard (by a court with jurisdiction)
Verdict. The decision or finding of a jury
Vicarious Liability. Situation where a superior may have to answer for the wrongdoing of a person under him or her (ie, in an employer-employee relationship)
Void. Not legally binding; null
Voir Dire. The process that precedes trial whereby prospective jurors are screened and selected for jury service

W
Waiver. Intentional or voluntary relinquishing of a right
Warrant. In criminal law, authorization from a court or magistrate directing a law officer to perform a certain act (usually make an arrest or search a premises)
Warranty. A legally enforceable promise often regarding the performance or quality of an item
Witness. One called upon to give testimony
Writ. A written order of an authority in the name of a state to compel an individual to perform an act mentioned in the writ

State Boards of Pharmacy

National Association of Boards of Pharmacy
700 Busse Highway
Park Ridge, IL 60068
847/698-6227
FAX # 847/698-0124
www.nabp.net

Alabama State Board of Pharmacy
1 Perimeter Park South
Suite 425 So.
Birmingham, AL 35243
205/967-0130
FAX # 205/967-1009
www.albop.com

Alaska Board of Pharmacy
PO Box 110806
Juneau, AK 99811-0806
907/465-2589
FAX # 907/465-2974
www.dced.state.ak.us/occ/ppha.htm

Arizona State Board of Pharmacy
www.pharmacy.state.az.us
Glendale Office:
4425 W. Olive Ave., Suite 140
Glendale, AZ 85302
623/463-2727
FAX # 623/934-0583

Tucson Office:
P.O. Box 13
400 West Congress
Tucson, AZ 85701
Pager: 520/218-4105
FAX # 520/296-0395

Arkansas State Board of Pharmacy
101 E. Capitol, Suite 218
Little Rock, AR 72201
501/682-0190
FAX # 501/682-0195
www.state.ar.us/asbp

California State Board of Pharmacy
400 R Street, Suite 4070
Sacramento, CA 95814
916/445-5014
FAX # 916/327-6308
www.pharmacy.ca.gov

Colorado State Board of Pharmacy
1560 Broadway, Suite 1310
Denver, CO 80202
303/894-7750
TDD: 303/894-7880
FAX # 303/894-7764
www.dora.state.co.us/Pharmacy
email: Pharmacy@dora.state.co.us

Connecticut Commission of Pharmacy
165 Capitol Avenue
Hartford, CT 06106
860/713-6065
FAX # 860/713-7242
www.ctdrugcontrol.com/rxcommision.htm

Delaware State Board of Pharmacy
P.O. Box 637
Dover, DE 19903
302/739-4708
FAX # 302/739-3071

District of Columbia Board of Pharmacy
825 N. Capitol Street, N.E.
Room 2224
Washington, DC 20002
202/442-9200
FAX # 202/442-9431

Florida State Board of Pharmacy
4052 Bald Cypress Way
Bin #C04
Tallahassee, FL 32399-3254
850/245-4292
FAX # 850/413-6982
www9.myflorida.com/mqa/pharmacy/
ph_home.html
email: MQA_Pharmacy@doh.state.fl.us

Georgia State Board of Pharmacy
237 Coliseum Dr.
Macon, GA 31217-3858
478/207-1686
FAX # 478/207-1699
www.sos.state.ga.us/plb/pharmacy

Hawaii State Board of Pharmacy
P.O. Box 3469
Honolulu, HI 96801
808/586-3000
www.state.hi.us/dcca/pvl/areas_pharmacy.html
email: pharmacy@dcca.state.hi.us

Idaho Board of Pharmacy
P.O. Box 83720
Boise, ID 83720-0067
208/334-2356
FAX # 208/334-3536
www.state.id.us/bop

Illinois Board of Pharmacy

Illinois Department of Professional
  Regulation
www.dpr.state.il.us
Springfield Office:
320 W. Washington
Springfield, IL 62786
217/785-0800
TDD: 217/524-6735
FAX # 217/782-7645

Chicago Office:
100 W. Randolph, Suite 9-300
Chicago, IL 60601
312/814-4500

Indiana Board of Pharmacy

402 W. Washington Street
Room W041
Indianapolis, IN 46204
317/234-2067
FAX # 317/233-4236
www.in.gov/hpb/boards/isbp

Iowa Board of Pharmacy Examiners

400 S.W. Eighth St., Ste. E
Des Moines, IA 50309-4688
515/281-5944
FAX # 515/281-4609
www.state.ia.us/ibpe

Kansas State Board of Pharmacy

900 S.W. Jackson Street
Room 513
Topeka, KS 66612-1231
785/296-4056
888-RXBOARD
FAX # 785/296-8420
www.accesskansas.org/pharmacy
email: pharmacy@ink.org

Kentucky Board of Pharmacy

23 Millcreek Park
Frankfort, KY 40601-9230
502/573-1580
FAX # 502/573-1582
www.state.ky.us/boards/pharmacy/
email: pharmacy.board@mail.state.ky.us

Louisiana Board of Pharmacy

5615 Corporate Blvd., Ste. 8E
Baton Rouge, LA 70808
225/925-6496
FAX # 225/925-6499
www.labp.com
email: labp@labp.com

Maine Commission on Pharmacy

Office of Licensing & Registraton
35 State House Station
Augusta, ME 04333
207/624-8620
FAX # 207/624-8637
Hearing Impaired: 207/624-8563
www.state.me.us/pfr/olr

Maryland Board of Pharmacy

4201 Patterson Avenue
Baltimore, MD 21215-2299
410/764-4755
FAX # 410/358-6207
www.dhmh.state.md.us/pharmacyboard/
email: mdbop@dhmh.state.md.us

Massachusetts Board of Registration in Pharmacy

239 Causeway Street, Suite 500
Boston, MA 02114
617/727-3074
FAX # 617/727-2197
www.state.ma.us/reg/boards/ph/default.htm

Michigan Board of Pharmacy

P.O. Box 30670
Lansing, MI 48909
517/373-1737
FAX # 517/335-4886
www.michigan.gov/cis

Minnesota State Board of Pharmacy

2829 University Ave. S.E., Ste. 530
Minneapolis, MN 55414-3251
612/617-2201
Hearing Impaired: 800/627-3529
FAX # 612/617-2212
www.phcybrd.state.mn.us
email: pharmacy.board@state.mn.us

Mississippi State Board of Pharmacy

625 North State Street
Jackson, MS 39202
601/354-6750
FAX # 601/354-6071
www.mbp.state.ms.us

Missouri Board of Pharmacy

3605 Missouri Boulevard
P.O. Box 625
Jefferson City, MO 65102
573/751-0091
TDD: 800/735-2966
FAX # 573/526-3464
www.ded.state.mo.us/regulatorylicensing/
   professionalregistration/pharmacy
email: pharmacy@mail.state.mo.us

Montana Board of Pharmacy

P.O. Box 200513
301 South Park, 4th Floor
Helena, MT 59620-0513
406/841-2355
FAX # 406/841-2343
www.discoveringmontana.com/dli/bsd/
   license/bsd_boards/pha_board/
   board_page.htm
email: dlibsdpha@state.mt.us

Nebraska Board of Examiners in Pharmacy

P.O. Box 94986
Lincoln, NE 68509
402/471-2115
www.hhs.state.ne.us

Nevada State Board of Pharmacy

555 Double Eagle Court, Ste. 1100
Reno, NV 89511-8991
775/850-1440
800/364-2081
FAX # 775/850-1444
http://glsuitewww.glsuite.com/nvbopweb
email: pharmacy@govmail.state.nv.us

New Hampshire Board of Pharmacy

57 Regional Drive
Concord, NH 03301-8518
603/271-2350
FAX # 603/271-2856
www.state.nh.us/pharmacy
email: nhpharmacy@nhsa.state.nh.us

New Jersey State Board of Pharmacy

124 Halsey Street
P.O. Box 45013
Newark, NJ 07101
973/504-6450
www.state.nj.us/lps/ca/brief/pharm.htm

New Mexico Board of Pharmacy

1650 University Blvd., N.E.
Suite 400B
Albuquerque, NM 87102
505/841-9102
800/565-9102
FAX # 505/841-9113
www.state.nm.us/pharmacy
email: Pharmacy.Board@state.nm.us

New York Board of Pharmacy

89 Washington Avenue
Second Floor West
Albany, NY 12234-1000
518/474-3817 ext. 130
FAX # 518/473-6995
www.nysed.gov/prof/pharm.htm
email: pharmbd@mail.nysed.gov

North Carolina Board of Pharmacy

P.O. Box 459
Carrboro Plaza
Carrboro, NC 27510
919/942-4454
FAX # 919/967-5757
www.ncbop.org

North Dakota State Board of Pharmacy

P.O. Box 1354
Bismarck, ND 58502-1354
701/328-9535
FAX # 701/328-9312

Ohio State Board of Pharmacy

77 S. High Street, Room 1702
Columbus, OH 43215-6126
614/466-4143
TTY/TDD: 800/750-0750
FAX # 614/752-4836
www.state.oh.us/pharmacy
email: exec@bop.state.oh.us

Oklahoma State Board of Pharmacy

4545 Lincoln Blvd., Ste. 112
Oklahoma City, OK 73105-3488
405/521-3815
FAX # 405/521-3758
www.state.ok.us/~pharmacy
email: pharmacy@oklaosf.state.ok.us

Oregon State Board of Pharmacy
State Office Building, Ste. 425
800 N.E. Oregon St., #9
Portland, OR 97232
503/731-4032
FAX # 503/731-4067
www.pharmacy.state.or.us

Pennsylvania State Board of Pharmacy
P.O. Box 2649
Harrisburg, PA 17105-2649
717/783-7156
FAX # 717/787-7769
www.dos.state.pa.us/bpoa/phabd/
    mainpage.htm
email: ST-PHARMACY@state.pa.us

Puerto Rico Board of Pharmacy
800 Avenida Robert T. Todd
Office #201, Stop 18
Santurce, PR 00908
787/725-8161
FAX # 787/725-8161

Rhode Island Board of Pharmacy
3 Capitol Hill, Room 205
Providence, RI 02908
401/222-2837
FAX # 401/222-2158
www.healthri.org/hsr/professions/
    pharmacy.htm

South Carolina Board of Pharmacy
P.O. Box 11927
Columbia, SC 29211-1927
803/896-4700
FAX # 803/896-4596
www.llr.state.sc.us/POL/Pharmacy
email: funderbm@mail.llr.state.sc.us

South Dakota State Board of Pharmacy
4305 S. Louise Ave., Ste. 104
Sioux Falls, SD 57106
605/362-2737
FAX # 605/362-2738
www.state.sd.us/dcr/pharmacy
email: dennis.jones@state.sd.us

Tennessee Board of Pharmacy
Davy Crockett Tower
500 James Robertson Parkway, 2nd Floor
Nashville, TN 37243-1149
615/741-2718
FAX # 615/741-2722
www.state.tn.us/commerce/boards/pharmacy
email: Kendall.Lynch@state.tn.us

Texas State Board of Pharmacy
William P. Hobby Building
Tower 3, Suite 600
333 Guadalupe Street, Box 21
Austin, TX 78701
512/305-8000
FAX # 512/305-8082
www.tsbp.state.tx.us

Utah Board of Pharmacy
P.O. Box 146741
Salt Lake City, UT 84114-6741
801/530-6628
FAX # 801/530-6511
www.dopl.utah.gov

Vermont Board of Pharmacy
26 Terrace Street, Drawer 09
Montpelier, VT 05609
802/828-2373
www.vtprofessionals.org/opr1/pharmacists
email: patkins@sec.state.vt.us

Virgin Islands Board of Pharmacy
Roy L. Schneider Hospital
Commissioner of Health Office
48 Sugar Estate
St. Thomas, VI 00802
340/774-0117

Virginia Board of Pharmacy
6603 W. Broad Street, 5th Floor
Richmond, VA 23230-1712
804/662-9911
TDD: 804/662-7197
FAX # 804/662-9313
www.dhp.state.va.us/pharmacy/default.htm
email: pharmbd@dhp.state.va.us

Washington State Board of Pharmacy
Department of Health
    Board of Pharmacy
P.O. Box 47865
Olympia, WA 98504-7863
360/236-4700
FAX # 360/263-4818
wws2.wa.gov/doh/hpqa-licensing/HPS4/
    Pharmacy/default.htm
email: hpqa.csc@doh.wa.gov

West Virginia Board of Pharmacy
232 Capitol Street
Charleston, WV 25301
304/558-0558

Wisconsin Pharmacy Examining Board

State of Wisconsin Department of
    Regulation and Licensing
1400 E. Washington Ave.
P.O. Box 8935
Madison, WI 53708-8935
608/266-2112
www.drl.state.wi.us
email: web@drl.state.wi.us

Wyoming State Board of Pharmacy

1720 S. Poplar, Ste. 4
Casper, WY 82601
307/234-0294
FAX # 307/234-7226
http://pharmacyboard.state.wy.us
email: wypharmbd@wercs.com

State Laws Affecting Pharmacy Practice

This appendix bears a reproduction of various aspects of state statutes and regulations pertaining to the practice of pharmacy. As has been noted elsewhere, pharmacists need to be concerned with laws, both statutes and regulations, emanating from two levels of government – federal and state. The federal government has authority to enact laws that impact professional practice through the authority conferred by the "Commerce Clause" of the United States Constitution, Article I, Section 8. Because the vast majority of pharmaceuticals and other items that the pharmacist deals with move via interstate commerce to reach the pharmacy, the authority of the federal government is invoked. Examples of this authority would include the regulation of medications and devices by the US Food and Drug Administration as well as the restrictions on distribution of controlled substances by the US Drug Enforcement Administration.

However, most direct authority over day-to-day pharmacy practice activities exists at the level of state government, usually seen through the actions of the state board of pharmacy or state-level controlled substances agency. The authority of state governments to put in place and enforce laws regulating the practice of pharmacy is rooted in the legal concept of "police power," the authority of government to make laws related to the public's health, safety, or welfare.

Because each state possesses its own authority to enact laws in this area, these laws, both statutes and regulations, vary from state to state. The National Association of Boards of Pharmacy (NABP) provides a valuable service to the profession by compiling these legal provisions in tables that facilitate both finding the relevant provisions on a particular topic in a certain state and comparing legal provisions among states. By special arrangement with NABP, their compilation of state law provisions is reproduced here.

National Association of Boards of Pharmacy

In compiling the information presented here, the NABP is dependent on the accuracy of the information provided by each of the state boards of pharmacy.

Survey of Pharmacy Law

Organizational Law
    I. Board Description, 816

Licensing Law
    III. Examination Requirements, 818
    IV. Practical Experience: Internship Hours, 820
    V. Registration for Interns/Preceptors/Training Sites, 824
    VI. Foreign Pharmacist Licensure, 826
    VII. Issuance of Initial Pharmacist Licensure, 828
    VIII. Licensure Transfer Requirements, 830
    IX. Issuance of Pharmacist Licenses Through Licensure Transfer, 833
    X. Pharmacist Licensure Renewal, 835
    XI. Continuing Pharmaceutical Education Requirements, 837
    XII. Discipline of Pharmacist Licenses, 841
    XIII. Status of Pharmacy Technicians, 843
    XIV. Pharmacy Technicians in Hospital/Institutional Setting, 847
    XV. Pharmacy Technicians in Community Setting, 850
    XVI. Pharmacy Licensure Requirements, 853
    XVII. Wholesale Distributor Licensure Requirements, 856
    XVIII. Drug Control Regulations, 858

Drug Law
    XIX. Drug Product Selection Laws, 860
    XX. Prescription Requirements, 862
    XXI. Facsimile Transmission of Prescriptions, 866
    XXII. Electronic Transmission of Prescriptions: Computer-to-Computer, 869
    XXIII. Patient Counseling Requirements, 871
    XXIV. Prescribing Authority, 873
    XXV. Dispensing Authority, 880
    XXVI. Possession of Non-Controlled Legend Drugs, 884
    XXVII. Possession of Controlled Substances, 888
    XXVIII. Miscellaneous State Pharmacy Laws, 892
    XXIX. Minimum Standards of Practice, 896
    XXX. Census Data, 897

I. Board Description

State	First Enactment	Board Designation/ State Agency	Rules and Regulations Made by	Number of Compliance Officers/ Inspectors	Board Fiscal Year
Alabama	1931	B	B	7	Oct. 1-Sept. 30
Alaska	1935	A	A	—	July 1-June 30
Arizona	1903	B	B	5	July 1-June 30
Arkansas	1891	B	B	4	July 1-June 30
California	1891	B	B	21.5	July 1-June 30
Colorado	1887	B, N	B	4	July 1-June 30
Connecticut	1881	C, L	C, L	12	July 1-June 30
Delaware	1883	B	B	9	July 1-June 30
District of Columbia	1906	A	A, T	5	July 1-June 30
Florida	1889	A	A	13	July 1-June 30
Georgia	1881	B, K	B	15	July 1-June 30
Guam	1982	F, I	B	1	Oct. 1-Sept. 30
Hawaii	1949	B, M	B	EE	July 1-June 30
Idaho	1889	A	A	4	July 1-June 30
Illinois	1881	B, D	B, D	7	July 1-June 30
Indiana	1899	AA	AA	4	July 1-June 30
Iowa	1880	BB	BB	3	July 1-June 30
Kansas	1885	B	B	3	July 1-June 30
Kentucky	1874	A	A	4	July 1- June 30 W
Louisiana	1888	A	A	4	July 1-June 30
Maine	1877	A, CC	A, CC	2	July 1-June 30
Maryland	1902	A	A	5 FF	July 1-June 30
Massachusetts	1885	E, P	E	2.5	July 1-June 30
Michigan	1885	A, J	A	EE	Oct. 1-Sept. 30
Minnesota	1885	A	A	5	July 1-June 30
Mississippi	1892	B	B	4	July 1-June 30
Missouri	1881	A	A	7	July 1-June 30
Montana	1895	A	A	1	July 1-June 30
Nebraska	1887	A, GG	A, GG	3	July 1-June 30
Nevada	1901	B	B	4	July 1-June 30
New Hampshire	1875	A	A	3	July 1-June 30
New Jersey	1877	A	B	4	July 1-June 30
New Mexico	1889	A	A	7	July 1-June 30
New York	1884	A, G	U	EE	July 1-June 30
North Carolina	1881	A	A	7	Oct. 1-Sept. 30
North Dakota	1887	B	B	4	July 1-June 30
Ohio	1884	B	B	8/15 DD	July 1-June 30
Oklahoma	1899	B	B	4	July 1-June 30
Oregon	1891	B	B	6	July 1-June 30
Pennsylvania	1887	B, R, S	B, V	6	July 1-June 30
Puerto Rico	1906	A, I	A	II	July 1-June 30
Rhode Island	1870	A, I	A, I	1	July 1-June 30
South Carolina	1876	A, Y	A, V	4	July 1-June 30
South Dakota	1899	B	B	2	July 1-June 30
Tennessee	1893	A, H	A	5	July 1-June 30
Texas	1907	B	B	11	Sep. 1-Aug. 31
Utah	1892	A, S	S	EE	July 1-June 30
Vermont	1894	A	A	1	July 1-June 30
Virginia	1886	A	A	4	July 1-June 30
Washington	1891	B	B	10	July 1-June 30 W
West Virginia	1881	A	A, V	4	July 1-June 30
Wisconsin	1882	O, Q	O	9	July 1-June 30
Wyoming	1886	B	B	2	July 1-June 30

I. Board Description *(cont.)*

Method of Financing the Board		
State Board Account	**Special Fund in State Treasury**	**State General Revenue Fund**
Yes	—	—
Yes	—	—
—	Yes	—
Yes	Yes	No
Yes	—	—
—	—	Yes
—	—	Yes
—	—	Yes
—	Yes	—
—	—	Yes
No	No	Yes
—	Yes	—
—	Yes	—
—	Yes	—
—	—	Yes
—	—	Yes
—	Yes	No
—	Yes	—
Yes	—	—
—	Yes	No
—	Yes	—
No	No	Yes
—	—	Yes
Yes	Yes	No
—	Yes	—
No	Yes	No
Yes	Yes	No
Yes	—	No
—	—	Yes
Yes	—	—
Yes	Yes	No
—	Yes	—
Yes	No	No
Yes	No	No
—	Yes	—
Yes	Yes	No
Yes	Yes	No
Yes HH	—	—
—	Yes	—
—	—	Yes
No	Yes Z	Yes X
Yes HH	—	—
—	—	Yes
—	Yes X	—
No	No	Yes
—	Yes	—
No	Yes	No
Yes	—	—
Yes	Yes	No
—	Yes	Yes
—	Yes	No

LEGEND

A — Board of Pharmacy.
B — State Board of Pharmacy. (AZ, PA – Board promulgates, others review and approve.)
C — Commission of Pharmacy.
D — Department of Professional Regulation.
E — Board of Registration in Pharmacy.
F — Board of Examiners in Pharmacy.
G — Department of Education.
H — Department of Commerce & Insurance.
I — Department of Health.
J — Department of Consumer and Industry Services, Bureau of Health Services.
K — State Examining Boards.
L — Department of Consumer Protection.
M — Department of Commerce and Consumer Affairs.
N — Department of Regulatory Agencies.
O — Pharmacy Examining Board.
P — Department of Consumer Affairs.
Q — Department of Regulation and Licensing.
R — Department of State.
S — Division of Occupational Professional Licensing. (PA – Bureau of Professional and Occupational Affairs.)
T — Mayor.
U — Board of Regents.
V — Must be approved by General Assembly. (PA – And various other regulatory review agencies.)
W — Budget is biennial.
X — Except for fines collected under Pharmacy Act.
Y — Department of Labor, Licensing and Regulation.
Z — For fines only.
AA — Health Professions Bureau.
BB — Board of Pharmacy Examiners.
CC — Department of Professional and Financial Regulation.
DD — Eight clinical and 15 non-clinical site inspectors.
EE — Centralized investigations pool.
FF — One compliance officer, five inspectors outside of Board control.
GG — Health and Human Services, Department of Regulation and Licensure, Credentialing Division.
HH — Licensure fees fund Board activities.
II — Pharmacy inspectors are under a different division of the local Department of Health.

III. Examination Requirements

State	Examinations NAPLEX®	MPJE®	Non-MPJE Law Exam	Other	Does State Participate in NAPLEX Score Transfer Program?	Validity Period for a NAPLEX Score Transfer?
Alabama	Yes	Yes	No	Interview	Yes A	None
Alaska	Yes	Yes	No	No	Yes	1 year
Arizona	Yes	Yes	No	No	Yes	1 year
Arkansas	Yes	No	Yes	No	Yes A	Not addressed
California	No	No	No	Yes J	No	N/A
Colorado	Yes	Yes	No	No	Yes	1 year
Connecticut	Yes	Yes	No	C, G	Yes	1 year
Delaware	Yes	Yes	No	—	Yes	1 year
District of Columbia	Yes	Yes	D.C. exam	No	Yes	1 year
Florida	Yes	Yes	No	No	B	N/A
Georgia	Yes	No	Yes	Yes H	Yes	None
Guam	Yes	No	Yes	Interview	Yes	Not addressed
Hawaii	Yes	Yes	—	—	Yes	90 days
Idaho	Yes	No	Yes	No	Yes A	1 year
Illinois	Yes	Yes	No	No	Yes	3 years
Indiana	Yes	Yes	No	Yes H	Yes	None
Iowa	Yes	Yes	No	No	Yes	1 year
Kansas	Yes	Yes	No	—	Yes D	1 year
Kentucky	Yes	Yes	No	Yes C, F, K	Yes	1 year
Louisiana	Yes	Yes	—	No	Yes A, D	1 year
Maine	Yes	Yes	No	No	Yes	1 year
Maryland	Yes	Yes	Yes S	Yes E, L	Yes E	1 year
Massachusetts	Yes	Yes	No	No	Yes	1 year
Michigan	Yes	Yes	No	No	Yes	None
Minnesota	Yes	Yes	No	Yes H, K	Yes A	Q
Mississippi	Yes	No	Yes	No	Yes A	1 year
Missouri	Yes	Yes	No	No	Yes A	Indefinite U
Montana	Yes	Yes	No	No	Yes	1 year
Nebraska	Yes	Yes	No	No	Yes	Not addressed
Nevada	Yes	Yes	No	—	Yes	1 year
New Hampshire	Yes	Yes	No	No	Yes	90 days N
New Jersey	Yes	Yes	No	No	Yes	None
New Mexico	Yes	Yes	No	No	Yes	1 year
New York	Yes	Yes	No	Yes H	Yes	5 years
North Carolina	Yes	No	Yes	Yes	Yes A, E	2 years
North Dakota	Yes	Yes	No	Yes F	Yes	3 years
Ohio	Yes	Yes	No	No	Yes	—
Oklahoma	Yes	No	Yes	No	Yes	1 year
Oregon	Yes	Yes	No	No	Yes	1 year R
Pennsylvania	Yes	Yes	No	—	Yes	6 months
Puerto Rico	Yes P	No	Yes O	Yes M	Yes	—
Rhode Island	Yes	Yes	No	No	Yes	6 months
South Carolina	Yes	Yes	No	No	Yes	1 year
South Dakota	Yes	No	Yes	No	Yes	1 year
Tennessee	Yes	No	Yes	No	Yes A	1 year
Texas	Yes	Yes	No	No	Yes A	2 years
Utah	Yes	Yes	No	No	Yes	90 days
Vermont	Yes	Yes	No	—	Yes	1 year
Virginia	Yes	No	Yes I	—	Yes	1 year
Washington	Yes	Yes	No	No	Yes	1 year
West Virginia	Yes	No T	Yes T	K	Yes A	1 year
Wisconsin	Yes	Yes	No	Yes	Yes	1 year
Wyoming	Yes	Yes	No	No	Yes	1 year

III. Examination Requirements *(cont.)*

Laws in all states, including the District of Columbia and Puerto Rico, require applicants for licensure to (1) graduate from an accredited first professional degree program of a college of pharmacy; and (2) pass an examination given by the board of pharmacy. All states, the District of Columbia, Guam, and Puerto Rico use the North American Pharmacist Licensure Examination™ (NAPLEX®), except California.

Candidate review guides for the NAPLEX and Multistate Pharmacy Jurisprudence Examination™ (MPJE®) are available free of charge on the NABP Web site at www.nabp.net.

LEGEND

A — Scores may not be transferred from Florida.

B — Scores **may** be transferred **from** Florida to some other state; however, scores **may not** be transferred **to** Florida from another state.

C — General Pharmacy Practice Examination, including Dispensing Laboratory Examination. (CT – Does not include Dispensing Laboratory Examination.)

D — State will score transfer on a reciprocal basis with any other state that will accept its scores.

E — Applicants licensed by score transfer must wait until the next exam administration to complete remainder of exam requirements. (MD – Maryland Laboratory Exam.)

F — Oral patient consultation examination.

G — Plus pharmaceutical calculations exam.

H — Practical exam.

I — Combined state/federal law exam.

J — California pharmacist licensure examination.

K — Errors and Omissions Exam.

L — Pre-screening exam of oral English competence.

M — Practice exam prepared by the Board.

N — Ninety days from the date the NH application is mailed by the Board office to the candidate.

O — State law exam prepared by the Board.

P — Candidate may choose to take the NAPLEX or an examination prepared by the Board.

Q — Until the next time the practical exam is given – twice a year: June and Jan.

R — Oregon will occasionally stretch the one-year validity period.

S — Score transfer candidates must take the MPJE. Reciprocity candidates must take non-MPJE law exam given monthly.

T — Plan to start MPJE in 2003.

U — State keeps transferred scores indefinitely.

IV. Practical Experience: Internship Hours

Table IV responds to the following questions:
1. Amount of practical experience required by the Board?
2. Total amount of time required after graduation?
3. What academic year does pharmacy internship/externship credit begin with the Board (BS program/PharmD program)?
4. Amount of college-supervised experience allowed by the Board?

State	1.	2.	3.	4.
Alabama	1500 B	400	first professional year	400 hrs. of the minimum total requirement must be obtained after completing the requirements of the third professional year. The 400 hrs. must be completed in a traditional setting, so emphasis is on distribution of medicines, prescriptions, and medical supplies. May be obtained through a college-structured or a non-structured program, all under the supervision of a registered preceptor.
Alaska	1500 B	None	third professional year	1500 hrs. internship required by Board. Max. of 1,000 hrs. completed in conjuction with educational requirement of the college of pharmacy.
Arizona	1500 B	None	first professional year	1500 hrs. required by regulation.
Arkansas	2000	None	after first professional year	Actual hours accepted for internship in conjunction with academic credit, 1500 hrs. for PharmD program. Additional internship credit accepted while enrolled in school, but not in class.
California	1500 C	1000 B Before taking exam	first professional year	Min. of 900 hrs. internship time in a pharmacy under a preceptor's supervision; 600 hrs. granted at Board's discretion, which may include 600 hrs. clinical clerkship.
Colorado	1500	None	first professional year	Max. 1100 hrs. may be obtained via accredited rotation program; other hours may be okayed through enrollment in approved school of pharmacy or via valid FPGEC certification. Up to 30 percent of the required hours may be obtained with a drug manufacturer and/or with a school of pharmacy in drug or drug-related research activities.
Connecticut	1500	None	after completing two years of college and while enrolled in college of pharmacy	1500 internship hrs. while enrolled in ACPE-approved college. Max. of 40 hrs. per week. Not more than 400 hrs. can be credited towards non-traditional experience.
Delaware	1500	None	first professional year	Full credit for college-supervised programs.
Dist. of Columbia	1500/1000 B	—	first professional year	1000 internship hrs. while enrolled.
Florida	2080 (varies) D	N/A	first professional year	Varies.
Georgia	1500 B	—	first professional year	480 hrs. internship in conjunction with academic credit. 480 hrs. for BS program, 700 hrs. for PharmD program.
Guam	1500 B, C	None	after completion of third academic year	1500 hrs.
Hawaii	1500 B	None	after successful completion of first professional year	1500 hrs.
Idaho	1500 B	None	first professional year	1500 hrs. internship required by Board.
Illinois	400 C	None	first professional year	400 hrs. internship in conjunction with academic credit.
Indiana	1500	None	upon enrollment in pharmacy school	The number of hours required by an ACPE- or Canadian Council on Pharmacy Accreditation (CCPA)-accredited college of pharmacy or other Board-approved experiential program. For those who have not graduated from such a program, 1500 hrs.
Iowa	1500 B	None	after one semester within a college of pharmacy	1000 hrs. internship in conjunction with academic credit; additional 500 hrs. required to be non-concurrent with academic training.

IV. Practical Experience: Internship Hours *(cont.)*

Table IV responds to the following questions:
1. Amount of practical experience required by the Board?
2. Total amount of time required after graduation?
3. What academic year does pharmacy internship/externship credit begin with the Board (BS program/PharmD program)?
4. Amount of college-supervised experience allowed by the Board?

State	1.	2.	3.	4.
Kansas	1500 B, C	None	first professional year	1000 program hrs. accepted by Board.
Kentucky	1500	None	admission to a college of pharmacy	Up to 960 hrs. for PharmD and up to 710 hrs. for BS college programs. Beginning Jan 1, 2001, Board will grant hour-per-hour credit to clinical experiential programs.
Louisiana	1 yr. C 1500 B	500 BS only	first professional year	BS – Minimum of 600 hrs. prior to structured program in order to receive 400 hrs. in structured program. 500 hrs. via internship after graduation or all 1500 hrs. after graduation. PharmD – mimimum of 400 hrs. prior to graduation. Structured program must include a minimum of 300 hrs. in a retail setting and a minimum of 300 hrs. in a hospital setting, for a maximum of 1100 hrs. in all settings.
Maine	1500	None	first professional year	1500 hrs. required by Board.
Maryland	1560/1000	None	first professional year	1560 hrs. required under supervision of licensed pharmacist OR 1000 hrs. in a school-supervised program, OR combination accepted on equivalent basis.
Massachusetts	1500	None	after completion of second year	Internship time while enrolled; 1500 hrs. required by Board including 400 hrs. clinical externship.
Michigan	1000	None	first professional year	40 hrs. a week while enrolled, but not in classes; 16 hrs. a week while attending classes; Board-approved practical experience within college program varies by college; up to 1000 hrs. clinical externship.
Minnesota	1600	None	after first professional year	400 hrs. while attending classes; 1600 hrs. allowed by Board. 800 hours must be actual dispensing hours.
Mississippi	1600	None	first professional year	Up to 800 hrs. while enrolled but not in classes; 800 hrs. in conjunction with academic credit.
Missouri	1500	None	after 30 hrs. of college of pharmacy credit	750 hrs. while enrolled but not in classes (externship); 10 hrs. per week while attending classes, max. of 500 hrs. (concurrent); 40 hrs. per week during summer or academic breaks (nonconcurrent).
Montana	1500 B	None	after first professional year	1000 hrs. (BS)/1500 hrs. (PharmD) in conjunction with academic credit.
Nebraska	1500 B	None	after completion of one week of pharmacy school	Up to 640 hrs. for a BS degree and up to 1300 hrs. for a PharmD degree in conjunction with academic credit. New regulations will allow Board to accept 1500 hrs. for PharmD programs.
Nevada	1500 C	None	first professional year	1500 hrs. required by board.
New Hampshire	1500 B, C	None	summer preceding first professional year	Actual hours worked.
New Jersey	1000 B	Varies	first professional year	Varies. 1000 hrs. required by regulation.
New Mexico	1500/2150 B	None	after 30 semester hrs. of college of pharmacy credit	1500 BS/2150 PharmD
New York	6 mos. B (1040 hrs.)	None	after first professional year	Graduates of registered or accredited programs leading to the doctor of pharmacy degree shall be considered to have completed the internship requirement.
North Carolina	1500	None	after second academic year	Actual hours worked.
North Dakota	1500	None	after first academic year	1500 hrs. required by rule.

IV. Practical Experience: Internship Hours *(cont.)*

Table IV responds to the following questions:
1. Amount of practical experience required by the Board?
2. Total amount of time required after graduation?
3. What academic year does pharmacy internship/externship credit begin with the Board (BS program/PharmD program)?
4. Amount of college-supervised experience allowed by the Board?

State	1.	2.	3.	4.
Ohio	1500 B	None	after successful completion of 48 semester hrs. or 72 quarter hrs. of college and enrollment in a college of pharmacy	Board-approved hours.
Oklahoma	1500	None	first professional year	Up to 1500 hrs. (PharmD)
Oregon	2000	None	first professional and third academic year	Board-approved hours. Up to 2000 hrs.
Pennsylvania	1500	None	A	Up to 750 hrs. in conjunction with academic credit.
Puerto Rico	1500	None	fourth year	Not specified in Rules. Board is currently accepting 540 hrs. in conjunction with academic credit.
Rhode Island	1500	None	first professional year	1500 hrs. required by Board
South Carolina	1500 C	None	three months prior to entering pharmacy school	Up to 500 hrs. (BS)/1000 hrs. (PharmD) in conjunction with academic credit.
South Dakota	1500 B	None	first professional year	Up to 640 hrs. allowed by the Board for college clinical rotation; 880 hrs. must be obtained in settings where training develops general pharmacist competencies.
Tennessee	1500 B	None	first professional year	1100 hrs. in conjunction with academic credit; 400 hrs. may be obtained through non-traditional programs.
Texas	1500 B	None	after completion of 30 credit hrs. towards a pharmacy degree	1500 hrs. allowed by regulation.
Utah	1500 C	None	after 15 quarter hrs. of professional pharmacy courses	900 hrs. in conjunction with academic credit. At least 120 hrs. each in community, hospital, and one other pharmacy practice setting.
Vermont	1500 C	None	first professional year	Up to 1000 hrs. in conjunction with academic credit.
Virginia	1000/1500	None	after first professional year	1000/1200 hrs. A minimum of 1500 hrs. of practical experience, of which at least 300 hours shall be gained outside of a school of pharmacy practical experience program, is required. Students enrolled in a school of pharmacy prior to January 1, 1999, are required to have a minimum of 1000 hrs., all of which may be gained within the college program. In addition, 300 hrs. must be in the area of prescription compounding and dispensing.
Washington	1500	None	after the first quarter/ semester of pharmacy education	1200 hrs. in conjunction with academic credit.
West Virginia	1500 C	None	upon pharmacy school enrollment	800 hrs. allowed by the Board.
Wisconsin*	1500 B	None	second year of pharmacy school curriculum	Up to 1500 pharmacy school hrs. for a PharmD program.
Wyoming	2000 B	None	after the first professional year	1600 hrs. of college-supervised clinical clerkship.

IV. Practical Experience: Internship Hours *(cont.)*

All jurisdictions require candidates for licensure to have a record of practical experience or internship training acquired under the supervision and instruction of a licensed practitioner.

LEGEND

A — Applicant must successfully complete two years of pharmacy college or an accredited program leading to transfer into the third year of a pharmacy college in which the applicant is enrolled or accepted.

B — Required by Rule or Regulation

C — Required by Statute

D — Applicants with ACPE-accredited PharmD received after January 1, 2001, are deemed to have met internship requirements for licensure.

*Pharmacy internship under the jurisdiction of the Pharmacy Internship Board, University of Wisconsin, 425 N Charter St, Madison, WI 53706.

NABP Internship Committee's definition of "concurrent time" as it applies to internship programs:

Concurrent time is defined as experience gained while a person is a full-time student. Further, a full-time student is defined as one carrying, in any given school term, at least 75% of the average number of credit hours per term needed to graduate within five years.

The 400 concurrent hours may be in any of the three areas or combinations of them 1) traditional internship supervised by the college; 2) clinical pharmacy programs; 3) demonstration projects.

In the event that the student is registered in a college-administered practicum, which involves the student in a 40-hour work week, (s)he is not to be considered as acquiring concurrent time in this situation. (S)he could be carrying three semester hours or less of didactic, academic work.

V. Registration for Interns/Preceptors/Training Sites

State	Does Board Require Licensure/Registration of: Training Sites?	Preceptors?	Interns?	Intern Initial Fee	Intern Renewal Fee	Intern Duration of Registration
Alabama	Yes	Yes	Yes	None	None	Intern duration
Alaska	No	No	Yes	$ 50 P	$ 50	1 year A
Arizona	No	No	Yes	$ 10	$ 10 B	6 years C
Arkansas	No	Yes	Yes	$ 15	$ 15	1 year O
California	No	No	Yes	$ 65	—	5 years V
Colorado	No	Yes	Yes	$ 41	$ 41	1 year (Sept. 1-Aug. 31)
Connecticut	No	No	Yes	$ 30	None	Intern duration
Delaware	No	No	Yes	$ 5	None	Intern duration
District of Columbia	No	Yes	No	$ 28	$ 28 D	Intern duration
Florida	No	No	Yes	None	None	Intern duration
Georgia	No	No	Yes	$ 25	$ 25	5 years A
Guam	No	Yes L	Yes	$ 40	$ 40	1 year
Hawaii	No	No	Yes	$ 10	None	Intern duration
Idaho	Yes	No	Yes	$ 15	$ 15	1 year
Illinois	No	No	Yes E	$ 40	$ 25	1 year
Indiana	No	No	Yes	$ 10	$ 10	6 years F
Iowa	No	No	Yes	$ 33	None	U
Kansas	No	Yes	Yes	$ 25	None	5 years G
Kentucky	No	Yes	Yes	$ 25	—	6 years
Louisiana	Yes	Yes	Yes	$ 10	None	Z
Maine	No	No	No	None	None	—
Maryland	No	No	No	None	None	—
Massachusetts	No	Yes	Yes	$ 95	None	Intern duration
Michigan	No	Yes	Yes	$ 35	$ 15	1 year post-grad
Minnesota	No	Yes	Yes	$ 20	—	Duration
Mississippi	No	No	Yes	$ 50	None	H
Missouri	Yes	No	Yes	$ 40	$ 25	X
Montana	No	Yes	Yes	$ 40	None	2 years post-grad
Nebraska	No	Yes S	Yes	$ 40	—	15 months post-grad
Nevada	No	No	Yes	$ 15	$ 15 B	4 years
New Hampshire	No	No	No	None	None	W
New Jersey	No	Yes	Yes	None	None	6 months post-grad
New Mexico	Yes	Yes	Yes	$ 15	$ 10	1 year
New York	No	No	Yes	$ 70	$ 70 D	5 years D
North Carolina	No	No	No	None	None	—
North Dakota	Yes	Yes	Yes	$ 10	$100 I	1 year
Ohio	No	No J	Yes	$ 22.50	$ 22.50	1 year A
Oklahoma	Yes	Yes	Yes	$ 50	—	5 years
Oregon	No	Yes	Yes	$ 30	$ 30	Up to 4 years
Pennsylvania	No	Yes	Yes	$ 30	—	6 years
Puerto Rico	T	K	Yes	None	None	Not specified
Rhode Island	No	No	Yes	$ 12.50	$ 12.50	1 year (July 1-June 30) A
South Carolina	No	No	Yes	$ 50	None	6 years A
South Dakota	No	No	Yes	$ 40	None	Intern duration
Tennessee	No	No	No	None	None	—
Texas Y	No	Yes	Yes	None	None	Intern duration
Utah	No	No L	Yes	$ 25	Q	4 years R
Vermont	No	Yes	Yes	None	None	Intern duration
Virginia	No	No	Yes	None	None	—
Washington	No	Yes	Yes	$ 20	$ 20	1 year
West Virginia	No	No M	Yes	$ 10	$ 10	4 years
Wisconsin	No	No	No	None	—	3 years N
Wyoming	Yes	Yes	Yes	$ 15	$ 10	Intern duration

V. Registration for Interns/Preceptors/Training Sites (cont.)

LEGEND

A — May be renewed. (AK – One time only.)

B — Biennial.

C — After six years, must be re-evaluated.

D — One two-year renewal permitted.

E — Registered as pharmacy technicians.

F — Plus one five-year renewal.

G — Except on Board approval.

H — Four years or until licensed as RPh, whichever is first.

I — Internship fee during the four-year professional program (Doctor of Pharmacy) is $100 per year. The initial $10 fee is for registration as a pharmacy intern by pre-pharmacy students after one successful academic year of pre-pharmacy program.

J — "Statement of Preceptor" form must be filed with the Board prior to obtaining practical experience.

K — Board "certifies" only preceptors with not less than three years of experience dispensing prescriptions.

L — However, Board approval required.

M — Must be licensed pharmacist.

N — Expires May 31 in the third year suceeding the year in which the license was issued.

O — Renewed annually up to one year prior to graduation.

P — Plus one-time application fee of $50.

Q — Not renewable.

R — Must surrender license within 60 days of not meeting regulations for licensure (student, resident).

S — Certified: Must be licensed six months, must apply to Department, and pass test, must receive notification of certification from Board/Department, and should be a member of a pharmacy association.

T — Board "certifies" only sites dispensing not less than 4,000 prescriptions per year.

U — Registration terminates upon earliest of any of the following: licensure to practice pharmacy in any state; laspe, exceeding one year, in pursuit of pharmacy degree; one year following graduation from college of pharmacy. May request extension beyond automatic termination; consideration granted for out-of-state pharmacists participating in Iowa fellowship or residency program.

V — Up to five years with extension possible for limited periods at discretion of Board.

W — A pharmacy student qualifies as an intern beginning three months immediately preceding the first professional year. Pre-pharmacy students must register with the Board as "technician."

X — Must maintain intern license until 1500 hours have been acquired plus renew annually.

Y — Internship hours may be used for the purpose of licensure for no longer than two years from the date the internship is completed.

Z — Registration expires one year after date of graduation unless licensed sooner.

VI. Foreign Pharmacist Licensure

State	Issuance of Licenses to Foreign-Educated Allowed	State Requirements for Foreign Pharmacist Licensure		
		FPGEC® Certification	Amount of Practical Experience	Board Appearance
Alabama	No	—	—	—
Alaska	Yes	Yes	1500 hrs. A	No
Arizona	Yes	Yes	1500 hrs. A	Optional
Arkansas	Yes	Yes	2000 hrs.	Yes
California	Yes	No H	1500 hrs.	No
Colorado	Yes	Yes	1500 hrs. E	No
Connecticut	Yes	Yes P	1500 hrs.	Yes
Delaware	Yes	Yes	1500 hrs.	No
District of Columbia	Yes	Yes	1500 hrs.	—
Florida	Yes	No H	500 hrs. B	No
Georgia	Yes	Yes	1500 hrs.	—
Guam	Yes	Yes	1500 hrs.	No
Hawaii	Yes	Yes	1500 hrs.	No
Idaho	Yes	Yes	1500 hrs. C	—
Illinois	Yes	Yes	400 hrs. D	No
Indiana	Yes	Yes	1500 hrs.	No
Iowa	Yes	Yes	1500 hrs. E, F	No
Kansas	Yes	Yes P	1500 hrs. C	No
Kentucky	Yes	Yes	1500 hrs. C	No
Louisiana	Yes	Yes	1500 hrs.	If appropriate
Maine	Yes	Yes	1500 hrs., 750 hrs. US	No
Maryland	Yes	Yes	1560 hrs.	No
Massachusetts	Yes	Yes	1500 hrs. C	Optional
Michigan	Yes	Yes	1000 hrs.	No
Minnesota	Yes	Yes	1600 hrs. C	No
Mississippi	Yes	Yes	1600 hrs.	Yes
Missouri	Yes	Yes	1500 hrs.	No
Montana	No	S	—	—
Nebraska	Yes	Yes	1500 hrs. C, F	No
Nevada	Yes	Yes	1500 hrs.	No
New Hampshire	Yes	Yes Q	1500 hrs.	No
New Jersey	Yes	Yes	1000 hrs.	No
New Mexico	Yes	Yes	1500 hrs. F	—
New York	Yes	Yes	L	No
North Carolina	Yes	Yes	1500 hrs.	No
North Dakota	Yes	Yes	1500 hrs.	Yes
Ohio	Yes	Yes	1500 hrs.	No
Oklahoma	Yes	Yes	500 hrs. B, I	Yes R
Oregon	Yes	Yes	2000 hrs.	No
Pennsylvania	Yes	Yes	1500 hrs. A	No
Puerto Rico	No G	N/A	N/A	N/A
Rhode Island	Yes	Yes	1500 hrs.	No
South Carolina	Yes	Yes	1500 hrs. A, K	No
South Dakota	Yes	Yes	1500 hrs.	Yes
Tennessee	Yes	Yes	1500 hrs. O	Yes
Texas	Yes	Yes	1500 hrs.	No
Utah	Yes	Yes	1500 hrs.	If appropriate
Vermont	Yes	Yes T	1500 hrs.	No
Virginia	Yes	J	1500 hrs. A, M	No
Washington	Yes	Yes	1500 hrs.	No
West Virginia	Yes	Yes	1500 hrs. N	No
Wisconsin	Yes	Yes	1500 hrs.	No
Wyoming	No	—	—	—

VI. Foreign Pharmacist Licensure (cont.)

A majority of jurisdictions has implemented provisions for licensing graduates of pharmacy educational programs outside the United States, Guam, and Puerto Rico. NABP provides the Foreign Pharmacy Graduate Examination Committee® (FPGEC®) Certification Program as the primary means of assisting boards of pharmacy in assessing the educational equivalence of foreign pharmacy graduates.

In the tripartite process of certification, candidates must document their educational backgrounds, and an evaluation of their academic program is performed to ascertain whether it meets certain minimum criteria of length and content. Candidates must then pass the Foreign Pharmacy Graduate Equivalency Examination™ (FPGEE®), a computer-based test of academic subject areas, as well as demonstrate English language proficiency by passing the Test of English as a Foreign Language (TOEFL) with a score of 550 and the Test of Spoken English (TSE) with a score of 50. To become licensed, the candidate must then complete experiential requirements and pass the licensing examinations, as domestic graduates are required to do.

FPGEC Certification is now accepted by the vast majority of NABP member boards. The *FPGEC Certification Program Application/Registration Bulletin* contains more information about the Program and is available from the NABP Foreign Pharmacy Department, 700 Busse Highway, Park Ridge, Illinois 60068.

LEGEND

A — In the United States.

B — In state.

C — After FPGEC Certification.

D — Clinical experience must be preapproved by the Board.

E — Internship credit shall be obtained following registration as an intern and following FPGEC Certification.

F — Credit for all or a portion of the 1500-hr. internship may be granted based on experience as a practicing pharmacist in the foreign country. Individuals must request and submit detailed information to justify the requested experiential credit.

G — Graduation from a school of pharmacy accredited by ACPE is specifically required.

H — Successful passage of FPGEE necessary but certification not required.

I — After FPGEC Certification and prior to licensure examination.

J — FPGEC Certification not specifically required but must have 1) NABP certification that foreign education meets standards for FPGEC Certification, 2) FPGEE score of at least 75, 3) TOEFL score of 550, and 4) TSE score of 50.

K — Internship credit shall be obtained following registration as an intern and following FPGEC.

L — 2080 hrs. (12 mos.).

M — If enrolled in college of pharmacy prior to January 1, 1999, 1000 hrs. in US. If after, 1500 hrs. in US.

N — One-third may be earned in foreign country.

O — When internship hours obtained outside of state, an additional 500 hrs. must be obtained in state. Candidates may officially obtain internship hours after they have applied for FPGEC Certification (TN).

P — Minimum TSE score of 55 required.

Q — FPGEC Certification is not required for graduates of Canadian colleges of pharmacy whose programs are accredited by the Canadian Council for Accreditation of Pharmacy Programs (CCAPP).

R — Must pass law exam and interview with Board.

S — Rule hearing to accept underway.

T — Canadian graduates now accepted without FPGEC Certification.

VII. Issuance of Initial Pharmacist Licensure

State	Board/Regulatory Agency that Issues Licenses	Age at Which Initial License Can be Obtained	Initial Certificate Fee	Temporary Licenses
Alabama	A	19	$ 60	None
Alaska	E	Not addressed	$180 N	Yes AA
Arizona	A	—	$ 20	None
Arkansas	A	21	$ 10	Yes
California	A	18	$115	None
Colorado	A	Not addressed	None	None
Connecticut	C, D	18	None	Yes AA
Delaware	E	Majority DD	R	None
District of Columbia	F	18	$ 20	None
Florida	F	18	$190	None
Georgia	A	18	None O	None
Guam	A	18	$100	None
Hawaii	A	18	P	Yes X
Idaho	A	Majority	None	None
Illinois	G	21	$ 75	None
Indiana	B	18	$100	Q
Iowa	H	—	U	None
Kansas	A	18	None	None
Kentucky	F	18	None	None
Louisiana	F	21	$ 75	None
Maine	F	21	None	None
Maryland	A	18	$100 CC	None
Massachusetts	J	18	$ 56	None
Michigan	B	18	$145	None
Minnesota	F	—	$105	None
Mississippi	A	—	$150	None
Missouri	F	21	$105 Z	Yes
Montana	A	Not addressed	$ 60	None
Nebraska	T	21	$ 300 I	None
Nevada	A	Not addressed	$150	Yes
New Hampshire	F	18	$265	None
New Jersey	A	Majority	$140	None
New Mexico	F	Majority	$100	None
New York	M	21	$155	None
North Carolina	F	Not addressed	None	None
North Dakota	A	18	$ 25	Yes
Ohio	A	18	None	None
Oklahoma	A	—	$125	None
Oregon	A	18	$120	None
Pennsylvania	A	21	$ 40	None
Puerto Rico	F	21	$ 10	None
Rhode Island	A	18	$125	None
South Carolina	F	Not addressed	$ 70	None
South Dakota	A	18	$ 35	None
Tennessee	F	21	$ 96	None
Texas	A	18	$227	None
Utah	K	Not addressed	$100 Y	None
Vermont	A, V	18	$110	None
Virginia	F	18	$ 50 W	None
Washington	L	18	$130	None
West Virginia	F	18	$255 S	None
Wisconsin	H	Not addressed	$378	None
Wyoming	A	Majority	None	None

VII. Issuance of Initial Pharmacist Licensure *(cont.)*

LEGEND

A — State Board of Pharmacy.
B — Department of Consumer and Industry Services.
C — Commission of Pharmacy.
D — Department of Consumer Protection.
E — Division of Licensing and Registration and approval of Board.
F — Board of Pharmacy.
G — Department of Professional Regulation.
H — Pharmacy Examining Board.
I — Plus a $1/yr LAP fee in odd years and $2 in even years.
J — Board of Registration in Pharmacy.
K — Division of Occupational and Professional Licensing.
L — Department of Health.
M — Department of Education.
N — Plus one-time application fee of $50.
O — One-time application fee of $75.
P — Initial license fee: even-year $170 (includes $50 application fee, $15 license fee, $70 compliance resolution fund [CRF] fee, and $35 for half-year renewal). Odd-year $100 (includes $50 application fee, $15 license fee, and $35 CRF fee).
Q — Only available to foreign-trained pharmacists meeting all requirements except for the completion of the FPGEE. Valid for up to one year.
R — $10 non-refundable application fee; $50 Delaware Jurisprudence exam; Prorated initial licensing fee; the renewal fee varies.
S — Includes application and state examination fee. $255 for reciprocity and score transfer; $125 for student applicants.

T — Health & Human Services, Department of Regulation and Licensure, Credentialing Division.
U — Included in exam or reciprocity fee.
V — Office of Professional Regulation.
W — Does not include state law examination fee, which is paid directly to the examination contractor and is currently $200 if exam is taken in VA, $250 if taken at a site outside VA. Examination fee includes copy of candidate study guide and law book covering applicable federal and state laws. Does not include price of NAPLEX, which is paid directly to NABP.
X — The issuance of a temporary license, although not necessary, is available to a licensed pharmacist from another jurisdiction in the US who does not have an uncumbered license, or any pending disciplinary action, or unresolved complaints and who is not eligible for licensure by reciprocity under Hawaii's laws and rules and upon passing of the jurisprudence examination.
Y — Plus $90 for Dispensing Controlled Substance License.
Z — Plus $36 fingerprint fee.
AA — For license transfer applicants only.
BB — Health Professions Bureau.
CC — $100 for Laboratory Exam.
DD — For reciprocity.

VIII. Licensure Transfer Requirements

State	Fee for Transfer of Licensure	Special Conditions/ Requirements	MPJE*	Non-MPJE Law Exam
Alabama	$300	A	Yes	No
Alaska	$230	A, C	Yes	No
Arizona	$300	B	Yes	No
Arkansas	$200	F	No	Yes
California	—	—	No	No
Colorado	$214	F	Yes	No
Connecticut	$100	A	Yes	No
Delaware	W	B	Yes	No
District of Columbia	$ 80	—	Yes	D.C. exam
Florida	$100	O	Yes	No
Georgia	$300	X	No	Yes
Guam	$100	A, C, F	No	Yes
Hawaii	I	A, B, C, G	Yes	—
Idaho	$250	A	No	Yes
Illinois	$200	C	Yes	No
Indiana	$100	B	Yes	No
Iowa	$160 EE	—	Yes	No
Kansas	$120 Z	E, Z	Yes	No
Kentucky	$250	A, C, F, J	Yes	No
Louisiana	$150	F, R	Yes	—
Maine	$150	K	Yes	No
Maryland	$200	B	Yes	Yes DD
Massachusetts	$150	A	Yes	No
Michigan	$145	—	Yes	Yes
Minnesota	$205	A, F	Yes	No
Mississippi	$200	K	No	Yes
Missouri	$350	F, M	Yes	No
Montana	$250	—	Yes	No
Nebraska	$250 T	F	Yes	No
Nevada	$420 N	A, C	Yes	No
New Hampshire	$265 Z	A, C	Yes	No
New Jersey	$125	A, B, C, F	Yes	No
New Mexico	$100	C	Yes	No
New York	$270 N	F	Yes	No
North Carolina	$400	F	No	Yes
North Dakota	$150	E, H, V	Yes	No
Ohio	$337.50	J	No	No
Oklahoma	$200	B	No	Yes
Oregon	$200 P	E	Yes	No
Pennsylvania	$ 40	R, C	Yes Q	No
Puerto Rico	$100	R	No	Yes BB
Rhode Island	$125	A, C	Yes	No
South Carolina	$300 P, Z	C	Yes	No
South Dakota	$150	E	No	Yes
Tennessee	$300	E	No	Yes
Texas	$250 P	A, C, R, S	Yes	No
Utah	$100 AA	A	Yes	No
Vermont	$110 N	—	Yes	No
Virginia	$ 50 U	Y	No	Yes CC
Washington	$330	A	Yes	No
West Virginia	$255	R, V, D	No L	Yes L
Wisconsin	$250	A, B	Yes	No
Wyoming	$200	G, B, C	Yes	No

VIII. Licensure Transfer Requirements (cont.)

The basic rule for pharmaceutic licensure transfer is: An applicant must have had the legal qualifications at the time of examination and registration in the state from which he or she applies, which would at that time have enabled him or her to qualify for examination and registration in the state to which he or she applies for licensure transfer registration.

Almost all jurisdictions that grant licensure by licensure transfer (all except California and Florida) require that a pharmacist who applies for such licensure furnish evidence of having acquired a license by examination in a state that grants licensure by licensure transfer. It is necessary that this license be in good standing, as the license by examination is the basis for transferring the license to other licensure transfer states.

LEGEND

A — Photographs, identification, and special forms furnished by state in addition to official NABP application. (HI, PA, UT, WI – No photograph required.)

B — There may be restrictions or special requirements for those licensed pharmacists who have not been actively practicing or for those who have been licensed for less than one year. Contact the State Board of Pharmacy office for details.

C — Licensure transfer applicant must have graduated and received a baccalaureate in pharmacy or a PharmD from a college of pharmacy whose degree program is accredited by ACPE (NH – or CCAPP) and approved by the Board. (KY, NH, NV, NM, PA, RI, TX – Or applicant must show proof of full FPGEC Certification. KY – FPGEC Certification must have been obtained after October 1992. SC – or applicant must show proof of FPGEC Certification prior to original licensure.)

D — Must take law exam.

E — "F" legend item (below) applicable only to licensees from those states that impose such a preclusion on licensure transfer applicants.

F — Pharmacists who have not been licensed one year are not eligible to be licensed by licensure transfer. (AR – Six months. CO – Unless it can be proved that the candidate met internship requirements the date they were first licensed in their exam state. KY – Applicants must also have engaged in active practice. NY – Pharmacists who have not practiced for one year.)

G — State of original licensure must have similar licensing requirements.

H — Graduates of foreign schools must have FPGEC certification.

I — $50 application fee plus $360 NAPLEX, and $130 MPJE exam fees, if applicable. (Effective January 1, 2003, NAPLEX fees will increase to $430 and MPJE fees will increase to $170.)

J — Standards at discretion of the Board.

K — Examination discretionary – usually none other than oral.

L — Plan to start in 2003.

M — "F" may be waived if internship is comparable to internship requirements of state.

N — Includes fees for application and initial license where such fees are applicable.

O — See Board Web site for specific requirements (www.doh.state.fl.us/mqa/pharmacy/ph_home.html).

P — Additional license fee.

Q — Unless licensed prior to January 26, 1983, or have taken the FDLE for the license that is the basis of the license transfer.

R — Applicant's state of initial licensure must grant reciprocal licensure to pharmacists licensed by examination in this state.

S — Licensure transfer applicant originally licensed after January 1, 1978, must show proof of having passed NABPLEX/NAPLEX or equivalent examination based on criteria no less stringent than the criteria in force in this state or demonstrate licensure in good standing for a period of two years immediately prior to the application for licensure transfer.

T — Plus Licensee Assistance Program fee of $1 in odd years and $2 in even years.

U — Does not include state law examination fee, which is paid directly to the examination contractor and is currently $200 if exam is taken in VA, $250 if taken at a site outside VA. Examination fee includes copy of candidate study guide and law book covering applicable federal and state laws.

V — Errors and Omissions Exam.

Legend continues on next page

VIII. Licensure Transfer Requirements *(cont.)*

LEGEND – (con't)

W — Pro-rated licensure fee to be determined.

X — Applicants who did not complete internship as required under GA law prior to original registration must furnish proof of one year's practice as a registered pharmacist.

Y — First professional pharmacy degree must be received from an ACPE-accredited school of pharmacy (either BS or undergraduate PharmD); otherwise, requirements for graduate of foreign schools of pharmacy apply.

Z — Plus $130 for MPJE, paid separately. (Effective January 1, 2003, NAPLEX fees will increase to $430 and MPJE fees will increase to $170.)

AA — Plus $90 for Dispensing Controlled Substance License.

BB — State law exam prepared by the Board.

CC — Combined state/federal law exam.

DD — Must take non-MPJE law examination given monthly.

EE — Plus MPJE and NABP licensure transfer fees.

IX. Issuance of Pharmacist Licenses Through Licensure Transfer

State	Is Board Hearing Required?	Hearings Per Year	Temporary License
Alabama	No L	12	No
Alaska	F	Upon request	Yes
Arizona	A	No	No
Arkansas	Yes	3 B	Yes
California	—	—	—
Colorado	Only if denied	Upon request	No
Connecticut	Yes	12 or as needed	Yes E
Delaware	No	As needed	No
District of Columbia	No	6	No
Florida	—	—	—
Georgia	C	5	No
Guam	No	—	No
Hawaii	No D	—	Yes E
Idaho	No	E	No
Illinois	No	—	No
Indiana	No M	—	No
Iowa	No	—	No
Kansas	No	Upon request	No
Kentucky	No	—	No
Louisiana	C	E	No
Maine	No	—	No
Maryland	Yes G	12	No
Massachusetts	No	As needed	No
Michigan	No	—	No
Minnesota	No	—	No
Mississippi	Yes	Any scheduled mtg.	No
Missouri	No	As needed	Yes
Montana	No D, M	4	No
Nebraska	No D, M	As needed	No
Nevada	No	—	Yes
New Hampshire	No K	—	No
New Jersey	No	When necessary	No
New Mexico	No	—	No
New York	No	—	No
North Carolina	Yes	6	No
North Dakota	No	4	Yes
Ohio	Yes I	12	No
Oklahoma	C	9	No
Oregon	No	As needed	No
Pennsylvania	No	As needed	No
Puerto Rico	No	N/A	No
Rhode Island	No K	—	No
South Carolina	Yes	7	No
South Dakota	No J	Upon request	No
Tennessee	No H	6	No
Texas	No	—	No
Utah	Individually determined	As needed	No
Vermont	No	Any scheduled mtg.	No
Virginia	No K	As needed	No
Washington	No	—	Yes
West Virginia	C	E	No
Wisconsin	No	0	No
Wyoming	No	—	No

IX. Issuance of Pharmacist Licenses Through Licensure Transfer *(cont.)*

LEGEND

A — If applicant has been disciplined by a Board of Pharmacy in another jurisdiction.

B — Plus special meetings, usually two.

C — Interview.

D — However, applications are subject to Board review and approval at regularly scheduled meetings.

E — Contact Board office for information.

F — Formal hearing not required, but applicant must appear before a Board member to take state law exam.

G — Law exam given monthly at Board meeting.

H — Law exam at each Board meeting.

I — Must appear before the Board.

J — However, applicant must meet with a Board member.

K — Unless application indicates grounds for denial.

L — Interview and MPJE.

M — May be required on rare occasions (ie, discipline in another jurisdiction).

X. Pharmacist Licensure Renewal

State	Renewal Schedule		Renewal Fee		License Renewal Schedule Expiration Date*		Mailing Date
Alabama	Annual		$ 60	A	Dec. 31		Oct.
Alaska	Biennial		$180		June 30		May 1
Arizona	Biennial	B	$145		Oct. 31		1 mo. prior
Arkansas	Biennial	E	$150		Dec. 31		Nov. 15
California	Biennial	D	$115		Cyclical	D	2 mos. prior
Colorado	Biennial	E	$218		Oct. 31	E	Sept.
Connecticut	Annual		$ 30		Jan. 31		30-45 days prior to expir.
Delaware	Biennial	F	Varies		Sept. 30	F	Aug.
District of Columbia	Biennial		$ 95		Feb. 28		Dec.
Florida	Biennial	E	$245		Sept. 30	E	July
Georgia	Biennial	F	$ 80		Dec. 31	F	Oct.
Guam	Biennial		$ 60		Sept. 30	E	June
Hawaii	Biennial	E	$140/$190	G	Dec. 31	E	Nov.
Idaho	Annual		$ 90	H	June 30		May
Illinois	Biennial	F	$150		March 31	F	Jan.
Indiana	Biennial	F	$ 80	V, C	June 30	F	April
Iowa	Biennial		$110		June 30		April
Kansas	Biennial	B	$150		June 30		May
Kentucky	Annual		$ 80	I, V	Feb. 28		Jan.
Louisiana	Annual		$ 75		Dec. 31		Nov. 1
Maine	Annual		$ 60		Dec. 31		Oct.
Maryland	Biennial	B	$150		Last day of birth month	B, D	—
Massachusetts	Biennial	F	$ 56		Dec. 31	F	Oct.
Michigan	Biennial		$ 70	J	June 30		April
Minnesota	Annual		$105		March 1		Jan.
Mississippi	Biennial	E	$155		Dec. 31	E	Oct.
Missouri	Biennial	W	$160		Oct. 31		Aug.
Montana	Annual		$ 55		June 30		60 days prior
Nebraska	Biennial		$200	L, M	Jan. 1	F	30 days prior
Nevada	Biennial	E	$150		Oct. 31	E	Sept. 15
New Hampshire	Annual		$ 75		Dec. 31		Nov.
New Jersey	Biennial	E	$140		April 30	E	March
New Mexico	Annual		$100	M	Last day of birth month		45 days prior to expiration
New York	Triennial	D	$200	Y	Variable	D	4 mos. prior
North Carolina	Annual		$110		Dec. 31		Nov.
North Dakota	Annual		$150	N	March 1		Jan.
Ohio	Annual		$ 97.50		Sept. 15		July
Oklahoma	Annual		$ 75		June 30		May
Oregon	Annual		$120		June 30		April
Pennsylvania	Biennial	F	$120		Sept. 30	F	July
Puerto Rico	Triennial		$ 15		Last day of birth month		90 days prior to birth month
Rhode Island	Annual		$ 62.50		June 30		May
South Carolina	Annual		$ 70		April 30		Feb.
South Dakota	Annual		$125		Sept. 30		Aug.
Tennessee	Biennial		$ 96	O	Cyclical		60 days prior
Texas	Biennial		$227		Last day of birth month		60 days prior P
Utah	Biennial	E, K	$ 50	Q	May 31	E	Feb. 28
Vermont	Biennial	E	$ 70		July 31	E	June 15
Virginia	Annual		$ 50	M	Dec. 31		Nov.
Washington	Annual		$135	R, S	Birth date		45 days prior
West Virginia	Biennial	X	$120	Z	June 30		May
Wisconsin	Biennial	F	$ 97	T	May 31	F	April
Wyoming	Annual		$ 75	U	Dec. 31		Nov. 1

X. Pharmacist Licensure Renewal *(cont.)*

LEGEND

*Excludes grace period, if any.

A — Controlled substances fee: $35.
B — Biennial, odd license numbers in odd years and even license numbers in even years.
C — Figures are per year. ($160 Total.)
D — Renew in pharmacist's birthday month.
E — Biennial, odd years.
F — Biennial, even years.
G — Odd-years – $190; even-years – $140.
H — Controlled substances fee: $60.
I — Inactive fee: $10.
J — Controlled substances fee: $75 for one year. In addition, renewal fees are $150 for two years.
K — The Board or committee recommends to the department, which has the function.
L — Plus $2 for Licensee Assistance Program.
M — Inactive fee: $35. (NE – One-time fee.)
N — Nonresident fee: $35. Fifty percent of the license renewal fees from in-state pharmacists are allocated to the state association.
O — Controlled substances fee: $40 every two years.
P — Statute requires at least 30 days prior.
Q — Controlled substances license: $90 initially, then $50 renewal every two years.

R — Retired fee: $20.
S — Inactive fee: $135.
T — If governor's budget passes.
U — May go inactive for CE requirement only, but must continue to pay the regular annual fee of $75. To be reactivated for practice in Wyoming, completion of all back-CE credit must be submitted for a maximum of five years.
V — Includes $10 that goes to pharmacist rehabilitation programs.
W — Effective with 2000 renewal period, changed from annual to biennial. Licenses renewed by Oct. 31, 2000, will bear an Oct. 31, 2002 expiration date with subsequent renewal every two years. Fee change reflects fee for a two-year period. No actual fee increase.
X — Beginning July 1, 2002.
Y — Includes $45 CE administration fee.
Z — Includes $20 fee for Pharmacist Recovery Network.

XI. Continuing Pharmaceutical Education Requirements

Fifty-two (52) boards of pharmacy require that pharmacists participate in continuing education activities as a prerequisite for relicensure. There are fairly uniform requirements regarding the types of programs that are recognized and the prescribed range of acceptable content matter.
One (1) board reports no activities related to continuing pharmaceutical education.
NOTE: One (1) continuing education unit, CEU, is equivalent to ten (10) contact hours (1 contact hour = 0.1 CEU).

Boards Requiring Participation in Continuing Pharmaceutical Education for Relicensure

ALABAMA
By January 1 of each year, every pharmacist must furnish proof of participation in not less than 15 hours of approved continuing education during the preceding year, 3 hours of which must be live exposure. Carry-over of no more than an excess of 12 hours credit is allowed.

ALASKA
Each pharmacist seeking renewal of a license shall obtain an average of 15 credit hours of continuing education per year offered by ACPE-approved providers during the previous licensure period. Only programs administered by ACPE-approved providers will be accepted by the Board of Pharmacy.

ARIZONA
Pharmacists must satisfactorily complete 3.0 CEUs biennially of continuing professional education activities sponsored by ACPE- or Board-approved providers. At least 0.3 CEUs shall be pharmacy law subjects. Satisfactory proof of participation should be retained by participants for five years. No carry-over of credit is allowed.

ARKANSAS
Beginning with the 2002-2003 biennium – for licensure in the 2004-2005 biennium, and in all future two-year periods – the requirements for continuing education will be as follows:
1. 30 hours of CE each biennium, as approved by the Arkansas Tripartite Committee on Continuing Education.
2. A minimum of twelve (12) CE hours, of the thirty (30) required hours, must be live contact hours as defined by the Committee. The live hours must be concerning drug therapy or patient care.
Continuing competency for certification for Authority to Administer Medications/Immunizations must be maintained. A minimum of one (1) hour of the fifteen (15) hour requirement for continuing education, every year, must be dedicated to this area of practice. Nursing Home Consultant pharmacists must annually obtain three (3) hours of CE specifically relating to his/her role as a consultant in a nursing home, in addition to the CE required for all pharmacists.

CALIFORNIA
Pharmacists must complete 30 hours of approved continuing pharmaceutical education every two years. All continuing pharmaceutical education providers must be ACPE-approved providers or recognized by the Accreditation Evaluation Service (AES). Providers who are not ACPE- or AES-approved may petition the Board for approval of courses. Pharmacists may independently petition as well. No carry-over of credit is allowed.

COLORADO
Pharmacists must obtain 24 hours of ACPE-approved continuing education prior to renewal date of Oct. 31 of odd-numbered years.

CONNECTICUT
Pharmacists are required to complete 15 hours of continuing education in the previous calendar year (Jan. to Dec.). At least five of those hours MUST be at a live presentation. Only courses that are ACPE, CME, CNE, or Commission approved are accepted. At least one of the live credits must be related to pharmacy law.

DELAWARE
Pharmacists must obtain 30 hours of continuing pharmaceutical education during each biennial renewal period. No carry-over of credit is allowed.

FLORIDA
Biennial renewal certificates require satisfactory proof that during the two years prior to the renewal application the licensee has participated in not less than 15 hours **per calendar year (30 hours/biennial period)** of approved continuing professional education programs. Five hours per year must be from an approved live program. In addition, 12 hours of consultant pharmacist coursework is required annually for *biennial* renewal of a consultant license. Additionally, 24 hours of nuclear pharmacist coursework is required for biennial renewal of a nuclear license. A Board-approved, 3-hour course on AIDS/HIV is required prior to licensure and a 1-hour update course on AIDS/HIV is required prior to renewal of licensure.

GEORGIA
Pharmacists must obtain 30 hours (3.0 CEUs) of continuing pharmaceutical education credit every two years as a condition of relicensure. All ACPE-approved providers giving a program in Georgia are required to submit a copy of the Program Description Form to the Georgia State Board of Pharmacy 60 days prior to the date of the program. Non-ACPE-approved providers must apply for and obtain a Georgia Board of Pharmacy I.D. number for each program and have a 60-day prior approval for their programs.

GUAM
Each pharmacist seeking renewal of a license shall satisfactorily complete one-and-one-half (1.5) continuing pharmacy education units (15 hours) in an approved continuing pharmacy education program or programs approved by the Board, unless he/she has passed an exam given by the Board.
Continuing pharmacy education programs attended by Guam-licensed pharmacists for purposes of satisfying licensure requirements of another state must be approved by the Guam Board of Pharmacy in order to be recognized for purposes of renewal of Guam license.

IDAHO
134. Amount of Continuing Education. The equivalent of one-and-one-half (1.5) continuing education units (CEU) shall be required annually of each applicant for renewal of license. One continuing education unit is the equivalent of ten (10) clock hours of participation in programs approved by the Board of Pharmacy.
(07-01-93)
01. ACPE, CME. At a minimum, eight clock hours (0.8 CEU) will be all or a combination of American Council on Pharmaceutical Education (ACPE) or Continuing Medical Education (CME) approved programs.
(12-07-94)

XI. Continuing Pharmaceutical Education Requirements *(cont.)*

02. Pharmacy law. One clock hour (0.1 CEU) must be Board of Pharmacy-approved jurisprudence (pharmacy law) programs.
(07-01-93)
03. Non-ACPE. A maximum of six clock hours (0.6 CEU) may be non-ACPE approved programs.
(12-07-94)
04. Live attendance. Three clock hours (0.3 CEU) of the required one-and-one-half (1.5) continuing education units (CEUs) must be obtained by attendance at live continuing education programs.
(07-01-97)

ILLINOIS
Pharmacists must obtain 30 hours (3.0 CEUs) of pharmacy continuing education from ACPE-approved providers during the two calendar years preceding expiration of certificate.

INDIANA
Pharmacists are required to complete 30 hours of approved continuing education every two years. No more than six hours of business- or computer-related CE is accepted. No carry-over of credit is allowed. At least half of total hours must be ACPE-approved; any other hours must be approved by the Board.

IOWA
Requires 30 hours (3.0 CEUs) of approved continuing pharmaceutical education every two years as a condition for license renewal. No carry-over of credit is allowed. Fifty percent of CE must be in drug therapy-related coursework from an ACPE-approved provider.

KANSAS
Requires 30 hours (3.0 CEUs) of approved continuing pharmaceutical education for biennial registration. No carry-over of credit is allowed.

KENTUCKY
Each licensee is required to complete a minimum of 15 hours (1.5 CEUs) annually in accredited programs. One hour must be earned from a Kentucky Cabinet for Human Resources-approved HIV/AIDS program every 10 years during the decennial year. Non-ACPE-approved programs must contain the Kentucky Board of Pharmacy I.D. number. Non-ACPE-approved courses given out-of-state are not reviewed for credit. Credit must be obtained between January 1 and December 31 each year. No carry-over credit is permitted.

LOUISIANA
Fifteen (15) hours (1.5 CEUs) of continuing pharmaceutical education from ACPE-approved providers must be completed annually as a prerequisite for relicensure. No carry-over of credit is allowed.

MAINE
Pharmacists must submit satisfactory proof of participation in not less than 15 hours of approved programs of continuing pharmaceutical education during the calendar year. No carry-over of credit is allowed.

MARYLAND
To qualify for biennial license renewal, pharmacists must have accumulated 30 hours of continuing education credit in approved programs by the last day of their birth month prior to obtaining licensure renewal. No carry-over of credit is allowed. Board, at its discretion, may grant extension, but pharmacist may not practice pharmacy until requirements are met.

MASSACHUSETTS
Pharmacists must complete 15 hours (1.5 CEUs) of continuing pharmaceutical education every year (30 hours [3.0 CEUs] per two-year renewal period). No carry-over of credit is allowed from year to year. Of the 15 hours required per year, at least 2 hours shall be in the area of pharmacy law, at least 5 hours shall be from live programs, and not more than 10 hours shall be credited through correspondence courses.

MICHIGAN
To qualify for biennial license renewal, pharmacists must have accumulated 30 hours of continuing education credit in approved programs. No carry-over of credit is allowed.

MINNESOTA
Requires at least 30 hours of credit from accredited continuing education programs every two years. Carry-over and splitting of program hours are not allowed.

MISSISSIPPI
Pharmacists are required to submit to the Board of Pharmacy evidence of completion of 20 hours (2.0 CEUs) in approved programs every two years. No carry-over of credit is allowed.

MISSOURI
Effective for 2002-2004 renewal, pharmacists are required to submit proof of 30 hours (3.0 CEUs) of continuing pharmaceutical education for biennial license renewal. No carry-over of credit is allowed.

MONTANA
Pharmacists are required to participate in 15 hours (1.5 CEUs) of approved programs each year following the first license renewal. A minimum of 5 hours (0.5 CEUs) is to be obtained in ACPE- or board-approved group (ie, live) programs. One-year carry-over of credit is allowed. CME acceptance pending.

NEBRASKA
Every two years, pharmacists will be required to complete 30 hours (3.0 CEUs) of continuing pharmaceutical education sponsored by ACPE-approved providers. Each pharmacist is responsible for keeping his or her own records. No carry-over of credit is permitted.

NEVADA
Pharmacists must submit proof of receiving 30 hours of continuing education credit within the two years preceding the current renewal period. In-state registrants must have 15 hours in accredited programs, including one hour in a jurisprudence program. Out-of-state registrants may submit 30 hours of acceptable continuing education. Carry-over of credits is not allowed.

NEW HAMPSHIRE
Requires 15 hours (1.5 CEUs) for annual relicensure. A minimum of 5 hours (0.5 CEUs) must be didactic (live presentation) hours. No carry-over of credit is allowed. Programs must be from ACPE-approved providers **OR** approved by any board of pharmacy **OR** AMA Category I-accredited.

NEW JERSEY
Effective April 11, 1995, legislation was enacted that transfers authority for continuing pharmaceutical education to the Board of Pharmacy.
Chapter 79, C. 45:14-11.11. Continuing education required of pharmacists. 1. The Board of Pharmacy of the State of New Jersey

XI. Continuing Pharmaceutical Education Requirements *(cont.)*

shall require each person registered as a pharmacist, as a condition for biennial certification pursuant to R.S. 45:14-11 and P.L. 1972, c. 108 (C.45.1-7), to complete 30 credits of continuing pharmaceutical education and submit proof thereof, as provided in section 2 of this act, during each biennial registration period. C.45:14-11.12. Standards for continuing education. 2. a. The Board shall: (1) Establish standards for continuing pharmaceutical education, including the subject matter and content of courses of study, the selection of instructors, and the type of continuing education credits required of a registered pharmacist as a condition for biennial certification; (2) Approve educational programs offering credit towards the continuing pharmaceutical education requirements; and (3) Approve other equivalent educational programs, including, but not limited to, home study courses, and shall establish procedures for the issuance of credit upon satisfactory proof of the completion of these programs. b. In the case of education courses and programs, each hour of instruction shall be equivalent to one credit. Effective May 1, 1995, the Board voted to automatically accept ACPE-approved continuing education credits. Programs presented by non-ACPE providers must apply to the Board for approval of these presentations for accreditation. There is a $50 fee for this review. Individuals attending non-ACPE programs who wish to receive continuing education credit can have these programs reviewed for a $10 fee. Non-ACPE courses must be issued a New Jersey number to be acceptable for continuing education credit.

NEW MEXICO
Pharmacists are required to submit evidence of 15 hours (1.5 CEUs) of continuing pharmaceutical education offered by ACPE-approved providers to renew their annual registration. A maximum of 15 hours, or one year of credit, may be accrued in excess and carried over to the next licensure year. One hour must be in the area of pharmacy law. Resident pharmacists must attend a program presented by the inspection staff **OR** take a 100-question exam and receive a score of 80% or better. The exam costs $100. Nonresident pharmacists may take an ACPE-accredited law course.

NEW YORK
During each triennial registration period, pharmacists must complete a minimum of 45 hours of acceptable formal continuing education with no more than 22 hours consisting of self-study courses.

NORTH CAROLINA
Requires 10 hours (1.0 CEUs) of continuing pharmaceutical education per year, with no more than 5 hours (0.5 CEUs) of non-contact (ie, correspondence/home-study) program credit.

NORTH DAKOTA
Requires 30 hours (3.0 CEUs) of continuing pharmaceutical education offered by ACPE-approved providers every two years for license renewal. One-year carry-over of credit is allowed.

OHIO
Requires that evidence of 6.0 CEUs of continuing pharmaceutical education offered by approved providers be submitted at intervals of three years. 0.3 CEUs must be in Board-approved jurisprudence. No carry-over of credit is allowed.

OKLAHOMA
Relicensure or licensure by reciprocity requires satisfactory proof of not less than 15 clock hours of participation in accredited continuing education programs per year. Carry-over of credit is not allowed.

OREGON
Each year pharmacists must satisfactorily complete 15 hours (1.5 CEUs) in approved continuing education programs. Eleven of the 15 hours **must** be in law and/or therapeutics; one hour **must** be in law; four hours **may** be in socioeconomic areas. No carry-over of credit is allowed.

PENNSYLVANIA
During each biennial renewal period, pharmacists must complete at least 30 contact hours (3 CEUs) of ACPE-approved continuing education. No carry-over of credit is permitted.

PUERTO RICO
Pharmacists must complete 35 hours (3.5 CEUs) of continuing pharmaceutical education for recertification every three years. No more than 15 hours may be obtained through professional journals, research, or CE presentations. Three hours on infection control and three hours on breastfeeding are required.

RHODE ISLAND
Pharmacists must complete 15 hours (1.5 CEUs) of continuing education offered by approved providers. Five (5) hours of credit must be obtained through participation in live programs. No carry-over of credit is allowed.

SOUTH CAROLINA
Pharmacists must complete 15 hours of ACPE-approved continuing education or CME Category I to be eligible for active license renewal. At least 6 hours of the total must be from live presentations. At least 7.5 hours must be concerning drug therapy or patient management. Excess credits may be carried forward one calendar year.

SOUTH DAKOTA
Pharmacists must provide evidence of completion of 12 hours of continuing education in approved programs in order to be eligible for annual relicensure.

TENNESSEE
Pharmacists must complete 30 hours of continuing pharmaceutical education every two years for license renewal. No carry-over of credit is allowed. At least 24 hours must be ACPE approved, and 15 hours must be obtained through ACPE-designated "live" contact programming.

TEXAS
Pharmacists must complete and report 24 hours of approved CE during a two-year license period. For licenses expiring on or after August 31, 2003, a pharmacist must complete 30 hours of approved CE during the previous two-year license period.

UTAH
Pharmacists shall complete 24 hours of continuing professional education approved by the division and the Board every two calendar years, beginning January 1, 1993. A minimum of 8 hours must be obtained through attendance at approved lectures, seminars, or workshops and a minimum of 6 hours must be in drug therapy or patient management. Continuing education hours for licensees who have not been licensed for the entire year will be prorated from the date of licensure at a rate of one hour for each month of licensure. No continuing education hours may be accrued as excess and carried forward to the succeeding reporting period. An approved provider is an individual, institution, organization, asso-

XI. Continuing Pharmaceutical Education Requirements *(cont.)*

ciation, corporation, or agency that has been approved by the American Council on Pharmaceutical Education (ACPE) and regional meetings sponsored by the Utah Pharmaceutical Association.

VERMONT
The licensee must complete at least 15 hours (1.5 CEUs), of which at least 0.5 CEUs shall be obtained during participation in a didactic session, for each full year since the date that the applicant's latest license was issued; for a total of 3.0 CEUs per renewal period.

VIRGINIA
§54.1-3314.1 Continuing education requirements; exemptions; extensions; procedures; out-of-state licensees; nonpractice licenses. A. Each pharmacist shall have obtained a minimum of 15 continuing education hours of pharmaceutical education through an approved continuing pharmaceutical education program during the year immediately preceding his license renewal date. B. An approved continuing pharmaceutical education program shall be any program approved by the Board. C. Pharmacists who have been initially licensed by the Board during the one year preceding the license renewal date shall not be required to comply with the requirement on the first license renewal date that would immediately follow. D. The Board may grant an exemption from the continuing education requirement if the pharmacist presents evidence that failure to comply was due to circumstances beyond the control of the pharmacist. E. Upon the written request of a pharmacist, the Board may grant an extension of one year in order for a pharmacist to fulfill the continuing education requirements for the period of time in question. Such extension shall not relieve the pharmacist of complying with the continuing education requirement for the current period. F. The pharmacist shall attest to the fact that he has completed the continuing education requirements as specified by the Board. G. The following shall apply to the requirements for continuing pharmaceutical education: 1. The provider of an approved continuing education program shall issue to each pharmacist who has successfully completed a program certification that the pharmacist has completed a specified number of hours. 2. The certificates so issued to the pharmacist shall be maintained by the pharmacist for a period of two years following the renewal of his license. 3. The pharmacist shall provide the Board, upon request, with certification of completion of continuing education programs in a manner to be determined by the Board. H. Pharmacists who are also licensed in other states and who have obtained a minimum of 15 hours of approved continuing educa-

tion requirements of such other states need not obtain additional hours. I. The Board shall provide for an inactive status for those pharmacists who do not wish to practice in Virginia. The Board shall require upon request for change from inactive to active status proof of continuing education hours equal to that which would have been required should the pharmacist have continued to hold an active license. No person shall practice in Virginia unless he holds a current active license.

WASHINGTON
Pharmacists are required to complete 15 hours (1.5 CEUs) of professional continuing education as a prerequisite for annual license renewal. No carry-over of credit is allowed.

WEST VIRGINIA
Fifteen hours (1.5 CEUs) required during previous year to renew license. Biennial renewal July 1, 2002. Two-year reporting period – 30 hours required. Two hours in end-of-life care including pain management required every two years.

WISCONSIN
Effective with the June 1, 2000 renewal, pharmacists will be required to complete 30 hours of continuing education every two years to renew their licenses.

WYOMING
Each pharmacist must complete a minimum of 12 credit hours (1.2 CEUs) of accredited continuing pharmaceutical education each year. Carry-over of credit is allowed for one year. Those who have been inactive must demonstrate completion of back-CE for a maximum of five years prior to reactivation.

Boards of Pharmacy Granted Legislative Authority to Promulgate Regulations:

DISTRICT OF COLUMBIA
Enabling legislation was passed by the city council, and the Board of Pharmacy published requirements for 1.5 CEUs for the 1991 renewal period to expand to 3.0 CEUs per renewal period.

States Reporting No Related Activities:

HAWAII

For additional information regarding specific requirements, contact the appropriate board of pharmacy.
     For additional copies of this report or information about the ACPE Provider Approval Program, contact:
American Council on Pharmaceutical Education, Division of Continuing Education, 20 N Clark St, Suite 2500, Chicago, Illinois 60602; 312/664-3575.

XII. Discipline of Pharmacist Licenses

From July 1, 2001 to June 30, 2002
Total Licenses:

State	Licenses Disciplined by	Suspended		Revoked		Reinstated	
Alabama	K	5		0		0	
Alaska	J	1		0		0	
Arizona DD	K	8		2		6	
Arkansas	K	84	B,W	21		10	
California	K	57	E	62	E		
Colorado	K	11	X	9	X	1	X
Connecticut	L	—		—		—	
Delaware	K	0		0		0	
District of Columbia	J, O	—		—		—	
Florida	J	23		13		4	
Georgia	K	47	B	1		N/A	
Guam	J	0		0		1	
Hawaii	K	0		0			
Idaho	K	2	A	2		3	
Illinois	K, M	—		—		—	
Indiana	J	9		1		6	
Iowa	S	3		1		1	
Kansas	J	1		0		0	
Kentucky EE	J	8		2		6	
Louisiana	J	24	FF	0	FF	30	FF
Maine	K, R	3		0		0	
Maryland	J	4	AA	0	A	3	AA
Massachusetts	N	6		1		5	
Michigan H	J	14	CC		CC	—	
Minnesota	J	3		0		4	
Mississippi	K	5		3		2	
Missouri	J	5		0		Not available	
Montana	J	3		1		0	
Nebraska	P	3	I	5	I	35	I
Nevada	K	1		3		2	
New Hampshire	J	2		2		3	
New Jersey	K	7		2		3	
New Mexico	J	15		2		1	
New York	Q	27		7		1	
North Carolina	J	25	GG	1		4	
North Dakota	K	2		1		0	
Ohio	K	25		8		10	
Oklahoma	K	14	HH	13		26	
Oregon	K	1		0		0	
Pennsylvania	K	10		2		9	
Puerto Rico	J	—		—		—	
Rhode Island	J, T	2		0		2	
South Carolina	J	11	D	2		15	
South Dakota	K	1		1		1	
Tennessee	J	0		21	B	17	
Texas C	K	34	BB	9	Y	3	F
Utah	U	7	G	14		3	
Vermont	J, Z	V		V		V	
Virginia	J	8		1		5	
Washington	K	9		3		6	
West Virginia	J	2		2	B	4	
Wisconsin	S	2		0		—	
Wyoming	K	—		—		—	

XII. Discipline of Pharmacist Licenses *(cont.)*

Revocation proceedings are specified in the state statutes of all states and territories listed. A statement of charges against the pharmacist must be furnished, and written notices are required. A hearing is required in all states and territories except for HI, IA, MD, MI, NH, SC, TN, TX, UT, WA, and WY, which require a hearing unless the licensee and Board agree to sanctions through an informal conference and an Agreed Board Order. Provisions for court review or retrial exist in all states with the following exceptions: ME provides for only original proceedings in court; RI provides for appeal to an adjudication officer. Contact the state Board office for more information.

LEGEND

A — 22 letters of reprimand. (Pharmacists only.) Does not include suspension of other practitioners' CS licenses.

B — Includes voluntary surrenders.

C — Sept. 1, 2000, to Aug. 31, 2001.

D — Plus 13 voluntary surrenders. (SC – Plus 6 voluntary surrenders.)

E — Plus 50 probations and 15 voluntary surrenders.

F — Included license reinstated under conditions followed by probated suspension under conditions.

G — Includes 5 surrenders, which are considered unprofessional conduct, plus 4 on probation.

H — Fiscal year Oct. 1, 2000, to Sept. 30, 2001.

I — Plus 3 censures, 1 voluntary surrender in lieu of discipline, 5 civil penalties, 6 probations, 8 letters of concern (non-disciplinary action), 9 pending actions.

J — Board of Pharmacy.

K — State Board of Pharmacy.

L — Commission of Pharmacy.

M — Department of Professional Regulation.

N — Board of Registration in Pharmacy.

O — Mayor.

P — Director of Department/Chief Medical Officer.

Q — Board of Regents.

R — Court Proceedings.

S — Pharmacy Examining Board.

T — Health Department adjudication officer.

U — Division of Occupational and Professional Licensing.

V — 3 revoked, 1 warning, 7 closed without charges.

W — Non-payment.

X — Also 18 placed on probation and 10 public admonitions.

Y — Includes revoked, retired, and canceled.

Z — Office of Professional Regulation.

AA — 2 voluntary surrenders plus 3 reprimands, 6 probations, 4 fines, 8 letters of education, 1 letter of admonishment.

BB — Plus 40 fines and/or reprimands.

CC — Plus 25 reprimands, 32 probations, 8 fines, and 6 limited licenses.

DD — Dates are from Jan. 1, 2001, to Dec. 31, 2001.

EE — Board took action against 137 licenses.

FF — 10 warnings and 10 reprimands.

GG — Plus 1 summary suspension, 31 reprimands, 4 voluntary surrenders, 27 letters of concern/caution/warning, 6 must obtain additional CE, of the 25 suspensions, 24 had probationary periods as part of the suspension period.

HH — Plus 3 reprimands, 12 fines, 9 probations.

XIII. Status of Pharmacy Technicians

State	Designation	Does State: License Technicians?	Register Technicians?	Certify Technicians?	Technician Registration Fee	Registration Renewal Schedule
Alabama	Pharmacy Technician	No	Yes	No	$ 20	Annual
Alaska	Pharmacy Technician	Yes	No	No	$100	Biennial
Arizona	Pharmacy Technician	No	Yes B	No	0	None U
Arkansas	Pharmacy Technician	No	Yes	No	$ 35	Annual
California	Pharmacy Technician	No	Yes	No	$ 50	Biennial
Colorado	Unlicensed Personnel, Unlicensed Assistant	No	No P	No	N/A	N/A
Connecticut	Pharmacy Technician	No	Yes	No	$50	Annual - 3/31
Delaware	Supportive Personnel	No	No	No	None	N/A
District of Columbia	Ancillary Personnel	No	No	No	–	–
Florida	Pharmacy Technician	No	No	No	N/A	N/A
Georgia	Ancillary Personnel	No	No	No	–	–
Guam	Pharmacy Technician	No	Yes	No	R, J	R, J
Hawaii	Pharmacy Technician	No	No	No	N/A	N/A
Idaho	Pharmacy Technician	No	Yes	No	$ 35	Annual
Illinois	Pharmacy Technician	No	Yes	No	$40 initial, $25 renewal	Annual
Indiana	Unlicensed Person, Technician	No	No	No	N/A	N/A
Iowa	Pharmacy Technician	No	Yes	No	$ 33	Z
Kansas	Pharmacy Technician	No	No	No	N/A	N/A
Kentucky	Pharmacy Technician	No J	No J	No J	N/A	N/A
Louisiana	Pharmacy Technician	Yes	No	No	$100	Annual
Maine	Pharmacy Technician	No	Yes	No	$ 20	Annual
Maryland	Unlicensed Person	No	No	No	N/A	N/A
Massachusetts	Pharmacy Technician J	No	Yes J	No J	$ 38	–
Michigan	Pharmacy Personnel	No	No	No	–	–
Minnesota	Pharmacy Technician	No	Yes	No	$ 20	Annual
Mississippi	Pharmacy Technician L	No	Yes Q	No	$ 25	Annual
Missouri	Pharmacy Technician	No	Yes	No	$ 10 W	Annual
Montana	Pharmacy Technician	No	Yes	Yes AA	$ 40	Annual
Nebraska	Pharmacy Technician	No	No	No	–	–
Nevada	Pharmaceutical Technician L	No	Yes	No	$ 40	Biennial
New Hampshire	Pharmacy Technician	No	Yes	No	$ 25	Annual - 4/01
New Jersey	Supportive Personnel	No	No	No	N/A	N/A
New Mexico	Pharmacy Technician N	No	Yes	No	$ 15	Annual
New York	Unlicensed Person	No	No	No	N/A	N/A
North Carolina	Pharmacy Technician	No	Yes	No	$ 25	Annual
North Dakota	Registered Pharmacy Technician	No	Yes	No	$ 35	Annual
Ohio	F	No	No	No	N/A	N/A
Oklahoma	Pharmacy Technician	No	Yes O	No	$ 40	Annual
Oregon	Pharmacy Technician	No	Yes	No	$ 35	1 year - Sept.
Pennsylvania	Pharmacy Technician	No	No	No	N/A	N/A
Puerto Rico	Pharmacy Assistant	No	Yes	Yes	–	–
Rhode Island	Pharmacy Technician	Yes	No	No	$ 25	Annual
South Carolina	Pharmacy Technician	No	Yes	Yes	$40 Initial, $25 renewal	Annual
South Dakota	Supportive Personnel	No	No	No	None	None
Tennessee	Technician	No	Yes J	No	$50-biennial	Cyclical
Texas	Pharmacy Technician	No	Yes G	No G	None	None
Utah	Pharmacy Technician	Yes	No	No	$ 50	Biannual
Vermont	Support Personnel	No	No	No	N/A	N/A
Virginia	Nonpharmacist Personnel	No	No V	No	N/A V	N/A V
Washington	Pharmacy Technician	No	No	Yes	$ 50	Annual
West Virginia	Pharmacy Technician	No	Yes	No	$ 25 X	Biennial
Wisconsin	Supportive Personnel	No	No	No	–	–
Wyoming	Registered Pharmacy Technician K	Yes*	Yes*	No	$ 35	Annual

* See "Footnotes (*)" on page 846.

XIII. Status of Pharmacy Technicians *(cont.)*

State	Technician Training Requirements	Technician CE Requirements	Can Technicians Check the Work of Other Technicians?	Maximum Ratio of Technician(s) to Pharmacist in an: Ambulatory Care Setting	Institutional Care Setting
Alabama	No	3 hrs/yr H	No	3:1*	3:1*
Alaska	Yes S	10 hrs/2 yrs	No	None	None
Arizona	Yes**	None	Yes A	2:1*	None
Arkansas	No	None	No	2:1	2:1
California	Yes	No	No	Varies*	2:1
Colorado	No	N/A	No	2:1	2:1
Connecticut	Yes**	No	No	2:1*	3:1*
Delaware	Yes	N/A	No	None	None
District of Columbia	No	—	—	—	—
Florida	No	None	No	3:1	3:1
Georgia	No	None	No	2:1	2:1*
Guam	No R, J	None R, J	No R, J	None R, J	None R, J
Hawaii	No	N/A	No	None	None
Idaho	Yes			2:1	2:1
Illinois	No J	No	No	None	None
Indiana	Yes	N/A	N/A	4:1*	4:1*
Iowa	Yes*	No	No	None	None
Kansas	Yes	N/A	No	2:1	2:1
Kentucky	No	None	No	None	None
Louisiana	No	10 hrs	No	2:1	2:1
Maine	Yes	No	No	3:1	3:1
Maryland	No	N/A	No	—	—
Massachusetts	Yes	No BB	No	3:1	3:1
Michigan	No			None	None
Minnesota	No	No	Requires variance	2:1*	2:1*
Mississippi	No I	No	Not addressed	2:1	2:1
Missouri	No	None	No	None	None
Montana	Yes**	Yes – PTCB	No CC	1:1	1:1*
Nebraska	Yes** I	—	No	1:1	2:1*
Nevada	Yes	No Y	No	2:1	2:1
New Hampshire	No	None	No	None	None
New Jersey	No	No	No	2:1	2:1
New Mexico	Yes**	None	No	4:1	4:1
New York	No	No	No	2:1	2:1
North Carolina	Yes	None	No	2:1*	2:1*
North Dakota	Yes*	Yes 20 hrs/2 yrs	Yes (but RPh ultimately respon.)	2:1	2:1
Ohio	No	No	No	None	None
Oklahoma	Yes	None	No	2:1	2:1
Oregon	Yes	No	No	2:1*	3:1
Pennsylvania	No	None	No	—	—
Puerto Rico	Yes*			None	None
Rhode Island	Yes	None	No	None	None
South Carolina	Yes DD	10hrs/yr EE	Yes T	2:1*	Varies*
South Dakota	No	None	No	2:1	2:1
Tennessee	No	None	No	2:1*	2:1*
Texas	Yes C	D	No	2:1*	None
Utah	Yes	8 hrs/2 yrs	No	3:1	3:1
Vermont	No	N/A	No	None	None
Virginia	No V	N/A V	No	1:1*	1:1
Washington	Yes	None	Yes E	3:1 M	3:1 M
West Virginia	Yes I	None	No	4:1	4:1
Wisconsin	No	—	—	4:1	4:1
Wyoming	Yes I	6 hrs	No	2:1	2:1

*   See "Footnotes (*)" on page 846.
** Contact the state board of pharmacy office to obtain requirements.

XIII. Status of Pharmacy Technicians *(cont.)*

LEGEND

A — But final check must be by RPh.

B — Pharmacist must "notify" Board of technician employees.

C — A person may be a technician trainee for no more than one year while seeking certification through PTCB. Contact the Board for specific on-site training requirements.

D — Same as PTCB requirements.

E — Unit dose only, meet certain requirements.

F — The use of pharmacy technicians is not addressed in state statutes or regulations.

G — Effective January 1, 2001, technicians must take and pass the national Pharmacy Technician Certification Board exam. Legislation that authorized registration began September 1, 2001; however, the project was not funded.

H — Effective January 1, 2002.

I — Training requirements developed by training pharmacies and approved by the Board.

J — The Board is proposing/developing regulations.

K — Designated as a "technician-in-training" prior to meeting requirements for licensure.

L — The term "Supportive Personnel" is also used.

M — A pharmacy may use more technicians than the prescribed 3:1 upon approval of the Board.

N — A "Pharmacy Technician" is a subset of "Supportive Personnel."

O — Technicians are not considered "registered" but are issued a "permit."

P — Pharmacy manager is required to file name and date of birth of any unlicensed assistant employed in the prescription drug outlet.

Q — As of January 1, 1999.

R — Not yet established.

S — On the job training by pharmacist-in-charge appropriate to technician's duties.

T — Check a technician's refill of medications if the medication is to be administered by a licensed health care professional in an institutional setting; check a technician's repackaging of medications from bulk to unit dose in an institutional setting.

U — Must notify Board on change of employment location.

V — New law passed will require technician registration no later than six months from date of final effective regulations to implement the law. Not effective at this time.

W — Plus a $36 fingerprint fee.

X — $25 initial; $30 renewal/2 years.

Y — However, technicians must complete 6 hours of in-service training per year.

Z — Biennial by birth month.

AA — PTCB certification required.

BB — However, "certified pharmacy technicians" must maintain certification.

CC — However, pilot project underway (hospital).

DD — An individual may be certified by the board as a pharmacy technician if the individual has: worked for fifteen hundred hours under the supervision of a licensed pharmacist as a registered pharmacy technician or has completed a Board of Pharmacy-approved pharmacy technician course as provided for in subsection (D); however, beginning July 1, 2004, to be certified as a pharmacy technician an individual must have worked for one thousand hours under the supervision of a licensed pharmacist as a technician and must have completed a Board of Pharmacy approved technician course as provided for in subsection (D); a high school diploma or equivalent; and passed the National Pharmacy Technician Certification Board exam or a Board of Pharmacy-approved exam and has maintained current certification; and fulfilled continuing education requirements as provided for in Section 40-43-130(G).

XIII. Status of Pharmacy Technicians *(cont.)*

EE — As a condition of registration renewal, a registered pharmacy technician shall complete ten hours of American Council on Pharmaceutical Education or CME I approved continuing education each year, beginning with the next renewal period after June 30, 2003. A minimum of four hours of the total hours must be obtained through attendance at lectures, seminars, or workshops.

Footnotes (*)

AL — 3:1 if one technician is PTCB-certified. All techs must be at least 17.

AZ — 3:1 if one technician is PTCB-certified and pharmacy space is adequate. Training – 18 years old, high school graduate or GED.

CA — In community pharmacy, the ratio is 1:1 for the first pharmacist on duty, then 2:1 for each additional pharmacist on duty. 2:1 if pharmacy services patients of skilled nursing facilities or hospices. A pharmacist may also supervise one pharmacy technician trainee gaining required practical experience. In addition to a pharmacy technician, a non-licensed person may type a prescription label, enter data into a computer record system, and obtain a prescription refill authorization.

CT — In a "licensed pharmacy," ratio is 2:1 except for those preparing IV admixtures and other sterile products, unit-dose and unit of use dispensing, and bulk compounding for which the ratio is 3:1. In an institutional outpatient pharmacy, ratio is 2:1. The pharmacist manager may petition the Commission to increase ratio to 3:1 in a licensed or institutional outpatient pharmacy. Inpatient pharmacy ratio is 3:1 generally, but pharmacy can petition for ratio of up to 5:1; satellite pharmacy 3:1, but can petition for up to 5:1.

GA — Board may consider and approve an application to increase the ratio in a hospital pharmacy.

IA — Technicians must be under the immediate and personal supervision of the pharmacist. Technician training must be documented and maintained.

IN — Technicians must be under the immediate and personal supervision of the pharmacist.

MN — Specific functions are exempted from the 2:1 ratio as follows: for intravenous admixture preparation, unit-dose dispensing, prepackaging, and bulk compounding, ratio is 3:1. One additional tech per pharmacy if that tech is PTCB certified.

MT — Ratio is 2:1 if both are performing the following procedures: IV admixture or sterile product preparation; filling of unit-dose cassettes; prepackaging; or bulk compounding. Licensee may ask board for variance based on established criteria.

NC — Ratio may be increased above 2:1 if additional technicians are certified

ND — Technicians must complete Board-approved academic program or on-the-job training program.

NE — Inpatient hospital only.

OR — With exceptions.

PR — 3,000 hours of internship under direct supervision of a registered pharmacist and passing an exam prepared by the Board are required for certification. 2,000 hours may be substituted by completion of a vocational or technical pharmacy assistant accredited course. Designated "Pharmacy Assistant Apprentice" until certified.

SC — Technician-to-pharmacist ratio may not exceed 3:1 employment ratio.

TN — 3:1 if technician is certified.

TX — 3:1 if at least one of the technicians is certified. Only one of the technicians may be involved in the compounding of sterile pharmaceuticals.

VA — 3:1 if all technicians are certified.

WY — "Technicians-in-Training" are registered until they meet the requirements for licensure. The technician-in-training permit is valid for no more than 2 years from date of issue.

XIV. Pharmacy Technicians in Hospital/Institutional Setting

State	May Pharmacy Technicians in the Hospital/Institutional Setting:					
	Accept Called-In Rx from Physician's Office?	Prepare Prescription Label?	Enter Prescription into Pharmacy Computer?	Enter Information into Patient's File?	Retrieve Medication from Stock?	Place Medication into Prescription Container?
Alabama	No	Yes	Yes	Yes	Yes	Yes
Alaska G	No	Yes	Yes	Yes	Yes	Yes
Arizona	No	Yes	Yes B	Yes B	Yes B	Yes B
Arkansas	No	Yes	Yes	Yes	Yes	Yes
California	No	Yes	Yes	Yes Y	Yes	Yes
Colorado	No	Yes	Yes	Yes	Yes	Yes
Connecticut	No K	Yes	Yes	Yes	Yes	Yes
Delaware	No	Yes	Yes E	Yes E	Yes E	Yes E
District of Columbia	Yes V	Yes	Yes V	Yes V	Yes V	Yes V
Florida	No	Yes	Yes	Yes	Yes	Yes
Georgia	No	Yes	Yes	Yes	Yes	Yes
Guam	No	Yes E, G	Yes E, G	Yes E, G	Yes E, G	Yes E, G
Hawaii	No	Yes E, G	Yes E, G	Yes E, G	Yes E, G	Yes E, G
Idaho	No	Yes	Yes	Yes	Yes	Yes
Illinois	H	Yes E	Yes E	Yes E	Yes E	Yes E
Indiana	No J	Yes	Yes	Yes	Yes	Yes
Iowa G	Yes	Yes	Yes	Yes	Yes	Yes
Kansas	No	Yes	Yes G	Yes G	Yes	Yes
Kentucky	No K	Yes E	Yes E	Yes E	Yes E	Yes E
Louisiana	No	Yes	Yes	Yes	Yes	Yes
Maine	No	Yes	Yes	Yes	Yes	Yes
Maryland	No	Yes G	Yes G	Yes G	Yes G	Yes G
Massachusetts	No	Yes	Yes G	Yes	Yes	Yes G
Michigan	Yes G	Yes G	Yes G	Yes G	Yes G	Yes G
Minnesota	No	Yes	Yes	Yes	Yes	Yes
Mississippi E, G	No	Yes	Yes	Yes	Yes	Yes G
Missouri	Yes E	Yes E	Yes E	Yes E	Yes E	Yes E
Montana	Z	Yes	Yes E	Yes E	Yes	Yes
Nebraska	No	Yes	Yes	Yes	Yes	Yes
Nevada	No	Yes	Yes	Yes	Yes	Yes
New Hampshire	No	Yes	Yes G	Yes	Yes	Yes G
New Jersey	No	Yes E, G	Yes E, G	Yes E, G	Yes E, G	Yes E, G
New Mexico	No	Yes	Yes	Yes	Yes	Yes
New York	No	Yes	Yes G	Yes	Yes P	Yes
North Carolina	Yes E	Yes E	Yes E	Yes E	Yes E	Yes E
North Dakota	Yes	Yes	Yes	Yes	Yes	Yes
Ohio	No	Yes	Yes	Yes	Yes	Yes
Oklahoma	No	Yes	Yes	Yes	Yes	Yes
Oregon	No	Yes	Yes	Yes	Yes	Yes
Pennsylvania G, E	No	Yes	Yes	Yes	Yes	Yes
Puerto Rico	N	N	N	N	N	N
Rhode Island	No J, V	Yes	Yes	Yes	Yes	Yes
South Carolina	Yes AA	Yes E	Yes E	Yes E	Yes E	Yes E
South Dakota	No	Yes G	No O	Yes G	Yes G	Yes G
Tennessee	Yes U	Yes G	Yes G	Yes G	Yes	Yes
Texas	No	Yes	Yes	Yes	Yes	Yes
Utah	No	Yes	Yes G, I	Yes G, I	Yes G, I	Yes G, I
Vermont	No	Yes E	Yes E	Yes E	Yes E	Yes E
Virginia	No	Yes G	Yes G	Yes G	Yes G	Yes G
Washington	No	Yes	Yes	Yes	Yes S	Yes
West Virginia	No	Yes B	Yes G	Yes G	Yes G	Yes G
Wisconsin	Yes	Yes	Yes	Yes	Yes	Yes
Wyoming E, G	No	Yes	Yes	Yes	Yes	Yes

XIV. Pharmacy Technicians in Hospital/Institutional Setting *(cont.)*

May Pharmacy Technicians in the Hospital/Institutional Setting:

State	Place Prescription Label on Container?	Prepare Medications in Cards for Nursing Homes?	Blister-Pack Medications for Future Use?	Reconstitute Oral Liquids?	Call Physician for Refill Authorization?	Compound Medications for Dispensing?
Alabama	Yes	Yes	Yes	Yes	Yes D	No
Alaska G	Yes	Yes	Yes	Yes	Yes D	Yes
Arizona	Yes B	Yes B	Yes B	Yes B	Yes B	Yes B
Arkansas	Yes	Yes	Yes	Yes	Yes D	Yes C
California	Yes	Yes	Yes	Yes	Yes	Yes
Colorado	Yes	Yes	Yes	Yes	Yes D	Yes
Connecticut	Yes E	Yes E	Yes E	Yes E	Yes D	Yes E
Delaware	Yes E	Yes E	Yes E	Yes	No	Yes F
District of Columbia	Yes V	Yes V	Yes V	Yes V	Yes V	Yes V
Florida	Yes	Yes	Yes	Yes	Yes	Yes
Georgia	Yes	Yes	Yes	Yes	No	No W
Guam	Yes E, G	Yes E, G	Yes E, G	Yes E, G	No	Yes E, G
Hawaii	Yes E, G	Yes E, G	Yes E, G	Yes E, G	No	Yes E, G
Idaho	Yes	Yes	Yes	Yes	Yes	Yes
Illinois	Yes E	Yes E	Yes E	Yes E	Yes E	Yes E
Indiana	Yes	Yes	Yes	Yes	Yes	Yes
Iowa G	Yes	Yes	Yes	Yes	Yes	Yes
Kansas	Yes	Yes	Yes	Yes	Yes	Yes G
Kentucky	Yes E	Yes E	Yes E	Yes E	Yes E, D	Yes E
Louisiana	Yes	Yes	Yes	Yes	Yes D	Yes E
Maine	Yes	Yes	Yes	Yes	Yes	Yes
Maryland	Yes G	Yes G	Yes G	Yes G	Yes X	Yes
Massachusetts	Yes	Yes G	Yes G	Yes G	Yes	Yes B, G
Michigan	Yes G	Yes G	Yes G	Yes G	No	Yes G
Minnesota	Yes	Yes	Yes	Yes	Yes	No
Mississippi E, G	Yes	Yes	Yes	Yes	Yes	Yes
Missouri	Yes E	Yes E	Yes E	Yes E	Yes E	Yes E
Montana	Yes G	Yes E	Yes E	Yes E	Yes	Yes L
Nebraska	Yes	Yes	Yes	Yes	Yes M	Yes
Nevada	Yes	Yes	Yes	Yes	Yes	Yes
New Hampshire	Yes	Yes G	Yes G	Yes G	No	Yes G
New Jersey	Yes E, G	Yes E, G	Yes E, G	Yes E, G	No	Yes E, G
New Mexico	Yes	Yes	Yes	Yes	Yes G	Yes
New York	Yes	Yes	Yes	Yes G	No	No
North Carolina	Yes E	Yes E	Yes. E	Yes E	Yes E	Yes E
North Dakota	Yes	Yes	Yes	Yes	Yes	Yes G
Ohio	Yes	Yes	Yes	Yes E	No	Yes E
Oklahoma	Yes	Yes	Yes	Yes	Yes D	Yes L
Oregon	Yes	Yes	Yes	Yes	Yes D	Yes
Pennsylvania G, E	Yes	Yes	Yes	Yes	No	Yes F
Puerto Rico	N	N	N	N	N	N
Rhode Island	Yes	Yes	Yes	Yes	Yes	Yes G
South Carolina	Yes E	Yes · E	Yes E	Yes E	Yes Z	Yes E
South Dakota	Yes G	Yes G	Yes G	Yes G	No	Yes G
Tennessee	Yes	Yes	Yes	Yes G	Yes G	Yes G
Texas	Yes E, G	Yes	Yes	Yes	Yes D	Yes E, R
Utah	Yes G	A	Yes G	Yes G	Yes D	Yes G
Vermont	Yes E	Yes E	Yes E	Yes E	No	Yes A, B
Virginia	Yes G	Yes G	Yes G	Yes E, G	Yes	Yes E, G
Washington	Yes	Yes	Yes	Yes	Yes D	Yes T
West Virginia	Yes G	Yes G	Yes G	Yes G	Yes D	Yes T
Wisconsin	Yes	Yes	Yes	Yes	Yes Q	Yes W
Wyoming E, G	Yes	Yes	Yes	Yes	Yes D	Yes G

XIV. Pharmacy Technicians in Hospital/Institutional Setting *(cont.)*

LEGEND

A — Activities not addressed in statutes or regulations.

B — Subject to approved policy and procedure manuals, supportive personnel training, and pharmacist final verification and initialing.

C — Except multiple additive IV solutions.

D — If there are any changes to the prescription and/or if professional consultation is involved, the pharmacist must handle the call.

E — Allowed activity must be under the **direct** supervision of a licensed pharmacist. (HI – "immediate supervision." KY – Direct supervision if technician is not certified by the PTCB; if certified, then technician may perform activity under indirect supervision. LA – "Direct and immediate" supervision.)

F — Compounding is the responsibility of the pharmacist or pharmacy intern under the direct supervision of the pharmacist. The pharmacist may utilize the assistance of supportive personnel under certain conditions. Contact Board for requirements.

G — Pharmacist must verify, check, and/or is responsible for allowed activities.

H — Not prohibited. Law and regulations are silent on this issue; however, the practice is discouraged. Pharmacists should exercise professional judgment.

I — Allowed activity must be under the general supervision of a licensed pharmacist.

J — Unless it is regarding a refill.

K — Allowed activity limited to pharmacist interns.

L — Bulk compounding allowed.

M — However, a technician cannot receive actual authorization to refill.

N — Pharmacy Act allows pharmacy assistants to perform the tasks assigned by the pharmacist under his/her direct supervision. PR Supreme Court has recognized that only pharmacists are prepared to do patient counseling.

O — May key-in but not enter.

P — May not select pharmaceutical to be dispensed; however, may take stock bottle of pharmaceutical from shelf per pharmacist's instructions.

Q — Only pharmacist may receive the oral prescription order.

R — Only certified pharmacy technicians may compound sterile pharmaceuticals, but must have special training. Contact the Board for training requirements.

S — Pharmacist must select if more than one generic is available.

T — Bulk compounding and IV preparation are allowed, but "extemporaneous" compounding is not allowed.

U — If technician is certified.

V — Pharmacist must verify, check, and/or is responsible for allowed activities; except in the case of Schedule II controlled substances, only a pharmacist may receive an oral prescription.

W — May compound IV admixtures only if pharmacist verifies the final product for accuracy, efficacy, patient utilization, and has a mechanism to verify the measuring of active ingredients added to the IV mixture.

X — Pharmacy technician may call for refills for prescriptions other than CDS. May not accept refill authorization that changes the order.

Y — May enter information in non-patient care area of patient file, but not in area designated as "MD orders."

Z — Can accept refills if no changes.

AA — Certified technicians only with supervising pharmacist authorization.

XV. Pharmacy Technicians in Community Setting

May Pharmacy Technicians in the Community Setting:

State	Accept Called-In Rx from Physician's Office?	Prepare Prescription Label?	Enter Prescription into Pharmacy Computer?	Enter Information into Patient's File?	Retrieve Medication from Stock?	Place Medication into Prescription Container?
Alabama	No	Yes	Yes	Yes	Yes	Yes
Alaska E	No	Yes	Yes	Yes	Yes	Yes
Arizona	No	Yes	Yes B	Yes B	Yes B	Yes B
Arkansas	No	Yes	Yes	Yes	Yes	Yes
California	No	Yes D, E	Yes	Yes	Yes D, E	Yes D, E
Colorado	No	Yes	Yes	Yes	Yes	Yes
Connecticut	No	Yes D, E	Yes D, E	Yes D, E	Yes D, E	Yes D, E
Delaware	No	Yes	Yes D	Yes D	Yes D	Yes D
District of Columbia	Yes S	—	Yes S	Yes S	Yes S	Yes S
Florida	No	Yes	Yes	Yes	Yes	Yes
Georgia	No	Yes	Yes	Yes	Yes	Yes
Guam	No	Yes D, E	Yes D, E	Yes D, E	Yes D, E	Yes D, E
Hawaii	No	Yes D, E	Yes D, E	Yes D, E	Yes D, E	Yes D, E
Idaho	No	Yes	Yes	Yes	Yes	Yes
Illinois	Q	Yes I	Yes I	Yes I	Yes I	Yes I
Indiana	No G	Yes	Yes	Yes	Yes	Yes
Iowa E	Yes	Yes	Yes	Yes	Yes	Yes
Kansas	No	Yes	Yes E	Yes E	Yes	Yes
Kentucky	No H	Yes D	Yes D	Yes D	Yes D	Yes D
Louisiana	No	Yes	Yes	Yes	Yes	Yes
Maine	No	Yes	Yes	Yes	Yes	Yes
Maryland	No	Yes E	Yes E	Yes E	Yes E	Yes E
Massachusetts	Yes R	Yes	Yes E	Yes	Yes	Yes E
Michigan	Yes E	Yes E	Yes E	Yes E	Yes E	Yes E
Minnesota	No	Yes	Yes	Yes	Yes	Yes
Mississippi D, E	No	Yes	Yes	Yes	Yes	Yes
Missouri	Yes D	Yes D	Yes D	Yes D	Yes D	Yes D
Montana	Y	Yes	Yes D	Yes D	Yes D	Yes D
Nebraska	No	Yes	Yes	Yes	Yes	Yes
Nevada	No	Yes	Yes	Yes	Yes	Yes
New Hampshire	No	Yes	Yes E	Yes	Yes	Yes E
New Jersey	No	Yes D, E	Yes	Yes D, E	Yes D, E	Yes D, E
New Mexico	No	Yes	Yes	Yes	Yes	Yes
New York	No	Yes	Yes E	Yes	Yes K	Yes
North Carolina	Yes E	Yes E	Yes E	Yes E	Yes E	Yes E
North Dakota	Yes	Yes	Yes	Yes	Yes	Yes
Ohio	No	Yes	Yes	Yes	Yes	Yes
Oklahoma	No H	Yes	Yes	Yes	Yes	Yes D, E
Oregon	No	Yes	Yes	Yes	Yes	Yes
Pennsylvania D, E	No	Yes	Yes	Yes	Yes	Yes
Puerto Rico	O	O	O	O	O	O
Rhode Island	G, R	Yes	Yes	Yes	Yes	Yes
South Carolina	Yes Z	Yes D	Yes D	Yes D	Yes D	Yes D
South Dakota	No	Yes E	No J	Yes E	Yes E	Yes E
Tennessee	Yes E, R	Yes E	Yes E	Yes E	Yes	Yes
Texas	No	Yes	Yes	Yes	Yes	Yes
Utah	No	Yes E	Yes E	Yes E	Yes E	Yes E
Vermont	No	Yes D	Yes	Yes	Yes	Yes
Virginia	No	Yes E	Yes E	Yes E	Yes E	Yes E
Washington	No	Yes	Yes	Yes	Yes	Yes
West Virginia	No	Yes B, D	Yes D, E	Yes D, E	Yes D, E	Yes D, E
Wisconsin	Yes	Yes	Yes	Yes	Yes	Yes
Wyoming D, E	No	Yes	Yes	Yes	Yes	Yes

XV. Pharmacy Technicians in Community Setting (cont.)

State	May Pharmacy Technicians in the Community Setting:					
	Place Prescription Label on Container?	Prepare Medications in Cards for Nursing Homes?	Blister-Pack Medications for Future Use?	Reconstitute Oral Liquids?	Call Physician for Refill Authorization?	Compound Medications for Dispensing?
Alabama	Yes	Yes	Yes	Yes	Yes M	No
Alaska E	Yes	Yes	Yes	Yes	Yes M	Yes
Arizona	Yes B	Yes B	Yes D	Yes B	Yes B	Yes R
Arkansas	Yes	Yes	Yes	Yes C	Yes M	Yes
California	Yes D, E	Yes D, E	Yes D, E	Yes D, E	Yes D	Yes D, E
Colorado	Yes	Yes	Yes	Yes	Yes	Yes E
Connecticut	Yes D, E	Yes D, E	Yes D, E	Yes D, E	Yes M	Yes D, E
Delaware	Yes D	Yes D	Yes D	Yes F	No	Yes F
District of Columbia	Yes S	Yes S	Yes S	Yes S	Yes S	Yes S
Florida	Yes	Yes	Yes	Yes	Yes	Yes
Georgia	Yes	Yes	No	Yes T	No	No
Guam	Yes D, E	Yes D, E	Yes D, E	Yes D, E	No	Yes D, E
Hawaii	Yes D, E	Yes D, E	Yes D, E	Yes D, E	No	Yes D, E
Idaho	Yes	Yes	Yes	Yes	Yes	Yes
Illinois	Yes I	Yes I	Yes I	Yes I	Yes I	Yes I
Indiana	Yes	Yes	Yes	Yes	Yes	Yes
Iowa E	Yes	Yes	Yes	Yes	Yes	Yes
Kansas	Yes	Yes E	Yes	Yes	Yes	No
Kentucky	Yes D	Yes D	Yes D	Yes D	Yes D, M	Yes D
Louisiana	Yes	Yes	Yes	Yes	Yes M	Yes D
Maine	Yes	Yes	Yes	Yes	Yes	Yes
Maryland	Yes E	Yes E	Yes E	Yes E	Yes W	Yes E
Massachusetts	Yes E	Yes E	Yes E	Yes E	Yes U	Yes E
Michigan	Yes E	Yes E	Yes E	Yes E	No	Yes E
Minnesota	Yes	Yes	Yes	Yes	Yes	No
Mississippi D, E	Yes	Yes	Yes	Yes	Yes	Yes
Missouri	Yes D	Yes D	Yes D	Yes D	Yes D	Yes D
Montana	Yes D	Yes D	Yes D	Yes D	Yes	Yes L
Nebraska	Yes	Yes	Yes	Yes	Yes X	Yes
Nevada	Yes	Yes	Yes	Yes	Yes	Yes
New Hampshire	Yes E	Yes E	Yes E	Yes E	No	Yes E
New Jersey	Yes D, E	Yes D, E	Yes D, E	Yes D, E	No	Yes D, E
New Mexico	Yes	Yes	Yes	Yes	Yes E	Yes
New York	Yes	Yes	Yes	Yes E	No	No
North Carolina	Yes E	Yes E	Yes E	Yes E	Yes E	Yes E
North Dakota	Yes	Yes	Yes	Yes	Yes	Yes E
Ohio	Yes	Yes	Yes	Yes D	No	Yes D
Oklahoma	Yes	Yes	Yes	Yes	Yes	Yes L
Oregon	Yes	Yes	Yes	Yes	Yes M	Yes
Pennsylvania D, E	Yes	Yes	Yes	Yes	No	Yes F
Puerto Rico	O	O	O	O	O	O
Rhode Island	Yes	Yes	Yes	Yes	Yes	Yes E
South Carolina	Yes D	Yes D	Yes D	Yes D	Yes Z	Yes D
South Dakota	Yes E	Yes E	Yes E	Yes E	No	Yes E
Tennessee	Yes	Yes	Yes	Yes E	Yes	Yes E
Texas	Yes	Yes	Yes	Yes	Yes M	Yes D, N
Utah	Yes E	A	Yes E	Yes E	Yes M	Yes E
Vermont	Yes	Yes	Yes	Yes	Yes	Yes A, B
Virginia	Yes E	Yes E	Yes D, E	Yes D, E	No	Yes D, E
Washington	Yes	Yes	Yes	Yes	Yes M	Yes P
West Virginia	Yes D, E	Yes D, E	Yes D, E	Yes D, E	Yes D, E	No
Wisconsin	Yes	Yes	Yes	No	Yes V	Yes B
Wyoming	Yes	Yes	Yes	Yes	Yes M	Yes E

XV. Pharmacy Technicians in Community Setting *(cont.)*

LEGEND

A — Activities are not addressed in laws or statutes.

B — Subject to approved policy and procedure manuals, supportive personnel training, and pharmacist final verification and initialing.

C — May reconstitute oral antibiotics only.

D — Allowed activity must be under the **direct** supervision of a licensed pharmacist. (HI – "Immediate supervision." KY – Direct supervision if technician is not certified; if certified by the PTCB, then technician may perform activity under indirect supervision. LA – "Direct and immediate.")

E — Pharmacist must verify, check, and/or is responsible for allowed activities.

F — Compounding is the responsibility of the pharmacist or pharmacy intern under the direct supervision of the pharmacist. The pharmacist may utilize the assistance of supportive personnel under certain conditions. Contact Board for requirements.

G — Unless it is regarding a refill.

H — Allowed activity limited to pharmacists and interns. (KY – Under direct supervision.)

I — Allowed activity must be under the supervision of a licensed pharmacist.

J — May key-in but not enter.

K — May not select pharmaceutical to be dispensed; however, may take stock bottle of pharmaceutical from shelf per pharmacist's instructions.

L — Bulk compounding allowed.

M — If there are any changes to the prescription and/or if professional consultation is involved, the pharmacist must handle the call.

N — Only certified pharmacy technicians may compound sterile pharmaceuticals but must have special training. Contact the Board for training requirements.

O — Pharmacy Act allows pharmacy assistants to perform the tasks assigned by the pharmacist under his/her supervision. PR Supreme Court has recognized that only pharmacists are prepared to do patient counseling.

P — Bulk compounding and IV preparation are allowed, but "extemporaneous" compounding is not allowed.

Q — Not prohibited. Law and regulations are silent on this issue; however, the practice is discouraged. Pharmacists should exercise professional judgment.

R — If technician is certified.

S — Pharmacist must verify, check, and/or is responsible for allowed activities; except in the case of Schedule II controlled substances, only a pharmacist may receive an oral prescription.

T — May reconstitute medications as long as a mechanism of verification is available for a pharmacist to check the final product.

U — Provided no change in therapy.

V — Only pharmacist may receive the oral prescription order.

W — Pharmacy technician may call for refills for prescriptions other than CDS. May not accept refill authorization that changes the order.

X — However, a technician cannot receive actual authorization to refill.

Y — Refills only with no changes.

Z — Certified technicians only with supervising pharmacist authorization.

XVI. Pharmacy Licensure Requirements

State	Number of Pharmacy License Categories*	Must Nonresident Pharmacies be Licensed/ Registered?		Initial Licensure/ Registration Fee	Renewal Fee	Renewal Schedule	Must Nonresident Pharmacists be Licensed?
Alabama	2	Yes		$225	$150	1 year	No
Alaska	3	Yes	A	$250	$200	2 years	No
Arizona	3	Yes		$400	$400	2 years	No
Arkansas	4	Yes		$200	$400	2 years	Yes H
California	3	Yes		$340	$175	1 year	No
Colorado	1	Yes	A	$250	$160	1 year	No
Connecticut	5	Yes	A, B	$600	$150	1 year	No
Delaware	1	Yes	D	$200	Varies	2 years	No
District of Columbia	4	No		$150	$150	1 year	—
Florida	14	Yes	A	$250	$250	2 years	No
Georgia	9	No		$100	$ 95	2 years	No
Guam	1	No		$ 50	$ 30	1 year	No
Hawaii	2	Yes		G, I	$220/$270 T	2 years	No
Idaho	6	Yes		$100 J	$100 J	1 year	
Illinois	5	Yes		$100	$200	2 years	No
Indiana	6	Yes		$100	$200	2 years	No
Iowa	4	Yes	A	$100	$100	1 year	No K
Kansas	1	Yes		$140	$125	1 year	No
Kentucky	2	Yes		$100	$100	1 year	No
Louisiana	8	Yes		$150	$100	1 year	No
Maine	3	Yes	B	$200	$200	1 year	No
Maryland	3	Yes		$300	$250	1 year	No
Massachusetts	5	No		$263	$263	2 years	No
Michigan	1	L		$180	$260	2 years	Yes
Minnesota	6	Yes		$165	$165	1 year	No
Mississippi	4	Yes		$250	$250	2 years	No
Missouri	10	Yes		$250	$400	2 years	No
Montana	1	Yes		$200	$100	1 year	No
Nebraska	2	Yes		$200	$200	2 years	No
Nevada	1	Yes		$425	$425 I	2 years	Yes
New Hampshire	1	Yes		$500 C	$250 C	1 year	No
New Jersey	2	No		$275	$175	1 year	No
New Mexico	2	Yes		$150	$150	1 year	No
New York	1	Yes	Q	$345	$260	3 years	No
North Carolina	3	Yes		$350	$175	1 year	
North Dakota	10	Yes		$175	$175	1 year	Yes
Ohio	9	Yes		$150	$150	1 year	No
Oklahoma	4	Yes	A	$200	$150	1 year	—
Oregon	2	Yes		$175	$175	1 year	No
Pennsylvania	1	No		$100	$ 75	2 years	No
Puerto Rico	1	R		R	$ 3	1 year	—
Rhode Island	4	Yes	A	$125	$ 62.50	1 year	No
South Carolina	1	Yes		$300	$200	1 year	No
South Dakota	2	Yes		$200 N, O	$200 N, O	1 year	No
Tennessee	6	Yes		$168	$168	2 years	Yes F
Texas	5	Yes	A	$363	$363	2 years	No
Utah	13	Yes	A	$100	$ 50	2 years G	No
Vermont	4	No		$270	$ 70	2 years	No
Virginia	1	Yes		$200	$200	1 year	No
Washington	1	Yes		$365	$265	1 year	No
West Virginia	1	Yes	A	$150	$100	1 year	—
Wisconsin	1	No		$ 53	$ 53	2 years	—
Wyoming	2	Yes		$100 resident $200 nonresident	$100 resident $200 nonresident	1 year	No

* See "Footnotes (*)" on page 855 for categories of pharmacy licenses for those states that issue more than one category. Contact the state board of pharmacy for specific information about these licenses.

XVI. Pharmacy Licensure Requirements *(cont.)*

State	Initial Controlled Substance Fee	Controlled Substance Renewal Fee	Controlled Substance Renewal Schedule
Alabama	$100	$100	1 year
Alaska	None	None	—
Arizona	None	None	—
Arkansas	None	None	—
California	None	None	—
Colorado	None	None	—
Connecticut	None	None	—
Delaware	$ 40	$ 40	2 years
District of Columbia	$ 50	$ 50	1 year
Florida	None	None	—
Georgia	None	None	—
Guam	$150	$120	1 year
Hawaii	$ 60	$ 60	1 year H
Idaho	$ 60	$ 60	1 year
Illinois	$ 5	$ 5	2 years
Indiana	$100	$100	2 years
Iowa	$ 50*	$ 50*	2 years*
Kansas	None	None	—
Kentucky	M	M	M
Louisiana	$ 25	$ 25	1 year
Maine	None	None	—
Maryland	$ 60	$ 60	2 years
Massachusetts	$113	$113	2 years
Michigan	$ 85	$160	2 years
Minnesota	None	None	—
Mississippi	$ 50	$ 50	2 years I
Missouri	None	None	—
Montana	$ 35	$ 35	1 year
Nebraska	None	None	—
Nevada	$ 70	$ 70	2 years I
New Hampshire	None	None	—
New Jersey	$ 20	$ 20	1 year
New Mexico	$ 60	$ 60	1 year
New York	None	None	—
North Carolina	None	None	—
North Dakota	None	None	—
Ohio	—	—	—
Oklahoma	None M	None M	M
Oregon	$ 25	$ 25	1 year
Pennsylvania	None	None	—
Puerto Rico	$200 S	$200 S	1 year
Rhode Island	$ 50	$ 50	1 year
South Carolina	$100	$100	1 year
South Dakota	$ 0	$ 0	3 years M
Tennessee	$ 40	$ 40	2 years
Texas	$ 25	$ 25	1 year P
Utah	$ 90	$ 50	2 years
Vermont	None	None	—
Virginia	None	None	—
Washington	$ 80	$ 65	1 year
West Virginia	$ 25	$ 25	1 year
Wisconsin	None	None	—
Wyoming	$ 10	$ 10	1 year

XVI. Pharmacy Licensure Requirements *(cont.)*

LEGEND

A — If pharmacy ships, mails, delivers, dispenses, and/or provides prescription drugs and/or devices to state residents. (TX – If pharmacy routinely provides such services. WV – If more than 10% of prescription volume is dispensed by mail.)

B — Registered, not licensed.

C — $150 for nonresident pharmacies.

D — Prorated initial licensing fee; renewal fee varies.

E — One licensed AR pharmacist required as pharmacist-in-charge for AR permit.

F — If acting as pharmacist-in-charge of a licensed out-of-state pharmacy.

G — Odd years. (HI – $295.)

H — State Department of Public Safety, Narcotics Enforcement Division.

I — Even years. (HI – $185.)

J — Mail Order Annual Fee – $250; Mail Order Initial Fee – $500.

K — Unless they enter state to provide pharmacy services.

L — Current law prohibits a pharmacist from dispensing a prescription by mail when the original Rx was received by mail.

M — Not handled by the Board of Pharmacy.

N — $200, community pharmacy and institutional full-time pharmacy.

O — $160, institutional part-time pharmacy.

P — Issued by Texas Department of Public Safety.

Q — New law requiring out of state reg. becomes effective as of March 18, 2003.

R — Not addressed in pharmacy act or Board regulations.

S — Required by the local Controlled Substances Act.

T — $220 – odd years; $270 even years.

Footnotes (*)

AK — Retail, institutional, drug room, out-of-state.

AZ — Community, hospital, limited service.

AR — Hospital, institutional, retail, charitable clinic.

CA — Community pharmacy, hospital pharmacy, exempt hospital.

CT — Community, nuclear, long-term care, infusion specialty.

DC — Retail, institutional, nuclear, special or limited use.

FL — Class I institutional (nursing home), Class II institutional (hospital), Modified Class IIA, Modified Class IIB, Modified Class IIC, community, special parenteral-enteral, special non-resident, special closed system, special end stage renal disease, animal shelter, nuclear. Special parenteral/enteral extended scope. Special assisted living facility.

GA — Retail, hospital, nuclear, prison, pharmacy school, pharmacy clinic, PBM, researcher, opioid treatment center.

HI — Pharmacy license and miscellaneous permit.

ID — Retail drug outlet, institutional drug outlet, parenteral, non-pharmacy drug outlet, limited service, out-of-state mail service pharmacy.

IL — Retail; off-site hospital, nursing home pharmacies; on-site hospital, nursing home pharmacies; nuclear; ambulatory care facility pharmacies and hospital or nursing home pharmacies providing services to the general public.

IN — Based on type of business conducted.

IA — General, hospital, limited-use, non-resident. Controlled substance registration not required for non-resident pharmacies.

LA — Community, institutional, industrial clinic, nuclear, parenteral/enteral, out-of-state, hospital, provisional.

ME — Retail, rural health center, mail order.

MD — Full service pharmacy permit; various waiver permits. Nonresident pharmacy permit.

MA — Hospital, clinic, retail, nuclear, restricted.

MN — Community/retail, hospital, parenteral-enteral/home health care, long-term care, nuclear, nonresident.

MS — Community, institutional, limited closed door, non-resident.

MO — Community ambulatory, hospital outpatient, long-term care, home health care, radiopharmaceutical, renal dialysis, medical gas, sterile product compounding, consultant services, and shared services.

NE — Pharmacy, dispensing practitioner.

NJ — Retail, hospital/institutional. Specialized permits where applicable.

NC — Pharmacy permits, limited service permits, out-of-state permits.

ND — Out-patient, home health care, nuclear, out-of-state, research, hospital, long-term care, mail order, governmental agency, office practice, telepharmacy.

OH — Retail, hospital, long-term care, fluid therapy/home health care, clinic, HMO, mail order, nuclear, specialty.

OK — Retail, hospital, non-resident, charitable.

OR — Retail, institutional, manufacturing, wholesale, nonprescription.

PR — Board issues licenses to pharmacies (community and institutional), wholesalers, manufacturers, non-pharmacy OTC drug outlets, and drug deposits.

RI — Retail (includes community, parenteral, nuclear), institutional (includes hospital, HMO, university, other settings).

SD — Full-time, part-time.

TN — Community, hospital, nursing home, home health care, nuclear, other.

TX — Community, nuclear, institutional, clinic, non-resident.

UT — Analytical laboratory, branch pharmacy, hospital pharmacy, institutional pharmacy, nuclear pharmacy, manufacturer, wholesaler, pharmaceutical teaching organization, retail pharmacy, veterinary pharmaceutical outlet, euthanasia agency, pharmaceutical administration facility, out-of-state mail service pharmacy.

VT — Retail, institutional, research and investigation, manufacturer.

XVII. Wholesale Distributor Licensure Requirements

State	Does State License Out-of-State Wholesalers?	Initial Wholesale Distributor Licensure/ Registration Fee	Renewal Fee	Renewal Schedule	State Agency Responsible for Licensing Wholesale Distributors
Alabama	Yes	$ 250	$ 250	1 year	Board of Pharmacy
Alaska	No	$ 250	$ 200	2 years	Board of Pharmacy
Arizona	Yes	$1,000 A	$1,000 A	2 years	Board of Pharmacy
Arkansas	Yes	$ 300	$ 150	1 year	Board of Pharmacy
California	Yes	$ 550	$ 550	1 year	Board of Pharmacy
Colorado	Yes B	$ 250	$ 250	1 year	Board of Pharmacy
Connecticut	Yes	$ 150 C	$ 150 C	1 year	U
Delaware	Yes	$ 200 D	D	2 years	Board of Pharmacy
District of Columbia	Yes	$ 100 L	$ 100 L	1 year	H
Florida	Yes	E	E	2 years	V
Georgia	Yes	$ 250	$ 195	2 years	Board of Pharmacy
Guam	No P	$ 50	$ 30	1 year	Board of Pharmacy
Hawaii	No M	$ 295/185 Q	$ 270/220 R	2 years	Board of Pharmacy Y
Idaho	Yes	$ 100	$ 100	1 year	Board of Pharmacy
Illinois	Yes	$ 200	$ 400	2 years	AA
Indiana	Yes	$ 100	$ 100	2 years	W
Iowa	Yes	$ 100	$ 100	1 year	X
Kansas	Yes	$ 300	$ 300	1 year	Board of Pharmacy
Kentucky	Yes	$ 100	$ 100	1 year	Board of Pharmacy
Louisiana	Yes G	—	—	—	S
Maine	Yes	$ 200	$ 200	1 year	Board of Pharmacy
Maryland	Yes	$ 500	$ 500	1 year	Board of Pharmacy
Massachusetts	No	$ 450 C	$ 450 C	1 year	Board of Pharmacy
Michigan	Yes	$ 160	$ 50 C	2 years	Board of Pharmacy
Minnesota	Yes	F	F	1 year	Board of Pharmacy
Mississippi	Yes	$ 250	$ 250	2 years	Board of Pharmacy
Missouri	Yes	$ 250	$ 400	2 years	Board of Pharmacy
Montana	Yes	$ 150	$ 75	1 year	Board of Pharmacy
Nebraska	No	$ 400	$ 200	1 year	BB
Nevada	Yes	$ 425	$ 425	2 years	Board of Pharmacy
New Hampshire	Yes	$ 250	$ 250	1 year	Board of Pharmacy
New Jersey G	No	—	—	—	CC
New Mexico	Yes	$ 300 C	$ 300	1 year	Board of Pharmacy
New York	Yes Z	$ 825 C	$ 520	3 years	Board of Pharmacy
North Carolina	Yes	$ 350	$ 350	1 year	Dept. of Agricult.
North Dakota	Yes	$ 150	$ 150	1 year	Board of Pharmacy
Ohio	Yes	$ 150	$ 150 C	1 year	Board of Pharmacy
Oklahoma	Yes	$ 200	$ 200	1 year	Board of Pharmacy
Oregon	Yes	$ 400 C	$ 400 C	1 year	Board of Pharmacy
Pennsylvania N	N	N	N	N	T
Puerto Rico	O	$ 30	$ 30	1 year	—
Rhode Island	Yes	$ 125	$ 93.75	1 year	Board of Pharmacy
South Carolina	Yes	$ 500	$ 500	1 year	Board of Pharmacy
South Dakota	Yes	$ 200	$ 200	1 year	Board of Pharmacy
Tennessee	Yes	$ 408	$ 408 C	Cyclical	Board of Pharmacy
Texas	Yes	Varies I	Varies I	1 year	H
Utah	No	$ 100 C	$ 50 C	2 years	Board of Pharmacy
Vermont	Yes	$ 400	$ 200	2 years	Board of Pharmacy
Virginia	Yes	$ 200	$ 200 C	1 year	Board of Pharmacy
Washington	Yes	$ 590 C	$ 590	1 year	Board of Pharmacy
West Virginia	Yes	$ 400	$ 400	1 year	Board of Pharmacy
Wisconsin	Yes	$ 53	$ 53 C	2 years	—
Wyoming	Yes	$ 200 K	$ 200 J, K	1 year K	Board of Pharmacy

XVII. Wholesale Distributor Licensure Requirements *(cont.)*

LEGEND

A — Full-service drug wholesaler licensure fees. Nonprescription drug wholesaler licensure fee: $500; renewal fee: $500 (biennial).

B — For controlled substances **only.**

C — Plus controlled substance registration fee. (CT – $150/yr. ID – $100/yr. MA – $113/yr. MI – $150/2 yrs. NM – $60/yr. NY – $1,200/2 yrs. OH – $37.50/yr, OR – $50/yr. RI – $50/yr. TN – $40/2 yrs. VA – $20/yr. UT – $90/yr ($50 renewal) WA – $115/yr. WI – 25/yr.)

D — Varies. Set by Division of Professional Regulation each calendar year.

E — The fee is $700 for prescription drug wholesaler; $600 for out-of-state prescription drug wholesaler; $100 for retail pharmacy drug wholesaler; $500 for compressed medical gas wholesaler. Fees are the same for biennial renewals.

F — Legend drugs – state licensure fee: $180; renewal fee: $180. OTC and/or veterinary drugs – state licensure fee: $155; renewal fee: $155. Medical gases – state licensure fee: $130; renewal fee: $130. If already licensed as a pharmacy – state licensure fee: $105; renewal fee: $105.

G — Wholesalers are regulated by another state agency.

H — Licensed by Department of Health.

I — In-state wholesale distributors vary depending on Gross Annual Volume (GAV). GAV less than $200,000 – fee is $400. GAV $200,000 to less than $20 million – fee is $650. GAV $200 million and over – fee is $850. Separate fee from Texas Dept. of Public Safety for controlled substances. Out-of-state – GAV less than $20 million – fee is $500. GAV greater than $20 million – fee is $750.

J — Manufacturer of controlled substances pays $150 for state licensure fee and for renewal fee. A distributor pays $100.

K — Wyoming has a separate registration for: 1) prescription drugs at $200/yr. (due to PDMA); 2) controlled substances – registration of manufacturers and distributors.

L — The fee is $200 annually for drug local wholesalers and $100 annually for out-of-state wholesale distributors. There is an additional annual fee of $50 for controlled substances, where applicable.

M — However, per Board's informal interpretation, if the out-of-state wholesaler has a vendor-managed inventory system within the state, a wholesale distributor license is required.

N — Wholesalers and distributors are regulated by another state agency.

O — Not addressed in Pharmacy Act or Board regulations.

P — However, legislation to require registration of out-of-state establishments, including the Internet, is pending.

Q — $295 – even years; $185 – odd years.

R — $270 – even years; $220 – odd years.

S — Board of Wholesale Drug Distributors.

T — Bureau of Drugs, Devices, and Cosmetics.

U — Department of Consumer Protection.

V — Bureau of Statewide Pharmaceutical Services.

W — Board of Pharmacy Health Professionals Bureau.

X — Board of Pharmacy Examiners.

Y — However, approved subject to satisfactory inspection by the Department of Health, Food and Drug branch.

Z — New law requiring out-of-state reg. becomes effective 3/18/03.

AA — Department of Professional Regulation.

BB — HHS, Regulation, and Licensure.

CC — Department of Health and Senior Services.

XVIII. Drug Control Regulations

	Does State Have:					
	Food, Drug and Cosmetic Act?	Dangerous Drug Law?	Controlled Substances Act?	Precursor Substances Placed in Controlled Substance Schedule?	Laws/Regs on Dispensing Prescription Medical Devices?	Laws/Regs on Dispensing Medical Oxygen?
Alabama	Yes A	Yes B	Yes B	Yes	Yes	Yes
Alaska	No	No	A	No	Yes SS	Yes SS
Arizona	No	Yes	Yes B	No C	No	No NN
Arkansas	Yes A	Yes	Yes D, E	Yes F	Yes	Yes
California	Yes	Yes	Yes	Yes G	Yes WW	Yes WW
Colorado	Yes E	No	Yes	Yes E	No	No
Connecticut	Yes H	Yes H	Yes H	No LL	ZZ	ZZ
Delaware	Yes A, I	Yes B	Yes E	Yes J	OO	No
District of Columbia	Yes A	Yes	Yes A, K	No	No	No
Florida	Yes A, I	Yes A, I	Yes A, I	Yes	No	No
Georgia	Yes	Yes B, JJ	Yes	No	No	No
Guam	Yes	Yes	Yes	No	Yes PP	Yes QQ
Hawaii	Yes E	Yes E	Yes C	C	D, E	Yes D, E
Idaho	Yes	—	Yes D	Yes F	Yes	Yes
Illinois	Yes B	Yes B	Yes B	Yes	Yes YY	Yes YY
Indiana	Yes	Yes	Yes	No	No	No
Iowa	Yes	No	Yes D	No W	Yes BBB	Yes BBB
Kansas	Yes	Yes B	Yes B	No	No	No
Kentucky	Yes	—	Yes	No	No	Yes
Louisiana	Yes AAA	No	Yes B	Yes	No	No
Maine	—	Yes	A	No	Yes XX	Yes XX
Maryland	Yes	Yes	Yes	No	ZZ	No Y
Massachusetts	No	No	Yes	Yes N, O	Not addressed RR	Not addressed RR
Michigan	Yes I	Yes	Yes D	No	Yes MM	No
Minnesota	Yes I	Yes	Yes D	Yes	No	Yes
Mississippi	No	No	Yes	Yes	Yes	Yes
Missouri	Yes	Yes K	Yes E	No	No	Yes
Montana	Yes	Yes P	Yes P	Q	No	No
Nebraska	Yes I	Yes	Yes R	No	ZZ	ZZ
Nevada	Yes L	Yes D	Yes D	Yes G	Yes D	Yes D
New Hampshire	—	—	Yes D	No	A, U	A
New Jersey	Yes I	Yes B	Yes E	Yes	No	T
New Mexico	Yes D, KK	No KK	Yes D	Yes F	Yes	Yes
New York	Yes	—	Yes - Legis.	Yes	Yes	Yes
North Carolina	Yes	No	Yes S	No	Yes	Yes
North Dakota	Yes T, U	Yes T, U	Yes B, U	Yes HH	Yes	No
Ohio	Yes D	Yes D	Yes D	No LL	No	Yes
Oklahoma	Yes I	Yes B	Yes V	No W	No	Yes TT
Oregon	Yes X	Yes	Yes	Yes	Yes	Yes
Pennsylvania	Yes M	Yes M	Yes M	Yes II	Yes II	Yes II
Puerto Rico	Yes E	Yes E	Yes E	A	—	—
Rhode Island	Yes	Yes P	Yes B	Yes	Yes	Yes
South Carolina	Yes B	Yes B	Yes E	No	No	Yes
South Dakota	—	Yes	Yes E	No	UU, VV	UU, VV
Tennessee	Yes	Yes	Yes D	No	No	No
Texas	Yes E	Yes D	Yes Z	No AA	Yes E	Yes E
Utah	No	No	Yes BB	No	No	No
Vermont	Yes	Yes	Yes E	No	E, U	E
Virginia	Yes CC	—	Yes D, CC	Yes	Yes	Yes
Washington	Yes	Yes	Yes D	Yes DD	No	No
West Virginia	No	Yes P	Yes I	Yes	Yes	No
Wisconsin	No	No	Yes B, EE	Yes	Yes	Yes
Wyoming	Yes F	Yes GG	Yes D, V	Yes HH	No	Yes

XVIII. Drug Control Regulations *(cont.)*

LEGEND

A — Same as federal regulations permit.

B — Uniform.

C — Jurisdiction: Narcotic Enforcement Division, Department of Public Safety.

D — Board of Pharmacy.

E — Jurisdiction: State Department of Health. (NJ and Kansas borviooo; LLI Public Health and Environment.)

F — Contact state Board office for list.

G — Immediate precursors.

H — Department of Consumer Protection.

I — State enabling act permits enforcement of federal act.

J — Immediate amphetamine precursors. Contact state Board office for list.

K — Dangerous Drug Law, including stimulants and hallucinogenics.

L — Department of Human Resources.

M — Food, Drug and Cosmetic Act is the "Controlled Substances, Drugs, Devices, and Cosmetic Act."

N — Scheduled in same schedule as controlled substance.

O — Non-controlled legend drugs are classified as Schedule VI.

P — Dangerous Drug Law is the "Controlled Substances Act."

Q — Department of Justice regulates under Non-Controlled Substance Reporting and Regulation Act.

R — Administered by Health & Human Services, Department of Regulation and Licensure, Credentialing Division and Division of Drug Control of Nebraska State Patrol.

S — Division of Mental Health, Developmental Disabilities, and Substance Abuse Services.

T — Department of Health.

U — State Board of Pharmacy.

V — Commissioner of Drugs and Substances Control.

W — Restrictions exist – contact Board of Pharmacy office.

X — Applicable to foods only.

Y — Although distributors must have a distribution permit.

Z — Department of Public Safety.

AA — Precursor sales records must be maintained.

BB — Division of Occupational and Professional Licensing.

CC — Combined into one act: the "Drug Control Act."

DD — Rule WAC 246-887-150 and WAC 246-889 for nonscheduled precursors. Ephedrine, pseudoephedrine, and phenylpropanolamine OTC sales limited to three packages per sale, three gram limit per package.

EE — Controlled Substances Board.

FF — Department of Agriculture.

GG — Pharmacy Act considers all prescription legend drugs as "dangerous drugs."

HH — Precursors listed same as those in CFR.

II — Department of Health regulates through the Drug, Device, and Cosmetic Board.

JJ — Lists all approved dangerous drugs.

KK — Dangerous Drug Law included in Food, Drug and Cosmetic Act.

LL — No state precursor statutes. Refer to federal laws and regulations.

MM — When it bears "Rx Only" legend.

NN — Only on distributing and manufacturing.

OO — Not under the jurisdiction of the Board of Pharmacy.

PP — State has statutory authority to write rules, but at present no specific rules have been written.

QQ — Title 10 of Guam Code Annotated, Chapter 40.

RR — If the device or oxygen bears the federal legend, the Massachusetts regulations would treat them as Schedule VI controlled substances.

SS — Regulation of prescription drugs and devices.

TT — Board rules require permits for medical gas supliers and distributors.

UU — Devices that are legend items require prescription from physician.

VV — Under the jurisdiction of the Department of Health, not the Board of Pharmacy.

WW — Medical device retailers may sell Rx devices and medical oxygen.

XX — Addressed in the Pharmacy Practice Act.

YY — Under the jurisdiction of the Home Medical Equipment and Services Board, not the Board of Pharmacy.

ZZ — Laws and regulations governing medical devices or medical oxygen are those governing legend drugs.

AAA — Department of Health and hospitals.

BBB — Medical oxygen and medical devices.

XIX. Drug Product Selection Laws

State	State Drug Formulary	Two-line Rx Format	Permissive or Mandatory*	How to Prevent Substitution	Pharmacy Record Required	Cost Savings Pass-on	Patient Consent**
Alabama	None	Yes	P	A	Yes	U	No
Alaska	None	No	P	B	Yes	T	Yes
Arizona	None	Yes	P	A	Yes	U	Yes
Arkansas	None	No	P	B	Yes	T	Yes
California	None	No	P	B, EE	Yes	T	Yes
Colorado	None	No	P	J	Yes	S	Yes
Connecticut	None	No	P	E, F	Yes	S	Yes
Delaware	Positive K	No	P	E	Yes	S	Yes
District of Columbia	Positive	No	P	B	Yes	T	Yes
Florida	Negative L	No	M	F	Yes	S	Yes
Georgia	None	No	P	C	Yes	N	Yes
Guam	None	No	P	G	Yes	T	No DD
Hawaii AA	Positive K	No	P	B	Yes	T	Yes
Idaho	None	No	P	D	Yes	T	Yes
Illinois	Positive KK	No	P	D	Yes	T	Yes
Indiana	None	Yes	P	A	Yes	O	Yes II
Iowa	None	No	P	I	Yes	X	Yes
Kansas	None	Yes (optional)	P	A, B	Yes	T	Yes
Kentucky	Negative	Yes (conditional)	M	B, H, Y	Yes	T	Yes
Louisiana	None K	No	P	R	Yes	MM	Yes
Maine	None	No	P	B, R	Yes	V	Yes
Maryland	Positive K	No	P	I	Yes	MM	Yes
Massachusetts	Positive K	No	M	B	Yes	T	No
Michigan	None	No	P	E	Yes	S	Yes
Minnesota	Negative	No	M	E	Yes	S	Yes
Mississippi	None	Yes	M	A	Yes	T	Yes
Missouri	Negative	Yes	P	A	Yes	T	Yes
Montana	None	No	P	B	Yes	S	Yes
Nebraska	Positive K	No	P	B	Yes	S	Yes
Nevada	Positive K	No	P	D	Yes	T	Yes
New Hampshire	Positive K	No	P	B	Yes	T	Yes
New Jersey	Positive	Yes	M	A	Yes	T	No
New Mexico	None	No	P	G	No	S	No
New York	Positive	No Z	M	D, H	Yes	T	Yes
North Carolina	None	Yes (optional)	P	A, B	Yes	T	No
North Dakota	None	No Z	P	B	Yes	T	Yes
Ohio	None	No	P	E	Yes	T	Yes
Oklahoma	None	—	W	—	—	—	W
Oregon	None	No	P	B	Yes	T	No
Pennsylvania	None K	No	M	C	Yes	T	Yes
Puerto Rico	Negative	No	M	LL	Yes	T, U	Yes
Rhode Island	None JJ	No	M, DD	C, GG	Yes	S	No
South Carolina	None	Yes	P	A	Yes	U	Yes
South Dakota	None K	No	P	B	Yes	U	Yes
Tennessee	Positive	Yes	P	A, E	Yes	S	No
Texas	None K	No	P	CC	Yes	T	Yes
Utah	Positive K	Optional	P	B, Q	Yes	U	Yes
Vermont	None K	No	P	D	Yes	V	Yes
Virginia	Positive	FF	P, HH	D	Yes	T	Yes
Washington	None	Yes	M	A	Yes	BB	No DD
West Virginia	K	No Z	M, O	B, F	Yes	S	Yes
Wisconsin	Positive K	No	P	B	Yes	T	Yes
Wyoming	None K	No	P	I	Yes	T	No

XIX. Drug Product Selection Laws *(cont.)*

LEGEND

* State laws either permit the pharmacist to substitute or mandatorily require the pharmacist to substitute a generic version of the prescribed drug if all prescription requirements are met.

** Yes – Includes states where consent is required and those that require the patient to be notified/
informed of substitution.

A — Prescriber's signature on appropriate line of two-line prescription

B — Prescriber expressly indicates do not DPS in some manner. (AR, MT, ND, SD – Prescriber must write in own handwriting other than signature "Brand Necessary." HI – Must handwrite "Do Not Substitute." MA – Must write "No Substitution." NH – Must handwrite "medically necessary" or, if oral prescription, must so specify.)

C — Prescriber's signature shall validate the prescription and, unless the prescriber handwrites "Brand Necessary" or "Brand Medically Necessary," shall designate approval of drug substitution by the pharmacist.

D — Prescriber must indicate "Dispense as Written" in the designated box.

E — Prescriber must write in own handwriting. "DAW" or "Dispense as Written."

F — Prescriber indicates "Medically Necessary" in own handwriting.

G — A licensed practitioner shall prohibit drug product selection by handwriting the words "No Substitution" or the diminutive "No Sub." on the face of the prescription.

H — "Brand Medically Necessary" to be handwritten on the face of the prescription by the prescriber for Medicaid patients, or product selection is allowed.

I — Prescriber must expressly indicate that substitution is not allowed.

J — Prescriber must hand write "Dispense as Written" or hand initial a preprinted box labeled "Dispense as Written."

K — Uses FDA Therapeutic Equivalency List ("Orange Book"). (HI – Plus deletions and additions by the legislature and/or the Food and Drug Branch. MD – Plus deletions and additions by the Department of Health and Mental Hygiene. MA – Plus "additional list" and "exception list." PA – Plus narrow therapeutic index.)

L — Each pharmacy is to develop DPS List.

M — Mandatory.

N — The pharmacist shall dispense the lowest retail priced drug product that is in stock, and which, in the pharmacist's opinion, is pharmaceutically and therapeutically equivalent to the prescribed drug.

O — Unless in the pharmacist's professional judgement.

P — Permissive.

Q — Allows use of preprinted "Do Not substitute" check-box.

R — Box must be checked to prevent DPS.

S — Full savings must be passed on to consumer.

T — Drug dispensed must be less or no more expensive than drug prescribed.

U — No cost savings pass-on requirement mentioned.

V — No more than usual and customary charge for prescribed drug.

W — O.S. (1961) states that it is unlawful for a pharmacist to substitute without the authority of the prescriber or purchaser.

X — Must pass on 50 percent of difference between brand name cost and generic cost.

Y — May indicate in manner of his or her choice on the prescription "Do Not Substitute," except that the indication shall not be preprinted on a prescription.

Z — One-line format.

AA — Product selection laws under jurisdiction of Department of Health, Food and Drug Branch.

BB — Must pass on 60 percent of difference between brand name cost and generic cost. Drug dispensed must be less expensive than drug prescribed.

CC — Beginning June 1, 2002, prescriber must indicate "brand necessary" or "brand medically necessary" in own handwriting or product selection is allowed.

DD — Patient may request that brand name be dispensed, but prescriber must authorize generic.

EE — Prescriber may indicate orally or in own handwriting "Do Not Substitute" or similar words. Allows use of a preprinted "Do Not Substitute" box, provided that the prescriber personally initials the box.

FF — Have a two "check box" format.

GG — Patient may request, in writing, that the brand name be dispensed.

HH — Pharmacist must dispense a "Virginia Voluntary Formulary" product if that box is checked or neither box is checked. However, most brands are also included in the formulary.

II — Patient must be informed/notified.

JJ — Director of Health designates items on Drug Product Selection List.

KK — Statute pending to add FDA "Orange Book" to current positive Illinois formulary in November 1999.

LL — Prescriber must write on the face of the prescription in own handwriting the phrase, "Do not interchange."

MM — Drug dispensed must be less expensive than drug prescribed.

XX. Prescription Requirements

State	Is Prescription Allowed for: Non-Controlled Substance Legend Drug from Out-of-State Prescriber?	Controlled Substance from Out-of-State Prescriber?	Is Rx Order Needed to Buy Syringes/ Needles?	Are Syringes/ Needles Restricted to Sale Only in Pharmacy?	Time Limit on Rx Refills?
Alabama	Yes	Yes	No	No	None
Alaska	Yes	Yes	No	No	1 year
Arizona	Yes	Yes	No	No	1 year D
Arkansas	Yes	Yes	No	No	1 year D
California	Yes	Yes	Yes G	No H	None I
Colorado	Yes	Yes	No	No	1 year D
Connecticut	Yes	Yes	Yes/No L	Yes	None D
Delaware	Yes	Yes M	Yes	No	1 year
District of Columbia	Yes	Yes	No	Yes	None
Florida	Yes P	Yes P	No Q	No	1 year
Georgia	Yes R	Yes R	No	Yes - and MDs	None
Guam	Yes T	No	No U	Yes	1 year
Hawaii	Yes W	No W, X	No W	Yes	1 year W, QQQ
Idaho	Yes	Yes	No	No	1 year D
Illinois	Yes	Yes	Yes	No AA, BB	1 year D
Indiana	Yes	Yes	No	Yes	1 year D
Iowa	Yes P, YYY	Yes P, YYY	No	No	18 months D
Kansas	Yes	Yes	No	No	1 year
Kentucky	Yes GG	Yes GG	No	No	1 year
Louisiana	Yes T, II	Yes T, II, JJ	No	No	1 year D
Maine	Yes	Yes	No	No	1 year
Maryland	Yes	Yes	No	No	1 year III
Massachusetts	Yes	Yes	Yes	Yes	None I
Michigan	Yes SSS	Yes DDD	No	No	1 year D
Minnesota	Yes	Yes MM	No	Yes	1 year I
Mississippi	Yes	Yes	No	No	1 year D
Missouri	Yes	Yes	No	No	1 year
Montana	Yes	Yes	No	No	1 year D
Nebraska	Yes AAAA	Yes QQ	No	No	1 year D
Nevada	Yes	Yes	No	No AA	1 year D
New Hampshire	Yes	Yes	Yes L, Q	Yes	1 year
New Jersey	Yes	Yes	Yes	Yes	1 year
New Mexico	Yes II	Yes II	No	No	1 year D
New York	Yes	Yes TT	No ZZZ	No ZZZ	None
North Carolina	Yes	Yes VV	No	No	1 year or PRN
North Dakota	Yes	Yes	No	No	1 year
Ohio	Yes	Yes	No	No	1 year I
Oklahoma	Yes	Yes	No	No YY	1 year
Oregon	Yes	Yes	No Q, BB	No	2 years D
Pennsylvania	Yes	Yes	Yes	No	1 year III, D
Puerto Rico	No	No	No EE	No	None D
Rhode Island	Yes	Yes	No	Yes	1 year
South Carolina	Yes	Yes T	No EEE	No AA	2 years D, FFF
South Dakota	Yes	Yes	No	No	None III
Tennessee	Yes	Yes	No	No	1 year
Texas	Yes	Yes JJJ	No	No	1 year D
Utah	Yes	Yes	No	No	1 year
Vermont	Yes	Yes	No	No	1 year D
Virginia	Yes II	Yes II	No	Yes	2 years D
Washington	Yes QQ	Yes QQ	No	No	1 year
West Virginia	Yes YYY	Yes YYY	No	No	1 year D
Wisconsin	Yes	Yes	No	No	1 year D
Wyoming	Yes	Yes	No	No	2 years

XX. Prescription Requirements *(cont.)*

State	Sell Schedule V Preparations OTC?	Does State: Have a Controlled Substance Prescription Monitoring Program?	Allow Use of Pre-Printed Rx Forms for Non-Controlled Prescriptions?	Require Expiration or Beyond Use Date on Rx Vial Labels in Community Practice?	How Long Must Prescription Records be Maintained?
Alabama	Yes A	No	Yes B	No	2 years
Alaska	Yes	No	Yes C	No	2 years
Arizona	Yes	No	Yes E	No	3 years
Arkansas	Yes	No	Yes F	No	2 years
California	No	Yes Sch. II	Yes J	Yes K	3 years
Colorado	No	No	Yes C	No	2 years
Connecticut	No	No	Yes F	Yes	3 years
Delaware	No A	No	Yes	No RRR	2 years
District of Columbia	Yes	No	Yes O	Yes	2 years
Florida	Yes	No	Yes F	Yes	2 years
Georgia	Yes S	No	Yes F	Yes	2 years
Guam	Yes V	No	Yes	Yes	5 years
Hawaii	Yes Y	Yes Y (narcotics)	Yes Y	Yes Y	5 years
Idaho	Yes Z	Yes XXX	Yes F	No	3 years
Illinois	Yes Z	ZZ	Yes B	No	5 years
Indiana	Yes Z	Yes NN, WWW	Yes CC, DD	No N	2 years
Iowa	Yes Z	No	Yes O	No	2 years
Kansas	Yes	No	Yes	Yes	5 years
Kentucky	Yes S, Z	Yes UUU	Yes F, HH	No	5 years
Louisiana	VVV	No	Yes	No	2 years
Maine	Yes	No	Yes KK	Yes	5 years
Maryland	No	No	Yes F, LL	Yes	5 years
Massachusetts	No	NN	Yes F	Yes	2 years
Michigan	Yes	OO	Yes F, P	Yes	5 years
Minnesota	No	No	Yes F	Yes FF	5 years
Mississippi	Yes	No	Yes F	No	2 years; 5 years
Missouri	No	No	Yes F	No	5 years
Montana	No	No	PP	No	2 years
Nebraska	No	No	Yes F	No	5 years
Nevada	Yes Z, RR	Yes	Yes F	Yes	2 years
New Hampshire	Yes A	No	Yes C	No	4 years
New Jersey	Yes S, Z	Yes	Yes F	No	5 years
New Mexico	Yes Z	No	Yes F	Yes	3 years
New York	No	TT	Yes F	No	5 years
North Carolina	Yes	No	Yes	Yes	3 years
North Dakota	No	No	Yes F	No	5 years
Ohio	Yes	No	Yes F, WW, XX	No	3 years
Oklahoma	Yes	Yes ZZ, NN	Yes F	No	5 years
Oregon	No AAA, BBB	No	Yes CCC	Yes	3 years
Pennsylvania	No	Yes MMM	HHH	Yes OOO	2 years
Puerto Rico	Yes SS	No	GGG	Yes UU	—
Rhode Island	No	Yes NN	Yes	Yes	2 years
South Carolina	Yes	No	Yes GGG	No	2 years
South Dakota	No	No	No KKK	No	2 years
Tennessee	Yes	Pending	Yes F	No	2 years
Texas	Yes AAA	Yes Sch. II	Yes	No	2 years
Utah	No	Yes	Yes	Yes	5 years
Vermont	VVV	No	Yes	No	3 years
Virginia	Yes	No	Yes F	No	2 years
Washington	Yes V	No	Yes DD	Yes	2 years
West Virginia	Yes	Yes TTT	Yes	Yes	5 years
Wisconsin	Yes	No	Yes LLL	No	5 years
Wyoming	Yes Z, RR, NNN, A	No	Yes	PPP	2 years

XX. Prescription Requirements *(cont.)*

LEGEND

A — Cough syrups containing codeine shall **not** be dispensed without a prescription. (DE – All C-V products require a prescription.)

B — Only controlled substances may **NOT** be preprinted.

C — No restrictions.

D — Six months for non-C-II controlled substance prescriptions.

E — For non-controlled prescriptions, **all** elements may be preprinted.

F — Only prescriber's signature may **NOT** be preprinted.

G — May sell without prescription for human use in the administration of insulin or adrenaline or for use on animals under the following conditions: 1) furnisher must be able to identify purchaser; 2) a record of the purchase must be made. May also sell for industrial use.

H — May be sold for animal, poultry, or industrial use, but must obtain a permit from the Board.

I — Six months for Schedule III and IV controlled substance prescriptions.

J — Prescriber's signature may **NOT** be preprinted, and pharmacist may only dispense one prescription drug on a noncontrolled substances multiple check-off prescription blank.

K — Requires expiration date.

L — May dispense up to a quantity of 10 without a prescription.

M — Must verify Medical Doctor's DEA number and receive positive (photo) ID from presenter of prescription.

N — Exception – sterile pharmaceutical products.

O — No law or regulation that prohibits preprinted prescriptions.

P — Some restrictions.

Q — Cannot sell to minors.

R — Only if written at the office of the prescriber, not if in transit through the state.

S — Check state requirements.

T — Pharmacist professional judgment.

U — Insulin syringes may be sold without a prescription if the pharmacist knows the patient.

V — Frequency more stringent than federal DEA rules.

W — Under jurisdiction of the Department of Health, Food and Drug Branch (328, Hawaii Revised Statutes).

X — Under jurisdiction of the Department of Public Safety (329, Hawaii Revised Statutes).

Y — Prescription drugs, labeling, and dispensing are under the jurisdiction of the State Department of Health, Food and Drug Branch. Narcotics and controlled substances are under jurisdiction of State Department of Public Safety, Narcotics Enforcement Division.

Z — Must be sold by pharmacist only in pharmacy.

AA — Also by veterinary suppliers.

BB — Check state requirements.

CC — Prescriber's signature and patient's name and address may not be preprinted.

DD — May not preprint signature, and form must comply with generic substitution law (ie, two signature lines).

EE — Paraphernalia provisions of the Controlled Substance Act prohibit selling syringes with criminal intention.

FF — If meaningful (ie, a two-week supply of medication would not need three-year dating).

GG — If prescriber is licensed in Kentucky.

HH — Must comply with KRS 217.216.

II — Must meet the same requirements as an in-state prescription. (VA – Except two check-box format.)

JJ — If the prescriber has an **individual** DEA number.

KK — May not preprint prescriber's signature and address.

LL — Although not prohibited by law, the Board believes that preprinted prescriptions are not good practice.

MM — Only from contiguous states.

NN — Electronic data transmission. (IN – C-II only. MA, OK – of C-II only. RI – of C-II and C-III.)

OO — A state form required for Schedule IIs except for methylphenidate.

PP — Issue not addressed.

QQ — Out-of-state prescriptions are limited to prescribers with full prescribing authority in this state (i.e., MD, DO, DDS/DMD, DPM, DVM). The prescribing authority for mid-level practitioners is so varied that it would be difficult for in-state pharmacists to be knowledgeable about the restrictions in the other 49 states.

RR — Cannot sell to minors.

SS — Federal restrictions for selling Schedule V preparation OTC apply.

TT — Schedule II and benzodiazepines must be on an official New York State prescription form.

Legend continues on next page

XX. Prescription Requirements *(cont.)*

LEGEND – (cont.)

UU — Required by Department of Consumer Affairs regulations.

VV — If licensed in North Carolina.

WW — May not preprint "DAW" or "Dispense as Written."

XX — One prescription order per blank if preprinted.

YY — Local restrictions exist.

ZZ — Utilizes an electronic data capture system.

AAA— Codeine-containing products must be prescription only.

BBB— Preparations containing opium (paregoric) shall be dispensed with prescription only.

CCC— Except dentistry. No rules for what may or may not be preprinted.

DDD— From land border physician prescriber.

EEE — Must be sold by pharmacist only in pharmacy or by a certified or licensed durable medical equipment provider.

FFF — Two years on PRN refill prescriptions; no time limit on prescriptions with a specified number of refills.

GGG— Signature may not be preprinted or rubber-stamped; definition of "written Rx" includes "signed by the prescriber." Only one drug and set of instructions for each blank preprinted.

HHH— Not known (Board of Medicine). Prescriber's signature and DEA number may not be preprinted.

III — No legal limit (except for controlled substances). One year by custom and standard of practice.

JJJ — Prescription must enter Texas as a written, signed prescription.

KKK— No, if furnished to a practitioner. (TX – After June 1, 2002, no longer prohibited.)

LLL — Specific pharmacy and language regarding substitution may not be preprinted.

MMM—Through the Office of the Attorney General.

NNN— Follows DEA guidelines exactly.

OOO— If drug's potency is less than one year.

PPP — Guideline only – not a law or regulation.

QQQ— After one year, pursuant to certain conditions and restrictions, a "PRN" prescription may be refilled by an in-state pharmacy for a subsequent three-month period.

RRR— Exception – intravenous products.

SSS — From physician prescriber.

TTT — Beginning Sept. 1, 2002 – all CII, III, and IV prescriptions electronically reported.

UUU— Electronic transmission of all scheduled prescriptions and special, secure prescription blank required.

VVV— Only antidiarrheals.

WWW—Prescription pad with security features required.

XXX— Electronic tracking of all Schedule II, III, and IV prescriptions. All written CS Rx's must be written on non-copyable paper and must provide positive ID of prescriber.

YYY— If licensed in a state or territory in the United States.

ZZZ— Effective January 1, 2001, pharmacists, certain health care facilities, and health practitioners who are otherwise authorized to prescribe needles and syringes in the scope of their practice, may sell or furnish 10 or fewer hypodermic needles or syringes to persons 18 years or older without a prescription.

AAAA—Must meet same scope of practice requirements as in state practitioners.

XXI. Facsimile Transmission of Prescriptions

State	Has State Adopted Prescription Fax Regulations?	Controlled Substances Allowed	Internal Security Code Required	Transmission Marked: "Faxed Copy"
Alabama	Yes	Yes	No	No
Alaska	Yes	Yes	No	No
Arizona	No A	Yes	No	No
Arkansas	Yes	Yes - Sch. III-V F	No	No
California	Yes	Yes - Sch. III-V G	No	No
Colorado	Yes	Yes Z	No	No
Connecticut	Yes	Yes - Sch. II-V F	No	Yes
Delaware	Yes	Yes	No	Yes
District of Columbia	Pending	—	—	—
Florida	Yes	Yes - Sch. III-V & Limited C-II	No	No
Georgia	Yes	Yes F	No	No
Guam	Yes E, I, J	Yes F	No	No
Hawaii	Yes K	Yes - Limited L	Yes M	No
Idaho	Yes	Yes F	No	No
Illinois	Yes A, N, P	Yes A, N, P	No	No
Indiana	Yes	Sch. III-V O, P	No	Yes
Iowa	Yes	Yes TN	No	No
Kansas	Yes	Yes P	No	No
Kentucky	No A, Q	Yes P	A	A
Louisiana	Yes	Yes	No	No
Maine	Yes	Yes	No	No
Maryland	Yes	Yes GG	No	No
Massachusetts	Yes	Yes F	No	Yes FF
Michigan	Yes	Yes	No	No
Minnesota	Yes	Yes	No	No
Mississippi	Yes	Yes	No	No
Missouri	Yes	Yes S, T	Yes	Yes
Montana	Yes	Yes	No	Yes JJ
Nebraska	Yes	Yes	oN	No
Nevada	Yes	Yes - Sch. III-V	No	Yes
New Hampshire	Yes	Yes	No	No
New Jersey	Yes	Yes - Sch. II-V B, EE	No	No
New Mexico	Yes	Yes	No	No
New York	Yes	No	No W	No
North Carolina	Yes	Yes	N/A	N/A
North Dakota	Yes	Yes X	No	Yes
Ohio	Yes	Yes P	Yes	No
Oklahoma	Board guidelines A	Sch. III-V only	No	No
Oregon	Board policy	Yes F	No	No
Pennsylvania	Yes	II	No	No
Puerto Rico	No	No	N/A	N/A
Rhode Island	Yes	Yes P	No	No
South Carolina	Yes	Yes U	No	No
South Dakota	Yes F	Yes	No	—
Tennessee	Yes	Yes F	No	Yes
Texas	Yes A, Q	Yes P	No	Yes
Utah	Yes AA	Yes	No	Yes
Vermont	Yes BB	No	—	—
Virginia	Yes	Yes	No	Yes
Washington	Yes	Yes	No	No
West Virginia	Yes DD	Yes F	No	No
Wisconsin	Yes	Yes F	No	No
Wyoming	Yes	Yes P	R	Yes

XXI. Facsimile Transmission of Prescriptions (cont.)

State	Must Prescriber Information Appear?	Signature of Prescriber's Transmitting Agent	Non-Fading Record – Legibility Time Requirement	Disposition of Original Prescription
Alabama	Yes	No	Yes	A, P
Alaska	Yes	Yes	Yes - 2 years	B
Arizona	Yes	No	Yes D	Not specified
Arkansas	Yes E	Yes	Yes	Not specified
California	Yes	No	Yes - 3 years	Not specified
Colorado	Yes	No	Yes - 2 years	Not specified
Connecticut	Yes E	No	Yes	H
Delaware	Yes	No	No	F (for C-II)
District of Columbia	–	–	–	–
Florida	Yes	No	No	J
Georgia	Yes	Yes	No	Not addressed
Guam	Yes	No	Not addressed HH	Not addressed HH
Hawaii	Yes	No - Prescriber only	Yes - 5 years	Not specified
Idaho	Yes	No	Yes	F
Illinois	No A	No A	Yes	A, N
Indiana	Yes	Yes - Name	Yes	Not specified T
Iowa	Yes	No	Yes - 2 years	Not specified T
Kansas	Yes	Yes	Yes - 5 years	Not specified
Kentucky	A	A	A	A
Louisiana	Yes	No	Yes D - 2 years	Not specified
Maine	Yes	No	Yes - 5 years	Board policy
Maryland	Yes R	No	Yes - 5 years	GG
Massachusetts	Yes	No	Yes	Not specified F
Michigan	Yes	No	Yes - 5 years	J
Minnesota	Yes	Yes	Yes - 5 years	B
Mississippi	Yes	No	Yes	B, I
Missouri	Yes	Yes	No	Retained by practitioner T
Montana	Yes	Yes	Yes - 2 years	Retained by practitioner
Nebraska	F	No	No	F
Nevada	Yes E	No E	Yes - 2 years	Not specified
New Hampshire	Yes	No	No	B, I, F
New Jersey	Yes	No	Yes	Not specified
New Mexico	Yes	Name required V	Yes - 3 years	Not specified F
New York	Yes	No	Yes - 5 years	Not specified
North Carolina	Yes	Yes	Yes	N/A
North Dakota	Yes	No	Yes - 5 years	I, P
Ohio	Yes	Yes - ID required	Yes Y	Retained by prescriber
Oklahoma	Yes	No	No	N/A
Oregon	Yes	Name or initials F	Yes	No
Pennsylvania	Yes	No	Yes - 2 years	II
Puerto Rico	N/A	N/A	N/A	N/A
Rhode Island	Yes	No	No	Not specified
South Carolina	Yes	No	Not addressed	Not specified
South Dakota	Yes	No	Yes	F
Tennessee	Yes	No	Yes	Not specified
Texas	Yes	Name required	Yes	Not specified
Utah AA	Yes	No	No	Not specified
Vermont	–	–	–	–
Virginia	Yes	No C	Yes CC	Retained by practitioner
Washington	Yes	No	Yes - 2 years	Not specified
West Virginia	Yes	No	No	Not specified F, D
Wisconsin	Same as written Rx	No	Yes	Not specified
Wyoming	Yes R	Yes, or initials	Yes	Patient files

XXI. Facsimile Transmission of Prescriptions *(cont.)*

LEGEND

A — A faxed prescription is handled in the same manner as a phoned-in prescription. (KY – "Oral" prescription. IL – Faxing of C-IIs is under the same restriction as telephone orders in emergency situations.)

B — Original, signed prescription must be presented before the faxed, filled prescription is released to the patient. (AK, IA, MD, MN, MS, NH – C-II prescriptions.)

C — Yes, if fax is used to transmit an oral prescription and prescription is not manually signed by the prescriber.

D — Must be reduced to hard copy if necessary that indicates mode of transmission and prescriber's phone number.

E — Prescriber's signature must appear.

F — Faxed prescriptions are permitted as per DEA regulation 21 CFR §1306.11. and 1306.21.

G — In handwriting of the prescriber for C-III-V.

H — Retained or destroyed by a practitioner.

I — Fax becomes original (not C-II).

J — If fax is prescriber-generated, fax is original. If fax is other-generated (patient), original to pharmacy before delivering to patient.

K — Jurisdiction: Department of Health, Food and Drug Branch.

L — Jurisdiction: Department of Public Safety, Narcotics Enforcement Division.

M — Practitioner oral code number.

N — Faxing allowed for all but C-II. Photocopying or immediately reducing prescription to writing is required in order to produce a non-fading record.

O — Schedule III-V may only be sent from an institutional facility by the authorizing practitioner or an authorized agent.

P — Schedule II permitted only for home infusion prescriptions, LTCF inpatients, and hospice patients. [AL - All other C-II prescriptions may be faxed, but original must be presented to pharmacist before medication can be dispensed. TX - The Schedule II prescription faxed must be a properly completed official prescription form. The prescriber must send completed official prescription to the dispensing pharmacy within 7 days.]

Q — However, the State Controlled Substance Act allows the faxing of C-II controlled substance prescriptions in certain circumstances.

R — Signature of prescriber; location from which the prescription was faxed, including address, phone number, and fax number; and pharmacy information must also include telephone number and fax number.

S — Bureau of Narcotics and Dangerous Drugs.

T — C-II requires original prescription at time of prescription pick-up except for prescriptions for long-term care patients and those written for parenteral narcotic drugs and emergency dispensing.

U — Hospice, long-term care, and home infusion patients only. For C-II prescriptions only.

V — For verbal confirmation.

W — Pharmacists are responsible for assessing authenticity.

X — No Schedule II prescriptions. All Schedule III, IV, and V prescriptions must be signed by prescriber within 7 days.

Y — Three years from date of last refill; maximum of four years.

Z — Pharmacist may accept an electronically transmitted order.

AA — Prescription must be transmitted by fax from site of origination to the dispensing pharmacy.

BB — A facsimile transmission is not a valid prescription in a retail setting.

CC — Two years from date of last refill; maximum of four years.

DD — Under regulations regarding electronic transmission of prescriptions.

EE — A prescription for a Schedule II drug written for a long-term care facility resident or hospice patient does not have to be in writing and signed by the practitioner if it is transmitted or prepared in compliance with the DEA regulations 21CFR §1306.11 (d), (e), (f), & (g).

FF — Must say "Electronically transmitted prescription."

GG — Fax prescriptions accepted as originals unless FDA or DEA restrictions apply, as in Schedule II in some instances.

HH — State is in the process of promulgating new regulations.

II — Board Regulation section 27.20 should be reviewed for the specific requirements and limitations.

JJ — Electronic copy.

XXII. Electronic Transmission of Prescriptions: Computer-to-Computer

State	Is Prescription Transmission from Out-of-State Prescriber Computer to Pharmacy Computer Allowed?	Is Prescription Transmission from In-state Prescriber Computer to Pharmacy Computer Allowed?	Is Prescription Transfer Between In-State Pharmacy Computers Allowed?	Is Prescription Transfer from Out-of-State Pharmacy Computer to In-State Pharmacy Computer Allowed?	Does Board Recognize Electronic Signatures for Non-Controlled Substance Prescriptions?
Alabama	Yes	Yes	Not addressed	Yes	No
Alaska	Not addressed	Not addressed	Not addressed	Not addressed	No
Arizona	Not addressed	Not addressed	Yes G	Yes G	Yes E
Arkansas	Yes	Yes	Yes	Yes	No
California	Yes	Yes	Yes	Yes	No
Colorado	Yes I	Yes I	Yes I, M	Yes I, M	Yes
Connecticut	Yes D, S	Yes D, S	Yes S	Yes S	Yes
Delaware	Yes	Yes	Yes F	Yes F	Yes
District of Columbia	No	No	No	No	No
Florida	Yes	Yes	Yes	Yes	Yes
Georgia	No	No	Yes F	Yes F	No
Guam	Not addressed E	Not addressed E	Not addressed E	Not addressed E	Not addressed E
Hawaii	No W	Yes W	Yes W	Yes W	Yes
Idaho	No	No	Yes F	Yes F	Yes
Illinois	Yes H	Yes	Yes M	Yes M	Yes S
Indiana	H	H	Yes	Yes	–
Iowa	Yes Y	Yes Y	Yes B, F, M	Yes B, F, M	Yes DD
Kansas	Yes	Yes	Yes	Yes	Yes
Kentucky	Yes I, J	Yes I, J	Yes K	Yes L	Yes
Louisiana	Yes	Yes	Yes B	Yes B	Yes
Maine	No	No	Yes F	Yes F	No
Maryland	Yes	Yes	Yes M	Yes M	Yes EE
Massachusetts	Yes N	Yes N	Yes N	Yes N	No
Michigan	Yes O	Yes	No	No	–
Minnesota	Yes	Yes	Yes	Yes	Yes
Mississippi	Yes	Yes	Yes	Yes	Not addressed
Missouri	Yes	Yes	Yes	Yes	Yes A
Montana	Yes	Yes	Yes	Yes	Yes
Nebraska	Yes	Yes	Yes	Yes	No
Nevada	Yes T	Yes T	Yes	Yes	Yes
New Hampshire	Yes	Yes	Yes F, O	Yes F, O	Yes E
New Jersey	No	No	No	No	No
New Mexico	Yes Z	Yes Z	Yes S, X	Yes S, X	Yes
New York	Yes P	Yes P	Yes P	Yes P	Yes
North Carolina	Yes	Yes	Yes	Yes	Yes
North Dakota	Yes	Yes	No	No	Yes
Ohio	Yes R	Yes R	Yes M	Yes M	Yes R
Oklahoma	Yes (Guidelines)	Yes (Guidelines)	Yes	Yes	Yes
Oregon	Not addressed	Not addressed	Yes M	Yes M	E
Pennsylvania	Not addressed C	Not addressed C	Yes	Not addressed	E
Puerto Rico	Not addressed	Not addressed	Not addressed	Not addressed	–
Rhode Island	Not addressed	Not addressed	Yes F	Yes F	Not addressed
South Carolina	No	No	Yes Q	No	Yes
South Dakota	No	No	Yes F	Yes F	Yes E, AA
Tennessee	Yes	Yes	Yes	Yes	Yes
Texas	Yes U	Yes I	Yes	Yes U	No BB
Utah	Not addressed	Yes	Yes	Yes	Not addressed
Vermont	P	P	P	P	Not addressed
Virginia	Yes	Yes	Yes V	Yes V	Yes
Washington	Yes	Yes	Yes N	Yes N	Yes
West Virginia	Yes S, T	Yes S, T	Yes S, T	Yes S, T	No
Wisconsin	Yes	Yes	Yes	Yes	Yes
Wyoming	Yes	Yes	Yes	Yes	Yes

XXII. Electronic Transmission of Prescriptions: Computer-to-Computer *(cont.)*

LEGEND

A — Electronic prescriptions recognized.

B — Regulations require pharmacist to perform certain functions.

C — Regulations are currently being considered and/or drafted.

D — Exclusive access or direct lines not allowed.

E — No rules at this time.

F — Only by pharmacies with a common electronic file.

G — Must comply with Rule R423-408.

H — Not prohibited.

I — No Schedule II substances allowed.

J — Prescriber must hold a Kentucky license. Treated the same as an oral prescription order.

K — Must fully comply with 201 KAR 2:165 and 21 CFR 1306.26, and must be on-line, real-time transmission.

L — Prescription must originate from a prescriber licensed in Kentucky. Must fully comply with 201 KAR 2:165 and 21 CFR 1306.26, and must be on-line, real-time transmission.

M — Must satisfy the requirements of state regulations for prescription transferral. Stores that access the same records electronically are not required to cancel the original prescription.

N — Prescriptions may be transmitted intrastate and interstate from pharmacy to pharmacy. If controlled substances, DEA rules must be followed.

O — For non-controlled drugs.

P — With assurances for confidentiality of the electronic message. No controlled substances.

Q — The transfer of prescription information for the purpose of dispensing authorized refills is permissible between pharmacies where all pharmacies are under common ownership and access prescription information through a common computerized data system, subject to subsection (G)(1)(c), (G)(2), (G)(6), (G)(7), (G)(8), (G)(9), and (G)(10).

R — Prescription not valid unless Board-approved system assures that only authorized prescribers have issued the electronically transmitted prescription.

S — Electronic transmission of prescription requires same verification as any oral or telephone prescription.

T — No access to the prescription information can be made by other than the practitioner and the pharmacy.

U — For dangerous drugs only.

V — Pharmacist to pharmacist "real time" communication of information found on or with prescription hard copy.

W — Under jurisdiction of Department of Health.

X — Only during normal business hours.

Y — Specific rules regarding electronic transmission computer to computer.

Z — Must comply with 16.19.23.6 of Board regulations.

AA — Allowed as long as pharmacist is satisfied with legitimacy of signature.

BB— Prescriber signature not required.

CC — If transmitted electronically; if hard copy given to patient, must be physically signed by prescriber.

DD — Electronic signature defined as "Confidential personalized digital key, code, or number used for secure electronic data transmissions, which identifies and authenticates the signatory."

EE — With proper security precautions.

XXIII. Patient Counseling Requirements

State	Is Patient Counseling Required for:				Must Patient Counseling be Performed Personally, Face-to-Face, by the Pharmacist?	Are Patient Profiles Mandated?
	Medicaid Patients?	All Other Patients?	New Prescriptions?	Refill Prescriptions?		
Alabama	Yes	Yes	Yes	A	Yes B	Yes
Alaska	Yes	Yes	Yes	No	Yes C	No
Arizona	Yes	Yes	Yes	Yes D	Yes	Yes
Arkansas	Yes	Yes	Yes	E	Yes	Yes
California	Yes F	Yes F	Yes F	No V	Yes	Yes
Colorado	Yes	No	No	No	Yes	No
Connecticut	Yes	No	Yes	No	Yes C, G	Yes
Delaware	Yes	Yes	Yes	No	Yes C	Yes
District of Columbia	Yes	No	Yes	No	Yes L	Yes G
Florida	H	H	H	H	Yes I	Yes
Georgia	Yes	Yes	Yes	Yes	Yes C	Yes
Guam	Yes	Yes	Yes	No	Yes	No
Hawaii	Yes J	No	J	J	Yes	Yes
Idaho	Yes	Yes	A	A	Yes K	Yes
Illinois	H	H	H	H	Yes I, M	Yes
Indiana	H	H	H	H	Yes A	Yes
Iowa	Yes	Yes	Yes	No	No N	Yes
Kansas	Yes	Yes	Yes	No	Yes B	Yes
Kentucky	Yes	Yes	Yes	No	Yes B	Yes
Louisiana	Yes	Yes	Yes M	Yes M	Yes B, M	Yes A
Maine	Yes	Yes	Yes	H	Yes	yes
Maryland	Yes	No	Yes	No	No	No
Massachusetts	H	H	H	E	Yes I	Yes
Michigan	Yes	Yes	Yes	E	Yes O	Pending
Minnesota	Yes	Yes	Yes	Yes A	Yes	Yes
Mississippi	Yes	Yes A	Yes A	Yes A	Yes B	Yes
Missouri	Yes	Yes	Yes	Yes	Yes L	P
Montana	Yes	Yes	Yes	E	Yes B	Yes
Nebraska	Yes	Yes	Yes	Yes	No	Yes
Nevada	Yes	Yes	Yes	E	Yes I, K	Yes
New Hampshire	Yes	Yes	Yes	No	Yes K	Yes
New Jersey	Yes	Yes	Yes	No	Yes K	Yes
New Mexico	Yes	Yes	Yes	Yes	Yes K	Yes
New York	Yes	Yes	Yes	Yes	Yes A, K	Yes
North Carolina	Yes	Yes	Yes L	E	Yes	Yes
North Dakota	Yes	Yes	Yes	Yes	Yes	Yes
Ohio	Yes H	Yes H	Yes H	Yes H	Yes I, L	Yes
Oklahoma	Yes A	Yes A	E	E	Yes B	Yes
Oregon	Yes	Yes	Yes	Yes Q	Yes B	Yes
Pennsylvania	Yes	Yes	Yes	No	Yes A	Yes
Puerto Rico	U	U	U	U	U	U
Rhode Island	Yes H	Yes H	Yes H	No	Yes K, L	Yes
South Carolina	Yes R	No H	No H	No	No B	Yes
South Dakota	Yes	Yes	Yes	Yes	Yes B, N	Yes
Tennessee	Yes	Yes	Yes	Yes	Yes	Yes
Texas	Yes	Yes	Yes	Yes S	Yes S	Yes
Utah	Yes	Yes	Yes	Yes	Yes I	Yes
Vermont	Yes	Yes	Yes	No	Yes B	Yes
Virginia	Yes	Yes	Yes	E	Yes B	Yes T
Washington	Yes	Yes	Yes	E	Yes B	Yes
West Virginia	H	H	H	E	Yes M	Yes
Wisconsin	Yes	Yes	Yes	Yes	Yes	Yes
Wyoming	H	H	H	No	Yes	Yes

XXIII. Patient Counseling Requirements *(cont.)*

LEGEND

A — When applicable/appropriate.

B — Face-to-face if prescription is delivered to the patient within the pharmacy; otherwise, by telephone or in writing. Required for all new prescriptions and as appropriate for refills. (KY – Required for all original prescriptions and as appropriate for refills. (LA and SC – Face-to-face when possible, otherwise by alternative method.)

C — Whenever practicable. (AK – When not possible, pharmacist must make reasonable effort to counsel by telephone, two-way radio, or in writing.)

D — If previously issued under different prescription number or with different directions or dose.

E — The pharmacist can use professional judgment in deciding whether or not to counsel.

F — When a patient is present in the pharmacy.

G — For Medicaid patients.

H — Only an offer to counsel is required. (SC – on new medication.)

I — Face-to-face if prescription is delivered to the patient or patient's agent within the pharmacy; otherwise, a written offer to counsel with toll-free telephone access to a pharmacist must be made.

J — OBRA requirements under the jurisdiction of the Department of Human Services, Health Care Authorization Branch.

K — In person, whenever practicable, or by telephone. (MA – Like New Mexico below, except only required on new prescriptions. NV – May also be in writing if the patient or caregiver is not present at the pharmacy. NM – If the patient or agent is not present when the prescription is dispensed, including but not limited to a prescription that was shipped by mail, the pharmacist shall insure that the patient receives written notice of his or her right to consultation and a telephone number to obtain oral consultation from a pharmacist. Required for all new and refill prescriptions. NY – If the patient or agent is not present when the prescription is dispensed; toll-free number required.)

L — The offer to counsel may be delegated by the pharmacist to non-licensed personnel. The actual counseling must be performed by the pharmacist or pharmacist intern/extern. (MO – By extern only under supervision of a pharmacist.)

M — Unless pharmacist deems counseling inappropriate or unnecessary, in which case it may be written, by telephone, or as considered appropriate.

N — If oral counseling is deemed not practicable, alternate forms of patient information may be used which also advise patient or caregiver that pharmacist is available for consultation at pharmacy, via toll-free telephone number or collect call. Combination of oral and alternative forms of counseling is encouraged.

O — In person to patient or patient's caregiver; if communication barrier prohibits oral communication, then providing printed material.

P — If offer to counsel is accepted, patient profile is mandated; however, if patient refuses offer to counsel, patient profile is not required.

Q — Counseling on refill prescriptions shall be such counseling as a reasonable and prudent pharmacist would provide and may include monitoring for compliance, intended or expected outcomes, adverse drug reactions, inquiries about OTC medications, generic changes, and the accuracy of the medication.

R — Health and Human Services Finance Commission Regulation.

S — Face-to-face if prescription is delivered to the patient within the pharmacy; otherwise in writing. Required for all new prescriptions, annually on refills for maintenance medications, and in the professional judgment of the pharmacist for all other refills.

T — Not specifically called "patient profile."

U — Not specifically addressed in Pharmacy Act or regulations.

V — Unless patient requests it or the pharmacist, in his/her professional judgment, believes it necessary.

XXIV. Prescribing Authority

State	Doctor of Homeopathy (Limited to Course of Practice)	Physician Assistant	Advanced Registered Nurse Practitioner	Clinical Nurse Specialist	Nurse Midwife
Alabama	D	H	H	E	H
Alaska	E	B	A*	E*	E*
Arizona	A*	B, H	A, B*	*	E*
Arkansas	A	D	B*	B	B
California	E	B	B	E	H*
Colorado	A*	B	A*	B	H
Connecticut	E	B, H	A*	E	A*
Delaware	D	B	A*	A*	A*
District of Columbia	D	B	A*	A*	A*
Florida	D	B*	B*	E	E
Georgia	D	B	B	E	B
Guam	A	H	E	H*	H*
Hawaii	D, E	H*	H	E	E
Idaho	D	B*	*	*	*
Illinois	E	B	B	B	B
Indiana	D	E	B*	B*	B*
Iowa	D	H*	A	E*	E*
Kansas	E	B	B	B	B
Kentucky	D	H*	H*	H*	H*
Louisiana	D	E	H	H	H
Maine	E	B	B	E	A
Maryland	E	B	B*	E	B*
Massachusetts	E*	B	B*	B*	B*
Michigan	D	B	B	B	B
Minnesota	D, E	B	B	B	A
Mississippi	D	B	B	C	B
Missouri	E	B*	B*	B*	B*
Montana	H	H	A*	H	H
Nebraska*	D	B	A*	A*	B*
Nevada	A	B	B	E	E
New Hampshire	E	A	A	E	E
New Jersey	D	B, H	B, H	E	B, H
New Mexico	E	D	A, H*	A, H*	A, H*
New York	D, E	B	A	E	E (see midwife)
North Carolina	E	B	E	E	B
North Dakota	D	B	A	A	A
Ohio	D	E	D*	D*	D*
Oklahoma	E	B, H	H	H	H
Oregon	D	B	A*	E	A*
Pennsylvania	D, E	H*	H*	E	E
Puerto Rico	E	E	H	E	E
Rhode Island	E	B	B	B, H	B
South Carolina	E	B*	B*	B*	B*
South Dakota	E	B	B	E	B
Tennessee	E	B	B*	B*	B*
Texas	D	B*	B*	B*	B*
Utah	D	B	A*	N/A	A*
Vermont	D	B	A*	B*	B*
Virginia	E	B, H	B, H	E	B, H
Washington	D	B	A *	—	A
West Virginia	E	B	H	E	H
Wisconsin	E	B	A	E	E
Wyoming	D	B	A*	E *	E *

* See "Footnotes (*)" on pages 876-879.

XXIV. Prescribing Authority *(cont.)*

State	Nurse Practitioner	OB/GYN Nurse Practitioner	Pediatric Nurse Practitioner	Psychiatric Nurse Practitioner	Certified Registered Nurse Anesthetist
Alabama	H	H	H	H	E
Alaska	E*	E*	E*	E*	E*
Arizona	E*	*	*	*	*
Arkansas	E	E	E	E	B
California	B	B	B	B	E
Colorado	B	B	B	B	B
Connecticut	A*	A*	A*	A*	A*
Delaware	A*	A*	A*	A*	A*
District of Columbia	A*	A*	A*	A*	A*
Florida	E	E	E	E	E
Georgia	B	B	B	B	E
Guam	H*	H*	H*	H*	H*
Hawaii	E	E	E	E	E
Idaho	*	*	*	*	*
Illinois	B	D, E	D, E	D, E	B
Indiana	B*	B*	B*	B*	E
Iowa	E*	E*	E*	E*	A*
Kansas	B	B	B	B	B
Kentucky	H*	H*	H*	H*	H*
Louisiana	H	H	H	H	H
Maine	A	A	A	A	E
Maryland	B*	B*	B*	B*	E
Massachusetts	B	B	B	B	E
Michigan	B	B	B	B	B
Minnesota	B	B	B	B	B
Mississippi	B	B	B	B	B
Missouri	B*	B*	B*	B*	B*
Montana	H*	H*	H*	H*	H*
Nebraska	A*	A*	A*	A*	A*
Nevada	E	E	E	E	E
New Hampshire	A	A	A	A	A
New Jersey	B, H	E	E	E	E
New Mexico	A, H*	A, H*	A, H*	A, H*	E*
New York	A*	A	A	A	E
North Carolina	B	B	B	B	E
North Dakota	A	A	A	A	A
Ohio	D*	D*	D*	D*	C
Oklahoma	E	E	E	E	H
Oregon	A*	A*	A*	A*	C
Pennsylvania	H*	H *	H *	H *	E
Puerto Rico	E	E	E	E	E
Rhode Island	B	E	E	E	E
South Carolina	B*	B *	B *	B *	E
South Dakota	B	B	B	B	E
Tennessee	B*	B*	B*	B*	E
Texas	B*	B*	B*	B*	B*
Utah	N/A	N/A	N/A	N/A	E
Vermont	B	B	B	B	B
Virginia	B, H	B, H	B, H	B, H	E
Washington	A	A	A	A	A
West Virginia	E	E	E	E	E
Wisconsin	E	E	E	E	E
Wyoming	E*	E*	E*	E*	E*

* See "Footnotes (*)" on pages 876-879.

XXIV. Prescribing Authority (cont.)

State	Midwife	Optometrist	Emergency Medical Technician Paramedic	Naturopathic Doctor
Alabama	E	H	C	D
Alaska	C, E	F, H	C	E
Arizona	E	A - Limited	E	H
Arkansas	E	A - Limited	H	F
California	E	H	C	E
Colorado	E	H*	E	E*
Connecticut	E	A	E	E
Delaware	E	A, G, H*	E	D
District of Columbia	B	A	C	E
Florida	E	A - Ltd. formulary	E	A*
Georgia	E	A - Ltd. formulary*	E	E
Guam	H*	H*	E	E
Hawaii	E	C, F, G	E	H*
Idaho	E	A	C	D
Illinois	D	F, G, H	E	E
Indiana	E	H- Ltd. formulary*	E	E
Iowa	E	A*	E	D
Kansas	E	H*	C	B
Kentucky	E	H*	C	E
Louisiana	H	H	E	D
Maine	A	H	C	H
Maryland	E	H*	E	E
Massachusetts	E*	H*	E	E
Michigan	E	C, F, H	E	D
Minnesota	E	H	C	D, E
Mississippi	C	H*	C	H
Missouri	E	E	E	E
Montana	E	A - Ltd. therapeutics	E	E
Nebraska	B*	A - Limited*	E	E
Nevada	E	H	E	E
New Hampshire	C	A*	C	H
New Jersey	D, II	H	E	D
New Mexico	A	A, H	E	E
New York	A*	A	C	E
North Carolina	B	A	E	E
North Dakota	A - Limited	H	E	D
Ohio	E	A - Limited	E	D
Oklahoma	H	A	E	E
Oregon	E	A - Limited	C	A*
Pennsylvania	E	F, G, H*	E	D, E
Puerto Rico	E	E	E	
Rhode Island	E	H	C	D
South Carolina	E	A - Limited*	E	E
South Dakota	E	A - Limited	E	E
Tennessee	E	A	E	E
Texas	C	A - Ltd. formulary	C	D
Utah	D	H	D, E	A*
Vermont	B*	G	C	H*
Virginia	E	A, H	E	E
Washington	C	F, G	C	H*
West Virginia	E	H	C	E
Wisconsin	E	H	E	E
Wyoming	E	H	C	D

* See "Footnotes (*)" on pages 876-879.

XXIV. Prescribing Authority (cont.)

Medical Doctors have unlimited, independent prescribing authority in every state.

Doctors of Osteopathy have unlimited, independent prescribing authority in all states, except Puerto Rico where they have no prescribing authority.

Doctors of Dental Surgery, Doctors of Podiatric Medicine, and Doctors of Veterinary Medicine have independent prescribing authority that is limited to their course of practice in every state.

Doctors of Chiropractic have no prescribing authority in any state.

LEGEND

A — Independent Authority.
B — Dependent Prescribing Authority.
C — Use Only.
D — Not Licensed.
E — No Prescribing Authority.
F — Diagnostic Only.
G — Therapeutics.
H — Limited Prescribing Authority.

Footnotes (*)

AK — Advanced Nurse Practitioners may prescribe and dispense within the scope of their specialty.

AZ — Homeopathic Physician has prescriber authority. Title of "Clinical Nurse Specialist" not used.

AR — "Advanced Practice Nurses" must be certified under rules promulgated by the Board of Nursing and Medical Licensing Board. When certified, they will have dependent authority. Must have collaborative agreement with physician and may only prescribe within the scope of the physician's practice.

CA — Dependent prescribing authority for **Certified** Nurse Midwife and **Certified** Nurse Practitioners. Dependent prescribing authority for Pharmacists in licensed health facilities, clinics, health maintenance organizations, and providers contracting with HMOs in accordance with policies, procedures, or protocols.

CO — Homeopathic Physicians have prescriptive authority if they are a Medical Doctor or Doctor of Osteopathy. A Naturopathic Doctor would have no such authority, except for vitamins, minerals, etc. Advanced Practice Nurses have independent authority if they are approved by the nursing board, have obtained a DEA number, and maintain a collaborative agreement with a physician licensed in Colorado whose background and active practice corresponds with that of the nurse. Optometrists may purchase, possess, administer, and prescribe certain

pharmaceutical agents for examination and treatment if they are therapeutically certified by the Optometric Examiners Board.

CT — Advanced practice nurses have independent authority if they are licensed as APRNs, have a obtained a DEA number, and maintain a collaborative agreement with a physician licensed in Connecticut whose background and active practice corresponds with that of the nurse practitioner, pediatric nurse practitioner, psychiatric nurse practitioner, and certified nurse anesthetist all fall under the category of advanced registered nurse practitioner.

DC — Only nurse practitioners, clinical nurse specialists, nurse midwives, and nurse anesthetists who are licensed by the DC Board of Nursing as an advanced practice registered nurse have independent prescribing authority.

DE — Advanced Practice Nurses must be licensed by the Board of Nursing and must submit a collaborative care agreement to the Joint Practice Committee. Optometrists must be therapeutically certified to prescribe.

FL — For Physician Assistants, there exists a limited formulary. Advanced Registered Nurse Practitioners may initiate orders under protocol. Naturopathic Doctors have unlimited prescribing authority.

GA — Optometrists may prescribe from a specific formulary.

GU — Optometrists may prescribe from a limited formulary. APRNs must have collaborative practice agreement with MD.

HI — Naturopathic Doctors may prescribe vitamins, minerals, amino acids, and fatty acids. Rules exclude the prescribing by PAs of controlled substances and also require that the supervising physician retain full professional and legal responsibility for PA performance, care, and treatment of patient. Pharmacists may adjust dosage regimens pursuant to

Legend continues on next page

XXIV. Prescribing Authority (cont.)

Footnotes (*) – (cont.)

prescriber authorization. Effective July 1, 1997, therapeutically certified optometrists shall not prescribe, dispense, or administer oral pharmaceutical agents except those available without a prescription. Only the use and prescription of topical therapeutic pharmaceuticals as established by the Joint Formulary Advisory Committee are allowed.

ID — Physician Assistants, Nurse Practitioners, Certified Nurse Midwives, Clinical Nurse Specialists, and Registered Nurse Anesthetists all have independent prescribing authority limited to scope of practice and must be approved to prescribe by their respective boards.

IN — "Advanced Practice Nurses" must be certified under rules promulgated by the Board of Nursing and Medical Licensing Board. When certified, they will have dependent authority. Must have collaborative agreement with physician and may only prescribe within the scope of the physician's practice. The state does not necessarily recognize each listed nursing specialty. Hospital and private mental institutional Pharmacists may adjust drug therapies pursuant to protocol and under the supervision of a physician. Optometrists must be certified by a committee of the Pharmacy Board and use formularies to prescribe. They may not prescribe for controlled substances.

IA — "Certified" Clinical Nurse specialists, "Certified" Nurse Midwives, and "Certified" Nurse Practitioners (Advanced Registered Nurse Practitioner classifications) have independent prescribing authority. PAs must have supervising physician and prescriptive authority; does not include CII stimulants or depressants. Three classes of Optometrists: 1) Plain Optometrists cannot use drugs at all; 2) Certified Optometrists can use some drugs for diagnostic purposes only; 3) Therapeutically Certified Optometrists can prescribe, but not dispense (except at no charge to commence a course of therapy), a select group of drugs including: a) topical and oral antimicrobial agents, b) oral antihistamines, c) oral antiglaucoma agents, d) topical pharmaceutical agents, and e) oral

analgesic agents; f) oral steroids (with limitations).

KS — Three separate licenses for Optometry; one allows prescriptive authority of topical, diagnostics, and certain oral medications. Naturopathic doctor may prescribe pursuant to a protocol with a physician.

KY — Pharmacists may initiate, continue, or discontinue drug therapy pursuant to an established collaborative care agreement. Pharmacists who enter into a collaborative care agreement with a practitioner may cooperatively manage a patient's drug-related health care needs. The agreement shall be limited to specification of the drug-related regimen and necessary tests; stipulated conditions for initiating, continuing, or discontinuing drug therapy; and directions concerning the monitoring of drug therapy and conditions warranting dose, dosage regimen, dosage form, or route of administration modifications. Advanced Registered Nurse Practitioners (ARNPs) who prescribe must enter into a written collaborative practice agreement with a physician that defines scope of prescriptive authority. ARNPs **cannot** prescribe controlled substances. Optometrists may prescribe diagnostic topical medications for use in the eye or its appendages. "Therapeutically Certified" Optometrists may prescribe oral medications, except C-I and C-II controlled substances, for any condition that an Optometrist is authorized to treat under KRS 320. The authority to prescribe C-III, IV, and V controlled substances shall be limited to prescriptions for a quantity sufficient to provide treatment for up to 72 hours. No refills of prescriptions for controlled substances are allowed. Physician Assistants cannot prescribe controlled substances.

MD — Certified Registered Nurse Practitioners (including specialties) and Nurse Midwives may only prescribe within their specialty. Nurse Midwives have a limited formulary. A therapeutically certified optometrist may prescribe under certain conditions.

Legend continues on next page

XXIV. Prescribing Authority *(cont.)*

Footnotes (*) – (cont.)

MA — Massachusetts only recognizes Registered
Nurse Practitioners. Clinical Nurse
Specialist prescribing authority is for
Psychiatric Nurse Specialists only. Nurse
Midwife prescribing authority is for
Certified Nurse Midwife only. Optom-
etrists may prescribe topical Schedule VI
drugs for use in the eye, but may not
prescribe glaucoma medications.

MS — Optometrists may prescribe topicals only,
for diseases of the eye and its adnexa.

MO — Must have a collaborative practice
arrangement with a physician.

MT — Nurse Practitioner, Pediatric Nurse
Practitioner, Psychiatric Nurse Practitioner, and Certified Nurse Anesthetist all fall
under the category of Advanced Registered Nurse Practitioner.

NE — Doctors of Homeopathy use naturopath
formulary. APRN, CNM, and CRNA must
be RNs. Optometrists may prescribe
topical ocular pharmaceutical agents and
oral medication that is within their scope
of practice.

NM — The Board of Nursing determines by
certification which specialties have
prescriptive authority. Certified nurse
midwives prescribe pursuant to Dept. of
Health rules. For pharmacist clinicians
only – in accordance with the New
Mexico Pharmacist Prescriptive
Authority Act.

NY — "Nurse Practitioners" are authorized to
issue prescriptions in accordance with
practice agreements and practice protocols between the physician and nurse
practitioner. Effective 1994, implementation of the Midwifery Practice Act
resulted in licensure of professional
Midwives.

ND — Pharmacist's prescribing authority based
on a collaborative practice agreement
with a physician.

OH — Advanced Practice Nurses licensed by the
Nursing Board may prescribe drugs under
certain conditions and within a limited
formulary.

OR — Nurse Practitioners may prescribe
independently, but only for drugs allowed
by formulary for their area of practice.
Naturopaths may only prescribe, administer, and dispense non-poisonous plant and
animal substances as determined by a
formulary council in therapeutic dosages;
they may administer select anesthetics,
antiseptics, and radiopaque substances.

PA — Physician Assistants and Nurse Practitioners based on formulary and written
agreement with supervising physician.
Please contact the Medical Board and/or
Nursing Board for specific requirements
and curent status of laws/regulations.
Optometrists – additional requirements for
a Board of Optometry therapeutic license.

RI — Nurse Midwives must be Certified Nurse
Midwives in order to prescribe, and
Nurse Practitioners must be Certified
Nurse Practitioners in order to prescribe.
Optometrists limited to topical
ophtholmics.

SC — Physician Assistants are certified by
Board of Medical Examiners for prescriptive authority and formulary. Extended
role of Nurse Practitioner certified by
Nursing Board; under approved protocol
from Nursing Board. Optometrists are
therapeutically certified by the Board of
Examiners in Optometry for limited
prescriptive authority.

SD — A statute passed in 1993 allows Pharmacists to initiate or modify drug therapy
by protocol or other legal authority
established and approved within a
licensed health care facility or by a
practitioner authorized to prescribe drugs.

TN — Certified Nurse Practitioners have
dependent prescribing authority.

TX — Physician Assistants and Registered
Nurses who have advanced training
may prescribe dangerous drugs per
protocol with a practitioner. Physician
Assistants must be recognized by the
Medical Board and have specialized
training and education. Registered
Nurses must be recognized by the
Nursing Board and have specialized
training and education. Pharmacists
may perform specific acts relating to
drug therapy management under
written protocol from a practitioner.

UT — APRNs can prescribe C-IIs and C-IIIs
with consultation. Naturopathic Doctors
must prescribe pursuant to a specific
formulary.

VA — In VA, nurse practitioners, including
nurse anethetists and nurse midwives as
well as other specializations of nurse
practitioners are licensed as "nurse
practitioners." "Prescriptive authority" is
an add-on to the nurse practitioner
license. As of July 1, 2000, nurse
practitioners with prescriptive authority
Legend continues on next page

XXIV. Prescribing Authority *(cont.)*

Footnotes (*) – (cont.)

will be able to prescribe and possess C-Vs only after they obtain a DEA registration. On January 1, 2002, C-IVs will be added. On July 1, 2003, C-IIIs will be added. "Prescriptive authority" is an add-on to the physician assistant license. As of July 1, 2001, physician assistants may prescribe and possess C-Vs after obtaining a DEA registration. On January 1, 2003, C-IVs will be added.

VT — Contact the Board of Nursing for specific prescribing requirements. Naturopaths may prescribe pursuant to their formulary.

WA — "Clinical Nurse Specialist" is not a recognized designation in this state. All other nurse practitioners are included in ARNP classification. ARNPs have independent authority for CV and legend drugs.

Collaborative agreement with physician required for CII-IV. Naturopathic Practitioners may prescribe a limited number of legend drugs, including vitamins, minerals, whole gland thyroid, Vitamin B_{12} prep, antibiotics, corticosteroids, etc. (List available from Washington State Board of Pharmacy.) They may not prescribe controlled substances.

WY — Prescribing authority only for those designated as Certified Advanced Nurse Practitioner. May be certified in specialty areas indicated with an asterisk (*). Certified Advanced Registered Nurse Practitioner may now prescribe controlled substances (CS II-V). Certification must be done with Nursing Board and requires additional education and testing to **regular** Advanced Nurse Practitioner.

XXV. Dispensing Authority

State	Medical Doctor		Doctor of Osteopathy		Dentist		Podiatrist		Veterinarian		Doctor of Homeopathy	
Alabama	Yes		Yes		Yes		Yes		Yes		No	
Alaska	Yes		Yes		Yes		Yes		Yes		No	
Arizona	Yes		Yes		Yes		Yes		Yes		Yes	
Arkansas	Yes	D	Yes	D	Yes		Yes	D	Yes		Yes	D
California	Yes		Yes		Yes		Yes		Yes		No	
Colorado	Yes		Yes		Yes		Yes		Yes		Yes	G
Connecticut	Yes		Yes		Yes		Yes		Yes		No	
Delaware	Yes		Yes		Yes		Yes		Yes		No	
District of Columbia	Yes		Yes		Yes		Yes		Yes		No	
Florida	Yes		Yes		Yes		Yes		Yes		No	G
Georgia	Yes		Yes		Yes		Yes		Yes		No	
Guam	Yes		Yes		Yes		Yes		Yes		Yes	B
Hawaii	Yes		Yes		Yes		Yes		Yes		No	
Idaho	Yes		Yes		Yes		Yes		Yes		No	
Illinois	Yes		Yes		Yes		Yes		Yes		No	
Indiana	Yes		Yes		Yes		Yes		Yes		No	
Iowa	Yes		Yes		Yes		Yes		Yes		No	
Kansas	Yes		Yes		Yes		Yes		Yes		No	
Kentucky	Yes		Yes		Yes		Yes		Yes		No	
Louisiana	Yes		Yes		Yes		Yes		Yes		No	
Maine	Yes		Yes		Yes		Yes		Yes		No	
Maryland	Yes	O	No		Yes	O	Yes	O	Yes		No	
Massachusetts	Yes	Q	Yes	Q	Yes	Q	Yes	Q	Yes	Q	No	Q
Michigan	Yes	R	Yes	R	Yes	R	Yes	R	Yes	R	No	
Minnesota	Yes		Yes		Yes		Yes		Yes		No	
Mississippi	Yes		Yes		Yes		Yes		Yes		No	
Missouri	Yes	R	Yes	R	Yes	R	Yes	R	Yes	R	No	
Montana	U		U		U		U		U		U	
Nebraska	Yes		Yes		Yes		Yes		Yes		N/A	
Nevada	Yes		Yes		Yes		Yes		Yes		Yes	
New Hampshire	Yes		Yes		Yes		Yes		Yes		No	
New Jersey	Yes		Yes		Yes		Yes		Yes		—	
New Mexico	Yes		Yes		Yes		Yes		Yes		No	
New York	Yes	H	Yes	H	Yes	H	Yes	H	Yes	H	No	
North Carolina	Yes		Yes		No		No		No		No	
North Dakota	Yes		Yes		No		No		Yes		No	
Ohio	Yes	R	Yes	R	Yes	R	Yes	R	Yes	R	No	
Oklahoma	Yes		Yes		Yes		Yes		Yes		No	
Oregon	Yes		Yes		Yes		Yes		Yes		N/A	
Pennsylvania	Yes		Yes		Yes		Yes		Yes		No	G
Puerto Rico	No	DD	No	DD	No	DD	No	DD	CC		No	DD
Rhode Island	Yes		Yes		Yes		Yes		Yes		No	
South Carolina	Yes	BB	Yes	BB	Yes	BB	Yes	BB	Yes	BB	No	
South Dakota	Yes		Yes		Yes		No		Yes		No	
Tennessee	Yes		Yes		Yes		Yes		Yes		No	G
Texas	Yes	EE	Yes	EE	Yes	EE	Yes	EE	Yes		No	
Utah	No		No		No		No		No		No	
Vermont	Yes		Yes		Yes		Yes		Yes		No	GG
Virginia	Yes	HH	Yes	HH	Yes	R	No		Yes		No	
Washington	Yes		Yes		Yes		Yes		Yes		Not licensed	
West Virginia	JJ		JJ		JJ		JJ		JJ		JJ	
Wisconsin	Yes		Yes		Yes		Yes		Yes		No	
Wyoming	Yes		Yes		Yes		Yes		Yes		No	

XXV. Dispensing Authority *(cont.)*

State	Physician Assistant	Advanced Registered Nurse Practitioner	Clinical Nurse Specialist	Nurse Midwife	Midwife	Nurse Practitioner
Alabama	Yes	Yes	No	Yes	No	Yes
Alaska	Yes	Yes A	No A	No A	No A	No A
Arizona	Yes	Yes	—	No C	No	Yes
Arkansas	No	No	No	No	No	No
California	Yes TT	Yes TT	No P	Yes TT	No	Yes TT
Colorado	Yes	Yes V	No	Yes B	No	No
Connecticut	Yes	Yes	No	Yes	N/A	Yes A
Delaware	Yes	Yes J	Yes J	Yes J	No	Yes J
District of Columbia	—	Yes UU	Yes UU	Yes UU	—	Yes UU
Florida	No E	Yes	No	No	No	No
Georgia	Yes K	Yes K	Yes K	Yes K	No	Yes K
Guam	Yes	Yes S	Yes S	Yes S	Yes S	Yes S
Hawaii	No	Yes L	No	No	No	No
Idaho	Yes	QQ	QQ	QQ	No	QQ
Illinois	Yes	Yes	Yes	Yes	No	Yes
Indiana	No	Yes NN	Yes NN	Yes NN	No	Yes NN
Iowa	No M	Yes	No N	No N	No	No N
Kansas	No	No	No	No	No	No
Kentucky	No	Yes V	No	No	No	Yes V
Louisiana	No	No	No	No	No	No
Maine	Yes	Yes	No	Yes	Yes	Yes
Maryland	Yes	Yes O	No	No	No	Yes O
Massachusetts	Yes Q	Yes Q	Yes Q	Yes Q	No	Yes Q
Michigan	Yes RR	Yes RR	Yes RR	Yes RR	No	Yes RR
Minnesota	Yes	Yes	Yes	Yes	No	Yes
Mississippi	No	No	No	No	No	No
Missouri	Yes T	Yes T	Yes T	Yes T	Yes T	Yes T
Montana	U	U	U	U	U	U
Nebraska	Yes V, W	Yes V, W	Yes V, W	Yes V, W	Yes V, W	Yes V, W
Nevada	Yes	Yes	No	No	No	No
New Hampshire	Yes	Yes	No	No	No	Yes
New Jersey	No	Yes	No	No	No	Yes
New Mexico	Yes	Yes	Yes	Yes	No	Yes
New York	Yes H	Yes H	No	N/A	Yes H	Yes H
North Carolina	Yes Y	Yes Y	N/A	Yes Y	Yes Y	Yes Y
North Dakota	Yes	Yes	Yes	Yes	No	Yes
Ohio	No	Yes R, O	Yes R, O	Yes R, O	No	Yes R, O
Oklahoma	No	No	No	No	No	No
Oregon	No Z	No AA	No	No AA	No	No AA
Pennsylvania	Yes PP	PP	No	No	No	PP
Puerto Rico	No DD	No DD	No DD	No DD	No DD	No DD
Rhode Island	Yes	Yes	MM	Yes	No	No
South Carolina	No	No	No	No	No	No
South Dakota	Yes W	No W	No	Yes W	No	Yes
Tennessee	Yes	Yes	Yes	Yes	No	Yes
Texas	Yes FF	Yes FF	Yes FF	Yes FF	No	Yes FF
Utah	No	No	No	No	No	No
Vermont	Yes	Yes	Yes	Yes	No	Yes
Virginia	No GG	—	No	No GG	No	No GG
Washington	Yes	Yes	OO	Yes II	No	Yes II
West Virginia	JJ	JJ	JJ	JJ	JJ	JJ
Wisconsin	No	Yes KK	No	No	No	No
Wyoming	Yes	Yes A, LL	No	No	No	No

XXV. Dispensing Authority *(cont.)*

State	OB/GYN Nurse Practitioner	Pediatric Nurse Practitioner	Psychiatric Nurse Practitioner	Optometrist	Naturopathic Doctor
Alabama	Yes	Yes	Yes	Yes	No
Alaska	No A	No A	No A	Yes B	No
Arizona	Yes	Yes	Yes	Yes B	Yes B
Arkansas	No	No	No	No	No
California	Yes TT	Yes TT	Yes TT	Yes	No
Colorado	No	No	No	No	Yes G
Connecticut	Yes A	Yes A	Yes A	Yes	Yes B
Delaware	Yes J	Yes J	Yes J	Yes J	No
District of Columbia	Yes UU	Yes UU	Yes UU	Yes	No
Florida	No	No	No	Yes	Yes
Georgia	Yes K	Yes K	Yes K	Yes	No
Guam	Yes S	Yes S	Yes S	Yes B	Yes
Hawaii	No	No	No	Yes	No I
Idaho	QQ	QQ	QQ	Yes D	No
Illinois	Yes W	Yes W	Yes W	No	No
Indiana	Yes NN	Yes NN	Yes NN	Yes B	No
Iowa	No N	No N	No N	No VV	No
Kansas	No	No	No	Yes B	No
Kentucky	Yes V	Yes V	Yes V	Yes B	No
Louisiana	No	No	No	No	No
Maine	Yes	Yes	Yes	Yes	Yes
Maryland	Yes O	Yes O	No	No	No
Massachusetts	Yes Q	Yes Q	Yes Q	Yes Q	No
Michigan	Yes RR	Yes RR	Yes RR	Yes SS	No
Minnesota	Yes	Yes	Yes	No	No
Mississippi	No	No	No	Limited	No
Missouri	Yes T	Yes T	Yes T	Yes R	No
Montana	U	U	U	U	U
Nebraska	Yes V, W	Yes V, W	Yes V, W	Yes	N/A
Nevada	No	No	No	Yes	No
New Hampshire	Yes	Yes	Yes	Yes B, X	Yes B
New Jersey	—	—	—	No	—
New Mexico	Yes	Yes	Yes	Yes	N/A
New York	Yes H	Yes H	Yes H	Yes H	No
North Carolina	Yes Y	Yes Y	N/A	No	No
North Dakota	Yes	Yes	Yes	No	No
Ohio	Yes R, O	Yes R, O	Yes R, O	Yes O	No
Oklahoma	No	No	No	No	No
Oregon	No AA	No AA	No AA	Yes	Yes
Pennsylvania	PP	PP	PP	Limited	No G
Puerto Rico	No DD	No DD	No DD	No DD	No DD
Rhode Island	No A	No A	No A	Limited, P	No
South Carolina	No	No	No	No	No
South Dakota	No	No	No	Yes	No
Tennessee	Yes	Yes	Yes	Yes	No G
Texas	Yes FF	Yes FF	Yes FF	Yes B	No
Utah	No	No	No	No	No
Vermont	Yes	Yes	Yes	Yes	Yes B
Virginia	No GG	No GG	No GG	No	No
Washington	Yes II	Yes II	Yes II	Yes	Yes
West Virginia	JJ	JJ	JJ	JJ	JJ
Wisconsin	No	No	No	No	No
Wyoming A	No	No	No	No	No

XXV. Dispensing Authority *(cont.)*

LEGEND

A — Any Nurse Practitioner must be **advanced** to dispense. (WY – And certified.)
B — Limited formulary.
C — "Yes" if also a Nurse Practitioner.
D — With special permit only.
E — Except may dispense samples.
F — Registered Nurse may dispense in clinic.
G — Not licensed by this state.
H — All prescribers are subject to restrictions on dispensing. Contact Board office.
I — Naturopathic Doctors are only allowed to prescribe and dispense prescription drugs that are vitamins, minerals, amino acids, and fatty acids.
J — Only if approved by the Board of Medical Practice.
K — Only by accordance with Pharmacy Board rules via a signed dispensing procedure and under the authority of a job description (PAs) or a nurse protocol.
L — Per ARNPs with prescriptive authority formulary.
M — Physician Assistants may only "supply" drugs.
N — However, "Certified" Clinical Nurse Specialists, "Certified" Nurse Midwives, and "Certified" Nurse Practitioner (Advanced Registered Nurse Practitioner classifications) may do so.
O — Under specified conditions, such as certain clinics.
P — Topical ophthalmics.
Q — A practitioner in Massachusetts may "dispense" a Schedule VI prescription drug pursuant to specific guidelines or for immediate treatment of his or her patient. Otherwise prohibited by State Controlled Substance Act.
R — May dispense only to his/her own patients.
S — Based on National Specialty Scope of practice.
T — Under authority of collaborative practice arrangement with doctor and limited to 72-hour supply.
U — MCA 37-2-104. **Dispensing of drugs by medical practitioners unlawful – exceptions.** (1) Except as otherwise provided by this section, it is unlawful for a medical practitioner to engage, directly or indirectly, in the dispensing of drugs. (2) Nothing in this section prohibits: (a) a medical practitioner from furnishing a patient any drugs in an emergency; (b) the administration of a unit dose of a drug to a patient by or under the supervision of such medical practitioner; (c) dispensing a drug to a patient by a medical practitioner whenever there is no community pharmacy available to the patient; (d) the dispensing of drugs occasionally, but not as a usual course of doing business, by a medical practitioner; (e) a medical practitioner from dispensing drug samples.
V — Samples only. (KY - noncontrolled substances.)
W — When acting as agent of physician.
X — Only TPA-certified Optometrists.
Y — Under rules of the Board of Pharmacy.
Z — Except emergency medications.
AA — Except in rural areas and student health centers and family planning clinics.
BB — May dispense drugs or devices that are the lawful property of the practitioner or a partnership or corporate entity which is fully owned by licensed practitioners. Drugs or medicine dispensed must comply with the labeling requirements of state and federal laws and regulations.
CC — Limited to veterinary products.
DD — Pharmacy Act allows only pharmacists to dispense prescriptions.
EE — Except for Veterinarians, dispensing is severely restricted. Contact the Board office.
FF — Physician Assistants (PAs) and Registered Nurses (RNs) who have advanced training may dispense their supervising physician's samples only. RNs must be recognized by the Nursing Board. PAs must be recognized by the Medical Board. Both must have specialized training and education.
GG — Except if allowed to prescribe, may dispense manufacturer's samples only of those drugs authorized to prescribe.
HH — Except for samples, must be licensed by Board of Pharmacy.
II — Included in Advanced Registered Nurse Practitioner classification. CII-IV limited to 72 hours.
JJ — State pharmacy law and Board regulations do not apply to these occupational groups. The Boards of Medicine, Osteopathy, Dental, Veterinarian, Registered Professional Nurses, and Optometry regulate these various occupational groups.
KK — Drug samples in towns with pharmacies; however, they can dispense prepackaged medicines that have been packaged by someone licensed to do so (i.e., Pharmacist) in rural settings where no pharmacy is available.
LL — Only if certified.
MM — If licensed to prescribe, may dispense only items on their protocol.
NN — "Advanced Practice Nurses" presumably have dispensing authority, although it is not explicitly authorized. The state does not necessarily recognize each listed nursing specialty.
OO — No such designation in this state.
PP — Limited, based on formulary and written agreement with supervising physician.
QQ — Certified Nurse Midwives, Clinical Nurse Specialists, Nurse Practitioners, and Registered Nurse Anesthetists may dispense (C-II only in an emergency).
RR — Under delegation and restrictions apply.
SS — Limited drugs.
TT — PAs and all NPs may provide medication pursuant to a protocol with a prescriber if prepackaged by the manufacturer, physician, or pharmacist.
UU — Only nurse practitioners, clinical nurse specialists, nurse midwives, and nurse anesthetists who are licensed by the DC Board of Nursing as an advanced practice registered nurse have dispensing authority.
VV — Therapeutically certified optometrist may supply without charge limited diagnostic and therapeutic agents.

XXVI. Possession of Non-Controlled Legend Drugs

State	Medical Doctor	Doctor of Osteopathy	Dentist	Podiatrist	Veterinarian	Doctor of Homeopathy
Alabama	Yes	Yes	Yes	Yes	Yes	No
Alaska	Yes	Yes	Yes	Yes	Yes	No
Arizona	Yes	Yes	Yes	Yes	Yes	Yes
Arkansas	Yes	Yes	Yes	Yes	Yes	Yes
California	Yes	Yes	Yes	Yes	Yes	No
Colorado	Yes	Yes	Yes	Yes	Yes	No
Connecticut	Yes	Yes	Yes	Yes	Yes	No
Delaware	Yes	Yes	Yes	Yes	Yes	No
District of Columbia	Yes	Yes	Yes	Yes	Yes	No
Florida	Yes	Yes	Yes	Yes	Yes	No
Georgia	Yes	Yes	Yes	Yes	Yes	No
Guam	Yes	Yes	Yes	Yes	Yes	Yes
Hawaii	Yes	Yes	Yes	Yes	Yes	No
Idaho	Yes	Yes	Yes	Yes	Yes	No
Illinois	Yes	Yes	Yes	Yes G	Yes O	No
Indiana	Yes	Yes	Yes	Yes	Yes	P
Iowa	Yes	Yes	Yes	Yes	Yes	No
Kansas	Yes	Yes	Yes	Yes	Yes	No
Kentucky	Yes	Yes	Yes	Yes	Yes	No
Louisiana	Yes	Yes	Yes	Yes	Yes	No
Maine	Yes	Yes	Yes	Yes	Yes	No
Maryland	Yes	Yes	Yes	Yes	Yes	No
Massachusetts EE	Yes	Yes	Yes	Yes	Yes	No
Michigan	Yes	Yes	Yes	Yes	Yes	N/A
Minnesota	Yes	Yes	Yes	Yes	Yes	No
Mississippi	Yes	Yes	Yes	Yes	Yes	No
Missouri	Yes	Yes	Yes	Yes	Yes	No
Montana	Yes	Yes	Yes	Yes	Yes	No
Nebraska	Yes	Yes	Yes	Yes	Yes	No
Nevada	Yes	Yes	Yes	Yes	Yes	No
New Hampshire	Yes	Yes	Yes	Yes	Yes	No
New Jersey	Yes	Yes	Yes	Yes	Yes	N/A
New Mexico	Yes	Yes	Yes	Yes	Yes	No
New York	Yes	Yes	Yes	Yes	Yes	Yes BB
North Carolina	Yes	Yes	Yes	Yes	Yes	No
North Dakota	Yes	Yes	Yes	Yes	Yes	No
Ohio	Yes	Yes	Yes G	Yes G	Yes G	No
Oklahoma	Yes	Yes	Yes	Yes	Yes	No
Oregon	Yes	Yes	Yes	Yes	Yes	No
Pennsylvania	Yes	Yes	Yes	Yes	Yes	No
Puerto Rico	Yes G	Yes	Yes G	Yes G	Yes O	BB
Rhode Island	Yes	Yes	Yes	Yes	Yes	No
South Carolina	Yes	Yes	Yes	Yes	Yes	No
South Dakota	Yes	Yes	Yes	Yes	Yes	No
Tennessee	Yes	Yes	Yes	Yes	Yes	No
Texas	Yes	Yes	Yes	Yes	Yes	No
Utah	Yes	Yes	Yes	Yes	Yes	N/A
Vermont	Yes	Yes	Yes	Yes	Yes	No
Virginia	Yes	Yes	Yes	Yes	Yes	No
Washington	Yes	Yes	Yes	Yes	Yes	No
West Virginia	Yes	Yes	Yes	Yes	Yes	No
Wisconsin	Yes	Yes	Yes	Yes	Yes	No
Wyoming	Yes	Yes	Yes	Yes	Yes	N/A

XXVI. Possession of Non-Controlled Legend Drugs *(cont.)*

State	Physician Assistant	Advanced Registered Nurse Practitioner	Clinical Nurse Specialist	Nurse Midwife	Midwife	Nurse Practitioner
Alabama	Yes	Yes A	No	Yes A	No	Yes A
Alaska	Yes	Yes B	Yes B	Yes B	Yes B, C	Yes B
Arizona	Yes A	Yes A	—	No	No	A
Arkansas	—	Yes A	Yes A	Yes A	No	No
California	Yes PP	Yes PP	No	No	No	Yes PP
Colorado	J	E	No	Yes E, K	No	No
Connecticut	Yes	Yes	No	— M	N/A	M
Delaware	Yes L	Yes L	Yes L	—	No	No
District of Columbia	—	Yes JJ	Yes JJ	Yes JJ	No	Yes JJ
Florida	Yes	Yes	No	No	No	No
Georgia	No	No	No	No	No	No
Guam	Yes N	Yes N	Yes N	Yes N	Yes N	Yes N
Hawaii	No	No	No	No	No	No
Idaho	Yes	NN	NN	NN	No	NN
Illinois	Yes	Yes	Yes	Yes	No	Yes
Indiana	P	Yes	Yes	Yes	P	Yes
Iowa	Yes	Yes	No Q	No Q	No	No Q
Kansas	No	No	No	No	No	No
Kentucky	Yes	Yes S	Yes S	Yes S	No	Yes S
Louisiana	No	Yes KK	Yes KK	Yes KK	Yes KK	Yes KK
Maine	Yes	Yes	No	Yes	Yes	Yes
Maryland	No	Yes	No	Yes	No	Yes
Massachusetts EE	Yes	Yes	No	Yes	No	Yes
Michigan	Yes T	Yes T	Yes T	Yes T	N/A	Yes T
Minnesota	Yes	Yes	Yes U	Yes V	No	Yes
Mississippi	No X	Yes X	Yes	Yes	Yes	Yes
Missouri	Yes S	Yes S	Yes S	Yes S	Yes S	Yes S
Montana	Yes Y	Yes	Yes	Yes	No	Yes
Nebraska	Yes G	Yes G	Yes G	Yes G	Yes G	Yes G
Nevada	Yes	Yes	No	No	No	No
New Hampshire	Yes	Yes	No	Yes	Yes	Yes
New Jersey	Yes	Yes	Yes	Yes	Yes	Yes
New Mexico	Yes	Yes	Yes	Yes	No	Yes
New York	Yes	Yes	No	No	Yes	Yes
North Carolina	Yes	No	No	Yes	No	Yes
North Dakota	Yes	Yes	Yes	Yes	No	Yes
Ohio	No	Yes FF	Yes FF	Yes FF	No	Yes FF
Oklahoma	Yes	Yes	Yes	Yes	No	Yes
Oregon	Yes	Yes	N/A	Yes	Yes	Yes
Pennsylvania	Yes DD	DD	No	No	No	DD
Puerto Rico	OO	OO	OO	OO	OO	OO
Rhode Island	Yes	Yes	Yes	Yes	No	Yes, B
South Carolina	No	No	No	No	No	No
South Dakota	Yes L, T	No	No	Yes L, T	No	Yes
Tennessee	Yes	Yes	No	No	No	Yes
Texas	Yes T	Yes T	Yes T	Yes T	Yes E	Yes T
Utah	Yes	Yes	Yes	Yes	N/A	Yes
Vermont	Yes	Yes	Yes	Yes	No	Yes
Virginia	Yes GG	—	No	—	No	Yes GG
Washington	Yes	Yes	LL	Yes M	Yes L	Yes M
West Virginia	Yes	Yes	—	Yes	No	Yes
Wisconsin	Yes	Yes	No	No	No	No
Wyoming	Yes	Yes D	No	No	No	No

XXVI. Possession of Non-Controlled Legend Drugs *(cont.)*

State	OB/GYN Nurse Practitioner	Pediatric Nurse Practitioner	Psychiatric Nurse Practitioner	Optometrist	Naturopathic Doctor	Pharmacist
Alabama	Yes A	Yes A	Yes A	Yes A	No	No
Alaska	Yes B	Yes B	Yes B	Yes	No	No
Arizona	A	A	A	A, E	E	Yes G
Arkansas	No	No	No	I	—	Yes G
California	Yes H	Yes H	Yes H	E	No	No
Colorado	No	No	No	L	No	J
Connecticut	M	M	M	Yes	No	No
Delaware	Yes	Yes L	Yes L	Yes L	No	Yes L
District of Columbia	Yes JJ	Yes JJ	Yes JJ	Yes	No	G
Florida	No	No	No	Yes	Yes	Yes G
Georgia	No	No	No	Yes	No	Yes
Guam	No	No	No	Yes AA, CC	No	Yes
Hawaii	No	No	No	Yes	Yes N	No
Idaho	Z	Z	Z	Yes	No	Yes G
Illinois	No	No	No	Yes I	No	Yes G
Indiana	Yes	Yes	Yes	Yes E	P	Yes
Iowa	No Q	No Q	No Q	Yes	No	No
Kansas	No	No	No	Yes E	No	No
Kentucky	Yes S	Yes S	Yes S	Yes L	No	Yes G
Louisiana	Yes KK	Yes KK	Yes KK	No	No	Yes G
Maine	Yes	Yes	Yes	No	No	No
Maryland	Yes	Yes	No	No	No	No
Massachusetts EE	Yes	Yes	Yes	Yes F	No	No G
Michigan	Yes T	Yes T	Yes T	A, E	N/A	Yes G
Minnesota	Yes	Yes	Yes	Yes	No	Yes G
Mississippi	Yes	Yes	Yes	Yes L	No W	No G
Missouri	Yes S	Yes S	Yes S	Yes G	No	No
Montana	Yes	Yes	Yes	Yes	Yes E	No
Nebraska	Yes G	Yes G	Yes G	Yes G	No	Yes G
Nevada	No	No	No	Yes	No	No
New Hampshire	Yes	Yes	Yes	Yes E	Yes E	Yes
New Jersey	No	No	No	Yes AA	N/A	Yes
New Mexico	Yes	Yes	Yes	Yes	N/A	Yes R
New York	Yes	Yes	Yes	Yes	Yes BB	Yes
North Carolina	Yes	Yes	Yes	Yes	No	Yes
North Dakota	Yes	Yes	Yes	Yes	No	Yes G
Ohio	Yes FF	Yes FF	Yes FF	Yes CC	No	Yes G
Oklahoma	Yes	Yes	Yes	Yes	No	No
Oregon	Yes	Yes	Yes	Yes	Yes	Yes
Pennsylvania	DD	DD	DD	Limited	No	Yes G
Puerto Rico	II	II	II	CC	BB	G
Rhode Island	Yes B	Yes B	Yes B	Yes L	No	Yes G
South Carolina	No	No	No	Yes	No	Yes
South Dakota	Yes L, T	Yes L, T	Yes L, T	Yes	No	Yes
Tennessee	Yes	Yes	Yes	Yes	No	Yes
Texas	Yes T	Yes T	Yes T	Yes E	No	No
Utah	Yes	Yes	Yes	Yes	Yes	Yes
Vermont	Yes	Yes	Yes	Yes	Yes E	No
Virginia	—	—	—	Yes D, E	No HH	Yes
Washington	Yes M	Yes M	Yes M	Yes L	Yes L	Yes
West Virginia	Yes	Yes	Yes	Yes	No	Yes G
Wisconsin	No	No	No	Yes	No	Yes
Wyoming	No	No	No	Yes	N/A	Yes G

XXVI. Possession of Non-Controlled Legend Drugs *(cont.)*

LEGEND

A — Those having prescribing authority.
B — If an Advanced Nurse Practitioner.
C — Very limited.
D — If certified or registered (WY – certified only).
E — Limited Formulary.
F — Topical non-federally controlled Schedule VI for treatment of conditions except glaucoma.
G — In the course of professional practice.
H — PAs and NPs can sign (**not** order) drug samples, and control (**not** own) drug stock.
I — Office use – diagnostics only.
J — Not independently.
K — Direct entry.
L — Limited.
M — See entry for Advanced Registered Nurse Practitioner.
N — Only those noncontrolled prescription drugs that are vitamins, minerals, amino acids, and fatty acids.
O — For animal use only.
P — Other practitioners are not specifically addressed in the law. There are cases where they may "possess" when acting as the agent of the licensed or authorized agent.
Q — However, "Certified" Clinical Nurse Specialists, "Certified" Nurse Midwives, and "Certified" Nurse Practitioners (Advanced Registered Nurse Practitioner classifications) may do so.
R — Pharmacist clinician.
S — Under authority of collaborative practice arrangement with a physician.
T — Under delegated authority.
U — In Psychiatric Mental Health Nursing.

V — Certified Nurse Midwife.
W — Not recognized.
X — Protocol.
Y — Certified Physician Assistant.
Z — Certified Nurse Midwives, Clinical Nurse Specialists, Nurse Practitioners, and Registered Nurse Anesthetists may possess.
AA — Only ophthalmic drugs.
BB — Only if they are a Medical Doctor.
CC — Listed in law and rules adopted by optometry board.
DD — Limited, based on formulary and written agreement with supervising physician.
EE — In Massachusetts, all non-federally controlled legend drugs are considered Schedule VI controlled substances and are regulated as controlled substances.
FF — If licensed to prescribe.
GG — Physician Assistants and Licensed Nurse Practitioners who have been certified to have some type of prescriptive authority may possess those drugs that they are allowed to prescribe only within the scope of their practice.
HH — No longer licensed in Virginia.
II — Not specifically addressed in the Pharmacy Act. Agents or authorized prescribers are allowed to "possess."
JJ — Only nurse practitioners, clinical nurse specialists, nurse midwives, and nurse anesthetists who are licensed by the DC Board of Nursing as an advanced practice registered nurse can have possession of non-controlled legend drugs.
KK — Advanced Registered Nurse Practitioner may distribute sample medication at no cost.
LL — No such designation in this state.

XXVII. Possession of Controlled Substances

State	Medical Doctor	Doctor of Osteopathy	Dentist	Podiatrist	Veterinarian	Doctor of Homeopathy
Alabama	Yes	Yes	Yes	Yes	Yes	No
Alaska	Yes	Yes	Yes	Yes	Yes	No
Arizona A	Yes	Yes	Yes	Yes	Yes	Yes
Arkansas	Yes	Yes	Yes	Yes	Yes	Yes
California	Yes	Yes	Yes	Yes	Yes	No
Colorado	Yes	Yes	Yes	Yes	Yes	No
Connecticut	Yes	Yes	Yes	Yes	Yes	No
Delaware	Yes	Yes	Yes	Yes	Yes	No
District of Columbia	Yes	Yes	Yes	Yes	Yes	No
Florida	Yes	Yes	Yes	Yes	Yes	No
Georgia	Yes	Yes	Yes	Yes	Yes	No
Guam	Yes	Yes	Yes	Yes	Yes	N/A
Hawaii K	Yes	Yes	Yes	Yes	Yes	No
Idaho	Yes	Yes	Yes	Yes	Yes	No
Illinois	Yes	Yes	Yes	Yes	Yes M	No
Indiana	Yes L	Yes L	Yes L	Yes L	Yes L	No
Iowa	Yes	Yes	Yes	Yes	Yes	No
Kansas A	Yes	Yes	Yes	Yes	Yes	No
Kentucky	Yes	Yes	Yes	Yes	Yes	No
Louisiana	Yes	Yes	Yes	Yes	Yes	No
Maine	Yes	Yes	Yes	Yes	Yes	No
Maryland	Yes	Yes	Yes	Yes	Yes	No
Massachusetts	Yes	Yes	Yes	Yes	Yes	No
Michigan	Yes	Yes	Yes	Yes	Yes	N/A
Minnesota	Yes	Yes	Yes	Yes	Yes	No
Mississippi	Yes	Yes	Yes	Yes	Yes	No
Missouri	Yes	Yes	Yes G	Yes G	Yes G	No
Montana	Yes	Yes	Yes	Yes	Yes	No
Nebraska	Yes	Yes	Yes	Yes	Yes	No
Nevada	Yes	Yes	Yes	Yes	Yes	Yes U
New Hampshire	Yes	Yes	Yes	Yes	Yes	No
New Jersey	Yes	Yes	Yes	Yes	Yes	N/A
New Mexico	Yes	Yes	Yes	Yes	Yes	No
New York	Yes	Yes	Yes	Yes	Yes	No W
North Carolina C	Yes	Yes	Yes	Yes	Yes	No
North Dakota	Yes	Yes	Yes	Yes	Yes	No
Ohio	Yes	Yes	Yes G	Yes G	Yes G	No
Oklahoma	Yes	Yes	Yes	Yes	Yes	No
Oregon	Yes	Yes	Yes	Yes	Yes	No
Pennsylvania	Yes	Yes	Yes	Yes	Yes	No
Puerto Rico	Yes X	Yes X	Yes G, X	Yes G, X	Yes G, X	W
Rhode Island	Yes	Yes	Yes	Yes	Yes	No
South Carolina	Yes	Yes	Yes	Yes	Yes	No
South Dakota	Yes	Yes	Yes	Yes	Yes	No
Tennessee	Yes	Yes	Yes	Yes	Yes	No
Texas	Yes	Yes	Yes	Yes	Yes	No
Utah AA	—	—	—	—	—	N/A
Vermont	Yes	Yes	Yes	Yes	Yes	No LL
Virginia	Yes	Yes	Yes	Yes	Yes	No
Washington	Yes	Yes	Yes	Yes	Yes	No
West Virginia CC	Yes	Yes	Yes	Yes	Yes	No
Wisconsin	Yes	Yes	Yes	Yes	Yes	No
Wyoming	Yes	Yes	Yes	Yes	Yes	N/A

XXVII. Possession of Controlled Substances *(cont.)*

State	Physician Assistant	Advanced Registered Nurse Practitioner	Clinical Nurse Specialist	Nurse Midwife	Midwife	Nurse Practitioner
Alabama	No	No	No	No	No	No
Alaska	Yes	Yes C, D	No C, D	No C, D	No C, D	Yes C, D
Arizona	Yes A, B	Yes A, B	—	—	—	—
Arkansas	No	Yes C	Yes C	Yes C	No	No
California	Yes R	Yes R	No	No	No	Yes R
Colorado	Yes C	Yes C	No	No	No	No
Connecticut	Yes	Yes	No	— I	N/A	I
Delaware	Yes	Yes E	Yes E	Yes E	No E	Yes E
District of Columbia	No	Yes EE	Yes EE	Yes EE	No	Yes EE
Florida	No	No	No	No	No	No
Georgia	No	No	No	No	No	No
Guam	No	No	No	No	No	No
Hawaii	No	No	No	No	No	No
Idaho	JJ	JJ	JJ	JJ	No	JJ
Illinois	Yes FF	Yes FF	Yes FF	Yes FF	No	Yes FF
Indiana	No N	Yes L	Yes L	Yes L	No	Yes L
Iowa	Yes	Yes	No O	No O	No	No O
Kansas	No	No	No	No	No	No
Kentucky	No P	No P	No P	No P	No P	No P
Louisiana	No	No	No	No	No	No
Maine	Yes	Yes	No	Yes	Yes	Yes
Maryland	No	No	No	No	No	No
Massachusetts	Yes H	Yes H	No	Yes H	No	Yes H
Michigan	Yes H	Yes H	No	Yes H	No	Yes H
Minnesota	Yes C	Yes C	Yes C	Yes C	No	Yes C
Mississippi	No	No	No	No	No	No
Missouri	Yes S	Yes S	Yes S	Yes S	Yes S	Yes S
Montana	Yes T	Yes	Yes	Yes	No	Yes
Nebraska	Yes G	Yes G	Yes G	Yes G	Yes G	Yes G
Nevada	Yes	Yes	No	No	No	No
New Hampshire	Yes	Yes	No	No	No	Yes
New Jersey	No	No	No	No	No	No
New Mexico	Yes	Yes	Yes	Yes	No	Yes
New York	Yes	Yes	No	No	Yes	Yes
North Carolina C	Yes	No	No	Yes	No	Yes
North Dakota	Yes Y	Yes	Yes	Yes	No	Yes
Ohio	No	Yes CC	Yes CC	Yes CC	No	Yes CC
Oklahoma	Yes	Yes	Yes	Yes	No	No
Oregon	Yes	Yes	N/A	Yes	No	Yes
Pennsylvania	Yes Y	PP	No	No	No	PP
Puerto Rico	OO	OO	OO	OO	OO	OO
Rhode Island	Yes	Yes	Yes F	Yes	No	Yes B
South Carolina	No	No	No	No	No	No
South Dakota	Yes	No	No	Yes	No	Yes
Tennessee	Yes C	Yes C	Yes C	No	No	Yes C
Texas	No	No	No	Yes Z	No	No
Utah	Z	—	—	—	—	—
Vermont	Yes A	Yes A	Yes A (endorsed)	Yes A	No	Yes A
Virginia	Yes Q	—	No	—	—	Yes PP, Q
Washington	Yes	Yes DD	II	Yes DD	No	Yes DD
West Virginia	Yes E	Yes E	Yes	Yes E	No	Yes E
Wisconsin	No	Yes	No	No	No	No
Wyoming	Yes	Yes T	No	No	No	No

XXVII. Possession of Controlled Substances (cont.)

State	OB/GYN Nurse Practitioner	Pediatric Nurse Practitioner	Psychiatric Nurse Practitioner	Optometrist	Naturopathic Doctor	Pharmacist
Alabama	No	No	No	Yes E	No	No
Alaska	Yes C, D	Yes C, D	Yes C, D	No	No	No
Arizona	Yes A, B	Yes A, B	Yes A, B	Yes E	E	Yes G
Arkansas	No	No	No	No	No	G
California	Yes R	Yes R	Yes R	Yes NN	No	No
Colorado	No	No	No	Yes E	No	Yes H
Connecticut	I	I	I	Yes	No	No
Delaware	Yes E	Yes E	Yes E	No	No	No
District of Columbia	Yes EE	Yes EE	Yes EE	Pending	No	Yes J
Florida	No	No	No	No	Yes	Yes J
Georgia	No	No	No	Yes	No	Yes
Guam	No	No	No	No	No	Yes
Hawaii	No	No	No	No	No	No
Idaho	JJ	JJ	JJ	Yes	No	Yes J
Illinois	No	No	No	No	No	Yes G
Indiana	Yes L	Yes L	Yes L	No	No	Yes L
Iowa	No O	No O	No O	Yes E	No	No
Kansas	No	No	No	Yes A	No	No
Kentucky	No P	No P	No P	Yes E	No	Yes
Louisiana	No	No	No	No	No	Yes G
Maine	Yes	Yes	Yes	Yes	No	No
Maryland	No	No	No	No	No	No
Massachusetts	Yes H	Yes H	Yes H	No	No	No G
Michigan	Yes H	Yes H	Yes H	No	No	Yes G
Minnesota	Yes C	Yes C	Yes C	Yes C	No	No G
Mississippi	No	No	No	No	No	No G
Missouri	Yes S	Yes S	Yes S	Yes G	No	No
Montana	Yes	Yes	Yes	Yes	Yes	No
Nebraska	Yes G	Yes G	Yes G	Yes G	No	Yes G
Nevada	No	No	No	No	N/A	No
New Hampshire	Yes	Yes	Yes	Yes V	Yes E, C	Yes
New Jersey	No	No	No	No	N/A	Yes
New Mexico	Yes	Yes	Yes	Yes	N/A	Yes KK
New York	Yes	Yes	Yes	No	No	Yes
North Carolina	Yes	Yes	Yes	Yes	No	Yes
North Dakota	Yes	Yes	Yes	No	No	Yes J
Ohio	Yes CC	Yes CC	Yes CC	No	No	Yes G
Oklahoma	No	No	No	Yes	No	No
Oregon	Yes	Yes	Yes	Yes BB	Yes	Yes G, J
Pennsylvania	PP	PP	PP	E	No	Yes G
Puerto Rico	OO	OO	OO	OO	W, X	G, X
Rhode Island	No D	No D	No D	No	No	Yes G
South Carolina	No	No	No	Yes	No	Yes
South Dakota	Yes	Yes	Yes	Yes	No	Yes
Tennessee	Yes C	Yes C	Yes C	Yes C	No	Yes
No	Yes					
Texas	No	No	No	Yes GG	No	No
Utah	—	—	—	Yes MM	—	—
Vermont	Yes A	Yes A	Yes A	Yes	BB	Yes G
Virginia	—	—	—	Yes HH	No	Yes
Washington	Yes DD	Yes DD	Yes DD	No	No	Yes
West Virginia	Yes E	Yes E	Yes E	Yes E	No	Yes G
Wisconsin	No	No	No	Yes	No	Yes
Wyoming	No	No	No	Yes	N/A	Yes G

XXVII. Possession of Controlled Substances *(cont.)*

LEGEND

A — Assuming the practitioner holds a valid DEA registration and is not under Board restrictions.

B — Those having prescribing authority.

C — If they are a DEA registrant.

D — If an Advanced Nurse Practitioner.

E — Limited. (KY – C-III-V only.)

F — Schedule IV only.

G — In course of professional practice.

H — Not independently.

I — See entry for Advanced Registered Nurse Practitioner.

J — Via pharmacy as a DEA registrant.

K — Jurisdiction over controlled substances lays with the Department of Public Safety, Narcotics Enforcement Branch.

L — Yes, if the practitioner holds a valid state registration.

M — Animal only.

N — Practitioner is not specifically addressed in the law. There are cases in which they may "possess" when acting as the agent of the licensed or authorized agent.

O — However, "Certified" Clinical Nurse Specialists, "Certified" Nurse Midwives, and "Certified" Nurse Practitioners (Advanced Registered Nurse Practitioner classifications) may do so.

P — Unless pursuant to valid medical order and for purposes of immediate administration.

Q — As of July 1, 2000, nurse practitioners with prescriptive authority will be able to prescribe and possess Schedule V controlled substances only after they obtain DEA registration. On January 1, 2002, Schedule IV will be added. On July 1, 2003, Schedule III will be added. As of July 1, 2001, physician assistants may prescribe and possess C-Vs after obtaining a DEA registration. On January 1, 2003, C-IVs will be added.

R — PAs and NPs can control drug stock (but not own it). DEA number required.

S — Under authority of collaborative practice arrangement with a physician.

T — If certified.

U — Homeopathic dosages only.

V — Only TPA-certified Optometrists and according to a limited formulary.

W — Yes, if they are a Medical Doctor.

X — If holding corresponding federal and state registration.

Y — Limited, based on formulary and written agreement with supervising physician. Schedule II prohibited.

Z — Under delegated authority.

AA — Any practitioner who holds a controlled substance license can possess controlled substances.

BB — Pursuant to their formulary.

CC — The affirmative answer is **only true** when these occupational groups have **prescriptive authority.**

DD — Independent authority for C-V and legend drugs. Collaborative agreement with physician required for C-II-IV controlled substances.

EE — Only nurse practitioners, clinical nurse specialists, nurse midwives, and nurse anesthetists who are licensed by the DC Board of Nursing as an advanced practice registered nurse can have possession of controlled substances.

FF — In all cases, must possess an Illinois controlled substance and DEA license. Supervising/collaborating physician must authorize Schedule III, IV, and/or V.

GG — Limited to drugs approved by the Optometry Board.

HH — May possess and prescribe only Schedule III controlled substances used in the treatment of ocular pain.

II — No such designation in this state.

JJ — Certified Nurse Midwives, Clinical Nurse Specialists, Nurse Practitioners, and Registered Nurse Specialists may possess if registered with the DEA.

KK — Pharmacist clinician.

LL — Not licensed in this state.

MM — Schedules IV and V only.

NN — Limited to hydrocodone with compounds and codeine with compounds.

OO — Not specifically addressed in Controlled Substances Act. Agents or authorized registrants are allowed to "possess."

PP — Limited, based on formulary and written agreement with supervising physician.

XXVIII. Miscellaneous State Pharmacy Laws

State	Does Board Allow Centralized Prescription Filling Facilities to be Utilized?	May Pharmacists Initiate, Modify, and/or Discontinue Drug Therapy Pursuant to a Collaborative Practice Agreement or Protocol?	Is Prescriber Ownership of a Pharmacy Prohibited?	May Pharmacists Administer Drugs?	Does Your State Have "Freedom of Choice" Legislation?
Alabama	Yes	No	No	Yes	Yes
Alaska	Not addressed	No	No	Yes	No
Arizona	Yes	Yes	Yes A	Yes B	Yes C
Arkansas	No	Yes	No	Yes S	Yes
California	Yes	Yes	Yes	Yes	Yes
Colorado	Yes	No	No E, F	Yes	No
Connecticut	No	Yes Y, restrictions	Yes	No	Yes G
Delaware	Yes	No	No	Yes	Yes
District of Columbia	No	No	No	No	No
Florida	Pending	Yes restrictions	No	No	No
Georgia	Yes	Yes	No L	Yes	Yes
Guam	Not addressed	Not addressed	No	Yes	No
Hawaii	Yes N	Yes	No	Yes I	No
Idaho	Yes KK	Yes	No	Yes	Yes
Illinois	Yes	Yes FF	No	Yes	Yes
Indiana	No	Yes	No	Yes N	Yes O
Iowa	No	No	Yes BB	Yes M	Yes
Kansas	Yes	Yes FF	No	Yes R	Yes (Limited)
Kentucky	Yes X	Yes	No	Yes S	Yes
Louisiana	No	No Z	No J	Yes	Yes
Maine	No	No	No	No	Yes
Maryland	Yes	No	Yes	No	Yes
Massachusetts	Not addressed AA	No	Yes	Yes K	Yes
Michigan	No	Yes	No	Yes	No
Minnesota	Yes	Yes	No	Yes D	No
Mississippi	Under review	Yes	No	Yes	Yes
Missouri	Yes	Yes	No	Yes N	Yes
Montana	Not addressed	Yes	Yes	Yes	Yes
Nebraska	Yes	Yes	No	Yes	Yes H
Nevada	Yes	Yes Y	Yes F	Yes T	No
New Hampshire	Yes	No	Yes	No	Yes
New Jersey	No LL	No LL	No	No	Yes
New Mexico	No	Yes MM	No	Yes K	No
New York	JJ	No	No L	No	Pending
North Carolina	Yes	Yes W	No U	Yes Q	Yes
North Dakota	Yes	Yes	Yes	Yes	Yes
Ohio	Yes EE	Yes DD	No	Yes EEE	No
Oklahoma	No	No	No	Yes	No
Oregon	Yes	Yes V	No	Yes	No
Pennsylvania	Not addressed LL	No NN	No CC	No NN	Unknown
Puerto Rico	—	—	No	No	Yes
Rhode Island	No	Yes P	No F	No	No
South Carolina	Not addressed	No	No	Yes	Yes
South Dakota	No Addressed	Yes	No	Yes	Yes
Tennessee	Not addressed	Yes	No	Yes	Yes
Texas	Yes GG	Yes	No	Yes S	Yes
Utah	Yes	No	No	No	No
Vermont	No	Yes	No	Yes	No
Virginia	No	Yes	No	Yes	Yes
Washington	Yes	Yes	No J	Yes	No
West Virginia	No	No	No	No	Yes K
Wisconsin	No LL	No	No	Yes V	Yes
Wyoming	Not addressed	Yes	No	No	Yes

XXVIII. Miscellaneous State Pharmacy Laws *(cont.)*

State	Does Board Allow Pharmacies to Maintain Electronic Reference Materials?	Does Board Require Pharmacies to Maintain Any Type of Continuous Quality Improvement Program to Monitor and Prevent Quality-Related Events?	Does Board Have Regulations Aimed at Relieving Pharmacist Workload?
Alabama	Yes	No	No
Alaska	Yes	Not addressed	No
Arizona	Yes	Y, OO	No
Arkansas	Yes	No	No
California	Yes	Yes	Yes
Colorado	Yes	No	No
Connecticut	Yes	Yes VV	No
Delaware	DDD	No	No
District of Columbia	No restrictions	No	No
Florida	Yes	Yes	No
Georgia	Yes	No	No
Guam	Not addressed	Not addressed	Not addressed
Hawaii	Yes	No	No
Idaho	Yes	No	No
Illinois	Yes	No	No
Indiana	Yes	No	No
Iowa	Yes	No	No
Kansas	Yes	No	No
Kentucky	Yes	Yes	No
Louisiana	Yes	No	No
Maine	Yes	No	Yes ZZ
Maryland	Yes	UU	No WW, UU
Massachusetts	No AAA	No BBB	No CCC
Michigan	Yes	—	No
Minnesota	Yes	No	No
Mississippi	Yes	No	No
Missouri	Yes	No	No
Montana	Yes	PP	Yes TT
Nebraska	Yes	No	No
Nevada	Yes	No	No
New Hampshire	Yes	No	No
New Jersey	Yes	No	YY
New Mexico	Yes	Yes	No
New York	Yes	No HH	Yes XX
North Carolina	Yes	Yes	Yes
North Dakota	Yes	No	No
Ohio	Yes	No	No
Oklahoma	Yes	No	No
Oregon	Yes	Yes Y	No
Pennsylvania	Yes	Not addressed	No
Puerto Rico	—	—	—
Rhode Island	Yes	No	No
South Carolina	Not addressed	No	No
South Dakota	Yes QQ	No RR	SS
Tennessee	Yes	No	Yes
Texas	Yes	Recommended	No
Utah	Yes	No	Yes
Vermont	Yes	No	No
Virginia	Yes	No	No
Washington	Yes	No	No
West Virginia	Yes	Yes	Yes II
Wisconsin	Yes	No	No
Wyoming	Yes	No	No

XXVIII. Miscellaneous State Pharmacy Laws *(cont.)*

LEGEND

A — Prescriber ownership of pharmacies is prohibited if prescribers are likely to benefit due to the prescriptions they write.

B — Definition of "dispense" includes "administer."

C — Limited to industrial accident prescriptions.

D — First doses and in medical emergencies.

E — A pharmacist may not work for a prescriber.

F — Prescriber(s) may own no more than 10 percent total interest in a pharmacy.

G — Does not apply to HMO or self-funded ERISA plans.

H — Health & Human Services, Department of Regulation and Licensure, Credentialing Division.

I — Pursuant to a licensed medical doctor's or osteopathic physician's order.

J — 1995 law prohibits self-referral of Medicaid patients when prescriber has ownership interest in pharmacy.

K — Have statutory authority but no rules/regulations. (DE – May not break skin, according to Attorney General opinion.)

L — Referral to pharmacies in which the prescriber has ownership interest is prohibited.

M — Anyone may administer drugs at the direction of a practitioner.

N — Not prohibited.

O — In the Division of Facilities' Standards, Department of Health.

P — Effective January 1, 2002, pursuant to regulations.

Q — Under the rules of the Boards of Pharmacy, Nursing, and Medicine.

R — Only when directed by a practitioner.

S — The definition of the "Practice of Pharmacy" includes "drug administration."

T — Conditionally with the written approval of the ultimate user. Immunizations by protocol.

U — Self-referral prohibited; limits ownership.

V — Under protocol with prescriber.

W — Rules effective 2001.

X — Refills only.

Y — In hospital settings only.

Z — Board has statutory authority to allow this, but regulations not yet promulgated.

AA — Patient would have to make a request for central fill, and the dispensing pharmacist would be required to follow Massachusetts prescription transfer requirements.

BB — As of April 23, 1981, existing pharmacies owned by prescribers were allowed, by rule, to continue operating for 25 years from the date of April 23, 1981.

CC — However, it shall be unlawful for one or more medical practitioners to have a proprietary or beneficial interest sufficient to permit them to exercise supervision or control over the pharmacist in his professional responsibilities or duties.

DD — Modify or discontinue only, if retail.

EE — If Board approved.

FF — Not addressed in laws or regulations but may do so if acting as an agent of the prescriber.

GG — Must comply with prescription transfer requirements.

HH — Encouraged, but no mandate at this time.

II — Must have technician help if filling more than 15 prescriptions/hour on average.

JJ — Currently under review; existing provisions do not appear to prohibit centralized filling if patients understand and agree to transfer of otherwise confidential information.

KK — Not specifically addressed; must follow laws and regulations governing all pharmacies.

LL — However, the Board is looking at this issue.

MM — "Pharmacist clinicians" only.

NN — Pharmacy Act has been amended to permit this, but regulations are not yet written.

OO — Currently under consideration.

PP — Under some circumstances.

QQ — But must also have a hard copy.

RR — Board recommends that such programs be addressed in the pharmacy policy and procedure manual.

SS — Statutory and regulatory interpretations allow for the temporary absence of a pharmacist working alone without closing the pharmacy or removing support staff.

TT — Variable technician ratios and mandatory pharmacist meal/rest breaks

UU — Regulations are in process.

VV — Statutory requirement for Board to adopt regulations to require such assessment; regulations currently pending approval with state authorities.

WW — Board is looking at allowing unlicensed persons to expand permissible tasks and work with less supervision in some areas.

XX — Amendments to rules and regulations allow for greater use of technology and unlicensed personnel.

YY — Board has established policy on allowing pharmacist work breaks without closing the pharmacy.

ZZ — Meal break provisions.

AAA— However regulations are proposed. Current Board policy allows if updated at least quarterly.

BBB— However regulations are proposed. Current policy requires medication error complaints to be followed up by USP/ISMP report of root cause analysis.

CCC— However, Board has meal break policy and Board is accepting pilot project proposals.

DDD— Supplements only. Hard copy must be available.

EEE— Limited to five immunizations.

XXIX. Minimum Standards of Practice

The *United States Pharmacopeia – National Formulary (USP-NF)* has been designated as the official compendia by the Congress of the United States through the federal Food, Drug, and Cosmetic Act.

Articles listed in the *USP-NF* are official and the standards set forth in the monographs apply to them when the articles are intended or labeled for use as drugs or medical devices and when bought, sold, or dispensed for these purposes whether or not the articles are designated *USP-NF*.

The designation *USP-NF* in conjunction with the official title on the label of an article is a reminder that the article purports to comply with *USP-NF* standards; it does not constitute assurances by the *USP-NF* that the article is known to comply with *USP-NF* standards.

An article is recognized in the *Pharmacopeia* when a monograph for the article is published in it, including its supplements, addenda, or interim revisions, and an official date is generally or specifically assigned to it.

XXX. Census Data* (As of June 30, 2002)

State	Number of Pharmacists Licensed by State	No. of Pharmacists with In-State Addresses	Practice Settings: Ambulatory/ Community Pharmacy	Hospital Pharmacy	Manufacturing/ Wholesale	Teaching/ Government	Other Capacities
Alabama	6,879	4,913	3,954	1,503	81	107	1,234
Alaska	577	388					
Arizona	7,687	4,587	2,883	674	12	239	491
Arkansas	3,506	2,524	1,614	565	21	107	217
California	30,845	22,588					
Colorado	5,217	3,567					
Connecticut S	4,393 D	2,946 D					
Delaware	1,314	564					
District of Columbia	1,564						
Florida	20,052						
Georgia	10,534	7,642					
Guam	71	69	N/A	N/A	N/A	N/A	N/A
Hawaii	1,449	860					
Idaho	1,530	1,480					
Illinois	13,151	9,978					
Indiana	8,597	5,759					
Iowa	4,993	2,825	1,697 F	517 F	12 F	91 F	187 F
Kansas	3,494	2,379					
Kentucky	4,746	3,634					
Louisiana	5,839	4,386	3,130	1,369	71	124	1,163
Maine	1,267						
Maryland	6,937	4,913					
Massachusetts	9,940	6,038					
Michigan	11,322	8,394					
Minnesota	5,853	4,393	4,020	1,480	130	238	1,735
Mississippi	3,483	2,525					
Missouri	7,123	4,561	2,397	1,030	1	54	341
Montana	1,463	885			340		
Nebraska	2,555	1,799	455	N/A	82		
Nevada	8,012	1,709					
New Hampshire	1,886	925					
New Jersey	16,245						
New Mexico	2,434	1,418			548		
New York	18,448	15,067					
North Carolina	9,397	7,345	3,792	1,486	132	75	1,186 M
North Dakota	2,089	741	499	122	10	30	20
Ohio	14,250	10,654	5,815	2,051	140	125	1,654
Oklahoma	4,713	3,241					
Oregon	4,079	2,843					
Pennsylvania	17,439	13,176					
Puerto Rico	3,573	2,216	1,629	314	143		130
Rhode Island	1,788	912					
South Carolina	5,052	3,451					
South Dakota	1,401	788	542	153	15	30	48
Tennessee	7,388	5,372					
Texas O	20,803	16,401	9,343	3,405	191	300	3,162
Utah	1,546						
Vermont	830	421			395	3	
Virginia	8,438	5,709					
Washington	6,718	5,143					
West Virginia	2,975	1,698					
Wisconsin	5,737	4,318					
Wyoming	1005	464					
TOTALS	**352,727**	**218,609**	**41,770**	**14,669**	**2,324**	**1,523**	**11,568**

* Information provided directly from the state boards of pharmacy. Blanks indicate that information is not available.

XXX. Census Data* (As of June 30, 2002)

State	Number of Pharmacy Technicians	Number of Pharmacies	Practice Settings/Categories of Licensure			
			Hospital/ Institutional Pharmacies	Independent Community Pharmacies	Non-Independent Community Pharmacies (Four or More)	Out-of-State or Non-Resident Pharmacies
Alabama	10,000	1,771	176	734	559	302
Alaska	575	127 G	14 H			156
Arizona	2,916 R	974	111	160	676	135
Arkansas	3,237	746	150	420	326	158
California	31,235	6,028	519			187
Colorado		821				252
Connecticut	2,926 D	582 D	45 D	165 D	417 D	235 D
Delaware	N/A	159	11	37	120	239
District of Columbia		123	13	27	61	0
Florida	Not available	6,567	2,097	4,098 A	A	341
Georgia	Not available	3,538	204	P	P	
Guam	0	32	N/A	N/A	N/A	N/A
Hawaii	Not available	213				131
Idaho	1,081	573	54	251 A, E		196
Illinois	22,500	2,451	342	2,183 A	A	296
Indiana	N/A	1,350	197			293
Iowa	4,109	1,198	130 F	786 A, F	A	265
Kansas	Not available	807	171	637 A		302
Kentucky	Not available	1,438	125	466	671	176
Louisiana	3,453	1,771	192	576	535	313
Maine		290	42			187
Maryland		1,384 I	70	250	698	263
Massachusetts	10,000 estimated	1,100 J	158	346	740	0
Michigan		2,505				125
Minnesota	5,354	1,409	137	521	526	229
Mississippi	3,906	962	130			220
Missouri	8,638	1,570 K	160	516	569	274
Montana	544	317	99			153
Nebraska	N/A	455	N/A			235 L
Nevada	3,104 T	702	47			252
New Hampshire	1,528	259	32	40	167	208
New Jersey		2,489				
New Mexico	1,862	612	61	298 A		283
New York	N/A	4,424	485	1,938	1,987	N/A Q
North Carolina	Not available	2,024 F	156	551	961	229
North Dakota	430	486	45	150	29	262
Ohio		2,875 N	224	483	1,471	275
Oklahoma	3,336	1,311	89 D	893 A	A	308
Oregon	4,798	1,061	120	300	413	232
Pennsylvania	Not available	3,166	293			0
Puerto Rico						
Rhode Island	1,307	191	20	41	150	227
South Carolina	3,860					
South Dakota		462	43	125	74	220
Tennessee		1,807	403	443	865	96
Texas O	Not available	5,676 B	587	1,654	2,310	252
Utah	2,036	734	107	415 A	A	235
Vermont	Not available	155	17	138		0
Virginia	Not available	1,513				378
Washington	5,689	1,502	222 C	358	710	214
West Virginia	2,041	826 J				270
Wisconsin	Not available	1,286			0	
Wyoming	269	128 F	30			248
TOTALS	**139,560**	**74,950**	**8,328**	**20,000**	**15,035**	**9,852**

* Information provided directly from the state boards of pharmacy. Blanks indicate that information is not available.

XXX. Census Data *(cont.)*

LEGEND

A — Chains included in independent community pharmacies figure.

B — Also licenses 873 nuclear, public health, clinic, ambulatory surgical center, and HMO pharmacies.

C — Includes 107 hospital, 17 nursing home, 25 home infusion, six nuclear, 42 HMO, and 19 other pharmacies.

D — Approximately

E — Plus 20 limited service and 52 parenteral admixture pharmacies.

F — In-state.

G — Includes nine wholesalers drug distributors.

H — Drug rooms.

I — Total includes other areas not listed: clinic, correctional, HMO, nursing home, IV, nuclear, research, and other. 89 pharmacies have waiver (specialty) permits. Board issued 582 distributor permits.

J — Total also includes home IV and mail-order pharmacies.

K — Includes the following pharmacy categories: 27 long-term care, 11 home health, 7 radiopharmaceutical, 2 renal dialysis, 2 sterile pharmaceuticals.

L — Nebraska "registers" out-of-state pharmacies.

M — Plus 336 who are practicing, but place is unknown.

N — Includes 263 nuclear, clinic, fluid therapy, mail-order, specialty, and pharmacies serving nursing homes only.

O — As of February 26, 2001.

P — 2,123 (2,085 independent and chain pharmacies, 12 nuclear pharmacies, 20 prison pharmacies, 4 clinic pharmacies, and 2 pharmacy schools).

Q — 14 Nuclear pharmacies.

R — PTCB Certified – Total number of technicians unknown.

S — As of July 14, 2002.

T — 2,689 technicians, 415 technicians-in-training.

Answer Key

REGULATION OF PHARMACEUTICALS

(1) e

(2) a

(3) b

(4) d

(5) e

(6) b

(7) a and c

(8) a

(9) a

(10) c

(11) a

(12) b

(13) e

(14) c

(15) d

(16) e

(17) d

(18) e

(19) b

(20) e

(21) a

(22) e

(23) c

(24) e

(25) a

(26) e

(27) Although the FDA suggests that the label of unit-dose drugs for hospital use include the information Frank mentions (as well as the drug's proprietary and generic names, the manufacturer's name, and any expiration date or warnings that apply), this information is not officially required. So Frank's idea is a good one, but Molly is not actually violating FDA regulations.

(28) Ipecac syrup is sold over-the-counter because its immediate availability is crucial in emergency situations (as a rapid emetic treatment in cases of poisoning). However, ipecac syrup must be dispensed in bottles containing no more than 30 ml (1 oz).

(29) Nora is right. Anyone dispensing ipecac syrup into a 1 oz bottle from a bulk container must never confuse ipecac fluid extract with ipecac syrup. The fluid extract of ipecac is far more concentrated than the syrup; if overdosed, it could cause death. The fluid extract of ipecac probably should not be stocked at all because it is almost never prescribed.

(30) The FDA Modernization Act of 1997 clarifies that compounding is appropriately regulated at the state level by state boards of pharmacy and medicine. The FD&C Act now specifically exempts pharmacists from the new drug application procedures, the current good manufacturing practices, and the misbranding provisions of the Act as long as certain conditions are met. Prior to these changes, the FD&C Act exempted pharmacy compounding only from the registration and inspection requirements.

(31) If there is no fraud evident or no evidence of unreasonable risk to health, drugs lawfully marketed in other countries may be imported into the US if the following criteria are met:
(1) The drug is not for commercial distribution and the quantity is not excessive (usually not more than a 3-month supply);
(2) The product is for personal use;
(3) The intended use of the product is clearly identified; and
(4) The patient declares it is for personal use and lists the practitioner in the US under whose care it will be used.

(32) "Full disclosure" in relation to promotional advertising and labeling (package inserts) of prescription drugs means that the advertising must include the conclusions of the National Academy of Sciences that a drug product is ineffective, possibly effective, probably effective, or effective as a fixed combination. Prescription drug advertisements require a "true statement of information in brief summary relating to side effects, contraindications, and effectiveness;" this is known as "fair balance."

(33) See the section on bans and prohibitions established by the Prescription Drug Marketing Act.

(34) Particular concerns have been raised regarding substituting generic drug products for brand name products that still have exclusivity over certain indications. One pharmacy organization wrote, "Although the various brands of propranolol may be equivalent/bioavailable, they are not equivalent in that only one brand has been approved by the FDA for post-myocardial infarction."

(35) A nonapproved drug may be defined as a drug banned from commerce because of its hazard or because it is ineffective or as a chemical or substance that has not been used previously in humans for the treatment of disease. If the banned substance or untried chemical is put to a drug use, it is an unapproved new drug or an investigational new drug. However, not every new drug is a nonapproved drug. An approved drug becomes a new drug when it is put to new medical use, but it still remains an approved drug and legally on the market for other medical uses.

(36) In marketing this supplement, the company is not allowed to make any claims about its potential effectiveness in treating arthritis symptoms because this would constitute a "health claim," which is prohibited by the Dietary Supplement Health and Education Act (DSHEA) of 1994. Manufacturers cannot claim that their dietary supplements are effective in treating any disease. However, they can make claims that describe the product's role in affecting the body's normal structure or function. When such a claim is made on the label, the following disclaimer must also appear: "This statement has not been evaluated by the Food and Drug Administration. This product is not intended to diagnose, treat, cure, or prevent any disease."

(37) Brock is right. Before OBRA 90, many courts refused to recognize that pharmacists had any legal duty to provide drug use review or counseling for patients even though many pharmacists provided those services. Because of OBRA 90, nearly all states now require pharmacists to perform these functions. OBRA has statutorily raised the legal standard of conduct required of pharmacists.

(38) The Hazardous Substances Act regulates household items such as bleach, cleaning fluids, antifreeze, and drainpipe cleaners, many of which are stocked in community pharmacies. Pharmacists selling these items must be sure they are sold only in the original containers, as labeled by the manufacturer or supplier with the required cautions and warnings. If these products are not sold in their original containers, the pharmacist must ensure that they are labeled as required by the Act.

(39) See the Hazardous Substances Act requirements for labeling.

(40) The Poison Prevention Packaging Act (PPPA) regulates certain substances (defined as "hazardous household substances") and requires that these substances be packaged for consumer use in special packaging that will make them difficult for children under the age of 5 years to open. One of the main purposes of the Poison Prevention Packaging Act is to extend the special "child-resistant" packaging requirements to both prescription and certain nonprescription drugs.

(41) This information is available from the Consumer Product Safety Commission or any of its regional offices. Also, announcements are published in the Federal Register, and news releases are issued (these may be published in the local press). In addition, journals and newsletters affiliated with pharmaceutical and medical groups, as well as the trade press, publicize these exemptions.

(42) Yes. The law does not preclude a pharmacist from honoring a specific request from a patient, preferably in writing, to have all of his or her medications placed in non-complying packaging.

(43) No. Nikisha may advise the customer that he has the option of having the prescription dispensed in noncomplying packaging, but the choice must be the customer's by specific request.

(44) Yes. Nikisha can dispense medication in noncomplying packaging based only on a physician's check indicating those directions on a prescription blank. However, the Consumer Product Safety Commission seeks to discourage physicians from using prescription blanks with such a box on the basis that this practice tends to encourage excessive use of noncomplying packaging.

(45) Pharmacists are required to dispense regulated prescription drugs in child-resistant packaging unless the consumer or prescribing physician stipulate that a noncomplying package be used. Pharmacists who violate this regulation may be criminally prosecuted. The penalties for each offense are imprisonment for not more than one year or a fine of not more than $1000, or both. For offenses committed with intent to defraud or mislead, or for a second or subsequent offense, the penalty will be imprisonment for not more than three years or a fine of not more than $10,000, or both. The Consumer Product Safety Commission could also seek court orders enjoining violators or authorizing seizures of noncomplying products supplied by manufacturers of consumer packages.

(46) If Nikisha is unable to provide the caller with the necessary emergency information or advise her as to the proper course of action, she should refer the caller to the Poison Control Center or the nearest hospital emergency room. The Poison Control Center phone number should be on or near the pharmacist's telephone, along with those of the fire and police departments. It would also be a good idea for Nikisha to suggest that the caller follow up with her physician.

(47) No. The two systems are separate. Pharmacists should not confuse the child-resistant packaging requirements with the FDA's tamper-evident packaging requirements for over-the-counter drugs. A child-resistant package is not necessarily tamper-evident. The FDA requires that evidence of tampering be visually determined on initial contact, whereas child-resistant packages have specific performance standards that must be met (for example, maintaining their child-resistance for the number of openings and closings customary during the life of the product).

(48) The unique provision of the Consumer Product Safety Act is its preemption of local and state consumer product safety standards unless these standards are identical with the federal standards or excepted by applicable federal regulations.

(49) The five sections of the Federal Anti-Tampering Act cover the following:
   (1) tampering with a consumer product that affects interstate or foreign commerce, with reckless disregard for the risk of death or bodily injury to another person;
   (2) tainting a consumer product with the intent of injuring a business;
   (3) communicating false information that a consumer product has been tainted;
   (4) threatening to tamper with a consumer product; and
   (5) conspiring to tamper.

(50) Alcohol is defined in the federal regulations as "spirits having a proof of 190 degrees or more when withdrawn from bond, including all subsequent dilutions and mixtures thereof, from whatever source or by whatever process produced." The term spirits is defined as "ethyl alcohol, ethanol, or spirits of wine." The term proof is defined as the ethyl alcohol content stated as twice the percent of ethyl alcohol by volume. Hospitals may obtain a permit to purchase and use tax-free alcohol only for medicinal, mechanical, and scientific purposes and for the treatment of patients.

(51) The purpose of the NPDB is to contribute to the improvement of the quality of health care by restricting the ability of incompetent and unethical practitioners to move from state to state without disclosure or discovery of their previous poor performance.

(52) In an HMO, health service is delivered by the HMO directly to the insured individual. Traditional health care insurance companies pay the insured individual's health care bills; they do not actually deliver care.

Critical Thinking Activities

(1) Table designs may vary, but all tables should include the following:

(a) FD&C Act Requirements for Prescription Labels
Name and address of dispenser (pharmacy)
Serial number of the prescription
Date of the prescription or date of its filling/refilling
Name of the prescriber
Name of the patient, if stated in the prescription
Directions for use, including precautions (if any)

(b) Additional Information That May Be Required by State Law
Address of the patient
Initials or name of the dispensing pharmacist
Telephone number of the pharmacy
Drug name, strength, and manufacturer's lot or control number
Beyond-use date, if any
Name of the manufacturer or distributor

(c) FDA Requirements for Manufacturer's Container
Name and address of the manufacturer, packager, or distributor
Ingredient information
Statement of identity (generic and proprietary names)
Quantity in terms of weight or measure applicable to drug
Net quantity of the package contents
Statement of dosage or reference to package insert for dose info
Expiration date of the drug
Lot number
National Drug Code (NDC) number (requested, not required)

(d) FDA Requirements for Package Inserts (must be listed under these heads and in this order)
Description (generic and proprietary names)
Clinical pharmacology
Indications and usage
Contraindications
Warnings
Precautions
Adverse reactions
Drug abuse and dependence
Overdosage
Dosage and administration
How supplied

Case Study 1: Drug Labeling

(1) A pharmacy may repackage or relabel under its own label OTC drugs purchased in bulk, but by doing so, the pharmacy takes legal responsibility for compliance with all the general and applicable specific labeling requirements of both federal and state law and for compliance with state law prohibiting the sale of adulterated or substandard drugs. The FDA's CGMP indicates that a pharmacy that repackages or relabels beyond the usual dispensing and selling of drugs at retail will face liability for registration and inspections as a manufacturer and must heed the detailed requirements of the CGMP. If the drug is intended for distribution to other pharmacies or locations, the CGMP regulations and FDA registration apply. If the drugs are sold at retail only from the pharmacy, these registration regulations do not apply.

(2) A retail dealer can escape criminal penalty for receipt in interstate commerce and subsequent sale of a misbranded drug if the sale was made in good faith and if, on request, he or she furnishes the FDA with records of the source of the interstate shipment. To protect themselves, Tim and Fahad should look for a guarantee that the drugs are not adulterated or misbranded on the invoice.

(3) A guarantee on drugs purchased interstate can be either a limited form for use on an invoice or bill of sale or a general and continuing form.

Case Study 2: Prescription Requirements

(1) While prescriptions written outside the specialist's realm of expertise are legally authorized, the pharmacist may want to scrutinize the prescription for any medical-legal concerns that apply in her state. A pharmacist who dispenses a drug on a prescription order that exceeds the legal limits of the practitioner may be in violation of the state pharmacy practice statutes because the prescription is not within the course of professional practice.

(2) It is possible for a pharmacist to be authorized to prescribe, under state powers, but this authorization should arise in the form of a statute for the state legislature, as opposed to a Board of Pharmacy regulation.

(3) A physician's nurse or assistant has no authority to authorize a refill of a prescription, nor can the physician legally delegate such authority. DEA regulations do permit an agent of the physician to communicate a prescription or refill authorization. However, any prescription or refill communication from anyone other than the physician is subject to risk.

(4) The FDA does not consider any prescription that puts no time limit on frequency of refilling, or specifies no length of time during which a prescription may be refilled, as a valid authorization for refilling a prescription. The law gives only a duly licensed physician authority to determine how much the patient should get. A physician cannot delegate that authority to someone else. The best advice to a pharmacist who receives a prescription so marked is to use care and professional judgment in handling it, to refill only with a frequency consistent with the directions for use, and to check with the physician after a reasonable time to make certain whether the physician wants the medication continued.

(5) If a legend drug is involved in this situation, the pharmacist should supply the patient with the minimum amount of the drug that is necessary until the prescriber can be contacted.

Case Study 3: Compounding

(1) Phil is probably in the least trouble, as long as he is consulting the physician on a patient-by-patient basis and carefully documenting the medical rationale for his particular variation. In certain circumstances, it may be appropriate for a pharmacist to compound a small quantity of a drug that is only slightly different than an FDA-approved drug that is commercially available. In these circumstances, patient-by-patient consultation between physician and pharmacist must result in documentation that substantiates the medical need for the particular variation of the compound.

(2) Ana can lose her status as a retail entity by compounding, providing, and dispensing drugs to third parties for resale to individual patients.

(3) The FDA may, in the exercise of its enforcement discretion, initiate federal enforcement actions against entities and responsible persons when the scope and nature of a pharmacy's activity raises the kinds of concerns normally associated with a manufacturer and that results in significant violations of the new drug, adulteration, or misbranding provisions of the Act. Jack's and Mary's activities are two examples of the kinds of acts that will most likely initiate such an action.

Case 4: Pharmacy Practice and the Health Care System

(1) Medicare is a two-part health insurance program: Part A is hospitalization insurance provided without charge to those eligible; Part B is medical insurance for which a beneficiary must pay a monthly premium. The premium is usually deducted from the beneficiary's social security check. Mrs. Jenkins' neighbor is correct: Those eligible for Part A are automatically enrolled in Part B, but may elect not to have it.

(2) Under Part A, Medicare covers drugs ordinarily provided by hospitals and skilled nursing facilities for the care and treatment of inpatients. With a few exceptions, Part B covers only prescription drugs furnished to a patient "incident to" a physician's services. Therefore, outpatient drugs are covered only if they cannot be self-administered by the patient, if they are administered by the physician on an outpatient basis, if they are reasonable and necessary, and if they are furnished as part of a physician's services. At times, Part B covers antigens, blood-clotting factors, immunosuppressive drugs, erythropoietin, drugs for osteoporosis, and oral anti-cancer drugs, as well as some drugs required for effective use of durable medical equipment.

(3) Refer to the list under "Health Maintenance Organization Regulations" in the "Pharmacy Practice and the Health Care System" section.

(4) Yes. A health maintenance organization is authorized, in connection with the prescription or provision of prescription drugs, to maintain, review, and evaluate a drug use profile of its members, to evaluate their drug use, and to provide instruction of its members and of health professionals in the use of prescription and nonprescription drugs.

Answer Key

CONTROLLED SUBSTANCES

(1)   Under the CSA, control is achieved through federal registration of all persons in the legitimate chain of manufacture, distribution, or dispensing of controlled drugs, except the ultimate user. However, even ultimate users are affected by the Act because it sets forth conditions under which they may possess controlled drugs. In contrast, the earlier Harrison Narcotic Act exerted control over narcotics by imposition of a tax and regulated only narcotics, whereas the CSA regulates both narcotic and nonnarcotic stimulant, depressant, and hallucinogenic drugs.

(2)   The Drug Enforcement Administration (DEA) is the federal agency responsible for enforcement of the Federal Controlled Substances Act (CSA); it is a unit of the Federal Bureau of Investigation (FBI) within the US Department of Justice.

(3)   e

(4)   a

(5)   d

(6)   b

(7)   c

(8)   d

(9)   These registered activities are:
    (1) Manufacturing controlled substances
    (2) Distributing controlled substances
    (3) Dispensing controlled substances from Schedules II through V
    (4) Conducting research with controlled substances in Schedule I
    (5) Conducting research with controlled substances in Schedules II through V
    (6) Conducting a narcotic treatment program using any narcotic drug listed in Schedules II through V
    (7) Importing controlled substances
    (8) Exporting controlled substances
    (9) Conducting chemical analysis with controlled substances

(10) d

(11) a

(12) Pharmacy registrants are required under the CSA to keep records of the following:
    • initial and subsequent biennial inventory records of controlled drugs
    • receipt of controlled drugs and records of their dispensing and disposal

(13) Records must contain the following:
    (1) the name of the controlled substance;
    (2) the dosage form;
    (3) the strength or concentration of the substance per dosage unit; and
    (4) the amount of dosage units per commercial container or volume per container.

(14) The third copy of an official order form (DEA Form 222c) will suffice as a record of Schedule II drugs, provided the pharmacist indicates the supplier's DEA registration number and records the number of commercial containers received and the date of receipt. A commercial invoice serves as a record of receipt for Schedules III, IV, and V drugs as long as the required information is contained therein. The pharmacist should place the actual date of receipt and the supplier's DEA registration on the invoice.

(15) Yes, Janice can use a computerized data processing system to keep refill records for Schedule III and IV drugs, as long as the following conditions are met:
   (1) For all prescription orders currently authorized for refilling, the system must provide immediate and complete online retrieval of both
      (a) the original prescription order information,
      (b) current refill history data, and
      (c) backup or verification documentation to show that the refill information is correct. This verification document must be maintained in a separate file for 2 years from the dispensing date.
   (2) The system must be able to provide the DEA, within 48 hours, a refill-by-refill audit trail for any specific dosage form of a controlled substance by brand name, generic name, or both.
   (3) The system must include a backup procedure for refilling prescriptions during computer down-time that will include the ability both to check refill authorizations and to collect and retain data for entry later.

(16) A pharmacy registrant can distribute to the original supplier of a controlled substance, according to 21 CFR §1307.12, provided that a written record is maintained.

(17) Normally, the pharmacist cannot be prosecuted unless it can be shown that she had knowledge or should have had knowledge that the prescriptions were not issued in the prescriber's usual course of professional practice. Normally, the pharmacist does not have this type of knowledge unless the prescriptions are (illegally) postdated or some indication alerts the pharmacist. Usually, if the pharmacist suspects an invalid prescription, checks with the prescribing physician and receives a satisfactory explanation, the pharmacist's duty is fulfilled under the law. That seems to be the case for Janice.

(18) Examples of qualified mid-level practitioners who may be eligible to prescribe controlled substances include, among others, nurse practitioners, nurse midwives, nurse anesthetists, clinical nurse specialists, and physician assistants who are authorized to dispense these substances in the state where they practice, as well as pharmacists in states where they are authorized to prescribe.

(19) The catch is that neither the CSA nor the DEA regulations confer authority to prescribe controlled substances on a person who did not otherwise have the authority to do so under either state or federal law.

(20) /s/Jeremy Castillo, MD

(21) c

(22) a

(23) d

(24) a

(25) a

(26) a

Critical Thinking Applications

(1) The CSA requires the DEA to request a scientific and medical evaluation from the Secretary of HHS before any substance may be added to a schedule, transferred between schedules, or removed entirely from the schedules.

(2) Given that Jackie's supervisor is right, Jackie's case is unique to that of many other pharmacists in her state in that pharmacists are subject to both federal and state drug control laws, *except* for those practicing exclusively in a federal facility, like this VA hospital.

(3) Both pharmacies can be right. In Roberto's case, the state law must have been more stringent than the federal one. In Becca's case, either the federal law was more stringent or the two laws simply could not consistently stand together, in which case, the state law must yield to the federal.

(4) Guidelines needed to create this table are found throughout the third section of this chapter titled "Registration Under the Controlled Substances Act."

(5) Table designs and layout may vary, but all tables should include the following key data for each form of controlled substance:

Controlled Substance Inventory Data	
Finished Form	Bulk Form for Compounding
Name of substance	Name of substance
Volume or number of units	Total quantity to nearest metric unit weight or total number of units of finished form
Dosage form; unit strength	Reason for maintenance of substance and whether substance is capable of use in manufacture of any controlled substance in finished form

(6) (a) Pharmacists may distribute by dispenser to other registrants under 21 CFR §1307.11, provided the registrant receiving these drugs furnishes the distributing registrant an executed order form. This allows distribution to both pharmacist and physician registrants.
   (b) Jack must have received a directive to register as a distributor because the number of dosage units he has distributed under this provision has apparently exceeded 5% of the total number of dosage units of all controlled substances he has distributed and dispensed in the last 12 months.
   (c) Jess is in trouble because he has *dispensed* (ie, through prescription) drugs for physician office use rather than *distributing*.

(7) Cases are found under "General Issuance Requirements" in the "Prescriptions" section.

(8) Anne is right. Although federal DEA regulations do allow for facsimile prescriptions for Schedule II drugs, in this case, they do not authorize a practitioner to prescribe, or a pharmacist to dispense the drug via faxed prescription unless expressly provided for under the state law in Anne and Carry's jurisdiction.

(9) In the case of these three pharmacists, for Phil and Anne to be doing this for "different reasons," one must be doing it on a first-time, one-time basis, while the other must share a real-time, on-line electronic database with the requesting pharmacy. The only explanation for Leo's exclusion would be that his dispensing the refill at this time would violate the one-time basis specified by law for this kind of transfer, and he apparently does not share a real-time, on-line electronic database with the requesting pharmacy.

(10) See cases for information.

Answer Key

PHARMACY INSPECTION

(1) d

(2) c

(3) a

(4) d

(5) a

(6) e

(7) e

(8) e

(9) b

(10) d

(11) e

Critical Thinking Activities

(1) Although actual researched student presentations will be much more extensive than this answer, these two cases initiated a whole new era of judicial thinking in the area of government inspection. Prior to 1967, the courts held the opinion that searches by administrative agencies were noncriminal in nature and that such searches presented only a minimal intrusion into personal privacy. Based on the decisions in these two cases, however, a search warrant is now required, as a general rule, when an administrative inspection is to be conducted, even if commercial premises are involved.

(2) The exclusionary rule has been enforced in pharmacy inspection, particularly in *United States v. Pugh*, 417 F. Supp. 1019 (W.D. Mich. 1976). The court ruled certain evidence inadmissible because it was seized by the DEA acting only on an inspection notice (Form DEA-82), when an inspection warrant was constitutionally required. A similar motion to suppress evidence was granted in *United States v. Anile*, 352 F. Supp. 14 (1973).

(3) In *Norman Bridge Drug Co. v. Banner et al*, the court rejected the claim that the DEA has a right to seize a pharmacist's stock of controlled drugs on a claim of "imminent public danger." In the case of *People v. White*, the court held that an inspection of areas on hospital premises open to the public was not subject to warrant requirements; it also held that an implied consent to warrantless inspection existed by acceptance of a license.

Case Study Questions

(1) Melanie should examine and ascertain the agent's credentials and purpose. She should write down the agent's name, agency, and badge number.

(2) If this FDA agent presents Form FD-482, he is entitled to entry and inspection because the FDA notice takes the place of the warrant if the inspection is limited in scope. If the FDA agent wants to conduct an accountability audit of a pharmacy, he will probably need an inspection warrant.

(3)   If the agent has no inspection warrant but insists on conducting a drug accountability audit, Melanie should not resist. The audit should be submitted after first asserting a demand for the inspection warrant. However, she may assert that the inspection is being allowed under protest.

(4)   If items are seized, Melanie should demand that a copy of the warrant should be left with her. She should also state verbally to the agent that the inspection is allowed under protest and upon reliance that the inspection warrant (or search warrant) is valid. In addition, the inspection or search can be contested later in a court action for emergency injunction quashing the warrant and suppressing any evidence seized.

(5)   Nothing. An individual's silence during interrogation cannot be used against her.

(6)   Melanie may tape record anything she says to the inspector because the law prohibiting interception of communications applies to illegal wire taps, not to a party to a conversation.

(7)   If Melanie is not a party to the conversation (by exercising her right of silence), she cannot tape record the inspection without permission, and the agent is not likely to give permission. Written observations can provide an accurate picture if it is needed later, and she has a right to do this.

(8)   Melanie does not have to sign anything without first conferring with an attorney, although it may be in her best interest to sign a receipt for drug samples taken by the FDA or a receipt for a state board inspection report. However, she should be wary of signing anything that looks like a waiver of rights.

Answer Key

BUSINESS LAW

(1) d

(2) c

(3) b

(4) e

(5) d

(6) d

(7) e

(8) b

(9) d

(10) e

(11) e

(12) e

(13) a

(14) c

(15) e

(16) b

(17) e

(18) Yes. Christine has some recourse for the reasonable value of the goods furnished if she did not know Theodore was insane or if the goods were necessities of life.

(19) Although the required written agreement cannot be changed verbally, in certain cases a written contract can be rescinded if it does not result in a retransfer of property. Rescission refers to the cancellation of a contract, with the involved parties placed in the positions that they held prior to making the contract. Although an oral rescission may be valid in some instances, scratching out a signature or otherwise defacing a written agreement will not serve as a valid rescission.

(20) Each state has a statute of frauds, which requires that certain agreements must be written and signed by the party to be charged (the party who wants to enforce the agreement). The purpose of the statute of frauds is to prevent fraud and to prevent the perjury of individuals who may lie about the terms of their oral agreements. If the subject matter of the agreement comes within the statute of frauds, unless it is in writing and signed by the party to be charged, the agreement is void, voidable, or unenforceable, depending on the particular state statute.

(21) A consignment sale is for the purpose of resale by a buyer, who may return any of the unsold goods. A sale on approval is a sale of goods for the buyer's own use with the privilege of return even if the goods conform to the contract terms.

(22) In these situations, employees usually allege that statements in the employee job manual, personnel handbook, or employment application serve as an implied promise prohibiting discharge except for cause.

(23) In such claims, the issue of comparable worth has failed to obtain judicial support even though some states have taken statutory initiatives in this area. The comparison of jobs that are substantially equal, not merely similar, is required to establish wage-based sex discrimination. Payment for traditionally female jobs at a salary rate that is less than that paid for traditionally male jobs is not evidence of discrimination even if the female jobs require more skill, effort, and responsibility. The mere predominance of persons of one sex in a job classification is not evidence of sex discrimination in setting wages.

(24) (a) Little legal or economic protection has been provided to individuals seeking employment. Job applicants do not have the benefits of collective bargaining agreements, nor do they possess the vested rights of an employee. It is not unusual for many employers to require pre-employment physical and medical examinations that include both blood and urine tests. One could argue that employers have greater latitude to conduct such exams on prospective employees because the applicant has implicitly consented to the intrusion as a condition of obtaining employment.

(b) Although the right to privacy is not directly articulated in the US Constitution, it permeates the Fourth Amendment. This constitutional right to privacy is not absolute and the courts must again balance a variety of competing interests. Some drug testing programs require employees to submit a urine specimen only under direct supervision to prevent counterfeit samples from being provided. The elimination of body wastes is one of the most private of human functions, and the mandatory observation by others has been held to constitute an invasion of privacy. While some courts have shown a great deal of sensitivity to these intrusive searches, others have given more weight to the employer's needs.

(25) The articles of incorporation usually include the name of the corporation, the period of existence (usually perpetual), the purpose for the information of the corporation, the location of the initial office, the name and address of the initial registered agent (the individual to whom legal papers may be served), the number of directors (in some cases, the names and addresses of the initial board of directors), the number and titles of the officers, and the number and type of shares of capital stock (eg, 100,000 shares of common stock).

(26) **Advantages:** If a sole proprietorship or partnership incorporates, the transfer of the proprietorship or partnership business property to the new corporation is tax-free if the proprietor or partners control the new corporation. Additional reasons for incorporation include limited liability, the perpetual existence of the corporation, and the flexibility of the transfer of interest (ownership is transferred by exchange of stock). A corporation can be a tax shelter, and qualified pension and profit-sharing plans can be established. Group life insurance and group health, accident, and medical insurance are advantages that a corporation can offer its employees. In a closely held corporation, the principal stockholder's estate can benefit from a stock redemption funded by life insurance proceeds, with the premium paid by the corporation, which is also the beneficiary.
Disadvantages: A corporation faces a double tax in that corporate income is first taxed to the corporation and then again when it is distributed as dividends to stockholders. Because the IRS looks very carefully at closely held corporations, the formalities of a corporation must be reasonably maintained or any tax advantages may be lost by reclassification of the firm by the IRS.

(27) (1) The corporation must be domestic (ie, it must exist under the laws of one of the states in the US).

(2) It must not be a member of an affiliated group (except as an inactive subsidiary).

(3) The corporation must not have more than 35 stockholders.

(4) It must have only one class of stock.

(5) It may have only individuals or estates as stockholders, although certain trusts may also qualify.

(6) The corporation must not have a nonresident alien as a stockholder.

(28) The potential liability exposure of a general partner in an L.L.P. is less than that of a general partner in a traditional partnership. Another difference is that the statutes that authorize L.L.P.s dictate that they be registered with the state government, something not required of a traditional partnership.

(29) Two possibilities exist:

(1) HMO enrollees receive pharmacy services only at outlets of a pharmacy chain if they want the HMO to pay for the medication (otherwise they must bear the expense out of pocket, giving up a significant benefit of enrollment).

(2) HMO enrollees are given a direct financial incentive to deal with pharmacies of the chain. Such arrangements have been upheld by the US Supreme Court and other federal courts.

(30) Fair trade laws or resale price maintenance is a practice in which a manufacturer or distributor of a brand name or trademarked product enters into agreements with retailers that prescribe a minimum resale price for the commodity. The purpose of a fair trade agreement is to allow the small-volume retailer the same competitive resale price as the large-volume retailer.

(31) In some states, the law prohibits a retailer or anyone else from selling an item below cost or 6 percent below cost. This practice is referred to as the "loss leader sale," in which the seller sells a brand name item below wholesale cost in order to attract customers who will probably buy other merchandise at the usual or above-average cost. Such sales are often prohibited by state fair trade laws. However, below-cost sales are permitted if:

(1) merchandise is on a bona fide clearance sale;

(2) merchandise is perishable and must be sold to avoid immediate loss;

(3) merchandise is imperfect or damaged;

(4) merchandise is sold to charities or government units; and

(5) merchandise is sold upon liquidation of the business.

Critical Thinking Applications

(1) (a) Stockholder insulation from corporate liability is not absolute. Stockholder liability is limited but not nonexistent. It is usually true that if an individual owns stock in General Motors, he or she will not be liable for any corporate mismanagement. The case may be different if that individual is a majority stockholder in a small corporation. In this case, Arman most likely was a stockholder in a small company.

(b) Stockholders will be held personally liable in the following situations:

(1) When stockholders treat the assets of the corporation as their own personal assets, taking from the corporation at will to the injury of creditors

(2) When stockholders personally sign or otherwise obligate themselves for corporate debts

(3) When stockholders substantially undercapitalize the corporation and actively participate in the corporate management

(2) A discussion of this issue and relevant court cases is found under "Price-Fixing and Third Party Payment Plans."

(3)   In a class action suit in 1994 in the US District Court in Chicago, the court ruled that the defendants unlawfully discriminated in price between community pharmacies and mail-order pharmacies by selling drug products of like grade and quality at different prices. A manufacturer can charge one price to a wholesaler and another price to a retailer because the two are normally not competitors, but this is not the case with a community and a mail-order pharmacy.

(4)   (a) Yes, the pharmacy can sue under a common law rule of restraint of trade. A conspiracy or a concentrated effort on the part of a group of retailers, manufacturers, or wholesalers to refrain from dealing with an individual or firm usually violates antitrust laws or, in some cases, the federal Civil Rights Act.

       (b) PPOs and HMOs will sometimes be interested in granting exclusive contracts for pharmacy services for health plan enrollees to one pharmacy chain, excluding all other pharmacies from the possibility of dispensing medications to plan enrollees. Some states have enacted statutory mandates that participation as providers in health insurance programs be open to "any willing provider." Sponsored by pharmacy groups in many states, such statutes require that the insurer accept any provider who is willing to abide by the program requirements pertaining to reimbursement, submission of claims, utilization review, and so forth. A closely related form of statute is that designated "freedom of choice laws." These statutes permit a person enrolled in a managed health care plan to be reimbursed for health care services even if the provider has not signed a contract with the managed care plan to be a participating provider. Typically, these laws require managed care plans to pay the same amount to a non-network provider chosen by the enrollee as would be paid to a participating provider, but this does not guarantee that the enrollee will incur the same out-of-pocket expense.

Case Study 1: Remedies on Breach

(1)   Liz can demand, in writing, that Jackie give adequate assurance of performance. This may consist of a promise on Jackie's part, or it may consist of correcting the delivery of nonconforming goods. The UCC requires adequate assurance within a reasonable time not exceeding 30 days.

(2)   Jackie can withhold further delivery of goods, stop delivery of goods in transit, and/or locate conforming goods that are not already committed and resell them. If any of the goods are unfinished, she may finish and resell them (exercising reasonable commercial judgment to avoid loss) or she may stop finishing the goods and resell them for scrap or salvage. She may resell the goods and sue for the difference between the resale price and the contract price plus incidental costs but less any expenses saved by buyer's breach. Jackie may sue for damages for repudiation by Liz or sue for the profit that would have been made from Liz's full performance. Finally, she may cancel the contract. In that case, Jackie retains any remedy for breach of whole or part of the contract, but she must notify Liz of the cancellation.

(3)   As long as Liz's rejection of the goods is justifiable (thus meaning that the seller is in breach of contract), she can cancel the contract and, in addition to recovering what has been paid, purchase substitute goods and recover damages. Or she can simply recover damages for nondelivery (measured by the difference between the market price when Liz learned of the breach and the contract price plus incidentals but less expenses paid). If the goods have been identified, Liz may recover them if Jackie becomes insolvent within 10 days after receipt of the first payment installment.

Case Study 2: Employment Screening

(1)   Yes. According to the Employee Polygraph Protection Act of 1988, private sector employers are prohibited from using a polygraph to test job applicants except in cases in which the employee will have direct access to controlled substances. Therefore, the hospital can require a polygraph test from prospective pharmacists who would be called upon to dispense controlled substances, but there are restrictions on when and how the test can be given.

(2)   No. Almost all experts agree that single-procedure methods are the least defensible in drug testing. Urine samples that test positive for drug use should be retested using a different procedure.

(3)   OTC cold medications may create a false-positive for amphetamine use; cough syrups containing dextromethorphan can result in a positive test for morphine; herbal tea, aspirin, or poppy seeds may result in a positive test for marijuana. False-positive test results could cause innocent employees to lose their jobs.

(4)   Maria is right. First of all, Alice's statement is wrong; the courts have generally not accepted the argument that submitting a urine sample does not constitute a search or seizure because there is no touching or invasion of the body. In general, they have ruled that a urine sample does constitute a search or seizure, just as a blood sample from an allegedly drunk driver does. Matthew is right in his assumption that he would have more Fourth Amendment protection in the public sector than in the private. However, he is not completely right; the Fourth Amendment prohibits only unreasonable searches and seizures, and employees who knowingly engage in work involving public safety are viewed by the courts as having lesser expectation of privacy. So, Matthew would most likely be confronted with drug testing in a public sector pharmacy as well.

Case Study 3: Partnership

(1)   In a general partnership, all the partners share in the duties, profits, and liabilities. The limited partnership consists of one or more general partners and one or more limited partners. The limited partners have limited liability, usually only to the extent of their dollar investment in the partnership; they usually cannot take an active part in the management and operation of the partnership.

(2)   Wallace and Julia would be jointly liable for the debts of the partnership in those states where the Uniform Partnership Act is in effect. However, the statutes of certain other states hold that the liability of partners for the debts and contract obligations of the partnership is both joint and several. A joint obligation means that all partners in the firm are liable as a group. If an obligation is joint and several, all the partners are liable together and each partner is liable individually for the entire debt or contractual agreement.

(3)   Generally speaking, a partnership is a separate entity, and it may be held liable for the criminal acts of a partner when those acts are committed within the scope of the partnership activity. However, criminal liability will not be imputed to the individual partners unless they have participated in the crime, have knowledge of it, and have consented to it, or have received benefit from it.

(4)   In cases of license violations, if the license is held in the partnership's name, each partner may be held liable for the violation of a copartner when it is committed in the usual course of partnership business. It would not matter whether Wallace had knowledge of Julia's act.

Case Study 4: Forming a Business Corporation

(1) The corporate promoter is the individual who brings about the formation of a business corporation by generating sufficient interest to invest in it. The promoter usually works prior to the formation of the corporation to circulate a capital stock subscription agreement, which binds the signers to purchase stock once the corporation is formed. The incorporator is the individual who executes the articles of incorporation, the initiating document of the corporation. The registered agent is the individual to whom legal papers may be served.

(2) Miguel, as incorporator, will call a meeting of the stock subscribers, who will name the initial board of directors. In some states, the initial board of directors may be named in the articles of incorporation, in which case the subscribers' meeting is bypassed.

(3) Listing the stock without par value gives the corporation more flexibility in that the board of directors is able to establish the stock value for sale purposes.

Answer Key

CIVIL LIABILITY

(1) e

(2) e

(3) d

(4) e

(5) b

(6) e

(7) d

(8) b

(9) c

(10) a

(11) e

(12) b

(13) b

(14) c

(15) e

(16) a

(17) e

(18) c

(19) d

(20) e

(21) c

(22) b

(23) a

(24) c

(25) b

(26) Malpractice is negligence performed by a professional person who, while acting within the scope of his or her profession, has performed in a fashion that is substandard and as a direct result, a person has suffered damages. Malpractice cases are usually subject to rules of evidence and procedure not applicable to allegations of ordinary negligence. The terms "mistake" and "negligence" are sometimes used interchangeably, but in the eye of the law, they are very different. To prove negligence, one must have all four required elements: duty, breach of duty, proximate cause, and damages. Moreover, there must be specified relationships between the facts of the case. Negligence is much more specific than the concept of mistake.

(27) Yes. Normally, the courts will defer to the members of a trade, occupation, or profession to establish the standards of performance in their field. However, if the members of that field allow those standards to slip, the courts will step in and establish standards for them.

(28) The rule known as statutory negligence or negligence per se can be used to establish duty. In order to satisfy the requirements of this doctrine, there must be a statute that

(1) is punitive in nature, that is, one for which an individual may be fined or incarcerated for violating;

(2) is designed to protect an identifiable group of people;

(3) is designed to protect them from an identifiable type of harm; and

(4) establishes an affirmative responsibility on someone to do something.

(29) Birgit is right. The Poison Prevention Packaging Act is a good example of how a statute can be used to establish duty because it:

(1) is punitive in nature (ie, a pharmacist who violates its provisions can be fined or incarcerated)

(2) is designed to protect an identifiable group of people (eg, children less than 5 years of age)

(3) is designed to protect from an identifiable type of harm (eg, from ingestion of dangerous household substances, including prescription drugs)

(4) establishes an affirmative responsibility upon the pharmacist (eg, using child-resistant closures on containers of prescription drugs unless the patient or prescriber requests otherwise).

(30) Overall, 83% of pharmacy lawsuits involve mechanical errors, in which the wrong drugs or wrong strength of drugs are dispensed. The other 17% involve intellectual errors, in which the correct strength of the correct drugs with the correct directions were dispensed, but the pharmacist did something else or failed to do something else that allegedly caused harm to the claimant.

(31) (a) The prescriber is in the best position to fill this role.

(b) Risk management is nonjudgmental, and it occurs after prescribing. Providing information concerning proper drug use and potential problems can lead to more successful therapy and to early recognition of adverse effects. By providing risk management information to a patient, the pharmacist helps to ensure that the patient uses a drug in a manner that maximizes the benefits and minimizes the risks.

(c) No. Because risk management does not result in a decision to forgo drug therapy, it does not interfere with the physician-patient relationship.

(32) This may be because they are applying risk assessment principles to risk management facts, but they also have chosen to deny the existence of a legal duty to warn in the pharmacist-patient relationship. There is a special relationship between pharmacist and patient, just as there is between physician and patient. A party in control has a legal obligation to keep the other from foreseeable harm.

(33) "Good Samaritan" laws establish that a physician, nurse, or other person cannot be civilly liable for negligence in rendering first aid at the scene of an accident.

(34) Generic substitution is the act of dispensing a different brand or an unbranded drug product for the drug product prescribed (ie, chemically the exact drug entity in the same dosage form, but distributed by different companies). Therapeutic alternates are drug products containing different therapeutic moieties but which are of the same pharmacological or therapeutic class and can be expected to have similar therapeutic effects when administered to patients in therapeutically equivalent doses. Therapeutic substitution is the act of dispensing a therapeutic alternate for the drug product prescribed.

(35) (a) Hospitals, HMOs, and third-party payers consider this process to be an aid in cost containment. While many hospital pharmacists have long engaged in therapeutic substitution, it is expected that this type of substitution will increase outside the hospital environment as more third-party payers realize financial benefits even when a single source drug is prescribed, because often a less expensive therapeutic equivalent could be dispensed in its place.

   (b) Research-oriented pharmaceutical manufacturers view therapeutic substitution as an additional threat beyond that presented by generic drug product selection. Pharmacists who wish to exercise their professional expertise in selecting therapeutically equivalent drug products have run head on into lobbyists for the pharmaceutical industry and medical groups who have established a formidable opposition.

   (c) The medical profession believes that therapeutic substitution is a "usurpation of the physician's professional prerogatives." Physicians argue that they are in the best clinical position to make critical decisions regarding a patient's drug therapy because they have access to the patient history, physical exam, and diagnosis.

(36) The hospital formulary system is a method whereby the medical staff of a hospital, working through a pharmacy and therapeutic (P & T) committee, evaluates, appraises, and selects from numerous therapeutic agents and dosage forms those which are considered most useful in the patient population. Under the hospital formulary system, the pharmacist has the authority to select the brand of medication dispensed unless the prescriber makes a specific notation to the contrary.

(37) These variables include the following:
   • The pharmacist must correctly follow the state product selection law (ie, substitute when permitted or required and in the exact manner set forth in the law).
   • The pharmacist must label the prescription so as to indicate whether a therapeutic equivalent or the brand name drug prescribed was dispensed.
   • The pharmacist should properly document whose generic drug was actually dispensed and note the lot number on the prescription document.

(38) The pharmacist can minimize liability exposure by always dispensing the exact brand name drug prescribed unless it is mandatory by state law to substitute a generic drug product. Pharmacists need not avoid performing drug product selection, even if not mandated by law, as long as they provide patients with high-quality pharmaceutical products at costs that benefit the consumer. Pharmacists should select a generic therapeutic equivalent marketed by a reputable manufacturer that has a product liability protection plan extending to the dispenser.

   In Wickline v. State of California, 228 Cal, Rptr. 661, the court noted that cost consciousness has become a permanent failure of the health care system and that cost-limitation programs must not be permitted to corrupt medical judgment. Third-party payers of health care services can be held legally accountable when medically inappropriate decisions result from defects in the design or implementation of cost-containment mechanisms (eg, when appeals made on a patient's behalf are arbitrarily ignored or unreasonably disregarded or overridden). Although the Wickline decision did not involve the practice of pharmacy, it is likely this case will be used by attorneys representing patients who have been injured by health care providers' compliance with cost-containment measures.

(39) Mark's liability would depend on whether his error or misinformation was a mistake in judgment (in contrast with carelessness or inadvertence) and, if it was a mistake in judgment, whether his judgment was reconcilable with the degree of skill and knowledge possessed by other pharmacists.

(40) Direct causation is one of the elements required to successfully establish a claim of professional negligence. This concept states that the breach of the duty must have led directly and without interruption to the damages.

(41) Warranty (expressed or implied) involves the sale of goods, whereas strict liability can exist whether or not a sale has occurred.

(42) Most pharmacists prefer to keep an entire family's medication records on one profile in order to save time and space. However, this practice can lead to embarrassing situations and legal encounters because all family members may have access to one another's medical records. This could cause a problem for minor children who do not wish their parents to know about certain medications they are taking. Other problems could arise between spouses, especially during the dissolution of a marriage or in child custody battles. Pharmacists should consider the possibility of creating separate profiles on each individual in the family, not only to protect a patient's right of privacy but also to improve the ease of monitoring drug therapy.

(43) In the unit dose system, tablet or capsule dosage forms are packaged in single-dose blister wrappers with the name, strength, and lot or control number on the label. In institutional practice, the system has substantially reduced dispensing errors. However, the system is bulky, expensive, and generally suitable only in institutional or hospital pharmacy practice. When hospitals do their own unit-dose packaging, there is the additional risk of mislabeling or misfilling. Therefore, adequate controls and documentation must be maintained to avoid packaging or labeling errors.

(44) This practice helps to reduce error. Somehow it seems to help the pharmacist concentrate better on what he or she is dispensing. In addition, if a question should arise several months or years later involving the prescription, the pharmacist will have no difficulty in identifying the drug dispensed because lot numbers are available from the manufacturer. The lot number can also trace a problem to a bad batch of drug products. Furthermore, Medicare participation standards require the recording of the lot number.

(45) In general, the purchaser must give the seller reasonable notice of the breach prior to commencing the suit. This notice allows the seller time to make necessary arrangements and to govern his or her conduct accordingly.

(46) Jack's admission may be used as grounds for a separate prosecution against him by federal or state authorities because double jeopardy does not attach to civil proceedings. Similarly, a plea of guilty to a drug law violation may subject a pharmacist to a license revocation or suspension action.

(47) No. However, the pharmacist in this situation can seek a postponement for one of the cases.

(48) Administrative agency action may be challenged on the grounds that
(1) the action exceeds the agency's statutory authority or jurisdiction,
(2) the agency has violated due process, or
(3) the decision of the board is clearly erroneous.

(49) (a) In Joanna's case, the board is performing a discretionary function.
(b) In Alan's case, the board is performing a ministerial function.

(50) Pharmacy board regulations must reasonably relate to issues of public health and safety. In a case similar to Alan's (*Board v. Peco*, 198 A. 2d 273), the courts held that such a regulation had no reasonable relationship to public health or safety.

(51) Alan has the following constitutional rights when accused in a pharmacy board disciplinary action:
(1) Right of notice: Alan has the right to be informed of the nature of the action and charges against him.
(2) Right of a hearing: Alan has the right to be heard before an impartial board with the essentials of a fair trial according to established rules.
(3) Right to counsel: Alan has the right to be assisted and represented by an attorney.
(4) Right against self-incrimination: Alan has the right not to be a witness against himself (the right to remain silent).
(5) Right to judicial review: Alan has the right to have a court determine whether the applicable rules of law and procedure have been followed.

(52) The basis for state action in requiring evidence of participation in continuing professional education is the police power of state governments. In order for an administrative agency, such as a board of pharmacy, to be authorized to require and enforce participation in continuing education as a condition for renewal of licensure, that authority must be assigned by the legislature. By using its power to protect the public's health, safety, and welfare, the legislature or pharmacy board may enact statutes or regulations requiring pharmacists to provide proof of continuing education. Although Alan's right to practice his profession is a valuable property right, no person has an absolute right to practice pharmacy or any other profession. Alan has only a conditional right that is subordinate to the police power of the state to protect and preserve the public health.

If Alan chooses to test the legality of mandatory continuing pharmacy education, the outcome might not rest so much on whether the pharmacist's license is a vested right or a personal privilege but whether it can be proven that the mandatory continuing education requirement is necessary to protect the public health and whether it can be determined to what extent a particular mandatory continuing education requirement is reasonable.

(53) The six basic standards and the JCAHO's interpretation of each standard are as follows:
(1) Standard I concerns the staffing of a pharmacy with competent and legally qualified personnel.
(2) Standard II concerns the space and equipment in a pharmacy and the storage of drugs.
(3) Standard III deals with the scope of pharmaceutical services.
(4) Standard IV involves the formulating of written policies and procedures for drug distribution within the hospital.
(5) Standard V treats drug administration policies and requires such policies to be made by the medical staff in cooperation with the pharmacy, nursing, and other departments.
(6) Standard VI requires that the pharmacy department's activities be monitored and evaluated in accordance with the hospital's quality assurance program.

Matching Answers

(1) c

(2) a

(3) d

(4) b

Critical Thinking Activities

(1)   See cases for information.

(2)   See section regarding the code of ethics for pharmacists.

Case Study 1: An Orientation

(1)   Mary, Ian, and Karen are all potentially right. While Karen seems to be hinting at the fact that negligence and a mistake are not the same thing, in cases where negligence is provable, a single act may violate administrative, criminal, and civil laws. In the case of a pharmacist dispensing the wrong drug, the pharmacist could be convicted criminally and could be sued by the patient for civil damages. A third consequence could be suspension or revocation of the pharmacist's license in an administrative action brought by the state for the licensing agency.

(2)   Karen's is a common misperception; it suggests that as long as one opts not to do something, he or she cannot be judged negligent. But Ian is right — one can be negligent in two ways: first, for omitting or failing to do something, and second, for doing something incorrectly.

(3)   The question here is how the plaintiff's attorney might most easily establish duty. In a lawsuit for negligence, the plaintiff could simply present a copy of the poison packaging act to establish negligence per se or statutory negligence. The testimony of professional peers would not be required in this case.

(4)   Mary is correct. Pharmacists must be prepared to face claims of breach of warranty and strict liability in the area of product liability. In such cases, pharmacists have been joined as defendants in the lawsuit not because of their failure to exercise due care in selecting the product, but because they are involved in the chain of the drug's distribution. When pharmacists select a drug product, they are also selecting a potential co-defendant manufacturer, and even though primary responsibility usually rests with the manufacturer, it is possible for the pharmacist to be "left holding the bag" if the manufacturer does not have adequate assets or insurance! Finally, there is even a remote possibility that a pharmacist could face a criminal charge for certain violations involving drug product selection.

Case Study 2: Elements of Negligence

(1)   One classic example of omission and negligence is in the pharmacist's maintenance of patient profiles. A pharmacist who fails to maintain patient profiles is not immune to charges of negligence, despite old popular opinion. Instead, such a pharmacist could be held liable for failure to detect potentially dangerous drug-drug interactions.

(2)   Opinions go both ways on the use of pharmacists who have limited or focused their practices in a way that gives them a special level of expertise. Although duty is ordinarily established or created by one's professional peers, just determining those peers may not be clear-cut. Even without specialization issues, evaluation of professional performance can be problematic, particularly with health professionals. It is not possible to measure the performance of practitioners in easily measured units, other than to have a reputable practitioner of the profession testify about how they would have handled the situation in question. The question of using a specialist when the defendant is not the same sort of specialist may warp the expected standard of performance.

(3)   (a) Irma has made an error of inadvertence.

       (b) She may be found guilty of breach of duty of due care.

(4)   In Cal's case, the manufacturer was sued on the basis of direct causation. In Amy's case, the patient was found to have been contributorily negligent.

(5) This patient has no chance of winning, despite Oscar's dispensing error because no damage was done: She did not use the medication and suffered no ill effects as a result.

Case Study 3: Minimizing Liability

(1) In a case like this, Garcia must decide upon the route of administration himself, based on patient data and knowledge he has of the prescriber's usual preferences. Although these assumptions increase liability exposure, if the patient will suffer from the delay, there is no reasonable alternative.

(2) Ivana should inform both the patient and prescribing physician immediately after discovering the error. In instances when the potential harm from the error is slight, she can inform the prescribing physician without alarming the patient and can simply call the physician for authorization to change the prescription. However, she cannot assume that any error is harmless; the prescriber should always be informed, and where harm may be substantial, the patient should be alerted immediately.

(3) One easy solution can be to tape-record the telephone conversations. As a rule, an individual may lawfully tape-record his or her own telephone conversations unless the purpose is to commit a criminal or injurious act, such as eavesdropping.

Case Study 4: Insurance Issues

(1) (a) Professional liability insurance insures pharmacists against allegations that they failed to exercise reasonable care in the practice of their professional duties. It can also provide all or part of the money to pay damages for an injury caused by the error or malpractice of the pharmacist. Liability insurance can also pay for all the legal costs of defense against a civil suit, even if the claim is fraudulent or without merit. It can provide supplemental coverage of the medical costs for an injury, regardless of fault.

(b) Commercial policies are purchased by employers or self-employed pharmacists to cover the business, pharmacy, or hospital but do not always protect the employed pharmacists. Individual policies do. Which type Maria chooses depends on what type of position she has.

(2) Individual policies are much less expensive than commercial ones. Commercial (business) policies are usually the primary ones, meaning they are the first level of protection and respond first. Individual policies are excess policies which respond after the commercial policy of the employer. Because they are purchased "just in case," they are relatively less expensive. Thus, Maria must be starting her own business or be in a position of authority to purchase commercial insurance, whereas Jamal is most likely currently employed by a pharmacy or hospital that he does not own.

(3) Pharmacists involved in consulting or independent contracting need additional insurance. As the terms are normally used, both are self-employed and need general liability coverage in addition to professional liability coverage. Self-employed consultants may also wish to explore an errors and omissions policy covering financial loss suffered by their clients caused by the pharmacist's alleged negligence.

Abbott Laboratories v. Gardner, 8

Abbott Laboratories v. Portland Retail Druggists Ass'n, 224, **584-585**

Abbott Laboratories; Jefferson County Pharmaceutical Ass'n v., 224, **588**

Abbott Laboratories; Wright v., **512**

Abbreviated New Drug Application (ANDA), 28, 31, 706
  for generics, 52-53, 66

Abbreviations for legal materials, 17

Abortive drugs/devices, 79

Abrams; Pharmaceutical Society v., **602-604**

Abrams; In re Westchester County Pharmaceutical Society v., 603

Abuse of discretion, 8

Acceptance of offer, 197-198

Accident, 550

Accountability audit inspection, 183

Adams v. American Druggist Insurance Co., 278, 284

Adams; Albertson's Inc. v., **350-351**

Addiction
  duty to warn re, 257, 332-333, 412-413
  liability for, 364-367
  opiate, 156-157
  to propoxyphene, 327
  treatments, 156-157

Adequate directions for use, 46, 58, 60, 378
  veterinary drugs, 61, 92-93

Adequate information for its use, 46

Adkins v. Mong, 252, **403-404**

Administration of drugs by pharmacists, 892

Administrative actions, 293-300. See also Boards of pharmacy
  challenges to, 295-299
  procedural and evidentiary rules, 246

Administrative agencies, 6. See also Boards of pharmacy
  authority of, 8-9, 293-294, 612
  exceeding authority/jurisdiction, 295
  FOIA request handling, 9
  powers and duties, 296
  rule changes by, 4
  searches by, 175

Administrative inspections, 176, 745-757
  warrantless, 752-753

Administrative inspection warrants, 176, 177, 183, 185, 187
  cases related to, 750-756

Administrative law, 6, 8-9

Administrative liability, 245-246

Administrative Procedure Acts, 8, 698-699, 711

Adulteration, 27-28, 49, 50, 53-55
  cases related to, 652
  dispensing and, 765-767
  Dotterweich case, 35-36
  exported drugs, 88
  FD&C Act provisions re, 49
  receipt of adulterated drugs, 59
  from repackaging, 35-36, 61

Advance PCS; United Healthcare Insurance Co. & AARP v., **573-574**

Advantage, interference with prospective, 522

Adverse reactions, 256, 332-333. See also Side effects

Advertising, 89-90, 90-91, 666-673. See also Marketing
  bait-and-switch, 231
  as basis of duty, 334-336
  cases related to, 666-673
  of compounded drugs, 700
  compounding services, 84
  to consumer, 90-91
  corrective, 230
  deceptive, 693
  dietary supplements, 707-708
  discounts, 671-673
  false, 90, 91, 230, 679, 692-693
  generic products and, 481-482
  negligent failure to print, 563-564
  as offer, 197
  off-label uses, 694-696
  otc drugs, 91
  overpromotion in, 691-692
  prices, 230-231, 643-644, 666-671
  prohibitions on, 10, 666-667, 690
  reminder, 90
  summary requirements, 90-91

Advocate Health & Hospitals; Williams v., **790**

Aerolone Solution, 39

Aerosols, 39

Aetna US Healthcare; Witt v., **581**

Affidavits, 530-531

Agbogun v. State of Texas, **705**

Age discrimination, 772

Age Discrimination in Employment Act, 208

Agency, law of, 217

AIDS, 212-213, 419

Aircraft, 159

Albany College of Pharmacy; Basile v., **580**

Alberto Culver Co.; Carpenter v., 289, 291

Albertson's; Bloching v., **461-462**

Albertson's Inc. v. Adams, **350-351**

Albertsons' Inc. v. Florida Department of Professional Regulation, **594-597**

Albuquerque Publishing Co.; State v., 755

Alcohol, 109-111
    drug interactions with, 257, 384-387, 413-
    414, 499-500

Alderman Drugs v. Metropolitan Life Insurance Co., **555-556**

Alexis v. GlaxoSmithKline, **529**

Alick's Drugs; Olson v., **773**

Allen v. Rose Park Pharmacy, 207

Allstate Insurance Co. v. Chicago Insurance Co., **475**

ALN Corp. d/b/a Gilbert Pharmacy; United States v., **722-723**

Altieri v. CVS Pharmacy, **477-478**

Alves v. Harvard Pilgrim Health Care, **607-608**

American Druggist Insurance Co.; Adams v., 278, 284

American Drug Stores v. Harvard Pilgrim Health Care, **607**

American Drug Stores; Chiney v., **330-331**

American Drugs; Wal-Mart Stores v., **604**

American Home Products; Kohl v., **527-528, 537**

American Home Products; McKee v., **404-405**

American Home Products Corp.; Batiste v., 275-276, 292, 380, 483

American Home Products Corp.; Foster v., **480-482**

American Medical Association (AMA), 66

American Pharmaceutical Ass'n; Federal Prescription Service, Inc. v., 77, **587- 588**

American Pharmaceutical Association (APhA), 66, 77, 587-588, 770

American Pharmaceutical Services, Inc.; Flores v., **768**

American Pharmacy Association (APhA), 301-302

American Prescription Plan; Preferred Rx v., **569**

American Society of Consultant Pharmacists v. Garner, **576**

American Society of Consultant Pharmacists v. Patla, **576**

American Stores Co.; United States v., 59

Americans with Disabilities Act (ADA), 210-211, 773-778

Amikar v. Drugs for Less, **540-541**

Anabolic steroids, 135, 731-732

Anabolic Steroids Control Act of 1990, 135

Anaeme v. Lovelace Health System, **784**

ANDA. *See* Abbreviated New Drug Application

Andrus; Guillory v., **417-418**

Anile; United States v., 176, 177, 180, **748-749**

Animal drugs, 92-93

Anonymous v. CVS, **419**

Anonymous; People v., 180

Anti-Drug Abuse Act of 1986, 166

Antitrust legislation, 4, 30, 63, 223-229
    cases related to, 584-601
    enforcement of, 229
    exemptions from, 602-604
    mail-order pharmacies and, 76-77

Any willing provider, 228, 583, 599, 606-607

APhA. *See* American Pharmaceutical Association; American Pharmacy Association

Apotex; Glaxo Group v., **711**

Appeals, 11, 14

Appellate courts, 9, 10

Approval process. *See* Drug approval process

Approved drug, 94

Approved Drug Products with Therapeutic Equivalence Evaluations, 70-72

Arbitrary and capricious standard, 8

Arbor Drugs; Baker v., **334, 335, 391**

Arenstein v. California State Board of Pharmacy, **631-632**

Arizona; Miranda v., 185-186

Arkansas Hospital Ass'n v. Arkansas State Board of Pharmacy, **592-593**

Arkansas State Board of Pharmacy v. Fenwick, **731-732**

Arkansas State Board of Pharmacy v. Patrick, **632-634, 664**

Arkansas State Board of Pharmacy v. Whayne, **664**

Arkansas State Board of Pharmacy; Arkansas Hospital Ass'n v., **592-593**

Arline; School Board of Nassau County v., 212

Armed Forces Retirement Home; Dillard v., **768**

Arraignment, 13

Arrest, 13, 179-180, 294
    for refusal of inspection, 184, 187

Articles of incorporation, 219

Assault, 514-515

Assent, mutual, 197-198, 207

Assistants. *See also* Pharmacy technicians
    delegation to, 267-268
    dispensing by, 613-614, 640-641, 662-663, 683-684
    permissible actions, 63, 73, 150, 618-619
    refill authorization, 73

Attorney fees, 552, 609

Attorney-client relationship, 15

Attorneys, 15

Aucoin v. Vicknair, **526-527**

Audits. *See* Inspections

Austermiller v. Dosick, **367-368**

Austin; State v., **664-666**

B*&C Family Center, Inc.; Moore v.,* 103

Baas v. Hoye, **439-440**

Bailey v. Johnson, 367

Baker v. Arbor Drugs, **334, 335, 391**

Baker; State v., 263

Baldridge; Liggett v., 680

Bales v. Wal-Mart Stores, **780-782**

Bancheri; Rudman v., 262

Banner; Norman Bridge Drug Co. v., 138, 180, **724-725**

Burad v. Stadnik, 299

Barber; Fuhs v., 372, **383-384**

Barber; Vuhs v., 257

Barlow v. DeVilbiss, 293

Barlow's Inc.; Marshall v., 175, 180-181, 182, 183, 188, 754

Bartee; United States v., 148

Basile v. Albany College of Pharmacy, **580**

Batiste v. American Home Products Corp., 275-276, 292, 380, 483

Battery, 476-477, 514-515

Bayer; United States v., 188

Bean; Burke v., 255, **346**

Beatty; RNH, Inc. v., **571-572**

Beckwith v. United States, 186

Becton, Dickinson & Co. v. FDA, 189

Beharry v. Mascara, **553**

Bell v. Supermarkets General Corp., **784-786**

Below-cost sales, 231, 604

Bengal v. Board of Pharmacy, 295

Bentex Pharmaceutical, Inc.; Weinberger v., 30

Berg; People v., 676

Bichler v. Willing, 276, 380, 483, **495-496**

Bickowicz v. Sterling Drug, Inc., **364-365**

Bill Lloyd Drug, **728**

Biloxi Regional Medical Center; Saucier v., **427-428**

Bioavailability, 64, 65, 67

Bioequivalence, 31, 33, 679
  consumer knowledge of, 65
  DPCPTRA requirements, 52
  FDA regulations, 67
  Orange Book listings, 71-72

Birth, wrongful, 274, 275

Biswell; United States v., 178, 179, 743, 748, 749, 755

Blatt; Griffith v., **511**

Blazy v. Ohio State Board of Pharmacy, **637**

Bloching v. Albertson's, **461-462**

Blood and blood derivatives, 51

Blue Cross v. Commonwealth, 226, **601-602**

Blue Cross Blue Shield of Tennessee; Reeves-Sain Medical v., **583**

Blue Cross of Western New York; Drug Emporium v., **600**

Board v. Peco, 296

Board; Feldman v., 295

Board of directors, 219-220, 223

Board of Pharmacy; Bengal v., 295

Board of Pharmacy; Herman v., 295

Board of Pharmacy; Hunter v., 295

Board of Pharmacy; Moretti v., 295

Board of Pharmacy; Rayburn v., 296, 298

Board of Pharmacy; Rosenthall v., 295

Board of Pharmacy; Thomas v., 295

Board of Pharmacy; Young v., **677-678**

Board of Pharmacy of State of California; Vermont & 110th Medical Arts Pharmacy v., **623-624**

Board of Pharmacy of State of New Jersey; Rite Aid Corp. v., **610**

Board of Regents of State of New York; McKaba v., 179, **740-741**

Board of Regents of State University of New York; Kramm v., 295

Board of Regents of State University System; Shermack v., **643-644**

Board of Regents of University of New York; Jay v., **639-640**

Board of Regents of University of New York; Moskowitz v., **732-733**

Board of Regents of University of New York; Urowsky v., 670

Boards of pharmacy, 293-295, 609. See also Administrative agencies
  centralized prescription-filling facilities, 892
  civil suits against, 297
  description, 815-817
  disciplinary actions, 298-299
  disciplinary hearings, 295
  drug therapy modification by pharmacists, 892
  electronic reference materials in pharmacy, 893
  immunity of members, 615-616
  inspectors, 186
  membership, 610
  pharmacist workload relief, 893
  physician dispenser regulations, 63-64
  powers and duties, 4, 74, 75, 611-614
  quality improvement requirements, 893
  state lists, 807-811

Bober v. Glaxo Wellcome, **695**

Boeck v. Katz Drug Co., **345-346**

Boller Beverages, Inc. v. Davis, 623

Bookman v. Ciolino, **339-340**

Borchardt v. Department of Commerce, **658**

Borough of Beaver; Hegner Pharmacy v., **660**

Boycotts, 224, 227, 604

Brand Name Prescription Drugs Antitrust Litigation, In re, **597-598**

Brannan v. Wyeth Laboratories, Inc., 206, **760-761**

Breach of contract, 762-764
  anticipatory, 203, 606
  benefit plans, 607-608
  buyer's remedies, 204
  damages for, 203-204
  employment contracts, 760-761
  insurance termination as, 555-556
  sales contract, 203-204
  seller's remedies, 203
  tort liability from, 337-338
  wrongful discharge as, 205

Breach of duty, 247-248, 268-272

Brener v. Diagnostic Center Hospital, 208

Brewer; George v., **792**

Brickell; Hosto v., **755-756**

Bristol-Myers Co. v. Gonzales, 66, **496-497**

Bristol-Myers Squibb Co. v. Shalala, **706**

Brockton Oaks C.V.S. Inc.; Cafaralle v., **397-398**

Brooks v. Wal-Mart Stores, **352-354**

Brown v. Commonwealth of Pennsylvania, **626-627**

Brown v. Glaxo, **457-458**

Brown v. Idaho State Board of Pharmacy, **647-648**

Brown v. Southern Baptist Hospital, **424-426**

Brown v. United States, 262

Brown Morris Pharmacy; Strickland v., **505**

Bruce Church, Inc.; Pike v., 75

Bulk drug products, labeling, 60-61

Bumgarner v. Carlisle Medical, **524-525**

Bumper v. North Carolina, 755

Buprenorphine, 157

Burbank & Jones; Ray v., 263

Burden of proof, 461-464

Burke v. Bean, 255, **346**

Burkes v. Fred's Stores of Tennessee, **547-548**

Burley v. United States Drug Enforcement Administration, **641-642**

Burns; United States v., **720**

Business
  closely regulated, 178, 179, 181, 182, 603
  sale of, 564-566, 582-583

Business Builders, Inc.; United States v., 178, 182

Business law, 197-232
  competition, regulation of, 222-232
  contracts. See Contracts
  employment law. See Employment law
  organization types, 216-222
  sales, 202-204. See also Sale

Business organizations, 216-222

Business, regular course of, 49, 60

Butler v. Louisiana State Board of Education, 264

Bycer; United States v., **737-738**

Bzdzuich v. Drug Enforcement Administration, **726**

Cackowski v. Wal-Mart Stores, **447-448**

Cafaralle v. Brockton Oaks C.V.S. Inc., **397-398**

California Board of Pharmacy; Rosenblatt v., 298-299

California State Board of Pharmacy; Arenstein v., **631-632**

California State Board of Pharmacy; Randle v., 36, 73, **629-630**

California, State of; Wickline v., 260-261

Camara v. Municipal Court, 175, 183, 746

Caperci v. Rite Aid, **764-765**

Caplin; Reisman v., 750

Caraway; Jeans v., **434**

Care, standard of. See Standard of care/conduct

Caremark; Slijepcevich v., **791**

Caremark, Inc.; K. Hefner, Inc. v., **598**

Carey v. Population Services International, **706-707**

Carey; Helling v., 251

Carlisle; United States v., 55, **688-689**

Carlisle Medical; Bumgarner v., **524-525**

Carlos; Schleiter v., 41

Carpenter v. Alberto Culver Co., 289, 291

Carter; Iowa v., **628**

Case law, 5, 16, 17

Causation
  actual cause, 347-348, 428-429
  direct, 272
  expert testimony to establish, 545-555
  intervening causes, 272-273, 368, 436
  negligence, 428-436
  plaintiff's wrongful conduct and, 468-471
  proximate cause, 272-273, 430-435
  unforeseeable consequences, 436

Caustic Poison Act, 53

Cavass v. Off, 298

Cease-and-desist order, 230

Census data, 897-899

Center for Biologics, 70

Center for Veterinary Medicine, 61

Centers for Medicare and Medicaid Services (CMS), 98, 99

Central Merchandise, Inc.; Nichols v., **406**

Centrus Pharmacy Solutions; New York State Teamsters Council Health & Hospital Fund v., **607**

Certiorari, 14, 297

CGMP. See Current Good Manufacturing Practices

Chambers v. G.D. Searle & Co., **496**

Charity Hospital of New Orleans; Hendricks v., **357-358**

Charleston Area Medical Center; Mace v., **782-784**

Charleston Community Memorial Hospital; Darling v., **331-332**

Chemical equivalents, 64

Chemicals
  bulk, 85-86
  listed, 158
  shipment/mailing of, 79

Chesteen v. State, **719**

Chicago Insurance Co.; Allstate Insurance Co. v., **475**

Child Protection Act, 101

Chiney v. American Drug Stores, **330-331**

Ciba Corp. v. Weinberger, 31

Ciba-Geigy; Docken v., 248, **497-498, 543-545**

Ciba-Geigy; Docken v. (1987), 543-544

Ciba-Geigy; Pilet v., **507**

Ciolino; Bookman v., **339-340**

Citations, legal, 15-18

Citizenship, diversity of, 9

City of ... . *See name of city*

Civil law, 5-6

Civil liability, 245-302. *See also* Contracts; Liability; Torts

Civil Rights Act of 1964, 208, 209, 228

Civil trial procedure, 10-13

Clair v. Paris Road Drugs, Inc., **365-367**

Clayton Antitrust Act, 223-224, 225
  enforcement, 229

Clinical pharmacy, 261-262

Clinical trials, 34, 45. *See also* Testing

Clodgo v. Kroger Pharmacy, **546**

CMS (Centers for Medicare and Medicaid Services), 98, 99

Code of Ethics (APA), 770

Code of Ethics for Pharmacists, 301-302

Code of Federal Regulations, 8, 17

Colburn; Winn Dixie of Montgomery v., **445-446**

Collaborative drug therapy management, 62-63

Collaborative practice agreements, 92, 892

Collateral attack, 296

Collier; State v., **721-722**

Collier; United States v., 147

Colonnade Catering v. United States, 178, 179

Colorado, State of; DeCordova v., **473-474**

Commerce Clause, 27, 75, 78, 812

Commerce, interstate. *See* Interstate commerce

Commerce, regulation of, 28, 29

Commissioner of Labor; Gewirtz v., **793**

Committees, legislative, 7

Common law, 4-5, 215, 246

Commonwealth v. Dravaecz, 186

Commonwealth v. Hovious, 675

Commonwealth; Blue Cross v., 226, **601-602**

Commonwealth; Intrieri v., **646**

Commonwealth of Pennsylvania; Brown v., **626-627**

Commonwealth of Pennsylvania, Department of State; Morris v., **625-626**

Community pharmacy, 261

Community pharmacy networks, 228-229

Commuoft Health Investment; Drennan v., **684**

Comparative negligence, 273, 276, 468

Competency, 198-199

Competition, regulation of, 222-232
  FTC's role, 229-232
  refusal to deal, 228-229
  rule of reason, 224
  state laws, 594-597
  unreasonable harm standard, 224

Compliance Policy Guides (CPGs), 61, 81-83, 698-699, 700-701

Compounding by pharmacy/pharmacist, 80-87, 698-701
  bulk, 81, 700
  bulk chemicals, 85-86, 698-699
  controlled substances for, 142
  FD&C Act exemptions re, 33-34, 80-81, 83
  new drugs, 700
  otc products, 85
  PET compounding, 32-33, 87
  regulation of, 80-81, 83

Compounding errors, 368

Comprehensive Drug Abuse Prevention and Control Act, 4, 131, 738

Comprehensive Methamphetamine Control Act of 1996, 158

Computers and computerized systems, 337
  controlled drug records, 142-143
  failure to perform, 556-557

Concord Wrigley Drugs, Inc.; Stebbins v., **401-403, 403**

Conduct, standard of. *See* Standard of care/conduct

Confidentiality, 419-422, 661-662. *See also* Privacy; Privileges
  attorney-client privilege, 15
  breach of, 246
  intrafamily, 267

Confiscation, 757-758. *See also* Seizures

Conglomerate, 229

Connors; Tombari v., 255

Consent
  to contract, 198
  to generic substitution, 65

Consent (cont.)
   implied, 179, 180
   informed, 45, 276
   to inspection or search, 176-180, 183, 184,
     748-749
     cases related to, 740-743, 751-752
     limited, 185
     refusal of, 185
   mutual, 197-198
   prior, 68-69
   to settle, 286
   voluntariness of, 176, 177
Consent orders, 229
Consideration, 198
Consignment sales, 202-203
Consolidated Supermarkets; Thatcher's Drugs v.,
   558-560
Constitutions, 3
Consultants, 286
Consultation. *See* Counseling
Consumer Product Safety Act, 102, 106-107
Consumer Product Safety Commission, 105-106
Containers, commercial, 38, 138, 142
Containers, sealed, 275-276
Contergan, 29-30
Continuing criminal enterprise, 162-163
Continuing education, 299-300
   for lawyers, 19
   requirements, 298, 837-840
Contraceptives, 39, 79, 706-707
Contract law, 6, 553-583
Contracts, 197-202, 288-293. *See also* Leases
   breach of. *See* Breach of contract
   cancellation of, 203-204
   changes to, 560-561
   electronic, 108
   elements of, 570-571
   employment, 204-205, 215, 760-761
   exclusive, 227, 228
   exclusive use agreements, 566-568
   exclusivity clauses, 566-568
   implied, 201, 204-205, 761-764
   of insurance, 283
   interpretation of, 566-568
   managed care agreements, 569
   by minors, 199
   modification of, 201
   mutual assent, 197-198
   noncompetition agreements, 558-560, 566-
     568, 575
   performance, 201
     adequate assurance of, 203
   performance of, 201, 203-204
   privity of, 293
   purpose/object of, 199
   requirements of, 197-199
   sales, 203-204, 288-289
   statute of frauds and, 199-201

Contracts, 197-202, 288-293. *See also* Leases
(cont.)
   types of, 201-202
   validity of, 197-199
   void, 199, 202
   voidable, 202
   writing requirement, 199-200
Contraindications, 401
Contributory negligence, 273, 465-468
Controlled drugs. *See* Controlled substances
Controlled premises, 185
Controlled substance analogs, 134
Controlled substances, 131-166, 713-723
   audits re, 144
   cases related to, 713-759
   compliance with law and regulations, 160
   conflicts of laws re, 759
   containers, 721-722
   DEA inspections, 182-183
   DEA role, 724-726
   dispensing, 136, 139, 147-148
   disposal of excess, 160
   distribution between registrants, 146
   diversion of, 728-730
   in emergency kits, 159
   illegal possession of, 166
   illegal use of, 647-648
   inspections, 740-757
   Internet and, 157-158
   inventory requirements, 735-738
   labeling, 138-139
   medical uses of, 134, 135. *See also* Legitimate
     medical purpose
   methadone, 156-157
   order forms, 140, 144-146
   penalties, 757-758
   polygraph testing for employees with access
     to, 213
   possession of, 888-891
   prescriptions for, 95, 140, 146-157, 726-728
     authority to prescribe, 149
     dating, 154-155
     filling, 154-155, 164-166
     hospital medication orders, 153-154
     manner of issuance, 150
     medical purpose for, 147-149
     quantity, 154
     refilling, 74, 155-156
     refusal to dispense, 150
     Schedule II substances, 150, 151-152, 156
   reclassification of, 720-721, 725-726, 732
   recordkeeping re, 139-146
     centralized systems, 142-143
     contents of records, 139-141
     disposal, 139, 140
     dosage form, 139, 141
     dosage units, 139, 141
     inventory, 139, 141-142
     name, 139, 141
     receipts, 139, 140

Controlled substances, 131-166, 713-723 (cont.)
    strength/concentration, 139, 141
    refills, 72
    return of, 146
    sale without prescription, 155
    schedules of, 133-135. *See also* Scheduled sub-
      stances
    state agencies, 812
    state laws re, 664-666, 759
    storage and security requirements, 159
    theft or loss of, 144
Controlled Substances Act (CSA), 6, 9, 131-133
    authority to prescribe under, 62
    consumer violations of, 166
    DEA guidance re, 131-132
    enforcement of, 161-166
    inspection warrants under, 176-177
    penalties for violation of, 161-163, 166, 757-
      758
    prescription authority, 62
    recordkeeping requirements, 37, 139-146, 726-
      728
    registration requirements, 136-138, 720
    violation of, 161-166, 715-716, 719
Cook County; Farooqui v., **790**
Cooper v. Missouri State Board of Pharmacy, **651-
652**
Copayments, 336, 569, 607-608
Cornell Prescription Pharmacies; Pedreyra v., 209
Corporate promoter, 219
Corporations, 216, 218-222
    formation of, 219-221
    incorporation advantages/disadvantages, 221
    liability of, 35-36, 362-363, 574-575, 631-632,
      674-675
    mergers, 229
Cos v. Laws, 293
Cosmetics, 93
Cost
    containment measures, 260-261
    estimated acquisition cost (EAC), 69
    maximum allowable costs (MAC), 64, 69
    Medicare/Medicaid coverage, 112, 113-114
Cottam v. CVS Pharmacy, **375-376**
Counsel, right to, 298, 653-655
Counseling, 100-101, 252
    accuracy of, 414-415
    duty of, 256-259
    prescribing distinguished from, 262-263
    refusal of, 377-378
    state law requirements, 871-872
Counterfeit drugs, 64
Counterfeit substance, 161
Counterprescribing, 262
Courier services, 79, 160
Courts, 9-14. *See also* Judicial system
    decision citations, 16

Courts, 9-14. *See also* Judicial system (cont.)
    functions of, 460-461
    imposition of duty by, 250-251
    statutory interpretation by, 5, 132, 614
Covenants not to compete, 207, 791-792. *See also*
    Noncompetition agreements
Cox; E.R. Squibb & Sons, Inc. v., **492-493**
Cox Medical Center; Schroeder v., 275, **444-445**
Coyle v. Richardson-Merrell, Inc., **500-501, 502-
503**
Crain v. Eckerd Corp., **525-526**
Crews; VanderLinden v., 297
Crime, conviction of, 625-629
Criminal law, 5-6, 245, 685
Criminal liability, 245
Criminal trial procedure, 13-14
Crippens v. Sav On Drug Stores, **455-457**
Crown Drug Co.; MacKay v., 282, **465-466**
Crown Drug Co.; McKay v., 273
CSA. *See* Controlled Substances Act
Current Good Manufacturing Practices (CGMP),
    48-49, 60-61
    application of, 48-49
    exemptions, 49
    inspections, 182
    manufacturers and, 85
    packaging, 108
    for PET compounding, 87
Custodial interrogation, 185-186
Customary practice, 147, 331-332, 334, 344
CVS; Anonymous v., **419**
CVS New York; Liberatore v., **767**
CVS Pharmacy; Cottam v., **375-376, 477-478**
CVS Pharmacy, In re (1988), **671-672**
CVS Pharmacy, In re (1989), **672-673**
CVS Revco; Vaughn v., **606**
Czarnowski; New York v., **629**

Daley v. Weinberger, 184, **749-750**
Damages, 436-443. *See also* Injunctions and
    injunctive relief
    for antitrust violations, 223, 225-226
    apportionment of, 457-460
    for breach of contract, 203-204
    from breach of duty, 247
    for bystanders, 452-457
    caused by negligence, 248
    compensatory, 245, 443-444
    contractual, 564
    for economic loss, 337
    judgment for, 13
    money, 14, 245, 283
    multiple theories for, 278
    for negligence, 273-275, 436-460
    noneconomic, 441-442

Damages, 436-443. *See also* Injunctions and
injunctive relief (cont.)
  punitive, 246, 274-275, 444-452, 517, 662-
  663
  recovery forms, 457
  substantial, 273-274
  treble, 223, 225-226
Danesh v. Rite Aid Corp., **792**
Daniel; United States v., **720-721**
Daniel Family Pharmacy, **728-729**
Dantonio v. Fontana, **564-566**
Darling v. Charleston Community Memorial Hospital, **331-332**
Dart Industries, Inc.; Hofherr v., **501-502**
Davidson v. Wee, 290-291
Davis v. Katz & Bestoff, Inc., **466-467**
Davis; Boller Beverages, Inc. v., 623
De Anda v. St. Joseph Hospital, 210
De Feese v. United States, 262
DEA. *See* Drug Enforcement Administration
Deal v. Rite-Aid of Alabama, In re, **541**
Death, wrongful, 275
Deceptive trade practices, 230-231, 549, 573-574,
705
Deck v. McBrien, 107
Declaratory judgment, 296
DeCordova v. State of Colorado, **473-474**
Defamation, 215, 246, 422, 508-509
  cases related to, 519-520, 760-761
Defendants, joinder of, 464
Defenses, 523
  in insurance policy, 286, 287
  to negligence claims, 248, 275-277
Delegation, 267-268
  of power, 295
*DeModena d/b/a Sixth Avenue Pharmacy v. Kaiser
Foundation Health Plan, Inc.,* 224, **588-589**
DeMoss Rexall Drugs v. Dobson, **538-539**
Dempsey v. Pease, **552**
Denatured alcohols, 109
DePanfilis v. Pennsylvania State Board of Pharmacy, **616-617**
Department of Commerce; Borchardt v., **658**
*Department of Consumer Affairs; Missouri Hospital
Ass'n v.,* **612**
Department of Health and Human Services
(DHHS), 53
Department of Professional Regulation; Sender v., **656-657**
*Department of Registration & Education; Hofmeister
v.,* **642-643**
Department of Registration & Education; Miller v., **646-647**

Department of Registration & Education; Talman v., 164-165
*Department of Registration & Education of State of
Illinois; Knop v.,* 271-272
Department of Veterans Affairs; Dunn & Ruiz v., **343**
Depositions, 10-12
Derby Center CVS; Polio v., **455**
Derwinski; Marten v., 211
Description, warranty by, 290
Desper; Ohio v., **756-757**
DeStefano; Nefris v., **420**
Detoxification treatment, 156
DeVilbiss; Barlow v., 293
DHHS (Department of Health and Human Services), 53
Diagnosis, 263
Diagnostic Center Hospital; Brener v., 208
Diberardinis-Mason v. Superfresh, **761**
DiDonna; Lewis v., **355**
Diet Drugs Products Liability Litigation, In re, **547**
Dietary Supplement Health and Education Act
of 1994 (DSHEA), 43-44
Dietary supplements, 43-44, 707-709
Diethylstilbestrol, 39-40
Digital Simplistics, Inc.; Rockport Pharmacy Inc. v., **337**
Dillard v. Armed Forces Retirement Home, **768**
Dillon Cos.; Thalos v., **776-777**
DiRe; United States v., 187
Directions for use, 48, 92-93. *See also* Labeling
Direct-to-consumer advertising, 90-91
Disability, 210-212. *See also* Handicap discrimination
Discharge from employment
  for cause, 205-206, 761-764, 773, 790, 795
    for misconduct, 761, 770-771, 793
  discriminatory, 786-788
  manuals, 205, 764
  retaliatory, 210, 765-767, 768-772, 782-784
  wrongful, 206-207
    for compliance with law/regulations, 768-
    770
    for personnel critiques, 772
    for refusal to violate law, 206-207, 770-
    771, 794-795
    for reporting illegalities, 765-767
Disciplinary actions, 298-299, 621-660. *See also*
License revocation; License suspension
  authority for, 659
  conviction of a crime, 625-629
  disciplinary procedures, 637-659
  examination denial, 637
  permit holder, 659
  prior, 624-625

Disciplinary actions, 298-299, 621-660. *See also*
License revocation; License suspension (cont.)
   settlements, 658-659
   unprofessional conduct, 621-625, 673, 677-678
   violation of statute or regulation, 629-636
Discovery, 10-12. *See also* Evidence
   cases related to, 538-542, 547-548
   misconduct in, 449
Discrimination
   age, 772
   AIDS, 212-213
   drug use screening, 214-215
   employment, 208-213
   in employment discharge, 210
   handicap, 210-212, 215, 773-778
   national origin, 786-788
   polygraph testing, 213
   price, 224-225, 584-585, 597-598
   public service obligations, 782-784
   racial, 784-790
   religious, 208, 790
   sex, 209-210, 784-786
   sexual harassment. *See* Sexual harassment
   wage, 209-210
Discriminatory pricing, 581-582
Dispensing, 61-78, 327, 683-684. *See also* Prescriptions
   adulterated drugs, 765-767
   to another practitioner, 146
   authorization, 6, 140, 880-883
   automated, 660-661, 710
   bad faith in, 164-165, 722-723
   controlled substance violations, 161
   controlled substances, 136, 139, 147-148
   expertise in, 328
   failure to dispense, 422
   FD&C Act regulation of, 28, 49
   by hospitals, 153-154, 225, 612
   over Internet, 157-158
   judgment re, 328
   for nonapproved uses, 95
   outdated drugs, 794-795
   by pharmacists, 28
   by physicians, 62, 63-64, 94, 605, 675-676,
     713-714
   prescription drugs. *See* Prescription drugs
   prescription requirements, 28, 61-78
   statutory authority for, 29
   by unlicensed personnel, 592-593, 640-641,
     662-663, 683-684
   as written, 64, 65, 69. *See also* Generic drugs
Dispensing errors, 253-254, 269-270
   concealment of, 346
   discharge from employment based on, 786-
     788
   reducing, 278, 279, 280-283
   wrong dosage or strength, 281-282, 355-359
   wrong drug, 343-355
   wrong labeling or directions, 359-361
   wrong route of administration, 361-362

Distractions, 280, 283
Distributors, 382-383
   wholesale. *See* Wholesale distributors
Diversity jurisdiction, 9
Division of Narcotic Control; 1962 Ford Thunderbird v., **757-758**
Dobson; DeMoss Rexall Drugs v., **538-539**
Docken v. Ciba-Geigy, 248, **497-498, 543-545**
Docken v. Ciba-Geigy (1987), 543-544
Documentation. *See* Recordkeeping
Doe v. Southeastern Pennsylvania Transportation Authority (SEPTA), **520**
Domestic corporation, 218
Dooley v. Everett, **388-389**
Dosage
   exceeding, 39
   form, 139
   labeling re, 48
Dosage equivalents, 695
Dosage units, 139
Dosick; Austermiller v., **367-368**
Dotterweich; United States v., 35-36, 674
Double D Drug; Rothenberg v., **771**
Double jeopardy, 245
Doubt, reasonable, 14
DPCTRA. *See* Drug Price Competition and Patent Term Restoration Act of 1984
Dravaecz; Commonwealth v., 186
Drennan v. Commuoft Health Investment, **684**
Drug
   definition of, 50
   legend. *See* Prescription drugs
Drug abuse. *See* Addiction; Controlled substances; Scheduled substances
Drug Abuse Treatment Act of 2000, 157
Drug accountability audits, 144, 182-183, 187
Drug approval process, 44-48, 52-53
Drug control regulations, state agencies, 858-859
Drug Diversion Act. *See* Prescription Drug Marketing Act of 1987
Drug Efficacy Study Implementation (DESI) project, 32, 70
Drug Emporium v. Blue Cross of Western New York, **600**
Drug Enforcement Administration (DEA), 4, 724-726, 812
   CSA enforcement by, 131-132
   forms, 136, 137, 140
     Form 222, 144-145
   powers, 161, 294, 720, 725-726
   web site, 131-132
Drug Enforcement Administration; Bzdzuich v., **726**
Drug information centers, 265

Drug interactions, 334, 383-393, 410-411, 685
  with alcohol, 257, 384-387, 413-414, 499-500
  duty to detect, 247
  duty to warn of. See Duty to warn
Drug names, 139, 281
Drug Price Competition and Patent Term Restoration Act of 1984, 32, 32-33, 52-53, 66, 70, 71
Drug product identification, 96
Drug product selection, 64-69, 259-262, 679
  defined, 66
  errors in, 271
  state laws re, 70, 860-861
  warranty and, 292
Drug Product Selection Act, 64, 65
Drug products. See Pharmaceuticals
Drug sample. See Samples
Drug use review programs, 100
Drug use screening, 214-215
Drugs for Less; Amikar v., **540-541**
DSHEA. See Dietary Supplement Health and Education Act of 1994
Duckworth v. State Board of Pharmacy, **652-653**
Duda, 646
Due process, 295, 652-653, 655-656
Duensing v. Huscher, 272, **662-663**
Duggan Drug Stores, Inc.; United States v., 137, **362-363**
Dunaway Drug Stores; Georgia State Board of Dispensing Opticians v., **709**
Dunn & Ruiz v. Department of Veterans Affairs, **343**
Durable power of attorney, 15
Durham-Humphrey Amendment, 29, 32, 55
Dutton Drugs, Inc.; State v., **462-463**
Duty, 248-268, 323-338. See also Duty of care; Duty to warn; Negligence
  of administrative agencies, 296
  changes to, 253
  court-imposed, 250-251
  delegation of, 268
  existence of, 327-334
  general, 256
  imputed, 423-426
  independent, 410
  limitations on, 427-428
  to nonpatient, 387-388
  rules re, 254-255
  specific, 256-268, 338-423
  statutory, 101, 252
  voluntary assumption of, 334-336
Duty of care, 247, 256
  breach of, 247-248, 268-272
  creation of, 513
  general, 330-331
  specific, 331

Duty of care, 247, 256 (cont.)
  voluntary assumption of, 334-336
Duty to avoid or prevent injury, 333
Duty to warn, 252, 256-259, 334-336. See also Warnings
  addiction potential, 332-333, 412-413
  adverse reaction monitoring, 410-411
  after-acquired knowledge of risk, 477
  allergies, 414-416
  birth defects, 406, 431-433, 512-513
  breach of, 271
  cases related to, 372-377
  contraindications, 401, 414-416, 434
  drug interactions, 257, 330-331, 333, 334-336, 383-393
  drug-disease contraindications, 405-406
  excessive dosage, 393-401
  foreseeability of injury, 387
  limitations on, 401-408
  manufacturers', 256, 486-494, 508-509
  physicians', 256
  of potential problems, 375-376, 411
  prescription drug dangers, 359-360
  prescription errors, 361-362
  of side effects, 378-383, 401-403, 406-408, 486-494
  standard of care/conduct re, 543-545
  unauthorized users, 407-408

East Jefferson General Hospital; Gassen v., **361-362**
East Jefferson General Hospital; Glassen v., 529
Eckerd; Sanderson v., **335**
Eckerd Corp.; Crain v., **525-526**
Eckerd Corp.; Sheils v., **534-535**
Education, 580-581
  continuing. See Continuing education
  patient, 228, 256. See also Counseling
  professional, 251, 252
Efficacy, 32, 50
  testing, 66
  veterinary pharmaceuticals, 92
Eldridge v. Eli Lilly & Co., 391, 404
Electronic/digital signatures, 108, 151. See also E-Sign
Electronic transmission (computer-to-computer)
  of prescriptions, 72, 869-870
Eli Lilly; Zeneca v., **692-693**
Eli Lilly & Co. v. Natural Answers, **712**
Eli Lilly & Co.; Eldridge v., 391, 404
Ellingsen v. Walgreen, **530-531**
Elsroth v. Johnson & Johnson, **478-479**
Ely; Reben v., 265, **438-439**
Ely; Stolfa v., **539-540**
Emergency kits, 159
Emotional distress, 246
  of corporate officers, 563-564

Emotional distress, 246 (cont.)
 intentional infliction of, 518-519
 negligent infliction of, 452-457
Empire State Pharmaceutical Society, Inc. v. Perales, **557-558**
Employee Polygraph Protection Act of 1988, 213
Employee Retirement Income Security Act (ERISA), 4, 606-608
Employees, 426
Employers
 insurance coverage, 283-284
 liability, 35-37, 50, 630, 662-663
Employment at will, 204-207, 762-763, 768-770
 cases related to, 761-770
 public policy exception, 761, 763, 766-767
Employment Department; Kaib's Roving R.Ph. Agency, Inc. v., **791**
Employment law, 204-215, 760-796
 breach of promise, 762-763
 cases related to, 760-796
 contracts, 204-205, 215, 760-761
 contractual issues
  breach of contract, 762-764
  express contract, 760-761
  implied contract, 761-764
  public policy retaliation, 768-772
  termination at will, 761-764
  termination for cause, 760-761
  whistleblowing, 765-767
 covenants not to compete, 207, 791. *See also* Noncompetition agreements
 discharge. *See* Discharge from employment
 discrimination laws, 208-213. *See also* Discrimination
 drug use screening, 214-215
 employment at will doctrine, 204-205, 207, 763
 overtime pay, 764-765, 792-793
 polygraph testing, 213
 workers' compensation, 215
Employment Security Department of State of Washington; Park v., **793-794**
Enserro; United States v., 177, **742-743, 752**
Entrapment, 632-633, 675
Entry, right of, 176. *See also* Inspections; Warrants
Equal Employment Opportunity Act of 1972, 208
Equal Employment Opportunity Commission (EEOC), 208, 778
Equal Pay Act of 1963, 209
Equity, 5, 297
E.R. Squibb & Sons; Hill v., 476, **490**
E.R. Squibb & Sons, Inc. v. Cox, **492-493**
E.R. Squibb & Sons, Inc.; Murphy v., **482-484**
ERISA. *See* Employee Retirement Income Security Act
Erwin v. Methodist Hospital, **795**

E-Sign, 108, 139, 151
Estinyl, 40
Estoppel, 201, 559, 762-763
Estrogens, 39-41
Ethics, 3
 codes of, 252-253, 301-302, 770
Ethyl alcohol, 109
Evans v. Rite-Aid Corp., **422, 661**
Everett; Dooley v., **388-389**
Evers; United States v., 95, **696-698**
Evidence, 12, 552
 admissibility standards, 398-400, 460, 678
 of claim elements, 248
 collection of, 750-751
 of crime, 750-751, 752-753, 756
 at hearings, 617
 illegally obtained, 177-178
 of negligence, 460-464
 oral, 200
 physical, 12
 plea as, 631-632
 proof standards, 13, 14, 245-246, 461-464. *See also* Burden of proof
 records as, 639-640
 sufficiency of, 428-429
Examination requirements, 637, 818-819
Exclusionary rule, 173-174
Exclusive contracts, 227, 228
Exclusive use agreements, 566-568
Executive branch of government, 7, 8-9
Executory contract, 201
Exhaustion, 8
Expert witnesses, 12, 249, 531
 cases related to, 542-550
 standard-of-care testimony, 248, 543-545
Expiration date, 80
Exporting, 87-89, 131
Express contract, 201, 760-761
Express Scripts v. Wenzel, **606**

Facsimile transmission of prescriptions, 72, 152, 866-868
Fact witnesses, 12
Fair Labor Standards Act, 764-765, 792-793
Fair Packaging and Labeling Act, 46
Fakhouri v. Taylor, **409-410**
False advertising, 90, 91, 230, 679, 692-693
False imprisonment, 515-518, 519
Falsehood, injurious, 521-522
Farooqui v. Cook County, **790**
Farr; Ramon v., **463-464**
Faryl's Pharmacy; Sullivan's Wholesale Drug Co. v., **562-563**
FD&C Act. *See* Food, Drug, and Cosmetic Act

FDA. *See* Food and Drug Administration

FDA; *Becton, Dickinson & Co. v.*, 189

FDAMA. *See* Food and Drug Administration Modernization Act of 1997

Federal Anti-Tampering Act, 107-108

Federal Caustic Poison Act (1927), 101, 102, 104

Federal Comprehensive Drug Abuse Prevention and Control Act, 131

Federal courts, 9-14, 16, 17

Federal Food, Drug, and Cosmetic Act. *See* Food, Drug, and Cosmetic Act

Federal Food, Drug, and Cosmetic Act (1938), 28

Federal government, 6-15
  powers, 4, 27

Federal Hazardous Substances Act, 101-103, 106

Federal Hazardous Substances Labeling Act, 101

Federal HMO Act, 115-116

Federal Insecticide, Fungicide, and Rodenticide Act, 102

Federal laws, 4, 75, 812. *See also* Statutes
  antitrust. *See* Antitrust legislation
  pre-emption by. *See* Pre-emption

Federal legend, 60

Federal Prescription Service, Inc. v. American Pharmaceutical Ass'n, 77, **587- 588**

Federal Register, 17

Federal Trade Commission (FTC), 228, 229

Federal Trade Commission Act, 229, 601

Feldman v. Board, 295

Feliciano; National Pharmacies v., **682**

Feliciano; Walgreen v., **682-683**

Fenwick; Arkansas State Board of Pharmacy v., **731- 732**

Ferguson v. Williams, 335, **414-415**

Fireman's Insurance Co. of New Jersey; Schwamb v., 286

First amendment. *See* Freedom of speech

Fisher v. Walgreens Louisiana, **536-537**

Fitness for purpose. *See* Warranty

Flores v. American Pharmaceutical Services, Inc., **768**

Florida Board of Pharmacy v. Webb's City, Inc., **667**

Florida Board of Pharmacy; Schwartz v., **638-639**

Florida Department of Professional Regulation; Albertsons' Inc. v., **594-597**

Florida State Board of Dentistry; Richardson v., 146, 147

Florida, State of; Olson v., 179, **742, 752**

Fontana; Dantonio v., **564-566**

Fontenot; Wainwright v., **443**

Food and Drug Administration (FDA), 8, 53, 812
  approvals by, 30, 34, 44-48
  authority of, 30, 31, 46, 50
  drug regulation, 132
  enforcement responsibilities, 49, 53, 294
  fast-track approval, 34
  fees charged, 33
  forms, 44
  inspection powers, 50, 182
  labeling requirements. *See* Labeling
  regulatory actions, 84

Food and Drug Administration Modernization Act of 1997 (FDAMA), 32, 33-36, 83-85, 694- 695, 700

Food, Drug, and Cosmetic Act (FD&C Act), 4, 6, 27-50
  1938 Act, 688
  amendments to, 29-30, 32-35, 688
  authority to prescribe under, 61-62
  background of, 27-28
  cases related to, 688-713
  efficacy proof, 30-32
  enforcement of, 49, 53
  exemptions from, 30, 83
  FDA inspections under, 182
  human drug regulation, 688-713
    compounding, 698-701
    dietary supplements, 707-709
    generic drugs, 705-706
    insulin, 704
    labeling, 701-704
    marketing of drugs, 691-696
    medical devices, 709
    misbranding, 688-689
    new drugs, 690
    nonprescription drugs, 706-707
    patents, 710-711
    personal use exemption, 712-713
    production of drugs, 690-691
    trademarks, 712
    unlabeled indications, 696-698
  liability under, 35
  manufacturing practices under, 49
  purposes, 49-50
  recordkeeping requirements, 37-39
  safety proof, 28, 30-32
  scope of, 46

Foods, regulation of, 43

Foreign corporation, 218

Forklift Systems, Inc.; Harris v., 209

Formulary standard, variation from, 28

Foster v. American Home Products Corp., **480- 482**

Fountain v. Oelshelgel, **637-638**

Fourth Amendment, 175, 180, 214-215,.740-745

Fowlkes; Richmond v., **580-581**

France v. State of New York, **368-369**

Franchisers, 501-502

Fraud, 198, 199, 535-536, 571-574
   disability claims, 572-573
   Medicaid, 114, 616-617, 649-650, 651-652
   Medicare, 114, 572
   re prescriptions, 732-735
   pricing and, 581-582
Fred's Stores of Tennessee; Burkes v., **547-548**
Freedom of choice laws, 227, 228, 598
Freedom of Information Act (FOIA), 9
Freedom of speech, 10, 668-671. *See also* Advertising
   commercial speech, 84, 89-90, 600, 670, 690
   FDAMA and, 89-90, 694-695, 700-701
   off-label treatment information, 34-35
French Drug Co., Inc. v. Jones, 255, **348-349**
Friedman; Washington Legal Foundation v., 694
Frost; Gorden v., **518-519**
Frye v. Medicare-Glaser Corp. (1992), 335, 373, **386-387, 390-391**
Frye v. Medicare-Glaser Corp. (1991), 386, **390-391**
FTC (Federal Trade Commission), 228, 229
FTC; *Novartis v.*, **693**
Fuhs v. Barber, 372, **383-384**
Fultz v. Peart, **458-460**

Galen Hospital; *Payne v.*, **400-401, 795-796**
Gardner; Abbott Laboratories v., 8
Garner; American Society of Consultant Pharmacists v., **576**
Garner; Southwest Drug Stores of Mississippi, Inc. v., **519-520**
Garrard Drugs; Lemire v., 293, **551**
Garrigus & Block; Nevada State Board of Pharmacy v., **621**
Gassen v. East Jefferson General Hospital, **361-362**
Gaston Drugs, Inc. v. Metropolitan Life Insurance Co., **554**
G.D. Searle & Co.; Chambers v., **496**
GDF; Providence Square v., **575**
General partnerships, 217
Generic drugs
   adoption of brand's representations, 481
   approval of, 32-33, 52-53
   cases related to, 705-706
   equivalency, 53, 481, 693
   interchange impropriety, 445-446
   laws promoting, 230
   marketing, 33, 66
   new drug status of, 30-31
   packaging, 281-282
   patents and, 711
   quality of, 66-67
   substitution of, 53, 64-72, 260, 260-261
      consumer consent to, 65

Generic drugs (cont.)
   labeling, 705-706
   liability re, 64-66, 292
   mandatory, 64, 260-261, 338
   therapeutic substitution, 66, 68
Generix Drug Corp.; United States v., 31
Gennock v. Warner-Lambert, **530**
George v. Brewer, **792**
Georgia Osteopathic Hospital v. O'Neal, **410-411**
Georgia State Board of Dispensing Opticians v. Dunaway Drug Stores, **709**
Gewirtz v. Commissioner of Labor, **793**
Gewirtz, In re, **793**
Gibson; Jacobs Pharmacy Co. v., 289
Givens v. Lederle, 490
Glassen v. East Jefferson General Hospital, 529
Glastonbury Towne Pharmacy; Reliable Refuse & Recycling v., **570-571**
Glaxo; Brown v., **457-458**
Glaxo Group v. Apotex, **711**
Glaxo Wellcome; Bober v., **695**
GlaxoSmithKline; Alexis v., **529**
Glossary, 799-805
Goldfine; United States v., 186, 188, **750-751**
Gonzales; Bristol-Myers Co. v., 66, **496-497**
Goods, title to, 203
Gorden v. Frost, **518-519**
Government, role of, 3
Governmental inspections, 176. *See also* Inspections; Pharmacy inspection
Grand jury, 13
Grand Union Co.; Kalman v., 206, **768-770**
Grandfather clause, 28, 30
Green Drugs; United States v., **726-727**
Greenberg; United States v., 176, **747, 748**
Greenblatt v. New Jersey Board of Pharmacy, 179, 188
Greenwald v. LeMon, **582-583**
Gregerson's Foods, Inc.; Moman v., **778-780**
Griffin v. Phar-Mor, **535-536**
Griffith v. Blatt, **511**
Grooming aids, 93
Group Health Plan, Inc.; Grouse v., 205
Group Life & Health Insurance Co. v. Royal Drug Co., 226-227, **585-587**
Grouse v. Group Health Plan, Inc., 205
Guarantees
   re misbranding/adulteration, 36, 59
   re otc drugs, 48
Guillory v. Andrus, **417-418**
Gumbhir v. Kansas State Board of Pharmacy, **619-620**

Guzzo; R.T. Cornell Pharmacy, Inc. v., **556-557**

Haas; United States v., **712-713**

Hacker; Martin v., **382-383**

Hale; United States v., 186, 188

Hamilton v. Hardy, 490

Hand v. Krakowski, 257, 258, 394, 402, **413-414**

Handicap discrimination, 210-212, 215, 773-778

Hannigan v. Sundby Pharmacy, **420-421**

Happel v. Wal-Mart Stores, **415-416**

Harco Drugs v. Holloway, 275, **341-342**

Hardy; Hamilton v., 490

Harold Donald Henry; United States v., **730**

Harrington v. Montgomery Drug Co., 291

Harris v. Forklift Systems, Inc., 209

Harrison Narcotic Act (1914), 28, 131

Harrow v. Prudential Insurance Co. of America, **570**

Harvard Pilgrim Health Care; Alves v., **607-608**

Harvard Pilgrim Health Care; American Drug Stores v., **607**

Hatten v. Price, **442**

Haver; Mutual Benefit Insurance v., **475**

Hay; Johnson v., **369-371**

Hayes; United States v., 147, 164, 165, 635

Hazardous substances, 102

Hazra v. National Rx Services, Inc., **786-788**

Health care practitioner, 89

Health Care Quality Improvement Act of 1986, 114

Health insurance, 97-98. See also Medicare

Health Insurance Portability and Accountability Act of 1996 (HIPAA), 97-99

Health maintenance organizations (HMOs), 115-116, 227, 606
    pricing and contracts, 227-228

Healthscript v. State, **686**

Healthy People 2000 objectives, 41

Hearings
    disciplinary, 295
    evidence in, 617
    preliminary (criminal), 13
    right to, 298
    timing of, 638-639

Hearsay rule, 639-640

Heath; State v., **649-650**

Heckler; Memorial Hospital/Adair County v., **589-590**

Hegner Pharmacy v. Borough of Beaver, **660**

Heller, In re, **622-623**

Helling v. Carey, 251

Hendricks v. Charity Hospital of New Orleans, 357-358

Henney; Mylan Pharmaceuticals v., **711**

Henney; Washington Legal Foundation v., 89, **694-695**

Henney; Watson Pharmaceuticals v., **710**

Henney; Western States v., 34

Henry; United States v., **730**

Henry's Drug Store; Pysz v., 257, 404, **412-413**

Heredia v. Johnson, **503-504**

Herman v. Board of Pharmacy, 295

Herman v. Smith Kline & French Laboratories, 293

Hill v. E.R. Squibb & Sons, 476, **490**

Hinze; Nebraska, State of v., **650-651**

HIPAA (Health Insurance Portability and Accountability Act of 1996), 97-99

HMOs. See Health maintenance organizations

Hoar v. Rasmussen, 256, **343-344**

Hobrecht; Malone & Hyde, Inc. v., **436-438**

Hoffman-LaRoche v. Weinberger, 31

Hoffman-LaRoche, Inc.; Woolley v., 205

Hofherr v. Dart Industries, Inc., **501-502**

Hofmeister v. Department of Registration & Education, **642-643**

Holbrook v. Rose, 278, **428-429**

Hollarnd; Walls v., **371**

Holloway; Harco Drugs v., 275, **341-342**

Hood; Walgreen v., **577**

Hook's Drugs, Inc.; Ingram v., 258, 328, **378-381**

Hook-SupeRx Inc.; McLaughlin v., **327-329**

Hook-SupeRx Inc.; Rodgers v., **514-515**

Hooper v. Perry Drugs, **391-392**

Hooper v. Thrifty Payless, **377-378**

Horizontal merger, 229

Horner v. Spalitto, **400**

Hospital formularies, 68, 69

Hospital medication orders, 153-154

Hospital pharmacies, 113, 270-271, 300-301
    controlled drug records, 140
    retail, 613
    unit-dose packaging by, 278-279

Hospitals
    accreditation standards, 300-301
    controlled drug dispensing by, 153-154
    liability of, 331-332
    Medicare participation, 112-113

Hosto v. Brickell, **755-756**

Houston; Pennsylvania Pharmacists Ass'n v., **576-577**

Hovious; Commonwealth v., 675

Howard University; Park v., 778

Howell; Jones v., **577-578**

Hoye; Baas v., **439-440**

Hueseman; Malon v., **658-659**

Huggins v. Longs Drug Stores, 252, **452-453**

Huggins v. Longs Drug Stores California, Inc., **454**

Hughes; United States v., **730-731**

Human drugs, regulation of, 688-713. *See also* Regulation of pharmaceuticals

Hundley v. Rite-Aid of South Carolina, **449-450**

Hunter v. Board of Pharmacy, 295

Huscher; Duensing v., 272, **662-663**

Hutchinson; Kinney v. (1985), 385

Hutchinson; Kinney v. (1984), 380, 384-385

Hutton; State v., **686-687**

Hynson, Wescott & Dunning; Weinberger v., 30

Idaho State Board of Pharmacy; Brown v., **647-648**

Immorality, gross, 637-638, 642-643, 646-647

Immunity
    grant of, 641-642
    of pharmacy board members, 615-616
    sovereign/governmental, 297, 471-474
    state recovery limits, 473-474

Implied consent, 179, 180

Implied contract, 201, 204-205, 761-764

Implied warranty, 59, 278, 290, 292-293, 409

Import Drug Act of 1848, 27

Importing, 88-89, 712-713
    controlled substances, 131, 158
    reimportation, 50, 51

Imprinting, 96

Imprisonment, false, 515-518, 519

In personam jurisdiction, 16

In rem jurisdiction, 16

In re ... . See name of party

Inadvertence, 269

Incorporator, 219

IND. *See* Investigational New Drug

Independent contractors, 286, 791

Indictment, 13, 715-716

Individual practitioner, 139, 147, 149

Inexperience, 269

Infliction of mental distress, 518-519

Information distribution, 40. *See also* Labeling; Package inserts

Information for use, 48. *See also* Directions for use; Labeling

Informed consent, 45, 276

Ingraham; Roe v., **716-717**

Ingram v. Hook's Drugs, Inc., 258, 328, **378-381**

Injectables, 80

Injunctions and injunctive relief, 5, 246, 294, 547-548
    violation of, 650-651

Injurious falsehood, 246, 521-522

Innovation, 251

Inspection warrants, 747. *See also* Search warrants; Warrants

Inspections, 50, 740-757
    administrative, 176, 745-757
    CGMP regulations and, 48, 49
    court orders prohibiting, 749-750
    Fourth Amendment issues, 740-745
    pharmacy. *See* Pharmacy inspection

Insulin, 704

Insurance
    antitrust laws and, 227, 585-587, 601-602
    audits, 554
    conditions, 287
    coverage, 284-285, 286-287, 550-551
    defenses clauses, 286, 287
    definitions in policy, 285
    exclusions, 286-287
    health, 97-98. *See also* Medicare
    malpractice, 253, 286, 475
    notice of claim, 288
    occurrence vs. claims-made basis, 284-285
    participating providers, 555-556, 583
    prescription drug programs, 4
    pricing and, 581-582
    prior acts coverage, 285
    professional liability, 283-288
    settlement clauses, 286
    specialty policies, 285
    types of clauses, 285-288

Insurance Commissioner of Maryland; Lubman v., **560-561**

Intellectual errors, 253-254, 269, 271-272

Intended use, 50-61

Intent, 50, 162-163, 245, 246

Intentional torts, 246, 514-523
    defamation. *See* Defamation
    defenses, 523
    false imprisonment, 515-518, 519
    infliction of mental distress, 518-519
    injurious falsehood, 246, 521-522
    interference with prospective advantage, 522
    interference with the person, 514
    invasion of privacy. *See* Privacy
    libel and slander, 246, 520
    malicious prosecution, 521
    outrageous conduct, 519
    slander, 246, 266, 520

Interactivity, warnings re, 333

Interference with business relationship, 563, 605

Interference with prospective advantage, 522

Interference with the person, 514

Internet
    controlled substances and, 157-158
    FDAMA information on, 33
    legal information on, 17
    sales via, 443-444. *See also* Mail order

Interns
    hours required, 820-823
    registration, 824-825
Internship hours, 820-823
Interrogatories, 12
Interstate commerce, 27, 29, 75-76, 812
    advertising and, 91
    burden on, 75-76, 77-78, 595-596
    compounded products in, 83
    drugs in, 53, 85-86, 95, 131
    employment law application to industry in,
        208
Intrieri v. Commonwealth, 646
Invasion of privacy. See Privacy
Inventories, 37, 139, 141-142
    cases related to, 735-738
Investigational New Drug (IND), 44-45, 94-95,
    104
Invitees, 428
Iowa v. Carter, 628
Iowa Board of Pharmacy Examiners; Sloman v.,
    634-635
Ipecac, 96
Irvin; Jones v., 393-394
Irvine Drugs; Pressler v., 441-442
Irwin; Jones v., 257-258
Isopropyl alcohol, 110
Isuprel Hydrochloride Solution, 39
IV Services of America; Shiffrin v., 421

Jack Eckerd Corp. v. Smith, 516
Jack Eckerd Corp.; Walker v., 101, 396-397
Jack Eckerd Corp.; Wimm v., 359-360
Jack Edgar Burns; United States v., 720
Jacobs Pharmacy Co. v. Gibson, 289
James David Daniel; United States v., 720-721
January v. Peace, 433-434
Jay v. Board of Regents of University of New York,
    639-640
JCAHO. See Joint Commission on the Accredita-
    tion of Healthcare Organizations
Jeans v. Caraway, 434
Jefferson County Pharmaceutical Ass'n v. Abbott
    Laboratories, 224, 588
Johnson v. Hay, 369-371
Johnson v. Walgreen Co., 252, 335, 392
Johnson; Bailey v., 367
Johnson; Heredia v., 503-504
Johnson; Laws v., 509-511
Johnson; Taylor v., 515-516
Johnson & Johnson; Elsroth v., 478-479
Joinder, fraudulent, 525-530
Joinder, improper, 528

Joint Commission on the Accreditation of Health-
    care Organizations (JCAHO), 300-301
Jones v. Howell, 577-578
Jones v. Irvin, 393-394
Jones v. Irwin, 257-258
Jones v. Walgreen Co., 266, 356-357, 394
Jones; French Drug Co., Inc. v., 255, 348-349
Judgment, 13, 14
Judicial law, 5
Judicial review, 8, 296, 297-298
Judicial system, 9-14, 524
Jurisdiction, 9, 16, 524-530
Jury, 10, 14, 249, 460-461
    instructions to, 13, 348-349
    selection of, 12
Justice Department (U.S.), 229

K. Hefner, Inc. v. Caremark, Inc., 598
Kaib's Roving R.Ph. Agency, Inc. v. Employment
    Department, 791
Kaiser Foundation Health Plan, Inc.; DeModena
    d/b/a Sixth Avenue Pharmacy v., 224, 588-589
Kaiser Foundation Health Plan of the Mid-Atlantic
    States; Nichols v., 545-546
Kalman v. Grand Union Co., 206, 768-770
Kansas State Board of Pharmacy v. Wilson, 611
Kansas State Board of Pharmacy; Gumbhir v., 619-
    620
Kasin v. Osco Drug Co., 335
Kasin v. Osco Drugs, 373
Kaspirowitz v. Schering Corp., 486
Katz & Bestoff, Inc.; Davis v., 466-467
Katz Drug Co.; Boeck v., 345-346
Kefauver-Harris Amendment, 30, 32, 52
Kershman; United States v., 163
Kevadon, 30
Key Enterprises v. Venice Hospital (1990), 592-
    593
Key Enterprises of Delaware v. Venice Hospital
    (1989), 590-592
Key Pharmaceuticals; Young v., 542-543
Kick-backs, 114, 562-563, 646-647
Kim; United States v., 685
Kimball; Tremblay v., 255-256, 271
King; Silves v., 392-393
Kingery; Patterson Drug Co. v., 667-669
Kinney v. Hutchinson (1985), 380, 385
Kinney v. Hutchinson (1984), 384-385
Kirk v. Michael Reese Hospital & Medical Center,
    387-388, 390, 499-500, 508
Kirk v. Porter Drug Store, 418
Kirkwood Drug Store Co.; Welkener v., 484-485

Kiser; Spry v., 65

Klingel's Pharmacy v. Sharp & Dohme, 228

Klingenstein v. State of Maryland, **745**

K-Mart; Van Hatem v., **460-461**

K-Mart Corp.; Perkins v., **772**

Knickrehm; Wal-Mart Stores v., **577**

Knoll Pharmaceutical v. Sherman, **690**

Knop v. Department of Registration & Education of State of Illinois, 271-272

Knowingly, 163

Knutson, Krueger v., 257, **372-373**

Koderick v. Snyder Bros. Drug, Inc., 248, **533-534**

Kohl v. American Home Products, **527-528, 537**

Kollenberg v. Ramirez, **521-522**

Krakowski; Hand v., 257, 258, 394, 402, **413-414**

Kramm v. Board of Regents of State University of New York, 295

Kroger Pharmacy; Clodgo v., **546**

Krueger v. Knutson, 257, **372-373**

Krug v. Sterling Drug, Inc., **486-487**

KV Pharmaceutical v. Missouri State Board of Pharmacy, **690-691**

Label, 46

Labeling, 46. See also Misbranding; Packaging; Warnings
    adequate directions for use. See Adequate directions for use
    bulk chemicals, 86
    bulk drug products, 60-61
    cases related to, 685, 701-704
    claims in, 38
    commercial containers, 38
    compounded products, 86
    consumer packaging, 46
    controlled substances, 138-139
    customized medication packages, 43
    dietary supplements, 44
    disease claims, 44
    Drug Facts panel, 47
    expiration date, 80
    FD&C Act/FDA provisions re, 34, 38, 46-48
    generic products, 481, 705-706
    habit-forming drugs, 34
    hazardous substances, 102-103, 107
    inpatient, 280
    ipecac, 96
    liability for, 291-292
    manufacturer's/distributor's container, 38
    MedGuide rules, 41-42
    mislabeling. See Misbranding
    NDC in, 38
    negligence in, 492-493
    otc drugs, 46-48, 49, 291-292
    package inserts, 38-39
    patient package inserts, 39-43

Labeling, 46. See also Misbranding; Packaging; Warnings (cont.)
    patient-directed, 702-704
    by physician dispensers, 63
    physician requirements, 63
    poisons, 104-105
    prescription drugs, 46, 48, 49, 58, 60
    promotional, 90. See also Advertising
    proposed, 45
    relabeling, 48-49
    repackaging and, 48, 60-61
    special, 46
    state/local requirements, 107, 259
    structure/function claims, 44
    truthfulness in, 46
    unapproved/nonapproved uses, 94, 95
    unit-dose, 42-43, 61, 80
    veterinary drugs, 46, 61
    violations, 28

Labeling errors, 270-271, 281

LaGarde; Tarlton v., 266

Langford v. Rite-Aid of Alabama, **581-582**

Lanham Act, 599-600

Lannett Co.; United States v., 31

Lasley v. Shrake's Country Club Pharmacy, Inc., 253, **332-333**

Law, 3-6
    administrative, 6, 8-9
    business. See Business law
    case, 5, 16, 17
    changing, 4
    civil, 5-6
    common, 4-5, 215, 246
    compliance with, 160, 768-770
    contract, 6, 553-583
    criminal, 5-6
    employment. See Employment law
    exactness of, 3
    federal pre-emption. See Pre-emption
    finding and reading, 15-18
    forms of, 3-5
    judicial, 5
    rules of, 338
    state. See State laws
    substantive versus procedural, 5
    tort, 6
    violation of, 35-37

Law schools, 18-19

Laws v. Johnson, **509-511**

Laws; Cos v., 293

Lawson; United States v., 163

Lawsuits
    in equity, 297
    plaintiff's wrongful conduct and, 468-471
    right to file, 277
    time for filing, 10

Learned intermediary rule, 492, 508-513, 529

Leases, 566-568, 575

Lederle; Givens v., 490
Lee v. United Church Homes, **598-599**
Lee; Wilson v., 274
Leesley v. West, **508-509**
Lefkowitz; Pharmaceutical Society of State of New York v., 64
Legal citations, 15-18
Legal systems, 6-15
Legend, 34
Legend drugs. *See* Prescription drugs
Legislative branch of government, 6-8
Legitimate medical purpose, 147-149, 155, 634-635
LeJeune v. Trend Services, **338**
Lejune v. Trend Services, 260
Lemire v. Garrard Drugs, 293, **551**
LeMon; Greenwald v., **582-583**
Leone; State v., 296
Lewis v. DiDonna, **355**
Liability, 35
    for addiction, 364-367
    administrative, 245-246
    for advertising, 231
    bases of, 253, 255
    civil, 245-302
    clinical pharmacy, 257-258
    corporate, 35-36, 362-363, 574-575, 631-632, 674-675
    criminal, 245
    for drug product selection, 64, 259-262
    employer, 35-37, 50, 630, 662-663
    for generic substitution, 64-66, 292
    hospitals, 331-332
    individual, 574-575
    joint, 350-351, 431, 457-460, 628
    for labeling, 291-292
    limited, 218
    minimizing, 280-283. *See also* Risk management
    parents, 199
    partners, 218
    partnerships, 37, 218, 222
    patient profiles and, 266-267
    personal, 525-527
    premises, 514
    products. *See* Strict liability
    reducing, 265
    of retailer, 231-232
    for sexual harassment, 209, 778-780
    sole proprietors, 37
    stockholders, 220, 656-657
    strict. *See* Strict liability
    successor, 551
    tort, 218, 337-338
    vicarious, 36, 263-264, 423-426
    without fault. *See* Strict liability
Liability suits, 253

Libel, 246, 520
Liberatore v. CVS New York, **767**
Liberatore v. Melville, **765-767**, 767
License revocation, 245, 295
    bases for, 645-648
    cases related to, 621-624, 629-630, 643-644, 677-678
License suspension, 616-617, 625-626, 644-645
    bases for, 651-652, 658, 659
Licensees, 428
Licensing. *See also* Licensure
    for alcohol sales, 109
    federal requirements, 61-62
    for practice of pharmacy, 632-634, 660
    requirements for, 618-619
    rights in, 298-299, 626-627
    state laws and requirements, 434, 818-859
    supportive personnel, 267, 618-619
Licensing exception, 179
Licensure, 79, 245, 826-836
    continuing education and, 299
    controlled substance violations and, 163
    discipline re, 841-842
    foreign pharmacists, 826-827
    initial, 828-829
    issuance through transfer, 833-834
    pharmacies, 853-855
    prescription authority and, 62
    reciprocal, 74, 619-620
    renewal, 835-836
    requirements for, 619-620
    transfer requirements, 830-832
    wholesale distributors, 51, 856-857
Liggett v. Baldridge, 680
Limited liability companies (LLCs), 216, 222
Limited liability partnerships (LLPs), 216, 222
Limited partnerships, 218
Linder v. United States, 148
Loans, 582-583
Locality rule, 249-250, 354
Longs Drug Stores; Huggins v., 252, **452-453**
Longs Drug Stores California, Inc.; Huggins v., **454**
Long-term care facilities
    controlled drugs in, 151-152, 159
    Medicare participation, 112, 113
Loomstein v. Medicare Pharmacies, Inc., 205, **770-771**
Loorie; State of New York v., 181
Loss-leader sales, 231, 604
Lot numbers, 280, 283
Louisiana State Board of Education; Butler v., 264
Lovelace Health System; Anaeme v., **784**
Lubman v. Insurance Commissioner of Maryland, **560-561**
Lutheran General Hospital; Roth v., 212, **773-776**

Lying, 188

Mableton Parkway CVS, Inc. v. Salter, **542**

Maccabees Mutual Life Insurance Co.; Zwerin v., **572-573**

Mace v. Charleston Area Medical Center, **782-784**

Machin v. Walgreen, **467-468**

MacKay v. Crown Drug Co., 282, **465-466**

Madison; Marbury v., 133

Mahaffey v. Sandoz, 257

Mahoney v. Nebraska Methodist Hospital, **358-359**

Mail order, 75-77, 87-89
   cases related to, 587-588, 660, 709
   requirement of, 606

Mailing, 78-79

Maintenance treatment, 156

Makripodis v. Merrell Dow Pharmaceuticals, Inc., **408-409**

Malice, legal, 517

Malicious prosecution, 521

Malon v. Hueseman, **658-659**

Malone & Hyde, Inc. v. Hobrecht, **436-438**

Malpractice, 247-248, 266. See also Negligence
   as accident, 550
   lawsuits for, 253
   statute of limitations for, 248, 534-535, 537

Malpractice insurance, 253, 286, 475. See also Insurance; Professional liability insurance

Managed care agreements/plans, 228, 569, 594-597

Mandamus, 297

Manufacturers
   CGMP compliance, 85. See also Current Good Manufacturing Practices
   duty to warn, 256, 476-484, 508-509
   negligent misrepresentation by, 480-482
   packaging negligence, 492-493
   pharmacies as, 505-506
   registration requirements, 80-81, 85
   strict liability of, 493-494, 496-500

Manufacturing, 81, 690-691
   adulteration during. See Adulteration
   compounding as, 80-81
   controlled substance quotas, 160-161
   defects, 482-485
   illegal, 161
   otc drugs, 60
   registration for, 50, 60

Mapp v. Ohio, 177

Marbury v. Madison, 133

Marc's Variety Store, Inc.; Rite Aid of Ohio, Inc. v., **566-568**

Marigold Drug Co.; Sanders v., 272

Marijuana, 134

Marion Merrell Dow; Rhone-Poulenc Rorer Pharmaceuticals v., **679**

Mark v. Williams, **615-616**

Marketing, 32, 89-91. See also Advertising
   under ANDAs, 31
   cases related to, 691-696
   exclusive rights, 53
   FDA list of marketed drug products, 70
   generic drugs, 33, 66, 71
   NDA approval and, 45
   off-label uses, 89-90

Marshall v. Barlow's Inc., 175, 180-181, 182, 183, 188, 754

Marshall; Weyerhauser Co. v., 187, 189, **753-755**

Marten v. Derwinski, 211

Martin v. Hacker, **382-383**

Martin v. Nyquist, In re, 644

Martin; Texas Board of Pharmacy v., 296

Maryland Board of Pharmacy v. Sav-A-Lot, Inc., 669

Maryland Pharmacists Ass'n v. Office of Attorney General, **604**

Maryland, State of; Klingenstein v., **745**

Mascara; Beharry v., **553**

Massachusetts v. Stop & Shop Cos., Inc., **572**

Mast Advertising, Inc.; Pittman v., **563-564**

Matthews; State v., 295

McBrien; Deck v., 107

McCarran-Ferguson Act, 585

McClellan; Ye Olde Apothecary v., **675-676**

McClure v. Walgreen, **450-452**

McComb City Drug Co.; White v., 266

McEwen v. Ortho Pharmaceutical, 66

McKaba v. Board of Regents of State of New York, 179, **740-741**

McKay v. Crown Drug Co., 273

McKee v. American Home Products, **404-405**

McLaughlin v. Hook-SupeRx Inc., **327-329**

McLean v. State, **715-716**

McLean v. United States, **349-350**

McLeod v. Richardson-Merrell, Inc., **506-507**

McLeod v. W.S. Merrell Co., 379, 412, 483

McMellon v. Safeway Stores, **794-795**

Mechanical errors, 253, 269-271

MedGuides, 41-42

Medicaid, 99-100, 113-114
   drug cost under, 64
   fraud, 114, 616-617, 649-650, 651-652
   inspections, 183
   prescriptions, 69
   rebates, 579
   reimbursement rates, 577
   withdrawal from, 227

Medical devices, 40, 709

Medical Liability and Insurance Improvement
Act, 549
Medicare, 111-113, 114
    HMOs and, 115
    reimbursements under, 589-590
Medicare and Medicaid Patient and Program Pro-
tection Act of 1987, 114, 115
Medicare-Glaser Corp.; Frye v. (1992), 335, 373,
386-387, 390-391
Medicare-Glaser Corp.; Frye v. (1991), 386, **390-
391**
Medicare Pharmacies, Inc.; Loomstein v., 205, **770-
771**
Medication errors, 270-271
    reducing, 60, 279, 279-280
    reporting, 97
Medication orders, 153-154. See also Prescriptions
Medication profiles, 140
Medication-use process, 683-685
Medihaler-Iso, 39
Meeks v. Shuman, **371**
Melville; Liberatore v., **765-767, 767**
Memorial Hospital/Adair County v. Heckler, **589-
590**
Memorial Hospital of Gulfport; Moore v., **512-513**
Memorial Medical Center; Quinn v., **471-472**
Mental distress, Infliction of, 518-519. See also
    Emotional distress
Merchantability, warranty of, 290-291, 292
Merck-Medco Managed Care v. Rite Aid, **605**
Mergers, 224, 229
Meritor Savings Bank v. Vinson, 209
Merrell Dow Pharmaceuticals, Inc.; Makripodis v.,
    408-409
Methadone, 156-157
Methamphetamine, 158
Methamphetamine Anti-Proliferation Act of
    2000, 158
Methodist Hospital; Erwin v., **795**
Me-too drugs. See Generic drugs
Metropolitan Life Insurance Co.; Alderman Drugs
    v., **555-556**
Metropolitan Life Insurance Co.; Gaston Drugs, Inc.
    v., **554**
Meyer v. Missouri Real Estate Commission, 645
Michael Reese Hospital & Medical Center; Kirk v.
    ,**387-388, 390, 499-500, 508**
Michael v. Warner/Chilcott, 291, **488-489**
Michigan Department of Community Health; Pharm-
    aceutical Research & Manufacturers of America
    (PhRMA) v., **579**
Miller v. Department of Registration & Education,
    646-647
Miller v. State Board, 299

Mink v. University of Chicago, **476-477**
Minors, contracts by, 199
Miranda v. Arizona, 185-186
Miranda warnings, 185-186, 188
Misbranding, 8, 28, 53-54, 55-59. See also Labeling
    cases related to, 29, 647-648, 652, 688-689
    Dotterweich case, 35-36
    exported drugs, 88
    FD&C Act provisions re, 49
    prescription without authorization, 63
    receipt of misbranded drugs, 59
    from repackaging, 35-36, 61, 636
Mischa Tereschouk, In re, **660-661**
Mislabeling. See Misbranding
Misrepresentation, 198, 535-536, 571-572
    negligent, 470-472
Mississippi Board of Pharmacy; Riddle v., **653-655**
Missouri Board of Pharmacy; Tadrus v., **655-656**
Missouri ex rel. Nixon v. Stallknecht, **443-444, 660**
Missouri Hospital Ass'n v. Department of Con-
    sumer Affairs, **612**
Missouri Real Estate Commission; Meyer v., 645
Missouri State Board of Pharmacy; Cooper v., **651-
652**
Missouri State Board of Pharmacy; KV Pharma-
    ceutical v., **690-691**
Missouri State Board of Pharmacy; Simon v., **644-
645**
Mistake, 248, 266, 523
    causes of, 270, 271, 339-340
    in contract, 198
Mistake defense, 523
Model Business Incorporation Act, 219
Model Drug Product Selection Act, 230
Model Pharmacy Act, 181
Modern Pharmacy Consultants, Inc.; Peiper v., **762-
763**
Moman v. Gregerson's Foods, Inc., **778-780**
Mong; Adkins v., 252, **403-404**
Monopoly, 223, 224, 590-592, 599-600
Montayne; United States ex rel. Terraciano v., 178
Montgomery Drug Co.; Harrington v., 291
Moore v. B&C Family Center, Inc., 103
Moore v. Memorial Hospital of Gulfport, **512-513**
Moore v. Wyeth-Ayerst Laboratories, **528-529**
Moore; United States v., 676
Moore Drug Exchange; United States v., 59
Mores, 3
Moretti v. Board of Pharmacy, 295
Morgan, In re Appeal of, **682**
Morgan Pharmacy; Riff v., 258-259, **395-396, 403**
Morris v. Commonwealth of Pennsylvania, Depart-
    ment of State, **625-626**

Moskowitz v. Board of Regents of University of New York, **732-733**

Motions, 14

Mounts; Murphy v., **419-420**

Mowery v. Rite Aid, **780**

Municipal Court; Camara v., 175, 183, 746

Municipal inspections, 186

Murdock v. Walker, **465**

Murphy v. E.R. Squibb & Sons, Inc., **482-484**

Murphy v. Mounts, **419-420**

Mutual assent, 197, 207

Mutual Benefit Insurance v. Haver, **475**

Mylan Pharmaceuticals v. Henney, **711**

Narcotic Addict Treatment Act of 1974, 157

Narcotics, 3-4, 28, 79. *See also* Controlled substances

Narcotics Penalties and Enforcement Act of 1986, 166

National Association of Boards of Pharmacy (NABP), 77, 78
   compilation of state laws, 812, 813-899
   continuing education endorsement, 299

National Association of Chain Drug Stores (NACDS) v. Thompson, **550, 578**

National Association of Controlled Substance Authorities, 132

National Council on Patient Information and Education (NCPIE), 42

National Drug Code (NDC), 38, 96-97, 280

National Pharmacies v. Feliciano, **682**

National Practitioner Databank (NPDB), 114-115

National Rx Services, Inc.; Hazra v., **786-788**

Natural Answers; Eli Lilly & Co. v., **712**

NCPIE (National Council on Patient Information and Education), 42

NDA. *See* New Drug Application

NDC. *See* National Drug Code

Nebraska Methodist Hospital; Mahoney v., **358-359**

Nebraska, State of v. Hinze, **650-651**

Nebulizer solutions, 39

Necessity, 523

Necessity defense, 523

Nechy; United States v., **756**

Nefris v. DeStefano, **420**

Negligence, 246-277. *See also* Malpractice
   breach of duty, 323-338
   causation, 272-273, 428-436
   comparative and contributory, 273, 276, 465-468
   customary practice, 334
   damages, 273-275, 436-460

Negligence, 246-277. *See also* Malpractice (cont.)
   defenses, 248, 275-277
   duties, specific, 338-422
   duty. *See* Duty; Duty of care
   elements of, 247, 248-275
      breach of duty, 248, 268-272
      damages, 248, 273-275, 436-460
      duty, 248-268, 327-329
      proximate cause, 248, 272-273, 430-435
   evidence (proof) of, 460-464
   foreseeability of injury, 245-246
   in information provision, 266
   intervening, 329
   by manufacturers, 492-493
   per se, 252, 263, 266, 368
   recovery for. *See* Damages
   res ipsa loquitur doctrine, 277-278, 549
   standard of care/conduct. *See* Standard of care/conduct
   strict liability distinguished, 476-478
   in supervision, 450
   tortfeasors, joint. *See* Tortfeasors, joint

Nelms v. Walgreen Co., **448**

Nerber; United States v., 188

Networks, 599, 600, 605, 607

Nevada State Board of Pharmacy v. Garrigus & Block, **621**

New Animal Drug Application (NADA), 92

New Drug Application (NDA), 28. *See also* Drug approval process
   need for, 31-32, 87
   supplemental, 34

New drugs, 83, 87, 690, 700
   animal drugs, 92
   definition, 30-31, 31-32, 94, 95

New England Grocers Supply Co.; United States v., 182

New Jersey Board of Pharmacy; Greenblatt v., 179, 188

New Jersey Board of Pharmacy; Newcomb Sales v., **613**

New London Pharmacy; Ostrow v., **435**

New Mexico Pharmaceutical Ass'n v. State of New Mexico, **613-614**

New Mexico, State of; New Mexico Pharmaceutical Ass'n v., **613-614**

New York v. Czarnowski, **629**

New York State Department of Education; Swartz v., **624-625**

New York State Department of Social Services; Pharmaceutical Society of New York Inc. v., **336**

New York, State of v. Loorie, 181

New York, State of; France v., **368-369**

New York, State of; Sheffield v., **683-684**

New York State Teamsters Council Health & Hospital Fund v. Centrus Pharmacy Solutions, **607**

Newcomb Sales v. New Jersey Board of Pharmacy, **613**

Nichols v. Central Merchandise, Inc., **406**

Nichols v. Kaiser Foundation Health Plan of the Mid-Atlantic States, **545-546**

1962 Drug Amendments, 32, 33

1962 Ford Thunderbird v. Division of Narcotic Control, **757-758**

Nipp; Stafford v., **363-364**

Nitroglycerin, 54

Nocerino; United States v., 149

Nolo contendere (no contest) plea, 13, 644-645

Nonapproved drug, 94-95, 260

Noncompetition agreements, 207, 558-560, 566-568, 575, 791-792

Non-controlled drugs, possession of, 884-887

Nondelegation doctrine, 8-9

Nonprescription drugs. *See* Over-the-counter (otc) drugs

Nonprofit Institutions Act, 224, 588

Nonprofit organizations, 216, 219, 232
  pricing by, 584-585, 588-589
  as retailers, 592-593

Norman Bridge Drug Co. v. Banner, 138, 180, **724-725**

North Carolina; Bumper v., 755

North Carolina Board of Pharmacy; Revco v., 670

North Carolina Board of Pharmacy; Revco Southeast Drug Centers, Inc. v., 9

North Carolina Board of Pharmacy; Sunscript Pharmacy v., **659**

North Carolina Board of Pharmacy; White v., **645-646**

North Dakota Board of Pharmacy v. Snyder's Drug Stores, Inc., 5, **679-680**

North Dakota Board of Pharmacy; Snyder's Drug Stores, Inc. v., **680-681**

Notice, right to, 298

Novartis v. FTC, **693**

NPDB (National Practitioner Databank), 114-115

Nyquist; In re Martin v., 644

Oakland Cannabis Buyers' Cooperative; United States v., 134, **759**

Objections, 12

Occupational Safety and Health Act, 181

Ocean vessels, 159

Oelshelgel; Fountain v., **637-638**

Off; Cavass v., 298

Offer, 197-198

Office of Attorney General; Maryland Pharmacists Ass'n v., **604**

Off-label treatment information, 34-35, 89-90

Ohio v. Desper, **756-757**

Ohio; Mapp v., 177

Ohio; Terry v., 180

Ohio State Board of Pharmacy v. Poppe, **635-636**

Ohio State Board of Pharmacy; Blazy v., **637**

Oken; Singer v., 289

Olson v. Alick's Drugs, **773**

Olson v. State of Florida, 179, **742, 752**

Omeprazole Patent Litigation, In re, **711**

Omnibus Budget Reconciliation Act of 1990 (OBRA), 99-101, 252, 336

On hand, 141

O'Neal; Georgia Osteopathic Hospital v., **410-411**

Open bidding laws, 228

Opiates, 156-157

Orange Book, 70-72, 710

Oresman v. Searle, 293

Organon, Inc.; Steele v., 248, **532-533**

Original jurisdiction, 9

Orr v. Wal-Mart Stores, **777-778**

Ortho Pharmaceutical; McEwen v., 66

Ortho Pharmaceutical Corp.; Pierce v., 207, 769

Ortho Pharmaceutical Corp.; Wells v., **431-433**

Orzel v. Scott Drug, **468-471**

Osco Drug v. Wisconsin Pharmacy Examining Board, 670

Osco Drug Co.; Kasin v., 335

Osco Drugs; Kasin v., **373**

Ostrow v. New London Pharmacy, **435**

Outrageous conduct, 519

Overdoses. *See* Dispensing errors

Over-the-counter (otc) drugs, 29, 46, 706-707
  adequate directions for use. *See* Adequate directions for use
  advertising of, 91
  compounding by pharmacy/pharmacist, 85
  labeling, 46-48, 49, 291-292
  Orange Book listings, 70
  packaging, 104, 107
  recommendations of, 48
  refills, 73
  veterinary, 61
  warranties re, 290-291

Overtime pay, 764-765, 792-793

Package inserts, 38-39, 490, 509-511. *See also* Labeling; Warnings
  as evidence of standard of care, 463-464
  as labeling, 46
  patient, 39-43

Packaging, 685. *See also* Labeling; Manufacturing; Repackaging
  child-resistant, 104-105, 439-440

Packaging, 685. *See also* Labeling; Manufacturing; Repackaging (cont.)
  commercial containers, 138
  customized, 43, 60-61
  negligence in, 492-493
  otc drugs, 104, 107
  by physician dispensers, 63
  physician requirements, 63
  PPPA requirements, 104-106
  prescription containers, 104, 138-139
  reuse of, 105
  similarity in, 281-282
  special, 105
  tamper-resistant, 104, 107-108, 478-479
Paris Road Drugs, Inc.; Clair v., **365-367**
Park v. Employment Security Department of State of Washington, **793-794**
Park v. Howard University, **778**
Park; United States v., 35, 36-37
Park Medical Pharmacy v. San Diego Orthopedic Associates Medical Group, **605**
Parke, Davis & Co.; Stevens v., 66, **691-692**
Parol evidence rule, 200
Parties, improper, 277
Partnerships, 216, 217-218
  liability of, 37, 218, 222
Pastor; Pennsylvania State Board of Pharmacy v., **666**
Patents, 66, 660-661, 710-711
  term, 33, 52
Patient counseling. *See* Counseling
Patient medication records, 101
Patient package inserts (PPIs), 39-43, 404-405
Patient profiles, 247, 261, 266-267
Patla; American Society of Consultant Pharmacists v., **576**
Patmore; Piedmont Pharmacy, Inc. v., **531-532**
Patrick; Arkansas State Board of Pharmacy v., **632-634, 664**
Patterson Drug Co. v. Kingery, **667-669**
Payment for services, 557
Payment plans. *See* Third-party plans; *see also* Insurance
Payne v. Galen Hospital, **400-401, 795-796**
PDMA. *See* Prescription Drug Marketing Act of 1987
Peace; January v., **433-434**
Pearson v. Shalala, **707-708**
Peart; Fultz v., **458-460**
Pease; Dempsey v., **552**
Peco; Board v., 296
Pediatric studies, 33
Pedreyra v. Cornell Prescription Pharmacies, 209
Peers, 248-249, 250

Peiper v. Modern Pharmacy Consultants, Inc., **762-763**
Pennsylvania Department of Public Welfare; Pennsylvania Pharmacists Ass'n v., **569**
Pennsylvania Pharmacists Ass'n v. Houston, **576-577**
Pennsylvania Pharmacists Ass'n v. Pennsylvania Department of Public Welfare, **569**
Pennsylvania State Board of Pharmacy v. Pastor, **666**
Pennsylvania State Board of Pharmacy; DePanfilis v., **616-617**
People v. Anonymous, 180
People v. Berg, 676
People v. White, 180
Peoples Service Drug Stores v. Somerville, **430-431**
Perales; Empire State Pharmaceutical Society, Inc. v., **557-558**
Perez v. Wyeth Laboratories, Inc., **512**
Performance, partial, 200
Perjury, 628
Perkins v. K-Mart Corp., **772**
Perry Drugs; Hooper v., **391-392**
Personal use, 88-89, 158
Personal use exemption, 712-713
Pesticides, 93
Petitions, 297
Pettigrew Rexall Drugs, **729**
Pettus v. Wal-Mart, **373-375**
Pfizer; United States v., 225
Pfizer; West Virginia v., 225
Pharmaceutical Manufacturers Association (PMA), 52
Pharmaceutical Research & Manufacturers of America (PhRMA) v. Michigan Department of Community Health, **579**
Pharmaceutical Research & Manufacturers of America (PhRMA) v. Thompson, **579**
Pharmaceutical Research and Manufacturers Association (PhRMA), 68
Pharmaceutical Society v. Abrams, **602-604**
Pharmaceutical Society of New York Inc. v. New York State Department of Social Services, **336**
Pharmaceutical Society of State of New York v. Lefkowitz, 64
Pharmaceuticals
  classes of, 92
  prescription drugs. *See* Prescription drugs
  regulation of. *See* Regulation of pharmaceuticals
Pharmacies
  hospital. *See* Hospital pharmacies
  independent, 594-597, 604
  licensure, 853-855
  long-term care facilities, 113

Pharmacies (cont.)
  operation of, 679
  ownership by prescriber, 892
  quality improvement programs, 893
  state laws re, 75-76, 892-895
Pharmacist-lawyers, 19
Pharmacist-patient relationship, 328
Pharmacists, 897
  collaborative practice agreements, 92, 892
  defined, 154
  discipline of licenses, 841-842
  drug administration by, 892
  examination requirements, 818-819
  as experts, 48, 401
  foreign, 826-827
  as health care practitioners, 89
  as health care professionals, 301
  internship hours, 820-823
  licensure of. See Licensure
  practical experience, 820-823
  prescribing by, 62, 262-264
  responsibilities of, 730-732
  rights of, 298-299
  rules of practice, 254-255
  state laws re, 892-895
  as therapeutic consultants, 264-266
  workload relief regulations, 893
Pharmacy as profession, 301, 602-604
Pharmacy board inspectors, 186
Pharmacy boards. See Boards of pharmacy
Pharmacy inspection, 50, 175-189
  accountability audit, 183
  administrative, 745-757
  cases related to, 740-757
  challenging unlawful, 188-189
  consent to. See Consent
  constitutional considerations, 175-181
  by DEA, 182-183, 185-186
  DEA forms, 187
  do's and don'ts during, 187-188
  exclusionary rule, 177-178
  by FDA, 182, 184
  FDA forms, 184, 187
  formats, 184, 184-187
  legality of, 176-177, 188-189
  licensing exception, 179
  Medicaid, 183
  municipal, 186
  OSHA inspections, 183
  probable cause and, 176-177
  under protest, 187, 189, 753-754
  public areas, 180-181
  refusal to allow, 185
  silence during, 188
  special situations, 183-184, 187
  by state board, 181
  types, 181-184
  warrantless, 178-179, 740-745
    constitutionality of, 742
    emergency, 180

Pharmacy practice, 660-661
  collaborative drug therapy management, 62-63
  criminal law and, 685
  definition of, 616-617, 664
  operation/ownership of pharmacy, 679-683
  regulated areas, 666-685
    advertising. See Advertising
    dispensing. See Dispensing
    drug product selection. See Drug product
      selection
    medication-use process, 683-685
    pharmacy operation, 679
    poisons, 679
    recordkeeping. See Recordkeeping
  scope of, 48
  state laws affecting, 812. See also Boards of
    pharmacy
  state regulation of, 609-687
  unauthorized, 664
Pharmacy practice acts, 62, 63-64, 69, 295, 610
Pharmacy regulation, 75-78
Pharmacy technicians, 262, 267-268
  census data re, 898
  in community settings, 850-852, 898
  controlled substance dispensing, 154
  in hospitals, 847-849, 898
  in institutions, 847-849, 898
  prescription verification by, 342
  registration of, 628
  status of, 843-846
Pharmanex, Inc. v. Shalala, **708-709**
Phar-Mor; Griffin v., **535-536**
Phelps Dodge Mercantile Co.; United States v., 53
Physician-patient relationship, interference with,
  258, 408-410
Physicians
  authority to prescribe, 62
  consent to drug product substitution, 68-69
  dispensing by. See Dispensing
  duty to warn, 256
  negligence of, 331-332
  nonapproved use prescriptions by, 94-95, 696-
    698
  nonresident, 713-714
Piedmont Pharmacy, Inc. v. Patmore, **531-532**
Pierce v. Ortho Pharmaceutical Corp., 207, 769
Pietrzyk v. River Oaks Sav-Mor Pharmacy, **434-
  435**
Pike v. Bruce Church, Inc., 75
Pilet v. Ciba-Geigy, **507**
Pioneer companies, 32-33
Pioneer drugs, 53, 66
Pittman v. Mast Advertising, Inc., **563-564**
Pittman v. Upjohn, **407-408**
Plarard; Suarez v., **422, 662**
Plea bargaining, 14
Plough, Inc.; Ramirez v., **701-702**

PMA (Pharmaceutical Manufacturers Association), 52

Poison Prevention Packaging Act (PPPA), 104-106, 252

Poisons, 183, 433-434, 679
    economic, 102
    labeling, 104-105
    regulation of, 28, 101-107

Police power, 4, 62, 263, 299, 611, 812

Polio v. Derby Center CVS, **455**

Polyeff; State v., **733-734**

Polygraph testing, 213

Poppe; Ohio State Board of Pharmacy v., **635-636**

Population Services International; Carey v., **706-707**

Porter Drug Store; Kirk v., **418**

Portland Retail Druggists Ass'n; Abbott Laboratories v., 224, **584-585**

Positron emission tomography (PET) compounding, 34, 87

Possession
    controlled substances, 141, 888-891
    non-controlled legend drugs, 884-887

Postal regulations, 78-79, 160, 759

Postal service, use of, 759

Poulin; United States v., **738**

Powers of attorney, 15, 144

PPIs. *See* Patient package inserts

PPOs (Preferred provider organizations), 228, 607

PPPA. *See* Poison Prevention Packaging Act

Practice standards. *See* Standards

Practitioners
    communication with, 38-39
    individual, 139, 149
    mid-level, 149
    scope of practice, 62

Precedent, 5, 246

Preceptors, registration of, 824-825

Pre-emption, 75, 103, 107, 526
    drug control laws, 132-133
    HIPAA and, 97
    recordkeeping requirements, 139
    of safety standards, 106

Preferred provider organizations (PPOs), 228, 607

Preferred Rx v. American Prescription Plan, **569**

Preferred stock, 221

Premarin, 40

Premises liability, 514

Premo Pharmaceutical Laboratories, Inc. v. United States, 31

Prendergast; United States v., 176, 183

Prescribing authority, 873-879

Prescription containers, 138-139

Prescription discount card initiative, 578

Prescription Drug Marketing Act of 1987 (PDMA), 50-52, 182

Prescription drugs, 29, 59-60
    adequate information for use, 46
    advertising, 90-91
    dispensing of, 58, 60, 674-677
    exporting, 87-88
    FD&C Act provisions re, 49
    HMO coverage, 116
    importing, 88-89
    labeling, 46, 48, 49, 58, 60
    Medicare/Medicaid coverage of costs, 112, 114
    non-controlled, possession of, 884-887
    packaging, 104
    sale, purchase, or trade, 50-52
    veterinary, 61, 92-93

Prescription Drug User Fee Act of 1992, 33

Prescription errors, 338-368. *See also* Dispensing errors
    classes of, 343-368
        compounding errors, 368
        wrong administration route, 361-362
        wrong dosage/strength, 355-359
        wrong drug, 343-355
        wrong labeling/directions, 359-361
    processing errors, 338-343
        environment, 339
        factors in, 338
        personnel, 338
        systems issues, 339-343
    refills, unauthorized, 362-368

Prescription plans, 226-227, 602-604, 607
    copayments, 569

Prescriptions, 683. *See also* Dispensing; Dispensing authority
    authority to issue, 873-879
    authority to prescribe, 29, 61-63, 149, 263-264
        pharmacists, 62-63
    benefits administrators, 574-575
    for children, 281
    for controlled drugs. *See* Controlled substances
    correction of, 150
    defined, 153
    discounts on, 671-673
    drug diversion/abuse, 728-730
    electronic, 108, 151, 157-158
    electronic transmission of, 72-78, 151, 869-870
    errors. *See* Prescription errors
    facsimile transmission of, 72-78, 151, 152, 866-868
    filling
        centralized authority for, 892
        controls over, 341-343
        freedom of choice re, 113
        partial, 151-152
        refusal to fill, 266
    foreign, 74-75, 712-713
    forged/fraudulent, 732-735

Prescriptions, 683. *See also* Dispensing; Dispensing authority (cont.)
    form of, 69
    labels, 46
    mailing, 160
    mail-order pharmacies, 75-77, 587-588, 660
    Medicaid, 69
    medical purpose for, 147-149, 155, 730-732
    monitoring, 403-405
    monitoring programs, 133
    need for, 330-331
    oral, 29, 282
    out-of-state, 74, 75-78
    ownership of, 266
    pharmacist responsibility re, 730-732
    by pharmacists, 62, 262-264
    record keeping, 726-728
    as records, 37
    refilling. *See* Refills
    requirements, 61-78, 644, 715-716
    self-prescribing, 160
    signature, 151
    state law requirements, 862-865
    transfers, 72
    validity of, 623-624, 732-735
    veterinary, 61
Pressler v. Irvine Drugs, **441-442**
Presumptions, 461-464
Price; Hatten v., **442**
Price discrimination, 224-225, 584-585, 597-598
Price-fixing, 223, 224, 226-227
    cases related to, 597-598, 601-602
    pharmacy agreements and, 585-587
Pricing, 30, 230-231, 589-590
    discriminatory, 227-228, 581-582
    preferential, 588-589
Prison services, 368-371
Privacy
    expectation of, 179, 181, 182, 183, 419
    HIPAA requirements, 98
    invasion of, 215, 246, 520, 554
    right to, 215, 267, 716-718
Privilege defense, 523
Privileges, 15, 420-422, 523, 551, 757
Privity of contract, 293
Probable cause, 176-177
    for search, 747
    for warrant issuance, 183, 754-755
Procedural law, 5
Product quality, 4
Product selection. *See* Drug product selection
Products liability. *See* Strict liability
Profession, 603
Professional associations, 76, 222, 557-558
    codes and standards, 248-249
Professional corporation, 218, 222
Professional custom. *See* Customary practice

Professional liability insurance, 283-288
Professionals & Patients for Customized Care v. Shalala, 82, **698-699**
Promissory notes, 582-583
Proof. *See* Evidence
Proof gallon measures, 111
Proof, standards of, 13
Property rights, 299, 626-627
Propranolol, 53
Propulsid Products Liability Litigation, In re, **505-506**
Prosecution, malicious, 521
Prospective advantage, interference with, 522
Providence Square v. GDF, **575**
Provident Life & Accident Insurance; Swisher-Sherman v., **550**
Proximate cause, 248
Prudential Insurance Co. of America; Harrow v., **570**
Prudential Life Insurance Co. of America; Texas Pharmacy Ass'n v., **599**
Public corporation, 218
Public Health Service Amendments of 1987, 115
Public interest, 75, 77
Public policy, 328
    agreements against, 199
    in employment discharge cases, 206-207
    exception, 761, 763, 766-767
Puffery, 290
Pugh; United States v., 177, 183, **751-752**
Purchase invoices, 37
Pure Food and Drug Act (1906), 27-28
Pysz v. Henry's Drug Store, 257, 404, **412-413**

Quality improvement programs, 893
Quasi contract, 199, 202
Quinn v. Memorial Medical Center, **471-472**

Racial discrimination, 784-790
Racketeer Influenced and Corrupt Organizations Act, 771
Radiopharmaceuticals, 87
Ralph Clayton Robinson; United States v., **720**
Ramirez v. Plough, Inc., **701-702**
Ramirez; Kollenberg v., **521-522**
Ramon v. Farr, **463-464**
Randle v. California State Board of Pharmacy, 36, 73, **629-630**
Rasmussen; Hoar v., 256, **343-344**
Rasmussen; State v., 74, 76, 133, **713-714**
Ray v. Burbank & Jones, 263
Rayburn v. Board of Pharmacy, 296, 298
Raynor v. Richardson-Merrell, Inc., **493-494**

Reardon; State v., **735-736**

Reasonable doubt, 14

Reasonable person standard, 247, 249, 331

Rebates, 579, 671-673

Reben v. Ely, 265, **438-439**

Recalls, 45-46

Recordkeeping, 37
    cases related to, 677-678, 726-728
    centralized systems, 142-143
    continuing, 739-740
    continuing records, 739-740
    re controlled substances. *See* Controlled substances
    electronic, 108
    failure in, 266
    improper, 726-728
    lot numbers, 280
    by mid-level practitioners, 149
    OBRA '90 requirements, 100
    prescription drugs, 50
    prescriptions, 726-728
    re refills, 73, 155
    for unit-dose drugs, 279
    violation of requirements re, 161-162

Records
    electronic, 139
    as evidence, 639-640
    inspection of, 183-184, 187-188
    readily retrievable, 141, 142-143

Recovery. *See* Damages

Red Owl Stores; State v., 294

Redhibition, 506

Reeves-Sain Medical v. Blue Cross Blue Shield of Tennessee, **583**

Reference drugs, 52, 71

Reference materials, electronic, 893

Referrals, 590-592, 593-594

Refills, 72-78
    authorization of, 73-74
    for controlled drugs, 142-143, 155-156
    excessive, 393-401
    information transfers for, 156
    labeling and, 139
    records of, 73
    refusal of, 327
    statutory authority for, 29, 49
    unauthorized, 29, 362-368

Refusal to deal, 228-229

Registration, 78, 85, 131
    applications, 628
    for controlled drugs, 131, 136-138
    CSA requirements, 136-138
    exemptions, 80, 137
    hospitals, 153
    interns/preceptors/training sites, 824-825
    repackaging and, 48, 50, 80-81
    revocation, 728-730

Registration fees, 136-137, 824-825

Regulation of pharmaceuticals, 27-117. *See also* Food and Drug Administration; Food, Drug, and Cosmetic Act
    authority for, 27
    dispensing. *See* Dispensing
    drug approval process, 44-48, 52-53
    FD&C Act, 27-50
    pharmaceutical products, 50-61
    postal regulations, 78-79
    prescriptions. *See* Prescriptions
    repackaging. *See* Repackaging
    uses. *See* Uses

Regulations, 4, 6, 8
    cases related to, 666-685
    challenges to, 8, 82-83
    DEA, 160
    finding and reading, 17
    HMOs, 116
    notice of change, 295
    subject of, 296

Rehabilitation Act of 1973, 210-211, 212, 215, 773-776

Reimbursement, 576-579, 602-604, 607
    Medicare, 589-590
    rates, 64, 577-578

Reisman v. Caplin, 750

Relabeling. *See* Labeling

Reliable Refuse & Recycling v. Glastonbury Towne Pharmacy, **570-571**

Religious discrimination, 208, 790

Remedies. *See* Damages

Reminder advertising, 90

Removal, 528, 530, 547-548

Repackagers, registration for, 50

Repackaging, 35-36, 48, 80-87
    CGMPs and, 48-49
    injectables, 80
    labeling and, 48, 60-61
    otc drugs, 60-61
    pharmacy compounding, 80-81
    prepackaging, 279
    unauthorized, 635-636
    unit-dose container expiration dating, 80

Replevin, 204

Reporting
    by manufacturers, 45
    to NPDB, 115
    problems and errors, 97

Res ipsa loquitur, 277-278, 549

Rescission, 201

Research incentives, 34

Respondeat superior, 35-37, 630

Restraining orders, 724-725

Revco v. North Carolina Board of Pharmacy, 670

Revco Southeast Drug Centers, Inc. v. North Carolina Board of Pharmacy, 9

Rexall Drug & Chemical Co.; Thomsen v., **347-348**

Reyes v. Wyeth Laboratories, Inc., 379

Rezulin Products Liability Litigation, In re, **528**

Rhone-Poulenc Rorer Pharmaceuticals v. Marion Merrell Dow, **679**

Richardson v. Florida State Board of Dentistry, 146, 147

Richardson-Merrell, Inc.; Coyle v., **500-501, 502-503**

Richardson-Merrell, Inc.; McLeod v., **506-507**

Richardson-Merrell, Inc.; Raynor v., **493-494**

Richmond v. Fowlkes, **580-581**

Riddle v. Mississippi Board of Pharmacy, **653-655**

Riff v. Morgan Pharmacy, 258-259, **395-396, 403**

Ripeness, 8, 557-558

Risk assessment, 258

Risk, assumption of, 276

Risk management, 258, 278-283

Rite Aid; Caperci v., **764-765**

Rite Aid; Merck-Medco Managed Care v., **605**

Rite Aid; Mowery v., **780**

Rite Aid; Washburn v., **421, 662**

Rite Aid Corp. v. Board of Pharmacy of State of New Jersey, **610**

Rite Aid Corp.; Danesh v., **792**

Rite-Aid Corp.; Evans v., **422, 661**

Rite Aid Corp.; Thomas v., **788-789**

Rite-Aid of Alabama, Ex parte, **541**

Rite-Aid of Alabama; In re Deal v., **541**

Rite-Aid of Alabama; Langford v., **581-582**

Rite Aid of Ohio, Inc. v. Marc's Variety Store, Inc., **566-568**

Rite-Aid of South Carolina; Hundley v., **449-450**

River Oaks Sav-Mor Pharmacy; Pietrzyk v., **434-435**

RNH, Inc. v. Beatty, **571-572**

Robbins; Wal-Mart Stores v., **447**

Roberson v. Wal-Mart Stores, **764**

Robinson v. Williamson, **537**

Robinson; United States v., **720**

Robinson-Patman Price Discrimination Act, 223, 224-225, 584-585, 588

Rockport Pharmacy Inc. v. Digital Simplistics, Inc., **337**

Rodgers v. Hook-SupeRx Inc., **514-515**

Roe v. Ingraham, **716-717**

Roe; Whalen v., **717-718**

Rose; Holbrook v., 278, **428-429**

Rose Park Pharmacy; Allen v., 207

Rosenblatt v. California Board of Pharmacy, 298-299

Rosenthall v. Board of Pharmacy, 295

Ross Laboratories v. Theis, **498-499**

Roth v. Lutheran General Hospital, 212, **773-776**

Rothenberg v. Double D Drug, **771**

Royal Drug Co.; Group Life & Health Insurance Co. v., 226-227, **585-587**

Rozas Gibson Pharmacy of Eunice, Inc., 183

R.T. Cornell Pharmacy, Inc. v. Guzzo, **556-557**

Rubbing alcohol, 109

Rudman v. Bancheri, 262

Ruiz v. Walgreen, **548-549**

Russell; United States v., **734-735**

S corporations, 216, 221

Safe and effective. See Efficacy; Safety

Safety, 32, 49
    proof of, 66
    veterinary pharmaceuticals, 92

Safeway Stores; McMellon v., **794-795**

Sale, 147-149, 197, 202-204
    alcohol, 109, 110-111
    of business, 564-566, 582-583
    contracts for, 203-204, 288-289
    foreign, 158
    loss-leader, 231, 604
    misbranded/adulterated drugs, 59
    poisons, 107
    returns, 52
    of samples, 182, 651-652
    warranties and. See Warranty

Sale on approval, 203

Salicylate preparations, 46

Salter; Mableton Parkway CVS, Inc. v., **542**

Samples, 51-52, 182
    sale of, 182, 651-652
    taken during inspection, 184
    warranty by, 290

San Diego Orthopedic Associates Medical Group; Park Medical Pharmacy v., **605**

Sanders v. Marigold Drug Co., 272

Sanderson v. Eckerd, **335**

Sandoz; Mahaffey v., 257

Saucier v. Biloxi Regional Medical Center, **427-428**

Sav-A-Lot, Inc.; Maryland Board of Pharmacy v., 669

Sav On Drug Stores; Crippens v., **455-457**

Scarf; Troppi v., 274, 275

Schedule I substances, 134, 146

Schedule II substances, 74, 134-135
    distribution, 146
    inventory records, 141
    mailing, 79
    prescriptions, 150, 151-152, 156

Schedule III substances, 135, 143

Schedule IV substances, 135, 143

Schedule V substances, 73, 92, 135
  record book, 183

Scheduled substances, 132, 133-135. *See also* Controlled substances
  inventory records, 141-142
  reclassification of, 720-721
  recordkeeping requirements, 141, 143

Schedules (drug), 9

Schering Corp.; Kaspirowitz v., **486**

Schiffman; United States v., 183, **752-753**

Schleiter v. Carlos, 41

School Board of Nassau County v. Arline, 212

Schroeder v. Cox Medical Center, 275, **444-445**

Schwamb v. Fireman's Insurance Co. of New Jersey, 286

Schwartz v. Florida Board of Pharmacy, **638-639**

Sciolino v. United States, **524**

Scott Drug; Orzel v., **468-471**

Search warrants, 175-176. *See also* Warrants

Searches, 175-178. *See also* Inspections; Pharmacy inspection
  consent to. *See* Consent
  drug testing as, 214
  illegal, 177-178, 745
  unreasonable, 175, 214
  warrantless, 175, 176, 178-179, 182, 184

Searle; Oresman v., 293

Seattle, City of; See v., 175, 176, 180, 183, 746, 750

See v. City of Seattle, 175, 176, 180, 183, 746, 750

Seizures, 50, 175, 214, 756-757

Selcke; Walgreen v., **618-619**

Self-incrimination, 298, 735-736

Sellers/suppliers, liability of, 485, 500-501, 502-503, 505-506

Sender v. Department of Professional Regulation, **656-657**

Servants, 426. *See also* Vicarious liability

Service of process, 10

Settlement, 10, 286

Severability, 84

Sex discrimination, 209-210, 784-786

Sexual harassment, 208-209, 778-782
  hostile work environment, 780-782

Shalala; Bristol-Myers Squibb Co. v., **706**

Shalala; Pearson v., **707-708**

Shalala; Pharmanex, Inc. v., **708-709**

Shalala; Professionals & Patients for Customized Care v., 82, **698-699**

Shalala; Syncor v., 87

Shalala; Warner-Lambert v., **693**

Shalala; Western States Pharmacy v., 84

Shared service operations, 49

Sharp & Dohme; Klingel's Pharmacy v., 228

Sheffield v. State of New York, **683-684**

Sheils v. Eckerd Corp., **534-535**

Shepard's Pharmacy v. Stop & Shop, **522**

Shermack v. Board of Regents of State University System, **643-644**

Sherman v. United States, 633

Sherman; Knoll Pharmaceutical v., **690**

Sherman Antitrust Act, 207, 223, 229, 587

Shiffrin v. IV Services of America, **421**

Shipping, 79, 87-89, 158

Shrake's Country Club Pharmacy; Lasley v., 253, **332-333**

Shuman; Meeks v., **371**

Side effects, 30. *See also* Adverse reactions
  duty to warn of, 378-383, 401-403, 406-408, 486-494

Signatures, electronic/digital, 108, 151

Siler Drug Store Co.; United States v., **674-675**

Silves v. King, **392-393**

Simon v. Missouri State Board of Pharmacy, **644-645**

Singer v. Oken, 289

Single entity products, 135

Sisters of St. Francis; Sullivan v., 96

Slander, 246, 266, 520

Slijepcevich v. Caremark, **791**

Sloman v. Iowa Board of Pharmacy Examiners, **634-635**

Smith; Jack Eckerd Corp. v., **516**

Smith Kline & French Laboratories; Herman v., 293

Snyder Bros. Drug, Inc.; Koderick v., 248, **533-534**

Snyder's Drug Stores, Inc. v. North Dakota Board of Pharmacy, **680-681**

Snyder's Drug Stores, Inc.; North Dakota Board of Pharmacy v., 5, **679-680**

Socony-Vacuum Oil; United States v., 223, 599, 601

Sole proprietors and proprietorships, 36, 37, 216-217

Somerville; Peoples Service Drug Stores v., **430-431**

Southeastern Pennsylvania Transportation Authority (SEPTA); Doe v., **520**

Southern Baptist Hospital; Brown v., **424-426**

Southwest Drug Stores of Mississippi, Inc. v. Garner, **519-520**

Spain; United States v., **725-726**

Spalitto; Horner v., **400**

Specific performance, 5, 204

Speech, freedom of. *See* Freedom of speech

Speer v. United States, **416-417**

Speevy v. United States, 255

Spirits, 110

Spry v. Kiser, 65

S.S. Kresge Co.; Tolan v., 281

St. Joseph Hospital; De Anda v., 210

St. Vincent Medical Center; Urfer v., **763**

Stadnik; Barad v., 299

Staffing, 300

Stafford v. Nipp, **363-364**

Stallknecht; Missouri ex rel. Nixon v., **443-444, 660**

Stamatiou v. U.S. Gypsum Co., 188

Stanack Sales Co.; United States v., **745-746**

Standard of care/conduct, 331-334. *See also* Duty of care; Ethics
  court-imposed, 250-251
  courts' view of, 255-256
  creation of, 248, 250, 252
  drug product selection, 259-261
  duty to warn, 543-545
  evidence (proof) of, 463-464
  expert testimony to establish, 248-249, 543-545
  local variations, 249-250, 354
  negligence, 329-334, 337-338
  under OBRA '90, 100-101
  professional, 389, 395, 413-414
  rules re, 254-255, 357
  supervisors, 423-426
  therapeutic consultants, 264-266

Standards, 254-255
  of care. *See* Standard of care/conduct
  dynamic nature of, 253
  ethical, 3
  evidence admission, 398-400
  JCAHO, 300-301
  labeling, 291-292
  of practice, 248-249, 336, 896
  of proof, 13, 14, 245-246
  reasonable person, 247, 249, 331
  recordkeeping violations, 161
  statutory, 252
  USP/NF, 54

Standing, 8, 76, 106, 277, 608

Stare decisis, 5

State; Chesteen v., **719**

State; McLean v., **715-716**

State Board; Miller v., 299

State Board of Pharmacy v. Weinstein, **609**

State Board of Pharmacy; Duckworth v., **652-653**

State Board of Pharmacy; Virginia Citizens Consumer Council, Inc. v., **669-670, 670**

State laws, 812, 813-899. *See also* Statutes
  boards of pharmacy. *See* Boards of pharmacy
  cases related to, 666-685

State laws, 812, 813-899. *See also* Statutes (cont.)
  competition, regulation of, 594-597
  conflicts with, 759
  re controlled substances, 132-133
  controlled substances, 664-666, 759
  counseling, 871-872
  dispensing authority, 880-883
  drug control, 858-859
  drug possession, 884-891
  drug product selection, 70, 860-861
  examination requirements, 818-819
  "freedom of choice" legislation, 892
  generic product substitution, 64-65
  re health insurance, 97-98
  interstate commerce and, 75-76, 77-78
  labeling, 58
  licensing, 434, 818-859
  OBRA '90 incorporation, 100-101
  patient counseling, 871-872
  pharmacist workload relief, 893
  pharmacists and pharmacies, 75-76, 609-660, 812, 892-895
  pharmacy practice, 609-687. *See also* Pharmacy practice acts
  possession of controlled substances, 888-891
  possession of non-controlled legend drugs, 884-887
  pre-emption by federal law, 4, 103
  prescribing authority, 61-63, 873-879
  prescription requirements, 862-865
  prescription transmission methods, 152, 866-870
  registration for interns/preceptors/training sites, 824-825
  trade-related, 601-605

State pharmacy boards. *See* Boards of pharmacy

State Uniform Controlled Substances Act, 132, 133

State v. ... . See name of other party

States, 27
  courts, 9, 11
  police power of, 4, 62, 263, 611

Statute of frauds, 199-201, 559

Statutes, 4, 5. *See also* Federal laws; Law; State laws
  appropriations to support, 7-8
  citation of, 16
  conflict with Constitution, 181
  enabling, 294, 610
  enactment of, 7-8
  interpretation of, 5, 132, 614, 742
  of limitations, 10, 37, 248, 276-277, 531-537
  pharmacy practice acts, 62, 63-64, 69, 295, 610
  retroactive application of, 626-627
  sections, 16
  titles, 16
  vagueness in, 634-635, 637-638
  violation of, 338
  wrongful death, 275

Statutory negligence, 252

Stebbins v. Concord Wrigley Drugs, Inc., **401-403, 403**

Steele v. Organon, Inc., 248, **532-533**

Steele v. United States, 264

Sterling Drug, Inc.; Bickowicz v., **364-365**

Sterling Drug, Inc.; Krug v., **486-487**

Steroids, 135, 731-732

Stevens v. Parke, Davis & Co., 66, **691-692**

Stock, corporate, 218, 220-221, 760-761

Stockholders, 220, 656-657, 679-680

Stolfa v. Ely, **539-540**

Stone v. City of Stow, 179, **744**

Stone; United States v., **627-628**

Stop & Shop; Shepard's Pharmacy v., **522**

Stop & Shop Cos., Inc.; Massachusetts v., **572**

Storage of drugs, 50, 300

Stow, City of; Stone v., 179, **744**

Stramonium, 92

Strickland v. Brown Morris Pharmacy, **505**

Strict liability, 35-37, 246, 277-278
    bases of, 478-479
    breach of warranty, 506-508
    cases related to, 35-37, 476-513
    for drug product selection, 260
    failure to warn, 495-505
    learned intermediary rule, 508-513
    of manufacturers, 493-494, 496-500
    manufacturing defect, 482-485
    negligence distinguished, 476-478
    negligent misrepresentation, 480-482
    of seller/supplier, 485, 500-501, 502-503, 505-506
    of service providers, 482-484
    statute of limitations for, 534-535
    warning defect, 476-484, 486-494

Students, 424-426, 580-581. *See also* Education

Suarez v. Plarard, **422, 662**

Subpoenas, 745-746

Subrogation, 278

Substance Abuse and Mental Health Services Administration, 156

Substances, controlled. *See* Controlled substances

Substantive law, 5

Successor liability, 551

Suicide
    as intervening cause, 329
    prevention, 416-418

Sulfanilamide Elixir, 28

Sullivan v. Sisters of St. Francis, 96

Sullivan; United States v., 28-29

Sullivan's Wholesale Drug Co. v. Faryl's Pharmacy, **562-563**

Sundby Pharmacy; Hannigan v., **420-421**

Sunscript Pharmacy v. North Carolina Board of Pharmacy, **659**

Superfresh; Diberardinis-Mason v., **761**

Supermarkets General Corp.; Bell v., **784-786**

Supervision, 267, 268
    ineffective, 271-272
    negligence in, 450

Supplements. *See* Dietary supplements

Supportive personnel. *See* Assistants

Supremacy Clause, 133

Survival statutes, 277

Swartz v. New York State Department of Education, **624-625**

Swisher-Sherman v. Provident Life & Accident Insurance, **550**

Syncor v. Shalala, 87

Tace, 40

Tadrus v. Missouri Board of Pharmacy, **655-656**

Take-home medications, 153-154

Talman v. Department of Registration & Education, 164-165

Tampering, 107-108

Tape-recording, 282

Tarlton v. LaGarde, 266

Taxation
    alcohol, 109, 110-111
    corporations, 216, 218, 221, 222
    exemptions, 660
    independent contractors, 791
    LLCs and LLPs, 222
    partnerships, 216, 217
    sole proprietorships, 216
    unrelated business income, 232

Taylor v. Johnson, **515-516**

Taylor; Fakhouri v., **409-410**

Tenth Amendment, 27

Teratogens, 29-30, 493-494

Tereschouk, In re, **710**

Tereschouk, Mischa, In re, **660-661**

Termination. *See* Discharge from employment

Terminology, 799-805

Terraciano, United States ex rel. v. Montayne, 178

Terry v. Ohio, 180

Testing, 44-45, 92
    accuracy of, 214
    animal data, 38
    CMS regulation of, 99
    for illicit drug use, 214-215
    risk assumption and, 276
    toxicity, 28

Texas; Wright v., **713**

Texas Board of Pharmacy v. Martin, 296

Texas Pharmacy Ass'n v. Prudential Life Insurance Co. of America, **599**

Texas State Board of Pharmacy; Young v., **640-641**

Texas, State of; Agbogun v., **705**

Thalidomide, 29-30

Thalos v. Dillon Cos., **776-777**

Thatcher's Drugs v. Consolidated Supermarkets, **558-560**

Theft, 144, 213, 793

Theis; Ross Laboratories v., **498-499**

Therapeutic alternates, 66

Therapeutic equivalents, 70-71

Therapeutic substitution, 66, 68-69

Third-party plans, 4, 226-227, 560-561, 585-587. See also Insurance

Thomas v. Board of Pharmacy, 295

Thomas v. Rite Aid Corp., **788-789**

Thompson v. Western States Medical Center, 34, 84, 85, **700-701**

Thompson; National Association of Chain Drug Stores (NACDS) v., **550, 578**

Thompson; Pharmaceutical Research & Manufacturers of America (PhRMA) v., **579**

Thomsen v. Rexall Drug & Chemical Co., **347-348**

Thrift Drug v. Universal Prescription Administrators, **574-575**

Thriftimart; United States v., 748

Thrifty Payless; Hooper v., **377-378**

Tigue; Wilmington Vitamin v., 296, 297

Timm v. Upjohn Co., **491-492**

Title, warranty of, 290

The T.J. Hooper, 250-251, 251

Tolan v. S.S. Kresge Co., 281

Tombari v. Connors, 255

Torsiello v. Whitehall Laboratories, 291, 476, **702-704**

Tort law, 6

Tortfeasors, joint, 350-351, 457-460, 464-474
   defenses, 465-474
   plaintiff's wrongful conduct and, 468-471

Torts, 246-278
   intentional. See Intentional torts
   liability for, 218, 337-338
   negligent, 246
   strict liability. See Strict liability
   willful, 636

Toxic substance, 102

Trade names, 217, 564-566

Trade or business, 232, 604

Trade practices. See Deceptive trade practices

Trademarks, 712

Training sites, registration of, 824-825

Transfer, licensure through, 833-834

Transfer warning, 138

Travia; United States v., **685**

Treaties, 3-4

Treble-damage suits, 225-226

Tremblay v. Kimball, 255-256, 271

Trend Services; LeJeune v., **338**

Trend Services; Lejune v., 260

Trespassing, 427-428

Trials, 10-14. See also Testing
   clinical, 34, 45

Troppi v. Scarf, 274, 275

Tying arrangements, 223, 593

Tylenol, 107

UCC. See Uniform Commercial Code

Ultra vires, 9

Unauthorized practice of medicine, 265-266, 650-651

Unemployment benefits, 793-794

Uniform Commercial Code (UCC), 197, 288
   partial payment under, 200

Uniform Limited Partnership Act, 218

Uniform Partnership Act, 217

Unit-dose labeling, 42-43, 61, 80

Unit-dose packaging, 80, 278-280

United Church Homes; Lee v., **598-599**

United Healthcare Insurance Co. & AARP v. Advance PCS, **573-574**

United States v. … . See name of other party

United States ex rel. Terraciano v. Montayne, 178

United States Drug Enforcement Administration; Burley v., **641-642**

United States Pharmacopeia-National Formulary (USP-NF), 54, 896

Universal Prescription Administrators; Thrift Drug v., **574-575**

University of Chicago; Mink v., **476-477**

Unprofessional conduct, 621-625

Unrelated business income tax, 232

Upjohn; Pittman v., **407-408**

Upjohn Co.; Timm v., **491-492**

Urfer v. St. Vincent Medical Center, **763**

Urowsky v. Board of Regents of Univ. of N.Y., 670

U.S. Gypsum Co.; Stamatiou v., 18

Use, directions for. See Directions for use; Labeling

Uses
   experimental, 94-95
   intended, 50-61
   new, 34
   off-label, 89-90, 694-696
   safe and effective. See Efficacy; Safety

Uses (cont.)
  unapproved/nonapproved, 34, 89-90, 94, 260, 696-698
  unauthorized, 407-408
USP-NF (United States Pharmacopeia-National Formulary), 54, 896

Van Bramer; Van Iperen v., 300, 381-382
Van Hatem v. K-Mart, 460-461
Van Iperen v. Van Bramer, 300, 381-382
VanderLinden v. Crews, 297
Vantreese Discount Pharmacy; Volner v., 461
Vaughn v. CVS Revco, 606
Venice Hospital; Key Enterprises v., 592-593
Venice Hospital; Key Enterprises of Delaware v. (1989), 590-592
Venue, 10
Verdict, 13, 14
Vermont & 110th Medical Arts Pharmacy v. Board of Pharmacy of State of California, 623-624
Vertical merger, 229
Veteran's Reemployment Rights Act, 783
Veterinarians, 149
Veterinary pharmaceuticals, 92-93
  labeling, 46, 61
  prescriptions, 61, 74, 139
Veto, 7
Vicarious liability, 36, 263-264, 423-426
Vicknair; Aucoin v., 526-527
Victim and Witness Protection Act, 628
Vinson; Meritor Savings Bank v., 209
Virginia Citizens Consumer Council; Virginia State Board of Pharmacy v., 10, 230
Virginia Citizens Consumer Council, Inc. v. State Board of Pharmacy, 669-670, 670
Virginia Citizens Consumer Council, Inc.; Virginia State Board of Pharmacy v., 670-671
Virginia State Board of Pharmacy v. Virginia Citizens Consumer Council, Inc., 10, 230, 670-671
Vitamin Industries, Inc.; United States v., 35
Voir dire, 12
Vollendorf v. United States, 423-424
Volner v. Vantreese Discount Pharmacy, 461
Vuhs v. Barber, 257

Wage discrimination, 209-210
Wainwright v. Fontenot, 443
Wainwright v. Walgreen Louisiana, 442-443
Waiver of constitutional rights, 180, 745-746
Walgreen v. Feliciano, 682-683
Walgreen v. Hood, 577
Walgreen v. Selcke, 618-619
Walgreen; Ellingsen v., 530-531

Walgreen; Machin v., 467-468, 548-549
Walgreen; McClure v., 450-452
Walgreen Co.; Johnson v., 252, 335, 392
Walgreen Co.; Jones v., 266, 356-357, 394
Walgreen Co.; Nelms v., 448
Walgreen Louisiana; Wainwright v., 442-443
Walgreens Louisiana; Fisher v., 536-537
Walker v. Jack Eckerd Corp., 101, 396-397
Walker; Murdock v., 465
Walls v. Hollarnd, 371
Wal-Mart; Pettus v., 373-375
Wal-Mart; Walter v., 351-352
Wal-Mart Stores v. American Drugs, 604
Wal-Mart Stores v. Knickrehm, 577
Wal-Mart Stores v. Robbins, 447
Wal-Mart Stores; Bales v., 780-782
Wal-Mart Stores; Brooks v., 352-354
Wal-Mart Stores; Cackowski v., 447-448
Wal-Mart Stores; Happel v., 415-416
Wal-Mart Stores; Orr v., 777-778
Wal-Mart Stores; Roberson v., 764
Wal-Mart Stores, Inc., In re, 792-793
Walter v. Wal-Mart, 351-352
Wantonness, 246, 275, 341
Warfarin Sodium Antitrust Litigation, In re, 599-600
Warner/Chilcott; Michael v., 291, 488-489
Warner-Lambert v. Shalala, 693
Warner-Lambert; Gennock v., 530
Warnings, 47
  re addictiveness, 332-333
  adequacy of, 702-704
  defects in, 476-484, 486-494
  re drug interactions, 333, 334
  duty to give. See Duty to warn
  re generic drugs, 481
  language of, 700-701
  learned intermediary rule, 256, 492, 497-502
  mandated, 410
  Miranda, 185-186, 188
  negation of, 691-692
  in patient package inserts, 39
  prescription drug dangers, 355
  re prescription errors, 361-362
  transfer, 138
Warrants, 175-176
  administrative inspection. See Administrative inspection warrants
  for audits, 755-756
  licensing exception, 179
  search, 175-176
  validity of, 745, 747, 753-755
  when required, 178-179, 740-745, 755-756
Warranty, 265, 289-290. See also Advertising
  breach of, 260, 495, 506-508
    notice of breach, 293

Warranty, 265, 289-290. *See also* Advertising
(cont.)
    drug product selection and, 292
    express, 91, 289-290, 292
    fitness for purpose, 290, 291, 292
    implied, 59, 278, 290, 292-293, 409
    merchantability, 290-291, 292
    otc drugs, 290-291
    removal of, 292-293
    title, 290
Washburn v. Rite Aid, **421, 662**
Washington Legal Foundation v. Friedman, 694
Washington Legal Foundation v. Henney, 89, **694-695**
Washington, State of; Wilson v., **772**
Watson Pharmaceuticals v. Henney, 710
Waxman-Hatch Act, 32
Webb's City, Inc.; Florida Board of Pharmacy v.,
    667
Wee; Davidson v., 290-291
Weeks v. United States, 177
Weinberger v. Bentex Pharmaceutical, Inc., 30
Weinberger v. Hynson, Wescott & Dunning, 30
Weinberger; Ciba Corp. v., 31
Weinberger; Daley v., 184, **749-750**
Weinberger; Hoffman-LaRoche v., 31
Weinstein; State Board of Pharmacy v., **609**
Welkener v. Kirkwood Drug Store Co., **484-485**
Wells v. Ortho Pharmaceutical Corp., **431-433**
Wenzel; Express Scripts v., **606**
West; Leesley v., **508-509**
West Virginia v. Pfizer, 225
*Westchester County Pharmaceutical Society v.
    Abrams, In re*, 603
Western States v. Henney, 34
Western States Medical Center; Thompson v., 34,
    84, 85, **700-701**
Western States Pharmacy v. Shalala, 84
Weyerhauser Co. v. Marshall, 187, 189, **753-755**
Whalen v. Roe, **717-718**
Whayne; Arkansas State Board of Pharmacy v., **664**
Whistleblowing, 765-767
White v. McComb City Drug Co., 266
White v. North Carolina Board of Pharmacy, **645-646**
White; People v., 180
Whitehall Laboratories; Torsiello v., 291, 476, **702-704**

Wholesale distributors, 50, 636
    licensure requirements, 51, 658, 857
Wickline v. State of California, 260-261
Wiley-Hepburn Act, 27
William Spain; United States v., **725-726**
Williams v. Advocate Health & Hospitals, **790**
Williams; Ferguson v., 335, **414-415**
Williams; Mark v., **615-616**
Williams; State v., **739-740**
Williamson; Robinson v., **537**
Willing; Bichler v., 276, 380, 483, **495-496**
Wilmington Vitamin v. Tigue, 296, 297
Wilson v. Lee, 274
Wilson v. State of Washington, **772**
Wilson; Kansas State Board of Pharmacy v., **611**
Wimm v. Jack Eckerd Corp., **359-360**
Winn Dixie of Montgomery v. Colburn, **445-446**
*Wisconsin Pharmacy Examining Board; Osco Drug
    v.*, 670
Witnesses, 12-13, 541. *See also* Expert witnesses
Witt v. Aetna US Healthcare, **581**
Woolley v. Hoffman-LaRoche, Inc., 205
Work hour limitations, 280
Workers' compensation, 215, **794-796**
Workload as error cause, 339-340
Wright v. Abbott Laboratories, **512**
Wright v. Texas, **713**
Writ of certiorari, 297
Writ of prohibition, 297
Wrongful death statutes, 275
W.S. Merrell Co.; McLeod v., 379, 412, 483
Wyeth-Ayerst Laboratories; Moore v., **528-529**
Wyeth Laboratories, Inc.; Brannan v., 206, **760-761**
Wyeth Laboratories, Inc.; Perez v., **512**
Wyeth Laboratories, Inc.; Reyes v., 379

Ye Olde Apothecary v. McClellan, **675-676**
Young v. Board of Pharmacy, **677-678**
Young v. Key Pharmaceuticals, **542-543**
Young v. Texas State Board of Pharmacy, **640-641**

Zeneca v. Eli Lilly, **692-693**
Zuchowicz v. United States, **398-400**
Zwerin v. Maccabees Mutual Life Insurance Co.,
    572-573

NOTES